90/net R.F.

Sociology
of Deviant Behavior

Sociology of Deviant Behavior

THIRD EDITION

Marshall B. Clinard

University of Wisconsin

Holt, Rinehart and Winston, Inc.
*New York   Chicago   San Francisco   Atlanta   Dallas
Montreal   Toronto   London*

*To my children from whom I have
learned a great deal*

MARSHA, STEPHEN, and LAWRENCE

A 7364/5

PREFACE

Some ten years have elapsed since this book first appeared, after being revised in 1963. It has been gratifying to learn that it has been well received. In this revision, the third, I have followed essentially the general format of the original work; namely, the analysis of certain behavior in terms of deviations from norms, the application of sociological and social psychological concepts and theory to deviant behavior, and the critical evaluation of nonsociological research and theories. Some revisions of textbooks constitute simply an updating of facts and the citation of more recent research articles. I do not agree with this idea of a "revision;" I believe it must also involve the incorporation of new ideas and the modification of old ones. Theoretical contributions are constantly being added to any scientific field, and an author must continually adjust his own thinking. In fact, the most difficult task in writing a textbook is the responsibility for judging the scientific relevance and validity of findings from available theoretical formulations and research, from articles, and from books, particularly newer ones. An author must not only incorporate some theories and reject others; he must also offer modifications and criticisms of them.

This third edition, then, constitutes a substantial revision. I have added chapters and dropped others. Three new chapters have been added on the sociology of the slum, a sociological discussion of the nature of poverty and the related theory of anomie, and a third chapter on deviant sex behavior. The number of chapters on delinquency and crime has been reduced from five to two, largely because some who have used previous editions have felt that there has been too much emphasis on this aspect of deviance. The discussion, however, has been thoroughly revised and strengthened; in doing so I have provided a more thorough analysis of types of criminal behavior which is in line with the present emphasis on typological analysis. The chapter on war and deviant behavior has been omitted largely because the material, derived for the most part from data from the Second World War, is now somewhat dated and because wars today seem more likely to be limited rather than total, which the discussion had assumed. Those who have found this chapter useful might wish to assign the material in the previous edition in the library.

Nearly all chapters have been thoroughly reorganized with the addition of new topics and the shifting of others. I have, for example, strengthened the discussion of norms. I have added considerable material on societal reaction and a critical analysis of theories built around it. I have also presented needed discussion of sources of data for studying deviant behavior. The chapter on drug addiction has been thoroughly revised to include recent research and developments in this area. The discussions of both the prevention and treatment of deviant behavior have been enlarged. In this connection, a more detailed study of the use of urban community development is included, emphasizing the stimulation of self-help—particularly in slum areas—if deviant behavior is to be effectively prevented and controlled.

In this revision, moreover, I have placed more emphasis on process in the analysis of deviant behavior and less on mere descriptions and isolated facts. In line with more recent developments in sociology, I have added considerable comparative material on deviant behavior from other societies. It is my hope that this addition will place a number of the issues presented in a wider perspective. My only regret is that more studies of deviant behavior in other societies are not presently available.

As the title indicates, this book presents a sociological approach to deviant behavior. It is written as a text for courses designated as "social disorganization," "social problems," "social pathology," "deviant behavior," or some similar term. I have tried to deal with certain deviations from social norms which encounter disapproval and to which theory and concepts derived from sociology and social psychology may be applied, and about which there is substantial sociological literature. Consequently, "social problems" primarily of concern to economics, political science, or public health are not taken up.

The book has been organized in three parts: Social Deviation, Deviant

Behavior, and Deviant Behavior and Social Control. Part I presents a general approach to social deviation, describing and defining various forms, and introducing a number of sociological and sociopsychological concepts. It also discusses the effects of contemporary urbanism, including particularly, the slum. In addition, various theories of deviant behavior which focus on the individual—the psychiatric, psychoanalytic, and personality trait explanations—are presented in the first part rather than throughout the book, thus avoiding repetition. Finally, there is a discussion and critical evaluation of the relation of poverty and anomie, particularly in relation to deviant behavior.

Part II presents a detailed analysis of a considerable number of forms of deviant behavior. In Part III, various types of proposed solutions to this behavior are dealt with at one time rather than after the analysis of each form of deviant behavior, so that the similarity of various approaches may be seen. Chapter 19, for example, deals with various group approaches, such as group therapy, and their application to such fields as alcoholism, mental disorder, drug addiction, and criminal behavior.

In Chapters 1 and 2, I have explained, in terms of deviant behavior, various concepts which are applied throughout the book. They have included social norms and values, subcultural groups, social differentiation, social structure, societal reaction, socialization, social status, self-conception, social roles, and the definition of the situation. In particular, I have stressed role theory. The wide use of these concepts is based on the premise that deviant behavior is social behavior, to which the same concepts can be applied in connection with *non*deviant behavior.

It is hoped that the opening chapters will help those who have not previously had an introductory course in sociology; for those who have, it will serve as a transition and review. It is possible that some courses may not include Chapter 2 as being superfluous and also omit Chapter 15, which deals with role status conflicts of old age, as not being exactly within the framework of deviant behavior, rather more of an analysis of a "social problem." All of the chapters end with a summary, and all conclude with an annotated list of selected readings. Extensive case material and personal documents are included throughout.

I have appreciated the help and suggestions of several persons who have read parts of the original or previous revision of the text, particularly Frank E. Hartung, Kingsley Davis, Arnold W. Green, Lyle W. Shannon, Simon Dinitz, Michael Hakeem, David Mechanic, Thomas J. Scheff, Eugene A. Friedmann, Orville G. Brim, Jr., Ersel E. LeMasters, Alfred Kadushin, Leslie A. Osborn, Donald W. Olmstead, Andrew L. Wade, and Torgny Segerstedt. For the third edition I should like particularly to express my appreciation to Harwin Voss, John C. Ball, and Donald R.

South for reading all or parts of the manuscript. I should like also to express appreciation to Alice Scudder who edited the first and second editions and who, at my personal request, was asked by the publishers to edit the third edition as well. Several graduate students have also furnished useful comments. I should like to acknowledge especially the help of my wife, Ruth, who has spent many long hours typing, retyping, and editing all editions of this book. She is one of those rare persons who, in carrying out many roles, makes it possible for college professors not only to teach and do research but also to write books.

Marshall B. Clinard
Madison, Wisconsin
March, 1968

CONTENTS

TABLES

Social Deviation

1

Social Deviation

Man's achievements in the area of social relationships have not equaled his achievements in physical science and technology. Within a few centuries, man has solved many of the mysteries of the world around him. His endeavors have progressed from the realm of folklore and magic to that of science. He has acquired an enormous amount of information about the earth, about life in all its forms, and even something about the vast areas of outer space. Scientific research today increasingly deals with such intricate problems as nuclear fission, electronics, changes in the human cell and control of the weather. This information has enabled him to build great dams and irrigation projects to prevent catastrophic floods and droughts and to open up marginal lands to cultivation. He has learned to control pestilence and many diseases so that his expected life span is greatly increased. In large parts of the Western world, at least, modern technical skills have provided food, clothing and shelter for most of the population. Man has even learned how to transplant the human heart.

Unfortunately these technological advances have not brought with them a comparable degree of conquest over man's problems of relationships with other persons. His success in social relationships generally has not approached his progress in dealing with his physical environment. Although the physical scientists have fathomed the very structure of energy and have made possible travel in outer space, man has been increasingly plagued with difficulties in his social relationships in cities and in the larger society.

Just as man has had to cope with mysticism and dogma in his understanding of the physical world, similar stumbling blocks have stood in his path as he has attempted to deal with problems in social relationships. Unscientific observations and theories of the behavior of man are as prevalent today as they were concerning the physical world in the medieval ages. Many falsely consider the behavior of man, his achievements as well as his problems, as a result of individual strength or individual perversity. The behavior of persons who constitute problems to themselves and to others is falsely attributed to individual biological weaknesses in inheritance, to feeble-mindedness, to body type, or even to racial origin, or is explained as the product of poverty or simply as the "moral" weakness of the individual.

Most people fail to realize that the scientific study of society, social behavior, and the social problems associated with them is fairly recent, though the basic discoveries which have culminated in the advances in the physical world go back many centuries. In fact, the basic knowledge for man's dramatic control of physical phenomena, resulting in the discovery of atomic energy, is the outcome of mathematical and other learnings accumulated over at least two thousand years. Until fifty to a hundred years ago scientific methods were applied for the most part to the physical world only, whereas human individual and group behaviors were chiefly subjects of philosophical and moral speculation. Scientific efforts in these areas have required the development of concepts and research tools for their study. Some of the more important concepts will be discussed briefly in the following sections.

SOCIETY AND GROUP RELATIONSHIPS

From birth man must depend upon other human beings. Physically and economically he is dependent on others for his survival; socially he relies on his fellow human beings for his personal development and his satisfactions. Man alone lives in true social groups. Like man, most animals form groups, and there may even be prolonged association, mutual dependence, and cooperation toward biologically common goals. The terms *society* or *social group*, however, can be applied to no animal other than man, for the ties which bind a human group together are not merely biological needs but abstract social relationships. Shared sets of common meanings or symbols, feelings of unity, and systems of mutual obligation characterize man's social groups. Some may attempt to read human counterparts into the life of other animals, but man alone has such social institutions as a political state, an economic system, and a religion. He alone has laws and moral judgments.

Social groups are more than simply a group or collection of persons. In a social group several persons are in interaction, there are social relationships among the persons, and, finally, there is a degree of consensus or concerted action. Social groups exist when there are *social relationships* among a number of persons. Social relationships, in turn, are a consequence of recurring or repeated *social interaction* between or among two or more persons. An individual, in his actions, takes into account what he considers to be the expectation of others, and his behavior, in turn, means that he expects others to act toward him in a certain way. These mutual expectations and a person's evaluation of them represent his *social role*, a term which will be more fully discussed in the following chapter.

> Sociology is the study of groups. There are many kinds of groups, and one inclusive way of conceiving of them is in terms of concerted action. . . . From birth to death each human being is a participant in a variety of groups, and neither he nor anything he does or experiences can be understood when separated from the fact of such participation. As John Donne so eloquently expressed it, "No man is an island, entire of itself." Human conduct is continually subject to social control. What one does often depends more upon the demands he imputes to other people than it does his own preferences.[1]

As a result of his group experiences, a human being becomes dependent on others. The importance of this dependence on groups, and man's need for human group relationships, can be demonstrated in situations where group contacts are removed. For example, prison officials have learned that solitary confinement, with its almost complete isolation from group relationships, is one of the most severe forms of punishment for any human being. A few days of this type of treatment usually will render the most defiant prisoner tractable. Admiral Byrd, the famous explorer of the Antarctic, voluntarily isolated himself for several months in uninhabited polar regions more that a hundred miles from the nearest human being of his expedition. He described his experiences of being alone and vividly showed how dependent the individual is on social groups when he is removed from such contacts.

> 10 P.M. Solitude is an excellent laboratory in which to observe the extent to which manners and habits are conditioned by others. My table manners are atrocious—in this respect I've slipped back hundreds of years; in fact, I have no manners whatsoever. If I feel like it, I eat with my

---

[1] Tamotsu Shibutani, *Society and Personality: An Interaction Approach to Social Psychology,* p. 61. © 1961. Prentice-Hall, Inc., Englewood Cliffs, N.J.

fingers, or out of a can, or standing up—in other words, whichever is easiest. What's left over, I just heave into the slop pail, close to my feet. Come to think of it, no reason why I shouldn't. It's rather a convenient way to eat; I seem to remember reading in Epicurus that a man living alone lives the life of a wolf.

A life alone makes the need for external demonstration almost disappear. Now I seldom cuss, although at first I was quick to open fire at everything that tried my patience. Attending to the electrical circuit on the anemometer pole is no less cold than it was in the beginning; but I work in soundless torment, knowing that the night is vast and profanity can shock no one but myself.

My sense of humor remains, but the only sources of it are my books and myself, and, after all, my time to read is limited. Earlier today, when I came into the hut with my water bucket in one hand and the lantern in the other, I put the lantern on the stove and hung up the bucket. I laughed at this; but, now when I laugh, I laugh inside; for I seem to have forgotten how to do it out loud. This leads me to think that audible laughter is principally a mechanism for sharing pleasure. . . . My hair hasn't been cut in months. I've let it grow because it comes down around my neck and keeps it warm. I still shave once a week—and that only because I found that a beard is an infernal nuisance outside on account of its tendency to ice up from the breath and freeze the face. Looking in the mirror this morning, I decided that a man without women around him is a man without vanity; my cheeks are blistered and my nose is red and bulbous from a hundred frostbites. How I look is no longer of the least importance; all that matters is how I feel. However, I have kept clean, as clean as I would keep myself at home. But cleanliness has nothing to do with etiquette or coquetry. It is comfort. My senses enjoy the evening bath and are uncomfortable at the touch of underwear that is too dirty.[2]

In social groups, as well as in the larger society, there are social structures involving systems of relationships among the members. Members have definite reciprocal rights and duties which are the result of each person's *social status* or social position. An individual's definition of the world around him depends largely on his social status, such as the class and subgroups to which he belongs. These interrelated status positions are based on such criteria as sex, age, race, family, and achievement. When status is based on one's position in the social structure at birth, regardless of personal attributes, it is referred to as *ascribed status*. When a person's social position is the product of achievement it is termed *achieved status*. In former times a person's status and role were clearly defined, and were largely fixed for life at the time of birth. In contemporary society it is possible that one's

---

[2] Richard E. Byrd, *Alone* (New York: G. P. Putnam's Sons, 1938), pp. 139–140. Reprinted by permission of the publishers.

position at birth can be much altered through achievement. Changes in statuses and roles may give rise to conflicts within the person as well as among groups, a situation we shall discuss frequently later.

Many people are as unaware of the great diversity and specialization among groups in modern society, and of the variations in their effects upon individual persons, as is a fish of the water around him. Groups, such as the neighborhood, village, or city, are based on physical proximity, and others, such as the family and larger groups of relatives, are based on kinship. Still others are based on congeniality, or on economic, technological, or other interests. The group nature of man is well indicated in Table 1.1, a list of groups based on interest.

Some social groups are informally organized and temporary, whereas others are highly formal and stable in their structure and in the specific duties and obligations of each member. The relatively permanent, stable, uniform, and formal manner in which social groups are interrelated produces what are termed *social institutions*. In addition, social institutions are generally distinguished by the fact that they encompass activities which are regarded as vital to certain ends, or as worthy in themselves by the society in which they exist.[3] For example, government, which is a social institution, is regarded as vital for the maintenance of order or peaceable relations in society. Other institutions include the family, and the economic, religious, and educational institutions. The *social structure of an institution* or other stable group consists of shared understandings concerning the duties and obligations of participants, the ways in which activities are to be carried out, the proper order of activities, ideas about what is desirable and undesirable or good and bad, and evaluations of the relative importance of the contributions of given participants and of the deference to be accorded by one participant to another. In addition, there are usually prescribed methods for recruiting participants, for training or indoctrinating them, and for expelling them.

Stated most simply, the social structure of an institution is merely the form in which group activities are to be carried out. However, the form is not "visible" or "tangible," but consists of systems of shared understandings in the minds of human beings as to their obligations, as in the case of the family. Changes in the specific functions and structures of institutions and in the relationship of one institution to another have an important bearing on social deviation. The stability of any society depends greatly on the functioning of its institutions and on their ability, through formal and informal means, to maintain social control.

---

[3] See George C. Homans, *Social Behavior: Its Elementary Forms* (New York: Harcourt, Brace & World, Inc., 1961), p. 5.

TABLE 1.1   **Social Groups Based on Interest**

Interests	*Groups*
Congeniality	Friendship groups Social clubs Taverns Purely social groups, boys' gangs, etc.
Economic interests	Corporations, partnerships Professional societies Associations of commerce Labor unions
Technological interests	Crafts Some athletic associations and teams Police departments
Religious interests	Churches Sects and other organizations
Aesthetic interests	"Schools" of painting, sculpture, literature, etc. Bands, orchestras, choirs, etc.
Intellectual interests (science, philosophy, the intellectual aspects of the humanities, etc.)	Research groups Learned societies
Educational interests	Schools Universities Study groups, etc.
Political interests	Political parties and machines Taxpayers' associations, etc.
Recreational interests	Philatelists' societies Yacht clubs Bridge clubs Some sports teams and clubs, etc.
Ameliorative interests	Charitable societies Community welfare organizations Alcoholics Anonymous Minority group associations, etc.

SOURCE: Adapted from John L. and John P. Gillin, *Cultural Sociology* (New York: The Macmillan Company, 1948), pp. 291–292. Some of these groups may arise through other factors than interests alone.

CULTURE AND SOCIAL NORMS

The concept of *culture* is closely related to the concept of social group, and others mentioned thus far, in that each of these concepts refers to phenomena which are constituted of the same basic social ingredients.[4] Culture may be distinguished from another concept, society, as involving primarily *normative standards* for conduct, rather than interaction and social relationships. Like society, culture arises out of the need of people to communicate about the meaning of things and to regulate social life. Culture is a system of symbols or meanings with three distinct properties. It is *transmittable, learned,* and *shared.* The fact that it is transmittable means that it is passed from one generation to another. The fact that it is learned means that it is not an innate or biological quality of persons, but that it is acquired and participated in by persons through association with others. The fact that it is shared means that there is a fair degree of consensus among a number of persons concerning what is proper and improper behavior, what meanings are to be attached to objects, situations, or events. It is only when such consensus exists that a group of persons can be said to be members of a "culture." Thus it is evident that culture has existed before the individual's birth and will continue, though probably with modifications, beyond his lifetime. It is more than merely a description of ways of acting. It is a system of standards and evaluations of how to act. Culture is a "blueprint for behavior," telling what a person must do, ought to do, should do, may do, and must not do.[5]

Social relationships and behavior are regulated through *social norms,* often referred to as standardized ways of acting, or expectations governing limits of variation in behavior. A norm is "any standard or rule that states what human beings should or should not think, say or do under given circumstances." [6] Such a view implies, first, that actual behavior may differ from the norm and, second, that it will differ from the norm unless some

---

[4] See Talcott Parsons, *The Social System* (New York: The Free Press, 1951), especially Chaps. 1 and 12.

[5] Robin M. Williams, Jr., *American Society* (New York: Alfred A. Knopf, Inc., 1954), pp. 22–23.

[6] Judith Blake and Kingsley Davis, "Norms, Values, and Sanctions," in Robert E. L. Faris, ed., *Handbook of Modern Sociology* (Chicago: Rand McNally & Company, 1964), p. 456. For a discussion of the role of norms see Torgny T. Segerstedt, *The Nature of Social Reality* (Totowa, N.J.: The Bedminster Press, 1966); Ephraim H. Mizruchi and Robert Perrucci, "Norm Qualities and Differential Effects of Deviant Behavior: An Exploratory Analysis," *American Sociological Review,* 27:391–399 (1962); and Williams, pp. 23–32.

force, such as a sanction, is imposed to bring about conformity. There is always room for the interpretation of norms; each norm has a history of what it means. The line of how and when behavior is to be interpreted as deviant or tolerated is always shifting according to public views and those of various groups.

Some social norms may be fairly widespread, whereas others are not. Some are temporary and some are fairly permanent. Some may have considerable force to support compliance with them, whereas others have very little. Many norms, but by no means all, are supported by a high degree of consensus and an intense reaction when violated. In every norm or rule there is the potentiality for deviance.[7]

Norms represent crucial mechanisms in the maintenance of order. They may be regarded either as ideal cultural norms or in terms of actual behavior in a statistical sense. One, for example, looks at sexual norms as cultural ideals or in terms of actual practices. Ideal cultural norms can be inferred from what people say or by observing what they support by sanctions in the form of rewards or penalties. "Cultural norms, as discovered by research, are statistical entities; that is, there is not a sharp line between normative and not normative, but a gradual shading from norms intensely supported by nearly everyone to those only casually accepted by relatively few." [8]

Norms may be classified according to the extent of knowledge, acceptance of the norm, the mode of enforcement of a given norm, the way the norm is transmitted, and the amount of conformity required by a given norm.[9] Cultural norms consist of technical or cognitive norms (for example, how to manufacture autos or how to make a cake), conventional norms (for example, etiquette), esthetic norms (for example, standards of taste and beauty), and moral norms (for example, laws forbidding murder, forcible rape, and so on).[10] Some are institutional norms, such as those regulating monogamy in the family, which are centered around a socially important complex of values and about which there is a high degree of obligation and permanence, as well as severe sanctions.

Moreover, the qualities of norms are important in any society; some have a definite quality of "ought" or "should," whereas others have a more permissive quality. Some of them are *proscriptive norms* in that the in-

---

[7] Albert K. Cohen, *Deviance and Control* (Englewood Cliffs, N.J.: Prentice-Hall, Inc., 1966), p. 4.

[8] Williams, p. 30.

[9] Richard T. Morris, "A Typology of Norms," *American Sociological Review*, 21:610–613 (1956).

[10] Williams, p. 25.

dividual is supposed to "not do this," that is, to avoid and desist from all forms of behavior such as those forbidden in the Ten Commandments. Others are *prescriptive norms* in that the individual is told to "do this or that," spelling out the forms of behavior to which a person must conform, such as the rules regarding the use of alcoholic beverages among Orthodox Jews. One study has shown that predominantly proscriptive norms are more likely than prescriptive norms to lead to extreme forms of reactions when deviation occurs.[11]

Social values are simply those things to which a society or cultural group attaches value, worth, or significance.[12] Social values are described by some as the goals or objectives of a given society or culture. They are not only shared; they are regarded as matters of collective welfare to which is often attached a high degree of emotional belief that they are important. The distinction between social norms and social values can be illustrated by the criminal law. Although criminal laws are simply legal norms regulating various types of behavior and are enforced by the coercion of the state, certain values or basic goals are involved in some of them. Murder, manslaughter, bigamy, rape, theft, and burglary are violations of legal norms, but the social values involved include the protection of human life, the protection of sexual and family life, and the protection of property.[13] Among the value orientations which Williams feels are the objectives of such a complex society, as, for example, American society, are achievement and success, activity and work, efficiency and practicality, progress, material comfort, humanitarianism, equality, nationalism-patriotism, and democracy and individual personality.[14]

Rarely are individuals consciously aware of the often arbitrary nature of the social norms and social values of a culture or subculture, for they are introduced to them in the ongoing process of living. Social norms are transmitted from one generation to another through groups, and each individual largely incorporates into his life organization the beliefs, ideas, and language of the groups to which he belongs. Men thus come to see the world around them not with their eyes alone, for if they did they would see the same things, but rather through their cultural and other group experiences. Even the moral judgments of man are not generally his alone, but those of the group or groups to which he belongs.

---

[11] Mizruchi and Perrucci, pp. 391–399.

[12] Homans, Chap. 3.

[13] Hermann Mannheim, *Criminal Justice and Social Reconstruction* (New York: Oxford University Press, 1946). He also included the values of protection against property, protection of labor, and protection against labor.

[14] Williams, pp. 388–442.

In the following passage Ellsworth Faris has brilliantly pointed out the significance of seeing the world through group experiences:

> For we live in a world of "cultural reality," and the whole furniture of earth and choir of heaven are to be described and discussed as they are conceived by men. Caviar is not a delicacy to the general. Cows are not food to the Hindu. Mohammed is not the prophet of God to me. To an atheist God is not God at all. Objects are not passively received or automatically reacted to; rather is it true that objects are the result of a successful attempt to organize experience.[15]

The process by which persons learn and incorporate cultural meanings and values is called *socialization*. The process of socialization continues throughout life. Rarely are individuals consciously aware of the often arbitrary nature of the social norms and social values of a culture, for they are introduced to them in the ongoing process of living. Social norms are transmitted from one generation to another through groups, and each individual largely incorporates into his life organization the beliefs, ideas, and language of the groups to which he belongs. Man develops a set of social norms and values as he develops a social environment, which consists of people with whom he comes into contact first in the family, then in his neighborhood and school, and later in his economic, religious, or educational groups, and his social class.[16]

SOCIAL DIFFERENTIATION AND SUBCULTURAL NORMS

An American child raised as a member of another culture, whether Eskimo, Chinese, or Hottentot, would adopt the norms and values of that culture, just as the immigrants to America adopted the more general norms and values of American culture. Similarly, a person in modern society tends to acquire the norms of those subcultural groups of which he is a part. Although a modern society has certain common norms and values, they may be differently regarded.[17] As one writer has stated, "Within such complex aggregates as modern nations many norms are effective only within limited subcultures, and there are wide differences in individual conformity and conceptions of normative structure." [18]

---

[15] Ellsworth Faris, *The Nature of Human Nature* (New York: McGraw-Hill Book Company, Inc., 1937), pp. 150–151.

[16] Muzafer Sherif, *The Psychology of Social Norms* (New York: Harper & Row, Publishers, 1936), p. 46.

[17] Frank E. Hartung, "Common and Discrete Values," *Journal of Social Psychology*, 38:3–22 (1953).

[18] Williams, p. 30.

Among more homogeneous peoples, such as primitive or folk societies, most norms and values are perceived in a somewhat similar, but by no means entirely so, way by various members of a society. Because of this fact members of the society come to share many common objectives and meanings. Modern societies are more complex and there is much *social differentiation*. In a highly differentiated society relatively distinct clutterings or groupings of persons will arise which have in common some socially assigned attribute or quality. Social clusterings arise around such attributes as race, occupation, ethnic background, religion, political party, residence, and many others. Modern societies are greatly differentiated by social class and into age or peer groups, into thousands of different occupational groups, often into a large number of religious groups, and even into rather distinct regional and neighborhood groups.

So diverse are the subcultural norms of most large societies that there are probably only a few norms which are accepted as binding on *all* persons. Sometimes social groupings which arise in the manner described may develop and share a set of values and meanings which are distinctive to some degree from the values and meanings shared by the society of which they are a part. When this occurs such a group may be called a *subculture*. A subculture is, simply speaking, a "culture within a culture." This implies that the subcultural group participates in and shares the "larger" culture of which it is a part, but also shares some meanings and values which are unique. A subculture is not necessarily in opposition to the larger culture, although some have suggested this in the term *contraculture*.[19] Some conflict may, however, arise between it and the larger culture.

Subcultural deviation has been referred to by Lemert as *systematic deviation* when group ties exist and there is communication of practices, rapport, and common rationalizations among deviants.[20] Systematic group deviation makes it possible to diffuse behavior in a way that individual deviants cannot do.

> Systematic deviation appears as a subculture or as a behavior system, accompanied by a special social organization and formalized status, roles,

[19] J. Milton Yinger, "Contra-Culture and Sub-Culture," *American Sociological Review*, 25:625–635 (1960). For a critical discussion and review of the general literature dealing with the concepts of subculture and contraculture, see Marvin E. Wolfgang and Franco Ferracuti, *The Subculture of Violence: Towards an Integrated Theory in Criminology* (London: Tavistock Publications, 1967).

[20] Edwin M. Lemert, *Social Pathology* (New York: McGraw-Hill Book Company, Inc., 1951), p. 44. He distinguishes systematic deviation from those that are individual or situational and cumulative situational. In the latter one may have considerable deviation, such as stealing towels from hotels, without communication between those who steal.

morals, and morale distinct from the larger culture. A definite profession-alization of conduct by deviant group members develops, along with craft pride similar to that found among integrated occupational groups. Informal and formal social controls function to induce conformity by the "deviant deviants" within the group. In other words, all the characteristics of any social group are present, the chief conditioning factors of the behavior system being the degree of deviation in the core behavior, the amount of differentiation of the deviants, and the extent and nature of the disapproving societal reaction to them.[21]

Large modern societies consist of a variety of subcultures and social groups, each often with its own set of norms and values not only as to what constitutes proper conduct but also even as to the goals of life itself. Cohen has suggested that subcultures emerge in a highly differentiated society when, in effective interaction with one another, a number of persons have similar problems.[22] Sociological research has shown the existence of pronounced differences in normative structures of subcultures involving persons of different age groups, social classes, occupations, racial, religious, and ethnic groups, neighborhoods, and regions. In addition, there are some even more limited subcultures such as those among teenage gangs, prostitutes, alcoholics, drug addicts, homosexuals, and professional and organized criminals. Institutions for the treatment of deviants, such as prisons and mental hospitals, may develop subcultures with their own social systems.

The norms and values of *peer groups*—persons of similar generations or ages—may also differ considerably. For example, a peer group, such as teenagers in modern urban societies, often has standards of conduct and even goals which are quite different from those of other peer or age groups, and these may lead to misunderstandings and conflicts. The teenage sub-culture is characeried by particular norms of dress, music, language, ways of regarding society and adults, and recreation.[23] Sometimes stealing, car

---

[21] From *Social Pathology*, p. 44, by Edwin M. Lemert. Copyright 1951 by McGraw-Hill Book Company. Used by permission of McGraw-Hill Book Company.

[22] See, for example, Albert K. Cohen, *Delinquent Boys: The Culture of the Gang* (New York: The Free Press, 1955), p. 59. While Cohen discussed this theory of the origin of subcultures primarily in connection with delinquent gangs, a more appropriate illustration might be the emergence of the subcultures of the "beatniks" and "hippies" of the 1960s. See Ned Polsky, *Hustlers, Beats, and Others* (Chicago: Aldine Publishing Company, 1967). See also Fred Davis, "Why All of Us May Be Hippies Someday" and Bennett M. Berger, "Hippie Morality—More Old Than New," in *Trans-Action*, 5:10–19 (1967).

[23] See, for example, "The Teen-Age Culture," *The Annals*, Vol. 338 (1961), for a description of the characteristic norms of teenagers in our culture as well as those of teenagers in Europe. There is also a discussion of the Italian-American,

theft, illegal sexual behavior and vandalism become accepted norms among certain parts of the teenage subculture.

Racial and religious discrimination may be greater in one part of a society than in another, depending on subcultural regional norms. Neighborhoods in the larger American cities often have distinct behavioral norms and values. The social norms and values in one neighborhood may contribute to the development in teenage boys of stealing as forms of recreation and status, whereas in another the norms and values may encourage teenage participation in scouting programs and similar community-directed youth activities which lead toward nondelinquent behavior. Neighborhood norms may define policemen in one area as "enemies" and in the other as symbols of respect for law. Similarly, prostitutes, professional criminals, drug addicts, organized criminals, and similar groups may have a series of social norms and values distinct from those of the larger society. An understanding of this condition of highly differentiated and often conflicting norms as part of the way "modern" societies are organized is essential to a meaningful analysis of social deviation. A set of norms is not always supported in the same way by different subcultural groups. Even groups of deviants have their own sets of norms as to what constitutes moral behavior and deviations within their groups. Such rules which result in "deviant deviants" are found, for example, among professional thieves, [24] among members of Alcoholics Anonymous, [25] and among drug addicts.

> In common with normal groups, deviant groups have morals and a morale of their own. The morals of deviant groups tend to be segmental and specialized rather than generally differentiated from those of other groups. As in normal groups it is possible to mark out a range of norms, embracing positive cultural compulsives, a spread or area of permissive behaviors, and at the other end of the hypothetical continuum a cluster of increasingly strong taboos. It is important to note that the mores of the deviant group overlap and coincide at many points with the mores of groups having more acceptable general status in the community. For example, professional shoplifters apparently have taboos against the use of narcotics which are at least as strong as, if not stronger than, those found

---

Jewish, and Negro teenage cultures. See also James S. Coleman, *The Adolescent Society* (New York: The Free Press, 1961). See, too, David Gottlieb and Charles Ramsey, *The American Adolescent* (Homewood, Ill.: The Dorsey Press, Inc., 1964); and T. R. Fyvel, *Troublemakers: Rebellious Youth in An Affluent Society* (New York: Schocken Books, 1962).

[24] Edwin H. Sutherland, *The Professional Thief* (Chicago: University of Chicago Press, 1937).

[25] Irving Peter Gellman, *The Sober Alcoholic* (New Haven, Conn.: College and University Press, 1964).

among law-abiding groups. The rationalizations for this common morality, of course, differ in the former case, the argument against using drugs is that a member of the organization when he is arrested can be forced too easily to divulge information if he is deprived of his narcotics by the police.[26]

There is a tendency for diversity of norms between groups to increase in a highly differentiated society. Often groups in such a society do not develop norms which are radically different from one another; the norms simply differ in emphasis. Nevertheless, if a person belongs to a number of groups in such a society, and if each group either holds different norms or emphasizes them differently, considerable personal conflict may ensue. The norms and social roles a person secures from the family group may not necessarily always agree with the norms and social roles of the play group, age or peer group, work group, or political group. Certain groups may become more important to an individual's life organization than others and, consequently, he may tend to conform to the norms of the groups with which he is more closely identified. The family, although important, is only one of many groups which may be related to a person's behavior, whether deviant or nondeviant. Among other important sources of norms and social relationships are social class, occupational, neighborhood, schools, and religious groups, and the gang or clique.

All this means three things: (1) that within a modern society there may be almost as pronounced differences among various groups about the norms of accepted behavior as there are between large cultures; (2) that to explain logically how members of certain deviant subgroups in a society come to act the way they do can be explained in the same way, for example, that an Eskimo becomes culturally an Eskimo; and (3) that even when we speak of the norms of a given family we are likely to be referring actually to the social class, occupational, or some other subcultural group to which the family belongs.

SOCIAL STRATIFICATION AND DEVIANT BEHAVIOR

Modern societies are socially differentiated in many ways: probably none is greater than the variations in behavior among the social classes in a society. Social class can be viewed as a hierarchical system by which large groups of families in society are ranked into lower, middle, and upper classes, according to a social position of inferiority, equality, or superiority.

---

[26] From *Social Pathology*, p. 49, by Edwin M. Lemert. Copyright 1951 by McGraw-Hill Book Company. Used by permission of McGraw-Hill Book Company.

Ranks may be based on six levels of stratification: prestige, occupation, possessions, interaction, class consciousness, and value orientations.[27] Studies of class structure have shown how value orientations, patterns of family life, and behavior in general not only represent but actually integrate class ways of life.

So different are the social norms and other behavior of, for example, American social classes, that these differences are probably actually greater than those between members of the same social class but, say, from some other Western European or even Asiatic societies. The norms of longshoremen, for example, may differ markedly from those of doctors or professors. Kinsey and others, for example, have shown the existence of great class differences in sex behavior and even in the nature of the sex relation itself. Studies by Green,[28] Davis,[29] and others have shown that even family rearing patterns of the lower and middle classes are greatly different. The use of physical punishment, for example, is an acceptable form of disciplining children in lower-class families. The middle-class boy is more likely to be whipped if he fights; the lower-class boy, if he does not or if he loses. Studies have shown great differences in the norms, behavior, and family structure of teenage youth by social class.[30] The norms and values of the middle class and the lower class have been characterized in the studies by Miller and Cohen.

Although a useful characterization of general lower-class norms and values, particularly in larger cities, there are great variations within these broad categories. The way of life of many lower-class families resembles, to some extent, working-class norms and values. In fact, Sydney Miller has suggested, using family stability and job security, that there are four types of the lower class.[31] Moreover, the lower class should not be confused with the working or "blue-collar" class.[32] This group, consisting of skilled and semi-

---

[27] Joseph A. Kahl, *The American Class Structure* (New York: Holt, Rinehart and Winston, Inc., 1957), pp. 8–13.

[28] Arnold W. Green, "The Middle-Class Male Child and Neurosis," *American Sociological Review*, 11:31–41 (1946).

[29] Kingsley Davis, "Mental Hygiene and the Social Structure," in Arnold Rose, ed., *Mental Health and Mental Disorder* (New York: W. W. Norton & Company, Inc., 1955).

[30] August B. Hollingshead, *Elmtown's Youth* (New York: John Wiley & Sons, Inc., 1949). Also see Coleman.

[31] Sydney M. Miller, "The American Lower Class: A Typological Approach," *Social Research*, 31:1–22 (1964).

[32] Herbert J. Gans, *The Urban Villagers: Group and Class in the Life of Italian-Americans* (New York: The Free Press, 1962), pp. 229–262.

skilled workers, has more stability of employment, although the orientation may be largely toward "getting by." Family life plays a more important role as does educational improvement; deviant behavior is likely to be less.

Lower Class (Miller)	*Middle Class* (Cohen)
Concern with "trouble" involving official authorities or agencies of middle-class society	Cultivation of manners and courtesy
Toughness, such as physical prowess, masculinity, fearlessness, bravery, daring	Control over physical aggression
Ability to outsmart others and to gain money by "wits"	Respect for property of others
Excitement of thrills, risk, and danger	Desire for wholesome recreation
Belief that people are favored by fate, fortune, and luck	Ambition; postponement of immediate goals for long-time objectives
Resentment of external controls of authority but at the same time dependence on them	Individual responsibilty

SOURCES: Walter B. Miller, "Lower Class Culture as a Generating Milieu of Gang Delinquency," *Journal of Social Issues,* 14:5–19, No. 3 (1958); and Albert K. Cohen, *Delinquent Boys: The Culture of the Gang* (New York: The Free Press, 1955), pp. 88–91.

Much of the research on social stratification has directly or indirectly contributed to the understanding of deviant behavior. There are great differences in the incidence and nature of different types of *reported* deviant behavior by social class.[33] Behavior may be approved in one class and disapproved in another. Class status may represent, for the individual, different neighborhood norms and different patterns of interpersonal relations, particularly between parents and children. The greater incidence and effects of more serious juvenile delinquency, such as burglary and robbery, among the lower class have been shown in many sociological studies.[34] Other types of less serious delinquency appear to be increasingly common among the mid-

---

[33] In fact, on the basis of these differences one theory of deviant behavior, anomie, has been advanced by Robert Merton. This theory will be discussed in Chapter 5.

[34] See, for example, Terence Morris, *The Criminal Area: A Study in Social Ecology* (London: Routledge and Kegan Paul, Ltd., 1957). Also see Albert J. Reiss, Jr., and Albert Lewis Rhodes, "The Distribution of Juvenile Delinquency in the Social Class Structure," *American Sociological Review,* 26:720–732 (1961); and Lee N. Robins, Harry Gyman, and Patricia O'Neal, "The Interaction of Social Class and Deviant Behavior," *American Sociological Review,* 27:480–492 (1962).

dle class.[35] The type and nature of sex offenses by juveniles appears to be related to social class.[36] Nearly all crimes of violence, such as murder and forcible rape, are committed by lower class adults, and the nature of lower class subculture seems to offer an explanation. Prostitution appears to be consistently more prevalent among the lower classes. The more overt types of crime, such as burglary, are rare among members of the middle and upper classes, who become more often involved in types of crimes to which the term *white-collar crime* has been applied. Sociological studies have shown the existence of wide-scale violations of law by persons in the upper and middle classes, politicians, government officials, businessmen, labor union leaders, doctors, and lawyers.[37]

Probably in no area have social class differences been reported to be shown more pronounced than in the area of mental disorder. Schizophrenia, a common form of mental disorder, has been reported as being nine times more prevalent among those of the lowest social class.[38] There were even class differences in the type of the neuroses. The incidence of suicide is related to occupation and social class, usually being highest at the two extremes, the poor and the well-to-do. This has been established by several studies, including Sainsbury's study of London suicides.[39]

SOCIAL DEVIATION AND SOCIETAL REACTION

Deviations grow out of rules or norms of a society. Each society has sets of norms and variations in attitudes toward deviation from various normative rules. Reactions to deviations from social norms can vary in the direction of approval, tolerance, or disapproval. Modern societies encourage a certain amount of nonconformity, provided it is in an approved direction. Deviations which society approves may be rewarded by admiration, prestige, money, or other symbols. Some deviations in the form of new mechanical

---

[35] Edmund W. Vaz, ed., *Middle-Class Juvenile Delinquency* (New York: Harper & Row, Publishers, 1967).

[36] Albert J. Reiss, Jr., "Sex Offenses: The Marginal Status of the Adolescent," *Law and Contemporary Problems,* 25:309–334 (1960).

[37] Edwin H. Sutherland, *White Collar Crime* (New York: Holt, Rinehart and Winston, Inc., reissue 1960) and Marshall B. Clinard, *The Black Market: A Study of White Collar Crime* (New York: Holt, Rinehart and Winston, Inc., 1952).

[38] August B. Hollingshead and Frederick Redlich, *Social Class and Mental Illness* (New York: John Wiley & Sons, Inc., 1958). Also see Jerome K. Myers and Bertram H. Roberts, *Family and Class Dynamics in Mental Illness* (New York: John Wiley & Sons, Inc., 1959).

[39] Peter Sainsbury, *Suicide in London* (London: Chapman & Hall, Ltd., 1955).

inventions, new styles in architecture, painting, literature, music, and fashions may, on occasion, meet with general approval. Approved deviations may also include behavior which is more industrious, ambitious, pious, patriotic, brave, or honest than is called for by the norms of a particular situation. Everyone is supposed to be a careful driver, for example, but rewards are sometimes given for the driver who has never had an accident over a long period of years. A certain degree of heroism is expected of everyone, civilian or soldier alike, but medals or other forms of recognition are given to soldiers, and occasionally to civilians, who are particularly heroic and risk their own lives.

In general, however, a society is probably more concerned with punishing with sanctions disapproved deviations from norms than with rewarding compliance with norms.[40] Deviations may be reacted to with varying degrees of disapproval. What specific behavior is disapproved and the point at which disapproval will be expressed depend largely on the content of the norms of the given society in question. Deviations which are disapproved may be reacted to with disgust, anger, hate, gossip, isolation, and ostracism, or even physical punishment. Deviations from orthodox political and religious thinking, approved sexual behavior, or certain legal codes may encounter strong disapproval.

Generally speaking, the norms of a given society or group may be known not only by observing what people do, but by observing when and how sanctions, both positive and negative, are applied. "Social groups create deviance by making the rules whose infraction constitutes deviance." [41] It is by observing what behavior is socially punished that we learn what behavior is disapproved and is therefore in violation of the norms. By observing what behavior is socially rewarded, or esteemed, we learn what behavior more nearly expresses the ideals embodied in the norms. Thus it is by observing the operations of sanctions, or in other words, *social control,* that we can infer the nature and the limits of acceptable and nonacceptable behavior implicit in given norms.

What constitutes social deviation is not something universal or "natural" but varies according to what a society wishes to make rules about. Behavior which is disapproved at one time may later become approved. This implies that ideas of what is proper or improper normative behavior may

---

[40] Jack P. Gibbs, "Sanctions," *Social Problems,* 14:147–159 (1966).

[41] Howard S. Becker, *Outsiders: Studies in the Sociology of Deviance* (New York: The Free Press, 1963), p. 9. Becker describes the forces and groups, for example, in the United States that were behind the enactment of the 1937 federal law making it a crime to sell or possess marihuana.

change. Over the years scientists who have challenged traditional beliefs have been scorned, ridiculed, ostracized, or even punished. Copernicus, Galileo, and many others who were regarded as deviants in their day would undoubtedly be regarded today with the same approval as was accorded Einstein. Within comparatively recent times there was strong disapproval of women's smoking, drinking alcoholic beverages, particularly in public, using make-up, wearing one-piece bathing suits, or engaging in political activity. Many religious offenses of various types, such as engaging in recreation on the Sabbath, were formerly considered crimes. Professional boxing matches or "prize fights" were generally a criminal offense during most of the nineteenth century in the United States. New York, for example, did not legalize prize fighting until 1896 and subsequently changed the law several times so that present legalization of professional fighting actually dates from as late as 1920.

> It was a crime in Iceland in the Viking age for a person to write verses about another, even if the sentiment was complimentary, if the verses exceeded four strophes in length. A Prussian law of 1784 prohibited mothers and nurses from taking children under two years of age into their beds. The English villein in the fourteenth century was not allowed to send his son to school, and no one lower than a freeholder was permitted by law to keep a dog. The following have at different times been crimes: printing a book, professing the medical doctrine of circulation of the blood, driving with reins, [selling] coins to foreigners, having gold in the house, buying goods on the way to market or in the market for the purpose of selling them at a higher price, writing a check for less than $1.00. On the other hand, many of our present laws were not known to earlier generations—quarantine laws, traffic laws, sanitation laws, factory laws.[42]

This means, of course, that the norms which define deviant behavior are not necessarily the same in various cultures, nor are they the same in a given culture over a period of time. Homosexual behavior, prostitution, or drunkenness does not constitute deviant behavior in some societies today. Some Scandinavian countries, for example, have such different interpretations of sexual norms that many delinquent and criminal acts in American society would not be regarded as such there. Changed attitudes in the United States over the past fifty years toward tobacco smoking by juveniles are an indication of how normative standards can be redefined in time.

---

[42] Reprinted by permission from *Principles of Criminology*, p. 16, by Edwin H. Sutherland and Donald R. Cressey, published by J. B. Lippincott Company, Copyright © 1924, 1960, 1966 by J. B. Lippincott Company.

Formerly there was great preoccupation with smoking among juveniles, laws were passed forbidding it, and often were strictly enforced. Smoking was thought to be related to a variety of other social problems.

Deviations vary in the *intensity* of the reaction to the deviation, as well as in the *direction* of approval or disapproval. Some deviations from norms in a society are not only approved but encouraged. Likewise, disapproved deviations may encounter various degrees of sanction, varying all the way from a certain amount of tolerance to mild and even strong disapproval. Certain behavior of the "idle rich," of actors, musicians, and artists, or of extreme religious sects, although not approved, may be tolerated. Deviations from norms of politeness, dress, table manners, and cleanliness, as well as the telling of risqué stories in public may encounter mild disapproval in the form of ridicule or scorn. Lying and malicious gossip may be more strongly disapproved, while certain behavior, such as murder, burglary, and robbery, may be punished by the political state through fine, imprisonment, or even death.

Norms have varying degrees of strength, or "resistance potential," in the event of a disapproved deviation from them, "a power which may be measured in degrees of what the group regards as the severity of the sanction." [43] Each norm can be thought of as having a *tolerance limit,* that is, the ratio between violations of the norm and a society's willingness to tolerate it or suppress it.[44] Deviations from sexual norms, for example, have different tolerance limits, depending on the society. Over the centuries, prostitution has been approved, tolerated, or disapproved, depending on cultural norms. Today in many European, Latin American, African, and Asian countries prostitution may be illegal; but is not actively suppressed. Some communities in the United States tolerate prostitution by ignoring its presence and by not fully enforcing the laws; other communities may take a strong position and attempt to wipe it out. The concept of "tolerance limit" is in some respects, however, misleading, for it implies a definite and absolute point at which norm violations will involve a reaction. Actually the relation between norm violation and the societal reaction is not as simple as this and may depend on the nature of the situation or on the social status of the deviant.

One study, using 180 subjects selected by a quota formula to produce variation in age, sex, education, occupation, religion, race, and census region, has thrown light on the societal reaction as seen through public

---

[43] Thorsten Sellin, "Culture Conflict and Crime" (Bulletin 41; New York: Social Science Research Council, 1938), p. 34.

[44] Courtland C. Van Vechten, "The Tolerance Quotient as a Device for Defining Certain Social Concepts," *American Journal of Sociology,* 46:35–44 (1940).

stereotypes to various forms of deviant behavior.[45] Such a large range of behavior was regarded as deviant that one conclusion was that "there may be only one sense in which deviants are alike: very simply the fact that some social audience regards them and treats them as deviant." [46] To the question "What is deviant?" the most frequent response was "Homosexuals" followed closely by "Drug addicts" and "Alcoholics," and then dropping sharply to "Prostitutes" and "Murderers."

TABLE 1.2   **Most Frequent Responses to the Question "What Is Deviant?"**

Response	*Percent*
Homosexuals	49
Drug addicts	47
Alcoholics	46
Prostitutes	27
Murderers	22
Criminals	18
Lesbians	13
Juvenile delinquents	13
Beatniks	12
Mentally ill	12
Perverts	12
Communists	10
Atheists	10
Political extremists	10

SOURCE: J. L. Simmons, "Public Stereotypes of Deviants," *Social Problems*, 13:224 (1965). Reprinted by permission of The Society for the Study of Social Problems.

SOCIETAL REACTION AND THE DEVIANT LABEL

The reaction of society to an act that results in a person's being labeled as a deviant is an important process in understanding the nature of deviant behavior. A crime is not made by the act itself but by society's reaction to the act; society holds against a man not the crime but the fact that he has been imprisoned.[47] To illustrate the effect of societal reaction in giving the deviant a label, imagine a possible classroom situation. If a student were to admit publicly that he had stolen a car or had committed a burglary but

---

[45] J. L. Simmons, "Public Stereotypes of Deviants," *Social Problems,* 13:223–232 (1965).

[46] Simmons, p. 225.

[47] The first statement is attributed to Gabriel Tarde, the French sociologist and criminologist; the second was made by Edwin H. Sutherland, the American criminologist.

that nothing had happened or the act was never known, the reaction by the others to such an admission would be different from the reaction to his admitting the act and then adding that he had been placed on probation for two years or sent to jail or to prison. The act would have been the same, but others would be reacting to the official labeling of deviance by society. In fact, official apprehension for one deviant act may mean that an individual will be regarded as deviant or will be regarded as displaying other undesirable characteristics.

Much of what has been said about delinquency and crime applies as well to becoming known as one who has been committed to a mental hospital, arrested for the use of drugs or committed to a drug treatment center, or arrested or "known" as a homosexual. The consequences of labeling are not always the same, but in general they can make the deviant act assume a greater importance to the individual than the mere act itself. Labeling as a deviant can transform the "offender" into what Cohen has termed a "deviant character." [48]

By emphasizing the label one shifts from an interest in how deviant behavior originates to the problem of societal reaction that is "attached to persons and the effective consequences of such attachments for subsequent deviation on the part of the person." [49] The official labeling of the deviant as delinquent, criminal, homosexual, drug addict, prostitute, or "insane" may have serious consequences for further deviation. The label, once attached, sets off a further sequence of events leading to subsequent deviation. If we designate the initial act, such as an act of prostitution, as primary deviation, we are likely to get a spiraling effect leading to a deviant career:

> (1) primary deviation; (2) social penalties; (3) further primary deviation; (4) stronger penalties and rejection; (5) further deviation, perhaps with hostilities and resentment beginning to focus upon those doing the penalizing; (6) crisis reached in the tolerance quotient, expressed in formal action by the community stigmatizing of the deviant; (7) strengthening of the deviant conduct as a negative reaction to the stigmatizing and penalties; (8) ultimate acceptance of deviant social status and efforts at adjustment on the basis of the associated role.[50]

Labeling a person as a "deviant" in a general sense may result in a "self-fulfilling prophecy"; because he is labeled a deviant he continues in acts of deviance, and develops a deviant career or becomes a secondary de-

---

[48] Cohen, *Deviance and Control.*

[49] Edwin M. Lemert, *Human Deviance, Social Problems and Social Control* (Englewood Cliffs, N.J.: Prentice-Hall, Inc., 1967), p. 17.

[50] From *Social Pathology*, p. 77, by Edwin M. Lemert. Copyright 1951 by McGraw-Hill Book Company. Used by permission of McGraw-Hill Book Company.

viant.[51] It sets in motion a process which tends to shape the individual into the image people have of him. He tends to be cut off from participation in conventional groups and he moves into an organized deviant group.

> In the first place, one tends to be cut off, after being identified as deviant, from participation in more conventional groups, even though the specific consequences of the particular deviant activity might never of themselves have caused the isolation had there not also been the public knowledge and reaction to it. For example, being a homosexual may not affect one's ability to do office work, but to be known as a homosexual in an office may make it impossible to continue working there. Similarly, though the effects of opiate drugs may not impair one's working ability, to be known as an addict will probably lead to losing one's job. In such cases, the individual finds it difficult to conform to other rules which he had no intention or desire to break, and perforce finds himself deviant in these areas as well. The homosexual who is deprived of a "respectable" job by the discovery of his deviance may drift into unconventional, marginal occupations where it does not make so much difference. The drug addict finds himself forced into other illegitimate kinds of activity, such as robbery and theft, by the refusal of respectable employers to have him around.[52]

> A final step in the career of a deviant is movement into an organized deviant group. . . . Moving into an organized deviant group has several consequences for the career of the deviant. First of all, deviant groups tend, more than deviant individuals, to be pushed into rationalizing their position. . . . The second thing that happens when one moves into a deviant group is that he learns how to carry on his deviant activity with a minimum of trouble. All the problems he faces in evading enforcement of the rule he is breaking have been faced before by others. . . . Thus, the deviant who enters an organized and institutionalized deviant group is more likely than ever before to continue in his ways. He has learned, on the one hand, how to avoid trouble and, on the other hand, a rationale for continuing.[53]

DEVIANT BEHAVIOR

There are several ways of looking at and defining deviant behavior. One is a *statistical* definition, namely, that deviant behavior constitutes variations from the average. The difficulty with this is that it can lead to some confusing conclusions if, for example, the majority are found to be deviants. Others have tried to define deviant behavior as a *pathological* phenom-

---

[51] See the discussion on pages 69–72.
[52] Becker, p. 34.
[53] Becker, pp. 37–39.

enon something on the order of a universal disease or an "unhealthy" deviation from some assumed universal norm of behavior. Those who take this view regard most deviations as some form of "mental illness" or psychological disorder. Consequently, starting with a few behaviors, the concept of mental illness and therefore deviations has been broadened by some to include "anything and everything in which they could detect any sign of malfunctioning, based on no matter what norm . . . Homosexuality is illness because heterosexuality is the social norm. Divorce is illness because it signals failure of marriage." [54] Likewise, delinquency and crime have all been regarded as "illness" or "pathological." This approach is invalid, first, because norms are relative and there are few norms whose violation can be universal. Deviant behavior is not an illness in the physiological sense but a violation of social norms.[55]

Starting with the correct assumption that societal reaction and labeling often have important consequences for subsequent deviant behavior, others, particularly Becker,[56] Erikson,[57] and Kitsuse,[58] have defined deviation exclusively in terms of the *effects of labeling*. In this definition acts can be identified as deviant only in reference to the reaction to them by society and its agents of social control. Viewed in these terms deviant behavior does not arise from some natural inherent quality of the act a person commits. Rather, according to Becker, it is a "consequence of the application by others of rules and sanctions to an 'offender.' The deviant is one to whom the label has successfully been applied; deviant behavior is behavior that people so label." [59] To constitute deviant behavior an act must first be known to others and second be reacted to by formal, or sometimes informal, agencies of social control. "A sociological theory of deviance must focus specifically upon the interactions which not only define behaviors as deviant but also organize and activate the application of sanctions by individuals, groups, or agencies." [60] In this connection the same writer has stated that "forms of deviant behavior *per se* do not differentiate deviants from non-deviants; it is the responses of the conventional and conforming members

---

[54] This statement is from a criticism of this view by Thomas Szasz, *The Myth of Mental Illness* (New York: Paul B. Hoeber, Inc., 1961), p. 45.

[55] This approach is discussed in more detail on pages 174–175.

[56] Becker, *Outsiders,* and his *The Other Side: Perspectives on Deviance* (New York: The Free Press, 1964).

[57] Kai T. Erikson, *Wayward Puritans: A Study in the Sociology of Deviance* (New York: John Wiley & Sons, Inc., 1966).

[58] John I. Kitsuse, "Societal Reaction to Deviant Behavior: Problems of Theory and Method," in Becker, *The Other Side,* pp. 87–102.

[59] Becker, *Outsiders,* p. 9.

[60] Kitsuse, p. 101.

of the society who identify and interpret behavior as deviant which sociologically transform persons into deviants." [61]

Deviant behavior, however, cannot be defined in such a limited or exclusive way as "behavior that people so label." (1) Such an emphasis shifts us away from norms and their violation to the problem of how they are reacted to, which is a subsidiary question. It does not explain why some person commits a given act and others do not; the fact that some persons encounter reactions to their deviation does not explain why they committed the acts in the first place. (2) There is admittedly little concern in the definition for the factors that account for deviation. Consequently the contention that deviation is produced by the character of reactions to certain acts does not explain the fact that the incidence of deviant behavior varies by the characteristics of population. "If two populations have the same legal and social definition of armed robbery and even if instances of the crime are reacted to in exactly the same way, it is still possible for the armed robbery rate to be much higher in one population than in the other." [62] (3) Societal reaction and labeling alone does not always mean that persons automatically continue or progress in deviation. Persons, after societal reaction, may reassess their behavior and alter it, as do a large proportion of women shoplifters who, when apprehended and labeled as "thieves," are likely to discontinue further deviants acts.[63] In other cases labeling may be interpreted by some deviants as helpful interventions, by others as a temporary reaction, and by some as a permanent punishment reaction. (4) Persons may continue committing deviant acts, such as homosexual behavior, without ever having been apprehended; in cases of other deviant acts they may even increase in seriousness, as in the case of mental disorder, without strong societal reaction. (5) Finally, the writers who have adopted this definition are not clear as to how much societal reaction constitutes effective labeling, in other words, how harsh must the reaction be to label or define a person as a deviant. One might ask if labeling is to be by formal agencies and if so how severe to penalty (arrest, imprisonment, and so on) and whether informal controls, such as family and neighborhood reactions, also have an effect. Those who define deviant behavior in this manner "have not specified what kind of reaction identifies behavior as deviant.[64] Commenting on this ap-

---

[61] Kitsuse, p. 97. Also see Kai T. Erikson, "Notes on the Sociology of Deviance," *Social Problems,* 9:308 (1962).

[62] Jack P. Gibbs, "Conceptions of Deviant Behavior: The Old and the New," *Pacific Sociological Review,* 9:12 (1966).

[63] See, for example, Mary Owen Cameron, *The Booster and the Snitch: Department Store Shoplifting* (New York: The Free Press, 1964).

[64] Gibbs, p. 12.

proach, another has stated that "with a few notable exceptions, there has been remarkably little explicit investigation of public attitudes toward deviant behavior." [65]

Deviant behavior is essentially violation of certain types of group norms; a deviant act is behavior which is proscribed in a certain way. It cannot be satisfactorily defined in either statistical, pathological, or labeling terms. Societal reaction leading to labeling is an important aspect in the study of deviant behavior, but it is a contingent and unnecessary element in a definition.

Obviously, deviations from norms which are tolerated or which provoke only mild disapproval are of little concern to a society. *Only those deviations in which behavior is in a disapproved direction, and of sufficient degree to exceed the tolerance limit of the community, constitute* deviant behavior *as it will be used here.*[66] This includes such deviations from norms as delinquency and crime, prostitution, homosexual behavior, drug addiction, alcoholism, mental disorders, suicide, marital and family maladjustment, discrimination against minority groups, and, to a lesser degree, role problems of old age.[67] Obviously the extent and the degree of disapproval in a particular instance are dependent on the nature of the situation and the community's degree of tolerance of the behavior involved. Rules—for example, those regulating the young about juvenile delinquency—are made by certain groups to order sanctions against others. A given situation of deviation depends, therefore, on the reaction of others and to some extent on the reaction of the deviant.

---

[65] Simmons, p. 223.

[66] Cohen has termed such behavior "violation of institutional expectations." See Albert K. Cohen, "The Study of Social Disorganization and Deviant Behavior," in Robert K. Merton, Leonard Broom, and Leonard S. Cottrell, Jr., *Sociology Today: Problems and Prospects* (New York: Basic Books, Inc., 1959), p. 462.

[67] For some other deviations from norms one might adopt Merton's distinction between two types of deviation: aberrant behavior and noncomformity. Aberrant behavior resembles much of what we have termed deviant behavior, such as crimes where individuals violate the norms in pursuit of their own ends and do not seek to change the norms. The nonconformer, such as beatniks, hippies, and often political offenders, announces his dissent publicly, challenges the legitimacy of the norms and laws he violates, aims to change the norms he is denying in practice, is acknowledged by conventional members of the society to depart from prevailing norms for disinterested purposes and not for what he personally can get out of it, and also lays claim to a higher morality and to ultimate values rather than to the particular norms of the society. See Robert K. Merton, "Social Problems and Sociological Theory," in Robert K. Merton and Robert A. Nisbet, eds., *Contemporary Social Problems* (2nd ed.: New York: Harcourt, Brace & World, Inc., 1966), pp. 808–811.

Deviant behavior and *social problems* are not necessarily the same thing. Not all social problems are instances of deviant behavior. For example, soil erosion, flood damage, and forest destruction have for decades been considered as social problems. Yet these problems can hardly be considered as instances of deviant behavior. To be sure, soil erosion may exemplify a variation from ideal standards of soil productivity; yet this variation is not a consequence of social behavior. The same could be applied to social problems involving disease or physical handicaps, such as cancer, heart disease, blindness, and crippling, as well as urban smog and traffic problems. Such conditions, when dealt with in textbooks on "social problems," are completely in order. It is only suggested here that they are not instances of deviant behavior within the definition stated above.

TYPES OF DEVIANT BEHAVIOR

In the chapters which follow, a number of types of deviant behavior, or, as they have been termed, "strongly disapproved deviations from norms," are discussed. The following discussion presents a brief description of each of these types of deviant behavior, including the nature of the norms involved and, in some cases, definitions of a few important terms which it is necessary to understand in connection with a particular type of deviation. These terms will be used often in subsequent discussions.

Most sociologists are skeptical of loose terms, such as "socially maladjusted," "antisocial," "emotionally disturbed," "abnormal," "mentally ill," "sexually deviant," and even an omnibus category, such as "delinquency," unless the norms are stated.[68] The definition of excessive drinking and alcoholism, for example, involves norms, such as the amount of alcohol consumed, the purpose and meaning of the drinking, the social handicap to the individual, and the degree of inability to refrain from excessive drinking. Even the norms involved in mental disorder need to be so stated that we can determine with some precision who is mentally ill and who is not, whom we are to treat, and whom not to treat.

Delinquency and Crime

Among the norms whose violation usually exceeds the tolerance limit of the community in even a highly differentiated society are the legal norms. To emphasize their importance and to force compliance with them, a series of penalties has been established by the political state. Enacted laws represent varying degrees of tolerance for the behavior outlawed. Some legal

---

[68] Marshall B. Clinard, "Contributions of Sociology to the Understanding of Deviant Behavior," *British Journal of Criminology*, 3:110–129 (1962).

norms forbidding certain behavior are supported by nearly all segments of a society, the behavior in question being regarded as inimical to group welfare, whereas norms embodied in other laws have little support. Deviant behavior, such as murder, kidnapping, sexual abuse of young children, or incest, may be overwhelmingly and strongly disapproved. Other behavior, while disapproved legally, may have less public disapproval. Although persons differ about the validity of individual legal norms, there may be agreement that there is need for "obedience of the law" in general.

Most criminal behavior represents a conflict between the norms of particular groups or individuals and those norms which the law represents. Much juvenile delinquency, organized prostitution, gambling, traffic in narcotics, and homosexuality, for example, arise from the growth of subgroups which, although in physical contact with the rest of the society, may have different norms. Norms of subgroups which conflict with legal norms may be those of certain age groups, social classes, occupations, neighborhoods, or regions.

Property crimes, such as larceny, burglary, automobile theft, and robbery, constituted 91.7 percent of all major crimes reported to the police in the United States in 1960. Murder and nonnegligent manslaughter, which are *personal crimes,* accounted for only 0.5 percent of the total. There is also a large group of *offenses against public order,* including vagrancy, disorderly conduct, prostitution, and gambling.

Certain types of offenses are often not included in the statistics for ordinary crimes. These include *occupational crimes,* that is, crimes committed in connection with a legitimate occupation, particularly high-status, white-collar occupations. *White-collar crimes* are violations of laws by those with high status, such as businessmen, professional men, and politicians, in connection with their occupations. Their law violations are not usually tabulated as "crimes," even though the effect on society as a whole may be far more serious than that of a typical burglary. These offenses include embezzlement and other trust violations, falsified income tax returns, political corruption, violations of food and drug laws, violations of banking and security laws, fee splitting by doctors, and violations of countless other regulations affecting persons of the white-collar class.

Antisocial acts committed by persons under a certain age, usually sixteen to eighteen, which are considered to be injurious to the person or to society are classified as *juvenile delinquency.* Generally "delinquents" are not punished by the criminal law but are treated in other ways. Antisocial acts of juveniles include not only those which would be crimes if committed by adults but many other offenses which are peculiarly juvenile, such as truancy, incorrigibility, and vandalism. Although these latter acts are dis-

turbing to community norms and are of increasing concern to American society, they are not generally included in national figures of "crimes" which
have been committed. While minors and adults are handled differently
under the law, many of the offenses of juveniles are behaviorally the same
as adults and can be explained in much the same frame of reference. (See
Chapter 8.)

Homosexual Behavior

Homosexual behavior represents sex relations with members of one's
own sex. In nearly all Western European countries and in other parts of the
world, homosexual acts between consenting adults, if not carried out in public, are not considered as crimes but are generally regarded with varying
degrees of tolerance as non-conformity. In the United States, with the exception of Illinois, and in a number of other countries such acts are considered as crimes and are often punished severely. Normatively the behavior
is considered inappropriate for one's sex. The negative attitude toward
homosexuality is based partly on the view that heterosexual intercourse is
necessary for procreation and is thus linked with institutional mechanisms
that guarantee the bearing and rearing of children.

Prostitution

Prostitution is sexual intercourse on a promiscuous and mercenary basis
and with emotional indifference. Acts of prostitution as well as soliciting
are strongly disapproved under Anglo-American law and are disapproved
with varying degrees of tolerance today in most other parts of the world.
Prostitution is opposed on a number of grounds, including the high degree
of promiscuity without the element of procreation, the willingness to commercialize sexual participation with emotional indifference, the effects on
women who participate, the threat to public health through the transmission
of venereal disease, and the fact that it affronts public morals by being generally a form of overt sexual solicitation.

Drug Addiction

The use of morphine, heroin, opium, cocaine, and occasionally marihuana, other than for medicinal purposes, is considered as a deviation from
cultural or legal norms not only in the United States but also in many other
Western societies. The use of drugs is disapproved because most of them
are habit-forming. Their use tends either to decrease mental or physical
activity or to overexcite and sustain such activity. Where a habit has been
established, there may be excruciating physical and mental symptoms when
the drugs are not used. Furthermore, drug addiction may become extremely

expensive for a person who has been addicted for some time and has built up an increased tolerance for the drugs. Some addicts even commit thefts or engage in prostitution to finance their addiction.

Alcoholism

The use of alcohol as a beverage is widespread in Western civilization and, by the majority of the population at least, its use in moderation is generally approved. Where alcohol is consumed mainly for purposes of conviviality or ceremony it is termed *social or controlled drinking*. The *social drinker* is able to control his drinking and rarely becomes intoxicated. Drinkers who deviate from the norms of the drinking patterns of a culture, and from such legal norms as those prohibiting drunkenness and driving while intoxicated, are referred to as *excessive drinkers*.

Excessive drinkers use alcohol for purposes of intoxication and some may even become completely dependent upon its effects. The *heavy drinker* uses alcohol more frequently than does the social drinker. He has occasional sprees of drunkenness, but in general his drinking does not seriously deviate from drinking norms. *Alcoholics* are those excessive drinkers who deviate markedly from drinking norms by the frequency and quantity of their consumption of alcohol and by the unconventional times and places selected for the drinking. Such excessive consumption of alcohol tends to disturb their interpersonal relationships in their family, occupational, and social groups. The alcoholic is unable to control consistently, or stop at will, either the start of drinking or its termination once started. Most deviant of all are those whose alcoholism has become chronic. *Chronic alcoholics* almost completely lose control over their drinking and become "compulsive" drinkers. They become so dependent upon alcohol that they live to drink and drink to live. Some of their characteristics are solitary drinking, morning drinking, and general physical deterioration.

Mental Disorders

Mental disorders must be thought of in terms of the norms violated and the social context in which they occur. The rule breaking in mental disorder has been termed "residual rule breaking" as distinguished from other types of violations of norms.[69] According to this view there are definite norms covering crime, sexual perversions, drunkenness, and bad manners and what is left is "residual" with no specific label. Violations of norms termed mental disorder, therefore, would include withdrawal from contact with others, hallucinations, delusions, peculiar language construction, aggressiveness,

---

[69] Thomas J. Scheff, *Being Mentally Ill: A Sociological Theory* (Chicago: Aldine Publishing Company, 1966).

muttering, compulsive behavior and hypochondria, posturing, and auditory states. Some mentally disordered persons have difficulty in relating to others and in sharing the norms and objectives of others in given situations. Every society tolerates a range of behavior and a certain amount of ec- centricity, but mental disorders often exceed the "limits of eccentricity."

Traditionally psychiatrists have classified mental disorders into the neuroses and the psychoses. Neurotic conditions are not as noticeable to other persons generally as is psychotic behavior. In mild forms they may even be recognized as a problem only by the individual, his immediate fam- ily, or his friends. Neurotic conditions include hypochondria, compulsions, phobias, and hysteria. Compulsive disorders comprise repetitive or ritualistic behavior, such as excessive hand washing or dressing in a precise manner. Phobias represent obsessive fears about something, such as high places, death, the loss of one's mind, or illness. If the individual is a hypochondriac he is unduly, and usually needlessly, concerned about the state of his health. Hysterical symptoms—which are without a physical basis—include fainting spells, tics or tremors, or the loss, for example, of the ability to write.

Psychotic individuals disturb other persons because it is difficult to interact with them, and the individual with a severe mental disorder may find it increasingly difficult to participate at all in a society. Psychoses are of two types, organic and functional. *Organic psychoses* are presumed to have some connection with disturbances in the physical organism. They in- clude the senile psychoses or mental disorders of old age; alcoholic psy- choses, which are related to alcoholism; and paresis, which is caused by syphilis. The *functional psychoses* are those in which the mental disorder cannot be attributed to organic disturbances. The chief disorders of this type are schizophrenia, characterized by withdrawal from reality, hallucina- tions, and delusions; manic-depressive psychoses, with symptoms of extreme elation, deep depression, or both; and paranoia, characterized by illusions of grandeur and extreme beliefs of persecution. That these types are not disease entities in the sense of physical illness is shown by the fact that psy- chiatrists vary in their diagnoses of cases.

Suicide

Many persons in Western civilization take their lives each year, but in no Western society is this action approved. There may be feelings of sympathy for the personal difficulties in certain cases of suicide, but this sympathy does not constitute approval. Norms opposed to suicide have a long historical background, including particularly strong attitudes against it in Christian theological doctrine. Also a factor is the general implication of cowardice in retreating from life through suicide and of disgrace to the family and even the associates of the suicide. This extreme and complete form of "social withdrawal" has long interested social scientists and others who consider suicide to be related to social and group factors in a society.

Conflicts in Marital and Family Roles

All societies recognize the importance of marriage and family relationships. Although great variations exist in marital and family systems, it is generally assumed in most Western European societies that marriage and family relationships have a high degree of permanence and are capable of satisfying the expectations of the marital partners. Marriage and family unity prevail where the roles and expectations of the members are satisfactorily achieved. If conflicts in marriage or family roles develop, the marital or family relationship is impaired.

Separation, desertion, and divorce, as they represent varying degrees of dissolution of the family, are generally widely disapproved of in Western societies. So also is wife beating or similar forms of physical violence. As scientific research has advanced in recent years, the concept of marital maladjustment has been broadened. Increasingly it is being regarded as embracing those situations in which the marital partners display little marital affection, slight dependence on one another, and no sharing of satisfactions and decision making. Where these are present there may be indifference, dissatisfaction, and incompatibility between the marital partners and a situation deviating from the behavior expected by each partner in marriage.

Obviously the actual extent of the breakdown of interaction in the marital or family situation cannot be determined. Generally divorce statistics are cited as an objective, though limited, indication of the extent of role conflicts in marriages. In addition, many families are broken by legal separation or by desertion, either temporary or permanent, of one or the other marital partner, more frequently the husband. Even these figures on broken homes, however, do not indicate the full extent of marital and family role conflicts in the United States. Studies of married persons have revealed that a considerable proportion of marriages in certain samples are unhappy even though the marriage has not been physically or legally dissolved.

Role and Status Conflict in Old Age

In growing older a person is faced with making adjustments so that his expectations and his evaluations of his social roles are in harmony with those of persons with whom he interacts. The roles of the aged are not clearly defined in contemporary society, and often the aged person experiences conflicts where his expectations are based on roles which were formerly appropriate. Many older persons in modern societies are unhappy in their daily living, feel frustrated in their relationships with other persons, and may even develop senile psychoses. To the extent that the aged person's behavior exhibits conflicting roles which are unsatisfactory to himself and to society it is deviant. This definition of certain behavior among the aged as social deviation is admittedly weak. A more precise statement is difficult until the status and roles of the age in contemporary society are more clearly defined.

Discrimination Against Minority Groups

Over the past few centuries a set of norms has evolved relating to certain rights for persons regardless of their race, creed or ethnic derivation. These norms include political equality, due process of law and equal justice, freedom of opportunity to achieve economic and political success, and the right to express one's religious beliefs. A Universal Declaration of Human Rights embodying these norms was approved by the United Nations in 1948. A similar group of norms and values constitutes what is termed the American Creed.[70]

These norms and values in the United States developed out of the philosophy of the Enlightenment and the English, American and French revolutions, with their emphasis on the importance of the individual; the traditional judicial procedures of English justice; Christianity, with its concept of universal brotherhood; capitalism, with its belief that individual success is based on individual initiative; and, finally, American nationalism itself, with its emphasis on the racial, religious, and ethnic diversity of America. These values are reflected in the Declaration of Independence, in the Constitution and its amendments, and in numerous decisions of the Supreme Court, particularly those in recent years dealing with the illegality of laws upholding segregation or denying equal citizenship rights to all persons.

When a group is placed in a lower status on the basis of race, religion, or ethnic background, the action is considered *discrimination*. It takes many forms and involves suffrage and public office, the administration of justice, employment and business opportunities, education, public accommodation and housing, and every form of social participation. Social norms and values sanctioning discrimination, such as beliefs about racial superiority and anti-Semitism, have a long history. Such discriminatory norms are derived from various subcultural groups and in some historic periods or in certain areas have even been enacted into law.

---

[70] Gunnar Myrdal, *An American Dilemma* (New York: Harper & Row, Publishers, 1944), Chap. 1.

MEASURING THE EXTENT AND CHARACTERISTICS OF DEVIANTS

Deviant acts do not necessarily become known to society. Wide variations exist in the "social visibility" of negatively regarded acts of deviations, that is, the extent to which behavior comes to the attention of people within a society and the acts are defined as "deviant." Wilkins has pointed out that the definition of what is deviance is considerably modified by the content of available information about certain behavior, the amount, and the channel of information.[71] The social visibility of events in a society such as the number arrested or imprisoned for offenses will have much to do with public definitions of acts as crimes.

Certain crimes, such as kidnapping, violent sex offenses, murder, lynching, and armed robbery, for example, are highly visible and create much comment and action. Offenses such as occupational crime, illegal abortions, blackmail, homosexuality, and petty theft, are not as socially visible. Symptoms of mental disorder are not always interpreted as such and so do not become visible to members of a society. In some instances the person is considered simply as "eccentric," "odd," or "difficult." Generally, the physical symptoms of intoxication tend to be visible, as the intoxicated person usually displays such physical symptoms as thickened speech, flushed face, and unsteady gait, although certain physical illnesses may produce similar symptoms. It is the social behavior of the intoxicated person, however, which attracts the most attention from others and brings about the strongest reaction. Some persons can actually be quite intoxicated without exhibiting noticeable behavior patterns, but others may become quarrelsome, noisy, loquacious, silly, depressed or otherwise annoying to other people so that the drunken behavior becomes even more conspicuous than the physical symptoms.

The social visibility of many forms of deviant behavior varies by social class and by racial characteristics. Among the lower classes, or among a group of homeless transients, for example, drunkenness may provoke little comment, and an alcoholic may at times go largely undetected. On the other hand, drunkenness and alcoholism in a middle-class group may stand out like a fire on a hillside.

Not all deviant behavior becomes known by public agencies; hence official statistics are not an accurate picture of the amount of deviant behavior. Criminal statistics, for example, are based on recorded criminality, that is, offenses reported by individual citizens or through the action of

---

[71] Leslie T. Wilkins, *Social Deviance: Social Policy, Action, and Research* (Englewood Cliffs, N.J.: Prentice-Hall, Inc., 1965), pp. 45–104.

police patrols. Whatever is recorded is only a sample of delinquency and crime in the total criminality.[72] The amount of crime recorded varies according to the visibility of the offense, the type of offense, the circumstances surrounding it, and the attitude of the victim. Robberies are most likely to be reported because the victim gives up his possessions by the threat of force. Similarly, murders, robberies of banks or business establishments, purse snatching, check forgeries, and the theft of articles of considerable value are likely to be reported. On the other hand, small larcenies, fights and assaults where injury was not serious, and certain sex offenses are not as likely to be reported. Where only the general public or the government is a victim private citizens are less likely to report the offenses. These include violation of traffic or motor vehicle laws, gambling, or prostitution. Sometimes offenses are known only to the participants as in cases of homosexuality, illegal abortion, illegal heterosexual behavior, and the use of drugs, and therefore may not become publicly known.

Measures of deviant behavior vary according to the source. Police statistics on arrested persons, for example, are not as satisfactory as those based on crimes reported to them by citizens. Many persons are not arrested, the efficiency of police departments varies, and arrest policies change, as they do with prosecutions. For example, the number of persons arrested for given types of crime varies a great deal. In 1963, for example, some 91.5 percent of all reported cases of murder and nonnegligent manslaughter in our cities were cleared by arrest, only 18.8 percent of larcenies were cleared.[73]

In computing rates based on statistics of various forms of deviant behavior one must be careful to compute them on the population affected. For example, the well-known *Uniform Crime Reports* of the Federal Bureau of Investigation, which cover national, state, and local statistics on crimes reported to the police base their rates on the "total population" rather than on the composition of the crime-committing population.[74] Using a "standard population" one might more accurately compute rates based primarily on males aged sixteen to forty, which is the crime-committing age. What has been said here also applies to the adequacy of rates for drug addiction, alcoholism, mental disorder, and suicide.

Official action against deviants seems to have elements of contingency,

---

[72] Thorsten Sellin, "The Significance of Records of Crime," in Marvin E. Wolfgang, *et al., The Sociology of Crime and Delinquency* (New York: John Wiley & Sons, Inc., 1962, p. 59. Also see Thorsten Sellin and Marvin E. Wolfgang, *The Measurement of Delinquency* (New York: John Wiley & Sons, Inc., 1964).

[73] *Uniform Crime Reports, 1963* (Washington, D.C.: Federal Bureau of Investigation, 1964).

[74] See, for example, Sellin, "Significance of Records of Crime," p. 65.

chance, or categoric risk.[75] Despite their similar behavior, arrest defines some persons as criminals whereas others not arrested are not so defined. Similarly, some persons who exhibit deviant behavior involving mental disorder, homosexuality, drug addiction, and prostitution may be committed to an institution such as a mental hospital or prison whereas others exhibiting the same behavior are not committed to an institution.

Whether a person is selected and labeled as a deviant depends on such factors as social class, occupation, racial and ethnic background, age, past record of deviation, the situation out of which the behavior arises, the pressures of public reaction, and the resources available to apprehend or deal with the deviant. It has been suggested that the number of deviants a society can afford to recognize in a community is likely to remain relatively stable because the problem of identifying them is limited by available resources, a society has difficulty dealing with them once they are identified, and consequently most agencies of social control merely operate to keep certain deviance within bounds; a sufficient number of homosexuals, for example, may be arrested to show that there is some enforcement.

> A community's capacity for handling deviance, let us say, can be roughly estimated by counting its prison cells and hospital beds, its policemen and psychiatrists, its courts and clinics—and while this total cannot tell us anything important about the underlying psychological motives involved, it does say something about the manner in which the community views the problem. Most communities, it would seem, operate with the expectation that a relatively constant number of control agents is necessary to cope with a relatively constant number of offenders. The amount of men, money, and material assigned by society to "do something" about deviant behavior does not vary appreciably over time, and the implicit logic which governs the community's efforts to man a police force or maintain suitable facilities for the mentally ill seems to be that there is a fairly stable quota of trouble which should be anticipated.[76]

Whether or not then, an offender is arrested, prosecuted, convicted, or imprisoned, depends on available manpower. The resources are limited; all police departments have insufficient personnel to arrest, jails are limited in size, prosecutors and judges are few, prisons are small in comparison to

---

[75] Walter Reckless developed this concept of categoric risk in 1950. See Walter C. Reckless, *The Crime Problem* (New York: Appleton-Century-Crofts, Inc., 1950), pp. 56–74. For further elaboration see Lemert, *Social Pathology,* Chaps. 2, 3, and 4. Also see Homans, pp. 349–359; and S. Kirson Weinberg, *Social Problems in Our Time* (Englewood Cliffs, N.J.: Prentice-Hall, Inc., 1960).

[76] Kai T. Erikson, *Wayward Puritans: A Study in the Sociology of Deviance* (New York: John Wiley & Sons, Inc., 1966), p. 24.

the total offender population. Consequently some laws are more strictly enforced than others, some persons or groups are elected out for arrest while others are less likely to be apprehended and processed. A study has shown, for example, that arrests are often not made for trivial offenses (for example, drunkenness) or for conduct that is thought to reflect the standards of a slum community (for example, marital fighting). Arrests are not made if the victim does not or will not request prosecution, if the arrest would be inappropriate or ineffective (homosexual behavior), if it would cause loss of public support for the police (for example, social gambling), or if the arrest would cause harm to the offender (upper-class person) or to the victim (exhibitionism or statutory rape) that would outweigh the risk from inaction.[77] On the other hand, a person may be arrested who otherwise might not be properly respectful of the police (young offender talking back to the police, for example) and arrests may be made to maintain the public image of full enforcement (for example, prostitution) or to aid the investigation of another offense or another offender. When they come to prosecution some cases are dismissed and others may plead guilty to a lesser charge; [78] if convicted most offenders are placed on probation but a few go to jail or prison.

Although heavy drinking is often found in the higher socioeconomic groups, arrests for public intoxication tend to concentrate in the lower groups, whose members are then labeled "drunks." A Rochester study found a significant negative relationship between education and family income and the rate of arrests.[79] Moreover, nonwhites had a higher rate of arrests than whites.

Whether a person is committed to a mental hospital depends on the attitudes toward his behavior entertained by the next of kin, by a complainant, such as a neighbor or an employer, or by a mediator, such as the family doctor, a psychiatrist, the police, or a clergyman.[80] Many persons

---

[77] Wayne R. LaFave, *Arrest: The Decision to Take A Suspect Into Custody* (Boston: Little, Brown & Co., 1965). Also see Jerome H. Skolnick, *Justice Without Trial: Law Enforcement in a Democratic Society* (New York: John Wiley & Sons, Inc., 1966) and Egon Bittner, "The Police on Skid-Row: A Study of Peace Keeping," *American Sociological Review,* 32:699–715 (1967).

[78] See Donald J. Newman, *Conviction: The Determination of Guilt or Innocence Without Trial* (Boston: Little, Brown & Co., 1966).

[79] Melvin Zax, Elmer A. Gardner, and William T. Hart, "Public Intoxication in Rochester: A Survey of Individuals Charged in 1961," *Quarterly Journal of Studies on Alcohol,* 25:669–678 (1964).

[80] Erving Goffman, *Asylums* (New York: Doubleday & Company, Inc., 1961), pp. 134–137.

never encounter a complainant face-to-face living in either the domestic establishment, the work place, or a public area such as a store, street, or park. Other factors affecting commitment include a person's social status, the visibility of his offense, the proximity of a mental hospital, and alternative community treatment facilities. The police have considerable discretion, on an emergency basis, in apprehending and conveying to hospitals, those whom they perceive to be mentally ill.[81] Those admitted to a mental hospital are disproportionately those referred by a physician, those who are males, and those with a record of previous hospitalization.[82]

Prostitutes, homosexuals, and drug addicts may be arrested when their behavior becomes unusually conspicuous or when public pressure for their arrest is increased. In fact, societal reaction to homosexual behavior depends a great deal on whether or not the behavior of the person is imputed to be homosexual and the person becomes so defined.[83]

All this means that official statistics of deviant behavior are not accurate measures of the number and characteristics of deviants, regardless of whether the statistics deal with delinquency, crime, mental hospitals, or arrests for drunkenness or drug use.[84] Such records are obviously not complete records not only because of the selective processing of deviants but because of the changes in administrative recording procedures. This does not mean that these statistics have no use. In general, they give us an approximation of the volume of deviation; moreover, the rates of deviant behavior indicate who is selected out of a total population of deviants for specific actions by agencies of social control, that is, the social processing of deviants.[85] For example, for some forms of deviant behavior members of the lower class may be more likely than other groups to come to the attention of authorities; for other cases it may be largely males or young persons whose behavior is regarded as deviant.

To overcome some of the inadequacies in official statistics two major devices have been used: studies and surveys in which people are asked confidentially about the number of delinquencies or crimes they have committed or whether they have used drugs, displayed symptoms of alcoholism

---

[81] Egon Bittner, "Police Discretion in Emergency Apprehension of Mentally Ill Persons," *Social Problems,* 14:287–292 (1967).

[82] Elliot G. Mishler and Nancy E. Waxler, "Decision Processes in Psychiatric Hospitalization: Patients Referred, Accepted, and Admitted to a Psychiatric Hospital," *American Sociological Review,* 28:576–587 (1963).

[83] Kitsuse, *op. cit.*

[84] Sellin, "The Significance of Records of Crime"; and James E. Price, "Testing the Accuracy of Crime Statistics," *Social Problems,* 14:214–222 (1966).

[85] John I. Kitsuse and Aaron V. Cicourel, "A Note on the Uses of Official Statistics," *Social Problems,* 11:131–139 (1963).

or mental disorder, or other deviations.[86] Although these surveys have turned up evidence of the inadequacies of official statistics, there has been considerable question about the reliability, particularly the surveys of mental disorder in the general population. Another device is to ask people whether they have reported to the police certain knowledge of deviant behavior. For example, in a survey of unreported crime in the United States in 1965 the National Opinion Research Center asked 10,000 house-holders whether any member of the household had been a victim of a crime during the past year, whether the crime had been reported and, if not, why.[87] The survey showed that the reported amount of personal injury crime, as well as of property crime, was about twice the official statistics of these crimes reported to the police. Forcible rapes and burglaries were three and a half times the reported rate. The extent of failure to report to the police was highest for consumer fraud (90 percent) and lowest for auto theft (11 percent). The reasons given were that the police would do nothing, that it was a private matter, that the victim did not want to harm the offender, or, in the case of assaults and family crimes, that the victim feared reprisal.

FUNCTIONS OF DEVIANCE

To the layman social deviation is naturally "bad," weakening the social system and having no positive values. Some writers refer to the presence of deviation as "social disorganization" and to the society as being "disorganized." A state of disorganization is often thought of as one in which there is a "breakdown of social controls over the behavior of the individual" and a decline in the unity of the group because former patterns of behavior and social control no longer are effective.[88] There are a number of

---

[86] See, for example, James F. Short, Jr., and F. Ivan Nye, "Reported Behavior as a Criterion of Deviant Behavior," in Wolfgang, Savitz, and Johnston, eds., *The Sociology of Crime and Delinquency* (New York: John Wiley & Sons, Inc., 1962), pp. 44–49; Leo Srole, *et al., Mental Health in the Metropolis: The Midtown Manhattan Study* (New York: McGraw-Hill Book Company, Inc., 1962); Alexander H. Leighton, *My Name Is Legion* (Stirling County Study of Psychiatric Disorder and Sociocultural Environment; New York: Basic Books, Inc., 1959), Vol. I; and Harold A. Mulford, "Drinking and Deviant Drinking, U.S.A., 1963," *Quarterly Journal of Studies on Alcohol,* 25:634–650 (1964).

[87] *The Challenge of Crime in a Free Society,* A Report by the President's Commission on Law Enforcement and Administration of Justice (Washington, D.C.: Government Printing Office, 1967), pp. 20–22.

[88] Contemporary use of the concept "social disorganization" comes largely from W. I. Thomas and Florian Znaniecki, *The Polish Peasant in Europe and America* (New York: Alfred A. Knopf, Inc., 1927). For criticisms of this concept see John F.

objections to this frame of reference. (1) Disorganization is too subjective and vague a concept for analyzing a general society. Effective use of the concept, however, may be made in the study of specific groups and institutions. (2) Social disorganization implies the disruption of a previously existing condition of organization, a situation which generally cannot be established. Social change is often confused with social disorganization without indicating why some social changes are disorganizing and others not. (3) Social disorganization is usually thought of as something "bad," and what is bad is often the value judgment of the observer and the members of his social class or other social groups. For example, the practice of gambling, the patronage of taverns, greater freedom in sex relations, and other behavior do not mean that these conditions are naturally "bad" or "disorganized." (4) The existence of forms of deviant behavior does not necessarily constitute a major threat to the central values of a society. The presence of suicide, crime, or alcoholism may not be serious if other values are being achieved. American society, for example, has a high degree of unity and integration despite high rates of deviant behavior if one considers such values as nationalism, a highly developed industrial production, and goals of material comfort. (5) What seems like disorganization actually may often be highly organized systems of competing norms. Many subcultures of deviant behavior, such as delinquent gangs, organized crime, homosexuality, prostitution, and white-collar crime, including political corruption, may be highly organized. The slum sex code may be as highly organized and normative regarding premarital relations in one direction as the middle-class sex code is in the other.[89] The norms and values of the slums are highly organized, as Whyte has shown in his *Street Corner Society*.[90] (6) Finally, as several sociologists have suggested, it is possible that a variety of subcultures may contribute, through their diversity, to the unity or integration of a society rather than weaken it by constituting a situation of social disorganization.[91]

Deviation often interferes with the smooth functioning of a society and destroys people's willingness to play their part in an ongoing activity; but

---

Cuber, Robert A. Harper, and William Kenkel, *Problems of American Society* (New York: Holt, Rinehart and Winston, Inc., 1956), Chap. 22; Lemert, *Social Pathology,* Chap. 1; and Hartung.

[89] William F. Whyte, "A Slum Sex Code," *American Journal of Sociology,* 49:24–32 (1943).

[90] William F. Whyte, *Street Corner Society* (Chicago: University of Chicago Press, 1943). Also see Marshall B. Clinard, *Slums and Community Development: Experiments in Self-Help* (New York: The Free Press, 1967).

[91] See Robin Williams, Jr., "Unity and Diversity in Modern America," *Social Forces,* 36:1–8 (1957).

most serious of all is its impact on trust that others will also abide by the rules.[92] It is incorrect to assume, however, that deviation is naturally bad or has no positive functions. "If by 'social disorganization' we mean the dissolution of social bonds, the disintegration of social groups, or the disruption of organized social activities, deviance is not to be identified with social disorganization. Deviance, if not contained, is always a threat to organization. In limited quantities and under certain circumstances, however, it may make important contributions to the vitality and efficiency of organized social life." [93]

1. To begin with, as Durkheim pointed out, deviations are not necessarily "bad," "pathological," or "abnormal"; they should be regarded as *normal* within the context of a society.[94] A society, because of its rules and the functioning of its social systems, makes for deviations as well as nondeviation; both are normal. Durkheim remarked [that] crime is an integral part of all "healthy societies." [95] Deviations can be found in behavior expected by social institutions. Many deviations grow out of and are consequences of legitimate and conventional controls.[96] Sex, business practices, drinking of alcoholic beverages, can lead one way toward conformity with norms or away towards deviation. "The deviant and the conformist, then, are creations of the same culture, inventions of the same imaginations." Men who fear witches found them and burned them; men who sanctify the value of property find thieves everywhere. Witchcraft in Puritan New England was normal if one considers their beliefs in religious heresy and predestination of a religious value.[97]

2. The existence of deviations in a society serves to *unite the group* in much the same way as it unites against any common enemy. The presence of and hostility toward gang delinquents, criminals, drug addicts, and homosexuals gives a certain solidarity to a society. Deviations make other people alert to their common interests; it gives them a sense of common morality. A certain amount of deviance in a group can increase the sense of community among those who are conforming members and enhance the importance of conformity in the group, which might

---

[92] Cohen, *Deviance and Control,* pp. 4–5.

[93] Cohen, *Deviance and Control,* p. 11. Cohen regards social disorganization as chiefly occurring when the "rules of the game" are disturbed. Cohen, in *Sociology Today.*

[94] Emile Durkheim, *The Rules of Sociological Method,* translated by S. A. Solvaay and G. H. Mueller (New York: The Free Press, 1958) and Durkheim, *The Division of Labor in Society,* translated by George Simpson (New York: The Free Press, 1950).

[95] Durkheim, p. 67.

[96] Cohen, in Merton, Broom, and Cottrell, p. 474.

[97] Erikson, *Wayward Puritans,* pp. 21–23.

otherwise take it for granted.[98] In some situations, as was shown in a study of Quaker work camps, common concerns over a group's deviants, together with a degree of tolerance and acceptance can even strengthen a group.[99]

3. The recognition of "deviations" sets the outer *limits* of rules or norms, beyond which society will not tolerate violation, as in the case of child molesting. Each society or community has certain margins or boundaries for its way of life. The deviant is one whose activities have moved outside the margins of the group. The recognition of deviations shows how much diversity can be permitted before a group loses its identity. Agents of social control, such as criminal trials and psychiatric counseling, help to define these limits. Each time a society moves to censure a deviant in the form of what has been called "degradation ceremonies," such as a criminal trial, it sharpens the norms violated and reinstates the limits of rule toleration.[100]

4. A certain amount of deviance can serve as a "safety valve" for those who, if the rules were rigorously enforced, might attack the rules themselves. It prevents the excessive accumulation of discontent and thus takes some strain off the legitimate order. For example, it may be argued that "prostitution performs such a safety valve function without threatening the institution of the family" and without involving the emotional attachments outside marriage that might arise from premarital or extramarital relations.[101]

5. The presence of deviance may serve as a signal or warning that there is some defect in the social organization. The deviant can, by committing a deviant act, expose the inadequacies. Violations of impossible parking regulations as well as "truancy from school, AWOL's from the army, runaways and other disturbances in a correctional institution . . . reveal unsuspected causes of discontent, and lead to changes that enhance efficiency and morale." [102]

THE SCIENTIFIC STUDY OF DEVIANT BEHAVIOR

Many people believe that deviant behavior cannot be studied scientifically because scientific methods cannot be applied to them as they are to the physical sciences. Human behavior, they claim, is not the proper field for scientific research. This skepticism about the effectiveness of the social

---

[98] Lewis A. Coser, "Some Functions of Deviant Behavior and Normative Flexibility," *American Journal of Sociology,* 68:172–179 (1962).

[99] Robert A. Dentler and Kai T. Erikson, "The Functions of Deviance in Groups," *Social Problems,* 7:98–107 (1959), and Coser.

[100] Harold Garfinkel, "Conditions of Successful Degradation Ceremonies," *American Journal of Sociology,* 61:420–424 (1956).

[101] Cohen, *op. cit.,* pp. 7–8.

[102] Cohen, *op. cit.,* p. 10, and Coser.

sciences is due, in large part, to the extreme complexity of the data which the research worker in these fields must use. In fact, the nature of human behavior is thought by some to be so different from other data that they would restrict the term *science* to the so-called exact or physical sciences, such as biology, chemistry, and physics. They would even deny the use of the term *science* to such social or behavioral sciences as sociology, social psychology, anthropology, economics, and political science, upon which the solution of problems of deviant behavior ultimately depends. As Sellin has indicated, however, these "are important considerations, but they do not permit us to assume that social facts cannot be studied scientifically and laws of social life gradually established. They merely recognize that the social scientist has great hazards to overcome." [103]

Part of this confusion is a result of failure to consider the nature of the scientific method. The scientific study of human behavior assumes that the criteria of science can be applied to the data involved. This means that human behavior can be studied as a *natural process,* or as a sequence of events in which certain events follow from other events, in much the same way as the process through which a disease develops or a chemical process occurs. Whether events which follow are "caused" by preceding events cannot be determined by merely observing the order of occurrence of the events; they must be subjected to scientific investigation.

The scientific study of deviant behavior, like the scientific approach to any data, is an attempt to describe the *processes* associated with the behavior. Generalizations as to cause-and-effect relationships in such processes are the purpose of science. Such generalizations, if eventually achieved, are usually stated in terms of probabilities. A criminal career, for example, is generally found to have followed a long series of circumstances and incidents, usually beginning with juvenile delinquency and progressing to more serious acts. Likewise, the admission of a psychotic patient to a mental hospital is not the result of one experience but rather may be the culmination of many experiences. The series of steps which precede the chronic alcoholic's admission to the alcoholic ward may extend back for many years. A divorce is seldom the product of a single argument.

A science also tries to put some order into a series of heterogeneous data by reducing them to *types,* as, for example, when the zoologist or botanist classifies animals or plants into species. The scientific study of "criminals" has resulted in the discovery that not all criminals have the same characteristics, but that there are various types of criminal careers. Similarly, excessive drinkers are of various types. People suffering from mental disorders can also be subdivided into types, as can suicides.

---

[103] Sellin, "Culture Conflict and Crime," pp. 12–13.

The social scientist, as contrasted with those who make unscientific claims about human behavior, is willing to do three things. First, he is willing to subject his hypotheses to tests. Second, he avoids making generalizations which are not based on empirical studies. Third, he will state his confidence in a proposition according to the degree to which it has been verified by a test using experimental or empirical data.

The *scientific method* is nothing more than a description or guide to the logic of scientific inquiry. It is generally stated as a series of steps, which in its simplest form involve:

1. the formulation of a hypothesis referring to the phenomenon to be studied;
2. the observation and collection of data which will test the hypothesis;
3. the classification and analysis of the data obtained; and
4. the arrival at conclusions as to whether, from the results of the analysis, the hypothesis is confirmed or not confirmed.

A *hypothesis* is a statement of a relationship that appears to exist, as, for example, "Delinquency is produced by crime stories on television." In this hypothesis the social scientist would define how he uses such terms as *delinquency, crime stories,* and other variables. In order to *test* such a hypothesis, however, it would have to be stated in a form which is testable, as "A significantly greater proportion of juveniles who watch crime stories on television have been legally classified as delinquent than have those who do not watch such crime stories." He then *observes* as much as he can of the relevant data, using the *research techniques* most appropriate to the data studied. It is usually not feasible for the social scientist to use mechanical instruments similar to those used in the physical science laboratories. Instead, he may rely on questionnaires and interviews, case histories, and personal documents, such as diaries. In other types of studies he may use ecological techniques, such as spot-mapping, community studies, and, finally, the comparative studies of people living in different cultures.

In his research the social scientist must see that the group he uses for study is representative of the phenomena he is studying. In most instances he also compares the group he is studying with a control group. For example, in testing the hypothesis about the relation of delinquency to crime stories on television, the social scientist must select a *representative sample* of all juvenile delinquents. Since only relatively few juvenile delinquents are sent to correctional institutions, he might decide to select a random sample of those who had been arrested or had appeared before a juvenile court. It would also be necessary, as in most research studies on behavior problems, to compare the delinquents, or the *experimental group,* with a sample of nondelinquents, or the *control group,* in order to discover to what extent the latter also watch crime stories on television.

This hypothesis would be partially *verified* if the delinquents, or a statistically significant proportion of the experimental group, watched crime stories and the nondelinquents did not. The hypothesis would be rejected if no differences were found, or if the control group were discovered to have been watching crime stories as much as or more than the experimental group. Even after the conclusion of this study, a generalization should not be established until the study had been repeated on other samples of the delinquent and nondelinquent juvenile population.

Advances in any physical or social science are often made through efforts to predict or control real phenomena. Such efforts may reveal the inadequacies of scientific knowledge when applications fail to produce the expected results. On the other hand, applications may confirm and even extend scientific knowledge. In the physical world, for example, the application of astronomy to the problems of sea and air navigation resulted in improvements in both the theory of astronomy and the techniques of navigation. Efforts to control criminal behavior contribute not only to the field of criminology but also to the broader study of human behavior and society in general.

Fortunately, there have been increasing efforts recently to apply the theory and concepts of sociology to the control of concrete situations such as delinquency and crime, drug addiction, race relations, alcoholism, poverty, and the slum.[104] Such applications provide one of the most effective means of checking upon a research finding that, if proved to be inadequate, can then be revised or reconceptualized. As Sutherland has stated, if applied programs wait until theoretical and research knowledge is complete, "they will wait for an eternity, for theoretical knowledge is increased most significantly in the efforts of social control." [105]

Nevertheless, emphasis on the application, rather than on the discovery, of basic scientific knowledge can be carried too far. Generally speaking, application of knowledge is not the *goal* of a science, but rather a by-

---

[104] Alvin W. Gouldner and S. M. Miller, *Applied Sociology: Opportunities and Problems* (New York: The Free Press, 1965); Donald W. Valdes and Dwight G. Bean, *Sociology in Use: Selected Readings for an Introductory Course* (New York: The Macmillan Company, 1965); Arthur B. Shostak, ed., *Sociology in Action* (Homewood, Ill.: The Dorsey Press, 1966); Paul F. Lazarsfeld, William H. Sewell, and Harold L. Wilensky, eds., *The Uses of Sociology* (New York: Basic Books, Inc., 1967); and Alfred R. Lindesmith, *The Addict and the Law* (Bloomington: University of Indiana Press, 1965). Also see Marshall B. Clinard, "The Sociologist's Quest for Respectability," *The Sociological Quarterly*, 7:399–412 (1966).

[105] Edwin H. Sutherland, *Principles of Criminology* (4th ed.: Philadelphia: J. B. Lippincott Co., 1947), pp. 1–2.

product or consequence of scientific discovery.[106] Preoccupation with social welfare and social legislation, where it has not been simultaneously concerned with the scientific study of deviant behavior, has often hindered the development of basic knowledge in this area.[107] Unfortunately, in the past, attention was often concentrated on the control of delinquency and crime, alcoholism, racial discrimination and mental disorder without the accumulation and study of concepts, theories, and research upon which to base a program of control.

Increasing recognition is being given to the importance of systematizing knowledge about deviant behavior for without this systematization, knowledge cannot be effectively utilized in social control. The mere description of the characteristics of deviants is of little use without some explanation of the development of their behavior. With the extension and systematic application of scientific knowledge, there appears to be no reason why many types of deviant behavior cannot be dealt with successfully.

SUMMARY

Unlike animals, the ties that bind a human group together are not merely biological needs but also abstract social relationships. Society or social group refers to social relationships among a number of persons in which there are shared sets of common meanings or symbols, feelings of unity, and systems of mutual obligation. In social groups members have definite reciprocal rights and duties that are the result of each person's social status. The relatively permanent, stable, uniform, and formal manner in which groups are interrelated are termed *social institutions.*

Culture may be distinguished from society as primarily involving normative standards of conduct. Social relationships and behavior are regulated through social norms that are either standardized ways of acting or expectations governing limits of variation. Norms refer to rules for what persons should or should not say, do, or think under given circumstances. Norms vary in the degree to which they may be widespread or permanent, as well as in the intensity of reactions to violation. They may be classified according to the extent of knowledge, acceptance of the norm, mode of enforcement, the way the norm is transmitted, and the amount of conformity required. Some norms are proscriptive, while others are prescriptive. Social

---

106 In a similar way modern-day space explorations involve applications of previously discovered basic knowledge in such sciences as physics or astronomy, which, however, has been added to, confirmed, or revised by testing through space explorations.

107 Edwin H. Sutherland, "Social Pathology," *American Journal of Sociology,* 50:429–436 (May 1945).

values are those things to which a society or cultural group attaches value, worth, or significance.

Modern societies are complex; there is much social differentiation by race and ethnic background, social class, occupation, age, religion, neighborhood, and region. Such groups constitute subcultures when they come to share a set of norms and values that are somewhat distinct from the general culture. There are also limited subcultures such as those among teenage gang groups, professional and organized criminals, prostitutes, homosexuals, and drug addicts.

While modern societies are socially differentiated in many ways, probably none is greater than the variations in behavior among the social classes in a society. There are great differences in the incidence and nature of different types of reported deviant behavior by social class.

What constitutes social deviation is not something universal or "natural." The reaction of a society to deviation from norms can vary in the direction of approval, tolerance, or disapproval. Deviations vary in the intensity of the reaction to the deviation, as well as in the direction of approval or disapproval. Each norm can be thought of as having a tolerance limit, that is, the ratio between violations of the norm and society's willingness to tolerate or suppress it.

The reaction of society to an act that results in a person's being labeled as a deviant is an important process in understanding the nature of deviant behavior. By emphasizing the label, one shifts from an interest in how deviant behavior originates to the problem of societal reaction and the consequences of being labeled a deviant.

Deviant behavior is essentially the violation of certain types of group norms; a deviant act is behavior that is proscribed in a certain way. It cannot be satisfactorily defined in either statistical, pathological, or labeling terms. Societal reaction leading to labeling is an important aspect in the study of deviant behavior, but it is a contingent and unessential element in a definition. Obviously, deviations from norms that are tolerated or that provoke only mild disapproval are of little concern to a society. Only those deviations in which behavior is in a disapproved direction, and of sufficient degree to exceed the tolerance limit of the community, constitute deviant behavior. This includes such deviations as delinquency and crime; prostitution; homosexual behavior; drug addiction; alcoholism; mental disorders; suicide; marital and family maladjustment; discrimination against minority groups; and, to a lesser degree, role problems of old age. Obviously the extent and the degree of disapproval in a particular instance are dependent on the nature of the situation and the community's degree of tolerance of the behavior involved.

Deviant acts do not necessarily become known to society. Wide variations exist in the "social visibility" of negatively regarded acts of deviation, that is, the extent to which behavior comes to the attention of people within a society and the extent to which the acts are defined as "deviant." Not all deviant behavior becomes known by public agencies; hence, official statistics are not accurate pictures of the amount of deviant behavior. Measures of deviant behavior vary according to the source. Official action against deviants seems to have elements of contingency, chance, or categoric risk. Whether a person is selected and labeled as a deviant depends on such factors as social class, occupation, racial and ethnic background, age, past record of deviation, the situation out of which the behavior arises, the pressures of public reaction, and the resources available to apprehend or deal with the deviant. To overcome some of the inadequacies in official statistics two major devices, studies and surveys, have been used. In these, people are asked confidentially about the number of delinquencies or crimes they have committed or whether they have used drugs, displayed symptoms of alcoholism or mental disorder, or about other deviations.

The presence of deviation in a society does not constitute social disorganization. Deviance in limited quantities and under certain circumstances may make important contributions to the vitality and efficiency of a society.

The scientific study of deviant behavior involves the description of processes associated with deviant behavior and an attempt to arrive at generalizations in terms of probabilities. It also tries to develop types. The scientific method involves (1) the formulation of a hypothesis referring to the phenomenon to be studied; (2) the observation and collection of data that will test the hypothesis; (3) the classification and analysis of the data obtained; and (4) the arrival at conclusions as to whether, from the results of the analysis, the hypothesis is confirmed or not confirmed.

Advances in both the physical or social sciences are often made through efforts to predict or control real phenomena. Increasingly, efforts have been made to apply the theory and concepts of sociology to the control of deviant behavior. Generally speaking, however, the application of knowledge is not the goal of a science but a byproduct or consequence of scientific discovery. Increasing recognition is being given to the importance of systematizing knowledge about deviant behavior for, without this systematization, knowledge cannot be effectively utilized in social control.

SELECTED READINGS

Becker, Howard S. *Outsiders: Studies in the Sociology of Deviance*. New York: The Free Press, 1963. A systematic study of deviants based on the recognition that deviance is a reaction by society to behavior that departs from conventional norms rather than an inherent quality of the deviant himself.

Cohen, Albert K. *Deviance and Control.* Englewood Cliffs, N.J.: Prentice-Hall, Inc., 1966. A theoretical attempt to develop a general theory of deviance. Contains an excellent discussion of normative rules and the functions of deviance.

Erikson, Kai T. *Wayward Puritans: A Study in the Sociology of Deviance.* New York: John Wiley & Sons, Inc., 1966. The first section deals with the sociology of deviance in terms of societal reaction. The remainder of the book applies the theory to deviance in Puritan New England.

Goode, William J., and Paul K. Hatt. *Methods in Social Research.* New York: McGraw-Hill Book Company, Inc., 1952. An excellent discussion of the scientific method in the study of human behavior. Discusses scientific design and the techniques used primarily in sociological research.

Homans, George C. *Social Behavior: Its Elementary Forms.* New York: Harcourt, Brace & World, Inc., 1961. An analysis of social behavior based on data obtained from observations of behavior in small groups in industry, in laboratory settings, and in communities. The social behavior of given group members is seen to depend upon a number of variables, such as their status, their role, the probability of rewards for given acts, and so forth.

Kahl, Joseph A. *The American Class Structure.* New York: Holt, Rinehart and Winston, Inc., 1957. An analysis of the norms and behavior patterns of American social classes.

Kitsuse, John I. "Societal Reaction to Deviant Behavior: Problems of Theory and Method," in Howard S. Becker, *The Other Side: Perspectives on Deviance.* New York: The Free Press, 1964. A theoretical discussion in terms of societal reaction as applied to homosexual behavior.

Lemert, Edwin M. *Human Deviance, Social Problems, and Social Control.* Englewood Cliffs, N.J.: Prentice-Hall, Inc., 1967. A series of articles by Lemert dealing primarily with social control and its consequences for deviance.

———. *Social Pathology.* New York: McGraw-Hill Book Company, Inc., 1951, Chaps. 1–3. Discusses the nature of deviation and the societal reactions to deviations from norms. There is also an analysis of the concepts of social visibility as well as mention of the tolerance quotient.

Miller, Walter B. "Lower Class Culture as a Generating Milieu of Gang Delinquency," *Journal of Social Issues,* 14:5–19 (1958). A well-known description of some of the norms of the lower class in America.

Scheff, Thomas J. *Being Mentally Ill: A Sociological Theory.* Chicago: Aldine Publishing Company, 1966. A sociological theory of mental disorder in terms of norms or residual rules and role theory. Societal reaction is usually the most important determinant of entry into the role of mental disorder.

Sellin, Thorsten, and Marvin E. Wolfgang. *The Measurement of Delinquency.* New York: John Wiley & Sons, 1964. A comprehensive survey of the problem of measuring crime and delinquency. The book constructs an index of delinquency that rests on juvenile offenses against criminal law but is not dependent on the specific label given by the law to such offenses.

Williams, Robin M., Jr. *American Society.* New York: Alfred A. Knopf, Inc., 1954. Chapter 3 presents basic concepts and approaches in analyzing sociological phenomena, particularly a discussion of norms.

2

Deviant Behavior
as Social Behavior

Many people look upon such deviants as delinquents, criminals, mental patients, suicides, and alcoholics as strange varieties of human beings whose behavior arises in an entirely different way from that of the more balanced and respectable members of society. It is true that deviant behavior is one kind of human, or social, behavior, just as conforming behavior is another kind. However, the difference between conforming and deviant behavior does not mean that there are different physical or psychological qualities which the deviant, as compared with the conformist, possesses. This assertion is alien to the thinking of many persons. We often learn to look upon those who behave differently from the way "we" behave as possessing individual qualities unlike our own. We tend, furthermore, to believe that these "qualities" are the "causes" of the behavior involved. Thus we say a person is an alcoholic, or "drinks" excessively because he is "weak," "has no character," "has no will power," or has "bad heredity." We tend, therefore, to believe that the excessive drinking of which we disapprove is due to some lack of "character" within the person. In the same way, we attribute excessive "sex drives" to the sex offender and prostitute, or we say that they are "emotionally insecure" and are attempting to find love and affection in sexual release. We describe delinquents as "having a need to rebel," or as "releasing aggressive drives which they have suppressed too long," or as "having hostile, aggressive, and rebellious personality traits." [1]

In various ways, therefore, our mode of perceiving and interpreting the world and the things about us is conditioned by meanings and categories with which our culture has provided us. We see our world through a cultural mesh, and nowhere is this truer than in our perception of the implied real nature of social deviants.

This attitude that deviants are inherently different is built upon a series of false assumptions, for *all deviant behavior is human behavior.* By this is meant that the same fundamental processes which produce the "normal" person also produce the "abnormal," for both of them are human beings. If certain basic processes underlie the development of the normal person, the same processes and structures must be sought in the deviant. Common components of human nature are found in all types of normality and abnormality.

> One implication of the sociological approach to the study of human behavior is that men are always participants in joint enterprises of one sort or other and that all individualistic explanations of the things men do are necessarily incomplete. Men are rarely isolated and acting purely as independent agents. Respiration is essentially an involuntary organic process, but even that is subject to social control. Men deliberately check their panting if they do not wish to appear cowardly or weak, or they may sigh to indicate hopelessness. Even passive acquiescence and failure to act are social to the extent that such hesitation arises from the anticipated reactions of other people. Each person is involved in many transactions to which he may contribute and thereby modify but only in his capacity as a participant in them. This means that what a man does cannot be explained exclusively in terms of his personality traits, his attitudes, or his motives. People frequently do things they do not want to do. Human behavior is something that is constructed in the course of interaction with other people, and the direction it takes depends upon the inclinations of others as well as those of the actor.[2]

Differences in subprocesses exist; if they did not there would be no way to account scientifically for deviant behavior. The subprocesses affecting deviants, however, must operate within the general framework of a theory of human nature. The units of analysis, as well as the fundamental social processes in all human conduct, are the same whether the end prod-

---

[1] See Edwin M. Lemert, *Social Pathology* (New York: McGraw-Hill Book Company, Inc., 1951), Chaps. 3 and 4, for further elaboration of this problem.

[2] Tamotsu Shibutani, *Society and Personality: An Interaction Approach to Social Psychology*, p. 60. © 1961. Prentice-Hall, Inc., Englewood Cliffs, N.J. By permission.

ucts are inmates of correctional institutions or wardens, mental patients or psychiatrists, habitual criminals or ministers. Brown writes that deviant behavior is not something outside nature: "It is a naturalistic phenomenon, socially defined as undesirable, but nevertheless a naturalistic phenomenon that developed as all other human nature developed." [3]

Moreover, there does not appear to be any general personality pattern of conformity or nonconformity with social norms or values, although there might be general nonconformity to a given class or set of norms.[4] Persons may deviate from certain norms and comply with others.[5] Those who deviate from sex norms may not steal, for example, and many white-collar offenders may have a rigid sexual code. In most cases strongly disapproved deviations may be but a small proportion of a person's total life activities. Even where the deviations constitute a more organized subculture, as in certain types of crime, accepted conduct may coincide at many points with the norms and values of the larger community.[6] In the case of professional crime, for example, personal honor and "honesty among thieves" may be a reality because it would generally be inappropriate to depend on the police or other outside agencies for support.

Further confusion arises in the minds of some observers when they perceive that certain factors are associated with the occurrence of deviant behavior. They often jump to the conclusion that two phenomena are related when they may have no connection. When it is noted, for example, that delinquency and bad housing are often associated, a causal relationship may be presumed to exist. Others may perceive that delinquents watch crime programs on television, so they conclude that this is a cause of delinquency. In both instances, the observer has failed to take into account how such situations may cause delinquency. Most important, however, they may have failed to observe that these same factors—bad slum housing and televised crime programs—affect a large proportion of our population without necessarily producing deviant behavior. Although most delinquency occurs in so-called slum areas, where housing is poor, the relation has little

---

[3] Lawrence Guy Brown, *Social Pathology* (New York: Appleton-Century-Crofts, Inc., 1946), p. 62. This quotation has been used by permission of the publisher.

[4] Many psychiatrists and psychologists believe, however, that there is such a relationship. Talcott Parsons, a sociologist, has also suggested, without supporting evidence, that there is a relationship between a nonconformist personality pattern and deviant behavior. See *The Social System* (New York: The Free Press, 1951), Chaps. 7–9, and particularly pp. 256–267.

[5] Robert Harper, "Is Conformity a General or Specific Trait?" *American Sociological Review,* 12:81–86 (1947).

[6] Lemert, p. 49.

direct connection with any theory of human behavior and must be discounted as an error in perception. Moreover, delinquency does occur in areas of good housing; hence, if the same logic is used, this situation might be attributed to the adequacy of the housing situation. In studying deviant behavior it is always necessary to consider whether similar influences are affecting nondeviants; therefore, some *theory of human behavior* must be devised which will account for the differential effects, if they exist.

With this statement of the thesis that, fundamentally, both deviant and nondeviant persons have essentially the same components, some further discussion of these components is necessary. Here the interest is not so much in society, culture, or the group as in the individual. The discussion will begin by analyzing what relation a person's biological structure has to his actions and what the differences are between the biological nature of man and that of other animals.

BIOLOGY AND SOCIAL BEHAVIOR

Man has a biological nature and a social nature, but it is obvious that without a biological nature there could be no human nature. There is an interplay between the two rather than opposition. Man is an animal who must breathe, eat, rest, and eliminate. Like any other animal, he requires calories, salt and other chemicals, and a particular temperature range and oxygen balance. Man is an animal that is dependent on his environment and limited by certain of his biological capacities.

Biology is of little relevance, however, to the social or symbolic behavior of man.[7] There are no physical functions or structures, no combination of genes, and no glandular secretions which contain within themselves the power to direct, guide, or determine the type, form, and course of the social behavior of human beings. Physical structures or properties set physical limits on the activities of persons, but whether such structures will set *social* limits depends on the way in which cultures or subcultures symbolize or interpret these physical properties. Despite this, as we shall see later, there are some scientists and practitioners who claim that deviant behavior can be traced to man's so-called instinctive urges, to heredity, or to some physical anomaly. These beliefs have, in turn, had important consequences for the nature of some preventive and treatment programs. Those, for example, who believe in the sterilization of certain types of deviants are advocating a biological view of man's nature.

---

[7] For further discussion see, for example, Alfred R. Lindesmith and Anselm L. Strauss, *Social Psychology* (rev. ed.; New York: Holt, Rinehart and Winston, Inc., 1955), Chaps. 1 and 2.

Instincts

Instincts are innate tendencies, dispositions, or drives to action which arise from vital needs of the organism and are not expressed in activity based on the past experiences in the life of the individual. Instinctive patterns are quite complex; in insects almost all behavior is instinctive. In animals except man there are often some instinctive patterns of behavior such as those regulating sexual life, including varied courtship patterns.

Certain writers on deviant behavior, particularly psychoanalysts, have erroneously stressed the animal nature of man, especially with reference to the existence in man of an "unrepressed instinctive primitive" animal nature.[8] It is said that man has instincts and that many contemporary difficulties in social relations result from man's inability to overcome his "real" or original nature. Man has no primitive instinctive nature, however, for there are no universal or instinctive patterns of behavior common to all men and transmitted biologically from one generation to another. Man does have inherited reflex patterns, such as blinking, which are specific responses to stimuli, and some biologists refer to these as instincts, which is not, however, the sense in which the term is used here. Man does not have instinctively patterned behavior. Hunger can be satisfied by a variety of foods, many of which are injurious to man. Sex acts have no particular season, there is no inborn pattern of courtship, and no "natural" way of sexual intercourse. There is no instinct which makes man religious or irreligious, kind or cruel, a killer or a pacifist. In fact, man's behavior is so varied and complex, and is so influenced by socialization and by cultural and subcultural factors, that the concept of instinct has no meaning with man.

Heredity and Deviant Behavior

If human behavior is to be inherited, it must have a direct connection with the biological structure, such as the tissue of the brain, the nervous system, the glands, or the blood. Moreover, the specific factor or factors must be present when the ovum is fertilized by the spermatozoon. An inherited quality must be reasonably specific, and must be stable enough that it might be able to affect all members of the species. Regardless of these prerequisites, some biologists still believe that crime, alcoholism, certain types of mental illness, and certain sexual deviations can be carried as specific unit factors in biological inheritance. According to this biological theory, certain specific deviant behavior can be inherited in much the same manner as eye or hair color, through the genes and the chromosomes, at the time of fertili-

---

[8] See the discussion of psychoanalysis, pages 176–186.

zation of the ovum. Persons with this scientific orientation speak of "born criminals," "born alcoholics," or "inherited insanity."

The evidence today is overwhelmingly against such a view, as in the case of "inherited" crime. "It is obviously impossible for criminality to be inherited as such, for crime is defined by acts of legislature and these vary independently of the biological inheritance of the violators of the law." [9]

Although the evidence is incomplete and contradictory, the numerically important types of mental disorder do not appear to be biologically inherited.[10] The evidence on the inheritance of alcoholism was surveyed by Jellinek, a biologist, who combined fifteen studies of heredity made of 4372 clinical alcoholics, of whom, 2799, or 52 percent, were found to have had at least one inebriate parent. He found that the estimates of the several investigators as to the percentage of alcoholics who had a possible history of hereditary factors varied from a high of 83 percent to a low of 23 percent. In his conclusions Jellinek, having left out some of the studies which dealt exclusively with persons suffering from alcoholic psychoses in which other factors besides alcoholism might be present, stated that the studies surveyed showed that "the incidence of hereditary taint in the total group of alcoholics probably does not exceed 35 percent. This leaves us with a large alcoholic population in which inebriety has developed independently of any hereditary liability."[11] This is far too cautious a statement, for the presence of an alcoholic parent by no means represents necessarily a biological rather than a social influence.

In order to prove that deviant behavior is inherited, the nature of the inheritance must be stated in such precise terms as to suggest what part of the physical organism is affected or how the organism as a whole is affected. This has not been done. Attitudes derived from the norms of the culture cannot be inherited; hence deviant attitudes derived from other sources cannot be inherited. Likewise, deviant behavior cannot be hereditary because such a theory assumes that what constitutes disapproved behavior is the same in all societies, which is not necessarily true.

What many persons confuse as inheritance in behavior is the social transmission of somewhat similar ways of behaving from one generation to another in a culture, or from one family to another. Actually, none of this is hereditary, for there is no way in which so-called family traits or

---

[9] Reprinted by permission from Edwin H. Sutherland and Donald R. Cressey, *Principles of Criminology*, published by J. B. Lippincott Company, Copyright 1924, 1960, 1966 by J. B. Lippincott Company.

[10] This will be discussed in Chapter 12, "The Functional Mental Disorders."

[11] E.M. Jellinek, "Heredity of the Alcoholic," in *Alcohol, Science, and Society* (New Brunswick, N.J.: Quarterly Journal of Studies on Alcohol, 1945), p. 109.

culture can be inherited through the genes. The complexity of gene structure which would be required to transmit a culture or family attitudes and values as part of the biological heritage would be inconceivable. The inheritance of eye color is one thing; the inheritance of thousands of social norms and values is another. Anthropologists have demonstrated conclusively that there is no connection between culture and the biological features of race. A typical American Negro, for example, would have little in common culturally with an African Negro. The American Negro has no appreciable vestige of his African culture left today. The social organization, the language, the African gods, the food habits have all been supplanted by a Western European culture.

One of the reasons for the belief in constitutional differences was the error in perceiving the reasons for resemblances and differences in the trait structures of father and son, mother and daughter, and brothers and sisters. The experiences of no two children are exactly the same even for an hour or a day, let alone a month, a year, or more. The child learns to adapt to the world around him and to the people in the world. Thus it can be understood that the experiences of two brothers, particularly if there is a considerable age disparity, may be even more dissimilar than the experiences of the friends of either one. Among these differences in experiences are obviously the addition of siblings to the family, new playmates, new school classes, and new teachers. If the family has moved during the childhood of two brothers, as many families do, the neighbors and the general environment may be quite different. What is probably most important is the change in attitudes of the father and mother with additional children, as well as changes in social status and possibly in occupation. The method of treating an older and a younger child may be quite different because of changes in the parents' social situation.

The relevance of all this discussion to deviant behavior should be clear. If one can inherit only something which is carried physiologically—and no social norms or values of one's culture or subculture are thus transmitted—much of what are termed "family traits" is eliminated. It is obvious, however, that behavioral traits can be passed on from grandfather to father and son through sharing common experiences and attitudes without recourse to inheritance. Likewise, there is no way in which such deviant attitudes as disrespect for laws, sexual licentiousness, or, in mental illness, for example, difficulties in interpersonal relations such as difficulties in role playing can be inherited. It is intriguing to consider what might happen in each instance, if it were possible to cross such traits. Such possibilities include crossing a shoplifter's genes with a forger's genes, the genes of a person who likes people with those of one who does not, or those of a teetotaler with those of an alcoholic.

Neither moral behavior nor immoral behavior is biologically inherited. This would be impossible, for, as we have said above, the definitions of what constitutes such behavior vary not only among societies, but, as Kinsey showed about sex behavior, primarily by social class within a society.[12] Morality also varies by generation, as illustrated by the changes in norms designated in the criminal code each year. Thus the gene structure would have to be extremely variable to keep up with these changes in moral definitions. Moreover, as indicated before, any propositions about the inheritance of deviant behavior would have to apply as well to the nondeviant.

Physical Characteristics and Defects

Some persons claim that certain antisocial behavior is often produced by poor health, disease, or malfunctioning of the glands. In particular, there has been an interest in the relation of deviant behavior to brain pathology, glandular disturbances, infectious diseases, heart lesions, and such foci of infection as tonsils or teeth. Crossed eyes, facial deformities, such as a large nose or acne, and other physical defects, such as clubfeet, have also been said to have an important relationship to delinquency and crime. There is, however, no one-to-one relationship between physical defects and social maladjustment. There are undoubtedly criminals, for example, who are physically weak, have infected tonsils, or are cross-eyed, but there are many persons with these characteristics who are not criminals, and the incidence of these conditions may be even greater among the noncriminal population.

Some biological or physical characteristics, while not having a direct effect on social behavior, may have some indirect effect. "It has been said that if Cleopatra's nose had been a half inch longer, she would have had a different kind of influence on history. Certainly physique, including health, appearance, physical strength and coordination, skin pigmentation, growth rate, height, weight, etc., are important factors in developing the kind of attitudes that a person has about himself." [13] What is important is the individual's conception of people's attitudes toward his appearance. A physical handicap, such as crossed eyes, may cause a person *indirectly* to seek certain antisocial contacts and participate in criminal activity. The expected social roles of women are different, however, and the chance of

---

[12] Alfred C. Kinsey, Wardell B. Pomeroy, and Clyde E. Martin, *Sexual Behavior in the Human Male* (Philadelphia: W. B. Saunders Company, 1948) and Alfred C. Kinsey, Wardell B. Pomeroy, Clyde E. Martin, and Paul H. Gebhard, *Sexual Behavior in the Human Female* (Philadelphia: W. B. Saunders Company, 1953).

[13] Richard Dewey and W. J. Humber, *Development of Human Behavior* (New York: The Macmillan Company, 1951), p. 87.

their participation in serious crime for this reason may be limited. The fact that a male has what appear to be feminine characteristics may make his indulgence in homosexual practices more likely, even though homosexual behavior cannot possibly be inherited. Finally, a person who has a dark skin or other Negroid features is forced to assume a series of subservient roles in a culture and often must live in city slums where criminal norms are more prevalent, and where there is greater temptation to adopt delinquent and criminal patterns of behavior.

Some writers have sought a more specific explanation of certain forms of deviant behavior in the malfunctioning of certain glands of the human body, particularly the endocrine glands. Some have suggested that glandular malfunctioning accounts for some criminal behavior. Efforts have also been made to trace some forms of mental disorders and alcoholism to the improper functioning of certain glands, particularly the thyroid and adrenal glands. Others have suggested that malfunctioning of the gonads and abnormal secretion of the sex hormones produce not only the effeminate homosexual and the oversexed personality types but the prostitute. In spite of these claims, research on glandular structure has as yet produced no conclusive explanations in any area of deviant behavior, with the possible exception of certain unique cases. Even if there were evidence that disturbances in the endocrine glands were related to certain forms of deviant behavior, it would be difficult to establish the fact that the glandular disturbances preceded the deviant behavior. Incarceration in a prison or a long period of mental illness might upset the glandular functioning of an individual. The association of glandular deficiencies with the development of alcoholism is even more difficult, for alcoholics may consume large quantities of alcohol over long periods during which their diet is anything but balanced.

Intelligence

Although the limits of intelligence are probably set at birth, the development of intelligence is greatly dependent on such variables as social experience, language, and education. Intelligence tests measure only intelligence as liberated through specific environmental forces. They do not measure innate intelligence, for such a form exists only in the abstract. Intelligence existing in any individual (which present intelligence tests attempt to measure) is a product of both environment and potentialities. A succeeding chapter will present a discussion of intelligence and deviant behavior with largely negative conclusions.[14]

---

[14] See Chapter 6.

SOCIAL NATURE OF MAN

Despite the fact that man is an animal, little that has a meaningful relationship to the essential qualities of human behavior can be derived from the study of lower forms of animal life. No matter how anthropomorphic we are in seeing human qualities in ants, bees, mice, dogs, and horses, there are extremely important differences that cannot be bridged. The behavior of lower forms of animal life is largely controlled by a series of innate reflexes and instincts, whereas man's behavior patterns are transmitted by culture from one generation to another. Man alone among the animals possesses language with which to convey abstract meanings. He alone has the language and intelligence needed to convey highly technical ideas, such as mathematical concepts. Man alone has a self, plays a variety of social roles, and makes moral distinctions. Lower animals are not nearly as dependent on others of their kind as is man. The limitations on the possibility that animals can approach human beings in their behavior far outweigh the few similarities. Even some comparative psychologists have pointed out the fallacy of trying to derive valid knowledge about human beings from experiments on animals. A well-known psychologist has summed it up as "the price paid for overmuch experimentation with animals is to neglect the fact that human subjects are brighter, are able to use language —and probably learn differently because of these advances over lower animals. . . . Only if a process demonstrable in human learning can also be demonstrated in lower animals is the comparative method useful in studying it." [15]

Communication and Language

Without human communication through language there can be no abstract reasoning, no social interaction, no self or conception of self; without language the human animal cannot play social roles. The possession of language is the most important distinguishing characteristic separating man from other animals. No matter how many experiments reveal subhuman or pseudohuman qualities in the learning process of rats and apes, the dividing line between the two groups is impossible to bridge without language. Language enables the human being to deal with norms and values. Scientific, moral, and religious ideas are carried and expressed through language. "The absence of morality, religion, conscience, etc., among both adult apes and

---

[15] Ernest R. Hilgard, *Theories of Learning* (New York: Appleton-Century-Crofts, Inc., 1948), p. 329.

human infants is based upon the same inability to represent to oneself in terms of a human language, one's own goals, purposes, or principles." [16] Even terms like "criminal," "drunk," "mental patient," "Negro," or "Jew" take on abstract or stereotyped meanings in common language.

A child acquires the language of his parents; he also acquires cultural meanings or evaluations which are communicated principally through language.[17] Conceptual categories are merely our general modes of viewing or relating to things, but our more specific modes of perceiving and feeling are closely aligned with the linguistic categories we have acquired. For example, the white child who learns that "dirty Negro" refers to dark-skinned persons will probably perceive or see a dark-skinned person as "dirty" whether he actually is dirty or not. In addition, the child may thus learn to have a feeling of revulsion or disgust when he sees a Negro.

The human infant, whether he turns into a criminal or a noncriminal, is born into this world the most plastic of all animals. A few reflexes, some drives, such as hunger and sex, and a potentiality for human behavior are about all he has. In turn, a human being requires a longer time to mature than any other animal. The child becomes socialized through the use of language. In communication through language with others over a long infancy, childhood, and young adulthood the human being interacts with others and both his and other personalities become modified. One social psychologist has defined *social interaction* as the "process by which an individual notices and responds to others who are noticing and responding to him." [18] This reciprocal process of interaction with other persons and through them with culture and subculture enables the child or adult to develop a unique personality, whether deviant or not.

Conception of Self

Man is the only animal who has a "self" in the sense that he conceives of himself as a separate being, has an understanding of who and what he is, and is even able to talk to evaluate himself in ways which are sometimes laudatory and at other times reproving. The human being is not born with

---

[16] Lindesmith and Strauss, p. 25.

[17] Should the student doubt this he might ask himself how often he has heard the following phrases: "She's a nice prostitute," "He's a kind murderer," or "He's a very sincere thief." Such phrases have a peculiar sound—the adjectives "kind," "nice," and so on, are incongruent with the invidious images portrayed by the nouns "prostitute," "murderer," or "thief."

[18] Theodore M. Newcomb, *Social Psychology*, (New York: Holt, Rinehart and Winston, Inc., 1950), p. 21.

a self; he acquires one through social interaction.[19] Like other, but mature, animals, a young infant cannot distinguish between himself and others. He and everything else in the world are part of a confusing hodgepodge with little meaning except in the immediate present. As speech develops, he realizes that he has a self separate from others. He acts out roles or parts, such as a cowboy, a fireman, an Indian chief, a policeman, his father, or his mother. In this role playing it is not someone else who does the things that the child does, but he himself. This constitutes the "play stage" of personality growth where dolls, toys, and other similar objects become an indispensable part of this acting process. Later the child develops a further conception of self through playing games of various types where there must be an ability to shift roles by playing the parts of the other players. The growing child learns to internalize the roles of others and in so doing to distinguish his own role from that of others. When the internalization of these roles has been sufficiently developed to give the child a conception of a generalized "other" person to whom he can respond, he has also achieved what might be referred to as a generalized self. As George Mead has written: "No hard-and-fast line can be drawn between our own selves and the selves of others, since our own selves exist . . . only insofar as the selves of others exist." [20]

As the child learns he is a separate person, with his own name, he learns to think of himself as having certain attributes. He learns this not from himself alone, but from the reactions of others toward him, and eventually from these actions plus his interpretations of them. In effect he learns to apply to himself both the words and the attitudes of others. He may become unhappy because the phrase "bad boy" conjures up a thought image of something he has learned to dislike and fear, and the idea that he is said to be bad, which occurs in the momentary reflection of himself as others see him, arouses a feeling of fear, shame, and dislike all at once. This is what we mean when we say that the child's self-concept develops as he, by means of language, takes the attitude of others toward himself and then calls out in himself (in his symbolic response) the attitude of others. This process

---

[19] Perhaps some persons would rush to defend a pet dog and say that he not only conceives of himself as a separate being, but when punished he has been observed to sulk. We would be the last to disturb such a pleasant fantasy, but it might be well to suggest that two elements make this improbable: a dog has no way to refer himself to himself and he possesses no words with which to talk to himself about the errors of his ways.

[20] George H. Mead, *Mind, Self, and Society* (Chicago: University of Chicago Press, 1934), p. 164.

is instantaneous and is not at all prolonged, as our description might suggest.

The three steps involved in each phrase of this process, from the standpoint of the individual, are

Perception: Attending to the other's action
Interpretation: Attribution of meaning to the other's action
Response: Acting or feeling on the basis of the meaning attributed [21]

The normal person is able to call out the same responses in himself that he calls out in others. An organized and integrated self permits him to put himself in the place of another while still maintaining his own identity. This growth of self-realization can be illustrated by the development of children's moral ideas. In a study of lower-class children in Switzerland, Piaget showed that a child's ideas of fair play move from self-centered judgments to seeing them through the eyes of others.[22] Until about the age of five a child has an absolute idea of right and wrong, and from then until about the age of ten the child comes to realize that moral ideas are not real in themselves but are related to numerous group ideas. Finally, the child learns that the group can make exceptions to rules and that new rules can be made by the group. In this way the child learns to acquire abstract, generalized ideals. He is not born with "ntural" moral judgments; instead, children in the early years have abstract conceptions of justice and "fairness" which are not yet specific.

The self-concept is not static, but is subject to change and modification throughout a person's life. It changes as the others with whom one identifies change, or as the expectations of these others alter. The concept of self which one has as a child will be decidedly different from one's concept of self as an aged person.[23]

> In recent years more and more students of human behavior have come to recognize the importance of personal identity, for what a man does or does not do depends in large measure upon his conception of himself. Each individual is tied to a pattern of communal life by the manner in which he is identified. By virtue of being who he is, he assumes status in a group. He can locate himself and is recognized by others, and his relationship to each of the others is thereby defined. Far from being creatures

---

[21] Mead, Chaps. 1 and 2. Actually, the three steps above characterize all social behavior, in the sense that all action (or response) which is social is preceded by perception and interpretation (or definition).

[22] J. Piaget, *Moral Judgment of the Child* (London: Routledge and Kegan Paul, Ltd., 1932).

[23] See, for example, Zena S. Blau, "Changes in Status and Age Identification," *American Sociological Review*, 21:198–203 (1956).

of impulse, men generally inhibit their organic dispositions in order to live up to the standards of conduct that they set for themselves. They are constantly responding to what they believe themselves to be. . . . Many of the distinctive features of human behavior arise from the fact that men orient themselves within a symbolic environment and strive to come to terms with what they believe themselves to be. Men give their lives willingly for a variety of worthy causes; they deny themselves many joys in order to build gigantic political or industrial empires; they build up social barriers to protect their progeny against miscegenation; they plot vengeance for a wrong suffered long ago by their ancestors; they create monuments in their own honor; they push their children to "make a name" for themselves; lovers commit suicide when they are denied the right to marry; artists paint happily for "posterity," serenely indifferent to the fact that their contemporaries regard them as mad. Although men take these activities for granted as a part of human life, no other animal is known to engage in such conduct. It is unlikely that any creature without self-conceptions would do any of these things. Human behavior consists of a succession of adjustments to life conditions, but each man must come to terms with himself as well as with other features of his world. To understand what men do we must know something about what each person means to himself.[24]

   The self-conception, therefore, is an important aspect of the person, and whether one is dealing with deviant or nondeviant behavior it is necessary to recognize this. It is the image in our minds of the "self" (ourselves) that we try to enhance and defend, whether we are a judge or a criminal. When this self-image gets out of line with the conception which others have of a person, the result may even be the "great inventor" or similar figures found in mental hospitals. As a person's conception of himself changes, so may a large part of his personality, as is indicated in what is termed the "successful treatment" of mental patients, alcoholics, and delinquents. What, in part, happens is that the deviant comes to view himself differently, placing new expectations on his conduct, as well as new demands.

SOCIALIZATION AND SOCIAL ROLES

   Up to now the discussion has been about the fact that all social behavior is human behavior and that people have language and a conception of self that other animals do not have. This leads us to a further discussion of socialization and social roles. Social behavior has to be acquired. It is not there at birth but develops through socialization. Behavior becomes modified in response to the demands and expectations of others. Practically all be-

---

[24] Shibutani, pp. 247–248.

havior is a product of social interaction and is seen only in relation to other people. Words like "honesty," "friendliness," "shyness" have meaning only in relation to other people. Even expressions of emotionality, such as anger or depression, although they have physiological concomitants, are mostly the expressions of social reactions. They can be expressed, controlled, or accentuated according to a variety of social and cultural definitions.

Social Roles

Deviants and nondeviants play a variety of *social roles* which represent the behavior that is expected of a person in a given position or status within a group.[25] The activities of a human being in the course of daily life can be regarded as the performance of a series of roles which he has learned and which others expect him to fulfill. It is through the expectation of others that persons are assigned roles and statuses and are expected to engage in the behavior prescribed for these roles and statuses such as the roles played by a mother or a son. Social behavior develops not only as we respond in relation to other people, but also through *social interaction* as we anticipate the responses of other people to us and incorporate them into our conduct. When two or more persons interact, for example, all are more or less aware of the fact that each is evaluating the behavior of the others. In this process each person also evaluates his own behavior. A *social role* more specifically involves four parts: (1) the person's identification or conception of himself; (2) the appropriate behavior he displays according to his conception of the situation; (3) the roles which are acted out by other persons in response to his role; and (4) the evaluation by the individual of these roles.[26] The person's behavior, based on his estimate of how he should act, is called, *role playing,* and his idea of the other person's behavior is called *role taking.* A *role set* is a complement of role relationships which persons have by occupying a particular social status such as the role of a teacher to his pupils and to all the others connected with the school.[27] *Social control* becomes pos-

---

[25] See Bruce J. Biddle and Edwin J. Thomas, eds., *Role Theory: Concepts and Research* (New York: John Wiley & Sons, Inc., 1966), particularly Chap. 1, "The Nature and History of Role Theory."

[26] Lindesmith and Strauss, p. 166. There are a large number of concepts relating to role theory. For our purposes it has been felt unnecessary to go into more than those we have used in this chapter. See Edwin J. Thomas and Bruce J. Biddle, "Basic Concepts for Classifying the Phenomena of Role," in Biddle and Thomas, pp. 23–63.

[27] Robert K. Merton, "Instability and Articulation in the Role-Set," in Biddle and Thomas, pp. 282–287; and Robert K. Merton, *Social Theory and Social Structure* (rev. ed.; New York: The Free Press, 1957).

sible through the fact that persons acquire the ability to behave in a manner consistent with the expectations of others.[28]

Socialization largely represents the learning of roles, that is, it refers to the "process by which the individual acquires the skills, knowledge, attitudes, values, and motives necessary for performance of social roles." [29] It involves a process of learning in which an individual is prepared in larger and smaller groups to meet the status requirements that society expects in a variety of social situations. The required behavior (habits, beliefs, attitudes, and motives) are an individual's *prescribed roles;* the requirements themselves are the *role prescriptions.*[30] The role prescriptions or norm requirements are learned in interaction with others. What roles the child learns in the family and elsewhere, such as the male or female sex role, are largely dictated by the social structure or the society itself, although there often exist family variations in the degree to which the child is socialized into certain roles.

Groups, then, are multidimensional *systems of roles;* a group is what its role relationships are. In the interaction of any group there are various role relationships involving mutual attitudinal and behavioral responses to one another. The individual members of a group may change but the group may continue, as in the case of a delinquent gang, where the roles of the leader and other required roles in the gang may continue to be played despite changes in gang membership.

> What distinguishes one group from others is its members' behavior, and not just who its members are—that is, their names, faces, and personal idiosyncrasies. . . . Thus the role relationships within a group represent the ways in which its members adapt to their positional relationships with each other. From this it follows that if different persons, as members of different groups, have similar positions in their own groups,

[28] Shibutani, pp. 118–121, 197. Self-control is, in essence, social control, for persons see themselves from the standpoint of the group and thus try to maintain self-respect through achieving social respect by meeting the group's expectations. Also see S.F. Nadel, "Social Control and Self-Regulation," *Social Forces,* 31:265–273 (1953).

[29] William H. Sewell, "Some Recent Developments in Socialization Theory and Research," *The Annals,* 349:163–181 (1963). Also see Part X, "Learning and Socialization," in Biddle and Thomas, pp. 345–382, and Orville G. Brim, Jr., and Stanton Wheeler, *Socialization after Childhood: Two Essays* (New York: John Wiley & Sons, Inc., 1966).

[30] See Orville G. Brim, Jr., David C. Glass, David E. Lavin, and Norman Goodman, *Personality and Decision Processes: Studies in the Social Psychology of Thinking* (Stanford, Calif.: Stanford University Press, 1962). Also see Biddle and Thomas.

then we would expect role relationships to be similar in the different groups. And so it happens that role relationships between husbands and wives or between employers and employees have much in common the world around. And so it happens, also, that even though there is a complete turnover of individual members, as in the case of the United States Senate every forty years or so, the role relationships of its members remain much the same. It is for this reason that we feel justified in saying that the Senate remains the same body even though its members change.[31]

Although a great deal of socialization in role playing and role taking occurs in childhood it also continues into later life, a fact often not adequately recognized, as we shall see later, by psychologists and psychiatrists. Individuals learn new roles and abandon old ones as they pass through the life cycle and encounter new situations. Adolescence represents a period of adjustment to new roles; marriage represents the acquisition of new roles; entrance into professions or occupations requires new roles; and old age often becomes a major role adjustment.

Like the actor who plays many stage parts, even though they are exaggerated, persons fill numerous roles. Some roles are general and others are specific; some are idealized and others are actual roles. A person's social roles are linked with his position or status in society, and each of these has role prescriptions. There are age roles, sex roles, social class roles, occupation roles, and family roles. Such roles are, for example, those of an old or a young person, a man or a woman, a husband or a wife, a parent or a child, a private or a general, a doctor, a lawyer, a salesman, or an employer. There are deviant roles such as an alcoholic, a homosexual, a delinquent gang member, or a drug addict. The student and the professor play a series of roles in the lecture room, in the office discussing a subject or bargaining for a grade, and often in their greeting and demeanor toward one another on the campus. Negroes, in their relations with whites, often act out roles, and the problems arising from these interacting roles are an important aspect of what are called race relations. For example, in the South, there is often a "continued flow of agreement by the Negro while a white man is talking, such as 'Yes, Boss,' 'Sho nuff,' 'Well, I declare' and the like." [32]

> That we do not get more mixed up than we do in shifting from role to role is a fortunate consequence of our capacity for broad social learning. The variety of roles we must juggle reflects the fact that complex

---

[31] Theodore M. Newcomb, Ralph H. Turner, and Philip E. Converse, *Social Psychology: The Study of Human Interaction* (New York: Holt, Rinehart and Winston, Inc., 1965), p. 350.

[32] John Dollard, *Caste and Class in a Southern Town* (New Haven, Conn.: Yale University Press, 1937), p. 180.

social systems are compounded of a great variety of subsystems such as families, friendship groups, working groups, and other more or less organized collectivities of persons. Although none of us participates in anything like all the specific groups about us, the fact remains that all of us are required to participate in a substantial number. In each of such kinds of groups, one or more roles are prescribed for us. And each of them, taken as a system of roles, presupposes that its members can indeed manage to engage in behaviors appropriate to that particular system when the situation warrants.[33]

Persons occupying a given status position are influenced in their *role behavior* by the role prescription or the "script" they are supposed to play. A changed social position, belonging to a delinquent gang or to a group taking drugs, for example, may mean a changed social role. Actual role behavior may be somewhat different from the role prescription, however, for it is affected by a variety of influences, such as the behavior of others in the situation, belonging to groups whose role prescriptions are different, and so on.

Some role prescriptions are highly structured and clear; some persons play more roles than others. *Role strain* may arise in situations requiring complex role demands and where a person is required to fulfill multiple roles.[34] Many of the problems arising in systems of roles are due to the fact that (1) the role prescriptions are unclear and the person has difficulty in knowing what is expected of him, (2) the roles are too numerous for the individual to fulfill, with a resulting "role overload," and (3) they may conflict or be mutually contradictory so that the individual must play a role he does not wish to play, such as the subordinate role a Negro must often play in the United States or the marginal role played by adolescents. Parsons, in fact, has explained role conflict as the basis of deviant behavior. Such behavior is a response to a strain or conflict in institutional role expectations which the individual faces.[35]

Primary and Secondary Deviants

Human behavior fundamentally represents a series of social roles which may be deviant or nondeviant. Much of deviant behavior is directly expressive of roles. "A tough and bellicose posture, the use of obscene language, participation in illicit sexual activity, the immoderate consumption of alcohol, the deliberate flouting of legality and authority, a generalized dis-

---

[33] Newcomb, *et al.,* p. 393.

[34] Newcomb, *et al.,* pp. 393–427. Also see Part II, "The Conceptual Structure," in Biddle and Thomas, p. 62.

[35] Talcott Parsons, "Role Conflict and the Genesis of Deviance," in Biddle and Thomas, pp. 275–276; and Parsons, pp. 280–283.

respect for the sacred symbols of the 'square' world, a taste for marihuana, even suicide—all of these may have the primary function of affirming, in the language of gesture and deed, that one is a certain kind of person." [36] Professional thieves, for example, play a variety of roles. Punctuality in keeping appointments with partners and the code of not "squealing" on another thief are of particular importance in their profession. Social status or position among thieves is based on their technical skill, connections, financial standing, influence, dress, manners, and wide knowledge. Their status is also reflected in the attitudes which ordinary criminals have toward them as well as the attitudes of lawyers, the police, court officials, and newspaper reporters. The professional criminal may play different roles toward victim, friend, wife, children, father, mother, grocer, or minister.

Most of the "script" for these deviant roles, as for nondeviant ones, is derived from group experience and cultural or subcultural situations. On occasions, however, where appropriate roles are not provided they may be unique to the individual's own life experience. The diversity of social roles in modern urban society, as will be indicated later, is an important factor in the extent of social deviation in modern society. Because of this diversity and the lack of coordination of social roles, the actual behavioral responses of persons to certain situations fail to conform to what would ordinarily be expected. A person's own evaluation of his role is often not the same as that of others.

The status and role (or roles) which a person is assigned cannot be easily changed by his own desires: whether a person plays the role which society has assigned to him or not, his behavior is still interpreted by society as consistent with this role and its corresponding status. For example, the behavior of the former inmate of a prison in his home community may be interpreted in a manner consistent with real or imagined criminal "tendencies," even if he is making a determined effort to "go straight." The power of community interpretations in perpetuating a person's occupancy of a criminal status and role may have several consequences. Sometimes such persons will "give in" to the societal definition and actively play the role expected of them; thus the individual becomes a "self-fulfilling prophecy" by repeating as a delinquent, criminal, drug addict, alcoholic, or mental patient.

On the basis of social roles, therefore, deviants can be distinguished as to whether they are primary or secondary deviants.[37] Persons may engage in

---

[36] Albert K. Cohen, "The Sociology of the Deviant Act: Anomie Theory and Beyond," *American Sociological Review*, 30:13 (1965).

[37] Lemert, pp. 75–76 and Edwin M. Lemert, *Human Deviance, Social Problems, and Social Control* (Englewood Cliffs, N. J.: Prentice-Hall, Inc., 1967).

deviant behavior but continue to occupy a conventional status and role. Such deviant behavior constitutes *primary deviation* when it is rationalized and considered as a function of a socially acceptable role. A deviant act may not materially affect the person's self-concept or give him a deviant role. Deviant acts may remain primary; for example, repeated drunkenness may not represent a problem to a person; a homosexual act or taking a drug may have few consequences for the individual; taking money for sex purposes may not give a person a feeling that she is a prostitute.

On the other hand, the deviant role may be reinforced by others; deviant actions may be reacted to by arrest, imprisonment, or other formal and informal sanctions which stigmatize the person. The deviant then becomes socially isolated as a deviant. Consequently, the deviant has less opportunity to play conventional roles and comes to incorporate a societal image of himself as a deviant and plays a deviant role.[38] "Secondary deviation is deviant behavior, or social roles based upon it, which becomes means of defense, attack, or adaptation to the overt and covert problems created by the societal reaction to primary deviation. In effect, the original 'causes' of the deviation recede and give way to the central importance of the disapproving, degradational, and isolating reactions of society." [39]

Thus persons may commit delinquencies and crimes without becoming secondary deviants and without being regarded as "delinquents" and "criminals." Women may engage in sex acts under conditions similar to those in which the prostitute operates yet not consider themselves as such. There are persons who engage in homosexual acts but are not homosexuals in the sense of secondary deviation. A person may be a heavy drinker and not be an alcoholic. Once the person becomes a secondary deviant it has important consequences for further deviant behavior. *The secondary deviant develops a deviant role which involves greater participation in a deviant subculture, the acquisition of more knowledge and rationalizations for the behavior, and skill in avoiding detection and arrest.* The process of self-evaluation in secondary deviation also has several effects, including a tendency to minimize the stigma of deviation.

---

[38] See pages 23–25. While societal reaction may have much to do with the development of most secondary deviation, it has been overstated as a necessary factor in all cases. Some persons may develop secondary roles without having been arrested, as in the case of some young gang offenders, professional criminals, and even homosexuals. A study of typical women shoplifters showed that such behavior, even when pursued over a long period of time, tends to cease when they are first apprehended. See Mary Owen Cameron, *The Booster and the Snitch: Department Store Shoplifting* (New York: The Free Press, 1964).

[39] Lemert, *Human Deviance,* p. 17.

The value hierarchy of the degraded individual changes, in the process of which ends become means and means become ends. Conventional punishments lose their efficacy with loss of status. Experiences at one time evaluated as degrading may shift full arc to become rewarding. The alcoholic is an example; deeply ashamed by his first stay in jail, he may as years go by come to look upon arrest as a means of getting food, shelter, and a chance to sober up.[40]

Attitudes

Every individual has literally thousands of *attitudes* which provide the basis for his actions in many situations.[41] On the basis of acquired attitudes a flavored solution of a chemical called alcohol may be regarded as a delectable beverage by a habitual drinker, whereas that same chemical may not only have a highly disagreeable taste to a teetotaler but be regarded as poisonous and sinful to drink. A Negro may be thought of as quite similar in his personality to most white men or he may be thought of as shiftless, immoral, and oversexed; as a result, the behavior of others toward the Negro will vary. Objects or social norms in our culture are defined by a person's experiences, as the following case illustrates.

> A novel example is furnished by Fung Kwok Keung, born Joseph Rinehart of American parents living in Long Island, New York. At the age of three, his parents deserted him, and he was adopted by Chinese, taken to China and reared there for nineteen years. Recently he returned to the United States. He is Chinese in manner, speech, habit, outlook—in all ways but appearance.[42]

Most attitudes are developed through group associations rather than as a result of individual experience. Inasmuch as people are all, in one way or another, members of groups, attitudes generally represent shared meanings. Hence most attitudes are derived from cultural norms. Groups, then, to which the individual may belong serve as a frame of reference and undoubtedly influence his attitudes. A group in terms of whose norms a person orients his behavior is a *reference group*. Such groups are not necessarily

---

[40] Edwin M. Lemert, *Human Deviance, Social Problems, and Social Control,* p. 54, © 1967. Reprinted by permission of Prentice-Hall, Inc., Englewood Cliffs, N.J.

[41] "An individual's attitude toward something is his predisposition to be motivated in relation to it. . . . The attitude concept seems to reflect quite faithfully the primary form in which past experience is summed, stored, and organized in the individual as he approaches any new situation." Newcomb *et al.,* pp. 40–41.

[42] Quoted in William F. Ogburn and Meyer F. Nimkoff, *Sociology* (Boston: Houghton Mifflin Company, 1946), p. 8. As the groups to which a person belongs differ, so do his attitudes.

the same as *membership groups* to which a person is recognized as belonging.[43] A delinquent gang may be the reference group of a delinquent rather than such membership groups as family, church, and similar groups.

Although cultural experiences are often superficially similar, they are not the same in detail, nor are they experienced in the same way by two individuals. As mentioned above, attitudes are derived from social experiences, and thus may differ according to such variables as the country or part of the country in which we live, the part of the city or town in which we have been raised, the social class and occupation to which we belong, and the amount and quality of our education. These differences in attitudes have been reflected in numerous surveys of public opinion. People have been shown to differ a great deal in their attitudes toward things simply on. the basis of their religious training. The attitudes of a slum neighborhood toward crime, delinquency, the police, gambling, premarital sex relations, and prostitution are often quite different from those held in middle-class residential areas.

Of fundamental importance in the development of attitudes are those groups which are described as "primary." Primary groups include the family, the neighborhood, and various friendship groups, such as high school cliques and boys' gangs—all groups from which basic attitudes are acquired, particularly those attitudes involving social values. These *primary groups* are extremely important because social interaction tends to be intimate and "face to face," which makes a greater impression on the person than the less intimate type of group. These primary groups affect the individual early in life, presenting the child with the first ways of acting, and with the only possible "right" conception of a situation. Early attitudes become important, whether they are about foods, manners, and religion or about Negroes, Jews, and honesty. These attitudes are called primary not only because they develop first but because they have attached to them strong personal ties which are more difficult to modify later in life. Among deviants, for example, the corner gang may supply the child with a view of the world in general, including conceptions of such broad categories as the police and schoolteachers, or stealing and truancy in particular.

As distinguished from "primary group attitudes," there is another source, called *secondary groups*. These are somewhat later associations based on common interests, abilities, roles, and status position and include occupational groups, labor union or professional groups, and church, tavern,

---

[43] See, for example, Robert K. Merton and Alice S. Kitt, "Contributions to the Theory of Reference Group Behavior," in Robert K. Merton and Paul F. Lazarsfeld,, eds., *Studies in the Scope and Method of "The American Soldier,"* (New York: The Free Press, 1950), pp. 70–105.

club, or lodge groups. The group members may not be emotionally tied together and may not even know each other well. The norms which are present usually refer to a specific area of life and may not be those of all the members. It is in this sense that it is often possible to speak of a person as belonging to such a secondary group without really becoming a part of it. Although a person undoubtedly acquires many attitudes from secondary groups, they are not likely to be the first presented to him on such important questions of behavior as racial or sexual attitudes. Oftentimes primary groups, such as the family, tend to channel persons, particularly when young, into secondary groups with similar norms, and in such circumstances what may appear to be a continuous hold of the family on the individual turns out to be a partial illusion.

Although people secure most of their attitudes from the general culture and from subcultural situations that differ according to region, neighborhood, class, occupation, religion, and education, some attitudes are the result of unique personal experiences. An example is the favorable change in attitudes toward Negroes that sometimes occurs among soldiers under battle conditions. This method of acquiring attitudes through unique experiences is not common, but probably everyone has had such experiences. Most attitudes involving disrespect for law are acquired through group experiences but some persons who have had particularly brutal experiences in a correctional institution or in a so-called reformatory may have attitudes of disrespect turn into hatred for law and law officers.

A differential process of acquiring attitudes has been suggested by Sutherland, particularly in connection with his well known theory of criminal behavior, a theory which will be discussed later.[44] The theory can be applied in general, however, to the acquisition of many other forms of deviant behavior involving cultural norms. He has suggested that variables such as the following would account both for the difference in the development and for the continuance of delinquent and criminal deviant attitudes: (1) How early in life did the association with a certain deviant norm begin? (2) How many and how extensive were the facets of the person's life that were associated with the deviant behavior? Did the definition of a social situation include only one social role or all the person's activities? (3) How continuous was the contact with the deviations? Did the association continue over a period of years, or was it limited to only a brief period? (4) How important was the association with the person who furnished a deviant model? In this connection, how much did the person identify himself with the deviant model, whether it was a companion, a member of the family, a play group, or other models?

---

[44] See pages 254–255, for example, and Sutherland and Cressey, Chap. 4, "A Sociological Theory of Criminal Behavior."

Research on attitudes has brought out the fact that, while they may be relatively stabilized definitions of situations, they can and do change. Among the more important variables which change attitudes appear to be such factors as the following: first, the strength of a particular attitude in the presence of external influences; second, increased familiarity due to firsthand experience; and third, the prestige of the model presenting a given attitude. These three ideas can be illustrated by the resistance to the use of drugs on the part of a middle-class boy who has attended a high school where there is little drug use and who has been active in conventional groups. Suppose that a boy who has been taking drugs moves into his neighborhood. Under the personal influence of this boy the first youngster may tend to alter his attitudes. If the new boy is someone with considerable prestige and one whom he admires, there is an increased possibility that he himself may engage in drug use. If the prestige model in this example were reversed the boy taking drugs might become a nonuser.

Motivations

Even so-called *motives* are acquired as the result of social experience.[45] They are socially molded, usually in accord with the prevailing norms of particular groups to which the individual belongs. For example, the possession of an automobile and the status it would give might be so important a goal to a delinquent boy that he would steal one. If his goals were directed toward a status based on higher grades in school or on some conventional hobby the end results would be different.

Persons appear to vary in their emphasis on given motives, depending on cultural and subcultural norms, the definition of the situation, and the life organization of the individual. In the process of reaching goals, deviants and nondeviants may adopt what might appear to be different patterns of behavior, but in reality they may be achieving similar goals in their own way. Some boys may have fun playing baseball or indulging in other sports, whereas others may find even more fun stealing automobiles, slashing tires, wrecking a school, beating up a stranger, or taking drugs. Some may find companionship in a delinquent gang rather than in a boy scout troop; some people may prefer the fellowship of drinking companions in a tavern to the fellowship offered by a church. A young "punk" in a city slum may seek to gain a status of a far different kind from that sought by a college student. Some men would probably prefer to have the prestige and acclaim accorded them in an organized criminal syndicate or in professional crime than be president of a university. Businessmen and politicians have engaged

---

[45] For various theories of motivation see Charles N. Cofer and Mortimer H. Appley, *Motivation: Theory and Research* (New York: John Wiley & Sons, Inc., 1964).

in illegal behavior in order to secure funds with which to buy material goods which, in turn, bring them greater recognition in society. Much of deviant behavior is motivated by an expression of roles.

> A great deal of deviance that seems "irrational" and "senseless" makes some sense when we see it as an effort to proclaim or test a certain kind of self. . . . The use of marihuana and heroin, especially the early experimental stages; driving at dangerous speeds and "playing chicken" on the highway; illegal consumption of alcoholic beverages; participation in illegal forms of social protest and civil disobedience; taking part in "rumbles"—all these are likely to be role-expressive behavior. In order to recognize this motivation, however, one must know the roles that are at stake, and what kinds of behavior carry what kinds of "role-messages" in the actor's social world.[46]

DEVIANT BEHAVIOR AND THE INTERACTION PROCESS

Most deviant acts do not just happen; they develop over a period of time out of a process or a series of stages. Some deviant acts, such as vandalism or assault, often begin without the person's intending to commit the act. In some acts he may choose among two or more alternatives, depending on the situation presented. A deviant act, such as an act of stealing a car, is often "a tentative, groping, feeling-out process, never fully determined by the past alone but always capable of changing its course in response to changes in the current scene." [47] One stage in a deviant act may not be necessarily determined by an antecedent stage. Speaking of the process in the use of marihuana, Becker has written that "the variables which account for each step may not, taken separately, distinguish between users and nonusers. The variable which disposes a person to take a particular step may not operate because he has not yet reached the stage in the process where it is possible to take that step." [48]

In defining a situation for appropriate deviant or nondeviant actions, one assumes the standpoint of real or imagined others and imaginatively rehearses the action expected by these others of oneself. Role taking, or assuming the attitudes of others, is the elementary process involved in defining a situation. "The comprehension of what a man does requires a record of (1) his definition of the situation, (2) the kind of creature he believes himself to be, and (3) the audience before which he tries to maintain

---

[46] Albert K. Cohen, *Deviance and Control,* p. 99. © 1966. Reprinted by permission of Prentice-Hall, Inc., Englewood Cliffs, N.J.

[47] Cohen, *Deviance and Control,* p. 45.

[48] Howard S. Becker, *Outsiders: Studies in the Sociology of Deviance* (New York: The Free Press, 1963), p. 23.

his self-respect." [49] The *definition of the situation* is essentially a means by which an individual organizes his behavior. In order imaginatively to rehearse his own action, he takes into account the anticipated responses of others and organizes them into his own behavior.[50] In defining situations with which we are unfamiliar, we often look for "cues" which allow us to assess the present circumstances in terms of context with which we are more familiar.[51]

The particular definition a given individual makes will be influenced by all that he has known and experienced until that time. The latter would include the set of attitudes, norms, and values which the person has acquired or known, the particular set of statuses and roles he has occupied, or is familiar with, and the particular cumulation of experiences and situations he has known of or participated in. For example, if a teenager perceives a set of keys left in a car he may interpret the situation as an opportunity to steal it; another may pay no attention to the same situation. The presence of drugs in a pharmacy or in a doctor's office may be perceived by a drug addict as a possible supply to be obtained by burglarizing the premises. A difficult situation may be perceived in one way by a person contemplating suicide, and in a completely different way by someone else. The direction of a deviant act depends on past experiences and learning but also depends on the responses of others in the immediate situation, for it is these responses which the individual takes into account in defining the situation and which he organizes into his own behavior.

In many cases unanticipated consequences arise from events which were not even considered in the earlier stages of the deviant act, as often occurs in cases of criminal homicide.

> For example, a person might set out to burglarize a house. Quite unexpectedly, the householder may come home and attack the burglar with a deadly weapon. The burglar, to save his own life, kills the attacker. What started out as a burglary might end up as murder, due to a circumstance that was not necessarily implicit in the earlier stage of the act. However, although the arrival of the householder was a separately determined event, unforeseen and perhaps unforeseeable, the situation as a whole is partly a product of the actor's own doing.[52]

Whether a given deviant act (such as shoplifting, rape, exhibitionism, or embezzlement) will be considered as such depends a great deal on the

---

[49] Shibutani, p. 279.

[50] Shibutani, pp. 118–119.

[51] See Erving Goffman, *The Presentation of Self in Everyday Life* (New York: Doubleday Anchor Books, 1959), Chap. 1.

[52] Cohen, *Deviance and Control*, p. 103.

response of other persons, such as the victim. Much may depend on the response of those who witness the deviant act or are involved directly in it, and how serious they think the act is.

> Much of the literature that is concerned with the acquisition of and commitment to deviant roles is couched in essentially these terms: somebody, for any one of many reasons, does something that is in no sense "characteristic" or "distinctive" of him as contrasted to a multitude of other people. This behavior, however, lends itself to interpretation as a sign of a "deviant character." Whether it will be interpreted in this way, and the individual identified and labeled as that kind of person, depends on who sees it and whether he is motivated to take action. Whether the label will stick, and the actor invested with the role, will depend partly on the reputation he has previously established and partly on the authority of those who apply the definition.[53]

SUMMARY

The same fundamental processes are involved in deviant and nondeviant behavior. Differences in subprocesses exist; if they did not, there would be no way to account for deviant behavior. The biological structure of man is of little importance in accounting for deviant or nondeviant behavior, for he does not have instincts which could account for such behavior. Deviant behavior cannot be inherited. Physical defects do not distinguish the deviant from the nondeviant. Physical characteristics are not directly important, although they may have an indirect influence in some cases of deviant behavior.

It is the social rather than the physical nature of man which is important in studying deviant and nondeviant behavior. Man's behavior is a product of socialization. This includes the acquisition of a self-concept, social roles, attitudes, and motives. The fact that man has language and a conception of self makes him different from other animals. Attitudes, important components of social behavior, are acquired primarily through relations with others. They are secured from primary and secondary groups and from unique experiences.

All persons play a variety of social roles which involve the way a person conceives of himself, the behavior he displays according to this conception, the roles acted out by others in response to his behavior, and his own evaluation of his role. The fact that deviants as well as nondeviants play social roles must be recognized in analyzing deviant behavior. Particularly important in understanding deviant behavior is the difference between primary

---

[53] Cohen, *Deviance and Control*, p. 104.

and secondary deviation. A well-integrated set of roles may characterize some deviants, whereas others may be the product of conflicting roles. Deviant behavior grows out of an interaction process and deviant acts must be interpreted in these terms.

SELECTED READINGS

Biddle, Bruce J., and Edwin J. Thomas. *Role Theory: Concepts and Research.* New York: John Wiley & Sons, Inc., 1966. A systematic analysis of the various aspects of role theory with examples of its application. Particularly useful is the explanation of various concepts used in role theory.

Cressey, Donald R. *Other People's Money.* New York: The Free Press, 1953. This study is a sociopsychological analysis of embezzlement emphasizing particularly self-conception.

Goffman, Erving. *The Presentation of Self in Everyday Life.* New York: Doubleday Anchor Books, 1959. A discussion of the self and its importance in social interaction with others.

Lemert, Edwin M. *Human Deviance, Social Problems, and Social Control.* Englewood Cliffs, N.J.: Prentice-Hall, Inc., 1967. Chapter 3 deals with the concept of secondary deviation.

———. *Social Pathology.* New York: McGraw-Hill Book Company, Inc., 1951, Chap. 4, "Sociopathic Individuation." This is an excellent application of the concept of social role to the study of deviant behavior.

Lindesmith, Alfred R. *Opiate Addiction.* Bloomington: Indiana University Press, 1947. A sociopsychological interpretation of opiate addiction using many of the concepts presented here.

———, and Anselm L. Strauss. *Social Psychology.* Rev ed. New York: Holt, Rinehart and Winston, Inc., 1955. Discusses human nature, language, the self, and social roles. Chapter 13, "Deviant Behavior," is a sociopsychological discussion of a number of areas.

Newcomb, Theodore M., Ralph H. Turner, and Philip E. Converse. *Social Psychology.* New York: Holt, Rinehart and Winston, Inc., 1965. Deals with social interaction, self-concept, and role theory, and emphasizes particularly the importance of social interaction in group behavior.

Shibutani, Tomatsu. *Society and Personality.* Englewood Cliffs, N.J.: Prentice-Hall, Inc., 1961. Discusses the fundamental processes and concepts involved in socialization. An unusually clear and interesting discussion of social behavior.

3

Urbanization, Urbanism, and Deviant Behavior

City living has characterized some areas for centuries, but urbanization has spread with such acceleration over the past century as to
encompass hundreds of millions of people throughout the entire world.
This urban life has produced what some have called the "Mass Society."
It has greatly increased social differentiation, the clash of norms and social
roles, and the breakdown in interpersonal relations among persons. Modern
conditions have presented opportunities for the development of such a
"way of life" in nearly every part of the world on a tremendous scale.[1] Increasing urbanization has almost everywhere, whether in the United States,
Latin America, Africa, or Asia, been accompanied by a marked increase in
various forms of deviant behavior.

---

[1] See Rose Hum Lee, *The City: Urbanism and Urbanization in Major World
Regions* (Philadelphia: J. B. Lippincott Company, 1955), and Nels Anderson, *The
Urban Community* (New York: Holt, Rinehart and Winston, Inc., 1959). Also see
Philip M. Hauser and Leo F. Schnore, *The Study of Urbanization* (New York: John
Wiley & Sons, Inc., 1965); and Noel P. Gist and Sylvia F. Fava, *Urban Society* (5th
ed.; New York: Thomas Y. Crowell Company, 1964).

THE GROWTH OF WORLD URBANIZATION

Cities first appeared in the Near East, in Mesopotamia, in the region between the Tigris and Euphrates rivers, about 3500 B.C.[2] A few centuries later they also appeared in the Nile Valley of Egypt and the valley of the Indus River, in what is now West Pakistan. The emergence of the earliest cities according to Sjoberg, required (1) that the surrounding region have a climate and soil sufficiently favorable to support a large population, (2) relatively speaking, an advanced technology in both agricultural and nonagricultural spheres, and (3) a complex social organization, particularly in political and economic spheres.[3]

Thus cities have existed for thousands of years. Some cities, such as those of the Orient, were of considerable size. In general, however, only a small proportion of the people lived in them, as compared with urban population today, and few cities had over 100,000 persons. Athens, at its peak in the fifth century B.C., was estimated to have had between 120,000 and 180,000 persons; Rome had several hundred thousand; Florence in 1338, 90,000; and London in 1377, 30,000.[4]

Life in the large cities of several hundred years ago, both in Europe and in the Orient, was quite different from life in the same cities today. There were no forms of rapid or extensive communication and transportation, nor were there the means of distribution and preservation of food which modern inventions have made possible. Consequently, cities, even though large, tended to be actually clusters of villages. Urban populations were much more permanent and settled than they are today, there was less migration into the cities from rural areas, and because of this and because of the absence of media of mass communication as we have them today, people were able to know one another better than they do now.

In 1800 only about 3 percent of the world's estimated population of 906 million lived in places of more than 5000 persons. By 1950 this proportion has increased to about 30 percent. Whereas the world population had increased by nearly 165 percent during these one hundred and fifty years, the urban population of the world had risen by 2535 percent to what has been termed not merely a population explosion but a world "urban explo-

---

[2] Gideon Sjoberg, *The Preindustrial City: Past and Present* (New York: The Free Press, 1960), pp. 25–51. Also see Kingsley Davis, "The Urbanization of the Human Population," in *Cities* (New York: Alfred A. Knopf, Inc., 1965), pp. 3–24.

[3] Sjoberg, p. 27.

[4] See Kingsley Davis, "The Origin and Growth of Urbanization in the World," *American Journal of Sociology*, 40:429–437 (1955).

sion." In 1800 the proportion of the world's population living in cities of 20,000 or more was 2.4; in 1950 it was 20.9 percent.[5] Cities of 100,000 or more contained 1.7 percent of the total world population in 1800; in 1950 they contained 13.1. In 1800 there were fewer than 50 cities in the entire world with 100,000 or more, no cities had a million persons, a figure which is smaller than the number of cities in the million class today.

The increase in the proportion of urban population in the under-developed areas of the world, such as those in South America, Africa, and Asia, has been particularly great. In India, for example, which is thought of as a rural nation, 8.2 percent of the population in 1941 lived in cities of 20,000 or more, whereas in 1961, 17.8 percent lived in cities of that size. This amounted to over 75 million urban persons in India in 1961, or a number larger than the population of most countries of the world. Only 2 Indian cities had over a million population in 1941; by 1961 there were 6, and Davis estimates that by 1970 there will be 10.[6] In 1951 there were 77 cities with 100,000 or more persons; in 1961 there were 121.

Australia leads the world in the proportion of its population living in cities of 100,000 or more. (See Table 3.1) The United Kingdom with 51.0, Japan with 41.2, and Argentina with 39.5 percent follow in that order. The United States has 28.4 percent of its population living in cities of this size.

In 1950 there were over nine hundred cities of 100,000 or more persons and over forty-nine cities with more than a million inhabitants. In 1960 one in every ten persons in the world lived in a metropolitan area of a million or more, and one in five lived in a city of 100,000 or more. (See Table 3.2) One authority has predicted that by the year 2000 over 42 percent of the world's population will be living in metropolitan areas of 100,000 or more.[7] According to 1960 estimates, Tokyo is the largest city in the world, with nearly 10 million persons, or one in ten persons, in Japan.

Behind this growth of modern urbanization, particularly in the Western European world, have been many forces which can only be listed here: the breakdown of the feudal system and the loss of prescribed duties and obligations and integrated way of village life; the Commercial and later the Industrial Revolution, which produced a wide dispersion of the population, particularly to cities; the development of the factory system of production, and extensive occupational differences; the development of science, which brought a secular way of life by destroying many age-old traditions of

---

[5] Davis, "The Origin and Growth of Urbanization in the World."

[6] Kingsley Davis, "Urbanization in India: Past and Future," in Roy Turner, ed., *India's Urban Future* (Berkeley: University of California Press, 1962), p. 25.

[7] Homer Hoyt, *World Urbanization* (Technical Bulletin #43; Washington, D.C.: Urban Land Institute, 1962), Table XVII, p. 50.

TABLE 3.1   **Estimated Proportion of Population Living in Cities of 100,000 or More**

Country	Percent
Australia (1959)	57.4
United Kingdom (1958)	51.0
Japan (1959)	41.2
Argentina (1958)	39.5
Israel (1959)	34.3
Denmark (1958)	34.2
West Germany (1959)	30.7
United States (1960)	28.4
Union of South Africa (1960)	25.4
Sweden (1959)	24.7
Italy (1959)	23.9
USSR (1959)	23.5
United Arab Republic (1958)	22.2
Brazil (1959)	17.6
France (1954)	16.8
Indonesia (1959)	9.4
Ghana (1960)	7.3
India (1951)	6.6
Congo (1959)	5.9
Burma (1958)	5.3

SOURCE: Prepared from *United Nations Demographic Yearbook, 1960* (New York: 1960).

TABLE 3.2   **Percentage of Population in Metropolitan Areas in Different Size Groups, by Continents, 1960**

	One million and over	100,000 and over
North America	27.2	49.7
Latin America	14.7	27.4
Europe *a*	12.5	29.6
Asia	6.2	12.3
Africa	2.6	8.1
Oceania	23.6	43.3
World Total	9.6	19.9

SOURCE: Adapted from Homer Hoyt, *World Urbanization* (Technical Bulletin #43; (Washington, D.C.: Urban Land Institute, 1962), Table II, p. 26; also in Noel P. Gist and Sylvia F. Fava, *Urban Society* (5th ed.; New York: Thomas Y. Crowell Company, 1964), p. 68.
a Including all of the USSR.

thought, also produced new forms of transportation as well as improvements in agriculture so that millions of people were freed from immediate dependence on the land, and enabled to work and live in cities. The virtual disappearance of the large family and with it the loss of many family functions and responsibilities further weakened the ties of family members to the land. All these forces produced drastic changes in the interpersonal relations of those who moved to cities.

Also essential for this growth of modern cities are more specific conditions. The level of agricultural production must be sufficiently high to provide a surplus which will allow people to concentrate in areas for nonagricultural production. Sources of power, such as coal, electricity, or oil, are also necessary to provide large concentrations of persons with the means of industrial production. Electricity, for example, has become essential not only in such production but as part of mass communication through the telephone, radio, and television.

URBANIZATION IN THE UNITED STATES

The United States, following the Civil War, changed from a society of rural communities to one of the most urbanized in the world. So rapid and extensive has been this urbanization that it is now possible to refer to the United States as an "urban society." As Table 3.4 shows, in 1790 only 5.1 percent of the population lived in cities. By 1880 this proportion had increased to 28.2 and in 1920 approximately half the people were urban. Using a slightly different definition, in 1950 the urban population of the United States was 64 percent of the total, and in 1960 69.9. In 1960 this amounted to 125,268,750 persons. In nine states the percentage of urban population exceeds 75: in order they are New Jersey, Rhode Island, New York, Massachusetts, Illinois, Connecticut, Hawaii, and Texas.

Perhaps even more marked has been the increase in the United States in the number of places with 2500 population or over—from 236 in 1850 to 2262 in 1910. By 1940 this figure had increased to 3464, and by 1950 to 4284, although the latter figure represented, in part, a change in the definition of an urban place. The number of cities, however, gives no idea of the increasing concentration of population in and around a small number of places. The 132 cities of 100,000 persons and over contained more than one fourth (28.4 percent) of the total population of the United States in 1960. One in ten Americans lives in a city of 1 million or more. A measure of urbanization, namely "urbanized areas," which includes cities with a

TABLE 3.3   **The Fourteen Largest Urbanized Areas in the United States, 1960**

Area	Population in millions
New York–northeastern New Jersey	14.1
Los Angeles–Long Beach area	6.5
Chicago–northwestern Indiana	6.0
Philadelphia–New Jersey area	3.6
Detroit	3.5
SanFrancisco–Oakland area	2.4
Boston	2.4
Washington–Md.–Va.	1.8
Pittsburgh	1.8
Cleveland	1.8
St. Louis, Mo.–Ill.	1.7
Baltimore	1.4
Minneapolis–St. Paul	1.4
Milwaukee	1.1

SOURCE: *United States Census of Population, 1960. Summary of Number of Inhabitants* (Washington, D.C.: Bureau of the Census, 1961), pp. 1–50.

TABLE 3.4   **Growth of the Urban Population in the United States, 1790–1960**

Year	Percent urban	Percent rural
1790	5.1	94.9
1800	6.1	93.9
1810	7.3	92.7
1820	7.2	92.8
1830	8.8	91.2
1840	10.8	89.2
1850	15.3	84.7
1860	19.8	80.2
1870	25.7	74.3
1880	28.2	71.8
1890	35.1	64.9
1900	39.7	60.3
1910	45.7	54.3
1920	51.2	48.8
1930	56.2	43.8
1940	56.5	43.5
1950	64.0	36.0
1960	69.9	30.1

SOURCE: *United States Census of Population, 1960. Summary of Number of Inhabitants* (Washington, D.C.: Bureau of the Census, 1961), pp. 1–4. The definition of "urban" changed in 1950, so that the comparable figure for that year was 59.6 and in 1960, 63.1.

population of 50,000 or more and those persons residing in certain contiguous areas which are not part of the city, is now used. The fourteen largest urbanized areas in the United States in 1960 are shown, in descending, in Table 3.3.

Slightly more than one half of the total, and more than three fourths of the urban, population of the United States in 1960 were living in 213 urbanized areas. Of the 95.8 million persons living in urbanized areas, 58 million lived in the 254 central cities and 37.8 million lived in the urban-fringe area outside the city. The 16 urbanized areas with more than 1 million inhabitants had a combined population of 51.7 million, or more than half of the total population of the 213 urbanized areas.

URBANISM AS A WAY OF LIFE

The growth of modern cities has meant the development of a way of life much different from that of the rural world. Urbanism as a way of life is often characterized by extensive conflicts of norms and values, by rapid social change, by increased mobility of the population, by emphasis on material goods and individualism, and by a marked decline in intimate communication.[8] The relation of these factors to the size, density, and heterogeneity of an urban area can readily be seen in the schematic presentation in Table 3.5.

Cities vary in the extent or degree to which they are characterized by urban qualities. Some cities have much less norm conflict, social change, mobility, individualism, and impersonality than others. Likewise, great variations in such characteristics often exist among local areas of a given city. Moreover, certain cultural values in a society may increase the effects of urbanization. If a culture emphasizes material possessions as a central value, the impersonality of urban life will tend to increase that emphasis. Furthermore, in a culture where people are formal in their behavior and where the people are, as a cultural pattern, more self-contained, the impact of urban life may further intensify impersonality in relationships.

[8] See Louis Wirth, "Urbanism as a Way of Life," *American Journal of Sociology*, 44:1–24 (1938). Wirth's statement was based in part on Georg Simmel, "The Metropolis and Mental Life," in Paul K. Hatt and Albert J. Reiss, Jr., eds., *Reader in Urban Sociology* (New York: The Free Press, 1951), pp. 563–574; and Robert E. Park, *The City* (Chicago: University of Chicago Press, 1925). Other terms, such as *mass society* or *secular,* have been used which in general reflect the same process. For a discussion of secular societies, see Howard Becker, *Man in Reciprocity* (New York: Frederick A. Praeger, Inc., 1956). pp. 169–197.

TABLE 3.5 Schematic Version of Urbanism as a Way of Life

Size An increase in the number of inhabitants of a settlement beyond a certain limit bring about changes in the relations of people and changes in the character of the community.	Greater the number of people interacting, greater the potential differentiation (mobility). Dependence upon a greater number of people, lesser dependence on particular persons. Association with more people, knowledge of a smaller proportion, and of these, less intimate knowledge. More secondary rather than primary contacts—increase in contacts which are face to face, yet impersonal, superficial, transitory, and segmental. More freedom from personal and emotional control of intimate groups. Association in a large number of groups, no individual allegiance to a single group.
Density Reinforces the effect of size in diversifying men and their activities, and in increasing the structural complexity of the society.	Tendency to differentiation and specialization. Separation of residence from work place. Functional specialization of areas—segregation of functions. Segregation of people: city becomes a mosaic social world.
Heterogeneity Cities products of migration of peoples of diverse origin. Heterogeneity of origin matched by heterogeneity of occupants. Differentiation and specialization reinforces heterogeneity.	Without common background and common activities premium is placed on visual recognition: the uniform becomes symbolic of the role. No common set of norms and values, no common ethical system to sustain them; money tends to become measure of all things for which there are no common standards. Formal controls as opposed to informal controls. Necessity for adhering to predictable routines. Clock and the traffic signal symbolic of the basis of the social order. Economic basis: mass production of goods, possible only with the standardization of processes and product. Standardization of goods and facilities in terms of the average. Adjustment of educational, recreational, and cultural services to mass requirements. In politics, success of mass appeals—growth of mass movements.

SOURCE: Schematic version by E. Shevky and W. Bell, *Social Area Analysis* (Stanford, Calif.: Stanford University Press, 1955), pp. 7–8, derived from Louis Wirth, "Urbanism as a Way of Life," *American Journal of Sociology*, 44:1–24 (1938). Copyright 1938 by The University of Chicago.

All too frequently the shortcomings of urban life are emphasized. Cities have several advantages over rural areas. Certainly they have been the centers of industrial production and distribution and as such have contributed much to higher standards of living. Cities, to a greater degree than rural areas, have been centers for inventions and the modification of cultural patterns. This is partly due to the anonymity of the city and its diversity of cultural patterns which provide more freedom for creative thought than do rural areas. As a result, artistic and intellectual centers have developed in many larger cities. Cities have also been the centers of great public health advances, particularly in sanitation and the prevention of disease. In fact, without good sanitation it would be difficult for many cities to exist. City living, as a way of life, is associated with many aspects of "civilization."

> What we call civilization as distinguished from culture has been cradled in the city; the city is the center from which the influences of modern civilized life radiate to the ends of the earth and the point from which they are controlled; the persistent problems of contemporary society take their most acute form in the city. The problems of modern civilization are typically urban problems.[9]

City living does not, of course, directly result in deviant behavior, but many of the conditions associated with city life are, to a preponderant degree, conducive to deviation.[10] It should be kept in mind, however, that the set of variables associated with the concept of urbanism may be found independent of city environments. In other words, "urbanism" is not synonymous with "city." Whereas "city" refers to an area distinguished principally by population size, density, and heterogeneity, "urbanism" refers to a complex of social relationships. Although urbanism may more frequently arise within the city environments, this does not mean that it is limited to them. Rural areas in urban-industrial societies are also becoming "urbanized" as their way of life is experiencing such changes, but there are still pronounced differences between the two types. One's place of origin, whether rural or urban, for example, continues to exercise an influence on behavior later in life.[11] Some changes in rural society represent the spread

---

[9] Louis Wirth, "The Urban Society and Civilization," *American Journal of Sociology*, 45:744 (1940).

[10] For a discussion of rural and urban ways of life and the manner in which they may lead toward or away from various forms of deviation, see Eleanor Leacock, "Three Social Variables and Mental Illness," in Alexander H. Leighton, John A. Clausen, and Robert N. Wilson, eds., *Explorations in Social Psychiatry* (New York: Basic Books, Inc., 1957), pp. 308–338.

of behavior patterns emanating from cities, but much of the change in rural areas has come about as the result of new relations among people who live in these areas. Some of the conditions of an urban way of life will be discussed in the following sections.[12]

Norm and Social Role Conflicts

A major characteristic of urbanism is the diversity of interests and backgrounds of persons who at the same time live in close contact with one another. People living in urban communities vary in age, race, ethnic background, and occupation, and in their interests, attitudes, and values. Moreover, urban life is characterized by contrasts in wealth, abilities, and class structure. Large cities, in particular, have generally been cities within cities in the form of areas with their own subcultures, religious affiliations, or racial characteristics. These are often groups with different customs as well as separate languages.[13] Speaking of the contemporary heterogeneity of urban areas in Africa, one writer has stated:

> One of the most noticeable features of both African periurban areas and African areas inside the towns is the high degree of tribal mixture in the population. It is not unusual to find from twenty to forty different tribes represented in such urban areas, the residents of which are thrown together without regard to their varied cultural backgrounds. Their great heterogeneousness contributes substantially to a peculiar type of congestion, the formation of tribal settlements—little pockets of intense overcrowding where members of the same tribe live and find comfort in one another's presence in an otherwise alien environment.[14]

The heterogeneity of the population, the complex division of labor, and the class structure existing in the larger communities generally result in divergent group norms and values and conflicting social roles. In modern

---

[11] Leo F. Schnore, "The Rural-Urban Variable: An Urbanite's Perspective," *Rural Sociology,* 31:131–155 (1966).

[12] See Charles T. Stewart, Jr., "The Urban and Rural Dichotomy: Concepts and Uses," *American Journal of Sociology,* 64:152–158 (1958); and Richard Dewey, "The Rural-Urban Continuum: Real but Relatively Unimportant," *American Journal of Sociology,* 66:60–66 (1960). Also see Paul Hatt and Albert J. Reiss, Jr., eds., *Cities and Society* (New York: The Free Press, 1957), especially pp. 35–45, and Anderson.

[13] For example, see Noel P. Gist and Sylvia Fleis Fava, *Urban Society* (5th ed. New York: Thomas Y. Crowell Company, 1964), pp. 118–145.

[14] Peter C. W. Gutkind, "Congestion and Overcrowding: An African Problem," *Human Organization,* 19:130 (1960). Also see Hilda Kuper, ed., *Urbanization and Migration* (Berkeley: University of California Press, 1965).

urban societies, so differentiated and so conflicting have become the ends sought by different groups that individuals are often in the position of not knowing in many areas of life exactly what are the conventional ways of behaving and the proper social roles. Role stress often arises under urban conditions because individuals are typically incumbents of many and varied positions.[15] Persons who are conventional in their sexual behavior live alongside those who are sexually promiscuous. The city harbors those who respect the law and are honest in most of their social relationships as well as those who have little respect for laws, officials, or property. Variations exist in religious beliefs, family systems, and the means of achieving satisfying human relationships.

At the same time the impersonality of urban life tends to foster increased individual freedom of normative choice.[16] Norm and role conflicts, or diversities of norms and behavioral standards, create a situation where no single standard is likely to be upheld and where deviation from it is not met with penalizing sanctions. Individuals who have been taught to accept the supremacy of a single rule may become skeptical of its validity when they discover, under urban conditions, that breaking the rule does not bring about social ostracism or censure as supposed.

Rapid Cultural Change

Rapid social and cultural change, disregard for the importance of stability of generations, and untempered loyalties also generally characterize urban life. New ideas are generally welcome, inventions of mechanical gadgets are encouraged, and new styles in such arts as painting, literature, and music are often approved. Urban society has been characterized as a secular one or "one in which resistance to change is at a minimum or, to say the very least, where change in many aspects of life is quite welcome." [17] Consequently, elements which are traditional, or "sacred," dwindle in importance and "skepticism with reference to the alleged truths [has] become . . . characteristic of the modern [urban] sophisticated man." [18]

Urban life itself also tends to facilitate changes in norms and ideologies, as well as systems of behavior, which may greatly alter the nature of

---

[15] See Frederick L. Bates, "Some Observations Concerning the Structural Aspects of Role Conflicts," *Pacific Sociological Review*, 5:75–82 (1962).

[16] Arnold Rose, "The Problem of a Mass Society," in Arnold Rose, *Theory and Methods in the Social Sciences* (Minneapolis: University of Minnesota Press, 1954), p. 37.

[17] Howard Becker, *Through Values to Social Interpretation* (Durham, N.C.: Duke University Press, 1950), p. 67.

[18] Louis Wirth, "Ideological Aspects of Social Disorganization," *American Sociological Review*, 5:482 (1940).

the social structure and the relationships of people to one another. Some-times these changes appear to result partly from the practical exigencies of urban life; at other times they seem to be outgrowths of the failure of informal controls to uphold and maintain the older values and ideologies. Urban living has brought such great changes in the modern family, for example, that it has come to be called the urban family. The reduced size of the modern family has been both a characteristic and a result of urban life. Urban life has developed the concept of the equality of the sexes in marriage, a concept which has caused considerable conflict with rural defini-tions of family roles. The structuring of urban society into often fairly dis-tinct peer groups has resulted in the magnification of age differences and the widening of the gap between teen-age persons and older generations. Likewise, the emphasis on youthful values in urban life has meant that as people grow older they are faced with new definitions of roles which may necessitate considerable readjustment.

Mobility

An urban population exhibits considerable horizontal and vertical mobility. Horizontal mobility involves physical movement in connection with occupation and other activities, or it may mean change of residence within a community or to another. Vertical mobility involves changes in occupational and social status.

Modern transportation, particularly in urban areas, enables persons to move about rapidly and to come into frequent contact with many dif-ferent people. It has been said that less than a century ago a man might live a lifetime without ever going far from his home, and without seeing more than a handful of strangers. In fact, one writer has stated that speed is the most common characteristic of urban life. Time has become such an ex-tremely important factor that it is seldom possible for urbanites to relax. Transportation, job, meetings, recreation, home—all move in response to the clock. "In spite of many time-saving gadgets and devices invented to leave more and more minutes free from some drudgery or operation, the urban day is still too short." [19]

Figures of the United States Census reveal how frequently families move in contemporary society. The number of persons who move each year is approximately one in five. Each year about 30 million persons move (see Table 3.6), and of this number about 5 million cross county lines. Another 5 million move across state lines. Two in five move across regional lines as well, many of them one or two thousand miles. Younger persons are more

---

[19] Rose Hum Lee, *The City: Urbanism and Urbanization in Major World Regions* (Philadelphia: J. B. Lippincott Company, 1955), p. 459.

TABLE 3.6   **Internal Migration in the United States**

| | | *Persons moving their home* | |
YEAR	TOTAL NUMBER OF PERSONS	WITHIN SAME STATE	FROM ONE STATE TO ANOTHER
1948–49	27,127,000	22,783,000	4,344,000
1949–50	27,526,000	23,637,000	3,889,000
1950–51	31,158,000	25,970,000	5,188,000
1951–52	29,840,000	24,728,000	5,112,000
1952–53	30,786,000	25,264,000	5,522,000
1953–54	29,027,000	23,993,000	5,034,000
1954–55	31,492,000	26,597,000	4,895,000
1955–56	33,098,000	28,045,000	5,053,000
1956–57	31,834,000	26,758,000	5,076,000
1957–58	33,263,000	27,679,000	5,584,000

SOURCE: U.S. Bureau of the Census, *Current Population Reports; Population Characteristics.* October 13, 1958, Series P-20, No. 85, pp. 8–9.

mobile than older persons; yet a large number of persons age sixty-five and over also move. During the years 1951–1952, 38 percent of those between twenty and twenty-four changed their places of residence, and the proportion was almost as great for those between twenty-five and twenty-nine. Nearly 9 percent of those sixty-five and over changed their residence during this period.

Although urban societies generally tend to regard mobility favorably, such frequent moves may have unsatisfactory effects. They tend to weaken attachments to the local community, particularly among primary or face-to-face contacts, to make persons less interested in maintaining certain community standards, and to increase contact with secondary groups of diverse patterns, thus tending to weaken bonds which help to provide the basis for social control among members of local groups. As a person becomes more mobile he comes into contact with many different norms and begins to understand that other codes of behavior are different from his own. Mobility often means the loss of personal relationships, such as kinship ties, neighbors, and close friendships. For child and adult alike, it may be necessary to acquire new friends and new norms, to change social roles, and to reconcile old norms and roles with new ones.

As close relations with neighbors and relatives are severed, there is less control over the mobile person's behavior and a decline in the importance to him of having a "good reputation" in the eyes of these persons. Too, the standards by which reputation is judged may become more diverse and may depend less upon the specific ethical and moral qualities of the person than upon the "general impression" of him as a person. Children may have increasingly fewer contacts with their grandparents and other relatives. Largely because of this mobility it is likely that a large proportion of young people today, living under urban conditions in America, cannot give the names of great-grandparents on either side of the family. The identification of third cousins usually becomes impossible.

Materialism

External appearances and material possessions become of primary importance in an urban society, where people are more often known for their gadgets than for themselves. People increasingly come to judge others by how well they display their wealth, a display which Veblen has called "conspicuous consumption." Under urban conditions the type of clothes a man wears or the automobile he drives, the costliness of his home and its furnishings, the exclusiveness of the club or association to which he belongs, and the knowledge of his salary or the amount of his financial assets are often the sole means others have of judging him or his success in life. It is on the basis of readily "visible" criteria such as these that status is assigned. Some persons emphasize the importance of "status symbols" in urban society.[20]

Individualism

In modern urban societies two almost contradictory trends affect the position of the individual. On the one hand, the focus is on the individual, as urban persons have more and more come to regard their own interests as paramount in their social relationships.[21] Thus "I" feelings come to replace much of the cooperation characteristic of rural life. People feel that they must look after their own interests and increase their status through their own efforts. The urban person's strong belief in hedonism or personal happiness as the goal of life is increasingly reflected, for example, in modern marriage, the function of which is thought to be primarily personal happiness, all other functions being regarded as subordinate.

As individualism in urban society has increased, competition has also

---

[20] See Erving Goffman, *The Presentation of Self in Everyday Life* (Edinburgh: Universiy of Edinburgh Social Science Research Center, 1956), especially Chap. 1. Also see Vance Packard, *The Hidden Persuaders* (New York: Pocket Books, Inc., 1958).

[21] There is much emphasis on individualism within contemporary economic, political, religious, and philosophical thinking. This individualism is also related to the Protestant Reformation, the seventeenth- and eighteenth-century political revolutions of England, America, and France, and the development of the American frontier. For some examples see Abbott P. Herman, "Our Values of Individualism," in *An Approach to Social Problems* (Boston: Ginn and Company, 1949), Chap. 8.

been intensified. Each individual may feel that he is in ceaseless competition with the remainder of society, or at least with that part of the society in which he operates. The intensity with which the goals are striven for is, generally, in proportion to the values attached to them and the extent to which they can satisfy socially induced needs of the individual.

On the other hand, there is a contrary stress in the modern urban world away from this type of individualism and aptly referred to by Riesman as "The Lonely Crowd." [22] According to him, there are three types of personalities in modern societies, each one "directed" in a different way. The "tradition-directed" type almost unthinkingly conforms to the norms of his culture. "Inner-directed" persons have some degree of independence in their actions. Regardless of conflicts with society, such individuals do not necessarily follow what others do but try to ignore the environment or shape it to fit their needs. The third type is what might be thought of as the modern urban type of personality, who loses his individuality and constantly follows the dictates of others. He wishes to conform and to be like others, and consequently becomes what Riesman has termed an "other-directed" person, his action being directed not by himself but by others.

DECLINE IN INTIMATE COMMUNICATION AND MODIFICATION OF MECHANISMS OF INFORMAL SOCIAL CONTROL

Central to the problem of urbanization is the general decline of intimate communication among the members of a society. Although individuals may live or work where association with others is on a fairly personal basis, urbanized areas, particularly those where the population is dense and mobile, tend to create an extensive outside area of impersonality for the residents. Associations among people outside their immediate contacts are scarcely more than acquaintance with people in their segmental social roles. Human beings tend to be regarded categorically much like physical objects, often to be "manipulated" without much feeling and primarily for personal satisfaction. In urban settings associations with people tend to be brief and fragmentary, and to be stereotyped because of the impossibility of dealing with each association individually. Max Weber suggested that population density and the presence of large numbers of persons decrease the possibility of mutual acquaintanceships between individuals.[23]

The urban world is one of large areas of anonymity where there are few

---

[22] David Riesman, *The Lonely Crowd: A Study of Changing American Character* (New Haven, Conn.: Yale University Press, 1950).

[23] Max Weber, *The City* (translated by Don Martindale; New York: The Free Press, 1958).

ties or interests to bind a person to others. Urban conditions generally do not provide means for getting psychologically "close" to other persons, and the so-called blasé, sophisticated attitude of many big-city dwellers represents in part a way of protecting their privacy from the intrusions of others. When they encounter difficulties in their interpersonal relations they consequently must often turn to professional counselors or psychiatrists. In many of the transitory relationships encountered, the only things of interest are those directly pertaining to the situation; for example, whether a man will "stand" for a round of drinks or is a "good talker." This has helped to produce the loneliness of the urban world so well described by Auden:

> . . . This stupid world where
> Gadgets are gods and we go on talking,
> Many about much, but remain alone.
> Alive but alone, belonging—where?—
> Unattached as tumbleweed.[24]

Whereas "anonymity" is virtually impossible in a rural society, it is the "norm" in a predominantly urban society. This is in marked contrast to the close personal contacts of the less urbanized small town where the townspeople may know large numbers of people in the town by name or sight and know many of them even intimately.[25] This is why, in the absence of intimate personal acquaintances a person's status and character are judged by others from his "self-presentation," or the external indices of that self. Thus symbols of wealth, sophistication, or other forms of influence are of special significance to urban society.[26] Some have suggested that the breakdown of intimate communication in an urban society lies at the center of many urban problems in that the individual finds that he cannot easily communicate with his fellows and thus cannot orient his own values or put himself into harmony with the group.[27]

It has been said that as urbanism has increased and as man's conformity to social norms has become less affected by informal group controls, greater opportunities and inducements develop for behavior which deviates from

---

[24] W. H. Auden, *The Age of Anxiety* (New York: Random House, Inc., 1946), p. 44. Reprinted by permission of the publisher.

[25] Albert Blumenthal, *Small-Town Stuff* (Chicago: The University of Chicago Press, 1932). For example, in Mineville the average person knew nine tenths of the townspeople by sight or name and a large number intimately.

[26] See Goffman for a discussion of the way in which personal impressions are formed in a mass society. See also C. Wright Mills, *The Power Elite* (New York: Oxford University Press, 1956), especially pp. 71–93, for a discussion of "elites" (higher status persons) in modern society.

[27] Rose, p. 25.

accepted norms. Social control over people's behavior in urban areas is more likely to be through formal measures, such as the police and the courts. A report on the effects of African urbanization makes this point: "In the past, as it is in many rural areas today, the family or the tribal group was the centre of life and the focus of all social activities, whether economic, religious, political or educational. In areas undergoing social change, such familial institutions have been greatly weakened, and many reports from Africa have reported the importance of this factor with respect to the emergence of juvenile delinquency." [28]

URBAN CHARACTERISTICS A MATTER OF DEGREE

The description of the characteristics of the urban way of life presented here should be considered only as an abstract ideal type which can be compared with the characteristics of rural society. It does not mean that the life of all persons in a city is so characterized. One may have considerable personal relationships, for example, with others in a city. Studies have shown that primary group life survives in urban areas of both developed and less developed countries. Gans, for example, like Whyte, found that close intimate relations exist in the Italian communities of a large city,[29] and that this is effective over considerable segments. A Detroit study of family patterns found that neighborliness was widespread, with about 75 percent reporting that they got together with neighbors as well as with relatives; 55 percent got together with "other friends" once or twice a week or a few times each month.[30] In addition, only 11 percent had no relatives at all in the Detroit area, and 54 percent saw one or more related units of the family once or twice a week. Other studies in Chicago have shown that customer-clerk relations in smaller city stores can be quite intimate.[31]

---

[28] "Some Considerations on the Prevention of Juvenile Delinquency in African Countries Experiencing Rapid Social Change," *International Review of Criminal Policy,* No. 16 (New York: United Nations Publication, 61.IV.2), p. 43.

[29] Herbert Gans, *The Urban Villagers: Group and Class in the Life of Italian-Americans* (New York: The Free Press, 1962); and William F. Whyte, *Street Corner Society* (Chicago: University of Chicago Press, 1943).

[30] Cited in Harold L. Wilensky and Charles N. Lebeaux, *Industrial Society and Social Welfare* (New York: Russell Sage Foundation, 1958), p. 122. Also see Whyte. Sjoberg has stated that preindustrial cities of underdeveloped countries do not have as many of the characteristics of urbanism. Although there is a difference in degree, the characteristics of an urban way of life can be found in cities like those of India. See Marshall B. Clinard, *Slums and Community Development: Experiments in Self-Help* (New York: The Free Press, 1964), pp. 69–85 and 140–145.

[31] Gregory P. Stone, "City Shoppers and Urban Identification: Observations on the Social Psychology of City Life," *American Journal of Sociology,* 60:36–45 (1954).

As one study has suggested, the role of mobility and impersonality in urban life should not be overstated either in the local community or in the factory and other work situations.

> Whatever the mobility of the population, intimate contacts with relatives, neighbors, and friends are a universal feature of urban life at home and in the local community (as indeed they were in an earlier day among the Little Polands and Little Sicilies of the slum). Such contacts are also a universal feature of life at work. Even in the huge workplace where many thousands mass for the daily routine, the informal workgroup seems destined to go on performing its usual functions of controlling the workpace, initiating new members, deciding how far to go along with the boss, and making work a bit more like play. There is no evidence that human relations are any more atomized at work than in the local community and neighborhood, though the liveliness of informal groups may, of course, vary from place to place.[32]

Although the life of suburbia has been described among the young upwardly mobile middle class as often a transient superficial life,[33] others have pointed out that areas with single-family dwellings, particularly those with more factory workers, have considerable stability in their family life and local community relations.[34] Even where people move within the city some retain active friendships over the city in neighborhoods where they once lived. "Spatial mobility makes for city-wide ties; stability makes for local area ties; and most urban residents have both.[35]

Certainly a degree of intimate life does exist in any city, in both the local community, including slum areas, and the work place. However, in the city a person experiences almost daily large areas of impersonal relations where his personal identity is not recognized. The teeming streets of our large cities, filled with strangers, the numerous contacts with them on the way to work or to shop, the impersonal contacts with thousands at large recreational events give vivid evidence that the city as a whole is hardly the same as the small, local community. To admit the need for exercising cau-

---

[32] Wilensky and Lebeaux, p. 124. According to Janowitz, sociologists have failed to take into consideration that "impressive degrees and patterns of local community life exist within . . . metropolitan limits." Morris Janowitz, *The Community Press in an Urban Setting* (New York: The Free Press, 1952), p. 19.

[33] See William F. Whyte, Jr., *The Organization Man* (New York: Simon and Schuster, Inc., 1956).

[34] Flint City—Fringe Survey. Social Science Research Project, University of Michigan, Ann Arbor, 1955, as cited in Wilensky and Lebeaux, pp. 126–127.

[35] Joel Smith, William H. Form, and Gregory P. Stone, "Local Intimacy in a Middle-Sized City," *American Journal of Sociological*, 60:284 (1954). See also Peter H. Rossi, *Why Families Move: A Study in the Social Psychology of Urban Residential Mobility* (New York: The Free Press, 1956).

tion in order to avoid overstating the universal presence of urban characteristics does not minimize, however, their importance as a framework for
understanding much of contemporary life and deviant behavior.

The discusson to this point has been in terms of the world-wide growth
of urbanization and the development of urbanism as a way of life. If it can
be demonstrated that this frame of reference is useful in explaining the
incidence of deviant behavior, it will furnish overwhelming evidence against
the contention that deviant behavior is the product of biological or individual psychological forces. It will also help to explain the rising problems
of deviant behavior, such as crime and delinquency, in less developed countries undergoing rapid industrialization and urbanization.[36] The following
section will compare the incidence and prevalence of certain forms of deviant behavior in rural and urban areas, between cities of various sizes, and
within areas of a city. Such material should furnish some evidence for the
contention that urbanization and urbanism are related to the extent and
increase of deviant behavior in modern societies.

COMPARISONS OF CERTAIN FORMS OF DEVIANT BEHAVIOR IN RURAL AND URBAN AREAS

For centuries writers have been concerned about the debauchery and
moral conditions of the cities and have generally praised rural life.[37] Hesiod,
for example, wrote about the corrupt justice of the cities. The Greeks and
Romans compared the city with agricultural areas, noting the greater evils
and sources of criminality in the cities. One of the first systematic comparisons of rural and urban peoples was made by Ibn Khaldun in the
fourteenth century. This famed Arab historian compared life in the city
with that among the nomadic tribes. He found that the nomads had good
behavior, whereas evil and corruption were abundant in the city; that
honesty and courage were characteristic of the nomads, whereas lying and
cowardice were prevalent in the city; and that the city caused decay, stulti-
fied initiative, and made men depraved and wicked. In general, rural life
has been, and still largely is, a world of close personal relationships which
Burgess has thus described:

---

[36] See J. J. Panakal and A. M. Khalifa, *Prevention of Types of Criminality Resulting from Social Changes and Accompanying Economic Development in Less
Developed Countries,* Reports on the Second United Nations Congress on the Prevention of Crime and the Treatment of Offenders, London, August 1960 (New
York: United Nations Department of Economic and Social Affairs, 1960).

[37] See Pitirim Sorokin, Carle Zimmerman, and Charles Galpin, *A Systematic
Sourcebook in Rural Sociology* (Minneapolis: University of Minnesota Press, 1930),
pp. 27–52, 54–68.

But the main characteristics of small-town life stand out in clear perspective: close acquaintanceship of everyone with everyone else, the dominance of personal relations, and the subjection of the individual to continuous observation and control by the community. . . . This fund of concrete knowledge which everyone has of everyone else in the small town naturally emphasizes and accentuates the role of the personal in all relationships and activities of community life. Approval and disapproval of conduct, likes and dislikes of persons, play correspondingly a tremendous part in social life, in business, in politics, and in the administration of justice.[38]

Delinquency and Crime

The types, incidence, and reactions to rural crime, as with urban crime, are a function of the type of life and the various norms and values of the communities. Delinquency and crime rates today are generally much lower in rural areas than in urban. A study of crime in France and Belgium has shown similar major differences between rural and urban areas.[39] In Japan it is reported that the rate of urban crime is higher than that of rural areas, and that the general increase in crime is particularly noticeable in the largest cities.[40] In India an official report of the Intelligence Bureau observed that "it was found that juvenile crime in an acute form is confined to the cities, particularly the cities of India, and to some of the larger towns which have suffered from economic distress. It is not a problem of the rural areas." [41] Pronounced differences have been found in the incidence of delinquency and crime in the urban and rural areas of Latin-American and African countries.[42]

In general, the differences between rural and urban property crimes are greater than the differences in crimes against the person. Some delinquent and criminal acts committed in rural areas are dealt with informally and not officially reported, and there are undoubtedly more opportunities to commit offenses in urban as compared with rural areas. The differences be-

---

[38] Ernest W. Burgess, in Blumenthal, pp. xii–xiii.

[39] Denis Szabo, *Crimes et Villes* (Louvain: Catholic University of Louvain, 1960).

[40] Quoted in *Urbanization in Asia and the Far East,* Proceedings of the Joint UN/UNESCO Seminar, Bangkok, August 8–18, 1956 (UNESCO, 1958—SS.57.V7A), Chap. IX, p. 232.

[41] *Urbanization in Asia and the Far East,* p. 233. Also see *A Report on Juvenile Delinquency in India* (Bombay: The Children's Aid Society, 1956), p. 8.

[42] Philip M. Hauser, ed., *Urbanization in Latin America* (New York: International Documents Service, Columbia University Press, 1961) and *Social Implications of Industrialization and Urbanization in Africa South of the Sahara* (Lausanne: Imprimerie Centrale Lausanne S.A., 1956).

tween rural and urban rates, however, are so great that differential reporting or opportunity could, at most, account for only a small part.[43] Also, there is little evidence to support the theory held by some that the city attracts deviants from rural areas.[44]

TABLE 3.7   **Rates per 100,000 Population for Crimes Known to the Police in Rural and Urban Areas, United States, 1966**

	Rate	
OFFENSE	URBAN	RURAL
Murder and nonnegligent manslaughter	6.0	4.7
Forcible rape	14.2	8.9
Robbery	115.0	10.0
Aggravated assault	142.8	60.9
Burglary—breaking or entering	855.3	335.1
Larceny—theft ($50 and over)	573.7	188.2
Automobile theft	394.3	60.7

SOURCE: Derived from Federal Bureau of Investigation, "Crime in the United States," *Uniform Crime Reports 1966* (Washington, D.C.: Government Printing Office, 1967), pp. 96–97. The population figures used were based on the estimated 1966 census. Rates for the above are based on estimated 1966 census data. "Urban areas" include Standard Metropolitan Areas.

As Table 3.7 shows, burglary rates in the United States, as a whole, are generally two and a half times as great in urban areas as in rural, larceny is over three times as great, and robbery over ten times.[45] The rates for burglaries known to the police per 100,000 population in 1966 were, for

[43] See, for example, Marshall B. Clinard, "Rural Criminal Offenders," *American Journal of Sociology,* 50:38–45 (1944); William P. Lentz, "Rural-Urban Differentials in Juvenile Delinquency," *Journal of Criminal Law and Criminology,* 47:311–339 (1956); and Marshall B. Clinard, "A Cross-Cultural Replication of the Relation of Urbanism to Criminal Behavior," *American Sociological Review,* 25:253–257 (1960).

[44] See page 111.

[45] In such countries as France, Belgium, Switzerland, Holland, Germany, Sweden, Finland, Denmark, and Italy, the incidence of urban offenses, crimes known, and convictions per population has been reported as generally higher than among rural areas. Hans H. Burchardt, "Kriminalität in Stadt und Land," *Abhandlungen des Kriminalistischen Instituts an der Universität Berlin* (4. Folge, 4 Bd., 1. Heft [1936]). Louis Wirth and Marshall B. Clinard, "Public Safety," in *Urban Government* (Supplementary Report of the Urbanism Committee to the National Resources Committee; Washington, D.C.: Government Printing Office, 1939), I, 247–303. Denis Szabo, *Criminologie* (Montreal: University of Montreal Press, 1965), pp. 204–239.

example, 855.3 in urban areas and 335.1 in rural areas. Crimes such as murder, which are relatively infrequent as compared with property crimes, are about the same, with a somewhat higher rate in urban areas, where the rate is 6.0 as compared with 4.7 in rural. Rape rates are much higher in urban areas: 14.2 in urban as contrasted with 8.9 in rural.

Specific studies, rather than statistical comparisons, also seem to support the thesis that the urbanization of rural areas and an increase in crime go hand in hand. A study of the southern mountain villages showed that as the hill country was opened to outside contacts criminal activities increased.[46] The most important factor associated with this increase was the growing lack of community identification on the part of individuals as the villages became more urbanized. A study of rural inmates in an Iowa reformatory revealed that characteristics associated with an urban way of life played a significant role in their criminal behavior.[47]

Mental Disorders

Most contemporary data on mental disorders, but not all, show that the rates are generally higher in urban than in rural areas. As with crime, many writers feel that the expansion of urbanism is significant in the production of mental illness in our society. After a study of the prevalence of mental disorder among the urban and rural populations of New York State, Malzberg concluded that the rural regions of the state had less mental disorder than the urban.[48] In another study, Texas rates for all persons who became psychotic for the first time were found to be two and a half times greater in urban areas than in rural, a difference which was statistically significant.[49] The same differential held for the sexes and age-specific psychoses rates. The large rate differentials between urban and rural areas were not due to differences in the accessibility of psychiatric treatment facilities or to the type of psychiatric facilities available in the two areas.[50]

---

[46] M. Taylor Mathews, *Experience Worlds of the Mountain Peoples* (New York: Columbia University Press, 1937).

[47] Marshall B. Clinard, "The Process of Urbanization and Criminal Behavior," *American Journal of Sociology*, 48:202–213 (1942). Also see his "Rural Criminal Offenders," and "A Cross-Cultural Replication of the Relation of Urbanism to Criminal Behavior." Also see Harold D. Eastman, "The Process of Urbanization and Criminal Behavior: A Restudy of Culture Conflict." Unpublished doctoral thesis, University of Iowa, 1954.

[48] Benjamin Malzberg, "The Prevalence of Mental Disease among the Urban and Rural Populations of New York State," *Psychiatric Quarterly*, 9:55–88 (1935).

[49] E. Gartly Jaco, *The Social Epidemiology of Mental Diseases* (New York: Russell Sage Foundation, 1960). Also see Leacock, p. 314.

[50] Jaco.

Not all the evidence supports the conclusion that the incidence of mental illness is much less in rural areas. The differences may actually be smaller than they now appear to be because of the likelihood that rural families may keep mentally disturbed members at home rather than have them treated in clinics or have them hospitalized. For this reason it is possible that mental deviants in urban society may be somewhat more socially visible, and that both unofficial and official tolerance of the deviation will be less.

Alcoholism

The chances that rural persons will become chronic alcoholics are less than half as great as those for urban dwellers.[51] Urban commitments for alcoholic psychoses are reported to be three and a half times the rate for rural areas.[52] The principal reasons for this lower rate of alcoholism in rural areas are the social norms and the amount of social control at the personal level over drinking or excessive drinking. Farm people in the United States are much less likely to drink alcoholic beverages than are city dwellers. Both farm rearing and farm residence are associated with lower proportions of heavy drinkers. An Iowa study showed that 58 percent of drinkers in the city were either moderate or heavy drinkers as compared with 43 percent of the farm drinkers.[53] Moreover, the extent of drinking increased among the farm-reared who had migrated to the city but this increase was in moderate rather than heavy drinking.

Suicide

On the whole, persons living on farms and villages are less likely to take their lives than persons living in cities. In London the standardized rate, expressed as a percentage of that for the whole of England and Wales, is 115, for the county boroughs 106, for other urban districts 97, and for rural districts 88.[54] In Sweden, Denmark, and Finland wide differences in the suicide rates exist between farm and city. A detailed study of suicide in France showed that the chances that farm people and persons living in places of less than 2000 population would take their lives were considerably less than for city people.[55]

---

[51] E. M. Jellinek, "Recent Trends in Alcoholism and Alcohol Consumption," *Quarterly Journal of Studies on Alcohol,* 8:23 (1947).

[52] Carney Landis and James D. Page, *Modern Society and Mental Disease* (New York: Holt, Rinehart and Winston, 1938).

[53] Harold A. Mulford and Donald E. Miller, "Drinking in Iowa. II. The Extent of Drinking and Selected Socio-cultural Categories," *Quarterly Journal of Studies on Alcohol,* 21:34–35 (1960).

[54] Figures cited in Peter Sainsbury, *Suicide in London: An Ecological Study* (New York: Basic Books, Inc., 1956).

[55] M. Halbwachs, *Les Causes du Suicide* (Paris: Librairie Félix Alcan, 1930).

The differential in rural and urban suicide rates in the United States appears to be declining because of the tendency for an urban way of life to characterize rural areas. Fifty years ago the rural rate per 100,000 population was about two thirds of the urban rate; in 1960 the rates were about the same, the rural being slightly higher: 10.5 in the urban and 10.8 in the rural.[56] An analysis of 3081 cases of suicide in Michigan between 1945 and 1949 revealed that rural males exhibited higher suicide rates than urban males.[57] Although "farmers and farm managers" had a high suicide rate in Michigan, the majority of "rural" males who committed suicide were engaged in urban occupation and resided in urbanized fringe areas. It is possible that the high rural rate in this sample was due to two factors: as urban values become more widely disseminated in rural areas they create an intense personal conflict because of the disparity between urban and rural values as they affect behavioral alternatives; and the occupations of rural males who committed suicide are characteristic occupations of urban groups, thus suggesting exposure to conflicting values and norms. Although they lived in the country, these people were oriented to an urban way of life.

SOCIAL DEVIATION AND CITY SIZE

The higher incidence of certain forms of deviant behavior in urban communities has been, in general, demonstrated by a comparison of urban with rural rates, but several questions remain to be answered: (1) If urban rates for certain forms of deviation are, in turn, analyzed by the size of the community, is there a proportional increase as one proceeds from the small city to the great metropolis? (2) Do deviation rates vary according to the distance from a large community? (3) Within any city are there variations in the rates of deviation according to the degree of urbanism of the area?

Durkheim in France, some fifty years ago, maintained that crime increases directly with the volume and density of the population. A later study by Burchardt concluded that crime rates in European cities generally increase directly with the size of the city.[58] The only exceptions which he found were in the Netherlands and Austria, where the largest cities have the least crime, a situation which he explained as due to unique factors. A comprehensive study of crime in France and Belgium has shown major differences in rates of cities of different size. The study found, however, that

---

[56] W. Widick Schroeder and Allan J. Beegle, "Suicide: An Instance of High Rural Rates," *Rural Sociology*, 18:45–52 (1953).

[57] See Jack P. Gibbs, "Suicide," in Robert K. Merton and Robert A. Nisbet, *Contemporary Social Problems* (rev. ed.; New York: Harcourt, Brace & World, Inc., 1966), p. 302.

[58] Burchardt.

such rates are affected by the extent of industry and other social factors.[59] Comparisons in the United States of crime rates by city size show some startling differences and, in most crimes, even a continuous progression in rates as the size of the city increases. (See Table 3.8). In 1966 the rate per 100,000 population for burglaries reported to the police, for example, which is probably the best comparable index of crime, rose steadily from cities of less than 10,000, with a rate of 395.1, to cities over 250,000 population, with a rate of 1,233.2, or over twice as great. [60] Robbery rates were twenty times as great in the larger cities as compared with the smaller ones.

TABLE 3.8   **Rates per 100,000 for Crimes Known to the Police by City Size, United States, 1966**

POPULATION	MURDER AND NONNEGLI- GENT MAN- SLAUGHTER	MAN- SLAUGHTER BY NEGLI- GENCE	FORCIBLE RAPE	ROBBERY
I Over 250,000	9.9	5.5	24.6	242.5
II 100,000–250,000	6.9	4.8	14.2	83.5
III 50,000–100,000	3.6	3.8	9.3	55.1
IV 25,000–50,000	3.4	3.0	7.2	36.4
V 10,000–25,000	2.8	1.7	5.7	20.6
VI Under 10,000	2.1	1.2	4.6	11.9

POPULATION	AGGRA- VATED ASSAULT	BURGLARY: BREAKING OR ENTERING	*Larceny* $50 AND OVER	UNDER $50	AUTO THEFT
I Over 250,000	228.1	1,233.2	768.8	1,396.1	645.9
II 100,000–250,000	157.3	952.5	601.3	1,591.8	400.9
III 50,000–100,000	92.3	719.4	546.9	1,352.7	327.3
IV 25,000–50,000	81.1	603.1	496.3	1,196.9	237.3
V 10,000–25,000	72.4	497.1	351.9	1,128.4	157.3
VI Under 10,000	68.2	395.1	280.1	839.5	109.5

SOURCE: Federal Bureau of Investigation, "Crime in the United States," *Uniform Crime Reports—1966* (Washington, D.C.: Government Printing Office, 1967), pp. 96–97. Included in this report were 55 cities over 250,000 population; 98 cities from 100,000 to 250,000 234 cities from 50,000 to 100,000; 477 cities from 25,000 to 50,000; 1,093 cities from 10,000 to 25,000; and 2,020 cities under 10,000 population. Population figures on which these rates are based are those for the 1966 estimated population.

---

[59] Szabo, *Crimes et Villes.*

[60] Federal Bureau of Investigation, "Crime in the United States," *Uniform Crime Reports* (1966), pp. 96–97. The rates for reported burglaries appear to decline in cities of 500,000 or more population, which may be due to a saturation

It is interesting to note that rates by city size are often affected, however, by the cultural factors in the area in which the cities are located.[61] In fact, the regional location of a city seems often to be more related to the crime rate than is the extent of urbanization in the state. Some states, such as California, with a large proportion of urban population, also have high crime rates, whereas Massachusetts, which is also heavily urbanized, has a comparatively low rate. It is likely that the urban "way of life" in a more recently developed area like California is characterized by norm conflicts, rapid change, and other unsettling conditions, whereas in older areas, such as New England, these aspects of urbanism may be somewhat attenuated.

Although cities with a population over 100,000 have estimated rates for chronic alcoholism which are considerably higher than the rates for cities up to 10,000 population, the progression by city size is not continuous.[62] The percentage of drinkers in the adult population increases in the United States from 60 percent in areas of under and 69 percent in areas from 2500 to 9999 to 76 percent in areas of 500,000 or more. Problem drinkers were 6 percent of drinkers in places of less than 2500 increasing to 8 percent in cities from 2500 to 74,999 and 13 percent in cities over 75,000.[63] Suicide rates appear to increase with the size of the community, until cities of 500,000 and over are reached.[64] It has been noted that fast-growing cities tend to have a higher suicide rate.[65]

In larger urban communities, where contacts between racial groups become more impersonal and segmental, there is often a decline in discrimination in some areas and an increase in others. Compared with smaller communities there is likely to be less emphasis on patterns of subservience or etiquette and less segregation of public facilities. On the other hand, urban racial social violence has occurred in every geographic region in the United States, including such cities as Chicago, Detroit, Tulsa, New York, Washington, East St. Louis, and Atlanta. There are four patterns of urban racial violence: [66]

---

point in urbanization above which size burglary rates do not materially increase. See Wirth and Clinard, p. 265.

[61] Lyle Shannon, "The Spatial Distribution of Criminal Offenses by States," *Journal of Criminal Law, Criminology and Police Science,* 45:264–274 (1954).

[62] Jellinek.

[63] Harold A. Mulford, "Drinking and Deviant Drinking, U.S.A., 1963," *Quarterly Journal of Studies on Alcohol,* 25:640 (1964).

[64] Wirth and Clinard, p. 271.

[65] Henry Wechsler, "Community Growth, Depressive Disorders, and Suicide," *American Journal of Sociology,* 66:110 (1960).

[66] See Allen D. Grimshaw, "Urban Racial Violence in the United States: Changing Ecological Considerations," *American Journal of Sociology,* 66:110 (1960).

1. Spontaneous brawls among bystanders over an immediate disturbance.
2. The "mass, uncoordinated battle" occurring when groups of one race attack isolated members of the other. Mobs of one race seldom engage mobs on the other in open battle.
3. The "urban pogrom," which is the full-scale assault of one group, almost always white, upon Negroes, and which has occurred particularly where whites have assumed the tacit approval of local government. These "pogroms" have resulted in the flight of large numbers of the minority community.
4. Stray assaults and stabbings on the part of individuals or small groups of one's race upon individuals of another.

DISTRIBUTION OF DEVIANT BEHAVIOR WITHIN A CITY

According to the most generally accepted theory, the characteristic spatial pattern of cities in developed, industrial societies is a series of concentric circles, with each circle having certain distinctive characteristics moving out from the central business district into increasingly better areas of housing.[67] The ecological pattern of the city in terms of concentric zones leading out from the first circle are Zone I, the central business district; Zone II, an area known variously by a number of names, such as the slum, zone in transition, blighted area, "gray area," or "inner core" area; Zone III, an area of

---

A fifth pattern has been occurring within recent years in the United States. Instead of directing the assault directly against individual whites, Negroes have engaged in rioting and destroying stores and buildings largely in their own areas, particularly those owned by non-Negroes and in looting and attacking the police.

[67] Ernest W. Burgess, "The Growth of the City," in Robert E. Park and Ernest W. Burgess, *The City* (Chicago: The University of Chicago Press, 1925). This theory has been criticized particularly because it does not apply to the spatial pattern of cities of less developed countries. See Leo F. Schnore, "On the Spatial Structure of Cities in the Two Americas," in Hauser and Schnore, pp. 347–398; George A. Theodorson, *Studies in Human Ecology* (New York: Harper & Row, Publishers, 1961); and Sjoberg. Another theory based on city growth is that cities have a pattern of sectors like pieces of a pie. According to this theory, industrial areas follow river valleys, water courses, and railroad lines out from the city and become surrounded by workingmen's housing, with factories tending to locate even along the outer fringe of the city. According to the sector view, the best housing then does not fringe the entire city but only parts of it. The main industrial areas of the future may well be located on the outskirts of cities in new industrial towns and suburbs as in now taking place.—Homer Hoyt, *The Structure and Growth of Residential Neighborhoods in American Cities* (Washington, D.C.: Federal Housing Administration, 1939), pp. 75–77, and his "The Structure of American Cities in the Post-War Era," *American Journal of Sociology,* 48:475–481 (1943).

two- and three-family flats or dwellings; Zone IV, an area of single-family dwellings; and Zone V, the suburban or commutation area. These circles can be thought of as undergoing constant movement in the form of expansion outward, much like the movement taking place on the surface of water when a pebble is dropped into it. The central business district is constantly expanding, depending on how many persons living in each successive zone eventually move outward to another area. Although this theory implies equal expansion in all directions, few cities ever completely approximate a series of concentric circles. Rivers, mountains—or a lake, as in Chicago—interfere with this natural growth. Even so, there are some cities, such as Rochester in New York, which closely resemble this pattern. This abstraction of concentric circles is no different from the law of falling bodies in which the principle of an equal rate of fall between an iron ball and a feather is valid only if both are in a vacuum.

In each section of the city there are wide variations in age, sex, nationality and racial origin, occupation, social class, homeownership, condition of housing, literacy, and education. Differences in social class are one of the most important characteristics of various areas of a city. The shifting of persons under *ecological* pressures brings about an association of like with like and a tendency for population specialization in certain areas.[68]

The population of both the central business district and the slum is heterogeneous; the residents are chiefly unskilled workers and their families, and include migrants from rural and other areas, and various nationality and racial groups. Zone III has a more stable population, more skilled workers, and fewer foreign-born or racial groups. Second-generation immigrant groups moving out of the slum generally move here first. Zones IV and V largely consist of apartment houses, single-family dwellings, and commuters' houses, which means that they are chiefly upper-middle and upper class.

Over a century ago a few studies were made of the distribution of deviant behavior within a city,[69] but most of this type of research began with

---

[68] For many years botanists and geologists have been interested in studying the pattern of distribution and movement in space of plant and animal life, which they call plant and animal ecology. Following this, interest grew in human ecology, or the study of the distribution of man and his institutions in space, which includes the study of rural-urban differences as well as differences in city size and within cities. The study of the ecology or distribution of deviant behavior has largely developed in the past forty years.

[69] Yale Levin and Alfred Lindesmith, "English Ecology and Criminology of the Past Century," *Journal of Criminal Law and Criminology*, 27:801–816 (1937); and Alfred Lindesmith and Yale Levin, "The Lombrosian Myth in Criminology," *American Journal of Sociology*, 42:653–679 (1937).

the stimulation of sociological studies by Park, Burgess, and their students of the Chicago community in the 1920s. The spot-mapping of labeled deviants in larger cities by place of residence has revealed that, on the whole, certain types of social deviation tend to be concentrated in specific areas.[70] For example, conventional crime, delinquency, mental illness in general and schizophrenia in particular, suicide, prostitution, vagrancy, dependency, illegitimacy, infant mortality, as well as associated problems, such as high death and disease rates, have been found to vary with the areas of the city. The highest rates are in Zones I and II, and become successively lower out from this area. The evidence on alcoholism and the manic-depressive psychoses does not show quite this pronounced pattern for, although there are probably higher rates in Zones I and II, the differences are not as marked from one part of the city to another. White-collar crime, on the other hand, is greater in Zones IV and V of the city. Gambling and prostitution are prevalent not only in Zone II but sometimes beyond the suburban fringe of the city.[71]

Delinquent gangs were found by Thrasher to be largely concentrated in the slum areas.[72] The spot-mapping of some 60,000 cases of delinquency, truancy, and crime by Shaw and McKay showed a close correlation among the rates of all three groups, with wide variation in their distribution among the local communities of the city.[73] The slum area near the centers of commerce and industry had the highest rates, whereas those in outlying residential communities of higher economic status were uniformly low. In a later study of some 25,000 juvenile court delinquents, distributed over thirty-three years, Shaw and McKay reported additional evidence of the consistency of high rates of delinquency in Zone II.[74]

Findings similar to those in Chicago have been reported for eight other large metropolitan cities and eleven other cities, all widely separated

---

[70] For a discussion of the patterns in a smaller city see, for example, Lyle W. Shannon, "Types and Patterns of Delinquency in a Middle-Sized City," *Journal of Research in Crime and Delinquency*, 1:53–66 (1964).

[71] Walter C. Reckless, *Vice in Chicago* (Chicago: University of Chicago Press, 1933).

[72] Frederic M. Thrasher, *The Gang* (Chicago: University of Chicago Press, 1927).

[73] Clifford R. Shaw and Henry D. McKay, *Delinquent Areas* (Chicago: University of Chicago Press, 1929). Jonassen has criticized the limitations of data, the methodology, and the internal consistencies of the data. Christen T. Jonassen, "A Re-Evaluation and Critique of the Logic and Some Methods of Shaw and McKay," *American Sociological Review*, 14:608–614, (1949).

[74] Clifford R. Shaw, Henry D. McKay, *et al.*, *Juvenile Delinquency and Urban Areas* (Chicago: University of Chicago Press, 1942).

geographically, including Boston, Philadelphia, Cleveland, Richmond, Birmingham, Omaha, and Seattle.[75] Higher rates of delinquency were found in the inner zones and lower rates in the outer zones, and in all nineteen cities, except for Boston, Birmingham, and Omaha, the rates also declined from innermost to outermost zones. Even in these cities where rates in the outermost zones were somewhat higher than in the intermediate, as in Boston, the explanation may possibly be not only that the industrial areas are near the periphery, but that differences exist in the policies of the courts in the various areas. Similar findings have been reported in more recent studies in Baltimore, Detroit, and Indianapolis.[76] A study of Croyden, a large English city near London, revealed that the highest rates for delinquency were concentrated in areas of the city populated by unskilled and semiskilled workers' families.[77] Studies of Kanpur and Lucknow in India showed that juvenile delinquency, and crime are primarily associated with slum areas.[78]

The correlation of delinquency rates with economic factors should not be interpreted as indicating any direct relation to poverty or bad housing, as Shaw and McKay have indicated. They point out that in rural areas, there may be poverty but little delinquency. Poverty, moreover, does not produce a tradition of delinquency because of a lack of money in itself; rather, it may interfere with the realization of status or prestige. The explanation of delinquency, they believe, is to be found in the general social situations in delinquency areas.

The rate of arrests of adults per 10,000 population seventeen years of age and over was more than ten times as great in the central area of Chicago as in the outlying areas of the city.[79] The rates for nearly all 29 types

---

[75] Shaw, McKay, *et al.,* Automobile theft may often be somewhat of an exception to the generalization that delinquency tends to be concentrated in areas such as these.

[76] Roland J. Chilton, "Continuity in Delinquency Area Research: A Comparison of Studies for Baltimore, Detroit, and Indianapolis," *American Sociological Review,* 29:71–83 (1964); Bernard Lander, *Towards an Understanding of Juvenile Delinquency: A Study of 8464 Cases of Juvenile Delinquency in Baltimore* (New York: Columbia University Press, 1954); and David J. Bordua, "Juvenile Delinquency and 'Anomie': An Attempt at Replication," *Social Problems,* 6:230–238 (1958–1959).

[77] Terence Morris, *The Criminal Area, A Study in Social Ecology* (London: Routledge and Kegan Paul, Ltd., 1958).

[78] Shankar S. Srivastava, *Juvenile Vagrancy: A Socioecological Study of Juvenile Vagrants in the Cities of Kampur and Lucknow* (New York: Asia Publishing House, 1963).

[79] Ernest R. Mowrer, *Disorganization, Personal and Social* (Philadelphia: J. B. Lippincott Company, 1942), p. 143.

of crimes known to the police in Seattle, and arrests for these crimes during the period 1949–1951, showed a decline as one moved out in six one-mile concentric zones from the highest land value in the central business district.[80] There was a tendency for 23 out of the 29 types of crime known to the police to decrease more or less in direct proportion from the center of the city, in particular shoplifting, theft, arson, rape, sodomy, and burglary. Bicycle theft was the only crime known to the police which had a higher rate in Zone VI (149.5) than in Zone I (65.3). The differentials between inner and outer zones were relatively small for Peeping Toms, obscene telephone calls, indecent liberties, and carnal knowledge. Not a single category in the arrest series showed a higher rate in the peripheral zones. Arrest rates for fraud, rape, prostitution, lewdness, robbery, gambling, and common drunkenness showed the greatest difference, while auto theft and indecent exposure showed the least.

White-collar crime, as one might expect, follows a reverse pattern, with concentration in Zones IV and V of the city. In a study of wartime black-market offenders in the wholesale meat industry in Detroit, Hartung found that more than 80 percent of them lived in the most desirable areas of the city.[81] Of the ten who lived in the least desirable areas (4 and 5), three lived in good downtown hotels.

EXPLANATION OF DISTRIBUTIONS
OF DEVIANT BEHAVIOR WITHIN CITIES

Some have suggested that the explanation of variations in deviant behavior within cities is differential reporting in various areas to authorities. Actually, however, the official rate differences between various areas of a city are so marked—often being, two, five, and even ten times as great—that even if reporting errors were overcome the rates probably would be little changed. As Schmid has written after studying the spatial distribution of crime in Seattle, "In spite of crime statistics and distortion in the derivation of rates resulting from differentials in population mobility and composition, there is still a very considerable portion of the high incidence of crime in the central segment of the city that must be explained on grounds other than these circumstances." [82]

---

[80] Calvin F. Schmid, "Urban Crime Areas: Part II," *American Sociological Review;* 25:655–678 (1960). There also appears to be a remarkable constancy and uniformity in the spatial patterning of crime by gradients. A comparison of two series of offenses known to the police in Seattle, 1939–1941 and 1949–1951, shows a close correspondence with high correlations for burglary and robbery.—Schmid, p. 669.

[81] Frank E. Hartung, "White-Collar Offenses in the Wholesale Meat Industry in Detroit," *American Journal of Sociology,* 56:25–35 (1950).

[82] Schmid, p. 675.

The differences in social class subcultures in each of the areas appear to account in large part for the variations in the incidence of deviant behavior. The subculture of lower-class urban areas is characterized by norms conducive to high delinquency, crime, prostitution, drug addiction, and other deviant behavior. Different systems of norms, values, and social relationships associated with the different social classes may directly influence the degree of deviant behavior. Or it could mean that, whatever the differences in the values and norms of the different classes, the deviant actions of persons in certain social classes, particularly the lower classes, are more likely to be noticed and to be dealt with officially.

It has also been suggested that certain areas of the city attract rather than produce deviants. This "drift" hypothesis is supported by little evidence as far as areas other than the "Skid Row" of the city are concerned. People may migrate because of differences in economic or educational status or because their friends migrated and told them about a new place to live, but there is little evidence to indicate that persons migrate because they are deviant. For example, there is no indication of selective migration of deviants to Harlem in New York City, which has a high delinquency and crime rate. Furthermore, there are indications that deviant behavior is as common among those who were reared, for example, within certain areas of a city as among those who were migrants to them. Faris states that there is little evidence for the theory that persons with mental illness in a large city have migrated there after economic failure and concentrate in slum areas.[83] Instead, he contends that the slum produces its own mental disorder. Similarly, Dunham claims that mobility provides "no significant explanation for variations in the rate of schizophrenia in social structures." [84]

The distribution of deviant behavior, with high and low rates in certain areas, furnishes us with leads to the social factors which may produce given forms of deviant behavior. Consequently, treatment and prevention might be concentrated in certain local areas, such as the slum, where the rates are highest in much the same way as public health officers concentrate their work in certain areas of the city. The latter often use spot maps of the city showing typhoid, scarlet fever, and similar contagious diseases and, with this information, concentrate on measures like vaccination, quarantine, the control of carriers, and the institution of better hygienic practices. A similar approach to deviant behavior would not eliminate the problem but would tend to lower the overall urban rate.[85]

---

[83] Robert E. L. Faris, *Social Disorganization* (2d ed., New York: The Ronald Press Company, 1955), pp. 337, 339.

[84] H. Warren Dunham, *Community and Schizophrenia: An Epidemiological Analysis* (Detroit: Wayne State University Press, 1965), p. 222.

[85] See Marshall B. Clinard, *Slums and Community Development: Experiments in Self-Help* (New York: The Free Press, 1966).

Present-day trends in city growth emphasize suburbanization and decentralization, particularly in the location of plants outside the city. The factors contributing to this growth have been the greater mobility made possible by improved highways and lower taxes on the periphery. These general changes in city patterns are bound to influence current theories on the concentration of deviant behavior. Through decentralization, contacts with deviant forms of behavior may become less intensive, and clusters of deviation may come to assume different patterns.[86]

SUMMARY

The rapid growth of urbanization has become a world-wide phenomenon. Increasing urbanization has almost everywhere been accompanied by a marked increase in various forms of deviant behavior. Urbanism, with its mobility, impersonality, individualism, materialism, norm and role conflicts, and rapid social change, appears to be associated with higher incidence of deviant behavior. Some evidence has been presented here about the comparative incidence of crime, mental illness, alcoholism, and suicide in rural and urban areas, in cities of different size, and within cities.

Delinquency and crime rates, as computed from official statistics, are almost universally lower in rural as compared with urban areas. Other forms of deviant behavior also tend, in general, to be statistically more frequent in urban areas. There are area variations in rates within cities. These variations arise from differences in the way of life of persons residing in each area.

Some persons have attempted to explain these differences in the extent of deviant behavior as being almost entirely due to differences in reporting and official statistics. Others have suggested that the inner zones of the city attract deviants from the other zones or from rural areas, but little evidence exists for either of these contentions. Obviously, these great differences are not due to variations in the biological constitution of individuals. Consequently, the variation among the zones can be thought of as important in suggesting social and cultural explanations for deviant behavior as well as indicating what areas should receive the greatest attention in any effort to reduce it.

SELECTED READINGS

Anderson, Nels. *The Urban Community: A World Perspective*. New York: Holt, Rinehart and Winston, Inc., 1959. A view of the impact of urbanism in a world-wide perspective, including a discussion of the characteristics of urban-

---

[86] See, for example, Edmund W. Vaz, ed., *Middle-Class Juvenile Delinquency* (New York: Harper & Row, Publishers, 1967).

ism, its effect on the family and other groups, and a discussion of social change and conformity under urbanism.

Burgess, Ernest W. "The Growth of the City," in Logan Wilson and William Kolb, *Sociological Analysis*. New York: Harcourt, Brace & World, Inc., 1949, pp. 407–414. This is a reprint of the original article, which described the concentric patterns of the city, using data from Chicago.

Clinard, Marshall B. "The Relation of Urbanization and Urbanism to Criminal Behavior," in Ernest W. Burgess and Donald Bogue, eds., *Contributions to Urban Sociology*. Chicago: University of Chicago Press, 1965. A study of the incidence of the urban characteristics of mobility, impersonality, and contacts with differential norms among farm, village, and city criminal offenders.

Cities. A Scientific American Book. New York: Alfred A. Knopf, Inc., 1965. A series of articles by urban specialists dealing with various aspects of world-wide urbanization, the origin and evaluation of cities, and an analysis, particularly, of New York, Stockholm, and Calcutta.

Gist, Noel P., and Sylvia F. Fava. *Urban Society*. Fifth edition. New York: Thomas Y. Crowell Company, 1964. A comprehensive analysis of the growth of cities, urban ecology, and the organization and social psychology of urban life. Contains much comparative material on urbanization and urbanism.

Hauser, Philip M., and Leo F. Schnore. *The Study of Urbanization*. New York: John Wiley & Sons, Inc., 1965. A series of basic articles on urbanization and urbanism using data from various parts of the world.

Morris, Terence. *The Criminal Area: A Study in Social Ecology*. London: Routledge & Kegan Paul, Ltd., 1957. An ecological study of crime and delinquency in an English city. Has an excellent survey and critique of nearly all studies of the ecology of delinquency both in America and in foreign countries.

Riesman, David. *The Lonely Crowd: A Study of Changing American Character*. New Haven, Conn.: Yale University Press, 1950. An important discussion of "tradition-directed," "inner-directed," and "other-directed" personality patterns. Riesman states that the modern urban person is losing his individuality and tends to conform to the dictates of others.

Rose, Arnold. *Theory and Methods in the Social Sciences*. Minneapolis: University of Minnesota Press, 1954, "The Problem of the Mass Society," pp. 25–49. This is a discussion of the relation of social problems to the rise of urban or the "mass society" of today. There are also some suggestions for the solution of the difficulties presented by a "mass society."

Shaw, Clifford, Henry D. McKay, *et al*. *Juvenile Delinquency and Urban Areas*. Chicago: University of Chicago Press, 1942. A series of studies of the ecological distribution of juvenile delinquency in twenty large American cities.

Sjoberg, Gideon. *The Pre-Industrial City*. New York: The Free Press, 1960. A discussion of the historical development of the city and the differences between preindustrial cities of the past as well as those of less developed areas today and the industrial city.

Turner, Roy, ed. *India's Urban Future*. Berkeley: University of California Press, 1962. The most comprehensive analysis of the impact of growing urbanization and urbanism on a less developed country.

Wilensky, Harold L., and Charles N. Lebeaux. *Industrial Society and Social Wel-*

fare. New York: Russell Sage Foundation, 1958. Contains an excellent statement of the nature of urban-industrial society and its effects, particularly on juvenile delinquency.

Wirth, Louis. "Urbanism as a Way of Life," originally published in 1938 in the *American Journal of Sociology,* it has been reprinted in Paul K. Hatt and Albert J. Reiss, Jr., *Reader in Urban Sociology.* Second edition. New York: The Free Press, 1962. Also reprinted in a number of other books. It is the best-known statement of the characteristics of the urban way of life.

4

The Slum
and Deviant Behavior[*]

The slum is almost universally reacted to in a negative manner, something evil, dark, and strange. In fact, the word itself is thought to be derived from "slumber" because slums were thought by most people to be "unknown, back streets or alleys, wrongly presumed to be sleeping and quiet." [1] Even today emotional attitudes toward the slum are reflected in the more popular definitions and value-laden terms which emphasize the filth and squalor of the slum, the poor social conditions existing there, and the presence "of vicious and dangerous persons." In fact, it has been defined as a "street, alley, court, etc., situated in a crowded district or town or city and inhabited by people of a low class or by the very poor, or as a number of these streets or courts forming a thickly populated neighborhood or district of a squalid and wretched character." [2]

---

[*] Portions of this chapter are reprinted from Marshall B. Clinard, *Slums and Community Development: Experiments in Self-Help* (New York: The Free Press, 1966) by permission of the publisher.

[1] Eric Partridge, *Origins: A Short Etymological Dictionary of Modern English* (London: Routledge & Kegan Paul, Ltd., 1958).

[2] *The Oxford Universal Dictionary*, 1955 edition, p. 1921, where the earliest use of the word is given as occurring in 1812; "slumming" was a fashionable pursuit in 1884.

Because of this general characterization of the slum, the word has been avoided in recent years, in the United States, at least, and other terms have been substituted, such as "blighted," "renewal," "deteriorated," "gray," "low-income," or "inner-core" areas, or as a "lower-class neighborhood." Hunter has pointed out, however, that the word "slum" is a good, old-fashioned word that carries real meaning.[3]

Slum areas are generally characterized as being overcrowded and congested, having bad and run-down housing, and being deficient in all amenities. Although slums do vary considerably from one type to another, as will be pointed out later, these general patterns of living conditions are almost universal; and although these general patterns of physical characteristics are almost without exception typical of slums, it would be a serious mistake to view slums only in such terms. The slum actually is far more than this; it is a way of life. Sociologically, it represents a subculture with its own set of norms and values, which is reflected in poor sanitation and health practices, often a lack of interest in formal education, deviant behavior, and characteristic attributes of apathy and social isolation. In this sense "slums" may exist in areas of reasonably good physical facilities such as slum clearance projects. Slum residents have become isolated from the general power structure of the community and are looked upon as being inferior; in turn, they reflect, in their living and in their behavior, their own suspicions toward the world that they regard as the "outside."

With this frame of reference, therefore, it is not surprising that slums in today's world constitute the most important and persistent problem of urban life: they are the chief sources of crime and delinquency, of illness and death from disease, and of manifold other problems. Even in developing countries, where the physical aspects of the slum may often not be too distinguishable from other areas of the large cities, the worst slum areas are the sources of the most serious and difficult problems.

Slums are of all types, shapes, and forms. New York has its Harlem and its Lower East Side, Chicago has its Black Belt, London has its well-known East End, and Bombay has its multistoried chawls. Southeast Asian families in Bangkok crowd together in "pile villages," wooden shacks raised on stilts along the waterfronts. Tin shacks, bamboo huts, or straw hovels crowd small lanes of Calcutta, Dacca, and Lagos, all of them steaming with the high humidity and stinking from the open drains. The impoverished shanty-towns or squatter shacks of the slum dwellers cover the hillsides of Rio de Janeiro, Lima, Hong Kong, and other Asiatic, African, and South American

---

[3] David R. Hunter, *The Slums: Challenge and Response* (New York: The Free Press, 1964), p. 6. The term has wide acceptance in other countries, particularly in developing countries.

cities. Few slums, however, are more crowded than those of Hong Kong and Singapore, where single rooms house from ten to forty families, each family with only "bed space" and no element of personal privacy. In areas around Canton, Shanghai, and Hong Kong hundreds of thousands of families live in waterfront sampan or "floating" slums.

The world's slums are populated by millions of persons, and because they constitute the chief sources of deviant behavior in all places where they exist it is essential to understand the nature of the slum if one is to understand the reason for its relationship to deviant behavior. Slums differ in physical setting, degree of overcrowding, permanence of the inhabitants, degree of organization among the residents, and types of problems, such as deviant behavior, which they present.[4] They may, particularly in developing countries, lack even the most basic amenities and be constructed of nothing more than scraps, or they may be substandard tenement housing or even once the homes of middle-class or wealthy residents.

Some slums are the gathering points for large numbers of recently arrived rural or village migrants. Although they may exhibit considerable heterogeneity they may also sometimes maintain degrees of unity in their ethnic, religious, or tribal backgrounds. Others are populated by long-term residents whose families often have lived under slum conditions for many generations.

Slums differ in the degree of organization among their residents. In some, few ties exist beyond the immediate families, and even family ties may be weak. In other more stable slums, quite close group and family relationships have developed. In a sense they constitute real slum communities, with sets of norms and values that differ sharply from those of the outside world.

Certain slum groups are products of unique sets of circumstances, as in the Negro slums of the United States and South Africa. There the difficulties of slum living have been compounded by the ever-present imprint of slavery and discrimination. In the United States, the pre-existing social values of the slums to which the Negroes moved were combined with the shattering effects of their slave backgrounds; in South Africa, detribalization, apartheid, and slum living have all affected slum living conditions. In both cases, the results have been exceptionally high rates of crime and delinquency, family instability, illegitimacy, and violence.

Slums also differ in the specific problems they present. United States

---

[4] Slums and slum dwellers can also be classified in terms of social mobility and the reason for their involvement in the slum. See John R. Seeley, "The Slum: Its Nature, Use, and Users," *Journal of the American Institute of Planners*, 25:7–14 (1959); and Charles J. Stokes, "A Theory of Slums," *Land Economics*, 38:187–197 (1962).

and European slums often are associated with delinquency, alcoholism, and similar problems, including drug addiction and illegitimacy in the United States. Although these problems are also present in much of Asia, Africa, and Latin America, they do not constitute the major complications. There the major obstacles are more physical in nature—the totally inadequate building structures, excessive overcrowding, lack of facilities, poor sanitation, and high disease rates. Although these problems exist in the United States and Europe, they do not provoke the same major concern. At one time, however, they were nearly as difficult.[5]

PHYSICAL CHARACTERISTICS OF THE SLUM

Of all the characteristics of a slum, the physical conditions have been most often emphasized.

Housing Conditions

Slums have commonly been defined as those portions of a city where housing is crowded, neglected, deteriorated, and often obsolete. Much of these inadequate housing conditions can be attributed to poorly arranged structures, inadequate light and circulation, poor design and lack of sanitary facilities, overcrowding, and insufficient maintenance. In developing countries many cities have large squatter areas—shantytowns built of scrap materials on unauthorized land which provide minimal protection from the elements.

In terms of physical conditions and housing standards, it is important to keep in mind the comparative nature of the definition. A slum should be judged physically according to the general living standards of a country. Certainly slum housing in New York City or Chicago would be regarded as adequate, even good, in many parts of the world. The availability of running water, flush toilets, electricity, and cooking facilities, even though in limited supply, may make a slum not a slum in the physical sense in other parts of the world.

The United States Census Bureau classifies poor dwellings as dilapidated or deteriorated. Dilapidated housing does not provide safe and adequate shelter, and deteriorated housing needs more repair than would be provided in the course of regular maintenance. According to the 1960 Census, the United States had 3,684,000 urban slum housing units, of which 1,173,000 were "dilapidated urban units." [6] According to one estimate, this

---

[5] Clinard, p. 48.

[6] *United States Census of Housing: 1960* (Washington: Department of Commerce, Bureau of the Census), I, lxiii.

meant that 12,500,000 persons lived in slum areas.[7] If slums in the United States are to be defined according to such standards as dilapidated housing, lack of adequate sanitary facilities, overcrowding, or location in an extremely undesirable area, it has been estimated that over 5 million families, or one sixth of the urban population, reside in slum environments.[8]

There is a world-wide tendency to stress the physical aspects of the slum and to define it in these terms alone. In some cases there may be a partial relation between housing conditions and these problems, but the explanation is more likely to be a slum way of life. Low economic status or discrimination forces people to live in low-rent areas where certain values prevail. Morris found that even after the construction of new government housing projects in an English city the rates of delinquency remained high.[9] He concluded that an area's physical characteristics are of little relevance to crime and delinquency, except as an indirect determinant of the social status of the area. The assumed relation of slum housing to deviant behavior has resulted in the erroneous belief that all that needs to be done is to provide new housing in slum areas.

> We hear that decent housing means less crime, less juvenile delinquency, lower costs for police and fire protection, and fewer welfare cases. From these assertions we get the impression that all the community has to do is remove the slums, and by this act it will wipe out social ills and their human and material costs. A documentary film of some years ago describes the metamorphosis in idyllic terms. First we see a shocking slum area with filthy and dilapidated buildings, rats running along the gutters, dirty and poorly clothed children playing amidst refuse and debris, and traffic moving slowly and impatiently in a bumper-to-bumper procession on the congested streets. Then the change takes place. Bulldozers and giant cranes move in to tear down the old buildings while construction crews follow closely behind to put up the new. Out of the ashes rises the new Phoenix: bright and shiny apartments insulated from the traffic of the city streets, happy children romping about in orderly and supervised play areas, and neatly dressed mothers sitting on decorative benches sewing or chatting gaily with their neighbors.
>
> Several things are wrong with his picture. Certainly there is much evidence to substantiate the argument that the incidence of poverty, disease, vice, and crime is far greater in slum districts than in other parts of the metropolis. What the picture overlooks, however, is that the housing

---

[7] Hunter, p. 32.

[8] William G. Grigsby, "Housing and Slum Clearance: Elusive Goals," *The Annals*, 352:107–118 (1964).

[9] Terence Morris, *The Criminal Area: A Study in Social Ecology* (London: Routledge & Kegan Paul, Ltd., 1957).

problems of slum occupants are generally inseparable from family and community disorganization, poverty, and disease. Human lives as well as houses are blighted in these areas. Merely moving occupants into better dwelling units will not cure other physical and social ills. Empirical evidence, in fact, is accumulating to show that improved housing does not have many of the social benefits initially attributed to it. . . . Yet the belief that delinquency, prostitution, alcoholism, crime, and other forms of social pathology magically inhere in the slums and will die with their demolition continues to persist.[10]

Overcrowding and Congestion

A slum may be overcrowded with buildings, or the buildings overcrowded with people, or both. High density is not the same as overcrowding: areas may have high densities, as in high-rise apartments, but not be overcrowded. Congestion may be so great that a judgment about the physical condition of the buildings must often be made in terms of the high density per block, acre, or square mile. It has been pointed out, for example, that if New York City's population density were as high as some of the Harlem slum's worst blocks, the entire population of the United States could fit into three of New York City's boroughs.[11] Whyte stressed the importance of overcrowding as a criterion for slum conditions when he described how he chose Boston's North End for a slum in his well-known sociological study of "street corner society":

> I made my choice on very unscientific grounds: Cornerville best fitted my picture of what a slum district should look like. Somehow I had developed a picture of run-down three-to-five-story buildings crowded in together. The dilapidated wooden-frame buildings of some other parts of the city did not look quite genuine to me. To be sure, Cornerville did have one characteristic that recommended it on a little more objective basis. It had more people per acre living in it than any other section of the city. If a slum meant overcrowding, this was certainly it.[12]

People who live under these crowded conditions obviously have little privacy, a factor which may be of great importance, especially in its effects

---

[10] John C. Bollens and Henry J. Schmandt, *The Metropolis: Its People, Politics, and Economic Life* (New York: Harper & Row, 1965), pp. 255–256. The relation of housing is discussed more fully in Chapter 5, pp. 153–154.

[11] Michael Harrington, *The Other America: Poverty in the United States* (Baltimore: Penguin Books, Inc., 1962), p. 70.

[12] William F. Whyte, *Street Corner Society* (Chicago: University of Chicago Press, 1943), p. 283. Some Indian slum areas, such as those of Delhi, may have 400,000 persons to the square mile. Ten persons commonly live in a room ten by fifteen feet in Bombay tenements, and in Hong Kong five or six human beings share cubicles measuring forty square feet.

upon interpersonal relations. Frazier states that overcrowded housing probably explains why so many Negroes congregate on the streets of Negro neighborhoods. "So far as the children are concerned, the house becomes a veritable prison for them. There is no way of knowing how many conflicts in Negro families are set off by the irritations caused by overcrowding people, who come home after a day of frustration and fatigue, to dingy and unhealthy living quarters." [13] The ill effects of this feature of slum life are partially mitigated, however, through the greater use of outside space, including front stoops and sidewalks, hallways, alleys, and lanes. Most studies of lower-class and slum life have shown the importance of peer group relations developed by these very conditions, where slum streets and sidewalks, lanes and alleys become important places for promoting such contacts.[14] Hartman refers to this as an interplay of slum dwellers between "inside and outside," both in a physical and social sense.[15] The higher value that the middle class places on privacy tends to encourage orientation toward individual responsibility and achievement.

Neighborhood Amenities

Poor slum housing is invariably associated with poor amenities and community services. Along with the shabbiness and dilapidation, the park facilities are inadequate, the schools may be of poor quality, and public amenities are often insufficient. Streets and sidewalks often go unrepaired, and rubbish and garbage are infrequently collected, adding to the undesirable environment. These services may be especially neglected in slums inhabited by minority groups in the United States. In developing countries this lack of amenities is often stressed in defining a slum.

Poor Sanitation and Health

Slums have generally been dirty places. These factors have resulted in high death and disease rates, which have always been typical of slum areas where overcrowding and the presence of rats, cockroaches, and other pests complicate the problems of health and sanitation. One United States estimate is that on the average the slum areas of a city, which contain about 20 percent of the residential population, will have 50 percent of all its diseases.[16] In one section of Cleveland the influenza and pneumonia death

---

[13] E. Franklin Frazier, *The Negro in the United States* (rev. ed.; New York: The Macmillan Company, 1957), p. 636.

[14] See Jane Jacobs, *The Death and Life of Great American Cities* (New York: Vintage Books, Inc., 1961), pp. 55–73.

[15] Chester W. Hartman, "Social Values and Housing Orientations," *Journal of Social Issues*, 19:113–131 (1963).

[16] Hunter, p. 77.

rate was 44.7 per 100,000, compared with 29.7 for the city as a whole.[17] In New York City areas containing 27 percent of the total population are reported to account for 45 percent of the infant deaths. In the slum areas of developing countries the rates of disease, chronic illness, and infant mortality are exceptionally high. There is little application of proper sanitation and health practices.

DEVIANT BEHAVIOR

A high incidence of deviant behavior—crime, juvenile delinquency, prostitution, drunkenness, drug usage, mental disorder, suicide, illegitimacy, and family maladjustment—has long been associated with slum living.[18] In the Western world, particularly in the United States, the slum is closely associated with delinquency and crime. Hunter's survey of the evidence led him to estimate that in slums composing 20 percent of the population of an American city there occur approximately 50 percent of all arrests, 45 percent of the reported major crimes, and 55 percent of the reported juvenile delinquency cases.[19] A number of studies made over a period of several years in Chicago, for example, have revealed that conventional crime, delinquency, mental disorder in general, and schizophrenia in particular, suicide, prostitution, vagrancy, dependency, illegitimacy, infant mortality, as well as high death and disease rates, are largely concentrated in the slum.[20] A 1960 study of Milwaukee showed that the slum, or inner core area of the city, which had 13.7 percent of the population, had 69 percent of the arrests for burglary, 21 percent of the aggravated assaults and 47 percent of other assaults, 60 percent of the murders, 72 percent of the arrests for commercial vice, 22 percent of the drunkenness, and 72 percent of the narcotics arrests.[21] Similar findings have been reported in such cities as Cleveland,

---

[17] R. B. Navin, W. B. Peattie, and F. R. Stewart, *An Analysis of a Slum Area in Cleveland* (Cleveland: Metropolitan Housing Authority, 1934).

[18] See, for example, Oscar Lewis, *La Vida: A Puerto Rican Family in the Culture of Poverty—San Juan and New York* (New York: Random House, Inc., 1966); and Kenneth B. Clark, *Dark Ghetto: Dilemmas of Social Power* (New York: Harper & Row, Publishers, 1965).

[19] Hunter, p. 71.

[20] For a survey of the studies see Ernest R. Mowrer, *Disorganization, Personal and Social* (Philadelphia: J. B. Lippincott Company, 1942).

[21] "Milwaukee Study Committee on Social Problems in the Inner Core of the City." Final Report to Honorable Frank P. Zeidler, Mayor, City of Milwaukee (Milwaukee: Study Committee on Social Problems in the Inner Core of the City, 1960). Also see Charles T. O'Reilly, Willard E. Downing, and Steven I. Pflanczer, *The People of the Inner Core—North: A Study of Milwaukee's Negro Community* (New York: LePlay Research, Inc., 1965).

Jacksonville, Florida, and Indianapolis. A slum area in Cleveland, which contained only 2.5 percent of the city's population in its 333 acres, was responsible for 6.8 percent of its delinquency, 21 percent of its murders, and 26 percent of its houses of prostitution.[22] The rates for nearly all 29 types of crime known to the police in Seattle, and arrests for these crimes, during the period 1949–1951, showed a decline as one moved out in six one-mile concentric zones from the center of the city. Slum areas were higher in 23 out of 29 crimes and were particularly high in robbery, prostitution, rape, gambling, and common drunkenness.[23]

Crimes involving violence, such as criminal homicide, assault, and forcible rape, are concentrated in the slums. Two detailed studies of criminal homicide in the United States, one in Houston and the other in Philadelphia, have shown a concentration of these offenses in lower-class slum areas.[24] Similarly, criminal homicides, assaults, and other crimes of violence in London have the highest incidence in slum areas, violence being used to settle domestic disputes and neighborhood quarrels.[25] Forcible rape is almost entirely committed by persons living in the slums; in fact, areas with high rates of forcible rape have been found to correspond to areas having high rates of crimes against the person generally.[26] Violence may be used by younger persons in the slums to achieve sexual objectives.

Studies of Shaw, McKay, and Thrasher in Chicago several decades ago demonstrated the much higher rates of juvenile delinquency within slum districts.[27] Moreover, the Chicago slum areas had much higher rates in both 1900

---

[22] Navin, Peattie, and Stewart.

[23] Calvin F. Schmid, "Urban Crime Areas: Part II," *American Sociological Review,* 25:655–678 (1960).

[24] Henry Allen Bullock, "Urban Homicide in Theory and Fact," *Journal of Criminal Law, Criminology and Police Science,* 45:565–575 (1955); and Marvin E. Wolfgang, *Patterns in Criminal Homicide* (Philadelphia: University of Pennsylvania Press, 1958).

[25] F. H. McClintock, *Crimes of Violence* (London: Macmillan & Co., Ltd., 1963); and David J. Pittman and William Handy, "Patterns in Criminal Aggravated Assault," *Journal of Criminal Law, Criminology and Police Science,* 55:462–470 (1964).

[26] Menachem Amir, "Patterns of Forcible Rape," in Marshall B. Clinard and Richard Quinney, *Criminal Behavior Systems: A Typology* (New York: Holt, Rinehart and Winston, Inc., 1967).

[27] See Clifford Shaw, *Delinquency Areas* (Chicago: University of Chicago Press, 1929); Clifford R. Shaw, Henry D. McKay, and James F. McDonald, *Brothers in Crime* (Chicago: University of Chicago Press, 1938), especially Chap. V, "The Community Background"; Clifford R. Shaw, *The Natural History of a Delinquent Career* (Chicago: University of Chicago Press, 1931), especially Chap. II, "A Delinquency Area"; Clifford R. Shaw, *The Jack Roller* (Chicago: University of

and 1920, even though the ethnic composition of the area had almost entirely changed. Whether slum areas were occupied successively by Swedes, Germans, Poles, or Italians, the rates were high, as they are today with a primarily Negro population. Similar findings have been reported in the United States for eight other large metropolitan areas and eleven other cities, all widely separated geographically, including Boston, Philadelphia, Cleveland, Richmond, Birmingham, Omaha and Seattle.[28] A study of Croydon, a large English city near London, revealed the highest rates for delinquency were concentrated in areas populated by unskilled and semiskilled workers' families.[29] Indications are that with the growth of urbanization, the cities of developing countries are beginning to face similar problems in their slums.[30] Studies of Kanpur and Lucknow in India showed that juvenile delinquency, juvenile vagrancy, and crime were primarily associated with slum areas.[31]

The use of drugs and drug addiction are heavily concentrated in the slums of large cities. In New York City, for example, 83 percent of adolescent drug users were found to live in slum areas populated by 15 percent of the city's census tracts.[32] Their use for "kicks" is more often common among teenagers and youths partly because drugs are more readily available in slum areas. There is much talk of drugs in slum areas.

The existence of unconventional values in slum areas accounts for the high rates of deviant behavior, such as delinquency. Yet it should be recognized that not all persons residing in slum areas become deviant. In any slum area there exist simultaneously conventional value systems carried through certain individuals, schools, churches, the police, and other sources.[33] The interaction of the conventional and unconventional value

---

Chicago Press, 1930); and Frederic M. Thrasher, *The Gang* (Chicago: University of Chicago Press, 1927), especially Chap. I, "Gangland."

[28] Clifford R. Shaw and Henry D. McKay, *Juvenile Delinquency and Urban Areas* (Chicago: University of Chicago Press, 1942).

[29] Morris.

[30] See 1957 United Nations Report on the World Social Situation, *op. cit.,* and Marshall B. Clinard, "The Organization of Urban Community Development Services in the Prevention of Crime and Juvenile Delinquency, with Particular Reference to Less Developed Countries," *International Review of Criminal Policy,* 19:3–16 (1962).

[31] Shankar S. Srivastava, *Juvenile Vagrancy: A Socio-Ecological Study of Juvenile Vagrants in the Cities of Kanpur and Lucknow* (New York: Asia Publishing House, 1963).

[32] See, for example, Isidor Chein, Donald L. Gerard, Robert S. Lee, and Eva Rosenfeld, *The Road to H* (New York: Basic Books, Inc., 1964), p. 73. For a vivid description of the pervasiveness of drug use in a Negro slum see Claude Brown, *Manchild in the Promised Land* (New York: Macmillan Company, 1965).

[33] See, for example, Whyte.

systems, such as delinquent and criminal values, may have a differential impact on those living in slum areas.[34]

A disproportionate number of schizophrenics appear to come from slum areas. In a Detroit study of two local communities the bulk of the schizophrenic cases (78.1 and 62.5 percent) had lived in slum areas before establishing residence there.[35] A New Haven study of all persons who were patients of a psychiatric clinic or a psychiatrist or who were in a psychiatric institution on December 1, 1950, found that those in the lowest classes had the highest rates of a diagnosed mental disorder.[36] Those in the lowest class had almost twice the expected percentage based on population; schizophrenia was almost two and a half times as great. A survey of the prevalence of mental disorder in midtown New York revealed a higher rate among the lower class; in fact, 13 percent of the lower class were classified as being psychotic as compared with only 3.6 percent of those from higher-status groups.[37] The validity of this and the other studies depends, of course, upon the research procedures and criteria used to determine "mental health," "mental disorder," "neuroses," and "psychoses," and adequately to take into account variations in societal reaction to mental disorders based on social class.

It is important to realize that a great deal of deviant behavior not only involves persons from the slums but is committed against other slum residents. Much theft and other property offenses, such as robbery, are perpetrated against stores in the area. The victims of nearly all violence, such as criminal homicide and assault, are the wives, husbands, friends, and other nearby residents of the slum.[38] A London study showed that nearly all crimes of violence occurred in the slum areas and were perpetrated against

---

[34] Solomon Kobrin, "The Conflict of Values in Delinquency Areas," *American Sociological Review,* 16:653–661 (1951).

[35] H. Warren Dunham, *Community and Schizophrenia: An Epidemiological Analysis* (Detroit: Wayne State University Press, 1965). His community explanation of this phenomenon is a cautious one, tying it to several other factors including life chances. Also see Lloyd H. Rogler and August B. Hollingshead, *Trapped: Families and Schizophrenia* (New York: John Wiley & Sons, Inc., 1965). Schizophrenia was found to be related, in part, to the role conflicts present in slum neighborhoods.

[36] August B. Hollingshead and Frederick C. Redlich, *Social Class and Mental Illness* (New York: John Wiley & Sons, Inc., 1958).

[37] Leo Srole, *et al., Mental Health and the Metropolis: The Midtown Manhattan Study* (New York: McGraw-Hill Book Company, Inc., 1962); and Thomas S. Langner and Stanley T. Michael, *Life Stress and Mental Health* (New York: The Free Press, 1963).

[38] Wolfgang, p. 191.

other slum people. "This was predominantly so in cases of domestic strife and neighborhood quarrels but even in the attacks and fights in public houses, cafes and streets the victims were attacked by other working-class people in the same neighborhood."[39] The victims of forcible rape are almost entirely girls from the slum areas.[40] Moreover, forcible rapes are almost entirely an intraracial phenomenon rather than interracial involving the rape of a Negro girl by a Negro male or a white girl by a white male. The adolescents and others of the slum who take up the use of drugs complicate not only their own lives but others living in slum areas. A recent government survey of crime in the United States has concluded that the offense occurs in, and the victims and the offenders are most frequently from, slum areas.

> One of the most fully documented facts about crime is that the common serious crimes that worry people most—murder, forcible rape, robbery, aggravated assault, and burglary—happen most often in the slums of large cities. Study after study in city after city in all regions of the country have traced the variations in the rates for these crimes. The results, with monotonous regularity, show that the *offense,* the *victims,* and the *offenders* are found most frequently in the poorest, and most deteriorated and socially disorganized areas of cities.[41]

THE CULTURE OF THE SLUM

The slum has a culture of its own, and this culture is a way of life. This learned way of life is passed from generation to generation, with its own rationale, structure, and defense mechanisms which provide the means to continue in spite of difficulties and deprivations. One writer has commented as follows on the slum: "It is because people themselves produce blight, or more correctly, the cultural patterns operating through people produce blight. This distinction between people themselves and the cultural patterns operating through people is an important one, because people themselves produce neither slums nor well kept neighborhoods. It is the habits, customs, behavior patterns people have learned and which they hold that move them to act in particular ways."[42]

---

[39] McClintock, p. 44.

[40] Amir.

[41] *The Challenge of Crime in a Free Society,* A Report by the President's Commission on Law Enforcement and Administration of Justice (Washington, D.C.: Government Printing Office, 1967), p. 35.

[42] Quoted in Arthur Hillman, *Neighborhood Centers Today: Action Programs for a Rapidly Changing World* (New York: National Federation of Settlements and Neighborhood Centers, 1960), pp. 20–21. Statement by Mel J. Ravits,

This slum culture affects virtually every facet of a great number of the world's slum dwellers. It is largely a synthesis of the culture of the lower class and of what Lewis has referred to as the culture of poverty.[43] Nearly all slum dwellers are of the lower class, and, with few exceptions, they live at the poverty level, while not all lower class or poor urban people live in slums. The culture of the slum has a number of characteristics which vary only in degree.[44] Although these cultural patterns are typical of the slum in an overall perspective, they vary in detail from slum to slum, from society to society. Each individual in the slum is influenced in different degrees by the general slum culture.[45] Moreover, certain people may live in a slum area, and may even be poor, yet remain removed from the slum culture. Persons of higher social classes, for example, may reside in a slum, as in some Asiatic cities, and yet not become a part of its way of life. Others, such as students and artists, may simply seek cheap housing in the slum and never become a part of it. In addition, certain groups, like the Jews in Europe or the Japanese-Americans in the United States, have often resided in slum areas but have not necessarily shared the values of those who live there.

Life in the slum is usually gregarious and largely centered in the immediate area, where are found friends, shops, and possible credit. There is little privacy, and confusion and noise seldom abate; life, however, has more spontaneity, and behavior, whether in the home or on the street corner, is more unrestrained than in the middle class. Toughness is often regarded as virtuous, and frequent resort to violence in the settlement of disputes is

---

"Reevaluating Urban Renewal," National Council of Churches, *City Church*, 10:5 (1959).

[43] See particularly Oscar Lewis, *The Children of Sanchez: Autobiography of a Mexican Family* (New York: Random House, Inc., 1961), especially the Introduction and "The Culture of Poverty"; and *Trans-Action*, 1:17–19 (1963). Also see Oscar Lewis, *Five Families: Mexican Case Studies in the Culture of Poverty* (New York: Vintage Books, Inc., 1959). Also see Lewis, *La Vida*, Introduction.

[44] See Lewis, *The Children of Sanchez*, pp. xxv–xxvii; and his *La Vida*; Walter B. Miller, "Lower Class Culture as a Generating Milieu of Gang Delinquency," *Journal of Social Issues*, 14, No. 3:5–19 (1958); Jerome Cohen, "Social Work and the Culture of Poverty," *Social Work*, 9:3–11 (1964); Elizabeth Herzog, "Some Assumptions about the Poor," *Social Service Review*, 37:389–402 (1963); Joseph A. Kahl, *The American Class Structure* (New York: Holt, Rinehart and Winston, Inc., 1957); St. Clair Drake and Horace Cayton, *Black Metropolis* (New York: Harcourt, Brace & World, Inc., 1945); Whyte; and Herbert J. Gans, *The Urban Villagers: Group and Class in the Life of Italian-Americans* (New York: The Free Press, 1962).

[45] Herzog.

common. Initiation into sexual experiences, whether by marriage or otherwise, comes early, and middle-class standards of sex conduct are not widely followed. Above all, there is a greater tolerance of deviant behavior, a higher rate of delinquency and crime, and an ambivalence toward quasi-criminal activities committed against the "outside world."

Slum dwellers display an apathy about their present conditions, an apathy associated with an intolerance of conventional ambitions. Accompanying this sense of resignation is often an attitude of "fatalism" toward life. Throughout the slums such attitudes have led to the development of a generalized suspicion of the "outside world," which includes government and politicians, welfare groups, and the upper and middle classes generally. Slum people often fail adequately to utilize those very agencies, both public and private, which could be helpful to them, such as the health department, the educational facilities, or even the police. These services are often feared as being possible dangerous sources of interference in their everyday living. Their fears are frequently confused with their own failure to understand modern health or educational services or even to use such public facilities as schools, playgrounds, or parks.

Unemployment, underemployment, and low wages are the rule in the slums. There is the ever-constant struggle for economic survival. Work patterns are likely to be irregular, and lack of permanent employment often contributes to unstable family patterns. There is an almost complete absence of savings, or even of a desire to save, and there is little ability to plan for the future or to defer present gratification of the senses. Food reserves are often nonexistent, and frequently personal possessions are pawned or local moneylenders are visited. Any exploration of the slum solely as a product of poverty, however, is far too simple. Poverty is both an absolute and a relative term. In absolute terms, it means a lack of resources for specified needs; in relative terms, it refers to the extent of these resources in comparison to what other individuals in the society have. As societies vary in the degree of poverty characterizing them, individuals and the slum itself vary in the degree to which they are poor. Slum people in the United States have a higher standard of living than many in higher social classes among other peoples of the world. For example, the radio, television, electricity, processed foods, and other material possessions which the poor generally have in the United States today would have been considered luxuries years ago, and they are still not available to large numbers of people in many countries today. A poor person in the Western world may have infinitely more material goods than a poor person in India: a relatively poor family today may have technological possessions and education superior even to those of the upper socioeconomic classes in the eighteenth century. In other words, poverty must be defined in terms of the aspirations and expectations of a culture and its capacity to produce these goods; in these terms as an explanation of slum life it has serious limitations.

The social aberration among the poor of the slums, as well as their apathy, is a product of their being the poorest, rather than their being "poor," and their alienation, apathy, and withdrawal from the general society appears to be maximum under urban slum conditions. In rural areas the relative effects of poverty are counterbalanced by stronger traditions and group ties. In areas of extensive urbanization and also industrialization, where traditional and primary group ties are weakened, the lack of power and status among the poor, particularly those in urban areas, is much greater.

General categorizations of the relation of poverty to lower-class life, however, are too broad. Sydney Miller has indicated that there actually are four types of the lower classes, using as criteria family stability and instability and job security and insecurity; the stable poor (both familial and economic stability); the strained (economic stability and familial instability); the copers (economic instability and familial stability); and the unstable (economic instability and familial instability).[46] Such a classification makes it possible to consider cultural variations in the lower class. In any event, the lower class, which is associated with slum living, should not be identified with, or confused with, the "working class." [47] The working class, made up of communities of semiskilled and skilled workers, has more stability of employment, although the orientation may largely be one of "getting by." The working class is more concerned with educational improvement than is the lower class, but not as much as the middle class.[48] Organized family life plays an important role in the working class.[49] Although the working class is not concerned with manners and proper behavior to the same extent as the middle class, it does not generally have as high an incidence of deviant behavior as the lower class.

APATHY AND SOCIAL ISOLATION

A slum also represents an image in the eyes of the larger community. There is a societal reaction to slum dwellers. The nonslum dweller often associates the physical appearance and difficult living conditions of the slum

---

[46] Sydney Miller, "The American Lower Class: A Typological Approach," *Social Research,* 31:1–22 (1965).

[47] Gans, pp. 220–262.

[48] Gans, p. 246.

[49] Gans, p. 244.

with a belief in the "natural inferiority" of those who live there. Because the slum is an inferior place, those who live there are also inferior.

This reaction has important consequences for the social isolation of slum dwellers and their exclusion from power and participation in urban society. "The slums of virtually every American city harbor, in alarming amounts, not only physical deprivation and spiritual despair but also doubt and downright cynicism about the relevance of the outside world's institutions and the sincerity of efforts to close the gap." [50] Those who live in the slum lack an effective means of communication with the outside world because of apathy, lack of experience in communicating with outsiders, or from their own powerlessness to make their voices heard. "The common denominator of the slum is its submerged aspect and its detachment from the city as a whole. . . . The life of the slum is lived almost entirely without the conventional world." [51] The local politician often becomes the only "ambassador to the outside world," one who unfortunately tries to manipulate it frequently for his own benefit.[52]

Inevitably the slum dweller's conception of himself comes to reflect the attitudes of outsiders toward the slum and its inhabitants. Slum dwellers realize that they live under conditions which are physically, although not necessarily socially, inferior to those of the middle class. Sometimes they may take actions which, hopefully, can improve their lot, but far more often they apathetically accept the situation, do what they can with what they have, and feel little or no control over their surroundings. A research study of midtown Manhattan in New York City, for example, reported that lower-class tenement dwellers tend not to plan ahead, have a feeling of futility as well as a fatalistic outlook on life.[53] In a New Haven study members of the lower class were described as being fatalistic, tending to accept what life brought them.[54]

Slum people feel relatively powerless to alter their life situation.[55] This powerlessness is accompanied by long-standing patterns of behavior and beliefs which accept current realities about this weakness. As conditions of success, a person tends to see chance rather than effort, luck rather than plan-

---

[50] *The Challenge of Crime in a Free Society*, p. 60.

[51] Harvey W. Zorbaugh, *The Gold Coast and the Slum* (Chicago: University of Chicago Press, 1929), p. 152.

[52] Gans, p. 170.

[53] Srole, *et al.*,

[54] Hollingshead and Redlich.

[55] Warren C. Haggstrom, "The Power of the Poor," in Louis A. Ferman, Joyce L. Kornbluh, and Alan Haber, *Poverty in America* (Ann Arbor: University of Michigan Press, 1965), pp. 315–334. Also see, for example, the discussion of the power structure of the slum in Kenneth B. Clark, *Dark Ghetto: Dilemmas of Social Power* (New York: Harper & Row, Publishers), 1965.

ning, and favoritism rather than ability. One writer refers to this as the "feel" of a slum, the feel when an outsider is in a slum, the feel of things when one lives in the slum.[56] "The attitude of the slum dweller toward the slum itself, toward the city of which the slum is a part, toward his own chances of getting out, toward the people who control things, toward the 'system'—this is the element which as much as anything else will determine whether or not it is possible to 'do something' about slums. This is what makes slums a human problem rather than a problem of finance and real estate." [57]

Not all slum dwellers feel inferior or rejected, however. Studies of the more settled Italian slums in Boston have demonstrated that the residents found many satisfactions in their neighborhood and did not want to be moved from it. Firey, for example, found that the physical undesirability of the North End was outweighed by the advantages of living with people of similar background.[58] Whyte stated that while this area, the North End, was a mysterious, dangerous, and depressing place, it provided an organized and familiar environment for those who lived there.[59] Seeley, who lived in the Back of the Yards in Chicago in the early 1940's discovered that its inhabitants had many advantages not found in "better" parts of the city: possibilities of fulfillment of basic human needs, an outlet for aggressiveness, adventure, and sex satisfaction, for strong loyalties, and for a sense of independence. When the slum inhabitants were taken "slumming" into middle-class neighborhoods, they did not envy them.[60] Gans found in the West End of Boston much the same attitudes reported by Firey and Whyte in the North End: residents were satisfied with their neighborhoods and did not want to leave them for the suburbs or for other central city locations which offered "improved" conditions.[61]

THE SOCIAL ORGANIZATION OF THE SLUM

Because slum dwellers are largely a part of lower-class culture, they develop a characteristic style of life within their environment in the same manner as does the middle class. The fact that their patterns of life differ

---

[56] Hunter, p. 18.

[57] Hunter, p. 18.

[58] Walter Firey, *Land Use in Central Boston* (Cambridge, Mass.: Harvard University Press, 1947), p. 179.

[59] Whyte, p. xv.

[60] Seeley, p. 10.

[61] Gans. Also see Edward J. Ryan, "Personal Identity in an Urban Slum," in Leonard J. Duhl, ed., *The Urban Condition: People and Policy in the Metropolis* (New York: Basic Books, Inc., 1963), pp. 135–150.

does not necessarily imply that one is "better," or more acceptable, as a "standard" of life, as many authorities on social problems, unfortunately, seem to indicate through their use of middle-class standards as a measuring rod or "core culture" with which to compare other class cultures.[62] This tendency has led to some erroneous assumptions concerning the life of slum inhabitants. For example, one such belief or assumption has been that the slum is composed of a "disorganized" population whose members neither know nor care about others living in the immediate vicinity.[63] Because delinquency, use of violence, sex patterns, the spontaneity and enjoyment of sensual pleasure, and various other norms of behavior, such as a lack of emphasis on good sanitation, neat housing and industriousness, differ from those of the middle class, they have been attributed to a state of "disorganization."

Detailed descriptive studies of slum communities, however, often reveal a high degree of organization, with systematic and persisting features of social behavior.[64] Rather than being "disorganized," the slum often simply has its own organization, usually a type judged by the middle class to be unconventional. Miller states that lower-class culture is a cultural system in its own right, with its own integrity, set of practices, focal concerns, and ways of behaving, systematically related to one another rather than to corresponding features of middle-class culture.[65] Whyte has pointed out that in the American slum, behavior may be as highly organized, and social controls as effective, as in middle-class suburbia, except that the slum resident may not always conform to middle-class standards of proper conduct and respectability.[66] Formal governmental control may be ineffective and police and other government authorities may be held in disrespect, but this is replaced by some degree of informal control based on age, sex, occupation, or ethnic group. Sanitation and the health and child care beliefs and practices may also indicate a highly organized system, even though contrary to both scientific and middle-class beliefs. In fact, Cloward and Ohlin have theorized that slum gang delinquency in the United States has become more aggressive and violent as a result of the disintegration of traditional slum organization

---

[62] Walter B. Miller and Martin Loeb, "Implications of Status Differentiation for Personal and Social Implications," *Harvard Educational Review*, 23:168–174 (1953).

[63] See, for example, Robert E. L. Faris, *Social Disorganization* (New York: The Ronald Press Company, 1948), p. 203; and Svend Riemer, *The Modern City* (Englewood Cliffs, N.J.: Prentice-Hall, Inc., 1952), p. 148.

[64] See, for example, Whyte; Gans; and Thrasher.

[65] Walter B. Miller, "Implications of Lower Class Culture," *Social Service Review*, 33:219–236 (1959).

[66] William F. Whyte, "Social Organization in the Slums," *American Sociological Review*, 8:34–39 (1943).

due to massive slum clearance programs which have displaced entire slum neighborhood populations.[67]

Although some slums lack unity, this cannot be assumed to be a general phenomenon of the slum. Rather, each slum neighborhood must be examined in the light of its own type of subculture. In each case the particular subculture involved will be the dominant influence on the life patterns of its inhabitants, shaping their lives through the pressures of environmental and family backgrounds, cultural traditions, and major life concerns. Zorbaugh described the rooming-house slum as a district of little social interaction among neighbors, because people constantly moved in and out without ever really becoming a part of the neighborhood.[68] Ethnic slums in the United States, on the other hand, may maintain their common cultural ties through their lodges, neighborhood shops, and the taverns which serve as meeting places. As ethnic slums split up, and the more upwardly mobile move away, even these slums demonstrate a breakdown in the effectiveness of the neighborhood as a unit of social control, and the continuity of neighborhood traditions becomes broken.[69] Moreover, although ethnic and racial groups may live in close association with each other, there may be considerable isolation from other ethnic groups living geographically close together.[70]

Upper- and middle-class areas in the city are, however, quite different from slum areas in their ecology, their social structure and, above all, their ability to participate and utilize effectively the resources of the larger city. Middle- and upper-class groups, particularly in the Western world, live in a neighborhood, but their actual participating area, where they shop, visit, and pursue recreational and cultural activities is generally much larger. The world of slum people is much more fixed. It is centered in a smaller world which tends to create resentment and suspicion of the outside urban community. Slum dwellers spend most of their time in the immediate neighborhoods: their friends and relatives live there, whatever recreation they have is there, and what credit they can get is also there. Slum dwellers thus remain more fixed in residence, although in certain types of slums there may be considerable mobility—largely, however, to other slum areas. Movement outside slum areas may be regarded as disrupting people's life situations and forcing them into a strange environment, a situation which has been par-

---

[67] Richard A. Cloward and Lloyd E. Ohlin, *Delinquency and Opportunity* (New York: The Free Press, 1960), pp. 203–210.

[68] Zorbaugh, p. 82.

[69] Shaw, *The Natural History of a Delinquent Career,* p. 15.

[70] Charles E. Silberman, *Crisis in Black and White* (New York: Random House, Inc., 1964), p. 321.

ticularly true of new slum clearance housing projects. There are, of course, a small proportion of persons in any slum area at a given time who are upwardly mobile and who may leave the slum.

THE FUNCTION OF THE SLUM

The slum reflects the larger processes of industrialization and urbanization and is involved in a series of relationships not only with certain segment of the city's population but also with the city as a whole.[71] Throughout history the slum has met various needs and has served several useful functions for its residents. It has provided a cheap labor supply, cheap housing for the poor, has fostered group associations, has educated people in an urban way of life, and has given some of its residents a medium of anonymity.

Cheap Labor Supply

A large function of the slum is to serve as a labor market by furnishing a cheap labor supply and at the same time to supply the migrants' needs for jobs. The slum is a supplier of unskilled and semiskilled labor. The slum replenishes the labor supply of the city by attracting migrants. The work of tens of thousands of slum dwellers doing the worst-paid jobs upon which important industries are dependent is valuable to city growth.[72] In fact, slums have been useful to employers as places where employees could live at lower rentals and therefore on lower incomes. Slum dwellers, being poorly paid and with fluctuating employment, are likely to be more affected by changes in the price structure of commodities than are residents of other parts of the city.[73]

---

[71] Muriel Adler, "Slums, Slum Dwellers, and the City" (Chicago: Training Center, National Federation of Settlements and Neighborhood Centers, 1966), mimeographed.

[72] Peter Marris, "The Social Implication of Urban Redevelopment," *Journal of the American Institute of Planners,* 28:183 (1962).

[73] Charles A. Frankenhoff, "A Model for Slum Development Economics," Social Science Research Center, University of Puerto Rico, 1966, mimeographed. "We assume that the development of slums belongs to urban development as a natural part of its growth, not as a cancer on the body social. Slum development is accepted as a healthy social phenomenon. The slum community should be seen as a community in development, receiving its share of urban community services, and contributing its own services to the development of the greater urban area." Charles A. Frankenhoff, "The Economics of Housing Policy for a Developing Economy: Puerto Rico," Social Science Research Center, University of Puerto Rico, 1967, mimeographed, p. 150.

Housing for the Poor and the Migrant

The most common function of the slum has been to provide housing for the lowest-income groups in society. Slums have been havens for penniless rural migrants who need a first living base in the city at the lowest possible prices. In areas undergoing industrialization and urbanization, migrants to the cities in the past and today have found their first homes, at rents they can afford, or as squatters, in the city slums. By living in the slum it is possible for such low-income families to save enough for other purposes, as in the case of Italian immigrants to the United States who desired to save enough money to enable their families to join them or to provide eventually a better life for themselves and their children.[74] Similarly, the Jewish immigrants in New York's Lower East Side slum tried to save in order to send money to their families for their passages to this country.[75] Akin to these people are those who, by living in the slums, have managed to build up small businesses, or to save enough money by renting out rooms to be able to move to a more suitable neighborhood.[76]

Slums of urban-interstitial areas in the United States are much more stable than is often thought, according to a study of slum migration which found that "since about 17 percent of American families move each year, these figures suggest that the slum dwellers are if anything less mobile than most people." [77] In developing countries where vertical class mobility is severely restricted, the older and more settled slums and the large colonies of squatter shacks which spring up in and around large cities often become more or less permanent habitations for the poor. With low rents or no rents at all, their meager existence can be stretched indefinitely.

Despite cheap housing, landlords of slum dwellings tend to exploit those who must rent from them. Rents are usually exorbitant; it has been estimated that the rate of return on some American slum property to their absentee owners is several times that of real estate located in other sections of the city. This is made possible by subdividing old and spacious dwelling units and by neglecting repairs.

Group Associations

In many countries the slum serves as a place where group living and association on the basis of village, region, tribe, ethnic, or racial group may

[74] Lawrence Frank Pisani, *The Italian in America* (New York: Exposition Press, 1957), pp. 62–64.

[75] Moses Rischin, *The Promised City* (Cambridge, Mass.: Harvard University Press, 1962).

[76] Seeley.

[77] Marris, p. 183.

develop. The appearance of a slum can easily be quite misleading to an outsider. What the middle-class observer often sees as a neighborhood of filthy,
dilapidated, and overcrowded dwellings is thought of quite differently by
those who live there and understand the neighborhood and its residents. In
the West End of Boston, for example, the low rents, the sentiments of the
people, and their identification with the neighborhood, as well as their
strong kinship ties, built an attachment for a slum or a low-rent neighborhood which cannot be fully understood by a person with middle-class
values.[78] Whyte found an organized way of life in the slums which offered
many satisfactions to its residents.[79] Firey also found a strong identification
by many with the Italian communities and its distinctive values among
many of the Boston North Enders. For those who most fully identified
themselves with the Italian values, the overcrowded and run-down housing
was more than offset by the advantages of living with similar people in an
Italian neighborhood. The fact that many of these people could have moved
out had they so desired tended to demonstrate as invalid the conception of
the slum as a "product of compulsion rather than design." [80] John Mays,
writing of British slums, agrees with the need-satisfaction function of slum
life and adds the importance of close family and kinship ties to "the creation of a satisfactory social life and . . . a reliable source of domiciliary help
during times of illness or stress." [81]

Satisfaction for residents of the ethnic or regional slum arises from the
fact that, for them, the residential area is often an area in which a vast and
interlocking set of social networks is localized, and from the fact that physical area has meaning for them as an extension of their homes, various parts
of which are delimited and structured on the basis of belonging to an area.[82]
Even for those who have close relationships, familiar streets, the faces at the
window, personal greetings, impersonal sounds, and people walking by—all
"serve to designate the concrete foci of a sense of belonging somewhere and
may provide special kinds of interpersonal and social meaning to a region
one defines as 'home.' " [83] Thus, a feeling of belonging in or to a slum is,
in some cases, an important factor in the attitudes of slum dwellers toward

---

[78] Marc Fried and Peggy Gleicher, "Some Sources of Residential Satisfaction
in an Urban Slum," *Journal of the American Institute of Planners,* 27:305–315
(1961).

[79] Whyte, p. xvi.

[80] Firey, p. 179.

[81] John B. Mays, "Needs of Old Urban Areas," in Peter Kuenstler, ed., *Community Organization in Great Britain* (New York: Association Press, 1961), p. 33.

[82] Fried and Gleicher, pp. 305–315.

[83] Marc Fried, "Grieving for a Lost Home," in Duhl, p. 154.

their environment. Many like the human satisfactions of slum living, as is shown in these comments on the advantages of a Chicago slum.

> For an outlet for aggressiveness, for adventure, for a sense of effectiveness, for deep feelings of belonging without undue sacrifice of uniqueness or identity, for sex satisfaction, for strong if not fierce loyalties, for a sense of independence from the pervasive, omnicompetent, omniscient authority-in-general which at that time still overwhelmed the middle-class child to a greater degree than it does now.[84]

There are indications that earlier immigrants to American slums found more satisfaction in staying together in the slum than do newer immigrants and the Negro. "Recent in-migrants are more likely to stay together because there is no other place for them to go. Race prejudice keeps most of these in-migrants together even after they have become differentiated with regard to occupation, income, and status." [85] Social stratification in a community of this type is likely to produce divisiveness rather than neighborliness.

Education for Urban Life

Being both a port of entry and an area of transition for some, the slum performs a function as a type of "school" to educate newcomers to the city; thus it is a real "port of entry" for the city. It gives these newly arrived persons a place to become oriented upon their arrival, to find a first job, and to learn the ways of city life. In the United States it is a "kind of combination Ellis Island and training school for the receipt, training, and ultimate transshipment to the suburbia of underprivileged in-migrants." [86] This function is particularly important in developing countries, where the contrast between village and urban life is often great. Just as the immigrants of the past lived in the slums for a period of adjustment before many of them moved on to better neighborhoods, so today in large cities of the United States the slum houses the migrants from rural areas, the Negroes from the South, the Puerto Ricans, and the Mexicans. To some it has become a more or less permanent living area.

Demand for Anonymity

An important function of the slum is its offering a place of residence to those people who prefer to live anonymously. The urban slum has harbored both those on the way up and those on the way down, but this

---

[84] Seeley, p. 10.

[85] Svend Riemer, *The Modern City* (Englewood Cliffs, N.J.: Prentice-Hall, Inc., 1952), p. 144.

[86] John E. Bebout and Harry C. Bredemier, "American Cities as Social Systems," *Journal of the American Institute of Planners*, 29:68 (1963).

twofold character of the slum's social function has often been overlooked.[87] The slum accepts people who may be rejected elsewhere, and this function is important in preserving conformity in the remainder of the city. Some of the deviant behavior found in the slum does not originate there, but in more fashionable neighborhoods. After defeat in personal life, an individual may drift to the slum.[88] The Skid Row slum of the large cities of the United States provides an example of the anonymity offered people in all kinds of circumstances. Skid Row residents include migratory workers, bums, criminals, chronic alcoholics, and workers in illegal enterprises.[89] Only in the city, where rapid change is taking place, and often only in the slums of the city, can the disenfranchised and the deviant find genuinely important roles.[90] In addition, the artist often finds his start here, as may the poet, the jazz musician, or the intellectual radical. The slum also satisfies certain demands for vice and illegal activities, such as gambling, prostitution, and black-market trades. These demands will call forth the supply, and the question is not whether, but where, the supply will be met.[91] This accumulation of various deviant groups in slum areas should not necessarily be taken as serving no function in society or as being a highly disturbing or dysfunctional element, for deviant groups may play an important role in the introduction of innovations in any society.

SUMMARY

The great world-wide increase in urban population has produced a complex and difficult world in terms of the social relations of people. In particular, slums present a difficult situation in most major cities. Although they vary from one city to another, certain general patterns of slum life are universal. The slum is generally characterized by inadequate housing, deficient neighborhood amenities, overcrowding and congestion, but it is much

---

[87] Svend Riemer, "The Slum and Its People," in C. E. Elias, Jr., James Gillies, and Svend Riemer, *Metropolis: Values in Conflict* (Belmont, Calif.: Wadsworth Publishing Co., Inc., 1964), p. 251.

[88] Riemer, *The Modern City*, p. 147.

[89] Donald J. Bogue, *Skid Row in American Cities* (Chicago: Community and Family Study Center, University of Chicago, 1963), Chap. 2, "Who Lives in Skid Row and Why—Views of Resource Persons," pp. 46–77. In most cities in the United States the skid-row population is declining. See Howard M. Bahr, "The Gradual Disappearance of Skid Row," *Social Problems,* 15:41–46 (1967).

[90] Donald A. Cook, "Cultural Innovation and Disaster in the American City," in Duhl, pp. 87–93.

[91] Seeley, pp. 7–14.

more than this. It is also, sociologically, a way of life, a subculture, with a set of norms and values which are reflected in poor sanitation and health practices; often a lack of interest in formal education; deviant behavior such as delinquency, crime, and drug addiction; as well as apathy, social isolation, and powerlessness. In this sense "slums" may exist in areas of reasonably good physical facilities such as slum clearance projects.

Because the slum is an inferior place those who live there are felt to be inferior. People who live in slum areas are isolated from the power structure, and this isolation and inferiority are reflected in their behavior and their suspicions about the outside world.

The slum has a culture of its own that is a way of life and is largely a synthesis of the culture of the lower class and the culture of poverty. The behavior of slum dwellers, however, cannot be explained simply as a product of economic deprivation. Slum communities have a high degree of organization with systematic and persisting features of social behavior.

Throughout history the slum has met various needs and has served several useful functions for slum residents. It has provided a cheap labor supply, cheap housing for the poor, has fostered group associations, has educated people in an urban way of life, and has also given some of its residents the protection of anonymity.

SELECTED READINGS

Back, Kurt W. *Slums, Projects, and People: Social Psychological Problems of Relocation in Puerto Rico.* Durham, N.C.: Duke University Press, 1962. A social-psychological study which shows that slums are more than physical entities.

Brown, Claude. *Manchild in the Promised Land.* New York: The Macmillan Company, 1965. An account of the realities of slum life in New York's Harlem.

Clark, Kenneth B. *Dark Ghetto: Dilemmas of Social Power.* New York: Harper & Row, Publishers, 1965. An analysis of the social dynamics, the psychology, and deviant behavior of the slums of New York's Harlem. Also contains an excellent discussion of the power structure of the slum.

Clinard, Marshall B. *Slums and Community Development: Experiments in Self-Help.* New York: The Free Press, 1966. A world-wide analysis of the slum from a comparative point of view, including the nature of the slum, types of slums and slum dwellers, the slums in the United States and England in historical perspective, and possible solutions to the problems of the slum. Contains much material on the Indian slum.

Duhl, Leonard J., ed. *The Urban Condition: People and Policy in the Metropolis.* New York: Basic Books, Inc., 1963. Contains a number of articles on the sociological aspects of the slum. An article by Hollingshead and Rogler contrasts the appeals of the slum with the advantages of living in housing projects.

Gans, Herbert J. *The Urban Villagers: Group and Class in the Life of Italian-*

Americans. New York: The Free Press, 1962. Although the author claims that the Italian slum he analyzes is not actually a slum, it is one from the view-point of this chapter. An excellent analysis, including particularly the attitude of the slum dweller toward the outside world.

Haggstrom, Warren C. "The Power of the Poor," in Louis A. Ferman, Joyce L. Kornbluh, and Alan Haber, eds., *Poverty in America.* Ann Arbor: University of Michigan Press, 1965, pp. 315–334. Also in Frank Riessman, Jerome Cohen, and Arthur Pearl, eds., *Mental Health of the Poor.* New York: The Free Press, 1964, pp. 205–226. An excellent analysis of the concept of power-lessness primarily among urban slum dwellers.

Hunter, David R. *The Slums: Challenge and Response.* New York: The Free Press, 1964. Deals with various physical and social aspects of the American slum.

Jacobs, Jane. *The Death and Life of Great American Cities.* New York: Vintage Books, Inc., 1961. A critical view of the slum as a physical rather than a social phenomenon.

Lewis, Oscar. *La Vida: A Puerto Rican Family in the Culture of Poverty—San Juan and New York.* New York: Random House, Inc., 1966. A description and analysis of the norms and social relations of slums in Puerto Rico and New York.

Sexton, Patricia Cayo. *Spanish Harlem: Anatomy of Poverty.* New York: Harper & Row, Publishers, 1965. An analysis of the Puerto Rican slum in New York City.

Whyte, William F. *Street Corner Society.* Chicago: University of Chicago Press, 1943. A study of the norms and social relationships of an Italian slum in the United States.

Zorbaugh, Harvey W. *The Gold Coast and the Slum: A Sociological Study of Chicago's Near North Side.* Chicago: University of Chicago Press, 1929 (10th printing, 1963). This classic sociological study of the slums in Chicago compares them with adjacent apartment-house areas occupied by the wealthy.

5

Poverty, Anomie, and Deviant Behavior

Economic distress and social inequality have long been considered as the basic cause of society's ills. Economists and others, including some sociologists, have contributed many studies attempting to show that the underlying basic factors in social deviation originate in economic forces and social inequality. Among the approaches which might be termed economic are those relating deviant behavior to poverty and substandard housing. Many of these writers have recognized the fact that economic factors are extremely important in social life and that most modern societies are built around an essentially economic ideology. They believe that the explanation of deviant behavior lies in the failure of society to provide adequate goods and services for everyone. Thus it has seemed reasonable to them to correlate the incidence of social deviation with various economic indices. There have been exclusively economic explanations of delinquency and crime, alcoholism, prostitution, mental illness, race prejudice, and other social problems. Implicit in all these studies is the assumption that if "poverty" could be abolished we would then enter a social millennium largely devoid of all social deviation.

A somewhat similar related explanation has involved the concept of anomie to explain the apparent higher incidence of such deviant behavior among the lower classes. Modern societies emphasize status goals, such as wealth and higher levels of education, but provide limited means for everyone to achieve these goals legitimately, as among lower-income groups. This "strain toward anomie" puts pressure on lower-income groups to achieve the goals of society by illegitimate means, that is, by deviations. This frame of reference, involving the idea of restrictions on opportunity, is accepted by many today.

Others have attempted to explain deviant behavior as due to a "cultural lag," that is, a lag of the nonmaterial parts of a culture behind its technological development. Deviant behavior arises from the malfunctioning of the technological system in relation to broader mechanisms of adaptation. Both poverty and anomie, as well as the cultural lag theory, are, however, inadequate explanations for deviant behavior.

POVERTY

The Poor and Poverty

Poverty has many shades of meaning; insufficiency relative to standard of living, the inequality of income distribution, and a subculture of behavior patterns and attitudes.[1] Generally, it refers to insufficiency in the material necessities of life. Such insufficiency can involve a low level of subsistence, as in a country like India and in other less developed countries.[2] On the other hand, it may more generally be relative to the standard of living of others. It may represent the failure or inability to achieve the expected level of living in a given society at a particular time. Thus viewed, poverty is determined by the amount of income necessary for providing an adequate diet or for "providing standards of what is needed for health, efficiency, nurture of children, social participation, and the maintenance of self-respect and the respect of others."[3] From this point of view the poor will vary with the standard of living in both place and time. A poor person in America may have infinitely more material goods than a poor person in India or China; a relatively poor family today may have technological possessions and education superior even to those of the upper classes of the American revolutionary period. Poverty is defined in terms of the aspirations and expectations of a culture, and its capacity to produce these goods.

---

[1] For a discussion of different ways of defining and estimating poverty in the United States see Louis A. Ferman, Joyce L. Kornbluh, and Alan Haber, eds., *Poverty in America: A Book of Readings* (Ann Arbor: University of Michigan Press, 1965).

[2] Andrew Shonfield, *The Attack on World Poverty* (New York: Vintage Books, Inc., 1962).

[3] Definition used by the United States Bureau of Labor Statistics.

Thus television, radio, electricity, inside plumbing, central heating, an old car or a washing machine, canned foods, and so on, are material possessions the poor generally have, for example, in the United States but would have been considered luxuries years ago.

Poverty may be regarded as an inequality in the distribution of income; generally the poor would represent the lowest segment. People are poverty-stricken "when their income, even if adequate for survival, falls markedly behind that of the community." [4] Several cut-off points or levels have been set, varying in the United States from $1000 to $4000 for a family of four. In the early 1960s in the United States, approximately 1.8 million families had incomes of less than $1000 and another 3.25 million families had incomes which did not exceed $2000. Using the more accepted $3000 family figure and $1500 for an individual living alone or with nonrelatives, it was estimated in 1963 that there were 33.4 million persons below or at the level of "poverty." One in seven was a farm resident, and one case in three affected a child under eighteen.

Using a broader definition of minimal budgetary food requirements to maintain an adequate standard of living which, in 1963, was $3130 for a family of four persons and $1540 for unrelated individuals, plus $500 for each additional family member, there were approximately 34.6 million persons. Because of larger families, the decline in the proportion of farmers, and the increase in the ratio of families of the aged, the persons of this group would not necessarily be the same as those with a flat income level of $3000. With this definition children of the poor would increase by 1 million and the poor on farms would be only 1 in 11.[5] In terms of estimated need, the poor of the United States had only 60 percent of the incomes they needed or a deficit of $11.5 billion.[6] The Bureau of Labor Statistics in 1959 calculated that an overall budget covering all necessities for an adequate standard of living for an urban family of four was $6147. These figures were above minimum maintenance and below luxury and below the average of American families. Using a reduced variation of this figure, it has been estimated that between 40 and 50 million persons in the United States in 1959 had inadequate housing, medicine, food, and other necessities, or about 20 to 25 percent of the population of the United States.[7]

---

[4] John K. Galbraith, *The Affluent Society* (Boston: Houghton Mifflin Company, 1958), p. 251.

[5] Mollie Orshansky, "Consumption, Work, and Poverty," in Ben B. Seligman, ed., *Poverty as a Public Issue* (New York: The Free Press, 1965), p. 67.

[6] Orshansky, p. 69.

[7] Michael Harrington, *The Other America: Poverty in the United States* (Baltimore: Penguin Books, Inc., 1962), p. 194.

There is somewhat of a contradiction between these definitions. When one reviews poverty as an absolute concept of inequality of income rather than a relative concept based on standard of living there is apt to be confusion. The poor would always be with us.

> The absolute concept refers to the comparative distribution of the over-all resources of society. In our usage growing inequality means that the bottom 20 percent of income recipients receive a smaller *percentage* of the economic pie in one year than they receive in another. If the number of poor families increases as the poverty line moves up with improving standards of living in society, we cannot speak of increasing inequality. In this situation we are dealing with a growth in the number who are relatively poor, not necessarily in the aggregate income position of the poor relative to better-off groups in society. It is important to keep distinct the differences between poverty as the inability to obtain a specific level of living and inequality as the relative sharing of the economic and social output. The two can be moving in different directions. For example, fewer people may be living in poverty, but they may also receive less of the society's output than a similar number of people did in former years.[8]

There are still other views of poverty, namely that it should be regarded as a culture or subculture. In this sense poverty represents certain behavior and attitudes. "A group of individuals or families may be said to be in poverty when they *share* a distinctive set of values, behavior traits, and belief complexes that markedly set them off from the affluent groups in the society. This set is a *derivative* of prolonged economic deprivation, lack of adequate financial resources, and socialization in an environment of economic uncertainty. This 'culture of poverty' is characterized by an intergenerational persistence and transmission to the children of the poor."[9] The difficulty with this definition is that the "investigators are looking at *different* groups of the poverty-stricken in *different* geographical locations and in *different* opportunity structures. It may well be that we should refer to '*cultures of poverty*' rather than a single '*culture of poverty*.'"[10]

---

[8] S. M. Miller and Martin Rein, "Poverty, Inequality, and Policy," in Howard S. Becker, *Social Problems: A Modern Approach* (New York: John Wiley & Sons, Inc., 1966), pp. 436–437. Reprinted by permission of the publishers.

[9] Ferman, *et al.*, "Introduction," p. 5. Italics are the editors'. For a discussion of the subculture of poverty see Chapter 4 on the slums in Oscar Lewis, *Children of Sanchez: Autobiography of a Mexican Family* (New York: Random House, Inc., 1961); Hanna H. Meissner, ed., *Poverty in the Affluent Society* (New York: Harper & Row, Publishers, 1966), pp. 92–135; and Ferman, *et al.*, pp. 259–311.

[10] Ferman, *et al.*, p. 5.

Societal Reaction to Poverty

Reactions to poverty and being poor have varied in different times. So has the concern for the poor.[11] Within recent years the poor in the United States have been "rediscovered," both as a scientific and as a public policy problem.[12]

Poverty has not always carried a negative connotation, and where it has, the reaction has differed. In fact, poverty has on occasion been viewed as an "ideal state" and as an end in itself. There is much in the philosophy of Christianity and Buddhism in the past and even today that regards poverty as a virtue, as shown by the vows of poverty taken along with other religious vows, and by comments on the virtues of the poor generally. Giving alms to the poor has frequently been regarded as a "good deed." Consequently, the poor have been "used" by those who are richer as a stepping-stone to heaven.

Some feel that the poor are social failures. The famous English social philosopher, Herbert Spencer, writing in the 1850's, took the view, in opposing the poor laws, that poverty purifies society of those who are incapable of contributing effectively to it. "The poverty of the incapable, the distresses that come upon the imprudent, the starvation of the idle, and those shoulderings aside of the weak by the strong, which leaves so many 'in shallows and in miseries,' are the decrees of a large, far-seeing benevolence."[13]

Today the reaction to the poor takes various form.[14] Some feel that only selected segments are deserving of help and that others are satisfied with their lot and with charity and are unwilling to make the effort to change. The self-defeating poor are incompetent in the way in which they

---

[11] Meissner has a discussion of attitudes toward poverty in the United States during the nineteenth and early twentieth centuries.

[12] See Robert H. Bremner, *From the Depths: The Discovery of Poverty in the United States* (New York: New York University Press, 1964). Also see Harrington. Some years ago there were scientific studies of poverty, and books dealing with social problems nearly always had a chapter on the subject. (See, for example, John L. Gillin, *Poverty and Dependency: Their Relief and Prevention* [New York: Appleton-Century-Croft, Inc., 1921].) The "rediscovery" of poverty and the War on Poverty which began in the 1964s served to revive a scientific interest in this area. For a discussion, see Meissner, pp. 199–248.

[13] Herbert Spencer, "Poverty Purifies Society," in Robert E. Will and Harold G. Vatter, *Poverty in Affluence: The Social, Political, and Economic Dimensions of Poverty in the United States* (New York: Harcourt, Brace & World, Inc., 1965), p. 58. Also see Meissner, pp. 4–23.

[14] Miller and Rein, pp. 485–488.

deal with their problems and they must be rehabilitated. Others look at the poor as a victimized group at the mercy of unscrupulous landlords and employers, particularly in the slums.

Poverty and the poor today have been largely defined in terms of a negative societal reaction.[15] The "poor" are made up of all types of backgrounds, but the status assigned them is a status consisting of negative attributes, that is, in terms of a status the person does not have. The poor are not expected to make a contribution to society or to be capable of doing so. Poverty is, then, a socially recognized condition of a certain social status. It is a product of the social structure. "Historically the poor emerge when society elects to recognize poverty as a special status and assigns specific persons to that category."[16] In particular, the poor are likely to be those who are dependent, who are helped and assisted by others such as social workers, and thus have "a special career that impairs their previous identity and becomes a stigma which marks their intercourse with others."[17] To receive assistance means to be stigmatized; once assigned the status of the poor a person's social role is changed. It is the lack of economic means that makes one "poor" or places him in a condition of poverty, for if he continues his occupational role of, for example, a plumber, he is not "poor." To receive assistance declassifies a person from his previous occupation.

Types of Poverty and the Poor

One way to distinguish types of poverty is collective, cyclical, and individual. Collective poverty represents a somewhat permanent insufficiency of material means as in the case of large proportions of the population of India or in the urban slums of more developed countries. Cyclical poverty is more temporary but is widespread and may arise from an economic depression with mass unemployment, or, in more agricultural countries, from crop failure, which in the past was likely to lead to famine. Individual poverty arises from individual difficulties not largely associated with collective or cyclical conditions. These may be the result of age, disease, crippling, and blindness, or the result of alcoholism, drug addiction, or other difficulty. In modern industrial societies relief is often furnished such persons through welfare payments.

The poor can be divided into four types according to the importance of economic and cultural factors in producing the life styles of such per-

---

[15] Lewis A. Coser, "The Sociology of Poverty," *Social Problems,* 13:140–148 (1965) and Georg Simmel, "The Poor," *Social Problems,* 13:118–140 (1965).

[16] Coser, p. 141.

[17] Coser, p. 145.

sons.[18] From the point of view of family stability and job security, there are the stable poor, the strained, "the copers," and the unstable poor. The stable poor are those whose income, though low, is fairly secure and whose family life is secure. The children of such poor families are most likely to be occupationally and educationally mobile. The strained generally have economic stability but their family life is unstable because of personal and family problems. The copers have economic insecurity but the family stability that enables these families to stay intact in the face of adversity. These persons, both white and Negro, are often recent rural migrants to the slums. The unstable poor have neither economic security nor family stability.

Characteristics of the Poor

If "poverty" is defined as an income of $3000 or less for a family, and $1500 for a single person, in a country like the United States, the poor in the early 1960s constituted a diverse group.[19] Poverty is more a rural phenomenon, for about 70 percent of the poor lived in rural areas and cities with a population under 50,000. The twelve largest cities furnished 11 percent of poor families. As a government report states: "There is a growing legion of unskilled, uneducated workers who come to the city in search of something they may not find, better opportunities. Often they find they have accomplished nothing but a relocation of their poverty." Almost half of the poor lived in the South, where only 30 percent of the population reside.

From 25 to 33 percent of poor families are in the category of the aged. One third (30.9 percent) of all poor families were headed by a person 65 years or older. Many of the poor were always poor, but others have joined this category because other sources of income have declined.[20]

Poverty is more a problem of white persons, although the Negro is overrepresented. Nearly eight in every ten poor families were white. Although Negroes comprise 10 percent of the general population, about 21 percent of poor families are Negro. If the $3000 level is used, almost one half (47.1 percent) of all Negroes live in poverty as compared with one in five whites (19.4 percent). Although Negro migration to the North continues

---

[18] S. M. Miller, "The American Lower Classes: A Typological Approach," in Arthur B. Shostak and William Gombert, *New Perspectives on Poverty* (Englewood Cliffs, N.J.: Prentice-Hall, Inc., 1965), pp. 22–39.

[19] Much of the material in this section was derived from Miller and Rein, pp. 426–465.

[20] *The War on Poverty: A Congressional Presentation*, March 17, 1964, pp. 5–6. This document was organized by The President's Task Force on the War on Poverty that developed the legislation which became the Economic Opportunity Act of 1964.

to grow, about 70 percent of Negroes with incomes of less than $4000 lived in the South. It is likely that migration from the South will not solve some of the low-income problems of the Negroes: one estimate is that although 54 percent of the Negroes resided in the South in 1960, 42 percent of all Negroes will reside in the South by 1980.[21]

The unemployment risk for Negroes was twice that of whites; in 1963 the white unemployment rate was 5.1 percent and the Negro 10.9 percent. A quarter of all Negro youth in the labor force were unemployed.

About one fourth (23 percent) of all families below the $3000 income level in 1960 were headed by females. Families with children and a single parent constitute about one in two poor families. The proportion of families headed by females is greater in the $2000 income bracket, of which they constituted 27 percent. Almost four in every five such Negro families were poor, compared with about one half of white families headed by females. Such a family is extensive among Negro low-income families in the urban slum areas of the North and West.

> Among all nonwhite families with incomes below $3000, more than a fourth (27.6 percent) were headed by females. If we exclude families headed by persons over 65 and compute the percentage that female-headed families are of all families headed by persons under 65, this percentage increases sharply. Of families headed by persons under 65, about a third have female heads. Of poor urban families the percentage is 41 percent, and of urban families resident in the North and West it is almost half (48.6 percent). These figures contrast with the one-third of similarly located whites with incomes under $3000 in 1960.[22]

Two thirds of poor families at the $4000 level in 1960 were headed by persons who were working. At the $3000 level the figure is 60 percent working or actively looking for work.

> To interpret these labor force participation rates, it should be remembered that 35 percent of the families of the poor are headed by aged or disabled persons and an additional 10 percent are headed by single individuals, most of whom are female. The labor force participation rate of 66 percent for heads of family who have incomes under $4000 is high; it is not substantially less than the rate (78 percent) for all heads of American families (which have a smaller proportion of aged, disabled, and broken families than do the poor).[23]

---

[21] Herman P. Miller, *Rich Man, Poor Man* (New York: Thomas Y. Crowell Company, 1964), pp. 212–214.

[22] Miller and Rein, p. 458.

[23] Miller and Rein, p. 460.

Poverty and Deviant Behavior

Since the great economic writings of Adam Smith, economic explanations of deviant behavior have been advanced by many students of social problems. Such spokesmen of the classical economic theory as Smith, Ricardo, and others discussed the degrading role of poverty. Alfred Marshall, in the introduction to his now historic work in the field of capitalist economic theory (1891), wrote: "Although then some of the evils which commonly go with poverty are not its necessary consequences; yet, broadly speaking, 'the destruction of the poor is their poverty,' and the study of the causes of poverty is the study of the causes of the degradation of a large part of mankind." [24] Writers who mentioned social problems in the nineteenth and early twentieth centuries often stressed the need for socioeconomic surveys, settlement houses, philanthropy, and other economic uplift procedures, as well as socialism or communism, to deal with the moral decay of society. Writers such as Henry George, Karl Marx, Charles Booth, Jacob Riis, Jane Addams, and William Bonger felt that we should concentrate our efforts on eliminating poverty, correcting the maldistribution of income, and overcoming economic fluctuations, not only because they were bad in themselves but because they produced most of the vices and evils besetting the world.[25]

Marx felt that crime, prostitution, vice, and moral evils were primarily due to the poverty produced by the capitalistic system, with its ownership of the means of production by a few, the general maldistribution of wealth, and an inevitable class struggle. The solution to these problems would eventually come in the establishment, first, of a dictatorship of the proletariat (that is, world-wide communism), and, later of a classless society in which each person would contribute according to his ability and receive according to his needs.[26] Many writers of Marx's day were socialists and were thus strongly influenced by his classic statement. Today, this general position has swelled into a dynamic communistic doctrine carrying an economic explanation of the world's difficulties into the farthest corners of the globe.

---

[24] Alfred Marshall, *Principles of Economics* (8th ed.; London: Macmillan & Co. Ltd., 1936), p. 3.

[25] See Charles Booth, *Life and Labour of the People in London* (London: Macmillan & Co., Ltd., 1892).

[26] Karl Marx, *Das Kapital* (translated by S. Moore and E. Aveling; edited by F. Engels; Hamburg, Germany: Otto Meisner, 1890). See also Karl Marx and Friedrich Engels, *The Communist Manifesto* (edited by F. Engels; London: 1848). Also see Will and Vatter, pp. 54–58.

Not everyone who subscribes to the paramount importance of economic factors in societal development is a communist. In fact, ardent believers in capitalism imply another materialistic emphasis by insisting that a higher standard of living and the elimination of poverty will lead to the solution of most social problems. The same line of reasoning prompts philanthropists to assume that merely by distributing some of their wealth among the poor they will eliminate much deviant behavior.

Many studies have tried to show that poverty is the basic cause of social deviation. Probably the most widely known of all exponents of this view was William Bonger, a Dutch social economist who used European data to ascribe practically every form of deviant behavior to poverty.[27] Other later investigations have attempted to show that since most or a large proportion of delinquents, criminals, drug addicts, alcoholics, mental patients, and suicides are from the lower classes this proves that deviants are a product of poor living conditions. Since many poor live in the slum or under conditions of insufficient economic means and poor housing it is the conditions of these areas that account for deviations. For example, probably few people believe that inadequate housing, by itself, is a cause of deviant behavior, but many consider it to be one of the major causes. Considerable evidence has been submitted to indicate that sub-standard housing plays a major role in deviant behavior by indicating the correlation of areas of high deviation with areas of bad housing.

Evaluation of Poverty and Deviant Behavior

Without question, poverty has serious consequences for health, life expectancy, infant mortality, nutrition, housing, the quality of family life, and educational opportunity. Above all, it limits social participation, particularly in the political, social, and economic spheres. There are a number of objections, however, to poverty as a basic explanation of deviant behavior: the meaning of the concept of poverty itself is relative; studies of poverty have been derived from biased samples; noneconomic factors are often of primary importance in deviation; deviation may be reduced without a great deal of change in economic conditions; there is little evidence, with the exception of suicide, of a relationship between the economic cycle and deviant behavior; and there is little evidence to support any marked relationship between the quality of housing and deviant behavior.

> 1. *The entire emphasis on "poverty," "lower economic group," or "minimum standard of living" can be challenged by questioning the meaning of these expressions.* They cannot be regarded as absolute and

---

[27] William A. Bonger, *Criminality and Economic Conditions* (translated by Henry P. Horton; Boston: Little, Brown & Company, 1916).

timeless designations in terms of either money or material goods. If poverty is regarded as a relative term, both from the standpoint of other cultures and in time, it has little utility as a universal explanation of deviant behavior. In fact, it is of interest that even though there has been a constant increase in the living standards of Western European countries over the past century, there is no indication that deviant behavior has decreased.

2. *Many studies of the economic background of deviants represent biased samples.* Most economic studies, for example, have neglected to indicate that a considerable proportion of our nondeviant population also has a low income and also is poorly housed. A considerable number of American families in recent years have had an income below the minimum standards recommended for health and welfare by the Bureau of Labor Statistics.

It is likely that the proportion of deviants from lower socioeconomic groups would generally be much smaller if the samples were more representative. Probably a greater proportion of deviants among the lower socioeconomic group comes to the attention of authorities, both in detection and in commitment, than the proportion of deviants from the wealthier classes. Delinquents among the higher economic groups, for example, are often dealt with by informal means. Crime of the white-collar type among the upper classes is seldom prosecuted, and few persons of this group are imprisoned for it.

Alcoholics and mental patients from the upper socioeconomic groups are less likely to be included in many studies of alcoholics who come to the attention of public agencies, for they are often treated privately. A study of 2023 male patients from the Connecticut outpatient alcoholism clinics tends to contradict previous impressions of the alcoholic population.[28] According to this study, rather than being "alcoholic bums" and derelicts, "nearly two-thirds of the men were gainfully employed when they first came to the clinic; 56 per cent were known to have held steady employment on one job for at least 3 years; 25 per cent for at least 10 years. At least seven out of ten have held jobs involving special skills or responsibility."

Homosexuals appear to exist among all classes.

3. *Investigations have indicated that poverty is not an important factor in generally accounting for deviant behavior.* Even in such pronounced "economic behavior" as begging, which is found all over the world, economic necessity is not the entire explanation. Noneconomic factors are often of primary importance. The beggar is a cultural phenomenon, capitalizing on the contrast between his appearance and that of others, appealing to pity, and generally exploiting his low economic status. In a detailed study of beggars, begging was found to be generally

---

[28] Robert Straus and Selden D. Bacon, "Alcoholism and Social Stability," *Quarterly Journal of Studies on Alcohol,* 12:231–260 (1951).

a highly organized activity with general acceptance of a role of begging rather than working. Professional beggars know what types of begging are the most productive, such as exhibiting deformities or "hitting" young people on dates for a handout; and where to beg, as in crowds of persons in the theater district or going to or from church. Careful attention is paid to styles of dirty dress and the use of certain words and signs. Some of this knowledge is transmitted from generation to generation in begging families.

In the cities of India a common feature in many bazaar areas, as well as in the central shopping areas, temples, and railway stations, is the inevitable beggar who makes his daily rounds. Although a certain type of mendicancy, such as religious begging, has long been common in India, professional begging has become an urban phenomenon for the simple reason that it is a lucrative "trade." [29] One survey reported that in the city of Bombay alone there are about 10,000 beggars, some 47 percent of whom are able-bodied. The total beggar population of Delhi has been estimated at about 3000, 44.5 percent of whom are able-bodied. Many beggars "earn" more than the daily wage of nonbeggars.

4. *There are indications, moreover, that deviant behavior can be modified without changing the economic situation.* An area can be improved without major material changes. For example, in projects where neighborhood councils in the slums have dealt with problems of delinquency there appears to be a reduction in these rates without changing either economic or housing conditions.[30] Treatment in general and group methods in the treatment, in particular, of delinquency, crime, drug addiction, mental disorder, and alcoholism, for example, through Alcoholics Anonymous, do not necessarily require marked changes in the economic status of the individual.[31]

5. Cyclical poverty in the form of the business cycle in the modern sense is primarily a development which began in the nineteenth century. Modern society has been characterized by recurrent fluctuations in economic conditions, fluctuations commonly referred to as prosperity, reces-

[29] M. V. Moorthy, ed., *Beggar Problem in Greater Bombay* (Bombay: Indian Conference of Social Work, 1959), p. 14; and *The Beggar Problem in Metropolitan Delhi* (Delhi: Delhi School of Social Work, 1959).

[30] See Chapter 18. Also see Marshall B. Clinard, *Slums and Community Development* (New York: The Free Press, 1966); H. L. Witmer and E. Tufts, *The Effectiveness of Delinquency Prevention Programs* (Children's Bureau, United States Department of Health, Education, and Welfare, Publication 350, Washington, D.C.: Government Printing Office, 1954), p. 15. Also see Solomon Kobrin, "The Chicago Area Project: A 25-Year Assessment," *The Annals*, 322:19–29 (1959); and Anthony Sorrentino, "The Chicago Area Project after 25 Years," *Federal Probation*, 23:40–45 (1959).

[31] Marshall B. Clinard, "The Group Approach to Social Reintegration," *American Sociological Review*, 14:257–262 (1959). Also see chapter 19.

sions, and depressions. During periods of recession or depression there is an increase in unemployment and poverty, along with a general decline in morale. During the Great Depression, for example, in the United States in 1935 20 million, or about one third of the population, were receiving public relief. It is believed by some people that depressions are associated with increased juvenile delinquency, crime, prostitution, mental disorder, marital maladjustment, suicide, and racial tensions. On the other hand, many believe that prosperity is accompanied by "high" living and an increase in deviant behavior.

In the scientific study of these relationships, different rates of deviant behavior have been compared with various economic indices, generally utilizing measures of statistical correlation. *From the evidence available it can be concluded that the business cycle has little or no direct relation to most forms of social deviation, with the exception of suicide.* Urbanism and norm conflicts must be regarded as the basic factors in producing social deviation. Whereas deficiencies in given economic processes may intensify urbanism, they certainly are not the prime causes of our contemporary difficulties. It is likely that a balanced economic system would still have most of our contemporary problems because most of them involve conflicts in norms and difficulties in interpersonal relations rather than technological or strictly economic issues.

6. *An analysis of the high deviation rates of the slums does not indicate that either low economic status or bad housing is the explanation.* Low economic status or racial prejudice forces persons to reside in low-rent areas which are characterized by accentuated urban characteristics and norm conflicts. Although it is true that sociological studies of the ecological distribution of delinquency within cities have indicated that such deviation and poor housing are correlated, this fact in itself is not the important variable. Rather, the explanation of the deviation appears to be primarily a product of the social conditions of the area.[32]

Part of the difficulty in attempting to show such relationships has been the research techniques employed. The studies are based merely on large statistical comparisons, disregarding for the most part individual case studies where the meaning of the economic factors could be better understood. What sometimes appears to be significant is often a crude relationship at best. Some studies have attempted to prove that when housing is improved, general social conditions, including delinquency, also improve. It has been claimed, for example, that the juvenile delinquency rates in some housing developments dropped as a result of changes in housing facilities. There is question, however, as to whether in such situations housing accounted for the decline or whether it was due to changes in social conditions.

---

[32] For a discussion of the relation of slum housing to deviant behavior, see Chapter 4, pp. 118–120.

Finally, it has not always been demonstrated that the families which moved into a housing project had previously lived in the area. After studying an English city, Morris concluded that the physical characteristics of an area are of little relevance to crime and delinquency, except as an indirect determinant of the social status of the area. Even after the construction of new government housing projects the high rates of delinquency remained.[33] The continuation of high rates of delinquency in slum clearance projects has been a common phenomenon in cities in the United States, Puerto Rico, and elsewhere.[34]

ANOMIE AND DEVIANT BEHAVIOR

To some sociologists and others deviant behavior is a result of *anomie* or the clash between institutional means and cultural goals in the access to the success goals of a given society by legitimate means. In his widely known theory of *anomie,* Robert Merton stated, some thirty years ago, that modern urban-industrial societies, such as the United States, emphasize material achievements in the form of acquisition of wealth and education as the accepted status goals of the culture.[35] At the same time such societies provide limited institutional means or norms to achieve these goals by persons of the lower class, particularly lower class persons of certain racial and ethnic groups such as the Negro. This results in a situation of *anomie,* that is, a breakdown in the social structure occurring where there is an acute disjunction between the cultural norms and goals and the capacity of certain groups in society to achieve them.[36] Such persons are often referred to as *anomic* or *alienated*

---

[33] Terence Morris, *The Criminal Area: A Study in Social Ecology* (London: Routledge & Kegan Paul, Ltd., 1957).

[34] See, for example, Richard Cloward and Lloyd Ohlin, *Delinquency and Opportunity: A Theory of Delinquent Gangs* (New York: The Free Press, 1960).

[35] See "Social Structure and Anomie" (pp. 131–160) and "Continuities in the Theory of Social Structure and Anomie" (pp. 161–194) in Robert K. Merton, *Social Theory and Social Structure* (rev. ed.; New York: The Free Press, 1957). Also see Marshall B. Clinard, "The Theoretical Implications of Anomie and Deviant Behavior," in Marshall B. Clinard, ed., *Anomie and Deviant Behavior* (New York: The Free Press, 1964), pp. 1–56; Stephen Cole and Harriet Zuckerman, "Inventory of Empirical and Theoretical Studies of Anomie" and "Annotated Bibliography of Theoretical Studies" in Clinard, *Anomie and Deviant Behavior,* pp. 243–311; Albert K. Cohen, *Deviance and Control* (Englewood Cliffs, N.J.: Prentice-Hall, Inc., 1966). Durkheim used *anomie* in the different sense of "normlessness" in connection with the anomic type of suicide which will be discussed in Chapter 13. Emile Durkheim, *Suicide* (translated by John A. Spaulding and George Simpson; New York: The Free Press, 1951).

[36] Merton's formulation seems to bear little resemblance to Durkheim's concept and is more likely a combination of Max Weber's Protestant Ethic. See Marvin

in the same sense of powerlessness, estrangement, and isolation from society.[37]

American society, for example, is characterized by great emphasis on the accumulation of wealth as a success symbol without a corresponding emphasis on the constant use of legitimate means to achieve such a goal, means often becoming secondary to ends. The cultural success goals can be secured by legitimate means through regular employment, better-paid occupations, and access to more education. However, there are certain persons whose income, social class, or racial and ethnic status make it impossible to achieve these goals through *legitimate* means. They then may resort to illegitimate means or deviant behavior to attain them. Deviant behavior occurs in a society when "a system of cultural values extols, virtually above all else, certain common success-goals for the population at large while the social structure rigorously restricts or completely closes access to approved modes of reaching these goals for a considerable part of the same population." [38] The explanation of anomie assumes that there is evidence that rates of deviant behavior within a society such as ours vary markedly by income, social class, ethnic, or racial status, the highest rates and the greatest pressure for deviation occurring among the lower socioeconomic groups where opportunities to acquire material goods are fewer and the level of education is lower. It should be recognized that not all persons who have difficulty in achieving the goals of a society turn to deviation; rather, only those located in places in the social structure which are particularly exposed to stress may exhibit a strain toward anomie.

Adaptations

There are several possibilities or adaptations, which can be used where legitimate means are blocked in an effort to achieve culturally prescribed goals of success. They are chiefly rebellion, innovation, and retreatism.[39] A

B. Scott and Roy Turner, "Weber and the Anomic Theory of Deviance," *Sociological Quarterly,* 6:233–240 (1965).

[37] Gwynn Nettler, "A Measure of Alienation," *American Sociological Review,* 22:672 (1957); Melvin Seeman, "On the Meaning of Alienation," *American Sociological Review,* 24:783–791 (1959); and Dwight G. Dean, "Alienation: Its Meaning and Measurement," *American Sociological Review,* 26:753–758 (1961).

[38] Merton, p. 146.

[39] Merton also includes *conformity* to goals and legitimate means as an adaptation as well as *ritualism,* but since these hardly result in deviant behavior they are omitted here. Ritualism is the abandoning or scaling down of goals of wealth and social mobility to a point where aspirations are solved by ritualistic behavior and routine which avoids the frustrations of ambition. A different set of adaptations has been proposed by Dubin ("Deviant Behavior and Social Structure: Con-

particular adaptation is dependent on the individual's acceptance or rejection of cultural goals and his adherence to, or violation of, accepted norms. In *rebellion* persons turn away from conventional cultural goals and seek to establish a new or greatly modified social structure. They seek to set up new goals and procedures to change the existing social structure rather than trying to achieve the goals that society has traditionally established. Political radicals and revolutionaries represent this type of deviant adaptation. In another context Merton similarly distinguished between the nonconformist who challenges publicly the legitimacy of social norms, and the aberrant, such as the delinquent and the criminal, who acknowledges the legitimacy of the norms he violates.[40]

Innovation as an adaptation involves the use of illegitimate practices or socially disapproved means to achieve the status provided by monetary success or more education. Anomie theory claims that the use of such illegitimate means as theft, burglary, robbery, organized crime, or prostitution to achieve culturally prescribed goals of success, power, and wealth is common in a society such as that in the United States. Innovation is "a 'normal' response to a situation where there is little access to conventional and legitimate means for becoming successful."[41]

The adaptation of means to goals through *retreatism* explains a number of forms of deviant behavior. The individual has internalized the success goals but finds he cannot achieve them and does not wish to utilize illegitimate means of innovation, such as delinquency or crime. He then substantially abandons both the goals and the institutionalized means of securing them. The individual retreats from this goal and either engages in drug addiction or alcoholism or "escapes" through functional mental disorder, either psychotic or neurotic, or by suicide. The retreatist adaptation is particularly subject to strong societal reaction because it is nonproductive, nonstriving, attaches no value to the success goals of a society, and does not use institutional means. Retreatism tends to be a private rather than a group or subcultural form of adaptation. "Although people exhibiting this deviant behavior may gravitate toward centers where they come into contact with

---

tinuities in Social Theory," *American Sociological Review*, 24:147–164 [1959]). Parsons has extended Merton's formulation of anomie and incorporated it into a broader theory of interactional analysis. See Talcott Parsons, *The Social System* (New York: The Free Press, 1951) and Talcott Parsons and Edward A. Shils, eds., *Toward a General Theory of Action* (Cambridge, Mass.: Harvard University Press, 1951).

[40] Robert K. Merton, "Social Problems and Sociological Theory," in Robert K. Merton and Robert A. Nisbet, *Contemporary Social Problems* (2d ed.; New York: Harcourt, Brace & World, Inc., 1966), pp. 775–823.

[41] Merton, *Social Theory and Social Structure*, p. 145.

other deviants and although they may come to share in the sub-culture of these deviant groups, their adaptations are largely private and isolated rather than unified under the aegis of a new cultural code." [42]

Differential Opportunity

A reformulation of Merton's theory of anomie has been made by Cloward to include not only differentials in the availability of *legitimate means,* but variations in the access or opportunity for *illegitimate means,* such as are provided in slum areas.[43] In Merton's theoretical statement, deviant behavior is a product of differentials in the access to goals of success by the use of legitimate means. But Cloward points out that there are also differentials in access to illegitimate means, and that this differential opportunity plays a large part in the distribution of deviant adaptations. Different social strata, such as the lower and middle classes, provide varying opportunities for the acquisition of deviant roles, largely through access to deviant subcultures and the opportunity for carrying out such deviant social roles once they have been acquired. The access to such opportunities for deviant behavior will vary in the same way as differential access to legitimate means varies.[44] Actually, the individual, whatever his position in the social structure, does not have illegitimate means equally available, for much the same reason that legitimate means vary by social strata. Two things are implied when we refer to the term *means,* whether legitimate or illegitimate. "First, that there are appropriate learning environments for the acquistion of the values and skills associated with the performance of a particular role; and second, that the individual has opportunities to discharge the role once he has been prepared. The term subsumes, therefore, both *learning structures* and *opportunity structure.*" [45]

Within this context Cloward has sought to explain delinquency, crime, alcoholism, drug addiction, mental illness, and suicide. His view about some "retreatists," however, is different from Merton's. To the latter the retreatist, say a drug addict, is a person who does not wish to use illegitimate means such as innovation; to Cloward they are "double failures" in that they have failed in the use of both legitimate and illegitimate means. Many have failed in the conventional as well as the illegitimate world. Delinquency arises from the disparity between what lower-class youths are led to want

---

[42] Merton, p. 155.

[43] Richard A. Cloward, "Illegitimate Means, Anomie, and Deviant Behavior," *American Sociological Review,* 24:164–176 (1959).

[44] Robert K. Merton, "Social Conformity, Deviation and Opportunity Structures: A comment on the contributions of Dubin and Cloward," *American Sociological Review,* 24:177–189 (1959).

[45] Cloward, p. 168.

and what is actually available to them. Desiring such conventional goals as economic and educational success, they are faced with limitations on legitimate avenues of success to these goals. Being unable to revise their goals downward, they experience frustration and turn to delinquency if the norms or opportunities are available to them.[46] Some delinquent gangs use drugs and are made up of retreatists or "double failures" in that they have failed at legitimate and illegitimate means, such as stealing.

EVALUATION OF THE THEORY OF ANOMIE

The intriguing explanation of deviant behavior in terms of anomie is logical—on the surface. Despite attempts at reformulation, there are so many objections to the theory, however, that it cannot be accepted. It makes far too simple something that is much more complex. Only a few of the inadequacies can be pointed out here.[47]

> 1. *Anomie theory rests completely on the assumption that deviant behavior is disproportionately more common in the lower class.* Statistics and other official measures indicate that this is generally the case, but there is considerable evidence that lower-class persons and members of minority groups are labeled delinquents, criminals, alcoholics, drug addicts, and mental patients to a greater extent than others. *More studies of the incidence and prevalence of various forms of deviant behavior are needed before what is assumed by theory is accepted as fact.*
>
> Several studies of occupational and white-collar crime show that crime occurs in the highest social strata. Delinquency is found among the middle as well as the lower classes.[48] Alcoholism in the lower class may actually be as prevalent in the upper class, although the latter are less likely to be arrested as chronic inebriates or to use public treatment facilities. The distribution rates of drug addiction are so variable that it is difficult to come to any conclusions. Although rates may be high in

---

[46] Cloward and Ohlin. This theory of gang behavior will be discussed in Chapter 7. This theoretical approach has been applied since 1960 to a number of practical attempts to control delinquency, such as Mobilization for Youth in the lower East Side of New York City.

[47] For more detailed criticisms see Marshall B. Clinard, "The Theoretical Implications of Anomie and Deviant Behavior"; Edwin M. Lemert, "Social Structure, Social Control, and Deviation"; James F. Short, Jr., "Gang Delinquency and Anomie"; H. Warren Dunham, "Anomie and Mental Disorder"; Alfred R. Lindesmith and John Gagnon, "Anomie and Drug Addiction"; and Charles R. Snyder, "Inebriety, Alcoholism, and Anomie"; in Clinard, *Anomie and Deviant Behavior.* Also see Albert K. Cohen, "The Sociology of the Deviant Act: Anomie Theory and Beyond," *American Sociological Review,* 30:5–14 (1965).

[48] Edmund W. Vaz, *Middle-Class Juvenile Delinquency* (New York: Harper & Row, Publishers, 1967).

slum areas, the highest occupational rate is generally among medical doctors.[49] Drug addiction in the past was not primarily associated as it is today with urban male lower-class adolescents. As one article concluded, "If anomie accounts for the present pattern of rates, what accounted for the very different patterns of the previous century and why did the change occur?" [50] Cultural patterns of use and accessibility explain much of the incidence of drug use. The explanation of the high rate of addiction in Negro areas of large cities today lies primarily in the concentration there of the drug traffic. "If anomie is pronounced in the urban Negro slums so also are the drugs easily available there . . . If drug use occurred only in this situation the theory of anomie would be a rather impressive one. But one still needs to keep in mind that, however much the Negro residents of slums may be influenced by anomie and however available illicit drugs may be for them, the vast majority do not become addicted." [51] Although schizophrenia appears to be more common in the lower class, mental disorder occurs in all social classes and the degree of differences is as yet unclear. The rates may be in part a reflection of differentials in societal reaction.

2. *It is difficult to identify a set of cultural goals that are universally appreciated in most modern, complex industrial societies.* Actually individuals participate in many groups and their values may not agree with values in other groups. The all-pervading importance of monetary goals and the goal of education do not appear to be as universally accepted by all groups, as the theory would suggest. Moreover, the theory assumes a universality of what constitutes "illegitimate means" that is not the case. What constitutes delinquent and criminal acts varies in time and place. The use of drugs is not a deviation in many parts of the world today and largely was not in Western European society, including the United States, a century ago.

3. *The theory stresses position in the social structure as the important variable in explaining deviant behavior.* The demonstrated importance of deviant subcultures, deviant groups, and the important role of the characteristics of urban life as well as the role of the slum are not recognized. Many forms of deviant behavior, such as drug addiction, professional crime, occupational crime, prostitution, and homosexual behavior, are collective acts in which association with group-maintained values explains the behavior. Delinquent gang behavior by lower-class boys, for example, is more likely to be linked with status considerations involving position in the peer group than with the ultimate goals of a society.[52]

4. *The theory largely neglects the important role of social control*

---

[49] See pages 316–317.

[50] Lindesmith and Gagnon, p. 165.

[51] Lindesmith and Gagnon, pp. 173–174.

[52] James F. Short, Jr., and Fred L. Strodtbeck, *Group Process and Gang Delinquency* (Chicago: University of Chicago Press, 1965).

in defining who is a "deviant," that is, how the label comes to be attached to a person. What acts will be considered deviant and what persons will be defined as deviants vary. Active social control is a continuous process by which values are examined by agencies of social control, such as the police, as to what acts they will consider deviant and enforce. The use of drugs was outlawed in the United States as late as 1914, thus making drug addicts "criminals" only since then. The theory also neglects the effect of societal reaction in defining deviant careers. The societal elements isolating and reacting to deviants in terms of self-concepts and social roles are disregarded. The theory does not distinguish between primary and secondary deviants, or between career and noncareer deviants, nor does it distinguish other types. All are considered together as a group—"delinquents," "criminals," "drug addicts," the "mentally ill," and "suicides"— a procedure inconsistent with contemporary theory and research on the types of deviant behavior.

5. *Anomie theory does not recognize the nature of social behavior, social roles, and self-concepts.* The deviant is considered in the theory as making individual adaptations in the system as a result of "pressures" arising from his failure to achieve certain goals. Actually most deviant acts arise out of a process of interaction with others who may serve as a reference group for the individual. The individual deviant is often not a free agent in his choice but is restricted by the pressures of the groups to which he belongs. In a later discussion, for example, it will be pointed out that delinquent gang behavior and drug addiction are largely products of an interactive process with others. A deviant act is not an abrupt change due to the strain of anomie but is built up through a process of interaction. In fact, many deviant acts are a part of role expectations rather than representing a disjunction between goals and means.[53]

6. *The theory of the adaptation of means to goals through retreatism lacks precision and is an oversimplification of what is actually a much more complex process of how alcoholism, drug addiction, mental disorder, and suicide arise.* For example, to an alcoholic the securing of alcohol becomes an end or goal; drug addicts are not retreatists, for difficulties in securing the goal of drugs make an addict an "active" rather than a retreatist person. In fact, a substantial number of addicts carry on other occupations, such as medical doctors, and are "responsible members of society, . . . share the common frame of values, . . . have not abandoned the quest for success, and are not immune to the frustrations involved in seeking it." [54] There is little evidence to support the "double failure" explanation of drug addiction. In a comprehensive study of delinquent gangs, retreatist gangs using drugs, for example, were not found to exist in any number.[55] In fact, if he is able to keep his habit going and

---

[53] Cohen, "The Sociology of the Deviant Act: Anomie Theory and Beyond."
[54] Lindesmith and Gagnon, p. 178. Also see pages 316–317.
[55] Short and Strodtbeck.

secure an adequate supply of drugs, the drug addict is a "double success" rather than a double failure. The explanation of mental disorder, as we shall see later, is much more than a process of retreating from success goals and involves normative actions and role playing.

Moreover, a major criticism of retreatism as an adaptation is that it confuses the origins of the deviation with the actual effects of the deviation. Long periods of excessive drinking or drug use may impair a person's social relations and his ability to achieve certain goals in society; anomie thus confuses cause and effect.

TECHNOLOGICAL DEVELOPMENT AND THE CULTURAL LAG

The machine age and all its complexity have been blamed by a number of scientists, including sociologists, for the confusion and deviation of the world in which we live.[56] The scientific theory is based on the "cultural lag," a concept first suggested by Ogburn.[57] All social problems, according to him, result basically from social change, which creates maladjustments among various parts of a culture. Such unrelated social problems as unemployment and labor conflicts, inadequate medical care, educational problems, traffic casualties, adolescent instability, marital and family maladjustment, juvenile delinquency, crime, and mental illness have been attributed to a lag behind technological advance.

According to the cultural lag theory, various parts of modern culture are not changing at the same rate. Some parts, the technological, are changing more rapidly than the nontechnological aspects of society, such as the family, religion, and the political system. Since there are a correlation and an interdependence of parts among all social institutions, a rapid change in one part of a culture requires readjustments through changes in the various

---

[56] See, for example, Charles R. Walker, ed., *Modern Technology and Civilization* (New York: McGraw-Hill Book Company, Inc., 1962).

[57] William F. Ogburn, *Social Change* (New York: The Viking Press, Inc., 1922). For further elaboration of his theory, see William F. Ogburn, ed., *Recent Social Trends in the United States* (New York: McGraw-Hill Book Company, Inc., 1933); National Resources Committee, *Technological Trends and National Policy* (Washington, D.C.: Government Printing Office, 1937); William F. Ogburn, *The Social Effects of Aviation* (Boston: Houghton Mifflin Company, 1946); and William F. Ogburn and Meyer Nimkoff, *Sociology* (Boston: Houghton Mifflin Company, 1940). An earlier writing by the sociologist Charles Cooley stated the somewhat similar view that social problems grew out of the "formalism" of certain social institutions which became ossified or fixed, while others undergo transformations.— Charles Cooley, *Social Organization: A Study of the Larger Mind* (New York: Charles Scribner's Sons, 1919).

other correlated parts. Technological changes eventually cause alterations in other parts of the culture, but corresponding changes in the nonmaterial culture do not occur simultaneously with the changes in the material sphere.[58] This differential time sequence results in the cultural lag.

The nonmaterial aspects of culture change much more slowly than the material for several reasons: (1) there is more emotional opposition to change in the former; (2) improvements resulting from changes in the material culture are more readily received because they are more visible; (3) a materialistic emphasis is itself a supreme value in our society; and (4) habit, vested interests, and ignorance all combine to favor the maintenance of the *status quo* in the nonmaterial sphere. With the present-day emphasis on machines and the rapidity with which these material aspects are changing, the lag between the technological and the adaptive culture has become increasingly great. Steam power replaced hand power; electrical power and electronics, together with the gasoline engine, have made great inroads in the use of steam power; and now nuclear fission has become a source of power.

Evaluation of the Cultural Lag Theory

Regardless of whether cultural lag is restricted to the material-nonmaterial definition or is described as a lack of synchronization in social institutions in the general culture, those who hold this theory believe that cultural lag explains much deviant behavior. The proposed solution to the problem of cultural lag obviously lies in social planning in order to restore balance within the culture. Such planning would include a study of past changes in the material culture and a prediction of future changes and of the resistances in a society which prevent adjustment to technological change.

Despite the following that the cultural lag theory has had among social scientists, however, there are a number of serious objections to it. These include the fact that norms and values, other than technological and materialistic ones, are often involved in deviant behavior; moreover, consideration of the individual is omitted, and the term *cultural lag* is loosely used.

1. *The problems of modern society involve, fundamentally, conflicts of norms and values which are many and of diverse origins.* The cultural

---

[58] Ogburn, as well as others, in later writings tried to place less stress on technological changes and has implied that lags could take place between any two parts of the culture even if both were adaptive: "The strain that exists between two correlated parts of culture that change at unequal rates of speed may be interpreted as a lag in the part that is changing at the slowest rate, for the one lags behind the other." In another connection Ogburn has written that "the lag of social changes behind technological progress is simply a special case of the general phenomenon of unequal rates of change of the correlated parts of culture." —Ogburn and Nimkoff, pp. 886, 893.

lag theory, even though there have been recent attempts at modification, is essentially an overstatement of the role that technological and economic forces play in conflicts in a society. It assumes that the norm conflicts disturbing a society are largely derived from these sources. Undoubtedly some social change does originate in technological factors, but much social change has been brought about by ideas not connected with material culture. They include Christianity and other great religious doctrines, the growth of secularism, democracy, the humanistic philosophy, communism, individualism, equal rights for women, and the English concept of justice in law. Questions about the use of alcoholic beverages and drugs as well as conflicts stemming from racial and religious discrimination disturb modern societies a great deal, but only by the widest stretch of the imagination can they be brought within the lag concept. Actually most social change is a product of inextricably connected forces, both material and nonmaterial. As one critic said, "It seems to us unwarranted and also historically inaccurate to say that society must always hop when technology swings the rope." [59]

2. *"Cultural lag" is used so loosely that it often has little meaning.* Instead of a single concept to be applied indiscriminately to all types of change, there are two types of lags: those that are really delayed responses and those that are spurious, that is, are actually not lags at all.[60] Most of the examples of the social lag concept turn out, on close analysis, to be spurious lags. Examples of true lags are seen in the workmen's compensation laws, which followed considerably behind the development of machine technology, and the development of other measures to deal with unemployment arising from new inventions. Many supposed lags are not lags at all because the variables assumed to be closely related are actually not. It would be impossible to relate, for example, divorce rates as measures of marital difficulties and industrial production or other similar economic indices unless one had a rather unusual concept of what were basically the causes of such marital maladjustment.

3. *Actually, the existence of a lag and its direction rest inevitably on a question of values.* What is a lag to one scientist may not be to another. A large percentage of women working in industry may suggest that the family system is lagging behind the industrial system and that later adjustments will take women out of the economic system and back into the home. On the other hand, the same facts might as plausibly suggest that more industrial work should be provided for women because of equalitarian treatment of women, or because of the decline of various functions of the family. Similarly, how can we be assured, as some have suggested, that contemporary marriage ethics and sexual morals are lagging behind

---

[59] Wilson D. Wallis, in Letters to the Editor, *American Journal of Sociology,* 43:807 (1938).

[60] John H. Mueller, "Present Status of the Cultural Lag Hypothesis," *American Sociological Review,* 31:320 (1938).

industrial development, and if they are, is it known how much they lag? Persons with opposite value systems might reach opposite conclusions. Mumford, too, has pointed out that the idea implies that man must always make an adjustment to the machine, whereas on occasions what may be required is adjustment away from the machine: "In truth, interactions between organisms and their environments take place in both directions, and it is just as correct to regard the machinery of warfare as retarded in relation to the morality of Confucius as to take the opposite position." [61]

SUMMARY

Poverty has many shades of meaning: insufficiency relative to standard of living, the inequality of income distribution, and a subculture of behavior patterns. Reactions to poverty and being poor have varied in different times. Today the reaction to the poor even takes various forms. Poverty and the poor have been largely defined in terms of negative societal reaction. One way to distinguish types of poverty is collective, cyclical, and individual. The poor can be divided into types according to the importance of economic and cultural factors in producing the life styles of such persons.

Poverty does not have a definite relation to deviant behavior because (1) the entire emphasis on "poverty," "lower economic group," or "minimum standard of living" can be challenged by questioning the meaning of these expressions; (2) many studies of the economic background of deviants represent biased samples; (3) investigations have indicated that poverty is not an important factor in generally accounting for deviant behavior; (4) there are indications that deviant behavior can be modified without changing the economic situation; (5) from the evidence available it can be concluded that the business cycle has little or no direct relation to most forms of social deviation, with the exception of suicide; and (6) an analysis of the high deviation rates of the slums does not indicate that either low economic status or bad housing is the explanation.

In the light of all this evidence it appears that it is not poverty, the amount of income, or economic factors generally which are crucial for understanding the dynamics of social and personal deviation. The relation of economic factors to deviant attitudes, social roles, and norms must be demonstrated before much reliance can be placed on explanations based on economic factors. Although no one would imply that economic factors are not significant, they must have a demonstrated meaningful relationship to human behavior if they are to be considered as basic.

---

[61] Lewis Mumford, *Technics and Civilization* (New York: Harcourt, Brace & World, Inc., 1934), p. 317.

What is important is the urbanized setting in which economic factors function, and the interpretation given by the person and the group to the economic situation in which they find themselves. Poverty and deprivation, prosperity and depressions are important only in terms of the aspirations, needs, socially defined status, and cultural conditionings of the person.

Countries with much material welfare, such as the United States, have some of the highest deviation rates in the world, and these rates are extremely high during times of great economic prosperity. Comparisons of rural and urban deviation rates in most societies, including American, indicate much lower rural rates even though tenant farmers and farm laborers often may be generally poorer and live under housing conditions almost as unsatisfactory as those in large urban centers. In fact, there is some indication that juvenile delinquency, rather than being a product of poverty, may, if anything, be related to "the affluent society." Certainly there is some evidence for this in the increasing delinquency of Western society and, in particular, in such countries as the United States and Sweden.[62]

Actually the basic process through which social deviation increases appears to lie in the urban way of life found today in all countries, regardless of the economic system. Urbanism is present whether a society is capitalist, democratic socialist, communist, or fascist. Forces tending to emphasize urban ways of life are present in all systems, and their influences range from New York City and Chicago to Moscow, Madrid, Stockholm, and the cities of Latin America, Asia and Africa.

Anomie involves a clash between institutional means and cultural goals in the access to the success goals of a given society by legitimate means. This explanation of deviant behavior in terms of a strain toward anomie has a number of limitations. The theory rests completely on the assumption that deviant behavior is disproportionately more common in the lower class; it is difficult to identify a set of cultural goals that are universally appreciated in most modern, complex, industrial societies; the theory stresses position in the social structure as the important variable in explaining deviant behavior; it largely neglects the important role of social control in defining who is a "deviant"; it does not recognize the nature of social behavior, social roles, and self-conception; finally, the adaptation of means to goals through retreatism lacks precision and oversimplifies what is actually a much more complex process of how problems of social deviation arise.

The cultural lag theory assumes that deviant behavior arises from the maladjustments created by the more rapid change of the technological, as compared with the nontechnological aspects of the culture. Objections to this formulation include the fact that conflicts of norms and values, other

---

[62] Galbraith, pp. 256–258.

than technological, are involved: cultural lag is so loosely used, it has little meaning; the existence of a lag and its direction rest inevitably on a question of values.

SELECTED READINGS

Clinard, Marshall B., ed. *Anomie and Deviant Behavior*. New York: The Free Press, 1964. In this volume the theory of anomie is explained, analyzed, and critically evaluated in terms of empiric research on deviant behavior, particularly in the areas of gang delinquency, mental disorder, alcoholism, and drug addiction.

Cloward, Richard A. "Illegitimate Means, Anomie, and Deviant Behavior," *American Sociological Review*, 24:164–176 (1959). A reformulation of anomie theory, adding availability of illegitimate means, which seeks to explain most forms of deviant behavior within this frame of reference.

Ferman, Louis A., Joyce L. Kornbluh, and Alan Haber. *Poverty in America*. Ann Arbor: University of Michigan Press, 1965. A series of articles dealing with such areas as the definitions and prevalence of poverty, the characteristics of the poor, their cultural values, and the sustaining conditions of poverty.

Galbraith, John K. *The Affluent Society*. Boston: Houghton Mifflin Company, 1958. A somewhat different view of the role of economic factors and social problems, namely, that affluence, rather than poverty, is important.

Gilmore, Harlan W. *The Beggar*. Chapel Hill: University of North Carolina Press, 1940. A study of begging as a highly organized activity and not one primarily arising from economic need.

Merton, Robert K. "Social Structure and Anomie," and "Continuities in the Theory of Social Structure and Anomie," in Robert K. Merton, *Social Theory and Social Structure*. Rev. ed. New York: The Free Press, 1957. These two articles set forth the theory of anomie. The first is probably the most widely quoted article in American sociology.

Ogburn, William F. *Social Change*. New York: The Viking Press, Inc., 1950. This book is the classic statement of the cultural lag theory. Originally published in 1922, it was reprinted again in 1950 with a supplementary chapter.

Sutherland, Edwin H. "White-Collar Criminality," *American Sociological Review*, 5:1–12 (1940). In this well-known presidential address to the American Sociological Society, Sutherland stated that crime cannot be explained by poverty, for it occurs among the middle and upper socioeconomic groups as well. Criminological research should be conducted on broader samples of criminal offenders.

Walker, Charles R., ed. *Modern Technology and Civilization*. New York: McGraw-Hill Book Company, Inc., 1962. This book of readings explores the relationship between man and the machine, and assumes that the future of all civilizations is closely linked to the manner in which man may either use or misuse modern technology. It also explores the human problems and promises of the machine age in which man now lives.

6

Deviant Behavior Theories Focusing on the Individual

Approaching the problem of deviant behavior—either the general or the specific type of behavior—with a background of particularistic knowledge derived largely from their own specialties, some scientists have on occasion shown little or no grasp of the principles of human behavior. In this chapter the following theories will be discussed: that deviants are feeble-minded, have certain body types, can be explained entirely by psychiatric or psychoanalytic principles, or have certain personality traits.

In the analysis that follows it has been necessary to refer to "biological," "psychiatric," "psychoanalytic," "psychological," and "sociological" approaches to deviant behavior. Such disciplines undergo constant modifications in their theoretical approaches and not all persons belonging to a given field believe in its general approach. There are psychologists and psychiatrists with a sociological approach, and there are sociologists with a psychological approach. Consequently, it would have been more practical to use more neutral terms such as "position A," "position B," "position C," and so on, but this would have presented difficult problems. There are now indications that traditional particularistic approaches are being slowly abandoned and that research derived from the study of cultural and broader social factors is not only being increasingly utilized by psychologists and psychiatrists but being recognized by biologists. If this trend continues, the distinctions in the theoretical positions of psychiatry, clinical psychology, and sociology may diminish so that, for example, a psychiatrist may, as a psychiatrist, be applying a sociological approach to deviant behavior.[1]

DEVIANT BEHAVIOR AND FEEBLE-MINDEDNESS

In the past, and to some extent today, constitutional inferiority in the form of subnormal intelligence has been frequently advanced as one of the principal causes of certain forms of deviant behavior. Hundreds of studies of intelligence have been made of juvenile delinquents, criminals, prostitutes, alcoholics, and hoboes. The assumptions have been made that either low intelligence and deviant behavior are directly associated, or low intelligence is likely to lead a person into patterns of such behavior.[2]

The theory that there is a relationship between intelligence and deviant behavior is now on its way out of accepted literature. The reasons for this are based on actual intelligence scores of deviants, on the fact that certain data are largely derived from biased samples, and on the fact that a direct relationship between intelligence and deviant behavior is simply an assumption.

More careful study of the empirical evidence has not substantiated earlier beliefs about subnormal intelligence. Not only are there wide variations in the intelligence scores of deviants, but in general their scores do not appear to differ too much from those of the general population. Sutherland examined 350 studies of the intelligence of some 175,000 criminals and delinquents and found such great variations in the percentage of offenders diagnosed as feeble-minded that any relationship had little meaning.[3] He also found that if allowances were made for selective factors in conviction and imprisonment the scores did not differ materially from those of the general population. Studies of juvenile delinquents have not shown their intelligence to be markedly different from nondelinquents. As one recent survey of studies has concluded: "The early assertion that low intelligence was causally related to delinquency appears to have been based upon erroneous assumptions about the nature of both intelligence and juvenile delinquency.

---

[1] For a discussion of this issue see Marshall B. Clinard, "Contributions of Sociology to the Study of Deviant Behavior," *British Journal of Criminology,* 3:110–129 (1962). These issues also apply to social work, which has been greatly influenced to date by psychiatry and psychoanalysis.

[2] Goddard was one of the earliest writers to advocate this theory. See Henry H. Goddard, *Human Efficiency and Levels of Intelligence* (Princeton, N.J.: Princeton University Press, 1922), pp. 72–73.

[3] Edwin H. Sutherland, "Mental Deficiency and Crime," in Kimball Young, ed., *Social Attitudes* (New York: Holt, Rinehart and Winston, Inc., 1931), pp. 357–375.

Critical examination of existing research on the subject suggests that the obtained differences in intelligence scores between known delinquents and 'nondelinquent' controls may be mainly, if not entirely, accounted for on the basis of differences between such samples on variables other than delinquency." [4]

Several wartime studies of prostitutes for the United States Public Health Service have failed to confirm the belief that girls from such groups are necessarily feeble-minded.[5] The Kinsey report, as well as other similar studies which have indicated widespread sexual deviation on the part of the general population, would serve to confirm the idea that sexual promiscuity certainly cannot be directly associated with intelligence scores.[6]

Now that more extensive studies have been made of alcoholism and mental disorder in all social groups, the intelligence quotient is no longer considered to be significant in their etiology. One test group of 47 compulsive drinkers had a mean IQ of 114.9 which is somewhat above the average; their standard deviation was 14.3; and their range was 73–139 on the Wechsler-Bellevue Adult Intelligence Test. Halpern, who made the study, said: "In general, then, this group of alcoholic subjects showed no characteristic organization of mental abilities which would serve to distinguish them either from normal subjects or from other clinical groups. For this group there was no evidence of mental impairment or deterioration." [7] Bühler subsequently corroborated these findings in her study of 100 alcoholics. They had an average IQ score of 103.2, or well within the normal range.[8]

Evaluation of Deviant Behavior and Feeble-Mindedness

Most of the studies of the intelligence of deviants have been based on institutional populations or detected deviants, and the fact that the studies sometimes indicate that deviants may have a low intelligence may simply

---

[4] Nathan S. Caplan, "Intellectual Functioning," in Herbert C. Quay, *Juvenile Delinquency: Research and Theory* (Princeton, N.J.: D. Van Nostrand Company, Inc., 1965), p. 131.

[5] H. L. Rachlin, "A Sociological Analysis of 304 Female Patients Admitted to the Midwestern Medical Center, St. Louis, Mo.," *Venereal Disease Information,* U.S. Public Health Service, 25:267 (1944).

[6] Alfred C. Kinsey, Wardell B. Pomeroy, and Clyde E. Martin, *Sexual Behavior in the Human Male* (Philadelphia: W. B. Saunders Company, 1948).

[7] Florence Halpern, "Psychological Test Results," in Jane F. Cushman and Carney Landis, *Studies of Compulsive Drinkers* (New Haven, Conn.: Quarterly Journal of Studies on Alcohol, 1946), p. 83.

[8] Charlotte Bühler and D. Welty Lefever, "A Rorschach Study of the Psychological Characteristics of Alcoholics," *Quarterly Journal of Studies on Alcohol,* 8:197–260 (1947).

mean that the samples are biased. Various investigators agree that there are fewer mental defectives among randomly chosen schoolchildren than among the delinquents who get caught, and that institutionalized delinquents have an average IQ below that of schoolchildren.[9] If professional and white-collar criminals, persons who are seldom detected or go to prison, were added to the sample of persons in penal institutions, the intelligence scores would undoubtedly increase. There may be, however, a relation between intelligence and certain types of offenses, with the habitual petty offender generally having a lower intelligence than the white-collar or professional criminal. If alcoholics from the more educated groups were added to drunks tested in Skid Rows, the IQ distribution would be skewed upward. There is no evidence to support any relationship between intelligence, drug addiction, homosexual behavior, or mental disorder.

No one knows the actual components of innate intelligence because the effect of social experience on the latter is such that it appears to be impossible to measure. It is now generally agreed that the so-called intelligence test measures only "test intelligence" and not innate intelligence. Moreover, there is increasing evidence that the IQ can be somewhat modified by social experience. On logical grounds, moreover, there is nothing in the nature of subnormal intelligence that implies a relationship with either social attitudes or social roles. The idea that persons with low intelligence are likely to engage in deviant behavior must be regarded simply as an assumption, since one might also argue that low intelligence could lead to rigid compliance with traditional ways of acting and that higher intelligence could be associated with deviant behavior when traditional values are violated. In fact, studies show that some delinquents have a high intelligence.[10] The great proportion of persons with low intelligence scores undoubtedly are nondeviants, whereas there are large numbers of persons with above normal intelligence who are.

DEVIANT BEHAVIOR AND BODY TYPE

In the past the writings of Lombroso on crime and of Kretschmer on mental illness—and in more recent years of Hooton on crime and of Sheldon on mental illness, crime, and alcoholism—have tried to correlate deviant behavior with certain body types. These studies have aroused great controversy among those interested in deviation and have captured the imagination of many laymen. The public has been quick to accept these ideas,

---

[9] Maud A. Merrill, *Problems of Child Delinquency* (Boston: Houghton Mifflin Company, 1947), p. 162.

[10] David L. Haarer, "Gifted Delinquents," *Federal Probation,* 30:43–46 (1966).

for carried in the folklore of our culture is a common belief in the direct relationship between physiognomy and personality. Crippled hunchbacks appear in literature as stereotypes of evil or as court jesters, fat persons are presumed to be jolly, thin persons are sad and melancholy, and the red-haired are hot-tempered. Commonly cartoons and literature picture the criminal, for example, as of middle age, hard in appearance and often with a malformation in the ear and in general facial structure. The myth of racial superiority or inferiority has served to perpetuate in the popular mind these ideas about differences in the physical appearance of deviants.

Lombroso, in the latter part of the nineteenth century, made studies to show that most criminals had certain physical characteristics.[11] On the basis of his studies in Germany in the 1920's, Kretschmer believed that he could classify human beings into three rather distinct physical types which were differently associated with certain forms of mental illness.[12] The asthenic type, who had a thin, narrow build, particularly in the shoulders and chest, long thin arms and delicately shaped hands, was associated with schizophrenia, as was the athletic type. The latter, as the name indicates, was a strong, muscular, well-developed physical type with broad shoulders and a thick chest. The pyknic type, on the other hand, was round and fat in appearance and was associated with the manic-depressive psychoses.

Somewhat later, Hooton, a physical anthropologist, made an elaborate study in which he compared several thousand prisoners with a control group.[13] He attempted to revive in many respects the Lombrosian theory—which started the science of criminology—that most criminals are some sort of atavistic, "primitive" men with observable physical features. Hooton reported that criminals are more likely to have long thin necks and sloping shoulders, low and sloping foreheads, thinner beard and body hair, more red-brown hair, thin lips, compressed jaw angles, and a small, extremely protruding ear. He stated, in addition, that certain body types are connected with certain types of crime, tall, thin men tending to murder and rob; tall, heavy men to kill and commit forgery and fraud; undersized men

---

[11] See Chapter 7.

[12] E. Kretschmer, *Physique and Character* (London: Routledge & Kegan Paul, Ltd., 1925). Although Mohr and Gundlach, attempting to test Kretschmer's body types, found some agreement in their study of Illinois prisoners, they found the same distribution of physical traits among the noncriminal population.—George J. Mohr and Ralph H. Gundlach, "The Relation between Physique and Performance," *Journal of Experimental Psychology,* 10:117–157 (1927).

[13] E. A. Hooton, *Crime and the Man* (Cambridge, Mass.: Harvard University Press, 1939), and *The American Criminal: An Anthropological Study* (Cambridge, Mass.: Harvard University Press, 1939).

to steal and to commit burglary; and short, heavy persons to assault, rape, and commit other sex crimes.

Von Hentig went even further and suggested, on the basis of a study of western outlaws, that criminals who committed frontier depredations were primarily red-haired and that red-haired persons are physiologically more active, impulsive, and with "accelerated motor innervation." Hence he concluded "that the number of red-headed men among the noted outlaws surpassed their rate in the normal population." [14] Another writer has presented contrary evidence, indicating that of fifty-eight frontier bad men only two were red-haired.[15]

Sheldon has attempted to isolate three poles of physique, through the use of numerous anthropometric measurements and profile photographs delineated as the somatotypes or body types of the endomorph, mesomorph, and ectomorph, which correspond roughly to the pyknic, athletic, and asthenic types of Kretschmer.[16] These types—which may be thought of as the round, soft, and fat type; the muscular and big-boned type; and the thin, small, bony type—are by no means the distinct entities that they were to some of his predecessors. Rather, persons possess all three components, which are indicated by a subjective rating scale of 1 to 7. Thus the endomorph might be a 5–3–1 with 5 parts of endomorph, 3 of mesomorph, and 1 of ectomorph. Sheldon, moreover, goes far beyond either Kretschmer or Hooton in attempting to correlate psychological or temperamental factors with each body type. The somatotype, the psychological characteristics, and the culture interact to produce deviant behavior, with cultural factors occupying a minor position.

Generally, the mesomorphs with psychological characteristics of somatomania do not fare well. Sheldon's work dealt with a study of 200 delinquent boys in the Hayden Goodwill Inn, a Boston social agency. According to his findings, delinquents and criminals are heavy, insensitive, aggressive mesomorphs.[17] The Gluecks have employed the logic of Sheldon in their study of physical types and delinquency.[18] In their study, approxi-

---

[14] Hans von Hentig, "Redhead and Outlaw," *Journal of Criminal Law and Criminology,* 38:6 (1947).

[15] Philip J. Rasch, "Red Hair and Outlawing," *Journal of Criminal Law and Criminology,* 38:352–356 (1947).

[16] William H. Sheldon, S. S. Stevens, and W. B. Tucker, *The Varieties of Human Physique* (New York: Harper & Row, Publishers, 1940); William H. Sheldon and S. S. Stevens, *The Varieties of Temperament* (New York: Harper & Row, Publishers, 1942); and William H. Sheldon, *Varieties of Delinquent Youth* (New York: Harper & Row, Publishers, 1949).

[17] Sheldon, *Varieties of Delinquent Youth.*

[18] See Sheldon Glueck and Eleanor Glueck, *Physique and Delinquency* (New York: Harper & Row, Publishers, 1956); and Eleanor Glueck, "Body Build in

mately 60 percent of a group of 500 delinquent boys in a correctional train-ing school were classified as mesomorphs, and with traits of temperament and character associated with this body type, as compared with 30 percent of 500 boys in a control group. In a study of 312 psychotic cases Sheldon found that endomorphy and mesomorphy are correlated with manic-depres-sive behavior reactions, that mesomorphy was also associated with paranoid reactions, and that ectomorphy was related to certain schizophrenic re-sponses.[19] Neurosis was explained by Sheldon as a conflict arising primarily from a person's attempting to be different from what is expected "normally" from his somatotype and temperament. He also associated physique with certain degrees of alcoholism. According to Sheldon, alcohol agrees with fat, soft persons and they seldom become addicted to it. Even a moderate quan-tity of alcohol serves, however, to accentuate the personality traits of persons who are of a hard, athletic body build. In conjunction with other situational components, individuals with such a body type become chronic alcoholics. Finally, those persons who are primarily thin and who have flat chests and a generally weak physical constitution find alcohol unpleasant, for it increases strain and brings on fatigue and dizziness. Consequently, they generally dis-like alcohol and avoid its use.

Evaluation of Deviant Behavior and Body Type

These studies of the relation of physique to deviant behavior have been attacked on numerous grounds:

> 1. The theory has not actually demonstrated the relation between physique and behavior; inferiority is judged by the presence of deviant behavior. Even if an association were proved statistically between constitu-tional features and behavior—and it has not been proved—before the theory could be accepted, there would still be need for an adequate gen-eral theory of human nature which would incorporate such findings.[20]
> 2. Most of the argument involves, in general, jumping from certain anatomical characterictics to deviant behavior. In nearly all such studies cultural factors either are not considered at all or occupy a position sub-ordinate to physical factors.
> 3. The contention that certain physical characteristics are by their

---

the Prediction of Delinquency," *Journal Of Criminal Law, Criminology, and Police Science,* 48:577–579 (1958). For another study of appearance and criminal behavior, see Raymond J. Corsini, "Appearance and Criminality," *American Journal of Sociology,* 65:49–51 (1959).

[19] Phyllis Wittman, William H. Sheldon, and Charles J. Katz, "A Study of the Relationship between Constitutional Variations and Fundamental Psychotic Be-havior Reactions," *Journal of Nervous and Mental Diseases,* 108:470–476 (1948).

[20] Edwin H. Sutherland, "A Critique of Sheldon's *Varieties of Delinquent Youth,*" *American Sociological Review,* 16:10–13 (1951).

very nature "inferior" is simply an assumption and nothing more. The physical appearance of the organism is naturally neither "good" nor "bad." It is significant that Hooton and Sheldon reach opposite conclusions as to what is "inferior." According to the former the criminal is an inadequately developed, runty physical type, whereas Sheldon finds the criminal and the alcoholic inferior because they are a husky, athletic type.

4. These studies have been largely conducted on institutionalized populations, or very select groups, such as Sheldon's, which probably do not represent a normal sample of the total population. Their control groups were either inadequate or nonexistent.

THE PSYCHIATRIC THEORY OF DEVIANT BEHAVIOR

In recent years the theory that deviant conduct is a result of childhood experiences in the family has gained great popularity. This theory is supported by representatives of many academic disciplines and laymen. It is the view of causation which is most frequently displayed in popular magazines, the press, and other mass media of communication, and propounded by most social welfare workers and psychiatrists and many psychologists.

To a great extent this theory owes its ascendancy to the dissemination of psychiatric and psychoanalytic thought over the past several decades.[21] Yet it could be said that both this idea and, indeed, psychiatric thought itself derive from more fundamental values which are rooted in the traditions of our culture. Prominent among these values are the beliefs in the responsibility of parents for the training and preparation of children for adult life, and the relation between early training and adulthood.

Undoubtedly there is much solid common sense in the idea that childhood experiences may influence later behavior—*if* childhood is regarded as the primary arena in which culture is acquired. Robert Merton has suggested that whatever prominence childhood and family experience may be assigned is due to the fact that the family is the principal transmitting agency of culture to the child.[22]

---

[21] See Franz G. Alexander and Sheldon T. Selesnick, *The History of Psychiatry: An Evaluation of Psychiatric Thought and Practice from Prehistoric Times to the Present* (New York: Harper & Row, Publishers, 1966). Psychiatrists are medical doctors who have had specialized training beyond their M.D. degree in a medical school, generally from other psychiatrists. Psychoanalysts are nearly always medically trained persons who have received special training, usually in a psychoanalytic institute. The differences in psychiatric thinking are great and the discussion here does not deal with those psychiatrists who take a nearly biochemical or organic approach to human behavior.

[22] See Robert K. Merton, "Social Structure and Anomie: Revisions and Extensions," in Ruth N. Anshen, *The Family: Its Function and Destiny* (rev. ed.; New York: Harper & Row, Publishers, 1959), p. 275.

While many agree with Merton, the psychiatric position implies that *certain childhood experiences have effects which transcend all other social and cultural experiences.* These proponents suggest that certain childhood incidents or family relationships lead to the formation of certain types of personalities which contain within themselves seeds of deviant or conforming behavior, irrespective of culture. Thus childhood is the arena in which personality traits toward or away from deviance are developed, and a person's behavior after the childhood years is fundamentally the acting out of tendencies formed at that time. Thus essentially these proponents offer the following psychiatric or "medical model" for explaining deviant behavior.

1. All deviant behavior is a product of something in the individual, such as personal disorganization or "maladjusted" personality. Deviants are individuals who are psychologically "sick" persons. Culture is seen not as a determinant of deviant and conforming behavior but rather as the context within which these tendencies are expressed.

2. All persons at birth have certain inherent basic needs, in particular the need for emotional security.

3. Deprivation of those universal needs in men during the early years of childhood leads to the formation of given personality types of structure. The degree of conflict, disorder, retardation, or injury to the personality will vary directly with the degree of deprivation.

4. Childhood experiences, such as emotional conflicts, will determine personality structure and thus the pattern of behavior in later life.

5. Family experiences of the child almost exclusively determine the pattern of behavior in later life, whether deviant or nondeviant, by affecting the personality structure of the child. The need for the mother to provide maternal affection is particularly stressed.

6. A high degree of certain so-called general personality traits, such as emotional insecurity, immaturity, feelings of inadequacy, inability to display affection, and aggression characterize the deviant but not the nondeviant. Such traits are the product of early childhood experience in the family. It is argued that, because the first experiences of the child with others are within the family group, traits arising there form the basis for the entire structure of personality. Deviant behavior is often a way of dealing successfully with such personality traits, for example, "immature" persons may commit crimes or "emotionally insecure" persons may drink excessively and become alcoholics.

This, then, is the theoretical framework with which psychiatry largely explains deviant behavior. Each year are published many books and articles written by psychiatrists who attempt to explain such diverse problems as stealing, murder, sex offenses, delinquency, alcoholism, narcotic addiction, marital difficulties, the psychoses and the neuroses, as well as racial and religious prejudice.

THE PSYCHOANALYTIC EXPLANATION OF DEVIANT BEHAVIOR

One part of the general field of psychiatry is called psychoanalysis, which has in addition to the psychiatric frame of reference its own particular system of explaining deviant behavior. This, as we shall shortly point out, involves what psychiatrists call conflicts between the id and the superego, the masculinity-femininity conflict, infantile regression, and parent fixation. We shall discuss this approach in detail because its followers publish widely on deviant behavior and their approach has greatly affected not only American psychiatry in general but many social workers and others who deal with deviants.

Because of their emphasis on sex and symbolism, psychoanalytic works in particular make fascinating reading for both professional people and laymen, with the result that probably no approach to deviant behavior has a wider audience. Sigmund Freud, the Viennese psychiatrist who died in 1939, founded psychoanalysis, which has become an important part of the contemporary vocabulary and thinking of Western Europeans.

According to psychoanalytic writers, the chief explanation of behavior disorders must be sought in an analysis of the *unconscious mind,* which consists of a world of inner feelings that are unlikely to be the obvious reasons for behavior or to be subject to recall at will. Antisocial conduct is a result of the dynamics of the unconscious rather than of the conscious activities of mental life. Much of the adult's behavior, whether deviant or nondeviant, owes its form and intensity to certain instinctive drives and to early reactions to parents and siblings.

Method

Psychoanalysts generally rely on the use of lengthy free association and the analysis of dreams to infer unconscious experience and motivations. The analyst listens, often taking notes, while the patient, usually in a reclining position, rambles on, presumably verbalizing all the thoughts that come into his mind. Through this "free association" the patient is thought to be able to reveal words, phrases, and ideas ordinarily excluded from consciousness. The same principle hold in hypnosis, which is sometimes used but which has many physical disadvantages over free association.

Dreams are supposed to have an obvious meaning as well as a hidden one.[23] That part of the dream which one can recall is its obvious content,

---

[23] See, for example, Thomas M. French and Erika Fromm, *Dream Interpretation* (New York: Basic Books, Inc., 1964); and Calvin S. Hall and Robert L. Van de Castle, *The Content Analysis of Dreams* (New York: Appleton-Century-Crofts, Inc., 1966).

whereas the unconscious processes which give rise to the dream are its hidden meanings. Since the latter are generally not acceptable to the dreamer, they must be transformed in some symbolic way to be made acceptable. The "censor," a mechanism of importance in this scheme, decides what may come to the dreamer's conscious mind and what may not. It also transforms, condenses, elaborates, and dramatizes the hidden content, through symbols, into the obvious content. These symbols often have sexual connotations. In dreams the father may be said to be symbolized as a king and/or various animals, the mother thought of as nature, and procreation by sowing or tilling.

Conflicts of the Id and the Superego

In the psychoanalyst's scheme, personality is thought of as composed of three parts: the primitive animal *id,* the *ego,* and the *superego.* Psychoanalysis assumes that the conscious self is built over a great reservoir of biological drives. Although biology, in the form of basic animal drives, plays an important part in psychoanalytic theory, these drives are present in everyone and do not necessarily represent individual biological differences.

> 1. The *id* is the buried reservoir of unconscious instinctual animal tendency or drive. From the Freudian standpoint these instincts are of two major types: the *libido,* including chiefly sexual drives, but not exclusively limited to them, and the love or life-trend instincts; and the sadistic or destructive instincts. These instincts operate in every activity.
>
> 2. The *ego* is elaborated from the large tract of instinctual tendencies as a result of the contact of the individual with the outer social world. Freud postulated here a dualistic conception of mind: the "id" or internal unconscious world of native or biological impulses and repressed ideas, and the "ego," the self, operating on the level of consciousness. These two may sometimes be compatible but more often are incompatible, unless adjusted through some psychological mechanism. There may be constant conflict between the "ego," the conscious part of the mind representing the civilized aspect of man, and the "id," the unconscious or "primitive" in man.
>
> 3. The *superego,* on the other hand, is partly conscious, partly unconscious; it is the conscious part which corresponds to the conscience. It is man's social self, derived from cultural definitions of conduct.

Some writers on psychoanalysis have made almost synonymous with criminal behavior the unresolved conflicts between the primitive id and its instinctive drives and the requirement of society. According to this view, crime arises out of inadequate social restrictions which society has placed on what psychoanalysts assume to be the original instinctive, unadjusted nature of man, which is savage, sensual, and destructive. Criminal behavior is thought of as an almost necessary outcome or expression of the personality, and hence does not always necessitate contacts with a "criminal" culture. According to Karpman, all persons are born criminals in the sense that they come into the world unconditioned and unrepressed. Society, therefore, is the mechanism through which we are conditioned so as to repress our criminal tendencies: "To put it in other words, we are born selfish, hateful, spiteful, mean; and it is the culture that makes us devoted, loving, kind and sympathetic . . . criminality . . . [is viewed] as being expressive of the anti-social feelings that each of us carries within him. And it is out of this criminal basis our normal citizenry carried that our criminal population is evolved." [24] Zilboorg writes that crime results from the temporary overcoming of the resistance of the superego and then the ego by instinctive drives from the id.[25] After the discharge of such impulses and the consequent silencing of id drives, the superego reasserts itself and a sense of guilt is felt. According to Abrahamsen, murder arises from the expression of the individual's natural aggressions: "Murder has psychological root in the person's aggressions related to attack and defense. These are expressions of his fight for survival or maybe due to an erotic drive, no matter how distorted or concealed it may be." [26]

Psychoanalytic writers dealing with the problems of suicide have stressed the polarity principle of the life (love) and death (hate) instincts of the id.[27] According to this view, there is a strong desire in the id for self-destruction, such as mutilation or suicide, and at the same time a desire for self-preservation. The superego, in turn, contains various social and moral restrictions on personal violence or self-destruction. The forces pulling toward self-destruction and self-preservation are in constant interaction, and when the former overcomes the latter, self-inflicted death ensues. In the course of

---

[24] Ben Karpman, *The Individual Criminal: Studies in the Psychogenetics of Crime* (Washington, D.C.: Nervous and Mental Diseases Publishing Co., 1935), p. ix.

[25] Gregory Zilboorg, *Mind, Medicine and Man* (New York: Harcourt, Brace & World, Inc., 1943). A study of adolescent violence showed that violence resulted from the "emergence of primitive nonneutralized aggression with the violent acting out of conflict previously held in check by the defensive system of the ego." See Sherwyn M. Woods, "Adolescent Violence and Homicide," *Archives of General Psychiatry*, 5:528–534 (1961).

[26] David Abrahamsen, *Crime and the Human Mind* (New York: Columbia University Press, 1944), p. 148. Also see Karl Menninger, "Verdict Guilty—Now What?" *Harper's Magazine* 210:60–64 (1959).

[27] Karl Menninger, *Man against Himself* (New York: Harcourt, Brace & World, Inc., 1938). Also see James Hillman, *Suicide and the Soul* (London: Hodder and Stoughton, Ltd., 1964).

normal mental development toward maturity, the destructive drives are directed outward in the form of aggression or are sublimated. Failure to direct these tendencies outward results in the individual's fighting or destroying himself.

Psychoanalysts often find hidden motives behind suicides as, for example, self-mutilation or self-destruction in place of injury to another person. Menninger has described three varieties of suicide: the wish to kill; the wish to be killed, which may take the form of hypochondria or alcoholism, or exposure of oneself to diseases; and the wish to die. Accordingly to him, the death wish, which is part of the id, may occur in alcoholics where chronic drunkenness is in a sense a slower method of self-annihilation than some of the others customarily employed. Alcoholism may also be a means of self-punishment, the desire for which stems from guilt feelings created by incessant war between the id and the superego.

Some psychoanalysts have suggested that the conflicts between the id and the superego explain prejudice. In our modern complex society the natural drives and personal wishes of the id meet all varieties of blocks in the path of achievement. More and more frustrations being forced upon individuals result in greater inner tensions and anxieties. Yet there are no standard cultural means of relieving this pressure. Tensions must somehow be relieved, either directly or through "free-floating aggression" against persons and groups. Just as the mother or other disciplinarian becomes the object of conscious or unconscious hatred and hostility of the child, so "out-groups" and other people with assumed or real divergences in physical or other characteristics become objects of hate through the displacement mechanism, that is, hatred is shifted to a more convenient object and away from the persons and groups who stand in the way of one's fulfillment of goals.[28]

Prejudice against the Negro has been explained as resulting from the white man's desire for sexual relations with Negroes or from his envy of their so-called hypersexuality. According to this explanation, white people believe that Negroes are less inhibited and more passionate sexually, that Negro males have larger sexual organs than do white males, and that Negro females can experience more orgasms than can white women. White persons who do not have sexual relations with Negroes feel that they must repress their desires, whereas those who do have relations with Negroes experience marked guilt feelings.[29] One writer believes that southern whites

---

[28] For a discussion see George E. Simpson and J. Milton Yinger, *Racial and Cultural Minorities: An Analysis of Prejudice and Discrimination* (3rd ed., New York: Harper & Row, 1965), pp. 54–56.

[29] See discussion of this theory in Arnold and Caroline Rose, *America Divided* (New York: Alfred A. Knopf, Inc., 1948), p. 290.

think themselves somewhat lacking in sexual expression, while the Negro has a superabundance of such feeling.[30] Their jealousy of the Negroes and the need to repress the id desires toward them result in prejudice.

Masculinity-Femininity Conflict

Every person, psychoanalytically, has both masculine and feminine tendencies or, to put it another way, is naturally bisexual with homosexual and heterosexual components. Within each individual this fact results in a certain amount of conflict. Many psychoanalytic writers have emphasized the conflict of the masculine and feminine components which are a part of everyone's original make-up, the one being aggressive and the other passive. The rapist, for example, has a feeling of inferiority and fear of sexual inadequacy which prevents normal permanent sexual alliances. Murder may even be a defense against "feminine" traits which are abhorred by the murderer.

Some psychoanalytic writers believe that alcoholism in the male represents the direct expression of his homosexual drives. Drinking often enables him to be in male company exclusively, particularly in bars and taverns, and it also enables him to overcome his feeling of sexual impotency. Eventually the inebriate substitutes the consumption of alcohol for heterosexual contacts. After analyzing the hangovers of seven men and seven women alcoholics, Karpman has concluded that they reflect guilt over homosexual feelings.[31]

Infantile Regression

Psychoanalysts think of a normal personality as having developed through a series of four stages. The development of personality involves shifting interests and changes in the nature of sexual pleasure from the oral and the anal preoccupation of infant life, to love of self, love of a parent of the opposite sex, and, finally, love of a person of the opposite sex and other than one's parent. Some of these stages overlap and may go on simultaneously. Some persons do not progress through all these stages, have conflicts, and develop personality difficulties.

According to psychoanalysts, the newborn individual operates on a pain-pleasure principle, and the environment is viewed merely as consisting of desirable objects which serve to bring about bodily comfort and satisfaction, such as oral gratification through nursing and preoccupation with the

---

[30] Helen V. McLean, "Psychodynamic Factors in Racial Relations," *The Annals*, 244:164 (1946).

[31] Ben Karpman, *The Hangover* (Springfield, Ill.: Charles C Thomas, Publisher, 1957).

activities of elimination. This stage, from the point of view of the affectional or libidinal development, is one of preoccupation with one's own body. From the start, however, this interest becomes increasingly blocked by cultural controls and restrictions. The adult world insists on adjustment to social patterns and an increasingly greater restriction on freely expressed biological drives and fantasies.

Many psychoanalysts stress the fact that deviants are immature persons who have not developed into fully socialized adults. The activities of deviants unconsciously represent unresolved infantile desires to which they have returned. Others believe that the type of crime, the type of objects involved in the crime, and the person from whom something was stolen often indicate infantile regression. Stealing from superiors, for example, may be symbolic of original childhood envy of adult sexual organs. Burglary has been traced by one psychoanalyst to fixation in the oral stage of development, and arson has been explained as a regression to an infantile stage of development.[32] Foxe has even classified various types of crime in terms of trauma and fixation in childhood. Automobile theft is due to regression to the early oral stage; burglary, forgery, and embezzlement are due to regression to the late oral stage; and armed robbery and swindling are due to regression to the late anal.[33]

> Earliest training leaves its impress upon one's constitution and character and so it is not surprising that so many individuals in whom the training deviated considerably from average showed strong marks of primitive infantile patterns [anal-oral stage]. . . . That even crime should show such impression—the tooth-like dagger of the assaulter and the tooth-like sadistic pen of the forger, the anal explosiveness of the gun-holding robber—is not at all remarkable.[34]

Many psychoanalysts have concluded that the etiology of schizophrenia lies in the regression of the total personality to the stage in life in which the ego is not completely molded. It is, therefore, a retreat to a form of infantilism. The alcoholic has often been characterized by psychoanalysts as a passive, insecure, dependent, "oral" personality of an infantile type, with his latent hostility being thereby obscured. Homosexual behavior has been explained as due to regression to the oral stage. One writer has stated that

---

[32] Otto Fenichel, *The Psychoanalytic Theory of Neurosis* (New York: W. W. Norton & Company, Inc., 1945).

[33] Arthur N. Foxe, "Classification of the Criminotic Individual," in Robert M. Lindner and Robert V. Seliger, eds., *Handbook of Correctional Psychology* (New York: Philosophical Library, Inc., 1947).

[34] Arthur N. Foxe, "Criminoses," in V. C. Branham and S. B. Kutash, eds., *Encyclopedia of Criminology* (New York: Philosophical Library, Inc., 1949), p. 117.

"the genital organ similar to their own remains throughout life as an essential condition for their love." [35]

Parental Fixation and Conflicts

In infancy the mother becomes definitely an object of the child's libido. She is the first object to whom love impulses are directed, but since she is the first person who restricts pleasure she is also one to whom hate is first directed. Based on this early attachment to the mother, there arises an *Oedipus phase* in libidinal development in which the male child unconsciously becomes a rival of his father for the mother's sexual affections and therefore comes to hate his father. In the case of girls, the conflict with the mother over the father is called the *Electra complex*.[36] Psychoanalytic writers have tried to show that many social phenomena can be understood only when viewed in the light of the Oedipus complex, which produces significant manifestations in almost every sphere of human activity.

An outstanding example of this approach is the view held by many, but not all, psychoanalysts, that the Oedipus complex is universal in all cultures.[37] Sexual adjustments become heterosexual, with the love object outside the family. With the deviant, however, this conflict is not solved; there are guilt feelings over the incestuous desires for the parent of the opposite sex, and an unsatisfactory shift to other heterosexual persons. These guilt feelings are relieved by deviant behavior or by the punishment that arises from antisocial behavior.

Criminals and neurotics have much in common, for example, for both feel that they need punishment to relieve guilt feelings arising from an Oedipus situation. The individual may feel a need for punishment because of the hostility he has harbored against a member of his family. He may commit a crime and seek punishment by society, whereas another may seek self-punishment through a neurosis. Self-destructive tendencies may result in a murder's being committed in order to receive punishment.

Many psychoanalysts believe that the behavior difficulties associated

---

[35] Sandor Ferenczi, "The Nosology of Male Homosexuality," in Hendrik Ruitenbeek, ed., *The Problem of Homosexuality in Modern Society* (New York: E. P. Dutton & Co., Inc., 1963), p. 4. Also see Edmund Bergler, *Neurotic Counterfeit Sex* (New York: Grune & Stratton, Inc., 1951) and Irvin Bieber, *et al., Homosexuality: A Psychoanalytic Study of Male Homosexuals* (New York: Vintage Books, Inc., 1965).

[36] Another conflict may result from overattachment to the mother, which turns to violent dislike and is called the *Orestes complex*. All these terms have their origin in the characters and plots of the classic Greek plays.

[37] Many psychoanalysts use the Oedipus complex symbolically but do not regard it as universal.

with alcoholism lie in various Oedipus or Electra conflicts.[38] Alcoholism is interpreted as an escape valve from these intolerable inner battles.

Homosexuality in a man has been explained as a result of overattachment for the mother in an unresolved Oedipus complex which results in his rejecting sex relations with other women.[39] Psychoanalytic theories of prostitution often explain it as caused by the individual's failure to reach sexual maturity. Some psychoanalysts characterize the prostitute as a person who has been denied sufficient parental love, affection, and security in childhood and who therefore establishes liaisons because she wants to feel that she is wanted and needed. She also suffers from, or has never outgrown, her Electra complex for her father, and is often incapable of receiving real sexual gratification.

One psychoanalytic study sought to explain the high suicide rates of Sweden and Denmark and the lower rate of Norway as a product of childhood dependency reactions.[40] Using free association, dreams, and fantasies as a source, an American psychoanalyst used only a total of about 200 suicidal patients for his study in these three countries. He concluded that the Swedish rates were high because of frequent separation from the mother through the use of nurseries, and in Denmark because of two great a dependency on the mother. Suicide grows out of suppression of aggressive tendencies and in Sweden often "represents a destructive act aimed at both the patient and the mother." [41] The Norwegians' lower suicidal rate, on the other hand, is due to a highly independent, self-sufficient childhood; the child's personal freedom is not restricted, and there is no dependency gratification.

Some Specific Criticisms of Psychoanalytic Theory

1. *Contrary to psychoanalysis, evidence suggests that human behavior is a product of social experience and that it is not determined by an innate reservoir of animal impulses termed the* id. Depending upon his social and cultural experiences, a man can be either cruel or gentle, aggressive or pacifist, sadistic or loving. He can be either a savage Nazi Jew-baiter or a compassionate and tender human being like Albert Schweitzer or Mohandas Gandhi. No detailed refutation is necessary, therefore, to disprove a psychoanalytic theory that some forms of criminality, for example, should be

---

[38] Eva Maria Blum, "Psychoanalytic Views of Alcoholism: A Review," *Quarterly Journal of Studies on Alcohol,* 27:259–300 (1966).

[39] Aron Krich, ed., *The Homosexuals* (New York: The Citadel Press, 1954).

[40] Herbert Hendin, *Suicides and Scandinavia* (New York: Doubleday & Company, Inc., 1965).

[41] Hendin, p. 86.

envisaged as outbursts of unsocialized original animal impulses. What constitutes criminal behavior is a matter of social determination, and impulses secure their social meaning only through the medium of social interaction. There is no savage man lurking under a veneer of socialization. This belief in something resembling human instincts, which was common until the 1920's, has been completely refuted by a large number of studies by social psychologists, psychologists, and anthropologists. It is no longer even a debatable subject. Also see pages 61–62 for a discussion of the absence of instincts in man.

2. *There is no evidence to support the theory that sex represents an all-inclusive factor which explains a host of mental conflicts.* The psychoanalytic emphasis on sexual eroticism is a great overstatement of an important aspect of human behavior. Conflicts can arise in many areas of human experience, particularly through excessive competition. Likewise, religion, the achievement of status, and various conflicts in social roles—all constitute wide areas of possible mental conflict.

3. *The entire psychoanalytic scheme is bodily conscious rather than primarily socially conscious for the child's development is greatly influenced by social relationships which have little or no connection with bodily functions.* The evidence does not support the view that these rather presocial experiences involving oral and anal stimulation affect the entire course of human life. The idea that frustrations of the libidinal infantile drives universal in all human beings will necessarily affect personality has been rejected by one writer after an extensive survey of anthropological literature. In a study of various societies he considered the effects on personality of different methods of nursing, mothering, bowel training, and restraint of motion, and reached negative conclusions about their "specific invariant psychological effect upon children." [42] He concludes that parental attitudes which are derived from the culture are the chief variables. Sewell has also concluded, from a study of 162 farm children, that different methods of infant breast feeding, weaning, and bowel training have practically no subsequent effect on personality.[43]

4. *Psychoanalytic theory has assumed certain universal uniformities in human behavior as arising from the assumed uniformities in human biological drives, irrespective of cultural influences, or historical eras, or of variations in social structure.* Actually "drives," if they exist, have no inherent direction or aim; but the complex behaviors necessary to relieve the physical

---

[42] Harold Orlansky, "Infant Care and Personality," *Psychological Bulletin,* 46:1–48 (1949).

[43] William H. Sewell, "Infant Training and the Personality of the Child," *American Journal of Sociology,* 58:150–159 (1952).

tensions, which we term "drives," are learned through social experiences. For example, the stomach contractions which we refer to as "hunger" do not in themselves explain why Americans eat hamburgers, Koreans prefer rice, and Eskimos prefer seal blubber. The kinds of food eaten and the methods of obtaining and preparing them are culturally learned.

An outstanding example of this approach is the view that the Oedipus complex is universal in all cultures. One survey of Freudian concepts has stated that "Freud assumed the Oedipus relationship to exist universally, and while other investigations have found instances of it, no indications of a universal cross-sex parental preference have been discovered in either children or adults." [44] It appears that Freud overrated the uniformity of family patterns and failed to perceive that sexual definitions are products of the child's social relationships. Even in our own culture families do not exhibit a similar culture pattern, and there is considerable variability in the specific behaviors expected of persons in their family roles. In turn, if various family patterns throughout the world are examined, these patterns and roles become even more variable.

> It is a truism today that adult behavior is a function of the culture in which it was learned. Psychiatric thought had not gone so far at the beginning of the century, however, and Freud's notion of the universal Oedipus complex stands as a sharply etched grotesquerie against his otherwise informative description of sexual development. From the analysis of data relating to object choice, it is apparent that in this matter perhaps more than in any other the nature of the chosen object and the reactions to other similar or dissimilar objects are dependent on the early home environment of the child. So far we are in agreement with Freud. But, beyond this, Freud seeks a common or typical pattern of development. If such existed, it should come only from a common culture pattern, i.e., from a constant situation in which learning could take place in a uniform way.[45]

5. *Psychoanalysis is not a scientific explanation.* Most of psychoanalysis has not been verified, and for that reason it is possible to give a "symbolic" interpretation to almost anything.[46] Most psychoanalysts are not aware of the possible type of evidence that would refute their theories.[47] The em-

---

[44] Robert R. Sears, "Survey of Objective Studies of Psychoanalytic Concepts" (Bulletin 51; New York: Social Science Research Council, 1943), pp. 134–135.

[45] Sears, p. 136.

[46] Andrew Salter, *The Case against Psychoanalysis* (New York: The Citadel Press, 1963), pp. 75–76.

[47] Sidney Hook, "Science and Methodology in Psychoanalysis," in Sidney Hook, ed., *Psychoanalysis, Scientific Method and Philosophy* (New York: New York University Press, 1964), p. 214, 40, 52.

phasis on the unconscious, as exemplified by the concentration on dream analysis, has never been scientifically established; it is a "ghost in the machine." [48] A scientific theory must be stated so that it is verifiable; in the case of psychoanalysis "the theory is stated in language so vague and metaphysical that almost anything appears compatible with it." [49] As Nagel has written, "Can an adult who is recalling childhood experiences remember them as he actually experienced them or does he report them in terms of ideas which carry the burden of much later experience, including the experience of the psychoanalytic interview?" Psychoanalysts, according to some, often forget that their symbolic theory has never been scientifically verified and treat symbols not as part of theory but as a fact. Much reliance is placed on analyzing parallels between, for example, humans and other animals, between male and female physiology but this is not scientific proof.[50]

GENERAL EVALUATION OF THE PSYCHIATRIC AND PSYCHOANALYTIC EXPLANATIONS

Psychiatry and psychoanalysis have a large following in present-day society and their literature is extensive. Psychoanalysis has emphasized the meaningfulness of subjective experience and as a theory it has contributed to the understanding of various psychological processes through which the mind avoids certain painful experiences. The emphasis on the unconscious, on symbolic expressions, and on mental conflict has been noteworthy, even if overstressed in the explanation. Some have increasingly recognized the importance of the larger world of cultural definitions and interpersonal relationships in the development of deviant behavior. Moreover, the remarks presented here are focused on the *theoretical explanation, and not on therapy*. Certainly some favorable therapeutic results are achieved by psychiatrists and psychoanalysts working with deviants. Therapy, however, does not necessarily always follow the theory but may be improvised to fit an individual case. Moreover, the results achieved by therapy may be due to other factors, such as the intimate social relationship between practitioner and patient.

1. *Psychoanalytic as well as psychiatric theory has all too frequently assumed that adult behavior and personality are almost wholly determined*

---

[48] Ernest Nagel, "Methodological Issues in Psychoanalytic Theory," in Sidney Hook, ed., *Psychoanalysis, Scientific Method and Philosophy* (New York: New York University Press, 1964) p. 47.

[49] Nagel, p. 41.

[50] Corbett H. Thigpen, "Multiple Personality," in Stanley Rachman, ed., *Critical Essays on Psychoanalysis* (New York: Pergamon Press, 1963), p. 259.

by childhood experiences, most of them in the family, whereas the over-whelming bulk of evidence suggests that behavior varies according to situations and social roles and that personality continues to develop throughout life. Such early family influences have probably been greatly overemphasized, sometimes to the virtual exclusion of the effect on personality of other groups such as the peer group, and of occupation, neighborhood, marriage, and other later social situations. Even in early life the socialization of the child is greatly influenced by the play group, by street play in urban areas, by preschool and kindergarten activities, and by neighbors and others, such as relatives. The rigidity of character structure during the first year or two of life has been exaggerated, for life must be regarded as a continuous experience of social interaction which cannot be arbitrarily divided between infancy, childhood, and adult experience. Events occurring at forty years of age, for example, may be explained by some occurrence at age four. The theory of predetermination of adult behavior on the basis of heredity has largely disappeared; in its place is predetermination based on early family interaction. For the most part, the sociological approach to deviant behavior, while certainly recognizing the importance of the family, does not agree with this theory in even paramount or exclusive emphasis on the family or on parental models as necessarily the determinants of either deviant or non-deviant behavior.

2. *Despite their claims, the explanations of psychiatrists and psycho-analysts and their proponents concerning deviant behavior have not, for the most part, been scientifically verified.* The psychiatric and psychoanalytic approaches have generally failed, and even have often refused, to use experimental or more verifiable situations, or other more rigorous and controlled techniques, to test their hypotheses.[51] For evidence, there is reliance on verbal recall of childhood experiences, which are interpreted by the psychiatrist or psychoanalyst. Much of that evidence is derived from memories in which childhood experiences, particularly in the family, are likely to be recalled without their necessarily having much bearing on why a person acts as he does in later life. Much of this type of activity has been criticized for using imagination and guesswork too freely. Another person going over the same material might find some other equally valid and

---

[51] See, for example, Lyle W. Shannon, "The Problem of Competence to Help," *Federal Probation*, 25:32–39 (1961). He suggests a number of positive criteria in evaluating a professional person's ability to deal effectively with deviant behavior: (1) the ability to predict human behavior, (2) the ability to control or modify human behavior, and (3) the existence of a body of scientific research which tends to support the explanation of the professional group in question and with which the therapy in question appears to be consistent.

significant explanation which did not employ the theory.[52] Most psychiatric and psychoanalytic studies have been concerned only with deviant persons, and only a few studies have employed control groups of nondeviant persons. This is understandable if one considers that they specialize in treatment, but they frequently generalize without utilizing accepted scientific procedures, such as samples of sufficient size or representativeness. One important psychoanalytic volume, for example, covered only six cases and yet was called "roots of crime." [53]

3. *Psychiatric and psychoanalytic explanations of deviant behavior exemplify a blurring of the line between "sickness" and simply deviations from norms.* According to these explanations the presence of mental aberrations explains the occurrence of certain antisocial actions, such as crime. Thus, criminal or socially deviant behavior is itself made the criterion for the diagnosis of mental abnormality. In this sense, deviations from norms, or "sinful behavior," such as delinquency and crime, are used as the basis for inferring the presence of "sickness" or mental aberration. This tendency is similar to older attempts to link behavioral deviations with "possession by devils." [54]

4. *Some writers, after extensive investigations, have concluded that psychiatric and psychoanalytic diagnoses are often unreliable, and that there is absence of agreement among psychiatrists themselves concerning what objective criteria are to be employed in assessing degrees of mental well-being or mental aberration.*[55] To a great extent it is the very absence of objective criteria of either mental illness or mental health which is responsible for the psychiatrists' and psychoanalysts' tendencies to equate

---

[52] Many psychiatrists and psychoanalysts maintain that successes in therapy are proof of the validity of their theoretical systems. This is no more proof than the "cures" of patent medicine. Other factors, such as the subject's belief and acceptance of the interpretation, as well as his personal relations with the analyst, also enter into the so-called successful treatment.

[53] Franz Alexander and William Healy, *Roots of Crime* (New York: Alfred A. Knopf, Inc., 1935).

[54] Barbara Wootton, *Social Science and Social Pathology* (New York: The Macmillan Company, 1957), p. 207.

[55] See Wootton, especially Chap. 7; Michael Hakeem, "A Critique of the Psychiatric Approach to Crime and Corrections," *Law and Contemporary Problems,* 22:681–682 (1958); Michael Hakeem, "A Critique of the Psychiatric Approach," in Joseph Roucek, ed., *Juvenile Delinquency* (New York: Philosophical Library, Inc., 1958), pp. 79–112; Arthur P. Miles, *American Social Work Theory* (New York: Harper & Row, Publishers, 1954), pp. 122–130; Percival Bailey, "The Great Psychiatric Revolution," *American Journal of Psychiatry,* 113:387–406 (1956); and Clinard, pp. 110–129.

"sickness" with, for example, delinquency and crime. The reason is that, lacking such criteria, there is no way of distinguishing between those whose criminal acts are excusable on the basis of mental disorder and those who, though committing criminal acts, are not mentally disordered. Finding themselves unable thus to distinguish "mentally healthy" criminals from "mentally unhealthy" ones, psychiatrists and psychoanalysts use criminal behavior itself as a criterion of mental disorder, or of other abnormalities within the person. This dilemma, in essence, underlies the psychiatric explanation of deviant behavior and the psychiatric view concerning the treatment of deviants.[56]

PERSONALITY TRAITS

Much effort has gone into the attempt, primarily by psychologists, social psychologists, and psychiatrists, to isolate through various personality tests those personality traits that would distinguish deviants from nondeviants, particularly delinquents, criminals, prostitutes, homosexuals, alcoholics, and drug addicts. It is assumed that the basic components of any personality are individual personality traits or generalized ways of acting. Many personality traits have been identified, such as aggressiveness or submissiveness, intense display of emotions or the lack of such display, suspicion or the lack of it, and self-centered reactions, as opposed to those which are directed toward the welfare of others, withdrawal from contacts with other persons, as contrasted with a desire to be with others, and a feeling that one is regarded with affection rather than dislike. Although these traits have been enumerated as if they were distinct entities, in actuality most proponents assume that they shade between the two extremes.

Many scientists used to believe that personality traits were hereditary and that some persons were "naturally" aggressive or "naturally" shy.[57] This view is still held by many laymen today. Contemporary research has built up evidence, however, which reveals that such behavior patterns are primarily developed out of social experience. Present-day theory attributes personality patterning primarily to interaction in early childhood, particularly to early experiences in the family with the mother and father. It is argued that, since the first experiences of the child with others are primarily within the family group, trait structures arising there form the basis for

---

[56] See Wootton, and see also Hakeem for further elaboration of this problem. Also see Frank E. Hartung, *Crime, Law, and Society* (Detroit: Wayne State University Press, 1965).

[57] At one time the term *temperament* was used to encompass all these personality traits. Now the term is used much more specifically to indicate that some persons differ in their physical sensitivity to sights, sounds, and pain.

the entire structure of personality. Such traits are supposed to represent the patterning of attitudes in relation to others. As he adjusts to new situations, particularly in the family, the young child learns to adapt himself and to secure recognition for his needs by displaying anger, by withdrawing from contact with others, or by becoming aggressive. Feelings of affection for others, as well as recognition that others have affection for him, grow out of these early experiences. Feelings of adequacy or timidity are also related to the degree of affection he receives during the early years of life.

Dozens of tests, rating scales, and other psychological devices have been used to try to distinguish deviants from nondeviants. Traits are often ascertained and measured by a variety of pencil-and-paper type of test, such as the MMPI (Minnesota Multiphasic Personality Inventory) and the CPI (California Personality Inventory). The former is a lengthy questionnaire scale of 550 items in which the subject is asked to respond to statements that are true or false about himself. Fourteen scales are usually scored, four as validity scales indicating the subject's accuracy and reliability, and ten as clinical scales which are assumed to measure important phases and traits of personality. Projective tests are also widely used, such as the TAT (Thematic Apperception Test), which consists of a series of pictures about which the subject comments, and the Rorschach, which uses various cards containing standardized ink blots, to which the subject responds by telling what they mean to him.

Delinquent and Criminal Behavior

Many psychologists and psychiatrists have sought to type and explain nearly all forms of delinquent and criminal behavior in terms of abnormalities in the psychological structure of the individual. They believe that inadequacies in the individual's personality traits interfere with his adjustment to the demands of society. To establish this, a personality test is given to a group of delinquents or criminals; their scores are then compared with the test scores of a so-called control group of nondelinquents or noncriminals.[58] Studies have been made of emotional security, aggressiveness,

---

[58] For attempts to show the relationship of personality traits to delinquency, see particularly Starke Hathaway and Elio D. Monachesi, *Analyzing and Predicting Juvenile Delinquency with the MMPI* (Minneapolis: University of Minnesota Press, 1953); Elio D. Monachesi, "Personality Charcacteristic and Socio-economic Status of Delinquents and Non-delinquents," *Journal of Criminal Law, Criminology, and Police Science,* 40:570–583 (1950); Elio D. Monachesi, "Personality Characteristics of Institutionalized and Non-institutionalized Male Delinquents," *Journal of Criminal Law, Criminology, and Police Science,* 41:167–179 (1950); and Sheldon Glueck and Eleanor Glueck, *Unraveling Juvenile Delinquency* (New York: The Commonwealth Fund, 1950). Also see Herbert C. Quay, "Personality and Delinquency," in Quay, pp. 139–170.

conformity, conscientiousness, deception, self-assurance, social resistance, suggestibility, and others. Efforts have been made to make distinctions in moral judgments and ethical views. The assumption of this approach to criminal behavior is that if it were possible to ascertain the nature of trait structures which are related to criminal behavior, and if formation of these structures could be prevented, or if they could be treated successfully, most crime could be eliminated. To them, delinquent or criminal behavior, even of a group nature, consists mainly of the actions of separate individuals.

There are several major difficulties in distinguishing between the personality traits of offenders and those of nonoffenders. Samples of institutionalized offenders are customarily used, which are probably unrepresentative; moreover, the test performances may be unreliable. It is also possible that experiences, such as arrests, court appearances, or imprisonment, may so affect the personality traits of offenders that it is impossible to determine what they were like prior to such experiences. Comparisons of delinquents, who are of a certain age and often of a particular cultural background, with a general test norm may be misleading. Finally, very few studies of personality traits have distinguished among types of offenders.

Some evidence that there is no necessary relationship, however, between personality traits and criminal behavior has been shown in a survey by Schuessler and Cressey. They took all 113 known studies (up to 1950) which had compared the personality characteristics of delinquents and nondelinquents, criminals and noncriminals. Although 42 percent of the studies showed differences in favor of the nondelinquents and noncriminals, in 58 percent of the studies the results, for various reasons, were indefinite: "The doubtful validity of many of the obtained differences, as well as the lack of consistency in the combined results, makes it impossible to conclude from these data that criminality and personality elements are associated." [59]

One theory of the relation of personality traits and certain criminal behavior needs more detailed comment. The literature of many phases of deviant behavior has had references to the existence of a deviant personality type termed a "criminal psychopath" or a "psychopathic personality," a habitual antisocial deviant.[60] Although there has been considerable

---

[59] Karl F. Schuessler and Donald R. Cressey, "Personality Characteristics of Criminals," *American Journal of Sociology,* 55:476 (1950). Vold has commented: "This negative conclusion would be more impressive if it had been drawn from a comparison of carefully conducted studies only. Unfortunately, their survey threw together indiscriminately a jumble of well, badly, and indifferently controlled studies, so that percentages computed on the total are of quite uncertain meaning." Also, George B. Vold, *Theoretical Criminology* (New York: Oxford University Press, 1958), p. 216.

[60] Harrison Gough, "A Sociological Theory of Psychopathy," *American Journal of Sociology,* 53:365 (1948). There are few more unprecise psychiatric terms, or with a

dispute over the meaning of the term *psychopath,* some of the characteristics of a so-called psychopath are said to be that he is free from the signs or symptoms generally associated with psychoses, neuroses, or mental deficiency, and that he demonstrates poor judgment and an inability to learn by experience, which is seen in "pathological lying," repeated crime, delinquencies, and other antisocial acts.[61] "Patients repeat apparently purposeless thefts, forgeries, bigamies, swindlings, distasteful or indecent acts in public, scores of times." [62]

Although many believe that the concept of a psychopath is real and that such a personality type sufficiently explains numerous antisocial acts, the term is used imprecisely and with a variety of meanings by people who are not clear as to the developmental processes of a psychopath; hence its usefulness can be seriously questioned. In fact, the authors of one study have reported that they found some 202 different terms applied in one form or another to the psychopath.[63] After a study of several years the Committee on Forensic Psychiatry of the Group for the Advancement of Psychiatry issued a warning against the use of a term in statutes with such a wide variety of meanings as the word "psychopath." [64] The lack of precision in describing psychopathic traits has been shown by the wide differences in the diagnoses of "psychopathic" criminal offenders in various institutions and by research on the traits. One study isolated fifty-four traits commonly held to be characteristic of psychopaths and applied them to two groups who had been diagnosed as the least psychopathic and the most psychopathic.[65] Their findings were that nearly all the traits were not statistically significant in distinguishing between the two groups.

---

longer history, than the term *psychopath.* Originally the terms *moral insanity* and *moral imbecility* were used. In the trial of Charles Guiteau in 1881 for the assassination of President Garfield, the issue of "moral" insanity was raised by the defense. Koch is credited with originating the term *psychopathic personality* in 1888 when he referred to a group of patients having no proper class of mental disorder but who could not be considered as entirely sane.

[61] Hervey Cleckley, *The Mask of Sanity* (St Louis: The C. V. Mosby Company, 1950).

[62] Cleckley, p. 415.

[63] Halsey Cason and M. J. Pescor, "A Statistical Study of 500 Psychopathic Prisoners," *Public Health Reports,* 61:557–574 (1946). Also see their "A Comparative Study of Recidivists and Non-Recidivists among Psychopathic Federal Offenders," *Journal of Criminal Law and Criminology,* 36:236–238 (1946).

[64] Group for the Advancement of Psychiatry, Report No. 9. Also see *The Habitual Sex Offender,* Report and Recommendations of the Commission on the Habitual Sex Offender as formulated by Paul W. Tappan, Technical Consultant (Trenton: State of New Jersey, 1950), p. 38.

[65] Cason and Pescor.

The view that a person is a psychopath merely because he is a repeater or is persistent in his behavior is circular reasoning.[66] Writing on the characteristic of persistent antisocial behavior as a criterion of a psychopath, Sutherland stated: "This identification of an habitual sexual offender as a sexual psychopath has no more justification than the identification of any other habitual offender as a psychopath, such as one who repeatedly steals, violates the antitrust law, or lies about his golf scores." [67] Repeated offenses can be explained as the effects of labeling, by their already being thoroughly inducted into a subculture, or through the person's having developed, through frequent arrests or imprisonment, a strong negative attitude toward the law and the police.

Drug Addiction

Psychologists and psychiatrists tend to view the drug addict as one with pronounced personality traits of inadequacy and strong dependency needs.[68] Chein and his associates claim that certain personalities are predisposed to drug use and that its use serves to relieve various personal and interpersonal strains.[69] These strains arise primarily from unstable family interaction which results in weak ego functioning, difficulties in aspiration levels, and distrust of social institutions.

The major difficulty with these explanations is the assumption that such a personality pattern existed before drug addiction took place, an assumption that is fallacious scientific reasoning because it confuses cause with effect.[70] In a later discussion drug usage will be explained not in terms

---

[66] The question of the point at which persistent lying and evasiveness become psychopathic was an important issue in the Alger Hiss case when his defense attorneys sought to prove, by testimony of a psychiatrist, that the chief prosecution witness, Whittaker Chambers, was a psychopath. In relentless cross-examination, which at times became humorous, the prosecutor showed conclusively that the term "psychopath" lacked preciseness. See James Bell, "Your Witness, Mr. Murphy," *Life,* 28:41–42 (1950). Also see Alistair Cooke, *A Generation on Trial* (New York: Alfred A. Knopf, Inc., 1952).

[67] Edwin H. Sutherland, "The Sexual Psychopath Laws," *Journal of Criminal Law, Criminology, and Police Science,* 40:549 (1950).

[68] See, for example, Marie Nyswander, *The Drug Addict as a Patient* (New York: Grune & Stratton, Inc., 1956) and Dale C. Cameron, "Narcotic Drug Addiction," *American Journal of Psychiatry,* 119:793–794 (1963). Others have suggested that they are psychopathic personalities.

[69] Isidor Chein, *et al., The Road to H: Narcotics, Delinquency and Social Policy* (New York: Basic Books, Inc., 1964).

[70] See, for example, Donald Gerard and Conan Kornetsky, "Adolescent Opiate Addiction: A Study of Control and Addict Subjects," *Psychiatric Quarterly,* 29:457–487 (1955).

of the presence of predisposing trait structures but in terms of the availability of the drug, the process of drug usage, and the role of the drug subculture.

Excessive Drinking

Alcoholism is believed by some to be a consequence of personality maladjustment. According to this view, certain childhood experiences produce feelings of insecurity which, together with difficulties in interpersonal relationships of adult life, produce tensions and anxieties reflected in certain personalities. Because the use of alcohol reduces anxiety some persons may come to depend upon it. Over a period of years this dependence on alcohol as a way of escaping hidden or obvious difficulties with which the individual cannot deal increases.

This explanation, although widely held, has several limitations. In the first place, such a theory is largely dependent for evidence on the personality traits of alcoholics and the differences between them and nonalcoholics. The personality traits of an alcoholic are measured after usually some ten to fifteen years of drinking in which the individual has encountered many problems due to his drinking, problems not only with his family but with the police, his employer, and others, and has had experiences foreign to the nonalcoholic.

Although efforts have been made to sketch an "alcoholic personality," presumably applicable to all alcoholics, surveys have concluded that scientific reports to date do not permit us to define such an alcoholic personality, or even to come to any substantial agreement as to what it might be like.[71] For example, two reviews of all personality studies of alcoholics and nonalcoholics up to 1956, using projective and nonprojective tests, found that there was no reason for concluding that persons of one type are more likely to become alcoholics than persons of another type.[72] Moreover, it cannot be assumed that the personality traits displayed by the alcoholic were there *before* excessive drinking began. A number of studies derived from alcoholism scales based on the MMPI have been criticized, for example, as not

---

[71] Alcoholics, according to some psychiatric and psychoanalytic literature are, for example, often dependent persons. Interviews with 141 wives of alcoholics, however, could not demonstrate that dependency was causative in alcoholism.—Edwin M. Lemert, "Dependency in Married Alcoholics," *Quarterly Journal of Studies on Alcohol,* 23:590–609 (1962).

[72] Edwin H. Sutherland, H. C. Schroeder, and C. L. Tordella, "Personality Traits and the Alcoholic: A Critique of Existing Studies," *Quarterly Journal of Studies on Alcohol,* 11:547–561 (1950); and Leonard Symes, "Personality Characteristics and the Alcoholic: A Critique of Current Studies," *Quarterly Journal of Studies on Alcohol,* 18:288–302 (1957).

distinguishing between measures of alcoholism and of general maladjustment.[73] It is possible that a number of types, such as the person who takes pride in his ability to consume large quantities of alcohol without becoming drunk, have a susceptibility for alcoholism, but more research is needed before any definite conclusion can be reached.

Homosexual Behavior

Efforts have also been made to discover basic underlying personality traits of homosexuals. These efforts have not been successful. One revealing study gave a battery of attitude scale projection personality tests and life histories to thirty homosexuals who had not been in therapy nor in an institution. Two experts examined the results without knowing the subjects and had difficulty in distinguishing, on the basis of the records, between the homosexuals and the heterosexuals. Over half the homosexuals were rated as having a high degree of adjustment.[74]

Evaluation of Personality Trait Explanations

One can summarize several criticisms of the personality trait explanations that have been implied in the preceding discussion.

> 1. *An explanation of human behavior, deviant or nondeviant, through the concept of personality traits does not agree with the basic nature of human behavior.*[75] *Actually, human behavior consists primarily of social roles which are variable and socially determined and not static entities like a so-called personality trait.* People learn to adapt and play roles according to given social situations and in connection with these situations come to display various normative behavior, deviant and nondeviant. Thus persons learn to play the social roles of a delinquent, criminal, drug addict, alcoholic, prostitute, or homosexual. Moreover, a "personality trait" does not indicate how a person will act in a situation which is likely to be a result of a reciprocal pattern of interaction in role playing and role taking between two or more persons. Likewise, it does not explain how specific definitions of a situation, such as techniques of stealing, are acquired.
>
> 2. *It is almost impossible to isolate the effects of societal reaction and labeling on the behavior of deviants. One is never sure whether given personality traits were present before the deviant behavior developed or whether experiences encountered as a result of the deviation produced the traits.* Thus the fact that a criminal or a delinquent who has been con-

---

[73] Craig MacAndrew and Robert H. Geertsna, "A Critique of Alcoholism Scales Derived from the MMPI," *Quarterly Journal of Studies on Alcohol*, 25:68–76 (1964).

[74] Evelyn Hooker, "The Adjustment of the Male Overt Homosexual," in Ruitenbeek, p. 152.

[75] See Chapter 2.

victed of an offense or has been confined in a correctional institution exhibits emotional insecurity is no proof that this person was insecure prior to committing the offense or prior to confinement in the institution. The alcoholic or drug addict who is isolated may have developed this trait as a result of a long period of alcoholism or drug addiction.

3. *The control group of nondeviants has generally not been acceptable —one often having been labeled and the other not.* This fact makes comparisons with a control group difficult; under these circumstances it is surprising that so few differences have been shown to exist. In some cases one is not certain whether many members of the control group were actually nondeviant for little is usually done to ascertain that fact other than through an examination of official records.

4. *No evidence has been produced that so-called personality traits are associated with deviations from disapproved norms.* Comparisons with control groups have revealed that no series of traits can distinguish deviants from nondeviants in general. The studies do not show that all deviants have particular traits and that none of the nondeviants have them. Instead, practically all studies show an overlap in that a certain proportion of deviants have a given trait as do the nondeviants, and vice versa. Some deviants, for example, are "emotionally insecure," but some nondeviants are also "emotionally insecure." On the other hand, some deviants are "emotionally secure." It is difficult to interpret such mixed results without accounting for the fact that, though the proportions may vary, the same characteristics may be present in both deviant and nondeviant groups.

5. *The internal construction and the arbitrary methods of weighting many personality tests have been questioned.*[76] It is difficult to judge the real validity of many tests purporting to measure personality traits. "Few personality scales lend themselves well to interpretations in terms of a single numerical score to be taken by itself and independent of scores in related test areas. The nature of the performance in some one area of the test usually affects and changes the significance of the score performance in another area." [77]

6. *Finally, like the psychiatric and psychoanalytic approach, the personality trait explanation purports to show that the etiology of deviant behavior can be traced in the final analysis to family interaction, particularly the effect of early family experiences.*[78] The wider studies of socialization in later life and the use of role theory in the studies of adult life may result in the demonstration that early life situations, particularly those in the family, have less importance in the etiology of deviant be-

---

[76] See, for example, Vold, pp. 126–138.

[77] Vold, p. 127.

[78] Marshall B. Clinard, "Contributions of Sociology to Understanding Deviant Behavior," *British Journal of Criminology,* 12:124–125 (1962).

havior than the play group, local community, school, marriage, and occupation.[79]

SUMMARY

This chapter has discussed several theories of the cause of deviant behavior—feeble-mindedness, body type, childhood experience (the psychiatric and psychoanalytic explanation), and personality traits. The discussion was not directed primarily at any criticism of a discipline but at *general positions*. Although these theories have much support, for a number of reasons they do not offer a valid explanation of deviant behavior. Many of their inadequacies can be attributed to the training and background of the investigators. Because deviant behavior is seen and experienced from this frame of reference, more often than not the facts are interpreted as fitting the theory, rather than altering the theory to fit the facts. Satisfactory control groups of nondeviants have not been utilized in most of the studies. Fortunately, there are indications that the importance of broader social and cultural factors is becoming increasingly appreciated by psychologists and psychiatrists.[80]

On the whole, these theories tend to be explanations of the behavior of human beings, without fully considering the social nature of man or the nature of human behavior. That consideration is necessary if one is to attempt to explain behavior as it actually occurs within society, instead of in what Planck has called the "picture world," or the world of "other things being equal."

Many of the concepts of psychiatry and psychoanalysis have been valuable contributions to a science of human behavior. Despite the vociferous claims of the psychiatrists and the psychoanalysts, however, that their *general theory* offers a solution to deviant behavior, the theory is more of a system of beliefs than scientifically verified bodies of knowledge. Until psychiatry and psychoanalysis are supported by extensive research using accepted scientific methods they will continue to remain largely a body of intriguing speculation.

Superficially, the theories discussed in this chapter seem to be simple ways of dealing with deviant behavior. It is fortunate that there is so little

---

[79] Marshall B. Clinard, "Areas for Research in Deviant Behavior," *Sociology and Social Research,* 42:416–417 (1958). Also see Orville G. Brim, Jr., and Stanton Wheeler, *Socialization After Childhood* (New York: John Wiley & Sons, Inc., 1966).

[80] A recent psychiatric study of crime has included a chapter on sociological theories. Seymour L. Halleck, *Psychiatry and the Dilemmas of Crime: A Study of Causes, Punishment and Treatment* (New York: Harper & Row, 1967).

validity in them, however, for if they were valid it would be virtually impossible ever to control deviant behavior effectively. If feeble-mindedness or body type were associated with certain deviations, control would have to be achieved through selective eugenic breeding and sterilization. Both methods may be applicable to other animals, but for man it would be virtually impossible because of the extensive nature of deviations, the possibility of biological inheritance through recessive characteristics, the relatively free marriage selection system in modern society, and the democratic rights of each individual. The application of psychiatric and psychoanalytic principles on a large scale and the use of psychiatry and psychoanalysis as treatment devices for millions of deviants would be an extremely complex solution. If personality traits are important, and, as in the case of psychiatric problems, they are largely derived from early family interaction the control of such influences by the general society would be extremely difficult.

SELECTED READINGS

Alexander, Franz G., and Sheldon T. Selesnick. *The History of Psychiatry.* New York: Harper & Row, Publishers, 1966. A comprehensive analysis of the development of psychiatry and psychoanalysis and of the various schools of thought.

Glueck, Sheldon, and Eleanor Glueck. *Physique and Delinquency.* New York: Harper & Row, Publishers, 1956. A study of the physique of 500 delinquent boys in a correctional training school, as compared with a control group of boys.

Hakeem, Michael. "A Critique of the Psychiatric Approach," in Joseph Roucek, ed., *Juvenile Delinquency.* New York: Philosophical Library, Inc., 1958, pp. 79–112. A critical appraisal of the methods and evidence on which psychiatric theory is based.

Hook, Sidney, ed. *Psychoanalysis, Scientific Method and Philosophy.* New York: New York University Press, 1959. A series of essays criticizing psychoanalysis, particularly in terms of scientific method.

Monroe, Ruth L. *Schools of Psychoanalytic Thought.* New York: Holt, Rinehart and Winston, Inc., 1955, Chaps. 2, 3, 5, and 7. A comprehensive description of the concepts and methods of psychoanalysis, with critical comments. Chapter 7 deals with the theoretical explanations of certain deviant behavior and the use of psychoanalysis in treatment.

Schuessler, Karl F., and Donald R. Cressey. "Personality Characteristics of Criminals," *American Journal of Sociology,* 55:476–484 (1950). A survey of all studies which sought to differentiate the personality traits of delinquents and criminals, with a control group. The survey concluded that such differences have not been established.

Sewell, William H. "Infant Training and the Personality of the Child," *American*

Journal of Sociology, 58:150–159 (1952). An attempt to test empirically the effect of certain child-rearing practices on personality emphasized by the Freudians. The conclusions were negative.

Shannon, Lyle. "The Problem of Competence to Help," *Federal Probation,* 25:32–39 (1961). A discussion of the positive and negative criteria which should be used in evaluating a professional person, such as a psychiatrist, on his competence to help a deviant.

Szasz, Thomas S. *The Myth of Mental Illness.* New York: Paul B. Hoeber, Inc., 1961. A psychoanalyst states the view that what is considered to be mental illness has come to be defined as whatever psychiatrists say it is, and that psychiatry has, with increasing and misplaced zeal, called more and more kinds of behavior "illness."

Vold, George B. *Theoretical Criminology.* New York: Oxford University Press, 1958. Contains an excellent discussion and criticism of tests of personality traits and their validity.

Wootton, Barbara. *Social Science and Social Pathology.* New York: The Macmillan Company, 1959. Includes an appraisal of current psychiatric beliefs and concludes that there is little evidence that antisocial attitudes are due to lack of maternal affection in infancy. She particularly condemns the blurring of the line between "sickness and sin" for which she holds contemporary psychiatry responsible.

Deviant Behavior

7

Delinquent and Criminal Behavior

In the previous discussions, which have covered many forms of
deviant behavior, the air has been cleared of some fundamental
misconceptions about deviant behavior in general; urbanization has been
found to be a profitable overall frame of reference for the analysis of
deviant behavior; and, finally, several key concepts of considerable
utility have been presented. They include the society, culture, groups,
social norms, values, attitudes, socialization, conception of self, and social
roles. Beginning with crime and criminal behavior, these concepts will
be applied more specifically to a number of important forms of deviant
behavior.

For many hundreds of years men have been intrigued with crime and
criminals—if numerous songs, poems, and stories in the literature of many
cultures are any indication of this interest. Ballads dealing with thieves
and highwaymen, gaols and sheriffs, have been passed down from generation to generation. Today this interest in criminal offenders has come into
even greater prominence as evidenced in the subject matter of many contemporary novels, newspapers, magazines, television plays, and motion
pictures. In fact, so large is the proportion of popular mass communication devoted to criminal behavior that one is tempted to speculate

about the content of fictional literature in that millennium of a crimeless society.[1]

Despite these centuries of interest in crime, it is only within the past eighty-five years that men have sought to study scientifically the factors underlying criminal behavior.[2] Previously there had been considerable writing and speculation about the nature of crime, but little interest in the criminal. Near the end of the eighteenth century, several writers, notably Cesare Beccaria in Italy suggested that a crime was simply an act wherein the pleasure derived from illegal behavior exceeded the possible pain that might consequently be imposed as punishment.[3] This conception of crime was based on the principles of hedonistic psychology, which assumed that the behavior of all persons was completely a matter of individual responsibility and that their misbehavior was motivated by pain and punishment. It was not until 1876, however, that there was any really scientific study of criminals. It was begun by Cesare Lombroso, an Italian army doctor. The abstract methods of studying crime did not appeal to him; instead, he began the study of the anatomy of various criminals. Lombroso was influenced by some work he had done in taking various physical measurements of patients in mental hospitals and by the still controversial Darwinian theory of evolution, and its corollary, that contemporary man had antecedents in various forms of primitive man.[4] Becoming convinced that some criminals were characterized by certain physical features, he later classified criminals into two additional categories—insane and criminaloids—the latter being persons who were not born with physical stigmata but who actually had innate tendencies toward crime. Although Lombroso's theory was later shown to be invalid, his work did much to arouse an interest in the scientific study of criminals.

----

[1] So much space is devoted to the reporting of various crimes in the daily press of Western society that the difference between most papers and one like the *Christian Science Monitor,* which seldom prints crime news, is striking.

[2] For a survey of the scientific approach to criminal behavior and an examination of our present knowledge, see George B. Vold, *Theoretical Criminology* (New York: Oxford University Press, 1958) and Hermann Mannheim, *Comparative Criminology* (Boston: Houghton Mifflin Company, 1965). The latter is an examination of the literature on a world-wide basis. Also see Hermann Mannheim, ed., *Pioneers in Criminology* (Chicago: Quadrangle Books, Inc., 1960).

[3] Cesare Beccaria, *An Essay on Crimes and Punishments* (New York: Stephen Gould, 1809).

[4] Cesare Lombroso, *L'uomo delinquente* (Turin: Bocca, 1896–1897). Also see Gina Lombroso Ferrero, *Lombroso's Criminal Man* (New York: G. P. Putnam's Sons, 1911); and Cesare Lombroso, *Crime, Its Causes and Remedies* (translated by H. P. Horton; Boston: Little, Brown & Company, 1912).

CRIME AND SOCIAL CONTROL

All societies and groups develop ways of dealing with behaviors which fall outside the range of tolerance of given societal or group norms. These methods are ordinarily called "negative sanctions" because they impose penalties on those whose behavior has transcended the range of tolerance of the norms. "Positive sanctions," on the other hand, consist of special rewards, such as praise, recognition, or prestige which are bestowed on persons whose behavior has conformed, or has exceeded conformance, to prescribed norms.

Both negative and positive sanctions are categories of social control. Social control may, in turn, be classified as either "formal" or "informal." In general, formal controls are the *official* actions of a group or society in response to the behavior of group members, whereas informal controls, such as gossip or ostracism, consist of *unofficial* group actions. Official actions or formal controls, such as the criminal law, derive from the official group machinery set up to carry out the functions of the group or agency. These controls are, in effect, imbedded in the formal structure of the group. However, these formal controls are generally backed by certain beliefs, ideals, customs, convictions, attitudes, and opinions which in themselves are actually informal controls. Thus, in this sense, informal and formal controls cannot be considered as completely discrete categories.

The use of penalties through the criminal law is therefore but one of the formal methods of control and but a small part of the total system of social controls which operate to create and maintain order in society.[5] Likewise, crime, which is behavior defined by law or legal norms, is nevertheless relative to the legal norms of a given area, community, state, or nation.

> What is crime to one city, county, or nation, may not be to another. What was crime yesterday may not be today, and what people consider crime today may not be tomorrow. . . . Moreover, laws are but one facet of the regulations we impose on individuals which may vary all the way from ordinary customs, social convention such as good manners, rules and regulations of a church or lodge, the mores, to other rules such as those called public regulations and laws. All of them represent simply variations in norms and are all part of a continuum. Sometimes, in fact, we may punish some acts which are not crimes more severely than if they were. Examples

[5]Thorsten Sellin, *Culture Conflict and Crime* (Bulletin 41; New York: Social Science Research Council, 1938); and Donald J. Newman, "Legal Norms and Criminological Definitions," in Joseph S. Roucek, ed., *Sociology of Crime* (New York: Philosophical Library, Inc., 1961).

of such are public reactions to some unconventional manners, the punishment of illegitimacy, or the religious penalty of excommunication.[6]

Informal Controls

No effort is required on the part of the group to secure compliance with most of our group norms, for they are the spontaneous and unconscious ways of acting which characterize the bulk of the customs of any culture. Generally speaking, mechanisms of control, such as customs, mores, traditions, beliefs, attitudes, and ideals, are taught through prolonged interaction between persons. Likewise, *informal control* of behavior may be observed in specific behaviors, such as gossip, ridicule, reprimands, praise, criticism, gestural cues, glances of approval or disapproval, emotional expressions, denial or bestowal of affection, ostracism, verbal rationalizations, verbal expressions of opinion, and many other methods. These specific modes of responding to the behavior of group members are generally learned without conscious awareness through group participation. Moreover, because they have been incorporated into their behavior systems and outlooks they are used in a way which seems "natural" or "spontaneous" to the persons involved. Unlike formal controls, informal controls are not exercised through official group mechanisms. Gossip, as an example of an informal social control, is undoubtedly one of the most effective instruments yet devised for disciplining people. These controls are extremely important in any society, for they bulwark the more formal controls of law. They are extremely effective in a folk society and in rural neighborhood situations of primary personal relationships.

To summarize, the difference between formal and informal controls does not depend on the specific behavior necessary for their operation, but depends instead on the source of societal reaction to such behavior, whether the reaction derives from formal machinery and relationships or from informal personal relationships.[7]

Formal Controls

Formal controls involve organized systems of specialized agencies and standard techniques. There are two main types: those instituted by agencies other than the state, and those imposed by the political state. Rules of a more abstract nature are formulated and authority is given such agents as the clergy or police for their interpretation and application.

A series of specific actions is established to punish the transgressor and

---

[6] Marshall B. Clinard, "Criminal Behavior Is Human Behavior," *Federal Probation,* 13:24 (1949).

[7] See Robert Bierstedt, *The Social Order* (New York: McGraw-Hill Book Company, Inc., 1957), pp. 188–189.

to reward those whose compliance with the norms is equal to or beyond the expectation of the group. Curiously, nonpolitical agencies, such as business concerns and professional, religious, or social groups, probably use rewards more than penalties, which is just the reverse of formal governmental controls. Through promotions, bonuses, or some token of merit, business organizations frequently reward those who have made an outstanding contribution to the firm, who have never been absent, or who have an unusual safety record. Professional groups often reward outstanding service with election to office or with some citation. Religious groups reward faithful adherents by promises of a future state of euphoria, by positions of leadership, and by pins or scrolls given for faithful attendance at Sunday school or for similar activities. Clubs, lodges, fraternities, and sororities likewise offer a large number of prestige symbols for those who walk the path from neophyte to full-fledged member without reflecting dishonor on the group. Recognition of a type similar to military rewards is given to a small number of civilians each year in the United States through the Carnegie awards for outstanding heroism.

Nonpolitical groups also impose penalties, some of which may be more severe than punishments imposed for crimes. A business concern may fire a man from his job, [8] and a professional group or a union may suspend a member or even expel him from the group, which may mean a loss of livelihood. Baseball players who do not obey the rules of the league or the ball club are usually fined $50 or $100 for an infraction and may be suspended. Religious organizations may demand penance or withhold certain religious services, such as the wedding privilege or a religious service at death. They may even use what is, to members of a particular faith, the most drastic punishment of all—excommunication from the church. Clubs and similar groups generally utilize a scale of fines, withdrawal of membership privileges, or even expulsion as formal means of controlling their members.

The other type of formal control is exercised by the state through its political and legal institutions. Unfortunately, this control is seldom exerted through positive sanctions or rewards. Some cities occasionally give publicity to safe and courteous drivers, but the reward is seldom more than a pleasant notoriety. The citizen who goes through life obeying nearly all the requirements imposed upon him by law seldom receives any rewards. Of course, a man's good reputation may be of benefit to him in connection with certain occupational or community responsibilities, and if he should

---

[8] Joseph Bensman and Israel Gerver, "Crime and Punishment in the Factory: The Function of Deviance in Maintaining the Social System," *American Sociological Review,* 28:588–598 (1963).

be apprehended for violation of the law his past conduct may mitigate the punishment. An important exception to this failure of the state to use rewards as a means of control is the practice in our armed services of giving good-conduct ribbons, medals, or special leaves for faithful adherence to duty or for outstanding bravery, even though every soldier is supposed to do his duty.

Social control of civilians is characterized by a variety of punishments which may be imposed by the state. If a person is below the legal adult age, he comes under the jurisdiction of the courts as a "delinquent." If the offender has reached the legal age of adulthood he is subject to punishment under the criminal law. He can be put on probation, fined, imprisoned, or even condemned to death. In the past various other cruel and inhumane methods of punishing criminals have been authorized by governments.

The measures at the disposal of the state for the control of violations by its members are not confined to the penalties available through the criminal law. The state has many ways of compelling individuals, business concerns, and labor unions to obey the law. It may withdraw a doctor's, lawyer's, or druggist's right to practice, and it may suspend a tavernkeeper or a restaurateur from doing business for a few days, a year, or even permanently. If an individual or a company makes a product illegally, such as alcohol, or if a concern manufactures foods in violation of pure-food laws, the products may be seized and destroyed by the government without compensation. In settling claims for back payment of taxes or fraudulent returns on taxes, the government may require an additional payment which may be quite a severe penalty. If a business concern or a union is defying a law, the government may institute an injunction "to cease and desist" from further violations, and if further violations occur, contempt of court proceedings may be instituted. Many other examples of government penalties could be cited to indicate that the criminal law is not the only sanction used by political institutions to secure compliance with conduct norms.

WHAT IS A CRIME?

The nature of a criminal act may be considered from two points of view, either as a violation of the criminal law or as a violation of any law punished by the state, depending upon the particular assumption with which illegal behavior is approached.

A Violation of the Criminal Law

First, from a strictly legal position, an act is a crime only when the statutes so specify. These statutes, and the subsequent interpretations of them by the court, constitute the criminal law. Most of the conventional crimes, such as burglary and robbery, were crimes under the common law long before the enactment of any legislation. At some time norms of nearly every kind have been punished by the state under the criminal law, which has developed as a result of legislative and court action. Violations of the criminal law have included such behavior as engaging in recreational activities on the Sabbath, practicing witchcraft, smoking, failing to show proper respect to a noble, wearing one-piece bathing suits, listening to illegal radio programs, and selling alcoholic beverages. On the other hand, many acts punishable under the criminal law today, such as armed robbery, have a long history of being regarded under the common law as antisocial. When written criminal codes came into being, sanctions against these acts were included, since many of them had their origin in institutional norms and values. Violations of these laws, which have their origin and partial support in the mores, are referred to by lawyers as *mala in se.* Certain other types of behavior which constitute a considerable portion of the criminal law have no such basis in the mores or in common law. Lawyers refer to this general group of criminal offenses as *mala prohibita,* or bad simply because they have been prohibited. Most of these offenses have grown out of more recent technological and cultural changes in society. Many are associated with the automobile, building codes, misuse of trademarks, false advertising, the manufacture of impure foods and drugs, acts in restraint of trade, fraudulent or negligent acts of bank officials resulting in insolvency of banks, sale of fraudulent securities, and improper conduct of labor relations.

Although a person below eighteen is generally regarded as a delinquent rather than a criminal, it would be an error to assume that all or even a large part of delinquency is comparable to adult criminality, or that boys and girls who are picked up for delinquency or are sent to our state training schools are always "junior criminals." Actually the behavior covered by the term "delinquency" goes beyond any definition of crime; many acts, if committed by adults, would not come before the criminal courts. The delinquent child is not technically prosecuted in a court of law: the state is supposed to "act in the interest of the child" to prevent further difficulties. Penalties are not specific, and the judge is permitted great latitude in his judgment, although this latitude is not permitted beyond the delinquent's twenty-first birthday. In Wisconsin, for example, a delinquent child is "any child under the age of eighteen years who has violated any law of the state or any county, city, town or village ordinance, who by reason of being wayward or habitually disobedient, is uncontrolled by his parent . . . who is habitually truant from home or school, who habitually so deports himself as to injure or endanger the morals or health of himself." [9] The following

---

[9] *Wisconsin Laws Relating to Juvenile Delinquency* (Madison: State Department of Public Welfare, Division for Children and Youth, March 1952). For a discussion of the legal aspects of juvenile delinquency, see Donald J. Newman, "Legal

are some of the offenses for which juveniles are apprehended, a list which should certainly remove the erroneous impression that boys and girls picked up for delinquency or committed to training schools are all "junior criminals":

1. Violates any law or ordinance
2. Engages in immoral or indecent conduct
3. Knowingly associates with vicious or immoral persons
4. Knowingly enters or visits house of ill repute
5. Patronizes gambling establishments
6. Patronizes a tavern where intoxicating liquor is sold
7. Uses intoxicating liquors
8. Patronizes a public poolroom
9. Smokes cigarettes around public places
10. Is habitually truant from school
11. Is incorrigible and will not obey parents
12. Absents self from home without consent
13. Wanders in streets at night, not on lawful business (curfew)
14. Habitually wanders about railroad yards or tracks
15. Begs or receives alms
16. Engages in an illegal occupation
17. Is in occupation or situation dangerous to self or others
18. Deports self so as to injure self or others
19. Habitually uses vile, obscene, or vulgar language in public places
20. Jumps train or enters car or engine without authority

In the criminal law there has been a trend toward the wider use of probation, the suspended sentence, and the indeterminate sentence rather than imprisonment. Another trend has been the widespread enactment of sex-deviate laws which require the psychiatric examination of certain types of offenders and their indefinite detention for treatment.

Punishment under the criminal law, such as imprisonment, is based on a number of beliefs. According to one view, physical punishment exacts retribution; here we have *lex talionis* and vengeance—an "eye for an eye and a tooth for a tooth." The offender should pay his debt to society. Another view, similar to Beccaria's idea of long ago, is that the punishment

---

Aspects of Juvenile Delinquency," in Joseph S. Roucek, ed. *Juvenile Delinquency* (New York: Philosophical Library, Inc., 1958), pp. 29–56. For a comprehensive discussion of court procedures in dealing with juveniles, as well as suggestions for greater legal protection for the juvenile, see *Task Force Report: Juvenile Delinquency and Youth Crime,* The President's Commission on Law Enforcement and Administration of Justice (Washington: U.S. Government Printing Office, 1967).

of an offender deters others from similar acts. Then there is the concept that punishment restores the social equilibrium, which has been upset by certain crimes. In such cases the offender might be considered as expiating his offense through suffering. Finally, in addition to these theories of punishment, some people have felt that punishment reforms, something it can do only with difficulty. On the contrary, physical punishment, whether by imprisonment or otherwise, appears to produce a number of harmful effects: [10]

1. It tends to isolate the individual. Some have remarked that what society holds against a man is not the crime he committed but the fact that he has been physically punished, as by imprisonment.

2. Punishment may simply develop caution in the individual so that instead of changing his attitudes he may simply try harder not to be apprehended again.

3. It frequently creates new and undesirable attitudes in the individual, such as fear and lack of self-confidence.

4. Punishment may even give the offender a sort of status. Delinquents and adults who have been punished often occupy a higher position in the eyes of other deviants and sometimes even in the eyes of the general public simply because of the fact that they have been punished.

5. Any attempt to reform an individual must be a constructive process, but physical punishment is the opposite of this. In fact, in many instances the application of force may stop any efforts on the part of the individual to change his personal behavior voluntarily.

With the development of the idea of prisons, with the wider extension of equality before the law affecting noble and serfs alike, and with the greater respect for human life, there has been a gradual trend toward the abolition of capital punishment, which was widely employed throughout the world fifty or more years ago.[11] Part of this trend is due to the repeal of certain laws, but disuse of others is largely responsible for it. The nineteen countries that have abolished the death penalty include Belgium, Denmark, Great Britain, Holland, Iceland, Italy, New Zealand, Norway, Portugal, Sweden, Switzerland, Argentina, Brazil, Colombia, Peru, Uruguay, and Venezuela.[12] Although the Soviet Union has reserved the death penalty to cases of high treason, espionage, sabotage, terrorist acts, banditry, and premeditated murder under certain aggravated circumstances, it announced

---

[10] Edwin H. Sutherland and Donald R. Cressey, *Principles of Criminology* (7th ed.; Philadelphia: J. B. Lippincott Company, 1966), pp. 373–375.

[11] See George Rusche and Otto Kirchheimer, *Punishment and Social Structure* (New York: Columbia University Press, 1939).

[12] Clarence H. Patrick, "The Status of Capital Punishment: A World Perspective," *Journal of Criminal Law, Criminology, and Police Science*, 56:397–411 (1965).

in May, 1961 that the death penalty might also be applied to large-scale embezzlers of state property and to counterfeiters. The death penalty—all executions being by a firing squad—was also sanctioned for especially dangerous habitual offenders and for prisoners who committed violence in their place of confinement.[13] In 1962 the death penalty was further extended to certain public officials who receive bribes, to those who make attempts "under aggravating circumstances" on the life of a policeman or of a citizen-volunteer charged with maintaining public order, and to those who commit some types of forcible rape.[14]

In many parts of the United States persons can still be executed for such crimes as murder, kidnapping, treason, rape, and armed robbery. Thirteen states have abolished capital punishment: Alaska, Hawaii, Maine, Michigan, Minnesota, North Dakota, Rhode Island, Wisconsin, and, since 1964, Oregon, Iowa, Vermont, New York (except for killing a police officer acting in line of duty or prison inmates under life sentence who kill a prison guard or another inmate), and West Virginia (except for killing prison personnel or for an unrelated second offense). Puerto Rico and the Virgin Islands also do not have capital punishment. There has been a marked decline in the use of capital punishment, from an annual average of 167 between 1930 and 1939 to 80 per year for the period 1950–1953. Actually, capital punishment is largely disappearing from the United States more by disuse than through repeal. In the calendar year 1960, 56 prisoners were executed in this country, but by 1964, the number had declined to 15; in 1965, 7; and in 1966, 1.

In the United States the decline in capital punishment has been due to a number of arguments which have been lodged against it: (1) There appears to be little evidence that capital punishment has a deterrent effect. (2) The abolition of the death penalty has resulted in no consistent reaction. Sometimes there has been an increase in the number of murders and sometimes not. (3) Moreover, evidence indicates that juries are less willing to convict a person when the penalty is death. (4) Another argument against capital punishment is that if an injustice has been done it can never be remedied. (5) A disproportionate number of persons executed are Negroes, young people, and the poor. Of those persons executed for rape from 1930 to 1960, for example, 89.9 percent were Negroes. Over 60 percent of all those executed during 1960 were Negroes, and of these over three fourths were under thirty-five. (6) Finally, there is the debasing effect of executions on societies where the taking of human life is contrary to most religious and social beliefs. It is not in line with contemporary scientific thinking, which emphasizes the treatment and rehabilitation of criminals.

---

[13] As reported in *The New York Times,* May 7, 1961, p. 28.

[14] As reported in *The New York Times,* February 28, 1962, pp. 1, 5.

Any Act Punishable by the State

The definition of a crime solely in terms of the criminal law seems to be too restrictive, however, for an adequate explanation of criminal behavior. Many students of the problem feel that a crime should be defined not only in terms of the criminal law but in broader terms as any act punishable by the state, regardless of whether the penalty is a criminal one or is administrative or civil in nature. They believe that the strict legal definition of a crime solely under the criminal law is too limited and biased. See pages 269–272.

Lawbreaking is often divided into two neat categories: the conventional crimes, such as larceny, burglary, and robbery, which are usually punished under the criminal law; and those violations of law which have come to be known as "white-collar crimes," or perhaps more approriately as "occupational crimes," and which are seldom punished in this way.[15] They include violations of law by small and large businessmen, employees, farmers, politicians and government employees, labor union leaders, doctors, and lawyers in connection with their occupation.[16]

Many people believe, however, that such violations of law are not really crimes, and that "crime" and "criminal" should be arbitrarily restricted to the more overt acts of ordinary criminals which are punished by the criminal law that fits the common stereotype and which they themselves would never do. This arbitrary distinction is made not on the basis of illegal behavior but on the basis of how the judicial process—namely, the criminal law—reacts to it. Sociologically a crime is any act which is considered socially injurious and which is punished by the state, regardless of the type of punishment. The difficulty in limiting the definition of a crime in terms of the criminal law becomes evident when one compares the punishment of a fine, jail sentence, or probation given an apprehended burglar or bank robber with the different kind of punishment often given a person in legitimate occupations. A doctor who violates the law might be punished by having his license revoked, a lawyer by being disbarred, or a businessman by

---

[15] See Edwin H. Sutherland, "Is 'White Collar Crime' Crime?" in Marvin E. Wolfgang, Leonard Savitz, and Norman Johnston, eds., *The Sociology of Crime and Delinquency* (New York: John Wiley & Sons, Inc., 1962), pp. 20–27. Also see Richard Quinney, "The Study of White Collar Crime: Toward a Reorientation in Theory and Research," *Journal of Criminal Law, Criminology, and Police Science,* 55:208–214 (1964). Also see Marshall B. Clinard, "White Collar Crime," *International Encyclopedia of the Social Sciences* (New York: Macmillan Company, 1968).

[16] One might ask about college professors. There is the possibility of their accepting bribes for higher grades, but this has never been a part of the pattern of college teaching. If it were, the results would be chaotic.

being enjoined by the government, being required to pay civil damages, having his license to do business suspended, or, in some cases, having his product seized and destroyed. Unless a more inclusive concept of what constitutes "crime" is used, it is impossible to deal analytically with the different illegal activities which are punished according to occupation and social class.[17]

> Conviction in the criminal court, which is sometimes suggested as the criterion, is not adequate because a large proportion of those who commit crimes are not convicted in criminal courts. This criterion, therefore, needs to be supplemented. When it is supplemented, the criterion of the crimes of one class must be kept consistent in general terms with the criterion of the crimes of the other class. The definition should not be the spirit of the law for white-collar crime and the letter of the law for other crimes, or in other respects be more liberal for one class than for the other.[18]

SOURCES OF DELINQUENT AND CRIMINAL ATTITUDES

Thus far this discussion of crime has attempted to clarify the nature of delinquent and criminal acts. It has shown that behavior becomes criminal because it is socially harmful and subject to punishment by the state. Attention will now be focused on the sources of various conflicting norms which either are in opposition to laws forbidding certain behavior or fail to support them. Criminals and delinquents develop attitudes and definitions of situations through group association in the same fashion as do noncriminals and nondelinquents. This group experience involves not only the family about which we now hear so much, but also the play group, the school, the neighborhood, clubs, church, marriage, occupation—in fact, all life in its interaction with the culture and the subculture. Both criminality and noncriminality are "natural" in the sense that they are the outgrowths of processes of social definitions.

First of all, in a consideration of these group experiences, some of the factors in the general culture should be examined, including cultural ideologies which might enhance criminal behavior, the effect of law-enforce-

---

[17] This sociological conception of crime does not consider as crime behavior which is solely antisocial, injurious to society, unfair, or greedy but not necessarily illegal.

[18] Edwin H. Sutherland, "White Collar Criminality," *American Sociological Review,* 5:5 (1940), and Frank Hartung, "White Collar Crime: Its Significance for Theory and Practice," *Federal Probation,* 17:31–36 (1953). Also see Marshall B. Clinard, *The Black Market: A Study of White-Collar Crime* (New York: Holt, Rinehart and Winston, Inc., 1952), pp. 226–262.

ment agencies on criminal behavior, and the effects of such secondary influences as newspapers, television, and motion pictures.[19] The role of the neighborhood or the occupational group, the subculture of delinquent companions and gangs, and the role of the family will also be discussed. All these areas, it is contended, are potential sources of criminal attitudes and thus should be considered in developing any program to control delinquency or crime.

GENERAL CULTURAL PATTERNS

Societies generally have prevailing patterns and beliefs about other people's behavior that make for more or for less crime. One writer, for example, has indicated the following as important crime-producing influences in American culture.

1. Belief that Everyone has a Racket
2. Influence of Destitution or Relative Poverty
3. The Search for Something for Nothing
4. The Influence of Misrepresentation in Advertising
5. Influence of White-Collar Crime
6. Preferential Loyalties
7. Growing Acceptance of Violence
8. Discrimination Against Minorities
9. Popular Reliance on Punishment as a Deterrent [20]

In the discussion here we shall present three general cultural patterns that make for delinquency and crime in probably any society and, conversely, could make for less delinquency and crime. These are general disobedience to law, selective obedience to law, and the behavior of law-enforcement officers and agencies.

General Disobedience to Law

Many societies today are characterized by an extensive disobedience of norms regulated by the law. Although American culture, for example, professes obedience to law, there is extensive flaunting of these taboos on the part of the general adult population. There are indications that disobedience to law is far more widespread than reports of crimes committed show. To indicate a few examples, several studies have been made of the extent of unreported delinquency and crime. A comparison of a group of 337

---

[19] Marshall B. Clinard, "Secondary Community Influences and Juvenile Delinquency," *The Annals,* 261:42–43 (1949).

[20] Donald R. Taft, "Influence of the General Culture on Crime," *Federal Probation,* 30:19–22 (1966).

Texas college students with a group of 2049 delinquents who came to the attention of the Fort Worth juvenile court revealed that the delinquent acts of these college students had been as serious, although probably not as frequent, as those of the delinquents.[21] Although the college students had rarely appeared in court except for traffic offenses, everyone had committed other offenses for which he could have been charged. For example, on the average every 100 male students had committed 116 thefts before college and 36 thefts during college. Of 49 criminology students at a midwestern university, 86 percent had committed thefts, and about 50 percent had committed acts of vandalism.[22]

An interesting study was made of criminal behavior among the general adult population in metropolitan New York City.[23] Of 1698 persons who answered a questionnaire anonymously, 91 percent stated that they had committed one or more crimes after they were sixteen years of age. Sixty-four percent of the men and 29 percent of the women could have been convicted of felonies. The mean number of offenses committed by the men in adult life (over sixteen years of age) was eighteen and ranged from 8 percent for ministers to 20 percent for laborers. Between eight and nine of every ten men and women had stolen things; one in four of the men admitted stealing an automobile; and one in ten of this group had robbed someone. From this study it was concluded that "the number of acts legally constituting crimes are far in excess of those officially reported. Unlawful behavior, far from being an abnormal social or psychological manifestation, is in truth a very common phenomenon."

The Kinsey report on sexual conduct in American society—although the sample used was only partially representative—revealed the startling presence of various violations of criminal law of which the public had not been aware.[24] The study revealed that nearly all men with less than an eighth-grade education and about three fourths of those with college train-

---

[21] Austin L. Porterfield, *Youth in Trouble* (Fort Worth, Tex.: Leo Potishman Foundation, 1946), pp. 32–35.

[22] Unpublished material collected by the author.

[23] James S. Wallerstein and Clement J. Wyle, "Our Law-Abiding Law-Breakers," *Probation,* 25:107–112 (1947). The immediately following statistics are from this study.

[24] A. C. Kinsey, W. B. Pomeroy, and C. E. Martin, *Sexual Behavior in the Human Male* (Philadelphia: W. B. Saunders Company, 1948). The quotation is from p. 392. This study has been criticized for the lack of representativeness of the sample and for the inaccuracy of some of the data furnished by some of the subjects as well as for other flaws. See Paul Wallin, "An Appraisal of Some Methodological Aspects of the Kinsey Report," *American Sociological Review,* 14:197–211 (April 1949).

ing had had premarital intercourse, an offense which is punishable in many states as fornication; about one third of the sample had had homosexual experiences; and nearly three fourths had had relations with prostitutes. There were extramarital relationships in a third of the marriages, a violation of our laws relating to adultery. Kinsey concluded that "the persons involved in these activities, taken as a whole, constitute more than 95 per cent of the total male population. Only a relatively small proportion of the males who are sent to penal institutions for sex offenses have been involved in behavior which is materially different from that of most of the males in the population."

Few evidences of our lawless behavior would be more startling to people of another culture than the widespread indirect association of the American people with organized crime through their participation in organized gambling. In 1951 the Kefauver Committee found that widespread illegal gambling was being practiced in nearly every city of any size in the United States. People illegally bet billions of dollars through organized racketeers on policy and numbers rackets as well as on the outcome and point range of many amateur and professional athletic contests. Within recent years some athletes have become involved with the law either because they did not report an offer of a bribe or because they accepted one. From 1956 through 1961 twenty college basketball players were paid $44,500 in bribe money to fix forty-four games, according to statements and indictments by prosecutors in New York and North Carolina. Another six players were charged with accepting money in "softening-up" cash, as potential or actual contact men.[25]

In 1959 the shock of television scandals on several nationally televised "quiz shows" swept through the American public, an estimated fifty million of whom, in 1958, had been watching the three leading quiz programs. A number of programs were found to have been rigged by feeding the contestants answers in advance. On this basis one contestant, whose father and uncle each had won a Pulitzer Prize in literature, defeated thirteen opponents and therefore won $129,000. Others confessed to winning large amounts fraudulently, as much as $237,500 in one case and $98,500 in another. Altogether, ten contestants were brought before the courts on charges of perjury since they had denied the charges under oath before a grand jury. They were given suspended sentences, but were allowed to keep their "earnings."

---

[25] See Tim Cohane, "Behind the Basketball Scandal," *Look,* 26:85 (1962). Also see Paul H. Douglas, *Ethics in Government* (Cambridge, Mass.: Harvard University Press, 1952), pp. 9–10, and "Ethical Standards in Public Life," *The Annals,* Vol. 280 (1952).

Selective Obedience to Law

Much more common than general disobedience to law is the tendency of persons to obey laws on a selective basis. Instead of obeying all laws one disregards those types of law which directly affect his own occupation and social class. Some laws are obeyed, others are not, according to a person's own beliefs. Many businessmen believe that such laws as those regulating securities and banking procedures, tax collections, restraint of trade, labor relations, wartime price controls and rationing, and others of a similar nature, are not as binding on the individual as are our burglary and robbery laws. Some labor leaders see no reason for obeying laws prohibiting labor "racketeering" or laws affecting the conduct of labor relations and strikes if it is to their advantage to break them. Farmers have been known, too, to disobey the law selectively; examples include their failure to pay proper income taxes, their intimidation of farm auctioneers, and their dumping of milk trucks to keep up the price of milk.[26] Government officials operate in a situation where bribes and favors are on occasion offered by businessmen and where politicians, including congressmen, may exert influence in behalf of special interests. A political scientist had this to say about political corruption:

> The record indicates that the political morality reflects, rather than shapes, the society in which it operates and that, more pertinently, it is naïve in the extreme to expect from politicians a far different ethical standard from that which prevails throughout the country. Indeed, were today's politicians to adopt such a standard they would almost certainly be rejected by the voters as idealists, dreamers, crackpots, or visionaries.[27]

The implications of selective obedience to law can be seen more clearly if ordinary crimes are considered. Many persons who engage in such crimes as robbery and burglary consider some of our laws unjust and too severe, and they often have a number of rationalizations for these attitudes. They point to the general dishonesty of the public, the brutality of the police, and the corruption of public officials, including those in the courts. A professional confidence man who is smart enough to outtrick a "sucker" may contend that the law should not punish him, or in any event not as severely

---

[26] James O. Babcock, "The Revolt in Iowa," *Social Forces*, 12:369–373 (1934). During the middle 1960s, extensive violations of laws regulating public order as well as draft regulations took place in the United States. These violations of law were supported by the persons involved as being justified by their need to express opposition to the war in Vietnam and to war in general.

[27] H. H. Wilson, *Congress: Corruption and Compromise* (New York: Holt, Rinehart and Winston, Inc., 1951), p. 234.

as it does. A man with a prison record who has a dependent family, whose wages are too low, and whose record interferes with employment possibilities may advance such arguments as rationalizations for thefts or burglaries. Certainly ordinary criminals are acquainted with the effects of this selective obedience to law, and this attitude presents a major problem in the re-habilitation work of our correctional institutions. As the warden of one of our prisons said in 1946, "What am I supposed to do, retrain people to be honest in a dishonest world of black markets and frauds?" Perhaps Willy Sutton, a well-known professional bank robber, put it best when he told a group of New York reporters some years ago: "Others accused of defrauding the government of hundreds of thousands of dollars merely get a letter from a committee in Washington asking them to come in and talk it over. Maybe it's justice but it's puzzling to a guy like me."

Great inconsistency exists in modern urban society between the be-havior required of a child and that of an adult, and these differences are not clearly defined as a correlate of age. In fact, adults are permitted increasing transgressions of the conduct norms, whereas juveniles are expected to con-form to ideals. In many simpler societies the situation is reversed. It is the juveniles who have considerable freedom, whereas the behavior of adults is one of rigid conformity.[28] The inconsistent value patterns of the adult world can be seen particularly in the consumption of alcoholic beverages in the United States. Persons under twenty-one are frequently denied legal access to alcoholic beverages, even beer and wine, that are drunk freely by adults, a normative behavior that does not apply, for example, to most of Europe.

The Behavior of Law-enforcement Officers and Agencies

The general attitude of the American public toward law-enforcement officers is certainly not conducive to obedience. The American people gen-erally do not have the same degree of respect that the English have for their "bobbies," barristers, and judges. In general, legislative bodies, considered as corporate bodies and not as individuals, are regarded with suspicion and distrust, and the police are looked upon as harsh, corrupt, and inefficient. There is a more favorable public attitude toward the courts, but the higher courts are often ridiculed because of their corporate inefficiency; the lower courts, for their inefficiency and dishonesty.

Although there is much evidence of this disrespect for law-enforcement agencies, it is possible that it may represent simply a vicious circle in that

---

[28] For example, see Margaret Mead, *Coming of Age in Samoa* (New York: William Morrow & Company, Inc., 1928), and the works of Bronislaw Malinowski on the Trobriand Islanders.

what the American people expect their law-enforcement officers to be is actually what they often are. Certainly, numerous studies have indicated that the police and other law-enforcement agencies, instead of preventing the development of criminal attitudes and acts, actually constitute one of the chief sources of indoctrination in attitudes of disrespect for law.[29] The all too common practice of employing police personnel and electing judges who in no way exemplify the type of conduct required of those charged with enforcing the law adds both directly and indirectly to the production of delinquency and crime. Many judges do not merit the respect of juveniles, for their attitudes on the bench and the general atmosphere of their courtrooms often seem to indicate a lack of understanding. This situation is understandable when one realizes that most law schools and the legal system itself do not provide adequate, or indeed, any training for lawyers or judges in juvenile or adult rehabilitation work. Very few jurists apply scientific knowledge in the treatment of crime in the courts. Cases of political influence, bribery, and outright violations of law by jurists occur in American society in sufficient numbers partially to endanger the concept of "justice" which has come over to us from English law. The serious injuries in such cases lie not only in the crime but in its effects on the attitudes of youth and adult criminal offenders brought before the courts. The Kefauver Committee found that organized crime in American cities could not exist or flourish without extensive bribery of politicians, public officials, sheriffs, police officers and others.[30]

---

[29] William Westley, "Violence and the Police," *American Journal of Sociology,* 59:34–41 (1953). Also see Jerome H. Skolnick, *Justice Without Trial: Law Enforcement in a Democratic Society* (New York: John Wiley & Sons, Inc., 1966).

[30] "The evidence . . . is perhaps sufficient to indicate that a considerable portion of crime in our larger cities, and also its character, are reflections of, and are intimately bound up with, the kind and character of the political organizations that exist in these cities. The political machine, the gamblers and the gangsters, the police and the local ward heelers, the city magistrates and the court clerks, the lawyers who practice in the courts, the bondsmen, the local attendants, the 'fixers,' the hangers-on, the good fellows about the political clubs, the dispensers of favors and the securers of jobs, the people willing to 'go to the front' for the less fortunate who have been arrested, the givers of political jobs to honest political workers, are all intertwined into a system or, still better, a way of life, for that part of our community which occupies itself with the business of governing under the conditions that make this kind of governing both possible and necessary." Frank Tannenbaum, *Crime and The Community* (Boston: Ginn and Company, 1938), pp. 150–151. A distinguished criminologist once wrote the author that bribery of police and judicial officials is almost nonexistent in Sweden.

The methods of dealing with crime often constitute little subcultures for the transmission of criminal norms.[31] According to reports of state and federal inspectors, many American jails fail to meet standards of health and welfare. Conditions in many of our boys' training schools and reformatories are not much better. The large number of criticisms of such institutions can be summarized by stating that most of them, as now constituted, probably produce more crime in a society than they eliminate.[32] Although there are small islands of exceptions in the correctional systems, scientific studies, reports of inmates and wardens, the high percentage of repeaters, and the frequent prison riots by outraged inmates—all justify this conclusion.

Fortunately, there is evidence that this situation is improving. More often than in the past policemen are being selected on a merit basis and given training in proper police conduct. Some judges receive training at professional institutes which deal with delinquency and crime. Jail and prison conditions are slowly being improved, substitutes are being devised for prisons, and probation is being more widely employed.

MASS MEDIA

The amount and prominence of space devoted to crime stories in the newspapers and the amount of conversation based on them present a bewildering picture in most societies. Because they play up crime, it is likely that newspapers are important in making us a crime-centered culture. Crime often seems more prevalent than it really is. There is a difference between reporting a crime in simple, verifiable factual statements, as is often done in many countries, and loading a long, detailed crime story with emotionally charged words. Crime receives particular prominence in American newspapers because of the amount of space given to crime stories and because of their position on the front page. The proportion of crime stories to the rest of the news is not an adequate basis for comparison, for the front page sells the paper. There is general indifference on the part of the newspaper publishers to the serious moral implications of this almost universal practice. Admittedly such a statement raises the problem of the function of the newspapers. On the one hand, the concept of free enterprise condones the collection of sordid tales as a valuable vehicle for selling advertisements; on the other, the concept of social responsibility suggests that some newspapers might re-evaluate their role in a society.

---

[31]Donald Clemmer, "Observation on Imprisonment as a Source of Criminality," *Journal of Criminal Law and Criminology*, 41:318 (1950).

[32] For a complete discussion of prisons see Chapter 20.

The great interest of juveniles and adults in crime stories on television and in motion pictures has caused some people to overestimate their importance, whereas others tend to discount them in their explanations of delinquency and crime. A survey of television, covering such questions as types of programs, time spent watching televison, and the like, was conducted by a research team at the Stanford University Institute for Communication Research.[33] The findings of this survey were based on responses from 6000 children, 2000 parents, and 300 teachers. It was found that from the age of three to sixteen the average child devotes about a sixth of his waking hours to watching television, and more than half the children studied watch "adult" programs, such as crime plays, westerns, and shows featuring emotional problems. The investigators analyzed 100 hours of programs in the so-called children's hours, the period from 4:00 to 9:00 P.M. In those 100 hours they counted twelve murders, sixteen major gun fights, twenty-one persons shot, twenty-one other violent incidents in which one person slugged another, an attempted murder with a pitchfork, two stranglings, one stabbing in the back with a butcher knife, three successful suicides (and one unsuccessful suicide), four people pushed over a cliff, two attempts made to run over persons with automobiles, a raving psychotic loose in an airliner, two mob scenes (in one the wrong man was hanged), a horse grinding a man under his hoofs, two robberies, a woman killed by falling from a train, a tidal wave, an earthquake, a hired killer stalking his victim, and, finally, one guillotining. Although admitting the disturbing effects of such violence on children, they concluded that almost invariably delinquent children who blamed television for their crimes had other things wrong with their lives quite apart from watching television and that with few exceptions these children had difficulties before they learned anything about crime from television.

There is no question that the motion picture often presents a version of our culture emphasizing wealth, materialism, and immoral conduct, both criminal and sexual, which furnishes juveniles approved models conducive to delinquency.[34] A realistic appraisal of television and motion-picture programs indicates, however, that on the whole their direct influence on the juvenile only serves to aggravate whatever existent deviant attitudes and subcultural roles there may be. Schramm has stated that children both

---

[33] Wilbur Schramm, Jack Lyle, and Edwin B. Parker, *Television in the Lives of Our Children* (Stanford, Calif.: Stanford University Press, 1961). Also see Joseph Klapper, *The Effects of Mass Communication* (New York: The Free Press, 1960).

[34] For this reason, in Sweden, children under fourteen are not permitted to see most motion pictures, which are primarily American; moreover, certain crime films are censored for adults.

learn and are influenced by the various media of mass communication, but that what they receive from the mass media is first passed through another set of influences, such as family, school, and church, before it becomes a very important guide to actions. "We might say that what television does to children is less significant than what children do with television; and what children do with television . . . depend[s] on their homes, their schools, their peer group relations, and many other factors quite outside the mass media." [35]

This does not mean, however, that such media have no effect. In 1961 a Senate committee looked into the problem of the large proportion of television programs dealing with crime and violence. In general, the conclusion was reached that this material might have an indirect effect on many youths by presenting a distorted picture of approved American values. The vivid pictures of juvenile delinquents and criminal offenders presented on television serves to perpetuate a stereotype, in the minds of the public, of *all* delinquents and criminals as tough and vicious. Consequently, this makes it difficult to bring about changes in the punitive aspects of the criminal law and correctional programs and to utilize measures to bring about reformation.

It is unfortunate that few scientific investigations have been made of the influence of these various forms of entertainment on delinquency and crime. Certainly there has been only limited investigation of the millions of nondelinquent juveniles who avidly attend crime movies, nightly watch several television programs dealing with crime and violence, or read "comic" books regularly. In most cases the result of the preoccupation of the public with the effect on juvenile delinquency and crime of television, motion pictures, and comic books is merely to release the feeling that somthing should be done. The deeper question of why juveniles are interested in this entertainment raises issues which adults often do not wish to face because of their own interests in similar material. Likewise, this problem is evidence of a reluctance on the part of the adult world to deal effectively with factors basic to it—general disobedience to law, the presence of deviant influences in their local neighborhoods, political corruption, and certain emphases in our culture, such as materialism and extreme individuality. The existence of gangs of delinquent boys is a more important and more difficult immediate problem than television, motion pictures, or comic books, but few communities have the necessary vision to attack it. In dealing with social difficulties the public tends to take the easiest course. It is conceivable, however, that even if all these media were to disappear from a culture we probably

---

[35] Wilbur L. Schramm, ed., *Mass Communications* (Urbana: University of Illinois Press, 1960), p. 466.

would still have almost as much delinquency and crime as we now have. Certainly delinquency and crime existed before any of them were considered of consequence.

THE FAMILY

The family is an institution which has been undergoing great social change. The result of this change has been a decline in the importance of the family's role in general social life. Because many of the traditional functions of the family have declined, the socialization of young children is increasingly being done by other groups, such as the school and the street gang. As kinship ties become weaker and as the mother is increasingly employed outside the home, the urban child may spend less time with members of his immediate family. Among large sections of the urban population today the family no longer plays the dominant idealized role that certainly is in the minds of those who think of it as the primary factor in encouraging or preventing delinquency and crime. Second, a family tends to reflect the norms of the social class of which it is a part, the occupation of the father, and the area of the city where it resides. It is difficult to speak of a family as such without referring to its place in the social structure.

Some people believe that the chief source of delinquent behavior lies in unsatisfactory family influences. In fact, judges in some cities have been punishing the parents of delinquents, although they seldom specify the family influences that might be related to illegal behavior other than sometimes "lack of parental supervision." For a number of reasons it is difficult to indicate specifically what influence the family may have on delinquency and crime. There are, however, a number of family influences which should be examined in relation to delinquent and criminal behavior: the family as a source of delinquent patterns, the broken-home situation, and emotional insecurity within the family.[36]

There is the possibility that delinquent patterns of behavior may be derived directly from the family. Although there may be some direct tutelage in criminal acts by father, mother, or brother, current evidence indicates that this is of minor importance. The influence of siblings on one another is not common, however, for in many families only one or two children may be delinquent. It is more likely that the family, par-

---

[36] For a comprehensive survey of the literature, see Donald R. Peterson and Wesley C. Becker, "Family Interaction and Delinquency," in Herbert C. Quay, *Juvenile Delinquency: Research and Theory* (Princeton, N.J.: D. Van Nostrand Company, Inc., 1965), pp. 63–99.

ticularly those in the slums, may furnish other patterns, such as sexual immorality, drunkenness, and other socially unacceptable models of behavior which may or may not be conducive to specific acts of delinquency or crime. Certainly studies have revealed some families with deviant standards in regard to stealing, gambling, or sex relations, particularly a mother-daughter situation where the former is sexually promiscuous.

Nevertheless, it is probably the contemporaries of persons who engage in crime and delinquency who are the important influences. Even a higher incidence of delinquent patterns in a home does not mean that deviant standards could not have been acquired from the outside. The family can enhance the effect of deviant patterns or it can help to inhibit them, but those who regard the family as the exclusive source of social norms and therefore put the blame on the family fail to see that the family is simply a part of the larger culture and tends to reflect the norms of its neighborhood. The difficulty which any family encounters in trying to keep a child away from delinquent influences in a neighborhood well illustrates this point. Parental discipline is, of course, not the only factor in the dynamics of family interaction. Nye has attempted to study this and other factors, such as value agreement, mutual recreation, parental interaction, and rejection by parents, in the lives of a group of delinquents and nondelinquents.[37] The study was not conclusive but direct control techniques were found to have a greater influence for girls than for boys, and the father's behavior was more significantly related to delinquent behavior than was that of the mother.

Persistent efforts have also been made to link delinquency to homes broken by separation, desertion, divorce, or death, on the assumption that such a break in the family ties would lead the child to commit delinquent acts. It is not the broken family as such, however, that is important but the local community conditions surrounding the family. Although studies show that 30 to 60 percent of delinquents come from broken homes, these figures must be considered in terms of sex, age, race, and social conditions in the local community. The proportion, however, is greater among girls [38] than among boys, and greater among Negroes than among whites.[39] These figures have little meaning unless we compare them with control groups. Shaw and McKay, for example, found that when they compared boys of the same age and national derivation, 42.5 percent of the delinquent boys and

---

[37] F. Ivan Nye, *Family Relationships and Delinquent Behavior* (New York: John Wiley & Sons, Inc., 1958).

[38] Jackson Toby, "The Differential Impact of Family Disorganization," *American Sociological Review*, 22:505–512 (1957).

[39] Thomas P. Monahan, "Family Status and the Delinquent Child: A Reappraisal and Some New Findings," *Social Forces*, 35:250–258 (1957).

36.1 percent of a sample of schoolboys were from broken homes.[40] No effort was made, however, to check on the delinquency of the schoolboys. A Norwegian study found that 17.4 percent of the offenders and 12.7 percent of the nonoffenders came from broken homes.[41]

The effort to link delinquency with broken homes is probably a blind alley. There is considerable evidence that juveniles from broken homes are more likely to be arrested, convicted, and sentenced to a juvenile institution.[42] As noted earlier, it is not the broken family as such that is important but the local community conditions surrounding the family. The concept of a broken home is by means a constant factor, and the relationship of broken homes to delinquency has never been conclusively demonstrated: "The broken home does not always cause delinquency; how and when the home was broken and the effect upon family relationships and the attitudes of the children make a great difference." [43] There are certainly millions of families which are broken in one form or another but whose members are not delinquent. No one knows what the proportion, is but some idea of it can be gained from the fact that there are annually about 400,000 divorces. Some homes where there is friction between the parents may, as will be indicated, be improved by separation. How closely identified a child is with a particular parent is another question, for the effect of a broken home on one child may be quite different from its effect on another. Broken homes, for example, seem to have more relation to delinquency among girls.[44]

Several studies have suggested that the family's failure to provide the child with a proper degree of security and affection produces delinquency and crime.[45] The Gluecks, for example, have recommended a prognostic instrument to predict delinquency at about six years of age. It emphasizes the role of the family and consists of prediction tables which involve ade-

---

[40] Clifford R. Shaw and Henry D. McKay, "Social Factors in Juvenile Delinquency," National Commission on Law Observance and Enforcement, *Report on the Causes of Crime* (Washington, D.C.: Government Printing Office, 1931), II, 262–285.

[41] Nils Christie, *Unge norske lovovertredere* ("Young Norwegian Lawbreakers") (Oslo: Universitetsforlaget, 1960), pp. 105, 111.

[42] Nye, pp. 43–44, 47–48. Also see Philip M. Smith, "Broken Homes and Juvenile Delinquency," *Sociology and Social Research*, 39:307–311 (1955).

[43] Donald R. Taft and Ralph W. England, Jr., *Criminology* (4th ed.; New York: The Macmillan Company, 1964), p. 143.

[44] Toby.

[45] Sheldon Glueck and Eleanor Glueck, *Unraveling Juvenile Delinquency* (New York: Commonwealth Fund, 1951). Also see William Healy and Augusta F. Bronner, *New Light on Delinquency and Its Treatment* (New Haven, Conn.: Yale University Press, 1936). Also see Chapter 6.

quacy of discipline of boy by father, supervision of boy by mother, affection of father and mother for boy, and family cohesiveness.[46] An examination of their actual data leads one to the opposite of their conclusions, namely, that the family was not as important as other influences. Four fifths of the delinquents moved five times or more, as compared with two fifths for the nondelinquents, and their mobility may well have exposed them to more deviant patterns. Other equally startling differences between the groups were sneaking into motion-picture theaters (62%:4%), running away from home (59%:1%), gambling (53%:9%), hanging around street corners (95%:58%), truancy (95%:11%). Half of the five hundred delinquents belonged to gangs, as compared with only three of the non-delinquents. In the light of this one wonders whether the emotional setting of the family was really of such great importance.

NEIGHBORHOODS AND OCCUPATIONS

So far these comments about the inconsistency of cultural norms have referred to the social heritage as a whole. This section will describe the role of neighborhoods and occupations in transmitting criminal norms. The neighborhood or local community is primarily one of personal relationships, where people live and where their local institutions are located. It is an area of more personal social participation in which the activities of child and adult tend to be organized around agencies, such as the local stores, the school, the church, playgrounds, and sometimes even a motion-picture theater. This local world may include taverns, lodges, gangs, athletic teams, and sports organizations. The members of the neighborhood tend sometimes to share in other activities, such as weddings and funerals, picnics and carnivals. It is a world of meaningful experiences to the individual. At the same time, the neighborhood reflects some of the norms and evaluations of the outside world. A child who lives "back of the yards" or "across the tracks" develops a conception of himself as being different from children in other neighborhoods. As a major work on delinquency concluded, "the major effort of those who wish to eliminate delinquency should be directed to the reorganization of slum communities." [47]

---

[46] Sheldon Glueck and Eleanor Glueck, *Delinquents in the Making* (New York: Harper & Row, Publishers, 1952).

[47] Richard A. Cloward and Lloyd E. Ohlin, *Delinquency and Opportunity: A Theory of Delinquent Gangs* (New York: The Free Press, 1960), p. 211. They point out that whereas slum areas used to be organized, they are now becoming "disorganized" because of such factors as the decline of the local political power structure and new housing developments. Also see Chapters 4 and 18.

Neighborhoods often differ as to social class, in the variety of the composition of racial, ethnic, and religious groups, and in the stability of the population. Even more important, there may be pronounced differences in the social norms of the local community. There are local areas which are organized principally around conventional norms, and there are other areas in which unconventional standards predominate.[48] In either instance no local community has norms exclusively of one type or another; rather, conflicting standards are present in varying proportions. A person in a delinquent area may have close associations with persons who engage in, or encourage him to engage in, delinquency and at the same time have similar contacts with law-abiding persons.

Some local communities maintain the middle-class virtues of pride in family status, of obedience to the sexual mores, of respect for the police and law, at least insofar as the more overt crimes are concerned. These local communities have considerable stability and relatively little racial and ethnic diversity. These areas do not tolerate houses of prostitution, gambling, and "fences" for the disposal of stolen goods. Most of the boys and girls belong to such traditional groups as the boy scouts, and the adults are actively organized in conventional groups like the parent-teacher association. Other groups are patterned along conventional ways, engaging in woodcraft, hikes, and games. Occasionally there is some vandalism but there is little theft. The social norms of the community are largely conventional, and conventional institutions exist to support these norms. The moral responsibilities of the outside world and general culture are continually brought into the lives of juvenile and adult alike.

Many local communities have norms so different from those of middle-class neighborhoods that they might be a part of a separate culture. As noted in Chapter 4, a considerable proportion of our population lives in slum areas. There are also similar areas, "back of the tracks," in our smaller cities and towns.[49] The norms of conventional society are not nonexistent in these

---

[48] See Irving Spergel, "Male Adult Criminality, Deviant Values and Differential Opportunities in Two Lower Class Negro Neighborhoods," *Social Problems,* 10:237–250 (1963).

[49] See pages 103–105. In some places our farming areas are characterized by pockets of deviant values, as has been satirized in *Tobacco Road,* and suggested by differentials in the norms of owners and some farm labor. Farming districts and small towns probably do not have nearly as distinct local areas as do the large urban communities, because of personal relationships which transcend the immediate neighborhood. A study of one small city showed that although counterparts to delinquency areas in large cities produced crime, localizations of deviant values were not entirely confined to a neighborhood but rather were associated with membership in certain families and small groups with deviant attitudes. See Donald R.

areas, however, and they include some traditional organizations such as youth groups, lodges, and churches. There are families who have traditional virtues, and there are persons who live in the area but whose standards are not part of it. On the whole, however, these conventional organizations are not too effective. These neighborhoods are often insulated from much of conventional society and its norms.

Similar to the impact of neighborhood norms on the individual are those of certain occupations. In some, norms may be law-abiding, whereas in others they may not be. This will be discussed in detail in a more extensive presentation of occupational crime in the next chapter.

ASSOCIATES AND DELINQUENT GANGS

The role of deviant cultural, neighborhood, and occupational norms and values in the development of criminal attitudes has been discussed, but the method of transmittal to the individual delinquent or criminal has not been indicated. These attitudes are primarily acquired through companions and by participation in small intimate groups in much the same manner as law-abiding norms are transmitted. Companions who play a major part in the acquisition of these norms include a group or gang, siblings in the family, associates in one's occupation, and other persons. This view that most crime and delinquency arise from the adoption of deviant norms, particularly through the tutelage of others, has been supported by studies of petty thievery, of highly organized thievery, of organized crime, and of white-collar crime.[50]

Popular thinking about delinquency and crime is, for once, quite correct in its emphasis on the role of "bad companions" in this behavior. One national survey concluded that "the typical delinquent operates in the

---

Taft, "Testing the Selective Influence of Areas of Delinquency," *American Journal of Sociology,* 38:699–712 (1933). Even in middle-sized cities, however, one finds a concentration of delinquency in certain areas that is similar to that found in larger metropolitan areas. See Lyle W. Shannon, "The Distribution of Juvenile Delinquency in a Middle-Sized City," *The Sociological Quarterly,* 8:365–383 (1967).

[50] Clifford R. Shaw and Henry D. McKay, *Juvenile Delinquency and Urban Areas* (Chicago: University of Chicago Press, 1942); Edwin H. Sutherland, *The Professional Thief* (Chicago: University of Chicago Press, 1937); Edwin H. Sutherland, *White Collar Crime* (New York: Holt, Rinehart and Winston, Inc., 1949, reissued, 1961); and Clinard, *The Black Market.* The "new" immigrants to Israel from Africa and Asia, largely from North African cities, have a much higher crime rate than Jews of European ancestry. This seems to be largely a product of the deviant mores they bring with them. See Shlomo Shoham, *Crime and Social Deviation* (Chicago: Henry Regnery Company, 1966), pp. 72–85.

company of his peers, and delinquency thrives on group support. It has been estimated that between 60 and 90 percent of all delinquent acts are committed with companions. That fact alone makes youth groups of central concern in consideration of delinquency prevention." [51] Most delinquents are arrested in company with others, and it can be safely assumed that those who had no companions at the time of their arrest had at least one in the beginning of their delinquency. In one study of 5480 Chicago delinquents Shaw found that 81.8 percent of those brought into juvenile court had one or more companions.[52] Considering those with one or more companions, he found that 30.3 percent had one companion, 27.7 percent had two, 10.8 percent had three, 7.1 percent had four, and 5.9 percent had five or more.

Some persons are critical of the emphasis on neighborhood and associational factors on the ground that generally, only about one fourth of the boys even in the worst delinquency areas have appeared before the juvenile courts. One writer has attempted to answer this by pointing out that official delinquency, as measured by juvenile court statistics, represents only a small proportion of actual offenders.[53] If police records in Chicago are used, this figure increases to nearly two thirds. Boys in areas of high delinquency simultaneously exhibit socially approved and disapproved behavior; hence the term "nondelinquent" becomes a rather meaningless one. A substantial number of boys who engage in juvenile delinquency, however, presumably grow up to be law-abiding persons.

Most persons who consider the role of companions in crime have in mind only juvenile gangs or the more organized criminal syndicate. Many delinquent juvenile associations, however, are not with organized groups but instead with one or two companions. It is possible, of course, that some nongang offenders at one time had an association with a gang; yet many of the nongang associates are undoubtedly those who have acquired deviant attitudes through other sources, particularly through contact with someone who has been in a correctional institution. Differential association with criminals or delinquents by means of contacts with one or two persons appears to be more characteristic of rural and village areas than of urban ones. In urban areas larger group patterns of delinquency are the more typical method of association. In rural areas these companions are more often

---

[51] *The Challenge of Crime in a Free Society*, A Report by the President's Commission on Law Enforcement and Administration of Justice (Washington, D.C. U. S. Government Printing Office, 1967), p. 66. For a survey of various findings, see Thomas G. Eynon and Walter C. Reckless, "Companionship at Delinquency Onset," *British Journal of Criminology*, 2:162–170 (1961).

[52] Shaw and McKay, "Social Factors in Juvenile Delinquency," II, 195–196.

[53] Solomon Kobrin, "The Conflict of Values in Delinquency Areas," *American Sociological Review*, 16:653–661 (1951).

chance acquaintances. A study of rural offenders found that almost two thirds of them had not been associated with groups of boys who stole, and if this category is restricted to those who committed serious thefts, 87 percent had never had such previous association.[54] This apparent difference in the pattern of associates is due to the existence of a greater informal social control in farm and village areas.

Many studies, however, have shown the high incidence of gang membership among youthful offenders. Approximately two thirds, for instance, of a sample of Swedish criminal offenders had belonged to a group of boys who stole.[55] During later childhood and early adolescence nearly all normal children associate in groups. Some of these groups develop into conflict groups or gangs in the sense that they are in conflict with some other groups in society. Some of these gangs turn from mere conflict with other gangs, the family, or the school to conflict with the police, property, owners, and certain normative standards of a society.

Gangs tend to reflect neighborhood values. If located in certain areas, primarily middle-class, the members of these male groups may engage in harmless club activities. In other areas, on the other hand, gangs may bring the delinquent norms of these areas into intimate contact with the individual. Such gangs delinquency, in the form of stealing and vandalism, may be regarded as a natural adjustment not only to the social roles, behavior patterns, and norms of the group but to those of the neighborhood of which the group is a part.

Many delinquent groups in more urban areas have a long history; some have been in existence for many years, long enough so that their members may have older brothers or even fathers who were once members. Gangs which have directed their activities toward crime and delinquency for some time have an opportunity to furnish excellent training in criminal techniques. They teach new members how to empty slot machines, shoplift, obtain junk illegally, open freight cars, snatch purses, "roll" drunks, secure skeleton keys, purchase guns, steal automobiles, engineer holdups, sell stolen goods to "fences," and, finally, bribe a policeman or otherwise "fix" a case. New members may progress from truancy and stealing petty objects and junk to the more serious activities of breaking into freight cars, purse

[54] Marshall B. Clinard, "Rural Criminal Offenders," *American Journal of Sociology*, 50:38–45 (1944).

[55] Marshall B. Clinard, "A Cross Cultural Replication of the Relation of the Process of Urbanism to Criminal Behavior," *American Sociological Review*, 25:253–257 (1960). Also see Marshall B. Clinard, "The Relation of Urbanization and Urbanism to Criminal Behavior," in Ernest W. Burgess and Donald J. Bogue, eds., *Contributions to Urban Sociology* (Chicago: University of Chicago Press, 1964).

snatching, jack-rolling drunks, burglaries, automobile thefts, and even armed robbery.[56]

When the gang develops considerable skill and the individual stays with it for a long enough period of time, he may acquire a considerable knowledge of crime, moving from the more simple offenses to the serious rackets. Many gangs furnish the training in techniques and the social status that accrue to those who have developed skill in crime. The following account of the "copper-wire" gang is typical of a large city gang.

> Police held 10 Milwaukee boys Sunday night on suspicion of stealing 42 cars and forging near-perfect street car passes in water colors. The "copper-wire gang," so-called because it used copper wires to "jump" cars' ignitions, was taken into custody when a 16-year-old member was picked up in a stolen car, police said. Authorities said they would be charged with stealing 42 cars over a two months' period. Two 18-year-olds were being held by police and the eight younger members were at the detention home. The 16-year-old who was arrested Friday had two guns in the car with him, police said. They believed they were to be used in holdups. They said the 16-year-old had perfected the copper-wire technique and taught it to the others. Donald H_____, 18, was accused of counterfeiting street car passes in water color so well they could hardly be distinguished from the originals. He allegedly produced as many as 40 a week and sold them for a quarter apiece.[57]

The effectiveness of delinquent gangs in disseminating knowledge of crime lies in the fact that through mutual excitation the gang makes illegal acts attractive to the individual. Members enjoy the thrill of common intimate participation in interests involving conflict.

> When we were shoplifting we always made a game of it. For example, we might gamble on who could steal the most caps in a day or who could steal in the presence of a detective and then get away. We were always daring each other that way and thinking up new schemes. This was the best part of the game. I would go into a store to steal a cap, by trying on one and when the clerk was not watching walk out of the store, leaving the old cap. With the new cap on my head I would go into another store, do the same thing as in the other store, getting a new hat and leave the one and when the clerk was not watching walk out of the store, leaving

---

[56] See Gerald D. Robin, "Gang Member Delinquency in Philadelphia," in Malcolm W. Klein, *Juvenile Gangs in Context: Theory, Research, and Action* (Englewood Cliffs, N.J.: Prentice-Hall, Inc., 1967), pp. 15–24.

[57] *Milwaukee Journal*, March 27, 1950.

one hat at night. It was fun I wanted, not the hat. I kept this up for months and then began to sell the things to a man on the west side. It was at this time that I began to steal for gain.[58]

Each gang is a social system. Many common symbols and activities hold it together, and each of its members is assigned a social status or position. Common symbols include gang names such as the Dirty Dozen, the Purple Gang, So So's, the Onions, the Torpedoes, the Wolves, White Rocks, the Murderers, Bat-Eyes, Dukies and the Hawthorne Toughs. They have their own universe of discourse and argot, as well as songs and stories which have become traditional with them. Common activities of various types hold them together: gang fighting, raiding, robbing, defending a hang-out, getting "shagged" (group sexual activities), holding smut sessions, drinking, playing games and pranks, maintaining clubrooms, gambling, and committing acts of vandalism.[59] These common activities give a gang unity in its endeavors, and *esprit de corps*. Part of its integration comes from warfare with other groups which have different names and territories, or which are organized along different racial, religious, or ethnic lines. Gangs develop common traditions not only through conflict with other gangs but through warring with the police, who represent more conventional norms. Many juvenile gangs in larger cities have terms for various forms of gang fighting:

Sounding: A dirty or questioning look.
Roughing: A jostling of one member of a gang by a rival gang member.
Fair one: A fist fight between two boys.
Rumble: A gang fight of the less serious kind, sometimes produced by a "sounding."
Stomping: A gang fight in which the enemy is knocked to the ground and kicked while down.
Burn, waste, or go down: To hold a gang fight in which "blades" [knives] and "pieces" [guns] are used.
Call it on: To hold a prearranged grudge fight in which anything goes.[60]

The position or social status of gang members is measured in ways entirely different from those used by conventional youth groups. A gang member achieves high status by displaying courage and skill in the commission of a crime, by having a long record of delinquencies, and, better

---

[58] Chicago Area Project, "Juvenile Delinquency," A monograph prepared by the Institute for Juvenile Research and the Chicago Area Project (rev. ed.; Chicago: 1953), p. 5.

[59] Frederic M. Thrasher, *The Gang* (Chicago: University of Chicago Press, 1929, 1963), p. 277.

[60] *The New York Times,* May 15, 1955, sec. 4.

still, by having been incarcerated in a correctional institution. Each boy comes to be designated by a nickname which is somewhat indicative of his social status in the gang. As a result of this participation in gang behavior its members develop fairly uniform attitudes toward "opposition to authority, contempt for the traitor, recognition and prestige through delinquency, hero-worship, stigma of petty stealing, and control of the gang over its members." [61] Nowhere are these values of the gang better seen than in the gang leader who comes to exemplify them. His control over the gang depends on such qualities. It is he who helps to invoke the code of the gang and to punish and ridicule those who do not live up to the standards of conduct the gang demands. One leader of a delinquent gang has written:

> The boys I ran around with were just like me, steal anything they get their hands on. One boy would make plans for stealing money, and we would give him jiggers and help him out if he needed help, and the other boys would do the same. We would meet every Saturday night in the pool room and set down in the pool room and plan our schemes out for the following week. The leader of each group was supposed to be tough. He would take most of the money and split the rest of it with the rest of the boys. I was leader, and never did cheat the other fellows out of a dime, and they had me for their leader until I was sent to Eldora Training School. The gang then got them a different leader, and they continued to take part where I left off. Then in Eldora they came and seen me and told me I could be their leader when I was released, but I said I wasn't going to be another leader, and they called me names such as coward. Well, I couldn't very well take those names, so I was their leader again when I was released, but I wished I wouldn't of for it got me only in trouble again, while the other boys was released on probation. It didn't offer me nothing but bad luck.[62]

Rationalizations or techniques of verbalization for delinquent behavior are extremely important to justify deviant behavior in the face of adult disapproval and legal sanctions, and these are largely derived from gang associations.[63] These are "denial of responsibility" by blaming parents, and so on; "denial of injury," by claiming, for example, that the act was a prank or that the stolen car was "borrowed"; "denial of the victim," namely, that the delinquency was justified under the circumstances; "condemnation of

---

[61] Chicago Area Project, p. 5. For a discussion of recent research on group cohesion and member interaction in delinquent gangs see LaMar T. Empey, "Delinquency Theory and Recent Research," *Journal of Research in Crime and Delinquency,* 4:28–42 (1967).

[62] From a personal document.

[63] Gresham M. Sykes and David Matza, "Techniques of Neutralization: A Theory of Delinquency," *American Sociological Review,* 22:664–670 (1957).

the condemners," such as cruel police methods; and, finally, the "appeal to higher loyalties," association in gangs being more important than loyalty to the larger society. These rationalizations, together with the boys' associations with an inconsistent legal system and its agents, come increasingly to mean that they break their ties with the legal order and "drift into delinquency." [64]

Some boys' gangs disappear after a while, but others continue for many years. Although there is no hard-and-fast line of demarcation between a gang of younger offenders and one of older offenders, the latter tend to become involved in more serious crimes. The membership of older criminal gangs appears to be drawn chiefly from those juveniles who have had a record of incarceration in correctional institutions. Criminal gangs often become tied up with organized criminal rackets. They develop connections as part of criminal syndicates, work with political machines, and specialize in types of rackets.

THEORIES OF GANG DELINQUENCY

Although the delinquent subculture of the gang has generally been explained as a product of neighborhood values and the process of gang behavior itself, several theories have been advanced to explain gang delinquency in a larger theoretical context.[65] Gang delinquency is a world-wide phenomenon today and not confined to the United States. "The more important new type of juvenile delinquency found in nearly all parts of the world is the formation of juvenile gangs which commit delinquent acts." [66] They are reported to be extensive in places far apart, for example, England,

---

[64] David Matza, *Delinquency and Drift* (New York: John Wiley & Sons, Inc., 1964).

[65] For a brief survey of many of these theories, see Daniel Glaser, "Social Disorganization and Delinquent Subcultures," in Quay, pp. 27–62.

[66] *New Forms of Juvenile Delinquency: Their Origin, Prevention and Treatment,* General Report by Wolf Middendorff, Judge, Federal Republic of Germany, Second United Nations Congress on the Prevention of Crime and the Treatment of Offenders, London, August 8–20, 1960 (New York: United Nations Department of Economic and Social Affairs, 1960), p. 43. Fyvel has examined gang delinquency in a number of countries. See T. R. Fyvel, *Troublemakers: Rebellious Youth in an Affluent Society* (New York: Schocken Books, Inc., 1962). Also see a study of French gangs in Philippe Parrot and Monique Gueneau, *Les Gangs d'Adolescents* (Paris: Presses Universitaires de France, 1959); and Edmund W. Vaz, "Juvenile Delinquency in Paris," *Social Problems,* 10:23–31 (1962). A study has also been made of adolescent delinquents in Sweden. See Dick Blomberg, *Den Svenska Ungdomsbrottsligheten* (Stockholm: Falu Nya Boktryckeri AB, 1960).

South Africa, Sweden, Australia, the Federal Republic of Germany, France, Japan, and the Philippines. Group delinquency of a nongang type, largely involving mass rioting and other forms of antisocial behavior, is widespread in many countries where the juveniles, are known as "halbustarke" (the half-matured) in Germany, "blousons noir" in France, "teddy boys" in England, "vitelloni" in Italy, "hooligans" in Poland and Russia, "bodgies" and "widgies" (girls) in Australia and New Zealand, "tsotsio" in South Africa, "mambo" boys and girls in Japan, and "titres" in Puerto Rico.[67] The problems of youth gangs are not confined to the Western world, but have been reported in the Soviet Union and its satellite countries. "East Germany's Communist rulers acknowledged today their deep concern over widespread juvenile delinquency and 'hooliganism' in the country. . . . Gangs of youthful trouble-makers have been arrested in recent months in Leipzig, Dresden and other East German industrial centers. In some cases the youths, armed with clubs, knives or pistols, battled the police, attacked passers-by or committed robberies." [68]

Among the several theories about gang delinquency, the most important may be outlined as follows: (1) the characteristics of lower-class culture, (2) hostility and rejection of middle-class values, (3) differential opportunity, (4) conflict in the transition from adolescence to adult status, and (5) social processes and status striving with the gang.

Lower-Class Culture

Gang delinquency, according to Miller, is concentrated in the male members of the lower class and is a product of lower-class culture.[69] The chief concerns of the lower-class culture are trouble (getting into it and staying out of it), toughness, smartness, excitement, fate, and autonomy. "Toughness" is highly valued in the form of "masculinity," physical prowess, strength, and skill in athletics. The gangster, the boxer, the tough guy, or the "hard" teacher become models. "Smartness" is duping and outsmarting the other guy. Such models are seldom the teacher but the "con" man or the "fast-man-with-a-buck." "Excitement" relieves the dullness of hanging around drab areas. Taking a risk appeals a great deal and is evident in goading teachers and policemen, picking up girls, destroying public prop-

---

[67] Middendorff, *New Forms of Juvenile Delinquency*, pp. 35–36.

[68] *The New York Times*, February 12, 1961.

[69] Walter B. Miller, "Lower Class Culture as a Generating Milieu of Gang Delinquency," *Journal of Social Issues*, 14:9 (1958). Also W. C. Kvaraceus and W. B. Miller, *Delinquent Behavior: Culture and the Individual* (Washington, D.C.: National Education Association, 1959). For a chart showing differences between values of the lower and middle class see p. 18.

erty, participating in a rumble, stealing a car, and joyriding. "Fate" is responsible when one is caught because of bad luck. "Autonomy" is the desire to be bossed around by others in a gang even though the members say they want to be their own bosses. There is a testing of authority to see if it is strict enough. The lower-class boy, therefore, wishing to belong and to achieve status, often joins delinquent groups which express these values. Delinquent acts not only provide status but are means of satisfying those factors which dominate the way of life of the lower class. Gang theft can be explained as related to being a male, in middle adolescence, and of the lower class.[70]

In some ways the focal concerns of the lower class are a tautology; they are derived from the observation of gang behavior which they seek to explain.[71] Moreover, the lower-class theory neglects the fact that middle-class values and agents also impinge on slum boys through the law and in school. The lower class itself is not homogeneous but consists of many subgroups, some ethnic and others regional; the focal concerns described by Miller are probably experienced most in the slums of large cities and less elsewhere. Miller's theory has the advantage, however, of telling us what lower-class boys are for rather than against as in that of the middle-class theory.[72] Most of all he deals basically with the slum community and the nature of the adult lower class culture. His theory does not satisfactorily explain middle class delinquency.[73]

Hostility Toward Middle-Class Values

Another explanation has suggested that the behavior of such delinquent gangs is a consequence of hostility toward middle-class values.[74] Such pertinent middle-class values include ambition, self-reliance, the postponement of immediate satisfactions, good manners and courtesy, wholesome recreation, opposition to physical violence, and respect for property. Lower-class boys, according to this theory, resent such dominant values because they have not been part of their world. Consequently, they also resent middle-class people, such as their schoolteachers, who consider them to have

---

[70] See Walter B. Miller, "Theft Behavior in City Gangs," in Klein, pp. 25–37.

[71] David Bordua, "A Critique of Sociological Interpretations of Gang Delinquency," in Wolfgang, *et al., The Sociology of Crime and Delinquency.*

[72] Bordua, p. 298.

[73] Edmund W. Vaz, ed., *Middle-Class Juvenile Delinquency* (New York: Harper & Row, Publishers, 1967).

[74] Albert K. Cohen, *Delinquent Boys: The Culture of the Gang* (New York: The Free Press, 1955). This provocative approach to delinquent gang behavior will have to be affirmed or rejected by subsequent research, as Cohen does little more than suggest it as a hypothesis. For a chart listing middle class values, see p. xxx.

low status because they do not exhibit middle-class values. Lower-class delinquent gangs are a natural consequence of certain boys of this class coming together because of common hostilities. The subculture they form is the opposite of middle-class values and is characterized by a malice toward things that are virtuous, a versatility in types of delinquent behavior, short-run hedonism involving nonutilitarian types of "fun" rather than long-range goals, and, finally, group autonomy or opposition to social control other than control by the group itself.

This theory of middle-class values has been severely criticized as lacking supporting research, as being too rational in its attribution of motivations to lower-class boys, and for assuming that lower-class boys actually aspire to middle-class norms.[75] Some question whether a gang member actually rejects middle-class standards as is claimed, but, instead, rationalizes his deviant behavior by techniques of neutralization or rationalization.[76]

Differential Opportunity

Somewhat related is the theory of differential opportunity of Cloward and Ohlin, who believe that delinquent subcultures arise where legitimate means to the attainment of the success goals of the dominant society, such as economic and higher educational opportunities, are blocked.[77] "The disparity between what lower-class youth are led to want and what is actually available to them is the source of a major problem of adjustment. Adolescents who form delinquent subcultures, we suggest, have internalized an emphasis upon conventional goals. Faced with limitations on legitimate avenues of access to these goals, and unable to revise their aspirations downward, they experience intense frustrations; the exploration of non-conformist alternatives may be the result." [78] Whether this deprivation will result in

---

[75] J. I. Kitsuse and D. C. Dietrick, "Delinquent Boys: A Critique," *American Sociological Review,* 24:211–212 (1959).

[76] Sykes and Matza, "Techniques of Neutralization."

[77] Cloward and Ohlin. Also see discussion on pages 157–158 in Chapter 5. According to their definition of delinquent subcultures, certain forms of delinquent activity are essential requirements for the performance of dominant social roles provided and supported by the subcultures. Such delinquent subcultures are characterized by a great frequency of criminal acts, stability, and resistance to change, and the recognition by members of a system of rules as binding upon their behavior. Legitimacy has been withdrawn from certain norms of law whose violations are regarded as illegitimate by official agency representatives. To these authors the acts of delinquent subcultures are much more deliberate and rational than Cohen, for example, has contended.

[78] Cloward and Ohlin, p. 86.

delinquency as well as the three types of gang delinquency which may arise depends, however, on the opportunity or availability of illegitimate means to obtain their goals and consequent status. In integrated slum areas where adult criminal patterns serve as models and opportunity structures are available, the subcultures will be *criminal* gangs engaged in thefts, extortion, and similar activities to achieve an illegal income and status. In unintegrated areas, characterized by mobility, transiency, and instability, such as new urban housing developments, where criminal patterns and opportunity structures are unavailable, models for delinquent behavior to achieve status come from other adolescents and tend to take the form of a *conflict* gang engaging in violence and vandalism. Another type, the *retreatist* gang or subculture whose gang members live in the slum, uses drugs and engages in other sensual experiences because its members find both legitimate and other illegitimate means to success closed to them. This type refuses to accept the moral validity of illegitimate means to status and success exemplified by stealing and vandalism.

In the differential opportunity theory the success-goal aspirations of slum boys are not clearly stated, except the economic and educational goals, and the theory assumes that these goals are more uniformly appreciated by subcultures in a society than is warranted. A major criticism of this theory is that it confuses the justificatory function—deprivation—with its causation. Members of delinquent gangs often find occupational opportunities blocked but this is a result of a long experience in gang activities rather than of more conventional experiences. "In short, Cloward and Ohlin run the risk of confusing justification and causation and of equating the end with the beginning." [79] Research applying this framework to actual gang behavior, moreover, has been limited and unconvincing.[80] One study found that although gang boys in general felt blocked in their opportunities, as measured by opportunity scores based on discrepancy between boys' aspirations and fathers' occupational levels, it did not explain the variations in gang behavior.[81] For example, Negro gang members felt deprived but Negro nongang lower-class boys had higher deprivation scores and less

---

[79] Bordua, p. 300.

[80] One study has tried to show this but the methodology was poor. See Irving Spergel, *Racketville, Slumtown, Haulberg: An Exploratory Study of Delinquent Cultures* (Chicago: University of Chicago Press, 1964). For a more convincing but not conclusive study, see Elmer Luchterhand and Leonard Weller, "Delinquency Theory and the Middle-Size City: A Study of Problem and Promising Youth," *The Sociological Quarterly*, 7:413–423 (1966).

[81] James F. Short, Jr., "Gang Delinquency and Anomie," in Marshall B. Clinard, ed., *Anomie and Deviant Behavior* (New York: The Free Press, 1964), p. 107.

delinquency than gang members. Opportunity scores did not predict behavior. Gang boys appreciate middle-class values but what is important to
them is actually linked to more immediate contexts, such as being a male
member of a gang and the immediate, on-going processes rather than
detached, cultural goals as the differential opportunity theory maintains.
Moreover, the existence of separate types of gangs—criminal, conflict, and
retreatist—could not be substantiated in a study.[82] An English study in two
east London boroughs found that the Cohen and the Cloward and Ohlin
hypotheses did not offer a satisfactory explanation.[83] Illegal behavior, which
largely stems from a desire to secure adolescent goals associated with recreation, can be more credibly explained in the working-class context; delinquency is not a product of "alienation" or of "status frustration" but
rather a process of dissociation from middle-class-dominated contexts of
school, work, and recreation.

Adolescence and Social Status

A fourth explanation is that gangs arise out of the conflict created by
the transition from adolescence to adult status.[84] In urban society there
is no equivalent of the ceremonies and other "rites of passage," such as
puberty ceremonies, found among preliterate societies which symbolized
transition to adult status. Despite his aspirations and his physical readiness
for adult status, the adolescent is kept in a condition of social and economic
and legal dependency by the withholding of adult symbols, such as money,
personal autonomy, and sexual relations, thus creating pressure to engage
in deviant behavior to secure what adolescents regard as symbols of this
adult status. One method of gaining status is to form gangs whereby adolescents may attain among their peers the equivalent of adult status and a feeling of power through demonstrating that they are independent, tough, and
capable of flaunting adult authority.[85] In delinquent gangs this is expressed
to the full. As an illustration, possession of an automobile becomes among
adolescents a symbol of adulthood, and may often be used for sexual experiences as well. Some may steal automobiles for this purpose and to
demonstrate their toughness. In this connection some have suggested that
one solution to gang delinquency might be to find some really constructive

---

[82] James F. Short, Jr., and Fred L. Strodtbeck, *Group Process and Gang Delinquency* (Chicago: University of Chicago Press, 1965), pp. 99–100.

[83] David M. Downes, *The Delinquent Solution: A Study in Subcultural Theory*
(New York: The Free Press, 1966).

[84] Herbert Bloch and Arthur Niederhoffer, *The Gang: A Study in Adolescent
Behavior* (New York: Philosophical Library, Inc., 1958).

[85] For a similar but later formulation see Gerald Marwell, "Adolescent Powerlessness and Delinquency," *Social Problems*, 14:35–47 (1966).

work for adolescents to perform for themselves and for the community, so that they would be able more adequately and quickly to achieve adult status.[86] Others have suggested greater integration into the adult world rather than participation of the adolescent primarily in adolescent institutions such as the school and youth groups.[87] Bloch and Niederhoffer fail to show how the status deprivation of adolescence leads some to delinquency but not others.

Status Striving Within the Gang

An intensive study of Chicago gangs by Short and Strodtbeck found that the behavior of the delinquent gang is largely to be explained by processes within the group rather than by forces from outside.[88] They found that the behavior is largely a product of status strivings within the gang rather than a result of limitation on class mobility; the delinquent boys' self-concept in the context of the group is what is important. Some delinquent acts, in fact, have status-maintaining functions, as seen in the attempts of the gang leader to maintain his status when threatened. He does this by getting the gang to commit delinquent acts. Thus gang behavior is a rational balancing of immediate loss of status within the group and the risk of punishment.

Gang delinquency is not so much, then, a failure to achieve membership in the middle class or a failure to attain certain adult goals in society as it is a failure to achieve status within the context of adult, middle-class-dominated institutions, such as the school, the church, and economic and political institutions. The formation of the delinquent subculture involves the establishment of new groups with new rules by which members may compete successfully to obtain status. The solutions for lower-class boys

---

[86] Erik Erikson, *Childhood and Society* (New York: W .W. Norton & Company, Inc., 1950).

[87] F. Musgrove, *Youth and the Social Order* (Bloomington: Indiana University Press, 1965). Also see James S. Coleman, *The Adolescent Society: The Social Life of the Teenager and Its Impact on Education* (New York: The Free Press, 1963); and David Gottlieb and Charles Ramsey, *The American Adolescent* (Homewood, Ill.; The Dorsey Press, Inc., 1964).

[88] Short and Strodtbeck. Also see James F. Short, Jr., and Fred L. Strodtbeck, "The Response of Gang Leaders to Status Threats: An Observation on Group Process and Delinquent Behavior," *American Journal of Sociology,* 68:571–579 (1963); James F. Short, Jr., Ray A. Tennyson, and Kenneth I. Howard, "Behavior Dimensions of Gang Delinquency," *American Sociological Review,* 28:411–429 (1963); and James F. Short, Jr., and Fred L. Strodtbeck, "Aleatory Risks versus Short-Run Hedonism in Explanation of Gang Action," *Social Problems,* 12:127–140 (1964).

provided by delinquent subcultures are primarily status-rewarding rather than economically rewarding, as suggested by the differential opportunity explanation. Money acquired by gang boys tends to be spent for status rewards within the group, for example, twenty-dollar hats, and for "kicks," alcoholic beverages and drugs.

The concentration of Short and Strodtbeck on the dynamics of the gang offers a useful and sound approach to the social acts which constitute delinquency. On the other hand, their analysis largely neglects the norms of the local community in which the delinquent gang behavior tends to take place. It also fails to see the gang as an aspect of the larger youth culture and the clash between the values of youth and those of the larger urban social world particularly represented by adult legal norms.

SUMMARY

The chief sources of delinquent and criminal behavior appear to be the general culture, the neighborhood, and associates. Of particular importance in the culture as a whole are the general and selective disobedience to law. It is unlikely that any person, without previous deviant patterns, would engage in delinquency or crime only because of crime stories on television, in motion pictures, and influences arising from secondary sources. Delinquents who have already had association with deviant norms through other influences may be further stimulated by certain types of motion pictures and television programs.

The role of the family in delinquency and crime does not appear to be as important as many think. There is considerable variation in family integration, and there are now other institutions and influences which are also sources of deviant norms. There is little evidence to indicate that the family is the source of delinquent patterns, or that broken homes are significantly related to delinquency. Similarly, there is no conclusive evidence that the lack of emotional security in family relationships leads to delinquency and crime.

Present evidence seems to indicate that social norms, both deviant and conventional, are primarily acquired through personal experiences of a face-to-face nature. Neighborhood influences and certain occupational situations may furnish a setting favorable to the development of delinquent and criminal behavior. Delinquent companions are extremely important, as are delinquent gangs. Such gangs disseminate techniques of committing offenses, help the individual delinquent to progress in crime, encourage mutual excitation and common activities in connection with delinquency and crime, give social status to the delinquent, and develop in him opposition to authority.

Several theories of gang behavior have attempted to provide a central framework for explaining delinquency in terms of basic concepts such as social class, role, and status aspirations. But they are recent, and thus far little research has been done to prove or disprove them. Each seems to make a contribution, but each, as an all-inclusive explanation, is deficient. Most of them are actually attempts to explain the reasons for gang delinquency in lower-class areas in large urban communities of the United States. Whether such explanations are sufficient to explain the delinquency in middle-class or rural areas in the United States, or the delinquency of other countries with different values and class structures, is open to some question. Subcultural gang delinquency may be more accurately explained by the lack of communication among various age peer groups which has arisen with pronounced urbanism, with the consequent development of adolescent subcultures, together with the acquisition of deviant norms as forms of status and excitement, particularly in slum areas, but in other areas as well.

SELECTED READINGS

Bloch, Herbert A., and Arthur Niederhoffer. *The Gang: A Study in Adolescent Behavior.* New York: Philosophical Library, Inc., 1958. An analysis of the behavior of adolescents in a variety of cultures. Gang delinquency in American society, these authors maintain, results from the difficulty of adolescents in achieving adult status.

Bordua, David. "A Critique of Sociological Interpretations of Gang Delinquency," in Marvin E. Wolfgang, Leonard Savitz, and Norman Johnston, eds., *The Sociology of Crime and Delinquency.* New York: John Wiley & Sons, Inc., 1962, pages 289–301. An excellent critique of a number of the leading theories of gang delinquency.

Cloward, Richard A., and Lloyd E. Ohlin. *Delinquency and Opportunity: A Theory of Delinquent Gangs.* New York: The Free Press, 1960. An explanation of how delinquent gangs arise, recruit their members, develop law-violating ways of life, and persist or change. Basically the explanation follows anomie with the addition of the concepts of differential opportunity.

Cohen, Albert K. *Delinquent Boys: The Culture of the Gang.* New York: The Free Press, 1955. An analysis of delinquent gangs in terms of social class differences.

Downes, David M. *The Delinquent Solution: A Study in Subcultural Theory.* New York: The Free Press, 1966. A comparative examination of theories of gang delinquency using research conducted on delinquents in east London. The book also contains an excellent description and critique of the various theories of gang behavior.

Glueck, Sheldon and Eleanor. *Unraveling Juvenile Delinquency.* Cambridge, Mass.: Harvard University Press, 1950. A comparison of 500 delinquents and nondelinquents on a large number of factors. Probably the best-known study of delinquency chiefly in terms of the family and certain personality traits.

Klein, Malcolm W., ed. *Juvenile Gangs in Context: Theory, Research, and Action.* Englewood Cliffs, N.J.: Prentice-Hall, Inc., 1967. A group of more recent articles and research studies dealing with juvenile gang delinquency.

Kobrin, Solomon. "The Conflict of Values in Delinquency Areas," *American Sociological Review,* 16:653–661 (1951). A discussion of the social norms and values of areas of high delinquency.

Miller, Walter B. "Lower Class Culture as a Generating Milieu of Gang Delinquency," *Journal of Social Issues,* 14:5–19, No. 3 (1958). Juvenile delinquency is explained as a product of the way of life of lower-class subculture.

Schramm, Wilbur, Jack Lyle, and Edwin B. Parker. *Television in the Lives of Our Children.* Stanford, Calif.: Stanford University Press, 1961. An analysis of the effects of television in the lives of over 6000 children.

Short, James F., Jr., and Fred L. Strodtbeck. *Group Process and Gang Delinquency.* Chicago: University of Chicago Press, 1965. A study of juvenile gangs in Chicago in terms of self-conception, status within the gang, and group process.

Thrasher, Frederic M. *The Gang.* Chicago: University of Chicago Press, 1963. This study of 1313 gangs in Chicago, originally published in 1929, is one of the most widely known books in criminology.

Vaz, Edmund W., ed. *Middle-Class Juvenile Delinquency.* New York: Harper & Row, Publishers, 1967. This series of theoretical and research articles deals with middle class delinquency.

8

Types of Criminal Offenders

The terms *delinquent* and *criminal* do not refer to a homogeneous group and have little meaning except as they refer to lawbreakers. There are various types and kinds of delinquent and criminal offenders, depending on whether the offenders are classified by types of crime committed, by characteristics such as sex and age, or in terms of behavior systems. Classification by offense is useful in studying the legal definitions of offenses; classification by sex, age, and other characteristics of offenders is necessary in enumerations for statistical purposes. From a scientific or sociological point of view, however, offenders are best grouped according to their behavior patterns and the processes through which criminal behavior is developed. An adequate explanation of delinquent and criminal behavior should show how it applies to all delinquent and criminal behavior, and how it should be modified to explain various types.[1]

Among the many problems confronting the student of juvenile delinquency, for example, probably none is more perplexing or elusive than that designated "juvenile delinquency." The various definitions of this

---

[1] Marshall B. Clinard and Richard Quinney, *Criminal Behavior Systems: A Typology* (New York: Holt, Rinehart and Winston, Inc., 1967).

term found in recent textbooks and monographs attest to the lack of agreement as to what juvenile delinquency is. Not only has the concept been subject to a variety of definitions; it has become an omnibus designation. Thus, as currently employed, the term *juvenile delinquency* has the doubtful function of being an inclusive category, often applied indiscriminately to much juvenile behavior in general. This confusing situation has affected the type of research done in this area. A typological approach to delinquency permits concentration upon problems of limited scope and enables one to deal with manageable groups characterized by relatively homogeneous behavior.[2] To understand delinquency more fully the various career patterns and types of offenses of delinquents must be studied.

CLASSIFICATION BY CRIME, SEX, OR AGE

Criminal offenders are often classified, from a legal point of view, by the *type of crime*, such as murder, arson, and burglary. Such a classification enables us, presumably, to group offenders neatly according to what they did, and to show something of the tolerance limits of crimes as reflected in the different penalties of the criminal law. This method of grouping may be quite misleading, inasmuch as persons of extremely diverse types may commit the same type of crime; moreover, the seriousness of a criminal act is not always correlated with criminal behavior patterns in offenders. Distinctions based on misdemeanants and felons are also unsatisfactory.

The major legal division of crimes is into personal and property crimes. Personal crimes actually constitute a small proportion of all reported crime, less than 9 percent in 1965, with murders and nonnegligent manslaughter but a tiny fraction of all crime. During 1965 an estimated 2,141,037 major property crimes were reported to the police, but only some 238,978 personal crimes. (See Table 8.1.) There were 762,352 reported larcenies and 1,173,201 burglaries, as compared with 9850 murders and cases of nonnegligent manslaughter. The distribution of types of crimes varies somewhat between different countries and between developed and less developed countries.[3]

---

[2] Marshall B. Clinard and Andrew L. Wade, "Toward the Delineation of Vandalism as a Sub-Type in Juvenile Delinquency," *Journal of Criminal Law, Criminology, and Police Science,* 48:493–499 (1958). Also see Theodore N. Ferdinand, *Typologies of Delinquency: A Critical Analysis* (New York: Random House, Inc., 1966).

[3] *Prevention of Types of Criminality Resulting from Social Changes and Accompanying Economic Development in Less Developed Countries,* General Reports to the Second United Nations Congress on the Prevention of Crime and the Treatment of Offenders (London, August 8–20, 1960) by J. J. Panakal and A. M. Khalifa (New York: United Nations Department of Economic and Social Affairs, 1960).

TABLE 8.1   **Major Crimes Reported to the Police in the United States During 1965**

Crime index classification	Estimated number of offenses [a]	Percentage of total
Murder and nonnegligent manslaughter	9,850	0.4
Forcible rape	22,467	0.8
Robbery	118,916	4.3
Aggravated assault	206,661	7.4
Burglary	1,173,201	42.2
Larceny $50 and over	762,352	27.4
Auto theft	486,568	17.5
Total	2,780,015	100.0

[a] Based on reports to law enforcement agencies in 1965.
SOURCE: Federal Bureau of Investigation, *Uniform Crime Reports* (Annual Bulletin, 1965; Washington, D.C.: Government Printing Office, 1961), p. 51.

Delinquents and criminals may be classified according to *sex*. This distinction had more significance when nearly all offenses committed by women were prostitution and drunkenness, but women now engage in as wide a variety of offenses as do men, although not as frequently. Women are increasingly becoming involved in cases of embezzlement and forgery. They are also involved as associates of men in many cases of property crime, although they are rarely charged. During 1965 women committed about 12 percent of a selected group of major offenses in the United States. In cases of embezzlement and fraud, larceny and theft, and homicide their proportion was considerably greater. The ratio of arrests for embezzlement and fraud, larceny and theft, and murder is approximately 6 men to every 1 woman; assault, 7 to 1; robbery, 22 to 1; and burglary, 30 to 1.

Although it is increasingly difficult to distinguish clearly among offenses in terms of the sex of the offender, the apparently low ratio of crimes committed by women raises a number of questions. Some people have attributed this low ratio to factors other than the low criminality rate of women. Some have suggested that women offenders often play a part in crimes committed by men offenders but that they are not as easily detected in crime as men. Others have suggested that because women can engage in prostitution they need not turn to burglary or larceny. Even with these allowances, however, the low incidence of crime among women is indicative of the importance of social rather than personality factors in crime. Certainly there must be the same range of personality traits among women as among men and the former now participate sufficiently in the general society to be able to steal a car or burglarize a home. More significant is the fact that women do not as frequently belong to gangs and are more isolated from criminal norms. And it has been suggested that women more often develop a conception of themselves in terms of future parental responsibilities, making their participation in serious crimes less likely.

Another distinction often made is the classification of offenders by *age,* with younger and older offenders supposedly denoting different degrees of criminal development. Offenders committing the serious crimes are most frequently under twenty-five. (See Table 8.2.) The group with the highest arrest rate, excluding traffic offenses, contained those between fifteen through seventeen and was also the group with the highest arrest rate for larceny, burglary, and motor vehicle theft. The next highest age group was 18—20; after that the rates drop off directly with an increase in age. Although all types of crimes are committed by persons of all ages, there is a much greater probability of young persons being arrested for the most serious felonies. (See Table 8.3.) Although the age group 11–17 represents only 13.2 percent of the population, during 1965 approximately one in every two burglars arrested was under eighteen, two thirds (61.4) of all those arrested for auto theft were under eighteen, and over one fourth (28.0 percent) of all those arrested for robbery. Over two thirds (67.5 percent) of the persons arrested in 1965 for robbery and nearly three fourths (71.1 percent) of those arrested for larceny were under twenty-five, as well as nearly nine out of ten (87.8 percent) of the automobile thieves and three fourths of the burglars. If one combines larceny, burglary, and motor vehicle theft, one half (50.5 percent) of those arrested for these offenses were under eighteen and three fourths were under twenty-five (75.2 percent). One fifth of all forcible rapes are committed by those under eighteen and nearly two-thirds by those under twenty-five. A different picture is revealed for arrests for other offenses, particularly those involving drunkenness and gambling violations, homicide, aggravated assault, and white-collar and professional crime, which are largely committed by the older age groups. Two-thirds of all those who commit homicide, for example, are twenty-five or over.

In all probability the age at which ordinary crimes are committed is even lower than the figures suggest. In the first place, many of those in the age group 14–16 are not included, for the figures cited above are computed from fingerprint cards; moreover, juvenile offenders are often not fingerprinted or their fingerprints may not be reported to the FBI. In the second place, arrests tabulated in a given year *do not indicate the age at first arrest.* If it were possible to know when offenses *first* started, a greater frequency might be found even below fourteen years of age.

Classification of offenders by age has little merit, for the "hardness" of an offender has little relation to his age. An offender is "hardened" if he has definite antisocial attitudes toward laws, property, and the police, professional knowledge of the techniques used to commit crimes and avoid

TABLE 8.2   **Arrest Rates for Different Age Groups—1965**
(Rates per 100,000 population)

Age groups	Arrests rates for all offenses (excluding traffic)	Arrest rates for willful homicide, forcible rape, robbery, aggravated assault	Arrest rates for larceny, burglary, motor vehicle theft
11–14	3064.4	71.0	1292.3
15–17	8050.0	222.8	2467.0
18–20	7539.6	299.8	1452.0
21–24	6547.2	296.6	833.7
25–29	5366.2	233.6	506.7
30–34	5085.8	177.5	354.4
35–39	4987.4	132.5	260.4
40–44	4675.3	98.0	185.4
45–49	4102.0	65.3	131.9
50 and over	1987.4	24.2	55.2
Overall rate	3349.9	99.9	461.5

SOURCE: FBI, Uniform Crime Reports Section, unpublished data. Estimates for total U.S. population, as prepared and presented in *The Challenge of Crime in a Free Society*, A Report by the President's Commission on Law Enforcement and Administration of Justice (Washington, D.C.: Government Printing Office, 1967), p. 56.

prosecution, and a framework of rationalizations to support his conduct. These attitudes may be well developed in a boy of seventeen and yet be absent in a "criminal" of forty. For example, 68.9 percent of all robberies are committed by persons under twenty-five, an offense which is almost always preceded by other crimes, which usually involves the use of a gun, and which indicates definite antisocial attitudes.

In recent years the number of delinquency arrests has increased sharply in the United States, as it has in several Western European countries studied by the Commission. Between 1960 and 1965, arrests of persons under 18 years of age jumped 52 percent, for willful homicide, rape, robbery, aggravated assault, larceny, burglary, and motor vehicle theft. During the same period, arrests of persons 18 and over for these offenses rose only 20 percent. This is explained in large part by the disproportionate increase in the population under 18 and, in particular, the crime-prone part of that population—the 11- to 17-year-old age group.

Official figures may give a somewhat misleading picture of crime trends. Over the years there has been a tendency toward more formal records and actions, particularly in the treatment of juveniles. In addition,

Deviant Behavior

TABLE 8.3 **Percent of Arrests Accounted for by Different Age Groups 1965 (Percent of Total)**

POPULATION	Persons 11–17 13.2	Persons 18–24 10.2	Persons 25 and over 53.5
Willful homicide	8.4	26.4	65.1
Forcible rape	19.8	44.6	35.6
Robbery	28.0	39.5	31.4
Aggravated assault	14.2	26.5	58.7
Burglary	47.7	29.0	19.7
Larceny (includes larceny under $50)	49.2	21.9	24.3
Motor vehicle theft	61.4	26.4	11.9
Willful homicide, rape, robbery, aggravated assault	18.3	31.7	49.3
Larceny, burglary, motor vehicle theft	50.5	24.7	21.2

SOURCE: FBI, Uniform Crime Reports Section, unpublished data. Estimates for total U.S. population, as prepared and presented in *The Challenge of Crime in a Free Society*, p. 56.

police efficiency may well have increased. But, considering other factors together with the official statistics, the Commission is of the opinion that juvenile delinquency has increased significantly in recent years.

The juvenile population has been rising, and at a faster rate than the adult population. And an increasing proportion of our society is living in the cities where delinquency rates have always been highest.[4]

DELINQUENT AND CRIMINAL BEHAVIOR SYSTEMS

A more useful way of distinguishing between criminal offenders is a criminal typology based on *behavior systems*. This involves four aspects; the criminal career of the offender, the group support of criminal behavior, the correspondence between criminal and legitimate behavior patterns, and the societal reaction to the behavior.[5]

———

[4] *The Challenge of Crime in a Free Society*, A Report by the President's Commission on Law Enforcement and Administration of Justice (Washington, D.C.: Government Printing Office, 1967), p. 56.

[5] Clinard and Quinney, pp. 7–18. For a somewhat different and more detailed typology see Don C. Gibbons, *Changing the Lawbreaker: The Treatment of Delinquents and Criminals* (Englewood Cliffs, N.J.: Prentice-Hall, Inc., 1965).

Criminal Career of the Offender

The criminal career of the offender is determined by the extent to which he has moved from primary to secondary deviations. It includes playing a criminal role, conception of self, progression in crime, and the extent to which criminal behavior has identified with and become a part of the life organization of the offender.

Social Roles

Although individuals may commit offenses which are legally similar, this behavior actually has a different significance for each. In some individuals their delinquent and criminal activity may represent only a minor and relatively unimportant part of their social roles and life organization. Delinquency and crime may pervade the lives of others. This degree of incorporation of delinquent and criminal attitudes in life organization reflects, for one thing, the relative degree of development of criminal social roles and identification with an antisocial way of life. Thus offenders may play roles varying all the way from an amateur, an occasional offender to a "tough guy," a "young punk," a "smart operator," a "big shot," a "strong-arm man," and "the Big Boss."

> In many respects delinquency and criminal experience do to the person just about what athletic, theatrical, sales, military, and many other semiprofessional and professional experiences do to individuals. The experience inures and steeps. It becomes integrated into the life organization of the person, establishing habits and attitudes, determining consciousness of kind and conception of self, and fixing the development of a successful role or justification of a less successful one. The behavior trend line of a life organization built out of delinquency, crime, and allied experience is more delinquency, crime, and allied behavior. The problem is for the person to revise his scheme of life and reorganize himself on a different basis. This would be true if the person took a desk job in an office and left the road as a salesman or if a newspaper reporter became an undertaker or a university professor became a barker in a circus.[6]

Similarly the social role of a "delinquent" is often different from the legal category in which he is placed by the courts. The labeling "delinquent" may bring with it the playing of a definite social role, as Cohen and Short have indicated.

---

[6] Walter C. Reckless, *The Crime Problem* (New York: Appleton-Century-Crofts, Inc., 1950), p. 35.

But the category "delinquent" as a social "role" of everyday life is not identical with "delinquent" as a legal category. That is, the criteria by which the man in the street defines somebody as delinquent and the images, feelings and dispositions that the word arouses are not identical with the criteria and consequences in the world of the courts. The social role of delinquent entails consequences over and above those provided by law. If a boy is defined as delinquent in the world of everyday life, his whole social world may be transformed: the ways in which other people see him, how they feel toward him, their willingness to associate with him, the activities and opportunities that are open to him. In consequence of these changes, the way in which the boy sees, labels and evaluates himself, his estimate of his chances and prospects in the world of nondelinquent and conventional people, his notion of whether trying to avoid delinquency is worth the trouble, may be profoundly affected. It is quite possible, indeed, that being invested with the social role may so narrow a person's opportunities for the rewards and gratifications of nondelinquent society that it may strengthen his tendency to behavior that is delinquent in the legal sense.[7]

Conception of Self

Closely associated with identification with delinquency or crime is the conception of himself and of his social role which a delinquent or a criminal offender develops. He may feel that he is essentially a "good boy" who has really done nothing more than make a technical mistake from the legal point of view, or he may regard his activities as isolated transgressions. On the other hand, he may regard himself as tough, antisocial, or even criminal. In one study farm boys were found to have conceptions of themselves as "wild" and "reckless," whereas city offenders with more pronounced activities in crime spoke of themselves as "hard," "tough," "criminal," "mean," or "no good." [8] Lower- and middle-class delinquents have been found to have pronounced differences in their self-conceptions and these differences appear to be reflected in the greater extent and more serious delinquency of lower-class boys.[9]

A conception of oneself as a delinquent or a criminal may become so

---

[7] Albert K. Cohen and James F. Short, Jr., "Juvenile Delinquency," in Robert K. Merton and Robert A. Nisbet, *Contemporary Social Patterns* (New York: Harcourt, Brace & World, Inc., 1966), pp. 87–88.

[8] Marshall B. Clinard, "The Process of Urbanization and Criminal Behavior," *American Journal of Sociology,* 48:202–213 (1942).

[9] Leon Fannin and Marshall B. Clinard, "Differences in the Conception of Self as Male among Lower and Middle Class Delinquents," *Social Problems,* 13:205–214 (1965).

well developed that the individual believes he is at war with society and that he is constantly being mistreated and persecuted by the police. In fact, societal reaction in the form of law-enforcement agencies is related to the acquisition of one's self-conception as a delinquent or a criminal, and for this reason the first arrest or incarceration is of prime importance in an offender's life organization.

Once an offender has developed the conception of himself as a delinquent, prostitute, confidence man, robber, or forger, it is often hard to change it. The following comments show how a group of reformatory inmates looked upon themselves.

> The gang I went with was some older boys than me and some were younger than I was, and all of us thought we were very tough.
>
> I had the reputation of being a tough guy. I am afraid that if there was anybody that had anything that I wanted I would find some way to get it if I had to steal it.
>
> I got in so many fights that some people started calling me a roughneck.

Sociological studies have suggested differences in self-conception as the reason that certain children residing in a delinquency area do not become delinquents.[10] In a study of 125 "good boys" and 108 potential delinquents in this area, the authors concluded: "Conception of self and others is the differential response component that helps to explain why some succumb and others do not, why some gravitate toward socially unacceptable patterns of behavior and others veer away from them." [11] Additional research in this direction may furnish valuable insights into why so many middle- and upper-class boys do not engage in delinquency and may help to explain the differential response patterns of adults, including white-collar workers, to criminal norms.

---

[10] Reckless, Dinitz, and Murray; Walter C. Reckless, Simon Dinitz, and Ellen Murray, "The Good Boy in a High Delinquency Area," *Journal of Criminal Law, Criminology, and Police Science,* 48:18–25 (1957); and Walter C. Reckless, Simon Dinitz, and Barbara Kay, "Self-Component In Potential Delinquency and Non-Delinquency," *American Sociological Review,* 22:566–570 (1957). Also see Walter C. Reckless, Simon Dinitz, and Ellen Murray, "Self Concept as an Insulator against Delinquency," *American Sociological Review,* 21:744–746 (1956). For a critical survey of research on the self concept as a variable in delinquency, see Sandra S. Tangri and Michael Schwartz, "Delinquency Research and the Self-Concept Variable," *The Journal of Criminal Law, Criminology, and Police Science,* 58:182–191 (1967).

[11] Reckless, Dinitz, and Kay, p. 570.

Progression in Crime

The history of a criminal career type is a progressive series of steps in the acquisition of criminal techniques and knowledge. This progression varies with different types of crimes. Burglars and robbers, for example, show a progression from petty theft to more serious larcenies, to crimes such as ordinary burglary or automobile theft, and then on to highly skilled burglary or armed robbery. Criminality may proceed from trivial to more serious crimes, from being a sport to being a business, and from occasional crime to more frequent crime. Along with progression in crime the offender develops a philosophy of life which justifies his criminal actions.

Identification with Crime

The individual may gain considerable satisfaction from the acceptance of group norms and will orient his life around them. Thus if a boy identifies himself with the activities of a group of "young punks," this relationship may become as satisfying as if he identified his activities with a group of boy scouts. Yet mere membership in a group or contact with deviant norms does not tell us what such behavior means to the individual. Criminality is the result of a person's identification with others to whom his criminal behavior seems acceptable.[12]

Group Support Criminal Behavior

Although most crime is learned from association with others, there are variations in the extent to which the behavior of a criminal offender is supported by norms of the group or groups to which he belongs. Some of these may be companions, gangs, occupations, or local communities. This includes the differential association of the offender with both criminal and noncriminal norms, and the integration of the offender into deviant social groups.

Most delinquency and crime are learned as anything else is learned and are a product of *differential association* with criminal norms.[13] There

---

[12] Daniel Glaser, "Criminality Theories and Behavioral Images," *American Journal of Sociology,* 61:433–445 (1956).

[13] The theory of differential association was originally developed by Edwin H. Sutherland nearly thirty years ago and has become the leading sociological framework for explaining the development of criminal behavior. See Edwin H. Sutherland and Donald R. Cressey, *Principles of Criminology* (7th ed.; Philadelphia: J. B. Lippincott Company, 1966), pp. 77–100. The details of the theory have been criticized and slightly modified but remain essentially the same, namely, a learning theory of criminality. Some modifications have included the addition of the self-concept, reference groups, and differential identification. For a discussion see Donald R. Cressey, "Epidemiology and Individual Conduct: A Case from Criminol-

is differential association with the pushes and pulls of conventional and criminal norms; contacts with some norms tend to push the individual away from criminal behavior whereas others pull him toward it. An important part of an offender's role is the extent to which a lawbreaker acquires the techniques, rationalizations, and philosophy of a criminal career.[14]

Delinquency and crime are learned in interaction with other persons; intimate and personal associations undoubtedly have the greatest influence in the acquisition of delinquent and criminal norms. Most of these associations are likely to be of a group nature. Their effect depends on the frequency, duration, priority, and intensity of exposure to conventional and criminal norms. The *frequency* of such an association and its *duration* have much to do with the development of a delinquent or criminal career. Exposure to delinquent norms in such an association early in life gives them *priority* in determining whether or not a criminal career will develop. The *intensity* of the association is related to the prestige of persons with criminal norms with whom an individual associates and to his reactions to such persons.

Correspondence between Criminal Behavior and Legitimate Behavior

Criminal acts vary in the extent to which the criminal behavior is consistent with legitimate patterns of behavior in the society. This includes the extent to which criminal behavior corresponds to valued goals and means which are regarded as legitimate by the dominant or power segments of

---

ogy," *Pacific Sociological Review,* 3:47–58 (1960). Also see Robert L. Burgess and Ronald L. Akers, "A Differential Association-Reinforcement Theory of Criminal Behavior," *Social Problems,* 14:128–147 (1966); Melvin L. DeFleur and Richard Quinney, "A Reformulation of Sutherland's Differential Association Theory and a Strategy for Empirical Verification," *Journal of Research in Crime and Delinquency,* 3:1–22 (1966); Donald R. Cressey, "The Language of Set Theory and Differential Association," *Journal of Research in Crime and Delinquency,* 3:22–27 (1966); Albert J. Reiss, Jr., and A. Lewis Rhodes, "An Empirical Test of Differential Association Theory," *Journal of Research in Crime and Delinquency,* 1:5–18 (1964); Daniel Glaser, "Differential Association and Criminological Prediction," *Social Problems,* 8:6–14 (1960); Henry D. McKay, "Differential Association and Crime Prevention: Problems of Utilization," *Social Problems,* 8:25–37 (1960); Harwin L. Voss, "Differential Association and Reported Delinquent Behavior: A Replication," *Social Problems,* 12:78–85 (1964); and C .R. Jeffery, "Criminal Behavior and Learning Theory," *Journal of Criminal Law, Criminology, and Police Science,* 56:294–300 (1965).

[14] Frank E. Hartung, *Crime, Law and Society* (Detroit: Wayne State University Press, 1965), pp. 62–88.

the society. Businessmen who commit white-collar offenses, for example, have many rationalizations that they are contributing to the goals of society in making wealth and producing goods. The values of the political offender, such as the conscientious objector, who seeks to "improve" society by his actions are different in nature but similar to those of the total society. On the other hand, the correspondence between the goals of most conventional criminals and the norms of legitimate society is slight.

Societal Reaction

Finally, society regards most types of crime in different ways, reacting more strongly to one than to another. The reactions may take the form of informal censure or official, formal control, such as enforcement of the law through prosecution, conviction, and sentencing, or through civil or administrative action by governmental agencies. Occupational crime and organized crime are reacted to differently with different degrees of punishment. Likewise, offenders of certain types are not as likely to encounter enforcement measures. Labeling by arrest, conviction, or imprisonment has important effects on the self-conception of the criminal offender.

CAREER AND NONCAREER OFFENDERS

Placed in a broader perspective, criminal offenders can be classified according to whether or not they are career offenders or secondary deviants. The distinction between a criminal career and a noncriminal career involves the extent to which delinquent and criminal norms are incorporated in the person to produce delinquent and criminal acts and how this behavior is viewed by the person. Most personal offenders are of the noncareer type, or primary criminal deviants, whereas property offenders are more likely to be of the career type. The most highly developed criminal careers are professional and organized criminals.

A criminal career as distinguished from a noncriminal career involves a life organization of roles built about criminal activities, such as identification with crime, a conception of self as a criminal, extensive association with criminal activities, including other criminals, and, finally, progression in crime. Progression in crime means the acquistion of more complex techniques, more frequent offenses, and, ultimately, dependence on crime as a frequent or sole means of livelihood. Among career offenders group and subcultural factors are extremely important.

Career criminals make crime a definite part of their life organization. They maintain association not only with other criminals but with those persons, such as shady politicians, who may be helpful in the continuation of their way of life. They develop techniques, "a level of operation," and

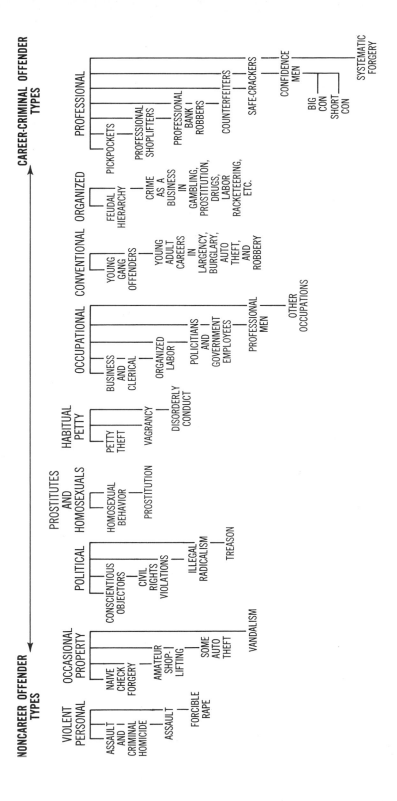

FIGURE 8.1 Selected Types of Delinquent and Criminal Behavior

a philosophy of life to go with it. Frequently it is a full-time occupation and their sole means of livelihood. These offenders often concentrate in certain fields of crime. In fact, the police often proceed on this assumption and develop a *modus operandi* file which frequently enables them to pick up burglars, forgers, counterfeiters, safe-crackers, or armed robbers. Professional criminal careers are developed almost entirely within the field of property crimes.[15] For example, in American society, murderers do not ordinarily make a career out of killing, although this practice exists in the Middle East, where one may hire a professional killer for a price. Likewise, rape and aggravated assault are seldom thought of as career crimes. Even persons with a history of a long series of criminal activities may not have a real criminal career.

Offenders can be divided into the following types along a continuum from noncareer to career and embodying the nature of the group support, the relation to noncriminal values, and the societal reaction. At one end of the continuum are violent personal criminals and occasional property offenders; at the other end are organized and professional offenders. In between are public-order offenders, political criminals, habitual petty criminals, occupational criminals, and conventional criminal careers.[16] (See fig. 8. 1.)

VIOLENT PERSONAL CRIMES

Those who commit criminal homicide, assault, and forcible rape constitute a single type termed *violent personal offenders.* All involve the use of violence to accomplish their objective, whether it is argument or personal dispute or sexual intercourse. The type of criminal homicide we shall discuss here consists of both murder and nonnegligent manslaughter, but does not include justifiable homicide, attempts or assaults to kill, or accidental deaths. Another type of criminal homicide also not included is negligent manslaughter, in which a death is attributable to the negligence of some other person than the victim. Technically "murder" is determined by the police and the court through a legal process. In aggravated assault there is an attempt to use physical force to settle an argument or a dispute. Nearly all criminal homicide represents some form of aggravated assault, the chief difference being that the victim died. Forcible rape or unlawful

---

[15] Walter C. Reckless, *The Crime Problem* (3d ed.; New York: Appleton-Century-Crofts, Inc., 1961), p. 153.

[16] Also see Clinard and Quinney, pp. 14–18.

sexual intercourse with a woman against her will is to be distinguished from statutory rape or sexual intercourse with or without her consent with a female under a specified age, generally sixteen or eighteen in the United States and fifteen abroad.

Offenders who commit criminal homicide, assaulters, and forcible rapists do not have criminal careers in such offenses. In fact, most murderers and assaulters do not conceive of themselves as being "criminals," for there is seldom identification with crime, and criminal behavior as such is not a meaningful part of their lives. Forcible rapists, on the other hand, are likely to have a record of other offenses, particularly property crimes.

General cultural and subcultural normative patterns seem to determine the frequency of violent crimes. Acceptance of the use of violence varies from country to country, from region to region, and from state to state. The use of violence also varies by neighborhood within a city, and by social class, occupation, race, sex, and age. These differences reflect what has been termed a *subculture of violence,* which is more commonly associated with the lower class.[17] Most acts of violence grow out of an interaction situation in which the act comes to be defined as requiring violence and in which the victim plays a part in precipitating it, whether it results in criminal homicide, assault, or forcible rape.

Criminal Homicide and Assault

Nearly all criminal homicide, like assault, is an outgrowth of personal disputes and altercations, some immediate and some long-standing in nature. Relatively few of these offenses are associated with the commission of other crimes such as robbery. The acceptance of the use of violence to settle disputes is related to general cultural patterns.

The acceptance of murder as a method of solving interpersonal conflicts varies a great deal in time, from country to country, from region to region, and from state to state. The use of personal violence to settle disputes, even though it results in assault and murder, appears to have been common in nearly all of Europe a few centuries ago, even among the upper classes. The Vikings of Scandinavia were not only the "scourge of Europe"; frequently they used violent methods on each other. Finland today, for example, has one of the highest homicide rates in the world, whereas the

---

[17] Marvin E. Wolfgang, *Patterns in Criminal Homicide* (Philadelphia: University of Pennsylvania Press, 1958); Marvin E. Wolfgang, "A Preface to Violence," *The Annals,* 364:1–7 (1966); and Marvin E. Wolfgang and Franco Ferracuti, *The Subculture of Violence: Towards an Integrated Theory in Criminology* (London: Tavistock Publications, Ltd., 1967).

rate is quite low in Norway, Sweden, Great Britain, and Canada.[18] Ceylon also has a high rate in Asia.[19] A study of personal offenses in Puerto Rico, for example, indicated that the high rates of these crimes in such Latin cultures are related to personal insult or honor.[20] In situations of personal vilification or marital triangles the culture may require the individual to attack the offender. Two thirds of the offenders were found to have had some personal association with persons who had also resorted to violence under somewhat similar circumstances. The regional differences in the United States are so wide that "a general murder rate for the United States as a whole has no very close relation to the actual rate of any specific area or section." [21] The homicide rates in the South are considerably higher than those in other regions.

Murder rates vary a great deal according to ethnic, racial, and class lines. Some indication of subcultural components in criminal homicide is the fact that of 489 cases in Houston, Texas, over 87 percent occurred in four areas, not far apart, located near the center of the city.[22] For the most part, outlying areas within the city had no homicides at all. Nearly all the homicides occurred in slum areas populated chiefly by Negroes and Spanish-Americans.

A study of 588 victims and 621 slayers in Philadelphia, between 1948 and 1952, has given us many insights into this subculture of violence.[23] Murder was found to be highest among Negroes, males, those in the age group 20–24 and 30–34, from the lower social classes, and in certain occupations. Nine in ten murderers were in lower-class occupations, laborers, for example, committing more homicides than did clerks. Most lived in slum

---

[18] Veli Verkko, *Homicides and Suicides in Finland and Their Dependence on National Character* (Copenhagen: G. E. C. Gads Forlag, 1951). The subcultural use of violence is also found particularly in Colombia, Mexico, and Sardinia. See Wolfgang and Ferracuti, pp. 275–281.

[19] See Jacqueline and Murray Straus, "Suicide, Homicide, and Social Structure in Ceylon," *American Journal of Sociology,* 58:461–469 (1953); and Arthur Wood, "Murder, Suicide, and Economic Crime in Ceylon," *American Sociological Review,* 26:744–753 (1961).

[20] Jaime Toro-Calder, "Personal Crimes in Puerto Rico." Unpublished master's thesis, University of Wisconsin, Madison, 1950.

[21] George B. Vold, "Extent and Trend of Capital Crimes in the United States," *The Annals,* 284:3 (1952). Also see H. C. Brearley, *Homicide in the United States* (Chapel Hill: University of North Carolina Press, 1932).

[22] Henry Allen Bullock, "Urban Homicide in Theory and Fact," *Journal of Criminal Law, Criminology, and Police Science,* 45:565–575 (1955).

[23] Wolfgang, *Patterns in Criminal Homicide.* Also see, for a summary, "A Sociological Analysis of Criminal Homicide," *Federal Probation,* 25:48–55 (1961).

areas.[24] Nearly one half of the offenders who had a previous arrest record of some type had been arrested for some form of assault more characteristic of lower-class behavior, such as wife beating and fighting.[25] Some indication of the relation of homicide to the pattern of life in certain areas of the city is suggested by the fact that 65 percent of all homicides occur during weekends, particularly on Saturday night. The rate among Negroes was four times that of whites, indicating the role of subculture and the isolating effects of segregation from the general norms of society. In fact, the rate was greatest among recent Negro migrants. The role of subcultural factors among the lower class in precipitating violence is that

> the significance of a jostle, a slightly derogatory remark, or the appearance of a person in the hands of an adversary are stimuli differentially perceived and interpreted by Negroes and whites, males and females. Social expectations of response in particular types of social interaction result in differential "definitions of the situation." A male is usually expected to defend the name and honor of his mother, the virtue of womanhood (even though his female companion for the evening may be an entirely new acquaintance and/or a prostitute), and to accept no derogation about his race (even from a member of his own race), his age, or his masculinity. Quick resort to physical combat as a measure of daring, courage, or defense of status appears to be a cultural expectation, especially for lower socio-economic class males of both races.[26]

Like those who commit criminal homicide, persons who commit assault are unlikely to have been involved in other types of crime. In a St. Louis study it was shown that the majority of the offenders had no prior arrest records, and relatively few of these were for crimes against the person.[27] A London study of "crimes of violence" found that the vast majority, eight out of ten, of London offenders convicted for a violent offense were convicted for the first time for this type of offense. In fact, the study concluded

---

[24] Thomas F. Pettigrew and Rosalind Barclay Spier, "The Ecological Structure of Negro Homicide," *American Journal of Sociology,* 67:621–629 (1962).

[25] Wolfgang, *Patterns in Criminal Homicide,* p. 178. His study of urban offenders, largely Negro, indicated a large previous arrest record: 68 percent of the males and 48 percent of the females. Of them, 66 percent had been arrested for offenses against the person (48 percent for aggravated assault, which is also included in this figure) and 34 percent for property and other offenses.

[26] Wolfgang, *Patterns in Criminal Homicide,* pp. 188–189.

[27] David J. Pittman and William Handy, "Patterns in Criminal Aggravated Assault," *Journal of Criminal Law, Criminology, and Police Science,* 55:462–470 (1964). Also see Richard A. Peterson, David J. Pittman, and Patricia O'Neal, "Stabilities in Deviance: A Study of Assaultive and Non-Assaultive Offenders," *Journal of Criminal Law, Criminology, and Police Science,* 53:44–49 (1962).

that "the analysis of crimes of violence according to their factual substance shows that most of the crime is not committed by criminals for criminal purposes but is rather the outcome of patterns of social behavior among certain strata of society." [28]

In the London study of crimes of violence, primarily assault, it was found that the majority of the offenders were unskilled or were casually employed and lived in slum areas.[29] The higher clerical and professional workers accounted for no more than 5 percent of the total. In a sample group of assaulters, four fifths of the offenders, as well as a like percentage of the victims, were from the working class. "The general neighborhood context is one populated by lower socio-economic groups, especially Negroes of this class." [30] The social background of a sample of London persons convicted of assault was not much different from that of those convicted of criminal homicide: both tended to have a lower-class slum background.[31]

Approximately one third (35 percent) of 588 male and female criminal homicides in Philadelphia were the result of general altercations; family and domestic quarrels accounted for 14 percent; jealousy 12 percent; altercation over money 11 percent; and, contrary to popular impression, robbery only 7 percent.[32] Of all homicides, 94 percent were within the same race. Close friends and relatives accounted for over half (59 percent) of all the homicides and four fifths of the women. In 28 percent of the cases the victim was a close friend of the murderer, in 25 percent a family relative, in 14 percent an acquaintance. In only one out of eight murders was the victim a stranger. Women, as contrasted with men, generally kill someone in their own family, or one in two of those murders committed by women in Philadelphia as compared with one in six committed by men. In all, one in five homicides represented husband or wife killings. Personal contacts have also been found to play a significant role in murders in Denmark and India.[33] In a Danish study it was found in nine out of ten cases that the murderer's victim was a relative or an acquaintance. Strangers were seldom the victims. Most murders in India occur within the same caste and

---

[28] F. H. McClintock, *Crimes of Violence* (London: Macmillan & Co., Ltd., 1963), p. 57.

[29] McClintock, p. 57.

[30] Pittman and Handy, p. 469.

[31] McClintock.

[32] Wolfgang, *Patterns in Criminal Homicide,* p. 191.

[33] Kaare Svalastoga, "Homicide and Social Contact in Denmark," *American Journal of Sociology,* 62:37–41 (1956); and Edwin D. Driver, "Interaction and Criminal Homicide in India," *Social Forces,* 40:153–158 (1961).

also frequently involve husband and wife. Nearly 80 percent of all homicides in the London study and "murderous assaults" (an English category of attempted murder) were committed against relatives or victims well known to the attacker.

Homicides and assaults are often precipitated by the victims. In one study, over one in four criminal homicides were precipitated by the victim in that the victim was the first to show or use a deadly weapon, or to strike a blow in an altercation.[34] Victim-precipitated homicides were found to be significantly associated with Negroes, victim-offender relationships involving male victims of female offenders, mate slayings, alcohol in the homicide situation or in the victim, and victims with a previous record of assault or arrest. Other homicides, not included in this figure, involved the infidelity of a mate or a lover, failure of the victim to pay a debt, use of vile names by the victim in such a way that the victim had a great deal to do with the homicide. Even in robbery the behavior of the victim may incite the robber to kill.

A period of social interaction between the parties takes place before any aggravated assault. In fact, Pittman and Handy, in their St. Louis study, reported that 70.5 percent of the 241 cases studied had been preceded by verbal arguments.[35] Such quarrels included primarily family arguments, but there were also disputes arising in a tavern, as well as in other places. Disputes arose primarily among persons of similar age group, sex, and race.

Most murder and aggravated assault represent a response, growing out of social interaction between one or more parties, in which a situation comes to be defined as requiring the use of violence.

> In order for such an act generally to take place, all parties must come to perceive the situation as one requiring violence. If only one responds in a dispute, it is not likely to become violent; likewise, if only one of the disputants is accustomed to the use of violence, and the other is not, the dispute is likely to end only in a verbal argument. On the other hand, when a cultural norm is defined as calling for violence by a person in social interplay with another who harbors the same response, serious altercations, fist fights, physical assaults with weapons, and violent domestic quarrels, all of which may end in murder, may result. In the process of an argument, A and B both define the initial situation as a serious threat, B then threatens A physically, A threatens B, and B then threatens A. By circular reaction, the situation can then rapidly build up to a climax

---

[34] Wolfgang, *Patterns in Criminal Homicide*, p. 252. Also see Hans von Hentig, *The Criminal and His Victim* (New Haven, Conn.: Yale University Press, 1948).
[35] Pittman and Handy, p. 467.

where one takes serious overt action, partly because of the fear of the one for the other. Consequently, the victim, by being a contributor to the circular reaction of an argument increasing in its physical intensity, may precipitate his own injury or death.[36]

Forcible Rape

Aggressive sex offenders are usually responding to culturally based patterns of aggression and situational factors. Forcible rape is generally committed by a young unmarried male, aged fifteen to twenty-five, who comes from slum areas.[37] Practically all rapes are intraracial involving only Negroes or only whites; usually the girl also comes from the same lower-class slum area. In a Philadelphia study of 1292 offenders, 90 percent of the offenders from both races belonged to the lower part of the occupational scale, one third belonging to the lowest part of the lower class. Offenders of the lower class used unnecessary violence in sex relations, due in general to the feeling that sex is more pleasurable if it is accompanied by some physical violence or by threats, or that the behavior of the girl warranted the use of force. Others came from patterns of gang delinquency where boys with other delinquent records wanted sex relations without considering the wishes of the female.[38] The Kinsey report showed that lower-class males had had considerably more frequent premarital sex experiences than those from other classes and were more likely to restrict their sexual contacts to the more direct form of sexual union rather than indulging in "petting" and other practices.[39] Moreover, lower-class males are likely to look with disgust on the indirect sexual gratification practices of the higher classes.

The role of subcultural group factors is also shown by the fact that areas with high rates of forcible rape have been found to correspond to areas having high rates of crimes against the person generally.[40] The slum

---

[36] Clinard and Quinney, p. 27. Also see Wolfgang, *Patterns of Criminal Homicide.*

[37] Menachem Amir, "Patterns of Forcible Rape." Unpublished Ph.D. dissertation, University of Pennsylvania, 1965. Also see his "Forcible Rape," *Federal Probation,* 31:51–57 (1967) and his "Patterns of Forcible Rape," in Clinard and Quinney, pp. 60–75.

[38] Another study of a sample of forcible rapists showed that this behavior is related to the more aggressive patterns of the lower class, particularly in sexual matters.—Paul H. Gebhard, John H. Gagnon, Wardell B. Pomeroy, and Cornelia V. Christenson, *Sex Offenders: An Analysis of Types* (New York: Harper & Row, Publishers, 1965).

[39] Alfred C. Kinsey, Wardell B. Pomeroy, and Clyde E. Martin, *Sexual Behavior in the Human Male* (Philadelphia: W. B. Saunders Company, 1948).

[40] Amir.

areas in Philadelphia where Negroes lived had the highest rates of forcible rape, the proportion of Negro offenders being four times that of the general population, as was the proportion of Negro victims. The role of group and subcultural factors in forcible rape is also indicated by the high prevalence of multiple rapes in which the victim was raped by more than one male. Of the 646 cases of forcible rape in the Philadelphia study, 43 percent were multiple rapes.[41] Altogether 912 offenders, or 71 percent, of the 1292 offenders were involved in multiple-rape cases. Group factors were also indicated by the fact that Negro offenders were more likely to be involved in a group rape, the group rape was generally an *intraracial* affair, and the older the offender the less likely was he to participate in group rape.

It has been demonstrated that the rape victim often has much to do with the actions leading to the forcible rape. Amir found in his Philadelphia study that 19 percent of the forcible rapes were victim-precipitated in the sense that the "victims actually, or so it was interpreted by the offender, agreed to sexual relations but retracted before the actual act or did not resist strongly enough when the suggestion was made by the offender or offenders." [42] The role of the victim was also crucial when she entered a situation in which sexual stimulation was pervasive or made what could be interpreted as an invitation to sex relations.

Societal Reaction

Societal reaction, as expressed in the law, is severe against murder, manslaughter, and forcible rape. They are punished severely primarily because of the strong middle-class attitudes toward the use of violence which are often supported by certain ideological views expressed in religion. In the United States, murder can carry with it the death penalty in thirty-seven out of fifty states, despite the fact that the murderer sociologically is often far less a "criminal" than are other offenders. Forcible rape is also punished by death in a number of states, but manslaughter and forcible rape are usually punished by a long period of imprisonment.

OCCASIONAL PROPERTY OFFENDERS

There are many offenders whose entire criminal records rarely consist of more than an occasional or infrequent property offense of some kind. Offenses are incidental to the way of life of occasional property offenders and are so rare that these people in no way make a living from crime and

---

[41] Amir.

[42] Amir, in Clinard and Quinney, p. 68.

do not play criminal roles. This type of criminal behavior is usually of a fortuitous nature, and the offense is often committed alone, with little in the way of prior criminal contacts. With the exception of an act of vandalism, the offender has little group support for his behavior, such as sustained contact with a criminal culture or with a slum area.

The occasional offender does not conceive of himself as a criminal. Most of them are able to rationalize their offenses in such a way as to explain it to themselves as a noncriminal act. The offenses show little sophistication in the techniques of crime; there is little knowledge about crime, and generally there is no need for it because his offenses are simple. There is also no vocabulary of criminal argot. To this type of offender the theft of an automobile is more like "borrowing" it and does not involve the techniques commonly associated with career types of offenders—selecting a special type of car, stripping cars, finding "fences," and so on.[43] The occasional offender makes no effort to progress to types of crimes requiring greater knowledge and skills.

It has been estimated that some 75 percent of all check forgeries are committed by persons who have no previous pattern of such behavior. Analyzing a small sample of twenty-nine cases, Lemert concluded that such persons generally do not come from a delinquency area, have no previous criminal record, or have had no previous contact with delinquents and criminals. They do not conceive of themselves as criminals. He suggests that the novice check forger, who generally comes from the higher socioeconomic groups, is a product of certain difficult social situations in which he finds himself, a certain degree of social isolation, and a process of "closure" or "constriction of behavior alternatives subjectively held as available to the forger." [44]

Nonprofessional shoplifting is a rather common offense, particularly among women; such persons steal for their own use rather than for sale to someone.[45] Generally they are respectable employed persons or housewives and do not conceive of themselves as criminals or their activities as constituting crimes. Rather, they regard themselves as "pilferers," and they rationalize their offenses on the basis that the things taken are generally of modest price and belong to large department stores which can absorb these losses. Few of these offenders have had criminal records; in one study

---

[43] See William W. Wattenberg and James Balistrieri, "Automobile Theft: A 'Favored-Group' Delinquency," *American Journal of Sociology*, 57:575–579 (1952).

[44] Edwin M. Lemert, "An Isolation Closure Theory of Naïve Check Forgery," *Journal of Criminal Law and Criminology*, 44:298 (1953).

[45] Mary Owen Cameron, *The Booster and the Snitch: Department Store Shoplifting* (New York: The Free Press, 1964).

92 percent of the women shoplifters who had been officially charged had never been convicted of such an offense previously.[46]

Vandalism includes many acts of destruction. They have been described as follows:

> Studies of the complaints made by citizens and public officials reveal that hardly any property is safe from this form of aggression. Schools are often the object of attack by vandals. Windows are broken; records, books, desks, typewriters, supplies, and other equipment are stolen or destroyed. Public property of all types appears to offer peculiar allurement to children bent on destruction. Parks, playgrounds, highway signs, and markers are frequently defaced or destroyed. Trees, shrubs, flowers, benches, and other equipment suffer in like manner. Autoists are constantly reporting the slashing or releasing of air from tires, broken windows, stolen accessories. Golf clubs complain that benches, markers, flags, even expensive and difficult-to-replace putting greens are defaced, broken or uprooted. Libraries report the theft and destruction of books and other equipment. Railroads complain of and demand protection from the destruction of freight car seals, theft of property, wilful and deliberate throwing of stones at passenger car windows, tampering with rails and switches. Vacant houses are always the particular delight of children seeking outlets for destructive instincts; windows are broken, plumbing and hardware stolen, destroyed, or rendered unusable. Gasoline operators report pumps and other service equipment stolen, broken, or destroyed. Theater managers, frequently in the "better" neighborhoods, complain of the slashing of seats, wilful damaging of toilet facilities, even the burning of rugs, carpets, etc.[47]

Acts of vandalism are committed largely by those without a criminal orientation toward themselves or what they do: their acts are regarded primarily as "pranks." [48] The fact that often nothing is stolen during acts of vandalism tends to reinforce the vandal's conception of himself as merely a prankster and not a delinquent. Some writers have pointed this out as a distinguishing characteristic of the vandal when compared with other prop-

---

[46] Cameron, p. 110.

[47] J. P. Murphy, "The Answer to Vandalism May Be Found at Home," *Federal Probation,* 18:8–10 (1954). This issue of *Federal Probation* contains a symposium on vandalism.

[48] Clinard and Wade. Also see Ferdinand; Don C. Gibbons, *Changing the Lawbreaker* (Englewood Cliffs, N.J.: Prentice-Hall, Inc., 1965), pp. 74–94; John M. Martin, *Juvenile Vandalism* (Springfield Ill.: Charles C Thomas, Publisher, 1961); Nathan Goldman, "A Socio-Psychological Study of School Vandalism," Final Report on Office of Education Contract No. SAE 181 (8453) (Syracuse: University Research Institute, 1959), pp. 349–353; mimeographed; William Bates and Thomas McJunkins, "Vandalism and Status Differences," *Pacific Sociological Review,* 5:89–92 (1962).

erty offenders, assuming that since nothing is taken vandalism has a non-utilitarian function. Property destruction appears to function for the adolescent as fun and excitement and as a protest against his ill-defined role and ambiguous status in the social structure. There is some evidence that vandalism appears to be increasing in middle-class suburbia.[49]

Vandalism is committed by a group, but the act does not derive from any subculture; in fact, acts of vandalism seldom utilize or even require prior sophisticated knowledge. They grow out of collective interaction of the movement; few are deliberately planned in advance.[50] Participation in acts of vandalism gives status and group interaction to each member; through direct involvement the individual avoids becoming a marginal member of the group. Vandalism is spontaneous behavior and the outgrowth of social situations in which group interaction takes place. Each interactive response by a participant builds upon the action of another participant until a focus develops and the group act of vandalism results. In the typical act of vandalism there are usually five stages: (1) waiting for something to turn up; (2) removal of uncertainty about what to do, resulting in an "exploratory gesture" to the act; (3) mutual conversion of each member of the group to participation; (4) joint elaboration of the vandalism; and (5) aftermath and retrospect.[51]

Societal Reactions

In most cases the societal reaction against occasional offenders is not severe: occasional offenders seldom have had any prior record. Generally the offender is dismissed or acquitted by the courts or placed on probation. It has been found that formal arrest of shoplifters, naïve check forgers, and vandals helps to redefine the act in their eyes as a "crime." For example an adult pilferer or shoplifter "does not think of himself, prior to arrest, as a thief and can conceive of no group support for himself in that role, his arrest forces him to reject the role" and conceive of himself as a law violator.[52] Provided the damage to property is not particularly serious, acts of vandalism by juveniles are likely to be viewed with a degree of tolerance; if by adults, a different view would be adopted. The juvenile is often regarded in an ambiguous role situation and as having not developed a responsible understanding of property rights and values.

---

[49] Edmund W. Vaz, ed., *Middle-Class Juvenile Delinquency* (New York: Harper & Row, Publishers, 1967).

[50] Andrew L. Wade, "Social Processes in the Act of Juvenile Vandalism," in Clinard and Quinney, pp. 94–109.

[51] Wade, pp. 99–108.

[52] Cameron, p. 165.

HABITUAL PETTY PROPERTY OFFENDERS

Habitual petty property offenders [53] constitute a large proportion of arrests, but since they do not often commit serious felonies they are commonly confined in city and county jails. Generally they begin their criminal activities while young and continue in petty crime, vagrancy, and disorderly conduct. These offenders have long criminal records, maintain extensive connections with a criminal underworld, and conceive of themselves as criminals. Habitual petty offenders do not, however, possess much sophistication about crime, do not employ elaborate techniques, and are not particularly effective at "fixing" their cases in court.

The criminal pattern of habitual offenders is complicated by their conception of themselves as failures in social adjustment. This self-conception has considerable basis in fact in their tendency to be lazy, shiftless, and irresponsible; moreover, they are likely to have been arrested not only for petty stealing but also for alcoholism, for the sale of or addiction to drugs, for vagrancy, or for other similar offenses. As a result they are more likely to be apprehended, and because they have little means of protection they continue to steal or get into other trouble, their reputations become known in the community, and they find it more and more difficult to find employment and to live without criminal activity.

OCCUPATIONAL OFFENDERS

Occupational offenders commit crimes in connection with their occupations.[54] Occupational crime does not include such crimes as murder or robbery, which could be committed by persons of any occupation, nor does it include illegitimate occupations such as prostitution or professional crime. Occupational offenders include small and large businessmen, politicians, government employees, doctors, pharmacists, and, of course, others. For those occupations of particularly high status the term *white-collar crime* is often used.

As has been pointed out in the discussion of crime, no act committed by members of occupational groups, however unethical, should be considered as crime unless it is punishable by the state in some way. For example, the deliberate sale of a pair of odd-lot shoes which are too small

---

[53] Here this term is being used to describe a behavior system and is not the legal term discussed on page 246.

[54] See Clinard and Quinney, pp. 130–132. Also see Richard Quinney, "The Study of White Collar Crime: Toward a Reorientation in Theory and Research," *Journal of Criminal Law, Criminology, and Police Science,* 55:208–214 (1964).

for a customer is unethical but it is not a crime; this is also true of advertising which is unethical but not necessarily illegal.

Many investigations by governmental committees, both state and federal, have revealed that crime among business concerns is extensive. These investigations have covered banking operations, the oil industry, stock exchanges, public utilities, munitions, real estate, insurance, and railways. Violations of law by businessmen include the illegal activities of reorganization committees in receiverships and in bankruptcies; restraint of trade such as monopoly, illegal rebates, infringements of patents, trademarks, and copyrights; misrepresentation in advertising; unfair labor practices; financial manipulations; and wartime crimes, such as black-marketeering.[55]

Employers seem to have extensively violated federal laws regulating wages, hours, and public contracts, as well as labor relations and trade practices.[56] A study covering seventy large corporations which, with two exceptions, are included among the two hundred largest nonfinancial institutions in the United States, found that they had had 980 decisions rendered against them for violations of government regulations, an average of 14 for each corporation.[57] After a careful analysis, Sutherland concluded that although 158 cases were dealt with by the criminal courts, in actuality crimes were committed in 779 out of the 980 cases, 583 being decisions by civil courts. Even if the analysis were restricted to the criminal courts, it would show that almost two thirds of the corporations had been convicted at one time or another and had an average of 4 convictions each.

Various offenses of a white-collar nature are committed by politicians and government employees. They include direct misappropriation of public funds or the illegal acquirement of these funds through padded payrolls, through relatives illegally on the government payroll, or through monetary "kickbacks" from appointees. Usually, however, the illegal activities are more subtle. Politicians and government employees may gain financially by furnishing some favor to business firms or to criminal syndicates. Favors for

[55] See Frank Gibney, *The Operators* (New York: Harper & Row, Publishers, 1960). This contains a good account, with many case histories, of unethical and illegal practices in business and politics.

[56] Robert A. Lane, "Why Business Men Violate the Law," *Journal of Criminal Law, Criminology, and Police Science,* 44:151–165 (1953).

[57] Edwin H. Sutherland, "Is 'White Collar Crime' Crime?" in Marvin E. Wolfgang, Leonard Savitz, and Norman Johnston, eds., *The Sociology of Crime and Delinquency* (New York: John Wiley & Sons, Inc., 1962), pp. 20–27; and Edwin H. Sutherland, *White Collar Crime* (New York: Holt, Rinehart and Winston, Inc., 1949, reissued, 1960).

which politicians may be rewarded by certain businessmen include illegal commissions on public contracts, issuance of licenses or certificates of building or fire inspections, and tax exemptions or lowered tax valuations. Criminal syndicates may share the proceeds of gambling or other profits with public officials who give protection from arrest.

Labor union officials may engage in a variety of criminal activities, such as the misappropriation or misapplication of union funds, defiance of the government by failure to enforce laws affecting their labor unions, collusion with employers to the disadvantage of their own union members, and the use of fraudulent means to maintain their control over the unions.[58]

Certain activities in the medical profession are not only unethical but illegal. They include giving illegal prescriptions for narcotics, performing illegal abortions, making fraudulent reports and giving false testimony in accident cases, and fee splitting. Fee splitting, in which a doctor splits the fee he charges with the doctor who referred the case to him, is against the law in many states because of the danger that such referrals will be based on the size of the fee rather than on the proficiency of the practitioner. This practice actually involves the very life of the patient if a doctor refers him to an inferior surgeon in order to secure a part of the surgeon's fee. One study reported that two thirds of the surgeons in New York City split fees.[59] Dr. Paul R. Hawley, director of the American College of Surgeons, declared that the American people would be shocked at the extent of this practice as well as at the amount of unnecessary surgery performed on patients throughout the country.[60]

Lawyers engage in such illegalities as misappropriating funds in receiverships, securing perjured testimony from witnesses, and "ambulance chasing" in various forms, usually to collect fraudulent damage claims arising from an accident.[61] When cases of these types are discovered the offender is more apt to be disbarred from practice than prosecuted.

The consideration of only conventional crimes gives an erroneous impression of the extent and effects of crimes on society as well as of the

---

[58] Malcolm Johnson, *Crime on the Labor Front* (New York: McGraw-Hill Book Company, Inc., 1950). See also Robert Kennedy, *The Enemy Within* (New York: Harper & Row, Publishers, 1960).

[59] Cited in Sutherland, *White Collar Crime,* p. 12.

[60] "Too Much Unneccessary Surgery," *United States News & World Report,* 34:47–55 (1953). Also see H. Whitman, "Why Some Doctors Should Be in Jail," *Collier's,* 132:23–27 (1953).

[61] Jerome E. Carlin, *Lawyers' Ethics: A Survey of the New York City Bar* (New York: Russell Sage Foundation, 1966).

nature of criminals.[62] Persons sentenced to prison are usually rather poor and relatively uneducated, whereas occupational criminals are generally well off and may even be in the higher income brackets. This is likely to be true of the white-collar criminal. There is considerable difference in the effect on society of ordinary crimes as compared with white-collar offenses. Sutherland has made these comparisons:

> The financial loss to society from white-collar crimes is probably greater than the financial loss from burglaries, robberies, and larcenies committed by persons of the lower socioeconomic class. The average loss per burglary is less than one hundred dollars, a burglary which yields as much as fifty thousand dollars is exceedingly rare, and a million-dollar burglary is practically unknown. On the other hand, there may be several million-dollar embezzlements reported in one year. Embezzlements, however, are peccadilloes compared with the large-scale crimes committed by corporations, investment trusts, and public utility holding companies; reports of fifty-million-dollar losses from such criminal behavior are by no means uncommon.[63]

The major difference between occupational crime and other forms of crime lies in the offender's conception of himself.[64] An occupational offender does not play as consistent a criminal role as do many other types of offenders. He may play a variety of other roles, such as that of a respected citizen; hence the degree of recognition of the conflict between this role and that of a criminal offender may vary with different individuals. Because he is likely to regard himself as a respectable citizen, at most he thinks of himself as a "lawbreaker" and not as a "criminal." In this sense he has the attitude of some offenders convicted of such crimes as statutory rape, nonsupport, or drunken driving. The higher social status attached to the legitimate occupation of such an offender makes it difficult for the general public, while not condoning their activities, to conceive of them as being associated with real criminal behavior, which is largely stereotyped as the

---

[62] Frank E. Hartung, "White Collar Crime: Its Significance for Theory and Practice," *Federal Probation*, 17:31–36 (1953). See also Donald J. Newman, "White-Collar Crime," in *Law and Contemporary Problems*, 23:735–753 (1958), and Marshall B. Clinard, "White Collar Crime," *Encyclopedia of the Social Sciences* (New York: Crowell-Collier and Macmillan, Inc., 1968).

[63] Edwin H. Sutherland, "Crime and Business," *The Annals*, 217:113 (1941). Also see Marshall B. Clinard, "Corruption Runs Far Deeper than Politics," *The New York Times Magazine*, August 1952, p. 21. The largest U.S. robbery was the 1950 Brinks robbery in Boston involving $2,775,395, of which $1,218,211 was in cash. The world's largest cash robbery was Britain's 1963 Great Train Robbery, when $7,000,000 was stolen.

[64] Sutherland, *White Collar Crime*, pp. 223–224.

more overt offenses. This attitude is, in turn, reflected in the conception that white-collar offenders have of themselves.[65]

In many areas of occupational crime there is often considerable organization. In fee splitting, for example, there must be a reciprocal relationship between the doctors. In political corruption there is an organized tie-up with businessmen or criminal syndicates. After studying the criminal behavior of seventy large corporations, Sutherland came to these conclusions: [66] (1) the criminality of corporations is persistent; (2) there is generally no loss of status by an offender among his business associates; [67] (3) in those areas which immediately affect white-collar offenders there is apt to be fairly general contempt for the government as a whole, the law, and the personnel who administer it; and (4) most white-collar business crimes are organized in the sense that the violation is a corporation affair or may extend to several corporations or subsidiaries.

In various occupations persons learn to violate the law with impunity. In some occupations a new man may learn the techniques by which the law can be violated, and he may build up a series of rationalizations such as "business is business" or "one cannot conduct a profitable business or

---

[65] Some people would therefore define behavior as really "criminal" only when it is considered so by general public opinion. According to such a definition neither violations of Prohibition laws, many types of gambling, nor similar kinds of illegal behavior should be considered as crimes. The same reasoning would be offered by those who feel that a crime has been committed only when an individual conceives of his offense as being criminal. According to this position, if persons do not think of their acts as violations of law either because of personal, situational, or occupational reasons, their acts would not be crimes, no matter what the law or public opinion felt. Thus a person who refuses to register for the draft because of religious reasons, as did thousands of Jehovah's Witnesses during World War II, would not be considered a criminal even though many were sentenced to prison. Nor would a person necessarily be a criminal if he held certain political beliefs that were opposed by the majority. Many feel that statutory rape is often not criminal, because these cases, which involve sexual intercourse with girls under eighteen, usually are with consent and seldom are the result of coercion. The same argument might apply to persons sentenced to prison for nonsupport of their families or for injuring someone through their neglect or because of drunken driving.

[66] Sutherland, *White Collar Crime,* pp. 217–220.

[67] In 1961 several high executives of the leading American electrical equipment companies were sentenced to jail for serious violations of law, some also receiving large fines. A number who resigned from their companies were within a short time appointed to positions of nearly equal executive responsibility in other companies.—*The New York Times,* June 23, 1961, p. 37. Also see Gilbert Geis, "White Collar Crime: The Heavy Electrical Equipment Anti-Trust Cases of 1961," in Clinard and Quinney, pp. 139–151.

profession in any other way." The diffusion of illegal practices is spread from a person already in the occupation to new persons entering it, and from one business establishment, political machine, or other occupational group to another. Sometimes the diffusion may be the result of an effort to meet illegal competitive activities of another business. How this diffusion of unethical and illegal behavior works is described by a person in the used-car business.

> When I graduated from college I had plenty of ideals of honesty, fair play, and cooperation which I had acquired at home, in school, and from literature. My first job after graduation was selling typewriters. During the first day I learned that these machines were not sold at a uniform price but that a person who haggled and waited could get a machine at about half the list price. I felt that this was unfair to the customer who paid the list price. The other salesmen laughed at me and could not understand my silly attitude. They told me to forget the things I had learned in school, and that you couldn't earn a pile of money by being strictly honest. When I replied that money wasn't everything they mocked at me: "Oh, no? Well, it helps." I had ideals and I resigned.
>
> My next job was selling sewing machines. I was informed that one machine, which cost the company $18, was to be sold for $40 and another machine, which cost the company $19, was to be sold for $70, and that I was to sell the de luxe model whenever possible in preference to the cheaper model, and was given a list of the reasons why it was a better buy. When I told the sales manager that the business was dishonest and that I was quitting right then, he looked at me as if he thought I was crazy and said angrily: "There's not a cleaner business in the country."
>
> It was quite a time before I could find another job. During this time I occasionally met some of my classmates and they related experiences similar to mine. They said they would starve if they were rigidly honest. All of them had girls and were looking forward to marriage and a comfortable standard of living, and they said they did not see how they could afford to be rigidly honest. My own feelings became less determined than they had been when I quit my first job.
>
> Then I got an opportunity in the used-car business. I learned that this business had more tricks for fleecing customers than either of those I had tried previously. Cars with cracked cylinders, with half the teeth missing from the fly wheel, with everything wrong, were sold as "guaranteed." When the customer returned and demanded his guarantee, he had to sue to get it and very few went to that trouble and expense: the boss said you could depend on human nature. If hot cars could be taken in and sold safely, the boss did not hesitate. When I learned these things I did not quit as I had previously. I sometimes felt disgusted and wanted to quit, but I argued that I did not have much chance to find a legitimate firm. I knew that the game was rotten but it had to be played—the law of the jungle and that sort of thing. I knew that I was dishonest and to

that extent felt that I was more honest than my fellows. The thing that struck me as strange was that all these people were proud of their ability to fleece customers. They boasted of their crookedness and were admired by their friends and enemies in proportion to their ability to get away with a crooked deal: it was called shrewdness. Another thing was that these people were unanimous in their denunciation of gangsters, robbers, burglars, and petty thieves. They never regarded themselves as in the same class and were bitterly indignant if accused of dishonesty; it was just good business.

Once in a while, as the years have passed, I have thought of myself as I was in college—idealistic, honest, and thoughtful of others—and have been momentarily ashamed of myself. Before long such memories became less and less frequent and it became difficult to distinguish me from my fellows. If you had accused me of dishonesty I would have denied the charge, but with slightly less vehemence than my fellow businessmen, for after all I had learned a different code of behavior.[68]

A study of World War II black-market dealings by businessmen involving violations of price and rationing regulations, showed them to have had their origin in behavior learned in association with others.[69] Unethical and illegal practices were circulated in the trade as part of a definition of the situation, and rationalizations to support these violations of law were transmitted by this differential association. Many types of violations were picked up from conversations with businessmen and from descriptions of violations in trade newspapers and the general press.

When one considers that the social background of persons engaging in white-collar crime is different from that of the habitual, conventional, or organized criminal, one might ask why exposure to illegal norms has any effect. A number of factors tend to isolate businessmen from unfavorable definitions of illegal activity.[70] Agencies of mass communication play up conventional crime as abhorrent but treat white-collar crime much more leniently. Also, businessmen are often shielded from severe criticism by government officials, many of whom either were formerly in business or accepted contributions from business sources. Finally, businessmen chiefly associate with other businessmen, both at work and in their social life, so that the implications of white-collar crime are shielded from objective scrutiny.

---

[68] Personal document in Sutherland, *White Collar Crime,* pp. 235–236. Copyright 1949 by Holt, Rinehart and Winston, Inc. Reissued 1961. Reprinted by special permission.

[69] Marshall B. Clinard, *The Black Market* (New York: Holt, Rinehart and Winston, Inc., 1952), pp. 298–313.

[70] Sutherland, *White Collar Crime,* pp. 247–253.

One of the most significant recent cases of white-collar crime involved conspiracy in price fixing as well as price-rigging violations of the federal antitrust laws by many of the leading electrical equipment concerns of the United States. Twenty-nine leading electrical equipment companies, including General Electric and Westinghouse and forty-five executives of the companies involved, were convicted in 1960 of illegalities in the sales of heavy electrical equipment amounting to $1,750,000,000 a year. Such violations meant that government and private purchasers of equipment had been deceived about the open competitive nature of bids and had to pay sums far in excess of a regular bid. In the end, such illegal behavior, when perpetrated against a government agency, costs the taxpayers. Consequently, the convictions were later followed by civil suits amounting to millions of dollars filed by various federal, state, and local agencies to recover damages from the illegal price fixing and price rigging.

Secret meetings had been arranged by representatives of the companies in hotel rooms. Participants were cautioned to conceal their bids in expense-account reports. At the secret meetings pricing schedules were arranged and arrangements were made for each company to submit the lowest bid for each of various contracts.

As an example of how the conspiracies worked, one of the most involved conspiracies, and also of longest duration, was in the switch-gear division, which handles the sale of electric circuit breakers and the like.[71] This conspiracy operated for a number of years and was well organized. Conspirators had their own lingo and operating procedures. Attendance lists at secret meetings of the companies were called "Christmas card lists"; meetings were known as "choir practices." The companies involved in this conspiracy—General Electric, Westinghouse, Allis-Chalmers, Federal Pacific, and I.T.E.—were given a code number which was used in the book price listings, and in communications between executives. The job of initiating memos on the subjects of jobs coming up, and on book price listings by each company, was rotated among executives, each performing this task for thirty days. Several times over a period of about eight years the conspiracy was given up because participants from the different firms tended to cheat on the "rules" of the conspiracy itself and attempted to "chisel" one another. However, slumps in profits and sales, combined with productive overcapacity, would generally force the executives to do something to remedy this situation. Since price fixing had succeeded before in solving the

---

[71] John Herling, *The Great Price Conspiracy: The Story of the Antitrust Violations in the Electrical Industry* (Washington, D.C.: Robert B. Luce, Inc., 1962), pp. 106–114. Also see Gilbert Geis in Clinard and Quinney, pp. 139–151, and Richard A. Smith, "The Incredible Electrical Conspiracy: I," *Fortune,* 63:139–151 (1961).

low-profit versus overcapacity dilemma, it was easily resorted to again. During slumps in profits and sales the division executives would be pressured from the central echelons to "do something" to raise profits and sales. This appeared to contribute to the decisions of lower-echelon executives to resume conspiracies. Through searching investigations, during which extensive records, including minutes, of the conspiracy meetings were obtained, the government was able to secure sufficient evidence to indict the forty-five executives. Moreover, executives of one company decided to cooperate with the government and submitted documents and other supporting evidence to the investigators.

One writer has suggested that in these cases a factor of major importance was the separation of business and personal ethics.[72] In the minds of the executives there was a cleavage between ordinary morals and business morals; what applied in one area did not in another.

Although many cases of white-collar crime can be satisfactorily explained by a theory of differential association, particularly if there had been continuous and intimate association with unethical and illegal differential norms and at the same time some isolation from other norms, such a general theory as an explanation for *all* cases has several limitations. Some individuals do not engage in such practices, even though they are familiar with the techniques and the rationalizations of violations and frequently associate with persons similarly familiar. It is doubtful if any businessmen could be in a given line of business for any length of time, either in peacetime or in wartime, without acquiring a rather complete knowledge of the illegalities practiced in it.

Persons tend, in part, to accept or reject opportunities for white-collar crime according to their orientations toward their roles and their attitudes toward general social values. Some of these factors are negative attitudes toward other persons in general, the relative importance attached to status symbols of money as compared with law obedience, and the relative importance attached to personal, family, or business reputations.[73]

---

[72] Smith, "The Incredible Electrical Conspiracy: II," *Fortune*, 63:161–164, 210–224 (1961).

[73] Clinard, *The Black Market*. See also Lane, pp. 161–163. Sutherland has stated, however, that he believes the variation in crimes of a group of corporations which he studied was not the result of personality factors.—Sutherland, *White Collar Crime*, p. 265. For example, corporations which have violated the antitrust laws have been doing so for over forty years. The presence of philanthropists and public-spirited citizens on boards of directors at various times has made little difference in the extent of violations. Moreover, the composition of boards of directors may vary from one concern to another and yet there are similar violations, indicating that personalities have little bearing on violation. These conclusions,

There are forms of occupational crime which are related to the structure of the occupation in which the offender is engaged and his occupational roles in it. A study of prescription violations by retail pharmacists, for example, showed that retail pharmacy consists of two divergent occupational role expectations: the professional training role and the business or profit role.[74] Because of this, pharmacists often have difficulty in adapting to one of several occupational role organizations, which in turn differ in the extent to which they produce tendencies toward prescription violations. Violations were found to occur more frequently among pharmacists whose role was that primarily of a businessman than among professional pharmacists, with pharmacists not oriented to either role being intermediate in frequency. The conclusion was that prescription violation is related to the structure of the occupation and the "differential orientation" of retail pharmacists to roles within the occupation.

Embezzlement, a form of occupational crime, is more common than most people assume. After studying 133 persons imprisoned for violations of trust as well as cases collected by others, Cressey has developed what he claims to be a universal explanation of trust violation. According to him, three elements are necessary in a trust violation and all must be present. First are the opportunity to commit a trust violation and the presence of what Cressey terms a nonsharable problem which, if revealed, would lose the individual the group's approval: "Trusted persons become trust violators when they conceive of themselves as having a financial problem which is nonsharable." [75] These difficulties include important obligations where the status of the individual might be interfered with, a feeling of personal responsibility, or a business reversal. Other difficulties are situations where the individual is isolated from others who might help him in his financial problems, situations where the person's general behavior is not approved by others, and unsatisfactory employer-employee relations where the individual feels underpaid or overworked or has a grudge. The second aspect of a violation is the knowledge of how to violate. Trust violators are aware "that this problem can be secretly resolved by a violation of the position of financial trust." Finally, the third necessary element of a violation is the presence of acceptable explanations "which enable [trust violators] to adjust

---

however, have been reached with only preliminary research and, while true in some cases, cannot be taken as evidence that individuals have little to do with the violations.

[74] Richard Quinney, "Occupational Structure and Criminal Behavior: Prescription Violation by Retail Pharmacists," in Clinard and Quinney, pp. 169–176.

[75] Donald R. Cressey, *Other People's Money* (New York: The Free Press, 1953), p. 30.

their conception of themselves as users of the entrusted funds or property." The potential trust violator defines the situation through rationalizations in terms which enable him to look upon the criminality as essentially noncriminal, such as merely "borrowing," as justified, as part of the "general irresponsibility" for which he is not completely accountable, or as due to unusual circumstances which are different in his case. Both the rationalizations and the techniques for violating are acquired through differential association. Indirectly the acceptance of a position of trust carries with it some idea of possible violation through the mere fact of being bonded; moreover, there are conversations with others about violations of trust, and observance of others who are dishonest.[76]

Societal Reactions

Punishments for occupational crimes vary considerably, and are in striking contrast to the punishment for ordinary crimes. There are several reasons for this difference. First of all, many acts of businessmen which are socially harmful were not made illegal until rather recently. Embezzlement and some forms of fraud, for example, were not designated as crimes until late in the eighteenth century, and it was not until after the beginning of the nineteenth century that the following acts were outlawed in this country: restraint of trade, false advertising, insolvency of banks due to fraud or negligence of officials, sale of fraudulent securities, and misuse of trademarks. This slow development was partly due to the fact that the philosophy of laissez faire and *caveat emptor* ("let the buyer beware"), which characterized the general social, political, and economic thinking, prohibited the development of certain needed legal prohibitions regardless of occupation or social class.

Second, there has been little organized public resentment against many socially injurious occupational crimes, and without great public pressures it has been difficult to get criminal laws passed against this behavior. As one writer has pointed out, white-collar crime differs from other crime, not only in the methods of dealing with it but in the status of the offender, the toleration of the public, and the support offenders may receive from other

---

[76] Some suggestions for the prevention of embezzlement have been given by Cressey, pp. 153–77, and by Norman Jaspan and Hillel Black, *The Thief in White Collar* (Philadelphia: J. B. Lippincott Company, 1960), pp. 233–254. Unfortunately, Cressey's study describes only the process of violation and not the characteristics of a person who violates a trust obligation. Moreover, it does not tell us what specific situations are likely to be more productive of violations. Perhaps future studies will enable us to predict with some accuracy who will violate, and what situations are more likely than others to lead to violations of trust.

groups in the society.[77] This confusion over white-collar crime is a reflection of the diversity of status systems in present-day society. The fact that white-collar crimes are usually more complex and are often diffused over a longer period of time than are simple and overt crimes, such as burglary, tends to obscure the essential criminality of the acts.[78] Furthermore, occupational crimes are publicized differently from ordinary crimes; consequently, they usually arouse less public resentment.

CONVENTIONAL CRIMINAL CAREERS

The conventional criminal career moves from juvenile gang associations to adult criminal behavior of a more serious type, primarily in burglary, automobile theft, or robbery. Such a career involves early group experience with delinquent behavior patterns as a member of a gang. The members adapt to a number of social roles and achieve high status through participation in gang activities. There is a continuous acquisition of techniques and rationalizations to explain their crimes as delinquent acts move from petty to more serious offenses. During this progression there are usually a considerable number of experiences with official agencies, including the police courts, juvenile authorities, juvenile institutions, reformatories and, finally, prison. Institutional experience adds to the offender's status and sophistication and helps mold his conception of himself as a criminal. The degree of development and sophistication in crime of an ordinary criminal career, however, is much less than among professional criminals. It is for these reasons that such careers are termed "conventional" criminal careers.[79] They usually terminate somewhere between the early twenties and the late twenties or early thirties. They are characterized by

    a. the use of strong-arm methods (robbery) of obtaining money.
    b. the sale of stolen articles, versus using for oneself, giving or throwing away, or returning stolen articles.
    c. stating, as a reason for continued stealing, "want things" or "need money" versus stealing for excitement, because others do it, because they like to, or for spite.[80]

A comparison of 32 Negro armed robbers with 368 other Negro offenders revealed a pattern which can be designated as an ordinary criminal

---

[77] Vilhelm Aubert, "White Collar Crime and Social Structure," *American Journal of Sociology,* 58:263–271 (1952).

[78] See Sutherland, *White Collar Crime,* pp. 50–51.

[79] Much the same distinction is made by Walter C. Reckless. See Chapter 9 "Ordinary and Professional Criminal Careers," in *The Crime Problem* (3d ed.).

[80] Albert K. Cohen and James F. Short, Jr., "Research in Delinquent Subcultures," *Journal of Social Issues,* 14:13, No. 3 (1958).

career.[81] As juvenile delinquents they frequently carried and used weapons of violence. Their arrest histories showed a mean of 18.2 arrests.

> An early patterning of stealing from their parents, from school, and on the street; truancy, and suspension or expulsion from school; street fighting, association with older delinquents, and juvenile delinquent gang memberships, all were usually evident in their social backgrounds. When compared with the men in the other criminal categories it was found that there was more destruction of property in their delinquent activities, and there were more frequent fights with schoolmates, male teachers, and delinquent companions. There was a higher incidence of "mugging" and purse snatching. They had more often been the leaders of delinquent gangs, and they claimed they were leaders because of their superior size and physical strength. . . . Criminal progression appeared to occur at a more rapid rate with an early trend toward crimes of violence—from petty thefts and playground fights, to the rolling of drunks and homosexuals, and on to holdups with such weapons as pistols and knives.[82]

One study has described five brothers with conventional criminal careers.[83] The two oldest brothers began their delinquency in company with a gang of twelve boys ranging in age from five to twelve. "Their playgrounds were the alleys, streets, and railroad yards; their activities were largely spontaneous, random, and unsupervised; simple forms of stealing were interspersed with nondelinquent activities with little realization of their moral implications." They stole all varieties of objects, most of them for fun. The more experienced and older delinquents furnished the models and encouraged the younger and less experienced to engage in more serious thefts. The three younger brothers became involved in this network chiefly through the indoctrination of their older brothers and other boys. All moved from truancy and petty stealing to stealing more valuable objects. Their contacts with conventional society were limited. They had intimate association with at least 250 known delinquents and criminals. Their associations gave them the moral sanctions to commit crime and to sell their stolen articles. "They lived in a social world in which delinquency served a dual purpose—on the one hand, it was a means by which they secured the friendly regard, approval, and approbation of their fellows, while on the other hand, it served as a source of economic gain." Edward was arrested at

---

[81] Julian B. Roebuck and Mervyn L. Cadwallader, "The Negro Armed Robber as a Criminal Type: The Construction and Application of a Typology," *Pacific Sociological Review*, 4:21–26 (1961).

[82] Roebuck and Cadwallader, p. 24.

[83] Clifford R. Shaw, Henry D. McKay, and James F. McDonald, *Brothers in Crime* (Chicago: University of Chicago Press, 1938). Quotations from pages 109 and 119.

twenty-one for stealing a car and at twenty-four for carrying a concealed weapon, James at seventeen was arrested four times for attempted or actual theft of autos; Michael at fifteen for robbery with a gun, burglary and larceny of cars, and Carl at thirteen for the theft of two cars. Nearly all of their crimes were committed in company with either a brother or a brother and other persons. All except one had terminated their criminal careers by the time they were twenty-five.

Societal Reaction

There is strong societal reaction to conventional offenders; punishments for those committing burglary and robbery are apt to be severe. These penalties in part represent society's desire to protect property and to punish harshly whenever violence is used, to obtain it. Because these offenders usually have extensive records as juveniles and young adults; prosecuting attorneys are likely to have a stereotyped view of such offenders and to secure from them a guilty plea to a lesser but still a severe charge.[84]

ORGANIZED CRIME

Organized crime is represented by criminal syndicates or rings whose members engage in criminal activities as a source of livelihood. Numerically, the number of persons involved is not large; the extent of their criminal activities and their effect upon society is, however, great. The public bestows the epithet "mobster" or "gangster" upon those active in organized crime, even though technically these terms should be reserved for those few individuals of this group who use force and violence. Criminal syndicates are usually well organized, and their operations are often of an intracity, intercity, or interstate character.[85] The characteristic features of organized crime are these:

1. Hierarchy involving a system of specifically defined relationships with mutual obligations and privileges.
2. Not confined by political or geographic boundaries. Intracity or intercity; intra- or interstate.

---

[84] David Sudnow, "Normal Crimes: Sociological Aspects of the Penal Code in a Public Defender Office," *Social Problems,* 12:255–276 (1965), and Donald J. Newman, "Pleading Guilty for Considerations: A Study of Bargain Justice," *Journal of Criminal Law, Criminology, and Police Science,* 46:780–790 (1956). Also see Donald J. Newman, *Conviction: The Determination of Guilt or Innocence Without Trial* (Boston: Little, Brown & Co., 1966).

[85] See Gus Tyler, ed., *Organized Crime in America* (Ann Arbor: University of Michigan Press, 1962).

3. Dependence upon
   a. the use of force and violence to maintain internal discipline and restrain competition;
   b. the securing and maintaining of permanent immunity from interference from law enforcement and other agencies of government.
4. Criminals operating for large financial gains and specializing in one or more combinations of enterprises which fall in the areas of social deviation where public opinion is divided.
5. Striving for either monopolistic control or establishment of spheres of influence between or among different organizations.

The most important characteristic of organized crime is its feudal pattern or "family." The structure of nearly all criminal syndicates is similar to that of the Mafia, which is here called La Cosa Nostra.[86] (See Figure 8.2.) Leaders of particular syndicates have the allegiance of several underlords who, in turn, have coteries of henchmen varying from lieutenants to what might be called "serfs." An organized crime syndicate is "held together by powerful leaders, by intense personal loyalties, by the gangsters' code of morals, by alliances and agreements with rival gangster chiefs, and by their common warfare against the forces of organized society."[87] There are interlocking relations between one syndicate and another and between one individual leader and another so that a given syndicate or a given leader may be engaged in several areas of crime.

Organized crime in the United States contains 24 groups operating in the large cities. "Their membership is exclusively Italian, they are in frequent communication with each other, and their smooth functioning is insured by a national board of overseers."[88] Each of the 24 groups, known as a "family," has a membership of as many as 700 and as few as 20. Most cities have only one such group; New York City has five. The wealthiest and most influential groups operate in New York, New Jersey, Illinois, Florida, Louisiana, Nevada, Michigan, and Rhode Island, but illegal activities in many other states are controlled from these places. Organized criminal groups operate in all sections of the country. "In response to a Commission survey of 71 cities, the police departments in 80 percent of the cities with over 1 million residents, in 20 percent of the cities with a population be-

---

[86] Robert T. Anderson, "From Mafia to Cosa Nostra," *American Journal of Sociology,* 81:302–310 (1965). Also see *The Challenge of Crime in a Free Society* (Washington, D.C.: Government Printing Office, 1967), p. 192.

[87] Ernest W. Burgess, "Summary and Recommendations," *Illinois Crime Survey* (Chicago: Illinois Association for Criminal Justice, 1929), Pt. 3, p. 1092.

[88] *The Challenge of Crime in a Free Society,* p. 192.

An Organized Crime Family

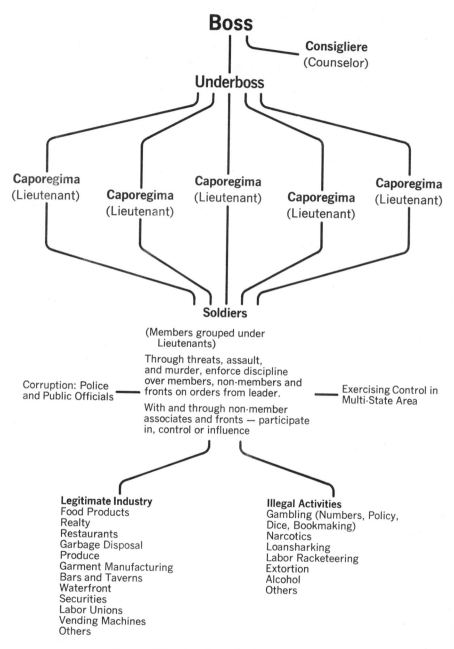

FIGURE 8.2 An Organized Crime Family

SOURCE: *The Challenge of Crime in a Free Society,* A Report of the President's Commission on Law Enforcement and Administration of Justice (Washington, D.C.: Government Printing Office, 1967), p. 194.

tween one-half million and a million, in 20 percent of the cities with between 250,000 and 500,000 population, and in over 50 percent of the cities
between 100,000 and 250,000, indicated that organized criminal groups
exist in their cities." [89]

Organized crime is more than a feudal hierarchy built to carry on
particular criminal activities; it is also organized to keep its members out
of legal entanglements. Connections with political machines or with
branches of the legal system, such as the police or the courts, bring almost
permanent immunity from arrest or, if there should be an arrest, make it
possible to apply the "fix." The Kefauver Committee reported in 1951 that
in New York City the Gross bookmaking empire had paid over $1,000,000
a year for police protection; in Philadelphia approximately $152,000 was
paid out each month in thirty-eight police districts.[90] The fix is not worked
out individually by each criminal when a need arises; instead, organized
criminal syndicates maintain such close political connections that local
immunity for their members is almost assured, especially for the top men
in the syndicate.

> The same pattern of organized crime found in large metropolitan
> areas exists in the medium-sized cities with similar evidence of official sanc-
> tion or protection. In some cases the protection is obtained by the pay-
> ment of bribes to public officials, often on a regular basis pursuant to a
> carefully conceived system. In other cases, the racketeering elements make
> substantial contributions to political campaigns of officials who can be
> relied upon to tolerate their activities. Sometimes these contributions will
> support a whole slate of officers in more than one political party, giving
> the racketeers virtual control of the governing body.[91]

Organized criminal syndicates maintain their close association with
political machines either through direct payoffs or through delivery of votes,
honest or fraudulent. The payoffs are used by politicians, police commis-
sioners, or police captains or lieutenants either as personal assets or as
contributions for the political machine. Both the contributions and the aid
in delivering votes, which possibly requires only the endorsement of the
party by the syndicate leader in local community areas, bring immunity,
either direct or indirect. Immunity also comes through the appointment

---

[89] *The Challenge of Crime in a Free Society,* p. 191.

[90] Third Interim Report of the Special Committee to Investigate Organized
Crime in Interstate Commerce, United States Senate, 82d Cong., 1st Sess., S.R. 307
(Washington, D.C.: 1951), pp. 1–2.

[91] Final Report of the Special Committee to Investigate Organized Crime in
Interstate Commerce, United States Senate, 82d Cong., 1st Sess., S.R. 725 (Washington, D.C.: 1951), p. 5.

of councilmen, police officers, prosecutors, judges, and other government officials who will cooperate with the leaders of organized crime and who will pass the word along that the syndicate is to be let alone. Frank Costello, leader of an organized criminal syndicate who was later sent to prison, was found in 1950 to have been friendly with many of the district leaders of the Democratic party and with many judges in New York City. Some political appointments were Costello's friends. Asked about them, Costello replied, "I know them, know them well and maybe they got a little confidence in me." [92]

Organized Crime as a Career

The feudal organization of a crime syndicate makes generalization about the backgrounds of its members difficult. Most of the members of the syndicates come from the slum, have a record of delinquencies, and have had some association with the Mafia or Cosa Nostra.[93] Many of their histories resemble the conventional criminal career, in which there is progression in a long series of delinquencies and crime and association with a tough gang of young offenders. Instead of ending their criminal careers in their twenties, however, they have continued their activities in association with some syndicate. One significant factor in this continuance is their habituation to crime, which means that they may attach themselves to criminal groups as conditions seem suitable. "Organized crime, manifesting itself in gangs and in the larger structures within which gangs function, may be regarded as the result of a process of sifting and selection whose final product is a criminal residue." [94]

The delinquent gang of the slum produces the adult gangster who uses strong-arm methods and is employed for this very purpose by the organized criminal groups. Gangsters usually come from our large cities, frequently have long criminal records of armed robberies, and have a conception of themselves as "tough." Those who are successful in the syndicate sometimes take it over.

> In many instances organized criminal machines have called upon the services of gangsters for protective or offensive operations only to have the gangsters take over the operations themselves. In other instances gangsters have been content to be on the payroll of a prosperous organization and to

---

[92] Third Interim Report of the Special Committee to Investigate Organized Crime in Interstate Commerce, p. 121.

[93] Anderson.

[94] Alfred R. Lindesmith, "Organized Crime," *The Annals*, 217:123 (1941). Also see life history of a gangster in John Landesco's "The Gangster's Apologia Pro Vita Sua," in *Illinois Crime Survey*, Pt. 3, pp. 1043–1057.

get a considerable cut of the profits without assuming full control. Gangsters are usually recruited from the slums of American cities. They have come up through the sand lots of crime and have made crime their career. Most of them have been members of small boys' gangs and have graduated to larger boys' gangs and later to affiliation with organized crime and political machines. They have made themselves useful to both political machines and organized crime. The gangster is the toughest of American criminals and invariably his is a blatant career of criminal activity.[95]

Organized Crime and Legitimate Behavior Patterns

Organized crime largely operates in those areas which are "moral problems," areas where public sentiment is divided over the actual immorality of such behavior.[96] As a result, organized crime finds less coordinated opposition from the general public and law-enforcement agencies in these areas.[97] Furthermore, because so many people want some of these illegal services, the revenues from them are large. It is thus possible for organized racketeers to make a substantial income and at the same time pay off properly those political officials without whose connivance no organized criminal activity could operate. Some of the more important areas in which organized crime has operated include liquor, prostitution, narcotics, gambling, union shakedowns, and industrial and business shakedowns. During Prohibition organized crime operated most extensively in supplying illegal liquor, which went out with the repeal of the Prohibition Amendment. Prostitution is a large area but not as large or as profitable as it was formerly. It now usually involves a syndicate of many prostitutes who are chiefly "call girls" and for whom the organized syndicate helps arrange the necessary "fix" or other overall business arrangements. Another area of organized crime has been, and still is, the drug traffic. Organized crime today finds that gambling and various forms of labor and industry racketeering bring the highest returns; hence it dominates their activities.

Control of Syndicate Enterprises

Organized crime also infiltrates legitimate businesses by investments and uses this legitimate control as a screen for its criminal activities. Too often, because of the reciprocal benefits involved in organized crime's dealing with the business world, or because of fear, the legitimate sector of

---

[95] Reckless (3d ed.), p. 203. Between 1964 and the end of 1967 forty-six gangsters were killed in gang warfare in Boston.

[96] Richard Fuller and Richard R. Myers, "Some Aspects of a Theory of Social Problems," *American Sociological Review*, 6:24–32 (1941).

[97] Gus Tyler, "The Roots of Organized Crime," in *Crime and Delinquency*, 8:325–338 (1962).

society helps the illegitimate sector. Investigations held by a U.S. Senate committee found that organized crime had infiltrated at least fifty legitimate business areas, including banking, insurance, liquor, loans, and juke boxes.[98] "Control of business concerns has usually been acquired through one of four methods: (1) investing concealed profits acquired from gambling and other illegal activities; (2) accepting business interests in payment of the owner's gambling debts; (3) foreclosing on usurious loans, and (4) using various forms of extortion." [99]

Second only to gambling in its attractiveness to organized crime is racketeering in labor unions and business. The term *racketeering* is often loosely used to refer to almost any criminal activity. In a strict sense, however, it refers to the use of organized force to maintain control over some organization, to extort money from it, or to force some services upon it. Racketeering has been used to maintain control of the members of a union or to defeat another union which is competing with it for members. In business racketeering, efforts are made to force concerns to pay tribute to "protect" themselves from violence, such as damaging clothes in a cleaning and dyeing establishment, or to maintain price fixing. Tribute may also be demanded to avoid a wildcat strike. Although racketeering activities have affected many industries, they have been particularly prevalent in the motion-picture industry, the building trades, liquor stores, laundry and cleaning establishments, and the waterfront, trucking, and loading businesses.[100] Senate investigations of the relation between certain union officials and organized criminals have in recent years brought this area of organized crime, particularly, to the public's attention.[101] The New York waterfront, for example, has a long history of domination by labor racketeers, and repeated attempts on the part of local and state officials to control this situation have proved unsuccessful.[102]

Racketeers in unions and businesses may use overt force in the form of property damage or physical violence to intimidate; or they may be more subtle and simply threaten a strike. A hierarchy of henchmen may maintain a certain leadership in control of a union, or may force certain retail outlets to pay a money tribute or to purchase a designated commodity, on the threat of destroying their merchandise or equipment. In re-

---

[98] U.S. Senate Special Committee to Investigate Organized Crime in Interstate Commerce, Third Interim Report, p. 171.

[99] *The Challenge of Crime in a Free Society,* p. 190.

[100] Malcolm Johnson, *Crime on the Labor Front* (New York: McGraw-Hill Book Company, Inc., 1950).

[101] See Kennedy.

[102] George C. Wright, "The Boss on the Pier: Waterfront Portraits," *The New York Times,* January 25, 1953.

turn for acquiescence to its demands the syndicate may offer to "protect" members of a given trade association not only from out ide forces but even from unfair competition in its own field, thus providing something in return for its exactions. Businessmen may be forced to join an "association" and pay dues to it in order to be protected from violence. In its more extreme form such an association may also control and fix prices in order to avoid price cutting. The Special Senate Committee to Investigate Organized Crime reported that in "some instances legitimate businessmen had aided the interests of the underworld by awarding lucrative contracts to gangsters and mobsters in return for help in handling employees, in defeating attempts at organization, and in breaking strikes."[103]

It is extremely difficult for law-enforcement officers to control such activities. Intimidation through fear of violence, the tie-ups among politicians, police, and organized criminals, the "fix," the difficulty of securing legal evidence, and inadequate laws interfere with the successful prosecution of racketeering. Occasionally businessmen have banded together to form a crime commission, as in Chicago, and to resist racketeering pressure more effectively through the threat of publicity.

Gambling

In 1951 a Senate committee found that organized criminals derive enormous profits from gambling. The "take" on a slot machine is about $50 a week; thus a mere two hundred machines would bring in about $10,000 weekly. A single one of the eight large policy wheels in Chicago made an annual net profit of over $1,000,000. In many large cities, as well as elsewhere, bookmakers, mostly associated with organized crime, specialize in bets on horse racing, professional boxing matches, baseball, hockey, and professional or amateur football and basketball games. Formerly the betting was concentrated on professional events, but college football and basketball games have drawn more and more of it.[104]

To wager money or anything else upon an outcome which depends largely on chance is gambling.[105] Gambling is illegal in nearly all parts of the United States, although most forms of gambling are legal in Nevada. There are wide variations in the attitudes of people toward private and public gambling. Gambling among friends for small stakes in such card

---

[103] Third Interim Report of the Special Committee to Investigate Organized Crime in Interstate Commerce, p. 5.

[104] See Chapter 7 for a discussion of the fixing of college basketball games by organized criminal syndicates.

[105] For a full discussion, see the series of articles on "Gambling," *The Annals*, Vol. 269 (1950). This issue dealt with the legal status, various forms of gambling, the gambler, and gambling in foreign countries.

games as poker, blackjack, and bridge is generally not regarded as gambling which is essentially bad. When gambling becomes public and commercialized so that its operation requires bets from a great many persons in an impersonal urban situation over which the individual has practically no control, public attitudes are divided over its social usefulness; moreover, it is an inviting situation for organized racketeers.

Generally, wherever opportunities are present for gambling, large numbers of persons are interested in participating, even though they may be publicly against it. There appear to be a number of reasons for this.[106] Gambling appeals because of the chance factor for success, regardless of the type of skill involved in it. In some societies, generally those where social status is achieved by, and depends upon, successful competition for money and material goods, the chance element is more important than in others. In Western European society it is very difficult to distinguish between situations in which there is a chance element called gambling and many other financial transactions which also contain a chance element and yet are not officially classified as forms of gambling.

Gambling also represents relief from the routine and boredom of contemporary urban life. Betting on something is often fascinating both to the participant and to the spectator. Whether one wins or not, for a while there is excitement over the possible result. The appeal of different forms of gambling varies according to social class, sex, and other differences, most gambling occurring among the lower and working classes. A study of lower-class gambling found that it appears to offer more than a means of recreation or monetary gain; it also serves the function of status rewards of success and recognition by others.[107] Chiefly it is a way of beating "the system" by picking a winner. Swedish gambling, like that in the United States, is predominantly among the lower class; it offers people an unrealistic "hope" for personal social betterment in seeking to fulfill their mobility aspirations.[108]

In some parts of Western society opposition to commercialized gambling seems to be based on the fact that gambling does not perform any socially productive economic function, for in a sense it is securing money without working to earn it. The odds in some forms of gambling, par-

---

[106] Herbert A. Bloch, "The Sociology of Gambling," *American Journal of Sociology,* 57:215–221 (1951); and David D. Allen, *The Nature of Gambling* (New York: Coward-McCann, Inc., 1952).

[107] Irving K. Zola, "Gambling in a Lower Class Setting," *Social Problems,* 10:353–361 (1963).

[108] Nechama Tec, *Gambling in Sweden* (Totowa, N.J.: The Bedminster Press, 1964).

ticularly organized gambling, are so great that the chances of winning are actually very small. Finally, because commercialized gambling must bribe law-enforcement officers and other public officials in order to secure the necessary "protection," it is opposed by many because of the effect of its methods. Gambling is legal in Sweden and a Swedish study of those who gambled on "football" (soccer) matches failed to show that gambling results in changes in the ordinary career of an individual.[109] Compared with non-gamblers, it did not affect their involvements with friends, dependence on families, and acceptance of family responsibilities. Gambling did not lead to unemployment, occupational apathy, and lack of initiative in work involvement. Gambling was not excessive, participation being proportionate to the individual income.

Commercialized gambling is of two types. In one, the person gambles in an establishment with such devices as roulette wheels, dice, or slot machines. In the other, bets are placed on larger events, such as illegal lotteries and "policy," the "numbers racket," horse or dog races, or various sports events. Policy is a variation of the lottery in that bets are placed on the drawing of numbers. The numbers racket involves a bet placed on the three digits of certain events, such as, for example, the daily United States Treasury balance of clearinghouse totals or racing pari-mutuels. In both policy and the numbers racket the amount of the wager, as well as the chance of winning, is small, but the odds paid are large.

The lucrative returns from gambling enterprises make them most attractive to organized crime. A considerable organization is required to distribute forms and collect bets. In the Detroit numbers racket, there were some thirty-five separate organizations, some of which were grouped into syndicates. These organizations had "cover banks" which underwrote the bets placed by the local gambling place as a protection against a run on a particular number. For efficient operation the gambling syndicate employed writers or runners, pick-up men or collectors of bets, cashiers, clerks, checkers, and operators. Tickets with winning numbers were redeemed by cashiers on the spot; if the holders were not present, the money was delivered by a runner.[110] There is also the "fix," as one New York bookmaker has stated: "The whole business is pretty damn complicated, let me tell you. I gotta worry about my runners so I gotta pay off beat cops, squad cars, detectives, everybody. In the last ten years I paid off $1 million to cops. It cuts into the profits, but, what the hell, a business is a business."[111]

---

[109] Tec.

[110] Gustav G. Carlson, "Number Gambling: A Study of a Culture Complex." Unpublished doctoral dissertation, University of Michigan, Ann Arbor, 1940.

[111] Roger Kahn and Richard Schaap, "The Mania to Bet on Sports," *Newsweek,* June 6, 1960, p. 41.

Gambling interests are protected through collusion between politicians and organized criminal syndicates. In 1951 the Special Senate Committee to Investigate Organized Crime reported that the most significant thing about organized criminal activities in gambling was "the extent of official corruption and connivance in facilitating and promoting organized crime." Top mobsters were found to be immune from prosecution, policemen and sheriffs were bribed, and political leaders were bought off. The committee gathered evidence of corruption of law-enforcement officers in practically all the many cities in which it held hearings.

Betting on horse races operates mainly in a complex urban environment, largely indulged in by millions of urban persons who seldom see horses, let alone horse races. Although several states permit pari-mutuel betting at race tracks, almost every state prohibits absentee betting through bookmakers. In many states, regardless of whether pari-mutuel betting is legal or not, absentee betting through organized criminal syndicates is a violation of law.

Societal Reaction

Although societal reaction is strong against organized crime as such, there have been few effective measures of control, and for a number of reasons: (1) difficulties in obtaining proof, (2) lack of effective resources to deal with nation-wide crime syndicates, (3) lack of coordination among local, state, and federal agencies, (4) failure to develop strategic intelligence, (5) failure effectively to use available sanctions in that sentences are frequently not commensurate with the financial rewards obtained from the illegal activity, and (6) finally, lack of public and private commitment.[112]

> The public demands action only sporadically, as intermittent, sensational disclosures reveal intolerable violence and corruption caused by organized crime. Without sustained public pressure, political office seekers and office holders have little incentive to address themselves to combatting organized crime. A drive against organized crime usually uncovers political corruption; this means that a crusading mayor or district attorney makes many political enemies. The vicious cycle perpetuates itself. Politicians will not act unless the public so demands; but much of the urban public wants the services provided by organized crime and does not wish to disrupt the system that provides those services. And much of the public does not see or understand the effects of organized crime in society.[113]

Much of organized crime has been illegal for some time; new laws, particularly federal attempts to control it by laws dealing with interstate

---

[112] *The Challenge of Crime in a Free Society,* pp. 198–200.
[113] *The Challenge of Crime in a Free Society,* p. 200.

commerce, have been tried, as well as other new laws, at the local, state, and federal levels.[114] In 1961, for example, three new federal laws made it illegal to use the mails to distribute the proceeds of gambling, prostitution, narcotics, or liquor sales; to carry or send across state lines, except when legal, records, tickets, or other materials used in gambling and to use teletypes or the telegraph for such information.

Some people believe that the solution to illegal gambling in the United States is to legalize it as in Nevada. Most countries have state lotteries, sweepstakes, or other forms of betting which bring in much revenue for the state after the winners are paid off. Sweden, for example, legalized betting on sports pools in 1934, the betting being supervised by a corporation consisting of members of several sports organizations. Some of the revenue is used for these organizations and for expenses, but the largest share goes to the government.

There is some question as to whether commercialized gambling could be legalized throughout the United States in the same manner as is done in many European countries. Many who have studied the problem believe that legalization is not the solution.[115] They argue that it would be too large an enterprise for the government and that legalized gambling in the United States might become infiltrated by the same criminal elements that now control illegal gambling, as has happened to a considerable extent in Nevada.[116] Moreover, politicians and public officials would be even more vulnerable than now to corruption. Finally, people, on the whole, do not participate in commercialized forms of gambling. Should it become legalized they might engage in it more extensively than they now do, or than is done in countries where gambling is legal, because it has been largely illegal in the United States.

Probably the most effective way to deal with gambling in the United States is to develop in the public a realization not only of the effects of commercialized gambling on law-enforcement personnel and other public officials but need for more enforcement of laws against commercialized gambling. The states will need help from the federal government, which can give it because commercialized gambling is interstate. Since 1951, for example, there has been a federal tax on bookmakers amounting to 10 percent of the gross bets each month and a $50 tax on those who accept bets. Finally, state and federal lotteries might succeed in diverting some illegal betting, but their use would present many difficulties.

---

[114] *The Challenge of Crime in a Free Society*, pp. 200–209.

[115] See, for example, Virgil W. Peterson, "Gambling: Should It Be Legalized?" *Journal of Criminal Law and Criminology*, 40:259–329 (1949); and Allen.

[116] See Estes Kefauver, *Crime in America* (New York: Doubleday & Company, Inc., 1951), pp. 229–237.

Despite legislative efforts to control it, organized crime continues, primarily because of its political and police tie-ups but also because it often provides a needed commodity, such as gambling, or serves to provide regulation in a union or to maintain monopoly prices in certain types of legitimate businesses. For this reason, and because of a certain degree of public tolerance toward organized crime, it is very difficult to enforce laws, Vold has concluded:

> Organized crime must be thought of as a natural growth, or as a developmental adjunct to our general system of private profit economy. Business, industry, and finance are all competitive enterprises within the area of legal operations. But there is also an area of genuine economic demand for things and services not permitted under our legal and social codes. Organized crime is the system of business functioning in this area. It, too, is competitive, and hence must organize for its self-protection and for control of the market.[117]

THE PROFESSIONAL OFFENDER

Of all criminal offenders, the "professionals" have the most highly developed criminal careers, social statuses, and skills. The use of the respected term "professional" to apply to criminal activities requires some explanation. The characteristics of any professional man, whether a doctor, an accountant, a lawyer, a professor, or a professional criminal, are the result of differential association, technical skill, consensus, organization, and status.[118] Because the professional criminal has all these attributes, the designation "professional" can be challenged only on the basis that a term carrying such high status is applied to an activity whose ends are hardly legitimate. Like other members of society the professional criminal has an occupation.

Professional criminals as a group engage in a variety of highly specialized crimes. The individual develops a great deal of skill in a particular type of offense. Activities include pickpocketing (cannon), shoplifting (the boost), sneak-thieving from stores, banks, and offices (the heel), stealing from jewelry stores by substituting inferior jewelry for valuable ones (pennyweighting), stealing from hotel rooms (hotel prowling), and a variety of miscellaneous rackets, such as passing illegal checks (hanging paper), and

---

[117] George B. Vold, *Theoretical Criminology* (New York: Oxford University Press, 1958), p. 240. Also see Robert K. Woetzel, "An Overview of Organized Crime: Mores Versus Morality," *The Annals*, 347:1–11 (May 1963).

[118] Edwin H. Sutherland, *The Professional Thief* (Chicago: University of Chicago Press, 1937), p. 197. Written by a professional thief and annotated and interpreted by Sutherland.

extorting money from others engaged in illegal activities (the shake). The specialized skills exhibited by the professional check forger are quite different from those of the amateur or naïve forger.[119] These professional criminals seldom use force in connection with their activities, as is done in the "heavy rackets," although occasionally certain of these, particularly bank robbers and safecrackers, are also professionals.

Confidence games are divided into the "short con" and the "big con." In the former, money is secured illegally from an individual directly and in a brief time, through the sale, for example, of false jewelry.[120] The big con usually requires a longer period of time and involves a larger sum of money, which is secured, for example, through the operation of a "money-making machine" or the sale of fraudulent securities. These professionals, particularly those operating in the big con, must be highly intelligent, well organized, and able to "fix" law-enforcement agencies. These abilities account, in part, for the fact that few confidence men ever go to prison or are even brought to trial.[121] A great asset for the con man is the fact that his victim is often also out to violate the law, either in accepting the illegal proposition of the confidence man or in engaging in illegal activity to raise money for the confidence game. Probably 90 percent of the victims, therefore, never complain to the police.

A special type of con man is the professional "hustler" who makes his living betting against his opponents, often with a backer, in various types of pool or billiard games and in so doing engages in various deceitful practices, such as hiding his own high degree of skill in the games. His conning involves an "extraordinary manipulation of other people's impressions of reality and especially of one's self, creating 'false impressions.' "[122] His concern about the evaluation of his behavior by others varies according to whether they are intended or actual victims, outsiders or colleagues.

The high status of professional criminals is reflected by the attitudes of other criminals and by the special treatment usually accorded them by the police, court officials, and others. This social status of the professional criminal is the result of several factors including "technical skill, financial standing, connections, power, dress, manners, and wide knowledge acquired

---

[119] Edwin M. Lemert, "The Behavior of the Systematic Check Forger," *Social Problems*, 6:141–149 (1958).

[120] Julian B. Roebuck and Ronald C. Johnson, "The 'Short Con' Man," *Crime and Delinquency*, 10:235–248 (July 1964).

[121] See, for example, Joseph R. Weil, *"Yellow Kid" Weil* (as told to W. T. Brannon; New York: A. S. Barnes and Company, 1948).

[122] Ned Polsky, "The Hustler," *Social Problems*, 12:3–15 (1964), and Ned Polsky, *Hustlers, Beats and Others* (Chicago: Aldine Publishing Company, 1967).

in his migratory life." [123] Offenders of lower-status groups tend to look up to the professional, whereas professional thieves are contemptuous of amateurs and have many epithets for them, such as "snatch-and-grab thief," "boot-and-shoe thief," and "best-hold cannon." A professional thief has nothing in common with those who commit forcible rape or child molesting crimes, and he would not even be courteous to them if he chanced to meet them in jail. He also has little in common with an occasional or a conventional offender, other than sympathy for a fellow lawbreaker, for they would seldom have common acquaintances or similar techniques of stealing.

Highly skilled criminal activities, however, do not alone make a criminal a professional, for even more important are other characteristics of his social role. In terms of social role, according to Sutherland, "a person who is received in the group and recognized as a professional thief is a professional thief." This role is the result of extensive contacts with others. Professional thieves have in common "acquaintances, congeniality, sympathy, understandings, agreements, rules, codes of behavior, and language." [124]

In comparison with other offenders, an extremely high degree of consensus exists among professional criminals, who develop common attitudes toward themselves, toward their crimes, and toward their common enemy, the police. These common attitudes include the support of other thieves in order to overcome the ostracism of conventional society. The group gives its members a cultural situation in which to carry on their social existence and a set of values held in common by all thieves. More specifically, the relationships among professional criminals are characterized by a "code of honor." In a sense this corresponds to the code of ethics and standards governing conduct in the more respectable professions. A professional thief, for example, is always punctual about his obligations and appointments. He must never "squeal" on another member of the profession.

Probably the best example of consensus in any profession, including professional crime, is the special language or argot by which members communicate with one another in a separate set of symbols. Various academic departments—sociology is one example—have separate symbols for conversation, as do the medical and legal professions. This language is not employed to hide anything, for its use in public would attract considerable attention among laymen. It is handed down from one generation to another; hence many of the terms used by professional criminals, like the terms used

---

[123] Sutherland, *The Professional Thief,* p. 200.
[124] Sutherland, *The Professional Thief,* p. 207.

by doctors, can be traced back several hundred years.[125] They give unity to the group and serve as a specialized language for specialized activities, as in any group, and other terms are adapted to their needs.[126] Hundreds of terms are used and understood by professional criminals, but rarely by other criminals. Their argot refers to other criminals, the rackets, the public, law-enforcement officers, and many other aspects of their lives.

> *Bandhouse* (n): House of correction or workhouse.
> *Boost* (n): The racket of shoplifting.
> *Cannon* (n): The pickpocket racket; a member of a mob engaged in the racket of picking pockets.
> *Fix* (v): Arrange immunity for a thief on a criminal charge.
> *Hang paper* (v): Write fraudulent checks.
> *Hook* (n): A member of a pickpocket mob who extracts the pocketbook from the pocket of the victim.
> *Poke* (n): Pocketbook.
> *Score* (n): Successful theft, referring to the value of the stolen property.
> *Sucker* (n): Victim; anyone who is not a thief.[127]

Although professional crime is not characterized by the same degree of formal organization as is organized crime, there is a system of extensive informal unity and reciprocal relations among thieves. In fact, the system consists of the whole complex of techniques, status, consensus, and differential association among thieves. Each professional thief, because of his extensive mobility, is known personally by a large number of professional thieves. He not only knows thieves in other cities but usually knows them by a nickname—Yellow Kid, Curly, or Chic. Information regarding methods and situations becomes known and shared by all professionals, as is illustrated by phrases such as "Toledo is a good town," "The lunch hour is the best time to work that spot," "Look out for the red-haired saleslady—she's double smart," and "See Skid if you should get a tumble in Chicago." Likewise, any thief will assist another if he is in difficulty. A professional thief may warn another, or he may take up a collection to help a thief who is in jail or to assist the man's family. Although these services may be reciprocal, they are not performed with this purpose in mind.

---

[125] Sutherland, *The Professional Thief*. Also see Eric Partridge, *A Dictionary of Slang and Unconventional English* (New York: The Macmillan Company, 1950).

[126] David W. Maurer, *The Big Con* (New York: Pocket Books, Inc., 1949), pp. 282–283.

[127] Sutherland, *The Professional Thief*, pp. 235–243 and David W. Maurer, *The Whiz Mob* (New Haven, Conn.: College and University Press, 1964), pp. 200–216.

The professional shoplifter or "heel" sells his stolen merchandise rather than stealing for consumption, as does the amateur. Generally they work in small "troupes," touring the country, staying long enough in a given place to clout (shoplift) and dispose of stolen merchandise. Their techniques are skilled, using "bad bags" (old printed paper bags from a store), "booster" skirts or bloomers, and "booster boxes" (boxes, for example, observably ready for mailing).[128]

The newcomer in the profession is first given preliminary instructions about the crime. He is trained by other professionals and frequently the techniques he uses have a long history.[129] His first efforts are made in a minor capacity, and he is given the kind of assistance he would later resent. If he does these minor assignments well, he is promoted to more important ones. During this probationary period he is taught the morality and etiquette of his profession. He acquires "larceny sense," learns how to dispose of stolen goods, and how to fix cases. He builds up associations with other criminals and the appropriate public officials. If successful, he is admitted to full status with other thieves. Frequently professional criminals are recruited from persons in their twenties who display potential skills but without necessarily having a record of previous delinquency or crime; for example, professional counterfeiters may recruit someone who works as an engraver.

Societal Reaction

There are not many professional criminals. The public tends to tolerate professional crime, such as confidence games, because of the collaboration with legitimate enterprise and the rather unusual nature of most crimes of this type. Various preventive devices have made professional forging more difficult and there is a possibility that it, as well as other types of professional crime, is declining. This may account for some of the lack of public concern.

Because of their highly developed skill, professional criminals are usually accorded special treatment by the police, the court, and other official persons. Sometimes they are able to buy protection and are able generally to arrange a fix to avoid punishment. They are often able to avoid conviction because of these informal processes; moreover, the fact of their not having a previous record does not fit the usual public stereotype of a highly developed offender. "Even perfect technique fails occasionally, but the advantage the professional shoplifter has (as with most professional

---

[128] Cameron, pp. 42–50.

[129] Arthur V. Judges, *The Elizabethan Underworld* (London: Routledge & Kegan Paul, Ltd., 1930).

thieves) over other shoplifters is to use his influence and 'know-how' in resolving a lengthy jail or prison sentence. An attorney will have been carefully selected for his 'right' connections (a condition rumored not to be too difficult to ascertain in many municipal courts)." [130]

SUMMARY

The terms *delinquent* and *criminal* have little real meaning, for actually there are many criminal types. Classifications of criminals based on the type of crime, age, or sex of the offender are useful for legal or statistical purposes, but for a scientific approach, behavior systems are a more satisfactory classification. Career criminals identify themselves with crime, have a conception of themselves as criminals, have extensive association with criminal activities, and have progressed in criminal techniques and in the frequency of offenses. Crime is a chief source of their income.

A behavior system involves the criminal career of the offender, group support of the criminal behavior, correspondence between criminal behavior and legitimate behavior patterns, and the societal reaction to the criminal behavior.

The criminal career of the offender consists of social roles, identification with crime, conception of self, pattern of differential association with others, progression in crime, and the degree to which criminal behavior has become a part of the life organization. Persons have associations which are criminal and noncriminal and whose effect seems to depend in part on their frequency, duration, priority, and intensity.

Violent personal offenses such as criminal homicide, assault, and forcible rape generally are not of the career type. They should be looked at, however, in the perspective of social behavior and as arising primarily from a subculture of violence. Occasional offenders do not have a conception of themselves as criminals, do not play a criminal role, and have little sustained group criminal support for their activities. Habitual petty offenders have had long criminal careers, but their criminal pattern is not highly developed. Occupational offenders are largely products of differential association, but in some instances it is also important to take into account their role organization. There is considerable organization in occupational crime. An occupational offender does not generally conceive of himself as a criminal Violations of trust appear to be products of opportunity and the existence of a nonsharable problem, along with the knowledge of how to violate and rationalizations about the violation.

In conventional criminal careers the offender moves from juvenile gang

---

130 Cameron, pp. 47–48.

associations to adult criminal behavior of a more serious type. There is a continuous acquisition of techniques and rationalizations about crime. Organized crime is a feudal structure involving widespread criminal operations, often of an interstate nature. There is a close relation between organized crime and political corruption. Areas of organized crime are largely those in which public sentiments are divided over the actual immorality of the behavior. Gambling today is one of the chief areas of organized crime. Professional criminals are characterized by a high degree of differential association, technical skill, consensus, organization, and status.

SELECTED READINGS

Bloch, Herbert A. "The Sociology of Gambling," *American Journal of Sociology,* 57:215–221 (1951). An analysis of the function of gambling in a society and the reasons for opposition to gambling in Western European society.

Challenge of Crime in a Free Society, The. A report of the President's Commission on Law Enforcement and Administration of Justice. Washington, D.C.: Government Printing Office, 1967. Contains a detailed discussion of youthful crime and organized crime.

Clinard, Marshall B. *The Black Market: A Study of White-Collar Crime.* New York: Holt, Rinehart and Winston, Inc., 1952. A study of price and rationing violations during World War II and an explanation of this white-collar crime.

———, and Richard Quinney. *Criminal Behavior Systems: A Typology.* New York: Holt, Rinehart and Winston, Inc., 1967. A discussion of typologies of criminal behavior and a more detailed analysis of most of the types of crime discussed here. The book also contains reports of research studies relating to those types, such as criminal homicide, forcible rape, vandalism, shoplifting, white-collar crime, and check forgery.

Cressey, Donald R. *Other People's Money.* New York: The Free Press, 1953. A study of 133 violators of trust, primarily embezzlers, in which a universal explanation was suggested for this kind of criminal behavior.

Gibney, Frank. *The Operators.* New York: Harper & Row, Publishers, 1960. A highly readable account of white-collar crime which originally appeared as a series in *Life* magazine.

Herling, John. *The Great Price Conspiracy: The Story of the Antitrust Violations in the Electrical Industry.* Washington, D.C.: Robert B. Luce, Inc., 1962. A detailed and comprehensive analysis of probably the most important case of white-collar crime. In this study of antitrust violations in the electrical industry use was made of Senate committee investigations, court records, and interviews.

Kefauver, Estes. *Crime in America.* New York: Doubleday & Company, Inc., 1951. A nation-wide investigation of organized crime was conducted by a United States Senate committee during 1951, many of the hearings being televised. Senator Kefauver, who was chairman of the committee, writes of the findings of this investigation.

Martin, John M. *Juvenile Vandalism.* Springfield, Ill.: Charles C Thomas, Publisher, 1961. One of the few studies of vandalism. Discusses the extent of vandalism. Several case histories are included.

Maurer, David W. *The Big Con.* New York: Pocket Books, Inc., 1949. Originally published in 1940 by Bobbs-Merrill Company. An excellent description of the activities of confidence men by a professor of English who had a particular interest in their special vocabulary.

Peterson, Virgil. *Barbarians in Our Midst.* Boston: Little, Brown & Company, 1952. An account by the operating director, Chicago Crime Commission, of organized crime in Chicago and its relation to politics.

Reckless, Walter C. *The Crime Problem.* 3d ed. New York: Appleton-Century-Crofts, Inc., 1961. The concept of a criminal career is discussed, and, in particular, ordinary types of criminal careers.

Shaw, Clifford R. *The Jack Roller.* Chicago: University of Chicago Press, 1930. A life history and analysis of a conventional criminal offender.

———. *The Natural History of a Delinquent Career.* Chicago: University of Chicago Press, 1931. A life history and analysis of a conventional criminal offender.

———, Henry D. McKay, and James F. McDonald. *Brothers in Crime.* Chicago: University of Chicago Press, 1938. In these well-known life histories the process of development of the conventional criminal career is outlined. Each life history is analyzed.

Sutherland, Edwin H. *The Professional Thief.* Chicago: University of Chicago Press, 1937. This account of stealing as a profession was written by a professional thief and analyzed by Sutherland.

———. *White Collar Crime.* New York: Holt, Rinehart and Winston, Inc., 1949, reissued 1960. Chapters 13 and 14 deal with white-collar crime as organized crime and present a general theory of white-collar crime.

Wolfgang, Marvin E. *Patterns in Criminal Homicide.* Philadelphia: University of Pennsylvania Press, 1958. Surveys the literature on homicide and studies nearly 600 cases of criminal homicide in Philadelphia, including both the offender and the victim. Presents the legal aspects of homicide, an analysis of race, sex, and age differences; methods and weapons used to inflict death; spatial patterns; relation to the use of alcohol; the degree of violence in homicide; and victim-precipitated homicide.

Wolfgang, Marvin E. and Franco Ferracuti. *The Subculture of Violence: Towards an Integrated Theory in Criminology.* London: Tavistock Publications, 1967. A comprehensive discussion of the concept of the subculture of violence, including the relation of values as well as comparative research, particularly on criminal homicide, on the subculture of violence in various countries.

9

Drug Addiction

According to the federal statutes, a drug addict is any person who "habitually uses a habit-forming narcotic drug as defined . . . so as to endanger the public morals, health, safety, or welfare, or who is or has been so far addicted to the use of such habit-forming narcotic drugs as to have lost the power of self-control with reference to his addiction." [1]

TYPES OF DRUGS

Although habit-forming narcotic drugs include many compounds, opiate addiction in the United States is generally from heroin or morphine, both of which are derived from opium. Other narcotic drugs of abuse are marihuana and cocaine.[2] From the standpoint of physiological effect, these drugs fall roughly into two categories, the depressants and the stimulants. As their names imply, depressants decrease mental and physical activity in varying degrees, depending upon the dosage, whereas the stimulants excite

---

[1] *Code of Laws of the United States of America,* Sec. 221, Title 21.
[2] John A. O'Donnell and John C. Ball, eds., *Narcotic Addiction* (New York: Harper & Row, Publishers, 1966), pp. 3–4.

and sustain activity and diminish symptoms of fatigue. The most important depressant drugs are marihuana, morphine, and heroin.

Marihuana (or marijuana), which is derived from the leaves and tender stems of the hemp plant, often known as "Indian hemp," is usually inhaled by smoking specially prepared cigarettes called "reefers." In spite of some controversy about the effects of marihuana, it is not usually considered by investigators in this country as a real form of drug addition in a physical sense although it may be psychological addiction. In fact, "tobacco may actually come closer to being truly addicting than does marihuana. Marihuana has a somewhat stronger psychological effect, though that effect seems to depend very much on the attitudes and beliefs of the user." [3] The usual effect is giggling and laughter, accompanied by a distorted sense of time and space, but there are no unpleasant aftereffects and little physical dependence upon the drug. Although the prolonged use of marihuana in this country is an exception rather than the rule, it may serve as a preliminary to heroin or morphine addiction, particularly for juveniles.[4]

The depressant drugs most commonly used are the *opiates,* heroin and morphine, which, together with semisynthetics and synthetics, such as ineperidine, with qualities similar to real opiates, account for the greatest proportion of drug addiction in the United States. A study of 3301 addict patients at the United States Public Health Service Hospital at Lexington, Kentucky, showed that heroin was the drug most often used.[5] Other drugs, including synthetic analgesics, are listed in Table 9.1.

---

[3]John A. Clausen, "Drug Addiction," in Robert K. Merton and Robert A. Nisbet, *Contemporary Social Problems* (2d ed.; New York: Harcourt, Brace & World, Inc., 1966), pp. 198–199.

[4]John C. Ball, "Marihuana Smoking and the Onset of Heroin Use," Proceedings of the Annual Meeting of the American College of Neuropsychopharmacology, 1966. A more recent study of 2,213 addict patients has shown that marihuana smoking is associated with the subsequent use of opiate drugs in high rise metropolitan areas of the East and West, but not associated with opiate addiction in twelve Southern states. See John C. Ball, Carl D. Chambers, and Marion J. Ball, "The Association of Marihuana Smoking with Opiate Addiction in the United States," unpublished paper presented at the annual meetings of the American Sociological Association, San Francisco, California, August 29, 1967.

[5] This institution, along with a second one at Forth Worth, Texas, was established by congressional action in 1929 for the confinement and treatment of narcotic addicts. They are now under the National Institute of Mental Health of the Public Health Service, Department of Health, Education, and Welfare. Comparing the representatives of the hospital population at Lexington with all addicts in the United States, Ball concludes that it appears to be fairly representative. "How do these 3301 patients compare with the total addict population of the nation? The

TABLE 9.1   **First Drug Diagnosis of 3301 Addict Patients at Lexington and Fort Worth Hospitals—1962**

DRUG DIAGNOSIS AT HOSPITAL	*Male*		*Female*		*Total*	
	NUMBER	PERCENT	NUMBER	PERCENT	NUMBER	PERCENT
I. *Opiates & Semi-Synthetics*						
Heroin	1753	64.6	329	56.0	2082	63.1
Morphine	242	8.9	69	11.7	311	9.4
Paregoric	202	7.4	44	7.5	246	7.5
Dilaudid	181	6.7	52	8.8	233	7.1
Codeine	116	4.3	24	4.1	140	4.2
Pantopon	17	0.6	7	1.2	24	0.7
Opium	4	0.1	4	0.7	8	0.2
Others	3	0.1	1	0.2	4	0.1
(I = 92.3%)						
II. *Synthetic Analgesics*						
Meperidine	95	3.5	41	7.0	136	4.1
Methadone	59	2.2	13	2.2	72	2.2
Other Synthetics	12	0.4	3	0.5	15	0.5
(II = 6.8%)						
III. *Other Diagnosis*						
Barbiturates	16	0.6	1	0.2	17	0.5
Marihuana	8	0.3			8	0.5
Observation	5	0.2			5	0.2
(III = 0.9%)						
Total	2713	100.0	588	100.0	3301	100.0

Difference between male and female drug diagnosis: $\chi^2 = 25.11$, P $<$ .001.
Note: Underline of last digit in total percent figure indicates that addition of the above column does not equal 100.0 due to rounding error.
SOURCE: John C. Ball, "Two Patterns of Narcotic Drug Addiction in the United States," *Journal of Criminal Law, Criminology, and Police Science,* 56:205 (1965).

Heroin and *morphine,* white powdered substances derived from opium are most frequently taken by injection, either subcutaneously or directly into the vein. Almost immediately after the injection of either drug the person becomes flushed and experiences a mild itching and tingling sensation. Gradually he becomes drowsy and relaxed and enters a state of reverie.

---

answer is that we do not know. We do not know for the simple reason that this larger group, all addicts, is a population with unknown parameters. Still, we do have various means of comparing this hospitalized population with other data pertaining to drug addiction, such as the File of Active Addicts maintained by the Bureau of Narcotics, or state and local health records." See John C. Ball, "Two Patterns of Narcotic Drug Addiction in the United States," *Journal of Criminal Law, Criminology, and Police Science,* 56:204 (1965).

Soon this state of euphoria is reached only with larger injections of the drug. Thus the addict builds up his *tolerance* for the drug as well as his dependence upon it. As this tolerance builds up, the addict becomes comparatively immune to the toxic manifestations of the drug. With morphine, for example, the tolerance may be as high as seventy-eight grains in sixteen hours, a dosage strong enough to kill twelve or more unaddicted persons. The safe therapeutic dosage of morphine given in hospitals is usually considered to be about one grain in the same period of time.

The heroin or morphine addict becomes dependent upon his injections over a varying length of time, usually quite short, the addiction increasing slowly in intensity thereafter. Authorities are generally agreed that this dependence is favored more by the regularity of administration than by the amount of the drug or the method of administration. The addict becomes as dependent on drugs as he is on food, and if he is receiving his usual daily supply he is not readily recognized as an addict. Even intimate friends and family may not know of the addiction. If the individual does not receive this daily supply, however, clearly characteristic symptoms, referred to as *withdrawal distress* or the abstinence syndrome, will appear within approximately ten to twelve hours. He may become nervous and restless, he may develop acute stomach cramps, and his eyes may water and his nose run. Later, he stops eating; he may vomit frequently, develop diarrhea, lose weight, and suffer muscular pains in the back and legs. During this period the "shakes" may develop, and if the addict cannot get relief by obtaining drugs he is in for considerable mental and physical distress. Consequently, an addict will go to almost any lengths to obtain a supply of drugs to relieve the suffering of withdrawal distress. Once the drugs are obtained, he appears normal again within about thirty minutes.

This physiological and psychological dependence on opiate drugs, with the stage always set for the withdrawal syndrome, makes this drug addict a particularly serious problem, both for himself and for society. As tolerance for the drug is developed and more and more must be taken to relieve the physiological and psychological symptoms of withdrawal distress, the habit is well established. It is difficult to break the habit.

Cocaine, the best-known stimulant drug, is not as popular now as it once was. Taken intravenously, this drug produces pleasurable sensations, described by addicts as similar to sexual orgasm. The pleasurable sensations, however, are so fleeting that repeated doses must be taken to recapture them. These cumulative dosages often produce such disagreeable symptoms as heavy perspiration, trembling hands, and even, occasionally, convulsions. Hallucinations may occur, and those who become addicted to this drug may develop delusions of persecution; hence the cocaine addict is potentially dangerous.

Barbiturates are sedatives and hypnotics that exert a powerful calming action on the central nervous system, and thus are of great value to those who suffer from nervous tension, high blood pressure, and epilepsy, as well as from a number of other physical and psychological conditions. These synthetic drugs, derived from barbital and produced in solution, tablet or capsule form, are legal when prescribed by a licensed physician. There are three general classifications: long-acting, slow-starting drugs like pheno-barbital; intermediates such as amobarbital sodium and butabarbital so-dium; and short-acting, fast-starters, pentobarbital sodium and secobarbital sodium. When properly prescribed and taken as directed, barbiturates have no lasting adverse effect. The patient's system will absorb the drug, make it harmless by liver or kidney action, depending upon the drug ingested, and eventually pass whatever residue may be left. If carelesssly used, however, barbiturates often lead to psychological dependency and physiological addic-tion. In their direct action on the body, they are potentially more dangerous than opiates, and an overdose may well lead to death because the drug can depress the brain's respiratory control to the point where breathing ceases. Under the influence of barbiturates addicts are confused and lose their sense of timing, thus they are prey to overdosages. Superficial signs of excessive barbiturate use are quite similar to the classic stages of alcohol intoxication: relaxation and increased sociability, then gloominess and irritability, then staggering, incoherence, and a lapse into deep sleep. Overdosage turns sleep into a coma, and if there is not prompt medical attention death may result.

Amphetamines, initially, work in the opposite manner, stimulating rather than relaxing the central nervous system. Sometimes they are com-bined with barbiturates to achieve a desired medical result. The combination is useful as a weight-reducing agent, but because it includes a barbiturate it might lead to dependency. Unlike barbiturates, amphetamines are not physically addictive. The body can build up tolerance to them, but users experience no physical withdrawal symptoms. Psychologically, however, these drugs are habituating; known as pep pills, they hide fatigue, create a feeling of euphoria, exhilaration, and unusual perceptiveness. Under their influence a state of mind can turn to a feeling of confidence and energy, but as the effect wears off a mild letdown occurs. Excessive use may lead to insomnia, and later exhaustion and deep depression. Overdoses of pep pills cause a loss of judgment, and the user may imagine himself capable of, and may sometimes actually attempt, impossible feats.[6]

The *hallucinogens,* or the "consciousness expanders," include the natural ones produced from certain mushrooms, morning-glory seeds, other plants, and LSD–25, a chemical synthetic mainly from lycergic acid. "The

_____

[6] The sections on the barbiturates and amphetamines is derived largely from *The Drug Takers,* Special *Time-Life* Report (New York: Time, Incorporated, 1965), pp. 108–109.

exact physiological workings of the hallucinogens are not clear. That they have a chemical effect upon the brain is obvious; how they do it remains a mystery. These drugs are thought to be neither addicting nor habituating physically, but the startling and sometimes pleasurable sensations they produce may lead to repeated use." [7] The effects of the natural hallucinogens, such as peyote, are not as great as those of LSD if not taken in prolonged overdoses, but LSD is a different matter. A tiny amount (1/300,000 of an ounce) of LSD–25 causes delusions or hallucinations, some of which are pleasant whereas other are terrifying. It tends to heighten sensory perceptions often to the point where they are wildly distorted. It is claimed, therefore, by some users that this has the effect of "opening up the mind," even to the extent of awakening latent talents. Research is currently under way to determine the immediate and long-term effects of LSD and to establish whether or not this drug has a legitimate medical function.

> After the cubes, containing 100–600 mcg (a microgram is one-millionth of a gram) each, are ingested a startling series of events occurs with marked individual variation. All senses appear sharpened and brightened; vivid panoramic visual hallucinations of fantastic brightness and depth are experienced as well as hyperacusis (abnormal acuteness of hearing). Senses blend and become diffused so that sounds are felt, colors tasted; and fixed objects pulsate and breathe. Depersonalization also occurs frequently so that the individual loses ego identity; he feels he is living with his environment in a feeling of unity with other beings, animals, inanimate objects and the universe in general. The body image is often distorted so that faces, including the user's, assume bizarre proportions and the limbs may appear extraordinarily short or elongated. The user is enveloped by a sense of isolation and often is dominated by feelings of paranoia and fear. If large doses are ingested (over 700 mcg) confusion and delirium frequently ensue. During LSD use, repressed material may be unmasked which is difficult for the individual to handle. Duration of the experience is usually 4 to 12 hours but it may last for days.[8]

SOCIETAL REACTION

People have used drugs for centuries and their use has not always been regarded as deviant behavior. The societal reaction has varied in time and place.

---

[7] *The Drug Takers,* pp. 110–111.

[8] *The Challenge of Crime in a Free Society,* Report by the President's Commission on Law Enforcement and Administration of Justice (Washington, D.C.: Government Printing Office, 1967), p. 215. Also see The President's Commission on Law Enforcement and Administration of Justice, *Task Force Report: Narcotics and Drug Abuse* (Washington, D.C.: U.S. Government Printing Office, 1967).

There seems little reason to doubt that, in terms of the available definitions of deviant behavior, a substantial part of marihuana and opiate use in the world today cannot be viewed as deviant behavior. In India, for example, where there is a strong, religiously associated aversion to alcohol in the higher castes, marihuana (bhang, ganja, and charas) not only is tolerated but is actually prescribed by social custom and religious usage. It is often expected, for example, that bhang (a liquid form of marihuana mixed with milk, fruit juices, etc.) be served at weddings, and the host is regarded as remiss in his social duties if he does not provide it. Priests, and especially Shaivite priests, are expected to use marihuana and also opium, and addiction on their part to the latter drug is not regarded as reprehensible or out of the ordinary. Indeed, frequent and liberal use of both of these substances might be taken as evidence of unusual religious devotion. . . . It may also be observed that opium was the prime therapeutic agent known to medicine for close to two thousand years, and has been recommended at one time or another for most human ailments. During these centuries there were unquestionably millions of persons who became addicts simply by following the advice of physicians or by acting in accord with widespread popular beliefs concerning the therapeutic power of opium and its derivatives.[9]

According to Lindesmith, the public's attitude in the United States toward drug users in the nineteenth century was different from that of today.[10] Although the use of drugs was not approved, there was considerable tolerance about it, drug addiction was regarded as a personal problem, and in general drug addicts were pitied. It was later that they came to be regarded as derelict characters, most people associating addiction with criminal behavior. This change in the public attitude was partly due to the prevalence of opium smoking among certain criminal elements in the nineteenth century.

Opium, which is easily grown from a poppy, was and is, in its various forms, the most widely used drug, not only in Europe and America but particularly in the Orient.[11] Its early use in medical treatment tended to spread

---

[9] Alfred R. Lindesmith and John H. Gagnon, "Anomie and Drug Addiction," in Marshall B. Clinard, ed., *Anomie and Deviant Behavior: A Discussion and Critique* (New York: The Free Press, 1964), pp. 162–163.

[10] Alfred R. Lindesmith, *Opiate Addicton* (Bloomington: Indiana University Press, 1947), p. 183. Also see Ball, "Two Patterns of Narcotic Drug Addiction in the United States;" and O. Marshall, "The Opium Habit in Michigan," in O'Donnell and Ball; and Roger Smith, "Status Politics and the Image of the Addict," *Issues in Criminology*, 2:157–176 (Fall 1966).

[11] According to a British government report, Hong Kong has an estimated 250,000 drug addicts, or one in every twelve of that British colony's population. A bill has been introduced into the Legislative Council to establish treatment centers

it. Two important drugs were derived from opium: morphine, a potent drug, in 1804; and heroin, about three times as powerful as morphine, in 1898. These drugs, as well as opium, which could be smoked or drunk, became widely used in the nineteenth century in America, particularly by women, who took them in patent medicines for "female disorders." At that time many of these drugs could be easily and legally purchased. The Harrison Act, passed in the United States in 1914, strictly regulated opiates and cocaine. This legislation, and subsequent statutes, made the sale and use of such drugs and marihuana illegal without a doctor's prescription.[12] Actually, it made drug users "criminals," and drugs something mysterious and evil, further influencing public attitudes against their use and making it difficult for persons to secure or use them without associating with other drug users.

Within recent years the use of drugs by juveniles in the United States has created even greater concern. In fact, the Federal Narcotics Control Act of 1956 imposes severe penalty for possessing, selling, bartering, or transferring any narcotic drug or marihuana, particularly to a person under eighteen. The sentence is not less than two nor more than ten years on a first offense of illegal *possession* of narcotics or marihuana, five to twenty years on the second offense, and ten to forty years on the third or later offense. In the case of illegal *sale* the penalty for the first offense is not less than five years nor more than twenty, and for subsequent offenses ten to forty years. Probation or parole are forbidden after the first offense in either possession or sale. The sale of, or conspiracy to sell, heroin to a person under eighteen is punishable by imprisonment from ten years to life. There are also various state laws punishing the possession and sale of narcotics, most of them rather severe.

EXTENT OF ADDICTION

It is impossible to know how many drug addicts there are in the United States today. Because the taking of drugs for nonmedical purposes is illegal, in all probability some addicts are neither reported officially as such nor

---

where an addict would be able voluntarily to obtain treatment. Under present legislation an addict would have to commit a crime to be arrested before being sent to a hospital. See Hong Kong Legislative Council, *The Problem of Narcotic Drugs in Hong Kong* (Hong Kong: S. Young, Government Printer, 1962); Albert G. Hess, *Chasing the Dragon* (New York: The Free Press, 1965); and R. N. Chopra, *Drug Addiction with Special Reference to India* (New Delhi: Council of Scientific and Industrial Research, 1965).

[12] See Donald J. Cantor, "The Criminal Law and the Narcotics Problem," *Journal of Criminal Law, Criminology, and Police Science*, 51:512–527 (1961).

arrested. Mose users carefully protect those who supply them so that to detect both users and suppliers requires great skill.

According to estimates of the Federal Bureau of Narcotics, on December 31, 1966, there were 59,720 active drug addicts, or 12,000 more than reported in 1960, an increase of about 4000 since 1964. Some estimates are much higher than this. Using the number of arrests of narcotic peddlers by the New York City Police Department, one study estimated that there were 90,000 addicts in that city alone.[13] Probably the most reasonable estimate for the United States is 60,000 to 100,000 addicts.[14] In several European countries, notably Great Britain and Sweden, there have been recent reports of increases in drug addiction, but the situation in Europe is, as yet, nothing like that in the United States.

> No other Western nation has as many as 5000 addicts and most have only a few hundred. Great Britain, France, and the Scandinavian countries all report addict populations of less than 1000. In western Europe only Germany has a sizable group of addicts—somewhat over 4000—but the nature of narcotics addiction in Germany is vastly different from that in the United States. For example, more than 95 percent of German addicts are over 30 years of age. The largest single occupational group represented consists of housewives, followed by medical personnel. The drugs used are largely synthetic counterparts of the opiates; heroin is almost nonexistent. . . . In some respects, the characteristics of the German addict population resemble those of American addicts 50 years ago.[15]

In 1963 the District of Columbia had the highest rate of addiction: 19.3 per 100,000 adult males; followed by New York, 14.4; Illinois, 11.5; and Puerto Rico, 12.2.[16] A study of the residences of 925 patients in 1962 at the United States Hospital at Lexington showed that the largest group of addicts—44.8 percent of the white males and 41.3 percent of the nonwhites

---

[13] New York City Mayor's Committee on Drug Addiction, *Report of Study of Drug Addiction among Teen-Agers* (New York: 1951).

[14] O'Donnell and Ball, p. 8. In the 1960's "glue sniffing" appeared among juveniles in some cities. Juveniles take airplane model glue, squeeze it on a cloth or into a paper bag, and inhale. These fumes precipitate a form of intoxication. See Stephen M. Allen, "Recent Trends in Substance Abuse: Glue Sniffing," *International Journal of the Addictions,* 1:147–149 (1966); and Gordon H. Barber and W. Thomas Adams, "Glue Sniffers," *Sociology and Social Research,* 47:298–310 (1963).

[15] Clausen, p. 206.

[16] Based on the residence of 39,743 male narcotic addicts in the active file of the Federal Bureau of Narcotics in 1963 and state of 2543 male addict patients admitted to the Lexington and Fort Worth Narcotic Treatment hospitals in 1963. See O'Donnell and Ball, pp. 8–9.

—were from New York State, nearly all from the New York City metropolitan area.[17] Among female white patient addicts, the largest group, 50.5 percent, were from the Western states, primarily California, with only 18.9 percent from New York. On the other hand, 38.2 percent of nonwhite females were from New York, followed by 22.5 percent from the Midwest.

Analysis of the medical records of 3301 addict patients discharged from the Lexington and Fort Worth hospitals in 1962 indicates two quite distinct patterns of opiate addiction in the United States. One pattern consists of heroin use among metropolitan youth who come predominantly from the minority groups in American society. The other consists primarily of middle-aged whites who use opiates other than heroin or synthetic analgesics, a pattern concentrated largely in the southern states.[18] There were reports in 1966 of a considerable increase in the use by college and high school students of marihuana and LSD–25. There seems to be no question that an increase has occurred but the extent is unknown and probably is exaggerated.

Drug addiction in the United States appears to be much more prevalent in large urban centers, particularly New York, Philadelphia, Washington, Baltimore, Chicago, Cleveland, Detroit, and Los Angeles.[19] In these cities drug addicts seem to come chiefly from the slum areas, although addiction is not entirely restricted to the lower socioeconomic classes. In fact, in a study of addicts in New York City, Chein and his associates found that most of the youthful drug users came from the most disadvantaged slum areas.[20] Eighty-three percent of the adolescent users were found to live in 15 percent of the city's census tracts, most of which were Negro and Puerto Rican slum areas. Ready access to drugs as well as talk of drugs is characteristic of these areas.

Contrary to popular opinion, drug addicts, male and female, are not more mobile from birth to the onset of addiction than the general U.S. population; moreover, they do not lead a transient way of life after their initial hospitalization.[21]

---

[17] See John C. Ball and William M. Bates, "Migration and Residential Mobility of Narcotic Drug Addicts," *Social Problems,* 14:56–69 (1966).

[18] Ball, "Two Patterns of Narcotic Drug Addiction in the United States," pp. 210–211.

[19] H. J. Anslinger and William F. Tompkins, *The Traffic in Narcotics* (New York: Funk & Wagnalls Company, 1953), p. 281. Also see John C. Ball, William M. Bates, and John A. O'Donnell, "Characteristics of Hospitalized Narcotic Addicts," *Indicators* (Washington, D.C.: U. S. Department of Health, Education, and Welfare, March 1966), pp. 17–26.

[20] Isidor Chein, Donald L. Gerard, Robert S. Lee, and Eva Rosenfeld, *The Road to H* (New York: Basic Books, Inc., 1964), Chap. 2.

[21] Ball and Bates.

As previous studies have indicated, narcotic addiction is essentially an urban phenomenon, concentrated in the largest cities of the United States. In these urban slums, narcotic drug abuse is most prevalent among the more disadvantaged minority group members, particularly Negroes and Puerto Ricans. The Negro addicts of the present study were second generation migrants to the northeastern metropolitan centers, whereas the Puerto Rican addicts were first generation migrants. In both instances, the addicts were not more mobile than their respective base populations— northern Negroes or New York City Puerto Ricans.

The white addicts were not only themselves stable in place of residence since birth, but there was considerable intergenerational stability. Among those white patients who did move, out-of-county migration was frequent; conversely, among the Negro patients, intracity mobility was the dominant change of residence noted. These racial differences in mobility patterns are similar, though more marked, than those of the U.S. population reported in the 1960 census.[22]

THE CHANGING NATURE OF DRUG ADDICTION

The nature of drug addiction is changing. Today addiction to opiates is heavily concentrated among young delinquent urban males from large cities of the lower socioeconomic groups and, in particular, among minority groups living in the slums, the Negroes and the Puerto Ricans. This is quite a different pattern from the one the nineteenth-century users of opiates presented.

> During most of the nineteenth century no similar concentration was noted. Approximately two-thirds of the users, according to a number of early surveys, were women. Most nineteenth century observers had the impression that addiction was less prevalent among Negroes than among whites, and slightly less prevalent in the lower than in the upper and middle classes. The usual concentration in the medical profession was noted. The average age of addicts was found to be from about forty to as high as fifty years, and some investigators observed that addiction was a vice of middle age usually taken up after the age of thirty.[23]

A comparison of the 3301 addict patients at Lexington and Fort Worth in 1962 with the hospital population of 1937 described by Pescor [24] revealed that marked changes have occurred during this twenty-five-year period. The male patients were younger by some eight years. The use of heroin prior to admission had increased whereas the use of morphine had decreased. The

---

[22] Ball and Bates, p. 68.

[23] Lindesmith and Gagnon, pp. 164–165.

[24] Michael J. Pescor, "A Statistical Analysis of the Clinical Records of Hospitalized Drug Addicts," *Public Health Reports,* Supplement No. 143 (1938), Appendix, p. 24.

proportion of the patients who come from northern metropolitan centers had increased notably. Nevertheless, high rates of hospitalization have continued from many of the southern states. "Thus, the major change has been the increasing preponderance of heroin addicts from the minority groups of our largest cities." [25]

According to reports of various governmental committees investigating the problem, drug addiction has been increasing among younger persons, although arrests for drug use constitute a small proportion of all arrests for persons in this age group. It has been estimated that about 60 percent of these young addicts use marihuana; the rest, heroin. The common sequence of events among a group of 121 Puerto Rican heroin users was marihuana use at sixteen or seventeen, heroin use at eighteen, and arrest for possession or sale of drugs at twenty.[26] Heroin use was a peer group phenomenon associated with delinquent behavior. The changing pattern of rates of drug addiction arrests in Chicago, beween 1934–1938 and 1951, is shown in Table 9.2. By 1951 the rates for younger age groups had become much higher.

TABLE 9.2 **Rates of Arrest for Narcotic Drug Law Violations (Chicago) per 10,000 Population for Different Age Groups**

Age group	1934–1938	1951
16–20	0.43	13.64
21–30	2.10	10.08
31 and over	1.09	1.48

SOURCE: Table from Harold Finestone, "Narcotics and Criminality," *Law and Contemporary Problems*, 22:70 (1957).

Approximately the same sex ratio—9 men to every 1 woman—exists for arrested addicts as for general crimes. Whereas about a fourth of those arrested for crimes in general are Negroes, this ratio is even higher for drug violations. A St. Louis study of a sample of the general Negro population, for example, found that one out of ten city-born Negro men had been addicted to heroin.[27] This study tended to confirm the accuracy of narcotics arrests as measures of drug addiction, for no regular user had escaped arrest, and 86 percent had been reported as addicts to the Federal Bureau of Narcotics. Very few men in this sample who denied drug use had narcotics arrest records.

[25] Ball, "Two Patterns of Narcotic Drug Addiction in the United States," p. 211.

[26] John C. Ball, "The Onset of Heroin Addiction in a Juvenile Population: Implications for Theories of Deviancy," Addiction Research Center, National Institute of Mental Health, Lexington, Ky., July 29, 1966, p. 6, mimeographed.

[27] Lee N. Robins and George E. Murphy, "Drug Use in a Normal Population of Young Negro Men," *American Journal of Public Health* (in press).

AGE AT ADDICTION AND LENGTH OF ADDICTION

The United States Public Health Service maintains hospitals for the treatment of committed and voluntary narcotic drug addicts at Lexington, Kentucky, and Fort Worth, Texas.[28] The age at addiction of 2213 addicted patients at the two hospitals indicated that approximately 50 percent of the male persons who became addicted did so before they were twenty, 75 percent before twenty-five, and 85 percent before 30 years of age. (See Table 9.3.) Women tended to become addicted at a later age; one third by age 20, two thirds by 25, and three fourths by 30.

TABLE 9.3   Age at First Opiate Use of 2213 Addict Patients Admitted to the Lexington and Fort Worth USPHS Hospitals in 1965, by Sex

	Male		Female	
AGE	NUMBER	PERCENT	NUMBER	PERCENT
19 or less	939	50.2	118	34.4
20–24	459	24.5	93	27.1
25–29	205	11.0	52	15.2
30–34	103	5.5	28	8.2
35–39	55	2.9	17	5.0
40–44	53	2.8	19	5.5
45–49	23	1.2	7	2.0
50–54	16	0.9	4	1.2
55–59	12	0.6	3	0.9
60 or over	4	0.2	1	0.3
Unknown	1	0.1	1	0.3
TOTAL	1870	100.0	343	100.0

SOURCE: Addiction Research Center, National Institute of Mental Health, Lexington, Ky.

Some two thirds of the drug addicts eventually appear to leave addiction or become inactive, according to 16,725 addicts who were originally reported in the records of the Federal Bureau of Narcotics as active addicts in 1953–1954 but were not reported in 1959.[29] A study made of those who were inactive in 1960 but had been active in 1955 involved 5553 men and 1681 women. Their ages ranged from 18 to 76, with average age of 35.1.[30] Addicts in this study included only regular users of opium derivatives, such

---

[28] See footnote 5, p. 303, for a discussion of representativeness of such patients.
[29] Study of Federal Bureau of Narcotics, cited in Charles Winick, "Maturing Out of Narcotic Addiction," *Bulletin on Narcotics,* 14:6 (1962).
[30] Winick.

as heroin and of synthetic opiates, such as meperidine (Demerol). (See Table 9.4.) The average length of addiction was 8.6 years, although some had been addicted for over fifty years. Inactivity increases cumulatively by age, with three fourths of the dropouts occurring by the age of 36.2. (See Table 9.5.) Inactivity takes place largely in the thirties, with 79 percent becoming inactive between twenty-five and forty-four. Statistical tests showed that

TABLE 9.4 **Age of Addicts Becoming Inactive, December 31, 1960**

Age	Number	Percent
18–19	6	0.1
20–24	373	5.2
25–29	1940	26.8
30–34	2172	30.0
35–39	1073	14.8
40–44	531	7.3
45–49	343	4.7
50–54	295	4.1
55–59	228	3.2
60 and over	273	3.8
Total	7234	100.

SOURCE: Derived from Charles Winick, "Maturing Out of Narcotic Addiction," *Bulletin on Narcotics,* 14:2 (1962).

TABLE 9.5 **Length of Addiction of Addicts Becoming Inactive, December 31, 1960**

Length of addiction (years)	Number of addicts	Percent
5	2473	34.2
6–7	1935	26.7
8–9	985	13.6
10–14	1168	16.1
15–19	262	3.6
20–24	136	1.9
25–29	126	1.7
30–34	60	0.8
35–39	45	0.7
40–44	23	0.4
45–49	15	0.2
50 and over	6	0.1
Total	7234	100.

SOURCE: Derived from Winick, p. 5.

this was not a statistical artifact, for the proportion of addicts becoming inactive in each group was not dependent on the proportion of addicts in that age group in the total active addict population. The reasons for leaving addiction are not clear; a number of hypotheses are that it is a function of the life cycle of juvenile addiction, the number of years of addiction itself, or that addicts leave the more youthful drug subculture as they grow older.

EDUCATIONAL LEVEL AND OCCUPATION OF DRUG ADDICTS

About one third of the drug addicts who undergo treatment at the United States Public Health Service Hospital at Lexington have had at least a high school education. The distribution for educational attainment was comparable to that of the general population. One can assume that most patients in private hospitals have an even higher average level of education.

Although there is a wide divergence in the occupations of narcotic addicts, certain occupations are known to offer more hazards. The medical profession, for example, has an excessive share of addicts.[31] The United States Commissioner of Narcotics estimated the incidence of opiate addiction among physicians as being about 1 addict among every 100 physicians, as contrasted to a rate of about 1 in 3000 in the general population.[32] The Federal Bureau of Narcotics reported that 1012 physicians were addicts, while 659 were found guilty of illegal narcotics sales or prescription activities from 1942 through 1956. Other countries have reported a substantial incidence of addiction among physicians. In England physicians are reported as being the occupational group most heavily represented among addicts, accounting for 17 percent of the addicts there. One report, summarizing United Nations data on the subject, stated that 1 physician in every 550 in England and 1 in every 95 in Germany were addicts.[33] A study of 457 consecutive admissions to the United States Public Health Service Hospital at Lexington, for meperidine ("Demerol," an opiate derivative) addiction, revealed that 32.7 percent of the cases of primary addiction were physicians and osteopaths.[34] Doctors can obtain drugs easily and rather inexpensively. Moreover, physicians have knowledge of what drugs can do for someone

---

[31] Charles Winick, "Physician Narcotic Addicts," *Social Problems,* 9:174–186 (1961).

[32] "Interview with Hon. Harry J. Anslinger," *Modern Medicine,* 25:170–191 (1957).

[33] Lawrence Kolb, "The Drug Addiction Muddle," *Police,* 1:57–62 (1957).

[34] Robert W. Rasor and H. James Crecraft, "Addiction to Meperidine," *Journal of the American Medical Association,* 157:654–657 (1955).

who is tense or tired, which is an important factor in their becoming addicted. Many of these physicians do not come to the attention of authorities because they can often maintain their addiction without detection.

In a study of 98 physicians who either were or had been opiate addicts, pronounced differences were found between them and the typical addict who buys drugs from a "pusher."

> The most obvious difference is that the age at which the physicians began to use drugs is just about the age that the typical addict stops using drugs, whether by "maturing out" or for other reasons. The "street" addict typically begins drug use in adolescence, while the physician begins when he is an established community and professional figure. The "street" addict takes heroin, while the typical physician addict took meperidine. The physician can get a pure quality of his drug, although it is not as strong as heroin. The "street" addict gets a diluted drug. He often starts with marijuana, although none of the physicians ever smoked marijuana.
>
> The physician is usually discovered by the indirect evidence of a check of prescription records, while the "street" addict is usually arrested because he has narcotics in his possession or has been observed making an illegal purchase. The physician is usually not arrested, while the typical "street" addict is arrested. Money to obtain drugs was not a problem for the physicians, as it usually is for the typical addict, who must steal in order to obtain money to buy drugs illegally. The physicians could use their professional access to narcotics to obtain drugs without much money. Even if they paid, the legal prices of narcotic drugs are very low.
>
> Most non-physician addicts associate with other addicts. In contrast, the physicians interviewed almost never associated with other physician addicts, or did not do so knowingly. They did not have any occasion for doing so, either for the purpose of getting drugs or for passing time, or for emotional support. They were solitary about their addiction. The "street" addict usually talks in a special jargon and often has a kind of wry insight into drug use, which stems from his extended discussions with his peers. The physicians did not talk in jargon and manifested very little insight into their drug use.[35]

Performers in the entertainment world, such as jazz musicians, sometimes become marihuana users, largely because such deviant behavior appears to be much less disapproved by their associates. The use of drugs has been studied among 357 jazz band musicians in New York City, 73 percent of whom were white. It was reported that 82 percent had tried marihuana at least once, 54 percent were occasional users, and one in four, or 23 percent, were regular users.[36] Heroin was used less than marihuana, but still

---

[35] Winick, "Physician Narcotic Addicts," pp. 178–179.

[36] Charles Winick, "The Use of Drugs by Jazz Musicians," *Social Problems,* 7:240–254 (1959–1960).

by a large proportion: 53 percent at least once, 24 percent occasionally, and by one in six, or 16 percent, regularly. Only 3 percent expressed any moral objections to the use of either marihuana or heroin by their musical colleagues, and although two thirds of the nonusers felt sorry for the drug users, the common reaction was, "It's their business if they want to do it."

Over a third of the sample believed that most jazz musicians think they play better when using marihuana, even if they actually are playing worse. Nearly one in five believed that it actually helps a musician to play better, but 31 percent felt that the musicians played worse. More specifically, marihuana seems to establish "contact high," a special kind of emotional group contagion, among those taking marihuana, resulting in "musical whimsy or humor," and can permit the musician to perceive new space-time relationships by altering his perception of time. In general the comments were much more negative in relation to heroin. No significant relation, however, could be found between the use of heroin or marihuana and the degree of professional success attributed to the musician by his peers.

A number of group factors are related to the musician's drug use. One was the extent of use by the band itself. About half (53 percent) felt that the use of drugs was related to upward or downward mobility. For example, a young musician may take a drug to accelerate his progress to the top. Drugs may be used to help tide a musician over when he is out of work. About one in five, especially by those over thirty, felt that drug usage was related to "one nighters" because this type of traveling is tiring for musicians. As one heroin user described it:

> "I was traveling on the road in 1952. We had terrible travel arrangements and traveled by special bus. We were so tired and beat that we didn't even have time to brush our teeth when we arrived in a town. We'd get up on the bandstand looking awful. The audience would say, 'Why don't they smile? They look like they can't smile.' I found I could pep myself up more quickly with heroin than with liquor. If you drank feeling that tired, you'd fall on your face." [37]

THE PROCESS OF OPIATE ADDICTION

Opiate addiction is learned just as other behavior is learned—primarily from association with others who are addicts.[38] The usual pattern is that of association for other reasons, rather than one person seeking another

---

[37] Winick, "The Use of Drugs by Jazz Musicians," p. 246.

[38] Some indication of this is the fact that although drug addiction used to be common among Chinese in the United States, by the 1960's this group had almost ceased to exist. See John C. Ball and M. P. Lau, "The Chinese Narcotic Addict in the United States," *Social Forces,* 45:68–72 (1966).

simply because the other person is an addict. "The process in which this pattern of opium addiction is taken over by an individual is not very much different from that in which other cultural patterns are transmitted. In a number of cases we found that the drug habit was started less for the effect of the drug than as a sign of identification with the group they happened to be in." [39] An addict must first learn how to use drugs. He must be aware of the drug, know how to administer it, and recognize its effects.

> Beyond this, one must have some motivation for trying the drug—whether to relieve pain, to produce euphoria, to please a loved person, to achieve acceptance in a group, or to achieve some other goal. The goal need have little to do with the specific effects of the narcotic. Moreover, the motivation or goal of initial drug use must be sharply distinguished from the motivation to maintain a drug habit. The latter is a product of learning which seems to depend on the interaction between drug effects, especially in the first experience of withdrawal, and the self-conception of the drug user.[40]

Whether one is referring to the physician, the jazz musician, the prostitute, or the juvenile in the slum, all have one thing in common: the availability or accessibility to a supply of illegal drugs. This may have much to do with the fact that rates are higher in these groups. The high addiction rate among Negroes is affected by the fact that the "concentration of the traffic in Negro ghettos made the drug particularly available in these areas and, as time passed, the number of Negroes experimenting with drugs such as marihuana and heroin apparently increased steadily." [41]

Finally, the process of drug addiction results in stigma and rejection as a product of societal reaction which, in turn, affects the self-image.

> The gradual immersion of most American addicts in a world of their own is inextricably connected with the general process by which they have been cast out of respectable society. The social definition of the addict as a criminal not only vitally influences his behavior but also significantly affects his self-image. Certainly the knowledge that one has become fully addicted must in itself have a profound impact on this self-image. At the same time it is noteworthy that although the physician-addict and the subcultural-type addict are addicted in precisely the same physiological sense, their self-images are likely to be strikingly different. Both may recognize themselves as addicts, yet the physician is most unlikely to consider himself a criminal. On the other hand, the addict who is driven to under-

---

[39] Bingham Dai, *Opium Addiction in Chicago* (Shanghai: The Commercial Press, 1937), p. 173.

[40] John A. Clausen, "Social and Psychological Factors in Narcotics Addiction," *Law and Contemporary Problems*, 22:38–39 (1957).

[41] Lindesmith and Gagnon, p. 172.

world connections and to crime in order to support his habit cannot help begin to feel that he is an enemy of society (or at least that society is *his* enemy). A self-fulfilling-prophecy cycle is set in motion from which it is very difficult for such an addict to extricate himself. He is aware that respectable people view him as a criminal, and he sees that he is beginning to act like one. Increasingly he must turn to the drug world for inter-personal support as well as for drug supplies. As the need to finance his habit occupies more and more of his time and energy, and as other worlds (such as those of work, family, and so on) recede into the background or fade away completely, addiction becomes a way of life.[42]

Sociological work in this field has challenged the general view that differences in personality traits or need for an escape mechanism accounts for addiction to opiates.[43] The work of Lindesmith, for example, explains addiction to opiates on the basis of the addict's association of the drug with the distress which accompanies the sudden cessation of its use. "If he fails to realize the connection between the distress and the opiate he escapes addiction, whereas if he attributes it to the opiate and thereafter uses the opiate to alleviate it he invariably becomes addicted. Addiction is generated in the process of using the drug consciously to alleviate withdrawal distress." [44]

Addiction is impossible without recognizing the withdrawal distress which may come several hours after a "shot" and in some cases may be difficult to detect, Lindesmith claims. Doctors may successfully prevent addiction by keeping patients unaware of the effects of the drug upon them. Patients who have experienced withdrawal distress without understanding the connection between it and the drug have therefore escaped addiction.[45] There are several crucial cases of persons who were receiving drugs without becoming addicted, but when they later took drugs and began to associate the taking of drugs with the fear of withdrawal symptoms they became addicted.

---

[42] Edwin M. Schur, *Crimes without Victims,* p. 145. © 1967. Reprinted by permission of Prentice-Hall, Inc., Englewood Cliffs, N.J.

[43] Addicts often exhibit other disturbances, but it is not sound reasoning to assume that such personality traits necessarily existed before addiction. In only a a few cases are comparisons made with the traits of the population as a whole, and there is some doubt as to whether the addicts studied are always representative of the entire population. See Donald Gerard and Conan Kornetsky, "Adolescent Opiate Addiction: A Study of Control and Addict Subjects," *Psychiatric Quarterly,* 29:457–487 (1955). Also see Chapter 6, pp. 193–194, 195–197.

[44] Alfred R. Lindesmith, "A Sociological Theory of Drug Addiction," *American Journal of Sociology,* 43:599 (1938).

[45] Animals and infants appear to become addicted without conscious motivation. Lindesmith implies that none of the lower animals respond to opiates in the same way that human addicts do.

This interpretation is supported by the fact that an addict seldom experiences the uplift of buoyancy attributed to the drugs unless he has been "taught" to expect it. Even the argot of addicts themselves in the word "hooked" indicates the process of addiction. The following case shows how a person begins to realize that he is addicted.

> Mr. G. was severely lacerated and internally injured in an accident. He spent thirteen weeks in a hospital, in the course of which he received opiates frequently both by mouth and hypodermically. He was unconscious part of the time and suffered considerable pain during convalescence despite the intake of opiates. He did not know what he was getting and noticed no effects except that his pain was relieved by the shots. He was discharged from the hospital but in several hours he began to feel restless and uncomfortable, without recognizing his condition. That night he became nauseated and vomited blood. Fearing that he was going to die, he summoned his family doctor. The physician did not realize what was the matter and administered a mild sedative. During the next day Mr. G.'s condition became steadily worse, and by the second night he was in such misery that, as he said, he began to wish that he would die. He again summoned his family doctor. This time the doctor began to suspect that Mr. G. was suffering from opiate withdrawal and prepared an injection of morphine. Mr. G. remembers nothing after the injection except that the doctor sat down by his bed and asked him how he felt. He replied that he noticed no effect, but the doctor said, "You will in a few minutes." Soon the patient fell asleep and continued in perfect comfort for many hours. When he awoke, he was informed of the true nature of the relieving dose by his wife and by the physician's comment: "Now we're going to have a hell of a time getting you off." The patient remained free of the drug for a few days and then purchased a syringe and began to use it himself.[46]

Lindesmith has summarized the evidence in support of his view that opiate addiction is a social psychological process associated with recognition of withdrawal symptoms; drug addiction is continued for fear of the pain or discomfort associated with withdrawal:

> (1) the fact that some addicts deny ever experiencing euphoria from the drug; (2) that persons may and do become addicts without ever taking the drug voluntarily; (3) that addicts can be deceived about whether they are under the influence of the drug or not; (4) that euphoria is associated primarily with the initial use of the drugs and virtually disappears in addiction; (5) that the addict maintains that his shots cause him to feel "normal," and (6) that marihuana and cocaine, which do not create

---

[46] Alfred R. Lindesmith, *Opiate Addiction* (Bloomington: Indiana University Press, 1947), p. 72. This extract and others reprinted from this work are used with the permission of the author and the publisher.

tolerance and physical dependence, are regarded as nonhabit forming and
that the habit-forming propensity of various substances seems to be roughly
proportional to the severity of withdrawal symptoms and not to the
euphoria they produce. One may say that the undoubted euphoria which
opiates often initially produce is the bait on the hook rather than the hook
itself.[47]

In becoming an opiate addict the individual changes his conception of
himself and of the behavior he must play as a "drug addict." These new
conceptions have both social psychological and sociological implications.
The more he associates with others who are "hooked" and finds that he
cannot free himself from dependence on drugs, the more he comes to play
the new role of the addict.

> It is evident that the drug addict assumes the group's viewpoint with
> respect to his experience of withdrawal distress by virtue of the fact that,
> prior to addiction, he has been a non-addict and a participating member
> of society. In view of the very use of language symbols, in terms of which
> the processes of re-evaluation which constitute addiction proceed, the addict
> necessarily shares the traditional heritage which includes knowledge of,
> and attitudes toward, the drug habit. Prior to addiction addicts acquire
> the attitudes of non-addicts, and when they become addicted they must
> adjust themselves to these attitudes.[48]

THE PROCESS OF USING MARIHUANA

There are two objections to the claim that the use of marihuana, which
actually does not cause addiction, is associated with personality traits.[49]
First, it is not known that marihuana users exhibit any uniform personality
traits; second, there is great variation in the use of the drug by a given
person. At one time the individual may be unable to use the drug for
pleasure, on a later occasion he may use it, and still later not do so.

To use marihuana for pleasure a person must learn to conceive of the
drug as something which can produce pleasurable sensations.[50] The user
of marihuana drugs must learn three things: (1) to smoke the drug in a

---

[47] Alfred R. Lindesmith, "Basic Problems in the Social Psychology of Addiction
and a Theory," in O'Donnell and Ball, pp. 102–103.

[48] Lindesmith, *Opiate Addiction,* p. 168.

[49] Howard S. Becker, "Becoming a Marihuana User," *American Journal of
Sociology,* 59:235–243 (1953). Also in Howard S. Becker, *Outsiders: Studies in the
Sociology of Deviance* (New York: The Free Press, 1963), pp. 41–59 and in John
A. O'Donnell and John C. Ball, eds., *Narcotic Addiction* (New York: Harper &
Row, Publishers, 1966).

[50] Becker, pp. 235–242.

way which will produce certain effects; (2) to learn to recognize the effects and connect the drug with them; and (3) finally, to enjoy the sensations he feels. These three steps occurred in the case of fifty marihuana users whom Becker studied. He claims that when a person first uses the drug he does not ordinarily "get high" because he does not know the proper technique of drawing on the cigarette and holding the smoke. Even after learning the technique he does not form a conception of the smoking as being related to pleasure. Even though there are pleasurable sensations, the new marihuana user may not feel that they are enough, or he may not be sufficiently aware of their specific nature to become a regular user. He learns to feel the sensations of "being high" as defined by others. With greater use he learns to appreciate more of the sensations of the drug.

Finally, one more step is necessary to continue the use of marihuana. The person must learn to enjoy the sensations he has experienced. Feeling dizzy, being thirsty, misjudging distances, or a tingling scalp may not of themselves be pleasurable experiences. He must learn to define them in this way. Association with other marihuana users helps to define sensations that were frightening into something pleasurable and to be looked forward to. An experienced marihuana user has described how newcomers are helped to define the use of the drugs as giving pleasurable sensations:

> "Well, they get pretty high sometimes. The average person isn't ready for that, and it is a little frightening to them sometimes. I mean, they've been high on lush (alcohol), and they get higher that way than they've ever been before, and they don't know what's happening to them. Because they think they're going to keep going up, up, up until they lose their minds or begin doing weird things or something. You have to like reassure them, explain to them that they're not really flipping or anything, that they're gonna be all right. You have to just talk them out of being afraid. Keep talking to them, reassuring, telling them it's all right. And come on with your own story, you know: 'The same thing happened to me. You'll get to like that after awhile.' Keep coming on like that; pretty soon you talk them out of being scared. And besides they see you doing it and nothing horrible is happening to you, so that gives them more confidence." [51]

THE SUBCULTURE OF DRUG ADDICTION

Much of drug addiction involves an elaborate subculture. The drugs must be imported illegally into the country and then distributed through suppliers or peddlers. There are "pushers" who help to indoctrinate new persons into addiction. Those who use the drugs are, to a large extent, also part of this subculture, since drug addicts must generally associate with

---

[51] Becker, p. 240.

peddlers and other addicts in order to secure their supply. Drug addiction involves an elaborate subculture supported by group norms which one writer calls a "survival system." [52] This involves the justification or ideology for drug usage and the "reproductive" system, namely, that addicted persons must continually recruit new members in order to sell them drugs to support their habit. There is also defensive communication with its own argot for drugs, supplies, and drug users, which must be learned by the initiates, and the "neighborhood warning systems" by which addicts are protected by others. The support of the habit requires a complex distribution network of the illegal drugs. Fiddle has termed this the "circulatory" system of the drug subculture: the system by which addicts learn to secure illegal drugs.

> Information about the coming of the police, or about the kind of heroin being sold, in different parts of the city is said to pass rapidly and accurately, with what is said to be greater safety than that furnished by the telephone. . . . Information is sifted out according to a consensus concerning the reliability of different individuals. In particular, there is a belief that informers can be spotted so that they can be excluded from the grapevine or sent onto a fake grapevine. In some periods, information can be so valuable that it is paid for by the addicted.[53]

To understand why this illegal trade in narcotics flourishes and why it is so difficult to wipe out, one must realize the potential large profit in the handling of illegal drugs. The price for a shot of heroin varies considerably, and is often what the traffic will bear. Although police often have little difficulty in apprehending the common addict who is searching restlessly for his next shot, it is much more difficult to track down the supplier or successive line of suppliers to the source. Many addicts would rather sweat out the "shakes" than disclose the name of their supplier, and often there is a high degree of organization among those who manage to get supplies of drugs illegally into the country.

---

[52] Seymour Fiddle, "The Addict Culture and Movement into and out of Hospitals," as reprinted in U.S. Senate, Committee on the Judiciary, Subcommittee to Investigate Juvenile Delinquency," *Hearings,* Part 13, New York City, September 20–21, 1962 (Washington, D.C.: Government Printing Office, 1963), p. 3156. Before 1914, when narcotics could be obtained legally, easily and cheaply, there was no drug subculture. After 1914 drugs could be obtained only with difficulty, but could be obtained through contact with addicts, and a subculture emerged. After 1940, the subculture no longer provided the only solution to the problem of obtaining drugs, and it has tended to decline. These conclusions were based on a measure of involvement in the subculture, and the changing associations, over time, of other variables with this measure. See John A. O'Donnell, "The Rise and Decline of a Subculture," *Social Problems,* 15:73–84 (1967).

[53] Fiddle, p. 3158.

The extremely high profits involved in the sale of illegal drugs can be seen from the return which is likely on one kilogram (approximately thirty-five ounces) of heroin. This amount of 86 percent pure heroin in Europe costs about $1000, and it might cost as much as $5000 more to smuggle it into the United States. However, this kilogram of heroin, which will be diluted as much as 90 percent with milk sugar, will eventually be made into about 20,000 capsules (at 437½ grains to an ounce and 1½ grains to a capsule of the cut product) which will sell for about $2 to $3 apiece. Thus the return on the original investment is up to $40,000 to $60,000. Where profits as high as this exist it is inevitable that well-organized techniques will be developed to protect them. It is also inevitable that such an enterprise should become a fertile field for organized crime.

Most drug addicts are knowingly initiated into drug usage, usually by a friend, acquaintance, or marital partner. Rarely does the use of drugs during illness lead to addiction. As for the large numbers who take them because of curiosity, there has usually been some association with persons already addicted. There is a desire to "try something once," especially if it happens to be something as frowned upon by society in general as is drug addiction. Some adolescents and others take drugs for the "kick" as something tabooed by "squares" and to heighten and intensify the present moment of experience and differentiate it from the routine of daily life.[54] The chain-reaction process of addiction has often been called a "sordid and tragic pyramid game" in which the average addict introduces several friends into the habit, often as a means of solving his own supply problem. Persons are often initiated at parties where the first several marihuana cigarettes or "shots" are "on the house" in order to initiate the beginner.[55]

Teenage addiction is group in nature. In their attempts to acquire status among their peers, adolescents in certain areas often appear to be willing to explore socially unacceptable areas of behavior. Drug use among juveniles, consisting primarily of heroin and marihuana, flourishes in the slum areas of large cities in the United States. In New York, for example, almost 90 percent of the cases are concentrated in only 13 percent of the census tracts.[56] In fact, in some of the tracts as many as 10 percent of the young men, aged sixteen to twenty, were known, during a three-year period, to be involved with drugs. In such areas the desire to enjoy life by having

[54] Harold Finestone, "Cats, Kicks, and Color," *Social Problems,* 5:3–13 (1957). This seems to be the chief reason for the use of drugs by beats, "hippies," and some college students during the 1960s.

[55] Chein, *et al.,* Chap. 6, and John P. Fort, Jr., "Heroin Addiction among Young Men," *Psychiatry,* 17:251–259 (1954).

[56] See Chein, *et al.,* Chap. 2, and Isidor Chein and Eva Rosenfeld, "Juvenile Narcotics Use," *Law and Contemporary Problems,* 22:52–69 (1957).

new experiences and taking chances means that there is a readiness to try
the drug, because, they are told, it will give them an immediate "kick" or a
"high" feeling. A study of male Puerto Rican addicts showed that they
smoked marihuana and associated with neighborhood boys who were known
addicts before starting to use heroin themselves. "The neighborhood addicts
who provided the drugs and technical knowledge to the neophyte were
invariably described by him as 'friends.' " [57] Great determination is required
to escape the pull or, rather, push of delinquent subcultures which are associated with the use of drugs. "The pressure to fall in with the fast, noisy
aggressive 'cats' is great. The derisive taunts of 'chicken,' 'yellow,' 'punk,'
and 'square' are powerful weapons to use against an adolescent boy." [58]

> In spreading to young persons, as it did, narcotics use made its in-
> roads within a distinctive and uniquely vulnerable social milieu, the world
> of the adolescent in the most disadvantaged areas of the city. Like their
> age-mates everywhere, these adolescents spontaneously form peer groups,
> which exert a significant influence upon their conduct. In other types of
> communities, however, particularly those of higher socioeconomic status,
> the control over behavior exerted by the peer group is subject to restraint
> by the obligations and loyalties binding the individual adolescent mem-
> bers to other conventional groups, such as the family and the school. By
> way of contrast, such competing obligations and loyalties fail to exert their
> limiting and moderating influences in the most disadvantaged areas, and
> the peer group assumes a virtually sovereign control over the behavior of
> the individual adolescent. Under such conditions, the introduction of a
> novel practice may lead to its rapid diffusion, and, because it is unchecked
> by pressures counter to those exerted by the peer group itself, go to ex-
> tremes that are not possible among adolescents elsewhere. In this milieu,
> narcotics use could spread more selectively and with somewhat greater
> difficulty, perhaps, but in a manner analogous to a new fashion in lan-
> guage, dress, or music. . . .
>
> It is evident from this description that there are significant influences
> originating in street-corner society itself that would be hospitable to ex-
> perimentation with narcotics. An orientation to life which gives zestful
> sanction to many forms of unconventional activity appears to have spread
> the welcome mat for narcotics use. Much of the behavior reported by these
> young addicts clearly indicates that they had actively sought out narcotics
> —and not only heroin, but every other substance of which they had
> heard which yielded a "kick" such as marijuana, cocaine, benzedrine, and
> the barbiturates. The activity centering around these narcotics had many
> of the characteristics of a fad—that is, the restless searching, the uncer-
> tainty and excitement and exclusive preoccupation with a novel expe-

---

[57] Ball, "The Onset of Heroin Addiction in a Juvenile Population," p. 8.
[58] Chein and Rosenfeld, p. 56.

rience, the pressures to "go along," and the final capitulation on the part of many, despite the existence of strong initial doubts and inhibitions.[59]

Teenagers in high delinquency slum areas, where drug use is also high, can be divided into four groups: (1) delinquents who use drugs, (2) delinquents who do not use drugs, (3) drug users who were not drug users prior to involvement with heroin, and finally (4), nondelinquent nondrug users. Not all delinquent groups engage in the use of drugs, a fact which appears to be related to the area where they are located. Finestone has suggested that the use of narcotics spreads to adolescents in those communities deficient in two essential types of social control: "first, controls originating in conventional institutions which define the limits of permissible behavior for adolescents; and secondly, the controls by means of which the community is enabled to resist encroachments by those espousing values to which it is strongly antagonistic." [60] In regard to lack of the first type of social control he writes:

> In the localities frequented by adult criminals, the notoriety, glamour, and symbols of material success that are sometimes associated with them enhance their attractiveness as role-models to members of street-corner society, who, as adolescents, may find it easier to identify with them than with conventional role-models. In a similar vein, interviews with young narcotic addicts in 1952 suggested the observation that in at least certain social circles where these youngsters sought status and recognition, adult addicts or "junkies" enjoyed a certain prestige. Many of these young addicts reported that they and others had tried to simulate the mannerisms and philosophy of life of addicts before they themselves had become addicted.[61]

As a study of Chicago juvenile gangs found, "extensive drug use is not a generally supported gang activity," although it tended to be more common among Negro than white gangs.[62] Most juvenile gangs that use drugs often try to set the limits of drug usage by their members. In a study of eighteen gangs it was found that 65 percent of the members were opposed to the use of heroin, or felt ambivalent about it, but very few gang members

---

[59] Harold Finestone, "Narcotics and Criminality," *Law and Contemporary Problems,* 22:73–74 (1957).

[60] Finestone, "Narcotics and Criminality," p. 74.

[61] Finestone, "Narcotics and Criminality," p. 75. For discussion of some group factors in younger drug addicts also see Alexander H. Leighton, John A. Clausen, and Robert N. Wilson, *Explorations in Social Psychiatry* (New York: Basic Books, Inc., 1957), pp. 230–277.

[62] James F. Short, Jr., and Fred L. Strodtbeck, *Group Process and Gang Delinquency* (Chicago: University of Chicago Press, 1965), pp. 1, 63–64, and 82.

had strong feeling about the use of marihuana.[63] Any leader who became a drug addict was demoted. Delinquent gangs are more tolerant of occasional use, but resist immoderate usage, on the ground that it interferes with their stealing or that it will get the gang into trouble. Some writers have referred to a type of delinquent gang which, in its inability to achieve the conventional goals of society, becomes preoccupied with the use of drugs rather than stealing except to get money for drugs.[64] A Chicago gang study could find little evidence that there were "gangs whose primary activities and norms were oriented around drug use." [65]

There is a widespread assumption that juvenile addicts are introduced to the drug habit by drug peddlers. One study has shown that the first shot of heroin came through some adult in only 10 percent of the cases.[66] Nearly all were introduced to the drug in the company of a boy their own age or in a group of boys. The first trial use of drugs was free to most. Only 10 percent had to pay for the first "shot" or "snort." The first dose was often taken in the home of one of the boys, although a large number tried it on the street, in a cellar, or even on a roof top. Frequently, it was taken before a party as a bracer to give poise and courage. Clausen reports: "There is general agreement that the great majority of these [marihuana and heroin] users were not tricked into addiction by drug peddlers." [67]

Once the adolescent becomes part of a group which is using drugs and becomes addicted, it is difficult for him to withdraw from the group. Later his whole life may revolve around maintaining a regular supply of "shots," and there is consequently less and less opportunity for him to have any contacts with acceptable groups. In these groups of youthful addicts loyalties become intensified because of the constant fear of being arrested and cut off from sources of supply. And the constant search for sources of supply compels them to seek the company of known adult addicts.

---

[63] Chein and Rosenfeld.

[64] Richard A. Cloward and Lloyd E. Ohlin, *Delinquency and Opportunity* (New York: The Free Press, 1960). Also see Finestone, "Cats, Kicks, and Color," pp. 3–14. In this study some fifty Negro male users of heroin in their late teens and early twenties were selected from areas of highest incidence of drug usage in Chicago, Through intensive interviews between 1951 and 1953, these drug users served as subjects to elicit expression of many common values, schemes of behavior and general social orientation, suggesting the existence of a social type, "the cat." It was concluded that "the cat" is a product of social change, representing a reaction to a feeling of exclusion from adequate access to the goals of our society. Therefore, measures, such as improved educational opportunities which put these means within his grasp, will hasten the extinction of this type.

[65] Short and Strodtbeck, p. 11.

[66] Chein and Rosenfeld, "Juvenile Narcotics Use," p. 58.

[67] Clausen, "Social and Psychological Factors in Narcotics Addiction," p. 40.

Suppliers and most addicts live in a world that often has its own meeting places and its own argot. Possibly nothing more clearly demonstrates the fact that addiction has cultural components than the argot which is used. It includes special names for the drugs, for those who supply the drugs, and for addiction. It also includes special descriptive terms for those who use drugs.

Selected Glossary of Terms Used by Addicts

Bang: The thrill in drug taking.

Burned out: A vein no longer useful for injection because of numerous puncture wounds.

Cold turkey: Complete and sudden withdrawal from drugs in jail.

Den: Place where several gather to use narcotics.

Drive: Addict's description of feeling good.

Goof ball: A pill or capsule of barbiturate used by addicts when they cannot get their supply of narcotics.

Hard stuff: Heroin, when compared to marihuana.

High: When an individual is under the effect of marihuana or other drugs.

Hooked: One who no longer can resist taking drugs.

Hophead: One who has become addicted to use of drugs.

Horse: Another name for heroin.

Hot shot: An overdose of drugs, sometimes fatal.

Joy popper: One who takes drugs only occasionally.

Junk: Any illegal drug.

Junkie: A drug addict.

Kick: Feeling of satisfaction after taking drugs (also lift).

Kicking the habit: Constant twitching of arms, legs, and feet, some twenty-four hours after last dose of morphine, during withdrawal.

Main-liner: Any addict who uses intravenous injections.

Reefer: Marihuana cigarette.

Shakes: Uncontrolled physical tremors of addict when withdrawn from drugs.

Sniffer: Inhalation of cocaine from thumbnail or match cover.

Snow: Slang for cocaine.

Stick: A marihuana cigarette.

Stuff: Any drug used illegally.[68]

---

[68] Derived from Lindesmith, *Opiate Addiction,* pp. 211–221; Anslinger and Tompkins, pp. 305–316; and "Children and Drugs," (Madison, Wisc.: State Department of Public Welfare, Division for Children and Youth, March 1952), pp. 23–25. Also see J. E. Schmidt, *Narcotics Lingo and Lore* (Springfield, Ill.: Charles C Thomas, Publisher, 1959). The use of LSD by "hippies" in the 1960's involved such terms as "drop acid" (take LSD) and "trip out" (experience the far-out effects of a hallucinogenic drug).

The argot of professional musicians makes use of many expressions which are widely known by addicts. They use terms and phrases to describe the music they like, such as "frantic," "it kills me," "wild," "crazy," "the end," "hip."[69]

> Since the 1920's, one popular procedure for combining musical expression with interest in drugs was to make records or perform pieces with thinly veiled references to narcotics in their titles: Hophead, Muggles, Reefer Song, Viper's Drag, Sweet Marijuana Brown, Weed Smoker's Dream, Chant of the Weed, Pipe Dream Blues, Kicking the Gong Around, You're a Viper, Reefer Man, Doctor Freeze, and Vonce, are among many such titles, some of which achieved considerable success. The lyrics as well as the title of many jazz pieces have dealt with narcotics, at least up to fairly recently.[70]

DELINQUENCY, CRIME, AND DRUG ADDICTION

Two questions are involved in the relationship between delinquency, crime, and drug addiction. First of all, the use of narcotics is so expensive that an addict must often engage in various illegal activities to maintain his supply. Second, the influence of drugs upon human behavior varies, and it is difficult to determine how much effect narcotics have on criminal behavior generally.

Once an individual becomes addicted to a narcotic drug, such as morphine or heroin, his dependence upon a continuous supply usually becomes the most important single aspect of his daily life. Although they took the drug earlier for pleasure or for an effect, most addicts soon take it to ward off withdrawal symptoms. The addict knows that conventional society is extremely hostile to his use of drugs, so he resorts to devious ways in his attempt to secure them. As his tolerance is built up and he requires more and larger dosages, it may cost as much as from fifteen to forty dollars a day to support the habit. This daily expenditure is generally much more than the addict earns, and thus he or she is literally compelled to engage in theft or prostitution in order to maintain an adequate supply.

Most crimes associated with drug addiction involve direct or indirect

---

[69] Winick, "The Use of Drugs by Jazz Musicians," pp. 249–250. "Drug users probably developed most of the key phrases in this jargon as outgrowths of various aspects of drug-taking activity. For example, the key concept of being 'hip' (a member of the in-group) derives from the slight atrophy of the hip which resulted from lying on one preferred hip and balancing opium on the other hip. A 'hip' person was thus originally an opium smoker."—"The Use of Drugs by Jazz Musicians," p. 250.

[70] Winick, "The Use of Drugs by Jazz Musicians," p. 251.

violations of narcotic laws. Drug addicts may engage in petty stealing, and occasionally robbery, to get enough money to buy their drugs, break into hospitals and doctors' offices to steal drugs, turn to prostitution, or sell drugs and become drug peddlers or "pushers." Drug addicts may also purchase a small supply of a drug from a peddler and then "water" down the powder with the addition of milk sugar before selling it to the next in line. By the time the last packet is bought by an addict it is mostly milk sugar. Doctors sometimes illegally prescribe drugs for an extra fee; indeed, some addicts have paid thousands of dollars to doctors for illegal prescriptions. One writer has thus described the young addict or "junkie" and the need to commit crimes in order to secure drugs.

> At the time when many of these young addicts were interviewed in 1952, most were still in the early stages of their addiction. They were "snatch-and-grab" junkies, supporting their habits through petty thievery, breaking into cars, shoplifting, and a variety of "scheming," such as "laying a story" on "a sucker" in the hope of gaining sympathy and some cash. Some enterprising ones actually had girls out "hustling" for them through "boosting" (shop-lifting) and "turning tricks" (prostitution). Despite the ragged state of their clothing and the harried nature of their existence, they regarded them-selves as the members of an elite, the true "down cats" on the best "kick" of them all, "Horse" (heroin). Many of them were still living at home, although they had long since exhausted the last reserves of patience of their families and "fenced" much of their movable property. Few, if any, of them had finished high school, and, on the average, they had little or no employment experience. Their attitudes towards work and the daily routine that steady employment presupposed were entirely negative. Their number-one hazard was the "man" (the police). Once they became "known junkies"—that is, known to the police—they were frequently picked up and sometimes sentenced—mostly for misdemeanors and, consequently, for short sentences. . . . The impression gained from interviewing them was that these addicts were petty thieves and petty "operators" who, status-wise, were at the bottom of the criminal population or underworld. It is difficult to see how they could be otherwise. The typical young junkie spent so much of his time in a harried quest for narcotics, dodging the police, and in lockups, that he was hardly in a position to plan major crimes.[71]

The second question is the relationship of drug addiction to crime in general. Of 1870 male addicts, 1679 (90 percent) had been arrested at some time. Of these 1679 addicts with an arrest history, 56.3 percent had been arrested before the onset of opiate use, 30.3 percent were arrested after the beginning of drug use, and 13.3 percent started opiate use and were arrested

---

[71] Finestone, "Narcotics and Criminality," pp. 76–77.

in the same year.[72] Among the female addicts, arrest was less common before opiate use (28 versus 51 percent), and they were less likely to have an arrest history. In a study of 266 white addicts residing in Kentucky, and with a rather rural background, a somewhat different criminal pattern was revealed.[73] Only one third of the men, and less than 10 percent of the women, had been arrested before addiction.

Most younger drug users from slum areas of cities appear to have engaged in prolonged delinquent activities either prior to their first arrest or prior to their first regular use of drugs. A report of a Chicago study states:

> With few exceptions known drug users engage in delinquency in more or less systematic form. Contrary to the widely held view that the delinquency of the young addict is a consequence principally of addiction, it was found that delinquency both preceded and followed addiction to heroin. Persons who became heroin users were found to have engaged in delinquency in a group-supported and habitual form either prior to their use of drugs or simultaneously with their developing interest in drugs. There was little evidence of a consistent sequence from drug use without delinquency to drug use with delinquency. Three observations may be made about the effect of addiction upon the delinquent behavior of the person: (1) The pressure of need for money to support his addiction impels the user to commit violations with greater frequency and with less caution than formerly. (2) Delinquents after becoming addicted to heroin do not engage in types of delinquency in which they are not already skilled. The post-addict delinquent, in other words, does not generally engage in more serious crimes than those he committed prior to his addiction. (3) Delinquents who as pre-addicts tended to engage in riotous behavior such as street fighting and gang attacks tend after addiction to abandon this kind of activity. Three elements are probably responsible for the change: (a) the sedative effect of the opiate; (b) the desire to avoid attracting the attention of public and police; and (c) the tendency for adolescents to become quieter in their conduct as they approach maturity.[74]

Some people erroneously believe that drug addiction is associated with crimes of violence. Actually, according to Chicago data, arrests for non-

---

[72] A study made by the Addiction Research Center of the National Institute of Mental Health at Lexington of the sequence of first arrest and first opiate use of 2213 addict patients admitted to the Lexington and Fort Worth hospitals in 1965.

[73] John A. O'Donnell, "Narcotic Addiction and Crime," *Social Problems,* 13:374–385 (1966).

[74] The Illinois Institute for Juvenile Research and Chicago Area Project, "Drug Addiction among Young Persons in Chicago." Summary Report of a Study Made by the Staff of the Chicago Area Project for the National Institute of Mental Health (Mimeographed: October 1953).

violent property offenses is proportionately higher among addicts, whereas arrest of addicts for violent offenses against the person, such as rape and aggravated assault, are only a fraction of the proportion among the population at large.[75] A group of young addicts was seldom found to have committed serious offenses against either persons or property, and those who did generally had committed similar offenses before becoming addicted, so that violence was only a part of the total picture. "Addiction, thus, appears to reduce both the inclination to violent crime and the capacity to engage in sophisticated types of crime requiring much planning." [76] Reckless concludes that there is little evidence to support the idea that addicts commit more violent crimes than do other criminals.

TREATMENT

The strong punitive societal reaction to drug use is probably the most significant factor in the development of a deviant career by the users of drugs.[77] In order to secure illegal drugs a male addict may engage in stealing and a female engage in prostitution. In a sense they come to fulfill society's image of them as being "criminals."

All studies of the results of treatment indicate that drug addiction, from the short-run point of view, is one of the most difficult forms of deviant behavior to treat effectively. The rate of relapse is high, particularly among juveniles and youths.[78] A follow-up study of 4776 addicts was made six months after their discharge from the United States Public Health Service Hospital at Lexington. Although the status of 39.6 percent of the patients could not be ascertained, it was revealed that 39.9 percent had relapsed, 7.0 percent had died after release, and only 13.5 percent had abstained from drugs.[79]

In a follow-up study of 1912 addict patients who had been discharged from the Lexington hospital between July 1942 and December 1955 and who were living in New York City, it was found that more than 90 percent of the patients discharged had become readdicted within five years of

[75] Chicago Police Department, *Annual Report*, 1951, p. 13.

[76] Walter C. Reckless, *The Crime Problem* (2d ed.; New York: Appleton-Century-Crofts, Inc., 1950), p. 356.

[77] Earl Rubington, "Drug Addiction as a Deviant Career," *International Journal of the Addictions*, 2:3–20 (1960).

[78] New York State, in 1966, passed a law making up to five-year "treatment" terms in institutions mandatory for drug addicts.

[79] Michael J. Pescor, "Follow-Up Study of Treated Narcotic Addicts," *Public Health Reports*, Supplement 170 (1943), pp. 1–18.

discharge.[80] Nearly one in three addicts admitted to the Lexington and Fort Worth hospitals is readmitted, and 5.1 percent of hospitalized addicts return five or more times, according to the United States Public Health Service data.[81]

Lindesmith attributes the high recidivism rate of the opiate addict to sociopsychological, rather than merely physiological, reasons. Recidivism in drug addiction is the result of long experience with the drugs and a conception of oneself as an addict, association with other addicts, and recognition of the importance of the drug in relation to withdrawal symptoms. It is often difficult to quit the use of drugs, or to abstain from beginning to use them again, because many friends and acquaintances are addicts. In addition, in large cities, particularly in the slums, a supply of drugs is not difficult to secure.[82] The feeling of boredom at being a nonaddict is also a factor in relapse. After the addict has been taken off drugs the old attitudes persist.

> The former user still believes in the efficacy of the drug. He still interprets the vicissitudes of life to some degree in terms of opiates and never again exhibits a feeling of disgust or moral indignation toward drug usage such as he may have had before addiction. These changes are produced by the influence of withdrawal distress, as has been demonstrated, but once formed, they are independent of the withdrawal symptoms.[83]

Addicts are generally not treated in their own homes or in general hospitals, for it is believed that they need constant specialized observation and treatment.[84] Most treatments of this type are given in only a few private sanatoriums, in some state and city hospitals, and in two federal hospitals, one at Lexington, Kentucky, and the other at Fort Worth, Texas. These

---

[80] G. H. Hunt and M. E. Odoroff, "Follow-Up Study of Narcotic Drug Addicts after Hospitalization," *Public Health Reports,* 77:41–54 (1962).

[81] See "Narcotic Addicts in U. S. Public Health Service Hospitals," *Indicators,* U. S. Department of Health, Education, and Welfare, March, 1966. Also see John A. O'Donnell, "The Relapse in Narcotic Addiction: A Critique of Follow-Up Studies," in Daniel M. Wilmer and Gene G. Kassebaum, eds., *Narcotics* (New York: McGraw-Hill Book Company, Inc., 1965).

[82] A study of white male southern addicts who were residents of Kentucky showed that only a minority had relapsed, although some had shifted to barbiturates or alcohol. A major reason for the abstinence was that there was no regular illicit source of narcotics in the area to which they had returned. See John A. O'Donnell, "A Follow-Up of Narcotic Addicts: Mortality, Relapse, and Abstinence," *American Journal of Orthopsychiatry,* 34:948–954 (1964).

[83] Lindesmith, *Opiate Addiction,* p. 139.

[84] For a description of specific methods of treatment, see Marie Nyswander, *The Drug Addict as a Patient* (New York: Grune & Stratton, Inc., 1956).

institutions were established by congressional action in 1929 for the confinement and treatment of narcotic addicts. They are now under the National Institute of Mental Health of the Public Health Service, under the Department of Health, Education, and Welfare. Although 80 percent of the patients are voluntary admissions at these institutions, many are under legal compulsion from local or state authorities.[85]

The optimum treatment period is from four to six months. A newly admitted drug addict is, first of all, given a thoroughgoing medical examination and treatment, which includes building up his general physical condition along with removal of drugs. The use of drugs is reduced gradually to minimize the severity of the withdrawal symptoms. Currently the most frequently used drug is a synthetic—methadon—for it has much milder abstinence symptoms than either heroin or morphine. The next step, removal of the patient's psychological dependence on drugs, is a much more difficult process. It usually involves psychiatric treatment, recreational and occupational therapy, and vocational training. It is also important that the addict receives follow-up supervision, as most relapses among addicts occur within the first two years after their release from the hospital.

New York and California have instituted "civil commitment" programs which provide for the suspension of criminal proceedings against defendants and their commitment to a specific rehabilitation program for drug addicts. Generally those who have had prior felony convictions or who have been involved in crimes of violence are excluded from these programs. With a view to preventing relapses, the total period of commitment is up to five years in New York and seven in California. Although such a program gets away from the legal stigma of criminal conviction, it is still a form of stigma and often "confinement" in the eyes of the individual and the public.

Being on drugs does not always markedly interfere with the individual's capacity to function effectively in society.[86] Experimental clinic programs in New York City have been directed, therefore, at keeping several hundred young addicts on drugs while efforts are made to bring about their rehabilitation.[87] In this way the addict is kept in free society, he can work,

---

[85] See Jerome Levine and Jack J. Monroe, "Discharge of Narcotic Drug Addicts against Medical Advice," *Public Health Reports,* 79:13–18 (1964).

[86] Lindesmith, in another connection, writes: "There are, for example, substantial numbers of addicts who are responsible and productive members of society, who share the common frame of values, who have not abandoned the quest for success and are not immune to the frustrations involved in seeking it, and who are not overcome by defeatism, quietism, and resignation." See "Anomie and Drug Addiction," p. 178.

[87] *The New York Times,* February 4, 1965, p. 63.

and he can even go to school. The addict comes to the clinic daily to receive a sufficient dose of methadon, the synthetic substitute for heroin, in a glass of orange juice. The results of this program have been encouraging.

In the United Kingdom, where a much different procedure from that attempted in the United States is in effect, drug addiction is considered a medical problem, a matter to be treated largely by outpatient care by physicians in hospitals, with prescription of drugs at low cost, often not as high as the price of cigarettes; physicians are supposed to prescribe a minimum dosage and to make prolonged attempts to cure the addict.[88] British officials, as well as the public, therefore do not regard the addict as a criminal. The addict does not have to steal, become a prostitute, or peddle drugs in order to secure them; thus British addicts appear to be relatively noncriminal. In nearly all the other Western European countries the program of narcotics control more or less resembles that used in Great Britain: addicts are permitted to have regulated access to legal supplies of drugs provided by physicians.[89] Frequently distribution is supervised by public health authorities; a register of known addicts is maintained and addicts must utilize only one doctor and one prescription pharmacy.

Other treatment methods employed in the United States have been carried out largely by groups of drug addicts themselves. These have included Addicts Anonymous and Synanon, both of which are discussed in Chapter 19.

CHANGING LEGAL ATTITUDES TOWARD DRUG ADDICTION

The United States is one of the few major countries which regards drug use as a crime rather than a medical problem. The penal regulation of drugs is based, first, on the assumption that addiction is harmful to the individual and to society, and, second, on the theory that "society may invade the domain of personal rights both to protect the general welfare and to prevent the individual from knowingly or unknowingly inflicting harm upon himself." [90]

The task of preventing unlawful trade in narcotics within the United States is assigned to the Bureau of Narcotics, a branch of the Treasury

---

[88] Because it is regarded as an illicit drug and is dealt with by the police, marihuana is not prescribed.

[89] Alfred R. Lindesmith, *The Addict and the Law* (Bloomington: Indiana University Press, 1965), pp. 179–188.

[90] David P. Ausubel, *Drug Addiction: Physiological, Psychological, and Sociological Aspects* (New York: Random House, Inc., 1964), p. 12.

Department, which administers the Harrison Narcotic Act.[91] This act requires the registration and payment of a graduated occupational tax by all persons who import, manufacture, produce, compound, sell, deal in, dispense, or give away narcotic drugs. In addition, it provides for a commodity tax imposed on the drug. The Bureau of Narcotics also administers the Marihuana Tax Act, which has regulatory features similar to those used in the control of narcotics. In 1966 there were 280 federal Bureau of Narcotics agents for the entire country, but they are aided by state and local enforcement officers. Uniform state drug control laws are now in operation in a large number of states, and there is increased cooperation among various enforcement agencies. There has been increased concern with enforcement problems connected with the use of marihuana by college students and with the use of LSD–25 and other hallucinogenic drugs, barbiturates, and amphetamines.[92]

Prior to 1966 a number of studies, particularly those by Lindesmith and Schur, presented evidence that drug addiction was a minor problem in Great Britain and tended to attribute this to the fact that the addict was dealt with differently.[93] It is, however, somewhat fallacious reasoning to assume that methods of control alone account for less drug addiction in Great Britain. Actually, patterns of drug use, particularly in slum areas, have not been common either there or in Europe generally. Moreover, there is evidence that the use of heroin and cocaine has within recent years increased greatly in Great Britain.[94] Modifications have been made in the originally highly permissive system. Government recommendations in 1967

---

[91] Two United Nations groups, the Permanent Central Opium Board and the Narcotic Drugs Supervisory Body, control the lawful traffic in drugs. In 1961, thirty-eight members of the United Nations agreed to a new, more rigid international regulation and control of drugs, subject to ratification by their home countries.

[92] See Richard Blum and Associates, *Utopiates—The Use and Users of LSD–25* (New York: Atherton Press, 1964); Arnold M. Ludwig and Jerome Levine, "Patterns of Hallucinogenic Drug Abuse," *Journal of the American Medical Association,* 191:92–96 (1965); and William H. McGlothlin and Sidney Cohen, "The Use of Hallucinogenic Drugs among College Students," *American Journal of Psychiatry,* 122:572–574 (1965).

[93] Alfred R. Lindesmith, "The British System of Narcotics Control," *Law and Contemporary Problems,* 22:141–142 (1957); Lindesmith, *The Addict and the Law,* pp. 162–188; and Edwin M. Schur, *Narcotic Addiction in Britain and America: The Impact of Public Policy* (Bloomington: Indiana University Press, 1962).

[94] See Thomas Bewley, "Heroin Addiction in the United Kingdom, 1954–1964," *British Medical Journal,* 2:1284–1286 (1965), and "Drug Addiction in the United Kingdom," *Bulletin on Narcotics,* 18:23–28 (1966).

would withdraw from individual British physicians the right to prescribe heroin or cocaine for addicts and would limit such rights to psychiatrists in hospitals. Treatment would be by either inpatient or outpatient services, but would not be forced.[95] These changes, however, do not carry the punitive character of drug legislation in the United States. The drug situation in Great Britain is still, however, nowhere near the problem that it is in the United States: these changes were recommended because heroin addicts in Great Britain had more than doubled in five years to 927 in 1963.

A different approach to this problem in the United States has been suggested by several authorities.[96] They believe that suppression has actually increased the difficulties of controlling the drug traffic because it has made necessary the development of an elaborate organization for illicit supply which seeks to extend itself by inducing nonaddicts to become users of narcotics. Because of their attempts to obtain enough money to buy illicitly—or to steal—high-priced drugs which could be obtained legally for a fraction of the cost charged by peddlers, crimes are committed by persons who would not otherwise commit them. "The policy of withholding legal satisfaction of the demand for narcotics inevitably leads to a profit-motivated and socially dangerous illicit market in drugs." [97] Drug users become "criminals" under these laws and drugs something mysterious and evil; the stigma of having an arrest record makes the rehabilitation of drug addicts more difficult. A "drug subculture" develops out of illicit efforts to secure a supply.

> Addiction itself is not a crime. It never has been under Federal law, and a State law making it one was struck down as unconstitutional by the 1962 decision of the Supreme Court in *Robinson v. California*. It does not follow, however, that a state of addiction can be maintained without running afoul of the criminal law. On the contrary, the involvement of an addict with the police is almost inevitable. By definition, an addict has a constant need for drugs, which obviously must be purchased and possessed before they can be consumed. Purchase and possession, with certain exceptions not relevant in the case of an addict, are criminal offenses under both Federal and State law. So is sale, to which many addicts turn to provide financial support for their habits. In many States, the nonmedical use of opiates is punishable, as is the possession of paraphernalia such as needles and syringes designed for such use. In other States, vagrancy statutes make it punishable for a known or convicted addict to consort with other

[95] *The New York Times,* January 31, 1967.

[96] See Lindesmith, *The Addict and the Law;* and Schur, *Narcotic Addiction in Europe and America.*

[97] Edwin M. Schur, "British Narcotics Policies," *Journal of Criminal Law, Criminology, and Police Science,* 51:619–630 (1961).

known addicts or to be present in a place where illicit drugs are found.

Thus the addict lives in almost perpetual violation of one or several criminal laws, and this gives him a special status not shared by other criminal offenders. Together with the fact that he must have continuous contact with other people in order to obtain drugs, it also gives him a special exposure to police action and arrest, and, in areas where the addiction rate is high, a special place in police statistics and crime rate computations.[98]

The Joint Committee on Narcotic Drugs (of the American Bar Association and the American Medical Association) has recommended that drug addiction be regarded primarily as a medical problem.[99] They have recommended a review of laws in order to abolish prison terms for addicts, to allow qualified doctors to dispense narcotics, and to establish experimental outpatient clinics, rather than hospitalization, for the care of addicts.

Opponents argue that the legalization and ambulatory treatment of drug addicts would not solve the problem. One writer, for example, argues that the assumption that the Harrison Narcotic Act causes addiction is "palpably false" because (1) there are other reasons, (2) such a procedure would increase drug addiction, and more narcotics would be added to the total amount in illicit channels while removing the deterrent value of the fear of the withdrawal syndrome, and (3) the drug addict could still be able to introduce others to the habit.[100] It is argued that the legal administration of a drug to known addicts would not decrease the number of addiction cases.

After a careful study of the problem, Lindesmith has summarized the aims of a more effective effort to control the use of drugs than is presently employed in the United States. Primarily he suggests that the power to control addiction now being exercised by legislators, lawyers, judges, prosecutors, and the police be transferred to the medical profession, which would deal with addiction as a medical problem, more or less as is done in Great Britain. Doctors would be given great freedom in dispensing drugs to addicts.

---

[98] *The Challenge of Crime in a Free Society*, p. 221.

[99] *Drug Addiction: Crime or Disease?* The Interim and Final Reports of the Joint Committee of the American Bar Association and the American Medical Association on Narcotic Drugs (Bloomington: Indiana University Press, 1960). The 1962 White House Conference on drug addiction proposed that the severe federal penalties be modified and regarded as a mistake the combining of penalties for the use of narcotics and for the more mild marihuana addiction in the same legislation. See White House Conference on Narcotic and Drug Abuse, *Proceedings* (Washington, D.C.: Government Printing Office, 1963).

[100] Ausubel, pp. 198–203.

Concerning the addiction problem as a whole, the following aims would probably be agreed upon as desirable by all parties in the current controversy:

1. Prevention of the spread of addiction and a resultant progressive reduction in the number of addicts.

2. Curing current addicts of their habits insofar as this can be achieved by present techniques or by new ones which may be devised.

3. Elimination of the exploitation of addicts for mercenary gain by smugglers or by anyone else.

4. Reduction to a minimum of the crime committed by drug users as a consequence of their habits.

5. Reducing to a minimum the availability of dangerous addicting drugs to all nonaddicts except when needed for medical purposes.

6. Fair and just treatment of addicts in accordance with established legal and ethical precepts, taking into account the special peculiarities of their behavior and at the same time preserving their individual dignity and self-respect.

Other aims and principles of an effective program which are of a more controversial nature but which are implied by the above are the following:

7. Antinarcotic laws should be so written that addicts do not have to violate them solely because they are addicts.

8. Drug users are admittedly handicapped by their habits but they should nevertheless be encouraged to engage in productive labor even when they are using drugs.

9. Cures should not be imposed upon narcotics victims by force but should be voluntary.

10. Police officers should be prevented from exploiting drug addicts as stool pigeons solely because they are addicts.

11. Heroin and morphine addicts should be handled according to the same principles and moral precepts applied to barbiturate and alcohol addicts because these three forms of addiction are basically similar.[101]

SUMMARY

Drugs consist of marihuana, the opiates, cocaine, barbiturates, amphetamines, and the hallucinogens. Societal reaction to drugs has varied in place and in time. At one time drug users were tolerated, even in the United States, where later the use of drugs was made illegal. The nature of drug addiction has changed in the United States, and there is increasing use by

---

[101] From Alfred R. Lindesmith, *The Addict and the Law* (Bloomington: Indiana University Press, 1965), pp. 269–270. Reprinted by permission of the publisher.

younger persons. Drug use appears to be much more prevalent in large urban centers. There are variations in drug use by age, sex, education, and occupation.

A person must be aware of the drug, know how to administer it, and recognize its effects. Drug addiction has a culture associated with it. This includes a system of sale and distribution of the drugs and the indoctrination of persons into the use of drugs by others who are already addicted. Drug addicts have an elaborate argot. Addicts often commit offenses in order to secure drugs or the money with which to purchase them.

There are two different approaches to the control of drug addiction. Some believe in rigid suppression, whereas others feel that this procedure has increased the deviant behavior by causing the development of an organization for illicit supply. They feel that drugs should be supplied to addicts through governmental and medical agencies.

SELECTED READINGS

Ball, John C. "Two Patterns of Narcotic Drug Addiction in the United States," *Journal of Criminal Law, Criminology, and Police Science,* 56:203–211 (1965). A study of the differences in two patterns of narcotic addiction: heroin use among metropolitan youth who come primarily from minority groups and use of opiates other than heroin or synthetic analgesics, which is principally found among the middle-aged in the southern part of the United States.

Becker, Howard S. "Becoming a Marihuana User," in John A. O'Donnell and John C. Ball, eds., *Narcotic Addiction.* New York: Harper & Row, Publishers, 1966, pp. 109–122. This study of a group of marihuana users describes the process of becoming a user. A good deal of case material is included.

Chein, Isidor, Donald L. Gerard, Robert S. Lee, and Eva Rosenfeld. *The Road to H: Narcotics, Delinquency, and Social Policy.* New York: Basic Books, Inc., 1964. A comprehensive study of drug addiction among youths in New York City. The discussion of the important role of social factors such as in the slum is excellent, but its attempts to link addiction to personality and family factors is weak.

Drug Addiction: Crime or Disease? Interim and Final Reports of the Joint Committee of the American Bar Association and the American Medical Association on Narcotic Drugs. Bloomington: Indiana University Press, 1960. Contains a comprehensive analysis of the drug problem in the United States by Morris Ploscowe, as well as a survey of drug control programs in Britain and European countries. The reports reveal widespread dissatisfaction with existing legislation and law enforcement among medical and legal authorities in the United States.

Law and Contemporary Problems. "Narcotics," Vol. 22, No. 1 (1957). Contains a series of articles on many phases of drug addiction, including the history of the development of narcotics, addiction and its treatment, social and psychological factors in narcotics addiction, juvenile narcotics use, narcotics and criminality, international control of narcotics, narcotic drug laws and enforcement policies, alternative solutions to the problem, and the British system of narcotics control.

Lindesmith, Alfred R.   *The Addict and the Law*. Bloomington: Indiana University Press, 1965. A detailed study of existing laws, regulations, and police practices relating to drug addiction in the United States. The author concludes that our present system of narcotics control not only is unjust to the addict but intensifies the problem. Comparative material on methods of drug addiction control in other countries is also presented.

————. "Basic Problems in the Social Psychology of Addiction," in John A. O'Donnell and John C. Ball, eds., *Narcotic Addiction*. New York: Harper & Row, Publishers, 1966, pp. 91–108. A more recent discussion by Lindesmith of a number of theoretical issues in the social psychology of opiate addiction.

————. *Opiate Addiction*. Bloomington: Indiana University Press, 1947. A socio-psychological study of the process of opiate addiction containing many cases.

————, and John R. Gagnon. "Anomie and Drug Addiction," in Marshall B. Clinard, ed., *Anomie and Deviant Behavior: A Discussion and Critique*. New York: The Free Press, 1964. A discussion of the sociological nature of drug addiction, in which it is maintained that drug addiction is not a consequence of personal or social failure.

O'Donnell, John A., and John C. Ball, eds. *Narcotic Addiction*. New York: Harper & Row, Publishers, 1966. A collection of articles dealing with the addict today and yesterday, causes and effects of addiction, and the treatment of the addict.

President's Commission on Law Enforcement and Administration of Justice, *Task Force Report: Narcotics and Drug Abuse*. Washington, D.C.: U.S. Government Printing Office, 1967. This detailed report presents a number of research papers dealing with mind altering drugs, drug legislation, and treatment, as well as detailed annotated material on narcotics and drug abuse.

————. *The Challenge of Crime in a Free Society*. Washington, D.C.: U.S. Government Printing Office, 1967. Chapter 8 deals with narcotics and drug abuse.

Schur, Edwin M.   *Crimes without Victims*. Englewood Cliffs, N.J.: Prentice-Hall, Inc., 1965. Contains a detailed discussion of the causes, enforcement, and treatment of drug addiction.

————. *Narcotic Addiction in Britain and America: The Impact of Public Policy*. Bloomington: Indiana University Press, 1962. A discussion of the nature of addiction and drug addiction policies in the United States and Great Britain. *In general* the difference in approach exists today, but restrictive policies have since been introduced in Great Britain.

10

Deviant Sexual Behavior

Sex deviations involve many different types of behavior, some of which are proscribed by law and some of which are negatively reacted to in other ways. They have in common the fact that they may violate the formal norms of a society, its legal codes, or both. Sex offenses which are considered deviations and punishable, for example, by law in American society consist, mainly, of rape, homosexual behavior (sodomy, fellatio, and so on), adultery, fornication, indecent exposure, incest (intercourse with a relative, as prohibited by law), and prostitution. Many of these offenses do little harm to other individuals and, in fact, the "victim" may have been a willing participant. The following is a *legal* classification of sex offenses by the nature of the deviant behavior.[1]

Sexual assault
  Mild sexual assault
  Serious sexual assault

---

[1] See Albert Ellis and Ralph Brancale, *The Psychology of Sex Offenders* (Springfield, Ill.: Charles C Thomas, Publisher, 1956), p. 31. One might add to these illegal abortions. See "Abortion" in Edwin M. Schur, *Crimes without Victims* (Englewood Cliffs, N.J.: Prentice-Hall, Inc., 1965).

Forcible rape
Statutory rape
Incestuous relations
Noncoital sexual relations with a minor
Exhibitory acts
Disseminating "obscene" material
Homosexual relations
    Homosexual relations with adults
    Homosexual relations with minors
Bestiality

Because of the wide variations in statutes geographically and temporally, it is often difficult to use a legal definition. In addition, some statutes are not enforced. In some societies acts such as homosexual relations between consenting adults are not crimes. On the other hand, sex deviations are not easy to delimit as sociocultural phenomena. One might say that a sex offense is an act contrary to sexual mores of the society in which it occurs. This has a number of limitations; here even it is difficult to draw a line, for some acts are only slightly at variance with the mores. Moreover, sexual mores vary widely, for the society or culture in the United States, as an example, consists of many subcultures such as class and ethnic groups, with their own distinct norms. What is an unimportant sexual act in one subcultural context may become a serious breach of law in another, as the following three situations illustrate.

1. A truck driver in a roadside cafe seats himself in a booth, gives the waitress his order, and, as she turns to depart, pats her on the buttocks. The other drivers who witness this are not offended, nor is the waitress, who is either inured to such behavior or interprets it as a slightly flattering pleasantry.

2. The same behavior occurs in a middle-class restaurant. The waitress feels that an indignity has been committed upon her person, and many of the waitresses consider it an offensive display of bad manners. The offender is reprimanded and asked to leave.

3. A man bestows the same pat upon an attractive but unknown woman on a city street. She summons a nearby policeman, some indignant witnesses gather to voice their versions of the offense, and the man is ultimately charged with a sexually motivated assault.[2]

Because of these difficulties, a recent large-scale study of sex offenders has developed the following definition of a *sex offense,* utilizing both a

---

[2] From *Sex Offenders* by Paul H. Gebhard, John H. Gagnon, Wardell B. Pomeroy, and Cornelia V. Christenson, p. 2. Copyright 1965 by the Institute for Sex Research, Inc. Reprinted by permission of Harper & Row, Publishers.

cultural and legal definition: "A sex offense is an overt act committed by a person for his own immediate sexual gratification which (1) is contrary to the prevailing sexual mores of the society in which he lives, and/or is legally punishable, and (2) results in his being legally convicted." [3] Using this definition, a classification of male sex offenders has been devised involving three independent variables or dimensions: whether the offense was heterosexual or homosexual in nature; whether the act was consented (consensual) or whether there was an element of force or intimidation; and whether the offense involved a child, a minor, or an adult.[4]

Sexual deviance can be divided also into broader types according to the *social dimensions of the activity* into acts involving "normal deviance," "pathological deviance," and deviance which generates a specific form of social structure.

> The first of these involves acts that are generally disapproved, but that either serve a socially useful purpose and/or occur so often among a population with such a low social visibility that only a small number are ever actually sanctioned for engaging in the behavior. This type would correspond to the second pattern of relations between law, mores, and behavior, or what has been called "normal deviance." The kinds of behavior that fall into this category include masturbation, premarital coitus, and heterosexual mouth-genital contact. All of these acts are performed by large numbers of people in our society, and they can all be construed . . . as articulating in some way with more fully legitimate expressions of sexuality. . . .
>
> The second type of sexual deviance corresponds to the general case where there is a high correlation between law, mores, and behavior. This type of deviance might be termed "pathological deviance." Examples include incest, sexual contact with children of either sex, exhibitionism, voyeurism, and aggressive or assaultive offenses. These types of deviance, unlike "normal deviance," involve very few persons, but are like it in that pathological deviance does exist without supportive group structures that serve to recruit to the behavior, train participants in it, gather partners together for its performance, or provide social support for the actors. . . .
>
> The third type of sexual deviation involves precisely those kinds of behavior that generate specific forms of social structure. Clearly, among those to be included in this type of deviance are female prostitution and both male and female homosexuality.[5]

---

[3] Gebhard, *et al.*, pp. 8–9.

[4] Gebhard, *et al.*, p. 11.

[5] From pp. 8–9, *Sexual Deviance* by John H. Gagnon and William Simon, ed. Copyright 1967 by the Institute for Sex Research. Reprinted by permission of Harper & Row, Publishers.

SOCIETAL REACTION

What is sexually normal or deviant behavior in a given society can be looked at from the point of view of societal reaction. Although there are variations in different cultures, most sex laws in American society govern four relationships: the degree of consent, such as forcible rape; the nature of the object, restricting legitimate sex objects to human beings of the opposite sex, of a certain age, of a defined distance in kinship, and to the spouse; the nature of the sexual act to certain behavior in heterosexual intercourse; and, finally, the setting in which the sex act occurs.[6]

> Sexual norms differ from others only by virtue of what they regulate, but this difference has important implications. First, the libidinal drive is powerful. It can be conditioned but not extinguished. Like other strong motives, it can disrupt orderly social interaction when left uncontrolled but, when controlled, can induce individuals to perform in socially advantageous ways. Second, though quite uniform in the sheer physiological mechanism of its gratification, the sexual urge is capable of an extraordinary amount of both situational and emotional conditioning. Third, this potentiality for conditioning is made especially complex and problematic by the fact that sexual gratification normally requires the direct, intimate cooperation of another person. . . . Consequently, the task of assigning rights in the means of gratification becomes extremely complicated. . . . Fourth, as if this were not enough, sexual intercourse is necessary for procreation and is thus linked in the normative system with the institutional mechanisms that guarantee the bearing and rearing of children. The sexual norms that guarantee the reproductive norms become intertwined, so to speak; to the possibility of illicit sexual expression is added the possibility of illegitimate parenthood.[7]

Some persons who have studied the operation of sex laws have maintained that the regulation of these laws is too wide and that only those sex acts should be punishable which involve (1) the use of force or duress, (2) adults who take advantage of a minor, and (3) public sex acts which are distasteful to the majority of those in whose presence they are com-

---

[6] Stanton Wheeler, "Sex Offenses: A Sociological Critique," in *Law and Contemporary Problems*, 25:258–259 (1960). Also see Morris Ploscowe, "Sex Offenses: The American Legal Context," in the same issue which is a symposium on sex offenses, pp. 217–225; and Morris Ploscowe, *Sex and the Law* (Englewood Cliffs, N.J.: Prentice-Hall, Inc., 1951).

[7] Kingsley Davis, "Sexual Behavior," in Robert K. Merton and Robert A. Nisbet, ed., *Contemporary Social Problems* (2nd ed.: New York: Harcourt, Brace & World, Inc., 1966), pp. 324–325.

mitted.[8] They maintain that it is questionable whether sex acts, other than those in which adults engage publicly, should be punished. Such a view would affect the legality of many present-day sex acts including much of unmarried adult heterosexual relations and adult homosexuality as has happened in many European countries like Sweden, Denmark, and more recently Great Britain. It has also been suggested that the age of statutory rape, or age of consent, be lowered from eighteen to fifteen, as generally obtains in Europe. Originally, in common law, the age of consent was under ten, but this age has been moved upward to a level that one leading legal writer claims is entirely unrealistic because of the voluntary nature of many sex relations in middle and late adolescence and the knowledge of sex relationships possessed by the girl. In the United States, "each such sexual contact may technically be rape under some law and may subject the male to ferocious penalties." In contrast to the United States, the age of consent is generally sixteen in England and Norway, fifteen in Sweden, Denmark, and France, and fourteen in Belgium and Germany.

SUBCULTURAL FACTORS AND SEXUAL DEVIATIONS

Although all societies have both formal and informal controls over sex behavior, there is a great diversity in emphasis in both the kinds of behavior controlled and the circumstances under which controls are imposed.[9] The criminal law of the seventeenth century did not include large areas of sex behavior which are now considered crimes. Similarly, the examination of research on sex offenders increasingly reveals evidence of the effect of the cultural and social structure on individual deviation from sexual norms. Patterns of cultural learning seem to account for a great deal of sexual behavior which, to many persons, is a product of some unique "personality disturbance." Some striking variations exist today in the norms of sex conduct, according to education, social class, race, religion, and region.[10] Sexual offenses may be the result of the influence of different subcultural definitions of sexual behavior. One study reported that when some southern rural families move north into more urban, middle-class areas, certain types

---

[8] Ellis and Brancale, pp. 88–89.

[9] Also see Clellan S. Ford and Frank A. Beach, *Patterns of Sexual Behavior* (New York: Harper & Row, Publishers, 1951), p. 130.

[10] Alfred C. Kinsey, Wardell B. Pomeroy, and Clyde E. Martin, *Sexual Behavior in the Human Male* (Philadelphia: W. B. Saunders Company, 1948); and Alfred C. Kinsey, Wardell B. Pomeroy, Clyde E. Martin, and Paul H. Gebhard, *Sexual Behavior in the Human Female* (Philadelphia: W. B. Saunders Company, 1953).

of sexual behavior which previously received little attention in the old permissive environment are looked upon as sex offenses.[11] Ethnic differences in rates of specific sex offenses show the effect of subcultural variables. In one study, for example, Negroes and Mexicans were overrepresented in the rape category and underrepresented in offenses against children.[12]

An Illinois report likewise referred to cultural factors in sex offenses. This report further indicated that the stability of sexual patterns is related to the stability of the social structure. "For example, the sex conduct of soldiers exposed to disorganized social conditions overseas varied widely from their sex conduct at home. Modern, industrialized, mobile, impersonal living has also affected traditional standards of sex behavior." [13] Sutherland has referred to cultural influences in the etiology of sex offenses:

> The absurdity of this theory (sexual psychopathy) should be evident to anyone who has an acquaintance with the variations in sexual behavior and sexual codes throughout the history of mankind; practically all of the present sex crimes have been approved behavior for adults in some society or other. Similarly within our society deviant cultures with references to sex behavior prevail in sub-groups. The manner in which juveniles are inducted into the cultures of these sub-groups in the toilets of schools, playgrounds, and dormiotries, as well as in other places, has been shown in many research reports on juvenile sex behavior.[14]

Sex violations, both heterosexual and homosexual, occurring among juveniles appear largely to take place with other juveniles rather than with adults and are the result of definitions of sexual behavior by the peer group.[15] The sexual behavior of adolescents is primarily peer-organized and peer-controlled.

> Adolescents themselves set standards for what is a violation of their sexual codes. The standards in these adolescent codes vary considerably according to the social status position of the adolescent and his family in

[11] *Report of the Governor's Study Commission on the Deviated Criminal Sex Offender* (Lansing: State of Michigan Printing Office, 1951), p. 31.

[12] *California Sexual Deviation Research,* January, 1953 (Sacramento: State Printing Office, 1953), pp. 32–35.

[13] *Report of the Illinois Commission on Sex Offenders,* to the 68th General Assembly of the State of Illinois (Springfield: State Printing Office, March 15, 1953), p. 10.

[14] Edwin H. Sutherland, "The Sexual Psychopath Laws," *Journal of Criminal Law and Criminology,* 40:549 (1950).

[15] Albert J. Reiss, Jr., "Sex Offenses: The Marginal Status of the Adolescent," *Law and Contemporary Problems,* 25:311 (1960). Also see Eugene J. Kanin, "Reference Groups and Sex Conduct Norm Violations," *The Sociological Quarterly* 8:495–505 (1967).

the larger society. A comparison of the prescribed heterosexual coition patterns of middle- and lower-status boys and girls may illustrate this variability. Among the lower-status white adolescent boys in our society premarital heterosexual intercourse is prescribed to secure status within the group, while it is not necessary to secure status within most middle-peer status groups, even though it does confer some status.[16]

Rather than think of the behavior of those who engage in aggressive sexual acts, such as rape, as sexually motivated in nature or regard them as "sick offenders," it would be better to view their "offenses as part of a broader system in which force may be used to attain their goals. It is the use of force, rather than any specifically deviant sexual motivation, that distinguishes these offenders from those who fall within the law." [17] The victim may also play a part in an act of rape because of similar subcultural sexual norms. "Consideration of the victim's role means that the offense can be viewed as a product of a social situation; its explanation cannot easily be reduced to a search for the childhood emotional disorders of the party who becomes labeled the offender." [18]

MISCONCEPTIONS ABOUT SEX DEVIANTS

In many ways the term *sex offender* or *sex deviant* is misleading. Sex is but one, and often a minor, aspect of a person's total life. It is not independent; rather, it is often an expression of other aspects of personality, so that to speak of a person as a "rapist" or as a "homosexual" or to use the general term "sex offender," tends to make one aspect of a person's life cover his entire life pattern. One writer has objected to the application of the label "sex offender" to juveniles.

> One technically violates the sexual conduct norm through behavior and thereby commits a *delinquent offense*. The term *sex offender* should perhaps signify no more nor less than this. Certainly, it should not imply that this is the only major kind of delinquent activity the person has committed. To classify a person as a sex offender may only serve to develop self and public definitions of the person as a sex offender.[19]

---

[16] Reiss, p. 312.

[17] Wheeler, p. 277. Also see Eugene J. Kanin, "Male Aggression in Dating-Courtship Relations," *American Journal of Sociology*, 63:197 (1957); and Menachem Amir, "Patterns of Forcible Rape," in Marshall B. Clinard and Richard Quinney, eds., *Criminal Behavior Systems: A Typology* (New York: Holt, Rinehart and Winston, Inc., 1967), pp. 60–75.

[18] Wheeler, p. 278. Also see Hans von Hentig, *The Criminal and His Victim* (New Haven, Conn.: Yale University Press, 1948). Also see Amir.

[19] Reiss, p: 257.

Many other misconceptions exist about sex offenders. Contrary to popular belief, a study of 300 convicted sex offenders revealed that the majority were rather harmless "minor" deviates rather than dangerous "sex fiends." [20] Of the sex offenders, 58 percent had committed relatively minor sex offenses. Only 10 in the entire group of 300 were considered to be dangerous in the sense that they had used force or duress. Moreover, aside from those convicted of statutory rape and incestuous relations, most sex offenders tend to be "sexually inhibited" rather than oversexed persons.

Another report on sex offenders has summarized a number of facts about them:

1. There are not tens of thousands of homicidal sex fiends abroad in the land.
2. Sex offenders are usually not recidivists (repeaters), at least in police and other official records.
3. Sex offenders do not progress to more serious types of sex crimes.
4. It is impossible at the present time to predict the danger of serious crimes being committed by sex deviates.
5. "Sex psychopathy" is not a clinical entity.
6. Sex offenders are not oversexed.[21]

After the elimination of statutory rape, incest, and the majority of homosexual cases, which as a general rule do not constitute a serious menace to females, there remains a relatively small number of violent sex cases in most countries. Sutherland estimated that in the United States there are annually about 5.7 sex killings of women and 4 of children.[22] He suggested that if these figures seem to be too low they could be multiplied fivefold or twentyfold and still not be large. He made a tabulation of all murders of women and of children as reported in *The New York Times* during the years 1930, 1935, and 1940, on the assumption that it would carry nearly all offenses of this type reported in the United States. He found that of the 324 murders of women reported, only 17 involved rape or suspicion of rape. Since the latter type of case would be more completely reported nationally, the ratio of such cases may be actually smaller. During these three years only 39 murders of children were reported and only 12 were indicated to be rape-murders.

Evidence indicates that sex offenders, contrary to common beliefs, have

---

[20] Ellis and Brancale, p. 32.

[21] Derived from *The Habitual Sex Offender*. Report and Recommendations of the Commission on the Habitual Sex Offender as formulated by Paul W. Tappan, Technical Consultant (Trenton: State of New Jersey, 1950), pp. 13–16.

[22] Sutherland, pp. 543–554.

a low rate of recidivism in comparison with other types of offenders. Out of a total of twenty-five kinds of crime reported in the FBI's *Uniform Crime Reports* for 1937, rapists ranked nineteenth as repeaters and the category "Other sex offenses" was seventeenth. Only 1 in 20 of 1447 males arrested in 1937 for rape had previously been convicted of rape. A special study of New York City juvenile delinquents revealed that only 3 boys in 108 brought in for sex delinquencies had subsequent appearances, none of which were sex offenses.[23] Between two thirds and three fourths of the sex offenders referred to the New Jersey Diagnostic Center were first offenders.[24] Of 1985 convicted English sex offenders over four out of five (83 percent) had no previous conviction for a sex offense.[25]

A California study covering sex offenders committed to correctional institutions during the five years 1945–1949 reported that one half of all sex offenders had a prior commitment record and one fifth a previous record. Recidivism was greater among the homosexuals than among any other group. On the other hand, sex offenders who had been committed to prison were found to be fairly good risks on parole. Only 31.8 percent of 568 California sex offenders committed another offense while on parole, as compared with 50.3 percent of all offenders.[26] Of these violators, less than 10 percent committed a serious offense.

Of 206 patients committed under the New Jersey sex offender law between June 1949 and April 1953, 57 were released on parole or discharged by this latter date, but no offender had violated his parole even though half had been out more than six months.[27] In Illinois, sex offenders have the lowest parole violation rate of any group of offenders, being about one third that of those committed for property offenses.[28] In England, of a group of 1985 convicted sex offenders who had been released for four years, 85 percent had no subsequent convictions.[29]

Sex offenders have often been erroneously labeled "psychopathic"—

---

[23] Lewis I. Doshay, *The Boy Sex Offender and His Later Career* (New York: Grune & Stratton, Inc., 1943).

[24] *The Habitual Sex Offender*, p. 24.

[25] Leon Radzinowicz, ed., *Sexual Offenses: A Report of the Cambridge Department of Criminal Science* (London: Macmillan & Co., Ltd., 1957), p. 137.

[26] *California Sexual Deviation Research*, pp. 21–22.

[27] *A Follow-Up Study of 206 Sex Offenders Committed to State Mental Hospitals in New Jersey* (Trenton: New Jersey Department of Institutions and Agencies, June 1953), pp. 1–2.

[28] *Report of the Illinois Commission on Sex Offenders*, p. 25.

[29] Radzinowicz, p. 268.

erroneously not only because this term is vague but because the percentage of these offenders diagnosed as such varies tremendously. Sutherland has concluded that the "concept 'sexual psychopath' is too vague for judicial or administrative use either as to commitment to institutions or as to release as 'completely or permanently cured.' " [30] Morris Ploscowe, a well-known legal authority, has written:

> Any revision of sex offender laws must also repeal much of the sexual psychopath legislation that is presently in force. These laws were passed to provide a means for dealing with dangerous, repetitive, mentally abnormal sex offenders. Unfortunately, the vagueness of the definition of sexual psychopaths contained in these statutes has obscured this basic underlying purpose. There are large numbers of sex offenders who engage in compulsive, repetitive sexual acts, which may be crimes, who may be mentally abnormal, but who are not dangerous. The transvestite, the exhibitionist, the frotteur, the homosexual who masturbates another either in the privacy of his bedroom or in a public toilet, the "peeping tom"—are typical of large numbers of sex offenders who are threatened with long-term incarceration by present sexual psychopath legislation. And what is even worse is that such legislation has not usually been implemented by facilities for treatment. The result is that many nuisance-type, nondangerous sex offenders have been imprisoned for long periods of time, without treatment, in those jurisdictions where such laws have been enforced. This is not to say that the compulsive nondangerous types of sex offenders should be immune from prosecution and punishment; but short sentences or probation are more than adequate to deal with these derelictions, unless better treatment facilities are provided.[31]

The remainder of the discussion will deal with two forms of deviant sex behavior: homosexual behavior and prostitution. In Chapter 8 we discussed forcible rape as a form of violent personal crime, partly because of its close etiological relation to other crimes of violence, such as criminal homicide and assault.[32]

---

[30] Sutherland, p. 551.

[31] Reprinted from a symposium, *Sex Offenses,* by permission from *Law and Contemporary Problems,* Vol. 25, No. 2 (1960). Published by the Duke University School of Law, Durham, N.C. Copyright, 1960 by Duke University. For a critical discussion of the concept of psychopath also see pages 191–193.

[32] Two other forms of deviant sex behavior might have been included here: illegal abortion and illegitimacy. See "Abortion" in Schur, pp. 11–66 and illegitimacy in Robert W. Roberts, ed., *The Unwed Mother* (New York: Harper & Row, Publishers, 1966) , and Clark E. Vincent, *Unmarried Mothers* (New York: The Free Press, 1961).

HOMOSEXUAL BEHAVIOR

The Nature of Homosexuality

Homosexual behavior represents sex relations with members of one's own sex, behavior which may be successfully carried out physically in a number of ways other than that possible in a complete heterosexual union. Many homosexual persons regard this form of sexual outlet as being more satisfactory than heterosexual relations. The label "homosexual," based as it is on a person's sexual proclivities, however, makes little sense when applied to a person; one is unlikely to speak of a nonhomosexual as a "heterosexual" or that person's behavior as "heterosexuality." Persons who engage in homosexual behavior come from all social classes, have varying degrees of education, are from a wide range of occupations and professions, have varied interests and avocations, and may be single or married.

A common myth is that male homosexuals can be readily recognized as physically effeminate persons. Most of them are indistinguishable physically from other people. Where they are socially visible, and many are, it is a matter of playing a feminine or homosexual sex role. An English study found only 17 percent with slight or pronounced feminine characteristics, but 66 percent said that they could be recognized by other homosexuals. In order of importance were the glance of the eyes, gestures, walk, voice, clothing, and vocabulary.[33] Another study maintains, however, that many male homosexuals display feminine traits because they believe they are "conforming to a stereotype"; they feel impelled to "adopt what they consider feminine characteristics" because of the traditional dichotomy between sex roles, because a male homosexual "construes his homosexual interest as evidence of a feminine component within himself." [34] Still the study showed that some "obviousness" as a homosexual for males with extensive homosexual experience varied from 27.6 to 59.7 percent.[35] There are sometimes subtle feminine mannerisms that can be detected by a homosexual only as a part of a total syndrome.

> These mannerisms are for the most part slight exaggerations of, or departures from, socially acceptable behavior or dress. Any single item has little significance, but if a number exist, they form a symptom-syndrome

---

[33] Gordon Westwood, *A Minority: A Report on the Life of the Male Homosexual in Great Britain* (London: Longmans, Green, & Co., Ltd., 1960), p. 62.

[34] Gebhard, *et al.,* p. 348.

[35] Gebhard, *et al.,* p. 652. The percentage of "some obviousness" has been added to the percentage of "obvious" in the figures given here.

that is quite diagnostic. Such subtle items are frequently associated with upper socioeconomic level tastes and behavior: over-meticulous dress, too well-groomed fingernails, a gentle, modulated voice, an interest in aesthetics, etc. Such things have, in our culture, a vague feminine significance: women pay attention to clothes, men are less concerned; women tend their nails, men are careless about them; women are supposed to have quiet, modulated voices, men are loud and assertive.[36]

Still, it is difficult to generalize about reversed sex roles, for there are many exceptions. Some evidence of the lack of physical differences in homosexuals is the evidence about leading historical figures.

> Socrates and Plato made no bones about their homosexuality; Catullus wrote a love poem to a young man whose "honeysweet lips" he wanted to kiss; Virgil and Horace wrote erotic poems about men; Michelangelo's great love sonnets were addressed to a young man, and so were Shakespeare's. There seems to be evidence that Alexander the Great was homosexual, and Julius Caesar certainly was—the Roman Senator Curio called Caesar "every woman's man and every man's woman." So were Charles XII of Sweden and Fredrick the Great. Several English monarchs have been homosexual. . . . About some individuals of widely differing kinds, from William of Orange to Lawrence of Arabia, there is running controversy which may never reach a definite conclusion. About others—Marlowe, Tchaikovsky, Whitman, Kitchener, Rimbaud, Verlaine, Proust, Gide, Wilde and many more—there is no reasonable doubt.[37]

In most Western European countries, and in other parts of the world as well, homosexual acts between consenting adults provided the acts are not carried out in public, are not considered crimes. They are in some countries including the United States, where, with the exception of Illinois, such acts are crimes in every state. In the United States, however, the acts involved in homosexuality are different from the stereotype of such crimes as theft or violence. Generally, they do not involve real injury to either property or person. Homosexuality is more likely to be disturbing to the community's sensibilities. Because the partner in homosexual behavior is likely to be a willing associate, this type of offense has been referred to as "crime without a victim." [38]

Some homosexuals live together as partners in a more or less per-

---

[36] From p. 348 *Sex Offenders* by Paul H. Gebhard, *et al.* Copyright © 1965 by the Institute for Sex Research, Inc. Reprinted by permission of Harper & Row, Publishers.

[37] Bryan Magee, *One in Twenty: A Study of Homosexuality in Men and Women* (New York: Stein and Day, 1966), p. 46.

[38] Schur, pp. 169–179. He also includes abortions and drug addiction.

manent union. For the majority of homosexuals, however, their sex life is likely to be highly promiscuous and their relations with other homosexuals confined to sexual encounters which are likely to be brief, and relatively anonymous. This means that not only are permanent relationships likely to be infrequent, "but even less lengthy affectional-sexual links tend to be over-shadowed in homosexual life by the predominant pattern of 'cruising' and relatively impersonal one-night stands." [39] Because the pattern of sex rela-tions is relatively impersonal, certain male juveniles, who are likely not to be homosexuals, make themselves available on a monetary basis.[40] Transitory sex relations may also be arranged with the homosexual pros-titute, the "hustler" for other homosexuals, who provides services which might be difficult to obtain without effort, particularly by those who are less attractive physically and older. The adult homosexual prostitute is a part of homosexual life; he learns to play the role in behavior, such as gesture, vocabulary, clothing and even makeup.[41]

Prevalence of Homosexuality

Various persons have attempted to estimate the size of the homosexual population in such countries as the United States and Great Britain. Kinsey reports that somewhere between adolescence and old age about 37 percent of the white male population has had homosexual experience and to the point of orgasm. Only half as many females as males have had homosexual experiences, but males have more frequent relations, continue their activi-ties for more years, and are promiscuous.[42] There is ample evidence that homosexual relationships exist to a considerable extent in our prisons and in other one-sex communities. Most homosexual relationships are of a transitory nature, occurring perhaps only once or twice over a number of years, or as a result of a unique social situation. Kinsey reports that 4 percent of his sample of males were career homosexuals. Basing his estimates partly on the Kinsey report, Lindner states that "treating the matter conservatively . . . the extent of genuine inversion in the United States appears to settle at a figure roughly 4 to 6 percent of the total male population over age 16 or around 3 million individuals." [43] A recent British study of homosexuality

---

[39] Schur, p. 89.

[40] Albert J. Reiss, Jr., "The Social Intergration of Queers and Peers," *Social Problems,* 9:102–120 (1961).

[41] John Rechey, *City of Night* (New York: Grove Press, 1963), p. 36.

[42] Kinsey, *et al., Sexual Behavior in the Human Male,* and Kinsey, *et al., Sexual Behavior in the Human Female.*

[43] Robert Lindner, "Homosexuality and the Contemporary Scene," in Hendrik Ruitenbeek, ed., *The Problem of Homosexuality in Modern Society* (New York: E. P. Dutton & Co., Inc., 1963), p. 61.

in men and women estimates it to be generally one in every twenty persons.[44] Many writers have estimated that homosexuality is not only widely prevalent but on the increase.

Estimates as to the incidence, prevalence, and increase of homosexuality are based, to date, on inadequate and unrepresentative data often accompanied by fallacious reasoning. After examining the literature, Schur has stated that "there are no satisfactory statistics regarding the prevalence of homosexuality . . . Estimates by individual homosexuals are not likely to be very accurate . . . many homosexuals have a psychological stake in exaggerating their number." [45] An English writer has concluded that he could not estimate the incidence because a homosexual's judgment "is biased by the greater or lesser ease with which he is able to find sexual partners." [46] "Homosexuality has existed in Great Britain . . . and all other European civilizations, but it is impossible to tell if this incidence has increased at different periods." [47] The authors of the Wolfenden Report dealing with homosexual behavior in Great Britain stated that "it is widely believed that the prevalence of homosexuality has greatly increased in this country. . . . In the general literature . . . there is a growing number of works dealing incidentally or entirely with this subject. . . . But it does not necessarily follow that the behavior which is so discussed is more widespread than it was before." [48]

Nature of the Societal Reaction

Although homosexual behavior is variant behavior in itself, it need not be deviant; it becomes deviant behavior when there is societal reaction. Deviance is not necessarily a quality essential to the homosexual act. On the basis of this assumption Schofield states that the disruptive influences of homosexuals in the community vary directly with the external constraints placed on the behavior. A homosexual may be well integrated in every way except in his sex life; others may be unintegrated because of the effects of societal reaction. "The social and economic value of the homosexuals in the community varies with the hostility shown them." [49]

Most societies have what are termed sexually appropriate and sexually

---

44 Magee, pp. 43–46.

45 Schur, p. 75.

46 Westwood, p. 62.

47 Westwood, p. 63.

48 Report of the Committee on Homosexual Offenses and Prostitution, *The Wolfenden Report* (New York: Lancer Books, Inc., 1964), pp. 40–41.

49 Michael Schofield, *Sociological Aspects of Homosexuality: A Comparative Study of Three Types of Homosexuals* (Boston: Little, Brown & Company, 1965), p. 211.

inappropriate roles according to a person's age, social status, and other criteria. In some societies homosexual roles and behavior are considered inappropriate for one's sex and in others it is condoned or even approved. There is ample evidence that cultural attitudes toward homosexual or one-sex behavior have differed from one period in history to another. In Greek and Roman times this behavior was prevalent, and in some societies homosexual practices were related to certain religious rites. Ford and Beach studied seventy-six folk societies and found that among forty-nine of them, or 64 percent, "homosexual activities of one sort or another are considered normal and socially acceptable for certain members of the community." [50] Some of the attitudes in parts of Western society that homosexuality is deviant behavior can be explained by certain aspects of the Christian tradition.[51]

The nature and extent of societal reaction to homosexuality in American society can be analyzed in two ways: actual studies of the reactions of others to homosexual behavior, and the legal statutes themselves. There have been few studies of attitudes toward homosexual behavior, possibly because it is obvious that it is stigmatized by the majority. A recent study, for example, of a fairly representative sample of 180 persons revealed that the persons considered to be "deviant" were most frequently the homosexuals.[52] Homosexuals were categorized, in order, as "sexually abnormal," "perverted," "mentally ill," "maladjusted," and "effeminate." Another researcher interviewed 700 university students, mostly undergraduates, and found that the reactions were not uniform; in fact, there were four basic reactions to "imputed" homosexual behavior in others the students had known.[53] These reactions were (1) explicit disapproval and immediate withdrawal, (2) explicit disapproval and subsequent withdrawal, (3) implicit disapproval and partial withdrawal, and (4) no disapproval and relationship sustained. Generally the reaction tended to be negative but it varied in intensity and generally did not take an extreme form. Consequently, "reactions to homosexuals in American society are not *societal* in the sense of being uniform within a narrow range; rather they are significantly conditioned by subcultural as well as situational factors. Thus not only are

---

[50] Ford and Beach, p. 130. Also see Ruth Benedict, *Patterns of Culture* (Boston: Houghton Mifflin Company, 1934).

[51] David S. Bailey, *Homosexuality and the Western Christian Tradition* (New York: David McKay Company, Inc., 1955).

[52] J. L. Simmons, "Public Stereotypes of Deviants," *Social Problems*, 13:223–332 (1965).

[53] John I. Kitsuse, "Societal Reaction to Deviant Behavior: Problems of Theory and Method," in Howard S. Becker, ed., *The Other Side: Perspectives on Deviance* (New York: The Free Press, 1964), pp. 87–102.

the processes by which persons come to be defined as homosexuals contingent on the behavior of others, but also the sanctions imposed and the treatment they are accorded as a consequence of that definition vary widely among conventional members of various subcultural groups." [54]

In the United States it is not a crime to be a homosexual; it is the homosexual acts such as sodomy, fellatio, and mutual masturbation which are the crimes, whether occurring among adults, adults and minors, and whether occurring in public or in private. Soliciting for such acts is also generally a crime. Such acts are between males, for although homosexual behavior is by no means uncommon among women, it is generally not punished by statutes.[55] The penalties on the statute books for such acts are severe. A large number of states provide up to ten or more years in prison; others, a five-year maximum. In addition, some states have sex deviate laws where an offender may be committed for "treatment" in excess of the period provided by the criminal statutes.

Although adults committing homosexual acts are subject to arrest in the United States (with the exception of Illinois), the likelihood of arrest, conviction, or prison sentence is probably not great. In cases where they do occur, the arrest and trial may be as damaging as conviction and sentencing in that they constitute a public degradation ceremony for the homosexual person.[56] In cases involving minors, however, or a particularly flagrant public act, the enforcement may be strict. There is often irregular harassment through entrapment by private detectives in such places as public toilets or by raids of "gay bars." What is more important in the lives of the homosexuals is that the threat of exposure to arrest may lead to blackmail by others. Persons may threaten to report them and even police officers may sometimes blackmail homosexuals. Consequently, homosexuals are generally ineligible for government service and may be dismissed when discovered because of their vulnerability to extortion and because of what is termed their "moral unsuitability."

There have been efforts in the United States—and these have been successful in Illinois—to remove homosexual acts, provided the persons involved are above a certain age, from the category of crimes, on the ground

---

[54] Kitsuse, p. 101.

[55] For a discussion of homosexual behavior among women, See Kinsey, *et al., Sexual Behavior in the Human Female;* Magee; and William Simon and John H. Gagnon, "The Lesbians: A Preliminary Overview," in Gagnon and Simon, pp. 247–282. Also see John H. Gagnon and William Simon, "Femininity in the Lesbian Community," *Social Problems,* 15:212–221 (1967).

[56] Public hysteria bordering almost on a "witch hunt" occurred a few years ago at the discovery of a number of cases of homosexual behavior among middle-class persons in Boise, Idaho. See John Gervassi, *The Boys of Boise: Furor, Vice and Folly in an American City* (New York: The Macmillan Company, 1966).

that it is a personal act. In fact, the Group for the Advancement of Psychiatry recommended, in 1965, that homosexual behavior be viewed from other approaches than the legal.[57] In Great Britain the Wolfenden Report recommended to Parliament in 1957 that "homosexual behavior between consenting adults in private be no longer a criminal offense." [58] In their opinion, private sexual acts, such as homosexual behavior between consenting adults, were not within the purview of the law if they did not interfere with public order and decency, if the protection of citizens from what is offensive or injurious was assured, and if it did not exploit others, particularly in younger groups. These recommendations changing the laws were finally adopted in 1967. Such a change in the law brought Great Britain into line with nearly all the remainder of western Europe; West Germany is almost the only country in Europe to consider homosexual acts between consenting adults to be a crime. In Great Britain the main arguments against the use of the criminal law against homosexuality have been summarized as follows:

1. The law discriminates irrationally against private male homosexuality, while leaving untouched female homosexuality and heterosexual misdemeanours, such as fornication and adultery, whose social consequences are probably more widely harmful.
2. The social consequences of the law are almost wholly bad. Many cases of blackmail and suicides have undoubtedly resulted from it, while it tends to increase rather than diminish homosexual promiscuity, instability and public misbehaviour by denying homosexuals the legitimate chance of establishing discreet permanent relationships.
3. Many homosexuals could be helped to a better adjustment if they felt freer to seek advice without incriminating themselves by doing so.
4. The present law does much to ensure that adolescents and young men who once become involved in homosexual practices will feel it far harder to escape than would otherwise be the case.
5. The lack of any distinction between homosexual behaviour committed in public or in private, or between those above or below an "age of consent," decreases the protection of the youth.[59]

---

[57] Group for the Advancement of Psychiatry, *Sex and the College Student* (New York: Mental Health Materials Center, Inc., 1966). In Illinois the homosexual acts between consenting adults must be in private and cannot involve persons who are under age.

[58] *The Wolfenden Report,* p. 48.

[59] From *Sociological Aspects of Homosexuality* by Michael Schofield, © Michael Schofield, 1965. Reprinted by permission of the author, Longmans, Green & Co., Ltd., London, and Little, Brown & Company, Boston. Also see R. O. D. Benson, *In Defense of Homosexuality: Male and Female* (New York: Julian Press, Inc., 1965).

The imputation of homosexuality may have great consequences for the individual: he may be treated as an object of avoidance or amusement; he may be dismissed from his employment and have difficulty in subsequent positions; the police may harass him and he may even be confined in jail or prison. The attributing of "homosexuality" does not necessarily follow from any specific behavior; rather, it is a consequence of the definition of others. A study of 75 subjects who had "known" homosexuals showed that categorizing such a person was complex, being based on indirect and direct evidence.[60] Regardless of the evidence of homosexuality, it is documented by retrospective interpretation of the deviant's behavior, which represents a review of past interaction with him in which a search is made for subtle cues and behavior which might give evidence to justify the attribution of the term *homosexual*. Indirect evidence is in the form of rumor, general representational information concerning the individual's behavior, associates, or sexual predelictions, or an acquaintance's experience with the individual. Generally such evidence is accepted without independent verification. Direct observation includes behavior "which everyone knows" as evidence of homosexuality, behavior which deviates from "behaviors-held-in-common" among members of the group to which he belongs, such as effeminate appearance and manners. Finally, there are behaviors which the person interprets as overt sexual propositions. In some instance the person comes to interpret the so-called deviant's behavior as progressively inappropriate in the course of interaction with him.

Normatively there have been a number of objections to homosexual behavior. It cannot lead to reproduction or to a normal family situation. In a sense, it distorts the general assignment of complementary sex roles to the members of a society. In fact, it is the reverse of sex roles on the part of homosexuals, particularly in homosexual pairs who may set up housekeeping; the feminine male and masculine female appear to be particularly disturbing to some. Still, because there have been changes in contemporary societies, such as a desire to have a lower birth rate, more equality of the sexes, and wider possibilities of heterosexual sex behavior, some have wondered why homosexuality should continue to be so strongly disapproved. On the other hand,

> In urbanized, mobile industrial societies, familial relationships seem to be particularly valued because they are virtually the only ones that are both personal and enduring; marital and parental ties therefore receive strong sentimental support. Furthermore, the differentiation of role as between the sexes shows a surprising persistence, even if less invidious than formerly. Homosexual relations are notoriously ephemeral by comparison;

---

[60] Kitsuse.

and, if they involve exclusive emotional commitment, they preclude marital and parental bonds except on a fraudulent basis. If homosexuality were to be generally approved, it would, like heterosexuality, have to be normatively regulated. The young would have to be protected against force, fraud, and economic enticement; the rights, obligations, and role differentiation of homosexual partners would have to be specified; a licensing or identification system would have to be utilized so that normal individuals would not innocently be deceived into marriage with homosexual ones. In short, an institutional system governing such relationships, paralleling the system governing normal sexual relations, would have to be evolved. As yet there is no sign that such an evolution will occur; the complications of the dual system would no doubt exceed even those that characterize the present single system.[61]

Primary and Secondary Homosexual Deviation

The various types of homosexuals are the overt versus the secret,[62] the adjusted and the maladjusted,[63] the jailhouse turnout and the true homosexual,[64] and the primary and the secondary.[65] It is important to distinguish between those who play a homosexual role under a variety of circumstances and those whose behavior is more likely to be the result of a situation. The behavior of the latter may be regarded as primary or situational and may occur frequently, for example, in one-sex communities such as prisons, the armed forces, prisoners-of-war camps, boarding schools, and other such one-sex communities. Likewise, there are those who have committed occasional homosexual acts, particularly in adolescence, and those who may commit homosexual acts only for money.

Most persons who commit homosexual acts are not homosexuals in a full sociological sense; they are not secondary deviants. Those who are secondary deviants tend to seek sexual gratification predominantly and continually with members of the same sex. They come to have a self-concept and play a homosexual role in connection with these acts. Such persons come to have the feelings of a homosexual. Goffman has limited the term

---

[61] From "Sexual Behavior" by Kingsley Davis in *Contemporary Social Problems* edited by Robert K. Merton and Robert A. Nisbet, © 1961, 1966 by Harcourt, Brace & World, Inc., reprinted with their permission.

[62] Maurice Leznoff and William Westley, "The Homosexual Community," *Social Problems*, 3:257–263 (1956).

[63] Evelyn Hooker, "The Adjustment of the Male Overt Homosexual," in Ruitenbeek, pp. 141–161.

[64] David Ward and Gene Kassebaum, "Homosexuality: A Mode of Adaptation in a Prison for Women," *Social Problems*, 12:159–177 (1964).

[65] Edwin M. Lemert, *Social Pathology* (New York: McGraw-Hill Book Company, Inc., 1951), Chap. 4.

homosexual to "individuals who participate in a special community of understanding wherein members of one's own sex are defined as the most desirable sexual objects and sociability is energetically organized around the pursuit and entertainment of these objects." [66] An important aspect of secondary deviation is participation in those establishments, such as bars, which are primarily attended by homosexuals in the larger cities of western Europe and America. Depending on the size of the city, there are a great variety of homosexual bars serving as a necessary locus for the male homosexual community.[67] They allow the individual not only to meet other homosexuals but to get away from the concealment he practices in the heterosexual world. There it is not necessary to conceal the stigma, and, in fact, the nonhomosexual may be subjected to some stigma. It is likely that the positive attraction for such meeting places is that they provide the homosexual with a positive self-image in the face of the pressures of societal reaction. Moreover, it is unlikely that such bars are sources for spreading homosexual behavior since nearly all of those who go there, other than the curious public, are already committed to homosexuality. In fact, some have suggested that these bars remove homosexuals from public view and out of other public places, and in this sense the spread of homosexuality is inhibited.[68]

Several studies have shown that there are homosexuals who, as secondary deviants, are fairly well adjusted to the homosexual role and experience little conflict. Hooker, for example, found that half her cases had a high degree of psychological adjustment and that homosexuality "may be a deviation in sexual patterns which is within the normal range psychologically." [69] They have developed their own identity. Rationalizations, the attitude of partners, and the homosexual subculture help. In fact, one writer maintains that "those who accept their homosexual impulses are less likely to get into trouble with the law and are more likely to be capable of establishing an emotional relationship with another man." [70]

Few studies attempt to indicate the stages through which a person moves from primary to secondary homosexuality. Schofield made a study

---

[66] Erving Goffman, *Stigma: Notes on the Management of Spoiled Identity* (Englewood Cliffs, N.J.: Prentice-Hall, Inc., 1965), pp. 143–144.

[67] Nancy Achilles, "The Development of the Homosexual Bar as an Institution," in Gagnon and Simon, pp. 228–244, and Evelyn Hooker, "The Homosexual Community," in Gagnon and Simon, pp. 167–184.

[68] Donald W. Cory and John P. LeRoy, *The Homosexual and His Society: A View from Within* (New York: The Citadel Press, 1963), pp. 122–123.

[69] Hooker, "The Adjustment of the Male Overt Homosexual," in Ruitenbeek. Also see Schofield.

[70] Schofield, p. 210.

involving six samples of fifty each: convicted homosexuals, homosexuals who had received psychiatric care, and homosexuals who had not been convicted nor had received psychiatric care.[71] The other groups were made up of those convicted of relations with boys under the age of sixteen and of two groups of nonhomosexuals. A homosexual was defined as a male over twenty-one but under sixty-one who "regarded himself as a homosexual and was prepared to say so to the interviewers." Most of the convicted homosexuals and patient homosexuals remained to a degree primary deviants in that they never seemed to come to accept their behavior as constituting to them a socially acceptable role; consequently, they expressed guilt feelings. This may have been a result of limiting their activities to occasional acts and therefore increasing the likelihood of getting into trouble. Those who had not been convicted and were not under treatment were more likely than the others to have close homosexual friends, to mix socially with other homosexuals, and to have a current affair, but less likely to have promiscuous relations. Their relationship with their partners was more likely to be a permanent liaison.

Social isolation tends to drive the homosexual underground into a subculture of homosexuals. Over a period of time the social ties that come to be important to him stem from his association with other homosexuals. He comes to speak their language and to accept their status systems. The homosexual becomes alienated from the conventional culture and this isolation makes it more difficult for him to participate in heterosexual activities. A four-stage progression has been sketched by Schofield. Some never go further than the first two stages, which can be regarded as primary deviation; others can stay in both the homosexual and the larger community. Involvement with the law may hasten progress through these four stages.

> 1. The first stage usually occurs in the late teens or early twenties. As his friends start to go out with girls and eventually marry, the homosexual finds other interests and drifts away from their company. Sometimes he is scarcely aware of his homosexual tendencies or has not come to terms with them, but gradually he becomes conscious of his isolation. Many young homosexuals have described their dismay when they discover that the sort of things which interest their friends hold no appeal for them.
>
> 2. Thus the young homosexual finds he is driven away from the company of ordinary men and women at just the time when he most needs their help. As he loses his friends he begins to regard himself as an outcast. He finds to his dismay that will-power and self-control are not the answer to his problem. The more extrovert homosexual will soon pass through

---

[71] Schofield.

this second stage and quickly make friends with other homosexuals. But others lead lonely lives, plagued by feelings of guilt and accepting the role of the social isolate.

3. At the third stage the young man meets other homosexuals and begins to go to their meeting places and joins a homosexual group. Some of them soon tire of this opportunity to mix in a group of like-minded individuals, but others accept the chance eagerly. Here a homosexual can feel at ease because he does not have to hide his true inclinations. Indeed, this is such a relief that much of the talk in these groups is about sex. It is here that the two worlds conflict. He must make sure that his friends from the other world do not meet his friends from the homosexual group. He has to explain his absences from the other world, think up convincing stories, and learn to lead two lives. Some homosexuals resolve this dilemma by moving on to the fourth stage.

4. At this last stage the homosexual way of life monopolizes his interests and absorbs all his time. He gives up his efforts to resolve the conflicts between the outside world and the homosexual way of life. He moves exclusively in a homosexual group and adopts a hostile attitude towards all those not in the group. He has, in fact, adopted all the characteristics of an introverted minority group.[72]

The Homosexual Subculture

Although our culture as a whole does not approve of this type of sex behavior, there exists a subcultural world or community of homosexuals who indoctrinate new individuals. Individuals who come to identify with it are socialized into a special social role and become secondary deviants. This subcultural world consists of a special language which serves to keep its members secret from the out-group. There are special words for this sex behavior, such as "gay," "straight," and "queen," which are "similar in some respects to that of the underworld; in others to that of the theater." [73] Recognition by other homosexuals appears to involve particularly gestures, walk, clothes, and a special vocabulary.[74]

There are subculturally defined ways in which homosexual relations are established. Many communities have special meeting places where homosexuals can gather, usually at certain street corners, parks, taverns, coffee

---

[72] From *Sociological Aspects of Homosexuality* by Michael Schofield, © Michael Schofield, 1965. Reprinted by permission of the author, Longmans, Green & Co., Ltd., London, and Little, Brown & Company, Boston.

[73] Donald W. Cory, *The Homosexual in America* (New York: Greenberg, Publisher, Inc., 1951), p. 90. Also see J. D. Mercer, *They Walk in the Shadow* (New York: Comet Press, 1959).

[74] Westwood, pp. 83–86.

houses, clubs, or lavatories.[75] After an intensive study of homosexuals in a large Canadian city the following conclusions were reached about the homosexual community.

> The homosexual community thus consists of a large number of distinctive groups within which friendship binds the members together in a strong and relatively enduring bond and between which the members are linked by tenuous but repeated sexual contacts. The result is that homosexuals within the city tend to know or know of each other, to recognize a number of common interests and common moral norms. . . . This community is in turn linked with other homosexual communities in Canada and the United States chiefly through the geographic mobility of its members.[76]

The homosexual community or subculture provides for its members what other communities do: a training ground for norms and values, a milieu in which people may live every day, and a social support as well as an information media for its members.[77] In the homosexual community, particularly through its gay bars, the individual learns about the rules of homosexual liaisons, the places to go, the things that are a part of homosexual life, and the necessity of watching for the police.

Problems of Self-Conception and Identity

The crucial point in the development of a homosexual pattern is how the individual comes to define homosexual acts as more pleasurable and significant than heterosexual relations and how he learns to define himself or herself as a homosexual. It involves the expectations of others, the degree of identity with the role models presented, and the reactions of others— the imputation of homosexuality. Likewise, official definitions of the individual as a "homosexual" by medical doctors, psychiatrists, or the police may have serious consequences. This labeling may have much to do with subsequent confirmed homosexuality.

The classification of a person by others as a "homosexual" may serve to develop a self-concept and public definition of the person as a sex offender. Although homosexuals may identify with other homosexuals, few regard themselves as "criminals" whose behavior is prohibited by law; their behavior is simply a form of sex gratification, some patterns of which may be carried out in heterosexual sex relations.

---

[75] For discussion see Gordon Westwood, *Society and the Homosexual* (New York: E. P. Dutton & Co., Inc., 1953), Chaps. 19–21; and Cory. Also see Westwood, *A Minority*, pp. 68–77.

[76] Leznoff and Westley, p. 263.

[77] Leznoff and Westley.

The negative societal reaction of large segments of heterosexual society affects the homosexual in many ways. In general, there is concealment of the fact of being a homosexual. Even with all the rationalizations available from the subculture, he often feels guilt and religious conflict, as well a fear of its effect upon his ambitions. Concealment from one's colleagues becomes important because of fear of forfeiting membership in the group. Humorous remarks about homosexuals made in the presence of hetero-sexuals may be damaging. Some positions are forbidden to them, as in certain branches of the government service and the armed forces. There is constant need to conceal their activities from the police. Possibly more im-portant than any of these is the negative effect of homosexuality on per-sonal ties, such as absence of people who stay conventionally close to them all of their lives—wives, husbands, and children—and this feeling of isolation becomes greater as homosexuals grow older.

> [The homosexual] may have plenty of gay companionship, and he may never lack company, but compared with what he sees most heterosexuals enjoying he feels an absence of deeply felt and, above all, *lasting* relation-ships, an absence of really tight and dependable loyalties that hold throughout life. These feelings may heighten, and be heightened by, a sense of being different, of not being like other people, of being the odd man out. They may be exacerbated by difficulty in finding a satisfactory partner on anything other than a pick-up level. It is one thing to go to a pub or bar or public lavatory in order to pick up a sexual partner—even someone who may come back home and stay for a few days—and quite a different thing to find someone to spend a lifetime with, as a man does a wife. There are few ways in which he can do this.[78]

The homosexual is aware of many of the attitudes and beliefs of the general society and may feel concern about his failure to meet its criteria of approval.[79] Identity problems plague many homosexuals even with group support. Homosexuals are generally aware, like other deviants, that the general society looks upon their behavior as odd. Even rationalizations, such as great men who were homosexuals, while effective are often insufficient. Because the stigma of homosexuality strikes at the 'heart of masculinity and femininity—important status labels—it is often even more disturbing than that associated with other deviations.

It is likely that homosexuals are found in nearly every occupation and among persons at all educational levels. Some evidence exists that homo-sexual behavior is more frequent among the more educated and in certain

---

[78] Magee, p. 118.
[79] Goffman.

occupations, but the evidence is inconclusive. Those who are apprehended for more overt homosexual acts are likely to come from lower occupations, whereas the secret homosexual, because of the added danger of exposure and the differential attitudes toward him by the police, is more likely to be a middle- or an upper-class person.[80] Schofield found that homosexuals in prison were generally not well educated and were from the less skilled occupations; on the other hand, those who had not been arrested and were not under treatment were more likely to be supervisors or nonmanual workers.[81] Some occupations may attract those who are homosexuals because they may not need to conceal their behavior for other persons tend to accept the peculiar nature of their occupational role. Others once in the occupation may come to accept the definition of themselves by others as "effeminate." Schur concludes that "for whatever reason it is in fact now probable that there is a higher proportion of revealed homosexuality in certain job categories—such as interior decoration, ballet and chorus dancing, hairdressing, and fashion design—than in others. The adjective *revealed* is important, because the true proportions for those occupations in which greater concealment is necessary are not known." [82]

Learning and Homosexual Behavior

Homosexual behavior is the adoption of certain sex practices which come to be defined as pleasurable, and the sex object, a person of one's own sex, as generally more sexually attractive than a member of the opposite sex. As one learns by association to define heterosexual sex behavior as pleasurable so does one learn homosexual patterns.

In every culture there are present in varying degrees both adolescent and adult persons who define homosexual relations as pleasurable. Likewise, large numbers of children engage in experimental sex play of a homosexual nature, particularly when such experimentation is difficult to achieve with members of the opposite sex. The very first homosexual experience among 127 homosexuals studied in Great Britain was usually with a school boy of the same age and generally constituted sex play, often in a school situation.[83] These experiences, however, did not necessarily lead to homosexuality as a pattern of sex behavior because such sex behavior among boys may have little emotional feeling. The first "significant homosexual experience" can be defined as one carried out with an adult or repeated acts carried out with

---

[80] Leznoff and Westley. Also see William J. Helmer, "New York's Middle-Class Homosexuals," *Harper's:* 226:85–92 (1963).

[81] Schofield, p. 209.

[82] Schur, p. 93.

[83] Westwood, *A Minority*, pp. 24–39.

the same boy over a year or so. Over two thirds of such experiences were with another boy. Only 18 percent were first introduced to homosexuality as boys by adults and a further 11 percent had no experience of any sort until they were adults, and in all such cases their partner was an adult. Contrary to the popular view, seduction is not an important factor. With most homosexuals there was a long period during which they fought against their homosexual activity before recognizing it as permanent behavior and assuming a conception of themselves as being homosexuals. Another study, however, showed that homosexuals are likely to have had sexual experiences with adult males even before puberty; in one study a third had been approached by men and 27 percent had had physical contact with men.[84]

Another study involving groups of 50 homosexuals each who had been convicted and were under treatment and those who were neither convicted nor under treatment showed the relationship of sexual contacts.[85] By the time they were adults nearly all the homosexuals had had at least one sex exposure. Three fourths (79 percent) of the men in all three groups had had their first homosexual exposure before the age of sixteen and 16 percent had had it with an adult. In the convicted group, for example, 32 had experienced homosexual relations before seventeen; in fact, 12 of the 31 who had had homosexual experiences with adults in their youth thought this had influenced their subsequent development. As one put it, "At first I wanted to find out what it was all about, but when it happened I seemed to take it for granted. As far as I can recall, I liked it. It seemed to please me." [86] When, however, comparisons were made with a nonhomosexual treatment control group, there were no significant statistical differences between the men who had taken part in homosexual activities before sixteen but the differences were statistically significant after seventeen. When homosexuals who had not been convicted or were not under treatment were compared with a control group, the homosexuals had had more statistically significant homosexual experiences before seventeen and fewer heterosexual experiences before twenty-one.

Another study found that approximately one half of all the homosexuals had had their first exposure before fifteen; one half of the control group, on the other hand, had had their first heterosexual petting experience before sixteen.[87] What was an even more important difference was that there was a far greater continuity in homosexual behavior and rejection of heterosexual behavior by unmarried male homosexuals than in a control group,

---

[84] Gebhard, *et al.,* p. 329.

[85] Schofield.

[86] Schofield, p. 33.

[87] Gebhard, *et al.*

that is, those who engaged in such behavior before twenty were more likely to continue it.[88]

At this time there are no definite answers as to why some persons who experience homosexual sex relations continue on through secondary deviation and others do not. It may be in some instances the favorable nature of the experience or the role model of the other person. In many cases it is probably the result of the negative reaction of others which develops a self-conception in the person that he is a homosexual. Another possibility is that one does not develop an adequate identification with his own sex role and instead adopts that of the other sex.

> In American culture, adolescents are expected to develop heterosexual interest. In fact, adolescence might quite properly be defined as a social role which includes, for the first time, the expectation of social and sexual interest in the opposite sex. This sharply distinguishes adolescence (a social role) from puberty (a set of physiological changes). That they correspond to some extent in age at onset is solely a matter of social convenience and is probably brought about by the association of puberty with the physiological ability to procreate. Social pressures and expectations of parents and peers generate the development of a social interest on the part of girls in boys, and a social and sexual interest on the part of boys in girls. Any individual who has learned an appropriate sex role will be strongly affected by these pressures toward heterosexual interest. Those (especially males) who have not established an appropriate role will not be affected in the same way. They may at this time develop socio-sexual interest in their own sex instead. It is easy to see from this analysis that it would be quite possible to develop homosexual interest as easily as heterosexual interest at this, or other, points.[89]

Sex roles are learned: the behavior patterns associated with masculinity and femininity are not inherited; they are learned as part of one's sex role. Homosexuality and heterosexuality may therefore be understood within three concepts: sex-role adoption, sex-role preference, and sex-role identification.[90] The former refers to the "actual adoption of behavior characteristic of one sex or the other not simply to desire to adopt such behavior." Sex-role preference is the desire "to adopt the behavior associated with one sex or the other or the perception of such behavior as preferable or more desirable." Finally, sex-role identification, which is crucial in homosexuality, is

---

[88] Gebhard, *et al.,* pp. 632, 636.

[89] J. Richard Udry, *The Social Context of Marriage* (Philadelphia: J. B. Lippincott Company, 1966), p. 107.

[90] David B. Lynn, "A Note on Sex Differences in the Development of Masculine and Feminine Identification," *Psychological Review,* 66:126–135 (1959).

"the actual incorporation of the role of a given sex, and to the unconscious [unthinking] reaction characteristic of that role." As Lynn has pointed out:

> Thus a person may be identified with the opposite sex but for expediency adopt much of the behavior characteristic of his own sex. He may even prefer the role of his own sex, although identified with the opposite sex role. One would expect such a person, being identified with the opposite sex, to have many unconscious reactions characteristic of the opposite sex role despite his adopting much of the behavior characteristic of the same sex role.[91]

Using these concepts, there is a possibility that career homosexuals are more likely to be those who have achieved inappropriate sex-role identification or sex-role assimilation in childhood.[92] Several studies have shown, for example, that the effectiveness of sex-role learning in children is associated with the sex of siblings, absence of father, and ordinal position in the family.[93] During childhood or adolescence the male homosexual has been presented with favorable feminine models (warm-nurturant) and with negative male models (cold and frequently absent) or with restrictions on playing male roles, some evidence for which has been given in studies by Gebhard and by Schofield.[94] Some male homosexuals come to choose other males as favorable sex objects because they have associated favorable sex-role preference with them. When individuals adopt the sexual aspects of the feminine role their behavior is consistent with their identification. Many potential homosexuals do not enter fully into the male subculture because of the negative sanctions that might be taken against them in view of their playing feminine roles. Those who drift later into a homosexual subculture are encouraged also to adopt a masculine role although they are not completely successful in this. Studies indicate that while adult homosexuals do often display feminine behavior they derogate femininity in their homosexual subculture and may often emphasize masculinity in their sex partners.[95] More-

---

[91] Lynn, p. 127.

[92] Barry M. Dank, "A Social Psychological Theory of Homosexuality and Sex Role Learning." Master's thesis in sociology, University of Wisconsin, 1966. The discussion as well as the materials presented here in support of this theory are derived from Dank's thesis.

[93] For example, see Orville Brim, "Family Structure and Sex Role Learning by Children," in Norman Bell and Ezra Vogel, *A Modern Introduction to the Family* (New York: The Free Press, 1960), pp. 482–496.

[94] Gebhard, *et al.*, and Schofield. Also see D. J. West, "Parental Figures in the Genesis of Male Homosexuality," *International Journal of Social Psychiatry*, 5:85–97 (1959).

[95] Westwood, *A Minority*, pp. 88–89, 118.

over, there seems to be evidence that there are not two types of homosexuals, the active and the passive, but rather that there is a great deal of role shifting, indicating that the role adaptations to femininity are fluid.[96]

PROSTITUTION

Although prostitution is virtually universal, it is generally disapproved in most societies. The extent of prostitution and the reaction to it has fluctuated over many years, but its definition has remained the same. Prostitution is sexual intercourse on a promiscuous and mercenary basis, with emotional indifference.[97] The patron pays for this intimacy, but the method of payment often clouds the definition of a true prostitute. "The reason for this lies in the broad gamut of female behavior in our culture containing elements of prostitution." [98] For example, when a customer "dates" a shopgirl for an evening dinner and show and later has sex relations with her, the relationship is often on a mercenary, emotionally indifferent basis; yet the girl may not be considered, nor consider herself, as a real prostitute. Such a girl may have a family, has a job, and may not make a practice of exchanging sexual favors for an evening's entertainment. There are "semiprostitute" roles involving the commercialization of sex behavior. For example, taverns and bars may have "B-girls" who induce male customers to drink and for their "companionship" receive a return from the management. "Selling her sexual favors may be a part of the role she plays, but both the societal and self-regarding attitudes differ in her case from those of a professional prostitute . . . where the ideal of a fair exchange for services rendered governs the relationship of the girl and the customer." [99]

Many women are promiscuous but are not prostitutes, for their sex relations have an element of affection, even if transitory. The prostitute "sells" her sex relations with an element of indifference. Although some prostitutes may be selective on the basis of race, age, economic status, or physical attractiveness of their customers, generally an act of intercourse may be carried out with almost anyone. With many prostitutes the sex act may

---

[96] Evelyn Hooker, "An Empirical Study of Some Relations between Sexual Patterns and Gender Identity in Male Homosexuals," in John Money, ed., *Sex Research: New Developments* (New York: Holt, Rinehart and Winston, Inc., 1965), pp. 24–52.

[97] In some countries, as well as in many states, it is not prostitution which is legally a criminal offense; rather, soliciting is the offense for which a prostitute is punished. See J. E. Hall Williams, "Sex Offenses: The British Experience," *Law and Contemporary Problems,* 25:334–360 (1960).

[98] Lemert, p. 238.

[99] Lemert, p. 239.

be purchased in varied physical forms, other than the usual form of hetero-sexual relations, such as both oral and anal sex acts, as well as sadistic, masochistic, and exhibitionistic acts of intercourse. So indifferent are most prostitutes to the emotional aspect of sex relations that they rarely expe-rience an orgasm with a customer, although they frequently do with their "pimp" or male consort.

Extent

The true prostitute might be considered as one who primarily makes her living from selling, for money, her sexual favors, but there is no way of ascertaining the number of these women.[100] Some of them have part- or full-time legitimate jobs which serve to cover up their real occupations. Usually statistical reports of prostitution are gathered from arrest figures, which themselves are not always reliable. Estimates have ranged from around 100,000 for the United States to as high as Reitman's estimate of 100,000 in 1931 for the city of Chicago alone.[101] It is likely that a much more conservative estimate than Reitman's figure is more nearly correct; probably over 300,000, in the United States, live by prostitution alone. About 69 per-cent of the total male population has had some experience with prostitutes, but a large majority of these have had only one or two experiences. Some 15 to 20 percent have relations more than a few times a year.[102] Prostitution accounts for less than 10 percent of the total nonmarital sexual outlet for males. Not more than 1 percent of extramarital sexual intercourse is with prostitutes.

There appears to have been a steady decline in prostitution throughout the past three decades, except for periodic increases in wartime. During World War II it was estimated that in the United States there were about 600,000 regular prostitutes and about an equal number who were engaged in prostitution but had other means of livelihood.[103] Kinsey states that the frequency with which American males go to prostitutes has been reduced by about one half of what it was prior to World War I.[104] Some have main-tained that prostitution has declined because of organized drives against prostitutes, elimination of red-light districts, and educational efforts regard-

---

[100] There are also male prostitutes in homosexuality, and Kinsey estimates their number to be as high in large cities as the number of female prostitutes.

[101] Ben L. Reitman, *The Second Oldest Profession: A Study of the Prostitutes' "Business Manager"* (New York: Vanguard Press, Inc., 1931).

[102] Kinsey, *et al., Sexual Behavior in the Human Male*, p. 597.

[103] Regulations of Vice," *Encyclopedia Americana* (1945 ed.; New York: Encyclopedia Americana), XXVIII, 58.

[104] Kinsey, *et al., Sexual Behavior in the Human Female*, p. 300.

ing the control of venereal diseases and prostitution. Others insist, however, that the decrease in prostitution is the result not of these factors but from the increased sexual freedom for women. Because young women have less restraint in their sexual relations, it is easier for men to have sex relations without recourse to prostitutes.[105] But even if prostitution continues to decrease there will probably always be a certain amount of it, for there will continue to be a group of men who are able to secure sexual satisfactions only if they pay for such services.

Function

A number of reasons for the existence of prostitution have been advanced.[106] Men go to prostitutes because they do not have enough other sexual outlets. It is simpler and often cheaper to secure extramarital intercourse through a prostitute than by dating. Likewise, there are no responsibilities for a resulting pregnancy. Married man also go to prostitutes for the sake of variety in methods of sexual intercourse, a variety often not otherwise available to married persons. Other men go because they may be ineffective in securing sexual relations with other women because these men are timid, deformed, deaf, blind, or otherwise physically handicapped. Even though they have stable relationships with a woman and have regular opportunities for sex relations, some married and unmarried men may resort to prostitutes when sexual expression is blocked by quarreling or other interpersonal difficulties. The impersonality of prostitution makes it useful for strangers absent from their families or their girls, for armed forces personnel, and for men attending meetings and conventions. "The prostitute's availability to the stranger is thus one of her appeals." [107] Davis has summarized the appeals of prostitution which, in part, is an attempt to regulate sex relations:

> In short, the attempt of society to control sexual expression, to tie it to social requirements, especially the attempt to tie it to the durable relation of marriage and the rearing of children, or to attach men to a celibate order, or to base sexual expression on love, creates the opportunity for prostitution. It is analogous to the black market, which is the illegal but inevitable response to an attempt to control the economy. The craving for sexual variety, for perverse gratification, for novel and provocative surroundings, for ready and cheap release, for intercourse free from entangling cares and civilized pretense—all can be demanded from the

---

[105] Kingsley Davis, "The Sociology of Prostitution," *American Sociological Review*, 2:744–755 (1937).

[106] Kinsey, *et al., Sexual Behavior in the Human Male*, pp. 606–609.

[107] Davis, "Sexual Behavior," p. 360.

woman whose interest lies solely in the price. The sole limitation on the man's satisfactions is in this instance not morality or convention, but his ability to pay.[108]

The nature of prostitution links it to many of the values of the "normal" society. The general culture stimulates the importance of sexual values in life and the satisfaction of these values may be difficult for many of the unmarried and some of the married. Prostitution, therefore, becomes a needed commodity for which there is widespread demand with often limited supply. The price of the service may vary from $5 to $500, depending on the supply and the characteristics of the prostitute. "Our laissez-faire economy and its integration through the price system allows the relatively free operation of supply and demand whether it be commerce in grain futures or sex service." [109]

Because of the functional nature of prostitution and its commercial aspects, prostitutes are following an occupation which parallels the goals of any other occupation.[110] In prostitution there are economic and cultural considerations common to the general society. Prostitution is an economic commodity, namely, the sale of sex privileges for monetary considerations. Full time, this illegal behavior is a gainful employment, often a highly lucrative one.

Societal Reaction

Attitudes toward prostitution have varied historically and today vary in different countries. The attitude toward, and the social status of, the prostitute, as Davis has suggested, varies according to three conditions: (1) if the prostitute practices a certain discrimination in her customers, (2) if the earnings are used for some socially desirable goal, and (3) if the prostitute combines with her sexual role others which are more acceptable.[111] In ancient Greece, for example, brothel prostitutes were given a different status from the hetaerae, who were educated in the arts and were often wealthy, powerful personages with great influence on many important leaders. Although prostitutes, they were generally highly respected. The devadasis, or dancing girls, were connected with the temples of India for centuries; be-

---

[108] From "Sexual Behavior" by Kingsley Davis in *Contemporary Social Problems* edited by Robert K. Merton and Robert A. Nisbet. © 1961, 1966, by Harcourt, Brace & World, Inc., and reprinted with their permission.

[109] Edwin M. Lemert, *Social Pathology* (New York: McGraw-Hill Book Company, Inc., 1951), p. 246.

[110] George B. Vold, *Theoretical Criminology* (New York: Oxford University Press, 1958).

[111] Davis, "Sexual Behavior," p. 360.

sides singing and dancing, they engaged in temple prostitution. In general, these girls were the only Indian women who had learned to read. Because the devadasi was one of a social group of religious prostitutes attached to the temple, payment was given to the temple and the act of intercourse was, to some extent, a religious ritual. Finally, the famous Japanese geishas can be cited as another example of women who could often engage in prostitution but still have high status in their society. They were trained in the arts, such as music, in conversation, and in social entertaining.

> In ancient cultures and in cultures of recent times, including our own in the nineteenth century, prostitutes have been a class set apart, with special locale and formally demarcated status symbolized in dress, manner, and speech. In Japan, special beautified quarters of its cities were designated as sites for prostitution. In Tokyo this quarter was one of the show places of the city. Japanese courtesans often were prominently displayed in cages on the streets; in genteel establishments they had their names and emoluments advertised on the equivalent of a marquee at the entrance. Special costumes and hair-dresses often have been symbols of the prostitute; for example, in ancient Rome prostitutes usually dyed their hair red or yellow. In some cultures these appurtenances were guarded and perpetuated by sumptuary laws. In the nineteenth and very early twentieth centuries in the United States, when prostitutes were quartered in red-light districts, they could be told apart from the respectable middle-class women of the community by their flamboyant clothes, abbreviated dresses, bobbed hair, rouged faces and lips, their use of tobacco, liquor, and profanity and general bold mien in public. In other words, the social cleavage between the "good" and "bad" women was not only sharp but could be quickly determined by cultural insignia. Today much of the behavior and morality of the prostitute has made its way upward and has been appropriated by the middle-class woman in her revolt against her traditional role.[112]

Prostitution, particularly soliciting, is strongly disapproved under Anglo-American criminal law. Such stringent attitudes toward prostitution were derived in part from the spread of syphilis and from the Protestant Reformation; even today, many Catholic countries, such as those in Latin America, have a rather tolerant view of prostitution. In prostitution,

> sex was a disruptive factor in the orderly pursuit of business and capital accumulation, and from this conviction there developed the puritanical strictures upon sexual thought and practice which have pervaded middle-class morality of the past. Oddly enough, and this point has frequently been ignored, the sex compulsives of the puritanical middle class have cen-

---

[112] From *Social Pathology* by Edwin M. Lemert. Copyright 1951 by McGraw-Hill Book Company, Inc. Used by permission of McGraw-Hill Book Company.

tered around the disapproval of overt and indiscreet sex behavior rather than the fact of sex indulgence outside of marriage or prostitution per se. This is borne out by the fact that many states and communities have had no laws against prostitution itself but, rather, have legislated against such things as disorderly conduct, vagrancy, soliciting, and pandering in conjunction with sex indulgence and prostitution.[113]

Where it is illegal, prostitution represents an effort to control certain private moral behavior by punitive social control. Undoubtedly only a tiny proportion of acts of prostitution are ever apprehended. Where apprehended, prostitution—or, under some laws, the act of solicitation—is generally punished with a fine or with a jail sentence of less than a year. If repeated misdemeanor convictions occur, the prostitute may be convicted of a felony and sentenced to a longer term. Great Britain has recently provided for a graduated system of fines and jail terms. Yet the Wolfenden Report, which recommended these changes, concluded about prostitution:

> It has persisted in many civilizations throughout many centuries, and the failure of attempts to stamp it out by repressive legislation shows that it cannot be eradicated through the agency of the criminal law. It remains true that without a demand for her services the prostitute could not exist, and that there are enough men who avail themselves of prostitutes to keep the trade alive. It also remains true that there are women who, even when there is no economic need to do so, choose this form of livelihood. For so long as these propositions continue to be true there will be prostitution, and no amount of legislation directed towards its abolition will abolish it.[114]

Prostitution is opposed on many grounds: because (1) it involves a high degree of promiscuity, particularly with strangers, rather than being the exclusive possession of one man; (2) the prostitute is willing to sell and commercialize her sexual participation with emotional indifference outside of marriage, one participating for pleasure and the other for money; (3) the social effects on the women who engage in the profession are unwholesome; (4) it is a threat to public health in that it facilitates the spread of venereal diseases; (5) it needs police protection in order to operate and thus reduces the quality of general law enforcement; and (6) sexual acts with a prostitute are generally such that there is no possibility of marriage and procreation and for this reason are different from ordinary premarital sex relations. In Great Britain, the Wolfenden Report stated rather clearly the reasons for British public attitudes toward prostitution, many of which would also apply in the United States.

---

[113] From *Social Pathology* by Edwin H. Lemert, pp. 257–258. Copyright 1951 by McGraw-Hill Book Co. Used by permission of McGraw-Hill Book Company.
[114] *The Wolfenden Report,* p. 132.

If it were the law's intention to punish prostitution *per se,* on the ground that it is immoral conduct, then it would be right that it should provide for the punishment of the man as well as the woman. But that is not the function of the law. It should confine itself to those activities which offend against public order and decency or expose the ordinary citizen to what is offensive or injurious; and the simple fact is that prostitutes do parade themselves more habitually and openly than their prospective customers, and do by their continual presence, affront the sense of decency of the ordinary citizen. In doing so they create a nuisance which, in our view, the law is entitled to recognize and deal with.[115]

Types of Prostitutes

Prostitutes can generally be classified according to their method of operation. There are the streetwalkers or common prostitutes operating alone, the inmate of an organized house of prostitution, the call girl, and the high-class independent professional prostitute.[116] These different types of prostitutes represent an adaptation to the characteristics of the available clientele. Similarly, "the modal tendencies in the organization and behavior systems of prostitutes must be interpreted in the light of the sexual requirements of the patrons of a class . . . Variations in the patterns of prostitution may be related to the variability in the socio-cultural characteristics of the clientele." [117]

The streetwalker procures her trade as she can, on the streets or in such places as bars and hotel lobbies. She takes her customers to a prearranged cheap rooming house or hotel. Sometimes she has no connection with organized crime, but often she must pay for her own protection from arrest; occasionally she is part of a more organized operation. Some prostitution is not strictly organized as such, but is knowingly permitted and even encouraged, through legitimate but often shady businesses, especially those in the commercial recreation industry, such as burlesque shows, night clubs, amusement parks, and the like. Taxi-dance halls afford many opportunities for the dancers to make later engagements with their patrons, either in a room hired for the occasion or in the dancer's own room or apartment.[118] Through a variety of techniques performers in cabarets or burlesque shows also recruit patrons for later dates.

Organized houses of prostitution, which flourished in the red-light districts, were more common a few decades ago than they are today. They vary

---

[115] *The Wolfenden Report,* pp. 143–144.

[116] For a discussion of types of prostitutes see Walter C. Reckless, *Vice in Chicago* (Chicago: University of Chicago Press, 1933). Also see Sheldon and Eleanor T. Glueck, *500 Delinquent Women* (New York: Alfred A. Knopf, Inc., 1934).

[117] Lemert, p. 245.

[118] Paul Cressey, *Taxi-Dance Hall* (Chicago: University of Chicago Press, 1932).

a great deal as to size, type of customers, and degree of respectability. New girls are "broken in" to the rules and regulations of the house, and each new prostitute soon learns various sex techniques. She learns how to handle a large number of customers without running the risk of losing them as patrons, how to deal with different types of men, and how to protect herself against venereal disease. The prostitutes are often exploited by the "madame," or the manager of the house, for they have small chance to protect themselves, and a high percentage of their earnings, from 50 to 60 percent, is deducted for the "house," for linens, medical examinations, police protection, and the like. Usually these houses are operated in conjunction with some type of organized crime, through which police "protection" is usually secured. They are also usually associated with taxicab drivers who receive commissions, and with pimps who solicit and who live off the girls' earnings. Often the house is controlled by an organized crime syndicate.

Another type of prostitution has become more and more prominent as societal reactions have changed and as police and health authorities have become more effective in doing away with street soliciting and with red-light houses. This is the so-called call girl, who in many ways is more adapted to the mobility of the urban areas, responding as she does to phone calls and other contacts.[119] The client may come to her room or apartment, or she may go to his. This type of prostitution allows for greater individ-ualization of operation and makes possible more part-time prostitution. The call girl usually depends upon some organization for recruiting her patrons, although she may operate independently and have her own list of patrons who call upon her services. More frequently these patrons are secured through the intermediary services of a bellhop, a hotel desk clerk, a taxi driver or other type of agent who, for a fee, will give her telephone number to the patron or arrange for her to come to his room or for him to go to hers. Call girls may work with lower-class hotels, but even some of the more ex-pensive hotels allow this type of prostitute to operate on their premises. The call girl has become widely known, particularly through her role at con-ventions and in entertaining out-of-town businessmen. In some New York City cases, patrons are reported to have paid large sums of money, reputedly as high as $500, for an evening's entertainment. Because this type of pros-titution is less visible than the "house" type, it gives more concealment to the prostitute and more anonymity to the patron. Frequently, however, she too must pay the police or others for "protection from arrest."

---

[119] For details and case studies of call girls, see Harold Greenwald, *The Call Girl: A Social and Psychoanalytic Study* (New York: Ballantine Books, Inc., 1958).

There is, finally, the independent professional prostitute who lives in her own apartment house or flat, often in an expensive part of the city, and caters to middle- and upper-class patrons. Most of her clientele is secured on an individual basis through referrals from taxicab drivers or others.

Characteristics of Prostitutes

Inasmuch as physical attractiveness and youth are a necessity for the successful prostitute, she is usually between seventeen and twenty-four; the peak earning age is usually twenty-two. Some prostitutes are older, but most of these have taken up the profession for special reasons, such as drug addiction or alcoholism, where their need for a continued supply of drugs or alcohol is expensive to support. Single girls constitute the largest proportion of prostitutes, although some prostitutes are divorced or separated from their husbands. Many of those who give their marital status as married either are living with or are married to pimps. On the whole, the professional common prostitute has less opportunity for marriage than the more "high-class" type of call-girl prostitute.

Other than the fact that prostitutes may primarily come from the lower socioeconomic groups and often from slum areas, there is no evidence that they enter this profession because of poverty even though they may desire to better their economic status. At one time there was probably a disproportionate number of prostitutes from various foreign-born groups; today there is a disproportionate percentage of racial minorities.[120] The prevalence of slum living conditions among Negroes and their cultural standards of less rigid sex mores have no doubt accounted for the higher proportion of Negro prostitutes.

Although the modern prostitute differs a great deal from her flamboyantly dressed and heavily made-up predecessor, they still have characteristics in common: they have often been indoctrinated into the profession by those who have been closely associated with it, they have usually been poorly integrated into socially acceptable groups, and they seldom develop a high degree of organization within their profession. Its very nature is competitive, each prostitute attempting to build up and keep her own clientele; hence there is little group solidarity except for cases where they must band together for protection from the police or from others who threaten their livelihood. Prostitutes have a limited argot or special language of their own, which is a mark of a degree of association and group cohesiveness.[121]

---

[120] Lemert, pp. 240–241.

[121] David Maurer, "Prostitutes and Criminal Argots," *American Journal of Sociology,* 44:546–550 (1939).

The Process of Prostitution

At one time, perhaps fifty years ago, it was rather widely believed in the United States that the prostitute was often the victim of a "white slaver" who had induced a sexually inexperienced girl to go into prostitution. The White-Slave-Traffic Act (The Mann Act) was aimed at eliminating what was called "white slavery." It was believed that girls were "seduced" into a life of prostitution. Another belief with very little substance to it is that women enter prostitution because of economic necessity. Perhaps some do, as is true of some female drug addicts, but actually, the earnings of most prostitutes, even allowing for deductions in payments to a madame, to a pimp, or for "protection" from the police, are higher than the earnings of most working women. The prostitute is paid for her loss of esteem through the negative societal reaction to the promiscuous selling of sexual intercourse. Because of the high income there is every economic incentive to enter prostitution. In fact, Davis concludes that "since the occupation is lucrative, the interesting question is not why so many women become prostitutes, but why so few of them do." [122]

Studies of girls who make their living in this way indicate that the process of becoming a prostitute is quite different from what it is supposed to be. Generally there is agreement that most girls of this type have lived in local communities, such as slums, where sexual promiscuity has been approved or at least condoned. Although most have had considerable previous sexual experience, either with or without marriage, this fact in itself does not account for the prostitution. Generally the important other factor is association with persons on the fringe of prostitution:

> In the United States, these contacts with persons in or on the fringe of prostitution are largely with women, practitioners of prostitution themselves. Although some prostitutes are exploited by pimps, this parasitism is not usually the mode. One should expect that those girls who acquire pimps do so after they have entered the trade. It is very rare to find a case in American prostitution in which a girl who has never been a prostitute was persuaded or forced into the business by a pimp.[123]

The developmental career of a call girl includes three stages: the entrance into the career, the apprenticeship, and the development of con-

---

[122] Davis, "Sexual Behavior," p. 361.

[123] Walter C. Reckless, *The Crime Problem* (2d ed.; New York: Appleton-Century-Crofts, Inc., 1950), p. 275.

tacts. The mere desire to become a call girl is insufficient for the assumption of this role; there must be training and a systematic arrangement for contacts. One call girl said, "You cannot just say get an apartment and get a phone and everything and say, 'Well, I'm gonna start business,' because you gotta get clients from somewhere. There has to be a contact." [124] One study has concluded that "the selection of prostitution as an occupation from alternatives must be sought in the individual prostitute's interaction with others over a considerable time span." [125] After having entered through personal contact with someone actually involved in the profession, like a pimp or other call girls,[126] most call girls serve an apprenticeship. In a Los Angeles study of thirty-three call girls only one had not been brought in through these sources.[127] Half of the girls in this study had had initial contact with a call girl, some over a long period of time, others for shorter periods. Some were solicited by a pimp with offers of love and managerial experience. When a call girl has agreed to aid a novice she assumes responsibility for her training; girls who are brought into prostitution by a pimp may either be trained by him or be referred to another call girl.

Once contact is made and the new girl decides to be a prostitute the apprenticeship begins. The "classroom" is typically an apartment more or less like the future workplace. Girls report spending up to 8 months in training, but the average is two to three months. The trainer controls all referrals and opportunities. The content of the training consists of the development of the value structure of the profession of prostitution and the other interpersonal "dos" and "don'ts" in problematic situations. The acquisition of a set of values serves to create "in-group" solidarity and to alienate the apprentice from the "square society." It helps the trainer and the pimp to maintain a personal control and an economic advantage. Values which are transmitted include beliefs and justifications to support and maintain the behavior. Among these are that prostitution is simply a more honest behavior than that of most people, that most men are corrupt or exploitative, and that a well-trained call girl can, in turn, exploit a man. That men are often "cheating" on their wives, or will cheat a prostitute, is supporting

---

[124] James H. Bryan, "Apprenticeships in Prostitution," *Social Problems,* 12:289 (1965).

[125] Norman R. Jackman, Richard O'Toole, and Gilbert Geis, "The Self-Image of the Prostitute," *Sociological Quarterly,* 4:160 (1963).

[126] For a discussion of the role of the pimp or male partner of the prostitute, see John M. Murtagh and Sara Harris, *Cast the First Stone* (New York: McGraw-Hill Book Company, Inc., 1957).

[127] Bryan, p. 289.

evidence. Other values include fairness with other call or "working girls" and fidelity to the pimp. The rules governing interpersonal contacts with the customers include what to say on the phone during a solicitation—a "line" such as needing money to pay the rent, a car, or doctor bills; social interaction in obtaining the fees; the nature of specific customers' preferences and what types of customers to avoid; how to converse with a customer; caution in the use of alcohol; and knowledge of physical problems associated with prostitution. Although prostitutes may be taught some things, such as not experiencing sexual orgasm with customers in general, little instruction is given about sex techniques.

Not all call girls, however, accept all the training in either the values or the techniques of interpersonal relations. One study showed that some "experience orgasms with the customer, some show considerable affect toward 'johns,' others remain drunk or 'high' throughout the contact. While there seems to be general agreement as to what the rules of interpersonal conduct are, there appears to be considerable variation in the adoption of such rules." [128]

A call girl must have access to a clientele of customers. An equally important aspect of training in prostitution, therefore, is the acquisition of contacts; this is done during the apprenticeship period. Although books or "lists" can be purchased from other call girls or pimps, some are unreliable. Most frequently names are secured through contacts developed during the apprenticeship period. For an initial fee of 40 to 50 percent, the trainer call girl refers customers to the apprentice and oversees her. This fee becomes the pay of the "teacher," along with the convenience of having another girl available to meet the demand or to take care of her own contacts. On the other hand, the new girl may have a rather high initial income because of the novelty of her newness to the business and this may serve as an incentive for her to continue. For her pimp it is important that a new girl develop a clientele.

The nonverbal skills acquired by a call girl, however, do not seem as developed or as complex as those demanded of the professional streetwalker. Most call girls look down on the streetwalker, perhaps because call work involves less physical effort and more verbalization. "The tasks of avoiding the police, soliciting among strangers for potential customers, and arrangements for the completion of the sexual contract not only require different skills on the part of the streetwalker, but are performances requiring a higher degree of professional 'know-how' than is generally required of the call girl." [129]

---

[128] Bryan, p. 293.
[129] Bryan, p. 296.

Self-Concept

It is difficult, of course, to discuss the self-concept of prostitutes because of the varied degrees of involvement in a career of prostitution. Societal reaction, arrests, and association with other prostitutes serve to increase the self-concept of the prostitute. On the other hand, if a prostitute's customers are more educated than she is and she moves in such a circle or she has another occupation, such as a secretary or a model, she is less likely to think of herself as a prostitute, particularly if such a concept refers to the "common prostitute" or streetwalker.

The self-image of the urban prostitute has been found to be related to the degree of social isolation, the more isolated girls tending to define their behavior in a more acceptable light.[130] As with other deviant behavior, prostitutes are aware of the legal values involved in their sexual acts but these are justified in three ways: (1) prostitutes are no worse than other people and often are less hypocritical; (2) prostitutes achieve certain of the dominant values in society as financial success and the support of others who are dependent on them;[131] and (3) prostitutes perform an important and necessary social function. Research on the philosophies of fifty-two call girls with an average age of twenty-two and length of experience of twenty-seven months found that virtually all respondents maintained that prostitution was important because of the varied and extensive sexual needs of men and the necessity to protect social institutions.[132] In their own view they serve sexually as outlets and therefore as protectors of society from more rapes, perversions, and broken marriages. Generally they also claimed that by furnishing friendship and giving physical comfort prostitutes help men who are embarrassed, lonely, or isolated. Prostitution is supported particularly by the theory that clients should be exploited and in exploiting them the prostitute is no more immoral than her customers and the rest of the world. Relations among prostitutes are much more genuine, loyal, and honest than those elsewhere. Another view is that in essence most interpersonal relationships between the sexes are acts of prostitution. Wives and others use deception and sex to achieve other objectives, whereas prostitutes are at least honest. The sex act may play a part in premarital courtship and even in some marriages that is analogous to the commercial exploitation of sex in prostitution. Women may exploit their "femininity" to male customers for commercial gain without engaging in actual sex relations, as do many sales girls, hostesses, secretaries, waitresses, and models.

---

[130] Jackman, O'Toole, and Geis, pp. 150–162. Intensive study was made of a sample of only 15 prostitutes.

[131] Jackman, O'Toole, and Geis, pp. 150–162.

[132] Bryan, pp. 287–297.

In actuality, however, such views are not held by many individual prostitutes, who know the ideology but do not support it. Prostitutes were asked to rate items on various ideological positions of themselves, other call girls, women in general, "johns," and men in general.[133] Correct individual predictions could not be deduced statistically from the accepted occupational ideology. For example, customers were evaluated by the call girl as being as worthwhile as herself and as significantly better than other call girls.

> Not infrequently, personal friendships with customers are reported: "Some of them are nice clients who become very good friends of mine." On the other hand, while friendships are formed with "squares," personal disputations with colleagues are frequent. Speaking of her colleagues, one call girl says that most "could cut your throat." Respondents frequently mentioned that they had been robbed, conned, or otherwise exploited by their call girls friends. Interpersonal distrust between call girls appears to be considerable.[134]

Reasons for this difference between the ideology of the deviants and their actual beliefs may be the relative lack of cohesiveness among prostitutes and possibly the fact that the stigma of the occupation is less than the ideology implies. However, in the first few months the ideology is important to the trainee, for she can counter a negative self-image and reduce moral conflicts by accepting the view that customers are exploitative, that other women are hypocrites, that prostitution provides a valuable social service, and that call girls' relationships are close: "while the professional ideology is learned and perhaps serves a function during this apprenticeship period, it is doubtful that it remains of equal importance throughout the call girl's career." [135]

Primary and Secondary Prostitution

An individual who engages in sex relations for monetary reasons, promiscuously and without much emotion, may still be a primary deviant or prostitute. The transition from primary deviation to professional or secondary deviation is accomplished as a person comes to acquire the self-conception, social role, ideology, and language of prostitution. It exists to the extent that the individual becomes identified with prostitution as a set of values and comes to accept the role definition accorded her by others. This can come about in a number of ways.

A girl may enter the profession by engaging first in a series of quasi-prostituting sex experiences and later become associated with a trainer,

---

[133] Bryan, pp. 287–297. A "john" is a customer of a prostitute.

[134] James H. Bryan, "Occupational Ideologies and Individual Attitudes of Call Girls," *Social Problems,* 13:445 (1966).

[135] Bryan, "Occupational Ideologies of Call Girls," p. 448.

usually an experienced prostitute. Instead of accepting gifts and entertainment in return for her "favors," she comes to perceive sex as a commercial act. When the prostitute sees the functional values of her role secondary deviation appears. Societal reaction is also important. It is the product of arrest and conviction; of a change to commercialized sex relations; of venereal infection and treatment with other prostitutes in a hospital or clinic; and of role-defining interpretations received from contacts with other prostitutes, pimps, and customers.

The exploitation of prostitutes also aids the development of secondary deviation.

> In the past the prostitute has been exploited and preyed upon from all sides. While there is less exploitation of vice today, still it supports or adds to the income of many persons and groups besides the direct participants. The madam in the house usually takes anywhere from one-third to one-half of the prostitute's earnings. If she works on her own, the cab driver or the bellhop have to be paid. The disreputable medical examiner and the abortionist take a portion of the prostitute's income, as do the attorneys who obtain her release when she is arrested. Apart from the attorney's fees, money has to go to the "fixer" who sees to it that she escapes prosecution or conviction. This might be a prosecutor, judge, or county chairman. The bail bondsman levies his toll, and often the policeman on the beat is not loath to practice crude extortion on the prostitute either in trade or money. . . . Customers are not above cheating the prostitute, and some take pleasure in inflicting physical cruelties upon her. If the woman is a drug addict and has turned to prostitution in order to earn sufficient money to purchase her costly opiates, she may be subject to the unscrupulous manipulations of the peddler from whom she obtains the drugs. . . .
>
> Real-estate owners and managers are able to earn far more on the investments and properties by renting to prostitutes or vice-resort operators than to other tenants. Better class hotels, along with the cheaper ones, owe part of their revenue to the prostitute, as well as taxicab companies, laundries, amusement parks, vacation resorts, and contraceptive manufacturers and distributors.[136]

After going into prostitution the girls tend to develop attitudes and behavior patterns which are a part of the social role they play. In this connection they develop an argot or special language for their work, special acts and services, patterns of bartering with their customers and an impersonal relationship with them, as well as a large number of rationalizations for their activities.

---

[136] From *Social Pathology* by Edwin H. Lemert, pp. 263–264. Copyright 1951 by McGraw-Hill Book Company, Inc. Used by permission of McGraw-Hill Book Company.

Many prostitutes are able to leave this occupation for marriage or for employment as waitresses, domestic servants, or salesgirls. A few others are able to achieve a high standard of living and maintain it. But for some of them, age, venereal disease, alcoholism, or drug addiction result in a derelict life, punctuated more or less regularly by arrests and jail sentences.

SUMMARY

Sexual deviance covers a wide range of behavior, some of which is punished by law and some of which is negatively reacted to in other ways. There are various ways of classifying deviant sex behavior. Subcultural factors play an important role in sex deviations. Many misconceptions exist about sex offenders.

Homosexual behavior represents sex relations with members of one's own sex. Societal reaction to such behavior varies by society, and even within a society there may be differences in attitude. The imputation of homosexuality may have great consequences for an individual. Homosexuals may be distinguished as to whether they are primary or secondary deviants. The homosexual subculture may play a particularly important role in secondary deviation. A crucial issue in the development of the homosexual pattern is how the individual learns to define such acts as pleasurable and to define himself as a homosexual. There are various theories about why some homosexual sex relations continue on to secondary deviations and others do not. One theory involves inappropriate sex role identification or sex role assimilation in childhood.

Prostitution is sexual intercourse on a promiscuous and mercenary basis, with emotional indifference. Prostitution has many functions in a society. Societal reactions to prostitution have varied historically and today vary in different countries. It is opposed on a number of grounds. There are several types of prostitutes, the streetwalker, members of an organized house of prostitution, call girls, and "high-class" independent prostitutes. The development of a call girl's career involves three stages: the entrance into the career, the apprenticeship, and the acquisition and development of contacts. Her self-image is an important aspect in the career of a prostitute. The transition from primary deviation to secondary deviation is accomplished as she comes to acquire the self-conception, social role, ideology, and language of a prostitute.

SELECTED READINGS

Bryan, James H. "Apprenticeships in Prostitution," *Social Problems,* 12:287–297
     (1965). A study of the developmental careers of 33 call girls.
Davis, Kingsley. "Sexual Behavior" in Robert K. Merton and Robert A. Nisbet,

eds., *Contemporary Social Problems*. 2d ed. New York: Harcourt, Brace & World, Inc., 1966. An analysis of prostitution and homosexual behavior primarily in terms of societal reaction and the functional relation of these forms of deviant behavior to society.

Gagnon, John H., and William Simon, eds. *Sexual Deviance*. New York: Harper & Row, Publishers, 1967. A selection of articles dealing with sexual deviance in general and, specifically, with prostitution and homosexuality.

Gebhard, Paul H., John H. Gagnon, Wardell B. Pomeroy, and Cornelia V. Christenson. *Sex Offenders: An Analysis of Types*. New York: Harper & Row, Publishers, 1965. A study of 1500 male sex offenders divided into fourteen categories according to whether their offenses involved a member of the same or opposite sex; whether the use of force or threat was involved; and whether the offense was committed against a child, a minor, or an adult. The study also included incest offenders, peepers, and exhibitionists. Although the study is fairly detailed, covers many facets, and used control groups, it is unfortunate that more attention was not paid to the sociological process through which the behavior developed.

Lemert, Edwin M. *Social Pathology*. New York: McGraw-Hill Book Company, Inc., 1951, Chap. 8. A comprehensive discussion of prostitution, including an analysis of the social visibility, societal reaction, and tolerance of prostitution.

Reckless, Walter C. *Vice in Chicago*. Chicago: University of Chicago Press, 1933. Although an older study, this is one of the best on prostitution. Includes case material.

Schofield, Michael. *Sociological Aspects of Homosexuality: A Comparative Study of Three Types of Homosexuals*. Boston: Little, Brown & Company, 1965. A sociological study of 150 English homosexuals divided into three equal groups of prison inmates, those under psychiatric treatment and those who had never been sentenced or undergone psychiatric treatment. They were in turn compared with their control groups.

Schur, Edwin M. *Crimes without Victims*. Englewood Cliffs, N.J.: Prentice-Hall, Inc., 1965. This book has a comprehensive discussion of homosexual behavior.

"Sex Offenses." Volume 25 (1960) of *Law and Contemporary Problems*. A symposium on the legal, anthropological, ethical, sociological, clinical, and medical-legal aspects of sex offenses. Includes also a study of British and Scandinavian experiences with sex offenders.

Westwood, Gordon. *A Minority: A Report on the Life of the Male Homosexual in Great Britain*. New York: David McKay Company, Inc., 1960. A study of 127 homosexuals, primarily with a sociological approach.

Wolfenden Report, The. Report of the Committee on Homosexual Offenses and Prostitution. New York: Lancer Books, Inc., 1964. An important study of homosexual offenses and prostitution in Great Britain. Its recommendations were largely accepted by Parliament.

11

Alcohol Drinking Behavior and Alcoholism

Problems related to the consumption of alcohol, the role of the tavern in a society, and the alcoholic are far from being unique to any culture or age. Researchers on the contents of the tombs of ancient Egypt and in the buried cities of Babylon reveal that as early in history as three thousand years ago the use of wine and beer was a subject of moral concern.

Socrates, Aristotle, Plato, Cicero, and others inveighed against intoxication as debasing the dignity of man. The Spartans and Carthaginians limited drinking among soldiers on active duty for reasons of efficiency. The Ethiopians, who were water drinkers, boasted of their long life and vigor in contrast to the shorter life span of their wine-using neighbors, the Persians.

The barbarian Gauls invading Roman territories reacted violently when they discovered the effects of wine. This was noticed by Roman leaders and by the Greeks, who avoided giving battle until the invaders were stuporous from drinking, then slaughtered them easily. But it should be noted that although Egyptian civilization attained a remarkably high level, both men and women gorged themselves with wine to the point of deep intoxication. The Spanish and Portuguese people, on the other hand, appear to have been remarkably abstemious.

Various attempts at regulatory controls of drinking appear in the ancient literature. In China during the Chou Dynasty (1134–256 B.C.) and the reign of the fourth emperor of the Yuan Dynasty, about A.D. 1312, laws against the manufacture, sale, and consumption of wine were established and repealed no less than forty-one times. Penalties for violation of the decrees were extremely severe.[1]

Today the use of alcohol represents a conflict of values, while excessive drinking and alcoholism may be considered as deviant behavior. The value conflicts over the use of alcohol actually represent a struggle between a Calvinistic tradition that it is the community's responsibility to supervise the individual's drinking and an individualistic tradition that regards drinking as a matter of free choice.

In 1959, 85.3 percent of the population of the United States resided in areas where alcoholic beverages were sold.[2] Local option was provided in many states so that the percentage of population living in "wet" areas was less than two thirds in many states: in Tennessee, 33.1; Georgia, 38.1; Kentucky, 42.5; Alabama, 51.1; Texas, 54.1; Kansas, 50.1; Arkansas, 57.0; and North Carolina, 57.1. Moreover, some counties in many states do not permit alcoholic beverages to be drunk where it is sold; that is, liquor is sold only in the bottle in privately or publicly owned liquor stores. In seventeen states, in 1966, the sale of distilled spirits by the bottle was controlled by a state board selling through states stores. The drinking of the stronger alcoholic beverages, such as distilled spirits, is prohibited in all states for those under 21 except New York and Louisiana, where the legal age is 18. It is illegal in 35 states for anyone under 21 to use regular beer (7 allow 3.2 percent), and 45 states prohibit the use of wine by those under age.

As a result of their continually conflicting claims and propaganda, temperance organizations and concerns manufacturing and distributing alcoholic beverages have done much to crystallize value judgments surrounding the use and misuse of alcoholic beverages. Frederick Lewis Allen in *Only Yesterday* wrote about the conflict during the Prohibition era:

> Whatever the contributions of the Prohibition regime to temperance, at least it produced intemperate propaganda and counter-propaganda. Almost any dry could tell you that Prohibition was the basis of American pros-

---

[1] Raymond G. McCarthy, ed., *Drinking and Intoxication* (New York: The Free Press, 1959), pp. 39–40.

[2] The Joint Committee of the States to Study Alcoholic Beverage Laws, *Alcoholic Beverage Control* (Washington, D.C.: 1960). The data for the states presented here were furnished the joint committee by the Distilled Spirits Institute. The 1966 data which follow are from *Summary of State Laws and Regulations Relating to Distilled Spirits* (Washington: D.C.: Distilled Spirits Institute, November, 1966).

perity as attested by the mounting volume of savings-bank deposits . . . or that Prohibition had reduced the deaths from alcoholism, emptied the jails, diverted the workman's dollars to the purchase of automobiles, radios, and homes. Almost any wet could tell you that Prohibition had nothing to do with prosperity but it caused the crime wave, the increase of immorality and of the divorce rate, and a disrespect for all law which imperiled the very foundations of free government. The wets said the drys fostered Bolshevism by their fanatical zeal for laws which were inevitably flouted; the drys said the wets fostered Bolshevism by their cynical lawbreaking. Even in matters of supposed fact, you could find, if you only read and listened, any sort of ammunition that you wanted. One never saw drunkards on the streets any more; one saw more drunkards than ever. Drinking in the colleges was hardly a problem now; drinking in the colleges was at its worst. There was a still in every other home in the mining districts of Pennsylvania; drinking in the mining districts of Pennsylvania was a thing of the past. Cases of poverty as a result of drunkenness were only a fraction of what they used to be; the menace of drinking in the slums was three times as great as in pre-Volstead days.[3]

The drys have concentrated their attack by upholding the home, family, children, religion, and morality, which they claim are endangered by the use of alcohol and the existence of taverns. Newspaper headlines inadvertently assist them in their attempts to show the deleterious consequences of the use of alcohol: "Stampede for Holiday Liquor"; "Paralytic Struck by Drunk Driver"; "Drunken Boys Jailed"; "Man Killed in Tavern Brawl"; "Drunken Father Beats Family"; "Drunken Driver Kills Three." A speaker at a convention of the National Temperance Movement stated:

> At the close of the first ten years of repeal a committee of fifty, after extensive research, reported that the use of liquor is responsible for 20 per cent of divorces, 20 per cent of fatal accidents, 25 per cent of insanity, 37 per cent of poverty, 50 per cent of crime, 75 to 90 per cent of venereal infection. My guess is that every one of these percentages is now greater after five additional years of repeal—with the possible exception of the one of poverty.[4]

---

[3] Frederick Lewis Allen, *Only Yesterday* (New York: Harper & Row, Publishers, 1931), pp. 254–255.

[4] Paul S. Rees, "Forward to Victory," a synopsis of his closing address at the Biennial Convention of the Convention of the National Temperance Movement in *The National Temperance Digest*, 3:5 (1949). For a study of the temperance movement in the United States, see Joseph R. Gusfield, "Status Conflicts and Changing Ideologies of the American Temperance Movement," in David J. Pittman and Charles R. Snyder, eds., *Society, Culture and Drinking Patterns* (New York: John

Although many of these claims cannot be supported, there is no question that the *excessive use* of alcoholic beverages costs industry huge sums of money in the form of absenteeism, inefficiency on the job, and accidents. As far back as 1945, for example, the total monetary cost of excessive drinking was estimated at nearly $800 million; it is, of course, impossible to estimate the indirect social cost.[5]

A comparison between a group of industrial workers who were problem drinkers and two control groups revealed that the problem drinkers had 2.9 times as many days absent and 2.5 times as many cases of illness or injury-caused absences of eight days or more than the control groups.[6] The cost of sickness payments was 3.3 times as great and, in the case of women problem drinkers, twice as great.

There are conflicts not only about the use of alcohol but also about the tavern as a public institution. An investigation in Wisconsin revealed that both patrons and nonpatrons of taverns differ within each group in their attitudes toward the tavern and drinking in general.[7] Some nonpatrons, for example, believe that the present-day tavern is a lesser evil than the speakeasy of the bootleg period and that there is no harm in an occasional drink with friends in a tavern, other nonpatrons think of the tavern as a place to relax and meet friends, but other nonpatrons view the tavern as an unmitigated evil related to drunkenness, unhappy home life, marital difficulties, and neglect of children. Regular tavern patrons were similarly divided in their opinions. Some believed that the tavern is useful because it provides a place for relaxation, a meeting place, and an orderly place for drinking as opposed to Prohibition days. Other regular patrons, however, believed that the tavern contributes to various types of crime, loss of jobs, domestic difficulties, highway accidents, and alcoholism.

The attitudes of certain groups in the population toward drinking and public drinking houses are also reflected in the rigid regulation of alcohol

---

Wiley & Sons, Inc., 1962). Also see Joseph R. Gusfield, *Symbolic Crusade: Status Politics and the American Temperance Movement* (Urbana: University of Illinois Press, 1963).

[5] Benson Y. Landis, "Some Economic Aspects of Alcohol Problems," *Memoirs of the Section on Alcohol Studies* (No. 4; New Haven, Conn.: Quarterly Journal of Studies on Alcohol, Inc., 1945), pp. 28–29.

[6] Observer (a pseud.) and Milton A. Maxwell, "A Study of Absenteeism, Accidents and Sickness Payments in Problem Drinkers in One Industry," *Quarterly Journal of Studies on Alcohol,* 20:302–312 (1959). Also see Harrison M. Trice, "Work Accidents and the Problem Drinker: A Case Study," *ILR Research,* 3:2–6, No. 2 (1957).

[7] Boyd E. Macrory, "The Tavern and the Community," *Quarterly Journal of Studies on Alcohol,* 13:609–637 (1952).

distribution through taverns.[8] These regulations imply that the tavern is the source of immorality, delinquency, and drunkenness and that a man of high moral character must be in charge if the community is to be protected. Regulations generally limit the number of taverns to a certain ratio of the population and specify high license fees, generally between $200 and $900 a year, regardless of the size of the establishment. Some states closely scrutinize prospective tavernkeepers' past histories for records of criminal or other immoral behavior. In some communities, the license of a tavern owner who knowingly employs a bartender with a criminal background is subject to revocation. Taverns must observe strict closing hours, they must generally remain closed on election days, on Christmas Eve, and on certain other holidays. They must not permit minors on the premises, are not allowed to obscure a full view of the interior from the outside, may not give "credit," and may not serve visibly intoxicated persons. Women, except relatives, are generally prohibited from working in taverns, although the employment of women is customary in Great Britain. In several states so-called dram acts make the tavern owner responsible for injuries incurred by a patron after leaving the tavern.

PHYSIOLOGICAL AND PSYCHOLOGICAL EFFECTS OF ALCOHOL

Alcohol is a chemical substance derived through a process of fermentation or by distillation. Although the process of distillation of alcoholic beverages from barley, corn, wheat, and other grains is fairly recent in human history, nearly all societies have made fermented beverages, such as wine, beer, and similar products, for thousands of years.[9] Following the intake of alcoholic beverages, a certain amount of alcohol is absorbed into the blood stream from the stomach, but most of it is absorbed in the small intestine. It is carried in the blood to the liver and then disseminated in diluted form to every part of the body. Because there can never be more than 1 percent of alcohol in the blood stream, it cannot directly cause organic brain damage, neither "corroding," "dissolving," nor in any way directly harming the brain cells.[10] In fact, all substances classed as volatile anesthetics, such as ether, can produce precisely the same reactions upon the

---

[8] See Marshall B. Clinard, "The Public Drinking House and Society," in Pittman and Snyder, pp. 270–292.

[9] Clarence H. Patrick, *Alcohol, Culture and Society* (Durham, N.C.: Duke University Press, 1952), pp. 12–39.

[10] Raymond G. McCarthy and Edgar M. Douglass, *Alcohol and Social Responsibility* (New York: Thomas Y. Crowell Company and the Yale Plan Clinic, 1949), pp. 89–93.

brain.[11] Alcohol is not physiologically habit-forming in the sense that certain narcotics are. One does not become a chronic drinker as the result of the first, twentieth, or even one hundredth drink. Moreover, it has never been demonstrated that the craving for alcohol is inherited.[12]

Actually the effect of alcohol is determined by the rate at which it is absorbed into the body, which depends upon the kind of alcoholic beverage consumed, the proportion of alcohol it contains, the speed with which it is drunk, and the amount and type of food in the stomach, as well as on certain minor physiological differences among individuals.[13] In moderate quantities alcohol has relatively little effect on a person, but large quantities disturb the activity in the organs controlled by the brain and cause the phenomenon known as "drunkenness." The effect on behavior of different kinds and quantities of alcoholic beverages on the human system of a 150-pound person is shown in Table 11.1.

As alcohol is consumed, it acts increasingly as a depressant and as an anesthetic.

> The prime action of alcohol in the body is its depressant action on the function of the central nervous system, the brain. This is an anesthetic action no different from that of ether or chloroform. The part of the brain affected and the degree of impairment depend on the concentration of alcohol in the blood and therefore acting on the brain. Although this action is entirely on the brain, disturbance in behavior is manifested in the organs controlled by the particular brain areas affected. Speech is thick, hands clumsy, knees sag, the person appears drunk—not because of the presence of alcohol in his tongue, hands or knees, but because it has depressed those parts of his brain controlling these organs.
>
> In a person of average size, 2 or 3 ounces of whisky present in the body will produce 0.05 per cent of alcohol in the blood. With this amount the uppermost levels of brain functioning are depressed, diminishing inhibition, restraint, and judgment. The drinker feels that he is "sitting on top of the world," many of his normal inhibitions have vanished; he takes many personal and social liberties as the impulse prompts; he is long-winded and has an obvious blunting of self-criticism. At a concentration

---

[11] See Howard W. Haggard, "The Physiological Effects of Large and Small Amounts of Alcohol," in *Alcohol, Science and Society* (New Brunswick, N.J.: Quarterly Journal of Studies on Alcohol, 1945), pp. 59–72.

[12] Anne Roe, "Children of Alcoholic Parents Raised in Foster Homes," in *Alcohol, Science and Society,* p. 124.

[13] McCarthy and Douglass, p. 89. This makes the problem of the measurement of the effects of alcohol, for example, on driving quite complex. See John A. Carpenter, "The Effects of Alcohol on Some Psychological Processes," *Quarterly Journal of Studies on Alcohol,* 23:274–314 (1962).

TABLE 11.1   **The Effect of Alcoholic Beverages**

Amount of beverage consumed	Concentration of alcohol attained in blood	Effect	Time required for all alcohol to leave the body
1 highball (1½ oz. whisky) or 1 cocktail (1½ oz. whisky) or 3½ oz. fortified wine or 5½ oz. ordinary wine or 2 bottles beer (24 oz.)	0.03%	No noticeable effects on behavior	2 hrs.
2 highballs or 2 cocktails or 7 oz. fortified wine or 11 oz. ordinary wine or 4 bottles beer	0.06%	Feeling of warmth—mental relaxation—slight decrease of fine skills—less concern with minor irritations and restraints	4 hrs.
3 highballs or 3 cocktails or 10½ oz. fortified wine or 16½ oz. (1 pt.) ordinary wine or 6 bottles beer	0.09%	Increasing effects with variation among individuals and in the same individuals at different times	Buoyancy—exaggerated emotion and behavior—talkative, noisy, or morose	6 hrs.
4 highballs or 4 cocktails or 14 oz. fortified wine or 22 oz. ordinary wine or 8 bottles (3 qts.) beer	0.12%	Impairment of fine coordination—clumsiness—slight to moderate unsteadiness in standing or walking	8 hrs.
5 highballs or 5 cocktails or (½ pt. whisky)	0.15%	Intoxication—unmistakable abnormality of gross bodily functions and mental faculties	10 hrs.

For those weighing considerably more or less than 150 pounds the amounts of beverage indicated above will be correspondingly greater or less. The effects indicated at each stage will diminish as the concentration of alcohol in the blood diminishes.

SOURCE: Leon A. Greenberg, "Intoxication and Alcoholism: Physiological Factors," *The Annals*, 315:28 (1958). Reprinted by permission of the American Academy of Political and Social Science.

of 0.10 per cent of alcohol in the blood, resulting from 5 or 6 ounces of whisky in the body, function of the lower motor area of the brain is dulled. The person sways perceptibly; he has difficulty putting on his coat; he fumbles with the key at the door; words stumble over a clumsy tongue.

The states so far described are popularly designated as mild intoxication or "feeling high." The significant feature of these states is depression and dulling of sensory and motor function and, contrary to popular belief, not stimulation. The illusion of stimulation is given by the increased tempo and altered quality of behavior occurring when the normally prevailing inhibitions and restraints are removed by alcohol. The effect may be compared to releasing the brakes rather than stepping on the accelerator. Notwithstanding this illusion there is actually measurable reduction in sensitivity, impaired discrimination, and diminished speed of motor responses. The drinker, however, often denies that this occurs; often asserts, on the contrary, that after a few drinks his reactions, perception, and discrimination are better. This is an important effect of alcohol; his judgment about himself and his own activities is blunted, allowing for an inflated feeling of competence and self-confidence.

With increasing concentrations of alcohol in the blood there is a corresponding progression of impairment of functions. At 0.20 per cent, resulting from about 10 ounces of whisky, the entire motor area of the brain is profoundly affected. The individual tends to assume a horizontal position; he needs help to walk or undress. At 0.30 per cent, from the presence of a pint of whisky in the body, sensory perception is so dulled that the drinker has little comprehension of what he sees, hears, or feels; he is stuporous. At 0.40 per cent, perception is obliterated; the person is in coma, he is anesthetized. At 0.60 or 0.70 per cent, the lowest, most primitive levels of the brain controlling breathing and heartbeat cease to function and death ensues. Throughout this entire progression the concentrations of alcohol in the body are far too low to cause any direct organic damage to the tissues. The disturbance is entirely one of nerve function and is reversible; short of death, when the alcohol disappears the effect goes with it.[14]

Alcohol has a number of psychological effects on emotional and overt behavior.[15] If taken in moderate amounts, alcohol can lessen tensions and worry, and in general may ease the fatigue associated with anxiety.[16] It presents an illusion of being a stimulant because it reduces or alters the cortical control over action. Under the influence of alcohol a person may

---

[14] Leon A. Greenberg, "Intoxication and Alcoholism: Physiological Factors," *The Annals,* 315:26–27 (1958). Reprinted by permission of the American Academy of Political and Social Science.

[15] For a review of the literature on psychological effects, see Carpenter.

[16] Haggard, p. 63.

become active, boisterous, aggressive, or silent, or he may even fall into a stupor—all as a result of this reduction in cortical control and not from stimulation. Alcohol has a negative effect on task performance, although this is dependent on the experience of the person, the complexity of the work, and whether the individual is emotionally tense. Those who have had little experience with alcohol may overact psychologically to its effects.

> The inexperienced drinker, however, is apt to overreact to the sensations of alcohol. He may be merely fulfilling what he perceives to be the socially expected behavior in response to drinking. Such a reaction is commonly seen in groups of young people who can behave as if hilariously intoxicated under the influence of very small amounts of alcohol (and sometimes without alcohol at all). Some drinking novices are so unaccustomed to even the mild sensations of a little alcohol that it may actually impede their task performance beyond the normal expectation for their level of blood alcohol concentration. This phenomenon contributes to a special concern over drinking and driving in young people who are neither experienced drinkers nor experienced drivers.[17]

Much has been made of the so-called alcoholic diseases, such as beriberi, pellagra, and cirrhosis of the liver. Although these diseases are found among nonalcoholics as well as among alcoholics, the continuous drinking of alcohol brings about a considerably diminished appetite, and, if this drinking is not curbed, disease may follow, not from the alcohol consumed but rather because of the nutritional deficiencies resulting from prolonged drinking. These deficiencies may produce an organic ailment called polyneuritis, or, less technically, beriberi, caused by a lack of vitamin B_1; or pellagra, caused by a deficiency of niacin. The fact that these deficiencies are present has caused some researchers to believe that alcoholism can be prevented or controlled by proper nutrition.[18] The disease which the man on the street most often associates with chronic alcoholism is cirrhosis of the liver. Although this disease occurs proportionately more often among inebriates than among nondrinkers, medical men state that it is not caused directly by alcohol but instead is due to some nutritional deficiency which has not yet been conclusively demonstrated.[19]

---

[17] Robert Straus, "Alcohol," in Robert K. Merton and Robert A. Nisbet, *Contemporary Social Problems* (2d ed.; New York: Harcourt, Brace & World, Inc., 1966), p. 244. Reprinted by permission of the publishers.

[18] Roger J. Williams, *Alcoholism: The Nutritional Approach* (Austin: University of Texas Press, 1959). This approach fails to take into account properly the sociological aspects of drinking.

[19] Norman Jolliffe, "Alcohol and Nutrition: The Diseases of Chronic Alcoholism," in *Alcohol, Science and Society*, pp. 76–77.

ALCOHOL AND DELINQUENCY OR CRIME

Some people believe that much delinquency or crime is committed under the influence of alcohol. On numerous occasions offenders have even excused their behavior as due to "one or two beers" or to "drinking." There is evidence that large numbers of arrests are for common drunkenness. Such drunkenness does have an important relation to misdemeanors and the police problem. When all offenses are examined, it is found that of all arrests, including misdemeanors as well as crimes, some one half or two thirds are for drunkenness, or for some related offense, such as disorderly conduct or vagrancy. In the United States in 1965 there were some 1,337,000 arrests for drunkenness in cities over 2500. Chronic drunkenness is a major problem and an alcoholic may be arrested and imprisoned as many as twenty to thirty times a year and have a total record of several hundred arrests.[20] Arrests for drunkenness among those under twenty-one is disproportionately smaller compared to older groups; arrests for violation of laws prohibiting the purchase of alcohol by minors may be disproportionately higher.[21] A St. Louis study showed that while persons ten through twenty-one make up 15 percent of the population, the percentage of alcohol-related offenses by this group was 11 percent.[22] This age group accounted for only 2 percent of arrests for public intoxication and 3 percent of the drunken driving arrests, but 23 percent of law violations relating to the purchase of liquor.

In *some* violent personal crimes—murder, aggravated assault, and forcible rape—drunkenness is undoubtedly of some significance.[23] After studying 588 criminal homicides in Philadelphia, Wolfgang concluded that there is a significant association between violent homicide and the presence of alcohol in the offender of either sex. "Approximately 60 percent of all offenders who committed homicide violently had been drinking prior to

---

[20] See David Pittmann and C. Wayne Gordon, *Revolving Door: A Study of the Chronic Police Case Inebriate* (New York: The Free Press, 1958) and David J. Pittman and Duff G. Gillespie, "Social Policy as Deviancy Reinforcement: The Case of the Public Intoxication Offender," in David J. Pittman, ed., *Alcoholism* (New York: Harper & Row, Publishers, 1967), pp. 106–124.

[21] Federal Bureau of Investigation, *Crime in the United States: Uniform Crime Reports, 1965* (Washington, D.C.: Department of Justice, 1966).

[22] Muriel W. Sterne, David J. Pittman, and Thomas Coe, "Teen-agers, Drinking, and the Law: A Study of Arrest Trends for Alcohol-Related Offenses," *Crime and Delinquency*, 11:81 (1965).

[23] See, for example, Julian Roebuck and Ronald Johnson, "The Negro Drinker and Assaulter as a Criminal Type," *Crime and Delinquency*, 3:21–33 (1962).

the crime, while 40 percent had not been drinking. On the other hand, among those who killed nonviolently, half had been drinking and half had not been drinking before the crime." [24] In Finland offenses of violence against the person are often committed in a state of intoxication.[25] It is estimated, however, that 43 percent of those who drink in Finland drink to a state of drunkenness once they begin to drink, indicating that only a small proportion of those who are intoxicated engage in acts of violence.

Drunken driving is particularly serious as far as criminality is concerned. In 1965 in cities in the United States of over 2500 population, there were slightly over 185,000 arrests for drunken driving. Some of these cases involved the injury or possible injury to persons, and, where death resulted, the drivers could be charged with negligent homicide.

The very volume of drinking by offenders and nonoffenders in the United States would suggest that there are other variables involved in the problems of crime and delinquency besides alcohol. There are about 200,000 taverns in the country, and about one in ten adults drinks heavily, more than one in three drink moderately. It is probable that in most cases where alcohol was associated with criminal behavior, it acted as a depressant and made the person temporarily less cognizant of the probable consequences of deviant behavior, or else less able to respond in terms of his ordinary system of values and norms. In a sense it simply "released" behavior patterns already there instead of "causing" them. Although alcohol may "release" an individual's criminal attitudes, such criminal activities, involving either property or personal crimes, might have taken place sooner or later irrespective of his alcohol intake. When murders and assaults are committed under the influence of alcohol, they usually represent long-standing quarrels or difficulties in relationships with others which may culminate in violence depending upon the definition of the situation and the response of the persons involved. Forcible rape may represent the enactment of definitions of sexual behavior already present.

DRINKING AS A SOCIAL PHENOMENON

Alcoholic beverages of one type or another have been widely used for centuries by most ancient and modern peoples.[26] The people of Western Europe, and those who first colonized America, were no exception.

---

[24] Marvin E. Wolfgang, *Patterns in Criminal Homicide* (Philadelphia: University of Pennsylvania Press, 1958), p. 166.

[25] Kettil Bruun, "Alcohol Studies in Scandinavia," *Sociological Inquiry,* 31:78–92 (1961).

[26] For a discussion of drinking practices of ancient Greece and Rome, the Far East, Central and South America, as well as France, England, Canada, and Russia, see McCarthy, pp. 39–179.

In New England and the Middle and Southern colonies along the eastern seaboard, beer and ale were part of the daily diet and believed necessary to maintain health. However, from the earliest days, drunkenness was frowned upon and punishments were imposed on those who consumed more than was considered seemly. During the late eighteenth century, rum, which has a far higher alcohol content than ale or beer, became an integral part of the economic and social life of the colonies. Numerous distilleries were established in all the population centers.[27]

Drinking patterns today appear to vary in terms of the beverage used, the circumstances under which drinking takes place, the time, the amount, and the individual's own attitude and that of others toward his drinking. All drinking patterns are learned, just as other behavior is learned. As one writer on alcohol has stated, there are no universal drinking patterns for John, the average citizen: "In any event, John will not drink like a Zulu or an Austrian or a Japanese; in fact, he will not drink like a New Yorker or a Californian or a ditch digger or a Yale man or a Kentucky mountaineer, unless he is or has been in socially significant contact with such a group." [28] Patterns of drinking come down to us from a long past in which alcohol has been used. The knowledge, ideas, norms, and values involved in the use of alcoholic beverages which have passed from generation to generation have thus maintained the continuity of an alcohol culture.

Drinking plays a significant role in everyday interpersonal affairs. Alcohol is used by many people to celebrate national holidays, such as Christmas and New Year's, and to rejoice in victories, whether those of war, the football field, or the ballot box. The bride and groom are often toasted, and the father may celebrate the birth of a child with a drink "all around." Promotions, anniversaries, and important special events of achievement by the family and close friends often call for a drink. Businessmen may negotiate contracts over a few glasses, and meeting an old friend is often the occasion for a drink. In many homes guests are welcomed with a drink or cocktails before dinner to help get the guests acquainted.

Even some religious ceremonies and, on occasion, the bereavement of death are accompanied by alcoholic beverages. On a more inclusive level, it has been said: "The custom of drinking together to symbolize common feeling and unity is almost universal in present-day culture. . . . Thus imbedded in the culture pattern is the notion that in alcohol is magic which, in sorrow and in joy, in elation and in depression, in rebellion against the misery of travail

---

[27] Raymond G. McCarthy, "Alcoholism: Attitudes and Attacks, 1775–1935," *The Annals,* 315:13 (1958).

[28] Selden D. Bacon, "Sociology and the Problems of Alcohol," *Memoirs of the Section of Studies on Alcohol* (No. 1; New Brunswick, N.J.: Quarterly Journal of Studies on Alcohol, Inc., 1946), pp. 17–18.

and the restraints which hem one in, frees the human spirit and permits it to soar into the heavens unhampered by the ills of the flesh." [29]

Drinking by teenagers is almost entirely a group activity and represents culturally patterned and socially controlled behavior.[30] Within the context of an age-graded social system drinking among teenagers represents peer group identification and status transformation into adult roles.[31] Drinking, for at least some teenagers, is related to the passage from youth into young male adult roles in our society. One study of adolescent drunkenness found that "in collectivities of high mutual attraction there is a tendency toward consensus in drinking behavior; that, if such consensus is attained, group standards arise to regulate and legitimate attitudes and behaviors related to alcohol usage; and that, if consensus is not achieved, cliques are less attractive and tend to reject the deviant member." [32]

There are also drinking patterns among college students. Dating often includes having a drink before or after a dance, show, or party. In some places college men have a tradition of drinking to celebrate the conclusion of examinations. "Bull sessions" often involve beer drinking, and some fraternities and other social organizations have drinking traditions. In European universities there were, and still are, "drinking fraternities" for which members qualified by their ability to consume a large quantity of wine, beer, ale, or other liquor. College drinking songs, expressing friendship and other deep feelings have at times attained great popularity. A detailed study of college drinking habits found that motivations for drinking, as given by men and women who drink, were approximately the same.[33] However, women more frequently felt that they drank in order to get along better on dates and they drank more often than men did to relieve illness and physical discomfort.

Despite the widespread use of alcohol in connection with many social

---

[29] Ernest R. Mowrer, *Disorganization: Personal and Social* (Philadelphia: J. B. Lippincott Company, 1942), pp. 263–264. Reprinted by permission of the publisher.

[30] Christopher Sower, "Teen-Age Drinking as Group Behavior," *Quarterly Journal of Studies on Alcohol,* 20:656 (1959).

[31] See George L. Maddox and Bevode C. McCall, *Drinking among Teen-Agers* (New Brunswick, N.J.: Rutgers Center of Alcohol Studies, 1964), pp. 77–78.

[32] C. Norman Alexander, Jr., "Consensus and Mutual Attraction in Natural Cliques: A Study of Adolescent Drinkers," *American Journal of Sociology,* 69:395 (1964).

[33] Robert Straus and Selden D. Bacon, *Drinking in College* (New Haven, Conn.: Yale University Press, 1953), p. 71. Also see C. A. Hecht, R. J. Grine, and S. E. Rothrock, "Drinking and Dating among College Women," *Quarterly Journal of Studies on Alcohol,* 9:252–259 (1948); and F. C. Berezin and N. R. Roth, "Drinking Practices of College Women," *Quarterly Journal of Studies on Alcohol,* 11:212–221 (1950).

functions, one writer has contrasted the value systems implicit in American drinking patterns with those in Europe:

> Traditionally, in European cultures, aside from past dietetic necessity, drinking has been a phase of a deeply rooted, stable and integrated social and recreational pattern. Among Europeans, drinking may remain a satisfying social practice rather than a vice or social problem, largely because it remains an element within otherwise integrated and participating recreational practices. . . . With Europeans, for example, drinking has traditionally been a phase of the occasion of the group's coming together; with Americans, conversely, coming together has all too frequently provided the occasion for drinking. In this distinction, and its historical evolution, appears to lie one of the salient factors in the more disturbing features of our drinking habits.[34]

PUBLIC DRINKING HOUSES AND SOCIETY

A large proportion of drinking is done in groups, much of it in public drinking houses, which are found in most of the world today under a variety of names: American taverns and bars, British pubs, French bistros, German beer halls, Italian wine houses, and Japanese bars. In the United States alone there are over 200,000 bars and taverns. In a study of a representative sample of 1268 adults in San Francisco 76 percent reported that they were drinkers and nearly one half of those who drank patronized a tavern, with 12 percent going once a week or more.[35] A Washington State survey found that most drinking is done either at home or in the homes of friends.[36] About 70 percent of the men and 83 percent of the women did their drinking at home, which meant that a relatively small proportion drank in taverns, cocktail lounges, clubs, or other places. Only 2.4 percent of the women patronized taverns as compared with 14.1 percent of the men.[37] In

---

[34] Herbert A. Bloch, "Alcohol and American Recreational Life," *American Scholar*, 18:56–57 (1949). References in fictional writings in the fifty-year period from 1900–1904 to 1946–1950 tended to present increasingly the use of alcohol in a more positive rather than negative view, seeing drinking as supportive and favorable relaxation. See Harold W. Pfautz, "The Image of Alcohol in Popular Fiction 1900–1904 and 1946–1950," *Quarterly Journal of Studies on Alcohol*, 23:131–146 (1962).

[35] Walter Clark, "Demographic Characteristics of Tavern Patrons in San Francisco," *Quarterly Journal of Studies on Alcohol*, 27:316–327 (1966). Similar findings were made by Macrory.

[36] Milton A. Maxwell, "Drinking Behavior in the State of Washington," *Quarterly Journal of Studies on Alcohol*, 13:224 (1952).

[37] This figure should be slightly larger because the study combined drinking in "clubs or cocktail lounges," which accounted for 7.9 percent of the women and 9.1 percent of the men.

a sample of Wisconsin replies from 872 men and 569 women, it was found that three fourths of the men patronized taverns, about half of them regularly, that is, once a month or more, whereas only about two fifths of the women went to taverns, only one in seven women being a regular patron.[38]

A tavern, as we shall refer to a public drinking house, is more than a place where alcoholic beverages are sold for consumption on the premises. There are several important characteristics of a contemporary tavern: (1) A tavern involves group drinking. (2) This drinking is commercial in the sense that the ability to buy a drink is available to all as opposed to the bars of private clubs. (3) A tavern serves alcohol, however, and can thus be distinguished from the modern soda fountains, the coffeehouses of the Middle East, or the teahouses of the Orient. (4) It has a tavernkeeper or a bartender who serves as a functionary of the institution and around whom, in part, the drinking gravitates. (5) There are many customs connected with a tavern, including the physical surroundings, types of drinks, and hours of sale.[39]

Taverns can be traced to Babylon, Greece, and Rome.[40] The inns of seventeenth- and eighteenth-century England, however, are more generally regarded as the forerunners of the modern tavern. There were two classes of "public houses" in England, the ale and the wine taverns, the latter being considered more "respectable than the ale taverns and catered to a wealthier clientele." [41] Although some people regarded taverns as dens of iniquity, others considered them as necessary public institutions. One writer has stated that many of the public drinking houses in London were the meeting places of politicians and traders and were "the only places of convenient sojourn and pleasant sociality." [42]

Taverns played a significant role not only in England, where they came from, but in colonial America. In part because they believed that drinking not done in public was likely to be excessive and that the sale of liquor in a tavern could be regulated, the Puritan authorities in Massachusetts in 1656 even enacted a law making towns liable to a fine for not maintaining an ordinary (tavern).[43] During Puritan times tavernkeepers

---

[38] Macrory, pp. 611–612.

[39] Clinard in Pittmann and Snyder.

[40] W. C. Firebaugh, *Inns of Greece and Rome* (Chicago: F. M. Morris, 1928).

[41] J. D. Rolleston, "Alcoholism in Medieval England," *British Journal of Inebriety*, 31:46 (1933).

[42] Frederick W. Hackwood, *Inns, Ales and Drinking Customs of Old England* (New York: Sturgis and Walton Co., 1911), p. 172.

[43] Eugene Field, *The Colonial Tavern* (Providence: Preston and Rounds, 1897), pp. 11–12.

enjoyed a rather high status, and attempts were made to attract the right kind of person into this occupation. Tavernkeepers were granted public land or pasturage and were often exempted from school taxes and church rates.[44] In colonial America taverns served as coach stations or wayside stops and as places of lodging for strangers in the community. They were used as schools, courthouses, public meeting houses, post offices, job markets, and as places for celebrations of weddings and national holidays.[45] One writer asserts that in colonial America the people found that "the tavern was their club, their board of trade, their 'exchanges,' and indeed, to most of the colonists it served as their newspapers." [46] In both England and the United States the coming of the railroads gradually eliminated the necessity for taverns as coach stations, and their number declined.

The Industrial Revolution brought thousands of migrants, particularly single men, to work in the factories. A new type of public drinking house, the saloon, replaced the wayside tavern. The saloon became common in urban areas and was characterized by strictly male patronage, drinking at an elaborate bar with free meals, and a special "family entrance." [47] Most saloons performed an important function by helping to relieve the poverty, loneliness, and monotony of city life, although some were centers of deviant behavior such as drunkenness, gambling, and prostitution. A sociological study of saloons in Chicago between 1896–1897 found that most saloons in this area were not centers of intemperance or vice.[48] In fact, the saloon was found to have many other functions:

> It [the saloon] is the workingman's club. Many of his leisure hours are spent here. In it he finds more of the things which approximate to luxury than he finds at home, almost more than he finds in any other public place in the ward. . . . But his demand for even these things is not fundamental, they are but the means to his social expression. It is the society of his fellows that he seeks and must have.[49]

---

[44] Herbert Asbury, *The Great Illusion* (New York: Doubleday & Company, Inc., 1950), p. 8.

[45] Simon Dinitz, "The Relation of the Tavern to the Drinking Phases of Alcoholics." Unpublished doctoral dissertation, University of Wisconsin, Madison, 1951.

[46] Field, pp. 232–233.

[47] Maurice Gorham and M. McDunnett, *Inside the Pub* (London: The Architectural Press, 1950), p. 68.

[48] Ernest C. Moore, "The Social Value of the Saloon," *American Journal of Sociology*, 3:1–12 (1897). Also see Raymond Calkins, *Substitutes for the Saloon: An Investigation Made for the Committee of Fifty* (Boston: Houghton Mifflin Company, 1901).

[49] Moore, pp. 4–5.

After enactment of the Eighteenth Amendment in the United States the saloon as a type became legally extinct. It was replaced by the illicit "speakeasy" with its select clientele, often adulterated alcoholic beverages, and an urban sophisticated setting. After the repeal of Prohibition the modern tavern made its appearance; more correctly, at least five different varieties of public places emerged, these types being largely associated with certain areas of the city. They were different from the saloon in that women in general were permitted, the surroundings were more attractive, and patrons more frequently drank while seated at tables rather than while standing at a bar. Contemporary taverns may be classified as Skid Row, the downtown cocktail lounge and bar, the dine and dance establishment, the night club, and the neighborhood tavern.[50] The Skid Row tavern is located close to the business district of urban centers. It offers little more than drinking and the blaring juke box. The bulk of its patrons are drifters, transients, and alcoholics. Drunkenness, prostitution, gambling, and violations of other state laws and ordinances are frequent. The regular patrons of cocktail lounges, however, are largely a higher-status group of regular patrons who engage in organized activities around which stable expectations of "proper" behavior are developed.[51] One study found that a major function is the facilitation of casual sexual affairs between middle- and upper-class married men and young, unattached women.[52]

The neighborhood tavern is the most numerous, constituting probably three fourths of all taverns. It is patronized by people, largely couples, in the neighborhood. It has many functions as a meeting place for regular patrons, offering them amusement, recreation, a chance to talk and to enjoy music, and general relaxation.[53] A neighborhood tavern tends to reflect the norms of the neighborhood.

Attitudes toward the tavern are influenced by a person's position in the social structure as well as by his tavern patronage. Although a large proportion of the general population in all social strata drink alcoholic beverages, not all go to taverns. Many consumers of alcohol, particularly those of the middle and upper classes, drink at home, at cocktail parties, or at the bars of private clubs, such as golf clubs. They may go to cocktail lounges or night clubs, but they seldom visit neighborhood taverns. Taverns

---

[50] Another classification has divided them into the convenience bar, the market-place bar, and the home territory bar. See Sherri Cavan, *Liquor License: An Ethnography of Bar Behavior* (Chicago: Aldine Publishing Company, 1966).

[51] Julian Roebuck and S. Lee Spray, "The Cocktail Lounge: A Study of Heterosexual Relations in a Public Organization," *American Journal of Sociology,* 72:388–395 (January 1967).

[52] Roebuck and Spray.

[53] Macrory, "The Tavern and the Community."

are often not even located in the immediate vicinity of their homes. On the other hand, neighborhood public drinking houses, as well as package liquor stores, are disproportionately concentrated in lower-class areas and constitute a highly visible symbol of the lower-class way of life.[54] In such areas there tends to be little distance between the place of residence and public facilities for alcohol consumption.

Drinking does not appear to be the actual reason for patronizing most neighborhood taverns.[55] The purpose of going to taverns is not primarily to drink, as was indicated in a study where only 20 percent of those who went to taverns reported that they drank beer or wine most frequently there or in restaurants and only 36 percent of the drinkers consumed distilled spirits most frequently there.[56] Rather, these taverns function primarily as a place for people to meet for the sake of establishing and maintaining social relationships.[57] Sociability is one of the main features of a tavern for it is one of the few places where the norms against speaking to strangers do not apply, interaction being available to all who enter.[58] People go to taverns to avoid loneliness and to relax from the cares and problems of the home and the factory, office, or farm. The neighborhood tavern also serves as a place for recreation, which includes such entertainments as card games, shuffleboard, pinball machines, juke boxes, or television. Finally, "sympathetic" tavernkeepers, bartenders, and others give the patron an opportunity to talk over his personal problems. Much the same reasons appear to account for the extensive patronage of British pubs (public drinking houses) and French bistros.[59] According to one study, British pubs are patronized not only for the sake of drinking but for the opportunities for sociability and recreation they provide.[60]

---

[54] Harold W. Pfautz and Robert W. Hyde, "The Ecology of Alcohol in the Local Community," *Quarterly Journal of Studies on Alcohol,* 21:447–456 (1960).

[55] Clinard, "The Public Drinking House and Society," and Margaret K. Chandler, "The Social Organization of Workers in a Rooming House Area." Unpublished doctoral dissertation, University of Chicago, 1948.

[56] Walter Clark, "Demographic Characteristics of Tavern Patrons in San Francisco," *Quarterly Journal of Studies on Alcohol,* 27:326 (1966).

[57] Macrory, pp. 630–636.

[58] Cavan, pp. 49–66.

[59] Joseph Wechsberg, "They Debate L'Alcoholisme—Over Their Drinks," *The New York Times Magazine,* March 26, 1961. Wechsberg remarks that the French bistros are the hub of French democracy and where the average Frenchman spends most of his leisure time. Also see Gabriel Mouchot, "France: Drinking and Its Control," in McCarthy, pp. 149–158.

[60] Mass-Observation, *The Pub and the People* (London: Victor Gollancz, Ltd., 1943), pp. 82–83. Authorities on British labor history, such as the Webbs, have shown that a significant portion of the old union budgets went to supply the mem-

No pub can simply be regarded as a drinking shop. It may be lacking in facilities for games and music, present no organized forms of social activity and its actual accommodation be of the crudest, but none the less the activities of the drinkers are not confined to drinking. . . . The pub is a centre of social activities—for the ordinary pub goer the main scene of social life. Worktown working people rarely meet in each other's homes for social activities in the way middle classes do. For some there is the social activity of politics, football, or cricket clubs. But participators in these activities are a small minority. The place where most Worktowners meet their friends and acquaintances is the pub. Men can meet and talk [out] of the way of their womenfolk.[61]

Finally, taverns have various "rituals" and customs.[62] There are, for example, rules about treating a person to drinks which differ for those already acquainted, merely acquainted, and the unacquainted. Neighborhood taverns exercise a degree of control over the drinking behavior of those who patronize it. As one writer who studied a number of them stated, "Each tavern seems to set its own norms as to what degree of inebriation it will tolerate. The old timers are allowed a certain freedom. In others, drunkenness and boisterousness are generally not acceptable." [63]
One study tried to test the hypotheses that there is a simple positive correlation between tavern frequency, amount of alcohol consumed, and drunkenness.

U.S. figures for per capita consumption and tavern frequency by state were examined, and it was found that the correlation approximated zero. The rate of arrest on charges of drunkenness and the number of pubs per 100,000 in the various counties of England and Wales also failed to show a positive relationship. As a matter of fact, the correlation in this case was slightly negative. In other words, there was a very slight tendency towards fewer arrests for drunkenness where tavern rates were high, and conversely, towards more arrests where taverns were fewer. In Ontario, convictions for drunkenness and tavern rates showed a quite markedly negative relationship when plotted through time.[64]

---

bers with ale and other drinks at meetings and social gatherings. Also see B. Seebohm Rowntree and G. R. Lavers, *English Life and Leisure* (New York: David McKay Company, Inc., 1951), pp. 159–198.

[61] Mass-Observation, p. 311.

[62] Cavan, pp. 112–139.

[63] David Gottlieb, "The Neighborhood Tavern and the Cocktail Lounge: A Study of Class Differences," *American Journal of Sociology*, 62:561 (1957).

[64] Robert E. Popham, "The Urban Tavern: Some Preliminary Remarks," *Addictions*, 9 (1962).

PREVALENCE OF DRINKING IN THE UNITED STATES

In the United States the drinking of alcohol, in order of amount consumed and cost, consists chiefly of beer, followed by distilled spirits, and wine fermented from grapes. Over the past eighty years there has been a downward trend in the drinking of distilled spirits and an increase in the consumption of beer. From the period 1860–1870 to 1960 the consumption of distilled spirits declined well over a third, while the consumption of beer almost doubled. (See Table 11.2.) In the year 1850 almost 90 percent of the absolute alcohol consumed, that is, the alcohol content of a beverage, in the United States was in the form of distilled spirits, and nearly 7 percent was beer. A century later only 38 percent was in the form of spirits; 51 percent was beer. In 1959 $9.6 billion was spent on alcoholic beverages of all types, representing, however, a decrease from 40 percent in 1950 to 3 percent of the total consumer expenditures. In the fiscal year 1964 the United States Treasury Department reported excise tax collections of $3.5 billion on alcoholic beverages, or one fourth of all excise taxes, and exceeding by far those collected on tobacco, automobiles, or gasoline.[65]

According to a 1963 study, approximately two thirds (65 percent) of the adult population over twenty-one, or 80 million persons, drink some type of alcoholic beverage during the year.[66] (See Table 11.3.) If one adds the 8 to 10 million younger persons, sixteen to twenty, who drink alcohol beyond isolated incidents there are about 90 million persons above fifteen who are users of alcoholic beverages.[67] A larger proportion of adult men drink than women: four in five men as compared with two in three women. There is considerable evidence, however, that with the increasing trend toward equality in the behavior of the sexes, drinking patterns may eventually become nearly the same. Comparisons of the prevalence of drinkers in 1963 with those in earlier studies revealed the prevalence rate of drinking to be slighly higher, not only in the total population but by sex, age, and education as well.[68] Although the trend is slight, the evidence suggests that the rate of drinkers is increasing. Each new generation tends to have a larger proportion of persons who drink and most of them remain drinkers throughout life. Some drinkers, however, give up drinking.

The number of taverns in the United States gives an additional indication of the extent of drinking, even though only about one third of all

---

[65] The federal excise tax rate on distilled spirits is $10.50 per proof gallon.

[66] Harold A. Mulford, "Drinking and Deviant Behavior, U.S.A., 1963," *Quarterly Journal of Studies on Alcohol*, 25:634–650 (1964).

[67] Robert Straus, "Alcohol," Merton and Nisbet, p. 251.

[68] Mulford, p. 649

TABLE 11.2   **Apparent Consumption of Alcoholic Beverages, per Capita (Age 15 and Over), United States, 1850–1960, in United States Gallons**

YEAR	Spirits		Wine		Beer		Total absolute alcohol
	BEVERAGE	ABSOLUTE ALCOHOL	BEVERAGE	ABSOLUTE ALCOHOL	BEVERAGE	ABSOLUTE ALCOHOL	
1850	4.17	1.88	0.46	0.08	2.70	0.14	2.10
1860	4.79	2.16	0.57	0.10	5.39	0.27	2.53
1870	3.40	1.53	0.53	0.10	8.73	0.44	2.07
1881–90	2.12	0.95	0.76	0.14	17.94	0.90	1.99
1906–10	2.14	0.96	0.92	0.17	29.27	1.47	2.60
1916–19	1.68	0.76	0.69	0.12	21.63	1.08	1.96
1940	1.48	0.67	0.91	0.16	16.29	0.73	1.56
1950	1.72	0.77	1.27	0.23	23.21	1.04	2.04
1960	1.90	0.86	1.32	0.22	21.95	0.99	2.07

SOURCE: Mark Keller and Vera Efron, *Selected Statistical Tables on Alcoholic Beverages, 1850–1960, and on Alcoholism, 1930–1960* (New Brunswick, N.J.: Quarterly Journal of Studies on Alcohol, Inc., 1961), p. 3. Used by permission of the publisher.

TABLE 11.3   **Proportion of United States Population Twenty-One Years and Over Who Drink Alcoholic Beverages**

Study	Total population %	Men %	Women %
Ley (1940) (U.S.)	57	60	34
Riley and Marden (1946) (U.S.)	65	75	56
Gallup (1947) (U.S.)	63	72	54
Maxwell (1951) (Washington State)	63	76	51
Mulford and Miller (1961) (Iowa)	59	67	52
Mulford (1963) (U.S.)	65	79	63

SOURCES: H. A. Ley, "Incidence of Smoking and Drinking among 10,000 Examinees," *Proceedings of the Life Extension Examiners,* 2:57–63 (1940); John W. Riley and Charles F. Marden, "The Social Patterns of Alcoholic Drinking," *Quarterly Journal of Studies on Alcohol,* 8:265–273 (1947); News Release (Princeton, N. J.: American Institute of Public Opinion, December 18, 1948); Milton A. Maxwell, "Drinking Behavior in the State of Washington," *Quarterly Journal of Studies on Alcohol,* 13:221 (1952); Harold A. Mulford and Donald E. Miller, "The Prevalence and Extent of Drinking in Iowa, 1961: A Replication and an Evaluation of Methods, *Quarterly Journal of Studies on Alcohol,* 24:46 (1963); and Harold A. Mulford, "Drinking and Deviant Drinking, U.S.A., 1963," *Quarterly Journal of Studies on Alcohol,* 25:634–650 (1964). The latter study was based on 1515 respondents chosen by modified random sampling procedures to represent the total non-institutional population of the United States age twenty-one and over. Sampling and field work was done by the National Opinion Research Center.

liquor sales are made in taverns. In spite of the value conflicts over the tavern, there are over 200,000 in the United States. Chicago has more than 9000; New York City alone has 12,000. Wisconsin has 14,000 taverns which sell beer, four in every five of them also serving distilled spirits.

The extreme of the drinking culture is probably found in France, where only 4 percent of the native French population are abstainers.[69] In the Netherlands the percentage of abstainers in the adult population is from 15 to 21 percent; for that 80 percent of the population which drinks, an alcoholic beverage is rarely drunk with meals, as is done in Italy.[70] A Polish survey on a representative sample of the population twenty years of age and over found 15.7 percent abstainers, with the percentage 25.1 percent among women and 7.6 percent among men.[71] Few teetotalers are found in Italy.

Frequency of Drinking

Statements about the proportion of the general population that drinks are often misleading, however, because they give no indication of the frequency of drinking. Using both an index of drinking frequency and the amount of alcohol consumed, a nation-wide study in 1963 found that 30 percent of the population are abstainers (22 percent of the men and 38 percent of the women), 28 percent drink infrequently (24 percent of the men, 32 percent of the women), not more than once a month and consume small amounts of alcohol at a single sitting (not more than 1.6 ounces of absolute alcohol).[72] Using three similar indices, the same study classified 32 percent as light drinkers (28 percent of the men, 36 percent of the women), 30 percent as moderate drinkers (37 percent of the men, 25 percent of the women), that is those who drank small or medium amounts of alcohol two to four times a month, and, at the extreme, 8 percent (13 percent of the men, 3 percent of the women) who drank three or more drinks two or more times a week. The national ratio was four men to one woman who are heavy drinkers. If one adds those who drink small amounts of alcohol

---

[69] Pierre Fouquet, "Facteurs Socio-Culturels et Economiques de L'Alcoolisme," Conférence Donnée au Cours Européan d'été sur L'Alcoolisme, Lausanne, Switzerland, June 1963. Also see David J. Pittman, "International Overview: Social and Cultural Factors in Drinking Patterns, Pathological and Nonpathological," in Pittman, pp. 12–13.

[70] Ivan Gadourek, *Riskante Gewoonten en Zorg Voor Eigen Welzijn* (Groningen: The Netherlands: J. B. Walters, 1963).

[71] Andrzej Swiecicki, "Survey on Alcohol Consumption in Poland," *Archives of Criminology* (Warsaw: Department of Criminology, Institute of Legal Science, Polish Academy of Science) 2:385–391 (1964).

[72] Mulford.

at one time (the slight and moderate drinkers) to the abstainers, this amounts to 81 percent of the United States population.

Another study of drinking behavior, with a sample of 2746 adults conducted during 1964–1965, found that 32 percent of the population were classified as "abstainers" because they said that they drank less than once a year, if at all. Most of the abstainers were lifetime abstainers; about one third of them had been drinkers at some earlier time. The remaining 68 percent of the adults in the United States said that they drank at least once a year. This total of 68 percent covered the continuum from the heaviest to the lightest drinkers, with each type blending into the next. Any division of this continuum would necessarily be arbitrary. The group of drinkers was divided into the heaviest-drinking (heavy drinkers), 12 percent of the population, based on quantity, frequency, and variability of intake (those who drank several times a week with usually three or more drinks per occasion, or nearly every day with five or more drinks at least once in a while) and the "infrequent" to "moderate" drinkers, 56 percent.[73]

Variations in Drinking Behavior

There are considerable variations in the frequency of drinking by age, education, income, size of community, marital status, and religion. In a national sample, approximately 79 percent of those between twenty-one and thirty-nine years of age drink, 70 percent between forty and fifty-nine, and 56 percent of those sixty years and older.[74] Generally those adults with a higher education drink more than those with less education, the percentage with seventh-grade or less education was 46; high school, 79; and college, 89. Drinking also increases directly with income, under $3000, 54 percent; $5000–$6999, 68 percent; and $10,000 and over, 87 percent. The proportion of drinking generally increases with the size of the community; among those living in areas under 2500 it was 60 percent whereas in cities over 500,000 it was 76 percent. Nearly four fifths (79 percent) of all single persons drink as compared with 72 percent of the married and 69 percent of the divorced. The proportion of those who drink is highest among the Jews (90 percent), followed by Catholics (89 percent), Lutherans (85 percent), and other large Protestant denominations (81 percent).

A large proportion of the younger age group drink. A survey of high

---

[73] Don Cahalan, Ira H. Cisin, and Helen M. Crossley, *American Drinking Practices: A National Survey of Behavior and Attitudes Related to Alcoholic Beverages* (Washington: George Washington University, Social Science Group Report No. 3, 1967).

[74] Mulford, "Drinking and Deviant Drinking, U.S.A., 1963." All the figures in this paragraph came from this study.

school drinking studies has concluded: "A considerable proportion of young people 14–18 years of age have had some experience with drinking. This has frequently been done with parental consent. However, drinking practices of young people can only be understood in terms of their social class, economic status, religious affiliation and drinking customs of their parents."[75] In a study of a highly urbanized and industrialized county in Wisconsin, two in three high school students reported that they consumed alcoholic drinks, almost entirely beer, on social and other nonreligious occasions.[76] There was a steady increase with age until the proportion who drank at the age of eighteen was four in five. Girls drank slightly less in most age groups, but there was little difference by seventeen or eighteen. Some 17 percent of the Kansas high school students in the urban Wichita area had had one or more drinks of alcoholic beverages, generally beer or wine, in the week before the survey was made, compared with 11 percent in Kansas rural counties.[77] The amount of drinking was small, 9 percent of the urban students and less than half of that percentage in the rural areas having had four or more drinks during the previous week. Although drinking among teenagers was positively associated with the frequency of drinking by the parents and with the fact that alcoholic beverages were kept in the home, the drinking patterns generally followed were those considered appropriate to the member of the group. A Michigan study of approximately 2000 teenage students found that 23 percent reported that they drank alcoholic beverages at least occasionally and 9 percent designated themselves as drinkers.[78]

A large proportion of college students, some 74 percent, drink alcoholic beverages, according to Straus and Bacon's survey of 15,747 students in twenty-seven American colleges.[79] Of the total group, 80 percent of the men and 61 percent of the women belong in this category. Actually these figures are misleading, for the drinking of college students varies a great deal by the type of institution, income, family drinking, religion, and ethnic

[75] Raymond G. McCarthy, "High School Drinking Studies," in McCarthy, *Drinking and Intoxication,* p. 205.

[76] John L. Miller and J. Richard Wahl, *Attitudes of High School Students toward Alcoholic Beverages* (New York: The Mrs. John S. Sheppard Foundation, 1956). This was a study of Racine County, Wisconsin.

[77] E. Jackson Baur and Marston M. McCluggage, "Drinking Patterns of Kansas High School Students," *Social Problems,* 5:317–326 (1958).

[78] Maddox and McCall.

[79] Robert Straus and Selden D. Bacon, *Drinking in College* (New Haven, Conn.: Yale University Press, 1953), p. 46. Also see Charles L. Maddox and Ernst Borinski, "Drinking Behavior of Negro Collegians: A Study of Selected Men," *Quarterly Journal of Studies on Alcohol,* 25:651–668 (1964).

background. In addition, the extent of drinking increases with each year in college. More students drink at private, nonsectarian colleges attended only by men or by women than at any other type. The least amount of drinking is done at private, coeducational, "dry" colleges. (See Table 11.4.) The frequency of drinking among college students who drink, however, is not great. Only 21 percent of the men and 10 percent of the women are reported to drink more than once a week, and two fifths of the men and more than half of the women drink no more than once a month.

TABLE 11.4   **Incidence of Drinking, by Type of College**

	Users of alcoholic beverages	
	Men (%)	*Women (%)*
Private, men or women only, nonsectarian	92	89
Private, coeducational, nonsectarian	92	84
Private, coeducational, "dry"	65	39
Public, coeducational, general	83	74
Public, coeducational, teachers	79	44
Public, coeducational, southern Negro	81	40

SOURCE: Robert Straus and Selden D. Bacon, *Drinking in College* (New Haven, Conn.: Yale University Press, 1953), p. 47. Reprinted by permission of the publisher.

TYPES OF DRINKERS

Persons learn in interaction with others to think and converse about alcohol in terms of what should be done with alcohol and what it will do to and for them. Drinkers can be classified in terms of the deviation from norms of drinking behavior within a culture and dependence on alcohol in the life organization of the individual. This includes the amount of alcohol consumed, the purpose and meaning of drinking as an aspect of role playing, the degree to which such drinking handicaps the individual in his interpersonal relations, and his ability to refrain from taking a drink. More specifically, the classification of types of drinkers involves the analysis of behavioral phenomena involving (1) the amount of consumption of beverage alcohol (2) in an excessive manner indicating preoccupation with alcohol which (3) interferes with the drinker's interpersonal relations.[80] One study has devised a scale to measure preoccupation with drinking so

---

[80] Harold A. Mulford and Donald E. Miller, "Drinking in Iowa. IV. Preoccupation with Alcohol and Definitions of Alcohol, Heavy Drinking and Trouble Due to Drinking," *Quarterly Journal of Studies on Alcohol,* 21:279–291 (1960). It was replicated on 1213 subjects in a later study with a high degree of similarity in the

that the differences between types of responses to the use of alcohol may be measured with Group I, representing the most highly preoccupied, and with IV, the least preoccupied, with alcohol. (See Table 11.5.)

TABLE 11.5 **The Iowa Scale of Preoccupation with Alcohol**

Item	Content of statement	Method of scoring
I	I stay intoxicated for several days at a time. I worry about not being able to get a drink when I need one. I sneak drinks when no one is looking.	Agree on any two.
II	Once I start drinking it is difficult for me to stop before I become completely intoxicated. I get intoxicated on work days. I take a drink the first thing when I get up in the morning.	Agree on any two.
III	I awaken next day not being able to remember some of the things I had done while I was drinking. I take a few quick ones before going to a party to make sure I have enough. I neglect my regular meals when I am drinking.	Agree on any two.
IV	I don't nurse my drinks; I toss them down pretty fast. I drink for the effect of alcohol with little attention to type of beverage or brand name. Liquor has less effect on me than it used to.	Agree on any two.

SOURCE: Adapted from Harold Mulford and Donald E. Miller, "Drinking in Iowa. IV. Preoccupation with Alcohol and Definitions of Alcohol, Heavy Drinking and Trouble Due to Drinking," *Quarterly Journal of Studies on Alcohol*, 21:281 (1960). The scale is cumulative in that with few exceptions respondents beginning with the bottom item agree to each item up to a point and then reject the remaining items.

There are several types of drinkers: the social or controlled drinkers, the heavy drinkers, the alcoholics, and the chronic alcoholics.

A *social or controlled drinker* drinks for reasons of sociability, conviviality, and conventionality. He may or may not like the taste and effects produced by alcohol. Above all else, he is able to desist from the use of

results. Harold A. Mulford and Donald E. Miller, "Preoccupation with Alcohol and Definitions of Alcohol: A Replication of Two Cumulative Scales," *Quarterly Journal of Studies on Alcohol*, 24:682–696 (1963).

intoxicating beverages when he chooses to do so. He drinks in a take-it-or-leave-it manner. There are two types of social drinkers, the occasional and the regular drinker. The former drinks sporadically and may have only a few drinks a year, whereas the regular social drinker may drink three or more times a week.

Not only does the *heavy drinker* make more frequent use of alcohol than the regular social drinker; in addition and occasionally, he may consume such quantities that intoxication results. Some studies have defined a heavy drinker as one who takes three or more drinks of liquor at a "sitting" more than once a week. He is sometimes, but not always, given to weekend binges or, at a party, may be drinking too heavily or just having a few more than anyone else in the place. Whatever else may be said about the excessive drinker, this type, in common with social drinkers, but with greater difficulty, may be able to curtail or completely cease drinking on his own volition. Depending upon circumstances, he may continue drinking in this manner for the rest of his life, he may later reduce the frequency and quantity of his alcohol consumption, or he may become an alcoholic. Approximately one in ten of all drinkers in a national survey reported themselves to be either heavy drinkers or as "having trouble due to drinking," or both.[81]

Alcoholics are those whose frequent and repeated drinking of alcoholic beverages is in excess of the dietary and social usages of the community and is to such an extent that it interferes with health or social or economic functioning. The alcoholic is unable to control consistently, or to stop at will, either the start of drinking or its termination once started.[82] Some of the elements in this definition are (1) reliance on alcoholic beverages, (2) repetitiveness or chronicity of the drinking in the sense that the drinking does not take place on rare occasions, (3) ill effects which derive from the drinking and not from other causes. The drinking must affect the drinker's life and not just society. These ill effects may be either definite ill-health, social or interpersonal ill effects, such as disruption of the family or ostracism which would not occur if the drinking were stopped, or economic effects, such as

---

[81] Mulford.

[82] See Mark Keller, "Alcoholism: Nature and Extent of the Problem," *The Annals,* 315:1–11 (1958) and his "Definition of Alcoholism," *Quarterly Journal of Studies on Alcohol,* 21:125–134 (1960). Some authorities feel that such definitions make it difficult for scientists to replicate research. Consequently, an operational definition of alcoholism in terms of community standards and societal reaction has been used involving frequent arrests for drunkenness, contact with social agencies, clinics, mental hospitals, or Alcoholics Anonymous. See William and Joan McCord, *Origins of Alcoholism* (Stanford, Calif.: Stanford University Press, 1960), pp. 10–11.

inability to keep a job, work efficiently, or take care of one's property as well as one could without the drinking.

Alcoholism is drinking behavior which is conceived of by others as an extreme deviation. Although the drinking of alcoholic beverages and heavy drinking are the necessary prerequisites, it should be regarded as a behavioral phenomenon and not as a biological or psychological entity. In terms of symbolic interaction, what a person does with an object is a function of what he has learned to think about it. In these terms an understanding of an alcoholic drinking behavior can come from a conceptualization and measurement of the relation between the drinking behavior of a person and "what alcohol does *to* him and *for* him and what he does *to* and *with* it." A preoccupation with alcohol scale has been developed to measure this and a close association between extent of drinking and problems has been found.[83] A scale of preoccupation with alcohol found that alcoholism probably fit in as responses to Groups I and II. (See Table 11.5.) A validation of the scale found a close association between extent of drinking and problems of various types.[84]

Chronic alcoholics characteristically have a "compulsion" to drink continually. Of particular importance are such other characteristics as solitary drinking, morning drinking, and general physical deterioration.

In the United States an estimated 3,760,000 men and 710,000 women, or a total of 4,470,000 were alcoholics in 1960.[85] This is equivalent to a rate of 4000 alcoholics per 100,000 adults age twenty and over,[86] which is equivalent to at least one in 15 adult persons who use alcohol. If corrections are made in the population for groups who do not generally have high rates of alcoholism, the rates can be extraordinarily high. If the total of alcoholics is assumed to be more than 6:5 million, a rate based on white urban non-Jewish, non-Italian, nonabstaining males age 25 years and over would prob-

---

[83] Mulford and Miller, "Preoccupation with Alcohol and Definitions of Alcohol."

[84] Mulford and Miller, "Preoccupation with Alcohol and Definitions of Alcohol."

[85] Mark Keller, "The Definition of Alcoholism and the Estimation of Its Prevalence," in Pittman and Snyder, *Society, Culture and Drinking Patterns.* Estimates of the number of alcoholics with complications (chronic alcoholism) are derived by multiplying the reported number of deaths from cirrhosis of the liver by a certain ratio, usually by three in the United States. To arrive at the estimated number of alcoholics in the United States, this figure is then usually multiplied by four.

[86] Mark Keller and Vera Efron, *Selected Statistical Tables on Alcoholic Beverages, 1859–1960, and on Alcoholism, 1930–1960* (New Brunswick, N.J.: Quarterly Journal of Studies on Alcohol, Inc., 1961).

ably involve one in five or six as alcoholics.[87] Chronic alcoholics (alcoholics with complications) were estimated to be 1,147,000 in 1953, or one fourth of the alcoholics. Of this total 971,000 were men and 176,000 were women. California and New Jersey had the highest rates, and South Carolina and Wyoming the lowest.

Although it is difficult to compare the alcoholism rates of various countries, the available figures indicate that in terms of total population the United States has the highest rate, or 4390, followed by France and Sweden. (See Table 11.6.) Rates for *chronic* alcoholism are highest in Switzerland, with the United States fourth.

During the past several decades there has been a great increase in the number of American women who drink, and although the rate of alcoholism has tended to increase there are indications that this increase has been small.[88] Several reasons appear to account for the differences between the rates of alcoholism among men and women. First, proportionately fewer women than men drink. Second, greater social stigma is attached to excessive drinking by women than by men. Third, a housewife does not face the same occupational drinking hazards that men face. Fourth, women are gen-

TABLE 11.6 **Estimated Rates of Alcoholism in Various Countries**

Country	Year	With complications (chronic alcoholism)	With and without complications (alcoholism)
Switzerland	1947	1590	2385
Chile	1946	1497	1500
France	1945	1420	2850
United States	1953	1098	4390
Australia	1947	671	1340
Sweden	1946	646	2580
Denmark	1948	487	1950
Italy	1942	476	500
Canada	1952	407	1630
Norway	1947	389	1560
Finland	1947	357	1430
England and Wales	1948	278	1100

SOURCE: Mark Keller and Vera Efron, "The Prevalence of Alcoholism," *Quarterly Journal of Studies on Alcohol,* 16:634 (1955). Reprinted by permission of the Journal.

[87] Mark Keller, "The Definition of Alcoholism and the Estimation of Its Prevalence," in Pittman and Snyder, p. 320.

[88] Edith S. Lisansky, "The Woman Alcoholic," *The Annals,* 315:73–82 (1958).

erally not as directly involved in the competitive economic struggle, and, since they have the responsibility for the care and upbringing of the children, are not as "free" to drink regularly as are men, especially in the lower classes. Fifth, a woman's self-image is not as seriously threatened. Because her role is more restricted, primarily to that of a wife and mother, failure in this role is less likely to be known to outsiders. "A man, on the other hand, can fail not only in his familial but also in his occupational role; the possibility that a man's self-image will be *publicly* deflated is greater." [89]

CHARACTERISTICS OF HEAVY AND PROBLEM DRINKERS

According to a study of a national sample of drinkers, heavy drinkers tend to be concentrated in the following social segments: males, the college-educated, the cities, the above-$5000-income group, the next-to-highest and the third-from-lowest status occupations, and the unmarried.[90] Among the religious categories the Protestants who did not specify a denomination have the highest rate of heavy drinkers, whereas the Methodist, Baptists, and Jews stand out with low rates. Drinkers over sixty have the lowest rates of both heavy drinkers and those having trouble due to drinking. Segments with the highest rates of heavy drinkers are generally the same as those having the highest rates of drinkers. A noteworthy exception to this is the Jews, who had the highest rates of drinkers of any religion, but, next to the Methodist, the lowest rates of heavy drinkers. This is consistent with the finding of the infrequency of alcoholism among the Jews.

Some idea of the characteristics of those who get into "trouble" because of alcohol use and who are likely to constitute a high proportion of alcoholics can be seen from a nation-wide survey. The most frequent difficulties involved complaints about the money spent for alcohol, followed by injury to health and by trouble with the police.

> Persons encountering trouble due to drinking occur most often among males who have had either the least or the most schooling. They also tend to be residents of the largest cities (over 75,000 population), and to be Baptists or members of "small" or unspecified Protestant denominations. They are also more frequent in the next-to-lowest income group, among divorced and unmarried persons, and in the three lowest-status and the two highest-status occupational categories. There is a hint in these findings that the drinker in a group where drinkers are less prevalent is more likely to encounter trouble because of his drinking. *This suggests the hypothesis that whether an individual's drinking leads to trouble depends as much or more upon the reactions of others as it does upon his own*

---

[89] McCord and McCord, p. 163.
[90] Mulford.

actions. On the other hand, there is the fact that males, the highest educational category, the next-to-highest if not the highest occupational categories, and the largest cities have relatively high rates of both drinkers and trouble-due-to-drinking as well as high rates of heavy drinkers.[91]

The research findings based on another national sample agreed somewhat with the other study. Heavy drinkers were found to be most likely white men and Negro women; men aged 40–49; men and women of lower status groups; men who had completed high school but not college; single, divorced or separated men and women, residents of large cities and Protestants of no established denomination, Catholics and those without a religious denomination.[92]

In a New York City study of the prevalence of alcoholism, as measured primarily by questions concerning difficulties associated with drinking, the most vulnerable subgroups in the population were found to be widowers (rate: 105 per 1000) and divorced or separated persons of both sexes (men, 68 per 1000; women, 19). Married men had a rate of 25 per 1000 and married women, 8 per 1000. Negroes had a higher rate (men, 37 per 1000; women, 20) than whites (men, 31 per 1000; women, 5) with Negro women seeming to be particularly susceptible. Except for the low rate among Jews, religion seemed to be less associated with alcoholism prevalence than was race: Roman Catholic, 24 per 1000; Jews, 2; Negro Baptist, 40; other Protestant, 20. The analysis of socioeconomic variables revealed some concentration of alcoholics among the group with least education (none to some grade school, 33 per 1000; high school graduate, 24; college graduate, 13). In addition, the alcoholics reported lower personal earnings, poorer housing, greater occupational and residential mobility, and more chronic physical illness than adults in general.[93]

THE DEVELOPMENT OF AN ALCOHOLIC SOCIAL ROLE

Shifts from the excessive drinking to the alcoholic stage with its social and often physical deterioration, and to the chronic alcoholic state are imperceptible transitions. One is never a full-blown alcoholic after a few ex-

[91] Mulford, p. 646. Italics mine.

[92] Cahalan, Cisin, and Crossley, *op. cit.*

[93] Margaret B. Bailey, Paul W. Haberman, and Harold Alksne, "The Epidemiology of Alcoholism in an Urban Residential Area," *Quarterly Journal of Studies on Alcohol,* 26:19–40 (1965). This survey of the prevalence of alcoholism was undertaken in the Washington Heights Health District in New York City. A two-stage stratified cluster sample was drawn, and interviews were conducted among 4387 families covering 8082 persons twenty years of age and over and representing 91 percent of the eligible dwelling units.

periences with the effects of liquor, for alcoholism means more than sporadic intoxication. It implies changes in the direction of other deviant behavior, in the nature of interpersonal relations with others, in attitudes toward drinking, in social roles, and in conceptions of the self, including increasing dependence on drinking, attitudes which are at variance with those held by others and which were developed through a marginal social existence, numerous rebuffs, social isolation, and physical deterioration.

> The really significant effects of inebriation do not lie in physiology but rather in social behavior. Thus excessive drinking is conjoined with other forms of behavior which run counter to the normal expectations of the sober community: traffic accidents, sexual immorality, obscenity, brawling and disturbing the peace, destruction of property, disregard of family and occupational responsibilities, misuse of money and credit, and petty crime. In some instances alcoholism brings on, or is associated with, psychotic disturbances making the person uncontrollable and necessitating forcible constraint and incarceration.[94]

The process in the development of an alcoholic role usually extends over a period of ten to twenty years of drinking, and can be sketched by the drinking symptoms of alcoholism in a group of 252 alcoholics.[95] These alcoholics became intoxicated for the first time at a mean age of 18.3 years, and within 11 years, or at age of 29.5 they had already experienced "blackouts," or amnesia during intoxication. By 35.6 years they were engaging in morning drinking, and at 36.1 they began to drink alone on a regular basis. At 37.8 they were first protecting their supply of alcohol, and by 38.6 years were first experiencing tremors. (See Table 11.7.)

Alcoholics, on the average, reach their lowest point and conceive of themselves as having reached this lowest point in their late thirties, and after one or two decades of drinking. In the interim they have tried to change their drinking patterns; have "gone on the water wagon"; have experienced daytime drunks, "benders," or prolonged drinking sprees; have begun taking drinks in the morning; have sought to escape their environment; and have begun losing working time, jobs, and friends. They also have irrational fears, resentments, and "remorse," the latter being par-

---

[94] From *Social Pathology: A Systematic Approach to the Theory of Sociopathic Behavior* by Erwin M. Lemert, p. 340. Copyright 1951 by McGraw-Hill Book Company, Inc. Used by permission of McGraw-Hill Book Company.

[95] Harrison M. Trice and J. Richard Wahl, "A Rank Order Analysis of the Symptoms of Alcoholism," *Quarterly Journal of Studies on Alcohol*, 19:636–648 (1958). Also see E. M. Jellinek, "Phases in the Drinking History of Alcoholics," *Memoirs of the Section of Studies on Alcohol*, No. 5 (New Brunswick, N.J.: Quarterly Journal of Studies on Alcohol, Inc., 1946).

TABLE 11.7   **Symptoms and Mean Onset Ages (Years) of 13 Selected Symptoms in a Wisconsin Study Group of 252 Alcoholics, 1955**

Symptoms	Mean age
First drink for self	17.6
First intoxication	18.3
First blackout	29.5
First frequent blackouts	33.6
First morning drinking	35.6
First "benders"	36.0
First daytime bouts	35.7
First loss of control	36.0
First drinking alone	36.1
First convulsions	37.6
First protecting of supply	37.8
First tremors	38.6
First drunk on less liquor	38.4

SOURCE: Derived from Harrison M. Trice and J. Richard Wahl, "A Rank Order Analysis of the Symptoms of Alcoholism," *Quarterly Journal of Studies on Alcohol,* 19:637 (1958).

ticularly characteristic. Alcoholics then often drink alone, "protect their supply," and experience tremors.

A more detailed description of the alcoholic process can be sketched in terms of early, middle, and late stages of alcoholism.[96] Many persons, of course, do not inevitably go on to the next stage. Each stage can be divided into physical symptoms and drinking roles. There is increasing impairment of effectiveness in adult social roles associated with the family, work, and even friendship patterns.[97]

> As the alcoholic drinks more and more with other heavy drinkers, an irreversible reaction by the general community segregates him from "normal" drinkers. At such a degree of deviation, the broad cultural value of self-reliance and self-control justifies a segregation which frees him even further from effective social controls over his drinking. In short, recurrent loss of self-discipline because of drinking calls for social avoidance and systematic rejection. The exclusion process, however, now gives the alcoholic deviant roles within highly stigmatized groups and encourages him to fulfill them.[98]

---

[96] Derived from Jellinek; Marty Mann, *A Primer on Alcoholism* (New York: Holt, Rinehart and Winston, Inc., 1950), pp. 18–57; and Dinitz.

[97] For a discussion of the impact of alcoholism on marriage and on work life, see Harrison M. Trice, *Alcoholism in America* (New York: McGraw-Hill Book Company, Inc., 1966), pp. 62–79.

[98] Trice, p. 5.

Excessive Drinking Stage

In the excessive drinking stage the drinker begins to lose control over his drinking, finding it difficult to stop at one or two drinks or from going on occasional weekend drunks. Blackouts frequently begin at this stage, although generally not until the end of a hard-drinking evening. He begins to gulp drinks, and he may take a drink *before* going to a party where there undoubtedly will be drinking, or *before* an appointment at which drinking would be quite in order. He feels the necessity of having drinks at certain regular times and the need for a certain amount of time spent in drinking before dinner, regardless of the inconvenience to others. He also needs to drink before special events, and he must have a drink for "that tired feeling," or for his "nerves," or to forget his worries or troubles for a while, or to avoid depression.

Middle or Alcoholic Drinking Stage

The prealcoholic at this stage begins to have ugly hangovers, which include physical near collapse, mental remorse and self-disgust, and a terrifying self-doubt because his schemes for control of his drinking no longer work. Nausea is still rare during drinking, but it now has become a frequent morning-after experience. Blackouts are increasing, and the time of their onset grows steadily earlier. He now passes out frequently, sometimes early in the course of an event to which he had genuinely looked forward.

His growing dependence on alcohol is indicated by the fact that he no longer seems able to function well without drinks, and apparently makes little effort to do so. He is less willing to talk about drinking, especially his own. The increasing use of alcohol often masks his real feelings toward himself and his role aspirations, as it also does toward increasing feelings of isolation and of "not belonging."

At this middle stage the alcoholic promises over and over again to stop drinking, but his drinking by now is so obviously different from other people's drinking that he lies about it to prevent discovery of this difference. He gulps drinks, makes sure of having enough "under his belt" before going anywhere, even to a scheduled drinking party, and to avoid any risks he carries his own supply. At this stage the alcoholic prefers to spend the allotted span of drinking time before meals at a tavern rather than at home,[99] and he often arrives home late. He must be "well away" for any special event, he is always "dog-tired and cannot go on without something

---

[99] One study, for example, found that tavern patronage was likely to be greater among heavy drinkers. See Clark. Another study also found that at this stage of excessive drinking persons spend more hours in taverns than previously and often at various times during the day. See Simon Dinitz, Unpublished Ph.D. dissertation, University of Wisconsin, Madison, 1953.

to drink." He is generally "nervous," plagued with worries and troubles, and life seems unbearable without drinks. His almost constant depression, often about his drinking, cannot be dealt with except by drinking.

The alcoholic at this stage now adds to the accepted drinking time, he may no longer care whether friends go with him, and he may prefer to sneak off-hour drinks. He keeps a bottle in his desk or hidden at home for purely private consumption, and signs of his drinking, even actual intoxication, begin to show up at the wrong time, such as at work or at gatherings where everyone else is sober. He no longer admits to having been drunk; he says he "wasn't up to par," "had eaten something," or was "under the weather." He does not usually admit having hangovers, an admission which might lead to inquiries about how much he has been drinking, a fact which he wishes to conceal carefully.

Episodes of drunkenness occur more and more often during this middle phase of alcoholism. Weekends are often real drinking bouts, with Sundays still reserved for "straightening out," but often matching Saturday in drinking intensity. Extravagance in buying drinks and other things for people and excessive tipping are characteristic of his drinking behavior. Some persons also commit various antisocial acts, such as fighting with others, vandalism in the form of malicious destruction, and practical jokes. Then the morning drink to "get going" increases rapidly in frequency as its efficacy becomes appreciated. As drinking behavior changes and the drinker's situation becomes more difficult, he starts, "going on the wagon," something he is able to do at this stage for extended periods of time. He has a false sense of power over his alcoholism during these periods of non-drinking, but he is noticeably irritable and his family, friends, and business colleagues label him as a "difficult" person.

Later or Chronic Alcoholic Stage

At the chronic alcoholic stage it is no longer a question of merely gulping drinks, either publicly or privately; there is now a pressing physical need to get and keep a certain amount of alcohol in the system at all times. Although hangovers are not now the usual morning-after discomfort known to social drinkers, they do make themselves felt in the peculiarly difficult form known to the chronic alcoholic. If at all possible they are immediately wiped out by drinks. An added problem, however, is nausea, and the morning drinks often do not stay down. Blackouts set in, and disappear, at any time, leaving unaccountable memory blanks possibly lasting for several days. Passing out also occurs at any time, and much of the alcoholic's sleep is actually no more than this.

The major psychological symptom is now an overwhelming compulsion to drink, and the greatest difficulty of all is the inability to control drinking. Drinking is apparently completely accepted as natural and inevitable. When sober, he does not admit or discuss his drinking, drunkenness, or behavior, although there are rare outbursts, usually when half-drunk, of horror and self-disgust, as well as the expression of a tragically real desire to "be like other people." His ordinary morning hangover is not allowed to occur, for round-the-clock drinking generally prevents it. A feeling of inferiority because of his drinking now frequently appears in an extreme form, contrasting sharply with equally extreme swings toward grandiosity.

The alcoholic now drinks to live and lives to drink. The full-fledged alcoholic's eating behavior is phenomenal: he seems to many people not to eat at all, a fact which is often quite true. He now maintains an adequate supply of liquor at all times in order to be able to "sneak drinks" because of the psychological need and desire for liquor during various parts of the day and night. It is almost impossible to describe adequately the terror that getting "caught short" holds for the addict, and the lengths to which he will go to prevent what to him would be a catastrophe of the most major proportions. Ingenious methods of safeguarding an ever-present supply indicate more clearly than almost anything else the compulsive need to drink experienced by the chronic alcoholic.[100]

Drunken behavior now usually, almost inevitably, takes place at the wrong time, drinking bouts occur regardless of the time of week, month, or year, their duration depending upon the financial and physical condition of the alcoholic, from a day or so to a week or longer. Even at this late stage, however, there may be times when the alcoholic manages his drinking well. Morning drinks and solitary drinking are indices of the chronic inebriate. He needs a few sips on awakening because he feels unsteady, has a headache, or has the "shakes" or tremors. This morning drink makes him "normal," if only psychologically so, and he feels he can meet his obligations for the day. In one novel the alcoholic is described as waiting for the corner tavern to open so that he can get his morning "shot."[101] This effect, unfortunately for the alcoholic, may wear off, and he is forced to resort to his hidden stock repeatedly during the day. "He may start utilizing techniques for the ingestion of alcohol which are beyond the pale of any conceivable development in the drinking usages of his group: starting off the day with 7 or 8 ounces of gin or whiskey; spending

---

[100] To keep a supply of alcohol available alcoholics devise many original schemes for hiding their bottles from the family. Some hang bottles just outside the window below the ledge on strings, others under their pillows, under porches, in stockings, and in every other conceivable place. One informant stated that he would return in the evening with a large supply of alcohol and since his wife anticipated this, he would hide one or two bottles in a conspicuous place so that his wife would find them. The remainder he hid more securely. When his wife located the decoys she would feel relieved and he would put on a most pitiable mien. Of course, what she did not know was that several times during the course of a night, when alcoholic tremors would awaken him, he would repair to his supply and after a few drinks would be quieted down enough to go back to sleep.

[101] Charles Jackson, *The Lost Weekend* (New York: Holt, Rinehart and Winston, Inc., 1948).

4 or 5 days of the ordinary work-a-day week doing nothing but ingesting alcohol; taking alcohol in such forms as mouth-wash, canned heat preparations, vanilla extract, and so on; in addition, he may omit such practices (if they were the norm in his group) as using ice, glasses, chasers, mixes." [102]

Periods of being "on the wagon" still occur, although less often unless the patient is under treatment. Complete drunkenness is his condition most of the time, although this is not always evident, and he has great difficulty on the job. This produces another unpleasant situation, the necessity for getting money to pay for drinks; this is often difficult, and ordinary borrowing soon deteriorates into the "touch." He often watches his family sink into destitution, or leave him, without showing any feeling about it. His behavior at this time shows an almost complete loss of time sense.

In areas other than drinking there develop socially unacceptable changes in his relations with others. Their strong societal reaction to him in turn causes further drinking. "Dishonesty, excessive rationalization, avoidance, and the other deviations, once perhaps even rare in his behavior, then noticeable where alcohol was concerned, now begin to appear in the family situation or perhaps in friendship groups or on the job. Accidents, job losses, family quarrels, broken friendships, even trouble with the law may take place, not just when he is under the influence of alcohol, but even when he is not. And such occasions quite usually set off further drinking." [103]

GROUP AND SUBCULTURAL FACTORS IN ALCOHOLISM

In some societies, such as the United States, Ireland, France, and Sweden, there is marked ambivalence about alcohol usage with conflicting and coexisting values.[104] In other societies, such as Italy, Spain, and Japan, and among Jewish groups, attitudes about alcohol are permissive, that is, they have a positive attitude about the use of alcohol. The differences between permissiveness and ambivalence about alcohol seem to be related to excessive drinking and alcoholism.

Rather than seek any universal explanation of alcoholism, either in the biological constitution or the personality trait structures, one should look for a variety of social and group situations under which alcoholism develops. Excessive drinking, for example, does not itself make the alcoholic. If it is continued over a long enough time he may increasingly become involved *in difficulties which arise from the drinking itself.* He may lose his job, his friends, and his wife because of his drinking, and he may even be arrested

---

[102] Selden D. Bacon, "Alcoholics Do Not Drink," *The Annals,* 315:62 (1958).
[103] Bacon, p. 63.
[104] Pittmann, *Alcoholism,* p. 8.

and placed in jail. Drinking may become a way of getting away from problems caused by drinking. He "is involved in a circular process whereby his excessive drinking creates additional problems for him which he can only face with the aid of further excessive drinking. The condition of true alcoholism has been established." [105] The Protestant ethic appears to play a role in this, since drunkenness is regarded as a lack of moral strength, will power, and devotion to the goals of personal discipline and work. The societal reaction to drunkenness may be expressed through the husband or wife, employer, work associates, parents, in-laws, neighbors, or church members. Some support for this is the fact that persons who encounter difficulty over drinking are often found to be members of larger groups where drinking is less prevalent.[106] In particular, repeated arrests by the police and incarcerations for drunkenness actually serve to reinforce the deviancy rather than to correct it.[107] In Japan, drunkenness does not seem to provoke quite the same societal reaction. It is largely regarded as a personal matter, often with good humor by other members of society. If anything, alcohol itself is generally considered to be the offender who occasionally misbehaves rather than the one who consumes it.[108]

Group associations and cultural factors, therefore, play an important part in determining who becomes an excessive drinker and who does not. There are differences not only in the drinking customs of societies but in those of subgroups within a modern society. Subgroups differ in the way in which alcohol is used, in the extent of drinking, and in attitudes toward drunkenness. The correlation of diverse drinking patterns with alcoholism can help us to test a number of hypotheses. Some believe that frequent drinking will lead to alcoholism; yet those groups with relatively high frequency of drinking, such as the American Jews, particularly the Orthodox, and the Italian-Americans, have low rates of alcoholism.[109] Still others say that frequency of drunkenness leads to alcoholism, and yet the Aleuts, the

---

[105] Expert Committee on Mental Health, "Second Report of the Alcoholism Sub-Committee" (Technical Report No. 48; Geneva: World Health Organization, 1952).

[106] See page 437.

[107] Pittmann and Gillespie, *Alcoholism,* pp. 106–124. Also see Pittmann and Gordon, *Revolving Door,* and Earl Rubington, "The 'Revolving Door' Game," *Crime and Delinquency,* 12:332–338 (1966).

[108] Robert A. Moore, "Alcoholism in Japan," *Quarterly Journal of Studies on Alcohol,* 25:143 (1964). There are indications that social changes in Japan since World War II have resulted in increasing arrests for drunkenness, reflecting a change in public opinion and in that of administrative authorities.

[109] See Charles R. Snyder, *Alcohol and the Jews* (New York: The Free Press, 1958); and Giorgio Lolli, Emilio Serianni, Grace M. Golder, and Pierpaolo Luzzatto-Fegis, *Alcohol in Italian Culture* (New York: The Free Press, 1958).

Andean Indians, and those of the northwest coast of America, among whom drunkenness is common, appear to have little alcoholism.[110] The Camba of Bolivia drink a particularly potent drink at fiestas, where mass drunkenness takes place, but they do not drink on other occasions.[111] All drinking is communal, and drinking and drunkenness become a means of acceptance rather than rejection of the person. Among Polynesians stigma is also rare for drinking, and no guilt develops over drunkenness even though it threatens other Polynesian values of friendship patterns.[112] Even with this ambivalence there is little alcoholism.

Ullman has stressed the role of the integration of drinking behavior patterns in low rates of alcoholism.[113] If conformity to drinking standards is supported by the entire culture or subculture, there will be low rates. If the individual drinker does not know what is expected or if the expected situation varies, he is in a position of ambivalence. Therefore, "in any group or society in which the drinking customs, values and sanctions—together with the attitudes of all segments of the group or society—are well established, known to and agreed upon by all, and are consistent with the rest of the culture, the rate of alcoholism will be low." [114]

---

[110] Chandler Washburne, *Primitive Drinking: A Study of the Uses and Functions of Alcohol in Preliterate Societies* (New Haven, Conn.: College and University Press, 1961). Also see, for example, Gerald D. Berreman, "Drinking Patterns of the Aleuts," *Quarterly Journal of Studies on Alcohol,* 17:503–514 (1956); William Mangin, "Drinking among Andean Indians," *Quarterly Journal of Studies on Alcohol,* 18:55–66 (1957); Edwin M. Lemert, *Alcohol and the Northwest Coast Indians* (University of California Publications in Culture and Society, Vol. 2, No. 6; Berkeley: University of California Press, 1954); and Ozzie G. Simmons, "Drinking Patterns and Interpersonal Performance in a Peruvian Mestizo Community," *Quarterly Journal of Studies on Alcohol,* 20:103–111 (1959).

[111] Dwight B. Heath, "Drinking Patterns of the Bolivian Camba," in Pittman and Snyder, pp. 22–36.

[112] Edwin M. Lemert, "Forms and Pathology of Drinking in Three Polynesian Societies," *American Anthropologist,* 66:361–374 (1964).

[113] Albert D. Ullman, "Sociocultural Backgrounds of Alcoholism," *The Annals,* 315:48–55 (1958).

[114] Ullman, p. 50. Also see Harrison M. Trice and David J. Pittman, "Social Organization and Alcoholism: A Review of Significant Research Since 1940," *Social Problems,* 5:294–308 (1958). Among folk societies prior to contact with Western Europeans, alcoholism appears to have been infrequent. The ceremonial use of alcohol to produce mass intoxication among male adults was permitted in many folk societies but drinking for personal reasons was rare and alcoholism virtually unknown.—Donald Horton, "The Functions of Alcohol in Primitive Societies," in *Alcohol, Science and Society,* p. 157. For a general discussion of group

Drinking in a Gond village in India was found, for example, to be moderate, for it was largely associated with religious ceremonies and in social situations with a communal setting. The study concluded that where conflict is present in a society there will be aggression; where conflict is absent friendly and sociable impulses will predominate during drinking.[115] Among the West African Kofyar beer has a ritual, ceremonial, and convivial use, being used as a medium of commercial exchange. Even in the conceptions of time the terms are related to a beer brewing cycle. Drinking is always regulated within a social setting; there is no solitary drinker.[116]

There is evidence that alcoholism is associated with culture where there is conflict over its use, where children are not introduced to it early, where drinking is done outside meals, and where it is drunk for personal reasons and not as part of the ritual and ceremony or part of family living. The general pattern of drinking in the United States seems to support this, as do studies of Jewish, Irish, Italian, and French drinking patterns, which will be discussed in a section following.

Companions and Excessive Drinking

In modern society, group patterns of excessive drinking, of companions, of social class, and of religious and ethnic groups are important.

> There seems to be a good deal of evidence to the effect that many problem drinkers are "processed" into it, that is, they are encouraged by informal drinking groups to use alcohol as a way to adjust to anxiety and difficulty. Having once been conditioned by such experiences to use alcohol as a way to manage the ever-present problems of living, it is a simple step to increase its use when these problems become larger, as they do at one time or another for all of us. To this group encouragement there is frequently added the reward of group recognition. Often the early symptoms of problem drinking are given prestige in such groups. For example, the ability to "drink 'em under the table" may provide the person so characterized with the esteem of a drinking group. At the same time, it may well signal a dangerous increase in the tolerance to alcohol. Furthermore, drinking groups have a subtle "limit" beyond which they believe a drinker gets "sloppy" and disgusting. At this point the rewards and recognition previously accorded tend to become rejection. This constitutes a further

association and cultural factors, also see Edwin M. Lemert, "Alcoholism and the Sociocultural Situation," *Quarterly Journal of Studies on Alcohol,* 17:306–317 (1956).

[115] Edward I. Jay, "Religious and Convivial Uses of Alcohol in a Gond Village of Middle India," *Quarterly Journal of Studies on Alcohol,* 27:88–96 (1966).

[116] Robert Netting, "Beer as a Locus of Value among the West African Kofyar," *American Anthropologist,* 66:375–384 (1964).

anxiety that must be met by a technique already well known: more alcohol. . . .[117]

Drinking generally takes place in small groups, and within these groups drinking norms tend to develop. In fact, the isolated drinker who drinks alone in the presence of others may be regarded somewhat as a deviant.[118] More than two thirds of the drinking occasions among men, for example, in rural Finland involve groups of two to four persons.[119] Moreover, while conformity between drinking habits and drinking norms is the rule in small groups, identification with a group is a variable on the basis of which it is possible to explain an individual's norms and his behavior.[120]

The drinking norms of an individual appear to conform closely to those of age contemporaries, and particularly of friends or the marital partner.[121] These individuals appear to be more influential than the drinking partners of the parental generation in determining how people drink. Scandinavian youth, for example, drink largely in the company of others, although they also drink in their homes; when they drink in the presence of their parents, however, they drink less than with their peer group.[122] In fact, wives of alcoholics have been found to have encouraged their husbands' alcoholism.[123] Another study has reported a close relation between the development of alcoholism and the type of companion with whom the indi-

---

[117] Harrison M. Trice, "The Problem Drinker in Industry," *ILR Research* (Ithaca: New York State School of Industrial and Labor Relations, Cornell University, June 1956), II, 11. Reprinted by permission of the New York State School of Industrial and Labor Relations.

[118] Robert Sommer, "The Isolated Drinker in the Edmonton Beer Hall," *Quarterly Journal of Studies on Alcohol,* 26:95–110 (1965). In this study it was found that there was no difference in the amount of drinking by isolated and group drinkers if allowance was made for time spent in the tavern.

[119] P. Kuusi, *Alcohol Sales Experiment in Rural Finland* (Helsinki: Finnish Foundation for Alcohol Studies, 1957).

[120] Eric Allardt, "Drinking Norms and Drinking Habits," in *Drinking and Drinkers* (Helsinki: Finnish Foundation for Alcohol Studies, 1957).

[121] John L. Haer, "Drinking Patterns and the Influence of Friends and Family," *Quarterly Journal of Studies on Alcohol,* 16:178–185 (1955).

[122] Kettil Bruun and Ragnar Hauge, *Drinking Habits among Northern Youth* (Helsinki: Finnish Foundation for Alcohol Studies; Distributors: Rutgers University Center of Alcohol Studies, New Brunswick, N.J., 1963).

[123] Samuel Futterman, "Personality Trends in Wives of Alcoholics," *Journal of Psychiatric Social Work,* 23:37–41 (1953); Thelma Whalen, "Wives of Alcoholics: Four Types Observed in a Family Service Agency," *Quarterly Journal of Studies on Alcohol,* 14:632–641 (1953); and G. M. Price, "A Study of the Wives of 70 Alcoholics," *Quarterly Journal of Studies on Alcohol,* 5:620–627 (1945).

vidual associates and drinks.[124] Of twenty-eight excessive drinkers under thirty-five, nearly all belonged to social groups in which regular drinking and drunkenness were accepted and approved.

Studying the work experiences in industry of problem drinkers, Trice found that their drinking was influenced by the fellow employees with whom they drank after work. In fact, fellow workers were first to notice the problem drinkers' developing loss of control. With their drinking problem becoming greater they tended to stop drinking with their work companions and to look for those whose drinking norms were more in line with their own.[125]

Drinking plays a major part in the lives of "homeless men," those in urban shelter houses, in flophouses, and on Skid Row. A study of several thousand shelter-house men in Chicago revealed that drinking is one of the most pervasive elements of their lives and that there were comparatively few teetotalers.[126] After studying 200 homeless men, Straus found that only 7 abstained entirely, and 17 were moderate drinkers.[127] Many homeless persons become excessive drinkers but by no means all become alcoholics. In a study of 444 homeless men, 10.6 percent were found to be nondrinkers, 16.9 percent moderate drinkers, 28.0 percent "heavy controlled" drinkers, 43.2 percent heavy "uncontrolled" drinkers or alcoholics; 1.3 percent were not classified.[128]

In one study alcoholic derelicts were found to spend over 65 percent of their income on alcohol, heavy drinkers 25–65 percent, and moderate drinkers 10–40 percent. Skid Row excessive drinkers can be classified into six types: "older alcoholics," "bums," "characters," "winos," "ruby-dubs," and "lushes," the last referring to the prestige group of alcoholics.[129] Among

---

[124] Marvin Wellman, "Towards an Etiology of Alcoholism: Why Young Men Drink Too Much," *Canadian Medical Association Journal,* 73:717–719 (1955).

[125] Harrison M. Trice, "Identifying the Problem Drinker on the Job," *Personnel Magazine,* 33:527–533 (1957).

[126] Edwin H. Sutherland and Harvey Locke, *Twenty Thousand Homeless Men* (Philadelphia: J. B. Lippincott Company, 1936), p. 113.

[127] Robert Straus, "Alcohol and the Homeless Man," *Quarterly Journal of Studies on Alcohol,* 7:360–404 (1946). Also see Robert Straus, "Some Sociological Concomitants of Excessive Drinking in the Life History of the Itinerant Inebriate," *Quarterly Journal of Studies on Alcohol,* 9:1–52 (1948).

[128] Robert Straus and Raymond G. McCarthy, "Nonaddictive Pathological Drinking Patterns of Homeless Men," *Quarterly Journal of Studies on Alcohol,* 12:601–611 (1951).

[129] W. Jack Peterson and Milton A. Maxwell, "The Skid Road 'Wino,' " *Social Problems,* 5:308–316 (1958). Also see Egon Bittner, "The Police on Skid-Row: A Study of Peace Keeping," *American Sociological Review,* 32:699–716 (1967).

those alcoholics with the most prestige on Skid Row, few are solitary drinkers. There are group definitions of behavior in the sharing of alcohol and, when drunk, in protecting each other from the police. Such alcoholics share in the financing of a bottle, and in drinking from a bottle to which all have contributed: "He should drink in turn, his turn being dictated by the size of his donation, and he should take only one gulp with each round." [130] So great are the group influences on Skid Row that if an individual is to deal effectively with his alcoholism he must leave.

Group life and cultural factors play a role among "winos" studied in Seattle's Skid Row (or Road). Winos are those who habitually get drunk on wine, with a consequent unpleasant characteristic odor, and who exhibit an extremely rundown appearance. They drink wine not only because it is the cheapest but because the subculture believes it to have the longest and the most deadening effect, to kill the appetite, and to be the easiest drink to keep down. The wino has association with small groups of men with whom he does almost all his drinking. Among the most imperative mores is the obligation to share: "Winos are not isolates. Instead, they are found to live as social beings within a society of their fellows. It is a society which prescribes and provides mutual aid in meeting the problems of survival: food, drink, shelter, illness and protection. But more than that it is a society which also provides the emotional support found in the acceptance by, and the companionship of, fellow human beings." [131]

A study of a random sample of 187 chronic police case inebriates, most of them from a predominantly lower-class background, showed that their drinking occurred in small intimate groups, less than 8 percent being usually solitary drinkers.[132] The major function of these drinking groups . . . is in providing the context, social and psychological, for drinking behavior. In reality we have subcommunities of inebriates organized around one cardinal principle: drinking. The fantasies concerning the rewards of the drinking experiences are reinforced in the interaction of the members, who mutually support each other in obtaining alcohol and mutually share it." [133]

---

[130] Joan K. Jackson and Ralph Connor, "The Skid Road Alcoholic," *Quarterly Journal of Studies on Alcohol*, 14:475 (1953). Also see Donald J. Bogue, *Skid Row in American Cities* (Chicago: Community and Family Study Center, University of Chicago, 1963), pp. 272–304.

[131] Peterson and Maxwell, p. 316. "For a wino to survive as a wino he needs someone to get him something to drink when he is sick and broke. Where it would be difficult for an individual to keep enough money for liquor coming in, two or three men bumming together can usually manage to keep enough money coming in for wine." P. 312.

[132] Pittmann and Gordon. Also see Earl Rubington, "Relapse and the Chronic Drunkenness Offender," *Connecticut Review on Alcoholism*, 12:9–12 (1960).

[133] Pittmann and Gordon, p. 71.

Class Differences in Excessive Drinking

Drinking customs and attitudes toward drinking vary in terms of the class structure. Dollard has shown, for example, that in the upper classes both sexes drink a good deal, and their drinking generally does not involve a moral issue, provided it is done "properly": One is condemned in the upper classes, not for drinking, nor for drunkenness, but for antisocial acts while drunk. Fighting is taboo; aggressive behavior is heavily penalized even when expressed only in verbal assaults." [134]

The lower-upper class is said to be distinguished from the other members of the upper class by the "cocktail set." In this particular group there is more alcohol drinking in general and some excessive drinking which may result from the fact that the persons in the lower-upper class, in striving to reach the top of the social ladder, feel more insecure. The role of the host varies with the structure of the cocktail party, the composition of the guests, and the objectives of the party.[135] Cocktail parties vary in the degree to which persons "responsible" for them can influence their course. At the large urban cocktail party, for example, the host tends to be relatively powerless, for such parties most often lack formal structure. The array of guests is heterogeneous, consisting of a wide cross section of persons of varying social statuses. Lack of space forces persons into little clusters where they may offer bits of polite small talk. Other persons, whose isolation is concealed by the unstructured nature of the group, may find solace in the food and drink. Such parties as these cannot be described as purely "sociable" occasions; rather, they are often "coming-out" parties for men, products, or ideas. Thus, the socially mobile couple who would not ordinarily give such a party, because of their lack of money and experience, may find themselves in a position which demands that they preside over such an affair.

On the upper-middle rungs of the success ladder, men drink at social gatherings and for business reasons. Women generally refrain from much drinking, however, and on the whole there seems to be a neutral attitude toward the consumption of liquor. Drinking parties seem to be increasing among middle-class groups who find escape, relaxation, and release through alcohol. A study of drinking parties, as compared with nondrinking parties, revealed that they were attended by white-collar groups who, among the men, found increasing tensions in the insecurity of their status in an era of high-speed industrial and commercial activity and high-pressure sales-

---

[134] John Dollard, "Drinking Mores of the Social Classes," in *Alcohol, Science and Society*, p. 99.

[135] David Riesman, Robert J. Potter, and Jeanne Watson, "The Vanishing Host," *Human Organization*, 19:17–28 (1960).

manship.[136] Members of the lower-middle class, striving desperately for recognition and status, and, in fact, for anything which would widen the gap between them and those whom they consider lower than themselves, have strong taboos against drinking, particularly among the women, because excessive drinking is associated in their minds with the behavior of the lower classes.

According to Dollard, the lower classes, in contrast to the lower-middle class, often do not exert restraints on drinking.[137] Both men and women may consume alcoholic beverages, and many, including primarily workers for whom drinking is in the norms, come, with few exceptions, to think of the tavern as the "poor man's club." The rates for military rejections during World War II for alcoholism were greater in the lower social strata of the population.[138] A study of a working class area in Santiago, Chile, found that 30 percent of the adult males have an episode of drunkenness every weekend, twice a month, or once a month.[139]

Occupation and Excessive Drinking

Social patterns call for more immoderate drinking in certain occupational categories than in others. This view has been supported by the finding that a heavy disproportion of alcoholic psychoses are found in jobs with relatively low income and prestige, a result of the acceptance of heavy drinking as a norm in certain lower-class occupational groups.[140] On the other hand, McCord and McCord, after studying a group of 254 persons, found that middle-class Americans were significantly more prone to alcoholism than were members of the lower-lower class.[141]

Some business occupations may be often associated with frequent and heavy drinking. "Organizations often informally stimulate the belief that drinking is an important part of performing a job. Thus work histories of sales managers, purchasing agents, and international representatives of labor unions who have become alcoholics strongly suggest that their organizations tacitly approve and expect them to use alcohol to accomplish

---

[136] Duane Robinson, "Social Disorganization Reflected in Middle-Class Drinking and Dancing Recreational Patterns," *Social Forces,* 20:455–459 (1942).

[137] Dollard, pp. 99–101.

[138] R. W. Hyde and L. V. Kingsley, "Studies in Medical Sociology: The Relation of Mental Disorders to the Community Socioeconomic Level," *New England Journal of Medicine,* 231:543–548 (1944).

[139] McCarthy, *Drinking and Intoxication,* pp. 99–105.

[140] Robert E. Clark, "The Relationship of Alcoholic Psychoses Commitment Rates to Occupational Income and Occupational Prestige," *American Sociological Review,* 14:539–543 (1949).

[141] McCord and McCord, p. 41.

their purposes effectively." [142] Taking prospective customers out to dinner and having a few cocktails before the meal is often regarded as a traditional way of doing business and is provided for in the expense account. A business executive in New York City has described how his daily luncheons are usually preceded by martinis, followed by the leisurely drinking of high-balls after the luncheon.[143] In addition, important negotiations are often conducted over a drink in a bar. The executives who commute generally leave the office early enough to have two or three "for the road" before boarding the train. When they arrive home they usually find that their wives have cocktails ready, or that they have been invited out for cocktails at the home of some acquaintance. Drinking is also a common practice among salesmen who travel in groups, drinking parties in hotel rooms being a particularly relaxing way to break monotony.

Seamen are an excellent illustration of occupational heavy drinkers. Life at sea for many becomes monotonous, frustrating, and socially isolating. Seamen have limited social outlets aboard ship, and often gain the satisfactions they need by looking forward to docking at the various ports of call in order to "have a good time." Enjoying oneself in port involves a good many things, and almost invariably excessive drinking. It is no wonder, then, that the percentage of seamen who eventually become alcoholics appears high. In the traditions of their trade, some form "bottle gangs," and tend to lose their individuality in these gangs. Often men in these gangs know little about each other, sometimes nothing more than their nicknames; yet in reference to norms such as excessive drinking and sexual promiscuity they may act as one.[144] Sailors often share their pay, for example, in order to continue drinking. During World War II an Alcoholic Seamen's Club was set up along the pattern of Alcoholics Anonymous. Treatment was directed toward breaking down the social isolation of the men and redirecting their desire for importance and recognition by letting them participate in more conventional social groups.[145]

Studies among seafarers in Sweden show that chronic alcoholism is common. One study involved the analysis of all seafarers registered in Sweden, and dying in 1945–1954, 1775 of whom were Swedish and 236 foreigners. Among the group of Swedes, 3.6 percent were alcohol addicts at the time they first signed on (their median length of service was 22.3 years),

---

[142] Trice, *Alcoholism in America,* p. 79.

[143] From a personal document.

[144] Anonymous, "Alcoholism—An Occupational Disease of Seamen," *Quarterly Journal of Studies on Alcohol,* 8:498–505 (1947).

[145] R. G. Heath, "Group Psychotherapy of Alcohol Addiction," *Quarterly Journal of Studies on Alcohol,* 5:555–562 (1945).

but 18.3 percent were chronic alcoholics when they last signed on. A significant number, therefore, had become addicted after they became seamen. In addition, among those who died in the Swedish alcohol addict group, an extremely high number of them, 41.1 percent, committed suicide.[146]

It is not surprising that drinking is almost universal among migratory workers, "hoboes," and "tramps," and that drunkenness is frequent. In his classic study of this group Anderson stated:

> The only sober moments for many hobos and tramps are when they are without funds. The majority, however, are periodic drinkers who have sober periods of a week, a month or two, or even a year. These are the men who often work all summer with the avowed purpose of going to some lodging-house and living quietly during the winter, but usually they find themselves in the midst of a drunken debauch before they have been in town more than a day or two. Rarely does one meet a man among migratory workers who does not indulge in an occasional "spree"; the teetotalers are few indeed.[147]

A large percentage of chronic police-case inebriates studied by Pittman and Gordon had experience with all-male institutional living, and this experience appears to have affected their heavy drinking patterns.

> The Army, the Navy, the work camp, the railroad gang, and the lake steamer, all are rich in drinking culture. In these groups the harsh, the monotonous and the protective but controlled routines are broken by the nights, weekends and lay-offs which offer opportunities to drink. Drinking is a preoccupation and conversations at work are filled with talk of drink. The imagery and love of drinking are built up through these talks and stories. Fantasy around future drinking episodes serves the function of reducing the impact of heavy jobs in heat and cold, and of alleviating dull

---

[146] This paragraph is derived from Pittmann, "International Overview: Social and Cultural Factors in Drinking Patterns, Pathological and Nonpathological," p. 19. Also see Anders Otterland, "Alcohol and the Merchant Seafarer," Twenty-Sixth International Congress on Alcohol and Alcoholism (Stockholm: August 1–5, 1960; *Abstracts,* pp. 206–207). An Italian study, on the other hand, found that Italian seamen have less alcoholism than any other occupational group. They explain that this may be due to a highly selective hiring process. Pittman suggests that the differences between Swedish and Italian seamen may be due to the former being ambivalent about alcohol and the latter permissive. For the Italian study see G. Bonfiglio and S. Cicala, "L'alcoholismonei marittinni italiani," from Records of the Center of Studies and Research for Health and Social Welfare of Seamen, CIRM (Rome: 1963), pp. 53–65.

[147] Nels Anderson, *The Hobo: The Sociology of the Homeless Man* (Chicago: University of Chicago Press, 1923; reissued by Phoenix, 1961), pp. 134–135.

routines, sexual deprivation, and the loneliness of the all-male group. Drinking becomes a symbol of manliness and group integration.[148]

On the other hand, drinking does not appear to constitute a major problem among domestic servants. The close supervision exercised in this occupation means that a developing alcoholic is quickly noticed and dismissed from his position as a domestic servant.[149]

Religious Differences in Excessive Drinking

Differences in drinking patterns also exist among religious groups. One study, for example, revealed that 41 percent of the Protestants, 21 percent of the Catholics, and only 13 percent of the Jews abstained from drinking.[150] Studies have indicated that in spite of the fact that drinking is quite pervasive among the Jewish people, their rates for alcoholism fall far below what one would expect.[151] Only 4 percent of Jewish students in one study experienced social complications on account of their drinking; Episcopalians, 39 percent; Methodists, 50 percent; and nonaffiliates, 57 percent.[152]

In a comparative study Orthodox Jews have been found to have less drunkenness than more secular Jews, and, in general, to use alcohol differently.[153] A number of subcultural factors seem to explain the low alcoholism rates for Orthodox Jews, among whom wine drinking is almost universal, since nearly all occasions, such as births, deaths, confirmations, and religious holidays, require it both by prescription and by tradition. Thus the Orthodox Jew becomes used to alcohol in moderation. He starts to use alcohol in childhood, later drinks with great frequency, but largely in a ritualistic context. Early socialization in the use of alcohol and ceremonial drinking is not as common among non-Orthodox Jews, who therefore use alcohol in less moderation. Patterns of Orthodox drinking and their ritualistic associations are further supported by a normative structure of ideas of drunkenness as a gentile vice. The strength of the taboo among Orthodox

---

[148] Pittmann and Gordon, p. 67.

[149] Robert Straus and Miriam Winterbottom, "Drinking Patterns of an Occupational Group: Domestic Servants," *Quarterly Journal of Studies on Alcohol,* 10:441–460 (1949).

[150] John W. Riley and Charles F. Marden, "The Social Pattern of Alcoholic Drinking," *Quarterly Journal of Studies on Alcohol,* 8:265–273 (1947).

[151] Charles R. Snyder, *Alcohol and the Jews* (New York: The Free Press, 1958); and Robert F. Bales, "Cultural Differences in Rates of Alcoholism," *Quarterly Journal of Studies on Alcohol,* 6:480–500 (1946).

[152] Jerome H. Skolnick, "Religious Affiliation and Drinking Behavior," *Quarterly Journal of Studies on Alcohol,* 19:452–470 (1958).

[153] Snyder, Chap. 6.

Jews against conspicuous or excessive drinking can be seen from an old folk saying sometimes heard: "Drunk he is, drink he must, because he is a gentile."

> Through the internalization of ideas and sentiments associated with Jewishness and the Jewish situation, and ideas of sobriety as a Jewish virtue, drunkenness as a Gentile vice, Jews bring to the drinking situation powerful moral sentiments and anxieties counter to intoxication. That these factors do not derive from the specific experience of drinking does not preclude their being a part of the normative orientation toward the act of drinking itself. We might say, then, that through the ceremonial use of beverage alcohol religious Jews learn how to drink in a controlled manner; but through constant reference to the hedonism of outsiders, in association with a broader pattern of religious and ethnocentric ideas and sentiments, Jews also learn how not to drink.[154]

The implications of these findings are great, as Snyder has suggested:

> More generally, the findings of this study indicate that the problems of alcohol which beset American society cannot be understood apart from a consideration of the broader sociocultural matrix in which drinking occurs. Drinking itself is obviously not the exclusive cause of these problems since Orthodox Jews clearly demonstrate that virtually every member of a group can be exposed to drinking alcoholic beverages with negligible departure from a norm of sobriety and without the emergence of drinking pathologies such as alcoholism. Still more important, these findings suggest that the emergence of drinking pathologies where drinking is prevalent cannot be explained by exclusive reference to individual psychology or to a mysterious "craving" for alcohol presumed to be physiologically determined. The possible role of psychophysical processes is not denied but social and cultural phenomena, especially those related to normative or cultural traditions regarding drinking, appear to be essential for the emergence of these pathologies. Where drinking is an integral part of the socialization process, where it is interrelated with the central moral symbolism and is repeatedly practiced in the rites of a group, the phenomenon of alcoholism is conspicuous by its absence. Norms of sobriety can be effectively sustained under these circumstances even though the drinking is extensive. Where institutional conflicts disrupt traditional patterns in which drinking is integrated, where drinking is dissociated from the normal process of socialization, where drinking is relegated to social contexts which are disconnected from or in opposition to the core moral values and where it is used for individual purposes, pathologies such as alcoholism may be expected to increase.[155]

---

[154] Snyder, p. 182.

[155] Snyder, p. 202. Reprinted by permission. Also see Charles R. Snyder, "Inebriety, Alcoholism, and Anomie," in Marshall B. Clinard, ed., *Anomie and*

In a limited study Methodists were found largely to disapprove of the use of alcohol and this fact predisposed those who drank, because of their childhood learning about the consequences of drinking, to show greater problems than did either Jews or Episcopalians.[156] Most of their drinking paralleled drinking among the Irish, who have high rates of alcoholism and whose drinking is done in the company of other males in commercial establishments. "The interpretation given to this finding is that abstinence teachings, by associating drinking with intemperance, inadvertently encourage intemperance in those students of abstinence background who disregard the injunction not to drink. However, frequent religious participation, even among students who drink, seems to diminish social complications." [157]

Ethnic Differences in Excessive Drinking

The extent and differences in drinking patterns of various ethnic groups are so pronounced that some people believe they have a biological rather than a cultural origin. The Irish, for example, have long been associated with traditions of excessive drinking. Studies indicate that their rates of chronic inebriety probably exceed those of any other single ethnic group.[158] The prevalence of the drinking habits in this group cannot be attributed, however, to any biological basis. Irish men drink because their culture permits drinking, particularly whiskey, probably more than many other ethnic groups permit it, although alcohol is not used in this group extensively for ceremonial purposes. After an examination of differences in Irish and Jewish rates of public drinking, one writer has suggested this as one of the chief reasons for the difference in the two groups.[159]

Bales has suggested that the explanation for the high rate of alcoholism among the Irish can be traced to a number of other factors.[160] In the 1840s the Irish farmer lived a marginal existence, the sexes were strictly separated, and because of economic conditions it was difficult to marry. The "older"

Deviant Behavior (New York: The Free Press, 1964), pp. 189–213; and Charles R. Snyder, "Culture and Jewish Sobriety: The Ingroup-Outgroup Factor," in Pittmann and Snyder, pp. 188–225.

[156] Skolnick.

[157] Skolnick, p. 470.

[158] William and Joan McCord, with Jon Gudeman, "Some Current Theories of Alcoholism: A Longitudinal Evaluation," *Quarterly Journal of Studies on Alcohol,* 20:746 (1959).

[159] D. D. Glad, "Attitudes and Experiences of American-Jewish and American-Irish Male Youth as Related to Differences in Adult Rates of Inebriety," *Quarterly Journal of Studies on Alcohol,* 8:452 (1947).

[160] Bales.

young men were expected to spend their spare time with others drinking in the tavern. When relatives met in the tavern it was a matter of obligation to "stand" a drink for the others, who then had to reciprocate. The tee-totaler was a suspicious character because he was not one of the "boys" in his drinking. Some of these drinking patterns have been carried on by immigrants who have left Ireland.

Italians in Italy have always had a tradition of using wine with their meals. Despite their extensive use of alcohol, the Italians have a low incidence of alcoholism.[161] In fact, the rate in the United States is eight times as great. Although the rate of alcoholism is also low among Italian-Americans, it appears to be higher than in Italy, even though the total consumption of alcoholic beverages was higher among the Italians. This was the problem of a unique joint research project on the use of alcohol in Italian culture among Italians and among first-, second-, and third-generation Italian-Americans conducted by the University of Rome and Yale University. In Italy milk is regarded primarily as a drink for children, whereas wine is for adults. Italians regard wine as healthful and as part of their tradition. Of 1459 adults interviewed in Italy, 79 percent said it was healthful to drink wine with the meals, 1 percent claimed it was not, and only one person expressed the fear that wine would lead to alcoholism.[162] Such an attitude appears, in part, to prevent alcoholic excesses and addiction. Most Italians first drink wine early in life, both men and women drink wine, and there is little opposition to the drinking of wine by young persons. Drinking is generally done in connection with meals. An interesting fact is that single persons appear to drink less wine, and "it would appear, therefore, that the use of wine—linked as it is with food events—loses much of its appeal for the unattached individual in the Italian culture, where alcoholic beverages are seldom used for 'escape' purposes."[163]

These drinking patterns were, in general, found to be present among Italian-Americans, although they are undergoing change. For example, 70 percent of Italian men, and 94 percent of the women, did all their drinking

---

[161] It has been suggested that the low rate of alcoholism in Georgia of the Soviet Union represents a situation similar to that of the Italian attitudes toward drinking and special customs connected with the use of wine. Vera Efron, "Notes from a Visit to the Soviet Union: Treatments and Studies of Alcoholism; Education about Alcohol; Drinking in Georgia," *Quarterly Journal of Studies on Alcohol,* 26:654–665 (1965). Also see Vera Efron, "The Soviet Approach to Alcoholism," *Social Problems,* 7:307–315 (1960).

[162] Lolli, *et al.* Also see Pierpaolo Luzzatto-Fegis and Giorgio Lolli, "The Use of Milk and Wine in Italy," *Quarterly Journal of Studies on Alcohol,* 18:355–381 (1957).

[163] Lolli, *et al.,* p. 79.

at mealtimes, in comparison with 7 percent of the first-generation Italian-American men and 16 percent of the women, and 4 percent of the men and 11 percent of the women in the second generation. All these factors, particularly drinking with the meals, tend to "inoculate" the Italian and Italian-Americans from alcoholism, and as they decline in importance alcoholism increases. Neither the cocktail hour, nor drinking after meals is a feature of Italian drinking; moreover, drinking with meals constitutes a safety factor for intoxication, as pointed out by Lolli:

> The relationship between the beverage used and the frequency of episodes of intoxication is outstanding. The occurrence of such episodes is lowest among the Italians, who drink almost exclusively table wine. The frequency increases among the first-generation Italian-Americans, who begin to drink more of other beverages. It is highest in the succeeding generations, who move still further away from the ancestral drinking customs and, presumably, the associated behaviors, attitudes and controls.[164]

Although persons in both Italy and France drink about the same large quantites of alcohol each day (900 cc to 1000 cc), the rates of alcoholism are much greater in France; in fact, this country has one of the highest rates of alcoholism in the world.[165] This difference can be explained by a number of factors: (1) Nearly all the alcoholic intake in Italy is wine consumed at meal-time. In France a substantial amount of the alcohol intake is in the form of distilled spirits and aperitifs between and after meals. In fact, in France, alcoholism rates are much lower in those parts of the country where wine is largely consumed and in connection with meals. (2) Exposure to alcohol in childhood is viewed quite differently. The French have rigid parental attitudes either favoring or opposing drinking among children. Nearly all Italians accept drinking of wine in childhood as a "natural" part of a child's development. (3) The Italians have a much lower "safe limit" for amounts of alcohol consumption than the French and tend to view drunkenness as a personal and family disgrace. (4) The French view drinking, particularly of copious quantities, as associated with virility, while the Italians do not. Alcoholism is high in Switzerland, and a study of Swiss alcoholics found that they had characteristics more similar to the drinking patterns of the French than of the Italians.[166]

---

[164] Lolli, *et al.*, p. 85.

[165] Roland Sadoun, Giorgio Lolli, and Milton Silverman, *Drinking in French Culture* (New Brunswick, N.J.: Rutgers Center of Alcohol Studies, 1965).

[166] Pierre Devrient and Giorgio Lolli, "Choice of Alcoholic Beverages among 240 Alcoholics in Switzerland," *Quarterly Journal of Studies on Alcohol*, 23:459–467 (1962). In order to reduce alcoholism in the United States, a five-year study by the Cooperative Commission on the Study of Alcoholism under a grant from the

Alcoholic beverages are widely used among the Chinese of New York City, but the incidence of excessive drinking or alcoholism is low.[167] The social control exercised by the Cantonese or Chinese subcultural pattern is such that alcohol is largely consumed as a part of social functions, public drunkenness is disapproved, and children are educated to observe these patterns. Unlike the Jews, frequent mild intoxication may occur, but statistics show low prevalence of alcoholism among Chinese-Americans.

Excessive drinking is a serious problem among Indians, and arrests for drunkenness generally seem greatly to exceed those for other groups. Drunkenness seems to be associated with many criminal acts, and the rate of arrests for alcohol-related crimes among Indians is twelve times greater than the national average.[168] The pattern of excessive drinking is not racially determined, for there is no evidence that the Indian is inherently more susceptible to intoxication or to alcoholism. The cause is a combination of historical, social, and cultural factors.[169] Most Indians had little familiarity with the use of alcohol before the coming of the white man. Later, federal laws were enacted, beginning with a rather general law in 1802 and a final, more specific one in 1893 and again in 1938, which made it an offense punishable by imprisonment and heavy fine to serve any intoxicants to an Indian. These laws were not repealed until 1953. Among the Navaho, as among most Indian tribes, when alcohol was illegal it was usually purchased secretly, at exorbitant prices, and the bottle was usually consumed by small groups until it was finished.[170]

Subcultural factors in the wide group use of alcohol as a form of recreation have contributed to high rates of drunkenness. "Many instances

---

National Institute of Mental Health recommended in 1967 a national policy of promoting drinking in a family setting and the reduction of the legal age for buying and public drinking of alcoholic beverages to 18 throughout the country. *The New York Times,* October 12, 1967.

[167] Milton L. Barnett, "Alcoholism in the Cantonese of New York City: An Anthropological Study," in Oskar Diethelm, ed., *Etiology of Chronic Alcoholism* (Springfield, Ill.: Charles C Thomas, Publisher, 1955), pp. 179–227. Also see Merrill Moore, "Chinese Wine: Some Notes on Its Social Use," *Quarterly Journal of Studies on Alcohol,* 9:270–279 (1948).

[168] Omer Stewart, "Questions Regarding American Indian Criminality," *Human Organization,* 23:61–66 (Spring 1964).

[169] Edward P. Dozier, "Problem Drinking among American Indians: The Role of Socio-cultural Deprivation," *Quarterly Journal of Studies on Alcohol,* 27:72–87 (1966). Beginning with 1960 this journal has contained several articles on drinking among Indians.

[170] Dwight B. Heath, "Prohibition and Post-Repeal Drinking Patterns among the Navaho," *Quarterly Journal of Studies on Alcohol,* 25:119–135 (1964).

of American Indian drinking behavior judged pathological by the dominant American society may not be so considered by the Indians who engage in it. Indeed, they may think of their drinking bouts as simply a form of recreation and relaxation and have no desire to eliminate such behavior." [171] Because of their minority status, it is probable that Indians are more likely than others to be arrested for drunkenness. Lemert has recently emphasized the need to determine whether a given situation is pathological in the view of the group studied or in the view of the dominant society of which the group is a part or of both groups. He cites a case from Polynesia which illustrates the point appropriately.

> [In cases of pathology] care must be taken to specify whose value hierarchies are being invoked when the costs of drinking are assessed.
>
> French authorities . . . are convinced that drinking is a very serious problem among their Polynesian peoples, primarily because they see earnings of the native population going for heavy weekend drinking and periodic, fete-type indulgence instead of into housing and other forms of material self-improvement. . . . Yet it is doubtful that Tahitians see their expenditures for liquor as sacrifices in the same sense as do the French, largely because as yet their commitment to material values is still quite tenuous. . . . Thus when one informant was asked why his fellows use their money for liquor instead of better housing and furniture, he laughed and said the Tahitian is likely to say: "If I spend money for those things I won't have any for beer and wine." [172]

Despite the fact that most studies suggest that alcoholism, as well as problem-drinking rates, is generally higher for American Negroes than for whites, there have been relatively few studies of drinking patterns and alcoholism among American Negroes.[173] There seems to be no question that Negro women have a higher rate of alcoholism, at least those hospitalized, than do white women. When controlled for education, hospitalization rates are three to six times greater, depending upon the level.[174] That this differ-

---

[171] Dozier, p. 83.

[172] Edwin M. Lemert, "Forms and Pathology of Drinking in Three Polynesian Societies," in Edwin M. Lemert, *Human Deviance, Social Problems, and Social Control,* © 1967. Reprinted by permission of Prentice-Hall, Inc., Englewood Cliffs, N.J., p. 180.

[173] For a survey of the literature see Muriel W. Sterne, "Drinking Patterns and Alcoholism among American Negroes," in Pittman, *Alcoholism,* pp. 71–74.

[174] See, for example, B. Z. Locke and H. J. Duvall, "Alcoholism among Admissions to Psychiatric Facilities," *Quarterly Journal of Studies on Alcohol,* 26:521–534 (1965); and B. Z. Locke, M. Kramer, and B. Pasamanick, "Alcoholic Psychoses among First Admissions to Public Mental Hospitals in Ohio," *Quarterly Journal of Studies on Alcohol,* 21:457–474 (1960).

ence is a real one is indicated by the fact that similar differences are found when inpatient and outpatient cases are considered.[175] Other studies have shown that the rates of arrest, conviction, or incarceration for public intoxication tends to be higher for Negroes than for whites.[176]

Earlier descriptions of alcohol use in southern Negro rural areas where most Negroes lived indicate that the use of alcohol was linked to

> 1. home celebrations on Christmas day; 2. the observance of Saturday as a day for marketing, idling, and drinking; and 3. where prohibition (most of the agricultural South was under local prohibition at this time) was not in effect, public social gatherings, camp meetings, and other religious gatherings. Intoxication is viewed permissively. The normative orientation toward drinking is distinctly convivial, with much treating and hilarity. Men form stable drinking groups of about six persons who divide a quart bottle of whiskey. The impression of conviviality is reinforced by distinctions made with respect to intoxication. Deep intoxication is not sought: "many get 'pretty full' but not many 'down drunk.' " [177]

Pronounced differences among lower-, middle-, and upper-class Negroes in alcohol-drinking behavior make it difficult to generalize about Negroes as a group. "The clearest variations in alcohol use by socio-economic status occur in the choice of public vs. private locales for drinking, elaboration of the drinking ritual and attention to the symbolic value of alcoholic beverages, and permissible behavior accompanying drinking—especially in regard to aggression." [178] A study of drinking in a South Carolina mill town of 4000, with a population one fourth Negro, found:

> Alcohol is pervasive in terms of the numbers of males and lower status females who use it, and in terms of its association with recreation, nonmarital sex behavior, and touchy behavior. Intoxication generally is not sanctioned negatively. Alcohol use is one of the axes along which social status is measured in a community whose access to individual recognition and achievement in the larger society is severely limited. Its use reflects some of the important values in the subculture, self-expression and self-indulgence or release. It has utilitarian functions for the personality in a subculture and society generating acute adjustment needs with some frequency. The network of sharing relationships in drinking groups functions

---

[175] M. B. Bailey, P. W. Haberman, and H. Alksne, "The Epidemiology of Alcoholism in an Urban Residential Area," *Quarterly Journal of Studies on Alcohol,* 26:19–40 (1965).

[176] Sterne, pp. 74–77. How much of this represents differences in societal reaction rather than actual behavior cannot be determined.

[177] Sterne, pp. 78–79.

[178] Sterne, p. 98.

to increase social integration; at the same time alcohol use abets social disruption by accentuating tendencies toward touchy behavior and aggression. Finally, in a community where few occupational opportunities are open to Negroes, the distribution of alcoholic beverages either through tavern operation or through bootlegging is a significant means of employment.[179]

Drinking in Negro slum areas of large urban communities, both in the North and in the South, appears to be extensive. Middle- and upper-class Negroes, either abstainers or more restrained in their drinking behavior, tend to regard lower-class drinking and the drunkenness and fighting associated with it as reflecting on the Negro.

SUMMARY

The problems related to the consumption of alcohol, the role of the tavern, and the alcoholic in modern society are far from unique to any culture and age. Today there are extensive value conflicts over the use of alcohol as well as over taverns. Alcohol acts physiologically as a depressant. The effect of alcohol depends on the rate at which it is absorbed, the kind of beverage consumed and the proportion of alcohol it contains, the amount and type of food eaten, and certain individual physiological differences. In moderate quantities alcohol does not appear to be harmful, but larger quantities can produce drunkenness.

Drinking is a social phenomenon. Group associations determine the kind of beverage and the amount used, the circumstances under which drinking takes place, the time of drinking, and the individual's as well as others', attitudes toward drinking. Most taverns are of the neighborhood type, and their chief functions appear to be to provide social relationships, recreation, and a place to talk over common problems.

Approximately two thirds of the adult population of the United States drink alcoholic beverages. The proportion who drink varies by sex, age, social class, education, religion, and type of community.

Those who drink can be classified in terms of deviations from norms of drinking behavior within a culture or subculture, and their dependence on alcohol in their life organization. This dependence includes the purpose and meaning of drinking, the degree to which such drinking handicaps the individual in his interpersonal relations, and his ability to refrain from taking a drink. On this basis drinkers can be classified as social or controlled drinkers, heavy drinkers, alcoholics, and chronic alcoholics.

---

[179] H. Lewis, *Blackways of Kent* (Chapel Hill: University of North Carolina Press, 1955), as reported in Sterne, pp. 88–89.

The excessive use of alcohol seems to be learned from others. Group associations and cultural factors are important in determining who will become excessive drinkers and who will not. The drinking norms of the individual appear to be associated with those of his associates. They learn to drink excessively because of the type of drinking behavior of their companions, social class, occupation, or ethnic status. Involvement in difficulties because of their excessive drinking leads some into a circular process of further excessive drinking.

SELECTED READINGS

Cavan, Sherri. *Liquor License: An Ethnography of Bar Behavior*. Chicago: Aldine Publishing Company, 1966. This study of the public drinking place includes types and patterns of behavior.

Clinard, Marshall B. "The Public Drinking House and Society," in David J. Pittman and Charles R. Snyder, eds., *Alcohol, Culture and Drinking Patterns*. New York: John Wiley & Sons, Inc., 1962. A comprehensive discussion of the tavern or public drinking house from the standpoint of the value conflicts involved, types of taverns, functions of taverns, and the relation of the tavern to alcoholism and delinquency.

Lolli, Giorgio, Emilio Serianni, Grace M. Golder, and Pierpaolo Luzzatto-Fegis. *Alcohol in Italian Culture*. New York: The Free Press, 1958. A comparative study of drinking patterns and attitudes of Italians in Italy and Americans of Italian extraction, based on interviews and dietary diaries. An analysis of the place of alcoholic beverages in the total pattern of eating and drinking behavior in Italian culture.

McCarthy, Raymond G., ed. *Drinking and Intoxication*. New York: The Free Press, 1959. A comprehensive selection of materials on historical and contemporary drinking customs, attitudes toward drinking, and methods of control of drunkenness from earliest times to the present.

Patrick, Clarence H. *Alcohol, Culture and Society*. Durham, N.C.: Duke University Press, 1952. A study of alcohol in a cultural context, including the influence of society on the use of alcohol and its effects on society.

Pittmann, David, J., ed. *Alcoholism*. New York: Harper & Row, Publishers, 1967. A collection of articles that place alcoholism in a cross-cultural perspective and discuss physical and psychosocial orientation and sociocultural aspects.

————, and C. Wayne Gordon. *Revolving Door*. New York: The Free Press, 1958. An intensive, systematic study of the men who are repeatedly jailed for drunkenness. Analyzes and interprets the family backgrounds, childhood and adolescent experiences, and criminal careers of men caught up in the circular process of arrest, imprisonment, and rearrest on charges related to public intoxication. Illustrated with cases.

————, and Charles R. Snyder, eds. *Alcohol, Culture and Drinking Patterns*. New York: John Wiley & Sons, Inc., 1962. A collection of articles, many of them original, by sociologists on various aspects of the use of alcohol, dealing with drinking in anthropological perspective; social structure, subcultures and drinking patterns and the genesis and patterning of alcoholics.

Sadoun, Roland, Giorgio, Lolli, and Milton Silverman. *Drinking in French Culture*. New Brunswick, N.J.: Rutgers Center of Alcohol Studies, 1965. A detailed study of French drinking patterns and a comparison with those of Italy.

Snyder, Charles R. *Alcohol and the Jews*. New York: The Free Press, 1958. A study of the influence of cultural norms on patterns of drinking behavior. Based on interviews with a random sample of adult Jewish men and on the results of a questionnaire study of the drinking practices of college students of various religious denominations.

Symes, Leonard. "Personality Characteristics and the Alcoholic: A Critique of Current Studies," *Quarterly Journal of Studies on Alcohol*, 18:288–302 (1957). This follow-up of an earlier survey by Sutherland and Tordella covers all studies from 1949 to 1956 which tried to differentiate the personality traits of alcoholics from nonalcoholics. Reaches a largely negative conclusion about the relationship.

Trice, Harrison M. *Alcoholism in America*. New York: McGraw-Hill Book Company, Inc., 1966. A comprehensive analysis of alcoholism, particularly in relation to its impact on family and work life. Compares alcoholism and opiate addiction.

12

The Functional
Mental Disorders

Mental disorders have long constituted a vast, mysterious, and challenging frontier in contemporary society. The basis of mental illness and the appropriate methods of preventing it are still frequently elusive. Only within recent times has society come to regard the mentally disturbed person as a "sick person." Yet this recognition has not completely eliminated the societal attitude of rejection of the mentally ill. Indeed, rejection is manifested in many ways, including often the disposal of society's "insane" to the "human dumping grounds" found in many state mental hospitals.[1] This situation has arisen largely from the different attitudes society holds toward physical as opposed to mental disorder. Toward the physically disordered there is generally a societal attitude of sympathy, perhaps because the features of physical disorders can be seen, felt, or objectively observed. On the other hand, mental disorders, which involve intangibles, such as feelings and ideas which are often incomprehensible to other persons, are ordinarily reacted to with fear, revulsion, and ridicule.

---

[1] *Action for Mental Health,* The Final Report of the Joint Commission on Mental Illness and Health (New York: Basic Books, Inc., 1961), pp. 56–63. "Insane" and "insanity" are legal concepts.

Despite this societal pattern of rejection toward the mentally ill, frank recognition of the problem of mental disorders constitutes the first step in its control.[2]

There are increasing scientific interest and research on mental disorders on the part of sociologists and anthropologists as well as psychiatrists and psychologists. The role which social and cultural factors play in the development of such disorders is of particular interest. Of concern also have been the effects of society on mental disorder, including the concepts of mental disorder held by society, the status and role of the mentally ill, and the changing nature of treatment.

CONVENTIONAL TYPES OF MENTAL DISORDERS

Conventionally, mental disorder has been classified by psychiatrists as the neuroses and the psychoses. Neuroses are considered to be the mildest and the most common type. Among psychotics, thoughts, feelings, expressions, beliefs, and acting deviate more markedly from approved norms. Psychotic behavior, as contrasted with neurotic, is more often characterized by a loss of contact with reality. Furthermore, the psychotic's ability to communicate intelligently with others may be partially or completely interrupted, a factor which is not generally characteristic of the neurotic. The essential feature of the neuroses is that they involve behaviors which deviate less markedly from societal norms than is true of the psychoses. They are therefore regarded as "less serious," and generally there is greater societal tolerance for them.[3]

Actually, it is much easier to recognize the behavior which is labeled psychotic because the deviation from norms is often more pronounced and visible. The so-called neuroses are much harder to designate and label. Role distortions or role inadequacies are not generally apparent. Consequently, among psychiatrists and others there is little agreement on the definition of a neurosis. This fact is shown by estimates of the number of neurotics in the general population. Some estimate as high as 40 percent; others, about 5 percent. Some have gone so far as to suggest that nearly everyone in a modern urban society is neurotic. Obviously, the concept becomes almost meaningless when used in this way.

---

[2] *Action for Mental Health.* Also see Ernest M. Gruenberg and Seymour S. Bellin, "The Impact of Mental Disease on Society," in Alexander H. Leighton, John A. Clausen, and Robert N. Wilson, eds., *Explorations in Social Psychiatry* (New York: Basic Books, Inc., 1957), pp. 341–364.

[3] *Action for Mental Health,* Chap. 3.

Organic Mental Disorders

According to *conventional classification of psychiatry,* there are two types of mental disorders: those having an organic basis, and those having a nonorganic, or functional, basis. Organic types of mental disorders are usually linked to some germ, to a brain injury, to other physiological disorder, or, in certain rare types of mental disorder, possibly to some hereditary factors. The three most important organic mental disorders are the arteriosclerotic senile psychoses, paresis, and the alcoholic psychoses, none of which is really hereditary.

The *senile or old-age psychoses,* which are generally classified as organic on the assumption that they are produced by certain physiological processes of aging, account for about a fourth of all admissions to state hospitals. Some of these cases are arteriosclerotic and result from changes in the circulatory system, but others are not. Senile psychoses are characterized by a loss of memory, particularly for recent events, inability to concentrate, or certain delusional thoughts. There is increasing evidence that many of the psychoses due to aging are the product of nonorganic conditions arising from interpersonal relations, such as social isolation and loss of status. The psychoses of old age will be discussed in greater detail in Chapter 15, which deals with sociological aspects of aging, pages 583–587.

A study of 1200 institutionalized and noninstitutionalized elderly persons found that lifelong extensive isolation is not necessarily conducive to the kinds of mental disorder that result in psychiatric treatment in old age but that lifelong marginal social adjustment may be conducive to the development of such disorder.[4] Late-developing isolation is apparently linked with mental disorder but is of no greater significance among those with psychogenic disorders than among those with organic disorders and may be a consequence rather than a cause of mental illness in the elderly. Finally, physical illness may be the critical antecedent to both isolation and mental illness.

Paresis, or dementia paralytica, is caused by syphilis, and accounts for about 4 percent of all state hospital admissions. This disorder begins at least ten years after the initial syphilitic infection, and there is often progressive degeneration in the brain of untreated patients. Although the symptoms of a paretic may not be different from those of many functional psychoses, the paretic may be relatively easy to diagnose through positive Wassermann and Kahn reactions. There may also be tremors, convulsive seizures, and a lack of coordination in bodily movements. The mental symptoms are often

---

[4] Margaret Fiske Lowenthal, "Social Isolation and Mental Illness in Old Age," *American Sociological Review,* 29:54–70 (1964).

a complete alteration in the personality traits: "The neat well-dressed individual becomes careless and slovenly; the efficient businessman shows poor judgment in the office; the moral, upright man suddenly becomes degraded." [5] Eventually memory about time and places may become defective and in some cases there is depression. As a rule, paretics do not live long. The elimination of syphilis would end paresis, and great advances have been made toward this goal. Today a number of factors have reduced not only the incidence of syphilis but, particularly, that of paresis. Widespread public health methods, including education, have reduced the incidence of syphilis; and drugs, including formerly arsenic and now the more effective antibiotics, which work on the nervous system, have helped to cure syphilis and thus prevent paresis.

The *psychoses resulting from alcoholism* are not as definitely organic as paresis, although they are usually classified as the same type. Relatively few alcoholics develop psychoses. There is some doubt as to how much mental disorder is organically produced by the alcohol and what proportion is the result of certain sociopsychological conditions.[6] The prolonged existence of chronic alcoholism, with its vitamin and nutritional deficiencies, may in some cases produce such deterioration in physical and psychological behavior that alcoholic psychoses may result. Some patients become rigid and develop terrifying hallucinations, others have tremors which are often referred to as delirium tremens or "D.T.'s," and still others show general progressive deterioration. Not all cases of D.T.'s indicate a psychosis, however, for many of these symptoms may be short-lived and without marked personality changes.

Functional or Nonorganic Mental Disorders

The disorders of primary interest to the social scientist are the functional disorders, those without an organic basis, which have been conventionally labeled as the neuroses, schizophrenia, the manic depressive psychoses, and paranoia. These functional disorders will be referred to as "mental disorder" in the sections which follow. The discussion will not include the organic psychoses.

According to many psychiatrists, the functional or nonorganic mental disorders "function" to adjust the individual to his particular difficulties; hence the term *functional*. The idea that such mental disorders are necessarily an adaptation to stress is difficult to prove, although in many cases this adaptation may play an important part. As yet no one has been able

---

[5] Roy M. Dorcus and G. W. Shaffer, *Textbook of Abnormal Psychology* (3d ed.; Baltimore: Williams & Wilkins Company, 1945), p. 278.

[6] See Chapter 11.

to demonstrate conclusively that functional disorders result from heredity, physiological disorders, or other organic deficiency. Although there have been reports of organic deficiencies in some cases, most leading authorities in psychiatry today agree that nothing of a universal nature has so far been established.

Such mental disorders should be regarded as a deviation from norms and can be understood only in terms of the societal reaction to certain behavior. What may be regarded as mental disorder—that is, beyond the tolerance limit of eccentricity—is therefore not necessarily the same from one culture to another.

Such a view conflicts with the general psychiatric tendency, which regards such behavior as clinical entities, as constituting a type of "sickness" which would, presumably, be the same in all cultures.[7] Because of their medical training, psychiatrists obviously look for disease entities and think in terms of a medical diagnosis.[8] In the case of mental disorder these diagnoses have come to be known as neuroses and psychoses, and the latter in turn have been divided into schizophrenia, manic-depressive disorders, paranoia, and other entities. They have come to be regarded as real disease entities which are important to the psychiatrist, who, being a physician, assumes that this enables him to deal with the "causes" and therefore to suggest treatment of the mental disorders. Rather than being disease entities they are actually *descriptions* of certain behavior.

These diagnostic categories themselves, and the adequacy of the diagnosis by psychiatrists, have been severely criticized by many writers. As Hollingshead has written: "Currently, psychiatry does not have a standard test which researchers may use to diagnose any of the functional mental illnesses. A standardized, valid, diagnostic test would enable a researcher to determine the presence or absence of functional mental illness in individuals. Until this problem is solved, research into mental illness will continue to be hampered."[9]

Being labeled or identified as mentally ill is not a simple and direct

---

[7] For a discussion of problems in cross-cultural psychiatric diagnosis and terminology, see Charles Savage, Alexander H. Leighton, and Dorothea C. Leighton, "The Problem of Cross-Cultural Identification of Psychiatric Disorders: II," in Jane M. Murphy and Alexander H. Leighton, eds., *Approaches to Cross-Cultural Psychiatry* (Ithaca, N.Y.: Cornell University Press, 1965), pp. 21–63, and Marvin K. Opler, *Culture and Social Psychiatry* (New York: Atherton Press, 1967).

[8] For a critical discussion of the implications of medical training for psychiatric treatment, see Erving Goffman, *Asylums* (New York: Doubleday Anchor Books, 1961), pp. 320–386.

[9] August B. Hollingshead, "The Epidemiology of Schizophrenia," *American Sociological Review*, 26:10 (1961).

outcome of "mental illness symptoms" even within the context of the same culture. Since there is no chemical or physical test for diagnosing functional mental illness, the diagnosis is dependent upon the clinician's judgment, which is, in turn, affected by his conception of mental disorder, the etiological doctrine he holds, and the values and attitudes of the patient. Other factors as the age, sex, race, religion, and social status of the patient may very well also enter into the diagnostic consideration.

The lack of reliability and validity of psychiatric diagnosis has been shown in a number of studies. For example, it has been reported by Hoch that the ratio of first admissions, with a diagnosis of manic-depressive in comparison with schizophrenia, reversed itself over a five-year period in one state hospital system. He attributed this reversal to a change in personnel and policy in the hospital system, not to a shift in the distribution of disease in the population of the state.[10] This report was supplemented by Pasamanick, with findings from another hospital where from one ward to another significant differences were found in the diagnostic classifications of patients with functional psychoses.[11] For example, on one ward the diagnoses changed with the change in the ward administrator. The diagnoses had been made by residents, as well as by the ward administrator, who was a trained psychiatrist. Whereas these data were based on reports of hospitalized patients, Leighton did research in which he attempted to assess the mental status of a nonpatient group. In his study six psychiatrists were asked to read the field protocols on fifty adult white males, and were instructed to assess whether each man was mentally "ill" or "well." Fifteen were placed in an equivocal category, and five were thought to be "well," although these five men diagnosed as "well" differed for each of the six psychiatrists. In fact, one psychiatrist's five "wells" had been placed in another's "sickest" group.[12]

One of the major difficulties in using psychiatric descriptions of mental disorders is that people do not necessarily reject a person who has such characteristics. It is necessary to distinguish those who are *publicly* defined as mentally ill and those who are *psychiatrically* defined. The severity of a psychiatrically determined illness may not be the reason for the rejection by others but, rather, its social visibility. Serious psychiatrically determined symptoms may be present without social visibility or strain. A study has

---

[10] Paul H. Hoch, in "Work Conference in the Mental Disorders" (Mimeographed; New York: February 15–19, 1959), pp. 145–146.

[11] Benjamin Pasamanick, in "Work Conference in the Mental Disorders," pp. 143–145.

[12] Alexander H. Leighton, in "Work Conference in the Mental Disorders," pp. 147–148.

shown, for example, that it is the visibility with which an individual deviates from customary role expectation that causes rejection.[13] Moreover, men are rejected more strongly than are women for such deviating behavior. In the case of former mental patients it was found that it was not so much the label but this fact plus the visibility of deviating behavior.

Having stated such criticisms, one might well question the relevance of including in the following section a description of various types of mental disorder. In fact, Scheff even claims that most of their symptoms are learned from the culture and are not biological in origin.[14] In the first place, they are terms widely used by psychiatrists, who are the persons mainly responsible for the treatment of mental disorders. Second, they are terms used by others. It is therefore necessary to become familiar with such terms and their use. Again, however, it should be understood that actually these are not clear-cut entities in the sense, for example, of tuberculosis. In fact, many persons exhibit the behavior described in each type, although in all probability to a lesser degree and in a manner which does not provoke much societal reaction. Probably all persons have, to some degree, exhibited such behavior as hallucinations, phobias, persecution complexes, and emotional extremes of elation and depression. For example, everyone will remember how many times during his lifetime he has had irrational fears, daydreams, flights of idea, and disorders of memory:

> . . . sense of inferiority, sublimation, imperception, illusion, hallucinations, delusions, disorders of judgment, disturbance of the train of thought, flight of ideas, nonessential ideas and thoughts, incoherence, retardation or inhibition of thought, disorders of orientation, disturbance of consciousness, clouding of consciousness, confusion, dream states, negativism, inaccessibility, obsession, fears, phobias, disorders of attention, disorders of memory, conflict, complexes compensation, symbolization, etc.—all of these are found operating in varying degrees in minds that are considered normal, as well as in minds that are disordered to such an extent that the case is diagnosed as insanity.[15]

The Neuroses

Some neurotic symptoms can be classified as dissociated behavior and others as compulsive disorders. In all of them the societal reaction to the behavior is not as great as with the psychoses. Hysteria, amnesia, and dis-

[13] Derek L. Phillips, "Rejection of the Mentally Ill: The Influence of Behavior and Sex," *American Sociological Review*, 29:679–687 (1964).

[14] Thomas J. Scheff, *Being Mentally Ill: A Sociological Theory* (Chicago: Aldine Publishing Company, 1966).

[15] Lawrence Guy Brown, *Social Pathology* (New York: Appleton-Century-Crofts, Inc., 1946), p. 62. Used by permission of the publisher.

turbances of speech, hearing, and sight are examples of dissociated behavior. It was once thought that hysteria, which was quite common, was a peculiarly feminine disease, because women were frequently given to "swooning." In addition to hysterical fainting, there may often be facial tics or uncontrolled movements. Ingenious tests have been devised, for example, to separate the person who is hysterically blind in one eye from the truly blind.[16]

Compulsive behavior is a form of neurosis where there are "irrepressible tendencies to do, say or think something in a particular way which persist in spite of strong contrary tendencies. In this situation anxiety reactions develop and their periodically rising intensity leads to indulgence, followed by temporary relief." [17] This behavior includes stepping on cracks in the sidewalk, excessive washing of the hands or bathing, counting telephone poles, dressing in a certain set manner, and requiring everything to be in a certain meticulous order, such as all drawers carefully closed or shoes or other objects lined up in order.

Often the compulsive behavior is not physical in nature but consists of obsessions or persistent ideas, emotional fears of objects, acts, or a situation. Some obsessions may be a more or less constant fear of death, of losing one's mind, or of losing one's friends, prestige, or job. A fairly common neurotic fear is anxiety about one's health, hypochondria, which may involve fears about one's general state of health or about nonexistent heart conditions, cancer, or tuberculosis. Sometimes neurotic obsessions are directed at destructive notions of injuring someone. Neurotic phobias are often of a general nature such as fear of confinement (claustrophobia) or its opposite, fear of open places, and fear of high places. Persons suffering from these fears are generally not only ashamed of this behavior but become perplexed and resentful of it as absurd and burdensome.[18]

Studies have shown that members of the upper class are more likely to be given the polite label "neurotic," whereas those in the lower class are labeled as psychotic or, more specifically, schizophrenic.[19] In this connection Clausen has stated:

---

[16] Red and green letters are put on a card so that the letters are alternately colored. On one there may be the red letters JHSOKN and the green letters ONHPIS. The subject is given glasses, through one lens of which he can see only the red letters, the other only green. If he reads "John Hopkins" it is apparent that he is using both eyes even if he reports he has vision in only one eye.

[17] Norman Cameron, *The Psychology of Behavior Disorders* (Boston: Houghton Mifflin Company, 1947), p. 12.

[18] Cameron, p. 281.

[19] See, for example, August B. Hollingshead and Frederick Redlich, *Social Class and Mental Illness* (New York: John Wiley & Sons, Inc., 1958).

Every community has some members who are regarded by their fellow citizens as "queer," "mean," "shy," "offensive," and the like. Many of these persons would be diagnosed by a psychiatrist as neurotic and some as psychotic, even though other community members may not regard them as mentally ill. It is not unlikely that many persons whose social background is grossly divergent from that of the psychiatrist (e.g., lower-class persons) will be seen as sicker than those whose attitudes and behaviors are close to the psychiatrist's own outlook.[20]

The Functional Psychoses

The functional psychoses are generally divided into three main types: schizophrenia, the manic-depressive psychoses, and paranoia. In all of these the social reaction tends to be greater than it is toward the neuroses. About 20 percent of all new admissions to state mental hospitals each year are diagnosed as schizophrenic. This disorder is sometimes referred to as dementia praecox, because it develops primarily between fifteen and thirty. Few persons develop schizophrenia after fifty. The manic-depressive psychotics constitute about 15 percent of all institutionalized patients, women making up roughly three quarters of all these cases. Only about 1 percent of all new admissions to state mental hospitals each year have a diagnosis of true paranoia.

Schizophrenic behavior. Partly because of its nature, social science research and writing on mental disorder are probably more concerned with schizophrenia than with any other disorder.[21] The most characteristic symptom of a schizophrenic is his withdrawal from contact with the world around him and his inability to play the roles expected of him. Even before the institutionalization becomes necessary, the schizophrenic may show a great deal of emotional indifference and inattention. He does not share the expectations and interest of the group, and there is a great indifference

---

[20] John A. Clausen, "The Sociology of Mental Illness," in Robert K. Merton, Leonard Broom, Leonard S. Cottrell, Jr., *Sociology Today* (New York: Basic Books, Inc., 1959), p. 494.

[21] See for example, Don D. Jackson, ed., *The Etiology of Schizophrenia* (New York: Basic Books, Inc., 1960); Alfred Auerback, ed., *Schizophrenia: An Integrated Approach* (New York: The Ronald Press Company, 1959); H. Warren Dunham, *Community and Schizophrenia: An Epidemiological Analysis* (Detroit: Wayne State University Press, 1965); Benjamin Pasamanick, Frank R. Scarpitti, and Simon Dinitz, *Schizophrenics in the Community: An Experimental Study in the Prevention of Hospitalization* (New York: Appleton-Century-Crofts, Inc., 1967); and "Mental Illness: Etiology, Treatment, and Future Trends," Chap. 15 in Russell R. Dynes, Alfred C. Clarke, Simon Dinitz, and Iwao Ishino, *Social Problems: Dissensus and Deviation in an Industrial Society* (New York: Oxford University Press, 1964).

to things previously considered important. In addition, the emotional tone is passive, often even negative, so that the patient has little interest in activities. Finally, his thought processes are so disturbed that he builds a world of his own imagination, including false perceptions and hallucinations of various kinds, such as ideas, voices, and forces which enter his daily living and which he cannot control. Schizophrenics have undergone a collapse in their personalities which involves a detachment of their emotional selves from their intellectual selves. It is for this reason that the term *schizophrenia* —or *split personality*, as it is often called—is used to refer to this illness.

Several subtypes of schizophrenia have been identified. A conventional distinction has been a fourfold classification of simple, hebephrenic, paranoiac, and catatonic schizophrenia. The symptoms of severe hebephrenics and catatonics are not seen as frequently today in institutions because of the use of tranquilizers. In simple schizophrenia, patients begin from early life to show increasing tendencies to withdraw, to daydream, and to be unable to concentrate. They become exceedingly careless of their personal appearance, manners, and speech, are listless and apathetic, and lose their interests and ambitions. There is little loss of memory and no serious mental deterioration, if any. Many of these cases are never institutionalized because they are not harmful to themselves or to others and because they may make some sort of adjustment to the world, inadequate as that adjustment may be.

Hebephrenic symptoms include a pronounced silliness of behavior with a great deal of situationally unwarranted smiling, giggling, odd mannerisms, gesturing, and incoherent speech and thought. There is pronounced mental deterioration with bizarre delusions and auditory and visual hallucinations.

Unlike those of the true paranoid, to be discussed shortly, the delusions of persecution of the schizophrenic paranoid are transitory and are based on his own social reality. Moreover, the schizophrenic with a paranoid reaction hears and sees varying images and noises and exhibits the characteristic emotional indifference of the schizophrenic. The following case illustrates a typical paranoid schizophrenic patient.

> A 46-year-old laborer admitted to the state hospital with complaint of feeling weak, mixed up, unable to work. Following admission to hospital he appeared shy, mixed poorly, and complained that someone was following him and wanted to get rid of him. He improved spontaneously, was discharged to his family, then readmitted seven years later. On readmission he had a crutch and cane, claimed he had not been working for several years because of a spinal injury. He offered various ideas of persecution and strange expressions, i.e., that he was surrounded by detectives who were trying to "run a secret world." He was being bothered by "radio tones." After a course of 23 electric shock treatments he discarded his cane and crutch and gave up his ideas about not being able to walk. He

has remained chronic with persistent delusions, some persecutory and other grandiose, e.g., identifying himself with Roosevelt and Truman, thinks he has done important "government work" in the past and that he is entitled to a large pension. He was well adjusted in the hospital.[22]

Catatonic schizophrenics have episodes of excitement and stupor. Because they live in a private world of their own, their behavior is characterized by apathy and impulsiveness. They display the most complete withdrawal from the social world of any mental patients. Many catatonics' withdrawal may be so complete that the muscular or waxy rigidity of the limbs and the stuporous appearance of the catatonic reminds an observer of a dummy. Such catatonics may sit for hours and days in the same position without movement or speech, and some have to be fed. One is able to lift the arm of many catatonics in such a stupor or place them in an uncomfortable position and for an indefinite time they will make no effort to alter their position. They seem to take no interest in things going on around them; yet they are often conscious of the most minute details in their surroundings. The catatonic syndrome also includes a manic state, with increased speech, muscular movements, and action. Gesturing and frenzy are also common. Probably most catatonics, but not all, alternate between these periods of severe depression, frenzied excitation, and stupor.

Some have suggested that some of the more bizarre reactions of hospitalized patients may, in fact, be reactions to their institutionalization and deprivation of civil rights. This might apply not only to the catatonic but to other types of patients as well.[23]

Manic-depressive behavior.   As the name implies, manic-depressive behavior may be extremely elated, in the manic stage, or depressed, although manic depressives do not necessarily pass through cyclical stages of mania and depression.[24] In the manic stage the patient is agitated and excited, elated and aggressive. He rapidly shifts from one topic, object, or activity, and there is a constant flow of manic talk, which, although continuous, is socially understandable. This method of talking is often filled with quips, rhymes, poems, and other witticisms, much with a personal reference. The manic patient sings or whistles, shouts, dances, walks, teases or clowns. He

---

[22] From a case record collected by the author.

[23] *Action for Mental Health*. See also M. Greenblatt, D. Levinson, and R. Williams, *The Patient and the Mental Hospital* (New York: The Free Press, 1957), pp. 438–471, 517–526.

[24] Thomas Rennie, "Prognosis in Manic-Depressive Psychoses," *American Journal of Psychiatry*, 98:801–814 (1942). In this study of 208 manic-depressive cases Rennie found that about one fourth had both manic and depressive attacks, although not as often in cycles.

may dress himself lavishly or prefer to go unclothed. Because he often disregards such bodily needs as food, rest, and elimination, he may be in need of immediate physical attention.[25]

In the depressed phase there is much brooding and unpleasantness, but little serious mental deterioration. Agitated depression involves restless overactivity and despair, whereas activity is minimized and stupor is not uncommon in retarded depression. This disturbance is generally characterized by feelings of dejection, sadness, and self-deprecation. The patient seems to have lost friends, home, family, and all purpose in life. He feels guilty about acts committed or omitted, and he believes he has grievously wronged or been wronged. Contact with reality is nonetheless maintained, as are memory and place-time orientation.

Not all depressed behavior is symptomatic of a manic-depressive psychosis. Neurotics may display secondary depression. Involutional melancholia is another fairly common mental disorder characterized largely by depression. This condition may occur among women during the menopause period and among men at a slightly older age. For example, it is difficult to distinguish schizophrenia from the extreme or manic phases of the manic-depressive disorders. In fact, today schizophrenia is apt to be a more popular diagnosis than formerly, and the manic depressives are likely to be largely the depressive cases.

Paranoia and paranoid behavior. At one time a large proportion of persons with mental disorders were diagnosed as suffering from paranoia, but today paranoia is not widely used as a diagnostic category. Most of those suffering from paranoid disorders are now considered to exhibit a form of schizophrenic behavior. Paranoids are thought to be extremely suspicious and to have ideas of persecution with an intellectual defense which often appears to have plausible reasons for it. Their delusions are usually limited to a few areas and may even be centered on a single person. The behavior of most people who are paranoid, however, does not seriously interfere with most of their life activities; their personalities do not deteriorate nor do they have hallucinations.

PROBLEMS OF DEFINITION

It is difficult to define adequately mental health and, consequently, mental illness or mental disorder. It is not easy to say who is mentally ill and who is not.[26] Mental health or mental disorder can be defined

---

[25] Cameron, p. 513.

[26] See Thomas S. Szasz, *The Myth of Mental Illness* (New York: Paul B. Hoeber, Inc., 1961).

in several ways—statistically, clinically, in terms of middle-class standards, and operationally in terms of societal reaction.

Statistical

Mental health is not the same as the statistically normal in terms of averages. According to this view, the mental health of the person in the "middle" would represent what might be termed "normality." It is difficult to measure the mental health of the average citizen in terms of averages, such as the mean, median, or mode, because there is no satisfactory frequency curve of mental health as is true of intelligence curves. A norm of this type would also mean one which changed with the state of mental health of a given population.

Clinical

In clinical medicine the terms *normal* and *health* are used in the same sense. The problem of definition of normality in organic medicine, although difficult enough, cannot quite compare with the complexities in behavioral disorders. From a clinical point of view, mental disorder is often regarded as behavior which does not "function according to design." [27] Thus a catatonic stupor would be clinically regarded as maladjusted behavior. It is difficult for the clinician to measure the signs of the beginning of mental disorder as distinguished from mental health. Hallucinations, for example, which are often considered to be signs of mental disorder, may be found in normal people. Catatonic stupor may be thought to be maladjustive in our society, but in Asia it might be associated with religious mysticism. As Redlich has written, there are three ideas which must be met before behavior can be labeled clinically as normal or abnormal.[28] (1) The motivation of the behavior must be taken into account, such as "normal" washing of the hands and a neurotic washing compulsion. (2) The context or situation in which the behavior occurs must also be considered. Wearing swimming trunks on a New England street in winter is one thing; on a summer bathing beach, another. (3) By whom is the judgment made that the behavior is clinically abnormal—the experts, such as the psychiatrist, or the general public? "As we do not possess a universal, rigorous science of man, many propositions on normality of behavior have a palpably low degree of validity and reliability and are apt to be challenged by a startled public,

---

[27] Psychoanalysts would regard mental health as freedom from anxiety and as a condition in which the rational replaces the irrational.

[28] Frederick C. Redlich, "The Concept of Health in Psychiatry," in Leighton, Clausen, and Wilson, pp. 145–146.

especially if scientific evidence for them is not particularly strong or runs counter to prevalent public opinion." [29]

The clinical definition of mental health gets us into the area of value judgments. Mental health is thus defined by listing certain traits, capacities, and relationships which are considered to be "normal." All kinds of criteria exist. Among the definitions which have been used by leading psychiatric writers are striving for happiness and effectiveness and sensitive social relationships, being free from symptoms, being unhampered by conflict and having the capacity to love other than himself, successfully integrating personality, and balancing instinctual and ego force. Karl Menninger, in a widely quoted definition, stated: "Let us define mental health as the adjustment of human beings to the world and to each other with a maximum of effectiveness and happiness. Not just efficiency, or just contentment, or the grace of obeying the rules of the game cheerfully. It is all of these together. It is the ability to maintain an even temper, an alert intelligence, socially considerate behavior, and a happy disposition. This, I think, is a healthy mind." [30]

With such criteria it is often difficult to see how anyone could be regarded as normal. A state of emotional health is thus regarded as par (to use the golf term) for the upper levels of health attainment.[31] They are ideals and are often contradictory. Actually, behavior contrary to such ideal values may often be considered normal in another society. Hysterical reactions, for example, are common and normal in many societies.

There have been several comparative studies of so-called mental disorders in a number of societies and within subcultures, such as ethnic groups within a society,[32] and the findings have a bearing on a clinical definition of mental disorders. Distinctions between beliefs in witchcraft and mental

---

[29] Redlich, p. 146. Also see Jurgen Ruesch and Gregory Bateson, *Communication: The Social Matrix of Psychiatry* (New York: W. W. Norton & Company, Inc., 1951). See also H. Warren Dunham, *Sociological Theory and Mental Disorder* (Detroit: Wayne State University Press, 1959); Joseph W. Eaton, "The Assessment of Mental Health," *American Journal of Psychiatry,* 108:81–89 (1951); and Marie Jahoda, *Current Concepts of Positive Mental Health* (New York: Basic Books, Inc., 1958).

[30] Karl Menninger, *The Human Mind* (New York: Alfred A. Knopf, Inc., 1946), p. 1.

[31] Leslie A. Osborn, *Psychiatry and Medicine* (New York: McGraw-Hill Book Company, Inc., 1952), p. 211. See Jahoda, pp. 5–9 and 65–80, for a critique of ideal definitions of mental health.

[32] Murphy and Leighton, *Approaches to Cross-Cultural Psychiatry.* Also see Marvin K. Opler, ed., *Culture and Mental Health* (New York: The Macmillan Company, 1959) and Opler, *Culture and Social Psychiatry.*

disorder are confusing, for example, in West Africa.[33] The Berens River Ojibwa in northern Canada, for example, have various fears about encounters with animals, as well as phobias about snakes and huge imaginary animals, such as toads.[34] The belief also exists that personal transgressions are related to disease. Finally, the most pronounced fear of these people concerns beliefs about the Windigo, or cannibals. Human beings can be transformed into cannibals, and this fact may be perceived by certain phenomena exhibited by individuals. To an outsider these fears appear to be "neurotic" mental disorder in the sense that there is no real danger and they arise from fantasies. Hallowell believes we should distinguish between individual fears and such culturally induced fears. This is a prevalent problem in the clinical diagnosis of mental disorder in more complex societies with various subcultures and social classes.

> The symptoms of mental disorder are ideational and behavioral. Therefore they reflect cultural emphases as well as disease processes. Many symptoms cannot be adequately interpreted without a knowledge of the norms of the subculture to which the individual belongs. For example, certain severe mental disorders are characterized by persisting delusions, such as believing oneself bewitched. In a culture in which most people believe in witches, however, such a belief cannot be considered delusional. It may be lacking in a scientific basis, but the same can be said of all beliefs in a supernatural realm. The culture not only provides the norms for assessing any given pattern of belief or behavior, but also provides the coloring or emphasis to the manifest symptomatology and the characteristic modes for dealing with such behavioral manifestations. Therefore it becomes extremely difficult to equate symptoms from one culture to another or even from one time to another.[35]

Middle-Class Values

Value judgments about mental health, moreover, often merely represent certain middle-class criteria, thus implying lower-class behavior to be the reverse. Frequently mental health is defined in middle-class terms, and an attempt is made to associate the definition with the Protestant ethic.[36]

---

[33] S. Kirson Weinberg, " 'Mental Healing,' and Social Change in West Africa," *Social Problems,* 11:157–169 (1964). Also see Weinberg, "Cultural Aspects of Manic-Depression in West Africa," *Journal of Health and Human Behavior,* 6:247–253 (1965).

[34] A. Irving Hallowell, "Fear and Anxiety as Cultural and Individual Variables in a Primitive Society: Ojibwa," in Opler, *Culture and Mental Health,* pp. 41–62.

[35] John A. Clausen, "Mental Disorders," in Robert K. Merton and Robert A. Nisbet, *Contemporary Social Problems* (2d ed.; New York: Harcourt, Brace & World, Inc., 1966), p. 31 Reprinted by permission of the publisher.

[36] Kingsley Davis, "Mental Hygiene and the Class Structure," *Psychiatry,* 1:55–64 (February 1938).

An analysis of the content of pamphlets attempting to improve the mental health of the general population has revealed these middle-class themes in the definition of the mentally healthy person: adjustment to group and prevailing norms by getting along with others, facing up to problems and then doing something about them, the value of work through enjoying it and getting satisfaction out of one's job, control of emotions, planning ahead without fear of the future, striving to achieve goals and community participation.[37] Such middle-class values often undoubtedly enter into the clinical diagnosis of psychiatrists, who are almost entirely from a middle- or upper-class background.

Residual Norms and Societal Reaction

Societies tend to have norms that designate as deviant behavior acts which are termed crime, sexual perversions, drunkenness, bad manners, and other more specific behavior. Mental disorder can be viewed as residual rule breaking or residual deviance in that it comes to cover deviant normative behavior that is left over, such as witchcraft, spirit possession, and what is termed various forms of "mental disorder."[38] The latter includes such behavior as withdrawal, hallucinations, muttering, posturing, depression, excited behavior, compulsions, obsessions, and auditory states. Such residual deviance must however, be regarded not only as normative behavior but also in terms of the social context in which the behavior occurs. Talking to spirits within the religious context of Spiritualism, for example, would not be residual deviance. Imputations of rule breaking in a social context may come from various sources, such as the family, school, or factory. The context of normative violations called mental disorder are therefore not within the individual but within the context in which they occur.

An operational definition of mental normality in terms of societal reactions means "normal for what" and "normal for whom."[39] This definition seems to be helpful in any adequate definition of mental disorder. The extent to which behavior, for example, can be tolerated by others may be different for a business executive and a person employed in a minor capacity

---

[37] Orville R. Gursslin, Raymond G. Hunt, and Jack L. Roach, "Social Class and the Mental Health Movement," *Social Problems,* 7:210–218 (1959–1960).

[38] Scheff. Also see Henry B. Adams, " 'Mental Illness' of Interpersonal Behavior?" *American Psychologist,* 19:191–197 (1964). Such deviant behavior should be viewed in terms of the prevailing cultural norms. See S. Kirson Weinberg, "A Cultural Approach to Disordered Behavior and Social Deviance," and S. Kirson Weinberg, "Disordered Behavior and Socially Deviant Behavior," in S. Kirson Weinberg, ed., *The Sociology of Mental Disorders: Analyses and Readings in Psychiatric Sociology* (Chicago: Aldine Publishing Co., 1967), pp. 163–166 and 166–172.

[39] Redlich.

in an industrial plant, both in terms of what is presumed to be "normal" and what is the societal reaction of others. "The self-perception of the person with the problem and the role assignment of all actors involved will determine subsequent labeling 'normal or abnormal with reference to certain tasks' and subsequent action." [40]

Operationally it is difficult, therefore, to draw a sharp line between mental health and mental disorder. What we really have is the problem of the social limits of "eccentricity," as an English writer has concluded: "It appears in fact that there is *no* clear-cut criterion of what constitutes a psychiatric case. Whether a person is regarded as in need of medical treatment is always a function of his behavior *and* the attitude of his fellows in society." [41] The person may be slightly, moderately, or severely impaired, depending upon the way his behavior is evaluated by others.[42] One prominent psychiatrist has even gone so far as to deny that mental disorder is an "illness" but rather represents merely defective strategies for handling life situations that are difficult for the individual.[43]

The more closely a person's behavior conforms to institutionalized expectations, the more favorably he will be evaluated by those around him. On the other hand, when his behavior is not within the expected range, he is likely to be segregated and evaluated negatively. Thus it is not necessarily the severity of the illness or the pathology of the behavior from a clinical view that leads to rejection of mentally ill individuals but rather the social visibility of the behavior. Indeed, it is generally agreed that persons who, by clinical standards, are grossly disturbed, and even overtly psychotic, may remain in the community for long periods of time without being "recognized" as "mentally ill." In a survey "The Public's Ideas about Mental Illness," Star, for example, found that of six case histories of mental deviants—paranoid, simple schizophrenic, alcoholic, anxiety neurotic, disturbed child, and compulsive phobic—only the most extreme one, the paranoid, was diagnosed as mentally ill by anything like the majority of the

---

[40] Redlich, p. 155.

[41] G. M. Carstairs, "The Social Limits of Eccentricity: An English Study," in Opler, *Culture and Mental Health*, p. 377. He shows historically how people have reacted in different ways to eccentricities. For a history of the norms and societal reaction involved in mental disorder in Europe during the seventeenth and eighteenth centuries see Michel Foucault, *Madness and Civilization: A History of Insanity in the Age of Reason* (Translated from the French by Richard Howard: New York: Pantheon Books, 1965).

[42] See August B. Hollingshead and Frederick C. Redlich, *Social Class and Mental Illness* (New York: John Wiley & Sons, Inc., 1958), Chaps. 1, 2, 6.

[43] Szasz.

public (75 percent).[44] Other researchers have similarly found that the public does not necessarily recognize certain clinical symptoms as seriously disturbed behavior.[45]

Collective action, then, on the part of a family, neighborhood, or community to hospitalize (that is, to label formally) an individual as being "mentally disordered" will always be, as Lemert points out, "an interactional product of the degree of stressful deviation and the tolerance of the group for the behavior." [46] Besides the variable of visibility of symptoms, such area phenomena as "the percentage of a given population living in family groups, the type of housing in an area, and physical characteristics of the neighborhood" also affect tolerance differentials. Then too, besides the characteristics of the individual deviant, as age, sex, marital status, and the presence or absence of children in families where they live, certain characteristics of the surrounding "society" also affect group tolerances for certain behaviors.[47] Ethnic background, socioeconomic status, educational level, and size of community, all affect the tolerance quotient, resulting in a measure of either high group receptivity or a limited group tolerance. One

---

[44] Shirley Star, "The Public's Ideas about Mental Illness." Paper presented at the annual meeting of the National Association for Mental Health, November 5, 1955 (mimeographed).

[45] Elaine Cumming and John Cumming, *Closed Ranks: An Experiment in Mental Health Education* (Cambridge, Mass.: Harvard University Press, 1957); B. Dohrenwend, V. Bernard, and L. Kolb, "The Orientations of Leaders in an Urban Area toward Problems of Mental Illness," *American Journal of Psychiatry,* 118:683–691 (1962); Paul Lemkau and Guido M. Crocetti, "An Urban Population's Opinion and Knowledge about Mental Illness," *American Journal of Psychiatry,* 118:692–700 (1962); and Jack Elinson, Elena Padilla, and Marvin E. Perkins, *Public Image of Mental Health Services* (New York: Mental Health Materials Center, Inc., 1967), pp. 20–30. When both lower- and upper-status groups define a pattern of psychological behavior as seriously deviant, lower status groups are less tolerant. Moreover, the relatively tolerant policy of upper-status groups appears to be a consequence of their generally more liberal orientation rather than of comprehension of the nature of psychopathology in psychiatric terms. Bruce P. Dohrenwend and Edwin Chin-Shong, "Social Status and Attitudes Toward Psychological Disorder: The Problem of Tolerance of Deviance," *American Sociological Review,* 32:417–432 (1967).

[46] Edwin M. Lemert, *Social Pathology: A Systematic Approach to the Theory of Sociopathic Behavior* (New York: McGraw-Hill Book Company, Inc., 1951), p. 406.

[47] Gerald Gurin, Joseph Veroff, and Sheila Feld, *Americans View Their Mental Health* (New York: Basic Books, Inc., 1960), p. 209; Phillips, p. 679; and Jack P. Gibbs, "Rates of Mental Hospitalization: A Study of Societal Reaction to Deviant Behavior," *American Sociological Review,* 27:788 (1962).

reason for this is that there is, in a complex society, differential access to existing "professional" knowledge of "mental disorder symptoms" and, therefore, awareness of it.

An operational definition depends also upon the societal reaction, including urgency of treatment as this is defined by society. Disorders may be divided into two groups.[48] One category is the severely mentally ill or psychotic, those cases in which the societal reaction to the behavior is strong and treatment is often urgent. Their behavior is regarded as social or antisocial in terms of the prevailing cultural norms and their level of social performance is not in conformity with norms current for persons of their particular age and status.[49] Such deviations are more easily recognized by the expert and the lay public with whom the persons are in contact, and they may even be treated without the consent of the patient. The second category represents those mild and transitory mental disturbances where there is little urgency and the problem is felt more by the individual than by others. The more moderately disturbed group includes those persons whose behavior deviates less markedly from the norms (of perception, belief, and feeling) and who may or may not be reacted to by most lay persons as "odd" or "peculiar." Professional persons would probably describe these persons with technical terms, such as the neuroses.[50]

> In evaluating the criteria by which visible symptoms might be judged, one practical basis is the extent to which the person failed to fulfill adequately expectations in performing his primary social roles (especially his familial and occupational roles), and the extent to which he violated legal and moral norms and highly important values of the group. Whether a definition of deviancy is made and acted upon will depend, largely, on how serious the consequences of this deviation are for the social group. Some deviant behaviors are rewarded and tolerated, others have some idiosyncratic function for the group as is often the case with the "comic," or the deviant may be thought of as "eccentric," "queer," or "strange" but not sufficiently so to merit a definition of illness. On the other hand, should the deviancy begin to have serious consequences, either in that it is damaging or harmful to the individual, a group, or both, or becomes so visible to external groups that the family suffers status loss, it might be redefined as "mental illness" and the person sent for treatment. In some groups, of course, the stigma attached to a definition of mental illness is sufficiently great to bring about group resistance to such a definition.[51]

---

[48] Redlich, pp. 154–158.

[49] Cameron, p. 8.

[50] See Hollingshead and Redlich, Chap. 6; and *Action for Mental Health*, Chap. 3.

[51] David Mechanic, "Some Factors in Identifying and Defining Mental Illness," in Thomas J. Scheff, ed., *Mental Illness and Social Processes* (New York: Harper & Row, Publishers, 1967), pp. 28–29.

A group of wives, for example, were found in one study to go through a "process of recognition" of what they defined as mental disorder symptoms in their husbands' sufficient to call for hospitalization.[52] Initially their interpretations of their husbands' behavior was not one of mental disorder and varied from nothing really being wrong to "character" weakness and "controllable" behavior (lazy, mean, and so on); physical problems; normal response to a crisis; mildly emotionally disturbed; "something" seriously wrong; and a serious emotional or mental problem.[53] How the wife comes to define the behavior as a problem and requiring hospitalization is a highly individualistic matter. "In some instances, it is when the wife can no longer manage her husband (he will no longer respond to her usual prods); in others, when his behavior destroys the status quo (when her goals and living routines are disorganized); and, in still others, when she cannot explain his behavior. One can speculate that her level of tolerance for his behavior is a function of her specific personality needs and vulnerabilities, her personal and family value system and the social supports and prohibitions regarding the husband's symptomatic behavior." [54] By the time of hospital admission there has been some shift in the nature of the problem behavior. (See Table 12.1.)

> We have attempted to describe the factors which help the wife maintain a picture of her husband as normal and those which push her in the direction of accepting a psychiatric definition of his problem. The kind and intensity of the symptomatic behavior, its persistence over time, the husband's interpretation of his problem, interpretations and defining actions of others, including professionals, all play a role. In addition, the wives come to this experience with different conceptions of psychological processes and of the nature of emotional illness, itself, as well as with different tolerances for emotional disturbance. As we have seen, there are also many supports in society for maintaining a picture of normality concerning the husband's behavior. Social pressures and expectations not only keep *behavior* in line but to a great extent *perceptions* of behavior as well.[55]

On the whole, people tend to reject a person as having a mental disorder according to the source of the "help" to which he turns. In one study the rejection scores given for identical descriptive cases of mental disorder by a sample of persons interviewed were lowest for those who sought no

---

[52] Marian Radke Yarrow, Charlotte Green Schwartz, Harriet S. Murphy, and Leila Calhoun Deasy, "The Psychological Meaning of Mental Illness in the Family," in Scheff, *Mental Illness and Social Processes*, pp. 32–48.

[53] Yarrow, *et al.*, p. 40.

[54] Yarrow, *et al.*, pp. 38–39.

[55] Yarrow, *et al.*, p. 47.

help, followed by receiving help from a clergyman, a physician, and a psychiatrist, and, finally, by going to a mental hospital.[56]

TABLE 12.1 **Reported Problem Behavior at Time of the Wife's Initial Concern and at Time of the Husband's Admission to Hospital**

	Initially		At hospital admission	
PROBLEM BEHAVIOR	PSY-CHOTICS N	PSYCHO-NEUROTICS N	PSY-CHOTICS N	PSYCHO-NEUROTICS N
Physical problems, complaints, worries	12	5	7	5
Deviations from routines of behavior	17	9	13	9
Expressions of inadequacy or hopelessness	4	1	5	2
Nervous, irritable, worried	19	10	18	9
Withdrawal (verbal, physical)	5	1	6	1
Changes or accentuations in personality "traits" (slovenly, deceptive, forgetful)	5	6	7	6
Aggressive or assaultive and suicidal behavior	6	3	10	6
Strange or bizarre thoughts, delusions, hallucinations and strange behavior	11	1	15	2
Excessive drinking	4	7	3	4
Violation of codes of "decency"	3	1	3	2
NUMBER OF RESPONDENTS	23	10	23	10

SOURCE: Marian Radke Yarrow, Charlotte Green Schwartz, Harriet S. Murphy, and Lelia Calhoun Deasy, "The Psychological Meaning of Mental Illness in the Family," in Thomas J. Scheff, ed., *Mental Illness and Social Processes* (New York: Harper & Row, Publishers, 1967), p. 39.

Controls for age, religion, education, social class, and authoritarianism failed to diminish the relationship, but controls for experience with an emotionally disturbed help-seeker and for adherence to the norm of self-reliance tended to specify it. Respondents who had had experience with a help-seeking relative deviated markedly from the pattern followed by the rest of the sample, as did respondents not adhering to the norm of self-reliance. Both of these groups rejected people seeking no help more

[56] Phillips, *op. cit.*

than they did those consulting a clergyman or a physician, and respondents with help-seeking relatives also rejected non-help-seekers more than those consulting a psychiatrist. Both groups rejected persons seeing a clergyman more than those seeing a physician.[57]

EXTENT OF MENTAL DISORDERS IN THE UNITED STATES

It is impossible to know the extent of mental disorder in the United States today. Even if one knew how many are so incapacitated mentally that they require hospitalization or have been released to home care, are being treated by psychiatrists, or are being counseled by their clergymen or by others, this total might well exclude many others who are regarded as mentally ill. The sources of knowledge about the extent of mental disorder have been chiefly from (1) data on patients in mental hospitals, (2) data from Selective Service examinations and the records of the armed forces, and (3) community surveys of the prevalence of mental disorders.[58]

Mental Hospital Population

In 1966 there were 452,329 mental patients in long-term mental hospitals in the United States, about 88 percent of them in public mental hospitals—state, county, or city. The movement of patients in and out of these hospitals during a given year is so extensive that the total is actually much higher, and on any one day of the year, patients in mental hospitals make up almost half of all the patients in all the hospitals of the United States. From 1955 to 1966 there was a marked decline of about one fifth in the resident population of mental hospitals, which has been thought to be due to the increased use of tranquilizers as well as to a spreading conviction that patients should, if possible, be treated without hospitalization.[59]

These figures are not an actual index of mental disorder because the proportion with mental disorders not hospitalized is not known. Also, there

---

[57] Phillips, "Rejection: A Possible Consequence of Seeking Help for Mental Disorders," in Scheff, *Mental Illness and Social Processes,* p. 77.

[58] These data have several limitations. They have largely not been made on random samples of the population, and they have not used "standardized methods of case finding, diagnosis, and classification, as well as comparable definitions of case and prevalence." See R. H. Felix and Morton Kramer, "Extent of the Problem of Mental Disorders," *The Annals,* 286:13 (1953). For a discussion of some of the difficulties in discovering the extent and characteristics of persons with mental disorders, see Richard J. Plunkett and John E. Gordon, *Epidemiology and Mental Illness* (Monograph No. 6 of the Joint Commission on Mental Illness and Health; New York: Basic Books, Inc., 1960).

[59] For a discussion of mental hospital populations see Chapter 20.

are considerable variations throughout the country: "Hospitalization rates are a resultant not only of the true incidence of mental disorder but of a number of factors such as availability of mental hospital beds, public attitudes toward hospitalization, and availability and use of other community resources for diagnosis and treatment." [60] These other resources include such facilities as general hospitals with psychiatric treatment services, psychiatric clinics, and private psychiatrists.

Selective Service Registrants

More Selective Service registrants were rejected during World War II for personality defects other than mental deficiency than for any other cause. Up to August 1, 1945, 900,000 men between eighteen and thirty-seven were rejected for military service and classed as nueropsychiatric casualties, a figure which represented 18 percent of all men rejected in the armed forces.[61] In a study of the prevalence of defects among those between eighteen and forty-four who were examined during the period 1940–1943, mental illness ranked sixth, with a rate of 55.8 per 1000 men. During World War II the armed services gave a medical discharge to about 460,000 men for neuropsychiatric reasons, or about 36 percent of all medical discharges. Such figures, high as they are, should not be taken as representative of the general male population of military age. Persons were deferred for a large number of reasons, others volunteered, and some of those with certain physical defects or low educational standards were not examined at all. Furthermore, the standards for military acceptance changed, and draft boards did not use identical methods in screening.[62] Moreover, the figures should be regarded with extreme caution because of inefficiencies in the general screening process for military service.

Surveys of General Population

Estimates of the incidence of mental disorder in the general population have been made, but it is difficult to know the true rate. Most of the estimates appear to be exaggerated. Those given here will be presented with

---

[60] Felix and Kramer, p. 12.

[61] United States Selective Service System, *Physical Examination of Selective Service Registrants* (Special Monograph No. 15; Washington, D.C.: Government Printing Office, 1948). This figure did not include those rejected because they were mentally deficient (feeble-minded) or those who were in mental hospitals.

[62] William A. Hunt and Cecil L. Wittson, "Some Sources of Error in the Neuropsychiatric Statistics of World War II," *Journal of Clinical Psychology*, 5:350–358 (1949). Also see Eleanor Leacock, "Three Social Variables and the Occurrence of Mental Disorder," in Leighton, Clausen, and Wilson, pp. 308–340. Leacock points out that a good proportion of those rejected as "neuropsychiatric casualties" were actually mentally deficient and/or illiterate.

this reservation. A community survey was made in the Eastern Health District, Baltimore, in 1936, and another in Williamson County, Tennessee, in 1938.[63] The Baltimore study found 3337 "active" cases of mental illness during the year in a population of 55,129, or 60.5 per 1000 population. The Williamson County survey found 1721 cases of mental illness in a population of 24,804. The two studies cannot be compared, however, because of demographic differences and the methods they used.[64]

One of the most intensive metropolitan surveys ever made in the field of mental health involved a cross-section of a heterogeneous midtown Manhattan residential population of 110,000 persons.[65] From interviews with 1660 residents the conclusion was reached that only 18.5 percent were free enough of emotional symptoms to be considered "well." A total of 58.1 percent were found to have mild to moderate symptoms, such as tensions, nervousness, and other indications of emotional disturbances, although not to the extent of impairing life functioning. Marked, severe, and incapacitating symptoms were found in 23.4 percent of the cases.

The validity of the study depends upon the criteria used to determine degrees of mental disorder, and these criteria have been severely criticized, particularly the methodology.[66] Questions were asked in the interviews, for

---

[63] Paul Lemkau, Christopher Tietze, and Marcia Cooper, "Mental Hygiene Problems in an Urban District," *Mental Hygiene,* 25:624–646 (1941), 26:100–119, 257–288 (1942), and 27:279–295 (1943). Also see William F. Roth and Frank Luton, "The Mental Health Program in Tennessee, I. Description of the Original Study Program; II. Statistical Report of a Psychiatric Survey in a Rural County," *American Journal of Psychiatry,* 99:662–675 (1943). It is unfortunate that the studies were not confined to mental illness, for the Baltimore study also included about 6.8 percent cases of mental deficiency, and the Tennessee study 8.2 percent. Feeble-mindedness, which represents a lack of intellectual development for organic or other reasons, is not considered here as a mental disorder. The distinction is often made between *amentia,* or the absence of mental faculties, and *dementia,* which is the disorder of such faculties. Occasionally feeble-minded persons develop disorders, but these generally have no connection with the feeble-mindedness. Feeble-minded persons probably have no more, and possibly even less, personality disorders than those with higher intelligence.

[64] In the former study, for example, "active" meant being a client of certain social agencies, whereas in the other "active" meant cases presenting both serious and mild personal problems.

[65] Leo Srole, *et al., Mental Health in the Metropolis: The Midtown Manhattan Study* (New York: McGraw-Hill Book Company, Inc., 1962). A large-scale 1963 New York City study involving interviews with adults living in each of the five boroughs, selected by a probability sample, has also shown existence of extensive mental health difficulties. See Elinson, *et al., Public Image of Mental Health Services,* pp. 29–30.

[66] For example, see Frank E. Hartung, "Manhattan Madness: The Social Movement of Mental Illness," *Sociological Quarterly,* 4:261–272 (1963); Jerome G.

example, about somatic disorders or feelings of "nervousness" and "restlessness" and difficulties in interpersonal relations. This information was then abstracted and given to a team of psychiatrists, who rated the person and the amount of impairment in psychiatric terms.

An intensive survey of Stirling County, Nova Scotia, using techniques similar to the Midtown Manhattan study, found that two thirds of the residents exhibited symptoms of mental disorder, most of them neurotic, but only a small proportion were urgently in need of care.[67] The highest incidence levels were among women, but although large numbers of persons had neurotic symptoms, the degree of impairment, most of the time, varied with life experiences. The Midtown Manhattan study and the study in Nova Scotia have such high estimates of mental disorder that many feel that either the research techniques were wrong or the results are meaningless.

A study in Texas has used a different measure: incidence of first cases of psychoses that came under diagnosis and treatment during the two-year period 1951 through 1952, whether private or public and whether in or outside a hospital, rather than merely hospitalization.[68] Jaco found the average number of Texans considered to be psychotic for the first time in their lives was 5649, or a crude annual incidence rate of 73.3 per 100,000. The age-adjusted rate was 68 for males and a higher rate of 78 for females. The median age was 44 for males and 40 for females. The incidence increased with each advancing age-group category in the total group and among males, although there were some slight exceptions among the female groups. As other studies have shown, highest standardized rates for psychoses were found among the divorced, followed in order by those who were single, separated, widowed, or married.

CULTURAL FACTORS IN MENTAL DISORDERS

Sociocultural factors have been shown in a variety of studies to play a significant role in the development of the functional mental disorders. These have included studies of mental disorders in comparative cultures and subcultures, social stratification and occupation, and ecological studies

---

Manix, Milton J. Brawer, Chester L. Hunt, and Leonard C. Kercher, "Validating a Mental Health Scale," *American Sociological Review,* 28:108–116 (1963); and Bruce P. Dohrenwend, "Social Status and Psychological Disorder: An Issue of Substance and an Issue of Method," *American Sociological Review,* 31:14–34 (1966).

[67] Alexander Leighton, *My Name Is Legion* (New York: Basic Books, Inc., 1959); and Dorothea Leighton, John S. Harding, David B. Macklin, Allister MacMillan, and Alexander Leighton, *The Character of Disorder* (New York: Basic Books, Inc., 1963).

[68] E. Gartly Jaco, *The Social Epidemiology of Mental Disorders* (New York: Russell Sage Foundation, 1960).

of distributions within cities.[69] Finally, another aspect has been the effects of mental hospital environment on the treatment of mental disorders.[70] Our knowledge is, as yet, only suggestive as to clues to the origins of the functional mental disorders. Most studies are fairly recent, and much more research needs to be done.

Cultural factors play an important role in mental disorders.[71] The incidence of mental disorder, for example, varies widely in different cultures, as is shown by Eaton and Weil's comparison of ten intensive studies of different societies.[72] These authors suggest that this variation is a product of the amount of stability and integrated cultural traits, consistent role-expectation, and close interpersonal, family, and community ties. Hindus, Chinese, and Malayans in Singapore, for example, have differing amounts and types of disorders, depending upon their cultural experiences.[73] In our own society differences in the nature of schizophrenic symptoms have been found between persons from Irish and Italian subcultures, the former favoring fantasy and withdrawal to the extent of paranoid reactions, while the Italian patients suffered from poor emotional and impulse control.[74] Jaco has found pronounced differences in the extent and nature of mental disorders among Spanish-Americans and Anglo-Americans in Texas.[75]

The relation of community social structure and culture has been studied among the Hutterites, members of a religious sect of European origin who have lived in South Dakota, North Dakota, Montana, Manitoba, and Alberta for over sixty years.[76] This group of 8542 persons was studied for any incidence of mental disorder, since commitment to a mental hospital had been reported as rare among the group. When they were studied, their incidence of diagnosed mental disorder was not too different from that of

---

[69] For a discussion of the ecological aspects of mental disorders, see Chapters 3 and 4.

[70] See Chapter 20.

[71] See Opler, *Culture and Social Psychiatry* and *Culture and Mental Health;* Leighton, *Approaches to Cross-Cultural Psychiatry;* and Saxon Graham, "Sociological Aspects of Health and Illness," in Robert E. L. Faris, ed., *Handbook of Modern Sociology* (Chicago: Rand McNally & Company, 1964).

[72] Joseph W. Eaton and Robert J. Weil, *Culture and Mental Disorders* (New York: The Free Press, 1955).

[73] H. B. M. Murphy, "Culture and Mental Disorder in Singapore," in Opler, *Culture and Mental Health,* pp. 291–316.

[74] Marvin K. Opler, "Cultural Differences in Mental Disorders: An Italian and Irish Contrast in the Schizophrenias—U.S.A.," in Opler, *Culture and Mental Health,* pp. 425–442.

[75] E. Gartly Jaco, "Mental Health of the Spanish-American in Texas," in Opler, *Culture and Mental Health,* pp. 467–489.

[76] Eaton and Weil.

other populations, but they tended to deal with it by unofficial means. Moreover, there were few cases of schizophrenia and little free-floating anxiety or physical aggression. Diagnosed manic-depressive behavior, nearly all of it depressive, was much more common than schizophrenia, or the reverse of data in most urban studies. Very few persons diagnosed as mentally disordered had ever been admitted to mental hospitals for treatment. In fact, only five persons had been admitted, and these five for a short time, ranging from a day to several months. The recovery rate among the Hutterites was also found to be very high—far in excess of that found for the general United States population with mental disorders. The explanation for the low incidence of hospitalized mental illness, both the neuroses and the psychoses, may be in the homogeneous and highly integrated social system of the Hutterites. Instead of rejecting and segregating their mentally ill by having them committed to public hospitals, the Hutterites attempt to keep these persons within their own group. Arrangements are made for necessary care, and the mentally ill person is given affection and understanding and offered a situation favorable to recovery.

Other cultural situations furnish illustrations of conflict. Many Andean Indians who migrate to coastal urban centers of Peru have pronounced psychiatric problems, in part because of the migrations but also because of "the extreme differences between the cultures of the Sierran Indians and the coastal urban populations which magnify the dimensions of change required of the Indian." [77] Mental disorders were increased among the Ifaluk of Micronesia as a result of culture conflict arising from the Japanese occupation during World War II.[78] Lack of cultural integration has been found to account for the higher incidence of schizophrenia among two groups of Japanese who migrated to Hawaii.[79]

The relation of research on culture and cultural situations to mental disorder has been summarized by saying that culture has been conceived as

1. determining the pattern of certain specific disorders, such as *lâtah* (in Malaya), *koro* (in China), and *witiko* (in the Indian cultures of Northeast America);

2. producing basic personality types, some of which are especially vulnerable to psychiatric disorder;

---

[77] Jacob Fried, "Acculturation and Mental Health among Indian Migrants in Peru," in Opler, *Culture and Mental Health,* p. 136.

[78] Melford E. Spiro, "Cultural Heritage, Personal Tensions, and Mental Illness in a South Sea Culture," in Opler, *Culture and Mental Health,* pp. 141–171.

[79] Kiyoshi Ikeda, Harry V. Ball, and Douglas S. Yamamura, "Ethnocultural Factors in Schizophrenia: The Japanese in Hawaii," *American Journal of Sociology,* 68:242–248 (1962).

3. producing psychiatric disorders (usually considered latent for a time) through certain child-rearing practices;

4. having a selective influence on a population's potential for psychiatric disorder as well as the pattern of disorder through types of sanctions and whether "shame" or "guilt" is engendered;

5. precipitating disorder in an otherwise adequately functioning personality by confrontation with stressful roles;

6. perpetuating disorder by rewarding it in prestigeful roles, such as holy man, witch doctor, or shaman;

7. precipitating disorder by changing more rapidly than personality systems are able to tolerate;

8. producing disorder through the inculcation of sentiments (beliefs and values) that produce emotional states damaging to personality, such as fears, jealousies, and unrealistic aspirations;

9. affecting the distribution of some kinds of disorders through breeding patterns; and

10. influencing the amount and distribution of disorder through patterns or poor hygiene and nutrition.[80]

SOCIAL STRATIFICATION AND MENTAL DISORDERS

There is evidence that *diagnosed* mental disorders are related to differences in occupation and social class. Mental disorder is not distributed either as a whole or by type randomly in the population. Most studies have found a higher incidence rate of first admissions to mental hospitals of those from the lower occupational categories.[81] Schizophrenic behavior appears to be most common among the lowest socioeconomic groups and communities, those who are in unskilled and semiskilled occupations, and among the unemployed.[82] On the other hand, manic-depressive behavior seems to be more prevalent among professional and socially prominent persons.

---

[80] Leighton, *Approaches to Cross-Cultural Psychiatry*, p. 10. Also see Opler, *Culture and Social Psychiatry* and the following articles in Weinberg, *The Sociology of Mental Disorders*—E. D. Wittkower and J. Fried, "Some Problems of Transcultural Psychiatry," Paul K. Benedict and Irving Jacks, "Mental Illness in Primitive Societies," and S. Kirson Weinberg, " 'Mental Healing' and Social Change in West Africa."

[81] See, for example, Robert E. Clark, "Psychoses, Income and Occupational Prestige," *American Journal of Sociology*, 54:433–440 (1949) and "The Relationship of Schizophrenia to Occupational Income and Occupational Prestige," *American Sociological Review*, 13:325–330 (1948).

[82] Paul M. Roman and Harrison M. Trice, *Schizophrenia and the Poor* (Ithaca, N.Y.: Cayuga Press, 1967), pp. 18–41. Also see Frank Riessman, Jerome

A fifteen-year study of a rural county in maritime Canada reported that the prevalence of symptoms of mental disorder increased as social status declined.[83] In a Texas study of persons coming under diagnosis or treatment, adjusted incidence rates for persons who became psychotic for the first time showed the highest rates among the unemployed, which might, in fact, reflect the fact that psychotic persons are often less likely to be employed.[84]

The Midtown Manhattan survey found that 30 percent of those in the higher socioeconomic status groups were rated "well"; less than 5 percent of the lowest strata were so rated. In the highest group only 12.5 percent were considered "impaired" while 47.3 percent of the lowest strata were rated as impaired.[85]

A study of all persons in New Haven, Connecticut, who were patients of a psychiatrist or a psychiatric clinic, or were in psychiatric institutions on December 1, 1950, revealed rather decided class differences.[86] The total group of 1891 patients was compared with a 5 percent random sample of the normal population, or 11,522. When both groups were divided into five classes and compared, with Class I at the top and Class V at the bottom, it was found that the lower the socioeconomic class the more prevalent the diagnosis of disorder. Class I contained 3.1 percent of the population and only 1.0 percent of the mental patients, whereas the lowest group, with 17.8 percent of the population, had almost twice as many mental patients. When sex, age, race, religion, and marital status were analyzed, social class was still found to be the important factor.

Cohen, and Arthur Pearl, eds., *Mental Health of the Poor: New Treatment Approaches for Low Income People* (New York: The Free Press, 1964).

[83] Dorothea C. Leighton, *et al.*, *The Character of Danger* (New York: Basic Books, Inc., 1963).

[84] Jaco, *The Social Epidemiology of Mental Disorders*, pp. 125–148. Among those who were employed at the time of the psychosis, the highest standardized rates of diagnosed illness were found among the professionals and semiprofessionals, followed by managerial, official, and proprietary occupations, clerical and sales workers, service workers, agricultural workers, and manual workers of all levels of skill. Jaco included public and private cases but maintains that this occupational difference does not reflect any bias in ability to pay.

[85] Srole, *et al.*, p. 138. For critical comments on this study, see page 469.

[86] Hollingshead and Redlich. Part of this difference was undoubtedly due to differential diagnosis on the part of the psychiatrist. Some studies have challenged the relation of schizophrenia to social class on the ground that there is little difference between classes if the cases are distributed not by the deviant's class but by that of his father. See Dunham, *Community and Schizophrenia;* and H. Warren Dunham, Patricia Phillips, and Barbara Srinivasan, "A Research Note on Diagnosed Mental Illness and Social Class," *American Sociological Review,* 31:223–236 (1966).

The diagnosis of neuroses was found to be more prevalent at the upper-class levels, whereas the psychoses were more frequent in the lower groups. Neurotics constituted nearly two thirds of all patients in the two upper-class levels, but among the lowest level, neurotics were less than 10 percent of the patients. A further analysis of the 847 diagnosed schizophrenic cases showed that in comparison with the normal population, the diagnosis of neurotic disorder is disproportionately high among the lower classes. In Class I this disorder was found to be only one fifth as great as it would be if proportionately distributed, whereas among those in Class V it was two and a half times as great. A contrary finding was made in another study using a survey where neurotic symptoms were found to be more frequent in the lowest occupational level.[87] This represents some evidence that the label "neurosis" may be a product of differential diagnosis of those who seek treatment and that class differences are not actually so pronounced.

Some comparison of the dynamic factors in the relation of social class and family dynamics to mental disorders was later made of a small sample of schizophrenics and psychoneurotics in Class III and Class V.[88] The schizophrenic patients, who were largely concentrated in Class V, were found to be withdrawn and submissive personalities, to have unstable parental relationships and home situations, and to lack parental interest and affection. On the other hand, the neurotics, mainly from Class III were thought to have more stable home environments, to have the presence of more affection and positive emotional attachment between parents and the family members, and to be characterized by greater rebellion than were the schizophrenics. Two values appeared to permeate all aspects of Class III— respectability and success; throughout life they reported being taught to focus their energies on social acceptance and upward mobility. Both these objectives were difficult for many who later developed mental disorders.

Using a different measure, others have found that the relative incidence of schizophrenia has been found to be directly related to the size of the discrepancy between education and occupational status.[89] Another study, however, found this discrepancy to be lower in some than in their fathers.[90] Instead of using occupation measures, measures of goal discrepancies between the goal aspirations and achievement of persons from low and high

---

[87] Leighton, *My Name Is Legion.*

[88] Jerome K. Myers and Bertram H. Roberts, *Family and Class Dynamics in Mental Illness* (New York: John Wiley & Sons, Inc., 1959).

[89] Jacob Tuckman and Robert J. Kleiner, "Discrepancy between Aspirations and Achievement as a Predictor of Schizophrenia," *Behavioral Science,* 7: 443–447 (1962).

[90] Dunham, Phillips, and Srinivasan, pp. 223–227.

status groups, such as certain racial and religious, have also been used.[91] Generally they have shown that low status persons tend to have greater goal discrepancies than high status persons which would tend to explain the higher rates of disorder in the low status groups.

Why a disproportionate number of schizophrenics are found in the lower class is still undetermined. As noted in the previous discussion, it may be a result of the conflicts in lower-class life itself, which will be discussed subsequently (pages 592–594); of family rearing patterns; or of a discrepancy between goal aspirations and achievements. Another view of social causation is that stresses of lower-class life resulting in downward mobility are associated with the development of schizophrenia. A study of 214 schizophrenic males dealt with factors associated with the presumed relationship between social class and schizophrenia.[92] Analysis of patients' occupations supported the typical finding of a substantially disproportionate number of schizophrenics in the lowest occupational category. In an attempt to determine the source of this overrepresentation, it was determined that the fathers of the patients were also overrepresented at the lowest prestige level, although to a lesser degree. This finding is consistent with the social causation hypothesis regarding the etiology of schizophrenia, but it appeared to make only a minor contribution to the overrepresentation. A detailed analysis of the occupational movement of patients relative to the position of their fathers clearly indicated that subject overrepresentation resulted primarily from downward mobility. An effort was made to distinguish the relative contributions of social selection (the failure of patients ever to attain expected levels) and social drift (the movement from higher-level to lower-level jobs within one's own career) to the observed downward mobility. Social selection accounted in largest measure for the downward shift, with social drift

---

[91] Thomas S. Langner, "Psychophysiological Symptoms and the Status of Women in Two Mexican Communities," in Murphy and Leighton; and Robert J. Kleiner, Jacob Tuckman, and Martha Lavell, "Mental Disorder and Status Based on Race," *Psychiatry*, 23:271–274 (1960).

[92] R. Jay Turner and Morton O. Wagenfeld, "Occupational Mobility and Schizophrenia: An Assessment of the Social Causation and Social Selection Hypotheses," *American Sociological Review*, 32:104–113 (1967). Also see Elliot G. Mishler and Norman A. Scotch, "Sociocultural Factors in the Epidemiology of Schizophrenia," *International Journal of Psychiatry*, 1:258–305 (1965); Dohrenwend; and E. M. Goldberg and S. L. Morrison, "Schizophrenia and Social Class," *British Journal of Psychiatry*, 109:785–802 (1963). One study has attempted to synthesize another explanation by combining the patterns of child socialization in the lowest socioeconomic stratum with the patterns of environmental stress, particularly occupational security, and disorganization among this group. See Roman and Trice, pp. 42–78.

making a relatively minor contribution. A study of a group of mentally ill urban Negroes with a control group in the Negro community reported that both the upwardly mobile and the downwardly mobile persons with mental disorder have greater status inconsistencies, greater goal discrepancies, and more stress than persons from the general community.[93]

MENTAL DISORDER AS A PROCESS

The description of the symptoms of neurotic and psychotic behavior which has been presented gives little insight into the developmental process in mental disorders. The mere description of mental disorders has, in fact, become an increasingly sterile approach to their understanding, prevention, or treatment. Although there are various biological, psychoanalytic, psychiatric, sociocultural, and other explanations of mental disorder, none as yet offer a fully adequate explanation of mental disorder.[94]

> Currently there are three general, theoretical perspectives from which it is possible to examine the nature of mental disorder. First, one can regard mental disorder, both specifically and generally, as resulting from some biological defect or deficit that has a genetic foundation. This view has been productive of a number of empirical studies in the past, and most texts in biology will have something to say about the evidence for this proposition, though such evidence cannot be regarded as conclusive. These studies will not concern us here. However, we call attention to their existence because of the marked tendency among sociologists to rule out biological considerations when they make interpretations of their findings. Second, mental disorder is regarded as the outcome of certain types of personality that have been forged out of conditioning and learning experiences. Such types display behavior that is inappropriate to situations, and they are triggered into social recognition by the impact upon them of various kinds of interpersonal relations and cultural patterns. This perspective represents a dualism wherein personality becomes an entity separated from its biophysiological base. A third possibility is to view mental disorder largely in behavioristic terms, and see it as a kind of behavior that becomes defined as deviant and unacceptable by the significant "others" that surround the person. Here, mental disorder as

---

[93] Seymour Parker and Robert J. Kleiner, *Mental Illness in the Urban Negro Community* (New York: The Free Press, 1966), p. 301.

[94] For a discussion of various theoretical approaches, see Franz Alexander and Sheldon T. Selesnick, *The History of Psychiatry: An Evaluation of Psychiatric Thought and Practice from Prehistoric Times to the Present* (New York: Harper & Row, Publishers, 1966); H. Warren Dunham, *Sociological Theory and Mental Disorder* (Detroit: Wayne State University Press, 1959), and Weinberg, *The Sociology of Mental Disorders*.

such becomes tied to the values and social preferences operating in a given cultural system. From this perspective it could easily be held that what passes for mental disorder in the society is extremely changeable, for it will tend to vary as cultural values, expectations, and preferences vary.[95]

We shall emphasize the sociocultural explanation, with the full realization that it is recent and requires much more research before it can be fully accepted. In a sociocultural framework, the functional mental disorders are primarily seen as normative behavior involving the product of a breakdown of effective communication between persons and defective role playing.[96] Although the psychoses may sometimes be more severe disorders than the neuroses, both arise from, and are perpetuated by, the use of the same inappropriate adjustive techniques in dealing with other persons and social situations in general.[97] Not everyone, of course, who has difficulties in dealing with other people and situations has a mental disorder, for many people, regardless of occasional erratic behavior, are effectual as social persons.

Mental disorders appear to be continuous, dynamic processes, and not a series of separate stages. Some have their origin in childhood; others develop in later life without childhood difficulties. All experiences which affect the person have a profound influence on his relationships with others and his self-reactions. The child or adolescent who does not know how to deal effectively with other people may become shy, and this shyness, in turn, may make him excessively obedient and submissive. It is out of such childhood experiences and later influences that some claim that the "shut-in," seclusive characteristics of many mental disorders develop, including the neurotically withdrawn person and the schizophrenic.

> The mothers of schizophrenics have been characterized as cold, perfectionistic, anxious, over-controlling, and unable to give spontaneous love and acceptance to the child. They often seem unwilling to accord the child any privacy, attempting to intrude even into its thoughts. . . . The net effect of most of the patterns noted is that they would make it

---

[95] H. Warren Dunham, "Anomie and Mental Disorder," in Marshall B. Clinard, ed., *Anomie and Deviant Behavior: A Discussion and Critique* (New York: The Free Press, 1964), pp. 130–131.

[96] A well-known psychiatrist stated that the objectives of psychiatry should be the study of processes that involve or go on between people: "The field of psychiatry is the field of interpersonal relations, under any and all circumstances in which these relations exist."—Harry Stack Sullivan, *Conceptions of Modern Psychiatry* (Washington, D.C.: William Alanson White Psychiatric Foundation, 1947). Also see Osborn.

[97] Cameron, p. 11.

difficult for a child to achieve an identity of his own, to be able to confront life situations with self-reliance and confidence.[98]

Clausen points out, however, that a major limitation of such findings is that families can only be identified and studied after schizophrenia has existed for some time and may well have affected family relations. Moreover, more careful studies do not sem to support the idea that schizophrenics come from families where the mother is dominant and the father submissive, but do show evidence that the family situation is "hostile" to the child, leading to some isolation of the child.[99]

Mental disorders generally have a history and are cumulative rather than products of a single circumstance or a few situations. Childhood experiences and those of early and later adult life have their influence. Difficulties in interpersonal relations and social roles, as well as faulty conception of self, may continue for years before there is the full-fledged development of a mental disorder. A depressed person, for example, may increasingly find more and more types of situations to depress him. This cumulative nature of mental disorder often makes its treatment a long and laborious process.

One study of schizophrenia, for example, has emphasized the distinctive effects of social relationships in many areas of life.[100] The reactions of the schizophrenic, his withdrawal, his attitudes of low self-worth, his anxiety concerning further social rejection, and his distorted meanings of reality all emerge from a series of social relationships. The weakening of the self-system is a product of social isolation and difficulties in interpersonal relations in the family, in peer relations, and with the opposite sex, as well as in work associations.[101]

Notwithstanding the cumulative nature of mental disorders, immediate

---

[98] John A. Clausen, "Mental Disorders," in Merton and Nisbet, pp. 67–68. Also see J. A. Clausen and M. L. Kohn, "Social Relations and Schizophrenia," in Jackson, pp. 295–320.

[99] Daniel J. Caputo, "The Parents of the Schizophrenic," *Family Process*, 2:339–356 (1963); and Stephen Fleck, "Family Dynamics and Origin of Schizophrenia," *Psychosomatic Medicine*, 22:333–344 (1960).

[100] S. Kirson Weinberg, "Social Psychological Aspects of Schizophrenia," in Lawrence Appleby, Jordan M. Scher, and John Cumming, eds, *Chronic Schizophrenia* (New York: The Free Press, 1960). Also see Lloyd H. Rogler and August B. Hollingshead, *Trapped: Families and Schizophrenia* (New York: John Wiley & Sons, Inc., 1965).

[101] S. Kirson Weinberg, "Sociological Analysis of a Schizophrenic Type," *American Sociological Review*, 15:605–606 (1950).

situations occasionally do have a bearing. They act as precipitants and bring the process to a climax. The effect of an immediate situation is particularly important in the manic-depressive disorders, where the anxiety builds up and tends to be set off by it. Although the underlying process would still be there, more study of precipitating situations might reduce the incidence or at least the recurrence of these disorders. A study of a group of manic-depressive cases, for example, revealed that nearly four fifths of them were precipitated by some particularly disturbing life situation, a marital disagreement, the death of someone, a crisis situation in a career, or a feeling of personal failure induced by harsh criticism.[102] These conditions cause particularly severe anxiety and tension. In most cases there had been a period of from one to six months in which anxiety and conflict had been built up.

Stress and Mental Disorder

In social living all persons frequently encounter circumstances in which their personal desires are not achieved. These conflicts may bring about stress, particularly if the situation is such as to threaten the person's self-image, roles, or values. An interference of one kind or another may prevent the adequate development or achievement of a person's desires. Some have felt that stress situations are associated with mental disorder. In fact, one theory of schizophrenia is that it arises from a situation called the "double bind," a situation in which no matter what a person does he cannot win; he is condemned whether or not he does something.[103]

A certain amount of conflict is a part of the normal process of social living. The individual is faced throughout life with conflicts, hazards, and overwhelming demands and perplexities. These tend to produce a certain amount of *anxiety,* which many claim plays an important part in mental disorder. In many ways anxiety resembles fear. Like fear, it is an emotional reaction produced by stimulation with which one is unable to deal, leaving the person with a feeling of possible loss of security and support. Unlike fear reactions, however, which call forth avoidance and even flight from a real danger when this is possible, in anxiety the emotional reaction does not go on to completion. Fear is overt but anxiety is covert, and leaves the person in an undefined emotional state with which he would like to cope but cannot. He is afraid, but since he is unable to identify what he fears he

---

[102] Rennie.

[103] Gregory Bateson, Don D. Jackson, Jay Haley, and John Weakland, "Toward a Theory of Schizophrenia," *Behavioral Science,* 1:251–264 (1956). Also see Paul Watzlawick, "A Review of the Double Bind Theory," *Family Process,* 2:132–153 (1963).

cannot eliminate it. As contrasted with overt fear reactions which can be identified, anxiety reactions are less visible and are often inaccessible both to the individual and to others.

In a nation-wide survey, anxiety, expressed through physical symptoms, has been found to be more prevalent in the lower-income groups where "low income" suggests current unhappiness and worries, no confidence in the future, and anxiety expressed through physical symptoms. On the other hand, psychological anxiety is more common at both extremes, the high and the low income, with middle-income groups expressing the least.[104]

A particular focus of the Midtown Manhattan study of 1660 men and women was stress. The number of stressful factors, but not their nature, was found to be associated with mental disorder.[105] The mental health condition in homes broken by death or divorce was found to be as good as that of people who lived with both parents through the age of sixteen. Low-status groups were found to encounter more stress, which the study suggested might be due to poor resistance and less ego strength. The development of psychophysiological symptoms has been found in another study to be related to the stress produced by the sharp and even moderate inconsistency between high ascribed status based on racial or ethnic rank and low achieved status.[106] A study of the relation of mental disorder among Negroes to goal-striving stress found that there was a higher degree of stress among psychotics than among neurotics.[107] Mentally ill persons were also found to set higher goals than they could achieve and to experience high levels of self-imposed goal-striving stress. Stress has been claimed to be related to high rates of psychoses among Italians in countries where they were a minority.[108]

If stress develops beyond the limits of the individual, there may be chronic anxiety reactions and even acute anxiety attacks. Not only do the

---

[104] Gerald Gurin, Joseph Veroff, Sheila Feld, *Americans View Their Mental Health,* Joint Commission on Mental Illness and Health (Monograph Series No. 4; New York: Basic Books, Inc., 1960), p. 218.

[105] Thomas S. Langner and Stanley T. Michael, *Life Stress and Mental Health,* Vol. II of the Midtown Manhattan Study (New York: The Free Press, 1963), pp. 147–157.

[106] Elton F. Jackson and Peter J. Burke, "Status and Symptoms of Stress: Additive and Interaction Effects," *American Sociological Review,* 30:556–564 (1965); and Elton F. Jackson, "Status Consistency and Symptoms of Stress," *American Sociological Review,* 27:469–480 (1962).

[107] David T. Schwartz and Norbett L. Mintz, "Ecology and Psychosis among Italians in 27 Boston Communities," *Social Problems,* 10:371–374 (1963); and Morris Rosenberg, "The Dissonant Religious Context and Emotional Disturbance," *American Journal of Sociology,* 68:1–10 (1963).

[108] Parker and Kleiner.

symptoms of anxiety continue for a long time; a person may be subject to very pronounced anxiety attacks and even panic reactions. With mounting anxiety the individual may reach the end of his tolerance limit and be subject to great fright. Such persons may become agitated, there may be nausea and salivation, dizziness, weakness in the knees, and hot flashes. He may feel that impending disaster is at hand—that he is going insane, is about to die, is on the verge of a heart attack, and so on. One patient described her anxiety attack after a hot, tiring day in which she had to deal with a domineering superior: "My heart suddenly stopped. Then it came up in my throat and turned over and quivered so fast you couldn't count it. I had a pain in my chest and down my arm. I was like in a tight vise; I couldn't breathe. It seemed like I was going to die." [109]

Neurotic compulsive behavior, such as orderliness and obsessional ideas, helps to relieve anxiety. The acts, words, and thoughts involved in the relief of the anxiety may include tapping, counting, saying a set word, recalling or imagining a certain scene, and even snapping the fingers. In hypochondria, for example, the individual's constant preoccupation with his health simply constitutes solutions in which this preoccupation diverts and releases anxiety. In fact, "the fruit of resistance to the compulsion is mounting anxiety, while the reward of indulgence is a temporary respite." [110] Although tendencies to compulsive neurotic behavior are an irritation and are opposed, the momentary feelings of anxiety lead to the behavior and the subsequent relief. The relief is always temporary, for eventually the anxiety begins to mount again and the patient has to give in to the compulsive behavior in order to reduce it. Moreover, the societal reaction of others to the bizarre behavior, whether neurotic or psychotic, may tend to increase anxiety.

In the schizophrenic disorders and depression, the individual may withdraw and find anxiety fended off as he retreats from threat and conflict to what Cameron calls a "protective shell of incapacity." The paranoid may relieve the prolonged excessive anxiety by focusing it on some individual or situation to which he can attribute his uncomfortable feelings. Manic behavior may constitute "an escape from insupportable anxiety into overt action," or, as often stated, constitute "an escape into reality." [111] Like depressions, this excitement begins after prolonged stress.

One must be careful, however, in explaining mental disorder in terms of stress. Stress-fed situations are not always reacted to in the same way, given situations being perceived differently. From studies of wartime civilian

---

[109] Cameron, p. 255.

[110] Cameron, p. 277.

[111] Cameron, p. 276.

bombing, of soldiers under combat, and of prisoners in concentration camps, it is clear that such stress alone does not generally produce mental breakdowns.

Self-Reactions and Communication

All persons have a self-reaction to their appearance, status, and conduct. They come to conceive of themselves not only as physical objects but as social objects as well. Likewise, human beings learn to express approval of themselves and are able to reproach themselves. This capacity of self-conception which all persons have plays an important part in mental illness. A study, for example, of a small group of emotionally disturbed young boys found that changes in one aspect of self, such as attitudes of others toward them, tended to be associated with other changes in themselves and with changes in overt behavior.[112]

Mentally disordered persons develop distorted self-conceptions or self-images which are reflections of difficulties in interpersonal relations and continuing anxiety. Other persons may come to think of them as "odd," "crazy," or "difficult." Some may become less confident and more preoccupied with themselves. Without logical reasons they may adopt egocentric ideas of being either a great success or a great failure. Where interpersonal relations have been difficult, the mentally ill person may learn to use his self-reactions in fantasy. He may dream of himself as someone he is not in order to overcome conflicts. A seventeen-year-old dishwasher who became mentally disordered built up a strongly organized role of fantasy so that she considered herself a "beautiful duchess, walked on her tiptoes, her mien proud and sweet, her gestures graceful and commanding." [113]

The schizophrenic's continued preoccupation with self and his lessened ability to share his experiences with others intensifies self-centeredness. His self-centered reactions obstruct his capacity to communicate and to relate to others, and this consequently magnifies his own concern about his symptoms and his conflicts, so that he is less able to act with emotional feeling. The reactions and interpretations of a schizophrenic to his hallucinatory behavior are illustrated by the following statement of a patient.

> When I first commenced hearing these voices I am hearing and having them unusual feelings in the arms I could tell by them feelings that I was having was caused by electric flashing and drawing through my body and head and them voices I was hearing about everything that I thought and I knew at the time that it was someone communicating with me in the way

---

[112] William R. Rosengren, "The Self in the Emotionally Disturbed," *American Journal of Sociology*, 66:454–462 (1961).

[113] Cameron, p. 101.

of having a short wave connected to me; and I knew that the short wave was working on my heart for every time I heard a voice my heart fluttered and pounded; and at night when I went to bed in the army barracks that electric would make me shake all over and I knew it was someone broadcasting to me in the way of having a short wave connected to me, but I could not figure out what they could have to do me them ways or who they was and when they first commenced talking to me.[114]

The paranoid's self-reaction is one of conceit and suspicion which affects his relations with others. The self-delusions of grandeur that develop out of this glorified self-conception are seen in extreme form in the paranoids who claim that they "own the entire world."

What a person does can result in self-approval or self-reproach. He can praise himself for what he has said or done, or he may be disturbed by what he has done and rebuke himself, producing frustration and conflict. For adults with a depressive psychosis, this self-punishment, representing an internalization of difficulties with their outside social situations, can become a "tragic melodrama, where the depressed self-accused lashes himself so mercilessly in talk and fantasy that death seems the one promise of penance and relief." [115] If the depressed person feels guilty, self-hostility may result in such a loss of self-respect and so much self-reproach that suicide may even result. In such mental disorders the self may become so detached from the individual that it becomes not a social object but a physical object to be mutilated and punished for "sin." In certain forms of neurotic behavior involving dissociation the person may even be able to forget his own identity. In some cases of hysteria and amnesia the person may even identify with a past role or with another self. In these cases there is an attempt to get away from one's conflicts by changing oneself. The new selves may be alternating or coexisting and one self may not be aware of the other.

Disturbances in language and in meaningful communication, which are often a part of the symptoms in schizophrenia, indicate rather clearly its connection with interpersonal relations.[116] A schizophrenic may be viewed as a person who is unable to discriminate the subtleties in an accurate sense

---

[114] As quoted in Weinberg, "Social Psychological Aspects of Schizophrenia," p. 82.

[115] Cameron, p. 101.

[116] See Julius Laffal, *Pathological and Normal Language* (New York: Atherton Press, 1965). One study has indicated that part of what is called disturbances in language or meaningful conversation of the mentally ill is actually a reflection of social class. See Lloyd H. Rogler and August B. Hollingshead, "Class and Disordered Speech in the Mentally Ill," *Journal of Health and Human Behavior*, 2:178–185 (1961).

in the communications from others and therefore is unable to respond adequately to others.[117] Although verbal imagination is perfectly normal, for without it books, poems, or great music could not be written, a person with a mental disorder, being socially isolated, verbalizes his thoughts and then becomes afraid of what he has created. The mentally disordered person is able to invent a world of his own through his thought processes with language. With language the neurotic is able to conjure up all types of evil thoughts of which he is afraid. The depressed person is able to talk himself into self-depreciation, the manic, into a frenzy. The schizophrenic is able to invent a world of private fantasy which lifts him in his own estimation. This expansion of fantasy, growing out of inadequate responses to shared social situations, continues until it no longer responds to the role taking of others in the culture. One interesting experiment which resulted in the modification of beliefs involved bringing together in group interaction three schizophrenic persons, each of whom believed he was Christ.[118] The disorders in thought processes are eventually expressed through his language and are a result of retreat from reality. The fact that the schizophrenic lives in a world of his own making, through verbal imagery, not only reflects and influences his thought processes but distorts his verbal reactions until they swing completely away from socially adequate responses. Language becomes private and not social; whether the other person understands it is immaterial.

The schizophrenic patient, living in his private world, invents his own common words and links them in such a fashion as to make his speech seem incoherent to others. In response to the question, "Why are you in the hospital?" one patient replied:

> I'm a cut donator, donated by double sacrifice. I get two days for every one. That's known as double sacrifice; in other words, standard cut donator. You know, we considered it. He couldn't have anything for the cut, or for these patients. All of them are double sacrifice because it's unlawful for it to be donated any more. (Well, what do you do here?) I do what is known as the double criminal treatment.
>
> Something that he badly wanted, he gets that, and seven days criminal protection. That's all he gets, and the rest I do for my friend. (Who is the other person who gets all this?) That's the way the asylum cut is donated. (But who is the other person?) He's a criminal. He gets so much. He gets twenty years' criminal treatment, would make forty years; and he gets seven days' criminal protection and that makes fourteen days. That's all he gets.[119]

[117] Rosengren.

[118] Milton Rokeach, *The Open and Closed Mind* (New York: Basic Books, Inc., 1960).

[119] Cameron, pp. 466–467.

MENTAL DISORDER AND SOCIAL ROLES

As has been indicated, we do not yet have, despite many claims, any final, definitive answers as to the causes of mental disorders. Role playing seems to offer, however, a profitable clue.[120] More specifically, difficulties in interpersonal relations found among persons with functional mental disorders appear to arise from role playing. As has been indicated, social roles are organizations of attitudes and responses to certain social situations. Roles must be played so that the points of view and expectations of others in society are shared. Some mental disorder is a product of inappropriate role playing; in other cases it may be actually the playing of a "mentally disordered role."

Social roles appear to enter into the functional mental disorders in several ways. (1) Some individuals may be unable to make the necessary shifts from one role to another as required in normal social relations. (2) There may be contradictions in role playing to which persons cannot adjust. (3) Persons may play the role of a mentally disordered person. To some extent these views of role playing are contradictory. In reality, some mental disorder may represent all three of these views.

Inability to Shift Roles

According to this view, the main characteristic of many persons who develop mental disorder appears to be an inability to shift from one social role to another. This difficulty, it is believed, largely arises from inadequate early childhood socialization. Some believe, in the case of schizophrenia, that there may be a hereditary predisposition. Schizophrenics have not had the kinds of social experiences needed to develop skills in shifting roles. As has been indicated, everyone normally plays many roles, even in a single day, depending upon the situation and the expectations of others. Thus mental disorder may come from having too few or having poorly differentiated sets of roles.[121]

An individual's inability to shift roles means that when "insurmountable personal difficulties arise (he) cannot abandon the non-adaptive perspective by shifting through roles to one that might offer a different solution." [122] Psychotic behavior in a group of married women, for example,

---

[120] For a discussion of role deficiencies in illness, see Talcott Parsons, "Definitions of Health and Illness," in E. Gartly Jaco, ed., *Patients, Physicians and Illness* (New York: The Free Press, 1960).

[121] John Cumming and Elaine Cumming, *Ego and Milieu* (London: Tavistock Publications, Ltd., 1964).

[122] Cameron, p. 94.

has been found to arise from the difficulty in making a transition from childhood to marital-parental roles; as a result of this poor role adaptation they faced much conflict.[123]

Paranoid behavior, according to Cameron,[124] appears to be a product of inappropriate role playing and role taking. Paranoids have an inflexible way of looking at things; they cannot shift roles or see alternative explanations for the behavior of others. Gradually a private world is built up in which the self as a social object becomes central and in which slights and discriminations, some real and some imagined, from the outside world are interpreted to fit the paranoid's preconceptions. He develops a "pseudo community" which is a product of his unique interpretation of "persecution" in the ordinary behavior of others toward him. He is unable to interpret accurately the roles of others and is therefore not socially competent to interpret their motives and intentions. His systematized paranoid or paranoiac delusions of discrimination and persecution develop out of his attempt to account for situations and happenings which are the products of his own lack of socialization and his fantasies. The pseudo community in which the paranoid lives is a private world which is real but not shared with others. In the earlier stages of paranoid behavior his private world seldom gives an overt indication of his thoughts. He may be socially acceptable in his manners, in courtesy, in personal conversation, and in community activities, but as his delusions grow in intensity the paranoid becomes more and more suspicious. On those rare occasions when he comes later to share his suspicions with others their ridicule makes him even more convinced that he is right. As a result he may suddenly decide that an extensive plot is being directed against him. The reactions of the real community in the form of restraint or retaliation for any of his vengeful or defensive overt behaviors make him convinced that the interpretations of his paranoid pseudo community are correct.

This interpretation of a "pseudo community" has been challenged by Lemert, who maintains, after studying a number of cases of paranoia, that the community to which the paranoid reacts is real and not a pseudo or symbolic fabrication.[125] He states that "while the paranoid person reacts differentially to his social environment, it is also true that 'others' react differentially to him and this reaction commonly if not typically involves

---

[123] Harold Sampson, Sheldon L. Messinger and Robert D. Towne, *Schizophrenic Women: Studies in Marital Crisis* (New York: Atherton Press, 1964).

[124] Cameron, pp. 466–467.

[125] Edwin M. Lemert, *Human Deviance, Social Problems, and Social Control* (Englewood Cliffs, N.J.: Prentice-Hall, Inc., 1967), Chap. 15, "Paranoia and the Dynamics of Exclusion."

covertly organized action and conspiratorial behavior in a very real sense." [126] Moreover, the reactions of the potential paranoid and those of "others" are reciprocal and result in exclusion. The delusions and associated behavior which develop must be understood in the context of a process of exclusion which disrupts his social communication with others.

One theory of schizophrenia for which there is considerable evidence is that the schizophrenic person often finds it difficult to play the roles expected of him in normal social relations and tends to be socially isolated.[127] He has never developed the necessary skill, when under stress, to be able to change his role in social situations. Situations which require social adjustment, and are easily handled by the average person, take on enormous proportions for the preschizophrenic. Shy and retiring as a child, he may not only be misunderstood by his more active peers but be the subject of their abuse as well. The so-called period of strain and stress of adolescence, when schizophrenic disorders begin to make their appearance, carries some of the elements of isolation. A detailed study of catatonic schizophrenics has shown that their solitary social roles prior to the onset of the illness were different from those of other boys in the community. These future patients could not establish intimate and informal relationships with others their age and as a result were unable to gain an adequate social conception of themselves.[128] In a study of fifty-three transitory schizophrenics, Weinberg found that their isolation resulted from the fact that they were unable to communicate their conflicts to others and assumed their characteristic role taking as a matter of self-protection.[129] By withdrawing they avoided the evaluation of others, building, in turn, a world which they did not share.

Although it is true that at the time of hospitalization very few schizophrenics have close ties, a fact that tends to support the isolation theory, the evidence is not conclusive. One study of the social aspects of the childhood and adolescence of schizophrenics and a matched control group of so-called "normal" persons found that only about a third of the schizophrenics were isolates from their peers early in adolescence.[130]

---

[126] Lemert, *Human Deviance,* p. 198.

[127] This concept of isolation was developed by Robert E. L. Faris and H. Warren Dunham in their *Mental Disorders in Urban Areas* (Chicago: University of Chicago Press, 1939).

[128] H. Warren Dunham, "The Social Personality of the Catatonic-Schizophrenic," *American Journal of Sociology,* 49:508–518 (1944).

[129] S. Kirson Weinberg, "A Sociological Analysis of a Schizophrenic Type," *American Sociological Review,* 15:609 (1950).

[130] M. L. Kohn and John A. Clausen, "Social Isolation and Schizophrenia," *American Sociological Review,* 20:265–273 (1955).

It has even been claimed that because of certain hereditary genes schizophrenics are persons who are vulnerable to certain social situations.[131] If the environment is favorable the genetic predisposition may not have an effect.[132] In this connection geneticists have attempted to demonstrate that heredity plays a leading part in schizophrenic disorders. For example, a number of studies in Sweden have indicated the possibility of genetic family patterns. Although the incidence of the disorder may be 1 percent in the general population, the incidence in those persons with schizophrenic parents is 10 to 15 percent.[133] This finding obviously does not refute the fact that social situations in a schizophrenic family may be the cause rather than heredity.

Kallman has been a leading proponent of the theory that schizophrenia is inherited, and the conclusions from his studies are often cited as proof that genetic factors predispose certain persons to schizophrenic behavior. He studied 1087 Berlin schizophrenic cases selected from 15,000 cases between the years 1893 and 1902; later, in New York, he made a study of pairs of twins of which one or both were diagnosed as schizophrenic.[134] He diagnosed the Berlin cases from information he secured and then compared them with the case histories of relatives. He found that 68.1 percent of the children whose parents were both schizophrenic developed schizophrenia. Where there was one such parent the chances were about one in six; with schizophrenic siblings, one in ten; nephews and nieces, one in twenty-five; and grandchildren, one in twenty. In the later study Kallman used 794 twin

---

[131] Dunham has suggested that mental disorder is a product of a broader conception of vulnerability of some persons to social situations. These include "genetic structure, the constitutional strength of the organism, disturbances in metabolism, physiological deficits, the role of the family in transmitting a culture, traumatic childhood experiences, and experiences with one's peers in the developmental years." Dunham, "Anomie and Mental Disorder," in Clinard, *Anomie and Deviant Behavior,* p. 155. Some researchers today, particularly Robert G. Heath of Tulane University, hold that schizophrenia is a biochemical abnormality and that if this abnormality could be identified the patient could be cured by correcting his body chemistry.

[132] See, for example, Clausen, "Mental Disorders," p. 69.

[133] J. A. Böök, "A Genetic and Neuropsychiatric Investigation of a North Swedish Population," *Acta Genetica et Statistica Medica,* 4:1–100, 133–139, 345–414 (1953).

[134] Franz J. Kallman, *The Genetics of Schizophrenia* (Locust Valley, N.Y.: J. J. Augustin, Inc., 1938). Also Franz J. Kallman, "The Genetic Theory of Schizophrenia," *American Journal of Psychiatry,* 103:309–322 (1946); reprinted in Clyde Kluckhohn, Henry A. Murray, and David M. Schneider, *Personality in Nature, Society, and Culture* (rev. ed.; New York: Alfred A. Knopf, Inc., 1959), pp. 80–100.

index cases, obtained over a nine-year period from New York mental hospitals, and compared them with the case histories of relatives. He also concluded that the more distant the relationship the less likelihood of schizophrenia and that "the predisposition to schizophrenia—that is, the ability to respond to certain stimuli with a schizophrenic type of reaction—depends on the presence of a specific genetic factor which is probably recessive and autosomal." [135] Although Kallman's is the leading study, others have tried to show that schizophrenia is hereditary. All of these efforts have been subject to severe criticism.[136]

1. Today Kallman's work is the single major source referred to by most authors writing on schizophrenia. In spite of this, Jackson made an exhaustive search of American and European literature of the past forty years and uncovered only two cases of twins who developed schizophrenia after having been allegedly reared apart. Considering the incidence of schizophrenia, these two cases could have occurred on a chance basis.

2. A joint study by a sociologist and psychiatrist who made a comprehensive survey of schizophrenic cases in the Greater New Haven area failed to show a significant number of relatives with schizophrenia.[137] Their cases consisted of all private and public mental hospital cases, as well as cases treated privately outside the hospital by psychiatrists. Of the 847 schizophrenic cases studied, only 25 percent had schizophrenic relatives.[138]

3. A truly Mendelian approach to the inheritance of schizophrenia cannot be carried out with human beings in the same manner as with plants and animals because human environments do not remain constant as is required in Mendelian studies.[139]

4. The problem of diagnosis is the greatest obstacle in the genetic study of schizophrenia. Often the diagnosis of schizophrenia is made on the basis of family history, a person being diagnosed as schizophrenic if someone in his family has been so diagnosed. There is a tendency even among clinicians to see twins as similar, whether they actually are or not.

5. Diseases may run in families, even physical ones, without having a genetic basis. For example, beriberi does so, but "what is 'inherited' is the pattern of preference for vitamin-poor foods which children pick up from their parents." [140] The fact that mental disorder may appear in a family line does not prove that it is inherited. These studies need to take into

---

[135] Kallman, "The Genetic Theory of Schizophrenia," p. 321.

[136] Don D. Jackson, "A Critique of the Literature on the Genetics of Schizophrenia," in Jackson, *The Etiology of Schizophrenia*, pp. 37–87.

[137] Hollingshead and Redlich.

[138] From a private communication from A. B. Hollingshead.

[139] Jackson, *The Etiology of Schizophrenia*.

[140] Jackson, *The Etiology of Schizophrenia*, p. 44.

account the effects on children of being reared in a family where one or both parents are mentally disturbed and the effect of the total environment.

6. The genetic mode of transmission has not been determined, and until this is done the genetic nature of schizophrenia will remain questionable.[141] Also, there has been no relationship established between hereditary taint, type of schizophrenia, age of onset, and outcome. Such studies do not tell us how the symptoms of mental disorder are related to hereditary transmission. In schizophrenia, for example, the person does not share reality with others, he has blunted emotional behavior, and he has disrupted role playing. Just how social behavior of this type is carried in the genes is not only not clarified; this crucial question is rarely raised. As Hollingshead has concluded about the inheritance of schizophrenia, "This theoretical approach has not been explored adequately; its validity remains in doubt." [142]

Contradictory Roles

The necessity for persons to play many and contradictory roles is perfectly normal. With normal activity an individual can meet this contradiction in roles. For example, a person plays one role with the marital partner and another with his parents. Individuals who cannot adjust to these changes often develop anxiety and mental disorder.

It has been suggested that a causal factor in the manic-depressive psychoses may be such intense group relationships and so many conflicting and contradictory roles that the resulting strain is enough to cause a breakdown. The individual who is all things to all people in his desire to please and to gain attention and prestige and who is continually participating in group activities may lose his basic and characteristic orientation. The demands and values of too many groups and too fervent participation leave him unable to incorporate them coherently into his life organization.

The hypothesis has been advanced by some writers, particularly in connection with the neuroses, that the intense striving for material goods and the competitive emphasis in present-day industrial urban society lead many persons to irreconcilable conflicts. Horney has suggested that contemporary life in modern Western societies is characterized by individualistic, competitive striving for achievement and social status and that as a result interpersonal relations are likely to be hostile and to promote insecurity.[143] This leads to conflicts between materialistic desires and the pos-

---

[141] Jackson, *The Etiology of Schizophrenia.*

[142] Hollingshead, "Epidemiology of Schizophrenia."

[143] Karen Horney, *The Neurotic Personality of Our Time* (New York: W. W. Norton & Company, Inc., 1937).

sibility of their fulfillment and between competitive striving and the desire for the affection of others, all of which tend to produce neuroses, particularly in urban males. Group contacts are maintained not for the social and personal gratifications to be derived from them, but because they may serve as steppingstones to getting ahead. Should prestige, status, class position, or material goods be threatened, the individual's world may collapse, leaving him with no supports. Economic competition, for example, operated in five hundred psychiatric cases as a factor in their mental illness.[144] The struggle for achievement liberated feelings of hostility in some patients. In others the culturally prescribed standards of success and prestige presented goals impossible of achievement and thus augmented already existing conflicts.

A more recent intensive study of schizophrenics and nonschizophrenics in a representative sample of lower-class husbands and wives, between twenty and thirty-nine, in the slums and housing projects *(caserios)* of San Juan, Puerto Rico, has presented evidence that such disorders cannot be explained by childhood experiences, social isolation, or occupational history, but rather on the basis of conflicts and problems associated with lower-class life and neighborhood situations.

> The husbands or wives who are schizophrenic present no evidence that they were exposed to greater hardships, more economic deprivation, more physical illnesses, or personal dilemmas from birth until they entered their present marriage than do the mentally healthy men and women. They had as many friends as the well persons; they viewed their friends and think they were viewed by their friends in the same terms as well persons think of their early peer relationships. The leisure time activities of the two groups were similar. There is no evidence that the sick persons were more prone to solitary activities than the well ones.
>
> In sum, systematic comparisons between the mentally healthy and the sick persons indicate that they are remarkably similar in their assumption of the appropriate social roles for each sex at the customary age. The life histories demonstrate that in childhood, youth, and early adult life there are only a few significant differences between the behavior of those who are now mentally healthy and those who are suffering from schizophrenia. One notable difference is the more frequent occurrence of nightmares during childhood among the sick than among the well persons. The occupational histories are almost identical in the two groups, with the exception that the schizophrenic women were gainfully employed at an earlier age than the well women.[145]

---

[144] Stanley A. Leavy and Lawrence Z. Freedman, "Psychoneurosis and Economic Life," *Social Problems,* 4:55–67 (1956).

[145] From Lloyd H. Rogler and August B. Hollingshead, *Trapped* (New York: John Wiley & Sons, Inc., 1965), pp. 404–405. This excerpt and those that follow are used by permission of the publisher.

What appears to be important are the role conflicts and personal problems which persons either solve successfully or become their victims. The schizophrenics had many more, as well as more severe problems, than the nonschizophrenics. The culture and their low socioeconomic status in the society present some persons with tension points. Such problems in this Spanish culture of Puerto Rico include courtship, woman's adjustment to sexual and other roles in marriage, the disparity between achieved and desired levels of living, conflict with neighbors, and the absence of privacy in the housing projects, as well as various problems of role fulfillment and performance. These problems continue to mount, imposing contradictory claims and leading to conflict, mutual withdrawal and alienation of neighbors, until the individual reaches a breaking point.

> The break in the life arc coincides with a complex of interrelated crises the schizophrenic person experienced during the 12 months preceding the perceived onset of his illness. He views these critical experiences as personal dilemmas with which he has to wrestle and, in some way, solve. His competence is called into question by the crises he faces. His adequacy in the performance of his basic social roles as a man and a husband, or a woman and a wife, is on trial. Coping with the difficulties that encompass him becomes the central issue in his life.[146]

The process finally moves on toward schizophrenic symptoms.

> The acceleration of problems in the life of the vulnerable persons and in the family, combined with the self-awareness of role failure, appears to be a factor in the development of the illness. A husband who inadequately fulfills the role demands required of him has this fact brought to his attention by his wife, relatives, or other persons outside the immediate family. As a consequence, his failure creates interpersonal difficulties in the home, on the job, and, often, in the neighborhood. The sense of inadequacy which results from a failure to fulfill normal role requirements becomes an intrinsic part of his very being. Relentless social pressures are converted internally into emotional stress. The besieged person, unable to cope with his external and internal crises, becomes physically and mentally distraught. He becomes the victim of his failure.[147]

> The sick men and the sick women change, as worry over their personal difficulties grips their thoughts both day and night. The afflicted person becomes tense; he prepares for attacks from persons and situations in his immediate environment and from within himself. He experiences an overwhelming fatigue that limits his capacity to fulfill everyday obligations. He begins to define himself as ill, but the unpredictability

---

146 Rogler and Hollingshead, *Trapped,* p. 409.
147 Rogler and Hollingshead, *Trapped,* p. 410.

of his aches and pains is puzzling. During this phase of his developing illness, the sick man is punished for his symptoms by his boss, work associates, neighbors, and relatives. He reacts to insults by fighting back in some instances and by withdrawal in others. In his search for a way out of the social and psychological labyrinth that enmeshes him, he begins to exhibit the behavior that the society defines as *locura* [insanity]. The ailing person is haunted by the dread of becoming a *loco* [crazy person].

The idiosyncratic, erratic, and hallucinatory person begins to disengage himself from normal social intercourse, as he fears the stigma of identification as a *loco*. Simultaneously, the social groups in which he has previously participated move away from him.[148]

A series of secondary problems come into existence. The ailing person has to cope with the crises that have come upon him; the internalized strains associated with his failure to meet his social obligations, the symptoms he reveals to his associates, and, finally, the heavily charged social definition of his illness. The problems encountered by the sick person overlap. The failure to solve one dilemma appears to condition the development of an additional one; a snowballing effect occurs until the person, enmeshed in insoluble difficulties, is overwhelmed. . . .

The person who decompensates into a schizophrenic solution to his personal difficulties, metaphorically speaking, is caught in a trap with two compartments: one is the intermeshed series of insoluble dilemmas he encounters in his failure to fulfill the role requirements of his society; the other is the culturally defined role of the *loco*. The sick man or woman fears, as he searches for a way out of his personal maze of problems, that he may spring the catch on the trap that will make him a *loco*. To be recognized and treated as a *loco* is to be truly an outcast in this society which places a mentally ill person outside the bounds of a normal social life.[149]

Playing the Role of a Mentally Disordered Person

According to Scheff, residual rule breaking is very common and may arise from diverse sources, such as organic difficulties, psychological problems, external stress, or willful volitional acts of defiance against some person or situation; consequently its origin is of little consequence.[150] At this level it appears to occur on a large scale, most of it being unrecorded. In fact, most residual rule breaking is of transitory significance and constitutes primary deviance. Most residual rule breaking is not recognized by others

---

[148] Rogler and Hollingshead, *Trapped,* pp. 411–412.

[149] Rogler and Hollingshead, *Trapped,* p. 412.

[150] Scheff, *Being Mentally Ill.* For discussion of residual rule breaking or residual deviance, see page 461.

or by the individual or tends to be rationalized away. One may have an illusion or auditory state and simply forget it.

Some persons may develop patterns of behavior in response to others' imputations that their behavior represents the playing of residual roles or the role of a person with a mental disorder or with a secondary deviation.[151] Others may come to define the rule breaking as deviant. Persons may take on the role of "insanity" when it is suggested that they are mentally ill. Many societies, such as that of the United States, popularly define certain behavior as "crazy"; people have shared concepts of what is meant by insanity or what Scheff has termed the "social institution of insanity." [152] Popular conceptions of mental disorder are perpetuated and reaffirmed in everyday conversations and in the mass media, such as comic strips, television, newspapers, books, and songs, even in advertising. One can learn from the culture the stereotyped imagery of what is mental disorder even in childhood, for children often "play crazy." [153] Adult persons know how to "act crazy."

A common stereotype of mental disorder was found in a systematic and large-scale content analysis of television, radio, newspapers, and magazines. "Media presentations emphasized the bizarre symptoms of the mentally ill. . . . In television dramas, for example, the afflicted person often enters the scene staring glassy-eyed, with his mouth widely ajar, mumbling incoherent phrases or laughing uncontrollably. Even in what would be considered the milder disorders, neurotic phobias and obsessions, the afflicted person is presented as having bizarre facial expressions and action." [154]

The symptoms of mental disorder are learned and are not of biological origin. Like the type-casting of actors, the playing of the role of a mentally disordered person can become stabilized because of the deference, expectations, and role taking received from others.

> Role imagery of insanity is learned early in childhood and is reaffirmed in social interaction. In a crisis, when the deviance of an individual becomes a public issue, the traditional stereotype of insanity becomes the guiding

---

[151] Scheff, *Being Mentally Ill.*

[152] Scheff, *Being Mentally Ill.* Also see Thomas Scheff, "The Role of the Mentally Ill and the Dynamics of Mental Disorder: A Research Framework," *Sociometry,* 26:236–453 (1963) and his "The Societal Reaction to Deviance: Ascriptive Elements in the Psychiatric Screening of Mental Patients in a Midwestern State," *Social Problems,* 11:401–413 (1964).

[153] Also see A. C. Cain, "On the Meaning of 'Playing Crazy' in Borderline Children," *Psychiatry,* 27:278–289 (1964).

[154] J. C. Nunnally, Jr., *Popular Conceptions of Mental Health* (New York: Holt, Rinehart and Winston, Inc., 1961), p. 74.

imagery for action, both for those reacting to the deviant and, at times, for the deviant himself. When societal agents and persons around the deviant react to him uniformly in terms of the traditional stereotypes of insanity, his amorphous and unstructured rule-breaking tends to crystallize in conformity to these expectations, thus becoming similar to the behavior of other deviants classified as mentally ill, and stable over time. The process of becoming uniform and stable is completed when the traditional imagery becomes a part of the deviant's orientation for guiding his own behavior.[155]

Where treatment tends to attach the label of mental disorder to a person it may enhance the stability of the role. In fact, labeled deviants under treatment may be "rewarded" by professional persons for "accepting" the fact that they are mentally ill. Moreover, labeled deviants may have difficulty in turning to another role and come to accept their deviant role as the only one available.

To recapitulate Scheff's theory of mental disorder, it consists of six propositions: [156]

1. *Residual rule breaking arises from fundamentally diverse sources.* Four distinct types of sources will be discussed here: organic, psychological, external stress, and volitional acts of innovation or defiance. (P. 40.)

2. *Relative to the rate of treated mental illness, the rate of unrecorded residual rule breaking is extremely high.* There is evidence that gross violations of rules are often not noticed or, if noticed, are rationalized as eccentricity. Apparently, many persons who are extremely withdrawn, or who "fly off the handle" for extended periods of time, who imagine fantastic events, or who hear voices or see visions, are not labeled as insane either by themselves or others. Their rule breaking, rather, is unrecognized, ignored, or rationalized. This pattern of inattention and rationalization will be called "denial." (Pp. 47–48.)

3. *Most residual rule breaking is "denied" and is of transitory significance.* The enormously high rates of total prevalence suggest that most residual rule breaking is unrecognized or rationalized away. . . . A person in this stage may "organize" his deviance in other than illness terms, e.g., as eccentricity or genius, or the rule breaking may terminate when situational stress is removed. (Pp. 51–52.)

4. *Stereotyped imagery of mental disorder is learned in early childhood.*

---

[155] Scheff, *Being Mentally Ill,* p. 82. A study of schizophrenia among lower-class persons in Puerto Rico seems also to support the role of cultural stereotypes in a person's definition of himself as "crazy" or "loco." See Rogler and Hollingshead, *Trapped.*

[156] Scheff, *Being Mentally Ill.* The specific pages for the six propositions are given following each proposition. Italics are Scheff's.

Although there are no substantiating studies in this area, scattered observations lead Scheff to conclude that children learn a considerable amount of imagery concerning deviance very early, and that much of the imagery comes from their peers rather than from adults. (P. 64.)

5. *The stereotypes of insanity are continually reaffirmed, inadvertently, in ordinary social interaction.* Although many adults become acquainted with medical concepts of mental illness, the traditional stereotypes are not discarded, but continue to exist alongside the medical conceptions because the stereotypes receive almost continual support from the mass media and in ordinary social discourse. (Pp. 67–68.)

6. *Labeled deviants may be rewarded for playing the stereotyped deviant role.* Ordinarily patients who display "insight" are rewarded by psychiatrists and other personnel. That is, patients who manage to find evidence of "their illness" in their past and present behavior, confirming the medical and societal diagnosis, receive benefits. This pattern of behavior is a special case of a more general pattern that has been called the "apostolic function" by Balint, in which the physician and others inadvertently cause the patient to display symptoms of the illness the physician thinks the patient has. (P. 84.)

This theory proposed by Scheff seems to have considerable evidence to support it. Whether the theory is valid and would apply to *all* forms of mental disorder, or to mental disorder in all other societies, will have to wait for further research.

SUMMARY

Mental disorder can be divided into the organic and the functional, the latter being primarily of interest to social scientists. Mental disorder may be defined statistically, clinically, in terms of middle-class values, and in terms of residual norms and societal reaction. Because of definition the extent of mental disorder is difficult to determine.

Sociocultural factors have been shown, in a variety of studies, to play a significant role in the development of functional mental disorders. There is evidence that diagnosed mental disorders are related to differences in occupation and social class.

Mental disorder can be viewed as a process. Stress has been emphasized in a number of studies. Self-reactions and problems in communication play a part.

Roles enter into the functional mental disorders in a number of ways. Some persons are unable to make the necessary shifts from one role to another as required in normal social relations, there may be contradictions in role playing to which persons cannot adjust, and some persons may play the role of a mentally disordered person.

SELECTED READINGS

Alexander, Franz G., and Sheldon T. Selesnick. *The History of Psychiatry.* New York: Harper & Row, Publishers, 1966. A discussion and evaluation of psychiatric thought and practice from early history to the present. Discusses various views of mental disorder historically and theoretically.

Cameron, Norman. *The Psychology of Behavior Disorders,* Boston: Houghton Mifflin Company, 1947, Chap. 4. One of the best discussions of role playing, language, and self-conception in relation to personality disorders. The author is both a psychiatrist and a psychologist.

Clausen, John A. "Mental Disorders," in Robert K. Merton and Robert A. Nisbet, eds., *Contemporary Social Problems.* New York: Harcourt, Brace & World, Inc., 2d ed., 1966. A critical discussion of the sociological aspects of mental disorder.

Dunham, H. Warren. *Sociological Theory and Mental Disorder.* Detroit: Wayne State University Press, 1958. A collection of both new and previously published papers on mental disorder. The author adds a new section on epidemiology and details the underlying assumptions of two current alternative conceptions of mental illness and health.

Eaton, Joseph W., and Robert J. Weil. *Culture and Mental Disorders.* New York: The Free Press, 1955. This is primarily a study of the limited extent of mental disorders among a religious sect, the Hutterites. In this joint study by a sociologist and a psychiatrist there is also a detailed comparison of ten other studies of mental disorder in various cultures.

Hollingshead, August B., and Frederick C. Redlich. *Social Class and Mental Illness.* New York: John Wiley & Sons, Inc., 1958. An analysis of the incidence and types of mental disorders in terms of social class.

Horney, Karen. *Our Inner Conflicts.* New York: W. W. Norton & Company, Inc., 1945. This study of neuroses, primarily in terms of reactions of going away from, against, or toward other people, is still one of the best.

Jahoda, Marie. *Current Concepts of Positive Mental Health.* Monograph Series; Joint Commission on Mental Illness and Health. New York: Basic Book, Inc., 1958. A discussion of the problems involved in attempting to define mental illness. The author does not resolve any of the issues her discussion raises, but she specifies the necessary considerations involved.

Leighton, Alexander H., and John A. Clausen, and Robert N. Wilson. *Explorations in Social Psychiatry.* New York: Basic Books, Inc., 1957. A collection of papers by representatives of several disciplines dealing with the issues, approach, and specific problems studied in social psychiatry.

Murphy, Jane M., and Alexander H. Leighton. *Approaches to Cross-Cultural Psychiatry.* Ithaca, N.Y.: Cornell University Press, 1965. A discussion by persons from various scientific disciplines of the ways of identifying the mentally ill in other cultures and of what kinds of sociocultural factors influence the origin, course, and outcome of psychiatric disorders.

Opler, Marvin K. *Culture and Social Psychiatry.* New York: Atherton Press, 1967.

This revision of his *Culture, Psychiatry, and Human Values* includes a discussion of the connection between culture and mental health, the perspectives of theory and research on cultural change and development, the migration of acculturating populations, and the resulting shifts in diagnostic and therapeutic problems brought on by the stresses of the modern world. Much of the discussion is cross-cultural.

Rogler, Lloyd H., and August B. Hollingshead. *Trapped: Families and Schizophrenia*. New York: John Wiley & Sons, Inc., 1965. A study of schizophrenia in the slums and housing projects of San Juan, Puerto Rico. The findings indicate that experiences in the childhood and adolescence of schizophrenic persons do not differ noticeably from those of persons who are not schizophrenic. A set of mutually reinforcing problems and role conflicts accounts for the mental disorder.

Scheff, Thomas J. *Being Mentally Ill: A Sociological Theory*. Chicago: Aldine Publishing Company, 1966. A sociological explanation of mental disorder in term of residual rule breaking, societal reaction, and the social institution of insanity. Most mental disorder is regarded as a social role, and societal reaction as usually the most important determinant of entry into that role.

————., ed. *Mental Illness and Social Process*. New York: Harper & Row, Publishers, 1967. A series of articles dealing with the categories and stereotypes that are called into play in the "recognition" of mental disorder, the judgmental processes that occur after a "diagnosis" of suspected mental illness has been made, and the social and psychological processes that are involved in psychiatric treatment and diagnosis.

Weinberg, S. Kirson, ed. *The Sociology of Mental Disorders*. Chicago: Aldine Publishing Company, 1967. This comprehensive series of articles deals with what the author terms "psychiatric sociology." It includes a discussion of the epidemiology of mental disorder, personality development and mental disorders, disordered behavior and social deviance, and cross-cultural aspects of disordered behavior and treatment. Also included is a discussion of the prevention and treatment of mental disorder.

13

Suicide

Generally, suicide refers to the destruction of one's self, self-killing, or, in a legalistic sense, self-murder. In one widely quoted definition, suicide is either "the intentional taking of one's life or the failure when possible to save one's self when death threatens." [1] Durkheim, the leading authority on suicide, defined it in a way as to include such acts of altruism as religious martyrs, "all cases of death resulting directly or indirectly from a positive or negative act of the victim himself, which he knows will produce the result." [2]

Two main forms of suicide may be distinguished.[3] One form is the definite desire on the part of a person to take his own life largely for this reason only. In the second form there is the additional desire to attract attention, to secure sympathy, or to revenge oneself on someone. Sometimes the same objective is then accomplished by a mere attempt at suicide.

Many persons commit suicide each year, although in comparison with

---

[1] Ruth S. Cavan, *Suicide* (Chicago: University of Chicago Press, 1928), p. 3.

[2] Emile Durkheim, *Suicide* (translated by John A. Spaulding and George Simpson; New York: The Free Press, 1951), p. 44.

[3] Ernest R. Mowrer, *Disorganization, Personal and Social* (Philadelphia: J. B. Lippincott Company, 1942), p. 332.

such forms of deviant behavior as crime or mental disorders, the number is small. During 1963 in the United States, 20,825 persons took their lives, a rate of 11.0 per 100,000 population. Probably at least another 125,000 made unsuccessful attempts to kill themselves.[4] Since 1950 the suicide rate in this country, per 100,000 population, has fluctuated from a high in 1950, of 11.4, to a low of 10.0 in 1952. (See Table 13.1.) Over a long period of time the fluctuation in suicide rates is more marked. The rate in 1900 in the United States was 10.2, 15.3 in 1910, 10.2 in 1920, and 15.6 in 1930. As has been previously indicated, suicide rates are responsive to marked economic changes being generally higher during periods of depression and lower during periods of prosperity.[5] Wars are usually characterized by a marked decline in suicide rates.[6]

TABLE 13.1   **Number and Rate of Suicides per 100,000 Population, United States, 1950–1963**

Year	Number	Rate per 100,000
1950	17,145	11.4
1951	15,909	10.4
1952	15,567	10.0
1953	15,947	10.1
1959	18,633	10.6
1960	19,450	10.8
1961	18,999	10.4
1962	20,207	11.0
1963	20,825	11.0

SOURCE: *Statistical Abstracts of the United States,* 1950–1963. Data for 1959 include Alaska; data for 1960–1963 include both Alaska and Hawaii.

SUICIDE AND SOCIETAL REACTION

So strongly is suicide condemned by Western European peoples that one might assume this attitude to be universal. Both today and in the past, however, attitudes toward self-destruction have varied widely. Moham-

---

[4] Harry Alpert, "Suicides and Homicides," *American Sociological Review,* 15:673 (1950). The statistical department of the Metropolitan Life Insurance Company estimates that the number of attempted suicides is six to seven for each actual suicide. Quoted in G. L. Williams, *The Sanctity of Life and the Criminal Law* (New York: Alfred A. Knopf, Inc., 1957), p. 272.

[5] See pages 150–151.

[6] See page 150.

medan countries strongly condemn suicide, the Koran expressly condemns it, and in actuality it rarely occurs there. The people of the Orient, however, do not normally disapprove of suicide. In fact, suttee, or the suicide of a widow on her husband's death, was common in India until well into the last century.[7] Priests taught that such a voluntary death would be a passport to heaven, atone for the sins of the husband and give social distinction to the relatives and children. Other aspects of Hindu philosophy, encouraged suicide for religious reasons and particularly the tendency to disregard the physical body. Suicide was regarded as acceptable in China; when committed for revenge it was considered a particularly useful device against an enemy because it not only embarrassed him but enabled the dead man to haunt him from the spirit world. Voluntary death has been given an honorable place in Buddhist countries, but for devout Buddhists there is neither birth nor death, the individual being expected to prepare himself to meet all types of fate with stoical indifference.

For many centuries suicide has been favorably regarded in Japan. Among all classes, but particularly among the nobility and the military, it was traditionally taught that one must surrender to the demands of duty and honor. Hara-kiri, originally a ceremonial form of suicide to avoid capture after military defeat and later to avoid disgrace or other punishment, was practiced even during and after World War II. The suicide compact of lovers who wish to terminate their existence in this world and to go to another is not unusual in Japan, nor is suicide for revenge or as a protest against the actions of an enemy.

The attitude of contemporary Western European peoples toward suicide originated mainly in the philosophies of the Jewish and later the Christian religions. The Talmudic law of the Jewish religion takes a strong position against suicide: respect should not be paid the memory of the suicide although comfort should be given to his family. Suicide and infanticide had been prevalent in ancient Rome, but with the spread and acceptance of Christianity came a change in the attitude toward human life. Basic to the Christian condemnation of suicide were the concepts that human life is sacred, that the individual is subordinate to God, and that death should be considered an entrance to a new life in which one's behavior in the old is important. Moreover, death was followed by Purgatory, in which an individual suffered in order to expiate some types of sins, but those who had committed such a sin as suicide were banished eternally to the torments of Hell. Death, to the Christians, unlike the pagans of Rome, was not something to look forward to without some misgivings. This con-

---

[7] Upendra Thakur, *The History of Suicide in India* (Delhi: Munshi Ram Manohar Lal, Publishers, 1963).

cept of life after death strengthened the position of the Church.[8] In addition, Christian doctrine looked upon life as an opportunity for moral discipline and resignation in the presence of pain and suffering endured in the hope of another and happier world.

Although at first Christians sanctioned suicide connected with martyrdom or the protection of virginity, eventually they disapproved of it for any reason and it became not only a sin in Christian countries but a crime against the state.[9] The property of a suicide might, for example, be confiscated and the corpse subjected to various mutilations. The laws of some European countries provided that the body of a suicide could be removed from a house only through a special hole in the wall, should be dragged through the streets, might be hung on the gallows, thrown into a sewer, burned, or even transfixed by a stake on a public highway as a sign of disrespect.

In the medieval ages church leaders denounced suicide, particularly Augustine, who stated, in the *City of God*, that suicide is never justifiable. He maintained that suicide precludes the possibility of repentance, that it is a form of murder prohibited by the Sixth Commandment, and that a person who kills himself has done nothing worthy of death. Similarly, Thomas Aquinas opposed it on the grounds that it was unnatural and an offense against the community. Above all, he considered it a usurpation of God's power to grant life and death. Generally, in both England and Scotland, as well as on the Continent, laws provided for special treatment of the bodies of suicides, often outside regular graveyards. Throughout the medieval ages and well into modern times the strong religious opposition, the force of condemnatory public opinion, and the severe legal penalties were so effective that few had the temerity to take their lives, despite infrequent sporadic outbreaks of mass suicide on certain occasions such as epidemics, religious fanaticism to gain martyrdom, or crises.[10]

These views did not go unopposed by later philosophers, particularly those of the Age of Enlightenment, who challenged many existing institutions and discussed the importance of individual choice, even of life and death. David Hume, in his *Essay on Suicide*, argued that man has the right to dispose of his life without the act being sinful. Other writers, such as Montesquieu, Voltaire, and Rousseau in France, challenged the laws on

---

[8] William E. H. Lecky, *A History of European Morals* (3d ed.; New York: Appleton-Century-Crofts, Inc., 1906), pp. 209–211.

[9] Donald McCormick, *The Unseen Killer: A Study of Suicide: Its History, Causes, and Cures* (London: Frederick Muller, Limited, 1964), pp. 36–51.

[10] Louis I. Dublin, *Suicide: A Sociological and Statistical Study* (New York: The Ronald Press Company, 1963).

suicide and the denial of individual choice about life and death. In Germany, however, Kant opposed such views and said that suicide was contrary to reason. Today both Catholics and Protestants are opposed to suicide, although the Catholic position is a stronger one and the rates in such Catholic countries as Italy, Spain, and Ireland are generally lower. (See Table 13.2.)

Suicide was punished as a felony or crime in England for centuries, and the suicide's property was forfeited to the Crown. In fact, these provisions were not abolished until 1870, although they had been largely in disuse since the eighteenth century. In his famous *Commentaries* on the law Blackstone had given these reasons for forfeiture: "The suicide is guilty of a double offense: one spiritual, in evading the prerogative of the Almighty and rushing into his immediate presence uncalled for; the temporal, against the King, who hath an interest in the preservation of all his subjects." [11]

TABLE 13.2   **Suicide Rates per 100,000 Population for Selected Countries, circa 1962**

Country		Country	
Hungary	24.9	Portugal	8.6
Austria	22.4	New Zealand	8.4
Finland	22.1	Bulgaria	8.0
Czechoslovakia	20.6	Chile	7.7
West Germany	18.7	Canada	7.2
Switzerland	18.2	Norway	6.6
Japan	17.3	Netherlands	6.6
Sweden	16.9	Panama	6.4
Denmark	16.9	Italy	5.6
France	15.1	Spain	5.5
Belgium	14.7	Colombia	4.8
Union of South Africa	14.2	Greece	3.4
(white only)		Guatemala	3.1
Australia	13.7	Costa Rica	2.4
United Kingdom	11.6	India	1.9
Uruguay	11.3	Ireland	1.8
United States	10.8	Peru	1.4
Ceylon	9.9	Dominican Republic	1.0
Iceland	9.4	Nicaragua	0.4
Luxembourg	9.3	Jordan	0.2
Poland	8.8		

SOURCE: *Demographic Yearbook* (New York: United Nations, 1964), Table 25.

---

[11] William Blackstone, *Commentaries on the Laws of England* (1765–1769), IV, 188.

To a certain extent, this concept, but without the law of forfeiture, was carried to America. In 1660 the Massachusetts law forbade burial of a suicide in the common burying place of Christians. Instead, burial was in some common highway, with a cartload of stones laid upon the grave, as a brand of infamy, and as a warning to others to beware of similar "damnable practices." This law was repealed in 1823, but it helped shape the attitude toward attempted suicide in America.

Attempted suicide is a crime in New Jersey and in North and South Dakota.[12] It is not against the law in any European country, including the Soviet Union. England had such a law from 1854 until its repeal in 1961. Prior to World War II in England, most attempted suicides were punished by a short period of imprisonment; for a second attempt, up to six months. From then until 1961 it was largely used only in those cases where there had been repeated attempts, where the would-be suicide threatened to try it again, refused treatment, or became an unnecessary nuisance.[13] Actually, in 1955, out of 5220 attempted suicides (a large number are not reported), only 535, or about 1 in 10, were brought before the courts. Of these cases, only 43 were sentenced to prison. Nearly all, however, were found guilty, and, as a result, have a criminal record.[14] There is no evidence that the law acted as a deterrent, and the pressure for repeal became great.[15] The Suicide Act of 1961 abrogated the law whereby it was a crime for a person to commit suicide, consequently attempted suicide ceased to be a misdemeanor. Because it was thought that repeal would encourage suicide pacts, the act made it a criminal offense to aid, abet, counsel, or procure the suicide of

---

[12] Attempted suicides raise an interesting legal problem, since by definition "a suicidal act is not punishable as an attempt unless it was intended to result in suicide."—Williams, p. 283. Some cases are genuine attempts; others are suicidal demonstrations where what is done is not really a serious attempt; finally, there are probably cases which fall in between. Many attempts, whether real or not, may endanger the lives of other persons or rescuers, as do those who resort to carbon monoxide gas in rooms or garages, who try to drown themselves, or who use firearms. Sometimes persons are prosecuted under other statutes. For example, in Oregon a woman jumped off a bridge in a definite suicide attempt, and a soldier jumped in to save her. He found himself in trouble with the current, and a third person jumped in and saved the woman while the soldier drowned. The woman was held under the misdemeanor-manslaughter law, to stand trial for manslaughter, not for "attempted suicide."

[13] Williams, p. 280.

[14] Kenneth Robinson, "Suicide and the Law," *The Spectator,* March 14, 1958, p. 317.

[15] Erwin Stengel, *Suicide and Attempted Suicide* (Baltimore: Pelican Books, 1964).

another person. As in England, there is a general rule in the United States, under common law, that in the case of a suicide the life insurance policy is not recoverable. Several states, however, have statutes providing that a suicide does not affect the policy if it occurs after a certain period of time, unless it can be proved that the insured intended to take his life when he took out the policy.

VARIATIONS BY COUNTRY

While for many years Japan had the highest suicide rate in the world, Hungary, followed by Austria, led all the countries in 1961 and 1962. (See Table 13.2.) The United States ranked sixteenth. Comparisons of the suicide rates of different countries indicate such great variations, however, that it is difficult to establish many uniformities. For example, among the Scandinavian countries, Denmark, Finland, and Sweden have high rates, but Norway's rate is quite low. Although the countries with the highest rates are industrialized and urbanized, the rates for the United States, England and Wales, and Canada were not as high as those of some countries which are less industrially developed. Predominantly Catholic countries were generally lower in the scale, but Austria, also a Catholic country, had the second highest rate in 1962. Asiatic countries had the lowest rates generally. Except for Japan, Ceylon had the highest rate of suicide in Asia, but it ranks seventeenth in the world.

ATTEMPTED SUICIDE

Suicidal attempts in the United States and the United Kingdom, particularly in urban areas, appear to be at least six to eight times actual suicides.[16] A study was made of 5906 attempted suicides as compared with 768 persons who did commit suicide in Los Angeles County in 1957.[17] They found that the typical (modal) suicide attempter was a female, Caucasian, in her twenties or thirties, either married or single, a housewife, native-born who attempted suicide by barbiturates and gave as a "reason" marital difficulties or depression. In contrast, the typical person who actually committed suicide was a male, Caucasian, in his forties or older, married, a skilled or unskilled worker, native born, who committed suicide

---

[16] Stengel, p. 75.

[17] Edwin S. Shneidman and Norman L. Farberow, "Statistical Comparisons between Attempted and Committed Suicide," in Norman L. Farberow and Edwin S. Shneidman, *The Cry for Help* (New York: McGraw-Hill Book Company, Inc., 1961), pp. 19–47.

by gunshot wounds, hanging, or carbon monoxide poisoning and who gave as a "reason" ill health, depression, or marital difficulties.

In a study of 1000 attempted suicides in Detroit, the rate per 100,000 population was nearly twice as great for females as that for males: 35.5 as compared with 18.4.[18] This fact invited at least two interpretations: women were less successful in committing suicide, or, more likely, that women more frequently use the threat of suicide to accomplish a certain goal.[19] Threats of or attempts at suicide must, however, be taken seriously, at least when made by men. Three fourths of a group of Los Angeles County male suicides had previously threatened or attempted to take their own lives.[20]

Most attempts at suicide are carried out in a setting which makes intervention possible or probable. Those who attempt suicide tend to remain near others and allow for the possibility of prevention.[21] Whether people will intervene is another matter.

Attempted suicides may result in a number of changes in the person's life, such as temporary hospitalization and treatment, an alteration of human relationships and modes of life, or a change in previous social isolation.[22] Depending upon the social situation, societal reaction on the part of others may result in the person's being temporarily or permanently labeled as "a person who has attempted suicide" with further isolating effects.

SOCIAL DIFFERENTIALS IN SUICIDE

Few forms of deviant behavior exhibit such pronounced differences in rates among various segments of the population as does suicide. Great differences can be found in rates, depending on sex, race, age, marital status, and religion. These differences in social factors have, in general, been found not only in Western societies but in Asiatic societies, as has been shown in studies of suicide in the Philippines, Ceylon, Singapore, and

---

[18] F. C. Lendrum, "A Thousand Cases of Attempted Suicide," *American Journal of Psychiatry*, 13:479–500 (1933). Also see Calvin F. Schmid and Maurice D. Van Arsdol, Jr., "Correlated and Attempted Suicides: A Comparative Analysis," *American Sociological Review*, 20:273–283 (1955).

[19] Mowrer, p. 339.

[20] Edwin S. Shneidman and Norman L. Farberow, "Clues to Suicide," in Edwin S. Shneidman and Norman L. Farberow, eds., *Clues to Suicide* (New York: McGraw-Hill Book Company, Inc., 1957), p. 9.

[21] For British data see Stengel, pp. 85–88.

[22] Stengel, pp. 89–96.

Hong Kong.[23] Many of these factors operate in the same fashion in these cultures.

Sex

Suicide is much more common among men than among women in Western European civilization, generally three to four times higher. In Finland almost four times as many men as women commit suicide; in

TABLE 13.3   **Male and Female Suicide Rates by Countries, circa 1960**

Country and Year	Suicide rate per 100,000 population		Ratio of male to female rate	Excess of male rate
	MALE	FEMALE		
Australia, 1960	15.0	6.2	2.4	8.8
Austria, 1959	35.8	15.2	2.4	20.6
Belgium, 1959	18.9	7.6	2.5	11.3
Bulgaria, 1960	10.5	4.7	2.2	5.8
Canada, 1960	12.0	3.0	4.0	9.0
Costa Rica, 1960	3.9	0.3	13.0	3.6
Denmark, 1959	28.7	13.5	2.1	15.2
England and Wales, 1959	14.2	8.9	1.6	5.3
Finland, 1960	32.7	8.9	3.7	23.8
France, 1960	24.0	8.0	2.9	15.8
Germany, West, 1960	25.7	12.6	2.0	13.1
Hungary, 1960	35.6	14.9	2.4	20.7
Iceland, 1960	9.0	6.9	1.3	2.1
Italy, 1959	8.9	3.6	2.5	5.3
Japan, 1959	26.6	18.9	1.4	7.7
Luxembourg, 1959	13.4	5.6	2.4	7.8
Netherlands, 1960	8.2	5.1	1.6	3.1
New Zealand, 1959 [a]	13.8	4.3	3.2	9.5
Norway, 1959	11.7	4.0	2.9	7.7
Panama, 1960	7.9	2.4	3.3	5.5
Portugal, 1960	13.6	3.7	3.7	9.9
Sweden, 1959	27.2	9.0	3.0	18.2
Switzerland, 1959	30.1	9.4	3.2	20.7
Union of South Africa, 1958 [b]	18.9	6.0	3.2	12.9
United States, 1960	16.6	4.7	3.5	11.9

[a] European population only.
[b] White population only.
SOURCE: *Demographic Yearbook, 1961* (New York: United Nations, 1962), Table 19.

----

[23] P. M. Yap, *Suicide in Hong Kong* (Hong Kong: Cathay Press, 1958).

Norway, South Africa, and France the ratio is 3 to 1.[24] (See Table 13.3.) In 1960 in the United States nearly 3.5 times as many men as women committed suicide. In the older age group the ratio of male to female suicides is even greater. On the other hand, the difference in adolescence is generally not nearly as great.

In Asia, however, women commit suicide much more frequently than they do in Western Europe and America. Hence, there the difference in the ratios is much less. In Japan the rate for males in 1959 was 26.6 and for females 18.9. In some areas of India the suicide rate for women is greater than that for men, as shown in a study of 1129 cases of suicide between 1952 and 1955 in Saurashtra in the state of Gujarat, where the rate was twice as great.[25] The reasons appear to lie in the conflicting roles and subordinate status of women in the Indian family, where nearly all marriages are arranged. Girls from poor homes have to suffer taunts, humiliation, and persecution for not bringing a handsome dowry. Even when the parents come to know that the daughter is unhappy in her husband's family, they are hesitant about taking her into their own home because of the loss of social prestige. The realization of their often difficult family role has become greater with increasing freedom for women.

Race

White persons in the United States generally have a much higher suicide rate than do nonwhite persons. In 1953, 15,307 white persons committed suicide, a rate of 10.7 per 100,000 population, or approximately three times as great as the nonwhite rate of 3.8, or 640 nonwhite suicides in the entire country. In 1959, of the total of 18,633 suicides in the United States, 17,719 were committed by white persons and 914 by nonwhites. This ratio increases in the older age groups. In a Chicago study Negroes had a rate of 7.7 as contrasted with 28.8 for native whites.[26] The rate for white females was 4.6 with only 1.3 for nonwhite females. There is some evidence, however, that suicide attempts are approximately twice as great among Negroes as among whites.[27]

The probable explanation for the differences between white and Negro suicide rates is the more rural background and traditions of Negroes, even city dwellers. This factor tends to inhibit suicide. Furthermore,

---

[24] Jean Daric, "L'Evolution de la Mortalité par Suicide en France et à l'Etranger" (Trends in Deaths from Suicide in France and Abroad), *Population*, 2, No. 4:673–700 (1956).

[25] Jyotsna H. Shah, "Causes and Prevention of Suicides." Paper read at the Indian Conference of Social Work, Hyderabad, December 1959.

[26] Cavan, p. 78.

[27] Lendrum.

Negroes, because of racial discrimination, are more accustomed to restrictions on their participation in the general society, so that crises are less likely to produce disastrous results. Higher status opportunities for Negroes have developed only recently; as a consequence there have been, in the past, few competitive status pressures at a high level. That the Negro rate may be expected to increase as Negroes experience greater equality and urbanization is indicated by the fact that the northern Negro suicide rate is much higher than that of the southern Negro.

Age

The older a person is, in the United States and generally in Western European countries, the more likely he is to take his own life. This likelihood progresses steadily with each age category. (See Table 13.4.) The rates in 1964 for those between forty-five and fifty-four were over three times as great as for those between fifteen and twenty-four. The rates for those over sixty-five in the United States were approximately twice as high as for those between twenty-five and thiry-four. Similar rates prevail in England and Wales.[28] Conversely, in Japan in 1956 the age group with the highest suicide was fifteen through forty-four, with a rate of 34.6, as compared with a rate of 31.0 for those forty-five through sixty-four.

Other variations can be seen in suicides by age and sex when one compares the rates in the United States and Japan, which has one of the

TABLE 13.4   **Suicide Rates in the United States, by Age, 1964**

Age	*Number*	*Rate*
BELOW 1 YEAR	—	0.0
1–14	92	0.2
15–24	1736	6.0
25–34	2623	11.8
35–44	3806	15.5
45–54	4446	20.5
55–64	3779	22.6
65–74	2519	22.1
75–84	1297	24.0
85 and over	262	25.3

SOURCE: *Vital Statistics of the United States* (Washington, D.C.: Department of Health, Education and Welfare), Vol II, Part A, 1964. In 1960 there were only 475 deaths, or a rate of 3.6 per 100,000 in the age category 15–19.

---

[28] Peter Sainsbury, "Social and Epidemiological Aspects of Suicide with Special Reference to the Aged," in Richard H. Williams, Clark Tibbits, and Wilma Donahue, eds., *Processes of Aging* (New York: Atherton Press, 1963), II, 153–175.

highest suicide rates in the world. The rates for both sexes in the United States show a steady rise, although much less for females. The suicide rate for Japanese males rises sharply through adolescence up to twenty-four, when it reached 60 per 100,000 in 1952–1954. It then fell to a rate of about 25 between thirty to fifty, and then rose steadily until at seventy it was 95. The rate for females follows a similar but lower pattern.

Adolescent suicides receive so much publicity that their number has been exaggerated in the popular mind. In 1964 there were only 1736 deaths, or a rate of 6.0 per 100,000 in the age category 15–24. The rate for those twenty-five through thirty-four was twice as great, and for every age group thereafter the rate increased, as shown in Table 13.4. Children under ten practically never commit suicide, and only occasionally are there suicides between the ages of ten and fifteen. No suicides were reported, for example, of children under ten during 1953. In the entire United States, during 1964 only 92 children under fifteen committed suicide. These figures do not mean that many children, as they grow up, do not on occasion, when encountering frustrating situations, "wish they were dead," as studies have shown. This is particularly the case following certain punishment situations. That these do not end in suicide seems partly the result of an incomplete formation of a self-identity, status, and social roles which are endangered by certain situations. Also, childhood crises are usually temporary, and there is seldom the long-term "brooding" which often occurs among adults.

Marital Status

In general, marriage, with its personal relationships, seems to be one of the best protections against the desire to commit suicide, although some situations produced by an unsatisfactory or a broken marriage may be conducive to it. Married persons have a lower rate than the single, the divorced, or the widowed. If age is not taken into account, variations sometimes occur. In general, for those over twenty the pattern is the same, although there is a much greater difference in the older age categories. Further evidence for this is the fact that in each age grouping over twenty the suicide rate is lower for married persons than for single persons of the same age group. About three times as many widowers and five times as many divorced men take their lives as do married men. Yet these comparisons should not minimize the fact that many married persons take their lives.

Another indication that the family has an important relationship to suicide is the fact that suicide appears to be greater among couples without children than among couples with children, who naturally have greater personal ties and feelings of responsibility that act as inhibiting factors.

Religion

Suicide rates among the main religious groups in Western European civilization vary greatly. In general, both in Europe and in America, Catholic rates are much lower than Protestant. Formerly the Jewish rate appears to have been lower than the Catholic, except that, on occasions when persecution made their situation particularly difficult or hopeless, waves of suicides occurred. Within recent years the Jewish suicide rate has risen considerably, perhaps reflecting changes in religious influence and greater participation in the general society. Both Catholic and Protestant rates have increased during the past century.

Religious differences in suicide rates have been interpreted as meaning in part the degree of integration of the various religious groups. Protestant religious groups tend to be more individualistic than Catholic. The Catholic position on suicide is more specific than that of most Protestant groups, at least in regard to the effect of suicide on the individual's afterlife and on the right to burial in consecrated ground.

Analysis of data from countries with large Catholic and Protestant populations, such as Germany and Switzerland, shows that even when all other factors are similar, fewer Catholics commit suicide. Catholic countries, such as Spain and Portugal, Ireland, and Italy, have low suicide rates, and predominantly Protestant countries, such as Denmark and Sweden, have high rates. (See Table 13.2.) Even this general rule does not explain the relatively low rate of Norway and Scotland.

It is difficult, however, to place too much emphasis on the factor of religious affiliation alone. The rate of Italian suicides for the period 1947–1951 in northern Italy is almost exactly twice as great as in the south, where economic conditions are poorer, there is less education, and adherence to Catholicism seems greater.[29] Most of the conclusions about the relation of religion, moreover, are based on large statistical categories and not on the effect of Catholicism at the individual level. Ferracuti has emphasized the possible role which the Catholic confession may play in furnishing a mechanism which might reduce the number of suicides.[30]

Occupation

In his classic study of suicide, Durkheim found that occupational status is linked to suicide, occurring more frequently in the upper ranks of various occupations as well as in positions of higher status. Suicides were found to

---

[29] Franco Ferracuti, "Suicide in a Catholic Country," in Shneidman and Farberow, *Clues to Suicide*, p. 74.

[30] Ferracuti, pp. 76–77.

be more frequent among army officers in proportion to population than among enlisted men, a fact which he attributed to the officers' feeling of status responsibility.[31] In a later study it has been found that United States Army officers are more likely to kill themselves than do enlisted men of the same race.[32] In a study of 955 persons who committed suicide in New Zealand between 1946 and 1951 the suicide rates were significantly greater among persons of high prestige, upper-class fathers producing more than their proportion of suicidal sons.[33] Moreover, suicide occurred more often when there was a pronounced mobility, downward and upward, on the prestige scale. A study of 103 white male suicides found that there was considerable downward mobility as seen in work, social class, reduced income, and unemployment.[34] In Hong Kong attempted and actual suicide rates are highest at the two ends of the economic scale—businessmen and the unemployed—with high rates also among entertainers and prostitutes. Lowest rates were among the police, farmers, and fishermen. The explanation given was that rates tend to be higher among groups subject to great economic insecurity and uncertainty, and lower among those groups with security of employment or among well-integrated groups.[35]

In the United States suicide rates are higher among those with high social status. Although suicides occur disproportionately among those at both extremes of the socioeconomic range, they are more numerous among those who are in higher-status occupational groups. The rate of suicides among pharmacists has been found to be twenty-four times that of carpenters.[36] As studies have shown, Londoners from the higher occupational status groups are more given to suicide. Those making the study attribute this to the fact that such groups not only are more subject to changes but are social isolates.[37] Gibbs has summarized the relation of occupation, social status, and suicide as follows: "High rates are often found in both the pro-

[31] Durkheim.

[32] Louis I. Dublin and Bessie Bunzel, *To Be or Not to Be: A Study of Suicide* (New York: Harrison Smith and Robert Haas, 1933), pp. 112–113.

[33] Austin L. Porterfield and Jack P. Gibbs, "Occupational Prestige and Social Mobility of Suicides in New Zealand," *American Journal of Sociology*, 66:147–153 (1960).

[34] Warren Breed, "Occupational Mobility and Suicide among White Males," *American Sociological Review*, 28:179–188 (1963).

[35] Yap, pp. 33–36.

[36] Elwin H. Powell, "Occupation, Status and Suicide: Toward a Redefinition of Anomie," *American Sociological Review*, 23:131–139 (1958).

[37] Peter Sainsbury, *Suicide in London: An Ecological Study* (London: Chapman & Hall, Ltd., 1955), p. 91.

fessional-managerial category and the category of unskilled laborers, with occupations ranking midway between these two in status having lower rates. The high rate that typically prevails among the unemployed and retired appears to fit the low income–low prestige pattern." [38]

SUICIDE AND THE TYPE OF SOCIETY

Suicide is related to the type of society, being more common in urban societies. Self-destruction is reported as not occurring among some folk societies. One observer who asked Australian aborigines about suicide stated that whenever he interrogated them on this point they invariably laughed at him, treating it as a joke.[39] A similar response was reported from natives of the Caroline Islands. A survey of some twenty sources dealing with the Bushmen and Hottentots of South Africa revealed no references to suicide among these people.[40] The Andaman Islanders in the Indian Ocean appear to have had no knowledge of suicide prior to their association with people from India and Europe. Nor has suicide been reported among such folk societies as the Indians of Tierra del Fuego and the Zuñi of southwestern United States.

It would be simple to analyze the problem of suicide in folk societies if other data were as consistent as those just cited. Suicide occurs among some folk societies, however, some having a much higher rate than others. Suicides have been reported among the natives of Borneo, the Eskimos, and many African tribes. It is also said to have been fairly common among the Dakota, Creek, Cherokee, Mohave, Ojibwa, and Kwakiutl Indians, and the Fiji Islanders, the Chuckchee, and the Dobu Islanders.

Because folk societies are generally well integrated, the problem of any suicides among them particularly interested the French sociologist Durkheim. As a result of his studies he classified suicides by type, and examined the different motives underlying suicide.[41] On the whole, according to Durkheim, suicide occurring among a folk people is considerably different from that in modern society. To him the extent of suicide was a measure

---

[38] Jack P. Gibbs, "Suicide," in Robert K. Merton and Robert A. Nisbet, *Contemporary Social Problems* (New York: Harcourt, Brace & World, Inc., 1966), p. 303.

[39] Edward A. Westermarck, *Origin and Development of the Moral Ideas* (London: Macmillan & Co., Ltd., 1908), II, 220.

[40] Robert E. L. Faris, *Social Disorganization* (New York: The Ronald Press Company, 1948), p. 198.

[41] Durkheim. Gibbs feels that although Durkheim's theory is important, he did not really test his data in terms of a set of rigorous criteria of social integration. See Gibbs, "Suicide," in Merton and Nisbet.

of the degree of social integration and regulation in a society, the amount of group unity, and the strength of ties binding people together. Suicide was not an individual phenomenon but was related to certain features of the social organization. A high or a low rate of suicide in a group may be related to the degree of its integration. Societies with a low rate of integration have a high rate of suicide. Suicide occurring in Western European countries is generally either *egoistic* or *anomic,* whereas nearly all suicide among folk people is of an *altruistic* nature.[42]

Altruistic Suicide

Among folk societies suicides tend to be altruistic in that a person takes his life with the idea that by doing so he will benefit others. The individual in such societies thinks primarily of the group welfare. When his actions or his continued living hurts the group he may turn to suicide so that the group will have one less mouth to feed or so that he may protect it from the gods. Suicides among folk peoples which may be classified as altruistic are those arising from physical infirmities, or connected with religious rites or with warfare, or in expiation for the violation of certain mores, such as tabus. Under such conditions suicide does not constitute a deviation; in fact, it would be considered a transgression to refrain from the act.

Suicides occur in certain primitive societies where limited food supplies make an old or infirm person a burden to the tribe. Among the Eskimos and the Chuckchee, for example, old people who can no longer hunt or work kill themselves so that they will not consume food needed by other adults in the community who produce it. On the death of certain persons in some folk societies, it is customary to commit suicide as part of a religious observance; women, for example, commit suicide on the death of their husbands, and relatives may kill themselves in order to propitiate the souls of the dead. Some suicide occurs in warfare when persons kill themselves

---

[42] Another type of suicide, fatalism, was mentioned by Durkheim, but he made little of it, and those who have commented on his theories have generally passed it by. Suicides of this nature result from excessive regulation in which futures are "pitilessly blocked and passions violently choked by oppressive discipline." A good example of fatalistic suicides would be the suicide of slaves. A recent article has maintained that altruistic and fatalistic suicides do not belong in Durkheim's scheme and that egoistic and anomic suicides are identical in that both deal with the level of integration. Consequently there is only one cause of suicide. See Barclay D. Johnson, "Durkheim's One Cause of Suicide," *American Sociological Review,* 30:875–886 (1965). For another formulation, see Bruce P. Dohrenwend, "Egoism, Altruism, Anomie, and Fatalism: A Conceptual Analysis of Durkheim's Types," *American Sociological Review,* 24:466–473 (1959).

to avoid capture and slavery or because of the disgrace of their failure as warriors. Probably the most common form of altruistic suicides among folk societies is the suicide committed as expiation for a violation of the mores, such as a tabu. In these cases the society itself feels that since it has been made unclean, the only recourse for the offender is death by execution or by his own hand to avoid public disgrace. Individuals who fail to commit suicide in atonement for these wrongs risk the imposition of other sanctions, such as perpetual public disgrace.[43]

In modern societies, occasionally in peacetime but more frequently during war, individuals may give their lives in order to accomplish some goal involving group values. Sometimes this behavior is approved as being heroic. These suicides in modern society resemble the altruistic type found among folk people. In peacetime people will give their lives to save others. Soldiers volunteer for dangerous missions knowing there is no chance of returning alive. The Japanese on many occasions during World War II engaged in what was termed suicidal behavior. Faced with certain death, large numbers of Japanese troops died to a man in suicidal banzai charges. In the latter days of that war Japanese kamikaze pilots became legendary for their disregard for their own lives. Loading their planes with explosives, they dived into Allied warships in order to make sure of destroying them completely. Because of the peculiar settings in which the altruistic type of suicide takes place in modern society, however, much of it cannot be classed with typical altruistic suicides in folk societies. Group attitudes and pressures in a military unit under battle conditions and the emotional nature of a peacetime crisis situation involving the saving of a human life are not found in most ordinary modern situations giving rise to suicide. Elderly or incurably sick persons may sometimes end their lives so as not to become a burden on others, but this type of altruistic suicide is generally not approved.

Egoistic Suicide

The types of suicide found in modern Western European society, egoistic and anomic, must be clearly distinguished from the group-oriented, altruistic type common among folk societies. Egoistic suicides are not the products of a tightly integrated society but of one in which interpersonal relations are neither close nor group-oriented. These suicides, which are the most common in modern societies, are a measure of identity with others

---

[43] Malinowski thus describes the motives of Trobriand Islanders, who generally commit suicide by climbing a palm tree, from which they give a speech before jumping to their deaths. See Bronislaw Malinowski, *Crime and Custom in Savage Society* (London: Routledge and Kegan Paul, Ltd., 1926), p. 97.

or a lack of group orientation. In such societies, individualistic motives for suicide are not unusual and are associated with such personal problems as financial difficulties. Durkheim cited the higher suicide rate among Protestant and single persons as evidence that weakened group ties create the likelihood of higher rates of suicide.

The Anomic Suicide

The anomic type of suicide occurs when the individual feels "lost" or "normless" in the face of situations where the values of a society or group are confused or break down.[44] In such instances the equilibrium of society has been severely disturbed. There exists a social void in which the social order cannot adequately satisfy the desires of the person, and he does not know which way to turn. Commonly such anomic suicides occur in modern society as an aftermath of severe and sudden economic crashes or depressions, such as the stock market crash in the United States in 1929, which was followed by a large number of suicides. A similar situation confronts people after a severe political crisis or a defeat in war. In Hong Kong the suicide rate for post–World War II immigrants, who were mainly refugees, was five times greater than the combined rate for prewar immigrants and those born in Hong Kong.[45] Similarly, sudden, abrupt changes in the standard of living of the wealthy, or the sudden breakup of a marriage by divorce or separation may produce a sense of normlessness and account for the higher rates of suicide among these two groups.

It is true that there are many altruistic suicides among folk societies, but it would be a mistake to assume that all suicides among such groups are of this nature. For example, although a study of suicide found little or no egoistic suicide among African tribes, it did find a moderate amount of anomic suicide: suicides committed by Africans who are not integrated satisfactorily into operating institutions.[46]

Suicide is not only related to the type of society; it is also related to conditions occurring in a society at a given time. For example, Durkheim noted, some sixty years ago, that suicide tends to decline during wartime.[47]

---

[44] This is a different use of anomie from Merton's in Chapter 5. Also see Marshall B. Clinard, "The Theoretical Implications of Anomie and Deviant Behavior," in Marshall B. Clinard, ed., *Anomie and Deviant Behavior: A Discussion and Critique* (New York: The Free Press, 1964), pp. 1–56.

[45] Yap, p. 76.

[46] Paul Bohannan, "Patterns of Murder and Suicide," in Paul Bohannan, ed., *African Homicide and Suicide* (Princeton, N.J.: Princeton University Press, 1960), pp. 262–264.

[47] Durkheim. Also see Fred Dubitscher, *Der Suicid* (Stuttgart: Georg Thieme, Verlag, 1957), pp. 80–115.

During World War II, from 1938 to 1944, the suicide rate declined from 20 to 50 percent in all nations which were at war.[48] In the United States the suicide rate per 100,000 declined by about one third: from 15.3 in 1938 to 11.2 in 1945. The number of suicides per year decreased, which meant that many more failed to take their lives, possibly as many as 25,000 during World War II. Moreover, there was a steady decline from year to year until the postwar years, when the rates increased. Several factors probably accounted for this decline. The feeling of unity in wartime is the opposite of the social isolation of the typical suicide. National solidarity and the "we" feeling of wartime probably make personal difficulties of less importance to the individual. War also brings increased economic opportunities, and it has already been indicated that the suicide rate is related to the business cycle. Wartime is a period of full employment, as well as high wages and profits, and thus less economic insecurity. Perhaps it would not be facetious to add that many persons would like to live to see the outcome of a war.

THE SUICIDE PROCESS

Although only a relatively few persons commit suicide, one writer claims that over half the people of the United States have contemplated it.[49] Death wishes are expressed in a variety of ways. One is the vague wish "never to have been born." Others occur in daydreams of death in which the person is likely to imagine himself dead and to speculate on the reaction of others to his death. By doing so the person lives out an experience which he desires but which he probably wishes will not occur. Similar death wishes are felt by those who wish for it but have no particular suicidal plans. Some persons may express a contingent wish for suicide about which they feel fairly safe, such as "If this thing happens, I will kill myself." Still others may make specific threats of suicide. In such cases if the threat is not effective, or the crisis is of long duration, suicide may result.

Suicides may be definitely planned without being carried to completion. Some persons may even have planned to kill themselves on a number of occasions, the final act being prevented by the removal of the original cause, an alternative solution, or the reinforcement of some attitude, particularly a strong religious one, opposed to self-destruction. A clinical investigation of material obtained from the psychiatric interviews of 100 attempted suicides confirmed the social isolation hypothesis in that it was found that suicides have had some difficulty in forming friendships.

---

48 See Sainsbury in Williams, *et al.,* p. 166.
49 Cavan, p. 178.

In addition, the study found that "the human being . . . wants to exist for somebody and for something . . . [he] wants his achievements to be accepted and acknowledged . . . he wants his place to be defined clearly by love and work." [50] The individual wants an accepted, useful role in a community which provides him with the means of satisfying his needs and desires. When such things are lacking he becomes demoralized and confused, life loses its meaning, and he resorts to suicide. Other persons may play a role in the potential suicide's definition of the situation.

> An individual comes to feel that his future is devoid of hope; he, or someone else, brings the alternative of suicide into his field. He attempts to communicate his conviction of hopelessness to others, in an effort to gain their assurance that some hope still exists for him. The character of the response at this point is crucial in determining whether or not suicide will take place. For actual suicide to occur, a necessary (although not sufficient) aspect of the field is a response characterized by helplessness and hopelessness.[51]

Various types and stages of the suicidal process have been identified. A distinction can be made between those suicides which are situational in pattern and those which represent an escape.[52] Situational suicides may range from those in which the act is impulsive and unpremeditated to those in which the individual deliberately plans to end his life. The former may be illustrated by adolescent suicides, which are usually impulsive actions after a broken infatuation, the denial of some privilege, or a severe rebuke. These situations may be of minor importance to an adult, but to the adolescent, suicide seems the only solution. Such adolescent suicides may be inspired by revenge or the desire for attention. Conversely, some persons, such as old people, may shrewdly calculate the balance between the difficulties of continued living and death. Situations such as ill-health and the loss of loved ones and friends may lead to suicide. Between the extremes of impulsive and planned suicides are others in which each of these patterns may play an important or a minor part. Most suicides among Africans, for example, appear to take place around domestic situations involving the husband and wife, or in status-linked situations.

> These additional, non-domestic situations in which men commit suicide in Africa are for the most part seen by Africans in terms of over-all status or rank in the society. The high suicide rates for Gisu, for example,

---

[50] Margarethe von Andics, *Suicide and the Meaning of Life* (London: William Hodge & Co., Ltd., 1947), p. 173.

[51] Arthur L. Kobler and Ezra Stotland, *The End of Hope: A Social-Clinical Study of Suicide* (New York: The Free Press, 1964), p. 252.

[52] Mowrer, pp. 357–365.

come at an age when a man's total status is in some doubt—in the years immediately following initiation, and in the years when a man should be settling down to assume the status of elder. The Luo, to take another example, phrase their loss or uncertainty of total social status in terms of shame. The loss of status or "face" may occur in institutional contexts of the traditional tribal system or of the modern system of Kenya, but can nonetheless be recognized as status problems.[53]

Other suicides represent escape patterns from the responsibilities of continued life. The individual does not wish to face reality and instead seeks a way out of a dilemma which may seem impossible of fulfillment or change. Such suicides may have a long history of continuous struggle against various circumstances.

Another type of escape pattern is exemplified by those suicides who take a calculated risk to achieve a goal. For example, after killing another person some commit suicide. In a Philadelphia study about 4 percent of those who committed homicide took their own lives. Other studies in America have shown an incidence of from 2 to 9 percent in such suicides.[54] In England and Wales the proportion is much larger: each year about one third of all murders are followed by suicide, one in every 100 suicides being of this nature.[55] Likewise, when a law violator escapes the consequences of his acts by committing suicide when caught, he does so in the same calculated manner in which he planned his illegal activities. Many swindlers, such as Ivar Kreuger, of Sweden, or embezzlers may take this way out of their predicaments.

Suicides have also been classified into types: those which result from an unidentified craving for a goal, from a recognized wish, from a specific wish, from mental conflicts, or from a broken life organization.[56] These types of suicidal processes represent interruptions or blocked desires which occur at different stages in some ongoing enterprise. Such suicidal processes are somewhat similar to any other behavior involving a social act which is blocked.

One type of suicidal process may simply be a general dissatisfaction with life or some unsatisfied need, or what might be termed an undefined craving. The idea of suicide is often vague and there is a high degree of restlessness, although the nature of this dissatisfaction is often not specified.

---

[53] Bohannan, p. 262.

[54] Marvin E. Wolfgang, *Patterns in Criminal Homicide* (Philadelphia: University of Pennsylvania Press, 1958), p. 274.

[55] Donald J. West, *Murder Followed by Suicide* (London: William Heinemann, Ltd., 1965).

[56] Cavan, pp. 148–177.

The person feels "disgusted with life," or "useless." Emotional tone is low, but there is "no sharp crisis, no mourning for something lost, no resentment toward anyone, no impassioned emotions, no self-judgment, but a strong desire to stop living, since life is flavorless." [57] A divorced man of fifty left this suicide note.

> To the Police—
>
> This is a very simple case of suicide. I owe nothing to anyone, including the World; and I ask nothing from anyone. I'm fifty years old, have lived violently but never committed a crime.
>
> I've just had enough. Since no one depends upon me, I don't see why I shouldn't do as I please. I've done my duty to my Country in both World Wars, and also I've served well in industry. My papers are in the brown leather wallet in my gray bag.
>
> If you would be so good as to send these papers to my brother, his address is: John Smith, 100 Main Street.
>
> I enclose five dollars to cover cost of mailing. Perhaps some of you who belong to the American Legion will honor my request.
>
> I haven't a thing against anybody. But, I've been in three major wars and another little insurrection, and I'm pretty tired.
>
> This note is in the same large envelope with several other letters—all stamped. Will you please mail them for me? There are no secrets in them. However, if you open them, please seal them up again and send them on. They are to the people I love and who love me. Thanks.
>
> George Smith [58]

Another case of this type was a wealthy, middle-aged businessman who had devoted his life to building up his company to achieve something he had always wanted, namely, a merger with a larger company. In this merger he retained the presidency of his own concern and became the vice-president of the larger company. After the agreement was concluded he immediately went into a depression. As the coroner commented, "The action was the reaction of a man who had built his business, makes the deal he wanted to make and then realizes he is no longer the direct owner of the business he spent his life building." He had no financial troubles, health problems, or marital difficulties to cause suicidal despondency.

Like the person with the unidentified craving, the individual with the specific need has not focused on a particular object or person. He is aware of how he feels and what he wants, but he is unaware of how this general need can be satisfied. The feeling may be one of loneliness, a wish for a better job, or something equally vague. Various situations are avail-

---

[57] Cavan, p. 149.

[58] From *Clues to Suicide,* Farberow and Shneidman, eds., p. 44. Copyright, 1957, McGraw-Hill Book Company, Inc. Used by permission.

able for the potential suicide. A married woman of twenty-four left this note.

> I've proved to be a miserable wife, mother and homemaker—not even a decent companion. Johnny and Jane deserve much more than I can ever offer. I can't take it any longer. . . . This is a terrible thing for me to do, but perhaps in the end it will be all for the best. I hope so.
>
> Mary [59]

The specific wish is at a more advanced level of needs, namely, a specific object or person. A person who is lonely may find other ways of overcoming his loneliness besides suicide. If he centers his interests on a specific goal or a love object which cannot be achieved, the situation becomes less one to which alternative solutions besides suicide can be applied. As attention is centered in a certain definite direction for a particular girl, man, or job, frustrated emotion tends to build up, until the suicidal process has moved decidedly from a condition of general dissatisfaction to a recognized wish. Any thwarted wish may take on the character of a "fixed idea" and become a predominant part of the person's life organization. Sometimes such suicides take the form of hate for the person who had been desired; suicide then becomes a form of revenge. In one case a husband wrote his reactions while taking gas because his wife had fallen in love with his brother.

> A young clerk twenty-two years old killed himself because his bride of four months was not in love with him but with his elder brother and wanted a divorce so that she could marry the brother. The letters he left showed plainly the suicide's desire to bring unpleasant notoriety upon his brother and his wife, and to attract attention to himself. In them he described his shattered romance and advised reporters to see a friend to whom he had forwarded diaries for further details. The first sentence in a special message to his wife read: "I used to love you; but I die hating you and my brother, too." This was written in a firm hand; but as his suicide diary progressed, the handwriting became erratic and then almost unintelligible as he lapsed into unconsciousness. Some time after turning on the gas he wrote: "Took my 'panacea' for all human ills. It won't be long now. I'll bet Florence and Ed are having uneasy dreams now." An hour later he continues: "Still the same, hope I pass out by 2 A.M. Gee, I love you so much, Florence. I feel very tired and a bit dizzy. My brain is very clear. I can see that my hand is shaking—it is hard to die when one is young. Now I wish oblivion would hurry"—the note ended there.[60]

Instead of a specific wish involving a person or an object, another type represents a conflict between two social roles which the individual holds

---

[59] *Clues to Suicide,* pp. 43–44.
[60] Dublin and Bunzel, p. 294.

and which he cannot reconcile. On the one hand, he may wish to be married, for example, but at the same time he has responsibilities to his family which make it necessary to postpone marriage. Conflicts growing out of participation in two different sets of cultural groups or sets of ethical norms are also examples of a situation which has potentialities for suicide.

Suicides as the result of a broken life organization represent those cases where individuals whose lives had previously been satisfactory encounter some crisis. If this crisis is associated with great emotional disturbance and no alternative action seems available they may feel they can no longer continue to face life. This type of suicide, in a broad way, resembles the anomic type of Durkheim, and includes crises like blindness, incurable illness, arrests, breaking up of a home, death of a marital partner, or sudden loss of a business. The individual is unable to reconcile his previous conception of himself with the change required by a new situation. The individual's life organization has collapsed through no fault of his own.

Prolonged frustrations and crises by no means always result in suicide, and it is not clear as yet just why some do. People face innumerable unpleasant crises in different ways. Some people may become drunk, others may seek religion, some will make light of the situation, and others will evade the issue or even consciously try to avoid it. The person who commits suicide is unable to find a satisfactory alternative solution.

Several factors probably play a significant role in a suicide. First, the desired goal may become so *dominant* that in many cases it becomes almost an obsession. A girl, for example, whose engagement has been broken may feel that nothing else—parents, career, or other interests—is of any consequence. Second, there is a *fixity* in the interest so that nothing else can satisfy it: "In the suicide, this non-adaptability seems unusually prominent. If he has determined upon a certain way to satisfy it he can consider no alternative way. If a system of relationships once found satisfactory is for any reason broken, he can conceive of no system doing the work of the old." [61] Third, a particular *lack of objectivity* on the part of those who commit suicide makes them see the difficulty only from their own point of view. A fourth factor is the *interpretation of the difficulty* by the person. Circumstances such as economic losses or other difficulties which may seriously disturb one person may have little effect on another. The need for the object desired or his loss of status may be interpreted by a suicide as destroying all future hope. A prosperous businessman who has lost his fortune and commits suicide may have felt that because of the loss of money his previous social status is irrevocably ended. Satisfaction and material comforts, the future of his family, and the plans for his old age have all come tumbling down at once and he has no desire to try to rebuild his

---

[61] Cavan, p. 173.

life. Sometimes persons commit suicide for some provocation which might seem unimportant or even trivial to others but which to the suicide has assumed tremendous proportions. The situation is defined as irremediable, intolerable, or even hopeless:

> The man who kills himself is through with life; he has literally died psychologically before his kills his body. Over and over again in the notes left by suicides appears the phrase, "I can't stand it any longer." It is a crisis which cannot be adjusted to—which ends in defeat. Externally, there may be little or even no evidence of the difficulty, but in his subjective life the person is enduring doubts, unsatisfied longings and finally hopelessness and inability to struggle longer.[62]

Persons who commit suicide are not generally "mentally deranged," or suffering from "temporary insanity." Such an idea has developed from the assumption that "no one in his right mind" would take his own life. To be considered a suicide resulting from a psychosis the patient generally must have been under treatment or there must exist some other demonstrable evidence of psychosis. Hearsay evidence from relatives cannot be accepted. Reliable studies indicate that at most only approximately 20 percent of suicides are suffering from a psychosis. In a study of 291 Chicago suicides, for example, only 58 were presumed to have had a psychosis.[63] Approximately 20 percent of 22,000 suicides among industrial policyholders of a large life insurance company were found to have had a recognized mental illness.[64] Severe depression, either involutional melancholia or manic-depressive psychosis, seems to be the most common form of psychosis associated with suicide. The percentage of psychotic disturbances, although not large, is great enough to account for concern, in most cases of attempted suicide, lest there be present some severe mental disorder which will lead to a repetition of the attempt unless the disturbance is discovered and treated. Likewise, psychiatrists must be on guard for such possibilities in patients suffering from severe depression.

On the other hand, a much larger percentage of suicides, at the time of the suicide, are in some way emotionally disturbed, although not to the point where their disturbance explains their action. In many instances they may have been agitated over a period of several days prior to the suicide.

---

[62] Cavan, p. 177. One study of a large sample of persons in New York City selected by probability samples found that 74 percent of the persons interviewed felt that suicide was mainly due to "illness." Jack Elinson, Elena Padilla, and Marvin E. Perkins, *Public Image of Mental Health Services* (New York: Mental Health Materials Center, Inc., 1967), p. 22.

[63] Cavan, p. 569.

[64] Dublin and Bunzel, p. 300.

Some of these undoubtedly have been "strange" or "queer." This is a different conception from that of suicide being basically a result of prolonged mental disturbance. Actually many suicides are rationally planned and carried out with no more evidence of mental disorder than would be found in the so-called normal person. The goals sought by most suicides, no matter how exaggerated, generally are real goals, the personal losses suffered are real losses, and are usually not the product of psychotic hallucinations or delusions having little or no basis in reality.

SUICIDE AND STATUS

An explanation of suicide and homicide within the framework of different adjustments to status frustrations which produce aggression has been offered by two sociologists, Henry and Short.[65] Suicide and homicide, they claim, can be differentiated in terms of the target of the aggression; in suicide the aggression is directed at the self, whereas in homicide it is directed at others.

> The sociological evidence suggests that suicide is a form of aggression against the self aroused by some frustration, the cause of which is perceived by the person as lying within the self. Failure to maintain a constant or rising position in the status hierarchy relative to others in the same status reference system is one—but by no means the only—important frustration arousing aggression. When this frustration is perceived as being the fault of the self, the aroused aggression may flow against the self. This is most likely when the person is relatively freed from the requirement that his behavior conform to the demands and expectation of others. Persons of high status and those isolated from meaningful relationships are most likely to blame themselves and commit suicide when frustration occurs, since their behavior is relatively independent of the demands and expectations of others.[66]

Suicide is related to three factors: (1) the strength of the relational systems of a given population; (2) this strength of relational system varies with the external restraints on the behavior of the population; and, finally, (3) the external restraints placed on the behavior of the members of a population vary inversely with their status position.

---

[65] Andrew F. Henry and James F. Short, Jr., *Suicide and Homicide* (New York: The Free Press, 1954). Suicide and homicide are related in that both respond to the business cycle and are, they claim, therefore simply common responses to frustration.

[66] Andrew F. Henry and James F. Short, Jr., "The Sociology of Suicide," in *Clues to Suicide*, p. 68.

As evidence of this relation Henry and Short explain the lower suicide rate of married persons, as compared with those who are single, divorced, or widowed, as due to the fact that married persons are involved in a stronger relational system in which they must conform more to the demands and expectations of others. The degree of involvement with other persons also explains the lower rates of rural areas, the high rates in the central parts of the city, and the general tendency for suicide rates to increase as the person grows older and has fewer close relations with others.

For some time it has been well established that suicide rates fluctuate with the business cycle. Henry and Short offer the explanation that status frustrations caused by the business cycle, such as depressions, result in different degrees of aggressive behavior in the form of suicide according to the status position of persons. Groups in higher-status positions react more violently to fluctuations in the business cycle, they claim, than do those in lower-status positions. The rate of male suicides reacts more to economic fluctuations than does that of women. Similarly, white suicide rates change more than Negro, and those in higher-income groups more than those in lower-income groups. The likelihood of suicide is thus related not only to the degree of interpersonal relations but also to the position in the status hierarchy. Here external restraint, demands, and expectations by those in higher-status categories operate to control the behavior of those of lower status and prevent suicide. Thus the lower suicide rate of the Negro and those in lower-status occupational categories, such as an employee, can be partly explained in this way. The higher the status category the less restraint imposed on a person if he desires to commit suicide. This general explanation of suicide in terms of status frustration is intriguing but does not seem to be proved by the evidence presented and is largely a theory read into certain broad statistical findings.

STATUS AND INTEGRATION

One of the most provocative hypotheses about suicide has been the view of Durkheim[67] that suicide is related inversely to the stability and integration of social relations. He cited many examples of evidence for this, including the lower suicide rate among Catholics as compared to that of Protestants, a fact he attributed to the greater social integration of the former. Somewhat related is another sociological theory which has attempted, using data on suicide differentials in the United States, to link suicide to a particular *pattern of status occupancy* or the degree of integra-

---

[67] Durkheim.

tion in a society.[68] Suicide varies inversely with the degree of status integration in the population. There is less suicide in populations where one status position is closely associated with other status positions and, consequently, the members are likely to experience less role conflict, are more capable of conforming to the demands and expectations of others, and are more capable of maintaining stable and durable social relationships. Status integration refers to the extent of association in the occupancy of statuses which is at a maximum in a society or other population where knowledge of all but one of an individual's statuses enables an observer to predict the remaining undisclosed status of an individual.[69] An example would be all the married persons with a certain occupation, age, sex, race, and religion. Societies with a high degree of status integration have lower rates of suicide. Likewise, within a society those status configurations, such as a particular sex, age, marital status, which are less numerous percentagewise have a high suicide rate. As an illustration, of the males in 1950 from sixty to sixty-four, 79.3 percent were married, 9.6 widowed, 8.6 single, and 2.5 percent divorced. The corresponding suicide rates for each of the four marital status groups was 36.2, 64.7, 76.4, and, finally, for the divorced, 111.1. This presumably indicates that, although its members belong to an older age group, the infrequently occupied status clusters, for example, the divorced, are assumed to be characterized by role conflict and consequently weak social relationships.

Two studies have challenged the status integration theory by reanalyzing the data used by Gibbs and Martin and by new data derived from other sources. One has concluded that "first, the logical structure of the theory is sufficiently faulty to raise serious doubts as to the theory's general value. Second, the utility of the operational definition of status integration employed is very questionable. Third, the authors' claim that the data tend to support the theory is contradicted by a more thorough analysis of their findings and by data from Seattle."[70] Another study concluded that "a major problem with the theory is the lack of congruence between the

---

[68] Jack P. Gibbs and Walter T. Martin, *Status Integration and Suicide: A Sociological Study* (Eugene: University of Oregon Books, 1964) and Jack P. Gibbs and Walter T. Martin, "A Theory of Status Integration and Its Relationships to Suicide," *American Sociological Review,* 23:140–147 (1958).

[69] Gibbs and Martin, *Status Integration and Suicide,* Chap. 2.

[70] William J. Chambliss and Marion F. Steele, "Status Integration and Suicide: An Assessment," *American Sociological Review,* 31:531 (1966). See reply by Gibbs and Martin in Jack P. Gibbs and Walter T. Martin, "On Assessing the Theory of Status Integration and Suicide," *American Sociological Review,* 31:533–541 (1966).

theoretical conception of status integration and its operational measurement. As indicated by examples cited, actual occupancy of a status configuration (which is the empirical referent of status integration) does not always reflect incompatibility or role conflict." [71]

Both the validity of the theory of suicide and status and that of status and integration rest on the analysis of official suicide rates. They are not studies of attempted or actual suicide cases. One study has taken the view that the suicide notes that people leave have significance for explanations of why people commit suicide, perhaps even more than official rates of suicide.[72] Such suicide notes were analyzed in terms of adopting the perspective of the suicide, what he experienced, how he viewed these experiences, the social constraints that restrained him from suicide, and how he succeeded in overcoming them.

SUMMARY

Suicide is strongly condemned among Western European peoples and in Mohammedan countries. The negative attitude in Western European civilization can be traced primarily to the attitude of the Christian and Jewish religious teachings on self-destruction.

Suicides appear to differ in their nature according to the type of society. Among folk societies most suicides are altruistic, whereas in modern societies they tend to be predominantly egoistic or anomic.

Rates of suicide fluctuate with the business cycle, being higher during periods of depression and lower at times of prosperity. Suicide rates for males are much higher than those for females. White persons in the United States have a higher rate than do nonwhites. Although suicide rates occur disproportionately among those at both extremes of the socioeconomic range, they are higher among those in higher-status occupational groups.

The likelihood of suicide increases with age. In general, married persons have a lower suicide rate than do single, divorced, or widowed persons. Rates for Catholics are, in general, lower than those for Protestants.

Suicides can be distinguished according to whether they are situational or escape patterns. They can be classified into those arising from an unidentified craving for a goal, a recognized wish, a specific wish, mental conflicts, and a broken life organization. Whether a person commits suicide

---

[71] Robert Hagedorn and Sanford Labovitz, "A Note on Status Integration and Suicide," *Social Problems,* 14:84 (1966).

[72] Jerry Jacobs, "A Phenomenological Study of Suicide Notes," *Social Problems,* 15:60–73 (1967).

appears to be dependent upon the dominance of the goal, the fixity, the lack of objectivity, and the interpretation of the difficulty.

One theory has attempted to associate social status frustration with suicide; another has sought to link suicide to a particular pattern of status occupancy and the degree of integration in a society. Neither study has presented sufficient evidence to support the theory. Durkheim's view of suicide as related to social integration is probably still the more valid.

SELECTED READINGS

Bohannan, Paul, ed. *African Homicide and Suicide*. Princeton, N.J.: Princeton University Press, 1960. A study of homicide and suicide among seven African tribes. Contains case materials and statistical comparisons with Western society.

Cavan, Ruth S. *Suicide*. Chicago: University of Chicago Press, 1928. Although an older study, its analysis of the suicide process has contributed a great deal to the understanding of suicide.

Dublin, Louis I. *Suicide: A Sociological and Statistical Study*. New York: The Ronald Press Company, 1963. A comprehensive study of suicide, using in particular Metropolitan Life Insurance Company data on suicides.

Durkheim, Èmile. *Suicide*. John A. Spaulding and George Simpson, trans. New York: The Free Press, 1951. This is one of the most important books by the famous French sociologist. Originally published in 1897, it has been translated into English for the first time. Contains a detailed discussion of egoistic, altruistic, and anomic types of suicide.

Gibbs, Jack P., and Walter T. Martin. *Status Integration and Suicide: A Sociological Study*. Eugene: University of Oregon Books, 1964. A study of status and integration, using suicide differentials in the United States.

Henry, Andrew F., and James F. Short, Jr. *Suicide and Homicide*. New York: The Free Press, 1954. An explanation of suicide and homicide primarily in terms of a theory of frustration and aggression. Contains a considerable amount of statistical data on suicides analyzed by race, sex, age, and income.

Sainsbury, Peter. *Suicide in London: An Ecological Study*. London: Chapman & Hall, Ltd., 1955. An ecological study of 409 suicides occurring in North London, analyzed according to residence, occupation, and other factors.

Shneidman, Edwin S., and Norman L. Farberow. *The Cry for Help*. New York: McGraw-Hill Book Company, Inc., 1961. A comprehensive study of a large number of suicides and attempted suicides in Los Angeles County.

Stengel, Erwin. *Suicide and Attempted Suicide*. Baltimore: Pelican Books, 1964. A British study dealing primarily with attempted suicides in which comparisons are made with those who actually commit suicide.

14

Conflicts in Marital
and Family Roles

At present one divorce is granted in the United States for every four marriages performed. Although this represents a decline from the peak immediately following World War II, when the ratio was 1 to 2½, there has been in general an increase over the past sixty years in the proportion of divorces to marriages. These statistics, however, do not give the full account of contemporary marital unhappiness. Many more applications for divorce are filed than are finally granted, and none of these figures include separations and desertions.

In general, marital unhappiness is taken as evidence of marital and family conflict. Conflict specifically refers to a situation where there is a discrepancy between the role expectations and role behaviors of family members in relation to one another. A conflict may thus be temporary or permanent. If it is temporary it may hasten or assist the ability of marital partners to develop role skills or to deal with problems which arise. Various studies have shown that a legally intact marriage is not necessarily a "happy" one, indicating that marital unhappiness is far more pervasive than divorce statistics alone reveal. In fact, the family where the internal dissolution has been great and where there is no longer a strong commitment to mutual role obligations but where they do not separate or divorce has been termed the "empty shell family."[1]

THE NATURE OF THE CONTEMPORARY FAMILY

As the character of American society has changed during the past century, so has the nature of family life been altered. Patterns which were once well adapted to the former type of society have become a source of marital conflict as ways of life have become more urbanized. As a result of the transfer of economic functions, the social and economic independence of women, and the changes in attitudes concerning marriage, the nature of the family has changed under urban conditions.

The modern urban family has lost many of its functions which formerly strengthened the unity of the group. The economic, religious, educational, and recreational functions of the family have diminished, and, with the development of various social services furnished by the state, it has lost much of the protective functions.

One of the greatest changes in family structure, brought about not only by the Industrial Revolution but by urban life, was the shift of economic functions from the family to other institutions. In contrast to the self-sufficient family of early rural America, the modern American family virtually produces nothing of its own. It now buys most of its clothes, household necessities, furniture, and various services. Most of its food is produced entirely outside the home and generally is even ready for serving. Thus the family has become primarily a consumption and distribution center, surrendering nearly all its productive functions to commercialized institutions. This function of consumption and distribution is important, however, and a failure to manage the family budget judiciously, especially in view of the numerous inducements to spend, may contribute to family instability. The family is increasingly a unit of consumption rather than production. Baking, canning, clothes-making, and various other operations formerly performed by the family are now largely carried out by specialized services and business establishments.

The religious activities of the family, which at one time included daily religious services at home, the saying of grace, and considerable religious instruction of the child, have been taken over by the Sunday school and the church. Training of the child in matters of moral conduct, hygiene,

---

[1] William J. Goode, "Family Disorganization," in Robert K. Merton and Robert A. Nisbet, eds., *Contemporary Social Problems* (2d ed.; New York: Harcourt, Brace & World, Inc., 1966), pp. 532–534.

home economics, manners, and skills used to be done mainly in the family household. Beginning with five-year-old children, in most communities, these functions have increasingly been taken over by the school. The teacher has become the substitute parent in many ways. In school the young child is taught how to read and write, as well as how to get along with others, how to use a toothbrush, and how to do many other things formerly taught exclusively in the home: "The school has thus taken over those elements in the social heritage which relate to practical knowledge, in addition to those less utilitarian elements which are assumed to make life more meaningful. The relative importance of the home and the school in the broad function of education has undergone a considerable change, with the home perforce the loser." [2]

Recreation has also moved toward largely nonfamily and commercial types. The increase in leisure time in urban areas has been followed by more demands for recreational facilities and opportunities, and the marked differences in the recreational interests of the children and even of the husband and wife have resulted in more individualized recreation, often of a commercial nature. Many of the activities of family groups, such as motion pictures or television, offer little opportunity for communication and social interaction.

The family has been modified in this urban setting. This new family no longer operates as a separate economic unit, and its role as a socializing agent, including its educational, religious, and character-building functions, has diminished. In addition, the family has largely lost its ability to confer status on the individual by reason of his simply being a member of it; nor is status now as easily acquired by marriage into another family.

In the light of these changes a number of frames of reference for the study of the family have evolved. They have included the functional-differentiation view of Parsons, [3] the companionship family of Burgess, and the orderly replacement versus the permanent-availability view of Farber. To Parsons the nuclear family tends to be highly independent, is a highly specialized group, is increasingly specialized in marital roles, but does not provide an institutional basis for having children. Children become an expression of personality needs. In terms of the companionship approach, the family is conceived as a continuum from a primarily institutional to purely companionship extremes; in the former it is supported by other institutions

---

[2] Andrew C. Truxal and Francis E. Merrill, *The Family in American Culture* (Englewood Cliffs, N.J.: Prentice-Hall, Inc., 1947), p. 351.

[3] Talcott Parsons and Robert F. Bales, *Family, Socialization and Interaction Process* (New York: The Free Press, 1955).

and the community whereas in the latter it is held together by the intimate association of husband and wife.[4] Providing affection and companionship is the chief integrative mechanism of the contemporary family. The loss of certain former functions does not constitute maladjustment but rather value conflicts over the success of the contemporary family and how it is achieving its new role.[5] Table 14.1 lists these distinctions between the former family of the rural type and the modern urban type:

TABLE 14.1   **The Nature of Marriage**

Former rural life conditions	*Modern urban life conditions*
1. Marriage a status of reciprocal rights and duties.	Marriage an interpersonal relation of compatibility.
2. Marriage largely arranged by parents (or by young people in accordance with parental standards of mate selection).	Freedom of young people in choosing a mate (ranging from predominance of romantic love to predominance of companionship as motives).
3. Separation of children and youth of the different sexes before marriage or only formal relations under strict chaperonage.	Increasing freedom of social relations before marriage with decline of parental supervision and control.
4. Love after marriage.	Love and companionship before marriage.
5. Emphasis upon the economic and legal aspects of marriage.	Stress upon the primacy of personnal relations.
6. Evaluation of children as potential workers and economic assets.	Appreciation of children as persons and interest in their personality development.
7. Marriage relatively indissoluble.	Divorce resorted to if marriage regarded as failure.

SOURCE: Adapted from Ernest W. Burgess and Paul Wallin, *Engagement and Marriage* (Philadelphia: J. B. Lippincott Company, 1953), p. 31.

In general, the urban family has tended to become an affectional companionship and democratic unit. There is considerable evidence that the nature of interpersonal contacts of urban life results "in the urge to find

---

[4] Ernest W. Burgess and Harvey J. Locke, *The Family: From Institution to Companionship* (2d ed.; New York: American Book Company, 1960).

[5] For a discussion of the changes in the family, see Arthur W. Calhoun, *A Social History of the American Family* (New York: Barnes & Noble, Inc., 1945), and Carle C. Zimmerman, *Family and Civilization* (New York: Harper & Row, Publishers, 1947), pp. 610–634.

love, affection, security and acceptance in a familial relationship." [6] One study of equalitarian, patriarchal, or matriarchal patterns in family decisions, for example, found no significant difference in the relative dominance of husband and wife among the families of white professors, white skilled workers, Negro professors, and Negro skilled works. Equalitarian patterns predominated in all these groups. Nonworking wives, however, tended to be more dominant in decisions than working wives. [7]

Some studies, however, have shown wide variations in marriage and family relations among social classes and occupational, educational, religious, and other groups. A number of studies, for example, of blue-collar or working-class families show differences between them and middle-class families. [8] A British researcher, for example, found that the traditional type of marital role relationship was more frequent among working-class families, whereas the companionship type was more frequent among those of higher social status. Yet the correlation was not perfect, for the companionship type was observed in some working-class families, and the traditional type in some of higher social status. [9] "If both husband and wife are highly educated, they are likely to have a common background of shared interests and tastes, which makes a [companionship] relationship easier to conduct." [10] A study of French urban society also found that there was far less willingness to accord equal status to women by lower-class men than among the middle class. [11]

The urban family is not necessarily "isolated," for members do retain many relationships with groups and families outside the family unit. But these groups and families are less likely, in the urban setting, to be connected or linked in some fashion with one another. Thus, although each group or family may exert control on some aspect of the family's activity,

---

[6] Robert F. Winch, *Mate Selection* (New York: Harper & Row, Publishers, 1958), p. 479.

[7] Russell Middleton and Snell Putney, "Dominance in Decisions in the Family: Race and Class Differences," *American Journal of Sociology*, 25:605–609 (1960).

[8] See, for example, Mirra Komarovsky, *Blue Collar Marriage* (New York: Random House, Inc., 1967); and Arthur B. Shostak and William Gomberg, eds., *Blue-Collar World: Studies of the American Worker* (Englewood Cliffs, N.J.: Prentice-Hall, Inc., 1965), pp. 59–120.

[9] Elizabeth Bott, *Family and Social Network* (London: Tavistock Publications, Ltd., 1957).

[10] Bott, p. 112.

[11] M. J. Chombart de Lauwe, "The Status of Women in French Urban Society," in S. N. Eisenstadt, ed., *Comparative Social Problems* (New York: The Free Press, 1964), pp. 215–237.

the social control of the entire family unit may be divided among many different sources. The result of this is that the urban family is often given greater freedom of individual choice and privacy in regulating its own activities. Hence, in cases such as these, marital partners are thrown more directly upon one another for emotional satisfaction and for carrying out family tasks.[12] Yet this situation cannot be described as applying to *all* urban families. It merely appears that urban living increases the probability of its occurrence.

A perhaps more realistic framework for understanding the contemporary family has been proposed by Farber: that the family should be regarded in terms of a lineage system or "orderly replacement" and the availability of individuals for marriage (permanent availability).[13] If orderly replacement is to occur, each family must provide for the continuance of its values and norms relating to patterns of family life and the socialization of children in terms largely of parental models. Each family then serves to transmit cultural patterns.

The orderly replacement or continuance of family values from one generation to another can be more readily carried out, of course, in a system where marriages are arranged or at least potential mates are restricted. Under such a situation the cultural transmission of family values, inheritance, and the maintenance of kinship relations are important. In urban, industrial societies the preservation of a marriage is increasingly more a personal than a kinship problem. When lineage considerations are increasingly unimportant each individual theoretically is available as a potential mate to individuals of the other sex.

There is continuing conflict in contemporary urban, industrial societies between these two aspects of the family. The family operating in terms of the universal, permanent availability of potential mates tends to have these characteristics:

1. The family tends to become a voluntary association in which a person's membership often continues only as long as he feels that his personal commitments are greater than those he could secure outside the family.

2. The individual attempts to maintain a high desirability as a potential mate by developing skills that make him attractive.

3. The socialization of the children is aimed at maximizing their market position as an occupation and as a potential mate.

---

[12] See Robert O. Blood and Donald M. Wolfe, *Husbands and Wives* (New York: The Free Press, 1960).

[13] Bernard Farber, *Family: Organization and Interaction* (San Francsico: Chandler Publishing Company, 1964).

4. Having children is a voluntary pledge by the parents to maintain their relationship and represents a compromise between orderly replacement of the family values and permanent availability of the mates.

CONCEPT OF MARITAL AND FAMILY CONFLICT

A marriage or family operates as a group in much the same manner as other social groups operate. Certain characteristics of such groups, however, make for a greater degree of interdependence, and hence interaction, than is true of most groups. The interlocking of the roles comprising the family group means that many of the actions of a family member deeply affect the other members. There are parallel intimate relations between many members, such as the parents' relations between themselves and with their children. Each of these conditions interacts with others and tends to intensify them.[14]

When the beliefs and expectancies about the bonds in a family remain fairly constant over a period of time and from situation to situation, the family is able to perform its functions, the individuals within the marital group are comparatively free of tension, and the interacting individuals form a "unity." [15] Thus when all these conditions exist, the family is organized: there is cooperation in the "process of building up organized attitudes in which all concur." [16] This set of mutually shared attitudes or expectations comprises what we call the organization or structure of the family, or the network of statuses and roles, common aims, and values, which make up the system of relationships. When family members share the same expectations and aims, and are able to act in accordance with them, the day-to-day needs of family members are generally met. Sometimes, however, obstructions to understanding or to role enactment may arise—either from within the family group or outside it. When this occurs, there may be a temporary conflict between the expectations of different family members. This conflict may, if it is permanent, affect the family

---

[14] Kurt Lewin, *Resolving Social Conflicts* (New York: Harper & Row, Publishers, 1948). See also Talcott Parsons, "The Social Structure of the Family," in Ruth Nanda Anshen, ed., *The Family: Its Function and Destiny* (rev. ed.; New York: Harper & Row, Publishers, 1959), p. 241.

[15] Ernest W. Burgess, "The Family as a Unity of Interacting Personalities," *Family*, 7:3–9 (1926). Some writers have suggested that the family, rather than a "unity," is more of an "arena" of interacting personalities.—Willard Waller, *The Family* (revised by Reuben Hill; New York: Holt, Rinehart and Winston, Inc., 1951), pp. 25–37.

[16] Annabelle Bender Motz, "Conceptions of Marital Roles by Status Groups," *Marriage and Family Living*, 12:136 (1950).

unit as a whole.[17] In the same manner, social changes occurring in the society of which the family is a part can impinge upon the family structure. For example, an economic depression may leave a father unemployed. Not only will this alter the father's breadwinning role; it will affect the attitudes and expectations of family members in relation to one another, and so affect, in varying degrees, the total network of relationships.[18]

Both interpersonal relations in marriage and family relations have many facets. Some involve intimacy of association, others influence the development of such an association, and still others affect the ability to meet these demands after association is developed.[19] The intimate relations of companionship can give great strength to the marriage relationship. Some of these intimate relations involve the development and expression of sentiment, such as love and affection; physical contact, such as sexual relations; and sharing of valued experiences and hopes.[20] Generally, it is supposed that marital happiness and stability are greater in a marriage characterized by affection, mutual dependence and compatibility, and shared satisfactions. On the other hand, it is believed that marital unhappiness and instability are more common where there is indifference, hostility, dissatisfaction, mutual independence, and incompatibility. Marital role relations may be predominantly "joint": that is, they may involve many shared or similar activities carried out by husband and wife together. Or they may be "segregated": that is, they may involve many independent activities carried out by husband and wife separately. But marital stability and happiness seem to occur with about equal frequency among "joint" and "segregated" marital role relations. Happiness and stability appear to be influenced more by the total social system of which the husband-wife relationship is a part than by the marital relationship alone.[21]

In the marriage situation a number of factors may operate to produce marital stability. In each instance, however, they may operate in reverse and contribute, instead, to instability in marriage. The similarities or differences in cultural backgrounds which each partner contributes to the marriage can make for harmony or for conflict. The development of interests and values likewise can strengthen the association through mutual

---

[17] Bott, p. 59.

[18] J. Cohen, R. Robson, A. Bates, *Parental Authority: The Community and the Law* (New Brunswick, N.J.: Rutgers University Press, 1958), p. 197.

[19] Ernest W. Burgess and Paul Wallin, *Engagement and Marriage* (Philadelphia: J. B. Lippincott Company, 1953), p. 418.

[20] Parsons.

[21] Bott, pp. 53–58, p. 219; and Carle C. Zimmerman and Lucius F. Cervantes, *Successful American Families* (New York: Pageant Books, Inc., 1960), pp. 35–55.

stimulation and complementary interests or it can take a course which may produce boredom and conflict. Domestic activities, including household tasks, the rearing of children, family activities, illness, friends, may be mutually shared or, as in some marriages, one partner may escape to activities outside the family circle. One study has even shown the importance of social approval from others in the adjustment of a married couple, particularly to new situations.[22]

The dynamics of a marriage are more, however, than the development of intimacy and association. Marriage also means decision making and adaptability. In such activities the marriage means not individuals making separate decisions but a couple deciding together. If mutual decisions are

TABLE 14.2   **Interpersonal Relations in Modern Marriage**

	Developmental and integrative	*Frustrative and disruptive*
I. Intimacy of Association:		
Love and affection	Mutual love, affection	Indifference, hostility
Sexual relations	Enjoyment and satisfaction	Dissatisfaction
Emotional interdependence	Mutual dependence	Emotional independence
Temperamental interaction	Compatibility	Incompatibility
II. Development of the Association:		
Cultural interaction	Assimilation and creativity	Accommodation and conflict
Interests and values	Stimulation and complementation	Boredom and conflict
Domesticity	Mutual enjoyment of home activities	Escape into outside activities
III. The Association in Operation:		
Decision making	Interdependent	Authoritarian and unilateral
Adaptability	Mutual adaptability	Unadaptability of one or both

SOURCE: Ernest W. Burgess and Paul Wallin, *Engagement and Marriage* (Philadelphia: J. B. Lippincott Company, 1953), pp. 418–419. By permission of the publisher. They include a factor "Expectations of Continuity," which is not discussed in this section.

---

22 Motz.

made about such things as expenditures and the children, they serve to integrate the marriage; if they are made in an authoritarian way or unilaterally they weaken it.

If the partners in a marriage adapt to one another, a marriage can be greatly strengthened. Adaptability represents a process of change. "In marriage, adaptability enables husband and wife to adjust successfully despite the conflicting facets of their personalities which reveal themselves in the exigencies of marriage, and to cope with changes in the social situation which impinge upon and affect their roles as husband and wife." [23] Although there are other facets, one of the most important is the determination that the marriage will succeed.

Burgess and Wallin have constructed an index of marital adjustment which stresses the need for consensus or common agreement, common interests and activities, demonstration of affection, satisfaction with marriage, and absence of feelings of unhappiness and loneliness. Their list of the developmental and integrative, as opposed to the frustrative and disruptive, forces in interpersonal relations in marriage appears in Table 14.2.

There are great differences in family structure by class, occupation, and ethnic and religious groups. There may also be marked differences in the family roles played by persons of different ethnic groups, religions, or occupations.

> Catholics, Jews, Mormons, and Quakers, to cite but a very few, have different expectations and must be understood in terms of them. The concepts of the good husband and good wife are variously defined by these groups. . . . For example, Jews, especially Orthodox Jews, tend to define the good husband more in terms of the good provider than do, let us say, the Quakers, who lay greater store by psychological factors. . . . When we turn to the influence of occupational factors on family behavior, we note that members of different professions, even those belonging to the same social class, religion, and ethnic group, may define proper family behavior differently. For example, the college professor's wife usually expects her husband to spend more time with her than does the doctor's wife. The minister's wife is expected to help her husband with his work more than the doctor's wife or the college professor's wife. The requirements of the professional lead to different expectations.[24]

---

[23] Burgess and Wallin, p. 623.

[24] Meyer F. Nimkoff, "Contributions to a Therapeutic Solution to the Divorce Problem: Sociology," in *Conference on Divorce* (Chicago: University of Chicago Law School, February 1952), p. 59. Also see Komarovsky and Shostak and Gomberg.

THE PROCESS OF MARITAL AND FAMILY MALADJUSTMENT

Every marriage or family has its breaking point, and it is possible to sketch the process through which marital and family conflicts may pass to their culmination in crisis. After the first aura of passion and the erotic newness of marriage have worn off, a monotonous pattern of day-to-day living may begin. Many withstand ripples of discontent and difficulties, finding more in the marital relation than any contemplated escape from it would provide. For others, however, small difficulties mount in frequency and intensity until one of the partners feels that there are more satisfactions to be gained outside marriage than within it. The period of conflict may extend over years; one study found a median period of two years.[25] There is a progressive withdrawal of affection and increasing irritation with the marital partner. While affection is being withdrawn there is at the same time a necessity to continue with the daily living connected with the marriage or the family. Each divorce is preceded by a series of clashes, withdrawal, coming back to the disagreements, and then further withdrawal. The steps in this process as it leads finally to divorce have been listed by Locke as follows:

1. Developing tensions and difficulties between family members
2. Debating the issues of the conflict within oneself
3. Overtly expressing the conflicts
4. Intermittently attempting to solve marital difficulties
5. Sleeping in different beds or in different rooms
6. Mentioning divorce as a possibility to the mate
7. Separating into different domiciles
8. Making a temporary reconciliation
9. Making application for a divorce
10. Getting the application dismissed
11. Reapplying for a divorce
12. Getting the application dismissed
13. Reapplying for a divorce
14. Securing the divorce
15. Trying to achieve emancipation from the mate
16. Adjusting to the crisis of the divorce [26]

Marital unhappiness may find a number of outlets short of annulment, separation, desertion, or divorce. Some persons resort to a world of fantasy

---

[25] William J. Goode, *After Divorce* (New York: The Free Press, 1956), p. 137.
[26] Derived from Harvey Locke, *Predicting Adjustment in Marriage* (New York: Holt, Rinehart and Winston, Inc., 1951), p. 71.

and daydreams to escape a difficult marital situation. Through their emphasis on romantic love, motion pictures, romantic stories, and particularly the "soap operas" of television furnish escapes. Chronic "illness" may also provide escape from an unpleasant marital situation. If either person feels neglected, dissatisfied, or unloved, he may resort to "illness" to obtain care and attention or to inflict discomfort on the other. Being constantly "tired" without a physical basis may be indicative of dissatisfaction with marriage. Studies have also shown that alcohol and other substitute satisfactions offer escapes from unsatisfactory marital situations. Some may take a more conventional outlet for such frustrations by minimizing interaction in the family and, instead, devote all their spare time to housework, their hobbies, or their jobs, or to golf, music, art, or club activities. Finally many parents who are not happy in their marital situation may project their frustrations through displaying excessive affection for their children and excessive interest in their children's goals.

DESERTION

Some couples separate without a divorce, maintaining the fiction of marriage but with two households. Some separations are temporary, but others may be permanent. The law may even recognize this fact by providing for a "legal separation." Separations may meet religious objections to divorce or be the result of one partner's refusal to grant a divorce. Some partners simply desert by leaving home without making provisions for financial or other responsibilities. It is usually the husband who deserts. This does not always mean that he is the more dissatisfied partner; rather, he is more mobile.

The number of separations and desertions can be but an estimate. However, some idea of the total may be obtained from the number of divorces granted for desertion, from the census enumeration which shows the number of husbands or wives absent from the household, and from child-support cases. The number of divorces granted for desertion in the United States has increased during the past several decades. Goode states that in 1960 there were 4.3 women whose husbands were absent and 3.8 divorced women per 1000 married women aged fifteen to fifty-four. For nonwhites, chiefly Negroes, the percentages were 20.3 and 5.8, respectively.[27] Estimates of the extent of separation and desertion may be found in census data which show that, in 1960, 929,387 men and 1,334,368 women were listed as "separated." These figures include only those legally separated,

---

[27] Goode, "Family Disorganization," p. 512.

those expecting to obtain a divorce, and those temporarily or permanently estranged. These data showed 1.9 percent of all married women to be separated from their husbands. Of nonwhite women only, chiefly Negro, 8 percent were separated from their husbands.[28] Over the past thirty years new desertion and nonsupport cases in Philadelphia were twice the number of divorce cases. In 1955, of the 2,600,000 children receiving aid-to-dependent children grants in the United States, the fathers of 1,400,000 were separated from their families.[29]

Desertion appears to be more frequent among groups where social controls are weaker, and where family groups may be presented with conflicting norms. Thus, it is observed that desertion occurs more frequently in "newer cities" which are presumably undergoing more rapid change, and in which associations may occur more frequently among heterogeneous groups.[30] Desertion is also more frequent among those religious groups for whom divorce is not acceptable. Among Catholics, for example, desertion is much more common than among Protestants. According to estimates, the desertion rate for Catholics in the United States exceeds that for the general population by about 40 percent.[31]

DIVORCE

Although many persons regard divorce as the only index of family disintegration, it is but one of many signs. Because it represents the legal dissolution of the marriage, it certainly is the final one. Two major types of legal divorce can be distinguished: absolute divorce, which restores marital partners to the status of single persons, completely absolving marital rights; and partial divorce, or legal separation, which gives legal status to separate maintenance without dissolving marital rights.[32]

---

[28] Bureau of the Census, *Population Characteristics, Marital Status, Economic Status, and Family Status:* March, 1957, *Current Population Reports,* Series P–20, No. 81 (March 19, 1958), Table 1.

[29] Jessie Bernard, *Social Problems at Midcentury* (New York: Holt, Rinehart and Winston, Inc., 1957), p. 383, from a report by the Commissioner of Social Security.

[30] Zimmerman and Cervantes, pp. 51–55.

[31] Thomas P. Monahan and William M. Kephart, "Divorce and Desertion by Religious and Mixed Religious Groups," *American Journal of Sociology,* 59:454–465 (1954).

[32] Mabel Elliott and Francis E. Merrill, *Social Disorganization* (New York: Harper & Row, Publishers, 1961), p. 390; and Paul H. Jacobson, *American Marriage and Divorce* (New York: Holt, Rinehart and Winston, Inc., 1959).

Extent of Divorce

The divorce rate is highest in the United States of any Western society. About 400,000 divorces and annulments are granted annually in the United States. The ratio of divorces to marriages is about one in four; moreover, about 4 percent of the children in the population who are under eighteen have been affected by divorce. In 1956 there were 2,418,000 divorced persons, 60 percent of whom were women. These figures do not include all persons who had been divorced, for about two thirds of divorced women and three fourths of divorced men eventually remarry.[33]

Divorce rates per 1000 marriages have increased in general, since 1890, in the United States, in most Western European countries where divorce is permitted, and in Australia. "It is therefore not merely an 'American' phenomenon, but is somehow related to the evolution of the family in Western society in general." [34] Divorce rates per 1000 marriages have increased markedly in many other countries besides the United States. Between 1930 and 1963 the change in England and Wales has been from a rate of 11.1 to 81; in Australia, from 41.2 to 91; in Germany, from 72.4 to 80; in France, from 68.6 to 96; and in Sweden, from 50.6 to 165.

Except during wartime, the number of divorces per 1000 marriages in the United States has, in general, increased, as it has in most Western countries. In 1890 the number of divorces was 55.6; in 1910, 87.4; in 1930, 173.9; in 1950, 231.7; and in 1963, 258.[35] Directly after a war there is generally a sharp increase in the divorce rate. Monahan lists three factors which affect the divorce rate. First, there is the historical trend. People who marry this year are more likely to become divorced than those who married twenty or thirty years ago because the attitudes and expectations of married couples, as well as the change in values, make divorce more acceptable. Second, situational factors, such as depression, affect the divorce rate at particular times. During the last depression the divorce rate dropped over 20 percent in three years. Finally, the last category concerns biographical aspects, or the time at which the marriage was contracted, as during wars, when there are many hasty marriages.

The increase in divorce rates in the past sixty years is no evidence that marital unhappiness has increased to the same extent, for there are other variables. Divorce laws have become increasingly liberal during this time, and the grounds for divorce have been broadened. South Carolina, for

---

[33] Elliott and Merrill, p. 391.

[34] Kingsley Davis, "Statistical Perspective on Marriage and Divorce," *The Annals*, 272:17 (1950).

[35] Goode, "Family Disorganization," p. 498.

example, did not permit divorce for any reason until 1949. Moreover, there
has been a decided change in public opinion about divorce. Many persons
who formerly continued unsatisfactory marriages, or separated, or were
deserted, now secure a divorce. Formerly a divorce often produced a strong
societal reaction, the divorced person was a deviant and the family disgrace
great. Now public attitudes are more tolerant, primarily because of increased securalization of society and the decline in the pressure from relatives and friends to avoid divorce. These changes in public opinion seem to
reflect more fundamental transformations in values and norms relating to
the nature of marriage and divorce.

Many countries of the Western world have been undergoing rapid
urbanization and industrialization, and in them there is increasing emphasis
on an independent conjugal unit, on the nuclear family, and on freedom
of action in choosing a mate, a practice which often results in divorce.
Formerly a man was independent of his wife for his own support; conversely, few women had sufficient training for employment, and disgrace
made it difficult to return to her family. Many of these forces can be seen
in contemporary India, where divorce is permitted but seldom resorted to
even in situations of great unhappiness. Commenting on the nuclear family
Goode has stated:

> This type of family system, characteristic of the West for several gen-
> erations, therefore requires that husband and wife obtain most of their
> emotional solace within the small family unit made up of husband, wife,
> and children; the extended kin network no longer serves as a buffer
> against the outside world. The conjugal family unit carries a heavier emo-
> tional burden when it exists independently than when it is a small unit
> within a larger kin fabric. As a consequence, this unit is relatively fragile.
> When husband or wife fails to find emotional satisfaction within this unit,
> there are few other sources of satisfaction and few other bases for common
> living. The specialization of service in an industrialized economy permits
> the man to purchase many domestic services if he has no wife, and the
> woman is increasingly able to support herself, even if she has no property
> and no husband. For these reasons, the independent conjugal family is
> not highly stable.[36]

Divorces are most likely to occur early in marriage, the majority before
the fifth year, and most frequently in the third.[37] Although slightly over

---

[36] From "Family Disorganization" by William G. Goode in *Contemporary
Social Problems* edited by Robert K. Merton and Robert A. Nisbet, © 1961, 1966
by Harcourt, Brace & World, Inc., and reprinted with their permission.

[37] Harold T. Christensen, *Marriage Analysis* (New York: The Ronald Press
Company, 1950), p. 13. Also see Jacobson, pp. 144–147.

half of the couples who are divorced in the United States have no children, many children are affected by a divorce. In 1955, about 343,000 children were involved in divorce and annulment cases, or an average of slightly less than two children per couple.[38] The proportion of children involved in divorces has continued to increase during the past twenty or thirty years. Actually in many cases a divorce may improve a family situation for the children, for continuous marital conflict may have greater affect upon children than a divorce of the parents.[39]

Differentials in Divorce Rates

All European countries allow for divorce except Italy, Spain, and Ireland, which permit only legal separations. A similar situation exists in a number of South American countries. All states of the United States now permit divorce. The legal grounds used in the divorce proceedings are seldom the real grounds for the proposed separation; the law permits divorce only for certain reasons and these reasons often do not fit the circumstances of a particular couple who wants a divorce. Usually the couple agrees to one of the generally "fictitious" legal grounds permitted by the state in which the pair resides. The grounds agreed upon are generally those least socially injurious to the other partner, and yet legally the most effective. Divorce is not regulated by a national law, and there are consequently great differences in state divorce laws. Some states require a minimum residence (six weeks in Nevada and Idaho) and allow a wide variety of grounds. This leads to migratory divorce from those states which have exceptionally severe grounds, such as, for example, South Carolina, where no divorce was permitted until 1949, and New York, where until 1966 divorce was permitted only on grounds of adultery. Consequently, many persons in some states who desire a divorce and have sufficient money to finance it, migrate to states with shorter residence requirements and less stringent grounds.[40] The woman usually files for the divorce, either for reasons of chivalry on the part of the husband, or because he may be unwilling to sever his ties with his children, whose custody the wife usually retains.

---

[38] Jessie Bernard, *Remarriage* (New York: Holt, Rinehart and Winston, Inc., 1956), pp. 301–303.

[39] See Harry Pannor and Sylvia Schild, "Impact of Divorce on Children," *Child Welfare,* 39:6–10 (February 1960), and Judson T. Landis, "A Comparison of Children from Divorced and Nondivorced Unhappy Marriages," *Family Life Coordinator,* 11:61–65 (1962).

[40] For a discussion of some of the legal and social problems which this presents those seeking a divorce, see Herbert F. Goodrich, "Migratory Divorce," in *Conference on Divorce* (Chicago: University of Chicago Law School, February 1952), pp. 82–87.

Divorced persons are generally more likely to marry than single persons of the same age. For example, divorced persons at age twenty-five have 99 chances in 100 to remarry, whereas single persons have about 88 chances in 100 to marry.[41] The time elapsing after divorce is relatively brief: both men and women tend to remarry within three years. Several studies have been made of remarriages and the conclusion is that "first marriages are the most stable, a marriage in which one partner is remarrying is less stable, while a marriage in which both have previous marriages is least stable and perhaps twice as likely to end in divorce." [42] Such a conclusion should probably be modified because of differences in the rate of divorce by social class; in fact, the differences would probably be slight if social class is held constant. Studies generally show that remarried persons believe their second marriages are better than their first, as do their friends.

In the United States considerable differences in divorce rates depend largely on area, religion, race, education, occupation, and number of children. In urban areas there is a much higher divorce rate than in rural areas, but the rural divorce rate is not markedly below the urban rate for the whole country. Some suggest that since 1940 the rural rates have shown a tendency to catch up with the urban rates. In Wisconsin, for example, the rural divorce rates have been about as high as the urban rates since World War II.[43]

Divorce rates are highest in the western part of the United States. The higher divorce rates for western states may be due in part to differences in religious composition and in legislation concerning divorce, as well as to the greater mobility of the population. In the northern and eastern states which have large Catholic populations, although divorce rates tend to be low, the number of desertions contributed by these states appears to be markedly in excess of the national average.[44]

Divorces and desertions are lowest for Jewish groups; divorces are more frequent among Protestants but desertion is highest among Catholics, exceeding the Protestant rate by about 100 percent and the Jewish rate by about 500 percent.[45] The divorce rate among Negroes, reflecting the influ-

---

[41] Jacobson, p. 82.

[42] J. Richard Udry, *The Social Context of Marriage* (Philadelphia: J. B. Lippincott Company, 1966), pp. 520–521.

[43] E. E. LeMasters, *Modern Courtship and Marriage* (New York: The Macmillan Company, 1957), p. 571. Also see Bernard, *Remarriage,* for a review of urban and rural trends in divorce.

[44] Monahan and Kephart.

[45] Monahan and Kephart. Also see Paul Glick, *American Families* (New York: John Wiley & Sons, Inc., 1957).

ence of common-law marriage during slavery and group differences in educational and occupational levels, is generally lower than the rate for whites because of the wider prevalence of desertion and of the fact that fewer are married or at least remarried. Possibly because of this, in contrast to the rate for whites, the higher the educational level, except for college graduates, the higher the divorce rate. There is an indication that as the Negro population has become "more assimilated into the dominant white culture, both their marriage and divorce behavior have become much like those of the whites." [46]

Divorce rates generally are less in the higher social classes and occupational groups. One author has indicated, for example, that available evidence demonstrates an inverse relationship between divorce rate and socioeconomic rank; thus, professional groups, which are highest in socioeconomic rank, have the lowest divorce rate, whereas service workers and laborers which occupy the lowest socioeconomic ranks, have the highest divorce rates.[47] Measures of proneness to divorce show a rate of 254.7 for service workers; 180.3 for laborers, except farm and mine; 68.6 for proprietors, managers, and officials; and 67.7 for professionals and semiprofessionals. Whatever the precise relation between divorce and occupation, data relating to these variables must be interpreted with caution. In the first place, before assessing the divorce rate, it is necessary to know how many persons within a given occupational category *marry*. In the second place, if we are examining the relative degree of family disintegration in various occupational groups and different categories of education, then it is necessary to know how many families in given occupational groups are broken by means other than divorce.

In general the more educated a person is the more likely he is to have a well-adjusted marriage and the less likely he is to become divorced than is the uneducated person. A similarity in education seems to be modestly related to marital adjustment, although it is not clear what is the relationship between educational similarity and marital stability.[48]

Other factors in the backgrounds of persons contribute to the greater or lesser likelihood of divorce. Several of them will be discussed in the sections on marital maladjustment which follow. They are summarized in Table 14.3.

---

[46] Goode, "Family Disorganization," pp. 513–514.

[47] Goode, *After Divorce*, p. 46 and Chaps. 4 and 5. For contrasting views, see also Thomas P. Monahan, "Divorce by Occupational Level," *Marriage and Family Living*, 17:322–324 (1955); and William M. Kephart, "Occupational Level and Marital Disruption," *American Sociological Review*, 20:456–465 (1955).

[48] Udry, p. 342.

TABLE 14.3   **Background Characteristics Associated with a Greater or Lesser Proneness to Divorce**

Greater proneness to divorce	*Lesser proneness*
Urban background	Rural background
Marriage at very young ages (15–19 years)	Marriage at average age (males, 23; females, 20)
Short acquaintanceship before marriage	Acquaintanceship of two years or more prior to marriage
Short engagement, or none	Engagement of six months or more
Couples whose parents had unhappy marriages	Couples with happily married parents
Nonattendance at church, or mixed faith	Regular church attendance, Catholics, and adherence to the same church
Disapproval of kin and friends of the marriage	Approval of kin and friends
General *dis*similarity in background	Similarity ("homogamy") of background
Different definitions of husband and wife as to their mutual role obligations	Agreement of wife and husband as to the role obligations

SOURCE: From "Family Disorganization," by William J. Goode, in *Contemporary Social Problems* edited by Robert K. Merton and Robert A. Nisbet, © 1961, 1966 by Harcourt, Brace & World, Inc., and reprinted with their permission.

CONFLICTING ROLES AND ROLE EXPECTATIONS IN MARRIAGE AND THE FAMILY

Marriage and family relations, like all group relations, involve role playing, and deficiencies and conflicts over role playing in the family situation have a leading part in breaking down relationships.[49] Role strain is as much a part of the empiric world of experience as is consensus and role interpretation.[50] In a sense marriage is a process in which continuous interaction and collective responses are made to an endless series of new stimuli, some of them representing cumulative circular interacton between each partner to the social roles they play.[51] Marital partners and other mem-

---

[49] If conflicts do result in marital unhappiness they may not always precipitate divorce or other forms of marital breakup. It is probable that many marriages do endure, despite conflict and unhappiness. There is little knowledge of the extent of unhappy but enduring marriages.

[50] William J. Goode, "A Theory of Role Strain," *American Sociological Review,* 25:483–496 (1960).

[51] Clifford Kirkpatrick, *The Family: As Process and Institution* (2d ed.; New York: The Ronald Press Company, 1963), pp. 491–495.
Roles," *Marriage and Family Living,* 21:1–11 (1959).

bers of the family may each have different aspirations and evaluations of the roles they play and expect of others in marriage and family relationships.[52] Much of this is a product of role differentiation and role strain. Conflicts in marriage and family roles may occur between marital partners over their duties and obligations.[53]

Difficulties in role playing on the part of husband, wife, and children, which have been accentuated by the changes that have taken place in the family and in urban living over the past century, are due to the fact that the roles of family members, particularly of the wife, are ambiguously defined in contemporary Western society. There is often no general agreement, for example, about the functions and responsibilities of a husband or father or about the role differentiation between wife and husband. In the rural family of the past, roles were well defined, with the father being largely a patriarchal figure. Women played a subordinate role and were largely concerned with household duties. Families were large, and children were expected to perform household duties and to be obedient to parents and to family traditions.

Role conflicts in marriage and family relations consist of four types: role conflicts between marital partners, role conflicts between marriage and other activities, role conflicts between parents and children, and role conflicts between marital partners and other relatives.

Role Conflicts between Marital Partners

Until quite recently a woman was dependent upon her family prior to her marriage; thereafter she relied upon her husband for support. Today about three fourths of all women work before marriage. In 1890 only 4.6 percent of married women were gainfully employed. In 1940 this percentage was 15.2, and by 1964 it was 37.0 percent, or one in four married women. Women's ability to work has made marriage for the sake of economic "security" less frequent; yet today a woman's lifetime chances for social status are still associated with marriage.[54] Because more women today have

---

[52] One study has measured differences between role performances and role expectations of husbands and wives and has constructed an index of marital strain. See Nathan Hurvitz, "The Measurement of Marital Strain," *American Journal of Sociology*, 65:610–615 (1960).

[53] See, for example, a study of husbands' and wives' expectations regarding their roles in the sexual relationship: Paul Wallin and Alexander Clark, "Cultural Norms and Husbands' and Wives, Reports of Their Marital Partners' Preferred Frequency of Coitus Relative to Their Own," *Sociometry*, 21:247–254 (1958).

[54] See Parsons, in Anshen; and David Riesman, "Permissiveness and Sex

had employment experience prior to marriage, divorce may not present the same difficulties that it once did. Yet divorce does introduce problems, usually of both an economic and a social-psychological sort. In the first place, the great majority of men and women in our society have different expectations about their future and their roles. For men, work or a job becomes the focus of self-identity and emotional investment, as well as of social status. On the other hand, women's socialization experiences are such that self-identity and emotional investment are intimately linked to successful wifehood. Thus, employment prior to marriage is regarded by most women as only temporary; after marriage it may serve other purposes.[55] The different societal attitudes which men and women incorporate in their own work roles are today reflected in societal practices which allocate differential salaries and statuses to male and female workers performing the same duties.[56]

The larger number of women employed today, which is in part a reflection of the "emancipation" of women occurring largely in this century, does not mean that women are no longer socialized differently from men. But the so-called emancipation of women has introduced additional roles for women. This does not mean that the old role of wife-mother is obsolete, but rather that today the wife-mother is subtly forced by social pressures to play additional roles. Some women may resist these pressures; others may regard them as a signal to abdicate the "drudgery" of wife-motherhood and become a full-fledged "careerist." Women today may feel ambivalent concerning their marital roles.[57]

Moreover, contrasted with the relatively limited education given them formerly, women today frequently go beyond high school, either to college or to business or secretarial school. This greater amount of education makes the wife a different kind of mate: she will tend to define her role in such a relationship differently, she does not respect her husband's position to the same extent, and she is more able to discuss things on an equal basis with her husband. The college-trained girl sets higher standards for her mate, and is less likely to accept a man with an education inferior to hers. As a result of both work experience and education, a woman is less likely than formerly to leave all decisions to her husband; more probably she will demand an equal share in this activity.

Some role conflicts involve the pattern played by the marriage partner

---

[55] Riesman.

[56] See Eli Ginsberg, *Woman Power* (New York: Columbia University Press, 1957).

[57] See Nora Johnson, "The Captivity of Marriage," *Atlantic Monthy*, 207:38–42 (1961).

in his marital and familial responsibilities. In some families, members may play their roles in a way which deviates markedly from that generally prescribed, so that any organization of roles becomes difficult. Sometimes, deviation in role playing in marriage is due to role expectations, as in the case of many adolescents, which are not even the same as those normally required for the marriage role.[58] The popular explanation that "neither was prepared to assume marriage and family responsibilities" probably best applies to these cases.

In other situations the role of one marital partner may be derived from a patriarchal or a matriarchal tradition, whereas the other partner may come from a more equalitarian or democratic background. One of the partners may then wish to assume entirely the major decision-making functions, such as the expenditure of money and the disciplining of the children. For example, a husband who was raised in a patriarchal family, and has expectations of playing a similar role in his own marriage, may marry a girl who has been supporting herself and making her own decisions. The husband can refer to families where the husband makes decisions, and the wife can refer to other families in which decisions are made on a democratic basis. In general, it has been shown that marital happiness and stability are more probable if the marital partners are from similar social backgrounds.[59]

A reverse situation may occur where "the woman plays the authoritative roles, ruling over her husband and children despotically. A man who has grown up in such a family will perhaps expect his wife to dominate him, but she may have had a family experience which prepared her for a submissive and dependent role. If such a man married such a woman, a struggle arises which is won by the person who forces the other to make decisions for the pair." [60]

Marital role expectations come from two major sources. It appears that in general the roles played by the marital partners largely reflect the marital roles played by the parents or other persons with whom each of the partners was intimately associated in childhood. Generally the girl derives hers far more from the mother than the boy does from the father.[61] The reason is that the parents or other "significant persons" are merely the "instruments"

---

[58] See Marie S. Dunn, "Marriage Role Expectations of Adolescents," *Marriage and Family Living*, 22:99–111 (1960); and Alvin Moser, "Marriage Role Expectations of High School Students," *Marriage and Family Living*, 23:42–43 (1961).

[59] See Winch.

[60] Waller, p. 285.

[61] David B. Lynn, "Sex Differences in Identification Development," *Sociometry*, 24:372–383 (1961).

through which societal attitudes, norms, and values regarding sex-associated roles are communicated to children. Married adjustment may be regarded in part as a process in which marriage partners attempt to re-enact certain systems or roles obtained in their own family groups. There are indications that there is greater dependence on the part of women on the family of orientation and that women's lesser emancipation from the family of orientation is a factor in marital discord.[62] The other source of role expectations in marriage is the general culture, including the mass media. Influenced by male subcultures, males come to marriage with interpretations of marriage that differ from those of females, namely, a view of male dominance and traditional roles for the wife.[63]

Differences about the need for children are reflections of conflict in the role playing of husband and wife. The husband may be influenced by his image of the traditional family, with the satisfactions derived from having many children around the house. If the woman has an occupation in which she is interested she may not want to give up her position in order to raise children. The man, on the other hand, may not want the obligation and expense which children bring.

Role Conflicts between Marriage and Other Activities

Role-playing difficulties may represent a conflict among family roles and those required in various outside activities. There may be a degree of incompatibility between the role of a man as a husband and father and the demands of his occupation, or between the role of a wife and mother and outside interests, whether connected with a job or with social activities. The qualities and status of a man or woman in their work may be quite different from the qualities required for successful performance in their home and family.[64] The difficulties the family faces in meeting other role demands have been accentuated in Western society by an urban way of life. In some instances these numerous demands may not represent conflict so much as the necessity for playing too many different roles; that is, the behaviors required of different roles may not actually be incompatible; yet the necessity of shifting to several roles during each twenty-four-hour period may seriously impede a person's skill in the playing of a single role.

Even when certain goals and conceptions of roles to be played are de-

---

[62] Mirra Komarovsky, "Functional Analysis of Sex Roles," in Eisenstadt, pp. 206–210.

[63] Dunn; and Debi Lovejoy, "College Student Conceptions of the Roles of Husband and Wife in Decision-Making," *Family Life Coordinator,* 9:43–46 (1961).

[64] Ronald Fletcher, *The Family and Marriage in Britain: An Analysis and Moral Assessment* (Baltimore: Penguin Books, Inc., 1962), pp. 171–174.

cided upon, society may make them difficult to carry out. The goal of becoming a professional man is highly rewarded by society; yet it makes early marriage difficult. A community may feel that having two or three children is desirable; and yet in housing and participation in social life it often rewards those without children. Parents may feel that their children have too much freedom; yet they offer them little "controlled" recreational facilities and permit commercial establishments to fulfill their recreational needs. A wife and husband may agree on the roles each is to play—for instance, companionship roles—but for economic reasons move to a small rural town which does not approve such roles. Thus, even if there is agreement as to the roles to be played in marriage, societal frustrations may prevent their being performed. If in the marital situation there is a failure to accept alternative conceptions of roles and goals, the potential unity is not realized.

Society has established, for example, no definite status for the working wife. It is undecided whether to reward or punish her for her emancipated form of living, especially the working wife in the middle classes.[65] As a result of his reaction to the uncertainty of others and the internal uncertainty he has learned, the husband is often ambivalent about his wife's working, particularly when it is not necessary. When the woman works from necessity there may be other difficulties in her role in the marriage.[66] This situation may be especially acute when the family lives in a community where many of the wives do not work. One study of married veterans on a college campus found that the employment status of wives was the most significant difference in the roles of husband and wife. The women who worked full time tended to have authoritarian conceptions of marriage, whereas those who worked only part time leaned toward the companionate conception of marriage.[67]

Role Conflicts between Parents and Children

There may be conflicts between the roles of children and parents. Such conflicts have been intensified by the democratic and individualistic training now given children in an urban world, training which increases

---

[65] See Riesman, for a discussion of how younger persons incorporate these societal attitudes toward their own working roles. Also see Ginsberg, for a discussion of how, in salaries and status, society reflects a differential attitude toward male and female workers.

[66] See *Work in the Lives of Married Women* (National Manpower Council Conference; New York: Columbia University Press, 1958); and Lee Rainwater, Richard Coleman, and Gerald Handel, *Workingman's Wife: Her Personality, World, and Life Style* (New York: Oceana Publications, Inc., 1959).

[67] Motz.

the adolescent conflict with a generation having different values and a different conception of the family roles. It has become increasingly difficult to impose authoritarian traditions of the last century on children of the present generation: Children have ways of influencing family decisions, in both small and large matters, by manipulating the reward structure in the family, by creating disturbances, and by making situations difficult for others.[68] Parents' expectations for their children frequently conflict with the children's desires. In an urban society children are often presented, through peers and others, with conflicting norms and values. As a result, younger persons may acquire attitudes which conflict with those of the parents, for the former have closer contacts with these emerging patterns and are more adaptable in learning them.

Role Conflicts between Marital Partners and Other Relatives

Relations of members of a family to other relatives may be still another source of difficulty arising from role playing. The fact that families in modern industrial societies tend to be nuclear rather than extended can be misleading in implying that there are few associations with relatives.[69] Migration studies indicate that prior location of relatives is the most important factor in determining the city of destination.[70] Studies in the United States and Great Britain have shown that kinship ties are likely to be most important in lower- and working-class families and least in middle-class and professional families where friendships are often more important than kinship ties.[71] Kinship ties in the United States have been shown generally to revolve around primarily mother-daughter associations. Maintaining kinship ties, moreover, is primarily the wife's responsibility and consequently, "most in-law problems are women's problems." [72] Studies have shown that women are more dependent on their parents than are men and the more

---

[68] Robert O. Blood, Jr., "The Measurement of Bases of Family Power: A Rejoinder," *Marriage and Family Living*, 25:475–478 (1963).

[69] See, for example, Leonard Blumberg and Robert H. Bell, "Urban Migration and Kinship Ties," *Social Problems*, 6:328–333 (1959).

[70] Marvin Sussman, "Relationships of Adult Children with Their Parents in the United States," in Ethel Shanas and Gordon F. Streib, eds., *Social Structure and the Family: Generational Relations* (Englewood Cliffs, N.J.: Prentice-Hall, Inc., 1965), pp. 62–92.

[71] Marvin B. Sussman, "Intergenerational Family Relationship and Role Changes in Middle Age," *Journal of Gerontology*, 15:71–75 (1960). Also see Herbert J. Gans, *The Urban Villagers* (New York: The Free Press, 1962); and Michael Young and Peter Wilmott, *Family and Kinship in East London* (London: Pelican Books, 1962).

[72] Udry, p. 381.

dependent a man or woman is on the mother the more trouble the marital partner will have with her. Udry has concuded from an analysis of the research literature that marital relations with in-laws are likely to succeed under conditions where there was parental approval of the marriage, a separate household, happiness in the parents' marriages, no religious differences, and a similarity in the cultural backgrounds of the marital partners."[73] The adjustment of satisfactory relationships with the in-laws of both families often presents a difficulty in many marriages. Patterns of respect for parents may conflict with the desire for freedom from them, and feelings of affection and obligation toward them may place the partner whose parent is in the home or living nearby in a peculiarly difficult position.[74]

Family difficulties may start between parents and their son or daughter as the former attempt to continue or to reassume the familiar protective role. The presence of in-laws may magnify difficulties which would normally be temporary.[75]

> Culture conflict, role incompatibility, and imperfect insight into the attitudes and roles of another seem to underlie occasional disharmony in the relationships between parents and their adult children. People are carriers of culture, but often of different and incompatible aspects of culture. Parents, by virtue of age grouping, immigration, migration, and vertical social mobility, may differ with their adult children on many family matters. There could be disagreement concerning child-rearing practices. The meaning of a kinship system might be a matter of dispute. Ascribed as compared with achieved status might also be an issue.[76]

CONFLICTS INVOLVING CULTURAL BACKGROUND AND INTERESTS

When members of a marriage or a family have backgrounds and social norms which are drastically different, this difference can be a source of a great deal of conflict and tension. In former rural societies in America, where the population within an area was quite homogeneous, an individual generally married someone who had grown up in the area and had accepted the ideas and norms of the community. The marital situation offered little opportunity for a conflict of fundamental norms and values.

---

[73] Udry, p. 381.

[74] For studies of generational relationships in developing and less developed societies see Shanas and Streib.

[75] Earl L. Koos, *Families in Trouble* (New York: King's Crown Press, 1946), p. 76.

[76] Kirkpatrick, p. 544.

Conflicting definitions of the marital situation, and especially of the relation of the marital group to outside group activities, have developed within modern urban society. One study has shown that residence in rural areas during childhood is a favorable factor in marital adjustment, whereas residence in a city is unfavorable.[77] Moreover, spatial and vertical class mobility have increased the possibilities of the marriage of persons with diverse backgrounds and interests. Cultural differentiation appears to occur when a family or an individual goes up or down in the scale of occupation or of social class.

In a comparative study of happily married couples and divorced couples, the importance of agreement between marital partners on certain fundamental activities was pointed out, such as "handling finances, recreation, religion, demonstration of affection, sexual relations, ways of dealing with in-laws, amount of time spent together, table manners, conventionality, and aims or objectives of the family." [78] These factors conform to common sense, for they refer to the general areas of interaction in marriage and represent typical areas of complaint against the marital partner.[79]

Similarity of family and cultural background is an important favorable factor in marital adjustment; a pronounced difference is unfavorable: Conflicts may often occur, for example, in a union where a rural person with orthodox religious values and attitudes marries a more cosmopolitan person having unorthodox religious views and liberal ideas and practices. It has been suggested that marital adjustment is easier for persons who have similar social backgrounds, and that marriage stability and success is more probable if both partners are from backgrounds with a strong set of values against divorce or other forms of disruption. Actually, the process of mate selection serves to bring together persons with similar backgrounds, for persons do tend in general to associate with, and to marry, others of similar social class, status, education, or religion.[80]

Some interests bind a marriage together, but others appear to have less influence. One study found that sports and games have little or no

---

[77] Ernest W. Burgess and Leonard S. Cottrell, Jr., *Predicting Success or Failure in Marriage* (Englewood Cliffs, N.J.: Prentice-Hall, Inc., 1939).

[78] Locke, p. 85. Also see a Swedish study by George Karlsson, *Adaptability and Communication in Marriage* (Totowa, N.J.: Bedminster Press, 1961).

[79] Numerous studies have been made of views of marital partners about the inadequacies of the other in various areas of marital life. See, for example, Judson T. Landis, "Social Correlations of Divorce or Nondivorce among the Unhappily Married," *Marriage and Family Living*, 25:178–180 (1963).

[80] For a partial bibliography of studies on "social homogamy" or common characteristics of marital partners, see Winch, pp. 5–7.

binding effect; friends, reading, and dancing have some effect; music, theater, and the church have more; but professional interests, active community service, and a common cause have great binding effect.[81] It is probable that agreement on a single factor or area of marriage interaction would not be of great significance in contributing to marriage success unless it were the outward expression of some more fundamental agreement —such as that concerning life values and goals.

SOCIAL SIMILARITY AND COMPLEMENTARY NEEDS

The bulk of evidence on marital selection suggests that similarity (or homogamy) of social characteristics is conductive to marital happiness and stability. This includes studies indicating that there is similarity in social class, education, and even physical characteristics such as height.

Other research has suggested, however, that whereas homogamous social characteristics may contribute to marriage stability, perhaps marriage partners are happier if certain of their psychological characteristics are *not* alike, but "complementary." [82] The theory of complementary needs is that "within the field of eligible persons [those] whose need-patterns provide gratification will tend to choose each other as marital partners." [83] For example, aggressive persons sometimes marry shy and retiring individuals; submissive persons may marry dominant ones.

In a test of this theory, Winch studied twenty-five married couples, all college undergraduates. The "needs" included dominance, submissiveness, receptiveness, and nurturance. "Nurturance" is the tendency or need to give support, aid, or care to a supposedly weak or helpless person. A woman who behaves maternally toward her husband, whom she regards as a "little boy" needing to be looked after, would be nurturant. The following are Winch's complementary need types: Ibsenian (husband dominant and nurturant; wife receptive and submissive), Thurberian (husband nurturant and submissive; wife receptive and dominant), Master–Servant Girl (husband receptive and dominant; wife nurturant and submissive), and Mother-Son (husband receptive and submissive; wife nurturant and dominant).[84] Sixteen of the twenty-five couples could be classified satisfactorily in one of these types, with nine couples being exceptions.

At present the evidence on psychological characteristics does not defi-

---

[81] Burgess and Wallin, p. 442.

[82] Winch.

[83] Robert F. Winch, *The Modern Family* (3d ed.; New York: Holt, Rinehart and Winston, Inc., 1963), p. 607.

[84] Winch, *Mate Selection*, pp. 212–233.

nitely support the notion of either complementariness or homogamy in mate selection. It is possible, of course, that there are general psychological characteristics and that some persons will be happier with mates who have dissimilar characteristics, whereas others would prefer mates with similar characteristics. The kind of mate a person seeks may depend upon his social background, which would tend to orient him toward one type of mate or another. It might be more appropriate to use the terms "expectations" or "role orientations," which clearly involve situational referents, rather than such static concepts as "trait" or "need." [85] There is also undoubtedly considerable variation in the response to deficiencies in needs.

> The stable marriage is likely to be one in which a range of the wife's and husband's needs are mutually gratified. An unhappy marriage leading to divorce may well be one in which some few needs are met, but others are frustrated or ignored, so that the union means a continued unhappiness for either or both persons. How far the adjustment of husband and wife to the reality of their situation is generally sufficient to tolerate this failure of need gratification is a question yet to be answered.[86]

SOCIAL PARTICIPATION

Because the family is a social group, one might well expect that the extent of social participation prior to marriage is related to marital happiness. According to some evidence, the number of friends, including those of the opposite sex, and the frequency of participating in social organizations are related to marital happiness.[87] The possession of many friends need not, of course, be related to marital happiness, but the presence of some satisfying relationships with other persons is probably a reflection of the manner in which an individual interacts with others. To the extent that a mode of interaction results in satisfying relationships prior to marriage it should also be conductive to later marital happiness.

Both American and British researchers have shown that the character of family friendship systems may contribute to marital stability or insta-

---

[85] See Nelson N. Foote and Leonard S. Cottrell, *Identity and Interpersonal Competence* (Chicago: University of Chicago Press, 1956).

[86] From "Family Disorganization" by William G. Goode in *Contemporary Social Problems* edited by Robert K. Merton and Robert A. Nisbet, © 1961, 1966 by Harcourt, Brace & World, Inc., and reprinted with their permission.

[87] Burgess and Cottrell, and Locke. Much of the data on these and the factors which follow have been derived from a number of studies which have tried to predict marital happiness from studies of factors associated with successful and unsuccessful marital adjustment. For a more detailed summary of the findings of such studies, a bibliography, and a criticism of this type of research, see Kirkpatrick, pp. 375–407, 673–678.

bility. In this case, it has been shown that it is not the number of friends which is significant so much as their similarity (in terms of values, goals, and so forth) to the particular family involved. Where friends of a family are similar, family disruption is much less frequent than when they are dissimilar.[88]

COMPANIONSHIP AND THE SEXUAL RELATION

Some older studies have suggested that marital happiness and the degree of companionship in marriage are positively associated. One study, for example, reported marital happiness to be related to close association as demonstrated by always or nearly always talking things over and by joint participation in all or almost all outside activities[89] More recent investigations by both British and American sociologists, however, have not supported the assertion that the degree of companionship in marital role relationships and happiness are necessarily correlated.[90] Instead, marital happiness occurs with about equal frequency in both the traditional and the companionship types of marital role relationship. There was a tendency toward greater stability in the traditional type and for the expression of somewhat greater happiness.

Despite rapidly changing sexual codes which have established a more equal approach to sexual gratification, sexual factors in marriage appear to affect men and women differently.[91] An unsatisfying sexual relationship is more likely to affect the views of a man about the success of the marriage, whereas with a woman there may be a low or a high degree of marital suc cess regardless of the quality of the sexual relationship.[92] Women tend to enter marriage with a lower sexual expectation, or their sexual response may be a more general, rather than specific, expression of affection for the husband. Among men there are high sexual expectations, with the sexual factor being dependent on the wives' sexual expression.

It is likely, of course, that marital happiness is the "cause" of sexual

---

[88] See Bott, and Zimmerman and Cervantes. The social characteristics referred to here included the proportion of kindred among the friend-families, the social backgrounds, as evidenced in region of origin, religion (ethical and moral views), income, and tastes. For further discussion of how the friend matrix of the family may operate as a means of social control, see Eugene Litwak, "Occupational Mobility and Extended Family Cohesion," *American Sociological Review*, 25:9–21 (1960).

[89] Locke, pp. 266–267.

[90] See, for example, Bott.

[91] See Edwin M. Schur, ed., *The Family and the Sexual Revolution* (Bloomington: Indiana University Press, 1964); and Kirkpatrick, pp. 483–490.

[92] Burgess and Wallin, pp. 662–663.

compatibility, rather than the reverse, as many have supposed.[93] Sexual factors probably never operate in isolation and rarely of themselves break down a marriage. Sexual difficulties have been found to be secondary expressions of conflicts arising from disagreements of various types. When sexual difficulties do seem to be a primary cause they may be an expression of tensions diffused from other conflicts or unresolved differences concerning the way each believes other conflicts should be settled. Sexual adjustment is to a large extent an effect or a reflection of success in other areas of the marriage relationship, but the effect varies according to the marital partner. One writer, after surveying the research, has concluded:

> For each sex then, there is the same *correlation* between marital adjustment and sexual adjustment, but the main direction of correlation is opposite for the two sexes. For a man, the level of sexual adjustment has a causal effect on his marital adjustment with little reciprocal effect of general marital adjustment on his sex life; for a woman, the level of general marital satisfaction has an effect on the sexual adjustment with little reciprocal effect of the sexual adjustment on her general satisfaction with the marriage.[94]

ECONOMIC FACTORS AND MARITAL STABILITY

A number of economic circumstances constitute a major adjustment difficulty in marriage, including "the unemployment of husband, living within a small income, disposal of income, to save or not to save, and the wife working after marriage." [95] Contrary to many statements of married couples, however, such economic factors do not appear to be the real reasons for disturbances in family unity. The economic relationship, like the sexual relationship, is secondary in comparison with other factors, such as social roles, cultural backgrounds, social participation, and affection. The attitude of the marital partner toward economic factors appears to be dependent upon other factors. Members of a family play more than one role. Often tensions engendered in other roles express themselves in the family relationship. The family is often a vehicle for tensions arising in other parts of the society. Business and industry, for example, may en-

---

[93] Goode, "Family Disorganization." He suggests that sexual expectations of persons entering marriage are probably not as great as they were following the decline of Victorianism and the emancipation of women, that young people today are better prepared for sex in marriage, and that their expectations are likely to be more realistic.

[94] Udry, p. 415.

[95] Burgess and Wallin, p. 609.

courage "supervisor anxiety." [96] This anxiety is often carried home from the plant or office, and the marital partner may be used as a scapegoat.

Loss of earning power may also create family tensions. Often a man's salary is part of the image a woman marries, and with a loss in earning power due to illness or depression, a part of this image disappears, weakening the affectional bond between the two members. Numerous studies have shown that both depressions and unemployment sometimes tend to increase family problems.[97]

SUMMARY

With the growth of industrialization and urbanization the family has undergone pronounced changes. A number of frames of reference for the interpretation of changes in the family have evolved. They have included functional differentiation, companionship family, and orderly replacement versus permanent availability.

Divorce rates appear to have increased rapidly in Western society, although the rate varies greatly among different groups within a society. Most divorces occur early in marriage, the legal grounds for divorce being rarely the real reasons. A large proportion of divorced persons eventually remarry.

Role conflicts play a particularly important part in marital and family problems. They represent conflicts between marital partners over their duties and obligations; conflicts between family roles and roles outside the family; conflicts in the roles of the children, particularly with parents; and, finally, conflicts between marital roles and those of other relatives.

Conflicts of cultural background and interests may also produce marital instability. Disagreements over values and goals in the marriage are the most significant. Similarities in norms are important in marital stability. Sexual and economic difficulties in marriage appear to be largely an expression of incompatibility in other areas of the marriage.

SELECTED READINGS

Bott, Elizabeth. *Family and Social Network*. London: Tavistock Publications, Ltd., 1957. A study of urban British families which examines the relationships between family roles and norms and the social matrix in which the family functions. The manner in which the social matrix acts as a medium of social control is thoroughly described.

---

[96] John J. Honigmann, "Culture Patterns and Human Stress: A Study in Social Psychiatry," *Psychiatry*, 13:25–34 (1950).

[97] Ruth S. Cavan and Katherine Ranck, *The Family and the Depression* (Chicago: University of Chicago Press, 1938).

Burgess, Ernest W., and Leonard S. Cottrell, Jr. *Predicting Success or Failure in Marriage*. Englewood Cliffs, N.J.: Prentice-Hall, Inc., 1939. One of the major prediction studies in which difficulties in role playing are emphasized. A study of 526 Illinois couples primarily from Chicago. There is extensive case material.
————, and Harvey J. Locke. *The Family: From Institution to Companionship*. Rev. ed. New York: American Book Company, 1960. A comprehensive analysis of marriage and family relations emphasizing the shift from an authoritarian to a democratic family system.
————, and Paul Wallin. *Engagement and Marriage*. Philadelphia: J. B. Lippincott Company, 1953. A detailed study of 1000 engaged and 600 married couples. In addition to statistical material there are numerous quotations from interviews and personal documents. The book also includes an extensive analysis of nearly all similar studies.
Farber, Bernard. *Family: Organization and Interaction*. San Francisco: Chandler Publishing Company, 1964. An analysis of the family in terms of orderly replacement of cultural values and the availability of individuals for marriage.
Fletcher, Ronald. *The Family and Marriage in Britain: An Analysis and Moral Assessment*. Baltimore: Penguin Books, Inc., 1962. A sociological study of the effects on the family of industrialization in Great Britain and the nature of contemporary family relationships.
Foote, Nelson N., and Leonard S. Cottrell, Jr. *Identity and Interpersonal Competence*. Chicago: University of Chicago Press, 1955. An examination of family and marriage from a symbolic interactionist view. Theoretical issues in family study are discussed and a new approach to family research is suggested. Such concepts as "compatibility," "adjustment," "maladjustment," and many others are critically evaluated.
Goode, William J. *After Divorce*. New York: The Free Press, 1956. A study of divorce and subsequent patterns of behavior.
————. *Women in Divorce*. New York: The Free Press, 1965. A study of differentials in divorce.
Locke, Harvey J. *Predicting Adjustment in Marriage*. New York: Holt, Rinehart and Winston, Inc., 1951. A comparative study of both divorced and happily married persons. In contrast to other studies which have generally studied college-educated persons, the sample is more representative of the general population.
Parsons, Talcott, and Robert F. Bales. *Family, Socialization and Interaction Process*. New York: The Free Press, 1955. A functional-differentiation view of relations in the nuclear family.
Udry, Richard J. *The Social Context of Marriage*. Philadelphia: J. B. Lippincott Company, 1966. A comprehensive sociological study of the family and problems of adjustment.
Winch, Robert F. *The Modern Family*. New York: Holt, Rinehart and Winston, Inc., 1952. An analysis of marriage and family relations with a sociopsychological emphasis. Chapter 15 deals with the theory of complementary needs.
Zimmerman, Carle C., and Lucius F. Cervantes. *Successful American Families*. New York: Pageant Books, Inc., 1960. A study of over 9000 American families

representing a cross section of social classes, ethnic and religious groups, and regions of the United States. The authors examine family friendship systems and find that the character of this system is one of the main determinants of family success or failure.

15

Role and Status Conflict in Old Age

The aged in many modern industrial societies have been likened to
a minority group because many encounter group discrimination,
not on the basis of racial, ethnic, or religious background but on the basis
of age.[1] There is often restriction on general social, economic, and political
participation, and this, in turn, makes their influence less than it should be
in terms of their numbers. The social roles of older people today are ambiguously defined. They have little place in most modern social structures,
for there are few regular, institutionally sanctioned opportunities for full
participation in an urban society. There is conflict between the role aspiration of older people and the actual role accorded them by our contemporary
society. In this sense their difficulties in role adjustments are similar to
those of the adolescent. Among both groups there is often a feeling of not
being useful, participating members of society as well as a feeling that their
desires are not fully recognized.

The composition of the aged population of a country such as the
United States is very diverse. One can only speak of such an age group in
general terms. There are aged who are urban and rural, healthy and sick,

---

[1] Milton L. Barron, *The Aging American* (New York: Thomas Y. Crowell Company, 1961).

wealthy and poor, native-born and immigrant. They are from all racial, ethnic, and religious groups. In 1963 those over sixty-five included more than 2 million persons working full time, nearly 1.5 million living on farms, over 12.5 million getting social security benefits, more than 3 million who migrated from Europe, over 2.3 million veterans, and 10,000 persons more than a hundred years old.[2]

PHYSIOLOGICAL CHANGES

Aging is accompanied by certain physiological changes [3] which are not necessarily the result of any disease. There is generally cellular atrophy and degeneration, as well as the more readily observable aspects of graying hair, baldness, wrinking of the skin, stiffness, and changes in bodily form. These general progressive changes due to age can be listed as follows:

1. Gradual tissue desiccation. Recent studies of electrolyte (salt) concentration in the tissue cells have cast some doubt as to the reliability of older experiments which formerly appeared to have established gradual tissue drying as part of the aging process.
2. Gradual retardation of cell division, capacity of cell growth, and tissue repair. This involves also a decline in capacity to produce the products of secretion, whether they be known substances such as pepsin or thyroxine or the less well identified antibodies involved in immunity.
3. Gradual retardation of the rate of tissue oxidation (lowering of the speed of living, or, in technical terms, the metabolic rate).
4. Cellular atrophy, degeneration, increased cell pigmentation, and fatty infiltration.
5. Gradual decrease in tissue elasticity, and degenerative changes in the elastic connective tissues of the body.
6. Decreased speed, strength, and endurance of skeletal neuromuscular reactions.

---

[2] President's Council on Aging, *The Older American* (Washington, D.C.: Government Printing Office, 1963), p. 1. For a comparative view of all aspects of aging and the problems associated with it, see Clark Tibbitts and Wilma Donahue, eds., *Social and Psychological Aspects of Aging* (New York: Columbia University Press, 1962) and Nathan W. Shock, *Biological Aspects of Aging* (New York: Columbia University Press, 1962). These constitute Volumes I and II of Aging around the World, Proceedings of the Fifth Congress of the International Association of Gerontology. Other volumes are *Social Welfare of the Aging* and *Medical and Clinical Aspects of Aging*.

[3] Leonard Z. Breen, "The Aging Individual," in Clark Tibbitts, ed., *Handbook of Social Gerontology* (Chicago: University of Chicago Press, 1960), p. 147. Also see Shock; and Kurt Wolff, *The Biological, Sociological and Psychological Aspects of Aging* (Springfield, Ill.: Charles C Thomas, Publisher, 1959).

7. Progressive degeneration and atrophy of the nervous system, impairment of vision, of hearing, of attention, of memory, and of mental endurance.
8. Gradual impairment of the mechanisms which maintain a fairly constant internal environment for the cells and tissues (a process known as homeostasis). It is evident that sufficient weakening of any one of the numerous links in the complex processes of homeostasis produces deterioration.[4]

These physiological criteria, however, must be properly interpreted, for they cannot be applied to all members of a given age group, such as some chronological age like sixty-five. No longer is the concept of aging based on "an assumption of general organic, functional and psychological deterioration beginning in middle life and proceeding rather rapidly until it becomes disabling and finally incapacitating."[5] Physiological aging is a gradual process which varies tremendously among individuals. Contrary to popular opinion, for example, sexual activity does not suddenly decline among males, for the decline is so gradual that it is not until the late seventies or eighties that there is complete impotency, and exceptions occur even then. In some activities one function may decline while another increases, as in the case of physical speed as contrasted with endurance.[6] Some have expressed the view that the physiological changes associated with age are not significant unless they affect either the older person's ability to maintain relationships with others, or unless they alter his appearance in such a way as to affect society's judgment of him.[7]

The physiological deterioration of the aged is real in some cases, but it has probably been overemphasized for the total group. There is no question that the incidence of certain ailments, such as heart disease and cancer, increases with age. For the year 1958, heart disease caused 747 deaths per 100,000 persons between the ages of fifty-five and sixty-four; the cancer deaths for this age group were 392 for the same base population. According

---

[4] Anton J. Carlson and Edward J. Stieglitz, "Physiological Changes in Aging," *The Annals,* 279:22 (1952).

[5] Clark Tibbitts and Henry D. Sheldon, "Introduction: A Philosophy of Aging," *The Annals,* 279:6 (1952). See also Breen, in Tibbitts, p. 146, and Hans Selye, "The Philosophy of Stress," in Clark Tibbitts and Wilma Donahue, *Aging in Today's Society* (Englewood Cliffs, N.J.: Prentice-Hall, Inc., 1960), p. 118.

[6] For example, the records for the 100-yard and 220-yard dashes are held by men from eighteen to twenty-two years of age, but the records for the long grind of the marathons are held by men between thirty-eight and forty-five. Some of the best mountain climbers are in their thirties and forties.

[7] Robert W. Kleemeier, "Behavior and the Organization of the Bodily and the External Environment," in James E. Birren, ed., *Handbook of Aging and the Individual* (Chicago: University of Chicago Press, 1959), pp. 400–447.

to the National Health Survey, over three fourths (78.7 percent) of those over sixty-five have some chronic health condition, which compares with 41.9 percent of those of all ages.[8] Of the aged, 45.1 percent were hindered in their activity because of these conditions and nearly one fourth were prevented from working or keeping house. One in six old persons are hospitalized during a year; both the costs and the hospital stay are likely to be twice as great as those for a younger person.

Chronological age is an unsatisfactory criterion for "old age" because of the great individual variation in the rate of physiological aging. Some people are relatively young at seventy or older, whereas some are quite aged physically at fifty. Some men have children in their eighties, some play golf and even ski at that age. Many farmers past seventy can outwork a younger man in the field. One of the more important concepts in the study of aging is that "physiologic age or biologic age is not the same as chronologic age. . . . Often biologic age is greater than chronologic age; sometimes it is less."[9] The attitude toward chronological age is well expressed by an eighty-year-old retired Army officer who had volunteered at seventy for Army service and was rejected because of age.

> Comes 1942 and World War II. I still held a hold-over commission as Captain in the United States Army, inactive reserve. I wrote a letter to the powers that be at the War Department asking that I too may be ordered to active duty. Come back instructions to present myself to the regular Army examining board in session at Fort Sheridan, Illinois for complete and final examination for active duty. . . . Could not imagine why I seemed to be the main attraction there, but I later learned that it was due to my age, only 70 and that I made the various tests with flying colors. I did not feel a day older than I did when I first enlisted in the Army 48 years ago. At the conclusion of the exam the commanding officer had me call at his office to congratulate me on the almost perfect score, and asked me the question asked me several times that day. This usually was, "What do you do to keep in such perfect physical trim?"
>
> Now I waited from day to day hoping, with each mail, to receive that order directing me to report to the commanding officer at so and so for active duty. But alas a letter came OK but it simply said that my physical condition was quite perfect but that due to my age I would not be allowed to serve my country. A nice letter of appreciation was enclosed. Thus ended my military career forever. Again I had the pain of completely separating myself from the military service. I have discovered this. That as we age we do not feel our hurts, both physical or emotional pains, as

---

[8] *Health, Education and Welfare Indications,* October 1962, p. xxi.

[9] Edward J. Stieglitz, *The Second Forty Years* (Philadelphia: J. B. Lippincott Company, 1946), p. 10.

keenly as we do in our younger days. This is because we are no longer as much alive. It is a melancholy fact that man begins to die the day he is born.[10]

It is clear that physiological age is not determined wholly by chronological age, but that these two variables are partially independent. Yet physiological deterioration alone does not define aging, for in addition there must be a societal reaction to such deterioration which defines it as symptomatic of aging. When a person's bodily functions become altered to such an extent that he begins to "look" old, the chances are great that he will increasingly withdraw from some groups with which he has been formerly associated.[11] To the extent that he does withdraw, his social and psychological adjustment will be affected, and he will validate society's judgment of a relationship between chronological age and deterioration. Although aging brings bodily changes, these changes do not account for the sudden behavioral changes or "breakdowns" noted in older persons following such events as retirement or widowhood; the latter are a result of social factors.

PSYCHOLOGICAL CHANGES

Psychological changes in aging relate to differences in sensory and motor functions, learning ability, memory, and to changes in performance on intelligence tests.[12] Sensory and motor functions of the aged show some marked differences. Hearing difficulties, particularly for the higher tones, increase with age, and there is less visual acuity where there is speed and poor contrast or dim illumination. Motor responses requiring speed generally decline. In fact, soon after maturity there is a decline in the swiftness of dealing a blow, in simple reaction time, and in strength of grip. Older persons generally may not be as fast in a given task, but they make fewer errors than younger persons. If an older person has retained his mechanical skill, however, he may be able to keep up with the speed of younger workers. A number of studies have shown that older persons are more expert at tasks which stress accuracy rather than speed.

There is some uncertainty about changes in learning abilities with old age. It would seem that learning *speed* declines slowly past the age of thirty and more rapidly past the age of fifty. However, studies in learning

---

[10] From a personal document.

[11] Breen, in Tibbitts, p. 152.

[12] Oscar J. Kaplan, "Psychological Aspects of Aging," *The Annals,* 279:32–42 (1952). Also see Tibbitts and Donahue, *Social and Psychological Aspects of Aging,* pp. 725–896.

power, that is, grasp or comprehension, show that it declines at a much slower rate, with some persons showing no apparent decline even in their eighties.[13] It is difficult to draw definite conclusions because of the artificial nature of many of the experiments on speed of learning and age. According to Kaplan, the continuance of an occupation or interest and motivation probably affect learning ability a great deal.[14] One of the primary difficulties in drawing conclusions from studies dealing with the relationship of age and learning stems from the fact that such factors as motivation, speed of performance, and physiological status are intimately correlated with age and exert a definite influence on learning task performance.[15]

Loss of memory, particularly the ability to recall present events, is often part of the popular characterization of the aged. Unfortunately, the evidence is not too clear on the extent of this loss. In Kaplan's words, these memory changes appear to "vary with the complexity of the task, loss being smallest on simple memory tests such as one dealing with visual memory for digits. There is a tendency for those of superior intelligence to sustain less memory loss than those who are mentally dull." [16] Since memory is related to personality, the role of motivation should play an important part. The decline on memory tasks may be due to decline in perceptual speed in "grasping" the material to be recalled, rather than to an actual "loss" of memory.[17] There is no evidence that loss of memory is essentially a biological function.

At present, no definite conclusions can be drawn from studies dealing with the relationship of intelligence test performance and aging. In general, these studies have shown lowered performance with aging; yet this decline is particularly prominent on those test items which require visual acuity and motor agility.[18] This would suggest that the apparent intellectual deterioration of the older person may be partially due to sensory impairment rather than to decline of intelligence. Moreover, the lowered performance of the older person may be partially due to changes in schooling that have taken place and that may make him less able to perform at

---

[13] Irving Lorge, "Intellectual Changes during Maturity and Old Age," *Review of Educational Research,* 17:326–332 (1947).

[14] Kaplan, pp. 35–36.

[15] Edward A. Jerome, "Age and Learning—Experimental Studies," in Birren, p. 696.

[16] Kaplan.

[17] Harold E. Jones, "Intelligence and Problem-Solving," in Birren, p. 732.

[18] George K. Bennett, "Relationship of Age and Mental Test Scores among Older Persons," in Clark Tibbitts and Wilma Donahue, eds., *The New Frontiers of Aging* (Ann Arbor: University of Michigan Press, 1957), pp. 153–157.

a high level on present-day intelligence tests. Also the older person may not be interested in the items on an intelligence test, and thus not be motivated to respond to them.[19] In addition, the speed factor, which is involved in all intelligence tests, creates a handicap for the older person.

SOCIOLOGICAL CHANGES

Neither the physiological nor the psychological characteristics of old age seem adequately to explain the differences in the status and role of older persons in various types of societies. Likewise, they do not sufficiently explain the difficult adjustment problems of older persons in contemporary society. Actually old age is a sociological process which is only partly determined by age; yet it occurs in the middle years in other cases. As a sociological concept, it may be regarded as "that point in an individual's life at which he ceases to perform all those duties, and enjoy all those rights, which were his during mature adulthood, when he begins to take on a new system of rights and duties." [20] This new system of rights and duties, or the status and role of the older person, is largely determined by the societal definitions of the nature of age and of the older person. From this point of view, aging is understood and interpreted "in terms of the behavior characteristics of persons designated by the society as aged." [21] *The adjustment of the older person, which is the degree to which his behavior corresponds to the societal role expectations, depends upon the clarity with which his roles are defined, the compatibility of the roles, the degree of preparation for assuming the roles, the consistency with which other persons allow him to play these roles, and the extent to which motivations of older persons can be realized.*

The process of sociological aging does not arbitrarily begin at any set age. Unlike chronological and biological aging, which takes place fairly continuously throughout life, sociological aging varies with societal definitions of age and the responses of individuals to changed age status. In this sense, chronological and physiological age are independent of the societal reaction, whereas sociological age is not. Thus, the aged person may not regard himself as aged, as was indicated when 499 men and 759 women, whose median age was 73.5 and 71.7, respectively, were asked whether they considered themselves middle-aged, elderly, old, or aged.[22]

---

[19] Jones, p. 722.

[20] B. Hutchinson, *Old People in a Modern Australian Community* (Melbourne: Melbourne University Press, 1955), p. 1.

[21] Breen, "The Aging Individual," in Tibbitts, p. 149.

[22] Robert J. Havighurst, "Social and Psychological Needs of the Aging," *The Annals,* 279:16–17 (1952). For a more lengthy personal document describing what

Only a small proportion regarded themselves as "old" or "aged." About half the men defined themselves as middle-aged, and in the age group sixty to sixty-four, two thirds put themselves in this category. In fact, not until they reach the seventies do most men and women have a conception of themselves as elderly. One woman in her eighties remarked, "I feel old only when I look at myself in the mirror."

Role and Status of the Aged in Nonurban Societies

The lower status of aged persons in urban society today is not dependent upon chronological or physiological age; rather, it is a reflection of the values of the culture. In many cultures older persons occupy positions of high status. In a study of a large group of folk societies, Simmons has reported that almost without exception older people have such an enviable position that, rather than fearing old age, many look forward to it.[23] Among certain groups, such as the Palaung of North Borneo, who attribute long life to a person's virtue in a previous existence, the aging years of life are regarded as the best.[24] Although this is partly a reflection of the fact that few of these people ever reach old age, even though it is chronologically defined as younger than it is in urban society, social values appear to play the leading role in the status of the old.

In folk societies the old person usually has a fixed role to play. For example, he is likely to be the dominant member of the family group, controlling its property and acting as leader for the kinship group. In fact, among many groups, such as the Australian aborigines, older males have preference in the selection of younger women for wives. This, in turn, enables them more effectively to continue their hold on family ties. Even very old people have a place in the family and community life. There is seldom idleness, but rather always a feeling of being useful, no matter how small the task. The following excerpt describes how the Hopi Indians of northeastern Arizona regard their aged:

> Old men among the Hopi tend their flocks until feeble and nearly blind. When they can no longer follow the herd, they work on in their fields and orchards, frequently lying down on the ground to rest. They also make shorter and shorter trips to gather herbs, roots, and fuel. When unable to go to the fields any longer they sit in the house or kiva where

it is like to be old, see Aldena Carlson Thomason, "We Who Are Elderly," in Arnold M. Rose, ed., *Aging in Minnesota* (Minneapolis: University of Minnesota Press, 1963), pp. 182–298.

[23] Leo W. Simmons, *The Role of the Aged in Primitive Societies* (New Haven, Conn.: Yale University Press, 1945).

[24] Leo W. Simmons, "Social Participation of the Aged in Different Cultures," *The Annals*, 279:43 (1952).

they card and spin, knit, weave blankets, carve wood, or make sandals. Some continue to spin when they are blind or unable to walk, and it is a common saying that "An old man can spin to the end of his life." Corn shelling is women's work but men will do it, especially in their dotage. Old women will cultivate their garden patches until very feeble and "carry wood and water as long as they are able to move their legs." They prepare milling stones, weave baskets and plaques out of rabbit weed, make pots and bowls from clay, grind corn, darn old cloths, care for children, and guard the house; and when there is nothing else to do, they will sit out in the sun and watch the drying fruit. The old frequently express the desire to "keep on working" until they die.[25]

One of the most important roles that old people play in folk societies is that of being the leading person in knowledge and decision making. Where there is no writing the old become the source of knowledge about many specialized techniques, religious rites, ethics, and physical ailments. Medicine men and priests are almost always old people. In fact, aged persons who have special qualifications in knowledge, wisdom, and experience find many opportunities to use their influence in the more formalized ceremonies, magical rites, and religious practices. Often they officiate at such events as child naming, initiations, weddings, funerals, and memorial ceremonies.

Old men in folk societies also exercise great political power: "Political, judicial and civil preferments and positions are often also the normal outcome of such personal growth in the lifetime acquirements of knowledge, wisdom, and sound judgment. The titles and often the offices tend to be lifelong. Old men may serve long and well as lawmakers, judges, and administrators of justice. Moreover, as leaders in exclusive societies and in initiating rites, the aging quite generally exercise the powers of discrimination and receive considerable deference." [26]

Role and status problems connected with old age have generally been minimized, at least in the past, in those areas of the world, such as India, and many parts of Asia and Africa, where the family and not the individual is the unit of social status and action. It is axiomatic that wherever a predominantly traditionalistic social system flourishes, old age and aging are largely not problematic. The reason is that the role and status of aged persons are clearly defined by the traditional values. In addition, there are generally a series of preparatory roles preceding assumption of the aged

---

[25] Leo W. Simmons, "Attitudes toward Aging and the Aged: Primitive Societies," *Journal of Gerontology,* 1:79 (1946).

[26] Simmons, "Social Participation of the Aged in Different Cultures," p. 49. See also P. M. Yap, "Aging in Underdeveloped Asian Countries," in Tibbitts and Donahue, *Social and Psychological Aspects of Aging,* pp. 442–453.

role. In this situation, the aged generally occupy positions of high status. Peasant China of some years ago, when the large-family system still predominated, was a classic example of a society where aged people were an asset rather than a problem. Because of their Confucianist philosophical and religious orientation, others in the Chinese culture were obligated to care for, obey, and revere the old. Filial piety was a chief commandment in this culture and one which was part and parcel of the larger value systems. The longer one lived, the more he had to look forward to in the way of psychic and social gratifications.[27]

It would be incorrect to leave an impression that the aged of Asia and Africa do not have problems related to age. Elderly women often lose status on the death of their husbands, many feel a degree of dependence on their children, particularly when they cannot work, and they are sometimes neglected in the larger family activities.[28]

Most older persons have a much more satisfactory status in rural societies than in urban. In the country almost everyone has a place in the cooperative activities of producing agricultural and household goods. The aged contribute in good measure, for they possess much of the rural society's technical skill and managerial experience. Furthermore, the integrated family system of rural areas gives the older person a continuing high place in the society. The individual is part of a group and rarely is in an individualistic setting. Old people are a part of this group, "the moving, directing, and controlling agents in this old rural type of collective entity. Because of this their status in such a society is greatly enhanced over that [which] they are privileged to enjoy in societies where familism does not persist." [29] In the larger rural families an extra person or two do not constitute the burden they may in an urban society. Moreover, the larger and more diverse rural household offers opportunity for much more interesting and productive work than does a household in the cities. The status of elderly persons in rural areas is also linked to the important roles they play as heads of households and in religious activities. Thus it is not likely that the older person's opinions and ideas will be scornfully disdained.

---

[27] Max Weber, *The Religion of China* (translated by Hans W. Gerth; New York: The Free Press, 1951). Also see Olga Lang, *The Chinese Family and Society* (New Haven, Conn.: Yale University Press, 1946).

[28] See, for example, Robert A. LeVine, "Intergenerational Tensions and Extended Family Structure in Africa," in Ethel Shanas and Gordon F. Streib, eds., *Social Structure and the Family: Generational Relations* (Englewood Cliffs, N.J.: Prentice-Hall, Inc., 1965), pp. 188–204.

[29] Lynn Smith, "The Aged in Rural Society," in *The Aged and Society* (Champaign, Ill.: Industrial Relations Research Association, 1950), p. 46.

Social Roles and Status in Urban Industrial Societies

Several factors account for the lowered status and undefined role of the aged in contemporary urban industrial societies. Burgess has stated that the problems of the aged population are relatively new problems and apparently are among the by-products of economic development which characterizes Western civilization.[30] The economic and sociological problems of old age found in the United States are also present in many other highly industrialized nations such as those of Northern Europe.[31] In a sense these problems are the result of urbanism, with its rapid social change and the tendency to emphasize youth and activity. Urbanized societies seem to regard older persons as having already had their turn at living and at experiencing the gratifications of life. Old people no longer have the same claim on kin for role, support, and social participation that they formerly did. Rarely is their advice given consideration, even if proffered, because their experiences and values are often out of line with those of the modern urban world. Some have therefore described the fundamental problem of the aged as involving role transition to a socially nonfunctional role which is only ambiguously defined.[32]

In an urban society as a whole, and in the family group as well, the aged are often marginal people. The smaller family unit no longer has a place for the aged person, for the modern democratic family is organized around the interests, wishes, and activities of its young and active members, who are more highly valued in the urban culture. Older persons may be left to their own devices, but rarely are they given equal status. Studies in a highly urbanized country like the Netherlands, for example, have shown increased isolation and loss of status for the aged. On the basis of these

---

[30] Ernest W. Burgess, ed., *Aging in Western Societies: A Survey of Social Gerontology* (Chicago: University of Chicago Press, 1960), Chapter 1.

[31] Arnold M. Rose and Warren A. Peterson, *Older People and Their Social World* (Philadelphia: F. A. Davis Company, 1965), p. 11. Also see Ethel Shanas, Peter Townsend, Dorothy Wedderburn, Henning Friis, Poul Milhoj, and Jan Stehouwer, *Old People in Three Industrial Societies* (New York: Atherton Press, 1967).

[32] See B. S. Phillips, "A Role Theory Approach to Adjustment in Old Age," *American Sociological Review*, 22:212–217 (1957); and H. L. Orbach and D. M. Shaw, "Social Participation and the Role of the Aging," *Geriatrics*, 12:241–246 (1957). For a discussion of a general theory of role change see Arnold M. Rose, *Theory and Method in the Social Sciences* (Minneapolis: University of Minnesota Press, 1954), p. 23. Also see the section on old age in S. Kirson Weinberg, *Social Problems of Our Time* (Englewood Cliffs, N.J.: Prentice-Hall, Inc., 1960).

Dutch studies a number of hypotheses have been advanced about the status of the aged in Western society.

1. Where the local society loses the character of a closed society, the status and role of the aged will decrease. The number of institutional roles played by aged people increases in the absolute sense, but decreases relatively. Lowered status and decreased role, though not always perceived as such by the aged themselves, cause frustration among older people.

2. As the individual grows older, he attaches a higher value to prestige and harmonious interaction and communication in his extended-family group, but breakdown of the local community reduces the importance of the extended family and increases the importance of the nuclear family. Thus, the elders lose their main point of support not only for their needs of self-maintenance, but also for self-development.

3. Older people's feelings of frustration and uncertainty will grow stronger as communities become more modern because of the factors discussed above.[33]

In urban areas today "what was good enough for father is not good enough for me." Present-day vertical class mobility has meant that the son may acquire more material goods, education, and status than his father had. The older person is thought to have lost his close touch with the dynamic occurrences and changes in everyday existence and undoubtedly he has to some extent. But this depends, of course, upon the older person himself. In times of rapid social change, each generation, in a sense, becomes a sort of subculture with its own set of values and motivations. This situation creates social distance between age groups. In rural communities social change is less rapid, and there is less friction between generations. The old person has met most of the problems his progeny face. This picture is often reversed, however, in urban areas, where the tempo of life is so accelerated that an older individual has increased difficulty adapting to the pace. New norms are constantly appearing, and what mother said ten years ago about the "correct" way to bring up children, handle money matters, and run the household is often almost as dated as last year's top tunes. At the same time, attitudes and patterns of behavior are often extremely rigid among older persons. Habits are difficult to alter at any time in life, but this statement is especially true of old age.

Many studies of the aged have indicated that elderly people regard

---

[33] Gerrit A. Kooy, "Social System and the Problem of Aging," in Richard H. Williams, Clark Tibbitts, and Wilma Donahue, *Processes of Aging,* II, 59. Reprinted by permission of the Publishers, Atherton Press. Copyright © 1963, Atherton Press, New York. All right reserved.

the later years of life as difficult and unrewarding.[34] This general characterization of the status of older people is by no means equally applicable to all classes or to all occupations, for there are many individual exceptions. More recent studies, based largely on those with a higher educational and occupational level than that of the general population, suggest that this conclusion may require revisions, for there appear to be many aged persons who have a positive or an ambivalent attitude toward their period of life.[35] The tendency for older persons to play a reduced status role is undoubtedly greater among the lower socioeconomic groups than among the upper classes, whose position and wealth continue to give them status even into advanced age. Likewise, in certain professions, such as law and medicine, an elderly person may even have increased status.

Many immigrants to America, in particular, have experienced conflicts upon reaching later maturity. With their predominantly rural background, they have a heritage of strong family ties and high status for the aged. Not receiving the status and care their early training led them to anticipate in their old age, they feel resentful and neglected. Old age often becomes a trying existence for them, especially because of the difficult relations with their children.

The basic difficulty seems to be the conflict between the behavior patterns which older people are supposed to display in urban society and the aspirations of older persons themselves.[36] They still have the same wishes and motivations as other persons for response, recognition, security, and new experience; yet there is increasing evidence that contemporary urban society and the newer, rather undefined cultural definitions of the status and role of the aged are unsatisfactory to them and to their peer generation. Consequently, personal adjustment among the aged appears to be the exception.

In modern society old age has become associated with a feared loss of physical attractiveness. Strenuous efforts are made to preserve this physical attractiveness on the assumption that to most people "to look young

---

[34] For a summary of the literature, see Robert Kastenbaum and May Durkee, "Elderly People View Old Age," in Robert Kastenbaum, ed., *New Thoughts on Old Age* (New York: Springer Publishing Cmpany, 1964), pp. 250–262.

[35] See, for example, Nathan Kogan and Florence C. Shelton, "Beliefs about 'Old People': A Comparative Study of Older and Younger Samples," *Journal of Genetic Psychology*, 100:93–111 (1962). Such studies have indicated that there are aged in the higher-status groups who are alert, independent, and financially secure and who participate actively in the social scene.

[36] Ruth S. Cavan, Ernest W. Burgess, Robert J. Havighurst, and Herbert Goldhamer, *Personal Adjustment in Old Age* (Chicago: Science Research Associates, Inc., 1949), pp. 18–29.

is to be young." Some observers have remarked that styles of clothing and other apparel are geared primarily to the youthful and not to the older person. Havighurst has recognized this fear in his discussion of the social and psychological needs of the aged person.

> Most of us, men as well as women, learn to place a high value upon our beauty and our strength. At the very least, we value highly our physical and mental vigor, our ability to do a hard day's work. In addition, most of us value our manliness or womanliness—the things that make us attractive to the other sex. Against these values the advancing years wage war. They rob a woman of her ability to have children, usually before she is fifty. Many women interpret this as a sign that they have lost much of their worth as women. Men do not fare much better. Already in their forties most of them lose much of their hair, grow fat in awkward places, and have to wear bifocal glasses. . . .
>
> These insults to the self usually strike us in vulnerable places. We express it by saying that we do not like to grow older—but what we really mean is that we have invested a great deal of emotional capital in our physical attractiveness, and this investment is going bad on us.[37]

One study found that a large proportion of older persons had feelings of unhappiness which seemed, on the whole, to increase as they grew older.[38] Older people vary considerably, however, in their responses to their changing situations. Riesman has suggested three different responses.[39] There are those who have psychological resources of self-renewal, lose little of their ability to enjoy life, and are relatively independent of the attitudes of the larger society. The majority have few resources of self-renewal, but at the same time do not decay because of their previous attitudes derived from work and other activities. Their adjustment, however, can be disturbed by a considerable change in their social situation. Others have neither inner resources nor the background of adequate social experiences and simply decay with old age and its problems. Which of these responses an individual makes seems to depend upon his past experiences and the social context surrounding transition to the aged role.

Societal values are closely linked to retirement in that it is an assumption by government and other private agencies of a method of insuring the welfare of the citizens of a society. Retirement is a product of modern industrial society: generally such a system has not existed in preliterate

---

[37] Havighurst, p. 11. Reprinted by permission of *The Annals* of the American Academy of Political and Social Science.

[38] Cavan, *et al.,* pp. 58–59.

[39] David Riesman, "Some Clinical and Cultural Aspects of Aging," *American Journal of Sociology,* 59:379–384 (1954).

and in predominantly rural societies today. The development of institutionalized retirement results from a complex of social, political, and demographic changes in modern society.

> By virtue of its productive capacity, modern society can readily support a non-working segment of its adult population; the political organization of the national state can provide structural apparatus for the operation of universal retirement systems; the demographic revolution has created an aged population, a large number of which will live far beyond their years of maximally potential economic life; and the changing social relationships which have arisen as a consequence of the industrial system have rendered untenable the types of social and economic accommodations which previous societies had created for their older people.[40]

EMPLOYMENT AND OLD AGE

Work has more function and meaning than simply a source of income.[41] It also represents an expenditure of time and energy devoted to doing something and thus helps to prevent boredom. Work provides identification and status through a definition of role and a way of achieving recognition or respect from others. Association with others at work means having friends and contacts with members of one's peer or age group generation. According to the nature of the work, it may provide a source of meaningful life experience through creativity, new experience, or service to others. The findings of some recent studies have shown that work in American society has lost some of its function as a central life activity, and that its value has shifted somewhat from being an end in itself to a means.[42] Yet these studies also show that work continues to be a primary focus of self-identification and role conception. These latter factors may explain why loss of work, as occurs at the time of retirement, is associated with problems of adjustment. The increased amount of leisure in the lives of the aged indicates a lack of a functional role.[43]

---

[40] Harold L. Orbach, "Social Values and the Institutionalization of Retirement," in Williams *et al.*, *Processes of Aging*, II, 391–392. Reprinted by permission of the Publishers, Atherton Press. Copyright 1963, Atherton Press, New York. All rights reserved.

[41] Eugene A. Friedmann and Robert J. Havighurst, *The Meaning of Work and Retirement* (Chicago: University of Chicago Press, 1954), pp. 1–9.

[42] See Robert Dubin, "Industrial Workers' Worlds," in E. Larrabee and R. Meyersohn, eds., *Mass Leisure* (New York: The Free Press, 1958), pp. 215–228; and David Riesman, "Leisure and Work in Post-Industrial Society," in Larrabee and Meyersohn, pp. 363–385.

[43] See Robert W. Kleemier, *Aging and Leisure: A Research Perspective into the Meaningful Use of Time* (New York: Oxford University Press, 1961).

Many workers look forward to the time when, at sixty-five, there will be no more clock punching, when they can engage in activities of their choice or travel if they wish. Retirement, however, may not be a pleasant experience, even when social security or retirement payments are adequate.[44] For a person who has worked eight or more hours a day, five or six days a week, for thirty or more years, enforced idleness and the loss of opportunities to use developed skills often produce a crisis situation. Such an individual finds himself with little to do that is constructive, day in and day out; he has lost many companions, particularly those with whom he has worked; and with the additional loss of other social contacts he becomes bored and lonely. New habits must be developed, and this is difficult at any age. Just as students often soon tire of long-awaited summer vacation and wish for a return to the "grind" or routine of the college year, so the older person may at first be delighted by the "vacation," but in time fervently desires to return to some socially useful role. Riesman suggests that it is not work, but having a job, which is important to the individual.[45] Many authorities are now of the opinion that the concept of "retirement" is perhaps unfortunate and that most persons should be retained indefinitely at some work, even in an industrial society.

For many, retirement today indicates that one is "aged." "Realizing on one hand the importance of occupational activity for stabilizing the individual's environment and inner self and, on the other hand, the fact that retiring is the social act which today marks the beginning of the social status 'aged,' the problem is clear: today old age, in its social sense, means, for the majority of the working population, foregoing one of the most significant means of stabilizing environment and personality. In this connection it must not be overlooked that most of the aged do not retire because they are old and incapable, but because social regulations relegate them to the status of old age." [46] As important, from the standpoint of personal and social adjustment, as the loss of employment or household duties is the loss of certain social roles which a person has played during the greater part of his mature life.[47] A person's job determines many of his

---

[44] Clark Tibbitts, "Retirement Problems in American Society," *American Journal of Sociology,* 59:301–309 (1954).

[45] Riesman, "Leisure and Work in Post-Industrial Society," in Larrabee and Meyersohn.

[46] Rudolf Tartler, "The Older Person in Family, Community, and Society," in Williams, *et al., Processes of Aging,* I, 72. Reprinted by permission of the Publishers, Atherton Press. Copyright 1963, Atherton Press, New York. All rights reserved.

[47] Aaron Lipman, "Role Conceptions of Couples in Retirement" in Tibbitts and Donahue, *Social and Psychological Aspects of Aging,* pp. 475–485.

extrafamilial associations, and may offer opportunities for satisfaction of needs not met within the family. For men, earning a living is regarded in our society as the most appropriate mode of life. The job is the basis of status in the eyes of the family and associates. It is also a source of reference groups which come to function as an anchor of self-identity.[48] Thus, when they are unable to maintain an independent existence in an urban society, the aged tend to lose self-respect. They are often forced to relinquish authority in the family because they no longer contribute to its economy. If they live with their children, the latter often become head of the households, and the older persons no longer, as they once did, have the status of the head of an economic unit such as a farm. Since the aged person seldom owns a farm or other property of consequence he cannot maintain status through the possibility of transmitting it by inheritance.

The role of the retired old person is especially difficult where no other roles carrying equal status are available. The loss of the social function, through loss of jobs and forced or voluntary retirement, usually brings with it lowered social status and a diminution of self-esteem. Where the individual has been prepared to accept the new status, however, and has developed hobbies, interests, and a new and self-embracing image to fit the new roles and status, the situation may be somewhat different.

Increasing unemployment among older persons in an urban industrial world results from many factors, including their numbers, changes in skills, automation, the growing emphasis on youth, and compulsory retirement at an arbitrary chronological age. Their employment difficulties do not arise primarily from mere physical impairments due to age. The emphasis on youth and the arbitrary retirement at a certain age are partly a reflection of the impersonality of modern urban life and the categoric contacts between large numbers of persons. It is possible today to shelve people arbitrarily, irrespective of a particular individual's physical, mental, and social qualities. Rather than adjusting work speed and capacity to older persons, society asks the older person to adjust to the machine. Methods in industry change so rapidly that an older worker who has not been retrained often finds himself at a distinct disadvantage when competing with a new worker. There is increasing evidence that older persons, if given a chance, can adjust much better to industrial work than society thinks they can, and that they often have qualities, such as conscientiousness, carefulness, and precision, which younger workers do not have. This situation differs from that in many rural societies, where the young must learn from the older men the traditional ways of doing things. At no time

---

[48] Wilma Donahue, Harold L. Ohrbach, and Otto Pollak, "Retirement: The Emerging Social Patterns," in Tibbitts, *Handbook of Social Gerontology*, p. 377.

in history have the skills of the aged been so rapidly discarded as today in urban society.

The consequences of a reduced income or of unemployment go far beyond mere figures. Between 1948 and 1957, the money incomes of older persons increased, although their incomes tended to remain below those of persons in the age groups from twenty to sixty-four. Although this increase was substantial, it was nevertheless smaller than the 54 percent increase in the median income of all men for this same period. Of the approximately 14.1 million persons sixty-five and over in July 1957, some 3.9 million were employed, their work being the chief source of their income. Approximately 6.7 million, or 47.3 percent, were supported principally by Old Age and Survivors Insurance benefits. About 10 percent, or 1.4 million reported no income, or income only from public social insurance programs, or from other than earnings.[49] The amount of money received from various outside sources by no means makes up for the loss of regular wages.[50] A 1962 survey of the aged in the United States showed that the median income of two-person families over sixty-five was $2875, whereas the 1960 income of those under sixty-five was $5314. Comparable figures for unmarried men were $1365 and $3371, and for unmarried women $1015 and $2152.[51] According to the standards of the United States Bureau of Labor Statistics, 72 percent of elderly couples have sufficient income but only 32 percent of single men and only 17 percent of single women, have an adequate income, the latter being mostly widows.

What the economic future of the aged will be like is difficult to predict. One prediction, made in 1966, stated:

> Certainly the small incomes of elderly women will improve as more women earn social security benefits in their own right. Both men and women in future decades will retire after having earned higher wages for longer periods of time than is true for those retiring today, and after having built up greater social security and pension benefits. These factors are operating to raise retirement income, but other factors are operating to

[49] Current Population Survey of the Bureau of the Census, as quoted by Margaret S. Gordon, "Aging and Income Security," in Tibbitts, *Handbook of Social Gerontology*, p. 209.

[50] John W. McConnell, "Aging and the Economy," in Tibbitts, *Handbook of Social Gerontology*, pp. 490–491, 502–503.

[51] See comparative figures in Bernice L. Neugarten, "The Aged in American Society," in Howard S. Becker, ed., *Social Problems: A Modern Approach* (New York: John Wiley & Sons, Inc., 1966), p. 183; and Lenore A. Epstein, "Income of the Aged in 1962," *Social Security Bulletin*, 27:8 (1964). Also see Harold L. Ohrbach and Clark Tibbitts, eds., *Aging and the Economy* (Ann Arbor: University of Michigan Press, 1963).

depress it. For instance, more workers are retiring before age 65 and taking reduced benefits; the cost of living is rising; in the next two decades, probably fewer than a third of the aged will enjoy private pension benefits; and finally, the elderly population is growing fastest in those age brackets where the lowest incomes are found. More and more elderly widows will be added to the aged population; and although their incomes may be expected to improve, there is little likelihood that they will improve enough in the foreseeable future to meet a "modest but adequate" budget for independent living.

From a long-range perspective, unless there is some major reversal of social values, the aged in American society may be expected to gain a more equitable share of the goods and services of the economy. They are likely in the long run to benefit somewhat more than younger groups if the war on poverty is successful and if the society as a whole becomes more affluent.[52]

OLD AGE AND THE FAMILY IN AN URBAN SOCIETY

Aged persons in the United States live under a variety of different family situations. In 1961 only 23.1 percent of those sixty-five and over were living with a relative other than their spouse and 3.7 percent were in institutions.[53] Of the remainder, 50.9 percent were living with the spouse, and 22.3 percent were living alone or in a lodging. The percentage of women living with a relative other than the spouse was much greater, 17.1 percent for women as compared with 6.0 percent for men. The gerontic family has come to refer to the fifteen to seventeen years during which the husband and wife are the remaining members of the household. "The significance of the gerontic family can perhaps be assessed by noting that the post–child-rearing period for older couples is now approximately two-thirds as long as the child-rearing period itself. It is then followed by a long period of widowhood, especially for women who, because of their disproportionate number, do not remarry at the same rate as men. (Approximately 25 percent of men but 55 percent of women are widowed in the age group 65 and over." [54]

About one third of the men sixty-five and over are married, as contrasted with only 18 percent of the women, who were generally younger than their husbands and who tend to outlive them. Some of the others

---

[52] Bernice L. Neugarten, "The Aged in American Society," in Howard S. Becker, ed., *Social Problems: A Modern Approach* (New York: John Wiley & Sons, Inc.; 1966), pp. 185–186. Reprinted by permission.

[53] *Health, Education and Welfare Indicators,* November 1962, p. xv.

[54] Neugarten, p. 187.

who live with their children have satisfying relationships, whereas others do not. Likewise, some who live apart from their children are happy, others unhappy.[55] The old and the young may work out a mutually satisfying relationship in the family group, but these adjustments, if any, are usually made in spite of the difficulties imposed upon the unity of the family rather than because of them. Grandparents are generally younger than those of preceding generations, and their roles are somewhat different.[56]

The urban housing situation often limits the inclusion of aged persons within the household, although many would not wish to be included. If a family living in an apartment, which seldom has more than two bedrooms, includes an old person, the arrangements have the effect of limiting the number of children or they create crowded living conditions in which widely separated generations do not make good adjustments unless there are strong ties between the individuals and a feeling of mutual responsibility. On the other hand, urban housing situations have often been used as rationalizations for not including the aged in the household when actually there are other reasons, such as the desire to maintain an independent household. In fact, Moore maintains that there is considerable crowding in rural housing.[57]

OLD AGE AND MENTAL DISORDERS

The older person may often work out ways of dealing with his unhappiness which may be inappropriate in terms of satisfactory interpersonal relationships. When faced with difficulties, old people often "respond by petulance, bitterness, exaggerated efforts to secure attention, and sometimes by hysterical symptoms." [58] Havighurst calls some of these symptoms "irrational defenses." [59] In some cases the aged person may retreat into a world of neurotic behavior, fantasies, and even psychoses, wherein the self is satisfied by past beauty or success in business or on the job. Another defense is loss of hearing, sight, and memory, a loss which is not genuine

[55] Ernest W. Burgess, "Family Living in the Later Decades," *The Annals,* 279:110–112 (1952). Also see Peter Townsend, *The Family Life of Old People* (London: Routledge and Kegan Paul, Ltd., 1957).

[56] Bernice L. Neugarten and Karol K. Weinstein, "The Changing American Grandparent," *Journal of Marriage and the Family,* 26:199–204 (1964).

[57] Wilbert Moore, "The Aged in Industrial Societies," in *The Aged and Society,* p. 36.

[58] Stuart A. Queen and Jeannette R. Gruener, *Social Pathology* (New York: Thomas Y. Crowell Company, 1940), pp. 100–101.

[59] Havighurst, pp. 15–16.

and which takes them, in the eyes of others, out of situations they wish to avoid. Some develop psychotic behavior but not all such behavior is actually psychotic. Havighurst explains why some old people escape through hallucinations:

> Sometimes a woman who has lost her husband or a man who has lost his wife will go on talking to the absent loved one. Why not? It is a pleasure to have someone to talk to. So why not go on talking to the people one loved? If one listens carefully, one may hear them reply; and so a person living alone may converse a great deal with absent persons. Then when someone—a son or daughter—notices this, that person becomes disturbed and goes to a doctor and says, "My old mother (father) is having hallucinations." Yet when a child discovers what we call an imaginary playmate, which often happens with only children or first children, and carries on long conversations with that imaginary person, the parents are often quite proud, and they say, "My, what a good imagination that child has!"[60]

There are two major types of senile psychotic mental disorders. The first is probably strictly organic in origin, resulting, it is believed, from a shrinkage or "hardening" of the blood vessels in the brain, arteriosclerosis, which in extreme instances causes an almost complete destruction of brain tissue. Such physiological deterioration may not always be accompanied by a mental disorder, but where the latter does occur there is a sudden upset by convulsions or an epileptic seizure, severe headaches, emotional outbursts, instability, and varied episodic confusion.[61] There is the usual memory loss, particularly for recent occurrences. Some senile psychoses have an organic basis in that there is a shrinkage of the brain tissue, but they differ from arteriosclerosis in that there is no sudden onset. However, the evidence concerning the presence of arteriosclerosis and "shrinkage" of brain tissue is, in the majority of studies, based only upon hospitalized and diagnosed cases, without an attempt to discover how frequently these same neurological changes occur in nonhospitalized and nonpsychotic cases. For this reason, the assertion that senile psychosis and arteriosclerotic degeneration and other brain changes are inevitably associated must be interpreted with caution.[62]

---

[60] Havighurst, p. 16. Reprinted by permission of *The Annals* of the American Academy of Political and Social Science.

[61] David Rothschild, "Senile Psychoses and Psychosis with Cerebral Arteriosclerosis," in Oscar Kaplan, ed., *Mental Disorders in Later Life* (rev. ed.; Stanford, Calif.: Stanford University Press, 1956).

[62] Rothschild, p. 292. See also Eugene A. Confrey and Marcus S. Goldstein, "The Health Status of Aging People," in Tibbitts, *Handbook of Social Gerontology,* p. 183.

Although brain damage may produce psychotic behavior in older persons, there is considerable evidence that psychotic conditions in a large number of older persons are not proportional to the amount of brain deterioration. Lewis, for example, indicates that in most post-mortem examinations the pathologist can tell whether or not a brain is that of an old person, but cannot tell whether the person was normal or was mentally ill.[63] Many individuals who exhibited great mental deterioration in their actions, which were thought to be due to biological old age, show little pathological changes of the brain at autopsy.[64] In addition, it should be pointed out that although such diagnoses as "senile psychosis" are frequently given to older persons referred for commitment to mental hospitals, they are ordinarily given without conclusive evidence of senile neurological damage. Rather, a growing body of evidence suggests that such diagnoses are given on the basis of the patient's *age* status, and not on the basis of specific organic changes associated with age.[65]

The functional disorders of paranoia, depressive behavior, and involutional melancholia appear to be common among institutionalized senile patients, although it is difficult to determine the precise extent. Functional mental disorders among the aged are probably an outgrowth of difficulties in interpersonal relations that characterize any such disorders regardless of age.[66] In this sense there are no truly "senile" functional psychoses; rather, there are functional disorders among the aged.

Manias and schizophrenic disorders are comparatively rare among senile patients, whereas depressions and paranoia are most common.[67] Perhaps the rarity can be explained by the hypothesis that the aged are too physically and socially feeble to revolt against an environment which they regard as oppressive. It is also possible and even probable that because of the wide breadth of experiences in the lifetime of the average person of later maturity he need not completely withdraw from the world of reality

[63] Nolan D. C. Lewis, "Applying Mental Health Principles to Problems of the Aging," in George Lawton, ed., *New Goals for Old Age* (New York: Columbia University Press, 1943), p. 91.

[64] Robert B. McGraw, "Recoverable or Temporary Mental Disturbances in the Elderly," *Journal of Gerontology*, 4:234–245 (1949).

[65] Evidence concerning the influence of sociological factors on commitment of older persons is given in the Technical Report, New York Department of Mental Hygiene, Mental Health Research Unit, 1958 (Albany: State Department of Mental Hygiene), p. 82.

[66] Moses M. Frohlich, "Mental Hygiene of Old Age," in Clark Tibbitts, ed., *Living Through the Older Years* (Ann Arbor: University of Michigan Press, 1949).

[67] Norman Cameron, *The Psychology of Behavior Disorders* (Boston: Houghton Mifflin Company, 1947), p. 572.

through schizophrenia, but merely retreats periodically to the recollection of those situations which have occurred during his lifetime and from which he has always derived satisfaction and can still do so. A study of ninety-nine patients of sixty and older revealed that the cumulative effects of social isolation arising from a variety of reasons account for the final schizophrenic breakdown in old age.[68]

Depressions among senile patients may result from excessive brooding over the lowered status, functions, and roles imposed upon them by the society, from the lack of satisfying outlets, and especially from the conflicts of the wish to quit living as against the desire to continue to live. Paranoid reactions are fairly common psychotic difficulties among older persons: "Depending on their previous modes of reaction, people may extrude the knowledge that they are growing older and their resentment of the younger generations which are making them aware of it, and attach their feelings to others about them. They become suspicious and even paranoid, feeling that they are persecuted and treated unfairly. There may be some truth in this at times, and they make the most of it." [69] Cameron has tried to show that the proportionately higher commitment rates of paranoia in old age may partially stem from the fact that those close to the senile person find it easier to tolerate a sad and self-reproachful attitude than an aggressive and other-accusing one. On the other hand, the person who suffers impairment of his sense organs often tends to become suspicious and anxious. At the same time, restrictions are placed on the aged, and these, coupled with the sense organ handicaps of the old, are "optimal conditions for the development of paranoid reactions." [70]

However, there is considerable evidence that the higher rates of commitment of older persons to mental hospitals in recent years are related to structural changes in society. Among these changes are those affecting family organization, housing conditions, and concepts of family responsibility. According to some authors, children today are more willing to deal with the mental problems of older parents by placing them in mental hospitals.[71] A study in Syracuse, New York, analyzed the socioeconomic status of patients admitted to mental hospitals because of alleged senile psychosis or arteriosclerosis. It was found that the area of the city with the

---

[68] D. W. K. Kay and Martin Roth, "Schizophrenias of Old Age," in Williams, *et al.*, I, 402–448.

[69] Frohlich, p. 88.

[70] Cameron, p. 572.

[71] R. H. Felix, "Mental Health in an Aging Population," in Wilma Donahue and Clark Tibbitts, eds., *Growing in the Older Years* (Ann Arbor: University of Michigan Press, 1951), pp. 23–44.

highest admission rate had the highest number of unemployed or disabled persons, the highest proportion of widowed and divorced, multiple-dwelling structures, tenant occupancy, and one-person households.[72] This would suggest that aside from any specific behavioral pathology, there are sociological factors which may condition or affect the societal reaction to the older person such as to result in commitment.[73]

In summary, psychic disturbances of the aged seem to be a product of cultural factors, a breakdown in customary channels of communication, and an interruption of routinized ways of living.[74] All of this is tied up with social changes in the status of the aged, their economic livelihood, and the nature of their family relations. Comparisons of older patients who came to the hospital for psychiatric disorders and a sample of the "normal" older person in the community showed that although the family roles and living arrangements were remarkably similar, there were notable differences in regard to family social contacts and in the extent of contacts with friends and acquaintances.[75] Three fourths of the hospitalized, as compared with one third in the community, had had a decrease in their informal social life after they were fifty. Mental disorders of later maturity among males would appear to be at a minimum if the continuity between generations is maintained, if spatial and social mobility is at a minimum, and the person's status is not abruptly lowered.[76]

ROLE ADJUSTMENT OF THE AGED

The problems of adjustment which older persons in our society face stem largely from the fact that aging involves a *change of roles as well as a change in the statuses associated with these roles.* Adjustment, or conformity

---

[72] Confrey and Goldstein.

[73] See also Robert H. Kleemeier, "The Mental Health of the Aging," in Ernest W. Burgess, ed., *Aging in Western Societies* (Cihcago: University of Chicago Press, 1960), pp. 265–266; and George Rosen, "Health Programs for an Aging Population," in Tibbitts, *Handbook of Social Gerontology,* pp. 530–531; and L. S. Rosenfeld, F. Goldmann and L. A. Kaprio, "Reasons for Prolonged Hospital Stay," *Journal of Chronic Diseases,* 6:141–152 (1957).

[74] See H. Warren Dunham, "Sociological Aspects of Mental Disorders in Later Life," in Oscar Kaplan, ed., *Mental Disorders in Later Life* (Stanford, Calif.: Stanford University Press, 1956).

[75] Marjorie Fiske Lowenthal, "Some Social Dimensions of Psychiatric Disorders in Old Age," in Williams, *et al.,* II, 224–246.

[76] Ivan Belknap and Hiram J. Friedsam, "Age and Sex Categories as Sociological Variables in the Mental Disorders of Later Maturity," *American Sociological Review,* 14:367–376 (1949).

to changed role expectations, is complicated if the new role is poorly defined, or if there is inadequate preparation for it. Unfortunately, in modern urban society, in contrast to folk and rural societies, both of these complicating factors are present for older persons.

Viewed as the acquisition of new roles, aging is primarily a process of disengagement in which the individual continuously withdraws from association with the members of various groups.[77] Beginning in middle age, there is an anticipatory socialization to the role of an aged person involving a restriction on participation and various other aspects of roles.

Several factors seem to be related to more adequate adjustment among older persons; yet the evidence concerning them must be interpreted with caution. For one thing, what is defined as "adequate adjustment" will vary for different subcultures, as will the factors taken as indices of "adjustment." [78] Some earlier studies suggested that such factors as these were conducive to adequate adjustment: new friends, new interests in civic and community affairs, new leisure-time activities and hobbies, and the avoidance of too much reminiscing over the past.[79] From adjustment scales, these studies found that good adjustment among older persons was associated with "the fields of good health, the maintenance of marital and family relations and of friendships, leisure-time and other activities, membership in at least one organization, no discrimination or unhappy period in life, conception of oneself as middle-aged rather than elderly, old, or aged, feeling of permanent economic security, no lowered social status, plans for the future, church attendance and belief in an after-life." [80]

One of the most extensive studies of adjustment and old age found that certain factors may be positively related to adjustment in one socioeconomic group, and negatively related to another.[81] In this study, a measure of "morale" (adjustment) was used, and persons of high, medium, or low morale were compared on a number of variables, after they had been divided into high and low socioeconomic groups. On the variable "health," the morale of those in the high socioeconomic group tended to be high whether their health was "good" or "poor." Yet surprisingly, the morale

[77] Elaine Cumming and William E. Henry, *Growing Old: The Process of Disengagement* (New York: Basic Books, Inc., 1961).

[78] Raymond G. Kuhlen, "Aging and Life Adjustment," in Birren, p. 890.

[79] Havighurst, pp. 16–17.

[80] Ernest W. Burgess, "Personality and Social Adjustment in Old Age," in *The Aged and Society*, p. 147.

[81] B. Kutner, D. Fanshel, Alice M. Togo, and T. S. Langner, *Five Hundred Over Sixty: A Community Survey on Aging* (New York: Russell Sage Foundation, 1956).

of those in the low socioeconomic group tended in the low direction for those with "good" and those with "poor" health. On self-image, the same relationship appeared, with those of high socioeconomic status tending toward high morale, whether their self-image was "positive" or "negative," and those of low socioeconomic status showing the opposite tendency. In general, similar relationships were observed for the variables "social isolation," "visiting with children," and "visiting with friends," with those of high status tending toward high morale, whether socially isolated or not, and regardless of the frequency (or absence) of visits with children and friends.[82]

These findings raise questions concerning the universality of factors previously assumed to indicate good adjustment. Although the married tended to have higher morale than the divorced, widowed, or single, this may vary by social class. In addition, greater income was associated with an increase in morale only among those who were employed. Among those retired, greater income was not associated with a rise in morale.

There is some evidence that a conception of self as "younger" is associated with more favorable adjustment.[83] Some have suggested that identification with a younger age tends to "insulate" the aged individual against the impact of role transition.[84] There is evidence, however, that self-conception is conditioned by situational or social factors. Blau found, for example, that socially isolated aged persons tended to regard themselves as "old" more readily than did those aged persons who were not socially isolated. Aged persons who participated in friendship cliques tended to conceive of themselves as more youthful than did nonparticipants.[85]

Many studies suggest that retirement entails greater adjustment problems for men than for women.[86] However, as one writer notes, "evidence is not consistent as to which sex is generally happier and better adjusted

---

[82] This study, unlike previous ones, was based on an adequate sample of older persons, and the measure of morale avoided circular reasoning in the definition, for the indices employed in the measurement of morale were independent of the attributes included in its definition.

[83] Kuhlen, p. 890; Burgess, "Personality and Social Adjustment in Old Age," p. 147; and Zena Smith Blau, "Changes in Status and Age Identification," *American Sociological Review,* 21:198–203 (1956).

[84] Kuhlen.

[85] Blau.

[86] Kutner, *et al.;* Blau, "Social Constraints on Friendship in Old Age," *American Sociological Review* 26:429–439 (1961); Peter Steiner and Robert Dorfman, *The Economic Status of the Aged* (Berkeley: University of California Press, 1957), pp. 148–152.

in old age."[87] Some data show that widowhood may pose especially difficult adjustment problems for women, but not for men.

These findings concerning sex differences in the response to circumstances associated with aging raise many significant questions which bear on the problem of *role change*. It is possible that, for either sex, an event or circumstance will not complicate adjustment to aging unless it deprives the individual of his primary role: that role which serves as an anchor of self-identity, status, and is the pivot of an entire "way of life." It may be that for most men in our society, work, or making a living, constitutes a primary role, whereas for women, generally, being a wife has similar value.

When we consider each sex separately, however, we find that retirement or widowhood has a different impact, depending upon social class. For example, it was shown that widowhood has more consistent *adverse* effects on friendship participation among lower-class women than among middle- and upper-class women.[88] This is due, apparently, to the fact that the latter have developed social ties independent of their husbands prior to widowhood. Thus, by drawing upon these resources, the upper- and middle-class women are more readily able to find significant substitute roles following widowhood. This again seems to emphasize that the impact of the change of roles associated with aging will be eased if there are available satisfying substitute roles for which there has been some previous preparation.

In one study comprehensive statistical data and extensive case studies were gathered on 168 elderly men and women, who were then divided into the most, less, and least adjustment to successful aging, being measured according to the amount of activity, ability to engage in activity, satisfaction with life, and maturity or integration of personality.[89] Life satisfaction or keeping active did not appear as important as the factors of autonomy in contributing to the social system of others, persistence in achieving objectives, the clarity of life style in relating to family and work, and flexibility in dealing with life situations.

SOCIAL PARTICIPATION OF THE AGED

There is evidence that social participation among the aged is related to satisfactory role adjustment. Yet in contemporary society, opportunities for such participation are apparently difficult. A study of 499 men and 759

---

[87] Kuhlen, in Birren, p. 890.

[88] Blau, "Structural Constraints on Friendships in Old Age," p. 439. The greater tendency of middle- and upper-class women to foster associations was also pointed out in Robert L. Havighurst and Ruth Albrecht, *Older People* (New York: David McKay Company, Inc., 1953).

[89] Richard H. Williams and Claudine Wirths, *Lives Through the Years: Styles of Life in Successful Aging* (New York: Atherton Press, 1965).

women primarily from large cities found that the companionship of friends decreases with increasing years.[90] Including their spouses, only about 50 percent of the males had a high degree of companionship at sixty to sixty-four, and this proportion declined to about 33 percent in the subsequent years. There is a curious contradiction in the fact that although old age means increased leisure it also seems to mean decreased social participation. According to one study, the age group sixty to sixty-four had a low degree of social participation (28 percent), but this low degree of participation increased to 35 percent among those sixty-five to sixty-nine.[91]

Evidence has shown that the number of friendships an older person has will be influenced by status changes, such as retirement or widowhood, which affect his location in the age, sex, and class structure of a given community. For example, a comparison of friendships of older persons in two different communities revealed that either widowhood or retirement decreased a person's friendships *if* it placed the individual in a different position with respect to his peers. Yet neither widowhood nor retirement had a detrimental effect on friendships if both these changes were also relatively prevalent among a person's peers.[92] These data suggest that aging as such does not necessarily adversely affect social participation, but that status changes which normally occur in the later years may adversely affect participation if they place an individual in a position different from that of his peers.

Because of the tendency in urban-industrial societies for associations to form along peer group lines, elderly persons tend increasingly to interact largely with one another. This is tending to create a subculture of the aged with their own groups, norms, and customs.[93] Although it is true, as Weinberg suggests, that loss of friends through death or dispersion is more probable with advancing age,[94] the creation of "retirement villages" and apartment communities for older persons both in the United States and abroad, would seem increasingly to provide living arrangements which would offer

---

[90] Cavan, *et al.*, p. 48.

[91] Cavan, *et al.*, p. 49. In this study nine types of participation were included: daily informal activities, hobbies, plans for the future, listening to the radio an hour or more daily, attendance at group meetings two or more times a month, holding club office, employment, attendance at church at least once a week, and voting in last election. High degree of participation indicated seven or more activities; moderate degree, five or six activities; and low degree, four or fewer activities.

[92] Zena Smith Blau, "Structural Constraints on Friendships in Old Age." See also Zena Smith Blau, "Old Age: A Study of Change in Status." Unpublished doctoral dissertation, Columbia University, New York, 1957.

[93] Arnold Rose, "The Subculture of the Aging: A Topic for Sociological Research," *The Gerontologist*, 2:123–127 (1962).

[94] Weinberg, p. 515.

significant opportunities for social participation among aged peers.[95] In addition, so-called Golden Age Clubs, where older persons get together at some community center, are becoming more common.[96]

A number of studies have shown that social participation among older persons is influenced by their social class. These studies show that in the United States, persons of upper and middle social classes generally participate more in both formal and informal associations than do those of lower-class status. This trend has been observed among the rural aged as well as among those in urban areas.[97] Some have suggested that lower-class status among the aged is associated with severe economic handicaps which necessitate a restriction of social participation.[98] In general, the evidence shows that economic and retirement status are more important than age in influencing social participation or withdrawal. Others do not participate because they never did so when younger and now are so socially isolated that they do not know how to go about it.

Studies of the social participation of European aged do not uniformly support the findings of American studies, which show a marked decline of participation with age. One study conducted in Sweden, for example, found no significant differences in the extent of participation in associations between those aged eighteen to fifty-six and those fifty-seven and over.[99] Havighurst suggests that older working-class people in Sweden participate more in mixed-age associations than is true in the United States. In addition to mixed-age groups, there are in Sweden a significant number of "old people's clubs" whose membership consists predominantly of working-class persons. These clubs may foster some specific project or may exist primarily to promote informal social relations. Among the Swedish middle- and upper-class elderly people, traveling and visiting resorts are popular.

Although there is a general decline in the aged person's general social and community participation, some writers report that there is an increase

---

[95] See Ernest W. Burgess, ed., *Retirement Villages* (Ann Arbor: University of Michigan, Division of Gerontology, 1961), for a discussion of such living arrangements for older persons. See also I. L. Webber, "The Organized Social Life of the Retired: Two Florida Communities," *American Sociological Review*, 59:340–346 (1954), for data showing the greater participation among older persons living in retirement communities.

[96] See Chapter 19.

[97] Philip Taietz and O. F. Larson, "Social Participation and Old Age," *Rural Sociology*, 21:229–238 (1956).

[98] Blau, "Structural Constraints on Friendships in Old Age"; and Steiner and Dorfman, pp. 146–147.

[99] Cited by Robert J. Havighurst, "Life beyond Family and Work," in Burgess, *Aging in Western Societies*, pp. 305–306.

in favorable attitudes toward religion, in religious activities, and in a belief in an afterlife. One study stated: "Apparently, as the prospect of an earthly future fades, the belief in a future after death replaces it." [100] There is conflicting evidence, however, on this point. Other studies have suggested that religious feeling and religious participation do not necessarily increase with age.[101] It was found, for example, that women in all groups attended church much more often than did men, whose attendance declined with age. Among Protestants, only Negro men showed an increase in attendance with advancing age. Among Roman Catholics, attendance for men decreased with age, whereas for women it showed no change. Jews were the only group showing an increase in attendance for both men and women with increasing age. In addition to denominational and sex differences, religious participation seems definitely to be influenced by the type of community. Barron suggests that research data in general show greater religious feeling and church attendance among the aged in smaller communities but not in larger communities. This trend would probably also apply to other age groups.[102]

INCREASE IN AGED POPULATION

The magnitude of these problems of the aged in contemporary society can be more readily seen when it is remembered that for the past hundred years the older age groups have continued to be an increasingly large proportion of the population. This situation exists not only in the United States but in most Western European countries as well.

Several European countries exceed the United States in the proportions of persons sixty-five and over relative to total population. The greatest proportion of older persons in 1950 was to be found in France, with Great Britain, Sweden, and Germany following, in that order. The United States is fifth in rank, followed by Italy, Canada, and the Netherlands. (See Table 15.1.) In the United States, the proportion of those sixty-five and over has increased from 4.1 percent of the population in 1900 to 9.2 percent in 1960. (See Table 15.2.) Since 1900 there have been increases in all groups over thirty-five. (See Figure 15.1.)

---

[100] Cavan, *et al.*, p. 57.

[101] Harold L. Ohrbach, "Aging and Religion: Church Attendance in the Detroit Metropolitan Area." A paper read at the Annual Gerontological Society Meeting, Philadelphia, November 1958. Also see H. Lee Jacobs, *Churches and Their Senior Citizens* (Grinnell, Iowa: Congregational Christian Conference of Iowa, 1957), p. 2.

[102] Barron, p. 177. For a further discussion on religious participation among the aged, see Delton L. Scudder, *Organized Religion and the Older Person* (Gainesville: University of Florida Press, 1958).

TABLE 15.1   **Percentage of Population 65 Years of Age and Over in Eight Western Countries**

Country	1950	1900	1850
France	11.8	8.2	6.5
Great Britain	10.8	4.7	4.6
Sweden	10.3	8.4	4.8
Germany	9.3	4.9	—
United States	8.2	4.1	2.1
Italy	8.1	6.2	—
Canada	7.8	5.1	—
Netherlands	7.7	6.0	4.8

SOURCE: Reprinted from "Aging in Western Culture," by Ernest W. Burgess, ed., *Aging in Western Societies*, Table 29, p. 15, and Table 2, p. 35, by permission of the University of Chicago Press. Copyright 1960 by the University of Chicago.

TABLE 15.2   **Population of the United States, by Age, 1960, 1950, and 1900 (In millions)**

AGE	Number			Percent		
	1960	1950	1900	1960	1950	1900
0– 4	20.3	16.3	9.2	11.3	10.8	12.1
5–19	48.8	35.1	24.5	27.1	23.1	32.1
20–44	58.2	57.1	28.8	32.4	37.7	37.9
45–64	36.1	30.8	10.5	20.0	20.3	13.8
65 and over	16.6	12.3	3.1	9.2	8.1	4.1
Total (all ages)	180.0	177.1	76.1	100.0	100.0	100.0

SOURCE: U. S. Department of Commerce, Bureau of the Census, *Current Population Reports: Population Estimates*, Series P-25 Nos. 98, 114, 170, 187, 193, and 212. Figures given in mimeographed booklet, "Health, Education, and Welfare Trends" (Office of Program Analysis, Office of the Secretary, U. S. Department of Health, Education and Welfare; Washington, D.C.: Government Printing Office, 1961).

In 1960 the northeastern and midwestern states had the highest proportions of older persons, with percentages ranging from 10 to 12 percent. These proportions were lowest for the western states, with the exception of Oregon, and for the southern states, with the exception of Florida.[103] Some cities have a large percentage of older persons, for example, St.

---

[103] From the 1961 White House Conference on Aging, *Chart Book*, published by the Federal Council on Aging, Arthur S. Flemming, Chairman, p. 15.

FIGURE 15.1—Changing Proportion of Age Groups in the Population, 1900–1960

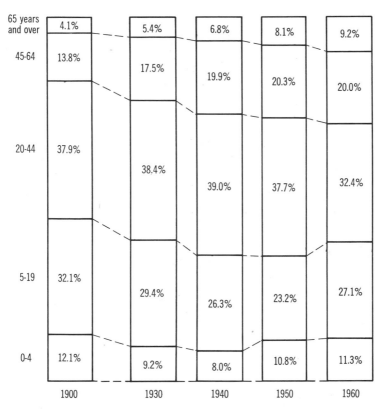

SOURCE: U. S. Department of Commerce, Bureau of the Census, *Current Population Reports:* Population Estimates, Series P-25, Nos. 98, 114, 170, 187, 193, and 212. Figures given in mimeographed booklet, "Health, Education, and Welfare Trends" (Office of Program Analysis, Office of the Secretary, U. S. Department of Health, Education and Welfare; Washington, D.C.: Government Printing Office, 1961).

Petersburg, Florida, where 22.2 percent of the population in 1950 was sixty-five or over.[104]

There has been a continuous increase in the life expectancy of both whites and nonwhites. Generally, white and nonwhite women live longer than men and therefore their percentage of the population increases with age. Life expectancy of white males under one year of age was 50.2 years in the period 1909–1911; by 1963 it had increased to 67.5 years. The corre-

---

[104] William H. Harlan, "Community Adaptation to the Presence of Aged Persons: St. Petersburg, Florida," *American Journal of Sociology,* 59:332–340 (1954).

sponding life expectancy of white females increased during this period from 53.6 to 74.4 years. Nonwhite males do not live as long as white males, the expectancy for nonwhite males under one year in 1963 being 6.6 years less and that for nonwhite women being 7.9 years less than that for white women.

This increased life expectancy, with the consequent rise in the proportion of the population in the older age groups, has been largely attributed to the industrial development of Western civilization over the past hundred years. The application of industrial techniques to agriculture has increased and improved the food supply. Industrialization has also brought, as one writer has suggested, increased emphasis on the values of health and longevity.[105]

One reason for this increased life expectancy has been the success in combating infant mortality, the dread childhood diseases, including diphtheria and scarlet fever, and such youth-killing diseases as tuberculosis. This triumph of medicine has vastly extended the life span of the population and has added millions of persons to the older age groups. Of all children born at the beginning of the century, less than 60 percent would have lived to be fifty; but by 1948 this percentage had increased to 86.[106] Until recently little progress has been made in increasing the average life expectancy by reducing the death rate from certain diseases of old age. The average life expectancy of white males forty-five years and older has only increased from 23.9 years in 1909–1911 to 27.2 years in 1963. So far there has been little improvement since 1850 in the life expectancy of persons reaching sixty or seventy years.[107] Since 1940, however, the development of the antibiotic drugs has made it possible to pull many older persons through otherwise fatal illnesses, and if similar advances are made in the effective control of such characteristic ailments of old age as cancer and heart disease a longer life span may be expected.[108]

In 1960 life expectancy was continuing to increase faster for women than for men, with the result that the excess of females to males has also increased. At approximately age forty, the number of women and men was

---

[105] Moore.

[106] Tibbitts and Sheldon, p. 5.

[107] Nathan W. Shock, *Trends in Gerontology* (rev. ed.; Stanford, Calif.: Stanford University Press, 1957).

[108] Even so, the only animal that normally lives longer than man is the giant tortoise. The longest that an elephant is known to have lived is sixty; fifty-four is the oldest for a parrot. Dogs of fourteen are about as old as an eighty-year-old man, and rats are old at four.—Carl V. Weller, "Biologic Aspects of the Aging Process," in Tibbitts, *Living through the Older Years,* p. 27.

about equal, but thereafter the number of women increasingly exceeded the number of men. Thus, for the ages forty-five to fifty-four, women exceeded men by about 5 percent, whereas for the group eighty-five and over, women were in excess by about 46 percent.[109]

Another factor of importance in producing this change in age composition has been the general decline in the birth rates throughout the Western European countries over the past century.[110] In the final analysis this decline in birth rate has been an expression of the increasing urbanization of the world.

Prior to the 1924 Immigration Act the United States received millions of immigrants, and for several years around the turn of the century the number was as high as a million a year. These newcomers were largely young, able-bodied persons in their teens and twenties when they came, but they are now in the older age groups and have had a marked effect on the composition of the population.

By 1975 it is estimated that there will be about 22 million Americans sixty-five and over compared with 16.6 million in 1960, even without further progress is medical science.[111] As of 1960 there were 34 persons eighty and over for every 100 persons sixty to sixty-four; by the year 2000 there will be 67.

SUMMARY

The aged are in an ambiguous position in contemporary American society. As a group, the aged in modern urban society not only are deprived of former traditional roles and statuses but are poorly integrated into the social structure. The shift to the ambiguous role and the lowered status of old age are the result of social changes stemming from industrialization and urbanization. This situation differs from that of older people in folk and rural societies, where the aged have generally occupied well-defined roles associated with high statuses.

Although physiological and psychological changes occur in old age, these changes in themselves do not account for the position or the behavior of aged persons. Old age is a sociological phenomenon which reflects the manner in which the social roles of the aged are defined, the amount of

---

[109] *Chart Book*, pp. 9–14.

[110] In recent years the birth rate in the United States has increased.

[111] Harold L. Sheppard, "Relationship of an Aging Population to Employment and Occupational Structure," *Social Problems*, 8:159–163 (1960). See also McConnell, "Aging and the Economy," in Tibbitts, *Handbook of Social Gerontology*, p. 491.

compatibility in these roles, the degree of preparation for assuming the roles, and the consistency with which other persons allow these roles to be played.

Problems of role adjustment in old age are associated with unemployment, retirement, difficult family relations, and lack of social participation. Mental disorder appears extensive among the aged.

The number and proportion of old people in Western European society have greatly increased over the past hundred years. During that period the proportion of those over sixty in the United States has grown, largely because of technical advances which have increased the food supply and have improved the nation's health. Infant mortality and childhood diseases have declined, thus adding to life expectancy. There are indications that recent improvements in medicine will also be reflected in an increase in life expectancy among older persons. The decline in the birth rate has also contributed to the proportion of older persons, and in some societies a large number of immigrants has tended to age the population.

SELECTED READINGS

Barron, Milton L.   *The Aging American*. New York: Thomas Y. Crowell Company, 1961. A comprehensive analysis of the problems associated with aging in American society.

Birren, James E., ed.   *Handbook of Aging and The Individual: Psychological and Biological Aspects*. Chicago: University of Chicago Press, 1959. A collection of articles dealing with physiological changes associated with age and suggestions for their possible effects on the social and psychological adjustment of the aged.

Burgess, Ernest W., ed.   *Aging in Western Societies: A Survey of Social Gerontology*. Chicago: University of Chicago Press, 1960. Reviews the trends in the phenomenon of aging in a number of Western European countries and Great Britain. Offers a wider perspective and basis of comparison of aging in the United States. Includes articles by leading authorities on social gerontology.

Cavan, Ruth S., Ernest W. Burgess, Robert J. Havighurst, and Herbert Goldhamer. *Personal Adjustment in Old Age*. Chicago: Science Research Associates, Inc., 1949. One of the first sociological studies of the aged. There are extensive case materials.

Friedmann, Eugene A., and Robert J. Havighurst.   *The Meaning of Work and Retirement*. Chicago: University of Chicago Press, 1954. A study of adjustment to retirement in a number of different occupations.

Kaplan, Oscar J., ed.   *Mental Disorders in Later Life*. Revised edition. Stanford, Calif.: Stanford University Press, 1956. A collection of articles of scholars from medical and social science fields, reviewing present research on the problems of mental illness among the aged, and suggesting important problems for future research.

Pollak, Otto. *Social Adjustment in Old Age*. New York: Social Science Research Council, Bulletin 59, 1948. A comprehensive analysis of the definitions of old age and of the psychological and sociological aspects of aging.

Shock, Nathan W. *Trends in Gerontology*. Stanford University, Calif.: Stanford University Press, 1957. This book is a series of articles dealing with a number of aspects of aging.

Simmons, Leo W. *The Role of the Aged in Primitive Societies*. New Haven, Conn.: Yale University Press, 1945. A study of the social position of aged persons in a large number of folk societies. In nearly every society they were found to have an important social position.

Tibbitts, Clark, ed. *Handbook of Social Gerontology: Societal Aspects of Aging*. Chicago: University of Chicago Press, 1960. A series of articles dealing with research on the phenomenon of aging as it relates to the changes in roles and status occurring with age, and the effect of these on behavior and adjustment.

———, and Wilma Donahue, eds. *Social and Psychological Aspects of Aging*. New York: Columbia University Press, 1962. A series of papers dealing with research primarily on the social psychological aspects of old age in various parts of the world.

Williams, Richard H., Clark Tibbitts, and Wilma Donahue, eds. *Processes of Aging*. New York: Atherton Press, 1963. Articles dealing with various sociological and social psychological aspects of aging.

16

Minority Groups

All societies have status systems which rank groups of people on the basis of birth, social class, wealth, or other criteria. Part of the reason for such social stratification is functional in order to accomplish certain societal tasks by a division of labor; partly the stratification is an instrument for maintaining power for those who, for various reasons historically, have already achieved a position of prestige. Some societies have more open stratification systems than others. In the more closed societies status is largely ascribed, that is, it is established at birth, as in the caste system of India or in the medieval feudal system; in others it is a class system or a class system with a majority-minority selection.

A *caste system* is characterized by descent. One is born into a caste system; one accepts, customarily, this status whether of high or low caste, and marriage is endogamous. The caste system is supported by various institutions, such as religion and the economic system. A caste system like the one in India, however, is undergoing changes; some Indians are opposed to it, and a certain amount of mobility is taking place in the system, largely outside the caste. In a more open system, based on *social class,* such as that of modern industrial societies, status is largely achieved and not fixed by descent, although there are some situations of hereditary wealth and family status. There is mobility in which persons may rise in the system; status is determined by the acquisition of wealth, education, and similar prerequisites, such as occupation. A *majority-minority system,* such as Negro-white relations in the United States, is in some ways similar to a caste system,[1] but should be considered a variation within a class system of social stratification.

> A minority-majority situation, on the other hand, tends to be similar to the caste situation on two counts and different on the other two. The rule of descent applies to both: one is "born into" a minority or majority group, just as he is born into a caste; and endogamy is the rule for both, although slightly less so for the minority-majority situation. Minorities, however, do not regard their situation as just and acceptable; nor does the discrimination implied in the concept of minority, the differential and unequal treatment, receive support from the basic institutions of society. There may be some support, but the fundamental rules of law and the basic religious ideology oppose discrimination. In these two respects, therefore, a minority-majority situation is similar to a class system.[2]

THE CONCEPT OF A MINORITY GROUP

Individuals in a society tend to be ethnocentric, that is, to identify positively with their own groups and to react negatively to others, whether they be Protestants or Catholics, Southerners or Northerners, Negroes or whites, or Jews or Gentiles. Association with one's group is related to satisfaction in membership, preference for association, solidarity, loyalty to its members, and belief in the rightness of its relationships.[3] Conversely, this is accompanied by a judgment of other groups in terms of the standards of one's own group. The acquisition of such ethnocentric normative standards is a result of cultural definitions and the behavior is characteristic of normal personalities in a social system.

The extent to which such normative behavior results in overt and pronounced discrimination against members of an outgroup which aspires to equality constitutes the essence of a majority-minority group problem. The United States has its Negro, Indian, Japanese, Chinese, Spanish-speaking,

---

[1] Several writers have maintained that the American racial situation is a caste system. See Gerald D. Berreman, "Caste in India and the United States," *American Journal of Sociology,* 66:120–127 (1960); and Allison W. Davis, B. B. Gardner, and M. R. Gardner, *Deep South* (Chicago: University of Chicago Press, 1941).

[2] From *A Minority Group in American Society* by J. Milton Yinger. Copyright 1965 by McGraw-Hill, Inc. Used by permission of Mc-Graw-Hill Book Company.

[3] Robin M. Williams, Jr., *Strangers Next Door: Ethnic Relations in American Communities* (Englewood Cliffs, N.J.: Prentice-Hall, Inc., 1964), p. 22.

and Jewish minority groups. South Africa and Rhodesia have an African minority, India its untouchables or Harijans, Japan the Eta or a large group something like the Indian untouchables. Much of South America has an Indian minority; Australia has its aboriginal group. Other minority groups also exist in various parts of the world, including Europe.

A minority group is simply a group of people who, because of their racial, ethnic, or religious origin, are discriminated against, are given lower status, and thus in a sense are "second-class citizens." Louis Wirth has defined a minority as a "group of people who, because of their physical or cultural characteristics, are singled out from the others in the society in which they live for differential and unequal treatment, and who therefore regard themselves as objects of collective discrimination." [4]

A minority group is subordinate to another group, restrictions are placed on their general social participation, and their power in the society is decreased. By "power" is meant the ability to influence the decisions of others and in being able to influence others in their decisions regarding one's own group. More specifically, a minority group situation is characterized by (1) discrimination against a certain *group* of people; (2) the clash of this discriminatory treatment of the minority group with other norms and values in the culture which would tend to give the groups equal status; (3) the recognition of this treatment as discriminatory by both minority and majority groups; and (4) an organized effort by the minority group to remove the discrimination.

A minority group cannot necessarily be regarded as smaller in number than the majority. In many counties of the South the Negro population greatly exceeds the white population. (See Figure 16.1.) Nearly a million Negroes live in Mississippi, or about one in every fifteen Negroes in the United States. Although the Negroes in Mississippi represent about 42 percent of the population of the state, most of the western counties along the Mississippi River or in the Delta country have Negro populations generally outnumbering the white populations—in some instances as much as four to one. The Spanish-speaking population of the Southwest, which for a century had a status generally inferior to that of the so-called Anglos, was until recently the larger group, and still is in many communities.

As used here, a minority group should not be confused with a colonial problem, a separate cultural minority, or simply any group which is numerically in the minority. Although the native group in a colonial society may occupy a more or less inferior status, these "natives" are usually re-

---

[4] Louis Wirth, "The Problems of Minority Groups," in Ralph Linton, ed., *The Science of Man in the World Crisis* (New York: Columbia University Press, 1945), p. 347.

FIGURE 16.1—Percentage of Nonwhite Population in Counties of Southern States

MINORITIES IN THE UNITED STATES

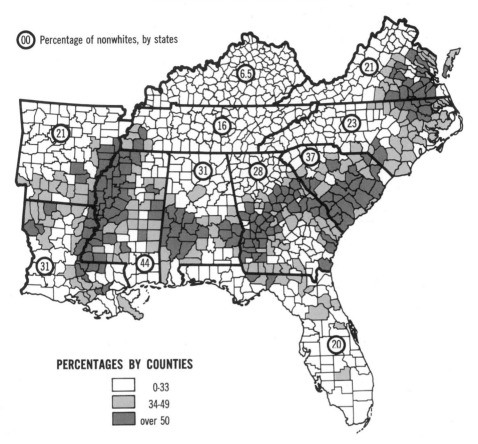

Percentage of nonwhites, by states

PERCENTAGES BY COUNTIES

☐	0-33
▨	34-49
■	over 50

SOURCE: Adapted from "Next Steps in the South: Answers to Current Questions," *New South,* Vol. II, Nos. 7, 8 (July–August, 1956). Used by permission of the Southern Regional Council, Inc.

garded as distinctly different from the ruling citizens. A separate status system exists for each. The American Indian of fifty years ago constituted a colonial problem rather than a minority problem. Within the past twenty-five years the 6 million natives of South Africa have been rapidly becoming transformed into a group which aspires to equal treatment instead of being segregated by the 2 million European whites of the dominant group.

In other parts of the world certain cultural groups may be referred to as minority groups because they have often been denied opportunities to maintain a separate culture, to preserve their own language, and to exercise a degree of political autonomy.[5] Minorities of this type, however, may actually not even desire to have equal status within the larger society. The Negro in the United States well illustrates the fact that a minority is not the same as a distinct cultural group. Most authorities agree that among American Negroes there are practically no vestiges of African culture,[6] and that generally they desire to be Western Europeans as much as do members of the white population. There has recently been, however, an increasing interest in Africa and African culture among large segments of the American Negro population.

NORMS OF EQUALITY AND THE AMERICAN CREED

To constitute a minority situation, there must be a set of norms against which discriminatory behavior may be arraigned. A classic study of the American Negro has been aptly titled *An American Dilemma,* the dilemma being the contradiction between the American creed of democratic values and the actual treatment of the Negro.[7] The American Creed gives expression to certain humanitarian ideologies and includes these fundamental beliefs, which apply regardless of race, creed, ethnic background, or any hereditary status: (1) the right of political equality, (2) the right of due process of law and of equal justice before the law, (3) freedom of opportunity to achieve economic and political success, and (4) the right to express one's religious beliefs.[8]

---

[5] United Nations Commission on Human Rights, *Definition and Classification of Minorities* (New York: 1950), pp. 2–3.

[6] A different point of view has been taken by Melville J. Herskovits, *The Myth of the Negro Past* (Boston: The Beacon Press, 1958).

[7] Gunnar Myrdal, *An American Dilemma* (New York: Harper & Row, Publishers, 1944).

[8] The General Assembly of the United Nations adopted in 1948 a universal declaration of these rights: "All human beings are born free and equal in dignity and rights" and "Everyone has rights without distinction of race, color, sex, language, religion, political or other opinions, national or social origin, property, birth or other status." Among the rights to which all persons are entitled are the following: (1) Life, liberty, and security of person; (2) equal treatment before the law; (3) opportunity to take part in the government, directly or through freely chosen representatives who are elected by universal and equal suffrage; (4) opportunity to work, equal pay for equal work, and an adequate standard of living; (5) freedom of thought, conscience, and religion, and (6) participation in the cultural life of the country.—United Nations Department of Public Information, *These Rights and Freedoms* (New York: 1950), pp. 170–176.

These beliefs permeate the American social scene, regardless of social class or geographic location. They are found expressed in such venerated documents as the Declaration of Independence, the Constitution, and the Bill of Rights, and, more explicitly, in countless Supreme Court decisions. The Creed is taught in schools and churches, and is regarded as a basic guiding principle by many organizations. It is symbolized in such national songs as "America," in the Statue of Liberty, and in countless stories, books, and plays dealing with the oppressed who sought freedom in America. Even those groups who experience discrimination believe in our American Creed, for, as Myrdal has written, "They, like the whites, are under the spell of the great national suggestion. With one part of themselves they actually believe, as do the whites, that the Creed is ruling America." [9]

Sources of the American Creed

The American Creed appears to have been derived from a number of sources, including the Philosophy of the Enlightenment, Christianity, English law, capitalism, and the nature of American nationalism itself. The so-called Philosophy of the Enlightenment, with its emphasis on the sacredness of the individual, came out of the English, American, and French revolutions and the writings primarily of Locke, Rousseau, and Voltaire. These beliefs were probably best expressed by Thomas Jefferson in this country. Such philosophical and political writings from earliest times have been important factors in the development of this basic heritage. Another and somewhat similar source of the American Creed has been the tradition of justice contained in English law, upon which the law of this country is based. These traditional beliefs in statutory enactments, fair trial, due process of law, and judicial interpretations expressive of humanitarian principles have time and again met conflict in discriminatory treatment of minorities.

Individual opportunity for economic success, regardless of race, creed, ethnic origin, or class position, is the cardinal principle of capitalism, success being presumed to be based on individual initiative, hard work, and private savings. Nothing in the capitalist ideology implies that success shall go, largely, to American citizens of the white race. Christianity, another source of these values, emphasizes the brotherhood of man and the essential dignity of the individual. Although in practice "brotherhood" frequently means one's own religion, from a strictly Christian point of view it includes Jew and Christian, Protestant and Catholic, and all races, regardless of the color of their skin.

Finally, American nationalism probably emphasizes the diversity of its

---

[9] Myrdal, p. 4.

people more than do most other countries, where common cultural or religious ideals, tribal separativeness, or military history is more often stressed. Many historians have pointed out that Americans have generally stressed their racial and ethnic diversity and have been proud of their nation's being a refuge for those discriminated against in other countries. In fact, the diversity of the American people is probably their most important distinguishing characteristic. Regardless of their skin color, religious heritage, or ethnic background, all Americans believe that America is made up of people drawn from the ends of the earth and that there should be true equality for all. A Negro leader has put it this way: "Every man in the street, white, black, red or yellow, knows that this is 'the land of the free,' the 'land of opportunity,' and 'cradle of liberty,' the 'home of democracy,' that the American flag symbolizes the 'equality of all men' and guarantees to us all 'the protection of life, liberty and property,' freedom of speech, freedom of religion and racial tolerance." [10] Whether all people believe that this is practiced is another question.

Discrimination and the Reinterpretation of the American Creed

Along with the American Creed there has always existed another series of social norms and values which have reflected racial ideas and the superiority of certain groups over others.[11] Consequently, these two series of norms and values have existed simultaneously, the American Creed generally permitting some degree of discrimination. The basic rights of minorities have been interpreted and modified according to circumstances; even slavery was at one time reconciled by many with this creed. This struggle between the American Creed and racism is strong in certain parts of the United States where racial doctrines are supported by certain norms. The simultaneous presence of contradictory norms within the same person has resulted in a situation which has been described as follows: "Although many Southerners today will agree that segregation is wrong in principle, the vast majority still fiercely defends it as right in practice. . . . The result is a war in the South's own soul which many Northerners, who see the South only as stubborn and narrow-minded, fail to understand." [12]

The American Creed cannot, therefore, be thought of as a stable system of norms, for, like the interpretations of the Constitution by the courts, the Creed has also undergone continuous interpretations. Not only have the "rights" of minority groups changed from one generation to another; within

---

[10] Ralph Bunche, as quoted, in Myrdal, p. 4.

[11] Robin M. Williams, Jr., *American Society* (New York: Alfred A. Knopf, Inc., 1954), pp. 438–440.

[12] "The U.S. Negro, 1953," *Time,* 61:55 (1953).

the population at a given time and in a given place there are pronounced differences of opinion as to what behavior on the part of a given minority should be approved or disapproved and still be in line with the Creed. Some of the conflict between the older and newer generations represents an outgrowth of these systems of differential norms.

This frame of reference has been termed the *race relations cycle*.[13] In this cycle successive stages of social interaction take place between subordinate and superordinate groups, and in each of them a series of temporary balances is established to avoid conflict. These levels become disturbed by new norms, and further new levels of adjustment arise among groups. More specifically, the parts of the race relations cycle are referred to as *conflict*, or the awareness of mutually exclusive ends; *accommodation*, or the establishment of a working arrangement in which reciprocal relations based on higher and lower status are accepted; and, as a final goal, *assimilation*, or the disappearance of accommodation and the establishment of an unconscious process of consensus or common norms. These processes are occurring simultaneously at various levels during the continuous process of conflict and redefinitions in a variety of areas. The following discussion will present, more or less specifically, the former conception of the American Creed at the outbreak of World War II, the new emerging definition, and possible future interpretations.[14] These statements should be regarded as only general comparisons.

Former interpretation of the American Creed. For some time before the outbreak of World War II most Americans of the majority group, as well as many of the minorities themselves, were in fairly general agreement about the following minimum "rights" and obligations of Americans in terms of the American Creed. Many of these rights were actually not in full agreement with the American Creed. Some of these limited rights, moreover, had been achieved after a long and arduous struggle.

1. Approval of *segregated but "equal"* education and other facilities as being in line with the American way of life.

---

[13] Robert E. Park, *Race and Culture* (New York: The Free Press, 1950), pp. 149–151. Also see Brewton Berry, *Race and Ethnic Relations* (2d ed.; Boston: Houghton Mifflin Company, 1958). Another useful set of processes characterizing minority-majority relations has been differentiating, sustaining, disjunctive, and integrative processes. See Tamotsu Shibutani and Kian M. Kwan, *Ethnic Stratification: A Comparative Approach* (New York: The Macmillan Company, 1965).

[14] Negroes, mainly from the West Indies, have come in considerable numbers to Great Britain since 1942. There have been conflict and some accommodation, processes which have been analyzed by Anthony H. Richmond in *Colour Prejudice in Britain* (London: Routledge and Kegan Paul, Ltd., 1954).

2. The right to a job, an unskilled or semiskilled one at the least, with adequate relief if no jobs are available.

3. The right to vote, except in certain areas of the South.

4. Some elementary school education for every American, including members of the lowest minority group.

5. Decent health standards for all minority groups and the reduction of their high infant mortality rate and the incidence of such diseases as tuberculosis.

6. The elimination of substandard housing, the agency not agreed upon.

7. Condemnation of lynching and the protection of minorities from such un-American practices.

Present "rights." The issues involved in granting full "rights" to minorities are now on a higher status level and many are of a different character from those accepted before World War II:

1. The elimination of the concept of "separate but equal" in education and in public facilities of an interstate nature.

2. The elimination of all forms of segregation including intrastate and municipal public facilities and in living areas.[15]

3. The right to vote even in the South; the right to full participation in public housing facilities, public recreational facilities, and professional athletics such as baseball, and in the armed forces.

4. The right to higher jobs, such as those of foremen and junior executive positions, as in personnel work.

5. Elimination of discriminatory provisions in union membership and in employment.

6. The right to membership in professional groups.

7. The right to social participation in fraternities, sororities, and general club organizations in most parts of the country.

Emerging "rights." Most people today would probably say that once conflict over the foregoing rights has been resolved, minority problems will have reached a stage of permanent accommodation. On the contrary, in terms of the American Creed, other issues involving new norms and values can be expected to arise. Some of these future "rights" include the elimination of slum living conditions, full political equality by election of minority group members to political offices, attainment of important positions in

---

[15] The elimination of segregation presents a problem for the Negro business and professional classes whose short-term status is based on being Negro businessmen, doctors, lawyers, teachers, or ministers. Negro enterprises, separate Negro churches, and higher status among the Negro group are endangered by the elimination of segregation.

business and finance, and election or appointment to positions of leadership in professional and other formal organizations:

1. The elimination of slum living conditions in both the North and the South, because minority groups are the most affected.

2. Full political equality in terms of both the appointment and the election of minority group members to high positions. This far transcends merely the granting of full suffrage. It would mean the election, in substantial numbers, of qualified Negroes, American Orientals, Spanish-speaking Americans, Indians, and others to municipal, state, and national offices and would enable minority group members to become governors, senators, cabinet members, Supreme Court members, Vice-President, or even President.

3. Right to position of high status in business and finance either as officers or as members of boards of directors. In the United States such a strategic position in the economy brings with it important power considerations.

4. Position of leadership and not merely membership in professional and other formal organizations.

These trends represent a reinterpretation of rights or norms, new conflicts, and new accommodations. They do not constitute the final goal of the social and cultural process, which is the elimination of superordination and subordination. In such a situation social relations, as well as political and economic activities, are conducted largely without regard to racial, ethnic, or religious status. In the earlier history of the United States certain groups, such as the Germans, and later to a large extent the Irish, were discriminated against. These groups have now largely reached a state of assimilation. In Brazil the Negro, once a slave, has now reached a stage where he is identified largely as a Brazilian and not commonly as a Negro Brazilian.[16] A great deal of assimilation has taken place in the so-called racial laboratory, Hawaii.[17] Here live over half a million persons of diverse

---

[16] Donald Pierson, *Negroes in Brazil* (Chicago: University of Chicago Press, 1942). A later study has challenged some of Pierson's findings. See Roger Bastide and Pierre Van Den Berghe, "Stereotypes, Norms and Interracial Behavior in São Paulo, Brazil," *American Sociological Review*, 22:689–694 (December 1957).

[17] Andrew W. Lind, *Island Community: A Study of Ecological Succession in Hawaii* (Chicago: University of Chicago Press, 1938). These nearly harmonious race relations, almost unique under the American flag, are the result of a long history of amicable race relations going back to the days before 1898, when Hawaii was a united, self-governing stopover on voyages across the Pacific. Formerly Hawaii, as an independent nation with a cultural pattern of harmonious relationships between races, was in a position to require white persons who desired to

ethnic and racial groups—203,455 Japanese, 69,070 Filipinos, 38,197 Chinese, 4943 Negroes, 472 Indians, and 11,405 "others," including Hawaiians. There are 202,230 white persons, and 430,542 nonwhites.[18] These people of Hawaii, who are even more racially mixed than the figures would indicate, live in a situation, even if not perfect, of harmony. School-teachers and principals are of all races. There are no public racial restrictions in accommodations or employment. Hawaii in 1961 had an elected Caucasian governor, both a Chinese and a Caucasian senator, and a Japanese congressman.

SEGREGATION AND THE AMERICAN CREED

Since to a minority group, the forced segregation of one group from another is probably one of the most important discriminations, the changing definition of segregation necessitates detailed discussion. Before 1941 there was consensus among the majority groups, as expressed through the Supreme Court, that, in general, segregation, at least for the Negro and similar groups, was in line with the American Creed. In pre-Civil War days the southern churches sanctioned segregation in the form of slavery, even citing Biblical passages in support of this practice. In the famous Dred Scott decision of 1857 the Supreme Court decided that Negroes were property, not citizens, and if freed they had no rights. Although segregation has a long history dating from the Negro freedmen group, it did not appear in the form of a real separation of the races until the 1890s and in the decades to follow, when more and more laws separating the races were enacted. Many of the laws relating to segregation, such as taxis and sports, were actually enacted much later. A city ordinance requiring Jim Crow taxis, for example, was adopted by Atlanta in 1940. After surveying the laws of segregation Woodward has concluded that most laws of segregation are neither as old nor as "natural" as some think. Racism as a legislative doctrine, to secure legal white supremacy and power, distinct from the inferior social position of Negroes, was much more recent.

> In a time when the Negroes formed a much larger proportion of the population than they did later, when slavery was a live memory in the minds of both races, and when the memory of the hardships and bitterness of

---

trade or live there to accede to a pattern of respect and nearly equal treatment. Subsequently, the introduction of many racial groups resulted in a blending of cultures and in racial hybrids which served to perpetuate the original situation of race contacts. Puerto Rico also is a situation where race and race mixture has little significance as factors in social relations.

[18] United States Bureau of the Census, *General Population Characteristics* (March 30, 1961), Bulletin PC (A2)–13.

Reconstruction was still fresh, the race policies accepted and pursued in the South were sometimes milder than they became later. The policies of proscription, segregation, and disfranchisement that are often described as the immutable "folkways" of the South, impervious alike to legislative reform and armed intervention, are of a more recent origin. The effort to justify them as a consequence of Reconstruction and a necessity of the times is embarrassed by the fact that they did not originate in those times. And the belief that they are immutable and unchangeable is not supported by history.[19]

Segregation in schools was maintained until recent years, sometimes unofficially, in communities in many northern and border states such as Illinois, Indiana, Missouri, Delaware, and West Virginia. Kansas did not completely abolish segregation until 1952. The Supreme Court had affirmed the belief that separate facilities constituted no violation of the American Creed, and in 1896 the Court, in a case involving segregation in transportation, stated: "We think the enforced separation of the races, as applied to the internal commerce of the state, neither abridges the immunities of the colored man, nor denies him the equal protection of the laws, within the meaning of the 14th amendment." [20] Segregation was not a badge of servitude nor did it mean the inequality of races. Public education and transportation were "social" rights and not rights of citizenship and, therefore, could be segregated. Such segregated facilities, however, must be "equal."

The belief of the Court in segregation as "right" and "natural" in terms of the American Creed is clearly indicated by this statement: "Legislation is powerless to eradicate racial instincts or to abolish distinctions based on physical differences." This 1896 decision did indicate, however, that there were some unreasonable limits to segregation. A city, for example, could not require white persons to walk on one side of the street and Negroes on another.

The Supreme Court redefined this interpretation in 1914, stating that

---

[19] C. Vann Woodward, *The Strange Career of Jim Crow* (rev. ed.; New York: Oxford University Press, 1966), p. 65.

[20] Plessy v. Ferguson, Supreme Court of the United States, 1896, 163 U.S. 537, 41 L. Ed., 256, 16 S. Ct. 1138. The only dissent from this decision was that of Justice Harlan, who maintained that "our Constitution is color-blind and neither knows nor tolerates classes among citizens." He also felt that segregation would create distrust and misunderstanding between the races. For a detailed discussion of the various Supreme Court decisions on segregation as well as the actual court decisions see Herbert Hill and Jack Greenberg, *Citizens' Guide to De-Segregation* (Boston: The Beacon Press, 1955) and Benjamin Munn Ziegler, ed., *Desegregation and the Supreme Court* (Boston: D. C. Heath and Company, 1958). Also see Jack Greenberg, *Race Relations and American Law* (New York: Columbia University Press, 1959).

these segregated facilities in interstate commerce must be "equal," as in the case of railroad coach travel. This belief in segregation but equality was approved by many, but by no means all, of the leaders of minority groups, such as Booker T. Washington. How "equality" was to be maintained in various services, in living accommodations, and in social interaction was not clearly stated.

An example of some of these controversial issues was the question of higher education. In 1938 the Supreme Court ordered Missouri to provide Lloyd Gaines, a Negro, with an education in law which would be substantially equal to that given white students.[21] In similar cases brought before the Court the ruling had favored "segregated but equal" facilities. Since few southern states provided graduate or professional training for Negroes, this redefinition of legal rights was extremely important.

In 1948 the Supreme Court ruled that if states did not provide equal separate facilities they must admit Negro students to white schools. In a desperate effort to avoid this step, some states set up makeshift separate facilities, and other southern states attempted to set up regional graduate schools to which Negroes from various southern states would be sent under a system of joint state expense. Others decided to admit a few Negro graduate students, but with various barriers to full participation. In Oklahoma, for example, one Negro graduate student was seated in an anteroom off the main classroom, and later in the same school had a small railing erected around his desk as a way of meeting the legal requirement of segregation. This was the situation existing in 1950, when the Supreme Court made a drastic redefinition of American rights.

The elimination of the concept of "separate but equal" facilities is probably one of the most important recent developments in race relations in the United States. Not only has actual "equality" been challenged as a fiction, but the maintenance of two types of facilities is thought to indicate second-class citizenship and to be harmful to the full dignity of the individual's personality. This is well illustrated in interstate travel. Before 1941 Negroes often had to ride in chair cars on trains because it was impossible to furnish separate Pullman cars for them. In a 1941 Supreme Court decision interstate railroads were ordered to provide first-class rail travel for everyone, which meant the admittance of Negroes to Pullman cars. A 1946 decision ordered segregation eliminated on buses in interstate travel. An important symbolic barrier was removed from interstate rail travel in 1950, when dining cars could no longer require the segregated seating of Negroes and whites at opposite ends of the car or utilize a curtain to screen one race from another.

---

[21] Missouri ex rel. Gaines v. Canada, Supreme Court of the United States, 1938, 305 U.S. 337, 83 L. Ed. 208, 59 S. Ct. 232.

The barrier of "partial equality" of higher education was also torn down by the Supreme Court in 1950. The Court unanimously agreed in the McLaurin and Sweatt cases that the universities of Oklahoma and Texas must accept graduate students on the same basis as whites.[22] In the Oklahoma case a Negro graduate student named McLaurin was segregated in seating and eating arrangements from the white students, and the Court ruled that this denied him equal protection before the law and that he must be admitted under the same conditions of participation as white students. The Supreme Court stated that the setting apart of a student impairs and inhibits "his ability to study, to engage in discussions, and to exchange views with other students."

Previously the Court had implied that a makeshift separate law facility provided by Texas in downtown Austin was suitable, but now it argued not only that this segregation was contrary to the rights of an American citizen but also that "equality" was an impossible fiction. In regard to Sweatt's petition to enter the University of Texas Law School rather than the separate Negro school the Supreme Court said:

> What is more important, the University of Texas Law School possesses to a far greater degree those qualities which are incapable of objective measurement but which make for greatness in a law school. Such qualities, to name but a few, include reputation of the faculty, experience of the administration, position and influence of the alumni, standing in the community, tradition and prestige.

The Supreme Court also felt that Sweatt, as a practicing lawyer, could not function in a setting in which most Texas lawyers were not the products of a segregated school.

> This law school to which Texas is willing to admit petitioner excludes from its student body members of the racial groups which number 85% of the population of the state and exclude most of the lawyers, witnesses, jurors, judges, and other officials with whom petitioner will inevitably be dealing when he becomes a member of the Texas Bar. With such a substantial and significant segment of society excluded, we cannot conclude that the education offered petitioner is substantially equal to that which he would receive if admitted to the University of Texas Law School.

Few Supreme Court decisions have been more drastic than that of May 17, 1954, which stated that segregation in public schools is unconstitu-

---

[22] McLaurin v. Oklahoma State Regents, Supreme Court of the United States, 1950, 339 U.S. 637, 94 L. Ed. 1149, 70 S. Ct. 851. Also Sweatt v. Painter, Supreme Court of the United States, 1950, 339 U.S. 629, 94 L. Ed. 1114, 70 S. Ct. 848.

tional.[23] The decision affected about 48 million persons, including some 10 million Negroes. It was a culmination of the series of previous decisions on higher education, but in its philosophy and effect was far more drastic than any one of them. In a unanimous decision the Court repudiated completely the "separate but equal" doctrine. The decision took into account the changes in the importance of education and the findings of psychological studies of children made since 1896. All children, to succeed, must have opportunities for equal education, and segregated but equal physical facilities are not "equal" in actuality.

> Education is perhaps the most important function of state and local governments. . . . It is the very foundation of good citizenship. . . . In these days, it is doubtful that any child may reasonably be expected to succeed in life if he is denied the opportunity of an education.
> To separate them [Negro children] from others of similar age and qualifications solely because of their race generates a feeling of inferiority as to their status in the community that may affect their hearts and minds in a way unlikely ever to be undone. . . . Separate educational facilities are inherently unequal.[24]

In 1955 the Supreme Court included recreation as a right of all citizens, ordering the end to segregation in public parks, playgrounds, and golf courses.[25] Each year since then additional desegregation decisions by the Supreme Court and other federal agencies, such as the Interstate Commerce Commission, have affected other facilities, such as bus travel and waiting rooms. In 1962 the Supreme Court ruled that *all* racial segregation in transportation facilities was unconstitutional. In the decision the Supreme Court said: "We have settled beyond question that no state may require racial segregation in inter-state or intra-state facilities. The question is no longer open: it is foreclosed as a litigable issue." Before 1899 just three states required or authorized Jim Crow waiting rooms, but within a decade almost all aspects of rail travel in the South had come under segregation laws. Later, interstate buses followed in the 1930s, until, finally, only the airplane escaped. As one historian has written, "even to the orthodox there was doubtless something slightly incongruous about requiring a Jim Crow compartment on a Lockheed Constellation or a DC-6." [26] Buses, streetcars, and trains throughout the South had separate seating arrangements for white

---

[23] For a series of court documents and commentaries on school desegregation, see Hubert H. Humphrey, ed., *School Desegregation: Documents and Commentaries* (New York: Thomas Y. Crowell Company, 1964).

[24] 347 U.S. 483.

[25] 350 U.S. 879.

[26] Woodward.

and for colored passengers; in addition, custom also required that Negroes wait until all white persons had boarded a bus or a streetcar before they themselves could enter. In 1959 thirteen southern states had laws requiring or authorizing segregated travel. In 1961, however, the Interstate Commerce Commission ordered the elimination of all segregated facilities in waiting rooms and eating places in railway and bus terminals serving interstate passengers. Also within the last few years the bus companies of several southern cities, beginning with Montgomery, Alabama, and Tallahassee, Florida, have been forced, through widespread boycotting of the services by Negroes and subsequent Supreme Court decisions, as well as by federal legislation, to integrate passenger seating.[27]

The redefinition of the American Creed underwent even more drastic modifications from 1963 through 1967. Incidents of strong opposition and violence in both South [28] and North, as well as pressure by interested groups, contributed a great deal to the rapidity and scope of the changes. These changes also reflected ideological changes in the society expressed in political leadership by President Kennedy's statement that civil rights legislation is "not merely for reasons of economic efficiency, world diplomacy and domestic tranquility but above all because it is right," or in President Johnson's view that he would be satisfied with "nothing less than the full assimilation of more than twenty million Negroes into American life." Federal legislation passed by Congress during this period included the guarantee of voting, equal access to public accommodations such as restaurants and motels, laws against racial barriers in employment and in labor union membership, the prohibition of discrimination in any state program receiving federal aid, and the authorization of the Justice Department to bring suit for desegregation of public schools. The 1965 Voting Rights Act, for example, eliminated illegal barriers to the right to vote by setting aside literacy tests and provided, where necessary, for citizens to be registered by officials of the federal government. Shortly after its enactment federal examiners were sent to register Negroes in seven southern states. Within a year the Negro voting strength in the South gained half a million, nearly as many as had been added in the previous five years altogether.

Still, these changes do not appear to have achieved the equality implied in the American Creed. Full equality both in terms of election and appoint-

---

[27] For a discussion of the important Montgomery bus strike in 1956 see Martin Luther King, *Stride toward Freedom* (New York: Harper & Row, Publishers, 1958); and C. U. Smith and Lewis M. Killian, *The Tallahassee Bus Protest* (New York: Anti-Defamation League of B'nai B'rith, 1958).

[28] See James W. Vander Zanden, *Race Relations in Transition: The Segregation Crisis in the South* (New York: Random House, Inc., 1965).

ment to political office and in terms of positions of importance in business and the professions is a major issue. The difference in the extent of Negro slum living, in poor housing, in the degree of education possible to them, and in the quality and quantity of their employment opportunities, as well as their general status, is still great. Many legal steps have been taken to redefine the American Creed to achieve equality; the implementation and social acceptance of the implication of the changes have still to be achieved. As one writer put it, "As a legal entity Jim Crow could at least be pronounced virtually a thing of the past. If Jim Crow was dead, however, his ghost still haunted a troubled people and the heritage he left behind would remain with them for a long time to come." [29]

SOCIAL CHANGES PRODUCING DESEGREGATION
AND ANTIDISCRIMINATION

Many forces operating in our society today have brought about these basic changes in attitudes toward segregation and minority discrimination:

1. The increasing urbanization and power of the urban majority in the United States. One writer has suggested that the movement toward racial equality in America has faced two political constituencies, one of which is essentially cosmopolitan, urban-oriented, and more in favor of equality whereas the other, essentially provincial and rural-oriented, seeks to maintain superiorities of the past based on race and religion. "White, Protestant, rural America pulls in one direction; urban America, with its diversity of religions and races, pulls in the other. The diffusing composition of the constituencies gives rise to different values." [30]

2. The increasing urbanization and industrialization of the South, which made the maintenance of many forms of segregation difficult.

3. The increasing power of the Negro vote in the cities of the North and in the South generally, a vote which often represents a balance of power in at least eight industrial states.

4. The general economic prosperity since 1940 which has diminished the Negro-white competition for jobs.

5. The cost of maintaining separate school systems, theaters, and other facilities, for example, becoming too difficult a financial burden.

6. The widespread use of nonviolence in the South and later the increasing militancy of the Negro in both North and South, particularly

---

[29] Woodward, p. 191.

[30] Alan P. Grimes, *Equality in America: Religion, Race, and the Urban Majority* (New York: Oxford University Press, 1964), p. ix.

in urban areas, becoming increasingly effective in producing change where initially there was little power.[31]

7. The increasing education of Negroes and the achievements of talented Negroes.

8. The growth of the white urban middle class in the South, with different vested interests, which has made them an important opposition to the rural oligarchic political pattern based largely on disenfranchisement of the Negro voter.[32]

9. Desegregation of the armed forces, which took place after the Korean conflict, with its effect upon the South, where there are a large number of military installations on which both Negro and white military and civilian personnel work and live without segregation.

10. The policy of the industrial type of labor union which includes members of both races in the South, and which has affected many social relationships formerly based on segregation.

11. The insularity of the Deep South, which has been broken by the more rapid desegregation in the border states,[33] by the mobility of Southerners and Northerners, and by such media as television, in which Southerners see, for example, Negroes participating in sports and political life.

12. The integration of the schools, which, although slow, has affected other forms of segregation.

13. Finally, the whole picture of segregation is increasingly being recognized as adversely affecting the international relations of the United States. Incidents like the following have hurt the appeal of American democracy, particularly in Asia, Africa, and parts of South America: A Hindu dance team canceled an appearance at Centenary College here [Shreveport, La.] today after a spokesman said that two nearby restaurants had refused to serve two dark-skinned members of the troupe. Tom Burrows, manager of the troupe, Indrani and her Hindu Dancers, said that the Indian embassy was studying whether the entire Southern tour should be canceled. . . . Mr. Burrows said that the group had previously been refused service in Charlotte, N.C. To avoid an incident in Bossier City, the troupe explained at two restaurants that two of the musicians were "dark-skinned." . . . The dance team appeared before President and Mrs. Kennedy earlier in its tour. The tour is supported and encouraged by the State Department.[34]

---

[31] James W. Vander Zanden, "The Non-violent Resistance Movement against Segregation," *American Journal of Sociology,* 88:544–550 (1963).

[32] Yinger, p. 51.

[33] Thomas Pettigrew and M. Richard Cramer, "The Demography of Desegregation," in Bernard E. Segal, ed., *Racial and Ethnic Relations: Selected Readings* (New York: Thomas Y. Crowell Company, 1966), pp. 354–366.

[34] *The New York Times,* November 21, 1961, p. 32-C.

MINORITIES IN THE UNITED STATES

The United States has been called a "nation of nations." [35] It should more aptly be called a nation of races, nations, and religions. The heterogeneity of the population is so great that it is difficult to think of a "typical American." Minority groups in the United States may be divided into three types, with primary emphasis on race, ethnic background, or religion.

Racial Minorities

Racial minorities in America represent slightly over 10 percent of the population. Negroes constitute the largest minority group, as they have for over a century, followed by the Indian, the Japanese, and the Chinese. Table 16.1 shows the racial minorities as they were in 1960.

TABLE 16.1 **Racial Minorities in the United States, 1960**

	Number	Percent of total population
Total population	179,323,175	100.00
Negro	18,871,443	10.5
Indian	523,591	0.29
Japanese	464,332	0.26
Chinese	237,292	0.13
Filipino	176,310	0.098
All other	218,087	0.12

SOURCE: United States Census of Population, 1960, *General Population Characteristics,* United States Summary, Final Report PC (1)-1B (Washington, D.C.: Government Printing Office, 1961), pp. 1–144 and Table 44.

The American Negro

The "Negro" is more of a cultural than a biological concept. He cannot always be physically identified, for in American society, in the North as well as in the South, persons known to have *any* Negro ancestry, no matter how small, are considered to be Negroes. United States census enumerators, for example, are given the arbitrary instruction that persons of mixed white and Negro "blood" should be classified as Negroes regardless of the proportion of Negro "blood." In some southern states this distinction has sometimes raised complicated legal questions. In those states

---

[35] Louis Adamic, *A Nation of Nations* (New York: Harper & Row, Publishers, 1944).

where the question has been raised the courts have not been unanimous as to the proportion of Negro "blood" a person must have to be classified as a Negro.[36] In Virginia in 1785, for example, the legislature changed the 1705 definition of a "Negro" as a person with one-eighth Negro blood to a person with one-fourth Negro blood and in 1930 to one with "any trace of Negro blood." The present definition of a white person is one who has "no trace of any blood other than Caucasian." [37]

This cultural norm can be contrasted with that of Brazil, where there are also millions of Negroes but where status is not based to any extent on color. Whereas in the United States one drop of known Negro "blood" makes a person a Negro, many Brazilians whose grandmothers were Negroes of pure African descent are listed in the census as white and are so considered by others.[38] Thus many individuals are considered white who have definitely Negroid physical features. Cultural norms define the Negro differently in the United States and in Brazil.

Beginning with the twenty Negroes who were first sold at Jamestown in 1619, the American Negro population has increased enormously as a result of natural increase and slave trade. In 1960 there were 18,871,443 Negroes, one in every ten Americans. About one in every five Southerners is a Negro, whereas only one in twenty of the population in the Northeastern and North Central states and only one in thirty-three in the West

TABLE 16.2 **Number and Percentage of Nonwhite Population in Some Southern States and the District of Columbia, 1960**

State	Number nonwhite	Percentage of total population
District of Columbia	418,693	54.8
Mississippi	920,595	42.3
South Carolina	831,572	34.9
Louisiana	1,045,307	32.1
Alabama	983,131	30.1
Georgia	1,125,893	28.6
North Carolina	1,156,870	25.4
Arkansas	390,569	21.9
Virginia	824,506	20.8

SOURCE: United States Census of Population, 1960, *General Population Characteristics*, pp. 1–164 and Table 56.

---

[36] Charles S. Mangum, *The Legal Status of the Negro* (Chapel Hill: University of North Carolina Press, 1940), p. 1.

[37] *The New York Times*, April 11, 1967.

[38] Pierson, pp. 127–128.

are Negroes. (See Table 16.4.) The distribution of the Negro population in states with the largest percentage is shown in Table 16.2. In 1960, 54.8 percent of the population of the District of Columbia was nonwhite, 42.3 percent of the population of Mississippi was nonwhite, as was 34.9 percent of the South Carolina population.

Although the Negro population has steadily increased, it has declined in proportion to the total population. The highest proportion of Negroes to whites occurred in the first census of 1790, when there were 757,000 Negroes, or 19.3 percent. The Negro population of the South has continued to decline, while that of the North and the Far West has increased. As late as 1910 almost 90 percent of the Negro population lived in the South, but during World War I the "Great Migration" of southern Negroes to the larger northern cities began. Manpower demands had increased in the North as a result of war production, and at the same time immigration from other countries had decreased to almost nothing. The needed labor supply came, therefore, chiefly from southern Negroes.

The high prosperity of the 1920s continued this northward movement to the cities, and although the depression of the 1930s temporarily reduced it, World War II brought about a great increase in migration not only to the North but to the West and to the industrial cities of the South. By 1940 the Negro population residing in the South had declined to 77 percent of

TABLE 16.3   **Number and Percent of Nonwhite Population in Selected Large Cities, 1960**

City [a]	Total Population [a]	Number nonwhite	Percentage nonwhite of total population
New York City	7,781,984	1,143,952	14.7
Chicago	3,550,404	837,895	23.6
Philadelphia	2,002,512	534,671	26.7
Detroit	1,670,144	487,682	29.2
Washington, D.C.	763,956	418,648	54.8
Los Angeles	2,479,015	416,475	16.8
Baltimore	939,024	328,658	35.0
St. Louis	750,026	216,008	28.8
Birmingham	340,887	135,332	39.7

[a] Data above refer to the 1960 census definition of "urban places." Roughly speaking, the area included in this definition corresponds to the central city and excludes the urbanized but unincorporated areas surrounding or lying adjacent to the city limits.
SOURCE: United States Census of Population, 1960, *General Population Characteristics*, pp. 1–176 and Table 63.

the total Negro population; after the extensive population movements of World War II continued to decline, reaching 59.9 percent in 1960. At that time nearly all the 6,474,536 Negroes in the North, and the 1,085,688 Negroes in the West, resided in large cities. Harlem, the largest Negro city in the world, has around a million people, and the so-called Black Belt of Chicago has over half a million in population. (See Table 16.3 for the nonwhite populations of the large cities of the United States.)

About three fourths of the Negro population now live in cities. The migration of the rural Negro to the cities has brought many problems. He finds barriers at every turn and is shunted into the slum areas of the city, where he often lives under crowded, unhygienic conditions. This urban physical and social situation in which the Negro migrant finds himself has resulted in extremely high rates of death, particularly from tuberculosis, and in high rates of such forms of deviant behavior as delinquency and crime.

TABLE 16.4   **Location of the Negro Population, by Region, 1790–1960**

	North *a*		South		West	
YEAR	NUMBER	PERCENT	NUMBER	PERCENT	NUMBER	PERCENT
1790	67,424	8.9	689,784	91.9	—	—
1860	340,240	7.7	4,097,111	92.2	4,479	0.1
1910	1,027,674	10.5	8,749,427	89.0	50,662	0.5
1940	2,790,293	21.7	9,904,619	77.0	170,706	1.3
1950	4,246,058	28.2	10,225,407	68.0	570,821	3.8
1960	6,474,536	34.3	11,311,607	59.9	1,085,688	5.8

a Includes Northeastern and North Central states.
SOURCE: Bureau of the Census, *Historical Statistics* (Washington, D.C.: Government Printing Office, 1949), and *Characteristics of the Population,* Pt. I, 1960 Census.

Because of these difficult conditions the majority often tends to view Negroes as if they constituted a single class. Negroes are socially stratified, and class relations within the group are important as well as those between its members and the majority group. For example, social class among Negroes is important in predicting the behavior in a given race-relations situation. The institutions and other activities of the Negro community can be understood only when studied in relation to the Negro class structure. Lower, middle-, and upper-class Negroes differ markedly not only in social characteristics but in behavior as well. For example, delinquency, criminal behavior, and sexual promiscuity are comparatively rare among middle-class Negroes. The Negro class system of northern cities has been thus described by Frazier:

The Lower Class

At the bottom of the class structure in the Negro community in the northern city is the lower class, which comprises about two-thirds of the Negro population. In the lower class are found the great body of unskilled workers who earn a precarious living and those who subsist on irregular employment and relief. In this class are many of the most recent migrants from the South, especially those who have little education or are illiterate. However, this class is set off from the middle class not merely because of occupation and low income or even illiteracy. The lower class is distinguished from the middle class because of certain forms of behavior which are associated with lower-class status.

The shiftlessness and irresponsibility of lower-class Negroes are due partly to their lack of education and partly to the lack of economic opportunity for the great masses of Negro men. Since emancipation the masses of Negro men have constantly been drawn from the southern plantations into a fluctuating labor market. Because of the uncertainty and seasonal nature of work in lumber and turpentine camps, many of them have become footloose wanderers. In the towns and smaller cities of the South, they have provided the cheap and casual labor which was needed. Their position in northern cities has scarcely been better except where there has been a demand for large numbers of unskilled workers. But usually the lower-class husband and father must share the economic burden with his wife, who often finds more secure employment in domestic service.

In the northern city the lower class tends to be concentrated in those areas where the Negro first gains a foothold in the city. In these areas the lower-class Negroes are crowded into tenements and dilapidated houses which are held for speculative purposes. In these deteriorated slum areas are found second-hand clothing stores, taverns, cheap movies, and the lighter industries. Moreover, these areas are characterized by the absence of what constitutes a real neighborhood. The public schools located in these areas not only reflect in their physical appearance the general deterioration but have scarcely any relation to the life of the residents. Even the church which plays such an important role in the life of the middle class is absent or is represented by the numerous "store front" churches. Consequently, the behavior of the lower class is free from the control of neighborhood influences and the control of other institutions.

The absence of neighborhood controls is associated with a general lack of participation in the institutions of the community. Various studies have shown that Negroes of lower-class status are not affiliated with many forms of organized activities. Even in their religious affiliations they tend to become associated with the "store front" churches and churches outside the regular denominations. In those churches they find escape from their poverty and frustrations in a highly emotionalized type of religious service. But such church affiliations have little influence on their morals and manners. . . .

There is an element among the lower class that is quiet and exhibits good manners in public. There are lower-class families that struggle to maintain stable and conventional family life. They may humbly accept the fact that they are poor in worldly goods as a part of God's plan but they believe that even the poor may live righteously. Or they may believe that by living honestly and justly and rearing their children properly, their children because of education will rise to a higher status.

The Middle Class

The emergence of a clearly defined middle class of any size and significance in the Negro community has coincided with the growing occupational differentiation of the population. Consequently, it is in the large urban communities of the North that a fairly large, well-defined middle class has appeared. In the northern city there is a large group of clerical workers, skilled industrial workers, responsible persons in the service occupations, and firemen, policemen, and other types of workers in protective service. There has thus come into existence a relatively large group of workers with a background of stable family life, a good elementary or high school education, and an income adequate to support a respectable way of living. Since the class structure in the Negro community is fluid, the upper layers of the middle class merge with the upper class, while the lower layers are hardly distinguishable from the lower class.

Because of their fairly secure and adequate incomes, Negroes of middle-class status are able to maintain what they regard as a desirable mode of life. This desirable mode of living includes, first, certain standards of home and family life. In the larger cities the middle class constantly struggles to escape from those neighborhoods inhabited by the lower class. This is often difficult because of rents and the restrictions upon the mobility of the Negro population. Nevertheless, the middle class endeavors to isolate itself from the environment of the lower class by moving into apartments occupied by people with similar standards. Since in middle-class families there is often a tradition of home ownership, which may have its roots in the South, Negroes of middle-class status endeavor to buy homes out of their savings. This ambition is generally thwarted because of the multiple dwellings in the large cities.

Even when Negroes of middle-class status cannot escape from an undesirable physical environment, they endeavor to maintain a stable and conventional family life. In the middle-class family, the husband and father assumes responsibility for the support of the family. He often takes pride in the fact that his wife does not have to aid in the support of the family. Both parents are usually interested in the welfare and future of their children. They are not simply interested in the physical welfare of their children but they want their children to conform to conventional moral standards. They want their children to avoid the behavior associated with lower-class status. Moreover, they want their children to take advantage of the educational opportunities which they themselves did not enjoy. . . .

The moral conduct and respectability of the middle class are bound up to some extent with its race consciousness. For the middle class is extremely race conscious. Failure to maintain respectability and moral conduct is a reflection upon the "race," i.e., the Negro. The race consciousness of the middle class is also tied up with the desire to rise in the world. Middle-class Negroes are ambitious for their children to get an education and to rise in the Negro world. At the same time they are ambitious to prove the ability of Negroes to rise in the white man's estimation if not in the white man's world.

The Upper Class

In the northern cities, the Negro professional man, especially the doctor or dentist, figures prominently in the upper class. Members of these two professional groups find in the large Negro community in the North a rich source of income as well as a relatively free environment. Likewise, the Negro lawyer, the more successful at least, will be found in the upper class. It is in the border and especially the northern cities that the Negro lawyer will find the most fertile field for the practice of his profession. Moreover, the position of the Negro lawyer in the northern city is supported by the political power of the Negro, whereas in the South his practice is restricted because of the traditional status of the Negro. Public school teachers are likewise found in the upper class. Where the Negro public school teachers are not numerous, they gain a certain prestige by the uniqueness of their position. But as their numbers have increased, their class position has been determined by a complex of factors, involving family, color, income, personal factors, and style of living. The same is true of the growing number of social workers. Negro public administrators who have recently made their appearance in the northern cities derive their social prestige partly from their occupations and partly from economic and social distinctions.

. . . The Negro businessman in the northern city has appeared in response to the varied needs of the large Negro communities in the North. . . . Although the more successful businessmen are at the top of the upper class, many of those in clerical occupations have gained admission to the upper class because their occupational status involves high educational qualifications and they are able to maintain certain standards of living. As among whites, in order to gain access to the upper class in northern cities, a Negro must have an income which will enable him to maintain a certain standard or style of living. . . .

Since income and pecuniary valuations are beginning to play such an important role in upper-class status, there has naturally arisen a conflict between economic and social distinctions, as a basis of upper-class status. In Negro communities, especially in the North, there has appeared a class of Negroes who are eligible for upper-class status from the standpoint of income but who have gained their wealth through "rackets" or other unlawful means and lack the family or educational background associated with upper-class status. . . .

Social ritual plays an important role in the life of the upper class. This social ritual, which is usually characterized as "social life," is focused upon entertaining and involves considerable expenditures. The numerous social clubs, in some of which there is much duplication of membership, are organized about cliques.[39]

The Negroes' historical background of slavery and plantation living is different from that of other minorities. Both elements in this background have left a mark on contemporary race relations. In 1860, slaves constituted 89 percent, or approximately 4 million, of the Negro population, the ancestors of most of them having also been slaves. Many families in the South did not have slaves, and most of those who did owned only a few. For example, only one third of the southern families in 1850 had slaves, the average number of their slaves being 8.6. In 1850, of the families who had slaves in the United States, about 17.4 percent had 1 slave, 29.5 percent had 2 to 5 slaves, 24.4 had 5 to 10, 17.4 had 10 to 20, and 11.3 had 20 or more slaves.

The position of the Negro in the United States cannot be understood without reference to the plantation, which, for centuries, was the home of nearly all members of this minority. In many ways the plantation was a forerunner of the present-day emphasis on mass production. With the use of a considerable amount of land, specialization in a commodity, a cheap labor supply, and an elaborate division of labor, it was possible to produce fairly cheaply certain agricultural products, chiefly for European export.

The complex division of labor on plantations involved the master or landowning class, the "poor-white" overseers, and the Negro slaves, who were divided into household or personal and domestic servants, skilled artisans, such as blacksmiths and shoemakers; and field hands, who were at the bottom of the social structure. The members of this biracial group lived a largely isolated existence on the plantation, but at the same time were in close physical proximity. In order to maintain a degree of separation, a system of social relationships developed, increasing social distance. These included beliefs about the racial superiority of the master class and the inferiority of the Negro, beliefs which were largely accepted by both groups, distinctive ways of addressing one another to indicate subservience on the part of the slaves, separate living quarters, a benevolence on the part of the master class toward the slaves, and legal penalties which, although

---

[39] Reprinted by permission of the publisher from *The Negro in the United States* by E. Franklin Frazier. Copyright 1957 by The Macmillan Company. Also see his *Black Bourgeoisie* (New York: The Free Press, 1957).

infrequently employed, were there to guarantee obedience and the separation of the races. Each generation inducted the other into the philosophy of rule by the master class and subservience on the part of the young slaves born into slavery, new slaves from Africa taking from older slaves the patterns of being "good slaves." Slavery was upheld by institutional norms in the South and was supported by most organized religions as being natural and decreed by God. Since slaves were not allowed to read or write, were seldom allowed to gather in large groups, to leave the plantations at night, or to have their own ministers, it was evident, however, that this accommodation or acceptance of servile status was not complete. After the Reconstruction period harsh laws or "Black Codes" were put into effect in most southern states in order to guarantee the separation of the races and the segregation of the Negro.

This long history of slavery on plantations affected the Negro people in many ways. As an authority on the Negro has written, "The pattern of race relations which developed on the plantation provided the traditional basis of future race relations in the South." [40] Plantation life, which broke the Negroes into small groups and maintained close physical proximity to the whites, destroyed the African cultures of the slaves within a relatively short period of time. This process was aided by the diversity of backgrounds of the slaves and their lack of a common culture. Consequently, African cultures have almost completely disappeared among the Negroes. The languages, religions, and other customs are no longer there, and the Negro is fully "American." This has meant that, as compared with other minorities, the Negro has lost his cultural identity. He is not discriminated against because of his religion—practically all Negroes, for example, are Protestants —or because of his customs, but because of his biological heritage.

Life on the plantation affected Negro and white relations in other ways. It left patterns of speech and manners, "tones of command" on the part of the whites, and a tendency on the part of the Negro to be servile and dependent. A large part of the hostility of many southern poor whites to the Negro is a carry-over from plantation days. The plantation often had the best land, and the cultivation of land on plantations was more efficient as a result of the division of labor. To the poor whites the Negro represented a cheap competitive labor supply, household servants were often cared for better than they were, the artisan slaves often had mechani-

---

[40] Frazier, *The Negro in the United States,* p. 44. Also see Edgar T. Thompson, "The Plantation: The Physical Basis of Traditional Race Relations," in Edgar T. Thompson, ed., *Race Relations and the Race Problem* (Durham, N.C.: Duke University Press, 1939), pp. 180–218.

cal skills which they did not possess, and the sick and aged Negro had a degree of security on the plantation. At the same time, the Negro, as a group, represented something for the poor white, despite a status lower than that of other whites, to look down upon.

Most Negroes today live in slum areas of large cities. The pre-existing norms of the slum have had pronounced effects on the Negro with his slave background and Southern rural heritage. During slavery, for example, legal marriage was largely impossible: as slaves Negroes could make no legal contracts. As a result, conditions of illegitimacy and sexual promiscuity were common, and the mother rather than the father was largely the center of what family life there was.[41] A study of one New York City Negro slum neighborhood in the 1960s showed that one third of the pupils in the schools came from family units in which there was no father, stepfather, or male guardian. Statistics on Negro families in Central Harlem, the slum district immediately north of Central Park in Manhattan, generally reflect the instability of family life among lower-class slum Negroes, where a third of the families had no fathers living at home and a third were on public-assistance rolls.[42] Only half the children under eighteen were living with both parents, as compared with 83 percent for New York City as a whole. Of the Central Harlem women, 29.7 percent and, of the Harlem men, 19.1 percent were listed as separated, compared to rates of 6.2 and 3.3 for New York City women and men, respectively.[43] The rate of aid to dependent children was 220.5 per 1000 youths under eighteen years of age, three times the rate (72) for New York City as a whole.

Rates for illness, infant mortality, and illegitimacy are also higher in Negro slum areas. In 1961 Harlem's infant mortality rate was 45.2 per 1000 live births, as compared to 25.7 for New York City as a whole,[44] the difference due largely to poor housing conditions, malnutrition, and inadequate health-care facilities. The venereal-disease rate for people under twenty-one was six times the city rate.[45] With respect to illegitimacy, it was found that 44.4 percent of the girls who dropped out of school did so because of pregnancy.[46] Low educational levels also contribute to the

---

[41] Jessie Bernard, *Marriage and Family among Negroes* (Englewood Cliffs, N.J.: Prentice-Hall, Inc., 1966).

[42] Harlem Youth Opportunities Unlimited, Inc., "Youth in the Ghetto" (Mimeographed: 1964), p. 109.

[43] "Youth in the Ghetto," p. 127.

[44] Kenneth B. Clark, *Dark Ghetto: Dilemmas of Social Power* (New York: Harper & Row, Publishers, 1965), p. 31.

[45] Clark, p. 87.

[46] "Youth in the Ghetto," p. 183.

problem of the Negro in the slum areas.[47] In 1959, 53 percent of the Central Harlem students in academic schools, and 61 percent in vocational schools, dropped out of school before receiving diplomas. In addition, as these students progress in school the proportion of them who perform below-grade levels of work increases.[48]

Juvenile crime in Negro slum areas has been described as the result of this depressing tangle of problems, in addition to the presence of gangs, the lack of organized community controls, discrimination in both educational and employment opportunities, and family problems.[49] The Negro slum youth witness frequent norm violations in the local community. Harlem's delinquency rate in 1962 was 109.3 per 1000 population, aged seven to twenty, whereas the rate for New York City as a whole was 46.5; the delinquency rate in Boston's Negro ghetto was four times that of the city as a whole.[50] Drug addiction has also increased greatly; the Harlem rate is almost ten times that of New York City.[51] Many studies of crime and violence in urban slum areas have revealed their extensiveness among the Negro urban population, which has a much higher arrest rate than do Negroes in rural areas. In 1960, the total urban Negro rate in the United States was about seven times that for rural Negroes.[52] Even if discrimination in arrests and in the judicial process is allowed for, the figures are still much larger than those for the white and general population.

The incidence of murder and assault appears to be particularly high among Negroes, mostly directed at other Negroes, relatives, and friends. The homicide rate in Harlem is nearly six times that of New York City; in one neighborhood the rate is fifteen times greater. A study of 462 homicides in one large urban county in Ohio between 1947 and 1953 showed that 76 percent were committed by Negroes, although only 11 percent of the population was Negro.[53] Wolfgang's study of criminal homicide in Philadelphia between 1948 and 1952 showed that the homicide rate among Negroes was

---

[47] See James B. Conant, *Slums and Suburbs* (New York: McGraw-Hill Book Company, Inc., 1961).

[48] Clark, p. 125; and "Youth in the Ghetto," p. 178.

[49] "Youth in the Ghetto," p. 178. Also see Ira L. Reiss, "Premarital Sexual Permissiveness among Negroes and Whites," *American Sociological Review*, 29:688–698 (1964).

[50] Clark, p. 87.

[51] Clark, p. 90.

[52] Department of Justice, Federal Bureau of Investigation, *Crime in the United States: Uniform Crime Reports, 1960* (Washington, D.C.: Government Printing Office, 1961), pp. 95, 101.

[53] R. C. Bensing and Oliver Schroeder, Jr., *Homicide in an Urban Community* (Springfield, Ill.: Charles C Thomas, Publisher, 1960), p. 41.

four times that among whites, emphasizing the role of subcultural factors in the slum and the effects of isolation from the general norms of society.[54] Assault is another crime in which Negroes in urban areas outdo the white population.

The Negroes in America have come a long way since plantation slave days and the largely penniless condition into which they were thrust after the Civil War. Practically all of the nearly 6 million Negroes of the North and West live under urban conditions and are engaged in industrial and other urban work; approximately one half the southern Negroes now live under similar conditions. This change to urban living represents both advantages and disadvantages to the Negro and has complicated his difficulties in competing satisfactorily.[55] Between 1940 and 1944 alone a million Negroes moved from farming to urban work. In 1960 over a million and a half Negroes belonged to labor unions, and increasingly they are moving from unskilled labor into positions of semiskilled and skilled employment. Negroes are also making increasing use of the power provided by the ballot.[56] In spite of the fact that pressures from whites, apathy, lack of leadership, and low economic and educational status keep the number of Negroes who register small, legislative changes and other factors have made it possible for the Negro to participate in primaries and to vote in all elections in increasing numbers in the South. The leading general Negro organizations are the National Association for the Advancement of Colored People (NAACP), which dates from 1909 and has spearheaded changes in legal statutes, and the National Urban League, established in 1910, which has as its chief goal the adjustment of Negroes to urban life. Within more recent years organizations interested in more direct changes have been formed, such as CORE (Congress of Racial Equality), SCLC (Southern Christian Leadership Conference), and SNCC (Student Non-Violent Coordinating Committee).

The American Indian

A majority of American Indians are still members of 200 reservations located in twenty-six states, most of them in the Far West. Half of them, however, live away from the reservations and are in the process of gaining

---

[54] Marvin E. Wolfgang, *Patterns in Criminal Homicide* (Philadelphia: University of Pennsylvania Press, 1958), pp. 31–33. Also see Thomas F. Pettigrew and Rosalind Barclay Spier, "The Ecological Structure of Negro Homicide," *American Journal of Sociology*, 67:621–629 (1962).

[55] See Charles E. Silberman, *Crisis in Black and White* (New York: Random House, Inc., 1964).

[56] See Anthony M. Orum, "A Reappraisal of the Social and Political Participation of Negroes," *American Journal of Sociology*, 72:32–46 (1966).

title to land. Thirteen states contain the bulk of the Indian population. Arizona has the largest number, with 83,387; Oklahoma is second with 64,689; and New Mexico third with 56,255.

It is difficult to generalize about the American Indian. Some Indians are almost completely assimilated, whereas others, with their superstition, poor hygiene, and opposition to Western European ways, are almost as "Indian" in their customs as they were in 1870. Nearly all of them are still farmers or livestock raisers, eking out additional incomes by selling curios or acting as tourist attractions and guides. Most of their reservations are marginal lands, and the Indians on them must often be supported by special governmental appropriations and relief. This governmental help amounted to $87 million in 1953.

Most of the Indians are unbelievably poor, although a few tribes are well-to-do. The average family income of the Sioux on the Standing Rock Reservation in North Dakota was $767 in 1955; it ranged from $730 to $855 among the Navahos. During the same year the average national family income was about $5300. Living conditions and health standards among the Indians are also far below the national average. On the Turtle Mountain Reservation in North Dakota, for example, as many as fifteen people live in a one-room cabin. The life expectancy for Papago Indian children in southern Arizona is seventeen years, as compared with sixty-nine years for the United States as a whole.

The difficulties which many present-day Indians face result from past policies and past contradictions. The original policy that "the only good Indian is a dead Indian" found expression in campaigns to exterminate them in many parts of the country. The program to place Indians on reservations began about 1850, and Indians were removed, often by force, to certain specified areas, to which they were given title. When land- and gold-hungry whites wanted these lands, the Indians were often moved farther West, from one reservation to another, until, finally, most of them had such poor lands that they had to be partially supported by government subsidies.

In 1887 the Dawes Allotment Act was set up to make "white men" out of the Indians by giving each an individual allotment of 160 acres from the reservation which had previously been commonly held by the tribe. After a certain number of years this land was finally to become the Indians' property. There was a provision that surplus reservation land could be homesteaded by whites. The Indians often sold these individual land rights, usually for very little, and between 1887 and 1928 they lost title to 87 million out of 137 million acres of land. In 1934 a new policy was instituted under the Indian Reorganization Act, which provided for the purchase of additional lands, for irrigation projects, and for self-government. Although these provisions strengthened the reservations, they continued segregation and expenditures of public funds for the special care of the Indians. About

1950 a new program was begun which will eventually mean the discontinuance of federal supervision over Indians and the gradual assumption of necessary services by the states. In addition, efforts are being made to eliminate reservations entirely by granting them complete autonomy over a period of years and by assisting Indians to leave the reservation permanently and to relocate in other areas, particularly large cities. The Menominee Indians of Wisconsin, after some delay, were first to be affected by this program, federal supervision ending in 1961. Two ways of dealing with the Indian situation are available.[57] One aims at a quick and intensive attempt to break down the special status of Indians and integrate them into the mainstream of American life. The other aims at maintaining Indian tribal integrity and special rights until such time as the Indians are ready and willing to dispense with federal supervision and control. On the whole, various Indian groups are so divided in their aspirations that they have not been too effective in working out a single national program. Some degree of pressure for an improvement in their situation, however, has been exerted on Congress and the general public through tribal representatives, the National Congress of American Indians, and an organization of persons interested in the Indian: American Association on Indian Affairs.

Japanese-Americans

Of the 464,332 persons of Japanese ancestry in the United States, 43.8 percent live in Hawaii and 33.9 percent live in California. Five states have 11.2 percent: in order, Washington, Illinois, New York, Colorado, and Oregon. The other states have only 11.1 percent. These Japanese are immigrants or descendants of immigrants who came to the United States largely between 1870 and 1920.[58] The Japanese Exclusion Act of 1924 eliminated all immigration of Japanese. Their exclusion was based on the erroneous

---

[57] See Oliver La Farge, "Termination of Federal Supervision: Disintegration and the American Indian," *The Annals,* 311:41–46 (1957). Some indications of the newer approach to their problems is the fact that in 1968 sixteen Arizona Indian tribes and one from California organized the Indian Development District, a self-help economic group that will eventually represent 160,000 Indians. "Immediate plans call for development of long-range economic growth plans, including land use and transportation forecasts, to increase Indian employment, facilitate economic planning and develop a wider economic base. . . . An application has been sent to the Economic Development Administration for funds to support the group's operation during 1968." *The New York Times,* January 8, 1968, p. 14–C. The Navajos, the largest of the Indian tribes, have also as a group, done much to improve their economic situation.

[58] See Forrest E. La Violette, *Americans of Japanese Ancestry: A Study of Assimilation in the American Community* (Toronto: Canadian Institute of International Affairs, 1945), p. 10.

belief that their industry, aggressiveness, and a high birth rate constituted a threat to the numerically superior dominant group. One writer summarized the opposition to them at that time.

> An anti-Japanese movement has been developing in the United States leading to differential race legislation. It has taken acutest form in the California Anti-Alien Land Law. Without attempting to characterize this movement adequately I may describe it as a movement partly economic, implicitly confessing fear of Japanese superior efficiency; partly racial, expressing scorn, disdain, and arrogance at the ambition and success of a people "instinctively" felt to be essentially inferior; partly political, furnishing opportunity to certain individuals and political groups to gain personal and party advantage by appealing to selfish interest and race prejudice against sections of the community politically helpless; and partly natural and inevitable, arising from numberless mistakes, misunderstandings, and misdeeds of individuals of different race groups speaking different languages and acting under different customs, ideas, and ideals.[59]

The Japanese in America have been characterized as having "a highly developed disposition of obedience and obligation, heavy self-demands involving the giving up of free impulse, a pride in name and the bringing of honor to one's family, an unusual cohesive organization of the group," and a generally dynamic aggressiveness.[60] In many ways, as Robert E. Park stated, the Japanese minority resembles the Jewish minority, for it is small in numbers, intimate, compact, and well organized. Both groups have great advantages in competition with a larger and less-organized community. The Japanese culture, however, affects this minority group in different ways, according to whether its members are Issei, Nisei, or Sansei. The Issei are those born in Japan, who, prior to 1952, were aliens because laws prevented their naturalization and, in the past, in California their ownership of land. The Nisei and the Sansei, who make up about two thirds of all Japanese, are the children and the grandchildren of the Issei. Although they are a part of both Japanese and American cultures, their acculturation is generally not complete.[61] The social separation of the Issei from the Nisei is very great because of differences in the degree of language facility and in

---

[59] Sidney L. Gulick, *American Democracy and Asiatic Citizenship* (New York: Charles Scribner's Sons, 1919), p. 22.

[60] R. A. Schermerhorn, *These Our People* (Boston: D. C. Heath and Company, 1949), p. 206.

[61] Before World War II there was a small group of Nisei called the Kibei, American-born Japanese who had been sent to Japan for part of their education and who were therefore often closer than the others to Japanese culture and traditions.

the extent of participation in American institutions. The Nisei, however, more than the Sansei, are a part of both cultures while not fully a part of either.[62]

At the time of World War II, nearly half of the Japanese in continental United States were engaged in agriculture.[63] The Japanese produced about a third of all truck crops grown in California. About two fifths of the non-agricultural Japanese workers were in business, a like proportion of these being in personal and commercial services. During World War II, the Japanese, most of whom were United States citizens, were subjected to one of the most extreme forms of discrimination in American history when they were ordered evacuated from the Pacific Coast and transferred to relocation centers. Several factors accounted for this action. The military officials in charge of the West Coast had a curious notion of the relation of race and culture; moreover, certain newspapers and politicians were opposed to the Japanese, many of whom were technically "enemy aliens." [64] These people were hurriedly uprooted and given only limited opportunities to protect their property, which many of them had to sell at a heavy loss when they could find no non-Japanese person to take care of it. The Japanese were incarcerated in camps behind barbed wire and under armed guards, in crowded institutional conditions and subject to tremendous psychological tensions.[65] During the war a large proportion were eventually released from the camps and relocated in states away from the Pacific Coast. After the war some 80 percent of them returned to the West Coast, three fourths of them to California. Actual income and property losses because of forced sales and damage during their absence have been estimated at $350 million.[66] Some 24,000 claims totaling $130 million were filed, and congressional legislation was passed permitting claims up to $100,000 to be settled without court litigation.

Since World War II a great many of the handicaps caused by relocation

---

[62] Jitsuichi Masuoka, "Race Relations and Nisei Problems," *Sociology and Social Research,* 30:456–457 (1946).

[63] Dorothy Swaine Thomas and Richard S. Nishimoto, *The Spoilage: Japanese-American Evacuation and Resettlement* (Berkeley: University of California Press, 1946).

[64] Thomas and Nishimoto. Also see Morton Grodzins, *Americans Betrayed* (Chicago: University of Chicago Press, 1949).

[65] Alexander Leighton, *The Governing of Men* (Princeton, N.J.: Princeton University Press, 1945).

[66] Leonard Broom and Ruth Riemer, *Removal and Return* (Berkeley: University of California Press, 1949), pp. 201–203. Also see Dorothy S. Thomas, *The Salvage* (Berkeley: University of California Press, 1952).

have been overcome, and Japanese-Americans are encountering less discrimination. The elevation of Hawaii to statehood in 1959 ended a long delay which was due, in part, to the many persons of Japanese and Chinese ancestry in its population. Their chief organization is the Japanese-American Citizens League (JACL), an association which unites Japanese-Americans and attempts to remove discrimination.

Chinese-Americans

Most of the Chinese now living in America are descendants of immigrants who came here from about 1850 and 1882, when the Exclusion Law barred further legal immigration. During the California gold rush few people would do the necessary menial tasks, and Chinese were imported as unskilled laborers. As the gold rush subsided and the whites returned to the cities, however, they competed with the Chinese for available jobs. As a result of a series of disturbances, the Chinese withdrew to segregated living in Chinatowns. This ghetto method of living kept the possibility of hostilities with the white population at a minimum, gave the Chinese certain limited specialized occupations, and enabled them to maintain their cultural unity. Their numbers were greatly increased from 1860 to 1882, when the western part of the transcontinental railroad was built and there was a need for cheap labor on the Pacific Coast. In some instances the Chinese laborers later returned to China. Although all immigration was officially banned until 1943, when a quota of 105 was permitted, some Chinese have illegally entered this country from Mexico and other places.

The number of Chinese in this country is still small, 237,292, as compared with 464,000 Japanese, largely because few Chinese women came here. Most of the Chinese immigrants came as young men, remained single, and often returned to China to live out their last years on the money made in the United States. Since they could not be citizens in California they, like the Japanese, were not allowed to own land there. As has been true of several generations, a large proportion of the Chinese in the United States is American-born. A small proportion have come more recently as immigrants from various Chinese communities outside of Communist China.

With the passage of years Chinatowns appear to be declining.[67] The movement of the central business districts is pushing Chinese inhabitants out and thus eliminating Chinatowns as distinct cultural entities; probably only those in San Francisco and New York will remain. As Chinatowns disappear and the Chinese-Americans become acculturated, their dispersions will be much like that of other small minority groups who have become

---

[67] Rose Hum Lee, "The Decline of Chinatowns in the United States," *American Journal of Sociology*, 54:422–433 (1949).

integral parts of the American society.[68] Because of their physical appearance they may still be treated as Chinese in one situation and as American in another. Thus they acquire a dual set of responses and many are never wholly free from the possibility of differential treatment. Incidents of prejudice and discrimination, although perhaps not frequent, do arise, evoking feelings of marginality, resentment, and dormant fears.[69]

Ethnic Minorities: Spanish-speaking Americans

Most immigrants to the United States prior to 1890 were minority groups at one time, such as the Swedish and German groups in the nineteenth century, but they have now become part of the majority group. On the other hand, many of the groups in the "new" immigration, such as the Italians and the Poles, might still be regarded as ethnic minorities today. They are rapidly changing their minority status as they move into the second and even third and fourth generations. The status of these groups is chiefly dependent on their social class and on the part of the country in which they reside.

One ethnic minority, the Spanish-speaking Americans, has a unique position. This group includes Mexican immigrants and Puerto Ricans, who are American citizens, and those persons descended from them, as well as those persons of Spanish-American and Mexican descent in the Southwest who have been part of the United States for a century and whom one can hardly regard as immigrants. Their number has been estimated at about 3.5 million, as of 1950, or somewhat less than 2 percent of the total population of the United States.[70] This minority group thus comes after Negroes and Jews in size. Most of the Spanish-speaking minority is concentrated in five southwestern states, Texas, California, New Mexico, Arizona, and Colorado, but many are found in the Middle West and the Northeast, chiefly in such cities as Chicago, Detroit, Kansas City, and New York. (See Table 16.5.)

Spanish-Americans

The Spanish-Americans, or "Hispanos," are primarily descendants of the early Spanish colonists who settled mainly in what is now New Mexico, ceded to this country in 1848 after the Mexican War. They have lived in

---

[68] Stanley L. M. Fong, "Assimilation of Chinese in America: Changes in Orientation and Social Perception," *American Journal of Sociology,* 71:265–273 (1965).

[69] Rose Hum Lee, *The Chinese in the United States of America* (Hong Kong: Cathay Press, 1960), p. 68.

[70] Paul A. F. Walter, Jr., *Race and Culture Relations* (New York: McGraw-Hill Book Company, Inc., 1952), p. 325.

the Southwest for over three hundred years, and most of them are sub-sistence farmers in small communities. For the most part they have remained as Spanish in custom as many persons in Spain or in South America. They are exceptionally attached to small, quaint, isolated communities in the Southwest not only because of their cultural background and language but because of the discrimination on the part of Anglos. They are generally poor, and their illiteracy rates and death rates are very high. Some refer to them as the Forgotten People because so few Americans outside the Southwest have much knowledge of them or their problems.[71] Although most of them are still in these areas, there has been a recent movement to cities where, together with persons of Mexican ancestry, they have generally set up a Spanish city within a city. Their adjustment to urban life has been a complicated one.

TABLE 16.5   **Estimated Spanish-speaking Population of the Southwest, 1950**

State	Total population	Spanish-speaking population	Percent Spanish-speaking
Texas	7,500,000	1,150,000	15.3
California	10,500,000	500,000	4.8
New Mexico	650,000	250,000	38.5
Arizona	750,000	160,000	21.3
Colorado	1,350,000	50,000	3.7
Total	20,750,000	2,110,000	10.2

SOURCE: By permission from *Race and Culture Relations* by Paul A. F. Walter, Jr., p. 329. Copyright, 1952, McGraw-Hill Book Company, Inc. Figures are approximate, to indicate roughly the proportion of Spanish-speaking people in each state. Since there are no precise statistics on the Spanish-speaking group, pretense at greater accuracy would be meaningless.

It is not the visibility of the Spanish-American minority that separates them from the majority group but their social and cultural differences. Although it is a heterogeneous group, it is largely a combination of a rural, folk way of life and a Spanish and partially an Indian culture. Between them and the Anglos or non-Spanish population there are a difference in language (the state documents in New Mexico are still being published in two languages), a difference in religion (the Spanish-Americans are nearly all Catholics), and frequently a difference in outlook on life. Their back-

---

[71] George L. Sanchez, *The Forgotten People: A Study of New Mexicans* (Albuquerque: University of New Mexico Press, 1940).

ground is nonindividualistic, is family- and village-centered, and has a relatively low technological development.

The world of the twentieth century is rapidly moving in on the Hispanos, who have found that their way of life of three hundred years ago cannot cope with it. The frequent feeling of futility is intensified by awareness of poverty and by ignorance, poor diet, inadequate landholdings, and discrimination. Although they and government agencies are making efforts to improve this situation, the road will not be short or easy for a people who have resisted change for so long a time.[72]

Mexican-Americans

A hundred years ago, when the Southwest became part of the United States, it was peopled largely by Spanish-Americans and Mexicans. The descendants of those Mexicans and of many others who came later, together with Mexican nationals living in the United States, will be discussed here as Mexicans. The largest part of the Mexican migration came during the period of World War I to the time of the depression, and again during World War II, when there was a great demand for labor but little opportunity for European immigration. Over half the Mexicans and persons of Mexican descent in the United States live in Texas, but over 600,000 live in California and 100,000 in Arizona. Los Angeles has 120,000 Mexicans; Chicago, about 25,000.[73]

Although Mexicans are increasingly being employed in industry, they are still mainly migratory laborers, planting and harvesting beet sugar and cotton, and picking the fruit crops of the West. Most of them are unskilled laborers, few are in business or the professions. They are a comparatively poor and illiterate people, usually living in segregated and poor slum areas.[74]

The discrimination against persons with a Mexican background arises from a number of factors. Some of the Spanish-Americans and most Mexicans have a mixed Spanish and Indian ancestry—mestizos. As a result, they are often physically visible enough to be distinguished from the non-Spanish population. Many have dual nationalistic ties which Spanish-

[72] John H. Burma, *Spanish-Speaking Groups in the United States* (Durham, N.C.: Duke University Press, 1954).

[73] Although they were for a long time a rural, agricultural people both in Mexico and in this country, over half of them now live, for at least part of the year, in urban areas. They often leave these urban areas for migratory agricultural work during the spring or summer. See Burma, p. 37.

[74] See Arthur J. Rubel, *Across the Tracks: Mexican-Americans in a Texas City* (Austin: University of Texas, 1966).

Americans do not have, and in the Southwest, particularly in Texas, they often encounter the latent century-old hostility of Anglos for Mexicans. Discrimination can also be explained by the fact that there is also often a difference in language, culture, and religion. Most of the Mexicans are poor. Many persons also tend to associate them with petty theft, personal violence, delinquency, and drunkenness, in all of which their rates are high but probably no higher than those for persons in a similar economic and cultural situation.

Several organizations set up by Mexicans and Spanish-Americans in recent years to help solve their problems have been concerned with discrimination against their group and other problems of adjustment which they encounter.

Puerto Ricans

By 1960 there were an estimated 900,000 Puerto Ricans living in the United States mainland, 690,000 of whom live in New York City, approximately one in four of all of them having been born on the mainland. Nearly three fourths of the Puerto Ricans live in "Spanish Harlem." Most Puerto Ricans have emigrated in the last twenty years because of overcrowding and economic conditions in Puerto Rico, as well as the appeal of a large city like New York. They have taken up residence in some of New York's most difficult slum areas, and while some of them have improved themselves economically many of them have a marginal existence and come to the attention of the welfare authorities. Their background in language and culture is largely Spanish, but some, because of their mixed white and Negro ancestry, encounter some of the same types of prejudice as do American Negroes. Because they come from a place where "race" has little meaning, this is difficult for them to understand and accept. Consequently, Puerto Ricans try to emphasize their Spanish language and customs. Their problems, particularly juvenile delinquency, will continue as long as the areas in which they reside contribute to deviant behavior and until, through cultural assimilation, they can change or move out of the slum areas.[75]

---

[75] Burma, pp. 176–187. Also see Morris Eagle, "The Puerto Ricans in New York City," in Nathan Glazer and Davis McEntire, eds., *Studies in Housing and Minority Groups* (Berkeley: University of California Press, 1960), pp. 144–177; and Clarence Senior, *Strangers Then Neighbors: From Pilgrims to Puerto Ricans* (New York: Freedom Books, 1961), and Patricia Cayo Sexton, *Spanish Harlem: Anatomy of Poverty* (New York: Harper & Row, Publishers, 1965). Also see Oscar Lewis, *La Vida: A Puerto Rican Family in the Culture of Poverty —San Juan and New York* (New York: Random House, Inc., 1966).

Despite the hardship of language for many and despite racial discrimination, Puerto Ricans come with a number of advantages. They are largely literate and many have a background of urban living. As a whole they are a youthful population, the sexes are about equally divided as compared with previous migrant groups, and they tend to marry early. Their birth rate is considerably higher than that of the general population of New York City. Their educational level is much lower than the level of New Yorkers in general, only one fifth of the adults over twenty-five having an eighth-grade education, as compared with three fourths of the New York population. Generally they are employed as semiskilled "operatives," sewing machine operators or service tradesmen, and not as domestic servants. In fact, these first two classifications accounted for two thirds of employed Puerto Rican men as compared with approximately one third of all men. Four fifths of the women were "operatives" as compared with one third of nonwhite and one fourth of white women.

Despite these conditions, Puerto Ricans as a whole do not feel that they are discriminated against; in fact, in one survey only 5 percent thought so, and 98 percent thought their families had been treated fairly well in New York City.[76] There are several reasons for this rather unusual attitude: (1) compared with wages, housing, and other living conditions in Puerto Rico, to them their situation here is not too bad, (2) their pride prohibits them from admitting discrimination, (3) there is little personal contact with those who are not Puerto Ricans, and (4) they are so concerned with economic matters that discrimination is a minor problem. Studies of intermarriages indicate that assimilation is taking place rapidly.[77] The principal organizations of Latin-Americans are the Alianza Hispano-Americana and the Political Association of Spanish-Speaking Americans.

Religious Minorities: The Jews

The United States Census does not enumerate a person's religious beliefs any more than it does his political affiliation. Thus the only statistics on religious groups must be obtained through the religious denominations, generally from church memberships. These figures are often misleading, particularly in the case of the Jew, for some persons are regarded by others and by themselves as Jews even though they may not attend any synagogue or may even belong to some Christian denomination.

The Jews are classified here as a religious minority, although they are not clearly a religious group. Having been discriminated against for two

---

[76] Eagle, in Glazer and McEntire, p. 186.

[77] See Joseph P. Fitzpatrick, "Intermarriage of Puerto Ricans in New York City," *American Journal of Sociology*, 71:395–406 (1966).

thousand or more years, they are the classic minority group of Western civilization. Christ was a Jew and the Christian Bible contains the history of the Jewish people and a large part of their traditional philosophy. Hence a Jewish author, Lewis Browne, wrote with irony, "How odd of God to choose the Jews." [78] They have endured generations of persecution and death in many lands and under many rulers, from Herod to Hitler and beyond. Anti-Semitism has been directed at forcing or holding the Jews in an inferior position by limiting their political, economic, and social rights. They were subjected to centuries of severe economic and personal restrictions in the European ghettoes and they were butchered under the Russian czars in countless pogroms. Between 1939 and 1945 the Nazis, regarding the Jews as a "race" personifying all evil, destroyed approximately six million, or nearly two thirds of all the Jews of Europe.[79] Anti-Semitic practices have been supported by all types of beliefs, including the view that they constitute a menace to Christians and to Christian society, offer unfair business competition, and are an inferior racial group. Anti-Semitic beliefs exist in the United States as part of the cultural heritage and various anti-Semitic organizations have from time to time overtly attacked the Jews. Still there are indications of a significant reduction in anti-Semitism since World War II. Most public opinion polls in the United States indicate that some 10 percent will make anti-Semitic statements.[80] In 1959 a public opinion survey asked persons whether they agreed with the view that Jewish businessmen were so "shrewd and tricky that other people cannot compete." [81] Of those who agreed, 43 percent had a grade school education, 28 percent a high school education, and 18 percent a college education.

Many people believe it is impossible to speak of Jews as a group because of the diversity among them in the United States and throughout the world. No concept would include all Jews, even in the United States. They are certainly not a race. Most Jews are white and so mixed that they constitute no distinctive subgroup; there are also Negro Jews and Chinese Jews. Nor are they a religion. Many persons are called Jews who are not

---

[78] Lewis Browne, *How Odd of God* (New York: The Macmillan Company, 1936).

[79] For an account of the persecutions of the Jews under Hitler and of the results of the extermination policies, see William L. Shirer, *The Rise and Fall of the Third Reich* (New York: Simon and Schuster, Inc., 1960).

[80] George E. Simpson and J. Milton Yinger, *Racial and Cultural Minorities* (rev. ed.; New York: Harper & Row, Publishers, 1965), p. 220.

[81] C. H. Stember, *Education and Attitude Change: The Effect of Schooling on Prejudice Against Minority Groups* (New York: Institute of Human Relations Press, 1961), p. 17.

Jews at all; moreover, there is considerable variation within each religious group. Some people feel that Jews do not have a distinctive culture because of the cultural and linguistic variations which distinguish those from America, Germany, Iraq, Yemen, Algiers, India, and other countries. Studies of Israel, which has become a haven of Jews from all lands, indicate that it contains one of the most diverse cultural groups existing today.[82] As one Jewish periodical has said: "We have not yet determined whether we are to use the term 'race,' 'religion,' 'nation,' or 'culture' to clarify the nature of our Jewish entity and identity." [83]

In sociological terms a Jew is simply a person who says he is a Jew or is considered by others to be a Jew. Several characteristics, however, give some unity to the Jews as a group despite the many exceptions: the nature of the Jewish religion, the high regard for learning, the biculturality or dual culture of many Jews, their long ghetto existence, and their urban and commercial background.[84] Many of these characteristics, if considered individually, would apply equally to groups other than the Jewish.

1. The religion of the Jews has been at the same time different from and similar to that of the Christians, among whom they have lived since A.D. 70, when the people of Jerusalem were dispersed by the Roman legions. The Old Testament, on which their religion is based, is also a part of the Christian religion; yet in their belief that Christ was not divine they have been almost the only distinctive religious group residing in Western European countries. This denial of the divinity of Christ was one reason for their persecution.

2. Learning has always been highly regarded among Jews. A large part of Jewish education has been based on the study of the books of the Talmud, in which the role of the scholar has been stressed: "Turn all thou hast into money and procure in marriage for thy son the daughter of a scholar, and for thy daughter a scholar." As a result of this emphasis, the medical, legal, and teaching professions, as well as the ministry and philosophy, have probably meant more to Jews as a group than to gentiles.

3. Jews can frequently be characterized by their possession of a somewhat dual culture. While usually taking on the customs of the people with whom they have lived, the Jews retained some of the customs of ancient Israel. This biculturality has meant a dual set of customs of education and etiquette. Because they have long had this dual culture the loyalty of many Jews to a national state has often been doubted.

---

[82] Rafael Patai, *Israel: Between East and West* (Philadelphia: Jewish Publication Society, 1953).

[83] *Reconstructionist,* June 23, 1944, as quoted in Schermerhorn.

[84] Schermerhorn, pp. 381–387.

4. The Jews' long ghetto existence constituted a severe form of segregation which has affected even those Jews who have never been forced to live in a ghetto.[85] These areas in medieval days, and even recently, were surrounded by walls and gates which were closed at night. Armed guards watched the gates but only a few Jews ventured out even on weekdays to transact business. Inside the ghetto were the synagogue, the burial place, and the tenements. Often there were pogroms and other invasions of the ghetto in which the Jews were slaughtered. The social effects of enforced segregation gave rise to an exaggerated cohesiveness and solidarity of the community (to outsiders, clannishness). It meant a temper of mind increasingly uneasy when too far from the organized forms of Jewish institutions and communal activities.[86] A study of Jews in three small communities in the United States has revealed the effect of this past and the difficulties of acceptance by the gentile community which make the Jew "the eternal stranger." [87]

> As a group the Jews find it very difficult to break with their past nor are they ever quite accepted into the larger society. Thus they remain, par excellence, the eternal strangers. In general, they live in two worlds—a little disillusioned in both. They have no real world of their own because the ideological system of the ghetto, which was responsible for the survival of the Jewish world in the first place, fails to solve the intellectual and moral perplexities by which the modern American Jew is beset. On the other hand, the world of the larger community is not quite their own because despite the fact that it may admire and tolerate them, it feels eternally irritated at their stubborn persistence in being different and treats them, at best, as guests. Being loyal and neighborly has not helped, living together in the same town for a hundred years has not helped, speaking the same language and venerating the same national heroes and institutions have not helped. Even when the lines between the Jewish and the Gentile communities become very thin, the Jews still find themselves far from constituting full-fledged members of the general community and their positions remain one of ambivalence.[88]

5. The Jews have traditionally been city persons from the time they left Israel, where they were pastoral nomads, until their present re-emergence as farmers in that country. Several factors account for this city background.

---

[85] Louis Wirth, *The Ghetto* (Chicago: University of Chicago Press, 1928).

[86] From R. A. Schermerhorn, *These Our People* (Boston: D. C. Heath and Company, 1949), p. 384. Extracts from this work are reprinted by permission of the publisher.

[87] Benjamin Kaplan, *The Eternal Stranger: A Study of Jewish Life in the Small Community* (New York: Bookman Associates, Inc., 1957).

[88] Kaplan, p. 156.

During medieval times they were forbidden by law to own land, they could not take the oath of fealty, and their religious customs did not permit their serving in armies, service which might have enabled them to acquire land. Consequently, over the centuries the Jew has been limited to an urban, commercial way of life which has affected his approach to social relationships. Of all immigrant groups in the United States, not only was he the most urban; he was the only one with such an exclusively urban background. So pronounced has been this characteristic that Rose has tried to explain anti-Semitism as an outgrowth of everyone's unconcious dislike of the frustrations and problems of urban life.[89] Since he is the most closely identified with city life, the Jew has received the overt expression of this dislike for the city.

6. The proportion of Jews engaged in commerce is, and has been, probably larger than that of any other group, as would be expected from their urban background. Moreover, during medieval times Christians were generally not permitted to lend money at interest; hence it was logical that some Jews assumed the banking function. Aware of this commercial background of the Jew, anti-Semites have often charged that Jews dominate the economy. Several studies of the occupations of Jews in the United States, although not conclusive because of the difficulties of making such studies, do not support any general Jewish dominance of the economy out of proportion to their numbers.[90] A few occupations do have disproportionate numbers of Jews. They are not, however, occupations of any particular power, being largely in light industries, such as the manufacture and distribution of clothing. Jews do not occupy a strong position in newspaper publishing; banking and investment; rubber, chemicals, and petroleum; transportation; or public utilities.

The Jews have come to the United States in approximately four more or less distinct groups: the Sephardic Jews of colonial days; the German Jews, from about 1800 to 1880; the east European Jews, from 1881 to 1924; and the refugees from the Nazis and the effects of World War II from all over Europe from 1933 to the present.[91] There were proportionately few Jews in the United States until 1848, when they numbered about 20,000 in a population of 20,000,000. A few German Jews—in general, small tradesmen and peddlers—started emigrating between 1800 and 1848; in the years

---

[89] Arnold M. Rose, "Anti-Semitism's Part in City-Hatred," *Commentary*, 6:374–378 (October 1948).

[90] William M. Kephart, "What Is the Position of the Jewish Economy in the United States?" *Social Forces*, 28:153–164 (1949).

[91] Jews from Germany and eastern Europe entered the United States during all these periods.

following the revolutionary movements which swept Germany in 1848, some 200,000 sought the political and economic freedom of the new land. They were chiefly political liberals as well as religious liberals who belonged to the Reform or liberal Jewish synagogue. On the whole, they did not tend to believe, as compared with Orthodox Jews, that kosher and other dietary laws were binding, that religious services need be conducted primarily in Hebrew, or that men and women need be seated separately during services. Because these Jews had enjoyed considerable freedom in their home country, they thought of themselves more as Germans than as Jews. Their political, religious, and social liberalism, which was not as strongly opposed to intermarriage with gentiles, together with their largely middle-class, educated background, made the German Jew assimilate American ways more readily. Although some German-Jewish groups were traditionalists or German separatists, by the time the eastern Jews began emigrating they were well on the road to economic prosperity and a considerable degree of assimilation and amalgamation.

Eastern Jews from Poland and Russia began coming in large numbers in 1881, eventually numbering approximately 2 million immigrants and now with their descendants constituting the majority of the American Jews. As a result of the pogroms in Russia and Poland begun by the czarist government as a political policy, various European Jewish groups outside Russia and Poland arranged to bring thousands of Jews, mostly as family units, to this country. These eastern European Jewish immigrants differed greatly from the German Jews because they had been confined to an almost medieval ghetto existence. The majority were poor, Orthodox even in style of dress, and almost a quarter of them were illiterate. The German Jews had dispersed to the smaller cities and many to the Midwest, but the eastern Jews concentrated in New York City, which today has almost half the Jews in the United States. Many of the Polish and Russian Jews, although poor, had been skilled laborers—tailors, hatmakers, milliners, and shoemakers—and their services were needed in the garment industry in New York.

The eastern Jews, emancipated suddenly from the ghetto, have had tremendous difficulties in adjustment. Thrown into a large industrial metropolis after living in small cities and towns, many of them were able to move from extreme poverty to moderate wealth. These changes in economic status greatly strained their family system, which was traditionally closely organized and patriarchal, and produced friction between the generations. They also resulted in conflicts between German and eastern Jews, the former often tending to look down upon the eastern Jews and avoid them. Despite its problems, the eastern Jewish group, on the whole, has been able to maintain a considerable degree of solidarity through its organization and centers. Some modifications of the Orthodox Jewish religion have been made, members of this movement being called Conservative Jews. Their modifications, however, have not gone as far as those of the liberal or Reform group.

TABLE 16.6 **Jewish Population, by Continents**

Continent	1939	1950	1960	Percent increase or decrease, 1950–60
United States and Canada	4,965,620	5,198,000	5,780,000	+8.0
South and Central America	524,000	621,930	681,150	+9.5
Europe	9,739,200	3,550,000	3,714,300	+4.6
Asia (including Israel)	771,500	1,374,350	2,057,650	+46.7
Australia and New Zealand	33,000	44,000	68,500	+55.6
Africa	609,800	702,400	543,180	−21.5
World Total	16,643,120	11,490,680	12,836,790	+10.1

SOURCE: Figures for 1939 and 1950 secured from *Monthly Bulletin of Statistics,* Office of the United Nations, August, 1950. Figures for 1960 are from the Jewish Statistical Bureau, as presented in *The World Almanac 1962* (New York: New York World-Telegram and The Sun, 1962), p. 258.

TABLE 16.7 **Jewish Population by Cities of the World, 1960**

City	Jewish population
New York City (greater)	1,940,000
Los Angeles (greater)	400,000
Tel Aviv-Jaffa	383,000
Philadelphia (greater)	330,000
Chicago	282,000
London (greater)	280,000
Paris	175,000
Haifa	174,000
Jerusalem	160,000
Boston	150,000
Montreal	102,000

SOURCE: Estimates given by the Jewish Statistical Bureau, as presented in *The World Almanac 1962*, p. 258.

The last wave of Jews came with Hitler's persecutions and the subsequent postwar adjustment. Between 1933 and 1944, about 160,000 to 200,000 Jews were admitted to the United States, almost all from Germany and Austria. In 1960 almost half of all the Jews in the world, 5,780,000, were in the United States and Canada, as contrasted with one third in 1939. (See Table 16.6.) The countries with the largest estimated Jewish populations in 1960 are the United States, 5,370,000; Soviet Union, 2,268,-000; Israel, 1,880,000; Great Britain, 450,000; Argentina, 400,000; and France, 350,000. New York City and Los Angeles are the American cities with the largest Jewish populations, with 1,940,000 and 400,000, respectively. (See Table 16.7.)

Because of these four distinct immigration periods, the American Jewish community has many differences, cultural and religious. An outstanding example of the latter is the division into Orthodox, Conservative, and Reform or liberal synagogues. The Orthodox membership, by families, is estimated to be 30,000; the Conservative, 250,000; and the Reform, 250,000. American Jews are now moving into the third and fourth generation with consequent differences in their attitudes toward many cultural values.[92] Despite their differences in background and religious customs, Jewish groups are well organized. In fact, they are probably the most effectively organized minority group. Some of their associations are the American Jewish Congress, established in 1917 to defend the political rights of Jews and active among middle-class persons interested in militant Jewish efforts; the Anti-Defamation League of B'nai B'rith, organized in 1913 to oppose discriminatory articles in the press; the Jewish Labor Committee; the Jewish Welfare Board; the Young Men's Hebrew Association; the Jewish War Veterans; the United Jewish Appeal; and many others devoted specifically to the aid of the Jewish state of Israel.[93]

SUMMARY

A fully developed minority group is one which is discriminated against by a certain group. This treatment clashes with other values in the culture which would tend to give the group equal status. Both the minority and the majority group recognize this situation as discrimination, and the minority group organizes itself to remove the discrimination. On the basis of this analysis there are a number of minorities in the United States. Some are racial minorities, such as the American Negro, the American Indian, the Japanese-American, and the Chinese-American. Others are religious minorities, such as the Jew, and still others are ethnic minorities such as

---

[92] Judith R. Kramer and Seymour Leventman, *Children of the Gilded Ghetto* (New Haven, Conn.: Yale University Press, 1961).

[93] For further discussions of the social characteristics of American Jews, see Marshall Sklare, *The Jews* (New York: The Free Press, 1958) and Albert I. Gordon, *Jews in Suburbia* (Boston: The Beacon Press, 1959).

the Spanish-speaking American. The present status of all these groups can be understood only in terms of a long series of historic relations among various groups.

SELECTED READINGS

Barron, Milton L., ed. *American Minorities.* New York: Alfred A. Knopf, Inc., 1957. A collection of readings in intergroup relations covering a wide range of topics.

Burma, John H. *Spanish-Speaking Groups in the United States.* Durham, N.C.: Duke University Press, 1954. A discussion of the background and problems of the Hispanos, Mexican-Americans, Filipino-Americans, and Puerto Ricans in the United States.

Davis, Allison, Burleigh B. Gardner, and Mary R. Gardner. *Deep South.* Chicago: University of Chicago Press, 1941. A study of whites and Negroes in a southern city and their relations with one another.

Drake, St. Clair, and Horace R. Cayton. *Black Metropolis.* New York: Harcourt, Brace & World, Inc., 1945. A study of the Negro area of Chicago and in particular the differences in social classes. Reprinted in 1965.

Frazier, E. Franklin. *The Negro in the United States.* Rev. ed. New York: The Macmillan Company, 1957. An analysis of the American Negro. Chapters 2 and 3 deal with slavery and the plantation as a social institution.

Kramer, Judith R., and Seymour Leventman. *Children of the Gilded Ghetto.* New Haven, Conn.: Yale University Press, 1961. A study of the values and difficulties in adjustment of third- and fourth-generation Jews.

Myrdal, Gunnar. *An American Dilemma.* New York: Harper & Row, Publishers, 1944. Probably the best-known book on minorities in America. It is a detailed study of the Negro by a large staff under the direction of the Swedish economist Gunnar Myrdal. The first chapter deals with the American Creed. A new twentieth anniversary edition was published in 1963.

Pettigrew, Thomas F. *A Profile of the Negro American.* Princeton, N.J.: D. Van Nostrand Company, Inc., 1964. An analysis of research dealing with the contemporary American Negro.

Segal, Bernard E., ed. *Racial and Ethnic Relations: Selected Readings.* New York: Thomas Y. Crowell Company, 1966. A collection of readings dealing with the theoretical aspects of ethnic and racial subcultural variations, southern and northern patterns of racial separation and subordination, desegregation, integration, attitude changes, and the search for Negro identity.

Sexton, Patricia Cayo. *Spanish Harlem: Anatomy of Poverty.* New York: Harper & Row, Publishers, 1965. A discussion of the problems faced by Puerto Ricans living in Spanish Harlem in New York City.

Silberman, Charles E. *Crisis in Black and White.* New York: Random House, Inc., 1964. An analysis of contemporary Negro-white relations in terms of historical factors and recent trends.

Simpson, George Eaton, and J. Milton Yinger. *Racial and Cultural Minorities:*

An Analysis of Prejudice and Discrimination. Third ed. New York: Harper & Row, Publishers, 1965. The most comprehensive analysis of racial and cultural minorities. Contains a discussion of types of majority-minority situations and an analysis of minorities in the social structure. There are chapters on minorities and the American political and legal processes.

Southern Education Report. Southern Education Reporting Service. Nashville. Published ten times a year, it provides a comprehensive coverage of developments in the school integration picture in all the southern and border states. Its reporting is objective and factual. In additon to its regular reports, it reprints some of the more important documents, speeches, and proposals relevant to public school segregation and desegregation. Extremely useful in following current developments.

These Rights and Freedoms. United Nations Department of Public Information. New York: United Nations, 1950. Contains the full text of the Universal Declaration on Human Rights adopted by the General Assembly of the United Nations in 1948 as well as the various drafts of this declaration.

Vander Zanden, James W. *Race Relations in Transition: The Segregation Crisis in the South*. New York: Random House, Inc., 1964. A discussion of contemporary developments in interracial relations in the South.

Wirth, Louis. *The Ghetto*. Chicago: University of Chicago Press, 1928, reprinted, 1965. A well-known study which traces the ghetto historically and shows its effect on the contemporary Jew.

Woodward, C. Vann. *The Strange Career of Jim Crow*. Rev. ed. New York: Oxford University Press, 1965. A well-known American historian shows that racial segregation in the South is of relatively recent origin and describes the social and political mechanism of its establishment.

Yinger, J. Milton. *A Minority Group in American Society*. New York: McGraw-Hill Book Company, Inc., 1965. An analysis of the American Negro in terms of social stratification and minority-majority relations.

17

Discrimination and Prejudice

Discrimination can be defined as the denial of equality of treatment to an individual or to groups of persons who desire this equality.[1] Often it involves restrictions on social participation and on occupying positions of social status which give a degree of power in a society.

Although there can be many kinds of discrimination, such as by sex or social class, the discussion here will be limited to discrimination on the basis of race, ethnic background, or religion. Several forms of discrimination can be described and analyzed: (1) social conventions, (2) segregated living, (3) mass media of communication, (4) discriminations affecting health and life expectancy, (5) exclusion from organized groups, (6) discrimination in public accommodations, (7) discrimination and segregation in educational facilities, (8) discrimination in employment and business, (9) discrimination in suffrage and public office, and (10) discrimination in the administration of justice.

Several rather widespread misconceptions exist about the nature of discrimination against minority groups. Many people associate discrimination only with poor housing, menial positions, and the quality of segregated

---

[1] Gordon W. Allport, *The Nature of Prejudice* (Reading, Mass.: Addison-Wesley Publishing Company, 1954).

education among the Negroes. Many other forms are less overt and thus there is less awareness of them. Although the exclusion of a member of a minority group from voting would generally be recognized as discrimination, for example, not so readily regarded as discrimination is the fact that even though that individual has a vote it might be virtually impossible for one of his group to be elected to public office.

Discrimination is often thought of chiefly as a problem of the Negro, whereas many other minority groups are subject to it. Another misconception is to think of discrimination in the United States as existing chiefly in the South. Actually there is frequent discrimination in many forms against nearly all minority groups from coast to coast and from North to South. As it has been observed more than once, "The Northerner is all for equality for the Negro, provided it is in the South." In 1960 more than half the Negroes in the country lived outside the Confederate states, primarily in the Negro ghettos of the large cities of the North. As one writer has stated, the second half of the twentieth century will find solutions of Negro discrimination in the United States primarily hinging on the success of integration in the northern and western metropolises.[2] So far Negro citizens largely live as second-class citizens in these cities.

FORMS OF DISCRIMINATION

Social Conventions

Probably the most serious forms of discrimination for a society are those restrictions which affect the general social participation of minority groups. They include a wide range of customs involving social conventions, segregated living, and media of mass communication. All of them represent restrictions on the full participation of certain minority members in the society.

Certain social conventions may prohibit full social participation of members of minority groups. For example, they are often referred to as "nigger," "Injun," "kike," "darkey," "boy," or "uncle." Children learn to associate degrees of acceptance with such verbal symbols which are considered "bad." Such words become categories of ideas with emotional effect and are difficult to overcome by later relearning or by contact with the real objects.[3] Frequently members of minority groups are called by their first

---

[2] Harry S. Ashmore, *The Other Side of Jordan: Negroes Outside the South* (New York: W. W. Norton & Company, Inc., 1960).

[3] H. H. Smythe and Myrna Seidman, "Name Calling a Significant Factor in Human Relations," *Human Relations,* 6:71–77 (1958). Racial epithets are also referred to as "ethnophaulisms." See Erdman Palmore, "Ethnophaulisms and Ethnocentrism," *American Journal of Sociology,* 67:442–445 (1962).

names only and are not accorded such terms of formal address as "Mr." and "Mrs." Jokes about them also represent a subtle form of discrimination, for they tend to reinforce the social discrimination barrier.[4] Such characters as Rastus, Mandy, Abie, Ikie, and Mike are familiar examples of stereotypes.

Members of minority groups are often required by custom, not law, to use rear entrances, to remove their hats in the presence of a member of the dominant group, and to use the term "sir" freely in speech. Numerous social taboos further restrict social participation. In certain parts of the South, Negroes and whites do not eat together, swim together, or participate in nonprofessional sports together.

There may also be restrictions on entertaining members of minority groups or inviting them to dances, parties, picnics, or other informal activities. Even more prevalent are restrictions on such social relationships as dating, courtship, and marriage. In some states a member of a minority group seen in the company of a member of the majority group of the other sex may be arrested for disorderly conduct. Until 1967 there were more antimiscegenation laws (laws prohibiting marriage between certain races), than any other kind of discriminatory statute.[5] Such laws were in existence in sixteen states: Alabama, Arkansas, Delaware, Florida, Georgia, Kentucky, Louisiana, Mississippi, Missouri, North Carolina, Oklahoma, South Carolina, Tennessee, Texas, Virginia, and West Virginia. Several states have repealed such laws only within the last two decades: Oregon, 1951; Montana, 1953; North Dakota, 1955; Colorado and South Dakota, 1957, and Idaho, 1959. The California Supreme Court held its antimiscegenation law unconstitutional in 1948. Such laws not only prohibited Negro-white marriages but also often forbade the marriage of whites with persons of Asiatic ancestry, and they often declared the marriage void, with criminal penalties which may be quite severe. The couple might be ordered to leave the state, and their children might be declared illegitimate. The United States Supreme Court in a 1967 decision involving Virginia (Loving vs. Virginia, 388 U.S. 1967) declared all laws restricting marriage solely on the basis of race to be unconstitutional. They stated that such laws were in

---

[4] Milton Barron, "A Content Analysis of Intergroup Humor," *American Sociological Review,* 15:88–94 (1950). Also see John H. Burma, "Humor as a Technique in Race Conflict," *American Sociological Review,* 11:710–715 (1946); and Russell Middleton and John Mogland, "Humor in Negro and White Subcultures: A Study of Jokes among University Students," *American Sociological Review,* 24:61–69 (1959).

[5] Jack Greenberg, *Race Relations and American Law* (New York: Columbia University Press, 1960), p. 343. For a discussion of interracial marriage, see Albert I. Gordon, *Intermarriage: Interfaith, Interracial, Interethnic* (Boston: The Beacon Press, 1964).

violation of the equal protection clause of the Constitution and deprived persons of liberty without due process under the clauses of the Fourteenth Amendment.

Segregated Living

A large proportion of Negro and Spanish-speaking minority groups usually reside in segregated housing or slum areas. Housing, stores, motion-picture houses, taverns, and other facilities are often separate from the dominant group. One of the most difficult problems for a Negro, for example, is to try to live in a white neighborhood.[6] There is evidence that the degree of residential segregation between whites and nonwhites in both northern and southern cities has been increasing since the Civil War.[7] Older southern cities are less segregated, however, than newer ones.[8] Living in segregated areas has generally meant, for minority groups, poor housing conditions in cities or in shacks in rural areas.

Minority housing tends to be concentrated in old buildings in poor condition and where services and facilities are inadequate and rents are higher than those paid by comparable groups. It is common for several families to use the same toilet and kitchen facilities. The 1950 census showed that 60 percent of all urban Negro families lived in substandard dwellings which were either dilapidated or lacked proper sanitary facilities.[9] Only 20 percent of the white population lived in a comparable situation. Areas where Negroes live in Chicago, for example, which were built to have 20,000 persons per square mile, now have 90,000.[10]

Research in the fields of racial and ethnic prejudice has indicated three major effects of segregated housing in deteriorated areas: (1) it represents symbolically and in an observable form the subordination of certain peoples

---

[6] Although minorities live in segregated areas because of low income and for other reasons, property owners and real-estate boards seek to restrict the minority groups from living areas occupied by the majority group. The Supreme Court has outlawed restrictive covenants but the ruling has not put an end to their informal existence.

[7] Karl Taeuber, "Negro Residential Segregation," *Social Problems,* 12:42–50 (1964).

[8] Leo F. Schnore and Philip C. Evenson, "Segregation in Southern Cities," *American Journal of Sociology,* 72:58–67 (1966).

[9] See also, the Puerto Rican housing situation in New York City as described in Morris Eagle, "The Puerto Ricans in New York City," in Nathan Glazer and Davis McEntire, eds., *Studies in Housing and Minority Groups* (Berkeley: University of California Press, 1960), pp. 144–178.

[10] Harry J. Walker, *The Negro in American Life* (New York: Oxford Book Company, Inc., 1959), p. 22.

to those with more adequate housing; (2) when certain minority groups attempt to move into areas populated by a dominant group the resistance of the latter may increase tension and prejudice and even result in vandalism or race riots; and (3) it creates health problems. The exceptionally bad housing afforded Negroes may have an effect on their family system. Because of their economic situation, two or more Negro families may occupy the same set of rooms without any privacy. When the family lives separately, it may take in lodgers, a practice more frequent when the household is headed by a woman. These living arrangements may seriously affect family morale and sex patterns. "There is no way of knowing how many of the conflicts in Negro families are set off by the irritations caused by overcrowding people, who come home after a day of frustration and fatigue, to dingy and unhealthy living quarters." [11] In addition to poor physical surroundings, slum areas are characterized by high disease and infant mortality rates and by the presence of gambling, prostitution, and "honky-tonks," all of which create a difficult environment in which to raise families.[12]

Segregated living areas also interfere with free lines of conversation and social participation between minority and majority groups. One writer has thus described this restriction on social participation in reference to the Spanish-speaking people in Texas:

> It has been my observation that everywhere in the state the Spanish-speaking and Anglo groups have trouble in communicating with one another. It is an oversimplified but nonetheless accurate statement of the situation to say that Latins tend to talk mainly to other Latins and Anglos to other Anglos. There are many reasons why this is so. One is the "we" and "they" identification which I have already mentioned. All of us feel more comfortable with people like ourselves than we do with those we consider different. Another is the physical separation of the two groups resulting from separate residential and business sections, and, heretofore, separate schools. Still another is occupational separation which comes about because the Latins are channeled into relatively few occupations in which they make up the numerically dominant group. But whatever the reasons, it is an observable fact that, by and large, Spanish-speaking people tend to associate with other Spanish-speaking, English-speaking tend to associate with other English-speaking. There are few organizations in any community with mixed membership, few in which members of the two groups have an opportunity to talk across ethnic lines about matters of

---

[11] E. Franklin Frazier, *The Negro in the United States* (rev. ed.; New York: The Macmillan Company, 1957), p. 636.

[12] See, for example, Richard Hammer, "Report from a Spanish Harlem 'Fortress,' " in Bernard E. Segal, ed., *Racial and Ethnic Relations: Selected Readings* (New York: Thomas Y. Crowell Company, 1966), pp. 324–330.

common concern. There are Anglo churches and Latin churches; Anglo Parent-Teachers Associations and Latin Parent-Teachers Associations; Anglo fellowship organizations and Latin fellowship organizations; Anglo veterans' groups and Latin veterans' groups.[13]

Minority group members whose education and income have improved often find it difficult to move into areas of better housing in suburban areas. Landlords will often not rent to them, nor will real-estate agents sell them houses. In addition, the residents will often not welcome them. Although Jewish discrimination in housing is less a problem in suburbia than it was ten years ago and several hundred thousand Jews have moved into these areas, discrimination is still a problem.[14] A 1957 survey of the policies of the real-estate agents in suburban Detroit showed that one third indicated they did not wish to sell or rent to Jews and discriminated against them in one way or another.[15] The living situation in suburbia is partly a product of anti-Semitic attitudes and partly a product of Jews' having their closest friendships among other Jews of the same community, class, synagogue, and organizational interests. Similar discrimination against the Japanese-Americans, an economically successful, highly educated, upwardly mobile group, is a constant source of unhappiness, irritation, and deprivation.[16]

Media of Mass Communication

An important form of exclusion of minorities from participation in society is their relative omission from the media of mass communication. Negroes, Spanish-speaking people, or those of Oriental descent are infrequently cast as major actors in motion pictures and television. Magazine fiction also reflects majority and minority status. In an analysis made some years ago of about two hundred stories, 84 percent of the characters were identified simply as Americans, which usually implied white, Protestant, English-speaking, and Anglo-Saxon.[17] Of nine hundred identifiable characters, only sixteen were Negroes and ten were Jews. Articles about Negro

---

[13] Lyle Saunders. Address Delivered at the National Convention of the League of United American Citizens, San Antonio, June 11, 1949. (Report on the Study of Spanish–Speaking People, University of Texas.)

[14] Albert I. Gordon, *Jews in Suburbia* (Boston: The Beacon Press, 1959).

[15] Anti-Defamation League, *Reports on Social, Employment, Educational, and Housing Discrimination,* Vol. II, No. 5 (1959).

[16] Harry H. L. Kitano, "Housing of Japanese-Americans in the San Francisco Bay Area," in Glazer and McEntire, pp. 195–196.

[17] Bernard Berelson and Patricia J. Salter, "Majority and Minority Americans: An Analysis of Magazine Fiction," *Public Opinion Quarterly,* 10:168–190 (1946).

citizens who are not celebrities or about Negro social gatherings, weddings, and other activities seldom appear in widely read newspapers, and advertisements in magazines and on television seldom picture Negro families or individuals, except for an occasional Negro singer or athlete.[18]

Most school textbooks contain little deliberate bias, but there is often subtle discrimination through the omission of certain materials dealing with minorities. By omission and commission the written history of the Negro has helped to intensify the pattern of discrimination. The history of the United States, at least in school textbooks, is largely the history of the majority group.[19] Although the situation is improving, this still constitutes a basic form of discrimination. After studying a number of American history textbooks, Irving Sloan reported that the following facts were neglected or underplayed:

> that a high degree of civilization existed in Africa prior to the slave trade, such as the kingdoms of Ghana, Mali, and Songhay;
>
> that the first Negroes were here with Spanish explorers, so that their presence in America precedes the English colonists;
>
> that the Negroes who first arrived in English America came as indentured servants, not as slaves;
>
> that slavery as an institution was degrading to masters and slaves alike;
>
> that Negroes made significant contributions to the wars fought by the United States, including 200,000 who fought on the Union side in the Civil War;
>
> that the Reconstruction Period was not as evil as painted and "illiterate, money-grasping ex-slaves" did not run the South during this period;
>
> that between Reconstruction and the 1954 Supreme Court decision the American Negro did not disappear, as is the usual impression in textbooks; and
>
> that the civil rights movement should not be explained only in the light of this 1954 decision and the 1964 civil rights acts. Very few of the texts included in this study trace the economic, social, and political abuses endured by the Negro in both the North and South through the long years of his "emancipation." [20]

---

[18] Consequently, some two hundred Negro newspapers and magazines are published whose contents, including advertisements, are almost exclusively Negro and whose advertisements usually show Negroes. One magazine, *Ebony,* has a circulation of over a million.

[19] Report of the Committee on the Study of Teaching Material in Integroup Relations (Howard E. Wilson, director), *Intergroup Relations in Teaching Materials* (Washington, D.C.: American Council on Education, 1949).

[20] "Have U.S. History Texts Hurt Negroes?" *Wisconsin State Journal,* December 11, 1966; sec. 2, p. 5.

Health and Life Expectancy

Minority groups, such as Negroes, Spanish-speaking peoples, and Indians, generally have a higher death rate than has the white population in the United States. The higher death rate among Negroes is due to several factors, including poor health practices, insufficient medical care, poor living conditions, and their low economic level. In 1956 the death rate for whites was 9.3 (number of deaths per 1000 population) while the nonwhite rate was 10.1. In 1960 the nonwhites had a life expectancy of 61 to 66 years, or six to eight years less than that of whites. In 1900 the nonwhite life expectancy was between 32 and 35 years, or 16 years less than the whites. In the sixty years the nonwhite increase was twice that of the whites, indicating that "corrosive poverty and inadequate medical care were the reasons for his short life span in the past," and that the diseases affecting the nonwhites were unnecessary, treatable, and preventable.[21]

The higher death rate for the nonwhite population, which consists chiefly of Negroes, is predominantly due to communicable diseases and to accidents, primarily in industry rather than to accidents involving a motor vehicle. One example illustrates this differential. In 1959 in the United States approximately 30 percent of all deaths from pneumonia and influenza were Negroes. Better hospital and health facilities are an obvious need to correct these conditions.

Exclusion from Organized Groups

Nearly all organized groups have certain criteria for membership, such as occupation and education, and many persons who do not have these qualifications may often consider them discriminatory. "Discriminatory" will be restricted, however, to those members of racial, ethnic, and religious groups who are still not permitted to join even when they possess the necessary occupational or educational qualifications. Such discrimination restricts communication between groups and makes segregation seem "natural." "Restrictions and freedoms for intergroup contact and communication depend upon prevailing community definitions of what is appropriate and acceptable. These definitions emerge from shared social experience. Once interlocked into common expectations and interests, they set the boundaries for any given time, place, and situation for intergroup contact. But the experience of interaction, when it does occur, may in turn reinforce or modify

---

[21] Thomas F. Pettigrew, *A Profile of the Negro American* (Princeton, N.J.: D. Van Nostrand Company, Inc., 1964), p. 99.

the beliefs and norms that guide intergroup relations at the level where one man speaks to another." [22]

Many clubs and organizations, including organizations of a recreational nature, practice discrimination. Private golf clubs, for example, generally exclude Negroes and often Jews, or keep the number of the latter to a few. A survey of 250 cities in 1954 showed that in 82 percent of all northern cities and 75 percent of all southern cities the Rotary clubs neither permitted Negroes nor had established segregated clubs.[23] There was little difference in city size. Forty-two percent of northern cities over 100,000 made no provision for Negroes. Less than four out of ten southern local councils of churches were integrated. The YMCA and the YWCA had largely separate organizations in the South. In the Community Chest 29 percent of southern cities with populations over 100,000 had separate organizations and 21 percent under 100,000 had no provisions for Negro participation. In 79 percent of the cities Negroes belonged to segregated Masonic lodges. All American Legion posts in large southern cities were segregated.

A 1961 survey of 1152 social clubs in forty-six states and the District of Columbia found that 781, or 67 percent, practice religious discrimination. Of the 781 discriminating clubs, 691 excluded or limited Jewish membership, and 90 were Jewish clubs which excluded or limited Christian membership. The 1152 clubs represent a total membership of approximately 700,000 persons. Particular attention in the survey was paid to those clubs which were evaluated as enjoying maximum prestige in their communities. Of the 693 top American clubs, 60 percent practice religious discrimination, and of these discriminatory clubs more than 90 percent discriminate against Jews. The survey concluded: "If the thesis is accepted that many prestige clubs are factors in the power structures which influence greatly the political and economic life of the community, then the fact that 60 percent of the prestige clubs of the United States discriminate against Jews has serious implications for the Jewish group." [24] It was also pointed out that this type of discrimination against Jews is far greater than the levels of discrimination against them in other areas, such as education, employment, housing, and public accommodations.

---

[22] Robin M. Williams, Jr., *Strangers Next Door: Ethnic Relations in American Communities* (Englewood Cliffs, N.J.: Prentice-Hall, Inc. 1964), p. 141.

[23] Williams, pp. 122–124.

[24] "A Study of Religious Discrimination by Social Clubs," *Rights* (Publication of the Anti-Defamation League of B'nai B'rith), 4:83–86 (1962). Also see N. C. Belth, ed., *Barriers: Patterns of Discrimination against Jews* (New York: Anti-Defamation League of B'nai B'rith, 1958).

Although the situation is changing, many national college social fraternities and sororities exclude from membership, either implicitly or explicitly, those who are non-Christian or non-Caucasian. The exclusion may
be stated in the constitutions; if there are no constitutional provisions, the
exclusion is just as real—students from these minority groups are not asked
to join.[25] Consequently, this is one reason why Jewish and Negro students
have separate fraternities and sororities. Several universities within the past
few years have taken a strong position against this discrimination, which is
becoming a subject of frequent discussion among fraternities and sororities.
Occasionally a fraternity or sorority may defy the national organization
and pledge a member of a minority group.

Many professional fraternities and associations either exclude certain
minorities from membership or discriminate against them. In 1949 the
American Bar Association had only 13 Negroes among its 41,000 members.
Several national law fraternities exclude Jewish students as well. The
American Medical Association and the American Dental Association has
no national policy, but leaves the question of discrimination up to local
groups, with the result that many qualified Negro doctors and dentists do
not belong; hence Negroes have their own separate national medical,
dental, and legal associations. Even where members of minorities are accepted in the organization they are seldom elected or appointed to positions
in the organization they are seldom elected or appointed to positions of
leadership. In 1949 the American Medical Association, for example, named
a Negro to its policy-making body for the first time in its 103-year history.

About 98 percent of all Negroes attend exclusively Negro churches.
Consequently, some Negro church organizations are very large, as is the
African Methodist Church. Other Negroes may belong to separate Negro
religious sects. Some of this separation is the choice of the Negroes and is
a result of other forms of segregation, principally segregation in housing.
In other instances separation in worship is the result of a church's not
allowing Negro attendance, failing to encourage it, or requiring separate
seating arrangements. Various church groups have opposed these discriminatory practices and some have made a positive effort to end them.

The exclusion of minorities from formal organizations hinders general
social communication with other groups. It may also mean exclusion from
groups with high social status and consequently the denial of opportunities
for "prestige" membership in the society. This exclusion often indirectly
results in serious economic discrimination in certain occupations. Membership in certain social and professional fraternities, and even clubs, may

---

[25] See Alfred McClung Lee, *Fraternities without Brotherhood* (Boston: The
Beacon Press, 1955).

mean associations and contacts which may furnish a definite business or professional advantage.[26]

Public Accommodations

Discrimination also takes the form of *informally* denying minorities access to certain hotels, motels, resorts, and the like throughout most of the South as well as in parts of the North. Claims may be made that accommodations are unavailable, that the reservation was lost, or that the price may be increased. Throughout the United States many restaurants, particularly the self-styled better ones, often discourage the patronage of Negroes, American Indians, or Spanish-speaking persons. Discrimination may be accomplished by discouraging admittance to such persons, by asking them to leave, by refusing or delaying service, or by serving them unpalatable food. In the South Negroes may find that they are unwelcome at a theater, a concert, or a motion-picture or drive-in theater, or they are permitted to occupy only the least desirable section. Otherwise they must attend motion-picture theaters patronized largely by Negroes. Even though against the law, in the South and sometimes in the North, parks, playgrounds, swimming pools, and beaches may be in fact operated on a segregated basis. This discrimination is not limited to Negroes, for the Mexicans and Mexican-Americans in the Southwest may encounter similar difficulties.

Discrimination in vacation resorts may exist for many minority groups, including Jews, even where the practice is illegal. A 1957 national survey of 933 resort establishments found that 22.9 percent clearly discriminated against Jews.[27] Even where discrimination is illegal, members of certain minority groups even encounter difficulty in finding hotel or motel accommodations on the highways. The denial of the opportunity to take a vacation in a particular area or place because of an individual's or a family's race, religion, or ethnic background is a severe type of discrimination.

---

[26] "The exclusion of Jews from 'Greek letter' fraternities and sororities parallels their exclusion from social clubs and is similarly motivated [for social power]. It is silly to speak of college fraternities as though they were the end-product of some instinctive process by which like-minded individuals are sorted into special categories. Freshmen are rushed for the most specific and tangible reasons: social standing, wealth, family connections, special talents, athletic ability, and so forth. Fraternities, like clubs in later years, are the pools and generators of social power and prestige: those with it enter them, those entering them, heighten their potency. Social alliances formed in college naturally tend to carry over into adult life."— Carey McWilliams, "Does Social Discrimination Really Matter?" *Commentary*, 4:411 (1947).

[27] Belth, pp. 37–120.

Educational Facilities

The accumulated knowledge of a culture is principally transmitted through its educational institutions, and discrimination in the extent and quality of any group's education may affect the cultural adjustment, social status, and personal enjoyment of its members. As groups, Negroes, Spanish-speaking people, and Indians receive less education than members of the majority group, the dollar cost of their education is less, the quality of their school buildings is poorer, and their teachers are often less educated and more poorly paid than other teachers. Negro children in many parts of the South, as well as children of Spanish-speaking migratory workers, have fewer required days in school per year than do white children. A 1963 study of the schools on the Dakota Indian Reservation found many parallels to the situation existing in Negro urban slum areas. Scholastic achievement was low and dropouts were high, the major loyalties were to the peer group, and the children were taught by teachers who saw Indian children as inadequately prepared, uncultured offspring of an alien and ignorant folk.[28]

The Negro situation has improved considerably, and even more can be expected in the future because of the Supreme Court decision of 1954 ordering the end of segregation in education. At the time of that decision seventeen southern and border states, in addition to the District of Columbia, had complete segregation in their elementary and secondary schools, with the exception of a few communities with only a few Negro children to educate. Four states outside this region, Arizona, Kansas, New Mexico, and Wyoming, allowed some local segregation contrary to law. Sixteen states prohibited by law any segregation, although not all of them enforced these statutes. Eleven other northern and western states had no laws dealing with this matter.

The present status of school segregation-desegregation in the southern and border states as of 1966–1967, twelve years after the Supreme Court decision, is shown in Table 17.1. In six states there was between 50 and 100 percent integration, in six states there was 10 to 50 percent integration, and in the five states of Louisiana, Mississippi, Alabama, Georgia, and South Carolina there was only 2 to 10 percent integration.

As of December 1966, in 11 southern states an average of only 12.5 percent of Negro schoolchildren were attending schools with less than 95 percent Negro enrollment, the range being from 2.4 percent in Alabama to 34.6 percent in Texas.[29] At the same time in the same states, 75.6 per-

---

[28] See "Formal Education in an American Indian Community," supplement to *Social Problems,* Vol. 11, Spring 1964.

[29] This figure was, however, twice the percentage (6 percent) at the same time in 1965.

cent of the Negro schoolchildren, or 2,571,540, were enrolled in all-Negro schools.

In the five border states, as of December 1966, an average of 45.1 percent of the Negro pupils were attending schools with less than 95 percent Negro pupils, the range being from 40.5 percent in both Maryland and Oklahoma to 88.5 percent in Kentucky. In the border states there were only 32.2 percent of the Negro pupils attending all-Negro schools.

Residential segregation in large cities generally means that, in both the North and the South, many schools are in fact segregated. Because

TABLE 17.1 **Percentages of Negro Pupils Attending All-Negro Schools and Those Attending Schools with Less than 95 Percent Negro Pupils, December 1966**

	Negro pupils attending schools less than 95% Negro		*Negro pupils attending schools 100% Negro*	
	%	NUMBER	%	NUMBER
TOTAL 17 States	17.3	589,620	75.6	2,571,540
Southern States	12.5	363,290	83.1	2,410,000
Alabama	2.4	6,570	95.3	260,900
Arkansas	14.5	17,140	83.4	98,650
Florida	14.7	41,120	79.2	221,550
Georgia	6.6	22,610	90.1	308,450
Louisiana	2.6	6,850	96.5	254,050
Mississippi	2.6	6,840	96.8	254,700
North Carolina	12.8	44,850	84.4	295,650
South Carolina	4.9	12,120	94.0	232,550
Tennessee	21.9	40,600	68.3	126,550
Texas	34.6	117,050	52.7	178,250
Virginia	20.0	47,540	75.2	178,700
Border States	45.1	226,330	32.2	161,540
Delaware	84.8	20,440	0	0
Kentucky	88.5	38,230	11.5	4,980
Maryland	40.5	88,980	36.0	79,150
Missouri	26.7	34,710	35.8	46,540
Oklahoma	40.5	24,950	44.3	27,290
West Virginia	83.4	19,020	15.7	3,580

SOURCE: U. S. Office of Education National Center for Educational Statistics, December 9, 1966.

FIGURE 17.1   Percentage of Negroes in Schools with Whites.

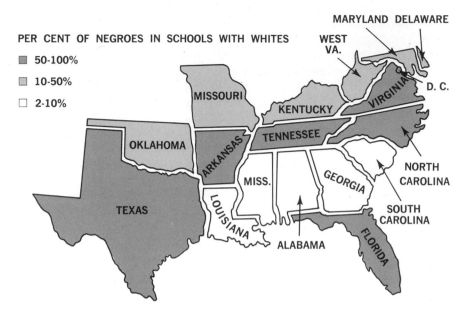

SOURCE: *A Statistical Summary, State by State, of School Segregation-Desegregation in the Southern and Border Area from 1954 to the Present,* (Nashville: Southern Education Reporting Service, February, 1967).

pupils are required to attend schools in the neighborhoods in which they live, the schools in Negro areas will virtually have all-Negro pupils. Even Negro teachers are generally assigned in the North to schools located in the Negro areas. In 1959 the New York City Board of Education reported that 56.7 percent of the students in elementary schools throughout the city were attending segregated schools, defined as 90 percent or more from the same race.[30] This situation had improved, however, but until residential segregation is markedly changed, segregated schooling is likely to affect a large proportion of Negro students in northern and southern cities.

The effects of segregated schooling have been amply demonstrated through special studies made of pupils in desegregated schools. In Washington, D.C., and elsewhere it was found that when Negro students were integrated with whites, their educational level, in many cases, was generally inferior.

The majority of Negro college students, either in the North or in the South, still attend Negro colleges. In 1967 in the eleven southern states there were 789,230 students attending predominantly white colleges and

---

[30] Ashmore, p. 122.

universities. The total Negro enrollment in these schools was 20,788. In Alabama colleges, for example, there were only 295 Negroes; in Arkansas, 303; in Mississippi, 131; and in South Carolina, 169. In addition, there were 39,612 Negro students attending 28 predominantly Negro colleges. In the border states and the District of Columbia, 34,890 Negro students were attending predominantly white colleges and universities, with a total enrollment of 289,264. In the combined southern and border states, there were 1,078,494 students enrolled in predominantly white colleges and universities, while there were 85,362 Negroes enrolled—34,890 in predominantly white schools and 50,472 in predominantly Negro colleges and universities.[31]

In a 1957 study, southern Negro college students attending an interracial northern university placed general social participation (Negro fraternities, sororities, dances, and so on) as the greatest asset of their college.[32] On the other hand, they felt that its greatest handicap was the inferiority of their college as measured by reputation, faculty, and their own performance at the northern university.

In general, there is an increasing improvement in Negro education. The Census Bureau reported that a total of 28 percent of Negro adults twenty-five and over in the United States had completed four years of high school or more by 1966, as compared with only 20 percent in 1960.

Employment, Business, and the Military

Members of the Negro, Indian, and Spanish-speaking minorities are disproportionately employed in such unskilled or semiskilled jobs as common labor, farm labor, housework, gardening, fruit picking, and shoeshining. The subordination of Negro minority groups brings definite economic advantages to the white groups, as one study of differential earnings has shown.[33] About Spanish-speaking persons, Saunders, for example, has remarked: "If one were to attempt to characterize the condition of the Spanish-speaking Texans, he would be forced to say that, in general, and for nearly any index of socioeconomic status that might be devised, the Spanish-speaking people are found to occupy a less desirable position that the Anglos or the population as a whole."[34]

---

[31] *A Statistical Summary, State by State, of School Segregation-Desegregation in the Southern and Border Area from 1954 to the Present* (Nashville: Southern Education Reporting Service, February, 1967), p. 3.

[32] Marshall B. Clinard and Donald L. Noel, "Role Behavior of Students from Negro Colleges in a Non-segregated University Situation," *Journal of Negro Education,* 27:182–188 (1958).

[33] Norval D. Glenn, "White Gains from Negro Subordination," *Social Problems,* 14:159–178 (1966).

[34] Saunders, pp. 7–8.

Most unions have removed the constitutional restrictions that formerly barred Negroes. Some unions, however, still discriminate against Negroes by tacit agreement or through segregated auxiliary status.[35] Although no constitutional provisions affecting Negroes exist, it is difficult for a Negro, for example, to become admitted to full membership in a union as a carpenter, painter, bricklayer, or plasterer in many areas of the North and the South. He may sometimes, however, become a member of a subordinate affiliated union. It is equally hard for a Negro in the North or the South to become an electrician or a plumber. Some unions put Negroes in a sort of Jim Crow status by allowing them to pay dues but to have little voice in the organization. This discriminatory situation has improved with the advent of the industrial union, the short labor supply in some trades from the beginning of World War II, the pressure of state fair employment practices commissions and the FEPC laws, and the Civil Rights Act of 1964. In 1960 Negro union members numbered 1.5 million.[36] The average wages of nonwhite males had increased in the past twenty years from 41 to 58 percent of what white workers get. In this same period the percentage of Negroes in professional and skilled work doubled.

These improvements have not necessarily meant complete equality for the Negro workers, however, for one of the most persistent forms of discrimination in employment involves opportunities for advancement.[37] In 1966, as in 1964, nonwhites who make up 10.8 percent of the labor force, still provided 40 percent of the private household workers, 25 percent of the

---

[35] George E. Simpson and J. Milton Yinger, *Racial and Cultural Minorities* (3d ed.; New York: Harper & Row, Publishers, 1965), pp. 260–281. In 1967 Roy Wilkins of the NAACP attacked the widespread union discrimination against Negroes, citing examples that in Cleveland in 1966 of 1258 electrical workers in one local union, only two were Negroes; in a plumbers local of 1483 members, three were Negroes, pipefitters local with 1319 had one Negro, and a sheetmetal workers union of 1077 had 45 Negroes. Reported in the *Wisconsin State Journal,* December 19, 1967.

[36] Ashmore, p. 78.

[37] Robert C. Weaver, "Negro Labor Since 1929," *Journal of Negro History,* 35:20–38 (1950). Also see Gary S. Becker, *The Economics of Discrimination* (Chicago: University of Chicago Press, 1957). Even if racial discrimination in the job market were eliminated it would not eliminate racial differences in occupations immediately, since there are broad societal processes operating to the disadvantage of Negroes. Racial differences in occupation would decline sharply after only one generation in which discrimination was absent, although several generations would be necessary before parity was reached. Stanley Lieberson and Glenn V. Fuguitt, "Negro-White Occupational Differences in the Absence of Discrimination," *American Journal of Sociology,* 73:188–201 (1967).

nonfarm laborers, but "only 2.8 percent of our managers, officials, and proprietors." [38] The United States Equal Employment Opportunity Commission reported in January 1967 that in 406 textile mills in North and South Carolina more Negroes were being hired but that fewer were being promoted to other than menial jobs. Of 10,211 persons employed as officials or managers of textile mills in the Carolinas, 11 were Negroes. Of 2338 workers designated as professionals, 3 were Negroes. Of 2104 technicians, 13 were Negroes. The largest Negro representation in white-collar occupations was among office and clerical workers, where 149 out of 11,784 were Negroes.[39] Discrimination may affect promotion to engineer, supervisor, foreman, salesman, buyer, or executive.[40]

Negro employment in the federal government, has shown some gain although the gains have not been increasing markedly in the last few years. According to a survey conducted by the Civil Service Commission in 1966, there were 109,658 Negroes employed in the so-called white-collar occupations, as compared with 106,658 in 1965. Of these, 31,205, or 10.1 percent of the total, were employed in grades earning $5331 to $9183 a year, as compared with 9.6 percent in 1965. In the salary bracket with earnings of $10,270 to $25,890 there were 3363 Negroes, or 1.6 percent of the total employees in those earning categories, as compared with 2815, or 1.3 percent, in 1965.[41]

The transformation of the armed forces of the United States from a totally segregated to a fully integrated institution is an important achievement in planned social change in race relations. It occurred in a fairly brief period of time. Negroes had generally served in the Army as special all-Negro units, usually with white officers. In 1948 President Truman issued an executive order abolishing racial segregation in the armed forces and by the middle 1950s this was largely an accomplished fact. Variations still exist in the various services in the degree of distribution of Negro personnel, the Army, the Air Force, and the Marine Corps having the most and the Navy the least. This desegregation has been accompanied by more favorable attitudes toward integration on the part of white soldiers and by improved performance on the part of Negroes. Differences in combat service have

---

[38] *The New York Times,* May 5, 1967.

[39] See *The New York Times,* Jan. 9, 1967, p. 95.

[40] The Ford Foundation in December 1966 announced a series of grants to help Negroes play a larger part in both small business and large industry. One grant of $300,000, to be matched by industry, was to train up to 100 Negroes yearly in business administration and to prepare more Negroes for expanding executive opportunities in businesses.

[41] As reported in *The New York Times,* Jan. 10, 1967.

been largely eliminated.[42] Racial separation, however, is the general off-duty rule both in the United States and in service abroad. More careers at enlisted levels are becoming avenues of Negro mobility, but the proportion of Negro officers in all the services is far less than the proportion of Negroes in the enlisted ranks. Although in 1964 the proportion of Negro enlisted men in the armed forces was 13.4 in the Army, 10.0 in the Air Force, 8.7 in the Marine Corps, and 5.8 in the Navy, comparable percentages in the officer corps were 3.4, 1.5, 0.4, and 0.3. There was only one Negro general in the Air Force, none in the Army, and no admirals in the Navy. In fact, in 1962 the first Negro was appointed to command a warship. The proportion of Negroes in the officer corps, particularly in the higher ranks, is a product in part of the disproportionate number who have been through the service academies. Although West Point was established in 1802, the first Negro was graduated in 1877; five had been graduated by 1942; twenty-two by 1953; and thirty-eight through 1960. During the year 1959–1960, nine were attending the Military Academy, and two were graduated in 1961. The first Negro was graduated from Annapolis in 1949, the year in which the first Japanese-American entered the Naval Academy. From 1949 through 1959, fourteen Negroes were graduated from the Naval Academy, and three were enrolled at the Air Force Academy.

Suffrage and Public Office

Although some difficulties still exist in Negroes' exercise of the right to vote, there has been a tremendous growth in their voting during the past two decades. These advances have resulted from improved intergroup relations, federal and state legislation, and various decisions of the United States Supreme Court. Supreme Court decisions outlawed a number of the various devices which had earlier been passed to prevent the exercise of the ballot. One of these devices, the so-called grandfather clause, stated that one's grandfather had to have been capable of voting; another, the exclusive "white primary" provisions, outlawed in 1944, kept a Negro from joining the Democratic party and thus virtually prevented him in some places from casting a meaningful vote. The Southern Regional Council reported in 1967 that Negro voter registration in the South had increased 30 percent, to 2.8 million, from 1964 to 1967.[43] The power of this increasing access to, and use of, their votes have had significant influences in local, state, and national elections in the United States.

Even if all minorities could vote freely, a wide and significant area of

---

[42] Charles C. Moskos, Jr., "Racial Integration in the Armed Forces," *American Journal of Sociology,* 72:132–148 (1966).

[43] As reported in *The New York Times,* January 9, 1968.

discrimination would exist if qualified members of minority groups could not be freely appointed to important governmental positions or run for political office without the handicap of discrimination. Major political positions are largely held by the older native white stock, and a relatively minor role in national and state politics is played by millions of citizens from minority groups. Within recent years, however, Negroes have been appointed as directors of large state agencies in such states as Illinois and New York.

Change in Negro political power by 1966 was beginning to be apparent, although it was still far short of full participation. There was one Negro Cabinet member; one Negro senator, the first since 1875; six Negro congressmen (out of a total of 435); eight federal judges, four United States Ambassadors; the Solicitor General, and a number of other high-level federal and state appointments. In the 1966 elections Negro candidates captured over 300 elective offices, including nearly 100 in state legislatures, several of which were in the South. Many had run for elective office, and Negroes were elected in the South to important local offices. The first Negro sheriff since the 1870s was elected in Macon County, Alabama. In 1966 ten Negroes were members of the Georgia Legislature. At the local and state levels of government there has been increasing recognition of the right of minority members to be elected or freely appointed to public office. Negroes are occupying an increasingly significant place in the local political communities, being appointed or elected to school boards in several southern cities, serving on the state boards of education, and securing places on city councils. In 1967 the first Negro was appointed to the Supreme Court, the first Negroes were elected mayors of major cities, Cleveland and Gary, and the first Negro in recent times was elected to the Mississippi legislature.

Administration of Justice

It is a generally established fact that Negroes, as well as Spanish-speaking people, are, on the whole, arrested, tried, convicted, and imprisoned more often than others who commit comparable offenses.[44] This does not mean that minority group members who live in the slums of large cities do not actually have a higher delinquency and crime rate; what is being referred to here is discrimination in legal processing for an offense.[45] Certain minorities appear to be more frequently subjected to the illegal "third

---

[44] See, for example, Edwin M. Lemert and Judy Rosberg, "The Administration of Justice to Minority Groups in Los Angeles County, 1948" (Publications in Culture and Society, Vol. II, No. 1; Berkeley: University of California Press, 1948).

[45] Wayne R. LaFave, *Arrest: The Decision to Take a Suspect into Custody* (Boston: Little, Brown & Company, 1965).

degree" and other forms of police intimidation. A Negro or a Spanish-American offender may be dealt with more harshly by a judge or jury than will a member of a majority group. A study covering the period 1945–1965 showed that a Negro convicted of raping a white woman in the South had close to a 50 percent chance of receiving a death sentence, whereas someone convicted of raping a woman of his own race stood a 14 percent chance.[46] Part of this situation in the past has stemmed from discrimination in the appointment of members of minority groups to police forces and the courts or in their limited service on juries.

Mob lynchings rarely occur today, but they were once common. From 1900 through 1960, altogether 1992 persons had been lynched. In the 1890s, when the population was only about 40 percent of what it is today, lynchings averaged 154 a year; in the 1930s, 13 a year; and in the 1940s, 4 a year. In most recent years no lynchings have been recorded. Some attempted lynchings still occur, and it has been estimated by Tuskegee Institute that lynchings of about 200 Negroes were prevented from 1937 to 1946.[47] Although mob lynchings and lynching attempts have decreased markedly, there has been an increase in the flagrant and brutal killings of Negro as well as of white civil rights workers; the total number of these victims is not large, however.

Race riots involving Negroes and whites have occurred in several large cities, including Chicago in 1919 and Detroit and New York during World War II.[48] Within recent years a new type of Negro rioting, involving property destruction and looting in their own communities, has occurred in many cities. In the 1965 riot in the Watts section of Los Angeles alone, 34 persons were killed, 1032 injured, and 3952 arrested. Some 600 buildings were damaged, and some $40 million in property destroyed. "The principal objects of attack were most often just those people or institutions, insofar as they were within reach, that the rioters thought of as being their principal oppressors: policemen and white passers-by, or white-owned commercial establishments, especially those that charged high prices, dealt in inferior merchandise or employed harsh credit policies. Loan offices were a favorite target. Homes, schools, churches, and libraries were, by and large, let alone."[49] The U.S.

---

[46] Reported in *The New York Times,* Nov. 30, 1966.

[47] President's Committee on Civil Rights, *To Secure These Rights* (New York: Simon and Schuster, Inc., 1947), p. 24.

[48] See Stanley Lieberson and Arnold R. Silverman, "The Precipitants and Underlying Conditions of Race Riots," *American Sociological Review,* 30:887–898 (1965).

[49] *The Challange of Crime in a Free Society,* A Report by the President's Commission on Law Enforcement and Administration of Justice (Washington, D.C.: Government Printing Office, 1967), p. 37.

Senate Permanent Investigations Subcommittee reported on November 1, 1967 that a survey of 129 cities showed that in racial disturbances from 1965–1967 in the United States, 130 persons were killed in 76 cities, 3623 were wounded, and that there was a total property loss estimated at $210.6 million. The Committee reported that there were 28,939 arrests which resulted in 5434 convictions. Twelve police officers were killed, and 1199 were wounded.

> Although once underway some riots were exploited by agitators, they were not deliberate in the sense that they were planned at the outset; the best evidence is that they were spontaneous outbursts, set off more often than not by some quite ordinary and proper action by a policeman. They were deliberate in the sense that they were directed, to an extent that varied from city to city, against specific targets.[50]

Jewish cemeteries and synagogues have been defaced. In the first two months of 1960 there was an epidemic of 323 anti-Semitic acts directed against Jews in the United States.[51] About half of these acts involved the paintings of a Nazi swastika; other acts included, in order, anti-Jewish slogans, threats, physical damage, bombings, Nazi flags, cross burnings, and ambiguous markings.[52]

THE NATURE OF PREJUDICE

Thus far minority groups have been described and the extent and nature of the discrimination against them analyzed. To complete this discussion the basic sources of prejudice toward minority groups must be understood. As it is used here, "prejudice" is a negative emotional attitude of prejudgment toward a group of people. The "prejudgment" aspect of this definition means that prejudices exist only when they cannot be changed by new knowledge.[53] It is the quality of prejudgment and rejection of contrary evidence which indicates the emotional nature of prejudice.

---

[50] *The Challenge of Crime in a Free Society*, p. 37.

[51] David Caplovitz and Candace Rogers, *Swastika, 1960: The Epidemic of Anti-Semitic Vandalism in America* (New York: Anti-Defamation League of B'nai B'rith, 1961).

[52] Not all violence and acts of vandalism have been directed against Negroes and Jews. One such example was the Los Angeles "Zoot Suit Riot" in 1943, which involved brutality to young adult Mexican-Americans. See Carey McWilliams, *North from Mexico* (Philadelphia: J. B. Lippincott Company, 1948), pp. 244–258. Also see Ralph H. Turner and Samuel J. Surace, "Zoot-Suiters and Mexicans: Symbols in Crowd Behavior," *American Journal of Sociology*, 62:14–20 (1956).

[53] Allport, p. 9.

Although prejudice and discrimination are generally associated, one can have prejudice without showing it by discrimination, either because there is no opportunity or because other attitudes may prevent the free expression of prejudice. Also, some people practice discrimination without necessarily being prejudiced, simply because the situation may call for it. This is particularly true in parts of the South where a relatively unprejudiced person may still generally follow the discriminatory patterns. In fact, there are some five possible relations of prejudice and discrimination:

1. There can be prejudice without discrimination.
2. There can be discrimination without prejudice.
3. Discrimination can be among the causes of prejudice.
4. Prejudice can be among the causes of discrimination.
5. Probably most frequently they are mutually reinforcing.[54]

In fact, as Rose has indicated, the history and process of change in intergroup relations involving discrimination and segregation may be quite distinct from prejudice.[55] Since 1940, for example, intergroup relations between majority and minority groups have drastically changed, but prejudices have not always done so. The explanation appears to be in the differences in the legal, economic, political, and social forces that are operating.

Thus it can readily be seen that prejudice is not a simple concept. It is a complex social psychological state involving various degrees of negative attitudes toward minority groups. One does not, for example, have a single attitude toward Negroes, Jews, and foreigners, but one's opinions about them vary with respect to their social, political, and economic rights and aspirations. The same individual, too, may hold different kinds and degrees of prejudice toward the various minority groups.[56]

Prejudice is not limited to members of the majority group. Minority groups also have their prejudices. Negroes in America may be prejudiced against whites. Some white people may be prejudiced against Indians, but the latter also have strong dislikes for many whites. Many Jews are prejudiced against gentiles, and some Jews even have anti-Semitic attitudes toward other Jews.

Prejudices are not clearly formulated sets of interwoven attitudes and opinions. Moreover, prejudices exist in various degrees and are likely to be expressed in interaction in group situations where no minority members are present. Unless responses are later directed into some sort of intergroup

---

[54] Simpson and Yinger, p. 14.

[55] Arnold M. Rose, "Intergroup Relations vs. Prejudice: Pertinent Theory for the Study of Social Change," *Social Problems,* 4:173–176 (1956).

[56] Brewton Berry, *Race Relations* (2d ed.; Boston: Houghton Mifflin Company, 1958), p. 375.

action with minority members, it remains nonfunctional or disengaged.[57] Prejudice against minority groups is linked to a number of social characteristics, according to findings of the Cornell study of a sample of 1430 persons in four American cities located in different parts of the country.

1. The Southern sample exhibits the greatest frequency of social-distance prejudice. The Far Western city has the largest proportion of relatively tolerant or accepting individuals. The Northeastern and Midwestern samples fall in between.

2. Educational level is significantly associated with degree of prejudice: the higher the educational level, the less frequent are high degrees of prejudice toward Negroes, Jews, and Mexican-Americans.

3. Individuals who identify themselves with the upper class tend to be slightly more prejudiced than other white gentiles toward Jews. While the relationships between social-distance feelings toward Negroes and self-chosen class identity are not clear cut, there is some tendency for persons who say that they belong to the working class to be more likely than those who consider themselves to be upper class to maintain attitudes of aversion concerning close social contacts. In both instances, those who identify with the middle class fall in between these two categories in prejudice toward Jews and Negroes.

4. Persons who work in relatively high-status occupations tend to be more prejudiced toward Jews, whereas those in lower status occupations are more likely to have feelings of social distance toward Negroes and Mexican-Americans.

5. There are no large or consistent differences among the various Protestant denominations nor between Protestants and Catholics in the extent of prejudice toward Jews, Negroes, or Mexican-Americans.

6. Individuals who report that they *seldom* attend religious services tend to be more prejudiced than those who report that they *often* attend *or* those who say they *never* attend. The regular churchgoers are the group showing least frequency of social-distance reactions, followed by the non-attenders, whereas it is the infrequent attenders — perhaps the "imperfectly churched" or "conventionally religious" — who are most likely to show exclusionistic prejudice. It appears, however, that the observed differences are partly due to correlated differences in education.

7. Political party affiliation or preference is not strongly related to differences in prejudice, although in the cities studied there is a slight tendency for the greatest frequency of intolerance to appear among Democrats. Independent voters are most likely to be free of feelings of social distance toward racial and ethnic minorities.

8. Individuals who report membership in clubs and organizations tend to be consistently more tolerant of Negroes and Mexican-Americans than those who do not belong to such groups. (Organizational membership is

---

[57] Williams, p. 77.

not predictive of attitudes toward association with Jewish persons.) The apparent effects of organizational membership are confounded with, and may be largely reducible to, effects related to educational level and social class.

9. On the whole, there is a slight tendency among adults for the prevalence of prejudices against close social contacts with Negroes, Jews, and Mexican-Americans to be greater among older persons.

10. Females are slightly more likely than males to be prejudiced against the three minorities named.

11. Individuals who are either divorced, separated, or widowed tend to be slightly more often prejudiced than those who are married or single. No clear conclusions can be drawn from comparisons of single with married people.[58]

The frequency and kinds of contacts across minority lines vary greatly according to situational context, minority group, and the status characteristics of participants. Persons who are relatively unprejudiced are more likely to have such contacts.[59] Moreover, prejudice appears to be diminished by the frequency of interaction and the wider contacts with members of a minority group. Such persons are less likely to accept derogatory stereotypes, to feel sentiments of social distance, or to favor public discrimination. Any changes in intergroup relations as a whole, however, as a result of such associations are likely in the short run to be minimal; in the long run they may have important consequences if the traditional norms are flexible enough to permit substantial numbers of the minority group to have such associations.

It is not inevitable that race, ethnic group, or religion will serve as the primary form of differentiating between people. Studies have found, for example, that racial or religious prejudices do not prevent interaction between people where elements of proximity, interdependence, or common interests are involved.[60] On the other hand, strong prejudices, which are accompanied by group supports, can take priority over the influence of proximity and common interests. In fact, there can be extensive group discrimination even when the minority is too small and weak to contribute a political or economic threat.[61]

---

[58] Robin M. Williams, Jr., *Strangers Next Door: Ethnic Relations in American Communities,* © 1964, pp. 64–66. Reprinted by permission of Prentice-Hall, Inc., Englewood Cliffs, N.J.

[59] Williams, pp. 143–222. Also see Richard F. Curtis, Dianne M. Timbers, and Elton F. Jackson, "Prejudice and Urban Social Participation," *American Journal of Sociology,* 72:235–245 (1967).

[60] Williams, p. 359.

[61] H. M. Blalock, Jr., "A Power Analysis of Racial Discrimination," *Social Forces,* 39:57 (1960).

In the following sections three sources of prejudice will be analyzed: the cultural and social factors, the extent to which competitive factors exclude a minority group, and the view that prejudice arises from the personality needs of the individual. Finally, the effect that members of minority groups have on prejudice among the majority will be discussed.

CULTURAL AND SOCIAL FACTORS AND PREJUDICE

Racial prejudice cannot be understood as a reaction of individuals: it is related to group structures.[62] It is the clashes of groups organized on various status lines that form the basis of discrimination and serve to define the subordinate group. Cultural definitions of race and religion which define stereotypes become meaningful only as the result of social interaction which leads to the awareness of collective differences. Through these processes what was originally mere individual perception becomes a powerful functioning collectively of "Negro" and "white," "gentile" and "Jew," and subgroups within each of these groups.

> Ethnic prejudices do not really refer to *personal* likings (or preferences for association) at all, but rather to the acceptance of *shared (cultural) definitions and evaluations of social categories as such.* The crux of intergroup prejudice is not the fact that an individual white person wishes to avoid social visiting with a particular Negro. Indeed, it is very likely that there are white people with whom he does not wish close social interaction, and it may well be that he enjoys informal association with some Negro person who is exempted from the racial definition. Interpersonal likings and associational preferences that are oriented only to individual personality compatibilities could never form the *structural* alignments represented by the classification of some 18,000,000 varied human beings as "Negroes" in our society today.[63]

Studies of infants and preschool children indicate that they typically do not exhibit prejudice toward racial or ethnic groups. This finding is of great significance, for it was at one time believed that human beings were by nature negatively disposed toward those who were biologically different. Prejudice is learned and appears to develop when definitions of the nature of subgroups (racial, ethnic, and religious) become more precise. Although

---

[62] Herbert Blumer, "Race Prejudice as a Sense of Group Position," *Pacific Sociological Review*, 1, No. 1:6 (1958): "Historical records of major instances of race relations, as in our South, or in South Africa, or in Europe in the case of the Jew, or on the West Coast in the case of the Japanese show the formidable part played by interest groups in defining the subordinate racial group."

[63] Williams, pp. 113–114.

some studies have reported finding marked prejudice against Negroes in children of five,[64] others indicate that children do not begin to withdraw from Negroes until about the fourth grade, do not think of themselves as a separate group until the fifth grade, and even in the eighth grade have many associations across race lines.[65]

In its early stages of development prejudice is quite vague. The child begins with a rather undefined awareness of racial and religious differences, then develops hostility and avoidance of certain groups which later become more specific, and he may even, by ten or eleven, totally reject a minority group. Later this total rejection may be modified by democratic and other pressures in the society.[66] The child acquires prejudice in a gradual and subtle manner, so gradual that when he later finds he has antipathetic feelings toward certain groups he does not know why he feels in this way. From his culture the child learns many things which are related to prejudice, and he acquires from his culture beliefs about the nature of race and racial characteristics or marks. He learns the ways in which members of minority groups are supposed to act and what they are permitted and not permitted to do. He likewise learns that members of minority groups are supposed to exhibit fairly uniform negative characteristics of stereotypes. He early learns linguistic tags such as "nigger," "kike," "Jap," "Chink," and "greaser" which carry with them the idea of power for him and rejection and avoidance of members of minority groups. Lasker has stated that the pressures which mold the child's prejudicial beliefs are those which make for social conformity: the attitudes of the parents, playmates, and such social institutions as the school and the church.[67] The child learns that certain groups, such as Negroes, have a lower status, that he should not play with them, and that there are other restrictions on their social participation. This lower status is often indicated to the child by the shabby appearance of members of minority groups, their poor housing, and their relative absence from white-collar positions in stores, banks, and similar places. He also notices that members of minority groups are not invited into the intimacy of the family. These patterns of minority and majority group behavior soon become accepted by the child as "natural," and even by the age of ten or

---

[64] E. L. Horowitz, *The Development of Attitudes toward the Negro* (New York: *Archives of Psychology,* No. 194, 1936).

[65] Joan H. Criswell, "Racial Cleavage in Negro-White Groups," *Sociometry,* 1:81–89 (1937).

[66] Allport, pp. 297–310.

[67] Bruno Lasker, *Racial Attitudes in Children* (New York: Holt, Rinehart and Winston, Inc., 1929). Also see Mary Ellen Goodman, *Race Awareness in Young Children* (Reading, Mass.: Addison-Wesley Publishing Company, 1952).

eleven he may ascribe all favorable qualities to whites and none for Negroes, although at a later age he may modify this exclusiveness somewhat.[68]

Whether a person will or will not discriminate against a given minority is greatly influenced by the opinions of his family and his friends. A St. Louis study found this, for example:

> It appears that individuals may be socialized either to discriminate or not to discriminate by family and friends just as they are socialized to favor one political party, a certain religion (or, perhaps, no religion), or a particular way of life over others. Just as families and friends, by exerting pressures, attempt to enforce norms about voting, religion, and a way of life, they also attempt to enforce norms about how the individual should relate to members of another race. Interestingly enough, the results indicate considerable variation, considerable conflict in the norms enforced by different families and friendship groups. If these norms are considered mores, evidently there are two conflicting sets of mores in operation in the St. Louis area. Family and friends tend to enforce one or the other, but even the degree of enforcement varies.[69]

Cultural Stereotypes

Many things that the child learns about minority groups are learned through stereotypes, which are accepted as evidence that all members of any group have the same characteristics. Some of the common stereotypes which are culturally transmitted are these: "Certain minorities are lazy, irresponsible, and immoral"; "Certain minorities are more hard working and shrewd and get ahead too fast [Orientals and Jews]"; "People of minority groups are incapable of holding important positions in our society without the risk of a decline of our civilization"; "Negroes are Africans at heart, are a 'primitive, childlike people,' and expect to be treated as inferiors"; "Orientals are by nature crafty and cruel and cannot be trusted"; "Jews control business, banking, the press, motion pictures, and other important segments of society"; "Jews are noisy, vulgar, and aggressive in behavior." A nation-wide 1963 survey of white opinions of Negroes reported the findings shown in Table 17.2.

Some cultural stereotypes are mutually exclusive, although this fact does not prevent some prejudiced persons from believing both. For example, the cultural stereotypes that Jews are Communists and at the same time "international capitalist bankers" are mutually exclusive. Some minorities are also looked down upon because they are thought to be indolent and

---

[68] Allport, p. 309.

[69] Robert L. Hamblin, "The Dynamics of Racial Discrimination," *Social Problems,* 10:117 (1962).

TABLE 17.2   **White Stereotypes about Negroes, in Percentages**

Agree with statement:	Nation-wide	South	Previous social con-tact group *
Negroes laugh a lot	68	81	79
Negroes tend to have less ambition	66	81	56
Negroes smell different	60	78	50
Negroes have looser morals	55	80	39
Negroes keep untidy homes	46	57	31
Negroes want to live off the handout	41	61	26
Negroes have less native intelligence	39	60	23
Negroes breed crime	35	46	21
Negroes are inferior to whites	31	51	15
Negroes care less for the family	31	49	22

SOURCE: William Brink and Louis Harris, "What Whites Think of Negroes," in Bernard E. Segal, ed., *Racial and Ethnic Relations: Selected Readings* (New York: Thomas Y. Crowell Company, 1966), p. 223.

  * The "Previous Social Contact Group" represented those in the nation-wide sample who had had previous social contact with Negroes. They constituted 25 percent of the total and proved throughout the survey to be the most sympathetic to the Negro and his cause.

incapable of full participation in our society, whereas others, like the Jews, may be discriminated against because they are all thought to be excessively aggressive. Merton has referred to this illogical approach to in-group values as the "damned-if-you-do and damned-if-you-don't process of ethnic and racial relations." [70]

Although some aspects of a stereotype may be supported by facts, they are largely unscientific. In reality, they cannot be applied to all members of a minority group for a number of reasons, outlined by Simpson and Yinger:

1. The stereotype gives a highly exaggerated picture of the importance of some few characteristics—whether they be favorable or unfavorable.
2. It invents some supposed traits out of whole cloth, making them seem reasonable by associaton with other tendencies that may have a kernel of truth.
3. In a negative stereotype, personality tendencies that are favorable, that would have to be mentioned to give a complete picture, are either omitted entirely or insufficiently stressed.
4. The stereotype fails to show how the majority of other groups share the same tendencies or have other undesirable characteristics.

---

[70] Robert K. Merton, "A Social Psychological Factor," in Arnold M. Rose, ed., *Race Prejudice and Discrimination* (New York: Alfred A. Knopf, Inc., 1951), p. 515.

5. It fails to give any attention to the cause of the tendencies of the minority group—particularly to the place of the majority itself, and its stereotypes, in creating the very characteristics being condemned. They are thought of rather as intrinsic or even self-willed traits of the minority.

6. It leaves little room for change; there is a lag in keeping up with the tendencies which actually typify many members of a group.

7. It leaves no room for individual variation, which is always wide in human groups. One does not deal with a group average, but with specific individuals. One of the functions of stereotypes is shown by this failure to adjust to individual differences—to do so would be to destroy the discriminatory value of the stereotype.[71]

Cultural Misconceptions about Race

Racial beliefs and stereotypes are extremely important, for they not only give rise to prejudice and discrimination against minority groups but also help to support both. These beliefs and stereotypes are of several kinds and include the concepts that the majority group must defend its values, that subordination to the majority group is natural, that the minority has some biological or other inferiority, and that discrimination against members of the minority is in their best interests.[72]

Such *rationalizations* to help one avoid subjective conflict are extremely powerful instruments for maintaining prejudice and discrimination. The individual can call on a ready-made stockpile of rationalizing beliefs which the culture provides. If one erroneously believes that Negroes innately have a body odor he can also believe that any close social contact or intermarriage with Negroes is impossible. If a minority group is believed to be mentally inferior, it would be only a mockery to place persons belonging to it in places of political or economic power where they would endanger American society. If a minority group, on the other hand, is believed to have a higher intelligence and to be excessively competitive, it would be detrimental to society if educational quotas and other restrictions were not imposed.

A major source of prejudicial attitudes are the numerous culturally transmitted misconceptions about race. As the child grows up in a culture he is certain, sooner or later, to hear frequently many such statements as the following: "Racial prejudice is innate"; "Certain races are pure, ordained by God, and should not be mixed"; "Races are distinct groups and over the years have not changed"; "All mixtures of racial groups result in biologically and socially inferior human beings"; "Certain peoples are

---

[71] Simpson and Yinger, pp. 119–120. Reprinted by permission of the publishers.
[72] Berry, p. 118.

markedly inferior in their native intellectual qualities"; and "Certain peoples are more or less emotional than others." These beliefs, and many similar ones, represent folklore which has been transmitted in our culture without scientific evidence and largely below the level of conscious understanding. They often arise out of scientific half-truths or the misinterpretation of some actual historical facts. The evolution of man, for example, is expanded to include the false belief that the Negro is closer to the ape than is the white man. The historical fact that in many parts of the world slaves have been chiefly Negroes rather than Indians or Asiatics is enlarged to the belief in the world-wide natural inferiority of the Negro peoples.

Most of the beliefs about minorities are based on a misunderstanding of the scientific relation of race and culture. Race refers simply to biological subgroups distinguishable by certain physical characteristics, whereas culture refers to social norms and values which are nonbiological. There are Caucasian, Negroid, and Mongoloid races and various subgroups under each.[73] Racial groups have few clearly distinguishable race marks, for there are no sharp and stable lines of demarcation. Rather, each race is a hypothetical average of certain physical features, including skin color, head shape, facial angle, nasal index, lip form, body proportions, and other characteristics. Although skin color is of great cultural importance, it is one of the most unreliable indices of race. Many "white men"—for example, most of the people of India and Pakistan—are actually not white in skin color at all.

Strictly used, the term *race* refers to biological processes and is distinct from culture. The two differ not only in process but also in unit, transmission, method of change, and product, as indicated in the following outline.

	Race	Culture
Unit	genes and chromosomes	norms and values
Transmission	fertilization	communication
Method of Change	by mutation or amalgamation	by invention and diffusion
Product	biological individual	person (personality)
Examples	hair color, eye color, skin color, height, etc.	attitudes toward objects and ways of believing

---

[73] "A race is a sub-group of peoples possessing a definite combination of physical characters of genetic origin; this combination serves, in varying degree, to distinguish the sub-group from other sub-groups of mankind, and the combination is transmitted in descent, providing all conditions which originally gave rise to the definite combination remain relatively unaltered; as a rule the sub-group inhabits, or did inhabit, a more or less restricted geographical region."—W. M. Krogman, "The Concept of Race," in Ralph Linton, ed., *The Science of Man in the World Crisis* (New York: Columbia University Press, 1945), p. 49.

Today there are no "pure" races. Through thousands of years, and as a result of trade, wars, and migrations, there has been a constant mixing of the races. Linton pointed out in his *Study of Man* that it seemed "slightly ludicrous" for the main exponents of the theory of superiority of pure strains to come from Europe which is one of the "most thoroughly hybridized regions of the world": "Tribes have marched and countermarched across the face of this continent since before the dawn of history, and the ancestry of most of the present population is not even pure white. . . . The result of all this has been an extreme mixture of heredity in Europe and a perfect hodgepodge of varying physical types." [74]

By varying one or the other of these components in different situations it is relatively easy to show that racial and cultural characteristics are independent of one another, and not correlated. [75] On the one hand, there are situations where the culture is fairly homogeneous but the racial groups constituting it are quite diverse. This is true in the United States and in Brazil, where, in addition to the white race, there are large Negro groups as well as persons of Mongoloid racial background, such as Japanese, Chinese, and Indians.

On the other hand, there can be *relative* homogeneity of biological type and great cultural diversity. Before his Europeanization, the American Indian, who is biologically a subtype of the Mongoloid race, exhibited enormous cultural differences. The variations ranged from the Arctic and sub-Arctic culture of the Indians of northern Canada to the tropical culture of the Amazon jungles, and from the culture of the Plains and Forest Indians to the stone houses of the Pueblo Indians of the Southwest. Finally, there were the great cultures of the Aztecs, Mayas, and Incas, which were undoubtedly more advanced than those of the Britons and Gauls of the time of Caesar's *Commentaries.* Today in nearly every continent of the world the Negro exhibits enormous cultural diversity. There are Negroes who have largely American, British, Spanish, Portuguese, French, Belgian, and Dutch cultures, besides those who belong to a host of native African cultures. Another example of cultural diversity is found in the white race, which exhibits considerable cultural variety in Western Europe; moreover, the Arabs, the Egyptians, and the people of India and Pakistan, all of whom are white men, also have greatly differing cultures.

In other situations the racial group can remain relatively constant while great changes take place in its culture. The difference between the type of culture of Japan at the time of Commodore Perry's visit a century ago and

---

[74] Ralph Linton, *The Study of Man* (New York: Appleton-Century-Crofts, Inc., 1936), p. 35.

[75] See Edward B. Reuter, "Race and Culture" in Robert E. Park, ed., *An Outline of the Principles of Sociology* (New York: Barnes & Noble, Inc., 1939), p. 188.

modern Japan, with its Western industrial type of culture and its fondness for baseball, is an example. Furthermore, although no culture ever really dies out completely, there are a number of instances where the racial group has continued even though there has been little or no understanding of the meanings of the previous culture. Until certain scientific discoveries were made, neither modern Egyptians nor Mayans could read the hieroglyphics on their ancient buildings. The descendants of the Carthaginians, Babylonians, and Assyrians live on; their cultures are largely dead.

The cultural misconceptions of racial characteristics have made it possible to associate all types of cultural factors with certain biological features. Sometimes a group is even defined as a race when it is not a race at all biologically. The Jews, for example, are generally referred to as a separate race when actually they are members of the white race. They may have had more physical homogeneity when they inhabited ancient Israel, but it is impossible to tell today, in a large proportion of cases, whether a person is a Jew.[76] The so-called Jewish nose existed among non-Semitic peoples and only a relatively small proportion of Jews today have such a nose. Today there are so many variations in measurable characteristics among Jews in various parts of the world that they have no racial identity. In parts of Germany, for example, as much as half the Jewish population have blue eyes and appear as fair as their neighbors.[77]

A culture defines certain physiological traits as being superior or inferior, in addition to defining certain supposed biological marks as constituting a "race." Actually a hooked nose is not inferior to a straight nose, thin lips are not superior to protruding lips, and wavy hair has no natural advantage over kinky or straight hair, although many societies may think so. A white skin is not "better" than a black or yellow skin, the Mongolian slanting eye, which is actually only a fold of skin over the eye, is just as good as the straight Caucasian eye, and a narrow head is neither inferior nor superior to a round one.

Beauty and ugliness are also seen in terms of the culture, for there is nothing "natural" about the esthetic qualities of certain physical characteristics. Gleaming black skin and kinky hair, almond eyes and fat, tubby

---

[76] "Jews are a mixed people derived originally from Caucasoid stocks in the eastern Mediterranean area. Insofar as the original stock remains the basis of their inheritance, they can sometimes be identified as eastern Mediterranean peoples, but not as Jews. Since there are very few eastern Meditteranean peoples in the United States except Jews, their identification with this wider stock is not usually made."—Simpson and Yinger, p. 41.

[77] R. A. Schermerhorn, *These Our People* (Boston: D. C. Heath and Company, 1949), p. 32.

bodies are all regarded as being beautiful in particular cultures.[78] Livingstone is said to have remarked once, after having resided in Africa for some time among black-skinned people, that he felt almost ashamed of the paleness of his white skin.

Through the centuries various peoples have boasted of their biological superiority over others. Greeks, Egyptians, Romans, Arabians, Chinese, Incas, Tibetans, Vikings, Teutons, Anglo-Saxons, and Slavs have all proclaimed their superiority. There are a number of reasons, however, why no race or ethnic group can be shown to be superior over another.

1. *No one has yet been able to demonstrate the innate mental, temperamental, or emotional superiority of one racial group over another.* Members of some American minority groups today generally exhibit lower *average* test scores on intelligence tests. This can be understood as consequences of inferior social status and living rather than as biological causes of inferior status. A number of conclusions can be reached from the study of a large number of studies of Negro intelligence.

(1) In every large group there is wide variation in intelligence scores, ranging, in terms of I.Q., from under 50 to over 200. (2) Group means, therefore, are of little significance, since it is individuals who are given or denied opportunities. To oppose higher education or some other opportunity for a Negro with an I.Q. of 140 because "his group" has an average score of 90 compared with an average among whites of 100 or 105 makes no sense. (3) Even those who argue in favor of the thesis that there are important racial differences note the extensive overlap among races, although the interpretation of that overlap is sometimes obscure. A 25 percent overlap between Negroes and whites, for example, means that 25 percent of the Negro scores are above the *median* white score. (4) White groups vary extensively in average scores, and in a way are incapable of interpretation on national grounds, unless one cares to argue that the predominantly "Anglo-Saxon" South represents an inferior national stock. (5) Differences by group averages among young children are small, but they become progressively larger with age, particularly on those tests which rely more heavily on language. (6) Differences in group averages become progressively smaller as life conditions (income, residence, education, occupation, etc.) become more nearly similar. (7) Full equation of conditions is difficult because equivalent income and education do not protect many minority-group members, Negroes, for example,

---

[78] A Malay story of creation illustrates this point. In the beginning, so the story goes, man was created out of dough and baked in an oven. The first one was cooked too much, and he was a Negro. The second was pale and not done enough, and he was a white man. The third was cooked just right, a golden brown, and he was a Malayan.

from rebuffs and other ego-crushing conditions which lead to ". . . intellectually defeating personality traits that play a significant role in their ability to score on measures of intelligence." (8) Intelligence defined solely with reference to the usual tests scarcely gives an adequate picture. If intelligence is skillful adaptation to the stresses and possibilities of one's environment—a functional interpretation—Negro responses may measure up well. (9) Tests free of cultural and subcultural influences have yet to be designed—indeed are probably not possible to design.[79]

2. *Superiority would have to be defined.* Does it mean physical strength, military power, technological development? Or does it mean human happiness and the relative absence of social deviations? Does superiority imply the development of great religious philosophy, art, and literature? Although many nonwhite races cannot equal the development of machines and public sanitation, they may still have developed an emphasis on moral values, art forms, and cooperative living that may excel the technological developments of Western European civilization. The question of superiority in itself is an issue involving value judgments which, by their nature, may be incapable of solution. Can modern machines be compared with the complex system of reckoning kinship among the so-called inferior Australian aborigines? Can religious beliefs or art forms be compared in terms of any universal standards?

3. *Superiority cannot be considered without regard to time.* In different historical periods every racial group and most European national groups have excelled in warfare. At other times the Mongoloid peoples have been technologically superior to the white people. In fact, the idea of the superiority of a people is based on the belief that a given race actually produced all its culture. This assumption is contrary to the scientific position that most culture has been borrowed and spread by diffusion. As Linton has indicated, little of the average American's daily activity is exclusively a Western European invention or development.[80]

The Self-Fulfilling Prophecy

An important cultural aspect of prejudice is what might be termed the principle of cumulation, the self-fulfilling prophecy or the vicious circle. The view that a minority is inferior is a product of prejudice and discrim-

---

[79] Simpson and Yinger, pp. 156–157. Also see Sheldon Roen, "Personality and Negro-White Intelligence," *Journal of Abnormal and Social Psychology* (1960), p. 150, R. M. Dreger and K. S. Miller, "Comparative Psychological Studies of Negroes and Whites in the United States," *Psychological Bulletin,* September 1960, pp. 389–390, Otto Klineberg, "Negro-White Differences in Intelligence Test Performance: A New Look at an Old Problem," *American Psychologist,* April 1963, pp. 198–203; and Otto Klineberg, *Characteristics of the American Negro* (New York: Harper & Row, Publishers, 1944).

[80] Linton, pp. 325–327.

ination, but once it is established it becomes a part of the circle of inter-action. Where social forces, such as slavery, have been associated with a minority group that group will later be judged as "inferior": "By limiting the opportunities of a minority group, by segregating it, by putting it at every competitive disadvantage, the prejudice helps to create the very inferiority by which it seems 'justified' in the minds of the dominant group. Start out by saying that the colored man is inferior; use this as the reason for giving him poor schools, poor jobs, poor opportunities for advancement; and one soon proves himself correct by creating and enforcing that very inferiority. This, in turn, will deepen the prejudice, which, again, will further restrict the opportunities of the colored person." [81]

What Myrdal called the vicious cycle of race relations is considered by both Merton [82] and MacIver [83] as the "self-fulfilling prophecy." Even though the original meaning of a social situation is false, it may become so much a part of interacting forces as to make itself true. George Bernard Shaw once expressed this principle in his remark that in the United States "the white man makes the Negro shine his shoes and then, because he shines shoes, considers the Negro inferior." According to MacIver discrimination moves to conditions imposed by discrimination back to discrimination:

> In symbolic form the circle proceeds:
> $$D^1 \rightarrow C^1 \rightarrow D^2 \rightarrow C^2 \rightarrow D^3 \rightarrow C^3 \text{ etc.,}$$
> where D stands for discrimination and C for the sequent conditions rel-evant to it. The situation here symbolized is one of progressive discrimi-nation. Where discrimination is established and relatively constant, we have a circle in a stricter sense, as follows:
> $$D \rightarrow C \rightarrow D \rightarrow C \rightarrow D \rightarrow C \text{ etc.}[84]$$

PREJUDICE AND COMPETITION

The previous discussion has emphasized the cultural factors in prej-udice. Attempts have also been made to attribute prejudice and the minority problem exclusively to competition and conflict. The great differentiation of groups and social roles in our modern society has made possible extensive areas of conflict over social and economic status. Under these conditions, therefore, it is sometimes possible for one group to try to restrict the eco-nomic position of another group entirely, or even to eliminate it. These

---

[81] Simpson and Yinger, p. 122.

[82] Robert K. Merton, *Social Theory and Social Structure* (rev. ed.; New York: The Free Press, 1957), pp. 421–436.

[83] R. M. MacIver, *The More Perfect Union* (New York: The Macmillan Company, 1948), pp. 52–81.

[84] MacIver, p. 67.

intergroup tensions are more likely to develop in situations where there are more rapid and far-reaching social changes, changes that have resulted in increased cultural conflict between groups. Migrations of groups with different physical and social characteristics often increase prejudice, for these newcomers exert pressures on housing facilities, transportation, schools, jobs, and even general social status. The pressures vary according to the size of the migration in relation to the existing population and the rapidity of the influx of the migrants. This type of pressure, with the resulting tensions, appears to have been an important factor in the famous Chicago race riot of 1919 and the Detroit race riot during World War II.[85]

There can be little doubt that competition does intensify prejudice. History has demonstrated that for centuries prejudice has been used as a weapon in religious and political struggles in Europe, including particularly the numerous anti-Semitic purges and pogroms. At various times there have been groups in America who have sought to eliminate certain minorities from economic and social competition. These have included the Native American party of the 1830s, the Know-Nothing Order of the 1850s, and a variety of more recent groups. It has also been suggested that prejudice arises from unfair competition or the tendency of one group to exploit another.[86] One writer has stated that American history and our contemporary life clearly reveal the role of economic factors in maintaining Negro prejudice.[87] This Negro writer has concluded, after a lengthy study, that race prejudice is a social attitude engendered by certain classes who stigmatize a group as inferior in order to justify their exploitation of the group or its resources.[88]

Open conflict between groups also seems to vary according to how direct and successful the minority competition is in attaining wealth and prestige. The prejudice toward the Japanese exhibited in California by certain vested farming interests is an illustration of this point, and it contributed greatly to their removal from the West Coast at the outbreak of World War II.[89] Much of United States immigration policy has been directed

---

[85] For a report on factors which precipitate race riots, see Lieberson and Silverman.

[86] Alexander Lesser, "Anti-Semitism in the United States," *Journal of Negro Education,* 10:545–556 (1941).

[87] Oliver C. Cox, *Caste, Class and Race* (New York: Doubleday & Company, Inc., 1948).

[88] Oliver Cox, "Race Prejudice and Intolerance—A Distinction," *Social Forces,* 24:216 (1945). See also his *Caste, Class and Race.*

[89] Carey McWilliams, *Prejudice—Japanese-Americans: Symbol of Racial Intolerance* (Boston: Little, Brown & Company, 1944).

toward excluding first the Chinese, then the Japanese, later people from southern and eastern Europe, and, finally, the Mexicans, from competition with various groups in the society.

Certainly minorities experience discrimination in employment, wage scales, and occupational opportunities. The generally low status of unskilled labor, held at one time or other by most minority groups, has added to the prejudices against them, and interferes with their social participation in society.

Prejudice appears in several studies to be associated with efforts of a given social class to maintain jobs, property, and social positions. One study found that a major determinant of the tendency to discriminate is the actual or feared competition with minority group members for jobs, houses, schools, and recreational facilities.[90] Anticipated frustrations seem to be more important than actual frustration. There is considerable evidence to support the view that prejudice varies by social class, some studies showing that lower-class whites, for example, are more prejudiced than other classes against Negroes. There is some evidence, based on American samples,[91] that the downwardly mobile economically are more prejudiced, but a Swedish study did not show such differences, indicating the important role of cultural factors and general economic systems in prejudice.[92] No definite conclusions can be reached, however, because of methodological difficulties, such as controlling for the effect of region, religion, ethnic group, and education. Moreover, "higher class standing is not automatically associated with lower prejudice." [93]

This role of the competitive and individualistic nature of modern society in prejudice cannot be overlooked. An economic explanation of prejudice is far too simple, however, for such an explanation does not consider the varied role of cultural definitions nor the possible role of personality factors. Actually it does not explain prejudice; it only suggests an explanation of intensity in some cases. More specific arguments against such an explanation can be cited. As they grow older, children, for example, often

---

[90] Robert L. Hamblin, "The Dynamics of Racial Discrimination," *Social Problems*, 10:103–121 (1962).

[91] Bruno Bettelheim and Morris Janowitz, *Social Change and Prejudice* (New York: The Free Press, 1964). An exception was cited in a study which found the individual's attitude toward status-striving important: Fred B. Silberstein and Melvin Seeman, "Social Mobility and Prejudice," *American Journal of Sociology*, 65:258–264 (1959).

[92] Melvin Seeman, Dennis Rohan, and Milton Argeriou, "Social Mobility and Prejudice: A Swedish Replication," *Social Problems*, 14:188–197 (1966).

[93] Simpson and Yinger, p. 105.

exhibit prejudice under circumstances where there is little competition. Likewise, individuals of all groups may exhibit prejudice toward a given minority, whereas only a small number are in direct competition with the group. Upper-class southern whites, for example, may be prejudiced toward Negroes with whom they are in little competition, although they may benefit from having Negro servants. There may even be prejudice where there is almost no competition, as demonstrated by the attitudes of the whites of Australia toward the native aborigines. Simpson and Yinger have indicated the limitations of the competitive theory of prejudice as follows:

> Many contradictory forces are at work in any given expression of prejudice. Which one will predominate depends upon their relative strength and the setting in which they work. The "economic" element in prejudice is *least* likely to predominate where traditional definitions of roles are most stable, where economic classes are least self-conscious and organized, where the "intellectual climate" encourages the interpretation of individual frustrations in terms of personal opponents. The "economic" element in prejudice is most likely to predominate where traditional definitions of roles are being challenged, where large-scale organizations along class lines are most highly developed, and where group differentiation tends to correspond with differences in economic functions. The careful student will not accept a blanket statement of the *general* role of group conflict in prejudice, whether it be a statement that stresses or one that minimizes that role. He will, rather, seek to find the role of group conflict in *specific* situations as it interacts with the other forces at work in those situations.[94]

PREJUDICE AND PERSONALITY NEEDS

Various attempts have been made to explain prejudice almost exclusively in terms of personality needs. These explanations have taken two forms: that prejudice arises from frustrations and aggressions, and that there is a general prejudiced personality pattern, often referred to as a "conformist" or "authoritarian personality." Although some of these explanations appear useful if accompanied by proper emphasis on the cultural heritage, they are not complete explanations of prejudice.

According to the first explanation, feelings of hostility arising within the individual may be freed at one level or at all three. First, the individual may exhibit hostility in the form of free-floating aggression toward anyone or anything. Second, he may attach his hostility to the behavior of specific individuals and attribute his own inadequacies to their behavior. A com-

---

[94] Simpson and Yinger, p. 107. Reprinted by permission of Harper & Row, Publishers.

mon way to release hostilities is, however, the third type, wherein the aggression is deflected toward certain larger social categories, usually minority groups.[95] Dollard has probably developed this explanation more than anyone, particularly with reference to Negro-white relations in a southern town.[96] The frustrations of whites, arising out of the repressions placed by their culture on their free social and sexual relations, for example, serve to make them overtly and psychologically aggressive toward the Negro.

One form of the frustration explanation of prejudice, the "scapegoat theory," has had wide support among many writers on anti-Semitism who have sought to explain the centuries' old hatred for the Jew as a product of the frustrations of the gentile world. The Jew has been blamed for political failure, economic misery, and religious strife. In various historic periods other "safe goats," as Carey McWilliams has called them, have been scapegoats. According to Allport, a good scapegoat should have five characteristics: (1) The group should be highly visible in physical appearance, manners, or customs. (2) It should not be a weak group; yet (3) it should be an accessible one which is not strong enough to retaliate. (4) There must be some latent hostility toward the group. Finally, (5) the group should represent some ideological principle which the people resent.[97]

The frustration-aggression theory sounds extremely plausible, but it is too simple an explanation for minority prejudice in general. The political, economic, and social positions of some groups, such as the Indians and the Spanish-speaking peoples, are so inferior that it would be difficult to attribute prejudice toward these minorities as a scapegoat mechanism. Likewise, as one author has indicated, the Negro's social and economic status has been historically so inferior that one could hardly blame our troubles on him.[98] Many cultural and competitive factors other than frustration and aggression enter into the explanation of prejudice. Aggression may well intensify prejudice, but this is not the same thing as saying that it causes prejudice. This theory, moreover, does not adequately explain why one group rather than another is the object of prejudice. Most prejudice has a long cultural history independent of the frustrations of given individuals or of historical situations.

---

[95] Robin Williams, Jr., *The Reduction of Intergroup Tensions* (Bulletin 57; New York: Social Science Research Council, 1947), p. 52.

[96] John Dollard, Neal Miller, Leonard Doob, *et al.*, *Frustration and Aggression* (New Haven, Conn.: Yale University Press, 1939), and John Dollard, *Caste and Class in a Southern Town* (New Haven, Conn.: Yale University Press, 1937).

[97] Gordon W. Allport, *ABC's of Scapegoating* (rev. ed.; New York: Anti-Defamation League of B'nai B'rith, 1948), pp. 42–43.

[98] Bohdan Zawadski, "Limitation of the Scapegoat Theory of Prejudice," *Journal of Abnormal and Social Psychology*, 43:127–141 (1948).

A somewhat different approach in terms of personality needs is the work by psychologists and psychiatrists in the field of racial and religious discrimination which has sought to discover the general personality characteristics of prejudiced persons. This approach has been based on the hypothesis that a certain constellation of personality traits characterizes the prejudiced person and that there is a "prejudiced personality." The most comprehensive attempt to discover a basic prejudiced personality pattern is reported in *The Authoritarian Personality* by Adorno, Frenkel-Brunswik, Levinson, and Sanford.[99] The purpose of this study was to reveal the characteristics of the "authoritarian personality," that is, a specific syndrome which includes anti-Semitism, general ethnocentrism, and political-economic conservatism. Their sample consisted of 2099 persons, primarily professional, middle-class people. A smaller group of the most prejudiced and the least prejudiced was then selected for comparative study. They were given an elaborate set of questionnaires consisting of a scale to measure anti-Semitism, one to measure ethnocentricism, and one to measure conservative and fascist tendencies. Approximately 80 of the highly prejudiced were chosen for intensive interviews and projective testing.

This research study revealed marked differences in the characteristics of the least and the most prejudiced persons. The least prejudiced were liberal, whereas the most prejudiced tended to be authoritarian and conservative. The former were cooperative, permissive, and flexible in social relationships, whereas the latter were power-oriented, looked up to the strong, disclaimed the weak, and had a conventional rigid fear of new situations. The least prejudiced had had an affectionate childhood and had an equalitarian marriage, whereas the most prejudiced had had an exploitative parent and had a dependent attitude toward their wives.

Since *The Authoritative Personality* appeared, many studies have tested, re-examined, and qualified the view that prejudice is largely an expression of an insecure personality.[100] Many of these studies have been critical of the sampling, the research design, and the scale instruments used in the original study. A number of research studies, however, have pointed to such facets of a prejudiced personality as repression, threat orientation,

---

[99] T. W. Adorno, *et al., The Authoritarian Personality* (New York: Harper & Row, Publishers, 1950). For a general discussion and criticism of the concept of personality needs and traits, see Chapter 6.

[100] For a discussion of the literature see Simpson and Yinger, pp. 65–79. Also see Donn Byrne and Terry Wong, "Racial Prejudice, Interpersonal Attraction, and Assumed Dissimilarity of Attitudes," *Journal of Abnormal and Social Psychology* (1962), pp. 246–253; Milton Rokeach, *The Open and Closed Mind* (New York: Basic Books, Inc., 1960); and Ivan Steiner and Homer Johnson, "Authoritarianism and Conformity," *Sociometry* (1963), pp. 21–34.

a strong concern for power in human relationships, anti-intellectuality, and a lack of confidence in the future. A comprehensive study of race prejudice found that the greatest likelihood of prejudice "attaches to those persons who (1) believe in *strict and unquestioning obedience* of children to parents; (2) advocate *severe punishment* of sex criminals; (3) acquiesce in statements of *moralistic condemnation* concerning youths, old people, or people who 'do not live upright lives'; (4) manifest a *generalized distrust* of other people; (5) report feeling *uncomfortable about meeting strangers;* (6) indicate feelings of *personal frustration* and lack of secure group belongingness." [101]

The theory of a prejudiced personality pattern may be useful if it is interpreted only in terms of the possible intensification of group prejudice. It has limitations, however, if it is suggested as a universal or basic explanation of prejudice itself: "The evidence to date indicates that certain types of personality are prejudice-prone; that a wide variety of needs may, in appropriate social settings, be served by prejudice; that a person's relationships with those around him may strongly influence his attitudes and behavior toward the members of minority groups. These explanations must come into any total theory of prejudice. We must be alert, however, to the weaknesses of this approach. There has been a tendency on the part of many writers to interpret prejudice as if it served *only* the need for ridding oneself of fear, guilt, and hostility." [102]

Personality theories have not dealt sufficiently with the differential exposure to cultural norms concerning minority groups. Many studies have shown variations in levels of prejudice and authoritarianism and social characteristics of the population. Prejudice varies by social class, by group membership, by religion, by region, and by sex.[103] It is possible that "authoritarian" and "liberal," *rather than simply representing basic personality trait structures, simply denote certain norms which groups of persons display.*[104] It is likely that in most cases it is no more necessary to use psycho-

---

[101] Williams, *Strangers Next Door,* pp. 109–110.

[102] Simpson and Yinger, p. 79.

[103] See, for example, Thomas Pettigrew, "Personality and Sociocultural Factors in Intergroup Attitudes: A Cross-National Comparison," *Journal of Conflict Resolution,* 2:29–42 (1958). Also see Pettigrew, "Regional Differences in Anti-Negro Prejudice," *Journal of Abnormal and Social Psychology,* 59:28–36 (1959); and Edwin H. Rhyne, "Racial Prejudice and Personality Scales: An Alternative Approach," *Social Forces,* 41:44–53 (1962). For further references see Simpson and Yinger, pp. 76–78.

[104] "We have found, then, that persons who express social distance toward ethnic, racial, or religious outgroups tend rather consistently toward a meaningful pattern of personality characteristics or, if one prefers, *a consistent pattern of beliefs and values.*"—Williams, *Strangers Next Door,* p. 109. (Italics mine.)

logical factors to explain prejudice toward Negroes than it is to explain certain habits in eating or dress. Even the selection of groups for prejudicial treatment has a cultural explanation and may vary from society to society. It is likely that many persons with an "authoritarian personality" or something resembling it are not excessively prejudiced. Exposure to extremely anti-Semitic attitudes in the family or in other intimate social groups, with no unique psychological traits being present, could probably make a person a Jew-baiter.

> Before we can explain antiminority feelings in terms of a harsh, capricious, and unloving childhood, we must be aware of group structure and of variation in values among the subcultures of a society. If residents of Mississippi have a higher anti-Negro score than those of Minnesota, this does not prove that they are more authoritarian—i.e., more intolerant of ambiguity, more cynical, more rigid, less self-accepting. It may be that they simply express different cultural influences. Differences in agreement with the idea that there are two kinds of people in the world, the weak and the strong, may simply indicate differences in actual experience.[105]

PREJUDICE AND THE MINORITY

Prejudice can be related to the minority group as well as to the majority group. In the first place, it is likely that some relation between the behavior of the minority and prejudice exists. To many who are prejudiced this is a satisfactory explanation of their prejudices, and Allport has referred to it as the "earned reputation" theory.[106] Although it is far too simple an explanation, one writer has suggested that pronounced differences in behavior may cause prejudice and that prejudice is much more a product of interaction than solely a result of majority attitudes.[107] One study has shown, for example, that apparent ethnocentrism on the part of a minority group increases antipathy on the part of the majority group and entails measurable costs for the group in intergroup relations.[108] As yet there has been little research in this direction, but the approach looks feasible provided that

---

[105] George E. Simpson and J. Milton Yinger, "The Sociology of Race and Ethnic Relations," in Robert K. Merton, Leonard Broom, and Leonard S. Cottrell, Jr., *Sociology Today* (New York: Basic Books, Inc., 1959), p. 379. Also see William J. MacKinnon and Richard Centers, "Authoritarianism and Urban Stratification," *American Journal of Sociology,* 61:610–620 (1956).

[106] Allport, p. 217.

[107] Zawadski.

[108] William R. Catton, Jr., and Sung Chick Hong, "The Relation of Apparent Minority Ethnocentrism to Majority Antipathy," *American Sociological Review,* 27:178–191 (1962).

proper weight is given to the likelihood that the majority attitudes are far more important in establishing prejudice.[109]

Most minority group members are also prejudiced against the majority but there have been relatively few studies of the nature of these prejudices. Negro prejudice against whites seems to vary according to various social types: the "race men" who are generally the spearheads of Negro leadership in communities; the "whitewardly mobiles" of higher socioeconomic status who have increased identification with the Negro community; the "Uncle Toms" who accept minority status; and the "hostiles," those who are generally hostile because of their treatment by whites.[110] There are indications that some members of a minority group are prejudiced against each other. Notable examples are Negro-Jewish groups and the Anglo-American and Mexican-American groups.[111] These various similarities between white and Negro groups in their prejudices about social factors far outweigh the differences. There was no difference between Negroes and whites regarding social-distance prejudice and sex, age, education, marital status, interracial contact, and authoritarianism. In contrast, occupational status and social participation, such as church and organizational membership, relate negatively to anti-Negro prejudice but are not significantly related to antiwhite prejudice. The participation difference can be explained by Negro and white differences in the extent of education and the nature of religious participation. The occupational status differences in prejudice are explainable in terms of race-class variations in exposure to out-group competition.

> Among whites competition with Negroes is inversely related to occupational status owing to the skewed distribution of Negroes in the class structure. Among Negroes, however, professionals and proprietors as well as skilled and unskilled workers are generally exposed to out-group competition while white-collar Negroes are generally insulated from such competition. Thus within each race the greater the probability of out-group economic competition, the greater the probability of out-group prejudice.[112]

More evident is the effect of prejudice and discrimination on the behavior of minority members. First of all, prejudice and discrimination are

[109] Allport, p. 217.

[110] Robert B. Johnson, "Negro Reactions to Minority Group Status," in Segal, pp. 251–270.

[111] Richard L. Simpson, "Negro-Jewish Prejudice: Authoritarianism and Some Social Variables as Correlates," in Segal, pp. 184–192, and Ozzie G. Simmons, "The Mutual Images and Expectations of Anglo-Americans and Mexican-Americans," in Segal, pp. 193–205.

[112] Donald L. Noel and Alphonso Pinkney, "Correlates of Prejudice: Some Racial Differences and Similarities," *American Journal of Sociology*, 69:621 (1964).

interpreted by members of minority groups in different ways according to the nature of the contact, the cohesiveness of the minority, the region of the country, and the education, income, occupation and social class, personality, skin color, and the individual's early training for minority-majority relations. In general, discrimination results in a feeling of inferiority on the part of the individual minority member, but may be expressed in other ways as well.

Minorities may deal with prejudice and discrimination by acceptance or submission, withdrawal or avoidance, or aggression.[113] Some minority members may avoid difficulties by accepting their place in the white man's world, as did many "folk" or rural, subservient Negroes in the South.[114] In the North, as well, some Negroes may accept the limitations placed on their participation, as was found in a study of approximately 200 Negroes in a town of 10,000.[115] They do not challenge their role and may look with disfavor on those who do. Such acceptance may arise from a real feeling of inferiority and apathy or it may give the person a feeling of security, acceptance, and pride in the approval with which he is received by an employer or other member of the majority group.

Avoidance can come in a number of ways. The member of the minority group may simply withdraw from it as do some mulattoes who pass as white persons or some Jews who hide their identity. There are indications that there even exists self-hatred among minority members, particularly anti-Semitism among some Jews.[116] Upper-class members of a minority—as do some Negro professional people—may simply isolate themselves from the problems of the lower-class members of their group. Another way to avoid some forms of discrimination is by living, for example, in all-Negro or all-Jewish communities. This withdrawal is only partly successful, simply because Harlem and similar segregated parts of a city are not completely self-contained and the minority member encounters prejudice in the outer world. Others may simply go out of their way to avoid contacts or incidents with members of the majority group. The rejection of the "white man's world" has been part of a number of American Negro movements, most

---

[113] Simpson and Yinger, *Racial and Cultural Minorities,* pp. 158–178. Also see Peter I. Rose, *They and We: Racial and Ethnic Relations in the United States* (New York: Random House, Inc., 1964), pp. 130–145.

[114] Charles S. Johnson, *Patterns of Negro Segregation* (New York: Harper & Row, Publishers, 1943), pp. 256–257.

[115] Frank F. Lee, *Negro and White in Connecticut Town* (New Haven, Conn.: College and University Press, 1961).

[116] Kurt Lewin, *Resolving Social Conflicts* (New York: Harper & Row, Publishers, 1948), pp. 186–200.

recent of which are the Black Muslims, who reject efforts of integrationists to work out a compromise with whites. Instead they work for racial and economic separation, Black unity, and similar separatist programs.[117]

Resort to aggression and hostility may be another and increasingly common form of adjustment to prejudice and discrimination. Aggression may also take the form of mass demonstrations, protest marches, and even rioting. Other aggression may be in the form of civil disobedience, "sit-ins," and "freedom rides," as well as in many subtle ways such as stereotyped humor and jokes about the majority, working slowly or leaving a job if the treatment is offensive, and failure to observe various forms of deference and ordinary etiquette. Still another weapon of aggression is the use of the boycott against municipal government, such as the school systems, or the withdrawal of patronage from certain white business concerns.

> The strength of the Negro protest movement which developed, arbitrarily we shall say, after the school-desegregation decision of 1954, has in many ways been surprising. It has involved more people, in more settings, seeking more goals than was thought at all likely when it began. This is testimony, we believe, to the fact that resentment against segregation and discrimination had always been strong, that many earlier forms of response were deflected and disguised aggression, that direct protests had been inhibited by powerlessness and fear of reprisals. Now "the lid is off;" attacks on the system are direct, and it seems highly unlikely that they will abate short of substantial change in America's race relations patterns.[118]

SUMMARY

Discrimination is the denial of equality of treatment to an individual or group of persons who desire this equality. Discrimination may take several forms, including the following: (1) social conventions, (2) segregated living, (3) mass media of communication, (4) discrimination affecting health and life expectancy, (5) exclusion from organized groups, (6) discrimination in public accommodations, (7) discrimination and segregation in educational facilities, (8) discrimination in employment and business, (9) discrimination in suffrage and public office, and (10) discrimination in the administration of justice.

Prejudice is a negative emotional attitude of prejudgment toward a group of people. Although prejudice and discrimination are generally associated, one may be prejudiced without discriminating or discriminate with-

---

[117] C. Eric Lincoln, *The Black Muslims in America* (Boston: The Beacon Press, 1961).

[118] Simpson and Yinger, *Racial and Cultural Minorities*, p. 165.

out being prejudiced. There are three sources of prejudice: the cultural heritage, the need for competitive advantages and, to a limited extent, the personality needs of the individual. The cultural source is basic to prejudice, and personality needs, as well as competitive advantage, appear merely to intensify it. Majority members also may be prejudiced against the majority group as well as against other minority groups. Minorities may deal with discrimination by acceptance or submission, by withdrawal or avoidance, or by aggression.

SELECTED READINGS

Adorno, T. W., Else Frenkel-Brunswik, Daniel J. Levinson, and R. Nevitt Sanford. *The Authoritarian Personality*. New York: Harper & Row, Publishers, 1950. The most important study which has attempted to show that prejudice is primarily a result of a certain type of personality. The methodological sections are particularly good.

Allport, Gordon W. *The Nature of Prejudice*. Reading, Mass.: Addison-Wesley Publishing Company, 1954. A comprehensive analysis of the group differences and psychological and sociocultural factors involved in prejudice. Part V discusses the manner in which the child acquires prejudice.

Ashmore, Harry S. *The Other Side of Jordan: Negroes Outside the South*. New York: W. W. Norton & Company, Inc., 1960. It is the thesis of this writer and journalist that in the second half of the twentieth century the race problem in America is approaching its final focus in the great cities outside the South —New York, Detroit, Chicago, and San Francisco—where more than one third of the Negroes now live.

Barron, Milton L., ed. *American Minorities*. New York: Alfred A. Knopf, Inc., 1957. A collection of readings in intergroup relations covering a wide range of topics.

Berry, Brewton. *Race Relations*. Rev. ed. Boston: Houghton Mifflin Company, 1958. An analysis of the concept of race and racial differences as well as an excellent critique of the various theories of prejudice.

Boyd, William C. *Genetics and the Races of Man*. Boston: D. C. Heath and Company, 1950. A discussion of race and racial differences.

Johnson, Charles S. *Patterns of Negro Segregation*. New York: Harper & Row, Publishers, 1943. A study of the different ways in which Negroes react to discrimination and segregation. Contains material from personal documents.

Lee, Alfred McClung. *Fraternities without Brotherhood*. Boston: The Beacon Press, 1955. A study of racial and religious prejudice among fraternities.

Rose, Arnold M., ed. *Race Prejudice and Discrimination*. New York: Alfred A. Knopf, Inc., 1951. A collection of readings on intergroup relations. Particularly good is the section dealing with prejudice and discrimination.

Rose, Peter I. *They and We: Racial and Ethnic Relations in the United States*. New York: Random House, Inc., 1964. An analysis of discrimination and prejudice in the United States.

Segal, Bernard E., ed. *Racial and Ethnic Relations.* New York: Thomas Y. Crowell Company, 1966. A book of readings dealing with discrimination and the scope and amount of prejudice.

Simpson, George E., and J. Milton Yinger. *Racial and Cultural Minorities.* Third ed. New York: Harper & Row, Publishers, 1965. Chapters 3–5 deal with the cultural, competitive, and personality functions of prejudice.

Williams, Robin, Jr. *The Reduction of Intergroup Tensions.* New York: Social Science Research Council, Bulletin 57, 1947. A general survey of research on prejudice and discrimination and the techniques for their reduction.

————. *Strangers Next Door: Ethnic Relations in American Communities.* Englewood Cliffs, N.J.: Prentice-Hall, Inc., 1964. A theoretical analysis of prejudice and discrimination as well as a report of a large research project dealing with the nature of prejudice against various minority groups in four cities in various parts of the country. The study analyzed not only racial and ethnic prejudices but also the nature of interaction and avoidance of people in each city.

Deviant Behavior and Social Control

18

The Prevention of Deviant Behavior

Over a period of time a society may adopt a number of alternative ways of dealing with negatively regarded deviant behavior. Sometimes social deviations may produce continuous tension in a society. In other cases the society may come to accept the deviations, establish an uneasy equilibrium, or, in the more usual cases, try to eliminate the deviations by increased pressure.

It might be argued that reduction of deviant behavior must be delayed until the nature and causes of deviations have finally been scientifically established, and ways of dealing with them found. Yet in a democratic society this is not feasible, for both policy and action depend ultimately on public decision, and when practical problems present themselves, public decision cannot always await the scientist. There is generally a period in which public action takes the form of trial-and-error efforts to combat the perceived threat of deviancy, a belief that "something must be done." But this action, however "unscientific" its foundation, ties in directly with the efforts of scientists. It is through such action, regardless of its success or failure in reducing deviation, that public interest and concern are aroused. One notable consequence of this is that funds for scientific research are often made available to scientists concerned with deviation. Eventually, the results of such scientific study may contribute to the fabric of understanding with which legislators and citizens arrive at more adequate policy decisions. Sociologists as scientists are becoming more involved than before in doing applied research and acting as directors or consultants to action programs dealing with deviant behavior.[1]

On the other hand, within a social system there may ultimately be acceptance of deviations, as has occurred countless times in Western European society. Women's use of cosmetics and their smoking and drinking a century or less ago among certain social classes were almost infallible signs of immorality, and for many justified the assumption that a woman who indulged in any of these practices was a prostitute.

Deviations may constitute a condition of equilibrium such as exists with regard to certain deviant sex practices or gambling in the United States. Although many people may realize that gambling, for example, is an expensive and, for society, an unproductive form of behavior, their attitude is complicated by the fact that most people have, at some time or other, gambled. "Drawing up legislation which will penalize the unwarranted deviation without jeopardizing the status of the numerous casual participants is exceedingly difficult." [2]

Societies may try energetically to eliminate deviations. Such a reaction more often occurs "when the norms violated are highly compulsive and universal in the culture." [3] Such deviations as incest, witchcraft, and adultery, for example, have almost always been treated harshly among primitive societies. On the other hand, in frontier days of a century ago horse stealing was regarded as a much more serious crime than is automobile theft today. In modern societies there is strong reaction against brutal murders, kidnaping, and sex crimes of violence, particularly those involving children.

One method by which strong societal action can be taken against deviation from norms is to cut the deviant off from communication with the group. Generally, this takes the form of rejection and decreased interaction, denial of privileges which the group controls, lowering of status,

---

[1] See, for example, Marshall B. Clinard, "The Sociologist's Quest for Respectability," *The Sociological Quarterly,* 7:399–412 (1966). Also see Paul F. Lazarsfeld, William H. Sewell, and H. Wilensky, eds., *Uses of Sociology* (New York: Basic Books, Inc., 1966); Donald W. Valdes and Dwight G. Bean, *Sociology in Use: Selected Readings for an Introductory Course* (New York: The Macmillan Company, 1965); and Arthur B. Shostak, ed., *Sociology in Action* (Homewood, Ill.: The Dorsey Press, Inc., 1966).

[2] Edwin H. Lemert, *Social Pathology* (New York: McGraw-Hill Book Company, Inc., 1951), p. 60.

[3] Lemert, p. 63.

and, eventually, ostracism. As a result of this action, the deviant may leave the group voluntarily, or the group will collectively push him out.[4] Thus the individual who, as a member of a group, develops ideas or engages in behavior at variance with the group norms may be ostracized if initial communications directed at him are not successful in causing him to conform. If the individual perceives the group as at least as satisfying as his deviant ideas, and if he believes that the group will reaccept him if he renounces his ideas or behavior, he may do so.[5]

In a complex society, even though communication among members is not as direct and personal, there is still a considerable amount of collective hostility expressed toward deviants. Some of this is evidenced by societal stereotypes concerning deviants, such as the "delinquent," "sex deviate," "ex-convict," "chronic drunk," "dope fiend," "criminal," or "insane" person. These stereotypes are also communicated through newspapers, radio, television, and movies. For example, as newspaper accounts seize upon such terms in their headlines, mass media, in effect, play up the societal image of the deviant or law violator as one with defects of charactor, mentality, or intelligence. These stereotypes reflect societal attitudes concerning deviation as well as the tendency to reject, label, ostracize, and isolate the deviant. These same stereotypes form the base of many traditional methods of dealing with deviants. This is evident from the manner in which deviants are "cut off" or isolated from respectable society through consignment to prisons; mental hospitals; treatment institutions for drug addicts or alcoholics; reformatories; or other "protective" institutions.[6] In some instances, of course, deviants are not physically isolated, but are socially isolated through relegation to a degraded status. Garfinkel has pointed out that criminal judicial processes may be regarded as "status degradation ceremonies" from the prisoner's point of view.[7] Two aspects of such ceremonies are the destruction of the person's identity and the assignment of

---

[4] Stanley Schacter, "Deviation, Rejection, and Communication," *Journal of Abnormal and Social Psychology,* 46:190–207 (1951).

[5] For further discussion of this process, see John W. Thibaut and Harold H. Kelley, *The Social Psychology of Groups* (New York: Holt, Rinehart and Winston, Inc., 1959), especially Chap. 13; and George W. Homans, *Social Behavior: Its Elementary Forms* (New York: Basic Books, Inc., 1961), section on conformity, pp. 116–119 and 339–358.

[6] Lemert, pp. 44–47. These will be discussed in the next chapter. See also Austin L. Porterfield, "The We-They Fallacy in Thinking about Delinquents and Criminals," *Federal Probation,* 21:44–47 (1957).

[7] Harold Garfinkel, "Conditions of Successful Degradation Ceremonies," *American Journal of Sociology,* 61:421–422 (1956).

a new identity that is lower in the social scheme. When this occurs, the deviant's opportunities for finding employment and enjoying other societal privileges are markedly limited. He may, at this point, feel forced to seek the support of a deviant organization or subculture. Some suggest that this is one reason underlying the development of deviant groups, such as subcultures.[8]

If deviations become a subculture the difficulties of controlling such behavior are increased. Deviants of this type communicate knowledge among themselves about disapproved ways of conduct, and there is rapport among them. The members develop their own set of norms, distinct social roles, and a status system apart from that of the larger society. Some systematic deviation may have less organization, as is true of many delinquent gangs, than that of others, for example, organized and professional crime or traffic in drugs. Some type of deviant behavior—professional pickpocketing, begging, or prostitution, to name a few—have a long history. Many forms of professional crime, such as the techniques and language of pickpockets, can be traced back to Elizabethan times and earlier. Among such highly organized forms of deviant behavior "a definite professionalization of conduct by deviant group members develops, along with craft pride similar to that found among integrated occupational groups." [9] It is easier for members of such groups to indoctrinate others and at the same time more difficult for society to deal effectively with behavior supported by a highly organized subculture.

MORAL AND AMELIORATIVE PROBLEMS

Difficulties in dealing with deviant behavior are often complicated by the lack of public agreement over whether certain deviations constitute a problem and also by disagreement about the norms and values involved in the solution. In this connection Fuller and Myers have distinguished between ameliorative and moral problems.[10] *Ameliorative problems* include deviations such as the conventional crimes of robbery, burglary, and murder, as well as drug addiction, mental illness, and alcoholism. The existence of an ameliorative problem implies that if the situation were eliminated the deviant behavior would be "ameliorated" or made better. Although in ameliorative deviations there is more general agreement that

---

[8] Lemert, pp. 44–47.

[9] Lemert, p. 44.

[10] Richard Fuller and Richard R. Myers, "Some Aspects of a Theory of Social Problems," *American Sociological Review*, 6:24–32 (1941). Also see John F. Cuber, Robert A. Harper, and William F. Kenkel, *Problems of American Society: Values in Conflict* (3d ed.; New York: Holt, Rinehart and Winston, Inc., 1956).

the situation is undesirable, there is disagreement as to the value of the corrective means or proposed solutions. This situation exists because the corrective means either interfere with other values of individuals or groups, or are believed to be inefficient. The solutions proposed frequently involve habits and attitudes which might have to be altered, and which currently provide a source of satisfaction for the individuals concerned. For example, few would say that mental disorders or such ordinary crimes as burglary and larceny and other than "bad." The solution of these problems, however, presents a different issue entirely, for it might mean changing, for example, some aspects of urban life.

In *moral problems* there is not only disagreement over the proposed solution to the problem but disagreement as to whether or not the situation is undesirable and should be changed. There may be disagreement over whether such "moral" conditions as divorce, discrimination against minority groups, occupational and white-collar crime, and gambling, actually constitute deviant behavior. To some, divorce is a serious moral transgression; to others, it is a solution to a problem which would be infinitely more serious if divorce were not permitted. Racial and religious discrimination is not "bad" to some people. They see the protection of vested interests, the preservation of so-called biological superiority or white supremacy, "natural law," and a host of others as reasons why it is, if not necessarily a good thing, certainly not a social problem. Others believe that discrimination is a serious contradiction of the American Creed of human rights, democracy, and freedom of opportunity. Some people regard white-collar crime as real crime and a serious form of deviant behavior in society, whereas others do not. Gambling and political corruption are abhorrent to some; to others they are not social problems but "normal" situations in contemporary urban life. Obviously there are similar difficulties about solutions when there is disagreement over the existence of a problem.

GENERAL PUBLIC EDUCATION

Many people feel that public education is basic to any program attempting to prevent certain types of deviant behavior. The underlying factors which account for the problems confronting modern society must be sought and dealt with on a broad basis. As some have noted, in order to find ways of combatting crime and delinquency, a necessary first step is to provide the public with more information about present problems and the successes and failures of methods used to deal with them.[11] Because in a

---

[11] Hugh P. Reed, "The Citizens' New Role in Combatting Crime," *Federal Probation,* 24:31–36 (1960).

democratic society operation of correctional and preventive measures rests ultimately on public support, it is imperative that the public be adequately informed. This information may be communicated not only through television, radio, the press, films, pamphlets, and books, but also through discussion. The type of education that seeks to provide such information will be discussed here.

All too frequently, however, the public receives misinformation about deviant behavior from these sources, which is almost as fallacious as having no information at all. Frequently the public receives information based on studies and opinions of psychiatrists and psychoanalysts about the etiology of delinquency, crime, and other forms of deviant behavior which are not scientifically accurate. In other cases the public is told that deviant behavior is a product of poverty. It is unfortunate that more effort is not made to dispense valid information about deviation, such as the increasing research showing the importance of sociological and cultural factors.

Delinquency and Crime

The public has been educated about delinquency and crime through those national, state, and local conferences and various legislative commissions or committees which have wide publicity. In 1965, for example, a Commission on Law Enforcement and Administration of Justice was created by executive order of the President. This commission made a detailed and comprehensive examination of crime and law enforcement in the United States and in its report in 1967 made many recommendations which were widely disseminated to the public in a report entitled *The Challenge of Crime in a Free Society*.[12] This report emphasized the role of citizens and their organizations in the prevention of crime.[13] It stressed the contribution that could be made by business, industry, labor unions, religious institutions, and community and professional organizations.

In 1959 the investigating subcommittee authorized by the Senate Judiciary Committee conducted widely publicized public hearings on the problem of juvenile delinquency. The objectives of the investigation were to

---

[12] *The Challenge of Crime in a Free Society*, A Report by the President's Commission on Law Enforcement and Administration of Justice (Washington, D. C.: Government Printing Office, 1967). This was followed by several volumes dealing with different segments, such as the police, in the fields of crime and law enforcement. A previous national study of crime and law enforcement, the Wickersham Commission, had issued a number of reports in the 1930s. See National Commission on Law Observance and Enforcement, *Reports* (Washington, D. C.: Government Printing Office, 1931).

[13] *The Challenge of Crime in a Free Society*, pp. 288–291.

examine (1) the extent of delinquency, its causes and contributing factors; (2) the adequacy of existing laws; (3) sentences and correctional action employed by federal courts; and (4) the extent of juvenile violation of federal narcotics laws.[14] The committee focused public attention on the problems it brought to light, and recommended measures considered to be helpful both in preventing juvenile delinquency and in rehabilitating delinquents and youthful offenders. The publicity which the findings of this subcommittee have received helped to arouse the public about the gravity of existing conditions and the difficulty of dealing with them.

One of the most famous of all congressional investigations of crime was the Special Committee to Investigate Organized Crime in Interstate Commerce, which was headed by Senator Estes Kefauver and which held nation-wide hearings during 1951.[15] These public hearings, the first senatorial hearings to be televised, enabled millions of Americans to see members of the Senate committee questioning organized criminals and their political allies about their activities.

In the past thirty years several congressional investigations have influenced public opinion about white-collar crime: the investigation of the Teapot Dome scandals of the mid-twenties; the various committees investigating business ethics during the 1930s; and the Truman Committee, which investigated graft and corruption in connection with war contracts during World War II.[16] Senator Paul H. Douglas headed a well-known committee which, in 1951, went into the question of preventing graft and corruption in government. This committee made several proposals to avoid corruption in government, including the disclosure of income and other transactions by government officials, the definition of improper or unethical conduct, and the imposition of specific penalties. Douglas also proposed that a commission on ethics in government be set up.[17]

Congressional investigations which have received much attention within recent years have dealt with unethical conduct in the labor and management field, and with manipulation of prices by business executives in a number of major industries. The Senate inquiry of 1956 into labor

---

[14] Senate Report of Juvenile Delinquency Hearings, 86th Cong., 1st Sess., S.R. 54, *Investigation of Juvenile Delinquency in the United States* (Washington, D.C.: Government Printing Office, February 12–13, 1959). See also reports dated during subsequent months.

[15] See pages 285–286

[16] See p. 577.

[17] Report of the Commission on Ethics in Government, Committee on Labor and Public Welfare, to accompany Senate Joint Resolution 107, October 9, 1951. Also see Paul H. Douglas, *Ethics in Government* (Cambridge, Mass.: Harvard University Press, 1952).

corruption revealed the penetration into manufacturing concerns by racketeers and gangsters known to be connected with several large labor unions. Further inquiry documented a succession of collusive arrangements between business organizations and some unions. In addition, numerous improper and illegal activities were revealed in some labor unions, including collusion with organized criminals, violence and beatings, pay-offs, blackmail, padded expense accounts, speculation in gambling, and other forms of vice.[18] These investigations led to the passage of laws requiring labor unions to make full reports of their administrative and financial affairs, and to hold fair election proceedings with secret ballots. Also, these laws restrict the use of union funds by providing criminal penalties for their misappropriation. Yet one of the most significant results of these investigations was the arousal of public attention and concern, and the recognition by lawmakers of the need for legal restrictions as well as their adequate enforcement.[19]

In more general terms, people appear to need to be educated to realize that a democratic society rests fundamentally on the premise that laws are to be obeyed. This concept differs somewhat from the currently accepted idea that it is the responsibility of government to force the citizens to obey the law through fear of being apprehended if they disobey it. Organized crime, for example, cannot be successfully controlled unless there is some agreement on the immoral consequences of widespread commercialized gambling by the public and its relation to the bribery of public officials and police officers. The public's definition of a criminal needs to be changed so that it will include not merely those who violate the criminal law but those who violate any law. Society cannot expect to control ordinary crime with one set of standards while at the same time allowing violations of law, such as organized or white-collar crime, to take place under another set of standards. The citizen's responsibility for society's laws can be strengthened through his wider participation in neighborhood, community, and welfare activities which will help him to understand social objectives. The presidential commission on law enforcement stressed the citizen's role in supporting law.

> The citizen's responsibility runs far deeper than cooperating with officials and guarding against crime, of course. Much more important is a proper respect for the law and for its official representatives. People who sneer at policemen; people who "cut corners" in their tax returns; landlords who violate housing codes; parents who set bad examples by their

---

[18] Robert F. Kennedy, *The Enemy Within* (New York: Harper & Row, Publishers, 1960), pp. 17–25.

[19] Kennedy, p. 300.

own disrespect for the law, or who wink at their children's minor offenses, contribute to crime. Delinquents—and adult criminals as well—often try to justify their actions by saying that the only difference between them and "respectable citizens" is that they were unlucky enough to be caught.[20]

An important area in the control of occupational and white-collar crime is the development of more effective ethics among the professional groups and various organizations.[21] More ethical standards need to be developed among politicians and government officials as well as among professional men and businessmen. There needs to be some agreement among the various groups in society as to what is proper conduct, how new members are to be indoctrinated with such a code of ethics, and how deviations are to be treated. This relationship of ethics to white-collar crime is illustrated by the difficulties encountered in controlling "sharp" practices in business:

> Control of sharp, evasive, and fraudulent practices in business will have to develop externally, that is, by boycotting and the reporting of white-collar violators by their victims (other businessmen, buyers, and consumers) as well as internally, that is, within the world of business and its various organizations and associations. The reporting of white-collar violations and bringing of action in the regular law enforcement channels rather than through investigations and action of administrative commissions and regulatory bodies is a matter of vital concern to crime control. Crystallized public sentiment against white-collar crime would be more of a preventive force, since one of the reasons that so much white-collar violation in the business world exists is that the public is really not vitally interested in the ethics of its businessmen just so long as it gets good service from them. Businessmen, through their own organizations and associations, must also become vitally concerned with the ethics of doing business and the ways of rendering service to the public. In several quarters of well-established and highly organized business, strong internal controls over members by associations are developing, whereby businessmen through their own collective pressure can hold their colleagues in line. Ethical business practices are what is needed to combat white-collar crime, although it is realized that this is difficult to bring about in some highly competitive enterprises, in wildcat operations, and in businesses that have not developed a strong association.[22]

---

[20] *The Challenge of Crime in a Free Society,* p. 289.

[21] Marshall B. Clinard, "Corruption Runs Far Deeper than Politics," *The New York Times Magazine,* August 10, 1952, pp. 20–21. Also see the special issue entitled "Ethical Standards in American Public Life," *The Annals,* Vol. 280 (1952).

[22] Walter C. Reckless, *The Crime Problem* (2d ed.; New York: Appleton-Century-Crofts, Inc., 1955), pp. 678–679.

Education about Mental Disorders

During the past decade, great strides have been taken toward educating the public about mental disorder. Such education is carried out largely through the mass media and through the efforts of three agencies—citizens' mental health organizations, federal and state agencies, and professional groups. The National Institute of Mental Health, an agency created by an act of Congress in 1946, is responsible for coordinating work dealing with mental disorder, including the dissemination of information to the public, community programs, research, and training of psychiatric personnel. State agencies generally function to assist public education through community services.

Voluntary citizens organizations are chiefly concerned with educating themselves and other members of the public about mental health. The work of these groups consists of such activities as gathering and documenting information about conditions affecting mental health, encouraging research on mental health, and trying to improve the number and quality of personnel in the field of mental health.[23] Much of their work is done through public speakers, motion pictures, television, and radio programs, and pamphlets. The professional organizations of certain applied disciplines, such as social work, medicine, and psychiatry, have assumed some of the responsibility for informing the public about mental disorder. Unfortunately, most of this information deals with an individualistic explanation of mental disorder rather than with sociological and cultural factors.

Despite such efforts as those described above, research evidence shows that the public generally continues to stigmatize mental disorder. A two-year poll of Americans' opinions of their own mental health showed that although one in four believed he had problems serious enough to seek help, only one in seven sought it.[24] A 1960 study, for example, found that relatives of former mental patients tend to expect that friends and neighbors will respond to them with rejection and disapproval.[25]

---

[23] George D. Stevenson, "Citizens Mental Health Movement," *The Annals,* 286:92–99 (1953).

[24] Gerald Gurin, Joseph Veroff, and Sheila Feld, *Americans View Their Mental Health* (New York: Basic Books, Inc., 1960). Also see Charles D. Whatley, "Social Attitudes toward Discharged Mental Patients," *Social Problems,* 6:313–320 (1959); and Howard E. Freeman and Ozzie G. Simmons, "Feelings of Stigma among Relatives of Former Mental Patients," *Social Problems,* 8:312–322 (1961).

[25] Freeman and Simmons. Also see Charlotte Green Schwartz, "Perspectives on Deviance: Wives' Definitions of Their Husbands' Mental Illness," *Psychiatry,* 20:275–291 (1957); and Robert H. Felix, "Social Psychiatry and Community Attitudes," *World Health Organization Technical Report* (Series 177; Geneva: World Health Organization, 1959).

There are indications that these attitudes are changing. A more recent survey in New York City of attitudes about mental illness, for example, showed that people do not regard mental disorder as a deviant phenomenon quite as much as they previously did.[26] While the majority felt that mental disorder tends to repel people, only a small minority admitted regarding themselves as being repelled by a person who was mentally ill. One out of ten said that they would be willing to have former mental patients as coworkers and neighbors, but less than one in four would be willing to share an apartment with a former mental hospital patient or to agree to the marriage of a family member with a former mental patient.

There is also evidence that public ideas about mental disorder are highly stereotyped. To the public, the term "mental disorder" often connotes bizarre, highly disturbed behavior.[27] Some suggest that such stereotypes may be fostered by mass media information which tends too often to present an oversimplified, distorted view of the subtleties involved in mentally disordered behavior.[28] It has also been shown that information distributed to the public about mental disorder is biased in the direction of middle-class values and norms, and that the picture the public receives may not represent the norms of mental disorder or mental health in the other social classes.[29]

One of the most significant proposals of the Joint Commission on Mental Illness and Health (which was authorized by Congress in 1955 to conduct a five-year study on aspects of mental health in the United States) was for public information of a *specific* kind on mental illness.[30] The commission noted that the continuing lag in treatment of the mentally ill reflects a basic pattern of social rejection. It stated that information to the public should aim specifically to counter this societal pattern of rejection of the mentally ill. Such information should focus on the major difference

---

[26] Jack Elinson, Elena Padilla, and Marvin E. Perkins, *Public Image of Mental Health Services* (New York: Mental Health Materials Center, Inc., 1967). Also see Bruce P. Dohrenwend and Edwin Chin-Shong, "Social Status and Attitudes Toward Psychological Disorder: The Problem of Tolerance of Deviance," *American Sociological Review*, 32:417–433 (1967).

[27] Shirley A. Star, "The Public's Ideas about Mental Illness." Paper presented to the annual meeting of the National Association for Mental Health, November 5, 1955.

[28] John Clausen, "Mental Disorders," in Robert K. Merton and Robert R. Nisbet, *Contemporary Social Problems* (rev. ed.; New York: Harcourt, Brace & World, Inc., 1966), pp. 26–84. Also see discussion in Chapter 12, pp. 494–495.

[29] Orville R. Gursslin, Raymond G. Hunt, and Jack L. Roach, "Social Class and the Mental Health Movement," *Social Problems*, 7:210–217 (1960).

[30] Report of the Joint Commission on Mental Illness and Health, *Action for Mental Health* (New York: Basic Books, Inc., 1961), pp. 275–282.

between physical and mental illness, that is, the differences in the reactions and attitudes toward the person by *others*. The commission report also noted a tendency for persons to react to the mentally ill persons with revulsion and ridicule. Public information should therefore make clear that public stereotypes of mental illness, as characterized by violent behavior, represent an exceedingly small proportion of all those who are mentally ill, and that these stereotypes inaccurately represent the overwhelming majority of mental patients.

Education about Alcoholism

Some of the most effective work in public education has been done with alcoholism. These accomplishments have been fairly recent but they have encouraged similar work in other areas of deviant behavior. Considering that extensive scientific efforts in this field are hardly more than twenty years old, the progress has been remarkable. As early as 1949 a study found that nationally about one in five persons had come to believe that alcoholism is a "sickness" and that alcoholics should not be punished.[31] There are indications that this belief is held much more widely today. Some suggest that this indicates progress in the field of alcohol education. This change in attitude on the part of the public has been largely due to the work of Alcoholics Anonymous, state bureaus of alcoholism, Yale University's Section on Alcohol Studies (now at Rutgers University), the National Committee on Alcoholism, which has many local chapters, school educational programs, industrial in-plant programs, as well as the continued cooperation of all types of media of mass communication.

Because the work of Alcoholics Anonymous will be discussed in the next chapter the remarks on alcohol education will be limited here to a few other programs. In nearly all states there are governmental programs on alcoholism which help to coordinate work in this area, furnish information on the subject to the public, and develop treatment and education programs. Practically all the states now require the teaching of alcohol education at some level in their school programs. More than sixty cities have information centers dealing with the problems of alcoholics, but many more are needed. Trained persons staff these centers, which are sources of information on alcoholism, including data on available treatment facilities—hospitals and sanatoria, medical specialists, Alcoholics Anonymous groups, and so on. Staffs not only help alcoholics work out some sort of treatment program but also help other persons who are interested in the problems of the alcoholic. Manuals devised for the use of schoolteachers cover many

---

[31] John W. Riley, Jr., "The Social Implications of Problem Drinking," *Social Forces,* 27:301–305 (1949).

of the important aspects of what has been learned about alcohol and alcoholism.[32] These school manuals have adult counterparts in a large number of books, pamphlets, and audiovisual programs, which have been developed for the adult citizen.

The public attitude, held increasingly by many, that alcoholism is a "sickness" may enable the alcoholic to receive sympathy and social support for his temporary occupancy of a "sick role." [33] To this extent, the alcoholic's rehabilitation may be enhanced, since his compulsive drinking seems to be due largely to perceived social rejection, ostracism, and isolation stemming from experiences of drinking of a noncompulsive nature.[34]

Education about Drug Addiction

Although there has been a great increase in public information about the use of narcotics, not all of it has been presented to the public in a scientific and instructive manner.[35] Much of this information, in fact, is still communicated in a sensational manner and with heavy moralistic overtones which create an erroneous conception of the drug addict. Like much of the publicity about mental disorders, it tends to develop public stereotypes. Ideally, educative efforts should be directed at what some suggest is the basis of the addiction problem in America: public attitudes toward addiction and the drug addict. So long as addicts are ostracized, rejected, stigmatized, and isolated from respectable society, their rehabilitation and the reduction of the drug problem are impeded.

Marriage and Family Education

Extensive work is being done now to dispense scientific information about marital and family relations. Many schools, particularly those dealing with higher education, have introduced courses in family relationships. High school courses are generally not designated as courses in family prob-

---

[32] See, for example, Joseph Hirsh, *Alcohol Education: A Guide Book for Teachers* (New York: Abelard-Schuman Ltd., 1952). For a general discussion of these programs see Raymond McCarthy and Edgar M. Douglass, *Alcohol and Social Responsibility* (New York: Thomas Y. Crowell Company and the Yale Plan Clinic, 1949).

[33] Lemert.

[34] See Edwin H. Lemert, "Alcoholism and the Sociocultural Situation," *Quarterly Journal of Studies on Alcohol,* 17:306–317 (1956) for some relevant comments. Also see David Mechanic and Edmund A. Volkart, "Stress, Illness, and the Sick Role," *American Sociological Review,* 26:51–38 (1961).

[35] *The Drug Takers,* Special *Time-Life* Report (New York: Time, Inc., 1965) and John A. O'Donnell and John C. Ball, eds., *Narcotic Addiction* (New York: Harper & Row, Publishers, 1966), are examples of a scientific approach.

lems; instead, the subject is treated in health, home economics, and social science courses. The first college course on marriage was given in 1926 at the University of North Carolina; marriage and family courses are now a regular part of the curriculum of many colleges and universities.

Numerous national and local organizations are interested in family relationships—so many, in fact, that they are sometimes referred to as "the family life movement." Some organizations are interested only in education, whereas other include counseling and discussion of proposed legislative changes affecting their programs. Utah, for example, has legislation requiring marital counseling for couples who have filed for divorce.

The National Council on Family Relations, organized in 1938, is probably the best known of the national private family organizations. Other national private organizations not affiliated with religious groups include the American Association of Marriage Counselors, the American Eugenics Society, the American Social Hygiene Association, the Family Service Association of America, and the Planned Parenthood Federation of America.

Reducing Discrimination

Efforts to reduce discrimination are now so extensive that it is possible to do little more than list them.[36] In 1956 there were 491 public or private national, regional, states, and local agencies, with paid staffs, exclusive of agencies of the federal government, working in the area of intergroup relations: 61 national private agencies, 63 regional agencies, 23 state public agencies, 48 state private agencies, 30 municipal agencies, and 266 local private agencies. In addition there were a large number of other groups with voluntary staffs.[37] Since 1947, groups working in this area have had a professional organization, the National Association of Intergroup Relations Officials (NAIRO), which has a membership of over 150 professional workers.

Of the national private agencies working in this area, the most important are the American Friends Service Committee, the American Jewish Committee, the American Jewish Congress, the Anti-Defamation League of B'nai B'rith, the Japanese-American Citizens League, the Jewish Labor Committee, the National Community Relations Advisory Council, the National Conference of Christians and Jews, the National Association for the Advancement of Colored People, the National Urban League, the Southern Christian Leadership Conference, the Congress of Racial Equality, The

---

[36] George E. Simpson and Milton J. Yinger, *Racial and Cultural Minorities* (3d ed.; New York: Harper & Row, Publishers, 1965).

[37] Material furnished by Research Department, National Association of Intergroup Relations Officials.

Student Non-Violent Coordinating Committee, the Southern Regional Council, as well as many Protestant and Catholic church organizations and Spanish-speaking and Indian groups.

Most significant of the post–World War II developments in inter-group relations have been not only the enactment of laws against discrimination in the fields of public accommodations, employment, housing, and education but the creation of government civil rights agencies to administer these laws. Twenty-five states have public agencies with authority ranging from purely advisory powers, as in Kentucky and Florida, to full-fledged regulatory powers, including the issuance of enforceable orders, as in sixteen of the northern states.

New York and Wisconsin were among the first states to enact fair-employment practices (FEPC) laws in 1945. In 1961 Illinois passed fair-employment practices laws to become the twenty-first state with such legislation. The first state fair-housing laws prohibiting discrimination in the sale, lease, and rental of dwellings were adopted by such states as New York, New Jersey, and Wisconsin in the late 1940s. All these early laws applied only to public or publicly assisted housing. In 1959, Colorado, Connecticut, Massachusetts, and Oregon passed the first fair-housing laws applicable to private housing as well.

Depending upon many complex factors, such as the population makeup and the climate of opinion toward human rights, state civil rights agencies vary considerably in organization, powers, functions, and budgets. The Governor's Commission on Human Rights was created by the Wisconsin legislature in 1947 ". . . to disseminate information and to attempt by means of discussion as well as other proper means to educate the people of the state to a greater understanding, appreciation and practice of human rights for all people. . . ." Without specific administrative responsibility or regulatory powers, the commission's program includes fact finding, education, community organization and relations, the handling of cases of discrimination, and recommendations of needed legislation. A broad approach utilizing existing agencies and resources is employed to remedy specific problems and to promote a climate of opinion favorable to equal opportunity for all minority groups.

Twenty states also have private agencies in intergroup relations. About twelve of them are councils on human relations in southern states organized through efforts of the Southern Regional Council to help particularly with tension growing out of school desegregation.

There has been an increasing development at the local level of community relations boards or mayors' committees. Some of them are quasi-public but most are primarily advisory. Of the more than thirty municipal intergroup relations agencies with paid staffs located in twenty-seven cities, some have fair employment practices responsibilities, and others work for the improvement of relations between various groups through education, persuasion, and consultation. Most are in large cities, such as New York, Boston, Chicago, Cincinnati, Cleveland, Denver, Philadelphia, Pittsburgh, Toledo, and St. Louis. In addition, there are 117 cities with local private agencies. Relatively few municipal committees with paid staffs exist in the South. In recent years a number of cities have established either official committees or permanent commissions. According to a 1961 survey, approximately one southern city in six with a population of over 10,000 had a biracial committee to deal with tensions and problems of desegregation.[38]

Educational methods include situations where members of different racial groups can associate freely, as they do in the camps conducted by the American Friends Service Committees. These camps bring together younger persons from various racial, religious, and national groups around a task not primarily concerned with majority-minority relations but which often influences them indirectly in a marked way. An increasing number of workshops in intergroup relations, generally about fifty each summer, have been held since the end of World War II. Many church groups, labor unions, and similar groups have been active in developing a local interest in discrimination and its consequences. Most colleges now have a course in minority problems, and many secondary schools deal with this topic in their social science or civics courses. Any permanent and large-scale solution to the problems associated with discrimination, however, must come through universal education at the elementary school level about the myths of racial differences, the nature of prejudice, and the consequences of discrimination.

It is difficult to say how effective these public and private programs of public education actually are. The very organization of these official and unofficial bodies is an indication that more citizens are assuming a larger share of the responsibility for these problems. This widespread awareness of group prejudices is evident in the results of surveys and in the extent to which the subject of racial and cultural relations has been featured in the press, television, radio, and motion pictures. That the subject of racial and religious discrimination is increasingly open and frank is in itself an indication of progress toward a solution. Some have even suggested that many difficulties in race relations can be partly ameliorated by greater dispersions of the Negro population not only within large cities but to smaller cities.[39]

---

[38] Charles Grigg and Lewis Killian, "The Bi-Racial Committee as a Response to Racial Tensions in Southern Cities," *Phylon*, 23:379–382 (1962).

[39] Morton Grodzins, "The Metropolitan Area as a Racial Problem," in Harry Gold and Frank R. Scarpitti, *Combatting Social Problems: Techniques of Intervention* (New York: Holt, Rinehart and Winston, Inc., 1967), pp. 141–150.

LOCAL COMMUNITY PROGRAMS

It is often difficult for the public to see that it is easier and less expensive, in the long run, to prevent the development of deviant attitudes and antisocial behavior through local community programs than to try to modify them later. Several different types of preventive agencies have been, or are in the process of being, established. Some current programs represent a general educational approach, whereas others deal more specifically with local communities. As in the case of information given to the general public, much of the information disseminated by, and programs of, local community agencies are based on the individualistic nature of deviant behavior rather than the significance of group or sociological as well as cultural factors.

The School

More and more schools have been recognizing that their duties extend beyond the transmission of knowledge. As the schools have taken over many responsibilities for character development which were formerly left almost entirely to the family and the church, some families have tended to attribute to them the difficulties their children develop. The training of teachers has increasingly emphasized problems connected with deviant behavior, and they have learned to recognize in the classroom situation many incipient behavior difficulties of children. Such children are referred to the counseling staff for guidance if the school has such a staff, or to an appropriate community agency.

So important has the school become that claims are made that dropouts from school are the chief source of delinquency and drug addiction. The actual evidence is somewhat contradictory. Many deviations are committed by those who attend school but dropouts are probably more likely to be apprehended; in addition, it is likely that the delinquent behavior, particularly of a group type, may facilitate dropping out of school. Part of the confusion lies in considering dropouts as a single group and assuming that all have the same capacities. As one study showed, they are of three types: the involuntary dropouts, the retarded dropouts, and the intellectually capable dropouts.[40] The involuntary dropouts are those who leave school as a result of some personal crisis, such as the death of a parent; the retarded dropouts are those who lack sufficient ability to handle academic subject matter and thus drop out prior to entering high

---

[40] Harwin L. Voss, Aubrey Wendling, and Delbert S. Elliott, "Some Types of High School Dropouts," *Journal of Educational Research,* 59:363–368 (1966).

school; and the capable dropouts are those who terminate their education prior to high school graduation in spite of the fact that they have the ability to do the required academic work.

> The prevalent stereotype of dropouts depicts them as persons lacking in intellectual ability, but the evidence indicates that many dropouts are capable of doing satisfactory work in high school. Further, the available data demonstrate that while some dropouts earn poor grades, are retarded in their grade placement, and are poor readers, many other dropouts do not face these particular problems.
>
> Many of the apparent contradictions in the findings concerning dropouts can be resolved by distinguishing between early and late dropouts. Students with limited ability generally leave school early, whereas capable dropouts tend to remain in school longer. Hence, the stereotype of the dropout emphasizes the characteristics of early dropouts, of whom a significant proportion are of limited intellectual capability, receive poor grades, are poor readers, and are retarded in their grade placement.[41]

Some school situations add to behavioral difficulties and to intergroup tensions, and may even contribute to truancy and to more serious delinquency. Many professional educators agree that schools are often places where juveniles are bored, subjected to monotonous routine, allowed to express little individuality, or thrown into needless competition with others instead of learning how to cooperate with them. In many urban areas the relation of teacher and pupil is impersonal. Nevertheless, the school situation is one of personal interaction, and too frequently those selected to educate others are themselves uninspiring and may even be seriously maladjusted. Teachers too often silence inquisitive, creative students by demands for obedience. As a result, it is no wonder that one of the functions of juvenile gangs is to furnish new experiences or the thrill of the cleverly executed act of vandalism or car theft.

After studying the problem of delinquency, Robert MacIver has recommended the following primary obligations of the school system:

> 1. Since the earlier the child's learning problems are observed, recognized, and treated, the better the chance of overcoming them, every school should establish a thoroughgoing early-identification program, beginning with kindergarten. Such a program might indeed be extended with considerable advantage into the preschool programs that are now developing.
>
> 2. All teachers should be trained, in their preparation for teaching or in in-service training, to identify problem children and to provide preliminary help and guidance through sympathetic understanding of their needs.

---

[41] Voss, Wendling, and Elliott, p. 367.

3. All schools should have available specially trained guidance counselors to whom more difficult cases should be referred.

4. To make this service possible, classes should, whenever possible, be limited to twenty or twenty-five pupils, and for particularly refractory or difficult groups to fifteen.

5. A far more intensive effort is essential for the proper instruction of disprivileged groups, particularly the in-migrant groups in urban centers, in order to help them adjust to the conditions of city life and overcome the educational deficiencies of their background. This is of high importance for their future as citizens and directly to prevent their lapsing into delinquent habits.

6. In substandard poverty-stricken urban areas the school cannot operate effectively as an educational agency unless it becomes a neighborhood institution, cooperating with the families of the area and the local welfare organizations and providing special services for the children in order to equip them for schooling. No less imperative is the need to anticipate the likelihood that certain pupils will become dropouts, to give special consideration to their needs and their difficulties, and to stimulate their families through friendly contacts to encourage them to remain in school.

7. For older pupils who have either no interest or too little ability to incline them to continue with the regular academic curriculum, it is eminently desirable that the school have a division providing work-experience courses directly related to the types of jobs on which they have a reasonable chance of being employed.

8. The schools in this country cannot rise to the high demand and challenge involved in the education of the young, and in the special and individual guidance that is the best assurance that children will overcome their difficulties and not fall into delinquent ways, unless the community comes to their aid and enables them to raise their standards, the qualifications required of teachers, the salary rates, and the whole status of the profession.[42]

Notwithstanding the problem presented by the school itself, the major reason for the ineffectiveness of schools in slum areas with high rates of deviation is the lack of real motivation for learning in the community itself and the failure to support the efforts of the school sufficiently. Slum parents

---

[42] Robert M. MacIver, *The Prevention and Control of Delinquency,* pp. 122–123, reprinted by permission of the Publishers, Atherton Press. © 1966, Atherton Press, New York. All rights reserved. Also see William C. Kvaraceus, *Delinquent Behavior: Principles and Practices,* Vol. II; and *Delinquent Behavior: Culture and the Individual,* Vol. I (Washington, D.C.: National Education Association, 1959); and William E. Amos, "Prevention through the School," in William E. Amos and Charles F. Wellford, *Delinquency Prevention: Theory and Practice* (Englewood Cliffs, N.J.: Prentice-Hall, Inc., 1967), pp. 128–149.

may wish an education for their children but do little to help. School programs and the motivation for learning cannot succeed without the support of the neighborhood people. As Conant has pointed out, "One needs only to visit a [slum] school to be convinced that the nature of the community determines what goes on in the school." [43]

The Church

Churches of all types are increasingly recognizing their community responsibilities for attempting to deal with, or prevent, alcoholism, mental disorder, and drug addiction. Religious organizations have been involved in various efforts for the prevention of delinquency and the rehabilitation of offenders. Some efforts are community-based whereas others are person-based; some are church-centered and others are not.[44]

It has been suggested that clergymen's activities in the area of mental health should be chiefly those of prevention. The clergyman, in particular, is in a position to intervene during times of crisis but he should be readily accessible to his parishioners. Like the medical doctor, the clergyman can detect potential problems in their early stages. One study found that 42 percent of Americans turn to clergymen for help with their problems, 29 percent to physicians in general, 18 percent to psychiatrists or psychologists, and 10 percent to social agencies or marriage clinics.[45] Numerically there are far more clergymen than psychiatrists in the United States. Many theological students are receiving training in counseling persons with problems of various types. In 1960 there were 343 programs in clinical pastoral training, counseling, or psychology offered by 212 Protestant seminaries; training is also provided in Catholic and Jewish theological schools. It is estimated that between 8000 and 9000 clergymen have taken formal courses in clinical pastoral training.[46] Some even spend some time studying the problems of patients in mental hospitals and clinics. By counseling their parishioners they supplement the work of the limited number of psychiatrists.[47]

A similar development has been the increase in pastoral premarital and marital counseling. Traditionally the church has also been the refuge of the

---

[43] James B. Conant, *Slums and Suburbs* (New York: McGraw-Hill Book Company, Inc., 1961), p. 20.

[44] George Edward Powers, "Prevention through Religion," in Amos and Wellford, pp. 99–127.

[45] Gurin, *et al.*

[46] Richard V. McCann, *The Churches and Mental Health* (New York: Basic Books, Inc., 1962).

[47] Thomas A. C. Rennie and Luther E. Woodward, *Mental Health and Modern Society* (New York: The Commonwealth Fund, 1948), p. 239.

aged in their loneliness. And for many years there has been a large inter-denominational program to deal with discrimination. This has included particularly the work of the National Conference of Christians and Jews. Other programs to make the church a center for community activities, particularly youth programs, have helped to deal with many of the problems created by urbanism. For example, the boxing programs of the Catholic Youth Organization (CYO), founded in Chicago in 1930, appear to have been particularly effective in the slum areas of larger cities. Thus churches can play an important role in forestalling juvenile delinquency through working with local community prevention programs.

Clinical and Counseling Facilities

Outpatient counseling and treatment clinics of various types have been established in many countries, the chief ones being community mental health clinics, child guidance clinics, alcoholic clinics, marriage and family counseling agencies, and clinics for the treatment of threatened suicides. Community psychiatric facilities, which have increased greatly since 1962, have stressed the prevention and early outpatient treatment of mental disorders. Community mental health facilities providing outpatient services include full- or part-time psychiatrists, clinical psychologists, and social workers who help with diagnosis and treatment.

Community psychiatric facilities have developed in an attempt to integrate the various health facilities in the community and to maximize the number of patients who remain in the community[48] The object is to treat the patients without requiring hospitalization.[49] What is today called "community psychiatry" received its greatest impetus from the proposals of the Joint Commission for Mental Health in 1961 and that of President Kennedy to Congress in 1963.[50] The Commission recommended that contemporary treatment should be directed at helping persons with mental disorders to

---

[48] William M. Bolman and Jack C. Westman, "Prevention of Mental Disorder: An Overview of Current Programs," *American Journal of Psychiatry*, 123:1063 (1967). Also Anita K. Bahn, "An Outline for Community Mental Health Research," and Gerald Caplan, "Community Psychiatry: The Changing Role of the Psychiatrist," in S. Kirson Weinberg, ed., *The Sociology of Mental Disorders: Analyses and Readings in Psychiatric Sociology* (Chicago: Aldine Publishing Company, 1967), pp. 310–314 and pp. 301–309.

[49] Leopold Bellak, *Handbook of Community Psychiatry and Community Health* (New York: Grune & Stratton, Inc., 1964), p. 5.

[50] See Joint Commission on Mental Illness and Health, *Action for Mental Health* (New York: Basic Books, 1961) and John F. Kennedy, "The Role of the Federal Government in the Prevention and Treatment of Mental Disorders," in Weinberg, pp. 297–300.

sustain themselves in the community and that those in hospitals be returned to the community as quickly as possible to avoid the isolating effects of hospitalization. Subsequently, Congress initiated a program, proposed by President Kennedy, involving the establishment, with federal aid, of comprehensive community mental health centers, along with other improvements in the treatment of mental disorders. These centers are located in the patient's own environment and emphasize prevention as well as treatment.

The writings of Menninger and others set the stage for the National Mental Health Act of 1948, which served to raise the problem of mental health to the status of public health and provided greater funds for research.[51] Such research covered community psychiatric experiments in other parts of the world. In Europe, programs like Querido's community psychiatry in Amsterdam, open-door hospitals in England, and auxiliary psychiatric units in hospitals and rehabilitative houses have broken the conventional and traditional concepts of mental illness as necessarily requiring social isolation, and have paved the way for taking a new look at treatment.

Bellak has warned, however, that such an approach may lead to reducing effective treatment of patients.[52] Community members may become apathetic to individual needs in the hopes that the individual will recover if he merely remains in the community and is not hospitalized. Second, a program that is designed to handle the problems of large numbers of people also requires greater staff. There is an inherent danger that such a requirement will demand the employment of less qualified personnel and thereby compound the problem. Dunham has also questioned the knowledge of most psychiatrists of the significance of the community and its implication for psychiatric treatment.[53]

Child guidance clinics have also been established as a community response to the problem of mental health.[54] Some are general clinics which take all types of children with behavioral disorders. Some are affiliated with hospitals; others in larger urban areas are often set up in connection with school programs. There are few adequate evaluations of clinics such as these, and their effectiveness in reducing deviant behavior is not definitely known. However, one of the few studies evaluating the effect of such clinics on

---

[51] H. Warren Dunham, "Community Psychiatry: The Newest Therapeutic Bandwagon," *International Journal of Psychiatry*, 1:562 (1965). Also see William Menninger, *Psychiatry in a Troubled World* (New York: The Macmillan Company, 1948).

[52] Bellak, p. 7.

[53] Dunham, "Community Psychiatry."

[54] George E. Gardner, "American Child Psychiatric Clinics," *The Annals*, 286: 129–135 (1953).

reducing delinquent behavior concluded that there was little indication of any effect.[55]

Special facilities for the treatment of alcoholics have been established in many cities. Although for most of the patients alcoholism has been a long and persistent difficulty, many are helped before it becomes worse. The recommended staff consists of a part-time psychiatrist, two full-time psychiatric social workers, an internist, and a psychologist. Such a clinic can deal with about 350 cases annually at a cost which represents a fraction of the cost of untreated alcoholism in most communities.[56]

The first marriage clinics were established in Austria in 1922 and about eight years later in this country in New York City, Los Angeles, and Philadelphia. Today there are many such counseling centers which deal with problems of marriage and family relations. Generally their work is diagnosis and treatment, and they use the services of such specialists as psychiatrists, psychologists, sociologists, urologists, and gynecologists. Many other agencies, such as family service, perform similar work along with their other activities.

A number of community agencies have been set up in various countries to prevent suicides by group counseling and to offer other assistance.[57] In Vienna most of the suicide prevention work is carried out through Caritas, a Catholic organization, which also works with a preventive clinic for attempted suicides at the Vienna hospital. A special suicide prevention telephone service is maintained to which a person contemplating suicide, or a relative or neighbor, might call and speak to someone about his problems. If the individual desires, a social worker will visit him in his home, or he may come for a visit.[58] Great Britain has an antisuicide Department in the

---

[55] H. Warren Dunham and LeMay Adamson, "Clinical Treatment of Male Delinquents: A Case Study in Effort and Result," *American Sociological Review*, 21:312–320 (1956).

[56] McCarthy and Douglass, p. 114.

[57] Norman Farberow and Edwin S. Shneidman, "A Survey of Agencies for the Prevention of Suicide," in Farberow and Shneidman, *The Cry for Help* (New York: McGraw-Hill Book Company, Inc., 1961), pp. 136–149. This volume also contains a discussion of the Los Angeles Treatment Center. A Center for Studies of Suicide Prevention was established by the National Institute of Mental Health and began publication in 1967 of a *Bulletin of Suicidology* which contains information on suicide and various preventive programs. For a discussion of the work of The Good Samaritans in preventing suicides in Great Britain, see Donald McCormick, *The Unseen Killer: A Study of Suicide, Its History, Causes and Cures* (London: Frederick Mueller, Ltd., 1964), pp. 157–170.

[58] G. Hofmann und E. Ringel, "Erfahrungen auf Einer Zentralen Entgiftungsstation," *Kongressberichte der 6 Psychiater-Tagung des Landschaftsverbandes* (Düsseldorf: Rheinlandverlag, 1965).

Salvation Army, as well as the Good Samaritans, a volunteer group combining religion and psychotherapy. Its twenty-eight centers have dealt with over a thousand cases in the ten months of the group's existence. In the United States the best-known organizations are the National Save-a-Life League, Inc., which was established in 1906; Rescue Incorporated, established in 1959, in Boston, to which persons can phone on a twenty-four-hour basis for psychological support and other help; and the Suicide Prevention Center founded in 1958 in Los Angeles. Some thirty-eight organizations deal with suicide prevention under a variety of names such as Suicide Prevention Service, Call-for-Help Clinics, Crisis Clinics, Crisis Call Centers, Rescue, Inc., Dial-a-Friend, and Suicides Anonymous, and were in existence in 1967 in eighteen states and the District of Columbia.

Street Corner Projects

One type of preventive program involves semiparticipant work with a group of deviants, such as delinquent gangs and drug addicts. One project has been the program for detached workers of the YMCA of metropolitan Chicago, where workers are assigned to make contacts with juvenile gangs and to try to change their delinquent patterns.[59] One similar project, for example, worked intimately with four Harlem street gangs from 1947 to 1950 in an effort to divert their activities into legitimate channels.[60] The gangs varied from thirty-five to over a hundred boys, ranging in years from nine to nineteen, all of whom had been engaging in such behavior as fighting in gangs, stealing, committing sex offenses, smoking marihuana, drinking liquor, and gambling.

A project worker was attached to each gang. As they established relationships with the boys in the gang, gradually won their confidences, and became accepted by them, they played several roles. One was a neutral role of observing and seeking information without displaying approval or disapproval; another was that of stimulating changes. They used such techniques as example-setting, delaying antisocial acts, and insight-inducing to make the boys aware of feelings they did not recognize. Through their associations they tried to encourage self-direction along the lines of new programs. They used various means to divert the boys' activities:

> 1. They organized baseball and basketball teams, obtained the use of school and church gyms for practice sessions, and participated in tournaments with the teams of former enemy gangs.

---

[59] James F. Short, Jr., and Fred L. Strodtbeck, *Group Process and Gang Delinquency* (Chicago: University of Chicago Press, 1965).

[60] Paul L. Crawford, Daniel I. Malamud, and James R. Dumpson, *Working with Teen-Age Gangs,* A Report on the Central Harlem Street Clubs Project (New York: Welfare Council of New York City, 1950), pp. 18–19.

2. They held a number of dances and block parties at which they sold refreshments and raffled off gifts. With the profits from these ventures some of the clubs were able to buy uniforms and equipment for their teams.

3. They organized a series of movie programs for their members and friends. The Project supplied the movie projector, but the boys ran the shows themselves—choosing the films, setting up chairs, collecting tickets at the door, and cleaning up afterwards.

4. They went on a number of overnight hikes, camping trips, and fishing and crabbing outings.[61]

Urban Community Development

The modern city, particularly the large metropolis, has produced a complex and difficult world of social relationships that are termed urbanism, with extensive conflicts of norms and values and a decline in informal controls; yet at the same time mechanisms of formal controls encounter difficulty. The characteristics of urbanism are products, first, of size, in which the increase in the number of inhabitants beyond a certain limit brings about changes in social and community relations. People encounter each other increasingly in daily life under impersonal conditions. Intimate personal groups like the family become less meaningful as an agent of social control. Formal controls, like law administered by the police, become ways of enforcing uniform normative standards in a city. Second, the great heterogeneity of the city is in part the product of the migration over many years of peoples of diverse origins and backgrounds. Large urban populations are a heterogeneous mass, a mixture of races, ethnic and regional groups, religions, social classes, and occupations. In some instances specific groups of persons are able to maintain some semblance of local unity but there is evidence that the population of cities in local areas is becoming more mixed as increased migration, housing pressures, and decrease in discrimination tend to scatter persons in larger areas. The heterogeneity of the cities means that individuals are confronted with conflicting standards of behavior.

Particularly characteristic of rapidly expanding urban areas has been the ever-increasing institutionalization of society and the individualization of man. Institutionalization is seen in the broad scope of governmental and nongovernmental city services, the inevitable result of larger and larger numbers of people concentrating in particular areas. As government has become larger, more specialists are required to take charge of varied services, and the active participation of individuals in the improvement of urban society has dwindled accordingly. Now and then even the lines of communication among the people, the city officials, and the politicians break

---

[61] Crawford, *et al.*, pp. 39–40.

down, and as a result the individual citizens feels less and less personally involved. Even private or voluntary agencies are often cut off from those whose needs they supposedly meet. Particularly bewildered is the new migrant to the city, who, along with the older urban resident, becomes completely confused by the bigness and impersonality of the city and even, at times, of the place where he works.[62]

Governmental and private welfare efforts seem powerless to cope effectively with the problems of the modern metropolis. The approach of urban community development is used increasingly in the United States as well as in many other countries of Europe, Asia, and Latin America.[63] It involves efforts to develop in a local community a realization that certain ways of life are inappropriate to effective urban living and a recognition that all citizens share in the solution of city-wide problems. The solution of urban problems, including those of the slum, depends largely on the development of effective local community feeling within an urban context as well as on individual initiative in seeking community integration and change. The development of a degree of self-help and initiative among urban dwellers is important to the solution of such problems as deviant behavior. More specifically, an approach to the problems created by the city, particularly in slum areas, through urban community development involves the following elements:

1. creation of a sense of social cohesion on a neighborhood basis and a strengthening of group interrelationships;
2. encouragement and stimulation of self-help, through the initiative of the individuals in the community;
3. stimulation by outside agencies when initiative for self-help is lacking;
4. reliance upon persuasion rather than upon compulsion to produce change through the efforts of the people;
5. identification and development of local leadership;
6. development of civic consciousness and acceptance of civic responsibility;

---

[62] See Marshall B. Clinard, *Slums and Community Development* (New York: The Free Press, 1966), p. 116.

[63] Clinard, *Slums and Community Development*. Also see Marshall B. Clinard, "The Sociologist and Social Change in Underdeveloped Countries," in Arthur B. Shostak, ed., *Sociology in Action* (Homewood, Ill.: The Dorsey Press, Inc., 1966), pp. 232–248; Marshall B. Clinard and B. Chatterjee, "Urban Community Development in India: The Delhi Pilot Project," in Roy Turner, ed., *India's Urban Future* (Berkeley: University of California Press, 1962); Marshall B. Clinard, "Perspectives on Urban Community Development and Community Organization," *Social Welfare Forum, 1962* (New York: Columbia University Press, 1963), pp. 65–85, and Peter Marris and Martin Rein, *Dilemmas of Social Reform: Poverty and Community Action in the United States* (New York: Atherton Press, 1967).

7. use of professional and technical assistance to support the efforts of the people involved;
8. coordination of city services to meet neighborhood needs and problems;
9. provision of training in democratic procedures that may result in decentralization of some government functions.[64]

This approach stresses the local neighborhood as an important area of action. An impressive amount of evidence in certain areas of social deviation indicates that often the neighborhood, rather than the individual or the family, is the locus of the urban problems. Research by social scientists in a number of cities has revealed that some neighborhoods have higher rates of deviations than others. This does not mean that deviations are nonexistent in some areas, but rather that if they are controlled in certain selected areas the total incidence can be materially reduced. There are great neighborhood variations in the rates for ordinary crime, delinquency, sexual promiscuity, family maladjustment, suicide, discrimination against Negroes, and anti-Semitism. Although alcoholism and certain forms of mental illness have not been characterized by such wide ecological differences, the incidence of schizophrenia may be several times greater—and the chances of getting early treatment much less—in certain areas.

The neighborhood is an area in which the family functions. To a large extent the kind of neighborhood determines the type of family life that will develop. Usually what a middle-class neighborhood claims as the personal virtues of the family are the reflection of groups of families and other institutions surrounding it. Conversely, there is a limit to what a single family with one set of norms can do if it is surrounded by other families with deviant norms and is in an area, such as a slum, where the institutions also cater to deviant norms. The family may come to reflect neighborhood approval or disapproval of conditions of stealing, prostitution, the use of personal violence, illegitimacy, marital infidelity, excessive drinking, or discrimination against certain groups. Neighborhoods and the children of neighbors help, more than is realized, to raise one's own children. The informal neighborhood education of a delinquent is frequently at odds with his more formal school education. There is often conflict between the neighborhood and the school in the definitions of what constitutes proper use of leisure time, and the attitudes toward legal codes.[65] Often the neighborhood play group can enforce more conformity than the school, and school programs which attempt, for example, to deal with juvenile delinquency cannot be effective without the active cooperation of the neighborhood. If there is a cleavage between school norms and neighborhood norms, the problems

---

[64] Clinard, *Slums and Community Development*, p. 126.
[65] Henry D. McKay, "The Neighborhood and Child Conduct," *The Annals*, 261:33 (1949).

of dealing with delinquency are greatly increased. Similarly, child guidance clinics and law enforcement must depend on neighborhood support. The people of a neighborhood can support or ridicule the work of psychiatrists and police officers. What their neighbors think is often the really important thing to people.

SLUMS AND COMMUNITY DEVELOPMENT

Many believe that the solution of deviant behavior lies in providing more agents of social control to apprehend deviants, such as the police, as well as more professional persons, such as psychologists and psychiatrists, and more institutions to treat them. Others believe that not only is it almost impossible for society to support and train personnel for such an enormous program but that it is unwise. In the first place, the stigma attached to a person by his being apprehended or treated for deviancy and the resulting effect on his self-concept may make the treatment results quite modest. The "deliquent role" is often reinforced by the actions of the police, the courts, and even by the professional social worker or probation officer.[66] The social worker is often regarded by the delinquent as an "outsider" of a different social class, as the enforcer of rules and regulations, and as a person who restricts his activities. Second, it is far easier to deal with deviant behavior by eliminating the principal source of deviance, such as the slum way of life, than to treat each generation of new deviants. Prevention of deviant behavior appears far more successful than treatment.[67]

Slums are areas with highly disproportionate rates of delinquency; conventional crimes of theft, burglary, and robbery; personal violent crimes such as criminal homicide, assault, and forcible rape; prostitution; drug addiction; mental disorder; and illegitimacy.[68] They also present the most difficult sanitation and health problems. In addition, slum dwellers generally have less desire for learning and give less support to the schools. They are generally apathetic toward their situation and feel powerless to change it. Despite the fact that persons who commit crimes are often from the slums, offenses generally take place there and the victim is another slum dweller.

Throughout the centuries many groups have lived in the slums and have moved out; others have stayed on. In most cities the slums have continued for centuries, in many instances either growing larger or spawning new ones. In this sense they can be said to be self-perpetuating, either re-

---

[66] William P. Lentz, "Delinquency as a Stable Role," *Social Work,* 11:66–70 (1960).

[67] MacIver and Amos and Wellford.

[68] See Chapter 4.

plenishing themselves from within or augmented by new ones created through migration from without the city. In the past, in the United States at least, it has generally taken about three generations for a substantial proportion of families to move from the tenements to middle-class areas. In developing countries this movement has hardly occurred at all, or if it has occurred it has done so over many generations. Such a "natural" method of moving people out of the slums has generally worked, but it has been inefficient, slow, sometimes barbaric, and wasteful of manpower and human talents. The problem is how to produce in one generation what might require three generations in more affluent societies and how to bring about change in developing countries in one or two generations which might otherwise require as many as five or more generations if it could be accomplished at all. Furthermore, since most large city slums contain not a few hundred or even a few thousand but hundreds of thousands and, in countries like India, even millions of people, some way must be found to produce widespread change.

The problem is more than moving people out of the slums; rather, it is one of change—even the complete eradication of the slum. In spite of welfare and other services through the years, slums have generally continued to resist efforts to change them, and they have remained largely unaffected by the multitude of agencies and services offered, even in developing countries. Thus far efforts have been directed toward ameliorating slum problems rather than eliminating the slum.

Slums cannot be rapidly changed simply by providing more professional help and guidance, greater economic and educational opportunities to overcome poverty, and more and better coordinated services.[69] Social workers have offered various services through settlement houses and welfare centers, for many humanitarian or liberally oriented persons have believed that the slum dwellers need help through charity, philanthropy, or other forms of "uplift." The past history, as well as the present status, of slum programs has indicated that such efforts alone have not been highly successful even though some slum dwellers may be changed. Slum people may even disdain to engage in activities yielding what appear to them to be the highest rewards.

Some feel that the slum problem, basically, stems from a lack of economic and educational opportunities.[70] If slum dwellers are given a chance

---

[69] For a more detailed discussion see Clinard, *Slums and Community Development*.

[70] Some with this approach have derived it, in part, from Robert K. Merton, *Social Theory and Social Structure* (rev. ed.; New York: The Free Press, 1957), and his "Anomie, Anomia, and Social Interaction: Contexts of Deviant Be-

to better themselves, by government agencies, the young people, at least, will individually take advantage of these services. Many slum dwellers, however, have limited aspirations and do not feel a desire for material wealth, education, or a fuller life strongly enough to make the effort to achieve them. Thus they may not take advantage of such proferred opportunities. Furthermore, any explanation based on lack of economic opportunity is too simple in view of the complexities of the slum problem.

It is questionable whether or not the so-called social psychological aspects of urban poverty—apathy, powerlessness, lack of planning, and hostility to outside agencies—can be directly attributed to the poverty of the slum. A given level of income does not necessarily produce certain psychological attitudes. In fact, subgroups among the urban poor may display reactions quite different from the psychological aspects of poverty. For example, very low-income families may have high levels of aspiration; leaders with strong motivation may be found among the poor; lower-middle-class families with high aspirations and little deviant behavior may actually have lower incomes than do many people receiving economic aid and benefits. Furthermore, Haggstrom claims that an increase in income among the poor in the United States has not altered these characteristics, nor has an increase in real per capita welfare and unemployment payments.[71] Differences in income and welfare payments among the various states do not appear to change the general characteristics of the slum and poverty.

There is no question, however, that measures to bring about improved economic conditions will be of great value to slum people. These include more adequate wages, guaranteed minimum incomes, undiscriminatory employment policies, accessible and inexpensive credit, programs to train or retrain youths and adults, more effective training for certain occupations, and increased social security and public assistance payments.[72] Education programs also have to be strengthened in order to turn out teachers of better caliber, children's reading skills must receive more attention, more tutoring services should be made available, and the school functions geared to the improvement of the community as a whole.

---

havior," in Marshall B. Clinard, ed., *Anomie and Deviant Behavior* (New York: The Free Press, 1964), pp. 213–242. Also see Richard A. Cloward, "Illegitimate Means, Anomie, and Deviant Behavior," *American Sociological Review*, 24:164–176 (1959); and Richard A. Cloward and Lloyd E. Ohlin, *Delinquency and Opportunity* (New York: The Free Press, 1960).

[71] Warren C. Haggstrom, "The Power of the Poor," in Frank Riessman, Jerome Cohen, and Arthur Pearl, eds., *Mental Health of the Poor* (New York: The Free Press, 1964), pp. 205–223.

[72] For a discussion see David Hunter, *The Slums: Challenge and Response* (New York: The Free Press, 1964), pp. 143–170.

Because slums have been so impervious to change and because the slum has been regarded primarily as a physical problem, one approach has been to destroy the slum through clearance and renewal programs. Within a new physical environment, it had been hoped, slum problems might disappear, but not only have slums usually not responded to such a simple solution; the problems of their inhabitants have even been accentuated. In developing countries, where urban housing is always in short supply, such an approach is unrealistic.

An adequate solution for the slum problem involves the development of community, self-help, and indigenous leadership. It assumes that change in the slum largely proceeds through the recognition, by those affected, of the need for change and their own assumption of responsibility and contribution. Its emphasis is on making and improving community ties, overcoming apathy and dependence, creating new aspirations, and changing self-concepts. In the process of developing a feeling of respectability and of importance, the slum dweller himself may find the slum way of life incompatible with his new self-image. The following detailed approach is essential in any successful effort to deal with the slums.

A Group Approach to Slum Problems

The problems that have developed in slum areas everywhere have generally originated in practices which have been condoned and continued by the group.[73] Thus the group may be used to produce effective changes in solving these problems. A group, rather than an individual, approach must be used, and slum people, as a group, must desire this change. A program will be effective only as a local community sees the need for change and as it, as a group, evolves and develops its own capacity for making the changes.

Creation of a New Type of Social Organization

Slum residents participate in organized groups to a minimal degree, particularly in comparison with similar participation by the middle class. Several characteristics of the lower- and working-class slum dwellers explain their relative lack of participation in community and neighborhood affairs.[74] In the first place, there is often a common set of self-defeating attitudes which act as a barrier to the slum resident's participation. Second, differences in racial and ethnic background often create feelings of antagonism which prevent cooperation. Another reason for the slum resident's failure

---

[73] See Chapter 4. For a fuller discussion of this and the other issues in the sections which follow see Clinard, *Slums and Community Development*.

[74] Hunter, pp. 17, 18.

to participate is that most organizations have been staffed or promoted by middle-class persons, and the average lower- and working-class slum dweller has not been able to see how such an organization will benefit him.

A type of *neighborhood organization* is needed if unity is to be brought about and effective change made for highly diverse slum people. The most likely approach is a geographic unit based on the local ties of residents. Organizations of this type may include a few hundred or a few thousand slum families organized into a council, with their own officers and committees. They would deal with local problems, develop neighborhood cohesion, or a sense of belonging in the area, as well as indigenous leadership capable of identifying neighborhood problems and acting upon them.[75] Such neighborhood organizations attempt to identify and support local needs, exert pressures on private and public authorities, and assume initiative for improving opportunities within the neighborhood. Where new local issues—the control of delinquency and crime, drug addiction, housing repairs, the cooperative development of a recreation area, mass cleanliness or immunization campaigns, for example—come under discussion, it is possible to obtain a degree of unity among people with diverse backgrounds.[76]

Group Perception of the Need for Change

Slum people will not necessarily change by being told what to do or by being furnished with the means for change, but people appear to be willing to participate in actions directed at adjusting or changing conditions in their neighborhoods if they perceive the need for change. This desire for change must precede any successful program of self-help. Permanent change is likely to come as a community sees this need, and as it develops the capacity for making the necessary changes.

The image of the Negro slum dweller, for example, must be modified not only through changes in opportunities but through self-instituted changes in the norms and values of the Negro slum areas relating to delinquency and crime, violence, illegitimacy, drug addiction, lack of family responsibility, and apathy toward educational opportunities. This change may, in turn, affect others' images of the "urban Negroes" and may facilitate the overcoming of discrimination and limitations on economic opportunity.

---

[75] For a discussion of the ways to organize slum areas into councils, see Clinard, *Slums and Community Development,* pp. 166–187; and Julia Abrahamson, *A Neighborhood Finds Itself* (New York: Harper & Row, Publishers, 1959).

[76] Coleman's studies of community conflict and organization around issues such as fluorine added to drinking water and urban renewal in the United States have suggested the same thing.—James S. Coleman, *Community Conflict* (New York: The Free Press, 1957).

Pursuance of Self-Imposed Change

Of great importance in social change is the slum person's direct role in changing the physical and social setting of his immediate surroundings and his day-to-day living. It is a curious contradiction that middle-class people whose community problems are not so serious often engage in far more self-help activities, either individually or collectively, than do the slum poor who have greater community problems. In this direct role slum people themselves may assume a direct role in dealing with delinquency and drug addiction in their areas. They may help to improve, maintain, and protect schools, parks, and other public facilities and they may take a direct part in learning which enables them to accept such modern advances as proper health and sanitation practices and to realize the importance of education.

Widespread and effective change in the slums requires the assumption of responsibility for, as well as the contributions by, the people who are directly affected. They must have a stake in the results and an appreciation of the need for change. "When change in custom is the immediate objective, the client community's cooperation is obviously essential." [77]

As they contribute to change by doing things for themselves, a total situation develops in which slum dwellers are likely to be more receptive to change as a whole. As Haggstrom has pointed out, the poor have found themselves at other times in a problematic situation and have themselves been moved to do something about their condition.[78] In early nineteenth-century England, for example, as part of the rising labor movement many working-class people began to educate themselves individually or in groups.[79]

Use of Traditional Groups for Change

Slum areas often have some traditional groups. They may be formal organizations such as a sports group, a local lodge, or a parent-teacher association.[80] They often have a degree of organization and carry on a cer-

---

[77] Ward H. Goodenough, *Cooperation in Change: An Anthropological Approach to Community Development* (New York: Russell Sage Foundation, 1963), p. 18.

[78] Warren C. Haggstrom, "Poverty and Adult Education," Mimeographed, Syracuse University, January 1965, p. 4.

[79] Edward P. Thompson, *The Making of the English Working Class* (London: Victor Gollancz, Ltd., 1963), pp. 711–713.

[80] See Nicholas Babchuk and C. Wayne Gordon, *The Voluntary Association in the Slum* (Lincoln: University of Nebraska Studies, New Series No. 27, 1962);

tain amount of self-help activities for the group, but generally they are poorly organized and functionally weak. In addition, their organization and functions often have been carried on without being re-examined in the light of changing social conditions. These groups can often be redirected to new goals which can do much to change slum conditions.

Change in Identity or Self-Image

A change in identity or self-image of the residents is vital to change in urban slum areas. In most instances, such a change represents a new sense of personal worth and organization based on reality. Most slum dwellers are characterized by an apathy and a lack of confidence in their own abilities that are due to their limited economic resources and their low social status. Confidence in themselves has to be developed if they are to feel their own importance and recognize the possibilities for changing conditions with only modest help from outside sources.

Much difficulty is encountered in attempting to bring about this new perception of personal identity, for the slum dweller, reinforced by the slum culture, is inclined to be suspicious of, or to reject, change from without. Expectations and actions that differ from tradition in any way may be rejected. Slum dwellers, who are often suspicious even of neighbors who cooperate with change agents from the outside world, may not try to avail themselves of what opportunities they have because they accept the view that it is impossible to change their present identities. Sometimes they build up rationalizations to protect a world that seems secure and comfortable.

The creation of a new self-image provides a possible motivating force for slum people to change their practices. Change in identity or self-image and recognition of a world of differing expectations are essential in any successful slum action program. Identity change under planned efforts includes the desire for change, new experiences and new criteria for self-appraisal, commitment to change in self-identity, and recognition of a new identity and new roles.[81] Successful important self-originated social actions, by increasing the force and number of symbolic or nonsymbolic communications, indicate to a slum dweller that he is a worthwhile person and help to overcome a feeling of powerlessness.[82]

In our society, in which inner worth is expressed in action and striving,

---

Clinard, *Slums and Community Development;* and Kenneth Little, *West African Urbanization: A Study of Voluntary Associations in Social Change* (New York: Cambridge University Press, 1965).

[81] Clinard, *Slums and Community Development,* pp. 301–307; and Goodenough, Chap. 9.

[82] Haggstrom, "The Power of the Poor."

the purpose of the struggle is to attain aspirations. If one is not successful, one is viewed as worthwhile so long, and only so long, as one struggles. The poor tend to be regarded as failures and not struggling, and hence as worthless. This perception of worthlessness is incorporated in the conception others have of the poor and also, to some extent, in the conception the poor have of themselves. One way in which the poor can remedy the psychological consequences of their powerlessness and of their image as worthless is to undertake self-help that redefines them as potentially worthwhile and individually more important.[83]

The importance of this change in identity has been particularly stressed in the Black Muslim movement in the United States.[84] Working largely in some of the worst lower-class Negro slums, this movement tries to develop a new image of the Negro. In their small mosques in neighborhood areas the Black Muslims place great stress on their proud African heritage and on the rejection of the appendages carried over from slavery. The new convert experiences a rebirth in self-image in which he changes his name (the names of most Negroes are those of their slave owners), his religion (Christianity was imposed by slavery), his idea of his African homeland, his moral and cultural values, and his very purpose in life. Among Black Muslims, pride in Africa means that new patterns of behavior must be practiced by the lower-class slum Negro if behavior and the new self-image are to be reconciled. A strict private and public morality is emphasized for the "new Negro"; crime, delinquency, drug addiction and illegitimacy no longer fit this new self-image. Family roles are also redefined; a patriarchal system is substituted for a matriarchal. Family responsibility is expected of the men, who must live soberly and with dignity, be honest, work hard, and devote themselves to their families' welfare. Women are to be treated with dignity and respect, given protection and security. In turn, their dress and behavior are to be circumspect, they are to learn modesty and thrift, and to set a "middle-class table" worthy of the "new Negro."

Although derived from a religious conflict sect, this general approach is highly suggestive for slum work elsewhere. Interest in Africa and its achievements on the part of American slum Negroes as a method of change has been developed by others than Black Muslims.

---

[83] Haggstrom, "The Power of the Poor," p. 220.

[84] See C. Eric Lincoln, *The Black Muslims in America* (Boston: The Beacon Press, 1961); and E. U. Essien-Udom, *Black Nationalism: A Search for an Identity in America* (Chicago: University of Chicago Press, 1962). In pointing out the efforts of Black Muslims to change their self-images there is no assumption that this constitutes an endorsement of the philosophy or the tactics employed by the group.

The complex process of identity change accounts for the lengthy procedures that are necessary to improve the self-images of slum people by modifying group practices and habits. It is not something that can be done on an individual basis, nor is it a change that can be successfully accomplished in a few months or even possibly in a few years. With some people it may never be accomplished. The process of identity change accounts for the difficulties of coping with slum sanitation problems in slum areas or with delinquency, drug addiction, and illegitimacy. It often takes a long time for people to see such behavior as a reflection on their new image of themselves.

Use of Indigenous Workers and Nonprofessional Leadership

Change in slum areas is unlikely to occur by itself: certain persons must act as agents of change to initiate the process of change. It has long been considered customary to use educated persons, generally professionally trained, as change agents in the slums. They have generally been known as social workers, community organizers, community workers, or urban extension agents. Certainly outsiders are an indispensable catalyst for change. "New forms and patterns of action have often come about only when an outside element has been added to the political chemistry." [85] A new trend is emerging, however: that efforts to bring about change should be carried out either through such professional persons working with indigenous persons in the area or through giving the entire responsibility for change to nonprofessional or indigenous leaders.[86] Such persons are viewed not merely as extensions of the professional worker but as having a distinct role themselves.

> Outside leaders have a definite but limited role. This approach to area reorganization places principal emphasis on the role of natural community leaders who are carriers of conventional conduct norms. Not only do such leaders serve as nondelinquent models for emulation by youngsters attracted to programs offered by projects of this type, but because these indigenous leaders have prestige in the local area, they easily attract adults, as well as children and youths, to project programs in the first instance. It is around natural community leaders, then, that legitimate social structures can be germinated and multiplied in delinquency-prone areas.[87]

---

[85] Nicholas Von Hoffman, "Reorganization of the Casbah," *Social Progress,* 3:33 (1962).

[86] See, for example, Frank Riessman, "The Revolution in Social Work," *Trans-Action,* 2:13–17 (1964); and Arthur Pearl and Frank Riessman, *New Careers for the Poor* (New York: The Free Press, 1965).

[87] John M. Martin, "Three Approaches to Delinquency Prevention: A Critique," *Crime and Delinquency,* 7:23 (1961).

Indigenous or nonprofessional persons have an advantage over outsiders in stimulating social change, for they are more closely linked to the people and their problems. Many indigenous persons are "significant others," with considerable power and influence. Being themselves a part of the problem-producing environment, they may be more able to establish effective communication patterns in the area. Many have more inside knowledge of traditional efforts to deal with the slum and can even change the professional workers' thinking about their problems, for the indigenous worker may perceive problems differently from the professional. This leadership also provides a large-scale supplementation of manpower resulting in a wider coverage of slum areas. Indigenous leadership also develops skills in dealing with various public agencies, such as the police, which adds to their confidence in dealing with community problems and may even lead eventually to attacks on more specialized and technical problems.

Representative Community Leadership

Slum people seldom participate in the decisions of the larger community and most do not expect to. The mobilization of slum people for effective action requires that they participate in leadership at both the local and city-wide levels. In the cities of most countries the boards of city and local welfare groups, including the police, education, health, welfare, library, and hospital boards and commissions consist primarily of what are called "public-spirited" citizens. Close inspection reveals that they often do not represent the larger population, for most of them come from the middle and upper socioeconomic groups. A similar situation is found with respect to committees appointed to deal with delinquency, mental disorders, and alcoholism. Exceptions can be found, of course, but the "people" of the slum remain in the minority although they often constitute a large proportion of the urban population with whose behavior such boards are mainly concerned.

All too often decisions and plans are made for the slum dwellers on the assumption that they are not competent. Decisions must be made by "successful people," and typical slum residents are by definition not successful. It should be quite apparent, however, that such leadership may not have the backing of the majority of slum residents. Encouraging their participation in community affairs has the beneficial effect of raising the perceived status of a slum dweller, thus paving the way for solving many slum problems. It also demonstrates to the low-income community that there is an interest in knowing their points of view, it provides "success models" for slum residents by demonstrating the mere fact of upward mobility, and it introduces new realism into community deliberations.

The Use of Conflict for Social Change: The Need for Power

Social conflict may have a positive function, as Simmel, and more recently Coser, have pointed out.[88] Conflict may help to establish or reestablish group unity and cohesion, serving as a binding element between parties which hitherto have had little relation to each other. The slum dweller's dilemma has been his own lack of power. Being lower in economic status, moving outside the sources of social and political power, and often apathetic or subject to political manipulation, he has become a pawn of others in the larger urban world. It has been suggested that slum dwellers need to reach some measure of unity among themselves, as well as some degree of militancy, if they are to be recognized as part of the power structure and their legitimate demands for services and opportunities met.[89]

Conflict as a means of change in slum areas raises some questions. In some situations conflict may be a prerequisite to overcoming apathy and a roadblock imposed from the outside; in other situations it may lead merely to more conflict as an end in itself within the slum neighborhood. Its use by slum dwellers is likely to result in strong negative reactions from the middle class, who may feel that lower-class people should not use such tactics as rent strikes or protest marches. Moreover, politicians and others are likely to feel uneasy as the slum dwellers, through the use of conflict, gain a sense of their independence and power rather than continue to depend on them.

The Use of Outside Assistance in Attaining Objectives

Urban people need help in recognizing their own needs and in organizing themselves to achieve their objective.[90] Although they may not be satisfied with many of the conditions under which they live, they have had little opportunity to express their feelings about their problems and their needs as a group.

---

[88] Lewis Coser, *The Functions of Social Conflict* (New York: The Free Press, 1964).

[89] See Saul Alinsky, *Reveille for Radicals* (Chicago: University of Chicago Press, 1946) and his *Citizen Participation and Community Organization in Planning and Urban Renewal* (Chicago: Industrial Areas Foundation, 1962). Also see Charles E. Silberman, *Crisis in Black and White* (New York: Random House, Inc., 1964), pp. 321–328.

[90] Ronald Lippitt, Jeanne Watson, and Bruce Westley, *The Dynamics of Planned Change: A Comparative Study of Principles and Techniques* (New York: Harcourt, Brace & World, Inc., 1958), pp. 86–88, 180–181.

If such outside intervention is to be at all successful the slum residents must accept it. Lower-class people are highly suspicious of "outsiders," and the middle class, city government employees, the police, and the neighborhood center workers are often viewed by the lower class and working class with suspicion and often hostility. Opportunities, temptations, and pressures of the larger society are evaluated in terms of their effect upon the ongoing way of life built around the family circle or the peer group, and any offer of outside help which threatens this pattern is likely to be rejected.

Decentralization of Some Governmental Functions

The modern metropolis is so large and sprawling that efficient management has become all but impossible, and the importance of direct contact between the people and their city services is frequently ignored. The very government designed to serve the people has become unwieldy. Political units, such as wards, are often too large and the problems too complicated for a single political representative, whether councilman, councillor, or alderman. This situation significantly affects those living in slums.

A controlled decentralization of civic authority in an urban setting might result in greater support for government and overcome some of the apathy and hostility of many urban citizens to government. Increased local governmental responsibility might well improve the work of the police by changing slum people's attitudes toward them, develop greater community interest in education and support for school programs, result in better cooperation on sanitation problems and public-health problems, and afford protection to various public facilities such as schools and parks.

One might, for example, foresee the possibility of decentralized lay panels to deal with local delinquents in place of the juvenile court judge, as is done in England and Sweden, or of local school districts in the slums with their own local school boards, coordinated, of course, with the large city school board.[91] There is need for local police commissions, library boards, local park boards,[92] and local public-health boards. The involvement of local citizens in positions of responsibility not only would facilitate a change in community self-image but would give local citizens responsibility for cooperation with the police, the school, the library, the parks, and the sanitation and health authorities.[93]

---

[91] As reported in *The New York Times,* December 1, 1967.

[92] As reported in *The New York Times,* April 29, 1967.

[93] Many a community in the United States with as few as 2500 persons administers and supports its own schools, police and fire departments, libraries, parks, and other public facilities.

Examples of Community Development in Slum Areas

Urban community development projects are being carried out in various slum areas in parts of the world, including, for example, the United States, where they are often called community action programs,[94] Colombia, Venezuela, Brazil, India, Pakistan, the Philippines, Hong Kong, and Yugoslavia.[95] Among the best known are the Chicago Area Project and the Delhi Project.

Chicago Area Project

The Area Project in the Chicago slums, beginning about 1930, has been one of the best known of the efforts at community development and self-help work. Although primarily organized to counteract delinquency, it has indirectly stimulated many attempts to solve other slum problems. Initially the project was instituted to reduce the high delinquency in three areas of the slum; since then the work has been expanded to include seven other areas. The project has the same purpose as have other agencies—the control of delinquency—but its methods are different.

> (1) It emphasizes the development of a program for the neighborhood as a whole. (2) It seeks to stress the autonomy of the local residents in helping to plan, support, and operate constructive programs which they may regard as their own. (3) It attaches special significance to the training and utilization of community leaders. (4) It confines the efforts of its professional staff, in large part, to consultation and planning with responsible neighborhood leaders who assume major roles in the actual development of the program. (5) It seeks to encourage the local residents to utilize to the maximum all churches, societies, clubs, and other existing institutions and agencies, and to coordinate these in a unified neighborhood program. (6) Its activities are regarded primarily as devices for enlisting the active participation of local residents in a constructive community enterprise, for creating and crystallizing neighborhood sentiment on behalf of the welfare of the children and the social and physical improvement of the community as a whole. (7) It places particular emphasis upon the importance of a continuous, objective evaluation of its effectiveness as a device for reducing delinquency, through constructive modification of the pattern of community life.[96]

---

[94] See "Community Action Guide Program," in Gold and Scarpitti, pp. 31–42. Also see Marris and Rein.

[95] Clinard, *Slums and Community Development,* pp. 159–165.

[96] Clifford R. Shaw and Jesse A. Jacobs, "The Chicago Area Project: An Experimental Community Program for Prevention of Delinquency in Chicago," (Mimeographed; Chicago: Institute for Juvenile Research, undated). Also see Anthony Sorrentino, "The Chicago Area Project after 25 Years," *Federal Probation:*

More specifically, programs of this type try first to develop a civic pride in the activity of its residents. The degree of participation in community activities seems, in part, to be a product of the individual's conception of his responsibility for improving social conditions. Second, the local committees try to develop recreational programs for the neighborhood children and to reach natural groups of children, such as gangs. Being citizen-led, these groups often have the advantage of knowing the delinquents personally, and they can enlist the support of persons with similar racial and ethnic backgrounds. Third, community groups assist in the rehabilitation of delinquent and criminal offenders by encouraging them to adopt conventional norms. This is often done by asking such people to serve on community committees: "By this method the parolee or ex-offender is introduced into a conventional group, his role in the community is thus redefined, which, in turn results in a redefinition of his own conception of himself. The vigor with which parolees and others with criminal records have worked to improve their own communities and to keep boys out of delinquency has been one of the most encouraging aspects of the Area Project program." [97] Variations of these projects, some with less citizen responsibility and more direction by the professional staff, have been adopted in other parts of the country.[98] A comprehensive evaluation of the Chicago Area Project reached these conclusions:

1. Residents of low-income areas can organize and have organized themselves into effective working units for promoting and conducting welfare programs.
2. These community organizations have been stable and enduring. They raise funds, administer them well, and adapt the programs to local needs.
3. Local talent, otherwise untapped, has been discovered and utilized. Local leadership has been mobilized in the interest of children's welfare.[99]

The Delhi Project

Beginning in 1958, the Delhi Project in urban community development in India, as a part of municipal government, has been a large-scale compre-

---

23:40–45 (1959); Solomon Kobrin, "The Chicago Area Project—A 25-Year Assessment," *The Annals,* 322:19–29 (1959); and Southside Community Committee, *Bright Shadows in Bronzetown* (Chicago: South Side Community, 1949).

[97] "Report of the Chicago Area Project, 1947–48" (Mimeographed; Chicago: Institute for Juvenile Research, 1949), p. 6.

[98] See Arthur Hillman, *Neighborhood Centers Today* (New York: National Federation of Settlements and Neighborhood Centers, 1960).

[99] H. L. Witmer and E. Tufts, *The Effectiveness of Delinquency Prevention Programs* (Children's Bureau, Department of Health, Education, and Welfare, Publication 350; Washington, D.C.: Government Printing Office, 1954), p. 15.

hensive effort to involve citizens through locally elected citizen councils or Vikas Mandals in dealing on a self-help basis with various slum problems.[100] Groups of several hundred slum families were organized in slum areas which, through self-help efforts, sought to improve physical conditions, environmental sanitation, health problems, education, recreational and cultural activities, economic conditions and delinquency control. Reliance was put on developing indigenous leadership and change in self-image.

As an experiment, the Delhi Pilot Project was planned to stimulate the active participation of citizens and encourage them in their efforts to cope with slum conditions and to prevent further deterioration in the city. It was designed as a realistic approach to the enormous problems presented by the city's slums; to try to bring about changes in large part through those resources most readily available: the thousands and thousands of hands and the limited financial resources of the people who live in the slums. It was directed toward limited physical improvements, such as repair of drains, lanes and houses, improvement of water and latrine facilities, as well as toward significant changes in the way of life of the people largely through their own efforts. It was not offered as a substitute for large-scale government action in improving economic opportunities, housing, and facilities; rather, it was limited to those areas in which self-help programs were feasible. Although the broad goals of the Delhi Project were to organize and stimulate community life and to identify and develop community leadership to handle problems on a mutual-aid and self-help basis, there were also some specific objectives:

1. development of communities, characterized by citizens' pride and sense of belonging;
2. development of self-help and mutual-aid programs to improve local communities and bazaars;
3. development of civic pride through stimulation of neighborhood interest in city-wide improvement campaigns;
4. preparation for democratic decentralization of some municipal services through the organization of citizen councils to foster indigenous leadership;
5. assistance to citizens in cooperating with municipal and other welfare agencies for the improvement of neighborhoods;
6. assistance to citizens in eliminating practices unsuited to urban living;
7. creation of the necessary climate for undertaking programs of economic

---

[100] See Clinard, *Slums and Community Development*, pp. 139–278; and Clinard and Chatterjee, in Turner.

betterment, based on maximum use of available community resources and local initiative.[101]

COMPREHENSIVE COMMUNITY PROGRAMS

Several attempts are now being made to deal with deviant behavior through comprehensive or inclusive programs. These attacks on the slum are broad-based and include greater economic self-sufficiency and employment, improved education, improved and better coordinated services, and community development, the latter generally being secondary to the other objectives.[102] Among these programs, most of which have been directed primarily at the prevention of juvenile delinquency and drug addiction, are Mobilization for Youth, Haryou Act (Harlem Youth Opportunities, Unlimited), Community Progress, Inc., in New Haven, and the Chicago Joint Youth Development Program.[103]

One of the largest of these programs, which began in 1962, involves an initial expenditure of $12.6 million to deal with juvenile delinquency and other problems of the lower East Side of New York City. The services provided through this Mobilization for Youth project, which is concerned with a sixty-seven-block slum area in Manhattan containing a population of 100,000, mainly Negro and Puerto Rican, are diverse. In addition to providing extensive training and job-placement and subsidizing the initial employment of some youths by employers who normally refuse to hire people without prior work experience, the project has an extensive "homework helper" program, preschool education, reading clinics, and guidance counselors. It also tries to bring together teachers and parents in common activities; to provide such other services as legal aid to the indigent, consumer education, apartment-finding help, clinical services for narcotic addicts and the mentally disturbed; to provide meeting places for adolescents; to organize unaffiliated adults into groups concerned with their common problems and to become politically active; and to provide a reintegration program for juvenile offenders released to the neighborhood from

---

[101] Clinard, *Slums and Community Development,* p. 146.

[102] For a broad attack on the slums, see Hunter.

[103] For a comprehensive discussion of these programs see Marris and Rein and James Cunningham, *The Resurgent Neighborhood* (Notre Dame, Ind.: Fides Publishers, Inc., 1965). Also see "Mobilization for Youth," in Gold and Scarpitti, pp. 360–370, Kenneth B. Clark, *Dark Ghetto: Dilemmas of Social Power* (New York: Harper & Row, Publishers, 1965), and George A. Brager and Francis P. Purcell, eds., *Community Action Against Poverty: Readings from the Mobilization Experience* (New Haven: College and University Press, 1967).

penal institutions. There are coffee shops operated by young people, and an adventure corps, for boys nine to fifteen, which provides marching bands, educational programs, athletics, and vocational training. It is hoped that such a "saturation" program in high-delinquency areas will prove the best possible method of crime prevention.[104]

MacIver has summarized a number of conclusions regarding the strategy of these comprehensive or inclusive programs.

> 1. Since delinquency, like many other social ills, takes various forms and results from the combined impact of a complex of adverse conditions, the attack on it should also be many-sided, the different lines being geared into an integrated program.
>
> 2. The locus of operation should be the neighborhood, to assure close relations between the people and the operating staff, and the whole field of action should be a reasonably well-demarcated region.
>
> 3. A many-sided program is likely to gain in concentration and efficacy if it gives a central place to some one important problem, say education for employment (social as well as academic and technical), and if it can focus its activities in each neighborhood around an appropriate school or community center.[105]

RESEARCH AND PREVENTION OF DEVIANT BEHAVIOR

Research on its nature is essential in order to deal effectively with deviant behavior, especially its prevention. Fortunately, within the past ten years much more social science funds have become available through various federal agencies, such as the National Institute for Health and the National Science Foundation, and through private foundations, to carry out needed research in the area. This has meant particularly that the application of sociological theory to research has increased markedly in such areas as delinquency, crime, mental disorder, alcoholism, drug addiction, and discrimination. It is likely that as more research occurs we will be in an even better position to devise more effective preventive programs. Soci-

---

[104] Also see Daniel Glaser, "New Trends in Research on the Treatment of Offenders and the Prevention of Crime in the United States of America," *International Review of Criminal Policy*, 23:8–9 (1965). In Mobilization for Youth and similar projects it remains to be seen whether attempts to change the slums through the people's own efforts will eventually receive due emphasis or whether efforts will continue to be mis placed on providing greater economic opportunity and services by outsiders.

[105] Robert M. MacIver, *The Prevention and Control of Juvenile Delinquency*, pp. 137–138. Reprinted by permission of the Publishers, Atherton Press. Copyright © 1966, Atherton Press, New York. All rights reserved.

ologists have also become increasingly interested in the evaluation of applied programs, an evaluation that is greatly needed.[106]

As a scientist a sociologist must attempt to discover processes about deviant behavior applicable to the 3 billion persons in the more than 100 nations in this world, or to propose modifications of such generalizations in the light of subprocesses found in other societies. He must not delude himself that research based on a college sample, or on a particular American city, state, or region, is a scientific generalization in the sense that it will predict beyond the limited data at hand. Little of the Protestant Ethic exists in a Hindu country; much of the communist world appears to de-emphasize individualistic goals; Sweden's high rate of delinquency and other deviant behavior appears to contradict the differential opportunity formulations of Cloward and Ohlin, a theory derived largely from the urban Negro slum in the United States.

Sociologists need to gather data from other societies and seek to explain contradictions in other cultures. Fortunately, there are indications that a comparative sociology is slowly emerging,[107] yet too many sociologists cling to the belief that the scientific generalizations about deviant behavior are primarily derived from a study of the behavior in America or, at most, Western European societies.

SUMMARY

There are a number of ways to deal with negatively regarded deviations, including acceptance, a condition of equilibrium, and the elimination of the deviation, particularly through social isolation of the deviant. Norm and value conflicts are involved not only in the definition of various forms of deviant behavior but in proposals for their solution.

Much can be done through public education to develop consensus on deviations and understanding of their nature. Local community agencies seeking to prevent deviant behavior include the school, the church, clinical and counseling agencies, and street corner projects. The prevention of de-

---

[106] See Donald W. Valdes and Dwight G. Bean, *Sociology in Use: Selected Readings for an Introductory Course* (New York: The Macmillan Company, 1965); Shostak; and Lazarsfeld, Sewell, and Wilensky. One of the chief problems in developing more meaningful research is the sociologists' need for more firsthand acquaintance with the data of social experience. Interest in methodology has often taken precedence over theory and research problems. See Marshall B. Clinard, "The Sociologist's Quest for Respectability," *Sociological Quarterly*, 7:399–412 (1966).

[107] Robert M. Marsh, *Comparative Sociology: A Codification of Cross-Societal Analysis* (New York: Harcourt, Brace & World, Inc., 1967).

viant behavior is handicapped by the frequent dissemination by public educational agencies, including those of the community, of information about the individualistic nature of deviant behavior. This incorrect information is largely derived from invalid theoretical approaches to these problems. Unfortunately, insufficient information about the group, sociological, and cultural factors in the causation of deviant behavior is made available to the public.

Urban community development tries to deal with the problems created by urbanism by encouraging local community feeling and initiative in dealing with ways of life inappropriate to effective urban living. Such an approach to the slums involves (1) a group approach to slum problems, (2) the creation of a new type of social organization, (3) group perception of the need for change, (4) the pursuance of self-imposed change, (5) the use of traditional groups for change, (6) change in identity or self-image, (7) the use of indigenous workers and leaders, (8) representative community leadership, (9) the use of conflict for social change: the need for power, (10) the use of outside assistance in attaining objectives, and (11) decentralization of some governmental functions. Some projects dealing with deviant behavior in slums use comprehensive community programs.

SELECTED READINGS

Action for Mental Health. Joint Commission on Mental Illness and Health. New York: Basic Books, Inc., 1961. Includes a detailed discussion of the role of public education in the prevention of mental disorder. Also a discussion of the part the school, the church, and clinical and counseling facilities can play in the prevention of mental disorder.

Amos, William E., and Charles F. Wellford. *Delinquency Prevention: Theory and Practice.* Englewood Cliffs, N.J.: Prentice-Hall, Inc., 1967. A comprehensive discussion of delinquency prevention including prevention through the family, religion, school, recreation, economic structure, police, judicial process, and community action.

Annals, The. Usually each year *The Annals of the American Academy of Political and Social Science* devotes one or more issues to some form of deviant behavior, considering it not only from the point of view of theory but from social action as well.

Barton, Rebecca Chalmers. *Our Human Rights.* Washington, D.C.: Public Affairs Press, 1955. A detailed description of how a governor's commission on human rights in a midwestern state operates to reduce discrimination. Contains numerous case materials.

Challenge of Crime in a Free Society, The. A Report by the President's Commission on Law Enforcement and Administration of Justice. Washington, D.C.: Government Printing Office, 1967. A comprehensive analysis of crime in the United States with suggestions for its prevention and treatment.

Clinard, Marshall B. *Slums and Community Development: Experiments in Self-*

Help. New York: The Free Press, 1966. Contains, in addition to an analysis of the slum, a comprehensive discussion of urban community development and its application to slum areas. The Delhi Project in the slums of India is discussed in detail.

Cuber, John F., Robert A. Harper, and William F. Kenkel. *Problems of American Society: Values in Conflict.* Third ed. New York: Holt, Rinehart and Winston, Inc., 1956. A discussion of the role of value conflicts in defining certain behavoir as deviant. Includes a discussion of the distinction between ameliorative and moral problems.

Cunningham, James. *The Resurgent Neighborhood.* Notre Dame, Ind.: Fides Publishers, Inc., 1965. A discussion of various efforts in the United States to stimulate comprehensive local community action.

Dean, John P., and Alex Rosen. *A Manual of Intergroup Relations.* Chicago: University of Chicago Press, 1955. A manual of principles and techniques for reducing racial and religious discrimination in a community.

Gold, Harry, and Frank R. Scarpitti. *Combatting Social Problems: Techniques of Intervention.* New York: Holt, Rinehart and Winston, Inc., 1967. A book of readings dealing with the prevention and treatment of deviant behavior, including juvenile delinquency, crime, drug addiction, alcoholism, mental disorder, and racial discrimination.

Hunter, David R. *The Slums: Challenge and Response.* New York: The Free Press, 1964. A comprehensive discussion of ways to deal with the slum.

Kobrin, Solomon. "The Chicago Area Project—A 25-Year Assessment," *The Annals,* 322:19–29 (1959). An evaluation of the work of the Chicago Area Project in preventing juvenile delinquency.

McCarthy, Raymond G., ed. *Drinking and Intoxication.* New York: The Free Press, 1959. Discusses public attitudes toward problems arising from the use of alcohol, programs of alcohol education, and alcoholic clinics.

MacIver, Robert M. *The Prevention and Control of Delinquency.* New York: Atherton Press, 1966. A theoretical discussion by a well-known sociologist of delinquency and delinquency prevention, including an appraisal of the role of the school, inclusive neighborhood and community programs, the police, the court, and custodial institutions.

Marris, Peter, and Martin Rein. *Dilemmas of Social Reform: Poverty and Community Action in the United States.* New York: Atherton Press, 1967. An analysis and evaluation of several comprehensive community programs in the United States, including the community action work of the Poverty program.

Sutherland, Edwin H., and Donald R. Cressey. *Principles of Criminology.* Seventh ed. Philadelphia: J. B. Lippincott Company, 1966. Chapter 29 is a discussion of the prevention of crime and delinquency, including the use of local community organizations, organized recreation, case work with near delinquents, group work with near delinquents, coordinating councils, and institutional reorganization.

Weinberg, S. Kirson, ed. *The Sociology of Mental Disorders: Analyses and Readings in Psychiatric Sociology.* Chicago: Aldine Publishing Company, 1967. Contains a discussion and four articles dealing with the role of community psychiatry in preventing mental disorder.

19

The Group Approach to Social Reintegration

Throughout the previous chapters the importance of the group in the development of deviant behavior has been emphasized. The group has been related to the acquisition of deviant norms and to difficulties in interpersonal relations, self-concept, and role conflicts. It has been seen that the deviant is a member of various types of social groups; that he plays a certain role in each of these groups; and that role conflicts may arise if participation in these groups exposes the deviant to competing demands and obligations. In addition, the deviant develops certain desires and attitudes through his group experiences which may conflict with the demands of the larger group, or "society." This recognition of the importance of group relationships is not confined to sociologists:

> The group factor in our civilization is receiving increasing attention. During the past decade there has been much interest in, and more understanding than previously of, the impact of the group on the individual, on the community, and on problem solving. The group in its various attributes—educational, therapeutic, recreational, and actional—is the object of study not only by social group workers but by educators, psychologists, and psychiatrists. Anthropologists and sociologists who have long been in-

terested in the group as an institution are gaining new insights into the power of the group factor in present-day culture.[1]

The importance of group relationships was revealed, for example, in studies of neuroses among members of the armed services during World War II. It was learned that integrating or nonintegrating forces in the immediate social environment of the soldier were far more important than his personality make-up, his family structure, or his previous history of personal maladjustment. The presence or absence of group supportive elements in the army, particularly identification with a group under conditions of stress, was found to be one of the most important keys to the development of mental disorder even among those who were supposed to have few tendencies in that direction.[2]

One commission of civilian psychiatrists who studied combat neuroses during World War II found that when "an individual member of such a combat group has his emotional bonds of group integration seriously disrupted, then he, *as a person,* is thereby disorganized. The disruption of the group unity is, in the main, a primary causal factor, not a secondary effect of personal disorganization."[3] William Menninger stated: "We seemed to learn anew the importance of the group ties in the maintenance of mental health. We were impressed by the fact that an individual who had a strong conviction about his job, even though his was a definitely unstable personality, might make remarkable achievement against the greatest of stress."[4] Such information, although limited, has suggested that neurotic

---

[1] Dorothea F. Sullivan, ed., *Readings in Group Work* (New York: Association Press, 1952), p. v. Also see Louis Wirth, "Clinical Sociology," *American Journal of Sociology,* 37:60 (1931); Stuart A. Queen, "Social Participation in Relation to Social Disorganization," *American Sociological Review,* 14:252 (1949), and his "The Concepts of Social Disorganization and Social Participation," *American Sociological Review,* 6:307–316 (1941).

[2] See Arnold M. Rose, "Factors in Mental Breakdown in Combat," in Arnold M. Rose, ed., *Mental Health and Mental Disorder* (New York: W. W. Norton & Company, Inc., 1955), pp. 291–313. It was found that the rate of neuropsychiatric casualty in army units during World War II was higher in units with low morale, and lower in units with high morale.

[3] L. H. Bartemeir, *et al.,* "Combat Exhaustion," *Journal of Nervous and Mental Diseases,* 104:370 (1946). In order to minimize mental breakdowns among members of U.S. armed forces in Korea an army psychiatrist in 1952 suggested that squads rather than individuals be rotated. The loss of a squad leader or disruption of friendships contributed to the breakdown of members left behind.

[4] William C. Menninger, "Psychiatric Experience in the War, 1941–1946," *American Journal of Psychiatry,* 103:581 (1947). Also see his *Psychiatry in a Troubled World* (New York: The Macmillan Company, 1948), Chaps. 5–6.

symptoms may occur among ordinarily stable persons if the group situation is disturbed and that it might be well to analyze similar situations in civilian life which cause mental breakdowns.[5]

Primarily during the past twenty years numerous developments have recognized the importance of the group and have applied group methods in the prevention and treatment of social deviation. Still other work has combined theory and application in the study of group dynamics in problem areas.[6] Although some group psychotherapy existed as early as 1906, much of the recent increase in this work resulted from its use during World War II, when the number of civilian and military neurotic and psychiatric casualties, as well as the need to rehabilitate military offenders, made it impossible to treat cases on an individual basis.

The group approach differs sharply from the relationship of a professional person with an individual patient—for example, the psychiatrist, the clinical psychologist, and the social worker and their clients, where the emphasis is on a person-to-person relationship rather than on a group-person therapy. Moreover, not all forms of "group work" can be described as applying a *group* orientation to the treatment of social deviation. Many forms of so-called "group work" are actually *individually* oriented and are based on the assumption that deviation is a consequence of a personality trait which is unique to an individual and not a kind of behavior developed in group relationships. Since this is assumed, the individual approach attempts to correct psychological malfunctions, believing that they, and not self-other relationships, are the causes of deviation.[7]

It is not the objective of the group approach merely to assist or supplement other forms of treatment, however. In essence, in this approach it is the *group* which is the instrument of change. The group approach views the *individual* as part of a broad stream of human relationships and within a complex network of roles and statuses. In a sense, any deliberate action which alters the relation of the individual to others in this network in an effort to change his behavior is an example of the group approach.[8]

---

[5] See S. Kirson Weinberg, "The Combat Neuroses," *American Journal of Sociology,* 54:465–478 (1946).

[6] See Kurt Lewin, *Resolving Social Conflicts* (New York: Harper & Row, Publishers, 1948). See also Dorwin Cartwright, "Achieving Change in People: Some Applications of Group Dynamics Theory," *Human Relations,* 4:381–392 (1951) and J. Douglas and Marguerite Grant, "A Group Dynamics Approach to the Treatment of Nonconformists in the Navy," *The Annals,* 322:126–135 (1959).

[7] See Donald R. Cressey, "The Nature and Effectiveness of Correctional Techniques," in *Law and Contemporary Problems* (Durham, N.C.: Duke University Press, 1958), pp. 754–771.

[8] For further discussion of this approach, see Edwin H. Sutherland and Donald R. Cressey, *Principles of Criminology* (7th ed.; Philadelphia: J. B. Lippincott Com-

There is evidence of growing recognition that the group approach is not distinguished by the number of persons involved, but by its particular perspective and theory.[9] There are today several variations of the group approach to social reintegration,[10] all of which conform to the definition above.

1. One form of group approach to problems of deviance is through the use of *community development* in which primarily local citizens deal with problems of the local area or neighborhood.[11]

2. *Citizen groups may work directly with deviants.* Both Great Britain and Sweden have citizen boards to deal with delinquents. Sweden uses local citizen boards to deal with cases of persistent drunkenness. The Soviet Union has trade-union brigade committeemen to help with the treatment of alcoholism. There are some 200,000 "comrade's courts" [12] in the Soviet Union which utilize citizens in industrial plants, housing projects, and collective and state farms to deal with petty offenders and acts of assault, drunkenness, or family neglect. These are sometimes referred to as "shame courts" because the trial is conducted at a public meeting. These comrade-ship courts may ask for a public apology to the injured party, issue a warning, issue a social reprimand which may be published in the press, order restitution to the victim, impose a fine not to exceed 10 rubles, or raise with the management the possibility of the offender's dismissal or assignment of fifteen days to a lower-skilled job, or recommend his expulsion from his

---

pany, 1966, pp. 378–380. Also see Donald R. Cressey, "Changing Criminals: The Application of the Theory of Differential Association," *American Journal of Sociology*, 61:116–120 (1955) and his "Contradictory Theories in Correctional Group Therapy Programs," *Federal Probation*, 18:20–26 (1954).

[9] This concept of the group approach agrees with the definition of the group in Chapter 1, page 4. See also Dorothy Fahs Beck, "The Dynamics of Group Psychotherapy Seen by a Sociologist, Part I: Basic Processes," *Sociometry*, 21:98–125 (1958).

[10] See M. Stranahan, C. Schwortzman, and F. Athens, "Activity Group Therapy with Emotionally Disturbed Delinquent Adolescents," *International Journal of Group Psychotherapy*, 7:425–436 (1957); Walter B. Miller, "The Impact of a Community Group Work Program on Delinquent Corner Groups," *Social Service Review*, 31:390–406 (1957); Lloyd W. McCorkle and Albert Elias, "Group Therapy in Correctional Institutions," *Federal Probation*, 24:57–63 (1960).

[11] See pages 723–724. Also see Marshall B. Clinard, *Slums and Community Development: Experiments in Self-Help* (New York: The Free Press, 1966).

[12] Harold J. Berman and James W. Spindler, *Soviet Comrade's Courts* (Cambridge, Mass.: Harvard University Press, 1963); and L. N. Smirnov, "Comradeship Courts and Related Innovations in the Soviet Union." Mimeographed paper, Third United Nations Congress on the Prevention of Crime and the Treatment of Offenders (tockholm: 1965).

apartment house. All decisions may be appealed to regular courts. Generally the purpose is to bring group pressure and offer group support to the offender to change his behavior which may be also accomplished by further conferences with him by members of the group.

3. Another type consists of *group therapy, or guided group interaction* sessions, which are usually employed with from four to twenty deviants, such as a group of mental patients or prison inmates, in an effort to change attitudes and other behavior. This method has been employed with deviants in institutions and in communities. In some cases role-playing techniques, such as psychodrama and sociodrama, have been used.

4. A fourth type consists of *activity or interest groups (group work)* which have been employed primarily with delinquents and older persons. In some instances, groups in their "natural settings," such as delinquent street groups, have been the focus of reintegrative efforts.[13]

5. *Halfway houses* use group methods, and the essential features of a *"therapeutic community"* have been applied to a number of institutions, such as mental hospitals.[14]

6. A sixth type of group approach is the *assumption by groups of deviants of the major responsibility for dealing with a common problem with which the members are personally concerned.* They are known by such names as Alcoholics Anonymous, Synanon, Narcotics Anonymous, and Recovery Incorporated. Such groups have been formed to aid in the rehabilitation of the alcoholic, the drug addict, former mental patients, and delinquents. In each instance the group helps to integrate the individual, to change his conception of himself, to make him feel again the solidarity of the group behind the individual, and to combat social stigma.[15] These group processes, it is felt, replace the "I" feelings with "we" feelings, give the individual a feeling of being a member of a group, and redefine certain norms of behavior.

GROUP APPROACHES TO ALCOHOLISM

Alcoholics Anonymous

Alcoholics Anonymous is probably the most widely known and presumably the most successful of all informal group approaches to social reintegration. There are more than 10,000 chapters—groups of alcoholics

---

[13] See Stranahan, Schwortzman, and Athens; Miller; and McCorkle and Elias.

[14] C. E. M. Harris, L. B. Brown, J. E. Cawte, "Problems of Developing a Group-Centered Mental Hospital," *International Journal of Group Psychotherapy,* 10:408–418 (1960); and F. Knobloch, "On the Theory of a Therapeutic Community for Neurotics," *International Journal of Group Psychotherapy,* 10:419–429 (1960).

[15] Marshall B. Clinard, "The Group Approach to Social Reintegration," *American Sociological Review,* 14:257–262 (1949), and Edward Sagarin, "Voluntary Associations Among Social Deviants," *Criminologica,* 5:8–22 (1967).

or "arrested" alcoholics—in the United States and in many other countries. The total membership in the United States consists of about 300,000 persons in 7500 chapters. In addition, a 1957 survey showed that "there were 257 hospital groups with 6000 members and 296 groups with 15,000 members holding meetings in jails, reformatories, prisons, and workhouses. Approximately 1000 seamen and 'lone' members in remote areas maintain a contact with each other by mail." [16]

Alcoholics Anonymous was founded in Cleveland less than thirty years ago by two alcoholics who felt that their mutual fellowship helped both of them with their drinking problems.[17] It is not an association or society in the accepted sense of the word, for it does not have a formal organization with officers or dues. However, it maintains a central office in New York and publishes a journal called *A.A. Grapevine.*

Although Alcoholics Anonymous is a voluntary association, it has a number of characteristics which distinguish it from other similar organizations.

1. Membership is comprised exclusively of social deviants.
2. Despite the deviant nature of its membership the organization has achieved the recognition and approval of the general society.
3. Membership is anonymous.
4. Membership is self-determined (by an expressed desire to stop drinking).
5. The deviant within the group, as defined by A.A. norms and values, is often supported, not rejected.
6. No authority exists to expel members.
7. Identification with the fellowship is neither secondary nor segmental. Alcoholics Anonymous is a "way of life" implying primary involvement.
8. The total organization, nationally and locally, is financially self-supporting. There are no fund-raising campaigns or solicitations from outside sources. In fact, such contributions are firmly and politely rejected when offered.
9. There are no dues or fees. All contributions from the members are made on a voluntary basis. No single donation may exceed $100.
10. There is no terminal point in view for the association. The goal of

---

[16] Harrison M. Trice, "Alcoholics Anonymous," *The Annals,* 315:111 (1958).

[17] For a history of this organization see *Alcoholics Anonymous Comes of Age: A Brief History of A.A.* (New York: Alcoholics Anonymous Publishing, 1957). Also see Irving Peter Gellman, *The Sober Alcoholic* (New Haven, Conn.: College and University Press, 1964), and Harrison M. Trice, "Alcoholics Anonymous," in Harry Gold and Frank R. Scarpitti, *Combatting Social Problems: Techniques of Intervention* (New York: Holt, Rinehart and Winston, Inc., 1967), pp. 503–511.

the program is to help alcoholics achieve and maintain sobriety, not to cure alcoholism. The A.A. member is a sober alcoholic but he must never think he is a cured alcoholic.[18]

Alcoholics Anonymous is quite the opposite from "total institutions"—prisons and mental hospitals which have been so aptly termed by Goffman.[19] Although both are large-scale efforts to deal with deviancy, A.A. does not have the characteristics of a total institution such as the status division between inmates and staff, the general isolation from society, bureaucratic rules, and relief from economic and social responsibility. In A.A. the members may continue to have family and work ties, handle their own deviancy, and are equal members of the organization; moreover, there is no professional staff.[20]

Alcoholics Anonymous is run by members only. No psychiatrists or other professional persons are directly associated with it. A potential new member must seek the help of the organization by admitting that he cannot deal with his drinking unaided. If he has been drinking unusually heavily for some time, attempts are made to get medical help for him and to tide him over the aftereffects of his excesses.

The emphasis is on mutual help. When norms and values conflict, there is a tendency to achieve some unanimity as to the goals and purposes of life and the relationship of alcoholism to them. The routine nature of life is diminished by participation in an outside activity in which the human element is stressed. Finally, and most important of all, the individual has a place to go, and a group with whose members he can talk, and where he can give and receive support.

The A.A. program breaks down the alcoholic's social isolation that has resulted from the stigma of his excessive drinking, by drawing him into a group in which he is accepted on face value as a past drunkard. This group is an intimate, primary one in which members can more easily reorient themselves. An alcoholic feels at home with other alcoholics who, like himself, have known degradation and the stigma of being an alcoholic.[21] The life stories told at meetings are helpful to the members, as well as is the reading of their basic book, *Alcoholics Anonymous,* which contains many stories of ex-alcoholics. The organization even has a common argot, includ-

---

[18] Gellman, pp. 172–173.

[19] Erving Goffman, *Asylums* (New York: Doubleday Anchor Books, 1961), pp. 1–124.

[20] Gellman, pp. 153–158.

[21] John F. Lofland and Robert A. LeJeune, "Initial Interaction of Newcomers in Alcoholics Anonymous: A Field Experiment in Class Symbols and Socialization," *Social Problems,* 8:102–111 (1960).

ing, for example, words like "slip" to describe a person who has returned to drinking, "twelfth-stepping" for working with other alcoholics, and "dime therapy" for a member who uses the telephone to help someone in the group avoid a "slip." [22]

Each new A.A. member is assigned to a sponsor, perhaps an old friend or drinking companion, although more often a complete stranger, who refers to him as his "baby." This sponsor is someone who has been successfully coping with an alcohol problem, and is ready at all times to help his charge. He often asks the man's wife or his employer to give their support and understanding to the new A.A. member, and he may even visit persons to whom the alcoholic may have given worthless checks or from whom he may have borrowed money, asking them to give the alcoholic an opportunity to get back on his feet.[23]

As soon as possible the sponsor will take his "baby" to A.A. meetings several nights a week. These meetings are of two types, the open meetings which family, friends, and other outsiders may attend, and the closed ones attended only by alcoholics. At open meetings a number of alcoholics may speak of their experiences and of their rehabilitation; in closed meetings experiences and problems are told in a more intimate situation. In these meetings the alcoholic takes up separately the so-called twelve steps which are discussed and interpreted by other alcoholics. These twelve steps are briefly outlined as follows:

> *Step One:* We admitted we were powerless over alcohol—that our lives had become unmanagable.
>
> *Step Two:* Came to believe that a Power greater than ourselves could restore us to sanity.
>
> *Step Three:* Made a decision to turn our will and our lives over to the care of God "as we understood Him."
>
> *Step Four:* Made a searching and fearless moral inventory of ourselves.
>
> *Step Five:* Admitted to God, to ourselves and to another human being the exact nature of our wrongs.
>
> *Step Six:* Were entirely ready to have God remove all these defects of character.
>
> *Step Seven:* Humbly asked Him to remove our shortcomings.
>
> *Step Eight:* Made a list of all persons we had harmed, and became willing to make amends to them all.

---

[22] Simon Dinitz, "The Therapeutic Effects of Alcoholics Anonymous." Unpublished master's thesis, University of Wisconsin, Madison, 1948.

[23] See H. S. Ripley and J. K. Jackson, "Therapeutic Factors in AA," *American Journal of Psychiatry,* 116:44–50 (1959), for a discussion of the roles of "sponsor" and "baby" and their importance. Sometimes the word "pigeon" is used in place of "baby."

Step Nine: Made direct amends to such people wherever possible, except when to do so would injure them or others.

Step Ten: Continued to take personal inventory and when we were wrong promptly admitted it.

Step Eleven: Sought through prayer and meditation to improve our conscious contact with God "as we understood Him," praying only for knowledge of His will for us and the power to carry that out.

Step Twelve: Having had a spiritual awakening as the result of these steps we tried to carry this message to alcoholics, and to practice these principles in all our affairs.[24]

These twelve steps, which are greatly emphasized in the program, can be roughly summarized in four principles: (1) relying on a power greater than themselves and recognizing that they are powerless to deal with alcoholism,[25] (2) making an inventory of their problems, (3) making amends to others, and (4) carrying the message to others. The "power greater than themselves" is not specifically related to a particular religion, for A.A. accepts men of all faiths and does not tolerate discussion of religious doctrines. However, such a belief tends to reduce the isolation of the alcoholic, which has involved building all sorts of glass houses filled with rationalizations.[26] This "something" helps the individual to identify with the group; in fact, so great is the identification that "the so-called religious emphasis in A.A. may be explained in terms of Durkheim's thesis that religion represents essentially the group and the feeling of getting outside of one's self by identification with others."[27] The concept of a greater power constitutes a symbol of future resources and hope for the individual.

The moral inventory of the twelve steps represents a sort of self-analysis and is closely related to the procedure of making amends to others for things done while drinking. The inventory helps alcoholics discover some of the sources of their problems: making amends is a way to resolve problems because it helps to bring about their reacceptance into society. Relating their life stories at meetings enables the alcoholics to review their past experiences in the presence of the group. In this way they are able to assert their new role as nondrinkers.[28]

---

[24] *Alcoholics Anonymous* (13th ptg.; New York: Works Publishing Company, 1950), pp. 71–72.

[25] For a discussion see Milton A. Maxwell, "Alcoholics Anonymous: An Interpretation," in David J. Pittman, ed., *Alcoholism* (New York: Harper & Row, Publishers, 1967), pp. 211–222.

[26] H. M. Tiebout, "Therapeutic Mechanisms of Alcoholics Anonymous," *American Journal of Psychiatry,* 100:468–473 (1944).

[27] Clinard, "The Group Approach to Social Reintegration," p. 262.

[28] Robert F. Bales, "Therapeutic Role of A.A. as Seen by a Sociologist," *Quarterly Journal of Studies on Alcohol,* 5:267–274 (1944).

In addition to attending these meetings, the alcoholic spends a great deal of time with other A.A. members, in the evenings or during lunch hours, in the late afternoon, and during weekends. Special programs are arranged for long weekends and holidays, when the temptation to drink may be extreme. Coffee and "cokes" are served in the clubhouse, where card games and other recreational activities are common; there are also picnics for the families. Frequently there are A.A. auxiliary groups composed of spouses of alcoholics, parents, relatives, children over twenty-one, and interested friends, those whose purpose is to understand the members of A.A. and to assist in therapy.[29] In 1960 there were 1308 A.A. auxiliary groups in the United States. In these groups there is considerable concern over the effect of alcoholism on the children of alcoholics, and a separate group for older children, Al-Teen, has been established for this purpose.

Carrying the message of A.A. to others is particularly important. In fact, Bales considers it the most important therapeutic aspect of the program. The relation of sponsor and "baby" and that of one member to another tends to create a series of reciprocal obligations toward others which result in greater solidarity or identification with the group. Alcoholics Anonymous involves a network of personal relationships and in this network each person is a focal point of interpersonal relations. This network of obligation is strengthened by the "carrying of the message." Bales has described it in this way:

> Further, his relationship to those whom he has brought into the group is strengthened by the expectation of each of his converts that he, who persuaded them that the program would work, will remain abstinent. He is, in fact, under obligation to each of these converts because of their dependence upon him. If he fails in his example to them, they may fail also. His failure cannot be a matter of purely personal concern, but involves the repudiation of accepted obligations. The success of each is to a peculiarly high degree contingent upon the success of the others in the group.[30]

The A.A. program allows the sponsor to see himself as he was before, in the image of the recently drunken "baby," or "pigeon," as the new members are sometimes called. Each is an image to the other, and the "baby" can call on his more successful sponsor for help on a twenty-four-hour basis. The "baby" is not only integrated into the group, but integrated in a strongly "antialcohol" group in which status is assigned according to the

---

[29] For a good discussion of A.A. groups, see Morris E. Chafetz and Harold W. Demone, Jr., *Alcoholism and Society* (New York: Oxford University Press, 1962), pp. 166–171.

[30] Robert F. Bales, "Types of Social Structure as Factors in 'Cures' of Alcohol Addiction," *Applied Anthropology*, 1:8 (1942).

degree that the person exhibits behavior that does not involve the use of alcohol. In this way the attitudes and motives of the alcoholic about the use of alcohol are replaced with new attitudes and motives, for "A.A. redefines self and role as that of an ex-alcoholic who cannot stand liquor." [31] By associating with other members the alcoholic is not under pressure to drink alcohol. The frequent stories told in A.A. meetings of the alcoholic binges of others remind the alcoholic of his former self and role. The *A.A. Grapevine,* their national official publication, contains chiefly stories and cartoons relating to the problem of alcoholics, which serve as constant reminders of success and the dangers of failure. Mottoes supply additional social pressures to conform and include the "24-Hour Plan" of keeping sober only for the day, and such clubhouse slogans as "But for the Grace of God . . ." and "This Clubhouse Keeps Us on the Beam."

The group therapy of A.A. appears to help overcome the forces which produced and reinforced the continuance of alcoholic drinking. As has been indicated, the alcoholic, through his drinking experiences, has built a conception of himself as a compulsive, uncontrolled drunkard. He has lost his self-respect, his friends have avoided him, and he himself has avoided groups except possible drinking groups. He wants acceptance, but conventional groups will not accept him. The A.A. member, through others' acceptance of him as he is, is offered an opportunity to learn new skills in interpersonal relationships. In addition, he acquires new goals: to keep sober and to reform other alcoholics. Thus, "the member sees in his prospective convert himself as he once was, and by teaching the other, becomes his own therapist." [32]

It is difficult to ascertain definitely the degree of success of Alcoholics Anonymous, but there is considerable evidence that there has generally been a high rate of recovery among the members.[33] One writer, for example, has stated that A.A. claims it has a recovery rate of 75 percent for those who really try their methods.[34] Such statements are difficult to verify, for

---

[31] Edwin M. Lemert, *Social Pathology* (New York: McGraw-Hill Book Company, Inc., 1951), p. 367. Alcoholics Anonymous does not take any stand on the general consumption of alcohol by others, but it does as far as alcoholics are concerned.

[32] Joseph A. Cook and Gilbert Geis, "Forum Anonymous: The Techniques of Alcoholics Anonymous Applied to Prison Therapy," *Journal of Social Therapy* 3:9–13 (1957).

[33] Oscar W. Ritchie, "A Socio-historical Survey of Alcoholics Anonymous," *Quarterly Journal of Studies on Alcohol,* 9:149 (1948); and J. Alexander, "Drunkard's Best Friend," *Saturday Evening Post,* 222:17–18, 74–79 (1950).

[34] Tiebout, "Therapeutic Mechanisms of Alcoholics Anonymous." For a discussion of the use of A.A. techniques in correctional work, see Cook and Geis. See

A.A. has no complete set of records, many A.A. members have a number of "slips" during the program, and many persons associate themselves with A.A. who are totally unsuited for it. Actual evaluation studies of A.A. are also limited because of the anonymity of the relatives. A study of 393 members of suburban A.A. chapters near a city of 220,000 by a member of A.A. found that over a seven-year period 47 percent had stayed sober at least a year, about 70 percent of those who stayed sober for one year continued to two years, and 90 percent of those sober for two years continued to three.[35] There are also indications that those who associate themselves with the A.A. program viewed their problem previously somewhat differently from those who had been exposed to A.A. but did not join it. In a study of 111 A.A. members compared with 141 nonmembers, a significant difference was found in that A.A. members tended to regard themselves, even before they ever attended a meeting, as persons who often shared their troubles with others. They tended less frequently to have known persons who they "believed" stopped drinking through will power. They had lost longtime drinking companions, and they had had exposure to favorable communications about A.A.[36]

Trice found initial experiences at the first meetings to be important.[37] The chances for joining were greater if an alcoholic had a real knowledge of what the meetings would be like, if he had a sponsor and group ties to keep in touch with him, if he had firm convictions about his drinking, and if he was not unduly sensitive to the social class differences found in A.A.[38] The effectiveness of these factors is increased if after a few weeks he finds that he can adjust to small informal and spontaneous groups, if his wife or his girl friend cooperates with the program, and if he is aware of the symptoms of alcoholism.

Certainly Alcoholics Anonymous has demonstrated that alcoholism is not primarily a result of a constellation of unique personality traits or an "alcoholic personality."

---

also H. M. Tiebout, "Alcoholics Anonymous—An Experiment of Nature," *Quarterly Journal of Studies on Alcohol,* 22:52–68 (1961).

[35] Bill C, "The Growth and Effectiveness of Alcoholics Anonymous in a Southwestern City, 1945–1962," *Quarterly Journal of Studies on Alcohol,* 26:279–284 (1965). (Bill C. is a pseudonym for an Alcoholics Anonymous member.)

[36] Harrison M. Trice, "The Affiliation Motive and Readiness to Join Alcoholics Anonymous," *Quarterly Journal of Studies on Alcohol,* 20:313–321 (1959).

[37] Trice, "The Affiliation Motive and Readiness to Join Alcoholics Anonymous."

[38] One study reports that initial activity is greatest where the A.A. group is relatively high and the newcomers are relatively low in social class. Loffland and LeJeune, "Initial Interaction of Newcomers in Alcoholics Anonymous."

Further evidence that alcoholism is not primarily an expression of personal pathology is found in the fact that the Alcoholics Anonymous organization has had some success in treating alcoholics. Although it can be argued that only the alcoholics without personal pathologies join the organization, those who do interact with ex-alcoholics gain asistance in overcoming their craving for alcohol. Alcoholics Anonymous has demonstrated that it is not necessary to attempt to find and treat some underlying defect in the alcoholic's personality.[39]

Halfway Houses

Hospitals have long been used for alcoholics. However, they are not of primary interest here, for their approach has often been typically individualistic and physiological. The type of center which is of interest here is generally called a "halfway house." The first were established several years ago in New York City, Long Island, and Boston. At present there are many such programs in different sections of the United States.[40] Halfway houses were begun in an attempt to rehabilitate the allegedly hopeless Skid Row type of alcoholic. These houses were established on the premise that the deviant subculture of the Skid Row alcoholic and its meanings to him must be considered if rehabilitation were to succeed. The halfway house was thus seen as a social milieu offering social support halfway between the deviant subculture and conventional society.

After entering a halfway house the alcoholic is expected to get a job, pay for his room and board, assist with maintenance tasks, and to stay sober. The staff, which frequently consists of recovered alcoholics, conducts counseling sessions with new residents. Perhaps the most powerful rehabilitative force is the group pressure from both staff and group members. In the halfway house group pressures operate to produce sobriety, whereas on Skid Row they operate to produce inebriety. The halfway house is a good example of the modification of the alcoholic's system of social relationships in an effort to change his behavior.[41] Preliminary reports of the reintegrative success of the halfway house program suggest that it provides an essential transitional period that allows the alcoholic to prepare to abandon his old ways of life for new ones. Yet complete success seems to depend upon the opportunities he has of being reaccepted into conventional society.

---

[39] Sutherland and Cressey, p. 176.

[40] Earl Rubington, "The Chronic Drunkenness Offender," *The Annals,* 315:65–72 (1958).

[41] Rubington.

Group Psychotherapy

Other group methods, such as group psychotherapy, have been employed with alcoholics. They have involved group discussions of a small number of alcoholics, usually led by a professional person.[42] An evaluation of 896 group therapy sessions for alcoholics held over a twelve-year period (1949–1961) in a mental hospital and involving 884 alcoholics found that there was a readmission rate to the hospital of 23.1 for males and 23.6 for females.[43] How many others continued to drink but were not readmitted to this hospital is a matter for conjecture, but the number was possibly low. Group therapy has also been used with the nonalcoholic wives of alcoholics with what have been claimed to be promising results; moreover, many of the women would not have participated in individual therapy.[44] Some persons have suggested that "therapeutic communities" or changes in hospital orientation, such as have been developed for mental patients, be organized in institutions for alcoholics.[45] (See pages 813–814.)

GROUP METHODS WITH DRUG ADDICTS

Narcotics Anonymous

Narcotics Anonymous was established in 1948 by Danny Carlson, a former drug addict. Similar to Alcoholics Anonymous in both its activities and its structure, it uses an informal organization in combating drug addiction. Carlson was fully aware of the difficulties faced by former addicts in keeping off drugs, and he founded Narcotics Anonymous in the belief that addicts would be more likely to stay off them if they could join some sort

---

[42] E. M. Scott, "A Special Type of Group Psychotherapy and Its Applications to Alcoholics," *Quarterly Journal of Studies on Alcohol,* 17:288–290 (1956).

[43] Albert C. Voth, "Group Therapy with Hospitalized Alcoholics: A Twelve-Year Study," *Quarterly Journal of Studies on Alcohol,* 24:289–303 (1963).

[44] John M. Pixley and John R. Stiefel, "Group Therapy Designed to Meet the Needs of the Alcoholic's Wife," *Quarterly Journal of Studies on Alcohol,* 24:304–314 (1963). Also see D. E. MacDonald, "Group Psychotherapy with Wives of Alcoholics," *Quarterly Journal of Studies on Alcohol,* 19:125–132 (1958); and W. W. Igersheimer, "Group Psychotherapy for Non-Alcoholic Wives of Alcoholics," *Quarterly Journal of Studies on Alcohol,* 20:77–85 (1959).

[45] See Lorant Forizs, "Therapeutic Community and Teamwork," *Research Conference on Problems of Alcohol* (New Haven, Conn.: Laboratory of Applied Biodynamics, Yale University, 1958), pp. 591–595; and Florence Powdermaker and Jerome D. Frank, *Group Psychotherapy* (Cambridge, Mass.: Harvard University Press, 1953), pp. 62, 67–69.

of group comprised of ex-addicts who could understand and help each other in dealing with their difficulties.[46] The strength gained from the mutual support of those interested in keeping away from drugs was felt to be the best answer to the problem of addiction.[47] During the first year there were eighty members in this group. Although handicapped by financial problems, due to minimal outside support, it has grown in size. At present branches exist in most large cities in the United States and Canada.[48]

Members of Narcotics Anonymous hold meetings twice a week. New members are recruited by getting in touch with addicts while they are hospitalized for withdrawal of the drugs, or while they are still in prisons or reformatories. As in Alcoholics Anonymous, new members are assigned to an older member upon joining the group, and the new member can call upon his "partner" when he is having a difficult time.[49]

The process in Narcotics Anonymous is similar to that of A.A., in that norms and attitudes favoring the use of drugs are replaced by norms and attitudes opposed to their use. This is evidenced by the fact that members who are actively on drugs are not retained in the group. They are given the assurance, however, that once they are off the drugs, they will be accepted. In this way group processes operate to change behavior from that of an addict to that of an ex-addict. In addition, N.A. members adhere to a set of prescribed steps similar in content to those of A.A. The first step, for example, requires that members admit that they are addicts and reads as follows: "We admit that we were powerless over drugs—that our lives had become unmanageable." [50] The N.A. steps, like those of A.A., seem to provide members with a kind of formal "guide" which assists them in making the difficult transition from addiction to postaddiction.

In general, Narcotics Anonymous has not been as successful as A.A. in terms of effecting permanent change. However, this group is still not highly developed, and accurate judgment of its potential value must await systematic investigation. Some believe that the comparative ineffectiveness of N.A. is due to the absence of public and community support. Others suggest that the public attitude toward addiction in the United States is

---

[46] Marie Nyswander, *The Drug Addict as a Patient* (New York: Grune & Stratton, Inc., 1956), p. 144.

[47] See Jerome Ellison, "These Drug Addicts Cure One Another," *Saturday Evening Post,* 227:22–23, 48–52 (1954).

[48] Nyswander.

[49] Nyswander. Also see John M. Murtagh and Sara Harris, *Who Live in Shadow* (New York: McGraw-Hill Book Company, Inc., 1959), pp. 178–179.

[50] Murtagh and Harris, p. 178.

responsible for the tremendous handicaps an addict faces in being reaccepted by society.[51] There is no doubt that the public attitude toward drug addiction is much more negative than it is toward alcoholism.

Synanon

A newer group method of dealing with drug addicts is Synanon, an organization of drug addicts—men and women—which was founded in California in 1958 by a member of Alcoholics Anonymous and a drug addict.[52] In 1965 there were Synanon establishments in Santa Monica, San Francisco, San Diego, Reno, and Westport, Connecticut. By 1965 more than 500 drug addicts had been involved in the program. The Synanon Foundation supports the work from donations received from thousands of persons all over the country. By their labor and contributions participants in the program also contribute to its support.

In a typical Synanon establishment drug addicts live voluntarily together in a number of buildings for the purpose of freeing themselves and each other from drug addiction. Some have been criminals and prostitutes before addiction, but many of them have had to engage in criminal activities and prostitution to support their habit. They manage their own offices and carry out the physical operations of the establishment. Membership in a Synanon group can be divided into three groups which represent stages in progress toward rehabilitation. In the first stage they live and work in the residential center; in the second they have jobs outside but still live in the house; in stage three persons graduate to living and working on the outside.

An important part of the program is that each evening members meet in small groups or "synanons" of six to ten members.[53] Membership is rotated so that one does not regularly interact in the small group with the same persons. The trend of the discussions is up to the members; no professional persons are present. The purpose of these group sessions is to "trigger feelings" and to precipitate "a catharsis." Because members of Synanon live together their behavior is under constant scrutiny by the others and affords material for every session. In the discussions there is an "attack therapy" or "haircut" in which members insist on the truth and cross-examination;

---

[51] See Nyswander, pp. 144–145, and Murtagh and Harris, pp. 179–181.

[52] Lewis Yablonsky, *The Tunnel Back: Synanon* (New York: The Macmillan Company, 1965); Rita Volkman and Donald R. Cressey, "Differential Association and the Rehabilitation of Drug Addicts," in John A. O'Donnell and John C. Ball, *Narcotic Addiction* (New York: Harper & Row, Publishers, 1966), originally published in *American Journal of Sociology*, 69:129–142 (1963).

[53] Synanon got its name from an addict who was trying to say "seminar."

hostile attack and ridicule are expected. "An important goal of the 'haircut' method is to change the criminal—tough guy pose." [54]

A study of the first fifty-two residents of Synanon found that they were not easy rehabilitation cases, for all had been in and out of jails and prisons throughout the United States.[55] The mean number of confinements was 5.5 for males and 3.9 for females. Half (54 percent) were from twenty-one to thirty; another 38 percent were from thirty-one to forty. Half had completed high school or had had some college training.

The program has been analyzed as essentially involving a number of theoretical ideas which unwittingly apply the differential association theory (see pages 254–255) to the treatment of drug addicts.[56]

1. Expressed willingness to submit . . . self to a group that hates drug addiction. . . . He must be willing to give up all ambition, desires, and social interactions that might prevent the group from assimilating him completely.
2. The addict discovers over and over again that the group to which he is submitting is anti-drug, anti-crime, and anti-alcohol. At least a dozen times a day he hears someone tell him that he can remain at Synanon only so long as he "stays clean," that is, stays away from crime, alcohol, and drugs. . . . A "haircut" is a deliberately contrived device for minimizing the importance of the individual and maximizing the importance of the group and for defining the group's basic purpose— keeping addicts off drugs and crime.
3. Cohesion is maximized by a "family" analogy and by the fact that all but some "third-stage" members live and work together. The daily program has been deliberately designed to throw members into continuous mutual activity. In addition to the free, unrestricted interaction in small groups called "synanons," the members meet as a group at least twice each day. After breakfast, someone is called upon to read the "Synanon Philosophy," which is a kind of declaration of principles, the day's work schedule is discussed, bits of gossip are publicly shared, the group or individual members are spontaneously praised or scolded by older members. Following a morning of work activities, members meet in the dining room after lunch to discuss some concept or quotation that has been written on a blackboard. . . . There are weekend recreational activities, and holidays, wedding anniversaries, and birthdays are celebrated. Each member is urged: "Be yourself," "Speak the

---

[54] Yablonsky, p. 241.

[55] Volkman and Cressey, p. 213.

[56] The following extracts are reprinted from Rita Volkman and Donald R. Cressey, "Differential Association and the Rehabilitation of Drug Addicts," *American Journal of Sociology*, 69:129–142 (1963), by permission of The University of Chicago Press.

truth," "Be honest," and this kind of action in an atmosphere that is informal and open quickly gives participants a strong sense of "belonging." Since many of the members have been homeless drifters, it is not surprising to hear frequent repetition of some comment to the effect that "This is the first home I ever had." . . . Holding addicts in the house once they have been allowed to enter is a strong appeal to ideas such as "We have all been in the shape you are now in," or "Mike was on heroin for twenty years and *he's* off."

4. The house has an explicit program for distributing status symbols to members in return for staying off the drug and, later, for actually displaying antidrug attitudes. The resident, no longer restricted to the status of "inmate" or "patient" as in a prison or hospital, can achieve any staff position in the status hierarchy. The Synanon experience is organized into a career of roles that represent stages of graded competence, at whose end are roles that might later be used in the broader community.

5. At Synanon, disassociating from former friends, avoiding street talk, and becoming disloyal to criminals are emphasized at the same time that loyalty to non-criminals, telling the truth to authority figures, and legitimate work are stressed. We have no direct evidence that haircuts, synanons, and both formal and spontaneous denunciations of street talk and the code of the streets have important rehabilitative effects on the actor, as well as (or, perhaps, even "rather than") on the victim. It seems rather apparent, however, that an individual's own behavior must be dramatically influenced when he acts in the role of a moral policeman and "takes apart" another member.

The nature of such a program, as well as the voluntary organization itself, makes it difficult to determine the degree of rehabilitation. The study of the fifty-two original residents showed that the average length of time on drug use was eleven years and 56 percent had not been off drugs for more than a month at a time. In a later survey twenty-seven (52 percent) of the fifty-two residents had abstained for at least six months: twelve of them had been "clean" for at least two years, and two had been off drugs for over three years.[57]

Of all the Synanon enrollees up to August, 1962, 108 out of 372 (29 percent) are known to be off drugs. More significantly, of the 215 persons who have remained at Synanon for at least one month, 103 (48 percent) are still off drugs; of the 143 who have remained for at least three months, 95 (66 percent) are still non-users; of the 87 who have remained at least seven months, 75 (86 percent) are non-users. These statistics seem to us to be most relevant, for they indicate that once an addict actually becomes a member of the antidrug community (as indicated by three to six months

[57] Volkman and Cressey, in O'Donnell and Ball, p. 231.

of participation), the probability that he will leave and revert to the use of drugs is low.[58]

Other Group Methods

Doubt has been expressed by some persons as to whether the kind of group therapy afforded by Narcotics Anonymous would have a permanent or even a marked effect on drug addicts.[59] Such skepticism is probably due, however, to the prevailing view among many authorities that the drug subculture and the "personality traits and psychological needs" of the drug addict make change by informal methods difficult. Yet the findings of one study definitely show that group-oriented methods were effective in reforming drug addicts.[60] In this study the prodrug subculture of the treatment ward was significantly changed to an antidrug subculture by reorganizing the status system and by reassigning prestige to those showing signs of abandoning drug use. As a result, addicts on this ward reformed, in contrast to other treatment wards where reorganization was not attempted. Some programs, as in San Juan, Puerto Rico, involve the employment of former drug addicts to induce drug addicts in the local community to engage in treatment programs and, as in New York City, their use in the treatment program itself.

This method has thus far been employed on a small scale; yet it is possible that its use will increase. Some persons, in fact, believe that drug addicts present special problems which may be resolved by changes in hospital orientation rather than by changes in individual addicts. One therapist reports a situation where the creation of a "therapeutic community" in a hospital for drug addicts resulted in a noticeable change in patients' attitudes.[61]

Group psychotherapy has been employed to some extent with addicts.[62] Generally, however, such attempts have used an individual approach, so that the effect of the group, if any, has been incidental. Until specifically

---

[58] Volkman and Cressey, in O'Donnell and Ball, p. 232. Some feel that abstinence from drugs is tied up with the residential program itself and that relapses may occur later after leaving. The data of this study seem to disprove this belief.

[59] Walter C. Reckless, *The Crime Problem* (2d ed.: New York: Appleton-Century-Crofts, Inc., 1955), p. 376.

[60] James J. Thorpe and Bernard Smith, "Phases in Group Development in the Treatment of Drug Addicts," *International Journal of Group Psychotherapy*, 3:66–78 (1953).

[61] See Arnold H. Zucker, "Group Psychotherapy and the Nature of Drug Addiction," *International Journal of Group Psychotherapy*, 11:209–218 (1961). For a discussion of various other hospital treatment methods, see Chapter 9, pages 334–335.

[62] Nyswander, pp. 143–144.

group-oriented psychotherapy is attempted on a wider scale, a definitive evaluation of its effectiveness will not be possible.

GROUP METHODS IN REINTEGRATING THE MENTALLY DISORDERED

Until recently the only major form of group treatment of mental patients was group psychotherapy. Within recent years there has been a fertile expansion of group approaches to reintegrating psychotic and neurotic deviants.

Recovery, Incorporated

In existence are a number of informal groups which function to assist former patients in becoming socially reintegrated. One of these national organizations, called Recovery, Incorporated, was founded in 1937 in Chicago by thirty recovered mental patients, with the help of a psychiatrist of the Psychiatric Institute of the University of Illinois Medical School, to help mental patients adjust to society in a satisfactory manner after their release from the hospital.[63] Thirty years later, in 1967, there were 600 groups, ranging in size from eight to thirty members, in forty states, with a total membership of 12,000. Those who belong may be either persons who have been previously in mental hospitals or under other treatment, or those who are disturbed about their mental difficulties and wish the help of the group.

The organization emphasizes self-help, and the members mutually support each other in the problems of their daily lives. Most of the social activities of the ex-patients are of an informal nature. Friendship patterns are established, the families of the recovered patients often become closely identified with each other, and there are group visits, picnics, and other activities.

The formal group meetings, usually scheduled several times a week, are largely discussion sessions led by a group leader, who must have once been a mental patient and who has been trained by the national organization. In this regard the meetings are quite different from those of A.A. The group sessions emphasize a realistic approach to difficulties through not avoiding discomforting situations as well as through tending to minimize individual efforts to reach perfection. There are some open meetings which patients, relatives, and friends attend and in which the families become familiar with

---

[63] A. A. Low, "Recovery, Incorporated: A Project for Rehabilitating Post-psychotic and Long-Term Psychoneurotic Patients," in W. H. Soden, ed., *Rehabilitation of the Handicapped* (New York: The Ronald Press Company, 1949), pp. 213–226.

the symptoms and behavior of mental disorders and learn how they can help the ex-patients. If a member should suffer a setback, he is instructed to call a veteran Recovery member, who will come to help him at any hour. If the illness becomes worse a neighborhood panel leader is summoned, and if he cannot help, psychiatric aid may be suggested. In order to keep them from being overly concerned about themselves, former patients are instructed not to indulge in self-diagnosis.

Other Informal Groups

Clubs whose membership is composed of former mental hospital patients, sometimes known as "social therapeutic clubs," have been established in many sections of the United States in recent years, and are growing in number and variety.[64] Such organizations provide patients with an opportunity to gain confidence in social situations through participating in group activities with others who have similar problems. In this way groups such as these function as "steppingstones" to permanent community reintegration. This type of organization is much more common in England, where these groups have been in operation for many years.[65]

Group Therapy

Group therapy became generally recognized as an acceptable method of treatment during World War II, and since then the number of persons who have experimented with various forms of group therapy has increased. The success of the armed forces with group treatment of neuropsychiatric patients, the greater awareness of the overcrowding in mental hospitals, the shortage of psychiatrists, and the high cost of individual therapy resulted in the adoption of group therapy as a part of the general treatment program. In addition, many feel that group therapy methods are more effective than individual therapy with many mental patients.

There are several different types of group therapy. In some cases lectures dealing with difficulties of adjustment are given to the patients, and are often followed by discussions. In the usual method of group therapy, however, a psychiatrist and from four to twenty patients hold frequent discussions as a group in which all participate and in which there is group sharing of experiences. Sometimes additional tools are employed, for ex-

---

[64] Milton Greenblatt, "The Rehabilitation Spectrum," in M. Greenblatt and Benjamin Simon, eds., *Rehabilitation of the Mentally Ill* (Washington, D.C.: American Association for the Advancement of Science, 1959), p. 19. See also pp. 229, 243.

[65] See J. Bierer, ed., *Therapeutic Social Clubs* (London: H. K. Lewis, 1948).

ample, the psychodrama in which conflict situations are acted out by a group on a stage.[66]

In some instances, hospitals have found it advantageous to provide special group therapy sessions for close relatives of their patients.[67] These group sessions are held for about an hour or two once or twice a week, and are limited to approximately ten people. Such relatives often have a feeling of isolation, disgrace, hopelessness, and even guilt, and the purpose of group therapy is to discuss such feelings and to provide a more positive approach to the problem. Some therapists take a passive role, encouraging the relatives to talk about their feelings and at the same time allowing relatives of the other patients to discover the resemblances to their own feelings. As a group, the relatives of mental patients often try to help one another and sometimes develop strong feelings of group identification. Other therapists, however, take a more active role, explaining the principles of psychiatry in relatives and talking about the care given to the patients.

Psychodrama is somewhat similar to discussion therapy, but it is carried out in a different setting. It had its origin in Vienna in 1922, when Moreno founded the psychodramatic theater to treat various mental disorders. As a result of his establishment of a psychodramatic institute later at Beacon, New York, this technique has been increasingly used in mental hospitals.[68] The essence of psychodrama and sociodrama [69] is the acting out of behaviors in imaginary situations which have previously proved difficult for patients. In this sense both psychodrama and sociodrama are role-playing techniques which offer an opportunity to acquire the social skills necessary to cope with certain situations. These techniques have been used in mental hospitals by both staff and patients as means of fostering communication and understanding. They have also been used to assist patients in acquiring social skills, both in relation to the hospital group and in relation to anticipated real-life situations with friends, family, and employers.[70] The

---

[66] Powdermaker and Frank, pp. 4, 5.

[67] W. D. Ross, "Group Psychotherapy with Psychotic Patients and Their Relatives," *American Journal of Psychiatry,* 105:383–386 (1948). Also see H. P. Peck, R. D. Rabinovitch, and J. B. Cramer, "A Treatment Program for Parents of Schizophrenic Children," *American Journal of Orthopsychiatry,* 19:592–598 (1959); and Erika Chance, *Families in Treatment* (New York: Basic Books, Inc., 1959).

[68] Jacob L. Moreno, ed., *Group Psychotherapy* (New York: Beacon House, Inc., 1945).

[69] There is no clear distinction between these concepts in the literature.

[70] M. Greenblatt, Richard H. York, and Esther L. Brown, *From Custodial to Therapeutic Patient Care in Mental Hospitals* (New York: Russell Sage Foundation, 1955), pp. 180–183.

usual procedure employed in psychodrama is to have patients and staff— usually but not always a small group—meet together and choose a problem situation to enact, members of the group assuming the necessary roles. The group may be seated in a semicircle, with or without a stage, and usually there is a "leader" appointed to take charge of the meeting. The problem situation may be drawn from some past or anticipated hospital occurrences: the recovering mental patient may be urged to re-enact some of the episodes leading to hospitalization. By re-enacting these experiences the patient is able to anticipate new behaviors which will enable him to cope more effectively with the recurrence of such experiences. A patient may have walked away from his work assignment, for example, and this incident may be enacted. Or a new staff member may have arrived on the ward, and the feelings of patients toward his reception might be dramatized.

In psychodrama various imaginary scenes with family, friends, and employers may also be enacted, so that the patient may be able later to cope with difficult situations outside the hospital. After the initial enactment of the problem the roles may be reversed, with the patients assuming the roles of staff members and staff members the roles of the patients. The audience in attendance acts as a sort of "jury" or "discussion panel," for criticism and comments are invited after the enactment. These comments may suggest how the problem might have been more adequately dealt with, and how the skills of the role players could have been improved. Frequently, these criticisms are difficult for both staff and patients, yet they seem to be helpful in enabling staff members to overcome professional blind spots and in assisting patients to grapple with situations which previously they have met with psychotic or neurotic deviation.[71]

Evaluations of group methods have challenged the traditional psychoanalytic view of the treatment of mental disorders. It has been suggested that the role of the therapist does not call for special medical or psychiatric training, that the therapist's role may be assumed by nurses, aides, and attendants.[72] Indeed, it has been suggested by some that the social distance between psychiatrists and patients creates a barrier to therapy of a nonorganic sort. In addition, it has been pointed out by others that group therapy can, and does, result in changes in attitudes, motives, and self-

---

[71] See Greenblatt, York, and Brown, pp. 180–190, and F. Knobloch, "On the Theory of a Therapeutic Community for Neurotics," *International Journal of Group Psychotherapy* 10:408–418 (1960). Also see Robert H. Hyde and Richard H. Williams, "What Is Therapy and Who Does It?" in M. Greenblatt, D. Levinson, and Richard H. Williams, *The Patient and the Mental Hospital* (New York: The Free Press, 1957), pp. 173–196.

[72] Hyde and Williams, "What Is Therapy and Who Does It?"

concepts. A sociologist has described group psychotherapy as the "deliberate creation of an artificial subculture and the manipulation of a special social system" to effect changes in behavior patterns.[73] The key to effectiveness of group therapy is seen sociologically to result from experience in playing new roles, and learning to deal with situations previously met with inappropriate role behavior.[74]

Although few really carefully controlled experiments have as yet been made on the results of group therapy in mental disorders, there is almost unanimous opinion among those who have been engaged in this work that group therapy is effective. Little fundamental research has been done on what takes place in such group sessions, but it seems possible that the encouraging results are explained not by the theoretical scheme of the group analysts but by the process of informal group adjustment. In group therapy with mental patients, "should an individual member express misgivings about his prospects of improvement, or about the need for resolving his problems, or about the worth of the group itself, he will be resisted by other members, for any group that strives to survive evolves a set of objectives. . . . In effective group psychotherapy the identity of the collectivity and its survival center around the improvement of its members." [75]

In group psychotherapy mentally disturbed patients appear to develop an identification with one another and a degree of group integration; sometimes the opinion of the group appears to change the personality pattern and attitudes of one of its members; and each member secures an opportunity to play new roles and to acquire a new conception of himself. In the light of the problems of others it is possible for the patient to see his own difficulties and to relieve his feelings of social isolation. As one psychiatrist states the problem, "It is the group itself that becomes the therapeutic agent as a result of the interaction between the individuals who form the group." [76] Weinberg has summarized the result of such a treatment program in this way: "He finds that other persons have problems somewhat similar to his own, that all want to be socially accepted and all want to improve. The collective morale and identity that emerge encourage the iso-

---

[73] Beck, "The Dynamics of Group Psychotherapy. . . ."

[74] Beck. Also see George Psathas, "Phase Movement and Equilibrium Tendencies in Interaction Process in Psychotherapy Groups," *Sociometry*, 23:177–194 (1960) and "Interaction Process Analysis of Two Psychotherapy Groups," *International Journal of Group Psychotherapy*, 10:430–445 (1960).

[75] Kirson Weinberg, *Society and Personality Disorders* (copyright, 1952, by Prentice-Hall, Inc., Englewood Cliffs, N.J.), p. 343. Reprinted by permission of the publisher.

[76] Bruno Solby, "Group Psychotherapy and the Method," in Moreno, pp. 50–51.

lated and timid person to increase his confidence, to become more socially active, and to feel that the therapeutic context is more real than in individual therapy." [77]

Other Group Methods

Certain other methods, such as dance and music therapy, have been used to engage otherwise isolated patients in group activities. Often square dancing and other group dances are used. It has been found that even catatonic patients, who were given special rhythmic exercises if they were seriously withdrawn, would stay together and participate in the program if they held hands in a circle, but would scatter immediately if they dropped their hands. Music therapy has involved singing and similar activities involving rhythm. It is felt that songs have personal meanings, are an outlet for self-expression, revive memories, and are therefore useful in the treatment of mental patients. Patients may be given wooden blocks or sticks and encouraged to clap them together in time with march music in two-four time. The music sessions also include the singing or humming of the national anthem, folk songs, or popular new songs. Group discussion often goes along with these activities. These methods seem to have had some success. It has been suggested that whatever value these activities have depends on their ability to foster interpersonal relationships, and that there is little intrinsic value in the activities themselves.

Family Care and Halfway Houses

Some procedures have attempted to reintegrate the mental patient under more "normal" group situations. The treatment for the mentally ill in Gheel, Belgium, for example, consists chiefly of incorporating mental patients into a small city. Here they are allowed, in the majority of cases, to live as part of the community rather than under the general scheme of institutionalization.[78] The people of Gheel have cared for the mentally ill since the medieval ages, when a shrine there became the object of frequent visits by mentally ill persons. A government mental hospital was established later. Among the 22,000 inhabitants of Gheel there are today over 2000 patients living with foster families. The town is divided into four wards, each with medical and nursing facilities, and the physician calls on the patients generally in the home. The mental hospital in the town is usually only a last resort. The objective of this plan is to absorb patients

---

[77] Weinberg, p. 357.

[78] See John D. J. Moore, "What Gheel Means to Me," *Look Magazine,* May 23, 1961, pp. 24–39 and Marvin E. Opler, ed., *Culture and Mental Health* (New York: The Macmillan Company, 1959), pp. 4–5. The author visited Gheel in 1955.

into both the home and the community. In addition, patients often perform various types of work, such as the care of children or farm work. Families receive a small remuneration for this patient-care from the Belgian government. It is believed that the value of this type of treatment lies in integrating patients into a normal, useful life, and freeing them from the social isolation of hospital wards. In addition, because Gheel residents are accustomed by tradition to caring for them, they are able to accept patients without fear or mistrust. This latter fact is believed to remove the stigma of mental illness so that patients can be reintegrated.

This method of placing patients in individual homes has been practiced in several other European countries extensively for some years. In Denmark, for example, there are as many patients living outside the hospital at Aarhus as within it. The United States does not have a history of family care programs comparable to those of Europe, and generally, when employed, they have been used only for chronic patients. At present family care programs are in operation in Maryland, Massachusetts, and a few other states.[79] Experience with family care programs in this country indicates that they have great, but unexploited, potential.

Halfway houses for mental patients are similar to those described for alcoholics. The objective of such houses is to provide a transitional living unit for ex-patients who need an opportunity to regain the social and vocational skills necessary for "life on the outside." Such houses as these are more common in Europe than in the United States.[80] Houses differ in the degree to which they are autonomous: some are run almost wholly by the former patient-residents, and others are dependent on hospital or social agencies. In 1956 a hospital in Vermont established a halfway house for thirty-five women, all chronic schizophrenics who had been hospitalized for an average of four years.[81] A housemother and a case worker were appointed, but the greater portion of responsibility for house maintenance and care was given to the patients themselves. Patients were able to make their own decisions and, as a group, were permitted to deal with the problems that arose. Many patients were assisted in finding employment. In addition, they were encouraged to participate in community social functions, in this way gradually regaining their place in the "outside." At the time of the study, twenty-seven of the thirty-five patients initially in the house were out

---

[79] M. Greenblatt and T. Lidz, "Some Dimensions of the Problem," in Greenblatt, Levinson, Williams, p. 515. Also see Greenblatt and Simon, p. 242.

[80] Greenblatt and Lidz, p. 514, and Greenblatt and Simon, p. 240.

[81] George W. Brooks, "Opening a Rehabilitation House," in Greenblatt and Simon, pp. 127–139, and Donald M. Eldred, "Problems of Opening a Rehabilitation House," *Mental Hospitals,* 8:20–21 (1957).

of the hospital. Of them, eleven were completely free of psychotic symptoms, were employed and socially active, and were thought to be making a superior adjustment. Another ten were making a satisfactory adjustment, were employed, less active socially, but retaining some delusions and other symptoms. Five patients were making marginal adjustments, most of them living with their families. Only one patient was reported to be relapsed, but living in the community.[82]

These various group treatments of mental disorders seem to suggest that mental illness cannot be adequately explained by individualistic theories which attribute mental illness to early childhood experiences, such as those often advanced by psychiatrists and psychoanalysts. Rather, a person's mental illness may develop out of difficulties that arise in his relating to groups in adult life without his having experienced exceptional difficulties early in life. One psychiatrist, in discounting the individual or personal problems of the patient, has stated that "since he [the patient] worked up his psychosis in the group, he can never be cured until he has worked out his recovery in a group." [83] As a research statement on the relation of mental disorder to socioenvironmental factors indicated, "the possible existence of group character structures, the stresses put on many by changing conditions or by the excessive demands of the culture, the sources of and the effect of loneliness and social isolation, and the techniques and effects of social esteem and social punishment on personality, these and many other problems need careful and continued investigation." [84]

GROUP METHODS IN REINTEGRATING THE AGED

Old People's Clubs

One of the most prominent group approaches to reintegrating aged persons consists of informal groups or social clubs. Many clubs run by and for older persons have been organized within the last thirty years. Some, such as the Townsend Clubs, grew out of the depression of the 1930s and the need for political organization to secure larger pension grants, but now they emphasize social relationships among old people. Some groups have

---

[82] Brooks reports that the thirty-five patients in this house had formerly been "dilapidated derelicts on the disturbed and semi-disturbed wards of the hospital—denuditive, smearing the walls of the seclusion rooms." He also reports that, as a result of this experiment, there had occurred in the hospital a marked increase in the status-value of the diagnosis "chronic schizophrenia," many hoping that they might be candidates for the halfway house.

[83] L. Cody Marsh, "Group Treatment of the Psychoses by the Psychological Equivalent of the Revival," *Mental Hygiene,* 15:341 (1931).

[84] R. H. Felix and R. V. Bowers, "Mental Hygiene and Socio-Environmental Factors," *The Milbank Memorial Fund Quarterly,* 26:134 (1948).

originated around social activities, such as Golden Age Clubs or Three-Quarter-Century Clubs, and for the most part they have been concerned with group activities for the aged. Some but not all of the Golden Age Clubs are directed by professional workers and financed by Community Chests or other groups.

Regardless of the original purpose of the clubs, they provide a place for old people to gather, to meet others of their own age, and to enter into activities in which they are mutually interested. They play games, talk, sing, or sew, and, as in the case of the Townsend Clubs, engage in political activities to promote their interests. All these activities give them something to do, a feeling of belonging, and also help to change their conception of themselves and their own problems because they see themselves through the eyes of others with similar, and perhaps even greater, difficulties.

GROUP METHODS WITH DELINQUENTS AND CRIMINAL OFFENDERS

Although sociologists have used the group approach in their explanation of delinquents and criminals in criminology perhaps more than in any other field, the verification of the findings through the practical manipulation of the social world of offenders, using group methods, has not been as extensively investigated. The use of group therapy in correctional programs has increased in recent years.[85] Yet most of these programs are of relatively recent origin and have not been adequately evaluated as to their effectiveness.

Individual clinical methods of treating potential or actual offenders, although quite commonly used, are often assumed to be effective, in spite of the fact that their success has not been demonstrated. One study of the effectiveness of clinical treatment with male delinquents in Detroit found, for example, that there was no significant difference in percentages of arrest for those receiving psychiatric treatment as compared with those not receiving such treatment. These researchers concluded that "psychotherapeutic treatment of juvenile delinquents in varying degrees does not serve to prevent them from becoming adult offenders." [86] A more recent study found no difference in outcome of a group of delinquent girls receiving intensive individual case work and therapy and a control group which did not receive such psychotherapeutic treatment.[87] In view of the question

---

[85] McCorkle and Elias.

[86] H. Warren Dunham and LaMay Adamson, "Clinical Treatment of Male Juvenile Delinquents: A Case Study in Effect and Result," *American Sociological Review,* 21:320 (1956).

[87] Henry J. Meyer, Edgar F. Borgatta and Wyatt C. Jones, *Girls at Vocational High* (New York: Russell Sage Foundation, 1965).

about the ineffectiveness of clinical and individual methods, some persons have suggested that rehabilitative efforts in correctional institutions should be more on a group basis. Consequently emphasis has been increasingly placed on group approaches to treatment.

> As to the "treatment" itself, it is suggested that the group relations which support criminality cannot be directly modified in a clinic in the way that the condition of a person suffering from syphilis can be modified in a clinic; they can be modified only by providing the criminal with new social relations or in some way changing the nature of present group relations.[88]

Informal Groups in Conventional Settings

As yet little on the order of Alcoholics Anonymous or Recovery, Incorporated, has been developed for juvenile and criminal offenders. Cressey has suggested that wide use be made of ex-criminals as agents for changing criminals, which will also aid in their own rehabilitation. "Criminals who have committed crimes and delinquencies by means of certain verbalizations, and who have rejected these verbalizations in favor of verbalizations making crime psychologically difficult or even impossible, should be more effective in changing criminals' self-conceptions than would men who have never had close familiarity with the procriminal verbalizations." [89] Cressey believes that ex-criminals could be used in a wide variety of ways, including serving as leaders in group therapy or in guided group interaction correctional programs.

Efforts have been made to work on problems of deviant attitudes on an informal group basis, incorporating, for example, an entitre delinquent group within a conventional framework. In one of these attempts the California Youth Authority, in cooperation with the War Department, in 1944 placed two groups of about 150 seriously delinquent boys in Army arsenals to work side by side with several thousand civilian men and women. The Army furnished barracks and provided otherwise for the boys. Attempts were made to change their roles by incorporating them into the norms and objectives of conventional society. The program seems on the surface to have made marked changes in the work habits of the boys, in their conception of themselves, and in group objectives.[90]

---

[88] Sutherland and Cressey, p. 379.

[89] Donald R. Cressey, "Social Psychological Foundations for Using Criminals in the Rehabilitation of Criminals," in Gold and Scarpitti, p. 327.

[90] Described in John R. Ellingston, *Protecting Our Children from Criminal Careers* (Englewood Cliffs, N.J.: Prentice-Hall, Inc., 1948), pp. 95–118. Also see J. Douglas and Marguerite Grant, "A Group Dynamics Approach to the Treatment of Nonconformists in the Navy," *The Annals*, 322:126–135 (1959).

In India a similar though community-based approach has been used in an effort to achieve social reintegration of the formerly "criminal tribes" of India. These groups consist of people who for centuries have lived by criminal means, such as stealing, robbery, and some types of pickpocketing. Frequently they sell women for prostitution, make alcohol illicitly, and fight with knives. Children born into the tribes acquire the deviant behavior patterns of their elders, with the result that the criminal traditions have been perpetuated. In recent years the Indian government has undertaken a rehabilitative program with these tribes. This program was begun when it was recognized that traditional methods, such as imprisonment, were largely ineffective. The objective of the present program is to achieve change in the behavior of these tribes by placing them in communities where they may gradually acquire noncriminal attitudes and norms. This is done by relocating groups within noncriminal villages or communities, and arranging special services to foster social interaction between local community members and members of the formerly criminal tribes.[91] A new experimental program has been started near Lucknow, where young children of these tribes are placed in a resident school on a voluntary basis. Here they receive a normal school program and have frequent associations with schoolchildren in the nearby noncriminal community. An effort is made to change not only their attitudes but their self-conceptions by insulating them from their former associates.

In Wisconsin, inmates of the county jails are permitted, under the Huber law, to work in free society during the day, as "day parole," returning to the jail in the evenings and on weekends. Deductions in their pay are made for their "lodging." The 1772 prisoners employed outside the jail during 1956 under this law earned $364,282.[92] Various prisons in the United States, Sweden, and elsewhere are now also utilizing a similar "work release" program for certain inmates. See pages 794–795.

Group Therapy and Guided Group Interaction

During World War II group therapy of a more specific nature was used with British military offenders. Later it was used in the United States at the Service Command Rehabilitation Center at Fort Knox, where the necessity for rehabilitating large numbers of persons far exceeded the

---

[91] B. H. Mehta, "Ex-Criminal Groups in India," *Indian Journal of Social Work,* Vol. 16 (1955); and P. N. Saxena, "Rehabilitation Work among Ex-Criminal Groups in India," *Social Welfare in India* (New Delhi: Planning Commission of the Government, September 1955), pp. 505–516.

[92] Sanger B. Powers, "Day-Parole of Misdemeanants," *Federal Probation,* 22:42–46 (1958).

supply of professional men available. In this group therapy work the "belligerent, over-assertive, anti-social rehabilitee is brought into line by his fellows and the asocial, shy, withdrawn person is drawn into the conversation." [93] Since World War II, more and more civilian correctional institutions have established group therapy as an aid to rehabilitation. Group therapy is extensively used at present in prisons and reformatories. In California, a group counseling program has been in operation since 1944.[94] Although there has been some use of sociodramas and psychodramas, for the most part the therapy has been mainly of the discussion-group type. These discussions may be guided either by a professionally trained leader, such as a sociologist, a psychologist, a social worker, or a psychiatrist, or by nonprofessional personnel with some in-service training.

In New Jersey group therapy in correctional institutions and halfway houses is called "guided group interaction" in an effort to avoid confusion with group therapy as practiced by psychiatrists, as well as the implication that inmates are "mentally abnormal." Such programs are also widely used in halfway houses in Pennsylvania, New York, Kentucky, California, and the District of Columbia. The following excerpt is taken from a discussion in a New Jersey correctional institution in which an inmate comes to see that his difficulties in living in various cell blocks are primarily from his own actions and not from those of other inmates.

S: Well, I might. But he wants me to adjust myself to the people in A Wing [cell block] and learn to get along in A Wing.

J: Why can't you get along in A Wing?

S: Because I can't.

J: What makes you think you can get along in another wing?

S: Because I'd be my myself then.

A: Can't you be by yourself in A Wing?

S: No.

J: Why can't you make those fellows leave you alone? You want to stay by yourself.

S: That is not the point. The point is they'll turn around and bother you anyhow. At least in one of the lock-up wings, if you don't want nobody around, you go in your cell and lock the door, and the hell with them. Right?

---

[93] Joseph Abrahams and Lloyd W. McCorkle, "Group Psychotherapy of Military Offenders," *American Journal of Sociology,* 51:458 (1946).

[94] Sutherland and Cressey, pp. 492–493, Norman Fenton, *A Brief Historical Account of Group Counselling in the Prisons of California* (Sacramento: State Department of Corrections, 1957); and G. Sterna, "The Correctional Officer as a Treatment Figure," *Group Counseling Newsletter,* California Department of Corrections, June 1958, pp. 9–10.

O: Sure.

B: Do you mean to tell me people bother you, S_____?

S: Yeah.

J: I think S_____ bothers people if I know S_____. I locked with you for three and a half months. If you come over to E–2 and pull the s_____ you pulled on B–3.

S: Well, any how, that what he said. I am just stating what he said, that's all.

Leader: Well, I think S_____ made a point. He said that really what determines whether or not a guy is ready to go out depends on his ability to get along in any kind of situation.[95]

Such discussions seem to set in operation group forces directed toward socially accepted goals, and which partially counteract the antisocial group conniving that goes on so extensively in correctional institutions. This process does not occur automatically; it extends over a long period of time. If the group atmosphere is one of true acceptance, respect, and non-censure, offenders seem to feel free to express their feelings and to share experiences of which conventional society would disapprove. Group accept-ance of mutual feelings thus enables offenders to examine their experiences and the reasons for their confinement. In addition, if in the therapy group the offenders are trusted and expected to abide by anticriminal norms, they may come to regard themselves as nonoffenders, or at least as potential nonoffenders. If such changes in self-concepts do occur, it is probable that offenders will then aspire to lead the lives of "respectable" law-abiding per-sons. If this point is reached, criminal attitudes and motives will have been replaced by noncriminal attitudes and motives.[96]

> . . . there seems to be an assumption that free discussion of an inmate's problems and personality characteristics by and with an inmate group and a therapist will both enable him and force him to "face the facts" of his case. . . . Inmates who have had experiences similar to his will not let him lie, bluff, or provide *ex post facto* justification for his criminal behavior. Presumably, the inmate . . . will accept his fellow inmates' friendly denun-ciations of his behavior and rationalizations more readily than he would accept the rejections and denunciations of the same behavior and ration-alizations by an outsider.[97]

---

[95] F. Lovell Bixby and Lloyd W. McCorkle, "Guided Group Interaction in Correctional Work," *American Sociological Review,* 16:458–459 (1951).

[96] Sutherland and Cressey, pp. 494–496. Also see Richard R. Korn and Lloyd W. McCorkle, *Criminology and Penology* (New York: Holt, Rinehart and Winston, Inc., 1959), Chaps. 23 and 24.

[97] Sutherland and Cressey, p. 555. In a rather unusual experiment in group therapy, two small groups of incorrigible prisoners in a North Carolina prison, one

A variation of guided group interaction which has been employed in some correctional institutions consists of "role training" or role playing as part of the therapeutic technique. One institution conducted an experiment in "role training" as a means of preparing inmates for the problems which would be encountered after release from the institution.[98] According to these experimenters, if an offender upon release is to play the role of a nonoffender and a law-abiding citizen, he must have experienced (1) knowledge of the expectations of the role, generally through intimate contact with nonoffenders which allows identification with persons occupying the role; (2) rehearsal in the role, either imaginal or incipient; and (3) actual practice in the role.[99] Results indicated that role training was successful in improving role-playing skills and attitudes. There were highly significant differences when these offenders were compared with a control group.

It is unfortunate that, instead of changing the attitudes of the inmate about various *social norms,* most correctional group therapy work is still directed at attempts to modify personality traits and allowing the individual to release some of his aggressions. The approach used may, of course, help the inmate adjust to the frustrations of prison life, but often it does not get at the basis of his criminal behavior. Because the inmate's attitudes are derived from the social groups to which he has belonged, and because he has not had normal relationships with more conventional groups, it is important that group therapy programs be based on a group, rather than on an individual, theory of criminality.[100]

One interesting recent group experiment in dealing with juvenile delinquency is known as the Provo (Utah) Experiment.[101] A group of ha-

---

from security isolation and the other from the yard, were selected for discussion therapy.—Richard McCleery, *The Strange Journey* (Chapel Hill: University of North Carolina Extension Bulletin, Vol. 32, No. 4 [March, 1953]). A more recent study of fifty prison "rats," or prisoners at odds with their fellow inmates, has examined some of these circumstances.—Elmer H. Johnson, "Sociology of Confinement: Assimilation and the Prison 'Rat,' " *Journal of Criminal Law, Criminology and Police Science,* 50:528–533 (1961).

[98] Martin R. Haskell and H. Ashley Weeks, "Role Training as Preparation for Release from Correctional Institutions," *Journal of Criminal Law, Criminology and Police Science,* 50:441–452 (1960).

[99] Haskell and Weeks, p. 441.

[100] Donald R. Cressey, "Contradictory Theories in Correctional Group Therapy Programs," *Federal Probation,* 18:20–26 (1954); also his "Changing Criminals: The Application of the Theory of Differential Association," *American Journal of Sociology,* 61:116–212 (1955) and his "The Nature and Effectiveness of Correctional Techniques," in *Law and Contemporary Problems.*

[101] LaMar T. Empey and Jerome Rabow, "The Provo Experiment in Delinquency Rehabilitation," *American Sociological Review,* 26:679–695 (1961).

bitual offenders, aged fifteen to seventeen, is assigned by the local court to join twenty others in daily group discussions. A control group is either placed on probation or sent to a correctional institution. The group discussions assume that delinquency is primarily a group phenomenon and the task of rehabilitation is one of changing shared delinquent characteristics. It involves discussions which (1) permit delinquents to examine the role and legitimacy of authorities in the treatment system; (2) give them the opportunity to examine the ultimate utility of conventional and delinquent alternatives for them; (3) provide the opportunity to declare publicly a belief or disbelief that they can benefit from a change in values; and (4) make peer group interaction the principal rehabilitative tool because it permits peer group decision making and grants status and recognition, not only for participation in treatment interaction, but for willingness to help others.

The Highfields Experiment

The use of halfway houses and residential treatment centers for delinquents and adult offenders will be fully discussed in the following chapter. A well-known experiment in a residential treatment center has been carried out at Highfields, which is part of the New Jersey correctional system and makes extensive use of guided group interaction and informal associations between staff and inmates in a fairly permissive, nonauthoritarian atmosphere.[102] It is a short-term detention facility located on the former estate of Charles Lindbergh in New Jersey, without bars or walls. The impact of the guided group interaction sessions, which are held five nights a week, appears to be reinforced by the group living experience.[103] In both guided group interaction and the living experience, the influence of the group is directed toward freeing the boys from delinquent associations and changing their conceptions of themselves from lawbreaking to law-abiding persons.

An evaluation made of the Highfields Project indicates that the delinquent boys aged sixteen and seventeen sent to Highfields have a lower rate of recidivism than those in the control group sent to the Annandale Reformatory.[104] In this study a control group of offenders, matched as to age, previous commitments, and so on, was sent for more conventional treatment to the New Jersey Reformatory at Annandale. A much lower percentage of boys from Highfields became delinquent after returning to

---

[102] Lloyd W. McCorkle, Albert Elias, and F. Lovell Bixby, *The Highfields Story* (New York: Holt, Rinehart and Winston, Inc., 1958).

[103] H. Ashley Weeks, ed., *Youthful Offenders at Highfields* (Ann Arbor: University of Michigan Press, 1958).

[104] *Weeks.*

the community than did the boys from Annandale, even when such factors as age, parents' marital status, race, parents' occupation, residence, and so on, were held constant. Also, comparison of Annandale boys with the Highfields boys on a number of scales designed to measure attitudes and value orientations reveals favorable changes among the latter. The conclusion of the evaluating committee was that Highfields had demonstrated greater success than the traditional type of institution in reintegrating delinquents.[105]

SUMMARY

Since evidence shows that deviant behavior is developed through group processes, group methods should help to bring about the social reintegration of deviants. Primarily during the past fifteen years, several different applications of group methods have been developed to treat mental disorders, delinquency and criminality, alcoholism, and old-age adjustment; these include community development, citizen groups working directly with deviants, group therapy or guided group interaction, group work, halfway houses, and groups of deviants dealing with a common problem. The latter include Alcoholics Anonymous and similar informal groups of mental patients, and narcotic addicts who are working out their problems more successfully together than they can alone.

Group methods appear to be more effective in reintegrating many social deviants than the individualized approach. The group approach to social reintegration affects the deviant in a number of ways which can be summarized as socialization into nondeviant behavior patterns through taking the role of a nondeviant person; sharing feelings and examining problematic past experiences in a permissive, noncensuring group setting; identifying with others who are beginning to regard themselves as nondeviants; establishing loyalty and allegiance to new group norms and values; and eventually reorienting attitudes and overt behavior. As the individual is socialized, or resocialized, a network of new interpersonal relations is established. Group identification is enhanced and a "we" feeling is developed by noting that others have similar problems. The group becomes an important link in helping its members to adjust. The individual is thus

---

[105] The Highfields Project actually did not evaluate group therapy alone, but also evaluated the difference between a small treatment institution with a permissive atmosphere and a reformatory. Although this study has shed some light on the value of group therapy, a more specifically directed research project is needed which would take inmates in the same institution and compare results in a group under such therapy with a control group which does not have such therapy.

enabled to gain a new conception of himself through group interaction. Finally, the operation of social pressures aids the establishment and maintenance of new social norms and values. This approach to the treatment of deviant behavior appears to offer unlimited possibilities for reintegrating deviants.

SELECTED READINGS

Alcoholics Anonymous.   New York: Works Publishing Company, 1950. This is the basic book used by members of Alcoholics Anonymous. It contains the stories of the founders, the general program, including the twelve steps, and a series of personal stories.

Bales, Robert F.   "The Therapeutic Role of A.A. as Seen by a Sociologist," in David J. Pittman and Charles R. Snyder, *Society, Culture and Drinking Patterns.* New York: John Wiley & Sons, 1963. The dynamics of Alcoholics Anonymous as seen by a sociologist who has studied it.

Bixby, F. Lovell, and Lloyd W. McCorkle.   "Guided Group Interaction in Correctional Work," *American Sociological Review,* 16:455–459 (1951). A theoretical analysis of the use of "guided group interaction" in the New Jersey correctional institutions. Contains several extracts from actual sessions.

Clinard, Marshall B.   "The Group Approach to Social Reintegration," *American Sociological Review,* 14:257–262 (1949). An analysis of the entire area of group approaches to reintegration. Indicates the theoretical implications of this work, particularly for sociology.

Gellman, Irving Peter.   *The Sober Alcoholic: An Organizational Analysis of Alcoholics Anonymous.* New Haven, Conn.: College and University Press, 1964. An analysis of the social organization of Alcoholics Anonymous and its historical development as a voluntary organization. Includes a description and analysis of various aspects of the A.A. program of therapy.

Korn, Richard R., and Lloyd W. McCorkle.   *Criminology and Penology.* New York: Holt, Rinehart and Winston, Inc., 1949, Chaps. 23 and 24. Contains a discussion of group methods in prisons.

Maxwell, Milton A.   "Alcoholics Anonymous: An Interpretation," in David J. Pittman, ed., *Alcoholism.* New York: Harper & Row, Publishers, 1967. A sociological view of Alcoholics Anonymous, including its program and subculture.

McCorkle, Lloyd W.   "Group Therapy," in Paul W. Tappan, ed., *Contemporary Correction.* New York: McGraw-Hill Book Company, Inc., 1951. A general statement on the use of group therapy in correctional institutions by one of the leaders in this area.

————, Albert Elias, and F. Lovell Bixby.   *The Highfields Story.* New York: Holt, Rinehart and Winston, Inc., 1958. A description of the plan, procedure, and operation of the experimental project for the group treatment of youthful offenders at Highfields.

Powdermaker, Florence B., and Jerome D. Frank.   *Group Psychotherapy.* Cambridge, Mass.: Harvard University Press, 1953. A research study of the therapeutic effect of group therapy on neurotic and schizophrenic patients of the Veterans Administration hospitals. Contains extensive material from actual group therapy sessions.

Trice, Harrison M. "Alcoholics Anonymous," in Harry Gold and Frank R. Scarpitti, eds., *Combatting Social Problems: Techniques of Intervention.* New York: Holt, Rinehart, and Winston, Inc., 1967. A comprehensive discussion of Alcoholics Anonymous and its implications for medical sociology.

Volkman, Rita, and Donald R. Cressey. "Differential Association and the Rehabilitation of Drug Addicts," in John A. O'Donnell and John C. Ball, eds., *Narcotic Addiction.* New York: Harper & Row, Publishers, 1966. A detailed analysis of the Synanon program as an application of differential association theory.

Yablonsky, Lewis. *The Tunnel Back: Synanon.* New York: The Macmillan Company, 1965. A detailed description of the Synanon program, and an analysis of its theories and techniques.

20

The Use of Total Institutions

Many people think that, in order to deal more effectively with certain deviant behavior, it is necessary to build more and better institutions to which delinquents, criminals, mentally ill persons, drug addicts, and alcoholics can be sent to be "cured." Actually, institutional treatment has limited possibilities. In the first place, the sheer size of the deviant population is so great that the cost of institutionalizing more than a fragment of all deviants would be prohibitive. For example, the prisoner population of state and federal institutions in the United States is over 250,000; the population of the mental hospitals over 500,000. Second, such places are "total institutions." [1] In other words, they are large-scale efforts to deal with deviancy, the inmates or patients are confined in "closed worlds," isolated from the larger society in a society or culture of their own, there are bureaucratic rules for whose violation the individual can be punished, the inmate or patient is confined and subservient to the social

---

[1] Irving Goffman, *Asylums* (Garden City, New York: Doubleday Anchor Books, 1959), pp. 3–124. Alcoholics Anonymous is a method of dealing with deviancy which is completely the reverse of a total institution. See Irving Peter Gellman, *The Sober Alcoholic* (New Haven, Conn.: College and University Press, 1964), pp. 153–158.

structure of the community of inmates and staff, and those confined are relieved of economic and social responsibility.[2] Although both mental hospitals and prisons may be regarded as total institutions, there is likely to be an avoidance of identification with inmate status and more turnover among mental patients than among prison inmates.[3]

CORRECTIONAL INSTITUTIONS

Although many people think that prisons are the only way to treat law violators, prisons as they are known today are a relatively recent invention, being hardly more than a century and a half old. Serious offenders —thieves, burglars, and robbers—except for those sent to the galleys, were formerly not imprisoned. Either they were executed or they were punished by being subjected to physical torture, branded, maimed, sent to the pillory, or transported to a penal colony, usually in another hemisphere. Penal servitude in the galleys was widely used from about 1500 until early in the eighteenth century.

Many factors affected the development of prisons—imprisonment in castle dungeons, the use of cell confinement by the church, houses of correction, and, most significant of all, the attitudes of the Quakers toward capital punishment. In America toward the end of the eighteenth century the Quakers of Pennsylvania became appalled at the brutal methods used on ordinary criminals, particularly the use of capital punishment for hundreds of crimes. The Pennsylvania legislature reduced the number of capital offenses to four, substituting fines, hard labor, and a relatively new idea for serious crimes—imprisonment—for all other offenses. The Walnut Street Prison in Philadelphia, built in 1790, was used for these offenders, who served their sentences in solitary confinement. The use of imprisonment as a punishment for crime spread throughout the world, and although there have been many modifications of the original idea, a sentence to prison is still one of the chief means of dealing with criminal offenders. In the United States there are approximately 230 state and federal prisons for adult offenders, but this number does not include such other places of incarceration as prison camps, workhouses, or farms. There are also approximately 1500 municipal jails, workhouses, and farms for offenders convicted of misdemeanors, 2500 county jails, workhouses, farms, and camps

---

[2] In addition to mental hospitals and prisons Goffman also discusses as "total institutions" army training camps, naval vessels, boarding schools, monasteries, and "old folks homes."

[3] Roland Wulbert, "Inmate Pride in Total Institutions," *American Journal of Sociology,* 71:1–9 (1965).

for misdemeanants, and about 200 correctional institutions for juveniles, over half of which are state institutions.

The average daily population of persons incarcerated in correctional institutions in the United States is about 425,000. The largest number— 201,220—are adults in state prisons; on an average day 141,303 adults are in local jails and workhouses. Federal prisons account for 20,377, thus making a total of 362,900 adults. A total 62,773 are in confinement, on the average day, in institutions primarily for juveniles: 43,636 in public training schools, 13,113 in detention homes, and 6,024 in local juvenile institutions.[4]

Objectives of Imprisonment

Originally the Quakers believed that meditation in prison would bring about reformation, but today public attitudes are extremely confused about the purpose of incarceration. Prisons seem to exist for such widely divergent purposes as retribution, deterrence, incapacitation, and rehabilitation. Some people regard the function of prisons as one of exacting retribution, *lex talionis:* "An eye for an eye and a tooth for a tooth." This principle, based on the concept that an individual is completely responsible for his actions, presumes that the punishment of an offender is in proportion to the injury to society that he has committed. Those who hold such an attitude regard prisons as places in which society may exact vengeance upon the wrongdoer.

Many persons view prisons as places whose very existence deters others from committing crimes. They assume that the knowledge that some are imprisoned for their crimes deters other citizens from committing crimes. Tappan has raised a number of objections to any belief that the mere threat of punishment has a uniform effect on individuals: (1) The restraining influences on crime are not as rational as punishment would suggest. (2) Deterrence from crime is not merely the result of punishment but also of many other factors, such as prestige in the community, moral training, attitudes toward authority, and the like. (3) The threat of punishment is probably greatest before a person is first convicted or incarcerated and declines thereafter: the stigma and ostracism associated with conviction and incarceration destroy the basis of this threat—a person's status as a "respectable citizen" or his self-esteem. (4) The certainty and speed of punishment seem to have

---

[4] As reported in *The Challenge of Crime in a Free Society,* A Report by the President's Commission on Law Enforcement and Administration of Justice (Washington, D.C.: Government Printing Office, 1967), p. 172. Also see the Commission's *Task Force Report: Corrections* (Washington, D.C.: U.S. Government Printing Office, 1967).

a more deterrent effect than the mere fact that punishment exists. (5) Finally, in many offenses of a circumstantial type the threat of punishment has slight deterrent effects.[5]

Still other persons look upon prisons as methods of getting offenders out of the way. Being imprisoned, they are unable to inflict further injury on society. This belief has two main flaws. Most of the people sentenced to prison not only are not dangerous but in all probability need more community participation rather than social isolation. A small proportion of men in prison, perhaps as little as 5 and not over 25 percent, are serious offenders. In the second place, nearly all prison inmates today are now released within from five to ten years, and it is highly unlikely that society would tolerate any incarceration for the actual life of many offenders, particularly since so many are committed when they are relatively young men. Thus prisons can only temporarily incapacitate persons from continuing their criminal activities.

For those who believe that the purpose of prisons is to rehabilitate, and these include practically all persons scientifically trained in correctional work, the idea of punishment is felt to be inconsistent. These people believe that prisons should be places where—after the social and psychological characteristics of prisoners have been studied by specialists, such as psychiatrists and psychologists, sociologists, and others—offenders are classified into various types and a program is devised for their institutional treatment. Confusion in the minds of the public, the nature of prisons as they exist after a century or more of punitive methods, and, in fact, the whole idea of incarcerating men like animals, however, have all worked against much success in this direction. Here and there can be found examples of an effective use of prisons as instruments of rehabilitation. Even in those places where theory is applied to practice, however, there are often so many negative factors present, including the artificial nature of prison life and the stigma of society, that much progress in reformation often appears difficult. Generally, prisons should serve primarily to prevent repetition of crime, by attempting to change prisoners' attitudes toward crime and their self-conceptions. The programs of such institutions should be directed toward changing offenders from law-violating to law-abiding persons, rather than providing custodial care as the majority of prisons presently still do.

------

[5] Paul W. Tappan, "Objectives and Methods in Correction," in Paul W. Tappan, ed., *Contemporary Correction* (New York: McGraw-Hill Book Company, Inc., 1951), pp. 8–9. For further discussion of this problem, see Donald R. Cressey, "Limitations on Organization of Treatment in the Modern Prison," in *Theoretical Studies in Social Organization of the Prison* (New York: Social Science Research Council, 1960), pp. 78–110.

Characteristics of Prison Life

In the United States and in other countries there is a great variety of prisons. Some are maximum security institutions, whereas others are medium and minimum. Some are small; others may have a population of thousands. Some have advanced programs; others are little more than custodial institutions. With this variety it is obviously difficult to generalize about prisons other than to discuss them in terms of the "average prison." Prisons provide little or no freedom comparable to that of the civilian life to which nearly all the inmates return. A prisoner cannot generally go where he wants to go, eat what and when he pleases, tune in on as many radio or television programs as he desires, or even take a bath at any time, let alone when he needs one. Although there is some choice of work, it is limited, and where a man is fortunate to have full-time employment his pay is rarely more than from ten to fifty cents a day. Few opportunities are given him to make decisions and permission to go anywhere is granted on much the same terms that it is granted a closely supervised child. In most prisons, inmates are marched everywhere, at night they are confined in cells hardly as large as lions' cages in the zoo, and at all times men on gun towers have lethal weapons ready to shoot. The attitude of some guards is impersonal, for they often operate almost mechanically in terms of the rule books. Life for the inmates becomes dull and monotonous.

What particularly lengthens the social distance between prison officials and inmates and negates rehabilitation are the endless prison rules which have been built up in the history of a prison. Some of the rules are necessary and result from the incarceration of thousands of men under maximum security in our larger prisons. There are many rules, however, which completely govern the inmate's behavior, prescribing such things as the care of cells, personal hygiene, eating, going to chapel, respect for officers, and obedience. Most rules are so petty that they could not be generally enforced in a free society, in an industrial plant, or even in a military establishment. Guards may display unwarranted authority over inmates because of the vague nature of many rules and the wide latitude with which they may be interpreted.[6]

In modern institutions infractions of rules largely result in the withdrawal of certain privileges, in counseling, and, in rare cases, in the use of solitary confinement. Some institutions, however, use more severe methods to secure compliance.

---

[6] See Vernon Fox, *Violence behind Bars* (New York: Vantage Press, 1956); and John Bartlow Martin, *Break Down the Walls* (New York: Ballantine Books, Inc., 1954).

The artificiality and social isolation of prison life and the multiplicity of rules are great hindrances to any program which attempts to deal with criminal attitudes. As long as prisons in general do not allow more social contacts with the outside world it is unlikely that institutional treatment can achieve much in the way of attitude changes or satisfactory emotional adjustment. To change attitudes there must be opportunities to assimilate those of the conventional culture. Prison confinement allows only rare outside social contacts; visits from the outside are infrequent and rigidly supervised, the general practice being only once a month; letters are limited in number and censored; and often choices of reading materials, radio programs, and movies are even restricted. The one-sex nature of prison communities results in great mental suffering and excessive discussion of sex, and the impossibility of heterosexual intercourse encourages homosexual practices among some inmates. The difficulties connected with the sex problem in prison communities make it one of the most serious and demoralizing features of prison life.

The institutional system is not the only reason why it is difficult to rehabilitate inmates through imprisonment. The public holds against a man not so much the crime for which he was convicted as the fact that he has been in prison. Perhaps if prisons were not the places they are, the public's reaction to imprisonment would not be as negative as it is. It is the prison experience which sets men apart and changes them, in the eyes of the public, into "dangerous convicts." Society vents its indignation against crime not on criminals but on "convicts." Once a man has been in prison the public attitude today is to stigmatize him in much the same way as a person who had been in a tuberculosis sanitorium was often formerly stigmatized. Ex-inmates frequently find it so difficult, after having left prison, to help their families face the stigma of the neighborhood, to get and hold a job, to participate in community activities, and even to have the right to vote again, that even those who at one time had intended to go "straight" return again to criminal activities, thanks to their post-prison experiences.[7]

The Prison Social System

The prison community and the prison code also generally work against reformation. Every prison has its subculture and a complex social system of officers and inmates; within the latter group is a social structure in which

---

[7] For further discussion, see Donald R. Cressey, ed., *The Prison: Studies in Institutional Organization and Change* (New York: Holt, Rinehart and Winston, Inc., 1961), Chaps. 1–3.

some inmates have higher status than others.[8] For example, some have found that prisoners and staff members differ markedly in whom they consider to be a "leader." [9] This inmate subculture exists alongside the formal prison system. The informal rules which reflect this subculture generally exert a greater effect on the prisoner's actual behavior than does the system of formally prescribed rules. "The value system of the prisoners commonly takes the form of an explicit code, in which normative imperatives are held forth as guides for the behavior of the inmate in his relations with fellow prisoners and custodians." [10] Violation of these norms, or informal rules, by any inmate evokes sanctions ranging from ostracism to physical violence. Some of these informal inmate rules are described in the following general maxims:

a. Don't interfere with the interests of inmates. Concretely, this means that inmates "never rat on a con," or betray each other. It also includes these directives: "Don't be nosey," "Don't put a guy on the spot," and "Keep off a man's back." There are no justifications for failing to comply with these rules.

b. Keep out of quarrels or feuds with fellow inmates. This is expressed in the directives, "Play it cool," and "Do your own time."

c. Don't exploit other inmates. Concretely, this means, "Don't break your word," "Don't steal from the cons," "Don't welsh on debts," and *"Be right."*

d. Don't weaken; withstand frustration or threat without complaint. This is expressed in such directives as, "Don't cop out" (cry guilty), "Don't suck around," *"Be tough,"* and *"Be a Man."*

e. Don't give respect or prestige to the custodians or to the world for which they stand. Concretely, this is expressed by "Don't be a sucker," and "Be sharp." [11]

---

[8] Donald Clemmer, *The Prison Community* (rev. ed.; New York: Holt, Rinehart and Winston, Inc., 1958); and S. Kirson Weinberg, "Aspects of the Prison Social Structure," *American Journal of Sociology*, 47:717–726 (1942). For a general article and bibliography, see Morris G. Caldwell, "Group Dynamics in the Prison Community," *Journal of Criminal Law, Criminology and Police Science*, 46:648–657 (1956). Also see Edwin H. Sutherland and Donald R. Cressey, *Principles of Criminology* (7th ed.; Philadelphia: J. B. Lippincott Company, 1967).

[9] Clemmer, pp. 134–137, and Clarence Schrag, "Leadership among Prison Inmates," *American Sociological Review*, 19:37–42 (1954). Also see Erving Goffman, "On the Characteristics of Total Institutions: The Inmate World," in Cressey, *The Prison*, pp. 15–67.

[10] Gresham M. Sykes and Sheldon L. Messinger, "The Inmate Social System," in *Theoretical Studies in Social Organization of the Prison*, p. 5.

[11] Sykes and Messinger, pp. 6–8. See also Gresham M. Sykes, *The Society of Captives: A Study of a Maximum Security Prison* (Princeton, N.J.: Princeton Uni-

In addition to these informal rules of behavior, inmates share a prison argot which expresses their code or value systems. By means of this argot, they communicate to one another stereotypes of prison officials and of the prison world. Guards are known as "hacks" or "screws," and are to be treated with distrust and suspicion. Inmates who conform to the values of the prison officials (by accepting the ideal of hard work and of submission to authority) are labeled "suckers." In addition, there is great preoccupation with "rats" who "squeal" on another inmate to gain favors. The "yard" serves as a place to talk about prison life, about crime, and about the vagaries of society. The inmate who tries to be part of the inmate subculture and at the same time tries to benefit from the professional and administrative staff generally finds himself playing contradictory social roles.[12] The control of the inmate subculture, as one writer has described it, is in the hands of "politicians" and "right guys." [13]

Depending upon the type of institution, this informal prison social system assigns appropriate roles and statuses to prisoners.[14] In general, a new prisoner is questioned by other prisoners as to his attitudes toward the prison system and his performance as an inmate is later evaluated. The inmate social system also sets up expectations of mutual care and protection. This system of reciprocal relations, however, is not supported by the prisoners who wish to go along with official prison policies. The system, while strong, is not invincible.

The nature of the inmate social system and culture tends to vary, however, with the type of correctional institution. In "treatment"-oriented institutions the entire inmate structure is less negative, and inmate leaders may serve as coordinators and interpreters for administration policies.[15] One study examined six public and private institutions for male delin-

---

versity Press, 1958); and for a more recent treatment of this same problem, see Goffman, "On the Characteristics of Total Institutions: The Inmate World."

[12] Lloyd E. Ohlin, *Sociology and the Field of Corrections* (New York: Russell Sage Foundation, 1956), pp. 34–37.

[13] Hans Reimer, "Socialization in the Prison Community," *Proceedings,* American Prison Association, 1937 (New York: The Association, 1937), pp. 152–153. In order to make this study, Reimer, a sociologist, arranged to have himself voluntarily committed to prison.

[14] Peter G. Garabedian, "Social Roles and the Process of Socialization in the Prison Community," *Social Problems,* 11:139–152 (1963).

[15] Bernard M. Berk, "Organizational Goals and Inmate Organization," *American Journal of Sociology,* 71:522–534 (1966); and David Street and Mauer Zald, "The Inmate Group in Custodial and Treatment Settings," *American Sociological Review,* 30:40–44 (1965).

quents.[16] Differing widely in goals, the institutions ranged from the primarily disciplinary to the educational to the treatment-centered organization. The research demonstrated that institutions vary systematically in such characteristics as power distribution, departmental structure, role definition, organizational conflict, staff perspectives on inmates, and staff systems of social control, and that all of these factors affect treatment effectiveness.

In recent years, studies of prison social structure have created an interest in the possibility of harnessing informal inmate groups in order to modify prison culture. As yet, there is insufficient knowledge of the kinds of social interactions occurring among prisoners, or of the specific mechanisms by which prison life alters inmate attitudes and loyalties. In order to reintegrate offenders effectively the informal system of relationships and controls needs to be utilized and directed toward conformity with conventional norms.

Some rudimentary beginnings toward modifying prison culture have been made in creating "honor systems," a kind of prison self-government in which prisoners are given responsibility and allowed to make choices. Honor systems have been used in prison camps for smaller groups of prisoners, and in some minimum-security, honor type of institution.[17] Evidence suggests that prisoners released from such institutions have lower recidivism and parole violation rates, perhaps due in part to the careful selection of prisoners for such institutions.[18]

Programs which effectively utilize all aspects of the inmate social system have not yet been devised, and promising programs which have been suggested have not been adequately applied. Some suggest that penal institutions, by their disciplinarian character, obviate the success of any such programs. Others suggest that though there are many obstacles to such programs, they are nevertheless possible, provided bold and imaginative steps are taken toward restructuring the formal system in such a way as to utilize the informal system. Cressey's "group relations approach," using programs involving groups, suggests a possible way of accomplishing this.[19]

---

[16] David Street, Robert D. Vinter, and Charles Perrow, *Organization for Treatment* (New York: The Free Press, 1966).

[17] Walter C. Reckless, *The Crime Problem* (3d ed.; New York: Appleton-Century-Crofts, Inc., 1961), pp. 524–528. Also see Kenyon Scudder, *Prisoners Are People* (New York: Doubleday & Company, Inc., 1952).

[18] Sutherland and Cressey. Some instances of inmate self-government have resulted in exploitation by "prison politicians."

[19] For discussions of prison social structure and group-centered programs, see Sutherland and Cressey, pp. 581–585; Johan Galtung, "The Social Functions of a

Evaluation of Imprisonment

Prisons are highly successful as a means of incapacitating persons for a period of time, but their successes in deterring them from becoming recidivists or repeaters is much less. If there is some deterrence it is probably not the length of the prison sentence but the element of incarceration itself. An examination of available data indicates that "the success of imprisonment as a means of reformation is very slight." [20] For example, probably the most comprehensive study of imprisonment was made of a representative sample of 1015 released inmates from United States federal prisons in 1960, one of the better systems in the world.[21] In this study Glaser found that one in three (35 percent) of the men could be classified as "failures" in that they had been returned to prison for a new offense as a parole violator, or were given a nonprison sentence for a felon type of offense. The real "successes" included 52 percent who had no further criminal record and an additional 13 percent who had been convicted of misdemeanors or arrested but not convicted on felony charges. Where there was reformation, all of it cannot necessarily be attributed to prisons but rather to changes in the life of the prisoner, such as marriage and new friendship patterns, which may often be a product of age and other circumstances.

The Future of Prisons

The predominance of certain bad features in prisons today raises questions about their future. Unfortunately, it appears that, because of society's attitude toward the offender, prisons will continue to exist for a long time. Meanwhile the main effort needs to be concentrated on keeping people out of prison by preventing delinquency and crime and by the wide use of adequately supervised probation. It is generally agreed that, from the standpoint of crime prevention, it is much wiser to concentrate on the widespread and effective use of probation than to attempt to change an offender's attitudes within the artificial confines of a jail or prison.

Probation

Probation is a suspension of sentence after conviction in which the offender is allowed, with some restrictions, to remain in free society rather than being imprisoned. To be effective, probation, of course, should be

---

Prison," *Social Problems,* 6:127–140 (Fall 1958); and Oscar Grusky, "Organizational Goals and the Behavior of Informal Leaders," *American Journal of Sociology,* 65:59–67 (1959).

[20] Sutherland and Cressey, p. 542.

[21] Daniel Glaser, *The Effectiveness of a Prison and Parole System* (Indianapolis: The Bobbs-Merrill Company, Inc., 1964).

well supervised and administered by a trained staff. In these circumstances it would be wise even to place an offender several times on probation rather than incarcerate him in a jail or prison. Not only is well-supervised probation likely to be more effective than prison treatment in preventing further crime; it is far less expensive even if administered by well-paid professional persons. It is estimated that one probation officer carrying a recommended case load of fifty cases can adequately supervise this number at about the cost of maintaining four or five men in a prison for a single year. In addition, a person on probation can make payments toward the support of his family as well as reparation and restitution to the victim.

> The advocates of probation do not insist that all offenders should be placed on probation, but rather that certain types of offenders will get along better and do less injury to society if they are placed on probation than if they are imprisoned or are dismissed without supervision. The probation policy enables these offenders to remain in the general society, which is the best situation in which to develop character, and at the same time to receive assistance in adapting themselves to the conditions of life, so that they will not not be so impotent in struggling against the conditions which produced the delinquency. . . .
>
> Probation officers, while assisting their charges, attempt to modify the family or neighborhood situations that are producing delinquency. Thus, by their own efforts, the cooperation of other agencies, and the public opinion which they develop, they are instruments for the prevention of crime. In this way, as well as by producing reformation in the probationers, probation should be regarded as one of the crime reducing agencies in modern society. Moreover, probation not only represents a change in the societal reaction to crime, but is producing a further change in that reaction.[22]

Changes in Jail and Detention Practices

Many persons get their start toward prison during their incarceration in lockups and jails, either awaiting hearing or a trial or serving a misdemeanor sentence. Many of these places are physically degrading, poorly managed, and breeding places for criminals who later show up in prisons. The federal government, for example, inspects county jails before deciding whether federal prisoners may be incarcerated in them. In 1959, of the 641 jails inspected in 45 states, 401 were rated "fair" or better and 241 less than "fair." [23]

---

[22] Reprinted by permission from *Principles of Criminology* by Edwin H. Sutherland and Donald R. Cressey, published by J. B. Lippincott Company. Copyright © 1924, 1960, 1966 by J. B. Lippincott Company, pp. 499–500 of the 1966 edition.

[23] U.S. Bureau of Prisons, *Federal Prisons, 1959* (Washington, D.C.: Department of Justice, 1960), p. 13.

These conditions could be changed by making improvements in the physical conditions and in the programs of the jails. Persons awaiting trial could be separated, for example, from convicted offenders. Bail and release on personal recognizance could be more widely used. In fact, efforts are now being made in some places to eliminate the requirement for bail, which falls heavily on the poorer person. Fines could be paid in installments instead of the term in jail ordered because of inability to pay a fine. Financial restitution to the victim in place of a jail or prison sentence and in connection with probation might be more widely employed than it is.[24] Courts could dispose of cases more rapidly to avoid lengthy jail incarceration. Those who are acquitted should be indemnified for financial losses suffered as a result of detention, a procedure which has existed in many European countries for a long time.

Improved Prison Practices

Prisons generally would be more effective, however, if certain practices were adopted:

1. *Work release programs of various types offer great possibilities for reformation.* This new type of approach is a combination of an institutional program with participation in free society during the day. Nearly all offenders, about 97 percent, sooner or later return to free society—most of them, in fact, after less than two to five years. In prisons and jails criminals associate only with criminals, but in work release programs they associate with noncriminals. There are several types of work release programs.

a. One such program encourages outside contacts by confining an inmate during the evenings and weekends but allowing him to work or to go to school in free society during the day. This means that the noncriminals with whom he works may have a greater effect in changing his attitudes and criminal self-conception than his former criminal associates. This type of program is being tried in a number of states and countries. Several states in 1966—California, Wisconsin, North Carolina, and Maryland—had work release laws, as did the federal government. These laws generally provide for payment of regular wages from which are deducted costs of food and clothing, travel, contributions to the support of the person's dependents, and payment of obligations. Even with these deductions, a man may leave the prison with a substantial sum instead of the usual ten dollars and a suit of prison-made clothes.

A Prisoner Rehabilitation Act was passed in 1965 in the United States for federal prisoners. This statute, which permits unescorted fur-

---

[24] Stephen Schafer, *Restitution to Victims of Crime* (London: Stevens & Sons, Ltd., 1960).

loughs and community employment, extends the type of confinement for offenders committed to the custody of the Attorney General. Both work release and furloughs are treatment techniques with unlimited potential in helping the offender to become reintegrated into the community. All institutions and facilities, with the exception of the two short-term detention centers, have secured approval of work release plans and have programs in operation. By the end of 1966, 1200 federal offenders had been in work release status. "They were employed in a variety of occupations, primarily in blue-collar jobs. Many work releasees have received vocational training in institutions, and others have taken jobs related to training undertaken in the institution. Work release has multiple benefits, such as providing funds to support dependents, pay legitimate debts, and accumulate a release 'nestegg.' A majority of those on the program who have completed their sentences remained employed on the same job after release. Only a small minority absconded from work release status and were programmed in the institutional setting." [25]

b. In other programs persons are released from institutions to what are termed "halfway houses," some run by government and others by private agencies. In this way a period of control, supervision, and assistance is provided.[26] The inmates receive residential treatment while they work or attend school outside. The federal government since 1961 has had federal prerelease centers for selected men. The Prisoner Rehabilitation Act of 1965 authorized the opening of adult halfway houses, or Community Treatment Centers. In 1967 there were six such centers, and the Bureau of Prisons asked Congress to appropriate funds for four more in fiscal 1967. The center residents are chosen from inmates of federal reformatories and correctional institutions who have about 90 to 120 days remaining before expiration of their sentences or paroles. The centers not only offer counseling in locating jobs, filling out job application forms, and participating in job interviews but also help with personal problems. They are staffed by a director, a casework researcher or an assistant director, one or two additional counselors, an employment placement specialist, two graduate students, and a secretary, as well as correctional counselors. They are geared chiefly to deal with youthful offenders who otherwise probably would not have been paroled. They have several goals: upon release the young offender should have a savings account, should have some experience in handling his own finances, should have a civilian wardrobe, and should have steady employment. They also try to make him feel familiar with the community, secure in his acceptance by the

---

[25] U.S. Bureau of Prisons, *Annual Report, 1966*, p. 3.

[26] Arthur Pearl, "The Halfway House: The Focal Point of a Model Program for the Rehabilitation of Low Income Offenders," in Frank Riessman, Jerome Cohen, and Arthur Pearl, eds., *Mental Health for the Poor* (New York: The Free Press, 1964), pp. 497–508.

community, and less anxious about being an ex-convict. If indicated, they also try to see that he is involved in Alcoholics Anonymous or Narcotics Anonymous, actively participates in socially acceptable leisure and recreational activities, and seriously tries to improve himself intellectually.

c. Another program is the "community treatment center," a day institution where offenders, instead of being committed to a conventional detention house, live at home and may have a job or be in school, but daily attend a center for intensive rehabilitation. One of the best known of these programs, using largely volunteer assistance, was the Provo (Utah) Experiment in which delinquent boys continued to live at home but were required to meet each day in the late afternoon.[27] Group counseling discussions were conducted, public school teachers assisted in remedial reading and handcrafts, and local college students transported the boys to and from their homes.

Still another program pays group-care foster homes for from four to ten delinquents. Wisconsin's program, a pioneer in this area, has been followed by similar ones in Minnesota, Ohio, and Michigan.

2. *The program of an institutional setup is directed at changing norms so as to make the offender into a law-abiding person.* Such a program relies on wider use of group therapy or guided group interaction, with a small group of similar offenders discussing such topics as the nature of criminal behavior and how it might be changed, a technique which has been discussed in the previous chapter.

3. *Correctional institutions need to be so diversified that their treatment programs can concentrate largely on offenders of a similar general type, programs being worked out for specific types of offenders within each type of institution.* One of the major problems in treatment has been that generally the same methods have been applied to all types of offenders. One study has proposed a specific treatment program for each type of criminal offender.[28]

4. *Correctional institutions should be small enough to permit intensive treatment programs and personal relations between staff and inmates.* The smaller the institution the fewer the necessary rules and the less rigorous the discipline. Generally a correctional institution should not be larger than 100 inmates, although, if that is financially too difficult, the prison population might be as large as 500.

5. *If correctional institutions are to be effective in changing a pris-*

---

[27] See LaMar T. Empey, "The Provo Experiment," in Harry Gold and Frank R. Scarpitti, eds., *Combatting Social Problems* (New York: Holt, Rinehart and Winston, Inc., 1967), pp. 371–404; and LaMar T. Empey and Jerome Rabow, "The Provo Experiment in Delinquency Rehabilitation," *American Sociological Review,* 26:679–695 (1961).

[28] Don C. Gibbons, *Changing the Lawbreaker: The Treatment of Delinquents and Criminals* (Englewood Cliffs, N.J.: Prentice-Hall, Inc., 1965).

oner's attitudes, they should be as relaxed and as much like normal life as possible. Less emphasis should be placed on discipline, rules, and an artificial institutional setting, all of which strengthen an inmate's conception of himself as a criminal.

6. *Brief home furloughs at periodic intervals would help to keep the offender in touch with his family and community and reduce homosexual behavior in prison.* These could be supplemented with emergency furloughs to go home in cases of illness or death there or to investigate post-release jobs. The 1965 federal prison act provides furlough leave up to thirty days for federal prisoners to attend funerals, visit dying relatives, interview prospective employers, and the like.

7. *In any institutional setup the staff should be stressed.* The members should be selected primarily in terms of how effective they can be in changing the attitudes of offenders. Of all the persons in authority in a correctional institution, probably the custodial officer or guard plays the most strategic role in that he is more frequently in contact with the offender. The guard is too frequently thought of as merely a custodial officer rather than as potentially a highly effective member of the treatment staff. Because his social background is generally much like that of most offenders, he has an advantage in communicating with them that a more highly educated officer does not have. In any event, all the staff members of the correctional institution should have had training in criminology and in their role of changing the attitudes of prisoners. Those in higher administrative and welfare posts need specific professional training that includes advanced courses in the behavioral sciences.

8. *Finally, there should be an effective selection of persons for parole and effective parole treatment for those released from prison.* Group therapy methods have been used with parolees. Residential treatment for those on parole has also been used for those whose conduct on parole requires a greater amount of programmed supervision.

After discovering that traditional methods did not work, Sweden in 1945 adopted a comprehensive rehabilitation program. This included small correctional institutions of usually not more than a hundred inmates in order to promote a high degree of group interaction with the staff, something that is virtually impossible in larger prisons.[29] In 1966 in Sweden

---

[29] Thorsten Sellin, *Recent Penal Legislation in Sweden* (Stockholm: Isaac Marcus Book Publishers, 1947), and his "The Treatment of Offenders in Sweden," *Federal Probation,* 12:14–18 (1948). Also see Wilfred Fleisher, *Sweden: The Welfare State* (New York: The John Day Company, Inc., 1956), Chap. 11; Ola Nyquist, "How Sweden Handles Its Juvenile and Youth Offenders," *Federal Probation,* 20:36–42 (1956); Torsten Eriksson, "Postwar Prison Reform in Sweden," *The Annals,* 293:152–162 (1954); and Gosta Rylander, "Treatment of Mentally Abnormal Offenders in Sweden," *British Journal of Delinquency,* 4:262–268 (1955). For an up-to-date appraisal of the Swedish system, see Norval Morris, "Lessons

there were eighty-eight prisons for the five thousand prisoners. Most institutions are open, with no walls, armed guards, or gun towers. All members of the staffs of correctional institutions are highly trained. Swedish prisoners work in highly diversified and skilled employment, may make several dollars a day in prison industries or in free employment, as compared to the 10 to 35 cents generally paid in the United States. In a new prison making prefabricated houses the inmates receive the prevailing free wage of about $10 to $12 a day. Board is deducted from this amount and the inmate must pay income taxes on it.

In addition, the Swedes allow most offenders short home furloughs of between forty-eight and seventy-two hours every four months, as well as special emergency furloughs and frequent visits and contacts with the outside world in order to change attitudes and to reduce sexual tensions leading to homosexual practices.[30] Because men in prison spend a great deal of time in their cells or rooms, Swedish inmates are allowed to furnish their rooms in a homelike way, with rugs, drapes, pictures, bedspreads, individual radios, as well as many flowers, plants, paintings, books, electric hot plates, and cups and saucers for coffee. Social participation in the community is, however, not stressed in Sweden to the same extent that it is in the famous Dutch prison at Utrecht, where, for example, a prisoner may often have dinner with a family in the community. The Swedish system, unfortunately, also places its main emphasis on industrial training rather than on guided group interaction and other methods of changing delinquent and criminal norms.

MENTAL HOSPITALS

Mental hospital appear to have two functions: the treatment of patients so that they will recover sufficiently to return to normal society and the provision of custody and care so that both patients and society are protected. Too often in many mental hospitals the function of custody appears to take precedence over treatment. A state hospital is "characteristically forbidding in appearance with its large masses of patients whose daily lives are

---

from the Adult Correctional System of Sweden," *Federal Probation,* 30:3–13 (1966); and John Conrad, *Crime and Its Correction: An International Survey of Attitudes and Practices* (Berkeley: University of California Press, 1965). During 1954 and 1955 the author studied delinquency and crime and their treatment in Sweden and has visited the country several times since.

[30] The U.S. Federal Bureau of Prisons has also recently initiated a furlough system.

scheduled and ordered to fit into institutional routines, its inadequacies . . . in such bare necessities as food and clothing, and its custodial and repressive atmosphere expressed in restraint, seclusion rooms, barred doors and windows." [31] The custodial atmosphere is in part a product of the size of such hospitals, which are often nothing more than a dumping ground for the aged, for the chronically ill, and for problem cases of the lower class. Other handicaps are the quality of personnel and the limited emphasis on psychotherapy.

Types of Mental Hospitals

Their functions are emphasized differently in the various types of mental hospitals in the United States: the large state mental hospital, the Veterans Administration Hospital, the smaller private hospital, and the psychiatric sections of general hospitals.[32] Each of these institutional types tends to differ in size, population composition, staff quality, training and orientation, and community relationships. These differences affect the introduction of treatment programs and services. It is so difficult to generalize about mental hospitals as a group that for the most part the discussion which follows focuses more on public mental hospitals, where most patients are be found.[33]

The custodial aspect of mental institutions primarily serves to protect the patient from those of the outside world who might not understand him and his problems as well as to protect him from harming others or himself. Most patients have not constituted a public menace. More often they are merely persons who have bizarre ideas, depressions, or suspicions of others. Few patients will actually harm others, in spite of the societal stereotype that mental patients are dangerous and to be feared. Some patients have become accustomed to institutional life and feel happier in custody than in free society because decisions are made for them and because life is routine. It is difficult to prepare such people for the changes in their interpersonal relationships which are necessary for a return to normal society. Where their care is good, they are often better fed and are cleaner and neater in dress and manners than they would be outside;

---

[31] Morris S. Schwartz and Charlotte C. Schwartz, *et al., Social Approaches to Mental Patient Care* (New York: Columbia University Press, 1964), pp. 102–103.

[32] Schwartz and Schwartz, pp. 102–103.

[33] There have been a number of studies of mental hospitals. The insights are valuable but unfortunately the research is still characterized by single case studies often done by one or two observers. In the future, we can expect more rigorously controlled studies using larger samples of hospitals and patients.

moreover, they usually do get some recreation and entertainment in institutions. In fact, it is these very features of custody which some people consider sufficient for the patients.

Veterans Administration hospitals tend to be smaller, better equipped, and better supported than public mental hospitals. There is a higher staff-patient ratio and the average expenditure is about twice that of the state hospital. All patients are males of a variety of backgrounds. Generally the hospitals are more progressive. The private mental hospital, which is generally small, lies at the opposite pole from the average state mental hospital. The treatment is advanced and expensive, the patients are of higher socioeconomic status, and more patients are diagnosed as "psychoneurotic." The psychiatric section of the general hospital is becoming increasingly important because of the greater stress on keeping the patient's local community ties. It emphasizes the rapid treatment of acute disorders, using various techniques such as shock therapy; consequently there is a high turnover, with few patients remaining longer than a few weeks at a time.

Extent and Cost of Mental Hospital Care

Today almost 88 percent of all hospitalized mental patients in the United States are in state and local mental hospitals. Nearly 10 percent are in veterans' hospitals, and slightly over 2 percent are in private hospitals. Whereas admissions to state and local mental hospitals have increased during the past few years, releases have also increased, reflecting a shortened length of stay for many patients. From 1955 to 1964 there was a consistent decline in the resident population of these hospitals. (See Table 20.1.) In 1966 there were 330,399 admissions to state and local hospitals, and an estimated 311,827 discharges. One study has concluded that this decline is not reflected in other types of hospitals, that it only represents a "shift in the flow and whereabouts of mental patients possibly reflecting in part the readily accepted conviction that, if at all possible, it is better for the patient and his prospect to keep him out of State hospitals" and also represents a policy of increased discharge rates, which is in part a reflection of savings in maintenance costs.[34] Much of the increase in discharge rates, however, has been possible through the use of tranquilizers and this has accounted for the decline in spite of the fact that admissions have greatly increased. Such drugs make it possible for a large number of patients to be managed as outpatients.

---

[34] *Action for Mental Health*, The Final Report of the Joint Commission on Mental Illness and Health (New York: Basic Books, Inc., 1961), p. 20. This commission was appointed by Congress to make a five-year study.

TABLE 20.1   **Resident Patients by Type of Hospital, 1955–1965**

Year	All hospitals	State, county, and city hospitals	Veterans' hospitals	Public Health Service hospitals	Private hospitals
1955	633,504	558,922	57,991	2001	14,590
1956	627,501	551,390	60,080	1935	14,096
1957	623,374	548,626	59,240	1965	13,543
1958	621,463	545,182	59,855	1955	14,471
1959	618,211	541,883	60,805	1827	13,696
1960	611,432	535,540	60,214	1883	13,795
1961	602,479	527,456	60,108	1896	13,019
1962	591,285	515,640	60,035	1854	13,756
1963	579,409	504,604	60,000	1824	12,981
1964	565,549	490,754	60,000	1795	13,000

SOURCE: Department of Health, Education, and Welfare, *Trends* (Washington, D.C.: Government Printing Office, 1966), p. 29. These are hospitals for long-term psychiatric care.

The cost of caring for the mentally ill is enormous. During 1950, state governments spent, in tax funds, about $520 million on capital costs and maintenance of their state mental hospitals and about $45 million for other mental health services. Yet the amount spent for patients in state mental hospitals is meager when compared with the amount spent for care in general or private hospitals. In 1961 the Joint Commission on Mental Illness and Health reported that the average amount spent for patients in state hospitals is $4.44 daily, whereas the average daily amount for patients in community general hospitals, largely private is $31.16, and for those in veterans' psychiatric or tuberculosis hospitals, $12.00.[35]

The Joint Commission reported in 1961 that overcrowding characterizes state hospitals in the United States today. Most state hospitals have from 2000 to 4000 patients.[36] The commission also found that the ratio of personnel to patients in state mental hospitals today is 0.32, as compared to a ratio of 2.1 for community general hospitals. In general, there is a short-

---

[35] *Action for Mental Health,* Chap. I.

[36] The commission strongly recommended that present state hospitals of 1000 patients or more "add not one" additional patient, and that no additional hospitals of more than 1000 beds be built. The commission further recommended a major reorganization of the existing method of treating the mentally ill, rather than simply increasing the size and populations of hospitals, as has been customary in the past.

age of psychiatrists in public mental hospitals. Although in 1956 there were 8713 psychiatrists in the United States, only about 1400 were employed full time in public mental hospitals.[37]

Methods of Hospital Treatment

Because of their large size, it is extremely difficult for state hospitals to give effective psychotheraputic treatment to their patients. Studies of treatment methods in hospitals have found that the choice of treatments for given patients by the physician in charge is not related to the patient's diagnosis so much as it is to his social characteristics, principally his social class. It was found that upper-class patients were much more likely to receive psychotherapy.[38] Thus, the majority of patients receive either no treatment or receive somatic treatments, usually in the form of drugs or electric shock, which can be administered to large numbers of patients in a minimum of time and with little effort.[39] These treatments help to reduce anxiety and the symptoms of the illness, but rarely deal with the "causes." Group psychotherapy, psychodrama, individual counseling, and occupational therapy, on the other hand, require a much greater effort on the part of the staff. The 1961 report of the Joint Commission on Mental Illness and Health concluded that 80 percent of the 277 state hospitals in the United States today are seriously lagging in the use of modern advances in the treatment of the mentally ill, and were providing custodial care rather than treatment. In only 20 percent of these hospitals was there evidence of some attempt to take advantage of these new techniques. The commission found that more than half of all patients in state mental hospitals receive "no active treatment of any kind designed to improve their mental conditions." [40]

The use of the shock therapies, electric and insulin, has been largely a development of the past thirty years and until the advent of tranquilizers some fifteen years ago were widely used. They still are used today, but

---

[37] *Action for Mental Health,* pp. 8–9, 144. In 1960 the American Psychiatric Association had 11,787 members, which although insufficient for the demand, were nearly three times the 4000 members in 1946.

[38] See Eugene B. Gallagher, Daniel Levinson, Iza Erlich, "Some Sociopsychological Characteristics of Patients and Their Relevance for Psychiatric Treatment," in M. Greenblatt, D. J. Levinson, and R. H. Williams, *The Patient and the Mental Hospital* (New York: The Free Press, 1957), pp. 371–373.

[39] Greenblatt, Levinson and Williams. Also see Alfred H. Stanton and Morris S. Schwartz, *The Mental Hospital* (New York: Basic Books, Inc., 1954), p. 69, and S. Kirson Weinberg and H. Warren Dunham, *The Culture of the State Mental Hospital* (Detroit: Wayne State University Press, 1960).

[40] *Action for Mental Health,* p. 23.

less frequently. Electric shock therapy, which produces temporary convulsions or coma, can be administered to many patients in a relatively short period of time. Although various theories, biological and psychological, have attempted to explain what happens in the shock therapies, so far none has been generally accepted. It has been difficult to come to a general theory in view of the fact that the results of this type of therapy vary greatly. The original claims of high success have been revised in more limited terms. Some patients do recover after a series of shock treatments and others are greatly improved. Most recoveries, however, are only temporary, and the relapse rate is high.

In general, relapse is greater where there is little follow-up treatment with individual psychotherapy. In one study of 380 patients who were given electric shock over a six-month period, 64.8 percent improved or recovered and 35.2 were unimproved.[41] Other studies which have used well-matched experimental and control groups and have employed rigorous research designs have found a much smaller percentage of improvement.[42] One sociological study has suggested that the extent of prior social participation is favorably associated with this treatment.[43]

Beginning in 1953, tranquilizing drugs, including chlorpromazine and reserpine, have been widely used to relieve some of the symptoms of mental illness. One report, in fact, refers to the present situation in treatment as "the tranquilized hospital." [44] Being used to tranquilize those patients who are excited, hyperactive, unmanageable, highly disturbed or highly disturbing, these drugs have changed somewhat the management of psychotic patients in mental hospitals. They have helped greatly to reduce, and in many cases almost eliminate, shock treatments and have given more freedom to the patients. They have helped to speed up release from mental hospitals. Between 1956 and 1965, for example, the rate of admissions to mental hospitals almost doubled but actual hospital populations declined by one fifth. In addition, they have made possible greater communication and, consequently, closer relations between staff and patients. These drugs, like

---

[41] S. Kirson Weinberg, *Society and Personality Disorders* (Englewood Cliffs, N.J.: Prentice-Hall, Inc., 1952), p. 435.

[42] See George H. Alexander, "Electroconvulsive Therapy: A Five-Year Study of Results," *Journal of Nervous and Mental Diseases,* 117:244–250 (1953); and Ugo Cerletti, "Electroshock Therapy," *Journal of Clinical and Experimental Psychopathology,* 15:191–217 (1954).

[43] Malak Guirguis, "Interpersonal Relationships as a Prognostic Factor in Electric Shock Therapy of the 'Functional Psychoses.' " Unpublished doctoral dissertation, University of Wisconsin, Madison, 1951.

[44] *Action for Mental Health.*

the shock therapies, cannot be thought as "curing" mental disorder in the sense of getting at the factors which produced it. An excessive reliance on drugs may make it more difficult to employ community psychiatric or other facilities that are designed to get to the precipitating factors of mental illness.[45]

The debate still continues, however, regarding the physiological and sociological results of these drugs. Some have predicted they would empty mental hospitals, while others have called them "clinical strait jackets." [46] A four-year study of the use of tranquilizers in New York State hospitals between 1955 and 1959 gives some partial, but by no means complete, answers.[47] It was concluded that restraint and seclusion of patients decreased markedly, and that, by 1959, 60 percent of all cases were given freedom of the grounds, or ten times the number who had this freedom in 1956. About half of the patients continued on drug therapy after leaving the hospital. The relapse, or rate of return to the hospital, was 35 percent, which was no higher than that of predrug days. The greatest gain in the release of patients was in the age group twenty-five through forty-four; there was little change in the rate of release of those over sixty-five. The drugs had little effect on the senile psychoses, which is the primary cause for admission to mental hospitals. Schizophrenic patients showed far greater benefit than did patients with other types of psychoses or organic brain disease, and these drugs may help to reduce chronic schizophrenic cases.

A survey of nearly 200 state mental hospitals found that special ward units for the treatment of alcoholics averaging 56 beds were in use in 31 percent of the hospitals; another 20 percent had special treatment programs without separate ward areas.[48] Alcoholics Anonymous was utilized in 88 percent of the hospitals while group psychotherapy, drug therapy, and individual psychotherapy were each used in over half. The estimated overall rate of improvement was 60 percent at discharge, 39 percent up to a year after discharge, and 33 percent for periods over a year after discharge. Lack of adequate after-care was probably a leading cause of the poor results.

---

[45] See Leopold Bellak, *Handbook of Community Psychiatry and Community Mental Health* (New York: Grune & Stratton, Inc., 1964), p. 6.

[46] *Action for Mental Health.*

[47] H. Brill and R. E. Patton, "Analysis of Population Reduction in New York State Mental Hospitals during the First Four Years of Large-Scale Therapy with Psychotropic Drugs," *American Journal of Psychiatry*, 116:495 (1959). According to the authors there was no change in the methods or standards for admitting or discharging patients during this period. Unfortunately, a control group was not used, so that their findings cannot be accepted as conclusive.

[48] Robert A. Moore and Thomas K. Buchanan, "State Hospitals and Alcoholism: A Nation-Wide Survey of Treatment Techniques and Results," *Quarterly Journal of Studies on Alcohol*, 27:459–468 (1966).

The Social Structure of the Mental Hospital

The social structure of mental hospitals may work for or against success in treatment, for a mental hospital is a unique community, with its own special social structure in terms of status and power to make decisions. (See Figure 20.1.) It is organized with the superintendent and professional staff, including psychiatrists, psychologists, occupational therapists, social workers, and similar personnel, at the top of the prestige hierarchy. Next come the clerical staff and, following it in social status, the attendants and utility workers. The patients make up the "lowest" status group.

One of the major difficulties of this social system of status and power relationships is that in the treatment of the mental patient there is often a breakdown in formal and informal communication between staff members and between staff and patients.[49] For example, in one situation described by Stotland and Kobler discord developed among staff members of a private hospital and many administrators left. This breakdown in administrative leadership, combined with a lack of interest in the staff on the part of the hospital director, led to a decline in the morale of the ward staff. A low morale in the ward staff, coupled with its already present low self-esteem and confidence, created helplessness and anxiety among the patients. The result was a rash of suicides and suicide attempts by the patients and a subsequent closing of the hospital.[50] As another example, status distance between nurse and patient occurs most frequently among staff of comparatively high position, who are obeisant toward their superiors and whose mobility aspirations are blocked. These factors are even more important where patients are of relatively low social standing.[51] This breakdown in the communication of information may lead to misunderstanding and interfere with the recovery of a patient. As one writer has stated, "When a hospital's system is principally designed to maintain the authority-power structure, conflict and concern over role relations are inevitable. Role rigidity is likely to result; function will be clearly tied to status and people will create barriers to protect their positions."[52]

Patients may be classified behaviorally in terms of the expectations of hospital staff members of the extent to which they will or will not re-

---

[49] Stanton and Schwartz, pp. 193–243.

[50] See Ezra Stotland and Arthur L. Kobler, *Life and Death of a Mental Hospital* (Seattle: University of Washington Press, 1965).

[51] Leonard I. Pearlin and Morris Rosenberg, "Nurse-Patient Social Distance and the Structural Context of a Mental Hospital," *American Sociological Review,* 27:56–65 (1962).

[52] Lawrence Appleby, "Milieu Therapy—A Dialogue," *Mental Hospitals,* 14:339 (1963).

cover. "Hopeful" patients are those whom the staff regards as having high chances of recovery and discharge. "Chronic" patients are those assigned lower chances of discharge, and who are expected to remain in the hospital for a long time. "Agitated" patients are those regarded as temporarily preoccupied with their illness and in need of special care, usually custodial. Patients may vacillate from "hopeful" to "agitated" and, conversely, from "chronic" to "agitated."[53] Patients of these three types are generally as-

FIGURE 20.1   Hospital Status Hierarchy

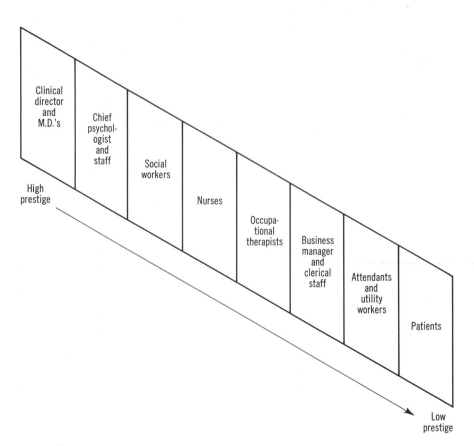

SOURCE: Derived from Martin B. Loeb and Harvey L. Smith, "Relationships among Organizational Groupings within the Mental Hospital," in Milton Greenblatt, Daniel J. Levinson, and Richard H. Williams, *The Patient and the Mental Hospital* (New York: The Free Press, 1957), p. 16.

---

[53] Weinberg and Dunham.

signed to a ward with others of the same type. Each of these wards—the hopeful, the chronic, or the agitated—has its own culture, with a set of norms and values which differs from those of other wards. For example, for patients in the hopeful ward, "going home" is a value highly esteemed. Thus, the ward norms prescribe behaviors which will achieve this value. There is great disapproval of patients who show childish or disturbed behavior, but approval of those who give evidence of "making it on the outside." On the other hand, patients in the chronic wards (called the "back wards" by patients) often seem resigned to remaining in the hospital for the rest of their lives. Many, after numerous disappointments and setbacks, have given up hope of achieving some life on the outside. In the chronic wards, therefore, behavioral norms are directed toward accepting and making the best of hospital life. This involves keeping out of trouble with attendants or other patients, doing their work, and making some sort of life for themselves within the hospital.[54]

Patients in mental hospitals may not have quite the same attitude toward the professional staff as have patients who are being treated by private psychiatrists or in private hospitals. The reason is that the contacts between patients and staff in the mental hospital are quite different in character. In the first place, patients have relatively little contact with their assigned physician: as many as a hundred or more patients may be under the same physician's care. Thus, for the most part, contacts between patients and doctors are impersonal and highly superficial, even though ideologically doctors believe in more personal relationships.[55] As one patient stated, "The doctor just comes through one door and goes out the other. He spends no time with the patients." [56] Other patients believe that because doctors can shorten or prolong an inmate's stay, in a sense doctors have entire control over their future. Patients try to cultivate the friendships of doctors and even learn to feign symptoms of recovery. One study showed that a woman patient's position in the status hierarchy of a psychiatric ward appears to be a function of (1) her access to prestigeful groups such as the staff, (2) her access to public and private knowledge of prestigeful groups such as the staff, and (3) the qualitative nature of her relation with others on the ward.[57]

---

[54] Weinberg and Dunham.

[55] See, for example, J. Cohler and L. Shapiro, "Avoidance Patterns in Staff-Patient Interaction on a Chronic Schizophrenic Ward," *Psychiatry*, 27:377–388 (1964).

[56] Weinberg and Dunham, p. 41.

[57] Robert Perrucci, "Social Distance Strategies and Intra-organizational Stratification: A Study of the Status System on a Psychiatric Ward," *American Sociological Review*, 28:951–962 (1963).

Social class factors are also related not only to the etiology of mental disorders but to their treatment.[58] Those from the lower socioeconomic groups are generally not as cooperative, as compared with more upper-class patients, in their treatment nor as highly motivated to recover.[59] They have little scientific knowledge about mental disorders and tend to think of them as a physical illness, requiring not therapy but "pills and needles." They are even secretive in giving information about mental illness in the family, attributing it to "bad blood," "a bump on the head," "too much booze," or to some physical defect. On the other hand, more upper-class patients stress fatigue and overwork, which tend to make them more amenable to treatment.

Even more important, lower-class patients tend not to think in the terms used by the psychiatrist and other professional workers, who are middle and upper class and frequently have middle- and upper-class family origins. Frequently there is almost complete lack of communication because of differences in the language used. To the psychiatrist patients with limited education often appear to be dull and stupid. They are worlds apart socially, and it is often difficult for the professional to think of them as friends in the same manner in which he might regard patients from a higher socioeconomic status. Psychotherapy becomes difficult, and shock therapy may seem to be the simplest form of treatment. When the lower-class patient fails to cooperate he is regarded as a "bad patient," particularly when he displays the violence characteristic of lower-class persons generally.

Much has been written about some of the attendant staffs of public mental hospitals: the inadequacy of their numbers, their frequent lack of proper motivation, their insufficient training, and the extensive turnover, largely because of poor pay. Fortunately, this situation has been improving. By far the greatest number of contacts of patients are their contacts with attendants.[60] However, the relationship of many attendants to the patients appears still to be largely a custodial one. The patients learn to comply with the demands of the attendants and to know which ones are friendly or are unfriendly. A study of staff-patient interaction on a schizophrenic ward found that attendants were more likely than other personnel to respond favorably to those patients whom they defined as the least self-sufficient

---

[58] August B. Hollingshead and Frederick C. Redlich, *Social Class and Mental Disorders* (New York: John Wiley & Sons, Inc., 1957). A partial replication of this study revealed a similar finding.—Robert H. Hardt and S. J. Feinhandler, "Social Class and Mental Hospitalization Prognosis," *American Sociological Review,* 24:815–821 (1959).

[59] See pages 449–452.

[60] B. E. Segal, "Nurses and Patients: Time, Place and Distance," *Social Problems,* 9:257–264 (1962).

and determined.[61] In another study it was found that ward attendants were more authoritarian than other staff members in their attitudes toward mental illness and the patient's treatment.[62] Strict enforcement of rules is often defended by attendants on the ground that the staff is too limited in size for other methods. One study found that resistance to the introduction of reform measures within a mental hospital came primarily from the attendants.[63] Despite in-service training, unscientific rationalizations and beliefs about patients and mental disorders persisted. They included, for example, the belief that patients are "children" and in reality are happy, and that female patients are wilder and stronger than male patients.

The Mental Patient's Career or Role

In the public mental hospital are brought together persons of all types —occupation, social position, education, age—but with hospital experience and societal reactions they come to develop a career or role and form a subculture. The career or role of the mental patient, according to Goffman, who studied patients in a large public mental hospital, is made up, first, of a status or life pattern as a public phenomenon and, second, of an image of self and felt identity.[64] The career of a mental patient includes the pre-patient phase, which covers the contingencies or factors that make a person likely or unlikely to end up in a hospital.[65] The inpatient phase is the experience in the hospital, but there is also an ex-patient phase. The formal agents of treatment in a mental hospital often appear to create certain unanticipated consequences by producing or stabilizing "mental illness" rather than eliminating it.

The newcomer to the mental hospital is introduced to a culture in which he is often expected to act out and accept the role of being mentally ill and a mental patient as part of his self-conception, all other roles being submerged.[66] This twenty-four-hour experience of being viewed and labeled as a mental patient encourages the acceptance of the "sick role." [67] This process of role assignment and role playing makes for the increased like-

---

[61] Cohler and Shapiro, p. 384.

[62] J. H. Williams and M. H. Williams, "Attitudes toward Mental Illness, Anomia and Authoritarianism among State Hospital Nursing Students and Attendants," *Mental Hygiene*, 45:418–424 (1961).

[63] Thomas J. Scheff, "Control over Policy by Attendants in a Mental Hospital," *Journal of Health and Human Behavior*, 2:93–105 (1961).

[64] Goffman, "The Moral Career of the Mental Patient," in *Asylums*, pp. 128–169.

[65] See pages 39–40.

[66] Thomas J. Scheff, *Being Mentally Ill: A Sociological Theory* (Chicago: Aldine Publishing Company, 1966), p. 86.

[67] Schwartz and Schwartz, *et al.*, p. 201.

lihood that a mental patient will come to develop a more or less stabilized identity as a mental patient, what Goffman and others have referred to as the "career" of a mental patient.[68] "Patienthood" becomes a form of organizational role and career of entering "student" and "inmate." [69]

Regardless of the path followed in getting into a mental hospital, the patient comes to adjust to the regimented regime, the reduction of free movement, the communal living, the living with others on a ward, and the imposition of authority in terms of his "helplessness"—a humbling experience that has an effect on his self-perception and is an attack on his self-image: he is a failure and the "reason" for it. Life often becomes a "sad" story rather than a success: staff meetings, case records—all re-emphasize this failure. He is constantly reminded that the reason for his being there is that he is "sick," and that he "must 'insightfully' come to take, or affect to take, the hospital's view of himself." [70] He must come to "develop a conception of self which gives meaning to the fact that [he] is, in an unavoidable public sense, a mentally ill person." [71] The patient becomes socialized about the hospital regime, he comes to accept with a degree of nonchalance the degradations, the deflation of self, the attempts to "reconstruct" his self. In order to leave the mental hospital he must often come to accept the hospital ideology and adopt the role it designs for him.

> In a psychiatric hospital, failure to be an easily manageable patient—failure, for example, to work or to be polite to staff—tends to be taken as evidence that one is not "ready" for liberty and that one has a need to submit to further treatment. The point is not that the hospital is a hateful place for patients, but that for the patient to express hatred of it is to give evidence that his place in it is justified and that he is not yet ready to leave it. A systematic confusion between obedience to others and one's own personal adjustment is sponsored.[72]

Patients in mental hospitals thus tend to generate patterned responses to their environment which come to be referred to as a patient society or a patient culture.[73] The nature of this patient society appears to depend a great deal on the general social structure of the hospital. In Goffman's

---

[68] Goffman, "The Moral Career of the Mental Patient," pp. 125–169.

[69] Daniel J. Levinson and Eugene B. Gallagher, *Patienthood in the Mental Hospital* (Boston: Houghton Mifflin Company, 1964).

[70] Goffman, p. 155.

[71] Levinson and Gallagher, p. 41.

[72] Goffman, p. 385.

[73] See, for example, Nathaniel H. Siegel, "The Impact of Patient Interaction on Behavior," *Journal of Hospital and Community Psychiatry*, 16:245–248 (1965); and Goffman.

study of a large public mental hospital the patients tended to respond to the more rigid staff control, the regimentation, and the assault upon self-findings by general resignation and acceptance of goals somewhat opposite to the staff objectives. In this way patients find a separate system of values and an organized pattern of relationships which enable them to preserve their self-respect.[74] That this situation does not always prevail is shown by studies of small, private psychiatric hospitals where patient groups were found to support staff values, to socialize new patients into the treatment objectives of the hospital, and to aid in the removal of dependence on institutional values prior to hospital discharge.[75] Other studies have indicated a variety of orientations by patient groups.[76]

Although increasing use is being made of occupational therapy and organized recreation, a considerable part of the mental patient's life in a public mental hospital is spent either in aimless boredom in the wards or in performing menial tasks around the institution, tasks which have no connection with therapy. Although there may be some therapy in it, most of the maintenance work around a public hospital is done by patients, whether or not it is good for them. Some resent this subordinate role, but others become so habituated to it that they become incapacitated for the outside world. As one patient said: "This hospital has been home to me for eleven years. I'm used to it. The work isn't hard and I know how to get along. It wasn't easy the first two years, but after being in and out three times, I can call this home." [77]

A study of the effect of "institutionalism" has been measured by the length of stay in a mental hospital.[78] With increase in the length of stay there was a progressive increase in apathy toward life outside the hospital. "Thus, 'institutionalism,' in the sense of a gradually acquired contentment in institutional life and apathy toward events outside the hospital, does seem to be a factor of major importance even in good mental hospitals." [79]

When the mental patient finally leaves the hospital he leaves under

---

[74] Goffman, pp. 172–235.

[75] H. B. Kaplan, Ina Boyd, S. W. Bloom "Patient Culture and Evaluation of Self," *Psychiatry*, 27:116–126 (1964); and Samuel W. Bloom, Ina Boyd, and Howard B. Kaplan "Emotional Illness and Interaction Process: A Study of Patient Groups," *Social Forces*, 41:135–141 (1962).

[76] Siegel.

[77] Weinberg, *Society and Personality Disorders*, p. 430.

[78] J. K. King, "Institutionalism in Mental Hospitals," in Thomas J. Scheff, ed., *Mental Illness and Social Processes* (New York: Harper & Row, Publishers, 1967), pp. 219–238.

[79] King, p. 236.

the care of a relative, an employer, or a guardian who has the legal authority to ask for his return at any time. Some people, such as a son or daughter, have power over him, a condition which had not previously existed.

The Future of the Mental Hospital

The size of the mental disorder problem, the unfavorable staff-patient ratio, and the numerous returns are a few of the difficulties of the state mental hospital. One comprehensive study has summarized the alternatives:

> One is to accept the mental hospital as the basic institutional form for helping psychotic persons and then to explore ways in which it can be radically altered to eliminate its untherapeutic features. The other is to abandon the mental hospital and to develop instead new institutions, social arrangements and processes that will provide a better fit between the social system and the patients' needs.[80]

Some, however, feel that by stressing the treatment and rehabilitative aspects of the state mental hospital we are not being realistic about its primary function. The more historical function is to protect the interests of society, groups, or families by removing individuals who exhibit certain kinds of socially disruptive behavior and providing custodial care for those who become mentally disordered.[81]

In spite of various limitations, mental hospitals might be more effective in treatment if the labeling process were reduced and an attempt made on the part of the staff not to regard the role of the patient as one of helplessness, dependency, and incompetence.[82] Hospitals with such an emphasis might interrupt the acquisition of a "sick role." The wider use of better trained nonmedical hospital personnel (attendants and nurses) in group and individual psychotherapy might help to deal with the problem of limited available medical and psychiatric personnel.

Patients also must have more visitors and other social contacts with the outside world. Often, in fact, a patient's chance of discharge does not depend on the state of his "illness," but on whether there is someone interested in him—and willing to help him—on the outside.[83] Visits

---

[80] Schwartz and Schwartz, p. 204.

[81] Robert M. Edwards, "Functions of the State Mental Hospital as a Social Institution," *Mental Hygiene,* 48:666–671 (1964); and Leonard Schatzman and Anselm Strauss, "A Sociology of Psychiatry: A Perspective and Some Organizing Foci," *Social Problems,* 14:3–16 (1966).

[82] E. Talbot and S. C. Miller, "The Struggle to Create a Sane Society in a Psychiatric Hospital," *Psychiatry,* 29:165–171 (1966).

[83] See Simon Dinitz, Mark Lefton, Shirley Angrist, and Benjamin Pasamanick, "Psychiatric and Social Attributes as Predictors of Case Outcome in Mental Hospitalization," *Social Problems,* 8:322–328 (1961).

particularly mean a great deal to mental patients; yet generally the longer a patient stays in a mental hospital the less likely is he to have many visitors. Visiting appears to vary according to the type of ward, those on "hopeful" wards receiving the most. The patient who has few visitors often loses prestige on the ward, feels that he is forgotten, and misses this way of breaking up the hospital routine.

The trial home visits of patients before release are crucial experiences for most mental patients. This is the test period of adjustment in the interpersonal relations of the patient with his family, friends, and neighbors, and unless they and the patient have been sufficiently prepared by the professional staff, particularly the psychiatric social workers, a relapse may occur. The readjustments necessary because of institutional living and the stigma of having been in a mental hospital are often too much for the patient unless he has help from others.

The stigma of having been in a mental hospital presents one of the most serious difficulties that changes in public attitudes might modify. Many released mental patients are conscious of this stigma, which interferes with recovery because it makes them feel that a barrier exists between themselves and others. To the public, institutional treatment often implies that the patient is different from others. The past reputation of public hospitals has not helped the conception that "insane persons" are confined much as prisoners are. Consequently, few persons wish to admit confinement in a mental hospital, although people may increasingly admit, without too much fear of the stigma, having been under treatment, outside a mental hospital, by a psychiatrist or a psychoanalyst. It may be some time before a person feels like talking as fully about hospitalization for mental difficulties as about hospitalization for some operation.

Possibly more effective is the fact that in recent years several mental hospitals both here and abroad have attempted a reorganization of their social structure in an effort to create what have been called "therapeutic communities" or "group-centered hospitals." [84] The rationale behind these attempts has been that the social environment or the system of social relationships imposed by the hospital structure is so overwhelming that therapy of any kind cannot succeed in reintegrating patients unless this

---

[84] See, for example, the discussion in Schwartz and Schwartz. This idea was pioneered by Maxwell Jones; for a later writing see his "Community Aspects of Hospital Treatment," *Current Psychiatric Therapies*, 1:199 (1961). Earlier mental hospital reformers in the first half of the nineteenth century, such as Dorothea Dix, made suggestions that today resemble the idea of a therapeutic community. See Henry Brill, "Historical Background of the Therapeutic Community," in Herman Denber, *Research Conference on the Therapeutic Community* (Springfield, Ill.: Charles C Thomas, Publisher, 1960).

environment is itself "therapeutic," or democratic. Thus the general changes attempted have been to "level" the rigid hierarchical status structure by giving patients more responsibility for themselves; giving attendants and other lower-status personnel greater status-giving roles; redefining the roles of doctors and psychiatrists so as to give them less power in making decisions for patients; creating "patient governments" and establishing hospital-wide discussion meetings; and introducing greater use of psychodrama, for both staff and patients, and group therapy sessions led by nurses, attendants, and other nonmedical personnel. Important corollaries of these changes have been greater interaction between staff and patients and between patients, and greater ease of communication.[85]

In general, creation of a therapeutic community changes the hospital into a more "democratic" organization, where all may participate in what goes on. This contrasts with the highly authoritarian climate of the great majority of mental hospitals, where power of decision is vested in the few at the top of the prestige hierarchy. In the therapeutic hospital "each patient is a citizen in the hospital community, having the privileges and responsibilities of a citizen." [86]

In an Australian mental hospital, for example, reorganization took place after community group discussions were introduced.[87] In these discussions patients and staff of all levels were expected to suggest changes to improve hospital functions and relationships. If people were able to defend their suggestions these were tried out experimentally in the hospital. When it became recognized that changes could be initiated by people at all levels, a change in the rigid hierarchical role and status system of the hospital became necessary. Such changes were implemented, to some extent, in later staff policy meetings. Some of these changes consisted of allowing patients of both sexes to mix, beginning group therapy sessions led by attendants and nurses where patients were allowed to answer their own questions, and increasing interaction between patients and between staff and patients.

Unfortunately, the successful application of the idea of a therapeutic community has been limited by the incorporation of certain features within

---

[85] Greenblatt, Levinson, and Williams, pp. 173–196.

[86] E. Talbot, S. C. Miller, and Robert B. White, "Some Anti-Therapeutic Side Effects of Hospitalization and Psychotherapy," *Psychiatry,* 27:176 (1964).

[87] D. Barker, L. B. Brown, J. E. Cawte, and J. Riley, "Revising the Patients' Day in a Mental Hospital," *Medical Journal of Australia,* 45:700–702 (1958); and C. E. M. Harris, H. L. Brown, and J. E. Cawte, "Problems of Developing a Group-Centered Mental Hospital," *International Journal of Group Psychotherapy,* 10:408–409 (1960). Also see H. Wilmer, *Social Psychiatry in Action* (Springfield, Ill.: Charles C Thomas, Publisher, 1958).

the framework of a traditional hospital system. For example, many hospitals have adopted a ward meeting of patients as an activity but without changing the ward's social organization. Patients may participate in the administration but have little power.[88] It is suggested that many of the therapeutic problems of mental hospitals grow out of their size and administrative practices rather than from their treatment orientation. Some limited studies maintain that the results of a milieu-oriented hospital are not much greater than those of a more conventional one.[89] What is suggested in these studies is that institutional treatment of mental patients, like the treatment in prisons, results in limited success, despite the methods employed. Institutionalization and separation from outside community relationships, as well as the stigma associated with them, markedly affect the situation. There are also problems in the application of the general concept and framework in actual situations.[90] Others have challenged the entire idea, indicating that the contrast between a mental hospital and the outside world is such that the emphasis on improved "communication" between them and similar recommendations are unrealistic.[91]

Wider placement of mental patients under home care plans would reduce the need for institutionalization. An important experiment has shown that mental hospitalization of schizophrenics, one of the most difficult groups to treat, can be provided through a program of combining drug medication and public-health nursing with care in the home of the patient. A careful evaluation of this home care program, involving 152 schizophrenic patients and a hospital control group, found that 77 percent of the home care patients remained outside the hospital over a period of from six to thirty months.[92] The study concluded that "in the absence of considerable deterioration, an acute episode, or grossly exaggerated symptoms, no special reason exists for keeping schizophrenic patients hospitalized." [93] Home

---

[88] John H. Vitale, "The Emergence of Mental Hospital Field Research," in George W. Fairweather, *Social Psychology in Treating Mental Illness: An Experimental Approach* (New York: John Wiley & Sons, Inc., 1964), pp. 14–15.

[89] See, for example, Stotland and Kobler.

[90] Robert N. Rapoport, *Community as Doctor* (Springfield, Ill.: Charles C Thomas, Publisher, 1960), pp. 68–77.

[91] Michael Etzion, "Interpersonal and Structural Factors in the Study of Mental Hospitals," *Psychiatry*, 23:16 (1960); and Charles Perrow, "Hospitals, Technology, Structure and Goals," in James G. March, *Handbook of Organizations* (Chicago: Rand McNally & Company, 1965).

[92] Benjamin Pasamanick, Frank R. Scarpitti, and Simon Dinitz, *Schizophrenics in the Community: An Experimental Study in the Prevention of Hospitalization* (New York: Appleton-Century-Crofts, Inc., 1967).

[93] Pasamanick, Scarpitti, and Dinitz, p. 255.

care also reduced costs, spread limited psychiatric and other professional manpower, and indicated that community mental health centers are a more effective approach to the problem than mental hospitals.

Even more promising is the trend toward preventive work through community psychiatric clinics in which emphasis is put on the prevention of further development of the disorder and on outpatient care. Likewise, there is a tendency to move toward small mental hospitals and psychiatric wards centrally located in metropolitan communities to supplement or replace the large, geographically isolated state hospitals. In this approach the large state hospital is not the only facility but a part of a larger comprehensive program. The state hospital might remain for those who need more long-term care, such as brain-damaged geriatric patients.

An unusual program to prevent admissions to mental hospitals has been developed in Amsterdam, as a municipal government service, and involves the treatment of patients in their own homes wherever possible.[94] Prospective admissions are seen by a city psychiatrist immediately, or within twenty-four hours, after a patient has been reported as disturbed by such persons as the family doctor or the police. By seeing the patient in his own home the psychiatrist can better determine the circumstances and assess the contributing causes more effectively. If clinical observation is necessary the patient may be sent to one of the psychiatric wards in Amsterdam. The city is divided into four sectors, and a "team," consisting of a psychiatrist and several social workers, is responsible for supervision in each sector. Supervision is carried out by visits to patients' homes, the frequency of the visits depending on the particular case. The number of cases per team is about four hundred. In addition, the psychiatrist visits clinics about four times weekly and mental hospitals less frequently. Each team is part of the "Consultation Bureau," a sort of central agency with a personnel of about forty-five. It may also give advice to other public agencies, such as public assistance departments, and may give other help, including aid in finding jobs. About 8000 patients are dealt with by this bureau each year.

It is reported that the program has succeeded in reducing the Netherlands mental hospital population. At present it meets the needs of about a third of all patients who would otherwise require hospitalization. Dr. Querido, who has done much to develop the Amsterdam program, points out the extreme importance of the patients' *first* contact with societal representatives. Because of the nature of the program he has felt that it has had an effect in changing the public's attitudes toward mental illness and

---

[94] A. Querido, "Social Psychiatry and the Legal Issue," *International Journal of Social Psychiatry*, 1:3–8 (1955).

also in changing the psychiatrists' approach to the nature of mental disorder.

SUMMARY

Total institutions, such as prisons and mental hospitals, are large-scale efforts to deal with deviancy; the inmates or patients are confined in "closed worlds" isolated from the larger society but with a culture of their own; there are bureaucratic rules for whose violation the individual can be punished; the inmate or patient is confined and subservient to the social structure of the community of inmates and staff, and those confined are relieved of economic and social responsibilities.

It is difficult, however, to treat deviant behavior adequately through institutions because of the large number of those needing treatment as well as because of their cost, the limited professional personnel available, the artificiality of institutional life, and the stigma associated with institutional confinement.

Studies on the effectiveness of treatment programs to deal with deviant behavior have shown the importance of the social structure and the subculture of both prisons and mental hospitals.

A number of programs to modify the conventional prison and mental hospital have been proposed as well as substitutes for institutional treatment.

SELECTED READINGS

Action for Mental Health. The Final Report of the Joint Commission on Mental Illness and Health. New York: Basic Books, Inc., 1961. This report contains an analysis of the state of mental hospitals, with recommendations for their improvement. The Joint Commission on Mental Illness and Health was set up by Congress to make a five-year study of mental hospitals in the United States and to make necessary recommendations.

Clemmer, Donald. *The Prison Community*. Revised edition. New York: Holt, Rinehart and Winston, Inc., 1958. A study of the prison as a social system, with particular emphasis on the inmates and their social relationships.

Conrad, John. *Crime and Its Correction: An International Survey of Attitudes and Practices*. Berkeley: University of California Press, 1965. A comparative study of correctional programs in Scandinavia, Great Britain, the Soviet Union, Netherlands, Canada, and parts of the United States.

Cressey, Donald, ed. *The Prison: Studies in Institutional Organization and Change*. New York: Holt, Rinehart and Winston, Inc., 1961. A series of articles on the organization of the prison, particularly its social system.

Glaser, Daniel. *The Effectiveness of a Prison and Parole System*. Indianapolis: The Bobbs-Merrill Company, Inc., 1964. A discussion of the effectiveness of prisons and the results of a series of studies attempting to evaluate the United States federal prison system.

Goffman, Erving. *Asylums.* New York: Doubleday & Company, Inc., 1961. An analysis of the characteristics of "total institutions," the moral career of the mental patient, and the nature of the mental hospital.

Levinson, Daniel J., and Eugene B. Gallagher. *Patienthood in the Mental Hospital.* Boston: Houghton Mifflin Company, 1964. A study of the role of the mental patient in a mental hospital.

Morris, Norval. "Lessons from the Adult Correctional System of Sweden," in *Federal Probation,* 30:3–13 (1966). A description and evaluation of the Swedish correctional system, which is considered one of the most advanced in the world.

Pasamanick, Benjamin, Frank R. Scarpitti, and Simon Dinitz. *Schizophrenics in the Community: An Experimental Study in the Prevention of Hospitalization.* New York: Appleton-Century-Crofts, Inc., 1967. A significant experiment and evaluation study of the substitution of community treatment for confinement in a mental hospital.

Scheff, Thomas J. *Being Mentally Ill: A Sociological Theory.* Chicago: Aldine Publishing Company, 1966. Contains a discussion of the stigma associated with hospitalization for mental disorder.

Schwartz, Morris S., and Charlotte C. Schwartz, *et al. Social Approaches to Mental Patient Care.* New York: Columbia University Press, 1964. A comprehensive examination of various types of mental hospitals and the social effects of such treatment.

Scudder, Kenyon J. *Prisoners Are People.* New York: Doubleday & Company, Inc., 1952. The story of the California Institution for Men, one of the most advanced prisons in the United States, by its first superintendent.

Stanton, Alfred H., and Morris S. Schwartz. *The Mental Hospital.* New York: Basic Books, Inc., 1954. A study of the mental hospital as a social system by a psychiatrist and a sociologist.

Sykes, Gresham M. *The Society of Captives: A Study of a Maximum Security Prison.* Princeton, N.J.: Princeton University Press, 1958. A sociological study of a prison, particularly the way informal rules of the inmate subculture control the behavior of its members.

Tappan, Paul W., ed. *Contemporary Correction.* New York: McGraw-Hill Book Company, Inc., 1951. A series of articles on various aspects of modern correctional work by some of the leading men in this area.

Von Mering, Otto, and Stanley H. King. *Remotivating the Mental Patient.* New York: Russell Sage Foundation, 1957. A description of efforts to treat patients by restructuring the social milieu of the hospital, with discussions of results in terms of patient improvement.

Weinberg, S. Kirson, and H. Warren Dunham. *The Culture of the State Mental Hospital.* Detroit: Wayne State University Press, 1960. A sociological study of a large midwestern public mental hospital. Contains much case and interview material.

Name Index

Subject Index